SOCIOLOGICAL THEORY

SOCIOLOGICAL THEORY

THIRD EDITION

George Ritzer

University of Maryland

McGRAW-HILL, INC.

New York   St. Louis   San Francisco   Auckland   Bogotá
Caracas   Lisbon   London   Madrid   Mexico   Milan   Montreal
New Delhi   Paris   San Juan   Singapore   Sydney   Tokyo   Toronto

This book was set in Palatino by Arcata Graphics/Kingsport.
The editors were Phillip A. Butcher and Ira C. Roberts;
the production supervisor was Denise L. Puryear.
The cover was designed by Rafael Hernandez.
R. R. Donnelley & Sons Company was printer and binder.

SOCIOLOGICAL THEORY

2 3 4 5 6 7 8 9 0   DOC DOC   9 0 9 8 7 6 5 4 3 2

ISBN 0-07-052971-X

Library of Congress Cataloging-in-Publication Data

Ritzer, George.
    Sociological theory/George Ritzer.—3rd ed.
      p.   cm.
    Includes bibliographical references and index.
    ISBN 0-07-052971-X
    1. Sociology.   2. Sociologists—Biography.   I. Title.
HM24.R4938   1992
301'.01—dc20   91–27818

PERMISSIONS ACKNOWLEDGMENTS

CHAPTER 2

Excerpts from Karl Marx, *The Economic and Philosophic Manuscripts of 1844,* ed. by Dirk K. Struik. © 1932, 1964. Excerpts from Karl Marx, *Capital,* vol. 1. © 1867, 1967. Both used by permission of International Publishers Co., Inc.

CHAPTER 4

Excerpts from Max Weber, *Economy and Society,* 2 vols., ed. by Guenther Roth and Claus Wittich, tr. by the editors and others. Copyright © 1978 by The Regents of the University of California. Used by permission of The University of California Press.

CHAPTER 5

Excerpts from Georg Simmel, *The Philosophy of Money,* ed. and tr. by Tom Bottomore and David Frisby. London: Routledge and Kegan Paul. © 1907, 1978. Used by permission of Routledge.

CHAPTER 7

Excerpts from Robert K. Merton, "Remembering the Young Talcott Parsons," *American Sociologist,* 15 (1980). Used by permission of The American Sociological Association.

Autobiographical sketch of Robert K. Merton, copyright © 1981 by Robert K. Merton. Used by his permission.

Figures 7.1 and 7.3 reprinted by permission of the publishers from *The American University* by Talcott Parsons and Gerald Platt, Cambridge, Mass.: Harvard University Press, copyright © 1973 by the President and Fellows of Harvard College.

Figure 7.2 from Talcott Parsons, *Societies: Evolutionary and Comparative Perspectives,* © 1966. Adapted by permission of Prentice Hall, Englewood Cliffs, New Jersey.

CHAPTER 9

Excerpts from George Herbert Mead, *Mind, Self, and Society,* ed. and introduced by Charles W. Morris. Copyright 1934 by The University of Chicago. Copyright 1962 by Charles W. Morris. Used by permission.

Excerpts from Leonard S. Cottrell, Jr., "George Herbert Mead: The Legacy of Social Behaviorism," in Robert K. Merton and Matilda White Riley, eds. *Sociological Traditions from Generation to Generation: Glimpses of the American Experience.* © 1980. Used by permission of Ablex Publishing Corp., Norwood, NJ.

CHAPTER 10

Excerpts from Charles Goodwin, "Notes on Story Structure and the Organization of Participation," in J. M. Atkinson and J. Heritage, eds., *Structures of Social Action,* © 1984. Used by permission of Cambridge University Press.

CHAPTER 11

Excerpts from George Caspar Homans, *Social Behavior: Its Elementary Forms,* © 1964, 1971. Used by permission of Harcourt Brace Jovanovich, Inc.

Excerpts from Peter Blau reprinted with permission of Macmillan Publishing Company, a Division of Macmillan, Inc., from *Exchange and Power in Social Life* by Peter Blau. Copyright © 1964 John Wiley & Sons, Inc.

Autobiographical sketch of George C. Homans used without objection of Nancy P. Homans and W. Lincoln Boyden of Ropes and Gray (Boston), executor to the estate of George C. Homans.

Excerpts from George Homans, "The Sociological Relevance of Behaviorism" and figures 11.1 and 11.2, from Don Bushell and Robert Burgess, "Some Basic Principles of Behavior," all in Robert Burgess and Don Bushell, eds., *Behavioral Sociology,* © 1969. Used by permission of Columbia University Press.

CHAPTER 12

Excerpts from Patricia Madoo Lengermann and Ruth A. Wallace, *Gender in America: Social Control and Social Change,* © 1985, pp. 141–144. Reprinted by permission of Prentice Hall, Englewood Cliffs, New Jersey.

CHAPTER 14

Figure 14.4 adapted from James Coleman, "Social Theory, Social Research, and a Theory of Action" in *American Journal of Sociology* 91 (1986). Used by permission of The University of Chicago Press.

Figure 14.5 from Allen E. Liska, "The Signifiance of Aggregate Dependent Variables and Contextual Independent Variables for Linking Macro and Micro Theories," in *Social Psychology Quarterly* 53 (1990). Used by permission of American Sociological Association and the author.

CHAPTER 16

Figure 16.1 from John Baldwin, *George Herbert Mead: A Unifying Theory of Sociology,* © 1986. Reprinted by permission of Sage Publications, Inc.

CHAPTER 17

Figure 17.2 adapted from Ronald Burt, *Toward a Structural Theory of Action: Network Models of Social Structure, Perception, and Action,* © 1982. Used by permission of Academic Press and the author.

PHOTOS

Page 8: Culver Pictures
Page 17: Culver Pictures
Page 32: National Library of Medicine
Page 36: Culver Pictures

Page 46: The Granger Collection, New York
Page 82: The Bettmann Archive
Page 112: The Granger Collection, New York
Page 158: The Granger Collection, New York
Page 198: Courtesy, University of Chicago
Page 204: Courtesy, American Sociological Association
Page 211: Courtesy, Howard Press
Page 240: The Granger Collection, New York
Page 256: Courtesy, Robert K. Merton
Page 297: UPI/Bettmann Newsphotos
Page 301: Laurent Maous/Gamma-Liaison
Page 317: Courtesy, Immanuel Wallerstein
Page 332: Courtesy, University of Chicago
Page 357: Courtesy, American Sociological Association
Page 376: Courtesy, Estate of Alfred Schutz
Page 426: Photo: Christopher Johnson
Page 464: Courtesy, Jessie Bernard
Page 476: Courtesy, Dorothy E. Smith
Page 528: Courtesy, Peter M. Blau
Page 558: Courtesy, Randall Collins
Page 600: Courtesy, Jeffrey C. Alexander
Page 662: Courtesy, George Ritzer

ABOUT THE AUTHOR

GEORGE RITZER is Professor of Sociology at the University of Maryland. His major areas of interest are sociological theory and the sociology of work. He has served as Chair of the American Sociological Association's Sections on Theoretical Sociology (1989–1990) and Organizations and Occupations (1980–1981). Professor Ritzer has been Distinguished Scholar-Teacher at the University of Maryland and has been awarded a Teaching Excellence award. He has held a Fulbright-Hays Fellowship and been Scholar-in-Residence at the Netherlands Institute for Advanced Study and the Swedish Collegium for Advanced Study in the Social Sciences.

In 1992 McGraw-Hill will publish the third edition of Professor Ritzer's basic text in sociological theory, *Contemporary Sociological Theory,* which has been adopted in many countries, as well as throughout the United States and Canada, in undergraduate and graduate courses in social theory. In addition, McGraw-Hill will also publish the first edition of his *Classical Sociological Theory.*

Dr. Ritzer's main theoretical interests lie in metatheory as well as in the theory of rationalization. In metatheory, his most recent book is *Metatheorizing in Sociology* (Lexington Books, 1991). Earlier books on this topic include *Sociology: A Multiple Paradigm Science* (1975, 1980) and *Toward an Integrated Sociological Paradigm* (1981). He has written a number of essays on rationalization as well as the soon-to-be published *Big Mac Attack: The McDonaldization of Society* (Free Press, 1992).

To David with Love

CONTENTS

LIST OF BIOGRAPHICAL AND AUTOBIOGRAPHICAL SKETCHES

PREFACE

SOCIOLOGICAL theory is undergoing dramatic changes and those changes are reflected in the substantial restructuring of the third edition of this book.

The most obvious change in this edition is in the overall structure of the book. The previous edition was divided into two parts—classical and contemporary sociological theory. In this edition there are three parts—classical sociological theory, the major schools of sociological theory, and the most recent developments in sociological theory discussed under the headings of integration and synthesis.

Part One, Classical Sociological Theory, remains largely intact, although discussions of new interpretations of classic theorists are scattered throughout these chapters. Part One opens with an overview of the history of sociological theory through approximately the close of the nineteenth century. The next four chapters deal with the work of the most important classical sociological theorists—Karl Marx, Emile Durkheim, Max Weber, and Georg Simmel.

Part Two, Sociological Theory: The Major Schools, deals with the major schools of sociological theory. All of these continue to be important today, but they are beginning to be overshadowed by the developments discussed in Part Three. Chapter 6 picks up the story of the history of sociological theory where Chapter 1 left off, and brings it up to the present moment with a discussion of the most recent developments in sociological theory. The rest of the section is composed of chapters dealing with the major schools of sociological theory.

Chapter 7 includes a discussion of structural functionalism (including an extended analysis of the work of Talcott Parsons), as well as of the conflict-theory alternative.

Chapter 8 deals with the main varieties of neo-Marxian theory—economic determinism, Hegelian Marxism, critical theory, structural Marxism, neo-Marxian economic sociology (including a new discussion of the debate over Fordism and Post-Fordism), and historically oriented Marxism (with a discussion of Immanuel Wallerstein's latest work on world systems theory).

Chapter 9, on symbolic interactionism, contains a much more elaborate discussion of the ideas of George Herbert Mead.

Chapter 10 (phenomenological sociology and ethnomethodology) includes a major addition to the discussion of the work of Alfred Schutz as well as substantial changes in the discussion of ethnomethodology based on recent work in that area.

Chapter 11 deals with exchange theory and behavioral sociology and is little changed from the last edition.

Chapter 12, on feminist theories, has been revised and updated by its two authors, Patricia Madoo Lengermann and Jill Niebrugge-Brantley.

Chapter 13 is a new chapter devoted to a wide range of structural sociological theories as well as to theoretical perspectives that stand as critiques of such theories.

Part Three, Recent Developments in Sociological Theory: Integration and Syntheses, is entirely new. The four chapters in this part reflect the fact that in the last few years sociological theory has begun to move away from the narrowness of the theories discussed in Part Two and toward more integrative and synthetic orientations. Integration involves the effort to integrate levels or domains of social analysis. Syntheses entail attempts to bring together ideas drawn from a number of different theories.

Chapter 14 deals with the largely American literature on micro-macro integration. In addition to a general discussion of this issue, the work of Ritzer, Alexander, and Wiley on levels of analysis, Coleman's contribution to micro-macro integration via rational choice theory, Collins's microfoundations of macrosociology, and interactor theory are discussed in some detail.

Chapter 15 covers the largely European literature on agency-structure integration. The relationship between this literature and that on micro-macro integration is discussed, and an overview of work on agency-structure is offered. This chapter allows us to cover in some detail Giddens's structuration theory, Archer's work on culture and agency, Bourdieu's integration of habitus and field, and Habermas's ideas on the colonization of the life-world.

Chapters 16 and 17 deal with synthetic efforts in sociology. Most of the theories discussed in Part Two are reviewed, this time from the point of view of the synthetic efforts emerging from them. In addition to such a review, there are discussions of important new synthetic developments in neofunctionalism, rational choice theory, postmodernism, and post-Marxist theory.

The book concludes with an Appendix, which includes a dramatically revised discussion of metatheorizing in sociology reflecting the current boom in interest in this topic. It also includes a discussion of the specific metatheoretical approach that undergirds the book as a whole.

A number of biographical sketches, held over from the previous edition, are presented throughout the text: Ibn-Khaldun, Auguste Comte, Sigmund Freud, Karl Marx, Emile Durkheim, Max Weber, Georg Simmel, Herbert Spencer, Robert Park, Pitirim Sorokin, C. Wright Mills, Erving Goffman, Talcott Parsons, Robert Merton, Louis Althusser, Nicos Poulantzas, Immanuel Wallerstein, George Herbert Mead, Alfred Schutz, George Caspar Homans, Jessie Bernard, Dorothy Smith, and Peter Blau. In addition, three new biographies of contemporary theorists have been included: Jeffrey Alexander, Randall Collins, and George Ritzer.

I would like to thank the McGraw-Hill staff, especially Phil Butcher, Sylvia Shepard, and Ira Roberts, for their encouragement and assistance with this revision. Thanks go to my son Jeremy who created the index to this book. Also to be thanked are a number of theorists who offered useful comments on part or all of this book: Robert Antonio, University of Kansas; John Baldwin, University of California, Santa Barbara; Deirdre Boden, Washington University; Ira Cohen, Rutgers University; Paul Colomy, University of Denver; Karen Cook, University of Washington; James Farganis, Vassar College; Gary Fine, University of Georgia; Robert A. Jones, University of Illinois; Stephen Kalberg, Harvard University; Frank J. Lechner, Emory University; Donald N. Levine, University of Chicago; Whitney Pope, Indiana University; George Psathas, Boston University; Steven Seidman, SUNY at Albany; and Jonathan H. Turner, University of California, Riverside. My assistant, Joanne DeFiore, was invaluable in helping with this revision.

George Ritzer

PART ONE

CLASSICAL SOCIOLOGICAL THEORY

A HISTORICAL SKETCH OF SOCIOLOGICAL THEORY: THE EARLY YEARS

A USEFUL way to begin a book designed to introduce the range of sociological theory is with several one-line summaries of various theories:

• The modern world is an iron cage of rational systems from which there is no escape.
• Capitalism tends to sow the seeds of its own destruction.
• The modern world has less moral cohesion than earlier societies.
• The city spawns a particular type of personality.
• In their social lives, people tend to put on a variety of theatrical performances.
• The social world is defined by principles of reciprocity in give-and-take relationships.
• People create the social worlds that ultimately come to enslave them.
• People always retain the capacity to change the social worlds that constrain them.
• In their social relationships, people often rely on tried and true "recipes" for how to handle such relationships.
• Society is an integrated system of social structures and functions.

This book is devoted to helping the reader to better understand these theoretical ideas, as well as the larger theories from which they are drawn.

INTRODUCTION

Part I of this book deals with classical sociological theory—theories developed mainly in the nineteenth and early twentieth centuries. Chapter 1 offers a historical overview of the early years of sociological theory. Chapters 2 through 5 are devoted to the ideas of the most important classical sociological theorists—Karl Marx, Emile Durkheim, Max Weber, and Georg Simmel. Part II focuses on schools of sociological theory and opens with Chapter 6, which gives an overview of the history of contemporary sociological theory. The remaining chapters in Part II deal with the full range of theoretical schools. Part III deals with the most recent developments in sociological theory- micro-macro integration, agency-structure integration and theoretical syntheses of various types.

As indicated above, Chapters 1 and 6 together provide an overview of the entire history of sociological theory.[1] The theories treated in these chapters, indeed in the entire book, are, as our definition suggests, concerned with the most important social issues and have implications for a wide range of social life. However, not all of the theories (and theorists) discussed in these chapters will be dealt with in the body of the book. Some will be omitted from more extended discussion for one of three reasons: because they do not have a *wide range* of application, because they do not deal with *centrally important social issues,* or because they have not *stood the test of time.*[2] Thus, a number of the theorists who are briefly discussed in Chapter 1 (for example, Herbert Spencer and Auguste Comte) will not receive detailed treatment later because they are of little more than historical interest. Other theorists (for example, Karl Marx, Max Weber, and Emile Durkheim) will be discussed in Chapter 1 in their historical context, and they will receive detailed treatment later because of their continuing importance.

Our focus is the important theoretical work of *sociologists* or the work done by those in other fields that has come to be *defined as important in sociology.* To put it succinctly, this a book about the "big ideas" in sociology that have stood the test of time (or promise to), idea systems that deal with major social issues and are far-reaching in scope.

---

[1] There is also an elaborate metatheoretical approach and schema that inform these two chapters as well as the rest of the book. That approach is outlined in the Appendix.

[2] These criteria constitute our definition of *sociological theory.* Such a definition stands in contrast to the formal, "scientific" definitions that are often used in theory texts of this type. A scientific definition might be that a theory is a set of interrelated propositions that allow for the systematization of knowledge, explanation, and prediction of social life and the generation of new research hypotheses (Faia, 1986). Although such a definition has a number of attractions, it simply does not fit many of the idea systems to be discussed in this book. In other words, most classical (and contemporary) theories fall short on one or more of the formal components of theory, but they are nonetheless considered theories by most sociologists.

Presenting a history of sociological theory is an enormous task, but because we devote only two chapters (1 and 6) to it, what we offer is a highly selective historical sketch.[3] The idea is to provide the reader with a scaffolding which should help in putting the later detailed discussions of theorists and theories in a larger context. As the reader proceeds through the later chapters, it might prove useful to return to these two overview chapters and place the discussions in that context. (It would be especially useful to glance back occasionally to Figures 1.1 and 6.1, which are schematic representations of the histories covered in those chapters.)

One cannot really establish the precise date when sociological theory began. People have been thinking about, and developing theories of, social life since early in history. But we will not go back to the early historic times of the Greeks or Romans or even to the Middle Ages. This is not because people in those epochs did not have sociologically relevant ideas, but because the return on our investment in time would be small; we would spend a lot of time getting very few ideas that are relevant to modern sociology. In any case, none of the thinkers associated with those eras thought of themselves, and few are now thought of, as sociologists. (For discussion of one exception, see the biographical sketch of Ibn-Khaldun.) It is only in the 1800s that we begin to find thinkers who can be clearly identified as sociologists. These are the sociological thinkers we shall be interested in, and we begin by examining the main social and intellectual forces that shaped their ideas.

SOCIAL FORCES IN THE DEVELOPMENT OF SOCIOLOGICAL THEORY

All intellectual fields are profoundly shaped by their social settings. This is particularly true of sociology, which is not only derived from that setting but takes the social setting as its basic subject matter. We will focus briefly on a few of the most important social conditions of the nineteenth and early twentieth centuries, conditions that were of the utmost significance in the development of sociology. We also will take the occasion to begin introducing the major figures in the history of sociological theory.

Political Revolutions

The long series of political revolutions ushered in by the French Revolution in 1789 and carrying over through the nineteenth century was the most immediate factor in the rise of sociological theorizing. The impact of these revolutions on many societies was enormous, and many positive changes resulted. However, what attracted the attention of many early theorists was not the positive consequences, but the negative effects of such changes. These writers were particularly disturbed by the resulting chaos and disorder, especially in

---

[3] For a much more detailed historical sketch see, for example, Szacki (1979).

6

FIGURE 1.1 Sociological Theory: The Early Years

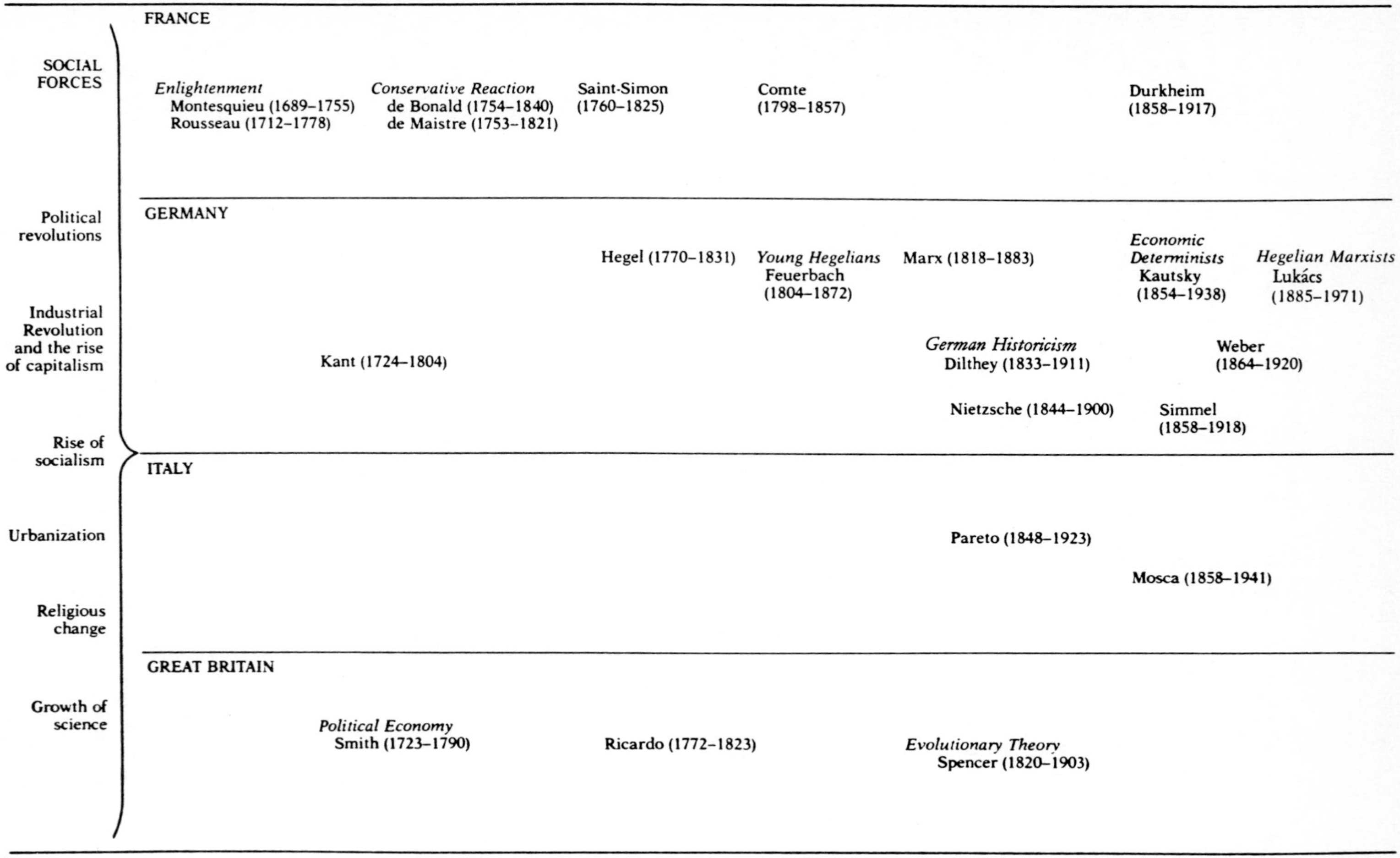

SOCIAL FORCES

Political revolutions

Industrial Revolution and the rise of capitalism

Rise of socialism

Urbanization

Religious change

Growth of science

FRANCE

Enlightenment
Montesquieu (1689–1755)
Rousseau (1712–1778)

Conservative Reaction
de Bonald (1754–1840)
de Maistre (1753–1821)

Saint-Simon (1760–1825)

Comte (1798–1857)

Durkheim (1858–1917)

GERMANY

Kant (1724–1804)

Hegel (1770–1831)

Young Hegelians
Feuerbach (1804–1872)

Marx (1818–1883)

German Historicism
Dilthey (1833–1911)

Nietzsche (1844–1900)

Economic Determinists
Kautsky (1854–1938)

Weber (1864–1920)

Simmel (1858–1918)

Hegelian Marxists
Lukács (1885–1971)

ITALY

Pareto (1848–1923)

Mosca (1858–1941)

GREAT BRITAIN

Political Economy
Smith (1723–1790)

Ricardo (1772–1823)

Evolutionary Theory
Spencer (1820–1903)

France. They were united in a desire to restore order to society. Some of the more extreme thinkers of this period literally wanted a return to the peaceful and relatively orderly days of the Middle Ages. The more sophisticated thinkers recognized that social change had made such a return impossible. Thus they sought instead to find new bases of order in societies that had been overturned by the political revolutions of the eighteenth and nineteenth centuries. This interest in the issue of social order was one of the major concerns of classical sociological theorists, especially Comte and Durkheim.

The Industrial Revolution and the Rise of Capitalism

At least as important as political revolution in the shaping of sociological theory was the Industrial Revolution, which swept through many Western societies, mainly in the nineteenth and early twentieth centuries. The Industrial Revolution was not a single event but many interrelated developments that culminated in the transformation of the Western world from a largely agricultural to an overwhelmingly industrial system. Large numbers of people left farms and agricultural work for the industrial occupations offered in the burgeoning factories. The factories themselves were transformed by a long series of technological improvements. Large economic bureaucracies arose to provide the many services needed by industry and the emerging capitalist economic system. In this economy, the ideal was a free marketplace where the many products of an industrial system could be exchanged. Within this system, a few profited greatly while the majority worked long hours for low wages. A reaction against the industrial system and against capitalism in general followed and led to the labor movement as well as to various radical movements aimed at overthrowing the capitalist system.

The Industrial Revolution, capitalism, and the reaction against them all involved an enormous upheaval in Western society, an upheaval that affected sociologists greatly. Four major figures in the early history of sociological theory—Karl Marx, Max Weber, Emile Durkheim, and Georg Simmel—were preoccupied, as were many lesser thinkers, with these changes and the problems they created for society as a whole. They spent their lives studying these problems, and in many cases they endeavored to develop programs that would help solve them.

The Rise of Socialism

One set of changes aimed at coping with the excesses of the industrial system and capitalism can be combined under the heading "socialism." Although some sociologists favored socialism as a solution to industrial problems, most were personally and intellectually opposed to it. On the one side, Karl Marx was an active supporter of the overthrow of the capitalist system and its replacement by a socialist system. Although he did not develop a theory of socialism per se, he spent a great deal of time criticizing various aspects of

---

ABDEL RAHMAN IBN-KHALDUN: A Biographical Sketch

There is a tendency to think of sociology as exclusively a comparatively modern, Western phenomenon. In fact, however, scholars were doing sociology long ago and in other parts of the world. One example is Abdel Rahman Ibn-Khaldun.

Ibn-Khaldun was born in Tunis, North Africa, on May 27, 1332 (Faghirzadeh, 1982). Born to an educated family, Ibn-Khaldun was schooled in the Koran (the Muslim holy book), mathematics, and history. In his lifetime, he served a variety of sultans in Tunis, Morocco, Spain, and Algeria as ambassador, chamberlain, and member of the scholar's council. He also spent two years in prison in Morocco for his belief that state rulers were not divine leaders. After approximately two decades of political activity, Ibn-Khaldun returned to North Africa, where he undertook an intensive five-year period of study and writing. Works produced during this period increased his fame and led to a lectureship at the center of Islamic study, Al-Azhar Mosque University in Cairo. In his well-attended lectures on society and sociology, Ibn-Khaldun stressed the importance of linking sociological thought and historical observation.

By the time he died in 1406, Ibn-Khaldun had produced a corpus of work that had many ideas in common with contemporary sociology. He was committed to the scientific study of society, empirical research, and the search for causes of social phenomena. He devoted considerable attention to various social institutions (for example, politics, economy) and their interrelationships. He was interested in comparing primitive and modern societies. Ibn-Khaldun did not have a dramatic impact on classical sociology, but as scholars in general, and Islamic scholars in particular, rediscover his work, he may come to be seen as being of greater historical significance.

---

capitalist society. In addition, he engaged in a variety of political activities that he hoped would help bring about the rise of socialist societies.

However, Marx was atypical in the early years of sociological theory. Most of the early theorists, such as Weber and Durkheim, were opposed to socialism (at least as it was envisioned by Marx). Although they recognized the problems within capitalist society, they sought social reform within capitalism rather than the social revolution argued for by Marx. They feared socialism more than they did capitalism. This fear played a far greater role in shaping sociological theory than did Marx's support of the socialist alternative to capitalism. In fact, as we will see, in many cases sociological theory developed in reaction *against* Marxian and, more generally, socialist theory.

Urbanization

Partly as a result of the Industrial Revolution, large numbers of people in the nineteenth and twentieth centuries were uprooted from their rural homes and moved to urban settings. This massive migration was caused, in large part, by the jobs created by the industrial system in the urban areas. But it presented many difficulties for those people who had to adjust to urban life. In addition, the expansion of the cities produced a seemingly endless list of urban problems—overcrowding, pollution, noise, traffic, and so forth. The nature of urban life and its problems attracted the attention of many early sociologists, especially Max Weber and Georg Simmel. In fact, the first major school of American sociology, the Chicago school, was in large part defined by its concern for the city and its interest in using Chicago as a laboratory in which to study urbanization and its problems.

Religious Change

Social changes brought on by political revolutions, the Industrial Revolution, and urbanization had a profound effect on religiosity. Many early sociologists came from religious backgrounds and were actively, and in some cases professionally, involved in religion (Hinkle and Hinkle, 1954). They brought to sociology the same objectives as they had in their religious lives. They wished to improve people's lives (Vidich and Lyman, 1985). For some (such as Comte), sociology was transformed into a religion. For others, their sociological theories bore an unmistakable religious imprint. Durkheim wrote one of his major works on religion. A large portion of Weber's work also was devoted to the religions of the world. Marx, too, had an interest in religiosity, but his orientation was far more critical.

The Growth of Science

As sociological theory was being developed, there was an increasing emphasis on science, not only in colleges and universities but in society as a whole. The technological products of science were permeating every sector in life, and science was acquiring enormous prestige. Those associated with the most successful sciences (physics, biology, and chemistry) were accorded honored places in society. Sociologists (especially Comte and Durkheim) from the beginning were preoccupied with science, and many wanted to model sociology after the successful physical and biological sciences. However, a debate soon developed between those who wholeheartedly accepted the scientific model and those (such as Weber) who thought that distinctive characteristics of social life made a wholesale adoption of a scientific model difficult and unwise. The issue of the relationship between sociology and science is debated to this day, although even a glimpse at the major journals in the field indicates the predominance of those who favor sociology as a science.

These are just a few of the major social factors that played key roles in the early years of sociological theory. The impact of these factors will become clear as we discuss the various theories and theorists throughout the body of the book.

Although social factors are important, the primary focus of this chapter is the intellectual forces that played a central role in shaping sociological theory. In the real world, of course, intellectual factors cannot be separated from social forces. For example, in the discussion of the Enlightenment that follows, we will find that that movement was intimately related to, and in many cases provided the intellectual basis for, the social changes discussed above.

INTELLECTUAL FORCES AND THE RISE OF SOCIOLOGICAL THEORY

The many intellectual forces that shaped the development of social theories are discussed within the national context where their influence was primarily felt. We begin with the Enlightenment and its influences on the development of sociological theory in France.

The Enlightenment and the Founding of Sociology in France

It is the view of many observers that the Enlightenment constitutes a critical development in terms of the later evolution of sociology (Hawthorn, 1976; Nisbet, 1967; Seidman, 1983; Zeitlin, 1981, 1990). The Enlightenment was a period of remarkable intellectual development and change in philosophical thought.[4] A number of long-standing ideas and beliefs—many of which related to social life—were overthrown and replaced during the Enlightenment. The most prominent thinkers associated with the Enlightenment were the French philosophers Charles Montesquieu (1689–1755) and Jean Jacques Rousseau (1712–1778). The influence of the Enlightenment on sociological theory, however, was more indirect and negative than it was direct and positive. As Irving Zeitlin puts it, "Early sociology developed as a reaction to the Enlightenment" (1981:10).

The thinkers associated with the Enlightenment were influenced, above all, by two intellectual currents—seventeenth-century philosophy and science.

Seventeenth-century philosophy was associated with the work of thinkers such as René Descartes, Thomas Hobbes, and John Locke. The emphasis was on producing grand, general, and very abstract systems of ideas that made rational sense. The later thinkers associated with the Enlightenment did not reject the idea that systems of ideas should be general and should make rational sense, but they did make greater efforts to derive their ideas from the real world and to test them there. In other words, they wanted to combine empirical research with reason (Seidman, 1983:36–37). The model for this was science, especially Newtonian physics. At this point, we see the emergence of

---

[4] This section is based on the work of Irving Zeitlin (1981, 1990). Although Zeitlin's analysis is presented here for its coherence, it has a number of limitations: there are better analyses of the Enlightenment, there are many other factors involved in shaping the development of sociology, and Zeitlin tends to overstate his case in places (for example, on the impact of Marx). But on the whole, Zeitlin provides us with a useful starting point, given our objectives in this chapter.

the application of the scientific method to social issues. At another level, not only did Enlightenment thinkers want their ideas to be, at least in part, derived from the real world, but they also wanted them to be useful to the social world, especially in the critical analysis of that world.

Overall, the Enlightenment was characterized by the belief that people could comprehend and control the universe by means of reason and empirical research. The view was that because the physical world was dominated by natural laws, it was likely that the social world was, too. Thus it was up to the philosopher, using reason and research, to discover these social laws. Once they understood how the social world worked, the Enlightenment thinkers had a practical goal—the creation of a "better," more rational world.

With an emphasis on reason, the Enlightenment philosophers were inclined to reject beliefs in traditional authority. When these thinkers examined traditional values and institutions, they often found them to be irrational—that is, contrary to human nature and inhibitive of human growth and development. The mission of the practical and change-oriented philosophers of the Enlightenment was to overcome these irrational systems.

Conservative Reaction to the Enlightenment   The theorist who was most directly and positively influenced by Enlightenment thinking was Karl Marx, but he formed his early theoretical ideas in Germany. On the surface, we might think that French classical sociological theory, like Marx's theory, was directly and positively influenced by the Enlightenment. After all, didn't French sociology become rational, empirical, scientific, and change-oriented? The answer is that it did, but not before it was also shaped by a set of ideas that was developed in reaction to the Enlightenment. In Seidman's view, "The ideology of the counter-Enlightenment represented a virtual inversion of Enlightenment liberalism. In place of modernist premises, we can detect in the Enlightenment critics a strong anti-modernist sentiment" (1983:51). As we will see, sociology in general, and French sociology in particular, has from the beginning been an uncomfortable mix of Enlightenment and counter-Enlightenment ideas.

The most extreme form of opposition to Enlightenment ideas was French Catholic counterrevolutionary philosophy, as represented by the ideas of Louis de Bonald (1754–1840) and Joseph de Maistre (1753–1821). These men were reacting against not only the Enlightenment but also the French Revolution, which they saw partly as a product of the kind of thinking characteristic of the Enlightenment. De Bonald, for example, was disturbed by the revolutionary changes and yearned for a return to the peace and harmony of the Middle Ages. In this view, God was the source of society; therefore, reason, which was so important to the Enlightenment philosophers, was seen as inferior to traditional religious beliefs. Furthermore, it was believed that because God had created society, people should not tamper with it and should not try to change a holy creation. By extension, de Bonald opposed anything that undermined such traditional institutions as patriarchy, the monogamous family, the monarchy, and the Catholic Church. To call de Bonald's position conservative is to understate the case.

Although de Bonald represented a rather extreme form of the conservative reaction, his work constitutes a useful introduction to its general premises. The conservatives turned away from what they considered to be the "naive" rationalism of the Enlightenment. They not only recognized the irrational aspects of social life but also assigned them positive value. Thus they regarded such phenomena as tradition, imagination, emotionalism, and religion as useful and necessary components of social life. In that they disliked upheaval and sought to retain the existing order, they deplored developments such as the French Revolution and the Industrial Revolution, which they saw as disruptive forces. The conservatives tended to emphasize social order, an emphasis that became one of the central themes of the work of several sociological theorists.

Zeitlin (1981) has outlined ten major propositions that he sees as emerging from the conservative reaction and providing the basis for the development of classical French sociological theory.

1 Whereas Enlightenment thinkers tended to emphasize the individual, the conservative reaction led to a major sociological interest in, and emphasis on, society and other large-scale phenomena. Society was viewed as something more than simply an aggregate of individuals. Society was seen as having an existence of its own with its own laws of development and deep roots in the past.

2 Society was the most important unit of analysis; it was seen as more important than the individual. It was society that produced the individual, primarily through the process of socialization.

3 The individual was not even seen as the most basic element within society. A society consisted of such component parts as roles, positions, relationships, structures, and institutions. The individuals were seen as doing little more than filling these units within society.

4 The parts of society were seen as interrelated and interdependent. Indeed, these interrelationships were a major basis of society. This view led to a conservative political orientation. That is, because the parts were held to be interrelated, it followed that tampering with one part could well lead to the undermining of other parts and, ultimately, of the system as a whole. This meant that changes in the social system should be made with extreme care.

5 Change was seen as a threat not only to society and its components but also to the individuals in society. The various components of society were seen as satisfying people's needs. When institutions were disrupted, people were likely to suffer, and their suffering was likely to lead to social disorder.

6 The general tendency was to see the various large-scale components of society as useful for both society and the individuals in it. As a result,

there was little desire to look for the negative effects of existing social structures and social institutions.

7 Small units, such as the family, the neighborhood, and religious and occupational groups, also were seen as essential to individuals and society. They provided the intimate, face-to-face environments that people needed in order to survive in modern societies.

8 There was a tendency to see various modern social changes, such as industrialization, urbanization, and bureaucratization, as having disorganizing effects. These changes were viewed with fear and anxiety, and there was an emphasis on developing ways of dealing with their disruptive effects.

9 While most of these feared changes were leading to a more rational society, the conservative reaction led to an emphasis on the importance of nonrational factors (ritual, ceremony, and worship, for example) in social life.

10 Finally, the conservatives supported the existence of a hierarchical system in society. It was seen as important to society that there be a differential system of status and reward.

These ten propositions, derived from the conservative reaction to the Enlightenment, should be seen as the immediate intellectual basis of the development of sociological theory in France. Many of these ideas made their way into early sociological thought, although some of the Enlightenment ideas (empiricism, for example) were also influential.

Although we have emphasized the discontinuities between the Enlightenment and the counter-Enlightenment, Seidman makes the point that there also are continuities and linkages. First, the counter-Enlightenment carried on the scientific tradition developed in the Enlightenment. Second, it picked up the Enlightenment emphasis on collectivities (as opposed to individuals) and greatly extended it. Third, both had an interest in the problems of the modern world, especially its negative effects on individuals.

We turn now to the actual founding of sociology as a distinctive discipline—specifically, to the work of three French thinkers, Claude Saint-Simon, Auguste Comte, and especially Emile Durkheim.

Claude Henri Saint-Simon (1760–1825) Saint-Simon was older than Auguste Comte, and in fact Comte, in his early years, served as Saint-Simon's secretary and disciple. There is a very strong similarity between the ideas of these two thinkers, and yet a bitter debate developed between them that led to their eventual split (Thompson, 1975). Because Comte is generally considered to be more important to the founding of sociology, we need say only a few words about Saint-Simon's thinking.

The most interesting aspect of Saint-Simon was his significance to the development of *both* conservative sociological theory (like Comte's) and Marxian theory, which was in many ways the opposite of conservative theory. On the conservative side, Saint-Simon wanted to preserve society as it was, but he did not seek a return to life as it had been in the Middle Ages, as did de Bonald and de Maistre. In addition, he was a *positivist* (Durkheim, 1928/ 1962:142), which meant that he believed that the study of social phenomena should employ the same scientific techniques as were used in the natural sciences. On the radical side, Saint-Simon saw the need for socialist reforms, especially the centralized planning of the economic system. But Saint-Simon did not go nearly as far as Marx did later. Although he, like Marx, saw the capitalists superseding the feudal nobility, he felt it inconceivable that the working class would come to replace the capitalists. Many of Saint-Simon's ideas are found in Comte's work, and we now turn to a brief examination of it.

   Auguste Comte (1798–1857)   Comte was the first to use the term *sociology*. He had an enormous influence on later sociological theorists (especially Herbert Spencer and Emile Durkheim). And he believed that the study of sociology should be scientific, just as many classical theorists did and most contemporary sociologists do (Lenzer, 1975).

   Comte's work can be seen, at least in part, as a reaction against the French Revolution and the Enlightenment, which he saw as the main cause of that revolution (1830–1842/1855). He was greatly disturbed by the anarchy that pervaded society and was critical of those French thinkers who had spawned both the Enlightenment and the revolution. He developed his scientific view, "positivism," or "positive philosophy," to combat what he considered to be the negative and destructive philosophy of the Enlightenment. Comte was in line with, and influenced by, the French counterrevolutionary Catholics (especially de Bonald and de Maistre). However, his work can be set apart from theirs on at least two grounds. First, he did not think it possible to return to the Middle Ages; advances of science and industry made that impossible. Second, he developed a much more sophisticated theoretical system than his predecessors, one that was adequate to shape a good portion of early sociology.

   Comte developed *social physics*, or what in 1822 he called *sociology*, to combat the negative philosophies and the anarchy that in his view pervaded French society. The use of the term *social physics* made it clear that Comte sought to model sociology after the "hard sciences." This new science, which in his view would ultimately become *the* dominant science, was to be concerned with both social statics (existing social structures) and social dynamics (social change). Although both involved the search for laws of social life, he felt that social dynamics was more important than social statics. This focus on change reflected his interest in social reform, particularly of the ills created by the French Revolution and the Enlightenment. Comte did not urge revolutionary change, because he felt the natural evolution of society would make things better. Reforms were needed only to assist the process a bit.

   This leads us to the cornerstone of Comte's approach—his evolutionary theory, or the *law of the three stages*. The theory proposes that there are three intellectual stages through which the world has gone throughout its history.

According to Comte, not only does the world go through this process, but groups, societies, sciences, individuals, and even minds go through the same three stages. The *theological* stage is the first, and it characterized the world prior to 1300. During this period, the major idea system emphasized the belief that supernatural powers, religious figures, modeled after humankind, were at the root of everything. In particular, the social and physical world was seen as produced by God. The second stage is the *metaphysical* stage, which occurred roughly between 1300 and 1800. This era was characterized by the belief that abstract forces like "nature," rather than personalized gods, explain virtually everything. Finally, in 1800 the world entered the *positivistic* stage, characterized by belief in science. People now tended to give up the search for absolute causes (God or nature) and concentrated instead on observation of the social and physical world in the search for the laws governing them.

It is clear that in his theory of the world Comte focused on intellectual factors. Indeed, he argued that intellectual disorder was the cause of social disorder. The disorder stemmed from earlier idea systems (theological and metaphysical) that continued to exist in the positivistic (scientific) age. Only when positivism gained total control would social upheavals cease. Because this was an evolutionary process, there was no need to foment social upheaval and revolution. Positivism would come, although perhaps not as quickly as some would like. Here Comte's social reformism and his sociology coincide. Sociology could expedite the arrival of positivism and hence bring order to the social world. Above all, Comte did not want to seem to be espousing revolution. There was, in his view, enough disorder in the world. In any case, from Comte's point of view, it was intellectual change that was needed, so there was little reason for social and political revolution.

We have already encountered several of Comte's positions that were to be of great significance to the development of classical sociology—his basic conservatism, reformism, and scientism, and his evolutionary view of the world. Several other aspects of his work deserve mention because they also were to play a major role in the development of sociological theory. For example, his sociology does *not* focus on the individual but rather takes as its basic unit of analysis larger entities such as the family. He also urged that we look at *both* social structure and social change. Of great importance to later sociological theory, especially the work of Spencer and Parsons, is Comte's stress on the systematic character of society—the links among and between the various components of society. He also accorded great importance to the role of consensus in society. He saw little merit in the idea that society is characterized by inevitable conflict between workers and capitalists. In addition, Comte emphasized the need to engage in abstract theorizing and to go out and do sociological research. He urged that sociologists use observation, experimentation, and comparative historical analysis. Finally, Comte was an elitist; he believed that sociology ultimately would become the dominant scientific force in the world because of its distinctive ability to interpret social laws and to develop reforms aimed at patching up problems within the system.

AUGUSTE COMTE: A Biographical Sketch

Auguste Comte was born in Montpellier, France, on January 19, 1798. Although a precocious student, Comte never received a college-level degree, and this had a negative effect on his teaching career. In 1818 he became secretary (and "adopted son" [Manuel, 1962:251]) to Claude Henri Saint-Simon, a philosopher forty years Comte's senior. They worked together for several years, but in 1824 they had a falling out because Comte believed that Saint-Simon was not giving him adequate credit for his contributions. Comte later wrote of his relationship with Saint-Simon as "the morbid lesson of his early youth with a depraved juggler" (Durkheim, 1928/1962:144). Despite his later hostility to Saint-Simon, Comte often acknowledged his great debt to him: "I certainly owe a great deal intellectually to Saint-Simon . . . he contributed powerfully to launching me in the philosophic direction that I clearly created for myself today and which I will follow without hesitation all my life" (Durkheim, 1928/1962:144).

In 1826, Comte concocted a scheme by which he would present a series of seventy-two public lectures on his philosophy of life. The course drew a distinguished audience, but it was halted after only three lectures when Comte suffered a nervous breakdown. He continued to suffer from mental problems and once in 1827 tried to commit suicide by throwing himself into the Seine River.

Although he could not get a regular position at the Ecole Polytechnique, Comte did get a minor position as lecturer there in 1832. In 1837, Comte was given the additional post of admissions examiner, and this, for the first time, gave him an adequate income. During this period, Comte worked on the six-volume work for which he is best known, *Cours de Philosophie Positive*, which was finally published in 1842. He outlined his view that sociology was the ultimate science. He attacked the Ecole Polytechnique in that work, and the result was that in 1844 his lectureship there was not renewed. By 1851 he had completed the four-volume *Système de Politique Positive*, which had a more practical intent of offering a grand plan for the reorganization of society.

Comte had a series of bizarre ideas. For example, he believed in "cerebral hygiene"; that is, Comte avoided reading the work of other people, with the result that he became hopelessly out of touch with intellectual developments. Comte also came to fancy himself as the high priest of a new religion of humanity; he believed in a world that eventually would be led by sociologist-priests. In spite of such outrageous ideas, Comte developed a considerable following in France as well as in other countries.

Auguste Comte died on September 5, 1857.

Comte was in the forefront of the development of positivistic sociology (Bryant, 1985; Halfpenny, 1982). To Jonathan Turner, Comte's positivism emphasized that "the social universe is amenable to the development of abstract laws that can be tested through the careful collection of data," and "these abstract laws will denote the basic and generic properties of the social universe and they will specify their 'natural relations'" (1985:24). As we will see, a number of classical theorists (especially Spencer and Durkheim) shared Comte's interest in the discovery of the laws of social life.

Even though Comte lacked a solid academic base on which to build a school of Comtian sociological theory, he nevertheless laid a basis for the development of a significant stream of sociological theory. But his long-term significance is dwarfed by that of his successor in French sociology and the inheritor of a number of its ideas, Emile Durkheim.

Emile Durkheim (1858–1917) Although for Durkheim, as for Comte, the Enlightenment was a negative influence, it also had a number of positive effects on his work (for example, the emphasis on science and social reformism). However, Durkheim is best seen as the inheritor of the conservative tradition, especially as it was manifested in Comte's work. But whereas Comte had remained outside of academia, Durkheim developed an increasingly solid academic base as his career progressed. Durkheim legitimized sociology in France, and his work ultimately became a dominant force in the development of sociology in general and of sociological theory in particular.

Durkheim was politically liberal, but he took a more conservative position intellectually. Like Comte and the Catholic counterrevolutionaries, Durkheim feared and hated social disorder. His work was informed by the disorders produced by the general social changes discussed earlier in this chapter, as well as by others (such as industrial strikes, disruption of the ruling class, church-state discord, the rise of political anti-Semitism) more specific to the France of Durkheim's time (Karady, 1983). In fact, most of his work was devoted to the study of social order. His view was that social disorders were *not* a necessary part of the modern world and could be reduced by social reforms. Whereas Marx saw the problems of the modern world as inherent in society, Durkheim (along with most other classical theorists) did not. As a result, Marx's ideas on the need for social revolution stood in sharp contrast to the reformism of Durkheim and the others. As classical sociological theory developed, it was the Durkheimian interest in order and reform that came to dominate, while the Marxian position was eclipsed.

In two books published in the late 1800s, Durkheim developed a distinctive conception of the subject matter of sociology and then tested it in an empirical study. In *The Rules of Sociological Method* (1895/1964), Durkheim argued that it is the special task of sociology to study what he called *social facts*. He conceived of social facts as forces (Takla and Pope, 1985) and structures that are external to, and coercive of, the individual. The study of these large-scale structures and forces—for example, institutionalized law and shared moral beliefs—and their impact on people became the concern of many later sociological theorists (Parsons, for example). Durkheim was not content simply to define the subject matter of sociology; he sought through sociological research to demonstrate the utility of such a focus. He chose as his subject suicide. In a book entitled *Suicide* (1897/1951), Durkheim reasoned that if he could link such an individual behavior as suicide to social causes (social facts), he would have made a persuasive case for the importance of the discipline of sociology. But Durkheim did not examine why individual *A* or *B* committed suicide; rather he was interested in the causes of differences in suicide rates among groups, regions, countries, and different categories of people (for example, married and single). His basic argument was that it was the nature of, and changes in, social facts that led to differences in suicide rates. For example, a war or an economic depression would create a collective mood of depression that would in turn lead to increases in suicide rates. As we will see in Chapter 3, on Durkheim, there is much more to be said on this subject, but the key point for our purposes here is that Durkheim developed a distinctive view of sociology and sought to demonstrate its usefulness in a scientific study of suicide.

In *The Rules of Sociological Method*, Durkheim differentiated between two types of social facts—material and nonmaterial. Although he dealt with both in the course of his work, his main focus was on *nonmaterial social facts* (for example, culture, social institutions) rather than *material social facts* (for example, bureaucracy, law). This concern for nonmaterial social facts was already clear in his earliest major work, *The Division of Labor in Society* (1893/1964). His focus there was a comparative analysis of what held society together in the primitive and modern cases. He concluded that earlier societies were held together primarily by nonmaterial social facts, specifically, a strongly held common morality, or what he called a strong "collective conscience." However, because of the complexities of modern society, there had been a decline in the strength of the collective conscience. The primary bond in the modern world was an intricate division of labor, which tied people to others in dependency relationships. However, Durkheim felt that the modern division of labor brought with it several "pathologies"; it was, in other words, an inadequate method of holding society together. Given his conservative sociology, Durkheim did not feel that revolution was needed to solve these problems. Rather, he suggested a variety of reforms that could "patch up" the modern system and keep it functioning. Although he recognized that there was no going back to the age when a powerful collective conscience predominated, he did feel that the common morality could be strengthened in modern society and that people thereby could cope better with the pathologies that they were experiencing.

In his later work, nonmaterial social facts occupied an even more central position. In fact, he came to focus on perhaps the ultimate form of a nonmaterial social fact—religion—in his last major work, *The Elementary Forms of Religious Life* (1912/1965). In this work, Durkheim examined primitive society in order to find the roots of religion. He believed that he would be better able to find those roots in the comparative simplicity of primitive society than in the complexity of the modern world. What he found, he felt, was that the source of religion was society itself. Society comes to define certain things as religious and others as profane. Specifically, in the case he studied, the clan was the source of a primitive kind of religion, *totemism*, in which things like plants and animals are deified. Totemism, in turn, was seen as a specific type of nonmaterial social fact, a form of the collective conscience. In the end, Durkheim came to argue that society and religion (or, more generally, the collective conscience) were one and the same. Religion was the way society expressed itself in the form of a nonmaterial social fact. In a sense, then, Durkheim came to deify society and its major products. Clearly, in deifying society, Durkheim took a highly conservative stance: one would not want to overturn a deity *or* its societal source. Because he identified society with God, Durkheim was not inclined to urge social revolution. Instead, he was a social reformer seeking ways of improving the functioning of society. In these and other ways, Durkheim was clearly in line with French conservative sociology. The fact that he avoided many of its excesses helped make him the most significant figure in French sociology.

These books and other important works helped carve out a distinctive domain for sociology in the academic world of turn of the century France, and they earned Durkheim the leading position in that growing field. In 1898, Durkheim set up a scholarly journal devoted to sociology, *L'année sociologique* (Besnard, 1983a). It became a powerful force in the development and spread of sociological ideas. Durkheim was intent on fostering the growth of sociology, and he used his journal as a focal point for the development of a group of disciples. They would later extend his ideas and carry them to many other locales and into the study of other aspects of the social world (for example, sociology of law and sociology of the city) (Besnard, 1983a:1). By 1910, Durkheim had established a strong center of sociology in France, and the academic institutionalization of sociology was well under way in that nation. (For an overview of more recent developments in French sociology, see Lemert [1981].)

The Development of German Sociology

Whereas the early history of French sociology is a fairly coherent story of the progression from the Enlightenment and the French Revolution to the conservative reaction and to the increasingly important sociological ideas of Saint-Simon, Comte, and Durkheim, German sociology was fragmented from the beginning. A split developed between Marx (and his supporters), who remained on the edge of sociology, and the early giants of mainstream German sociology, Max Weber and Georg Simmel.[5] However, although Marxian theory itself was deemed unacceptable, its ideas found their way in a variety of positive and negative ways into mainstream German sociology. Our discussion here is divided between Marxian and non-Marxian theory in Germany.

The Roots and Nature of the Theories of Karl Marx (1818–1883)   The dominant intellectual influence on Karl Marx was the German philosopher G. W. F. Hegel (1770–1831). Marx's education at the University of Berlin was shaped by Hegel's ideas as well as by the split that developed among Hegel's followers after his death. The "Old Hegelians" continued to subscribe to the

---

[5] For an argument against this and the view of continuity between Marxian and mainstream sociology, see Seidman (1983).

master's ideas, while the "Young Hegelians," although still working in the Hegelian tradition, were critical of many facets of his philosophical system. Among the Young Hegelians was Ludwig Feuerbach (1804–1872), who tried to revise Hegel's ideas. Marx was influenced by both Hegel's ideas and Feuerbach's revisions, but he extended and combined the two philosophies in a novel and insightful way.

Two concepts represent the essence of Hegel's philosophy—the dialectic and idealism (Hegel, 1807/1967, 1821/1967). The very complicated idea of the dialectic will be discussed in Chapter 2, on Marx, but a few introductory remarks are needed at this point. The *dialectic* is both a way of thinking and an image of the world. On the one hand, it is a way of thinking that stresses the importance of processes, relations, dynamics, conflicts, and contradictions—a dynamic rather than a static way of thinking about the world. On the other hand, it is a view that the *world* is made up not of static structures but of processes, relationships, dynamics, conflicts, and contradictions. Although the dialectic is generally associated with Hegel, it certainly predates him in philosophy. Marx, trained in the Hegelian tradition, accepted the significance of the dialectic. However, he was critical of some aspects of the way Hegel used it. For example, Hegel tended to apply the dialectic only to ideas, whereas Marx felt that it applied as well to more material aspects of life, for example, the economy.

Hegel is also associated with the philosophy of *idealism*, which emphasizes the importance of the mind and mental products rather than the material world. It is the social definition of the physical and material worlds that matters most, not those worlds themselves. In its extreme form, idealism asserts that *only* the mind and psychological constructs exist. Some idealists believed that their mental processes would remain the same even if the physical and social worlds no longer existed. Idealists emphasize not only mental processes but also the ideas produced by these processes. Hegel paid a great deal of attention to the development of such ideas, especially to what he referred to as the "spirit" of society.

In fact, Hegel offered a kind of evolutionary theory of the world in idealistic terms. At first, people were endowed only with the ability to acquire a sensory understanding of the world around them. They could understand things like the sight, smell, and feel of the social and physical world. Later, people developed the ability to be conscious of, to understand, themselves. With self-knowledge and self-understanding, people began to understand that they could become more than they were. In terms of Hegel's dialectical approach, a contradiction developed between what people were and what they felt that they could be. The resolution of this contradiction lay in the development of an individual's awareness of his or her place in the larger spirit of society. Individuals come to realize that their ultimate fulfillment lies in the development and the expansion of the spirit of society as a whole. Thus, individuals in Hegel's scheme evolve from an understanding of things to an understanding of self to an understanding of their place in the larger scheme of things.

Hegel, then, offered a general theory of the evolution of the world. It is a subjective theory in which change is held to occur at the level of consciousness. However, that change occurs largely beyond the control of actors. Actors are reduced to little more than vessels swept along by the inevitable evolution of consciousness.

Ludwig Feuerbach was an important bridge between Hegel and Marx. As a Young Hegelian, Feuerbach was critical of Hegel for, among other things, his excessive emphasis on consciousness and the spirit of society. Feuerbach's adoption of a materialist philosophy led him to argue that what was needed was to move from Hegel's subjective idealism to a focus not on ideas but on the material reality of real human beings. In his critique of Hegel, Feuerbach focused on religion. To Feuerbach, God is simply a projection by people of their human essence onto an impersonal force. People set God over and above themselves, with the result that they become alienated from God and project a series of positive characteristics onto God (that He is perfect, almighty, and holy), while they reduce themselves to being imperfect, powerless, and sinful. Feuerbach argued that this kind of religion must be overcome and that its defeat could be aided by a materialist philosophy in which people (not religion) became their own highest object, ends in themselves. Real people, not abstract ideas like religion, are deified by a materialist philosophy.

Marx was simultaneously influenced by, and critical of, *both* Hegel and Feuerbach. Marx, following Feuerbach, was critical of Hegel's adherence to an idealist philosophy. Marx took this position not only because of his adoption of a materialist orientation but also because of his interest in practical activities. Social facts like wealth and the state are treated by Hegel as ideas rather than as real, material entities. Even when he examined a seemingly material process like labor, Hegel was looking only at abstract mental labor. This is very different from Marx's interest in the labor of real, sentient people. Thus Hegel was looking at the wrong issues as far as Marx was concerned. In addition, Marx felt that Hegel's idealism led to a very conservative political orientation. To Hegel, the process of evolution was occurring beyond the control of people and their activities. In any case, in that people seemed to be moving toward greater consciousness of the world as it could be, there seemed no need for any revolutionary change; the process was already moving in the "desired" direction. Whatever problems did exist lay in consciousness, and the answer therefore seemed to lie in changing thinking.

Marx took a very different position, arguing that the problems of modern life can be traced to real, material sources (for example, the structures of capitalism) and that the solutions, therefore, can be found *only* in the overturning of those structures by the collective action of large numbers of people (Marx and Engels, 1845/1956:254). Whereas Hegel "stood the world on its head" (that is, focused on consciousness, not the real material world), Marx firmly embedded his dialectic in a material base.

Marx applauded Feuerbach's critique of Hegel on a number of counts (for example, its materialism and its rejection of the abstractness of Hegel's theory), but he was far from fully satisfied with Feuerbach's own position. For one thing, Feuerbach focused on the religious world, whereas Marx believed that it was the entire social world, and the economy in particular, that had to be analyzed. Although Marx accepted Feuerbach's materialism, he felt that Feuerbach had gone too far in focusing one-sidedly, nondialectically, on the material world. Feuerbach failed to include the most important of Hegel's contributions, the dialectic, in his materialist orientation, particularly the relationship between people and the material world. Finally, Marx argued that Feuerbach, like most philosophers, failed to emphasize praxis—practical activity—in particular, revolutionary activity. As Marx put it, "The philosophers have only *interpreted* the world, in various ways; the point, however, is to *change* it" (cited in Tucker, 1970:109).

Marx extracted what he considered to be the two most important elements from these two thinkers—Hegel's dialectic and Feuerbach's materialism—and fused them into his own distinctive orientation, *dialectical materialism*, which focuses on dialectical relationships within the material world.

Marx's materialism and his consequent focus on the economic sector led him rather naturally to the work of a group of *political economists* (for example, Adam Smith and David Ricardo). Marx was very attracted to a number of their positions. He lauded their basic premise that labor was the source of all wealth. This ultimately led Marx to his *labor theory of value*, in which he argued that the profit of the capitalist was based on the exploitation of the laborer. Capitalists performed the rather simple trick of paying the workers less than they deserved, because they received less pay than the value of what they actually produced in a work period. This *surplus value*, which was retained and reinvested by the capitalist, was the basis of the entire capitalist system. The capitalist system grew by continually increasing the level of exploitation of the workers (and therefore the amount of surplus value) and investing the profits for the expansion of the system.

Marx also was affected by the political economists' depiction of the horrors of the capitalist system and the exploitation of the workers. However, whereas they depicted the evils of capitalism, Marx criticized the political economists for seeing these evils as inevitable components of capitalism. Marx deplored their general acceptance of capitalism and the way they urged people to work for economic success within it. He also was critical of the political economists for failing to see the inherent conflict between capitalists and laborers and for denying the need for a radical change in the economic order. Such conservative economics was hard for Marx to accept, given his commitment to a radical change from capitalism to socialism.

Marx was not a sociologist and did not consider himself to be one. Although his work is too broad to be encompassed by the term *sociology*, there is a sociological theory to be found in Marx's work. From the beginning, there were those who were heavily influenced by Marx, and there has been a continuous strand of Marxian sociology, primarily in Europe. But for the majority of early sociologists, his work was a negative force, something against which to shape their sociology. Until very recently, sociological theory, especially in America, has been characterized by either hostility to or ignorance of Marxian theory. This has, as we will see in Chapter 6, changed dramatically in the last two decades, but the negative reaction to Marx's work was a major force in the shaping of much of sociological theory (Gurney, 1981).

The basic reason for this rejection of Marx was ideological. Many of the early sociological theorists were inheritors of the conservative reaction to the disruptions of the Enlightenment and the French Revolution. Marx's radical ideas and the radical social changes he foretold and sought to bring to life were clearly feared and hated by such thinkers. Marx was dismissed as an ideologist. It was argued that he was not a serious sociological theorist. However, ideology per se could not have been the real reason for the rejection of Marx, because the work of Comte, Durkheim, and other conservative thinkers was also heavily ideological. It was the nature of the ideology, not the existence of ideology as such, that put off many sociological theorists. They were ready and eager to buy conservative ideology wrapped in a cloak of sociological theory, but not the radical ideology offered by Marx and his followers.

There were, of course, other reasons why Marx was not accepted by many early theorists. He seemed to be more an economist than a sociologist. Although the early sociologists would certainly admit the importance of the economy, they would also argue that it was only one of a number of components of social life.

Another reason for the early rejection of Marx was the nature of his interests. Whereas the early sociologists were reacting to the disorder created by the Enlightenment, the French Revolution, and later the Industrial Revolution, Marx was not upset by these disorders—or by disorder in general. Rather, what interested and concerned Marx most was the oppressiveness of the capitalist system that was emerging out of the Industrial Revolution. Marx wanted to develop a theory that explained this oppressiveness and that would help overthrow that system. Marx's interest was in revolution, which stood in contrast to the conservative concern for reform and orderly change.

Another difference worth noting is the difference in philosophical roots between Marxian and conservative sociological theory. Most of the conservative theorists were heavily influenced by the philosophy of Immanuel Kant. Among other things, this led them to think in linear, cause-and-effect terms. That is, they tended to argue that a change in A (say, the change in ideas during the Enlightenment) leads to a change in B (say, the political changes of the French Revolution). In contrast, Marx was most heavily influenced, as we have seen, by Hegel, who thought in dialectical rather than cause-and-effect terms. Among other things, the dialectic attunes us to the ongoing reciprocal effects of social forces. Thus, a dialectician would reconceptualize the example discussed above as a continual, ongoing interplay of ideas and politics. It is admittedly difficult to get a feel for the complicated differences between Kantian and Hegelian philosophy, but the crucial point for our purposes is that these basic philosophical differences were an important source of the negative reaction of early sociological theorists to Marxian theory.

Many volumes have been written about the substance of Marx's theory, and we devote Chapter 2 to it. Marx published most of his major works in the middle third of the nineteenth century. Not only is there a great deal of his work, but it is a difficult body of work, not easy to summarize.

To oversimplify enormously, Marx offered a theory of capitalist society based on his image of the basic nature of human beings. Marx believed that people are basically productive; that is, in order to survive, people need to work in, and with, nature. In so doing, they produce the food, clothing, tools, shelter, and other necessities that permit them to live. Their productivity is a perfectly natural way by which they express basic creative impulses. Furthermore, these impulses are expressed in concert with other people; in other words, people are inherently social. They need to work together to produce what they need to survive.

Throughout history this natural process has been subverted, at first by the mean conditions of primitive society and later by a variety of structural arrangements erected by societies in the course of history. In various ways, these structures interfered with the natural productive process. However, it is in capitalist society that this breakdown is most acute; the breakdown in the natural productive process reaches its culmination in capitalism.

Basically capitalism is a structure (or, more accurately, a series of structures) that erects barriers between an individual and the production process, the products of that process, and other people; ultimately, it even divides the individual himself or herself. This is the basic meaning of the concept of *alienation*: it is the breakdown of the natural interconnection between people and between people and what they produce. Alienation occurs because capitalism has evolved into a two-class system in which a few capitalists own the production process, the products, and the labor time of those who work for them. Instead of naturally producing for themselves, people produce unnaturally in capitalist society for a small group of capitalists. Intellectually, Marx was very concerned with the structures of capitalism and their oppressive impact on actors. Politically, he was led to an interest in emancipating people from the oppressive structures of capitalism.

Marx actually spent very little time dreaming about what a utopian socialist state would look like. He was more concerned with helping to bring about the demise of capitalism. He believed that the contradictions and conflicts within capitalism would lead dialectically to its ultimate collapse, but he did not think that the process was inevitable. People had to act at the appropriate times and in the appropriate ways for socialism to come into being. The capitalists have great resources at their disposal to forestall the coming of socialism, but they could be overcome by the concerted action of a class-conscious proletariat. What would the proletariat create in the process? What is socialism? Most basically, it is a society in which, for the first time, people could

approach Marx's ideal image of productivity. With the aid of modern technology, people could interact harmoniously with nature and other people to
create what they needed to survive. To put it another way, in socialist society,
people would no longer be alienated.

**The Roots and Nature of the Theories of Max Weber (1864–1920) and
Georg Simmel (1858–1918)**   Although Marx and his followers in the late
nineteenth and early twentieth centuries remained outside of mainstream German sociology, to a considerable extent early German sociology can be seen
as developing in opposition to Marxian theory. In the view of some, this
explains a large part of the theory of the early giant of German sociology,
Max Weber. Albert Salomon, for example, claimed that Weberian theory
developed "in a long and intense debate with the ghost of Marx" (1945:596).
This is probably an exaggeration, but in many ways Marxian theory did play
a negative role in Weberian theory. In other ways, however, Weber was working *within* the Marxian tradition, trying to "round out" Marx's theory. Also,
there were many inputs into Weberian theory other than Marxian theory
(Burger, 1976). We can clarify a good deal about the sources of German sociology by outlining each of these views of the relationship between Marx and
Weber (Antonio and Glassman, 1985; Schroeter, 1985). It should be borne in
mind that Weber was not intimately familiar with Marx's work (much of it
was not published until after Weber's death) and that Weber was reacting
more to the work of the Marxists than to Marx's work itself (Antonio, 1985:29;
B. Turner, 1981:19–20).

Weber *did* tend to view Marx and the Marxists of his day as economic
determinists who offered single-cause theories of social life. That is, Marxian
theory was seen as tracing all historical developments to economic bases and
viewing all contemporaneous structures as erected on an economic base.
Although this is not true of Marx's own theory (as we will see in Chapter 2),
it was the position of many later Marxists.

One of the examples of economic determinism that seemed to rankle Weber
most was the view that ideas are simply the reflections of material (especially
economic) interests, that material interests determine ideology. From this point
of view, Weber was supposed to have "turned Marx on his head" (much as
Marx had inverted Hegel). Instead of focusing on economic factors and their
effect on ideas, Weber devoted much of his attention to ideas and their effect
on the economy. Rather than seeing ideas as simple reflections of economic
factors, Weber saw them as fairly autonomous forces capable of profoundly
affecting the economic world. Weber certainly devoted a lot of attention to
ideas, particularly systems of religious ideas, and he was especially concerned
with the impact of religious ideas on the economy. In *The Protestant Ethic and
the Spirit of Capitalism* (1904–1905/1958), he was concerned with Protestantism,
mainly as a system of ideas, and its impact on the rise of another system of
ideas, the "spirit of capitalism," and ultimately on a capitalist economic system. Weber had a similar interest in other world religions, looking at how

their nature might have obstructed the development of capitalism in their respective societies. On the basis of this kind of work, some scholars came to the conclusion that Weber developed his ideas in opposition to those of Marx.

A second view of Weber's relationship to Marx, as mentioned earlier, is that he did not so much oppose Marx as try to round out his theoretical perspective. Here Weber is seen as working more within the Marxian tradition than in opposition to it. His work on religion, interpreted from this point of view, was simply an effort to show that not only do material factors affect ideas but ideas themselves affect material structures. This interpretation of Weber's work obviously places it much closer to, in fact in line with, Marxian theory.

A good example of the view that Weber was engaged in a process of rounding out Marxian theory is in the area of stratification theory. In this work on stratification, Marx focused on social *class*, the economic dimension of stratification. Although Weber accepted the importance of this factor, he argued that other dimensions of stratification were also important. He argued that the notion of social stratification should be extended to include stratification on the basis of prestige (*status*) and *power*. The inclusion of these other dimensions does not constitute a refutation of Marx but is simply an extension of his ideas.

Both of the views outlined above accept the importance of Marxian theory for Weber. There are elements of truth in both positions; at some points Weber *was* working in opposition to Marx, while at other points he *was* extending Marx's ideas. However, a third view of this issue may best characterize the relationship between Marx and Weber. In this view, Marx is simply seen as only one of many influences on Weber's thought.

We can identify a number of sources of Weberian theory, including German historians, philosophers, economists, and political theorists. Among those who influenced Weber, the philosopher Immanuel Kant (1724–1804) stands out above all the others. But we must not overlook the impact of Friedrich Nietzsche (1844–1900)—especially his emphasis on the hero—on Weber's work on the need for individuals to stand up to the impact of bureaucracies and other structures of modern society.

The influence of Immanuel Kant on Weber and on German sociology generally shows that German sociology and Marxism grew from different philosophical roots. As we have seen, it was Hegel, not Kant, who was the important philosophical influence on Marxian theory. Whereas Hegel's philosophy led Marx and the Marxists to look for relations, conflicts, and contradictions, Kantian philosophy led at least some German sociologists to take a more static perspective. To Kant the world was a buzzing confusion of events that could never be known directly. The world could only be known through thought processes that filter, select, and categorize these events. The content of the real world was differentiated by Kant from the forms through which that content can be comprehended. The emphasis on these forms gave the work of those sociologists within the Kantian tradition a more static quality than that of the Marxists within the Hegelian tradition.

German sociology emerged in a complex interplay with Marxian theory and a variety of other intellectual currents. The foremost exponents of early German sociology were Max Weber and Georg Simmel.

Whereas Karl Marx offered basically a theory of capitalism, Weber's work was fundamentally a theory of the process of rationalization (Brubaker, 1984; Kalberg, 1980, 1990). Weber was interested in the general issue of why institutions in the Western world had grown progressively more rational while powerful barriers seemed to prevent a similar development in the rest of the world.

Although rationality is used in many different ways in Weber's work, what interests us here is a process involving one of four types identified by Kalberg (1980, 1990; see also Brubaker, 1984; Levine, 1981), *formal rationality*. Formal rationality involves, as was usually the case with Weber, a concern for the actor making choices of means and ends. However, in this case, that choice is made in reference to universally applied rules, regulations, and laws. These, in turn, are derived from various large-scale structures, especially bureaucracies and the economy. Weber developed his theories in the context of a large number of comparative historical studies of the West, China, India, and many other regions of the world. In these studies, he sought to delineate the factors that helped bring about or impede the development of rationalization.

Weber saw the bureaucracy (and the historical process of bureaucratization) as the classic example of rationalization, but rationalization is perhaps best illustrated today by the fast-food restaurant (Luxenberg, 1985; Ritzer, 1983, forthcoming a). The fast-food restaurant is a formally rational system in which people (both workers and customers) are led to seek the most rational means to ends. The drive-through window, for example, is a rational means by which workers can dispense, and customers can obtain, food quickly and efficiently. Speed and efficiency are dictated by the fast-food restaurants and the rules and regulations by which they operate.

Weber embedded his discussion of the process of bureaucratization in a broader discussion of the political institution. He differentiated among three types of authority systems—traditional, charismatic, and rational-legal. Only in the modern Western world can a rational-legal authority system develop, and only within that system does one find the full-scale development of the modern bureaucracy. The rest of the world remains dominated by traditional or charismatic authority systems, which generally impede the development of a rational-legal authority system and modern bureaucracies. Briefly, *traditional* authority stems from a long-lasting system of beliefs. An example would be a leader who comes to power because his or her family or clan has always provided the group's leadership. A *charismatic* leader derives his or her authority from extraordinary abilities or characteristics, or more likely simply from the *belief* on the part of followers that the leader has such traits. Although these two types of authority are of historical importance, Weber believed that the trend in the West, and ultimately in the rest of the world, is toward systems of *rational-legal* authority. In such systems, authority is derived from rules legally and rationally enacted. Thus, the president of the United States derives his authority ultimately from the laws of society. The evolution of rational-legal authority, with its accompanying bureaucracies, is only one part of Weber's general argument on the rationalization of the Western world.

Weber also did detailed and sophisticated analyses of the rationalization of such phenomena as religion, law, the city, and even music. But we can illustrate Weber's mode of thinking with one other example—the rationalization of the economic institution. This discussion is couched in Weber's broader analysis of the relationship between religion and capitalism. In a wide-ranging historical study, Weber sought to understand why a rational economic system (capitalism) had developed in the West and why it had failed to develop in the rest of the world. Weber accorded a central role to religion in this process. At one level, he was engaged in a dialogue with the Marxists in an effort to show that, contrary to what many Marxists of the day believed, religion was not merely an epiphenomenon. Instead, it had played a key role in the rise of capitalism in the West and in its failure to develop elsewhere in the world. Weber argued that it was a distinctively rational religious system (Calvinism) that played the central role in the rise of capitalism in the West. In contrast, in the other parts of the world that he studied, Weber found more irrational religious systems (for example, Confucianism, Taoism, Hinduism), which helped to inhibit the development of a rational economic system. However, in the end, one gets the feeling that these religions provided only temporary barriers, for the economic systems—indeed, the entire social structure—of these societies ultimately would become rationalized.

There is a great deal more to Weberian theory than this. For example, his work on rationalization has much more historical detail and innumerable theoretical insights. Beyond that, although rationalization lies at the heart of Weberian theory, it is far from all there is to the theory. But this is not the place to go into that rich body of material. Instead, let us return to the development of sociological theory. A key issue in that development is: Why did Weber's theory prove more attractive to later sociological theorists than Marxian theory?

One reason is that Weber proved to be more acceptable politically. Instead of espousing Marxian radicalism, Weber was more of a liberal on some issues and a conservative on others (for example, the role of the state). Although he was a severe critic of many aspects of modern capitalist society and came to many of the same critical conclusions as did Marx, he was not one to propose radical solutions to problems. In fact, he felt that the radical reforms offered by many Marxists and other socialists would do more harm than good.

Later sociological theorists, especially Americans, saw their society under attack by Marxian theory. Largely conservative in orientation, they cast about for theoretical alternatives to Marxism. One of those who proved attractive was Max Weber. (Durkheim and Vilfredo Pareto were others.) After all, rationalization affected not only capitalist but also socialist societies. Indeed, from Weber's point of view, rationalization constituted an even greater problem in socialist than in capitalist societies.

Also in Weber's favor was the form in which he presented his judgments. He spent most of his life doing detailed historical studies, and his political conclusions were often made within the context of his research. Thus they usually sounded very scientific and academic. Marx, although he did much serious research, also wrote a good deal of explicitly polemical material. Even his more academic work is laced with acid political judgments. For example, in *Capital* (1867/1967), he described capitalists as "vampires" and "werewolves." Weber's more academic style helped make him more acceptable to later sociologists.

Another reason for the greater acceptability of Weber was that he operated in a philosophical tradition that also helped shape the work of later sociologists. That is, Weber operated in the Kantian tradition, which meant, among other things, that he tended to think in cause-and-effect terms. This kind of thinking was more acceptable to later sociologists, who were largely unfamiliar and uncomfortable with the dialectical logic that informed Marx's work.

Finally, Weber appeared to offer a much better rounded approach to the social world than Marx. Whereas Marx appeared to be almost totally preoccupied with the economy, Weber was interested in a wide range of social phenomena. This diversity of focus seemed to give later sociologists more to work with than the apparently more single-minded concerns of Marx.

Weber produced most of his major works in the late 1800s and early 1900s. Early in his career, Weber was identified more as a historian who was concerned with sociological issues, but in the early 1900s his focus grew more and more sociological. Indeed, he became the dominant sociologist of his time in Germany. In 1910, he founded (with, among others, Georg Simmel, whom we discuss below) the German Sociological Society. His home in Heidelberg was an intellectual center not only for sociologists but for scholars from many fields. Although his work was broadly influential in Germany, it was to become even more influential in the United States, especially after Talcott Parsons introduced Weber's ideas (and those of other European theorists, especially Durkheim) to a large American audience. Although Marx's ideas did not have a significant positive effect on American sociological theorists until the 1960s, Weber was already highly influential by the late 1930s.

Georg Simmel was Weber's contemporary and a cofounder of the German Sociological Society. As with Marx and Weber, we will devote a chapter to Simmel (Chapter 5); here we place him within the historical development of sociological theory.

Simmel was a somewhat atypical sociological theorist (Frisby, 1981; Levine, Carter, and Gorman, 1976a, 1976b). For one thing, he had an immediate and profound effect on the development of American sociological theory, whereas Marx and Weber were largely ignored for a number of years. Simmel's work

helped shape the development of one of the early centers of American sociology—the University of Chicago—and its major theory, symbolic interactionism. The Chicago school and symbolic interactionism came, as we will see, to
dominate American sociology in the 1920s and early 1930s (Bulmer, 1984).
Simmel's ideas were influential at Chicago mainly because the dominant figures in the early years of Chicago, Albion Small and Robert Park, had been
exposed to Simmel's theories in Berlin in the late 1800s. Park attended Simmel's lectures in 1899 and 1900, and Small carried on an extensive correspondence with Simmel during the 1890s. They were instrumental in bringing
Simmel's ideas to students and faculty at Chicago, in translating some of his
work, and in bringing it to the attention of a large-scale American audience
(Frisby, 1984:29).

Another atypical aspect of Simmel's work is his "level" of analysis, or at
least that level for which he became best known in America. Whereas Weber
and Marx were preoccupied with large-scale issues like the rationalization of
society and a capitalist economy, Simmel was best known for his work on
smaller-scale issues, especially individual action and interaction. He became
famous early for his thinking, derived from Kantian philosophy, on *forms* of
interaction (for example, conflict) and *types* of interactants (for example, the
stranger). Basically, Simmel saw that understanding interaction among people
was one of the major tasks of sociology. However, it was impossible to study
the massive number of interactions in social life without some conceptual
tools. This is where forms of interaction and types of interactants came in.
Simmel felt that he could isolate a limited number of forms of interaction that
could be found in a large number of social settings. Thus equipped, one could
analyze and understand these different interaction settings. The development
of a limited number of types of interactants could be similarly useful in
explaining interaction settings. This work had a profound effect on symbolic
interactionism, which, as the name suggests, was focally concerned with interaction. One of the ironies, however, is that Simmel also was concerned with
large-scale issues similar to those that obsessed Marx and Weber. However,
this work was much less influential than his work on interaction, although
there are contemporary signs of a growing interest in the large-scale aspects
of Simmel's sociology.

It was partly Simmel's style in his work on interaction that made him accessible to early American sociological theorists. Although he wrote heavy tomes
like Weber and Marx, he also wrote a set of deceptively simple essays on such
interesting topics as poverty, the prostitute, the miser and the spendthrift, and
the stranger. The brevity of such essays and the high interest level of the
material made the dissemination of Simmel's ideas much easier. Unfortunately, the essays had the negative effect of obscuring Simmel's more massive
works (for example, *Philosophy of Money*, translated in 1978), which were
potentially as significant to sociology. Nevertheless, it was partly through the
short and clever essays that Simmel had a much more significant effect on
early American sociological theory than either Marx or Weber.

We should not leave Simmel without saying something about *Philosophy of*

Money, because its English translation has made Simmel's work attractive to a whole new set of theorists interested in culture and society. Although this macro orientation is clearer in *Philosophy of Money*, it always existed in Simmel's work. For example, it is clear in his famous work on the dyad and the triad. Simmel thought that some crucial sociological developments take place when a two-person group (or *dyad*) is transformed into a *triad* by the addition of a third party. Social possibilities emerge that simply could not exist in a dyad. For example, in a triad, one of the members can become an arbitrator or mediator of the differences between the other two. More important, two of the members can band together and dominate the other member. This represents on a small scale what can happen with the emergence of large-scale structures that become separate from individuals and begin to dominate them.

This theme lies at the base of *Philosophy of Money*. Simmel was primarily concerned with the emergence in the modern world of a money economy that becomes separate from the individual and predominant. This theme, in turn, is part of an even broader and more pervasive one in Simmel's work, the domination of the culture as a whole over the individual. As Simmel saw it, in the modern world, the larger culture and all its various components (including the money economy) expand, and as they expand, the importance of the individual decreases. Thus, for example, as the industrial technology associated with a modern economy expands and grows more sophisticated, the skills and abilities of the individual worker grow progressively less important. In the end, the worker is confronted with an industrial machine over which he or she can exert little, if any, control. More generally, Simmel thought that in the modern world, the expansion of the larger culture leads to the growing insignificance of the individual.

Although sociologists have become increasingly attuned to the broader implications of Simmel's work, his early influence was primarily through his studies of small-scale social phenomena, such as the forms of interaction and types of interactants.

The Origins of British Sociology

We have been examining the development of sociology in France (Comte, Durkheim) and Germany (Marx, Weber, and Simmel). We turn now to the parallel development of sociology in England. As we will see, Continental ideas had their impact on early British sociology, but more important were native influences.

Political Economy, Ameliorism, and Social Evolution   Philip Abrams (1968) contended that British sociology was shaped in the nineteenth century by three often conflicting sources—political economy, ameliorism, and social evolution.[6] Thus when the Sociological Society of London was founded in 1903, there were strong differences over the definition of *sociology*. However, there were few who doubted the view that sociology could be a science. It

[6] For more recent developments in British sociology, see Abrams et al (1981).

SIGMUND FREUD: A Biographical Sketch

Another leading figure in German social science in the late 1800s and early 1900s was Sigmund Freud. Although he was not a sociologist, Freud influenced the work of many sociologists and continues to be of relevance to sociologists (Carveth, 1982).

Sigmund Freud was born in the Austro-Hungarian city of Freiberg on May 6, 1856 (Puner, 1947). In 1859, his family moved to Vienna, and in 1873, Freud entered the medical school at the University of Vienna. Freud was more interested in science than medicine and took a position in a physiology laboratory. He completed his degree in medicine, and after leaving the laboratory in 1882, he worked in a hospital and then set up a private medical practice with a specialty in nervous diseases.

Freud at first used hypnosis in an effort to deal with a type of neurosis known as *hysteria*. He had learned the technique in Paris from Jean Martin Charcot in 1885. Later he adopted a technique, pioneered by a fellow Viennese physician, Joseph Breuer, in which hysterical symptoms disappeared when the patient talked through the circumstances in which the symptoms first arose. By 1895, Freud had published a book with Breuer with a series of revolutionary implications: that the causes of neuroses like hysteria were psychological (not, as had been believed, physiological) and that the therapy involved talking through the original causes. Thus was born the practical and theoretical field of *psychoanalysis*. Freud began to part company with Breuer as he came to see sexual factors, or more generally the *libido*, at the root of neuroses. Over the next several years, Freud refined his therapeutic techniques and wrote a great deal about his new ideas.

By 1902, Freud began to gather a number of disciples around him, and they met weekly at his house. By 1903 or 1904, others (like Carl Jung) began to use Freud's ideas in their psychiatric practices. In 1908, the first Psychoanalytic Congress was held, and the next year a periodical for disseminating psychoanalytic knowledge was formed. As quickly as it had formed, the new field of psychoanalysis became splintered as Freud broke with people like Jung and they went off to develop their own ideas and found their own groups. World War I slowed the development of psychoanalysis, but it expanded and developed greatly in the 1920s. With the rise of Nazism, the center of psychoanalysis shifted to the United States, where it remains to this day. But Freud remained in Vienna until the Nazis took over in 1938, despite the fact that he was Jewish and the Nazis had burned his books as early as 1933. On June 4, 1938, only after a ransom had been paid and President Roosevelt had interceded, Sigmund Freud left Vienna. Freud had suffered from cancer of the jaw since 1923, and he died in London on September 23, 1939.

was the differences that gave British sociology its distinctive character, and we will look at each of them briefly.

We have already touched on *political economy*, which was a theory of industrial and capitalist society traceable in part to the work of Adam Smith (1723–1790).[7] As we saw, political economy had a profound effect on Karl Marx.

[7] Smith is usually included as a leading member of the Scottish Enlightenment (Chitnis, 1976) and as one of the Scottish Moralists (Schneider, 1967:xi), who were seeking to establish the basis for sociology.

Marx studied political economy closely, and he was critical of it. But that was not the direction taken by British economists and sociologists. They tended to accept Smith's idea that there was an "invisible hand" that shaped the market for labor and goods. The market was seen as an independent reality that stood above individuals and controlled their behavior. The British sociologists, like the political economists and unlike Marx, saw the market as a positive force, as a source of order, harmony, and integration in society. Because they saw the market, and more generally society, in a positive light, the task of the sociologists was not to criticize society but simply to gather data on the laws by which it operated. The goal was to provide the government with the facts it needed to understand the way the system worked and to direct its workings wisely.

The emphasis was on facts, but which facts? Whereas Marx, Weber, Durkheim, and Comte looked to the structures of society for their basic facts, the British thinkers tended to focus on the individuals who made up those structures. In dealing with large-scale structures, they tended to collect individual-level data and then combine them to form a collective portrait. In the mid-1800s it was the statisticians who dominated British social science, and this kind of data collection was deemed to be the major task of sociology. The objective was the accumulation of "pure" facts without theorizing or philosophizing. As Kent (1981:187) argues, these empirical sociologists were detached from the concerns of social theorists. Instead of general theorizing, the "emphasis settled on the business of producing more exact indicators, better methods of classification and data collection, improved life tables, higher levels of comparability between discrete bodies of data, and the like" (Abrams, 1968:18).

It was almost in spite of themselves that these statistically oriented sociologists came to see some limitations in their approach. A few sociologists began to feel the need for broader theorizing. To them, a problem such as poverty pointed to failings in the market system as well as in the society as a whole. But most, focused as they were on individuals, did not question the larger system; they turned instead to more detailed field studies and to the development of more complicated and more exact statistical techniques. To them, the source of the problem had to lie in inadequate research methods, *not* in the system as a whole. As Philip Abrams noted, "Focusing persistently on the distribution of individual circumstances, the statisticians found it hard to break through to a perception of poverty as a product of social structure. . . . They did not and probably could not achieve the concept of structural victimization" (1968:27). In addition to their theoretical and methodological commitments to the study of individuals, the statisticians worked too closely with government policy makers to arrive at the conclusion that the larger political and economic system was the problem.

Related to, but separable from, political economy was the second defining characteristic of British sociology—*ameliorism*, or a desire to solve social problems by reforming individuals. Although British scholars began to recognize that there were problems in society (for example, poverty), they still believed in that society and wanted to preserve it. They desired to forestall violence and revolution and to reform the system so that it could continue essentially as it was. Above all, they wanted to prevent the coming of a socialist society. Thus, like French sociology and some branches of German sociology, British sociology was conservatively oriented.

Because the British sociologists could not, or would not, trace the source of problems such as poverty to the society as a whole, the source had to lie within the individuals themselves. This was an early form of what William Ryan (1971) later called "blaming the victim." Much attention was devoted to a long series of individual problems—"ignorance, spiritual destitution, impurity, bad sanitation, pauperism, crime, and intemperance—above all intemperance" (Abrams, 1968:39). Clearly, there was a tendency to look for a simple cause for all social ills, and the one that suggested itself before all others was alcoholism. What made this perfect to the ameliorist was that this was an individual pathology, not a social pathology. The ameliorists lacked a theory of social structure, a theory of the social causes of such individual problems.

But a stronger sense of social structure was lurking below the surface of British sociology, and it burst through in the latter part of the nineteenth century with the growth of interest in *social evolution*. One important influence was the work of Auguste Comte, part of which had been translated into English in the 1850s. Although Comte's work did not inspire immediate interest, by the last quarter of the century, a number of thinkers had been attracted to it and to its concern for the larger structures of society, its scientific (positivistic) orientation, its comparative orientation, and its evolutionary theory. However, a number of British thinkers sharpened their own conception of the world in opposition to some of the excesses of Comtian theory (for example, the tendency to elevate sociology to the status of a religion).

In Abrams's view, the real importance of Comte lay in his providing one of the bases on which opposition could be mounted against the "oppressive genius of Herbert Spencer" (Abrams, 1968:58). In both a positive and a negative sense, Spencer was a dominant figure in British sociological theory, especially evolutionary theory.

Herbert Spencer (1820–1903) In attempting to understand Spencer's ideas, it is useful to compare and contrast them with Comtian theory. Spencer is often categorized with Comte in terms of their influence on the development of sociological theory, but there are some important differences between them. For example, it is less easy to categorize Spencer as a conservative. In fact, in his early years, Spencer is better seen as a political liberal, and he retained elements of liberalism throughout his life. However, it is also true that Spencer grew more conservative during the course of his life and that his basic influence, as was true of Comte, was conservative.

One of his liberal views, which coexisted rather uncomfortably with his conservatism, was his acceptance of a laissez-faire doctrine: he felt that the state should not intervene in individual affairs, except in the rather passive function of protecting people. This meant that Spencer, unlike Comte, was not interested in social reforms; he wanted social life to evolve free of external control.

This difference points to Spencer as a *Social Darwinist* (G. Jones, 1980). As such, he held the evolutionary view that the world was growing progressively better. Therefore, it should be left alone; outside interference could only worsen the situation. He adopted the view that social institutions, like plants and animals, adapted progressively and positively to their social environment. He also accepted the Darwinian view that a process of natural selection, "survival of the fittest," occurred in the social world. (Interestingly, it was Spencer who coined the phrase "survival of the fittest" several years *before* Charles Darwin's work on natural selection.) That is, if unimpeded by external intervention, people who were "fit" would survive and proliferate whereas the "unfit" would eventually die out. Another difference was that Spencer emphasized the individual, whereas Comte focused on larger units such as the family.

Although there are important differences between Comte and Spencer, their shared orientations, or at least the similar ways in which they were interpreted, proved to be more important than their differences for the development of sociological theory.

Comte and Spencer shared with Durkheim and others a commitment to a science of sociology, which was a very attractive perspective to early theorists. Another influence of Spencer's work, shared with both Comte and Durkheim, was his tendency to see society as an *organism*. In this, Spencer borrowed his perspective and concepts from biology. He was concerned with the overall structure of society, the interrelationship of the *parts* of society, and the *functions* of the parts for each other as well as for the system as a whole.

Most important, Spencer, like Comte, had an evolutionary conception of historical development. However, Spencer was critical of Comte's evolutionary theory on several grounds. Specifically, he rejected Comte's law of the three stages. He argued that Comte was content to deal with evolution in the realm of ideas, in terms of intellectual development. Spencer, however, sought to develop an evolutionary theory in the real, material world.

Although Spencer is best remembered as an evolutionary theorist, his theory is highly complex, takes varied forms, and is often unclear and ambiguous (Haines, 1988; Perrin, 1976). However, it is possible to identify at least two major evolutionary perspectives in Spencer's work.

The first of these theories relates primarily to the increasing *size* of society. Society grows through both the multiplication of individuals and the union of groups (compounding). The increasing size of society brings with it larger and more differentiated social structures, as well as the increasing differentiation of the functions they perform. In addition to their growth in terms of size, societies evolve through compounding, that is, by unifying more and more adjoining groups. Thus, Spencer talks of the evolutionary movement from simple to compound, doubly-compound, and trebly-compound societies.

Spencer also offers a theory of evolution from *militant* to *industrial* societies. Earlier, militant societies are defined by being structured for offensive and

HERBERT SPENCER: A Biographical Sketch

Herbert Spencer was born in Derby, England, on April 27, 1820. He was not schooled in the arts and humanities, but rather in technical and utilitarian matters. In 1837 he began work as a civil engineer for a railway, an occupation he held until 1846. During this period, Spencer continued to study on his own and began to publish scientific and political works.

In 1848 Spencer was appointed an editor of *The Economist,* and his intellectual ideas began to solidify. By 1850, he had completed his first major work, *Social Statics.* During the writing of this work, Spencer first began to experience insomnia, and over the years his mental and physical problems mounted. He was to suffer a series of nervous breakdowns throughout the rest of his life.

In 1853 Spencer received an inheritance that allowed him to quit his job and live for the rest of his life as a gentleman scholar. He never earned a university degree or held an academic position. As he grew more isolated, and physical and mental illness mounted, Spencer's productivity as a scholar increased. Eventually, Spencer began to achieve not only fame within England but also an international reputation. As Richard Hofstadter put it: "In the three decades after the Civil War it was impossible to be active in any field of intellectual work without mastering Spencer" (1959:33). Among his supporters was the important industrialist Andrew Carnegie, who wrote the following to Spencer during the latter's fatal illness of 1903:

> Dear Master Teacher . . . you come to me every day in thought, and the everlasting "why" intrudes— Why lies he? Why must he go? . . . The world jogs on unconscious of its greatest mind. . . . But it will wake some day to its teachings and decree Spencer's place is with the greatest.
>
> (cited in Peel, 1971:2)

defensive warfare. While Spencer was critical of warfare, he felt that in an earlier stage it was functional in bringing societies together (through, for example, military conquest) and in creating the larger aggregates of people necessary for the development of industrial society. However, with the emergence of industrial society, warfare ceases to be functional and serves to impede further evolution. Industrial society is based on friendship, altruism, elaborate specialization, recognition for achievements rather than the characteristics one is born with, and voluntary cooperation among highly disciplined individuals. Such a society is held together by voluntary contractual relations and, more important, by a strong common morality. The government's role is restricted and focuses only on what people ought not to do. Obviously, modern industrial societies are less warlike than their militant predecessors. Although Spencer sees a general evolution in the direction of industrial societies, he also recognizes that it is possible that there will be periodic regressions to warfare and more militant societies.

But that was not to be Spencer's fate.

One of Spencer's most interesting characteristics, one that was ultimately to be the cause of his intellectual undoing, was his unwillingness to read the work of other people. In this, he resembled another early giant of sociology, Auguste Comte, who practiced "cerebral hygiene." Of the need to read the works of others, Spencer said: "All my life I have been a thinker and not a reader, being able to say with Hobbes that 'if I had read as much as other men I would have known as little' (Wiltshire, 1978:67). A friend asked Spencer's opinion of a book, and "his reply was that on looking into the book he saw that its fundamental assumption was erroneous, and therefore did not care to read it" (Wiltshire, 1978:67). One author wrote of Spencer's "incomprehensible way of absorbing knowledge through the powers of his skin . . . he never seemed to read books" (Wiltshire, 1978:67).

If he didn't read the work of other scholars, where, then, did Spencer's ideas and insights come from? According to Spencer, they emerged involuntarily and intuitively from his mind. He said that his ideas emerged "little by little, in unobtrusive ways, without conscious intention or appreciable effort," (Wiltshire, 1978:66). Such intuition was deemed by Spencer to be far more effective than careful study and thought: "A solution reached in the way described is more likely to be true than one reached in the pursuance of a determined effort [which] causes perversion of thought" (Wiltshire, 1978:66).

Spencer suffered because of his unwillingness to seriously read the works of other people. In fact, if he read other work, it was often only to find confirmation for his own, independently created ideas. He ignored those ideas that did not agree with his. Thus, his contemporary, Charles Darwin, said of Spencer: "If he had trained himself to observe more, even at the expense of . . . some loss of thinking power, he would have been a wonderful man" (Wiltshire, 1978:70). Spencer's disregard for the rules of scholarship led him to a series of outrageous ideas and unsubstantiaated assertions about the evolution of the world. For these reasons, sociologists in the twentieth century came to reject Spencer's work and to substitute for it careful scholarship and empirical research.

Spencer died on December 8, 1903.

In his ethical and political writings, Spencer offered other ideas on the evolution of society. For one thing, he saw society as progressing toward an ideal, or perfect, moral state. For another, he argued that the fittest societies survive, while unfit societies should be permitted to die off. The result of this process is adaptive upgrading for the world as a whole.

Thus Spencer offered a rich and complicated set of ideas on social evolution. His ideas first enjoyed great success, then were rejected for many years, and recently have been revived with the rise of neoevolutionary sociological theories (Buttel, 1990).

The Reaction against Spencer in Britain   Despite his emphasis on the individual, Spencer was best known for his large-scale theory of social evolution. In this, he stood in stark contrast to the sociology that preceded him in Britain. However, the reaction against Spencer was based more on the threat that his idea of survival of the fittest posed to the ameliorism so dear to most early British sociologists. Although Spencer later repudiated some of his more outrageous ideas, he *did* argue for a survival-of-the-fittest philosophy and against government intervention and social reform. He did say things like:

> Fostering the good-for-nothing at the expense of the good, is an extreme cruelty. It is a deliberate stirring-up of miseries for future generations. There is no greater curse to posterity than that of bequeathing to them an increasing population of imbeciles and idlers and criminals. . . . The whole effort of nature is to get rid of such, to clear the world of them, and make room for better. . . . If they are not sufficiently complete to live, they die, and it is best they should die.

> (Spencer, cited in Abrams, 1968:74)

Such sentiments were clearly at odds with the ameliorative orientation of the British reformer-sociologists.

Key Figures in Italian Sociology

We can close this sketch of early, primarily conservative, European sociological theory with brief mention of two Italian sociologists, Vilfredo Pareto (1848–1923) and Gaetano Mosca (1858–1941). These two sociologists were influential in their time, but their contemporary relevance is minimal. Few people read Mosca today. There was a brief outburst of interest in Pareto's (1935) work in the 1930s, when the major American theorist, Talcott Parsons, devoted as much attention to him as he gave to Weber and Durkheim. However, in recent years, except for a few of his major concepts, Pareto also has receded in importance and contemporary relevance.

Zeitlin argued that Pareto developed his "major ideas as a refutation of Marx" (1981:171). In fact, Pareto was rejecting not only Marx but also a good portion of Enlightenment philosophy. For example, whereas the Enlightenment philosophers emphasized rationality, Pareto emphasized the role of nonrational factors such as human instincts. This emphasis also was tied to his rejection of Marxian theory. That is, because nonrational, instinctual factors were so important *and* so unchanging, it was unrealistic to hope to achieve dramatic social changes with an economic revolution.

Pareto also developed a theory of social change that stood in stark contrast to Marxian theory. Whereas Marx's theory focused on the role of the masses, Pareto offered an elite theory of social change, which held that society inevitably is dominated by a small elite that operates on the basis of enlightened self-interest. It rules over the masses of people, who are dominated by nonrational forces. Because they lack rational capacities, the masses, in Pareto's system, were unlikely to be a revolutionary force. Social change occurs when the elite begins to degenerate and is replaced by a new elite derived from the nongoverning elite or higher elements of the masses. Once the new elite is in power, the process begins anew. Thus, we have a cyclical theory of social change instead of the directional theories offered by Marx, Comte, Spencer, and others. In addition, Pareto's theory of change largely ignores the plight of the masses. Elites come and go, but the lot of the masses remains the same.

This theory, however, was not Pareto's lasting contribution to sociology.

That lay in his scientific conception of sociology and the social world: "My wish is to construct a system of sociology on the model of celestial mechanics [astronomy], physics, chemistry" (cited in Hook, 1965:57). Briefly, Pareto conceived of society as a system in equilibrium, a whole consisting of interdependent parts. A change in one part was seen as leading to changes in other parts of the system. Pareto's systemic conception of society was the most important reason Parsons devoted so much attention to Pareto's work in his 1937 book, *The Structure of Social Action,* and it was Pareto's most important influence on Parsons's thinking. Fused with similar views held by those who had an organic image of society (Comte, Durkheim, and Spencer, for example), Pareto's theory played a central role in the development of Parsons's theory and, more generally, in structural functionalism.

Although few modern sociologists now read Pareto's work (one exception is Powers, 1986), virtually none ever read Mosca's. But his work also can be seen as a rejection of the Enlightenment and of Marxism. The important point is that Mosca, like Pareto, offered an elite theory of social change that stands in opposition to the Marxian perspective.

Turn of the Century Developments in European Marxism

While many nineteenth-century sociologists were developing their theories in opposition to Marx, there was a simultaneous effort by a number of Marxists to clarify and extend Marxian theory. Between roughly 1875 and 1925, there was little overlap between Marxism and sociology. (Weber is an exception to this.) The two schools of thought were developing in parallel fashion with little or no interchange between them.

After the death of Marx, Marxian theory was first dominated by those who saw in his theory scientific and economic determinism. Wallerstein calls this the era of "orthodox Marxism" (1986:1301). Friedrich Engels, Marx's benefactor and collaborator, lived on after Marx's death and can be seen as the first exponent of such a perspective. Basically, this view was that Marx's scientific theory had uncovered the economic laws that ruled the capitalist world. Such laws pointed to the inevitable collapse of the capitalist system. Early Marxian thinkers, like Karl Kautsky, sought to gain a better understanding of the operation of these laws. There were several problems with this perspective. For one thing, it seemed to rule out political action, a cornerstone of Marx's position. That is, there seemed no need for individuals, especially workers, to do anything. In that the system was inevitably crumbling, all they had to do was sit back and wait for its demise. On a theoretical level, deterministic Marxism seemed to rule out the dialectical relationship between individuals and larger social structures.

These problems led to a reaction among Marxian theorists and to the development of "Hegelian Marxism" in the early 1900s. The Hegelian Marxists refused to reduce Marxism to a scientific theory that ignored individual thought and action. They are labeled *Hegelian Marxists* because they sought to combine Hegel's interest in consciousness (which some, including the author of this text, view Marx as sharing) with the determinists' interest in the economic structures of society. The Hegelian theorists were significant for both theoretical and practical reasons. Theoretically, they reinstated the importance of the individual, consciousness, and the relationship between thought and action. Practically, they emphasized the importance of individual action in bringing about a social revolution.

The major exponent of this point of view was George Lukács (Fischer, 1984). According to Martin Jay, Lukács was "the founding father of Western Marxism" and the author of *Class and Class Consciousness*, which is "generally acknowledged as the charter document of Hegelian Marxism" (1984:84). Lukács had begun in the early 1900s to integrate Marxism with sociology (in particular, Weberian and Simmelian theory). This integration was soon to accelerate with the development of critical theory in the 1920s and 1930s.

SUMMARY

This chapter sketches the early history of sociological theory in two parts. The first, and much briefer, section deals with the various social forces involved in the development of sociological theory. Although there were many such influences, we focus on how political revolution, the Industrial Revolution and the rise of capitalism, socialism, urbanization, religious change, and the growth of science affected sociological theory. The second part of the chapter examines the influence of intellectual forces on the rise of sociological theory in various countries. We begin with France and the role played by the Enlightenment, stressing the conservative and romantic reaction to it. It is out of this interplay that French sociological theory developed. In this context, we examine the major figures in the early years of French sociology—Claude Henri Saint-Simon, Auguste Comte, and Emile Durkheim.

Next we turn to Germany and the role played by Karl Marx in the development of sociology in that country. We discuss the parallel development of Marxian theory and sociological theory and the ways in which Marxian theory influenced sociology, both positively and negatively. We begin with the roots of Marxian theory in Hegelianism, materialism, and political economy. Marx's theory itself is touched upon briefly. The discussion then shifts to the roots of German sociology. Max Weber's work is examined in order to show the diverse sources of German sociology. Also discussed are some of the reasons that Weber's theory proved more acceptable to later sociologists than did Marx's ideas. This section closes with a brief discussion of Georg Simmel's work.

The rise of sociological theory in Britain is considered next. The major sources of British sociology were political economy, ameliorism, and social evolution. In this context, we touch on the work of Herbert Spencer as well as on some of the controversy that surrounded it.

This chapter closes with a brief discussion of Italian sociological theory, especially the work of Vilfredo Pareto, and the turn of the century developments in European Marxian theory, primarily economic determinism and Hegelian Marxism.

KARL MARX

*T*HERE has long been an uneasy and often bizarre relationship between sociological theory and the work of Karl Marx (1818–1883). In some sectors of the world, at least until the recent (apparent) end of the "cold war," sociological theory was virtually identical with Marxian and neo-Marxian theory, and in others (most notably the United States) Marx had been virtually ignored (at least until recently) as a significant sociological thinker. In Eastern Europe Marx's influence was, at least until recently, overwhelming, with sociological theory largely reduced to various forms of traditional and neo-Marxian thinking. In Western Europe Marx's influence has been highly variable. Among some Western European sociologists, Marx has had a profound positive influence; others have fashioned their sociological theory specifically *against* Marxian theory. In the United States sociological theorists prior to the 1960s (with a few exceptions, like C. Wright Mills) tended to ignore, be ignorant of, or even be hostile to Marx's ideas. For example, in the book that revived grand theory in the United States, Talcott Parsons (1937, 1949) dismissed Marx's

41

work in a few pages but spent hundreds of pages on the work of Emile Durkheim, Max Weber, and the marginally significant Vilfredo Pareto. Most American theorists dismissed Marx as an ideologist who had little to contribute to the development of *scientific* sociological theory. However, in the 1960s young American sociologists—at least partly because of their personal experiences in the civil-rights, anti-Vietnam War, and student-rights movements—began to give serious attention to Marx as a sociological theorist. Reflecting this change was a book by Henri Lefebvre (1968) in which he argued that, although Marx was not simply a sociologist, there is a sociology in Marx's work. Since the late 1960s, a serious effort has been made to integrate Marxian and neo-Marxian theory into American sociological theory, while in the rest of the world Marx's influence has continued strong and even grown in strength in some areas. Although resistance to Marx remains among some American sociologists, many thinkers now are willing to accord Marx his rightful place among the giants of sociological thought.

With the recent failure of communist societies and their turn to a more capitalistically oriented economy, it is necessary to address what this means for the role of Marxian theory within sociology. On the surface it appears that these changes suggest that we will see a substantial decline in interest in Marxian theory among sociologists. In fact, this *is* likely to occur, especially as a result of the fact that new theorists are less likely to turn to Marx for answers to the problems of modern capitalistic societies. However, the retreat from Marxian sociological theory is likely to be limited for several reasons.

First, most sociologists who have adopted a Marxian perspective have a deep and long-term commitment to it that is not likely to be greatly modified by changes in societies that were very remote from Marx's principles and ideals. Second, and relatedly, many of Marx's ideas have been integrated into various sociological perspectives (see, for example, the integrated paradigm discussed in the Appendix), and they will not be excised merely because of failures in the communist bloc. Third, and most important, it is the thesis of this chapter that it is Marx's *sociological* theory, not his economic theory, that is of greatest importance. As we will see, Marx offered an abstract, coherent, and greatly satisfying sociological theory that can be used to analyze *any* society, not just capitalistic societies and their economic systems. Since that sociological theory was uninvolved in the creation of communist societies, and in fact was contradicted by them, it is unscathed by recent developments in the communist world. Sociologists will continue to be attracted to the scope and elegance of Marx's sociological theory.

Many students (and some academicians), both pro- and anti-Marx, might be surprised to find Marx mentioned as one of the major theorists in the history of the discipline. Students trained in an anti-Marxian tradition or influenced by a similarly oriented mass media are socialized to believe that Marx was a bloodthirsty radical whose ideological commitments prohibited him from producing a serious scientific theory. It is crucial to sound scholarship that this myth be dispelled, and there are two bases on which it can be attacked. Similarly, it must be demonstrated to pro-Marxian students that it is legitimate to consider Marx a sociologist.

Two basic arguments can be made to those anti-Marxists who reject Marx as a sociologist because of his ideological orientation. First, although it is true that Marx's approach is heavily influenced by his ideology, it is important to recognize that *all* sociological theorists have an ideological bias. This is as true for Comte, Spencer, Durkheim, Weber, and Simmel as it is for Marx. There is no such thing as a "value-free" sociological theory. In theorizing about social phenomena, sociologists find it impossible to be completely neutral, and this remains true whether or not they are willing to recognize it or to admit it. Thus it *is* true that Marx's sociological theory is ideological, but that is no reason to dismiss it, because this is also true of *all* other sociological theories. The *major* difference between Marx and other sociological theorists is that Marx made no effort to conceal the ideological character of his work; indeed, as we will see, it is built into the very structure of his theorizing.

Second, it is important to point out that although Marx was avowedly ideological in his theorizing, the widely shared view of Marx as a blood-crazed fanatic is not admissible. As we will see throughout this chapter, Marx was a humanist who was deeply hurt by the suffering and exploitation that he witnessed among the working class under capitalism. His humanism led him to call for a revolution that would overturn the economic system, which was exploitative of the vast majority of people, and that would lead to the creation of a more humane socialist society. Although he called for revolution, Marx did *not* believe that the change *had* to be bloody. It was possible for the transition to socialism to occur peacefully, and given Marx's humanistic proclivities, this would clearly have been the most desirable course of action to him.

Although these points might ease some of the doubts among readers with an anti-Marxian bias, they will not satisfy those who begin with a pro-Marxian orientation. Such students might object that to label Marx a "sociologist" is much too restrictive. In their view, Marx defies simple categorization, because he was also a philosopher, a revolutionary, a pamphleteer, a journalist, a political scientist, a dialectician, and so forth. It is true that Marx is a highly complex thinker whose work is attractive to people in a wide range of endeavors, but among the many labels that fit Marx *is* that of sociologist. We can deal with those elements of Marx's thought that are relevant to sociology as long as we recognize that he is also many other things to many other people.

There is another debate that must be addressed at this point, this one among various interpreters of Marx's work. There are a number of schools of neo-Marxian theory, and many of their differences stem from varying interpretations of Marx's theory. For example, some stress Marx's early work on human potential and see the rest of it as derived from, and consistent with, his earlier work (see, for example, Ollman, 1976; Wallimann, 1981; Wartenberg, 1982). Others stress Marx's later work on the structures of society, especially the economic structures, and see that work as separable, and even different, from his early, largely philosophical work on human nature (see

Althusser, 1969; Gandy, 1979; McMurty, 1978). This chapter is based on the premise that there is no discontinuity or contradiction between Marx's early work on human potential and his later work on the structures of capitalist society. After a general introduction to Marx's mode of thinking (the dialectic), we will look at Marx's work on human potential and then show its relationship to his later work on the larger structures of society.

THE DIALECTIC

Marx adopted the dialectical mode of logic from Hegel. However, whereas Hegel focused on a dialectic of ideas, Marx tried to embed his dialectical approach in the material world. This is a crucial transformation because it allowed Marx to move the dialectic out of the realm of philosophy and into the realm of what some consider a science of social relations as they exist in the material world. It is this focus on material social relationships that makes Marx's work most relevant to sociology, even though the dialectical approach is very different from the mode of thinking used by most sociologists (Ball, 1979; Friedrichs, 1972a, 1972b; Ollman, 1976; Schneider, 1971).

Two basic features of dialectical analysis contrast sharply with most sociological thinking. First, the dialectical method of analysis does not see a simple, one-way, cause-and-effect relationship among the various parts of the social world. For the dialectical thinker, social influences never simply flow in one direction as they do for cause-and-effect thinkers. To the dialectician one factor may have an effect on another, but it is just as likely that the latter will have a simultaneous effect on the former. For example, the increasing exploitation of the proletariat by the capitalist may cause the workers to become increasingly dissatisfied and more militant, but the increasing militancy of the proletariat might well cause the capitalists to react by becoming even more exploitative in order to crush the resistance of the workers. This kind of thinking does not mean that the dialectician never considers causal relationships in the social world. It does mean that when dialectical thinkers talk about causality, they are always attuned to reciprocal relationships among social factors as well as to the dialectical totality of social life in which they are embedded.

The second feature of dialectical analysis is even more at odds with most contemporary sociological thinking. In dialectical analysis, especially as Marx developed it, social values are not separable from social facts. Most sociologists believe that their values can and must be separated from their study of facts about the social world. The dialectical thinker believes that not only is it impossible to keep values out of the study of the social world but it is also undesirable because it produces a dispassionate, inhuman sociology that has little to offer to people in search of answers to the problems they confront. Facts and values are inevitably intertwined, with the result that the study of social phenomena is value laden. Thus to Marx, it was impossible, and even if possible, undesirable, to be dispassionate in his analysis of the two major classes within capitalism—the bourgeoisie (also called "capitalists") and the proletariat (the workers). In *Capital* (1867/1967), for example, Marx talked about the capitalists as werewolves and vampires who suck the blood out of the workers, and he was very sympathetic to the plight of the proletariat. But Marx's emotional involvement in what he was studying did not mean that his observations were inaccurate. It could even be argued that Marx's passionate views on these issues gave him unparalleled insight into the nature of capitalist society. A less passionate student might have delved less deeply into the dynamics of the system. In fact, research into the work of scientists indicates that the idea of a dispassionate scientist is largely a myth and that the very best scientists are the ones who are most passionate about, and committed to, their ideas (Mitroff, 1974).

Both of the above characteristics of the dialectic reflect Marx's view that there are no hard and fast dividing lines between phenomena in the social world. Marx believed that the various components of the social world blended gradually and imperceptibly into one another. Thus, to take two of Marx's major concerns, he would argue that the capitalists and the proletariat are not clearly separated but gradually blend into one another. This means that there are a large number of people who either exist in the interstices between the two classes or move from one class to another (the successful worker who becomes a capitalist; the capitalist who fails and drops into the working class).

Dialectical thinkers also take a *relational* view of the social world (Ollman, 1976). They focus on the relations within and among various aspects of the social world. Thus, in examining a bureaucracy, they look at the various social relationships that go into its construction. Relationships between individuals, between groups of people, and between various subunits within the organization (for example, the personnel department and the engineering department) all would come under the intense scrutiny of the dialectical thinker. In addition, a dialectician never would concentrate on one social unit in isolation from other social units. Thus, the relationship between a given bureaucracy and various other social units in the social world would be of chief concern to the dialectician.

Dialecticians are interested not only in the relationships of social phenomena in the *contemporary* world but also in the relationship of those contemporary realities to both *past* (Bauman, 1976:81) and *future* social phenomena. This has two distinct implications for a dialectical sociology. First, it means that dialectical sociologists are concerned with studying the historical roots of the contemporary world as Marx (1857–58/1964) did in his study of the sources of modern capitalism. In fact, dialectical thinkers are very critical of modern sociology for its failure to do much historical research. A good example of Marx's thinking in this regard is found in the following famous quotation from "The Eighteenth Brumaire of Louis Bonaparte":

Men make their own history, but they do not make it just as they please; they do not make it under circumstances chosen by themselves, but under circumstances

KARL MARX: A Biographical Sketch

Karl Marx was born in Trier, Prussia, on May 5, 1818. His father, a lawyer, provided the family with a fairly typical middle-class existence. Both parents were from rabbinical families, but for business reasons the father had converted to Lutheranism.

In 1841 Marx received his doctorate in philosophy from the University of Berlin, a school heavily influenced by Hegel and the Young Hegelians, supportive, yet critical, of their master. Marx's doctorate was a dry philosophical treatise that bore little resemblance to his later, more radical and more pragmatic work. After graduation he became a writer for a liberal-radical newspaper and within ten months had become its editor-in-chief. However, because of its political positions, the paper was closed shortly thereafter by the government. The early essays published in this period began to reflect a number of the positions that would guide Marx throughout his life. They were liberally sprinkled with democratic principles, humanism, and idealism. He rejected the abstractness of Hegelian philosophy, the naive dreaming of utopian communists, and those activists who were urging what he considered to be premature political action. In rejecting these activists, Marx laid the groundwork for his own life's work:

> Practical attempts, even by the masses, can be answered with a cannon as soon as they become dangerous, but ideas that have overcome our intellect and conquered our conviction, ideas to which reason has riveted our conscience, are chains from which one cannot break loose without breaking one's heart; they are demons that one can only overcome by submitting to them.
> (Marx, 1842/1977:20)

Marx married in 1843 and soon thereafter left Germany for the more liberal atmosphere of Paris. There he continued to grapple with the ideas of Hegel and the Young Hegelians, but he also encountered two new sets of ideas—French socialism and English political economy. It was the unique way in which he combined Hegelianism, socialism, and political economy that shaped his intellectual orientation. Also of great importance at this point was meeting the man who was to become his lifelong friend, benefactor, and collaborator—Friedrich Engels (Carver, 1983). The son of a textile manufacturer, Engels had become a socialist critical of the conditions facing the working class. Much of Marx's compassion for the misery of the working class came from his exposure to Engels and his ideas. In 1844 Engels and Marx had a lengthy conversation in a famous café in Paris and laid the groundwork for a lifelong association. Of that conversation Engels said, "Our complete agreement in all theoretical fields became obvious . . . and our joint work dates from that time" (McLellan, 1973:131). During this period Marx produced academic works (many unpublished in his lifetime) that were mainly concerned with sorting out his link to the Hegelian tradition (for example, *The Holy Family* and *The German Ideology*), but he also produced

directly encounterd from the past. The tradition of all the dead generations weighs like a nightmare on the brain of the living.

(Marx, 1852/1963:15)

Second, dialectical thinkers are attuned to the future directions of society. This interest in the future is one of the main reasons that dialectical sociology

The Economic and Philosophic Manuscripts of 1844, which better integrated all of the intellectual traditions in which he was immersed and which foreshadowed his increasing preoccupation with the economic domain.

While Marx and Engels shared a theoretical orientation, there were many differences between the two men. Marx tended to be a highly abstract thinker, a disorderly intellectual, and very oriented to his family. Engels was a practical thinker, a neat and tidy businessman, and a womanizer. In spite of their differences, Marx and Engels forged a close union in which they collaborated on books and articles and worked together in radical organizations, and Engels even helped support Marx throughout the rest of his life so that Marx could devote himself to his intellectual and political endeavors.

In spite of the close association of the names of Marx and Engels, Engels made it clear that he was the junior partner:

> Marx could very well have done without me. What Marx accomplished I would not have achieved. Marx stood higher, saw farther, and took a wider and quicker view than the rest of us. Marx was a genius.
>
> (Engels, cited in McLellan, 1973:131–132)

In fact, many believe that Engels failed to understand many of the subtleties of Marx's work. After Marx's death, Engels became the leading spokesperson for Marxian theory and in various ways distorted and oversimplified it.

Because some of his writings had upset the Prussian government, the French government (at the request of the Prussians) expelled Marx in 1845, and he moved to Brussels. His radicalism was growing, and he had become an active member of the international revolutionary movement. He also associated with the Communist League and was asked to write a document (with Engels) expounding its aims and beliefs. The result was the *Communist Manifesto* of 1848, a work that was characterized by ringing political slogans (for example, "Working men of all countries, unite!").

In 1849 Marx moved to London, and, in light of the failure of the political revolutions of 1848, he began to withdraw from active revolutionary activity and to move into serious and detailed research on the workings of the capitalist system. In 1852, he began his famous studies in the British Museum of the working conditions in capitalism. These studies ultimately resulted in the three volumes of *Capital,* the first of which was published in 1867; the other two were published posthumously. He lived in poverty during these years, barely managing to survive on a small income from his writings and the support of Engels. In 1863 Marx became reinvolved in political activity by joining the *International,* an international movement of workers. He soon gained dominance within the movement and devoted a number of years to it. He began to gain fame both as leader of the *International* and as the author of *Capital.* But the disintegration of the *International* by 1876, the failure of various revolutionary movements, and personal illness took their toll on Marx. His wife died in 1881, a daughter in 1882, and Marx himself on March 14, 1883.

is inherently political. It has an image of the future world, and it is interested in encouraging practical activities that would bring that world into existence. In trying to grasp the nature of this future world, dialecticians believe that much is to be learned from a careful study of the contemporary world. It is their view that social change is a coming to be of what potentially is, that the sources of the future exist in the present. To take an example from Marx, the proletariat of modern capitalism, which does not own the means of production, is a model of what all people will be like in socialist society. There is to be no private ownership of the means of production in socialism. This does not mean that people will not own clothes, television sets, and cars, but rather that one class will not own and dominate the industrial and corporate structure as it does in contemporary capitalism.

But in saying that the dialectical thinker believes that the future is the coming to be of what potentially is, we do *not* imply the deterministic view that the future course of the world is preset and unchangeable. The basic nature of the dialectic militates against a deterministic orientation. Because social phenomena are constantly acting and reacting, the social world defies a simple, deterministic model. The future *may* be based on some contemporary model, but not inevitably. Marxists hoped and believed that the future was to be found in socialism, but the proletariat could not simply wait passively for it to arrive. They had to work for it, and there were no ironclad guarantees that it would occur.

This disinclination to think deterministically is what makes the best-known model of the dialectic—thesis, antithesis, synthesis—a gross distortion. This simple model implies that a social phenomenon will inevitably spawn an opposing form and that the clash between these two will inevitably lead to a new, synthetic social form. *But in the real world, there are no inevitabilities.* Furthermore, social phenomena are not easily divided into simple thesis, antithesis, and synthesis categories. The dialectician is interested in the study of real relationships rather than grand abstractions. It is this disinclination to deal in grand abstractions that led Marx away from Hegel and would lead him today to reject such a great oversimplification of the dialectic as thesis, antithesis, synthesis. Marx analyzed the conflict between the capitalists and the proletariat, and although he foresaw a revolution and, ultimately, a new type of society, he did not see this as an inevitable process. The proletariat would have to work and fight for socialism if it were to occur. But even if the workers did strive for it, they were not assured that it would come to pass. Actions of the capitalists have made the working class more satisfied with their lot, and this has militated against the occurrence of a working-class revolt.

What is perhaps best known about the dialectic is its concern with *conflict* and *contradiction* (Elster, 1985). This leads to a number of by-products, including a concern for the process of change as well as a political program. But what is of importance here is that the dialectic leads to an interest in the conflicts and contradictions among various levels of social reality, rather than to the more traditional sociological interest in the ways that these various levels mesh rather neatly into a cohesive whole. Although Marx was aware of how the ideologies of the capitalists mesh with their objective interests, he wanted to concentrate on issues like the conflict between the large-scale structures created by capitalists and the interests of the proletariat.

Perhaps the ultimate contradiction within capitalism for Marx exists in the relationship between the bourgeoisie and the proletariat. In Marx's terms, the bourgeoisie produces the proletariat, and in producing and expanding that class, the capitalists are producing their own gravediggers. The capitalist produces the proletariat by forcing workers to sell their labor-time for very low wages. As capitalism expands, the number of workers exploited, and the degree of exploitation, increases. The escalating level of exploitation leads to more and more resistance on the part of the proletariat. Resistance begets more exploitation and oppression, and the likely result is a confrontation between the two classes, a confrontation that the proletariat, in Marx's view, is likely to win.

Despite the importance to Marx of the future communist society, he spent surprisingly little time depicting what this world would be like. In fact, he was critical of those utopian socialists who wrote book after book on their dreamlike images of future society. To Marx, the most important task was the critical analysis of contemporary capitalist society. He believed that such criticism would help bring down capitalism and create the conditions for the rise of a new socialist world. There would be time to construct communist society once capitalism was overcome.

Dialectical thinkers in general are also interested (as Marx was) in the structures of society and the actors within society, as well as with the dialectical relationship between actors and social structures. But the dialectical method is even more complex than this, because, as we have already seen, the dialectician considers past, present, and future circumstances, and this applies to both actors and structures. Figure 2.1 is a simplified schematic representation of this enormously complex and sophisticated perspective.

Marx made it abundantly clear throughout his work that he was working with a model like Figure 2.1. He was attuned to the ongoing interplay among the major levels of social analysis. For example, Marx and Engels said, "Circumstances make men *just as much* as men make circumstances" (1845–46/ 1970:59; italics added). Lefebvre was therefore quite accurate when he argued that the heart of Marx's thought lies in the relationship between people and

FIGURE 2.1   Schematic Representation of a Sociologically Relevant Dialectic

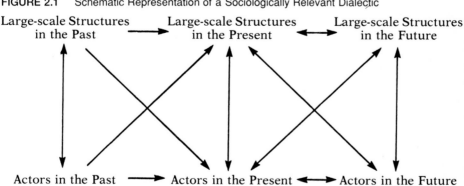

Large-scale Structures in the Past

Large-scale Structures in the Present

Large-scale Structures in the Future

Actors in the Past   Actors in the Present   Actors in the Future

the large-scale structures they create (1968:8). On the one hand, these large-scale structures help people to fulfill themselves; on the other, they represent a grave threat to humanity.

Despite his general commitment to the dialectic, in particular the dialectical relationship between large-scale structures and actors, Marx came to focus more and more of his attention on the structures of capitalist society. In part, this is traceable to Marx's political interests, which led him to examine and criticize the structures of capitalism in order to help bring about revolutionary change. By so doing, the transition to socialism could be expedited. A good portion of this chapter will be devoted to a discussion of Marx's analysis of the structures of capitalism. But before we can analyze these, we need to begin with Marx's thoughts on the more microscopic aspects of social reality. Marx built his critical analysis of the structure of capitalist society on his premises about actors, action, and interaction.

HUMAN POTENTIAL

The basis of much of Marx's thinking lies in his ideas on the potential of human beings (or what he called *species-being*). He believed that until his time in history, people had not even begun to approach what they ultimately could become. The nature of societies prior to capitalism had been too harsh to allow people to realize their potentialities. They were too busy trying merely to get enough food, shelter, and protection to develop their higher capacities. Although capitalism solved some of these problems, it was too oppressive an environment to allow most people to develop their human potential. It was Marx's hope and belief that communism would provide the kind of environment in which people could begin to express that potential fully. Thus Marx could not describe human potential in any detail, because it had yet to be allowed to develop to its fullest and to express itself adequately. Marx's critique of capitalist society was based in part on what he felt humans could become once they were freed from the shackles of capitalism and allowed to express themselves in the unfettered environment of communism.

Powers and Needs

The bases of Marx's conception of human potential were his ideas on the powers and needs of people (Heller, 1976; Ollman, 1976). *Powers* may be defined as the faculties, abilities, and capacities of people. In the Marxian system, human powers are not simply what they are now, but also what they were historically and what they can be in the future under changed social circumstances. *Needs* are the desires people feel for things that are usually not immediately available. Needs, like powers, are greatly affected by the social settings in which people exist. Even the most microscopic notions of human powers and needs cannot be discussed without taking into account the larger setting of society as a whole.

It is necessary to differentiate between natural powers and needs and species powers and needs. In brief, *natural* powers and needs are those shared with other animals, whereas *species* powers and needs are those that are uniquely human. Natural powers and needs per se are of little interest to us because, as Bertell Ollman argued, "natural" man is *"not yet* a man but still an animal" (1976:80). However, all natural powers and needs can be expressed in distinctly human ways. Sex, for example, is a behavior common to human beings and all other animals, but when it is expressed in peculiarly human ways, it moves into the category of species powers and needs.

Consciousness

The heart of the notion of human potential lies in Marx's view that people differ from animals in their possession of consciousness as well as in their ability to link this consciousness to their actions. The emphasis on consciousness is directly related to Marx's ties to Hegelian philosophy and its interest in the phenomenon. Although borrowing from Hegel here, Marx was critical of Hegel for discussing consciousness as if it existed independently of people rather than *focusing on the consciousness of real, sentient people.* The following is the famous quotation from Marx in which he acknowledged his ties to Hegel and laid out his basic point of departure from Hegel's orientation:

> Hegel makes man *the man of self-consciousness* instead of making self-consciousness the *self-consciousness of man,* of real man, man living in a real objective world and determined by that world. He stands the world *on its head* and can therefore dissolve *in the head* all the limitations which naturally remain in existence for *evil sensuousness,* for *real* man.
>
> (Marx and Engels, 1845/1956:254)

Thus, Marx was opposed to Hegel not only on intellectual grounds but also because his ephemeral image of self-consciousness was a barrier to the kind of political action that to Marx was imperative.

Marx went further than arguing simply in general terms that people are distinguished from other animals by their consciousness. According to Ollman (1976), Marx believed the following mental capacities set humans apart from other animals:

1 While animals just "do," people can set themselves off mentally from whatever they are doing.
2 Since they have a distinctive form of consciousness, human actors are able to choose to act or not to act. Furthermore, they are capable of choosing what kind of action to undertake.
3 The minds of human beings enable them to plan beforehand what their action is going to be.
4 Human beings possess both physical and mental flexibility.

5 Human beings are capable of giving close attention to what they are doing over a long period of time.

6 The nature of the human mind leads people to be highly social.

Consciousness is a characteristic of people, and it is shaped out of human action and interaction: "Consciousness is, therefore, from the very beginning a social product, and remains so as long as men exist at all" (Marx and Engels, 1845–46/1970:51). Out of people's activities, social relationships, and the production of material life comes an expansion of consciousness:

> Not only do the objective conditions change in the act of production . . . but the producers change, too, in that they bring out new qualities in themselves, develop themselves in production, transform themselves, develop new powers and ideas, new modes of intercourse, new needs and new language.
>
> (Marx, 1857–58/1974:494)

It is not just consciousness or self-consciousness that differentiates human beings from other animals but also the relationship of that mental capacity to the peculiar kinds of activities of which people are capable. Human beings are capable of *activity* of a distinctive kind, quality, and pace. It is the ability to control activities through consciousness that distinguishes people from animals. Marx is perfectly explicit on this point:

> The animal is immediately one with its life activity. . . . Man makes his life activity itself the object of his will and of his consciousness.
>
> (Marx, 1932/1964:113)

> A spider conducts operations that resemble those of a weaver, and a bee puts to shame many an architect in the construction of her cells. But what distinguishes the worst architect from the best of bees is this, that the architect raises his structure in imagination before he erects it in reality. At the end of every labor-process we get a result that already existed in imagination of the laborer at its commencement.
>
> (Marx, 1867/1967:178)

McMurty (1978) argues that to Marx the special property of human nature is its creative intelligence, the ability to raise a structure in one's imagination and then to erect that structure in reality. To Marx, at the most abstract level, consciousness and its ability to direct activity were the distinctive characteristics of human beings, at least potentially.

But the problem with this conception of human potential is that it is highly abstract, and Marx had to bring it down to the level of the real world. People, their consciousness, and their activities cannot exist in isolation; they must be related to the natural world. People require objectives for their thoughts and actions, and the most important of these objectives are other people and nature. Humans must act on something, and what they act on mainly, with all their creative powers and in interaction with other people, is nature. We can differentiate three components of the relationship between human beings and nature—perception, orientation, and appropriation.

Perception is the immediate contact that people have with nature through their senses. But a mass of unorganized perceptions is likely to leave actors quite disoriented. What is needed is a process of *orientation* that organizes, patterns, and imposes a framework on the various perceptions of the world. Once the world has been perceived and the perceptions organized, the stage is set for *appropriation,* in which actors use their creative powers on nature in order to satisfy their needs. The conscious, creative capacity of human beings only makes sense in Marx's view when it is seen in relationship to the perception, orientation, and appropriation of nature. Not only does the nature of people's powers and needs shape the form of perception, orientation, and appropriation, but the form that they take in a particular social setting affects, in turn, the nature of these powers and needs. This reinforces the idea that for Marx human nature was not carved in stone but was very much affected by the nature of the social setting.

Following Marx, we may differentiate three basic epochs in the relationship between human potential and the processes of perception, orientation, and appropriation—primitive society, capitalism, and communism.

In *primitive society* people used natural resources to produce the things that they needed (for example, boats and shelters). Because relatively few things were produced—and those rather inefficiently—we can say that people developed their capacities to only a slight degree. Because powers were expressed to only this slight degree, the needs of people remained at a minimal level in primitive society (Ollman, 1976:91). In earliest times, people were busy desperately trying to survive and, as a result, were able to develop and express only a limited number of needs: "In lowest stages of production . . . few human needs have yet been produced and thus few to be satisfied" (Marx, 1857–58/1974:398). The ability of people to think, their consciousness, was limited and amounted to little more than animal, "sheep-like," consciousness (Marx and Engels, 1845–46/1970:51).

Capitalism was viewed by Marx as an epoch in which the creative capacity of most human beings as it is expressed in the act of appropriation is virtually eliminated. Instead, most people are reduced to wanting to make enough money to be able to *own* the commodities they desire. Thus the goal becomes ownership rather than the expression of human potentialities. In comparing primitive society to capitalism, Marx noted, "The ancients provide a narrow satisfaction, whereas the modern world leaves us unsatisfied, or, where it appears to be satisfied with itself, it is *vulgar* and *mean*" (1857–58/1964:85).

Communism, however, was viewed as an era in which the structural forces leading to this distortion of human nature are overthrown, and people are allowed to express their human potential in ways never before possible. The meanness of primitive life permitted only a minimal expression of that potential, and the structures of capitalism (for example, division of labor, private property, and money), while freeing people from the limitations of primitive society, represent barriers to the expression of many species powers and needs. But capitalism was seen by Marx as an important stage, because it developed the *organizational* and *technological* forms that a communist society could use, although in radically different ways, to free individuals further from the kinds of limitations encountered in primitive society. They could then express their human capacities in new and unprecedented ways. To Marx, communism is an epoch in which human beings are able to "bring their species powers out of themselves" (1932/1964:151; Barbalet, 1983:47, 55). With a slightly different emphasis, Ollman contended that "communism is the time of full, personal appropriation" (1976:93).

Activity

Activity now can be viewed as the means by which people appropriate objects from nature. In discussing activity, we are moving out of the subjective realm of consciousness and touching on the objective realm. But because Marx's work, to its credit, is a dialectically related whole, it is virtually impossible to talk about one aspect of social reality without at least touching on the others.

It is important to note that Marx's use of activity is virtually indistinguishable from his concepts of work and creativity. Marx was most prone to use the idea of work but in a way that is much different from common usage. Ollman defined the Marxian notion of work as "conscious, purposive activity in the productive process" (1976:98). By this definition, then, work is an expression of people's distinctive abilities. In fact, work is not restricted to economic activities but encompasses all productive activities that use the creative capacities of the actor. Work, in turn, also serves to allow greater development of people's powers and needs.

Although Marx did not clearly differentiate among activity, work, and creativity, he tended to use different terms at different stages in his career. However, what is important here is that each of these terms highlights a different aspect of people's relationship to nature. *Activity* refers to the motions involved in purposeful endeavors; *work* refers to the process of material production; and *creativity* refers to the ability of people to make unique products (Ollman, 1976:102). In capitalism, work tends to be separated from activity and creativity; in communism, we are likely, in Marx's view, to find a situation where as far as possible work and activity fully involve the creative capacity of human beings.

Objectification   In the activity involved in appropriating the natural world, people, according to Marx, always engage in the process of *objectification,* which means that they produce objects (food, clothes, and shelters). The process of objectification was important to Marx for several reasons. First, it reaffirmed his materialist orientation, his interest in the real world of real actors. He was not merely concerned with work in the abstract or objectification in the realm of consciousness, as was Hegel, but with objectification in the real world. Second, Marx saw objectification as the true arena in which people express their human capacities. Human potential is actualized in the objectification of products.

This process of objectification is normal and expressive of human potential if it involves certain characteristics (Israel, 1971:39). First, the activity must involve the consciousness of the actors. Second, the actors must be able to express their capabilities in a comprehensive manner. Third, they must be able to express their inherently social character in the process of objectification. Fourth, the process of objectification must not merely be a means to some other end (that is, the earning of money). In its most general sense, this means that objectification must involve the creative capacities of individuals.

Labor   In the context of this image of truly human objectification Marx discusses work in capitalist society. For this type of society, Marx usually did not use the interrelated concepts of work, activity, and creativity. Pointedly, he was most likely to refer to *labor*. In one sense, as is clear from the following quotations, Marx used the idea of labor as an equivalent to these other concepts:

> Labor is a creator of use-value, . . . a necessary condition, independent of all forms of society, for the existence of the human race.
>
> (Marx, 1867/1967:42–43)

> Labor is . . . a process in which both man and Nature participate, and in which man of his own accord starts, regulates, and controls the material re-actions between himself and Nature. He opposes himself to Nature as one of her own forces, setting in motion arms and legs, head and hands, the natural forces of his body, in order to appropriate Nature's productions in a form adapted to his own wants. By this acting on the external world and changing it, he at the same time changes his own nature. He develops his slumbering powers and compels them to act in obedience to his sway.
>
> (Marx, 1867/1967:177)

There seems little doubt that Marx is using *labor* here to mean work, activity, and creativity. Clearly implied is appropriation, objectification, and the full expression of human potential. However, as will be made clear throughout this chapter, Marx saw labor in capitalist society as taking on some distinct and perverted forms. Instead of being an end in itself, an expression of human capabilities, labor in capitalism is reduced to a means to an end—earning money (Marx, 1932/1964:173). In capitalism, labor is *not* the equivalent of work, activity, and creativity.

Sociability

Another aspect of Marx's image of human potential is the idea that people are inherently *social*. Marx and Engels talked of "the need, the necessity, of intercourse with other men" (1845–46/1970:51). Elsewhere Marx wrote, "Man is in the most literal sense of the word a *zoon politikon*, not only a social animal, but an animal which can develop into an individual only in society" (1857–58/1964:84).

At one level, as we have already seen, this means that all other truly human capabilities make no sense in isolation; they must be related to *both* the natural and the social worlds. In Marx's view, people cannot express their humanness without nature and without other people. At another level, sociability is an integral part of human nature. That is, to Marx people are inherently social. They need to relate to other people both for the sake of relating and in order to be able to appropriate nature adequately (Mészáros, 1970:149).

Unanticipated Consequences

Finally, a little-discussed aspect of Marx's image of human nature is directly related to the development of capitalism. It addresses the issue of how people, endowed with at least potentially positive human characteristics, are able to produce a structure of capitalism that serves to distort their essential nature. This is the notion of *unanticipated consequences* (Elster, 1985:3). Although we most often associate this idea with the work of Max Weber, it seems clear that Marx too had a conception of unanticipated consequences: "Here, then, is the dialectical worm: while we are highly successful in bringing about the immediate results of our conscious intentions, we still too often fail to anticipate and forestall the undesired remoter consequences of those results themselves" (cited in Venable, 1945:76).

At the most general level, we can argue that capitalism was the unanticipated consequence of a large number of actions. People did not intend to create a structure that distorted humanity, but that is just what they did. It is also necessary to point out that the idea of unanticipated consequences, like other aspects of Marx's image of human nature, is tied to the social context. Although it is an integral part of past and present society, Marx probably would have argued (had he addressed the issue) that unanticipated consequences need not be a characteristic of society. That is, communism need not be subverted by unanticipated consequences. Yet the concept of unanticipated consequences is very useful in thinking about capitalist society. For example, capitalists believe that their actions are furthering their interests as well as the interests of the captialist system as a whole. But as Marx believed, many of the actions of capitalists create the conditions for the system's ultimate collapse. To take only one very broad example, capitalists believe that it is in their interest as well as in the interest of the system itself to extract every last ounce of productivity from the worker. Although in the short run this may create greater profits, in the long run, in Marx's view, it creates the class that will eventually destroy the capitalist system—the proletariat.

ALIENATION

Up to this point, we have been discussing a number of components of Marx's work at the microscopic level—human potential (species-being), powers, needs, self-consciousness and consciousness, activity, work, creativity, labor (perception, orientation, appropriation), objectification, sociability, and unanticipated consequences. This discussion has been derived mainly from Marx's early work. Marx rarely allowed himself the luxury later in his life of such philosophical analyses, for it was then that he wrote about the nature of capitalist society. In his early works, Marx called the distortions of human nature caused by the structure of capitalist society *alienation*. Although he shied away from this heavily philosophical term later in his work, it remained, in a different guise, one of his main concerns. As Barbalet says, "In *Capital* Marx seldom uses the term—although he clearly employs the concept—'alienation' " (1983:95). For in the end Marx was a humanist, and even as he explored the structure of capitalist society, he never lost sight of its impact on the actor (Wartenberg, 1982).

Although it is the actor who feels alienated in capitalist society, Marx's basic analytic concern was with the structures of capitalism that cause this alienation. Thus, contrary to the view of many interpreters who argue that he takes a social-psychological approach, Marx basically offered a theory of alienation rooted in social structure. It is social structure that acts to break down the natural interconnections that characterize human nature in an ideal sense. Of crucial significance here is the two-class system in which the capitalists employ the workers (and thereby own their labor-time) and own the *means of production* (tools and raw materials) as well as the ultimate products. In order to survive and to have access to tools and nature, workers are forced to sell their labor-time to capitalists. Although the workers then use the tools and apply them to nature in order to manufacture products, the natural interrelationships are shattered.

Components of Alienation

Alienation can be seen as having four basic components. First, the workers in capitalist society are alienated from their *productive activity*. In such a society they do not work for themselves in order to satisfy their own needs. Instead, they work for capitalists, who pay them a subsistence wage in return for the right to use the workers in any way they see fit. Both workers and capitalists come to believe that the payment of a wage means that the productive activity belongs to the capitalist. Because productive activity belongs to the capitalists, and because they decide what is to be done with it, we can say that workers are alienated from that activity. Instead of being a process that is satisfying in and of itself, productive activity in capitalism is reduced, Marx argued, to an often boring and stultifying means to the fulfillment of the only end that really matters in capitalism—earning enough money to survive.

Second, the workers are alienated not only from productive activities but also from the object of those activities—the *product*. The product of their labor does not belong to the workers, to be used by them in order to satisfy basic needs. Instead, the product, like the process that resulted in its production, belongs to the capitalists, who may use it in any way they wish. This usually means that the capitalists sell it for a profit. Not only do workers not have control over the product, but they do not even have a very good sense, in many cases, of what they are producing. They often perform highly specialized tasks and as a result have little sense of their role in the total production process. For example, automobile assembly-line workers who tighten a few bolts on an engine assembly may have little feel for their role in the production of the engine, let alone for their contribution to the production of the entire car. Assembly lines often are so long and involve so many steps that individuals are reduced to insignificant roles in the overall process. Playing such small roles in the process, workers often come to feel that it is the assembly line—rather than the people who work on it—that produces the final product.

Third, the workers in capitalism are alienated from their *fellow workers.* Marx's assumption was that people basically need and want to work cooperatively in order to appropriate from nature what they require to survive. But in capitalism this natural cooperation is disrupted, and people, often strangers, are forced to work side by side for the capitalist. Even if the workers on the assembly line, for example, are close friends, the nature of the technology makes for a great deal of isolation. Here is the way one worker describes his social situation on the assembly line:

> You can work next to a guy for months without even knowing his name. One thing, you're too busy to talk. Can't hear. . . . You have to holler in his ear. They got these little guys coming around in white shirts and if they see you runnin' your mouth, they say, "This guy needs more work." Man, he's got no time to talk.
> (Terkel, 1974:165)

But this social situation is worse than simple isolation; the workers are often forced into outright competition, and sometimes conflict, with one another. In order to extract maximum productivity and to prevent the development of cooperative relationships, the capitalist pits one worker against another to see who can produce more, work more quickly, or please the boss more. The ones who succeed are given a few extra rewards; those who fail are discarded. In either case, considerable hostility is generated among the workers toward their peers. This is useful to the capitalists because it tends to deflect hostility that otherwise would be aimed at them. The isolation and the interpersonal hostility tend to make workers in capitalism alienated from fellow workers.

Finally, and most generally, workers in capitalist society are alienated from their own *human potential.* Individuals perform less and less like human beings as they are reduced in their work to animals, beasts of burden, or inhuman machines. Consciousness is numbed and, ultimately, destroyed as relations with other humans and with nature are progressively severed. The result is a mass of people who are unable to express their essential human qualities, a mass of alienated workers.

Distortions Resulting from Alienation

Alienation, then, is the structurally imposed breakdown of the natural and total interconnectedness that is, to Marx, an essential part of life, at least in an ideal sense. Communism implies a reestablishment of the interconnections that have been broken in capitalism. Alienation, then, can be seen as the opposite of what people can be potentially (Barbalet, 1983:53). As Elster puts it, "Marx's discussion of alienation only makes sense against the background of a normative view of what constitutes the good life for man . . . a life of all-sided creative activity" (1985:51). As a result of alienation, work in capitalism is reduced to mere labor in which the individual "does not affirm himself but denies himself, does not feel content but unhappy, does not develop freely his physical and mental energy but mortifies his body and ruins his mind" (Marx, 1932/1964:110). Labor in capitalism is therefore very different from genuine human activity.

One of Marx's most beautiful examples of the perversion of humanity by capitalism is found in his discussion of *money*. Ideally, to Marx, people can be no more or less than they actually are, but in capitalism money can bestow on people powers and abilities that they do not actually possess. The following is Marx's penetrating statement on this point:

> That which is for me through the medium of *money*—that for which I can pay (i.e., which money can buy)—that am *I*, the possessor of the money. The extent of the power of money is the extent of my power. Money's properties are my properties and essential powers—the properties and powers of its possessor. Thus, what I *am* and *am capable* of is by no means determined by my individuality. I *am* ugly, but I can buy for myself the most *beautiful* of women. Therefore I am not *ugly*, for the effect of *ugliness*—its deterrent power—is nullified by money. I, as an individual, am *lame*, but money furnishes me with twenty-four feet. Therefore I am not lame. I am bad, dishonest, unscrupulous, stupid; but money is honored, and hence its possessor. Money is the supreme good; therefore its possessor is good. Money, besides, saves me the trouble of being dishonest: I am therefore presumed honest. I am *stupid*, but money is the *real mind* of all things and how then should its possessor be stupid? Besides, he can buy talented people for himself, and is he who has power over the talented not more talented than the talented? Do not I, who thanks to money am capable of *all* that the human heart longs for, possess all human capacities? Does not money, therefore, transform all my incapacities into their contrary?
>
> (Marx, 1932/1964:167)

Although money is capable of buying virtually anything in capitalism, it cannot perform that function in a truly human world. In such a world one can, for example, "exchange love only for love" (Marx, 1932/1964:119). Wealth is only a veneer that when stripped away leaves nothing but "the universality of needs, capacities, enjoyments, productive powers, etc., of individuals, produced in universal exchange. . . . What, if not the full development of human control over the forces of nature—those of his own nature—as well as those of so-called 'nature'? What, if not the absolute elaboration of his creative dispositions?" (Marx, 1857–58/1964:84–85).

The list of distortions caused by capitalist society is lengthy. First, the structure of manufacturing turns workers into "crippled monstrosities" by forcing them to work on minute details rather than allowing them to use all their capabilities (Marx, 1867/1967:360). Similarly, the natural interrelationship between head and hand is broken in capitalism so that only a few people are allowed to do headwork; most others do handwork that is devoid of mental components (Marx, 1867/1967:508). Then there is the monotony of doing the same specialized task over and over again. Engels underscored this problem: "Nothing is more terrible than being constrained to do alone one thing every day from morning to night against one's will . . . in such unbroken monotony, that this alone must make his work a torture . . . if he has the least human feeling left" (Venable, 1945:137). Then there is the point that human beings are no longer creative but are oriented solely toward owning and possessing objects. To Marx, private property makes people so "stupid and one-sided" that they feel that an object is only theirs when they possess it, that is, when it is "eaten, drunk, worn, inhabited," and so forth. For all these reasons, work in capitalism largely ceases to be an expression of human potential. In fact, in many ways it is the opposite. With human functions so highly alienating, a person is no longer able to satisfy human powers and needs and is forced to concentrate on natural powers and needs.

> As a result, therefore, man (the worker) only feels himself freely active in his animal functions—eating, drinking, procreating, or at most in his dwelling and in dressing-up, etc.; and in his human functions he no longer feels himself to be anything but an animal. What is animal becomes human and what is human becomes animal.
> (Marx, 1932/1964:111)

Perhaps this is the height of unanticipated consequences. People have produced a society that allows them to feel comfortable only when they function like animals.

Marx argued that capitalism is an inverted world, in which those who rightfully should be on top are relegated to the bottom, and those who deserve to be on the bottom rise to the pinnacle of society. Thus the people who Marx believed should be most important to society—the producers (the proletariat)—are near the bottom, scraping by on a subsistence wage and dominated by the capitalists. The capitalists, who produce nothing of their own but simply live off the labor of others, are the dominant force in society. Also inverted is the sense of what is real in society. For example, it is people who set prices, but they fail to see their essential role in this process. Rather, it appears as if it is the unreal "market" that sets prices. Finally, the reality of life in capitalism is hidden while illusion is seen as fact. For example, from Marx's perspective, the capitalists exploit the proletariat, but the dominant belief is that the abilities of the capitalist lead to success for the worker. We shall return to this theme later in a discussion of ideology in capitalism, but the key point is that in many ways, capitalism is an inverted and distorted social system.

Emancipation

Marx's critique of capitalist society is not an end in itself, of course, but an effort to help bring about the changes needed to create a society in which human potential can be adequately expressed. We can say that the goal of Marx's sociology lies in the ultimate emancipation of humanity from the enslavement of capitalist society (Mészáros, 1970:200). As Marx put it: "Human emancipation will only be complete when the real, individual man . . . has become a *species-being*" (cited in Bender, 1970:66). Vernon Venable catches the essence of the problem and the need for reform quite well:

> Hence human activity ought to be aimed . . . at their collective rescue from the pitiable, fragmentary, self-divided, craft-idiotic, class-enslaved state in which they find themselves. It should aim, in short, at the transformation of human nature. It should make man dignified, integrated, complete and free, so that the resources and potentialities that reside in him . . . may develop, expand, and find fruitful expression.
>
> (Venable, 1945:151–152)

Thus Marx's work on human potential led him both to a critique of capitalist society and to a political program oriented to overcoming the structures of capitalism so that people can express their essential humanity (Mészáros, 1970).

The transition to socialist society and emancipation is brought about endowed with at least potentially positive human characteristics, are able to must not be content with philosophizing about capitalism but rather must develop a critical intellectual stance that will help bring about the action needed to revolutionize society. This concept also is construed to mean that capitalism can be transformed only through concrete action. Thus the proletariat must act to bring about the transition to socialism; they cannot sit back and wait for it to collapse because of internal contradictions. Marx's usage of praxis was both political and theoretical.

The communist society that would be created by praxis "does not rule over the individuals and is nothing in itself beyond the concrete individuals in their social relation to each other" (Gould, 1978:166). This would serve to eliminate alienation ("the human condition in the pre-communist stage" [Barbalet, 1983:53]) and reunite people with their products, productive activities, other people, and themselves. The goal of emancipation is *species-being*. Another way of saying this is that the goal of emancipation is communism,[1] which is "the first real emergence, the actual realization for man of man's essence and of

---

[1] According to Berki, communism is "the *only thing* that is important about Marx's thought" (1983:1).

his essence as something real" (Marx, 1932/1964:187). In Avineri's view, "Marx's postulate about the ultimate possibility of human self-emancipation must be related to his philosophical premise about the initial creation of the world by man" (1968:65). In other words, we cannot understand communism without understanding species-being.

THE STRUCTURES OF CAPITALIST SOCIETY

We have spent many pages analyzing Marx's thoughts on actors, mental processes, and action, much of which is embodied in his work on human potential and its distortion (alienation) by the structure of society, in particular the structure of capitalist society. It is time now to turn to Marx's work on those large-scale structures that are the cause of alienation in capitalist society.

The first issue to be addressed is whether Marx thought of these social structures as "things," that is, as hardened structures. Another way of putting this is to ask whether Marx adopted the position taken by Durkheim (1895/1964) that social facts should be treated as if they were "things." Marx's views on large-scale social structures were shaped by his dialectical approach, especially his tendency to focus on social relations (Ollman, 1976). Marx thought of social structures as being composed of a large number of continuing social relationships. This dynamic, or dialectical, perspective stands in sharp contrast to the view of many neo-Durkheimians, who overlook Durkheim's warning to simply *treat* social facts as things and who regard them as things *in fact*. Although he held a dynamic view of social structures, Marx did regard the set of relationships in capitalism as external to, and coercive of, actors. This is not to say that this set of relationships is inevitable or eternal, but they certainly have achieved objective reality in capitalism, and they must be overthrown in order to move on to communism. We can see how this meshed with Marx's political commitments, because this more relational view makes social structures much more changeable than would a view of them as things.

Commodities

The basis of all of Marx's work on social structures, and the place in which that work is most clearly tied to his views on human potential, is in his analysis of *commodities*. As Georg Lukács put it, "The problem of commodities is . . . the central, *structural* problem of capitalist society" (1922/1968:83).

Marx's conception of commodity was rooted in his materialist orientation, with its focus on the productive activities of actors. As we saw earlier, it was Marx's view that in their interactions with nature and with other actors, people always produce the objects that they need in order to survive; objectification is a necessary and universal aspect of human life. These objects are produced for use by oneself or by others in the immediate environment—they are *use values*. The objects are the products of human labor and cannot achieve an independent existence because they are controlled by the actors. However, in capitalism this process of objectification takes on a new and dangerous form. Instead of producing for themselves or their immediate associates, the actors produce for someone else (the capitalist). The products, instead of being used immediately, are exchanged in the open market for money (*exchange values*). While people produce objects in capitalism, their role in producing commodities, and their control over them, becomes mystified. At first they are led to believe that these objects and the market for them have an independent existence, and then this belief turns into reality as the objects and their market *do* become real, independent phenomena. The commodity becomes an independent, almost mystical external reality (Marx, 1867/1967:35).

Fetishism of Commodities With the development of commodities comes the process Marx labeled the *fetishism of commodities*. The basis of this process is the labor that gives commodities their value. The fetishism of commodities involves the process by which actors forget that it is their labor that gives the commodities their value. They come to believe that value arises from the natural properties of the things themselves or that the impersonal operation of the market gives commodities value. Thus the *market* takes on a function in the eyes of the actors that in Marx's view *only* actors could perform—the production of value. In Marx's terms, "A definite social relation between men . . . assumes, in their eyes, the fantastic form of a relation between things" (1867/1967:72). Granting reality to commodities and the market, the individual in capitalism progressively loses control over them.

> A commodity is therefore a mysterious thing, simply because in it the social character of men's labor appears to them as an objective character stamped upon the product of that labor: because the relations of the producers to the sum total of their own labor is presented to them as a social relation, existing not between themselves, but between the products of their labor.
>
> (Marx, 1867/1967:72)

The beauty of Marx's discussion of commodities and their fetishism is that it takes us from the level of the individual actor and action to the level of large-scale social structures. That is, people endowed with creative minds interact with other people and nature to produce objects, but this natural process results in something grotesque in capitalism. The fetishism of commodities imparts to them and to the marketplace an independent objective reality that is external to, and coercive of, the actor.

Reification The concepts of commodities and fetishism of commodities would appear to be of limited sociological use. The concepts seem to be restricted to the economic realm—that is, to the end result of productive activity. Yet productive activity can—indeed must—be looked at more broadly if we are to grasp the whole of Marx's meaning as well as its application to sociology. We need to understand that people produce not only economic objects (food, clothing, shelters) but also social relationships and, ultimately, social structures. Looked at in this way, the fetishism of commodities is translated into the broader concept of reification (Lukács, 1922/1968). *Reification* can be thought of as the process of coming to believe that humanly created social forms are natural, universal, and absolute and, as a result, that those social forms do in fact acquire those characteristics. The concept of reification implies that people believe that social structures are beyond their control and unchangeable. This belief often comes to be a self-fulfilling prophecy. Then the structures actually *do* acquire the character people endowed them with. By using this concept, we can see that people reify not only commodities but also the whole range of social structures.

We can find the groundwork for a broader concept of reification in Marx's own discussion of labor. Basically, Marx argued that, as a *social* phenomenon, labor becomes a commodity under the peculiar circumstances of capitalism: "Labor-power can appear in the market as a commodity, only if, and so far as, its possessor, the individual whose labor-power it is, offers it for sale, or sells it, as a commodity" (1867/1967:168). Once we admit the possibility of one social phenomenon (labor) becoming reified, it becomes possible for a wide range of other social phenomena to take on the same characteristic (Lefebvre, 1968:16). Just as people reify commodities and other economic phenomena (for example, the division of labor [Rattansi, 1982; Walliman, 1981]), they also reify religious (Barbalet, 1983:147), political, and organizational structures. Marx made this point in reference to the state: "And out of this very contradiction between the individual and . . . the community the latter takes an independent form as the *State*, divorced from the real interests of individual and community" (cited in Bender, 1970:176).

Marx had a few things to say about the range of reified social structures, but he focused primarily on the structural components of the economy. It is these economic structures that Marx saw as causing alienation by breaking down the natural interconnectedness of people and nature.

Capital

The most general economic structural element in Marx's work is *capital,* or the capitalist system. As an independent structure, capital (through the actors who operate in its behalf, the bourgeoisie) exploits the workers, who were and are responsible for its creation. Marx talked of the power of capital appearing "as a power endowed by Nature—a productive power that is immanent in Capital" (1867/1967:333). Thus people tend to reify capital by believing that it is natural for the capitalist system to be external to, and coercive of, them. Workers are exploited by a system that they have *forgotten* they *produced* through their labor and have the capacity to change. "By means of its conversion into an automaton, the instrument of labor confronts the laborer, during the labor-process, in the shape of capital, of dead labor, that dominates, and pumps away, living labor-power" (Marx, 1867/1967:423). This is what led Marx to conclude that capitalism is an inverted world.

Before we get to a discussion of some of Marx's economic ideas, and later to a case study of Marx's economics, the reader should be reminded that this is a book in sociological, not economic, theory. Thus, the economic ideas are introduced in order to illustrate underlying and more basic sociological ideas.

Circulation of Commodities   Marx discussed not only the character of capital in general but also the character of more specific components of the capitalist system. For example, Marx examined the circulation of commodities, which he considered "the starting-point of capital" (1867/1967:146). Marx discussed two types of circulation of commodities. Both represent the sum total of patterned economic relationships that are external to, and coercive of, the actor. One of these types of circulation—Money-Commodities-Money (M-C-M)—is characteristic of capital; the other—Commodities-Money-Commodities (C-M-C)—is not.

In the simple circulation of commodities, the circuit C-M-C predominates. An example of C-M-C would be the fisherman who sells his catch and then uses the money to buy bread. In a society characterized by the simple circulation of commodities, exchange is accomplished by "the conversion of the commodity into money, and the reconversion of the money into a commodity" (Marx, 1867/1967:105). This circuit, however, does not exist in isolation; it is inextricably interrelated to similar circuits involving other commodities. This type of exchange process "develops a whole network of social relations spontaneous in their growth and entirely beyond the control of the actors" (Marx, 1867/1967:112).

The simple circulation of commodities that is characterized by the circuit C-M-C can be considered the second historical type of circulation of commodities. Barter is the first historical form. Both of these circuits eventually lead to the circulation of commodities under capitalism, which is characterized by the circuit M-C-M.

In the capitalist circuit, referred to by Marx as "buying in order to sell" (1867/1967:147), the individual actor buys a commodity with money and in turn exchanges it for money. Here our hypothetical fisherman buys new nets with his profits in order to increase his future profits. This circuit, similar to the circuit under the simple circulation of commodities, is characterized by two antithetical yet complementary phases. At one and the same time, one person's purchase is another's sale. The circulation of commodities under capitalism begins with a purchase (new nets) and ends with a sale (a larger catch of fish). Furthermore, the end of this circuit is not the consumption of the use value, as it is in the simple circulation of commodities. The end is money in an expanded form, money that is qualitatively identical to that at the beginning of the circuit but quantitatively different (Marx, 1867/1967:150).

The importance of the M-C-M circuit, from our point of view, is that it is an even more abstract process than C-M-C. The "real" commodity declines in significance, with the result that the essence of capital is reduced ultimately to the "unreal" circulation of money. This greater abstractness makes reification easier, with the result that the system is even more likely to become external to, and coercive of, actors.

Private Property

Marx also analyzed the process by which *private property* becomes reified in capitalism. In his view, of course, private property, like the other structural components of capitalism, is derived from the labor of workers. *"Private property* is thus the product, the result, the necessary consequence, of *alienated labor,* of the external relation of the worker to nature and to himself"* (Marx, 1932/ 1964:117). But workers lose sight of, and ultimately control over, this fact. Instead of controlling private property, the workers are controlled by it. As with all other structural components of Marx's work, his conception of private property was directly related to his early work on human potential and action as well as to his political goals. In relating private property to his earlier work, Marx made it clear that not only is private property the product of alienated labor but, once in existence, it in turn exacerbates alienation by imposing itself between people and the production process. If people are to realize their human potential, they must overthrow private property as well as all the other structural components of capitalist society: "The positive transcendence of *private property,* as the appropriation of *human* life, is therefore the positive transcendence of all estrangement—that is to say, the return of man from religion, family, state, etc., to his *human,* i.e., social existence" (Marx, 1932/ 1964:136).

Division of Labor

The division of labor is another structural component of capitalism that comes under Marx's scrutiny. Marx and Engels traced the origins of the modern division of labor to the early family, "where wife and children are the slaves of the husband" (1845–46/1970:52). Although Marx was obviously critical of these early forms of the division of labor, he was most critical of its particularly pernicious form within capitalism.

Marx's most basic view of the division of labor is set forth in his distinction between the owners of the means of production and those who must sell their labor-time to the owners in order to survive. More specifically, Marx was interested in the tendency to structure work so that people are forced to specialize in ever more minute tasks. Such specialization prevents actors from realizing and expressing their human potential (Marx, 1867/1967:350).

Marx offered a number of criticisms of the division of labor in capitalism (Venable, 1945). First, the existence of the division of labor artificially separates the individual from the community as a whole. Indeed, people come to focus almost totally on their own slots and ignore, or even fight against, the interest of the whole community. Second, the labor process is broken down so that functions that ideally would be integrated are separated. For example, intellectual functions are separated from manual tasks; work and enjoyment are separated; and the act of production is radically separated from the act of consumption. Third, the powers of the individual are reduced to simply another tool in the production process. Fourth, each person makes only a small contribution to the final product. The worker is disassociated from that product and everything that happens to it after it is produced. More generally, workers as a class lose control over *all* the things that they produce as well as the market for them. Finally, the narrow specialization has the effect on man of "stunting him, dehumanizing him, reducing him to a mere fragment of a man, a crippled monstrosity, an appendage to a machine" (Venable, 1945:124).

These criticisms of the structure of the division of labor led Marx to an inevitable political conclusion—that a society must be created in which people are *not* narrowly specialized:

> In communist society, where nobody has one exclusive sphere of activity but each can become accomplished in any branch he wishes, society regulates the general production and thus makes it possible for me to do one thing today and another tomorrow, to hunt in the morning, fish in the afternoon, rear cattle in the evening, criticize after dinner, just as I have a mind without ever becoming hunter, fisherman, shepherd or critic.
>
> (Marx and Engels, 1845–46/1970:53)

Although Marx probably never believed that such a society was totally possible, it does reflect his interest in eliminating the destructive effects of specialization. Marx was not saying that everyone can or will become good at everything. His point was that the division of labor has artificially prevented people, particularly the proletariat, from developing their abilities to the fullest. As David McLellan makes clear, Marx did not believe "that each should do the work of Raphael, but that anyone in whom there is a potential Raphael should be able to develop without hindrance. The exclusive concentration of artistic talent in particular individuals, and its suppression in the broad mass . . . is a consequence of division of labor" (1971:218). Thus in communism people will not all become, in Marx's view, poets or artists or lawyers, but the artificial barriers preventing people from developing to their fullest will be eliminated. Foremost among these barriers, and one that must be eliminated, is the division of labor.

Social Class

One other aspect of Marx's interest in social structure was social class (primarily the bourgeoisie and the proletariat). Although Marx actually spent very little time analyzing social class as a concept, it is clear that he viewed social classes as structures that are external to, and coercive of, people.

Although Marx himself offered us only hints, Ollman's interpretation of Marx is quite explicit about social class. Ollman emphasized that *social classes* are "reified social relations" or "the relations between men [that] have taken on an independent existence" (1976:204–205). He also linked the emergence of social classes to the previously discussed emergence of commodities in capitalism. *"Class and commodity are brothers under the skin"* (Ollman, 1976:205; italics added). Social classes arise out of the acts of production; people come to reify classes, and as a result these classes come to have a life of their own that constrains the actor. Marx did not make this explicit, but it makes sense, given the general thrust of his arguments.

In this section, we have examined Marx's views on large-scale social structures. We saw that he tended to view them relationally rather than as real, material structures. Nevertheless, they are external and coercive forces to Marx. All his views on such structures were rooted in his conception of commodities and the fetishism of commodities. Moving beyond the purely economic realm, Marx adopted the same view about social structures. But the bulk of Marx's work concerns the structures of the economy in capitalism—commodities, capital, private property, the division of labor, and social class. All these evolve out of the thoughts and actions of actors, and once in existence, they constrain the very processes that created them. Most of Marx's political attention was devoted to the question of how these structures could be overcome so that a communist society might be created.

CULTURAL ASPECTS OF CAPITALIST SOCIETY

Marx focused on the large-scale structures of capitalist society and their alienating impact on human beings. He did not have a great deal to say about the cultural domain, but a careful analysis indicates that he was not insensitive to the importance of this aspect of social reality. Marx's materialism led him away from a concern with culture, and it could be said that at times Marx went too far in his rejection of this domain, which he associated with the weaknesses of Hegelian philosophy. For example, in *The Critique of Political Economy* Marx wrote:

> The totality of these relations of production constitutes the *economic structure* of society, the *real foundation,* on which arises a legal and political superstructure and to which correspond definite forms of *social consciousness.* The mode of production of *material* life *conditions* the general processes of social, political, and intellectual life. It is not the consciousness of men that determines their existence, but their social existence that determines their consciousness.
>
> (Marx, 1859/1970:20–21; italics added)

Marx might be thought of here as talking about consciousness in a cultural sense (that is, talking about norms, values, or in Hegel's terms, spirit, or *Geist*) and not in the sense of mental processes and the social construction of reality. Given this interpretation, Marx seemed to be relegating the cultural level to the status of an "epiphenomenon" determined by social and economic structures. This seems to be confirmed when, slightly later in the same work, Marx appeared to reduce all social change to change of the material base on which is erected the cultural superstructure:

> Then begins an era of social revolution. The changes in the *economic foundation* lead sooner or later to the transformation of the whole immense *superstructure*. In studying such transformations it is always necessary to distinguish between the *material* transformation of the economic conditions of production, which can be determined with the precision of natural science, and the *legal, political, religious, artistic* or *philosophic—in short, ideological forms* in which men become *conscious* of this conflict and fight it out. *Just as one does not judge an individual by what he thinks about himself, so one cannot judge such a period of transformation by its consciousness, but on the contrary, this consciousness must be explained from the contradictions of material life.*
>
> (Marx, 1859/1970:21; italics added)

It is even clearer here that Marx was talking about the cultural level ("the legal, political, religious, artistic, philosophic—in short, ideological forms"). He even differentiated between individual consciousness and the consciousness of a "period." We must applaud Marx for this awareness and this clear differentiation, but we also must be highly critical of his tendency to reduce the cultural domain to an epiphenomenon, if that is in fact what he did.

However, contrary to these words from the preface to *The Critique of Political Economy*—which is, unfortunately, one of Marx's most simplistic statements— we are led by the thrust of his entire work and by his commitment to the dialectic to dismiss such deterministic statements. A commitment to the dialectic means a commitment to studying the interrelationships among phenomena; it is inherently antideterministic. It could be argued that the nature of capitalism led to the preeminence of the structural level, with the result that the other levels are under its sway. Although this is true to Marx's characterization of capitalism, he still did not simply dismiss the cultural level; he had a number of things to offer here, particularly in his discussions of class consciousness and false consciousness as well as ideology.

Class Consciousness and False Consciousness

The ideas of class consciousness and false consciousness are intimately related in Marx's work. Both refer to idea systems shared by social classes. In capitalism both capitalists and workers have incorrect assessments of how the system works and of their role and interest in it (*false consciousness*). In the evolution toward communism, there is the possibility that the proletariat will develop an accurate conception of how capitalism works and how it affects them (*class consciousness*).

What is characteristic of capitalism, for *both* the proletariat and the bourgeoisie, is false consciousness. We are not surprised to learn that workers have false consciousness, but it is sometimes startling to think of capitalists in this way. After all, they are presumably exploiting the system, and the proletariat, to their advantage. Georg Lukács (1922/1968), one of the foremost interpreters of Marx, pointed to a number of elements of the false consciousness of the bourgeoisie.The bourgeoisie is unaware of its own history and the role it played in the formation of capitalism. More important, it is unaware of the contradictions that exist within capitalism as well as of the role it is playing in contributing to those burgeoning contradictions. The bourgeoisie, like the proletariat, is unaware of the consequences of its actions. Its idea systems contain delusions about its control over the capitalist system. The fact is that its actions are contributing to the ultimate demise of the system that it believes it is serving to buttress. The proletariat's thought system is at least as deluded as the bourgeoisie's.

There is, however, a crucial difference here between the two classes. The bourgeoisie can never transform its false consciousness into true class consciousness; this is possible only for the proletariat. In Marx's view, the proletariat occupies this privileged position because as the propertyless class, it is the model for the future propertyless society. At the height of capitalism, the proletariat "is already a class in opposition to capital, but not yet a class for itself" (McLellan, 1971:155). It is not adequate for the proletariat to be a "class in itself"; it must become a "class for itself." If the proletariat is to take on its historic role in capitalism, "it must become a class not only 'as against capital' but also 'for itself'; that is to say, the class struggle must be raised from the level of economic necessity to the level of conscious aim and effective class consciousness" (Lukács, 1922/1968:76).

In talking about class (and false) consciousness, Marx was talking not about individual consciousness but about the consciousness of the class as a whole. Furthermore, the concepts of class consciousness and false consciousness are not, in Marx's hands, static but are rather dynamic idea systems that make sense only in terms of social change and development. False consciousness describes the situation throughout the capitalist epoch, whereas class consciousness is the condition that awaits the proletariat and that can help bring about the change from capitalist to communist society.

Ideology

The other major cultural dimension of Marx's analysis is ideology. An *ideology* can be defined as an integrated system of ideas that is external to, and coercive of, people (Lefebvre, 1968). Although Marx often talked of ideologies in the same way as he talked about class and false consciousness—that is, as mere reflections of the material base—it is clear that ideologies, too, take on an independent existence in his system. Some analysts make much of the apparent determinism of passages like the following, but it is the author's view that Marx was only offering one side of his multifaceted analysis here:

> The *ideas* [italics added] of the ruling class are in every epoch the ruling ideas, i.e.,
> the class which is the ruling *material* force of society, is at the same time, its ruling

intellectual force. The class, which has the means of material production at its disposal, has control at the same time over the means of mental production, so that thereby, generally speaking, the ideas of those who lack the means of mental production are subject to it. *The ruling ideas are nothing more than the ideal expression of the dominant material relationships* [italics added], the dominant material relationships grasped as ideas.

(Marx and Engels, 1845–46/1970:64)

At least three basic interrelated ideas are involved in Marx's conceptualization of ideologies. First, they certainly do represent the interests of the ruling class, but that is not to say that these ideas do not have a reciprocal impact on material interests. Second, they constitute an "inverted, truncated reflection of reality" (Lefebvre, 1968:64). Third, ideologies have an independent existence that is coercive of people. Lefebvre caught the essential point for us here in discussing the effect of ideologies on members of the oppressed class: "It is the role of ideologies to secure the assent of the oppressed and exploited. Ideologies represent the latter to themselves in such a way as to wrest from them, in addition to material wealth, their spiritual acceptance of this situation, even their support" (1968:76).

An ideological system functions to alter the thoughts and actions of members of the oppressed class. In this way, ideologies serve to foster the exploitation of the proletariat. Of course, ideologies do not function in a vacuum; they operate through agents who carry out their dictates. Thus ideologies affect the actions of agents of the ruling class, who, in turn, affect the thoughts and actions of the proletariat.

MARX'S ECONOMICS: A CASE STUDY

This chapter is devoted to an analysis of Marx's sociology, but of course it is his economics for which he is far better known. Although we have touched on a number of aspects of Marx's economics, we have not dealt with it in a coherent fashion. In this closing section, we will look at Marx's economics, not as economics per se, but rather as an exemplification of his sociological theory (Mazlish, 1984).[2] There is much more to Marxian economics, but this is the most relevant way to deal with it in a book devoted to sociological theory.

A starting point for Marxian economics is in the concepts, previously touched on, of use value and exchange value. People have always created use values; that is, they have always produced things that directly satisfy their wants. A *use value* is defined qualitatively; that is, something either is or is not useful. An *exchange value*, however, is defined quantitatively, not quali-

---

[2] *One* way of looking at Marx's economic theory (for example, the labor theory of value) is as a specific application of his more general sociological theory. This stands in contrast to G. Cohen's (1978) work, in which his overriding concern is the underlying *economic* theory in Marx's work. Although Cohen sees the "economic" and the "social" as being interchangeable in Marx's work, he clearly implies that Marx's economic theory is the more general.

tatively. It is defined by the amount of labor needed to appropriate useful qualities. Whereas use values are produced to satisfy one's own needs, exchange values are produced to be exchanged for values of another use. Whereas the production of use values is a natural human expression, the existence of exchange values sets in motion a process by which humanity is distorted. The entire edifice of capitalism, including commodities, the market, money, and so forth, is erected on the base of exchange values.

To Marx, the basic source of any value was the amount of socially necessary labor-time needed to produce an article under the normal conditions of production and with the average degree of skill and intensity of the time. This is the well-known *labor theory of value.* Although it is clear that labor lies at the base of use value, this fact grows progressively less clear as we move to exchange values, commodities, the market, and capitalism. To put it another way, "The determination of the magnitude of value by labor-time is therefore a secret, hidden under the apparent fluctuations in relative values of commodities" (Marx, 1867/1967:75). Labor, as the source of all value, is a secret in capitalism that allows the capitalists to exploit the workers.

According to Peter Worsley, Marx "put at the heart of his sociology—as no other sociology does—the theme of exploitation" (1982:115). The capitalists pay the workers *less* than the value the workers produce and keep the rest for themselves. The workers are not aware of this exploitation, and, often, neither are the capitalists. The capitalists believe that this extra value is derived from their own cleverness, their capital investment, their manipulation of the market, and so on. Marx stated that "so long as trade is good, the capitalist is too much absorbed in money grubbing to take notice of this gratuitous gift of labor" (1867/1967:207). In sum, Marx said:

> The capitalist does not know that the normal pace of labor also includes a definite quantity of unpaid labor, and that this very unpaid labor is the normal source of his gain, the category, surplus labor-time, does not exist at all for him, since it is included in the normal working-day, which he thinks he has paid for in wages.
>
> (Marx, 1867/1967:550)

This leads us to Marx's central concept of *surplus value.* This is defined as the difference between the value of the product and the value of the elements consumed in the formation of that product. Although means of production (raw materials and tools, the value of which comes from the labor involved in extracting or producing them) are consumed in the production process, it is labor that is the real source of surplus value. "The rate of surplus-value is therefore an exact expression for the degree of exploitation of labor-power by capital, or of the laborer by the capitalist" (Marx, 1867/1967:218). This points to one of Marx's more colorful metaphors: "Capital is dead labor, that, vampire-like, only lives by sucking living labor, and lives the more, the more labor it sucks" (1867/1967:233).

The surplus derived from this process is used by the capitalists to pay for such things as rent to landowners and interest to banks. But the most important derivation from it is profit. The capitalists can use this profit for private consumption, but that would not lead to the expansion of capitalism. Rather they expand their enterprise by converting it into a base for the creation of still more surplus value.

The desire for more profit and more surplus value for expansion pushes capitalism toward what Marx called the *general law of capitalist accumulation*. The capitalists seek to exploit workers as much as possible: "The constant tendency of capital is to force the cost of labor back towards . . . zero" (Marx, 1867/1967:600). Marx basically argued that the structure and the ethos of capitalism push the capitalists in the direction of the accumulation of more and more capital. In order to do this, given Marx's view that labor is the source of value, the capitalists are led to intensify the exploitation of the proletariat. Ultimately, however, increased exploitation yields fewer and fewer gains; an upper limit of exploitation is reached. In addition, as this limit is approached, the government is forced to place restrictions on the actions of capitalists (for example, laws limiting the length of the workday). As a result, the capitalists must look for other devices, and a major one is the substitution of machines for people. This substitution is made relatively easy, because the capitalists already have reduced the workers to laboring machines performing a series of simple operations. As mechanization proceeds, more and more people are put out of work and fall from the proletariat to the "industrial reserve army." At the same time, heightening competition and the burgeoning costs of technology lead to a progressive decline in the number of capitalists. In the end, Marx foresaw a situation in which society would be characterized by a tiny number of exploitative capitalists and a huge mass of proletarians and members of the industrial reserve army. In these extreme circumstances, capitalism would be most vulnerable to revolution. As Marx put it, the expropriation of the masses by the capitalists would be replaced by "the expropriation of a few usurpers by the mass of people" (1867/1967:764). The capitalists, of course, seek to forestall their demise. For example, they sponsor colonial adventures with the objective of shifting at least some of the burden of exploitation from the home front to the colonies. However, in Marx's view these efforts are ultimately doomed to failure, and the capitalists will face rebellion at home and abroad.

The key point about the general law of capitalist accumulation is the degree to which actors, both capitalist and proletarian, are impelled by the structure and ethos of capitalism to do what they do. Marx usually did not blame individual capitalists for their actions; he saw these actions as largely determined by the logic of the capitalist system. This is consistent with his view that actors in capitalism generally are devoid of creative independence. However, the developmental process inherent in capitalism provides the conditions necessary for the ultimate reemergence of such creative action and, with it, the overthrow of the capitalist system.

Now that we have discussed Marx's economic ideas in some detail, the reader should remember that we are not interested in those economic ideas per se; rather, we are interested in them for what they tell us about Marx's more basic sociological theory.

SUMMARY

Despite his overwhelming importance to sociology in both a positive and a negative sense, Karl Marx's work rarely has received its due in historical analyses of the development of sociological theory. It is one of the goals of this book to accord Marx his proper place in that history.

The chapter begins with a discussion of the dialectical approach that Marx derived from Hegel and that shapes all of Marx's work. An interest in the dialectic leads into complex philosophical issues, but our discussion concentrates on those elements of the dialectic that are most relevant to Marx's sociology and to sociological theory in general. The dialectic is contrasted with the causal logic that dominates much of sociological thinking. Among other things, the dialectic emphasizes that there are no simple cause-and-effect relationships among elements of the social world; there is no clear dividing line between fact and value; and there are no hard-and-fast dividing lines among phenomena in the social world. Further, the dialectic stresses that we should focus on social relationships; we should be oriented not only to the present but also to the past and future; we should resist the idea that there are social inevitabilities; and we should be concerned with conflicts and contradictions within the social world. Despite his political orientation toward the creation of a communist society, Marx devoted his attention to dialectical *and* critical analyses of capitalist society. It was his hope that such criticism would help bring about the overthrow of capitalist society and the coming of socialism.

In analyzing the substance of Marx's work, we begin with an analysis of the potential of human beings. This is Marx's image of human nature, but it is a human nature that is greatly affected by its social setting. Marx saw capitalism as a setting that distorts humanity, whereas communism would be a setting in which humanness would be allowed to express itself. Marx's actors are endowed with consciousness and creativity, which are expressed in various types of actions and interactions. Of utmost importance here is the need to interact with other people and with nature in order to produce the objects that people need to survive. It is significant that this natural process is subverted as a result of the unanticipated consequences of capitalism.

The distortions of humans caused by the structures of capitalism fall within the bounds of Marx's famous concept of *alienation*. People are naturally connected with their productive activity, their products, their fellow workers, and, ultimately, with themselves, with their inherent nature as human beings. But all these connections are severed by the structures of capitalism. On a political level, this led Marx to an interest in emancipating people from the oppressive structures of capitalism. On an intellectual level, it led him to examine the nature of the structures of capitalism and their oppressive impact on actors.

We examine various aspects of the structure of capitalist society. We discuss the central role played by commodities in capitalism and the way they are created by the process known as the *fetishism of commodities*. In effect, people endow commodities, and the market for them, with a life of their own. This concept is later expanded (by Lukács) to the idea of reification; that is, people make fetishes not only of commodities but also of many other structural components of capitalist society. In this context, we look at capital as the most general reified structure in capitalist society. Also, we examine a number of reified components in capitalist society, including private property, the division of labor, and social class.

Although Marx, especially in his later work, was particularly concerned with the structures of capitalism, he did have some things to say about the cultural aspects of capitalist society, especially class consciousness, false consciousness, and ideology.

We close the chapter with a discussion of Marxian economics as an illustration of Marx's overall sociological theory. Although for various reasons people have tended to ignore it, there is a very powerful sociological theory in Marx's work.

EMILE DURKHEIM

*E*MILE Durkheim's theoretical orientation, unlike that of many other major sociological thinkers, contains little ambiguity. He was deeply concerned with the impact of the large-scale structures of society, and society itself, on the thoughts and actions of individuals. He was most influential in shaping structural-functional theory, with its emphasis on social structure and culture. In light of this, our objective in this chapter is to describe Durkheim's theoretical perspective, with particular (but not exclusive) attention to its macrosociological concerns.

The development and use of the concept of a social fact lies at the heart of Durkheim's sociology. We will have a great deal to say about this concept in this chapter, but a brief introduction to it is needed at this point. In modern terms, *social facts* are the social structures and cultural norms and values that are external to, and coercive of, actors. Thus readers of this text, as students, are constrained by such social structures as the university bureaucracy as well as the norms and values of American society, which place such great importance on getting a college education. Similar social facts constrain people in all areas of social life.

To understand why Durkheim developed the concept of social fact and what it means, we need to examine at least a few aspects of the intellectual context in which he lived.

In Durkheim's (1900/1973:3) view, sociology was born in France in the nineteenth century. He recognized its roots in the ancient philosophers (Plato, Aristotle) and more proximate sources in French philosophers such as Montesquieu and Condorcet. For example, Durkheim noted, "It is Montesquieu who first laid down the fundamental principles of social science" (1893/ 1960:61). However, in Durkheim's view, Montesquieu (and Condorcet) did not go far enough: "They limited themselves to offering ingenious or novel views on social facts rather than seeking to create an entirely new discipline" (1900/ 1973:6). Durkheim (1928/1962:142) gave Saint-Simon credit for first formulating the notion of a science of the social world, but Saint-Simon's ideas were seen as scattered and imperfect. Those ideas were, in Durkheim's view, perfected by Comte, "the first to make a coherent and methodical effort to establish the positive science of societies" (1900/1973:10).

Although the term *sociology* had been coined some years earlier by Comte, there was no field of sociology per se in late nineteenth-century France. There were no schools, departments, or even professors of sociology. There were a few thinkers who were dealing with ideas that were in one way or another sociological, but there was as yet no disciplinary "home" for sociology. Indeed, there was strong opposition from existing disciplines to the founding of such a field. The most significant opposition came from psychology and philosophy, two fields that claimed already to cover the domain sought by sociology. The dilemma for Durkheim, given his aspirations for sociology, was how to create for it a separate and identifiable niche.

To separate it from philosophy, Durkheim argued that sociology should be oriented toward empirical research. This seems simple enough, but the situation was complicated by Durkheim's belief that sociology was also threatened by a philosophical school *within* sociology itself. In his view, the two other major figures of the epoch who thought of themselves as sociologists, Comte and Spencer, were far more interested in philosophizing, in abstract theorizing, than they were in studying the social world empirically. If the field were to continue in the direction set by Comte and Spencer, Durkheim felt, it would become nothing more than a branch of philosophy. As a result, he found it necessary to attack both Comte and Spencer (Durkheim, 1895/1964:19–20). He accused both of substituting preconceived ideas of social phenomena for the actual study of the phenomena in the real world. Thus Comte was said to be guilty of assuming theoretically that the social world was evolving in the direction of an increasingly perfect society, rather than engaging in the hard, rigorous, and basic work of actually studying the changing nature of various societies. Similarly, Spencer was accused of assuming harmony in society rather than studying whether harmony actually existed.

SOCIAL FACTS

In order to help sociology move away from philosophy and to give it a clear and separate identity, Durkheim argued that the distinctive subject matter of sociology should be the study of social facts. The concept of social fact has several components, but crucial in separating sociology from philosophy is the idea that *social facts are to be treated as things*. In that they are to be treated as *things,* social facts are to be studied empirically, *not* philosophically. Durkheim believed that ideas can be known introspectively (philosophically), but *things* "cannot be conceived by purely mental activity"; they require for their conception "data from outside the mind" (1895/1964:xliii). This empirical study of social facts as things sets Durkheimian sociology apart from the largely introspective theorizing of Comte and Spencer.

Although treating social facts as things countered the threat from philosophy (at least as far as Durkheim was concerned), it was only part of the answer to the problem of dealing with the threat coming from psychology. Like Durkheimian sociology, psychology was already highly empirical. To differentiate sociology from psychology, Durkheim argued that social facts were *external to,* and *coercive of,* the actor. Sociology was to be the study of social facts, whereas psychology was relegated the study of psychological facts. To Durkheim, psychological facts were basically inherited phenomena. Although this certainly does not describe psychology today (and was not a very accurate description of the subject matter of psychology even then), it did allow Durkheim to draw a clear differentiation between the two fields. Psychological facts are clearly internal (inherited), and social facts are external and coercive. As we will soon see, this differentiation is not so neat as Durkheim would have liked us to believe. Nevertheless, by defining a social fact as a *thing* that is *external to, and coercive of, the actor,* Durkheim seems to have done a reasonably good job (at least for that historical era) of attaining his objective of separating sociology from both philosophy and psychology. However, it should be noted that to do this, Durkheim took an "extremist" position (Karady, 1983:79–80), especially in limiting sociology to the study of social facts. This position was to limit at least some branches of sociology to the present day.

We know that a social fact is a thing and that it is external and coercive, but what else is a social fact? Actually, Durkheim differentiated between two broad types of social facts—material and nonmaterial. *Material social facts* are the clearer of the two because they are real, material entities, but they are also of lesser significance in Durkheim's work. As Durkheim put it, "The social fact is sometimes materialized so far as to become an element of the external world" (1897/1951:313). Architecture and the law would be two examples of what he meant by material social facts. We will encounter other examples in this chapter.

But the bulk of Durkheim's work, and the heart of his sociology, lies in the study of nonmaterial social facts. Durkheim said: "Not all social consciousness achieves . . . externalization and materialization" (1897/1951:315). What sociologists now call *norms* and *values,* or more generally culture (see Alexander, 1988), are good examples of what Durkheim meant by *nonmaterial social facts.* But this idea creates a problem: How can nonmaterial social facts like norms and values be external to the actor? Where could they be found except in the minds of actors? And if they are in the minds of actors, then are they not internal rather than external?

To clarify this issue, we must refine Durkheim's argument by contending that while material social facts are clearly external and coercive, nonmaterial social facts are not so clear-cut. (For a similar distinction, see Takla and Pope [1985:82].) To at least some extent, they are found in the minds of actors. The best way to conceptualize nonmaterial social facts is to think of them as external to, and coercive of, psychological facts. In this way we can see that both psychological facts and *some* social facts exist within and between consciousness. Durkheim made this clear in a number of places. At one point he said of social facts, "Individual minds, forming groups by mingling and fusing, give birth to a being, *psychological if you will,* but constituting a psychic individuality of a new sort" (Durkheim, 1895/1964:103; italics added). At another point, Durkheim said, "This does not mean that they [nonmaterial social facts] are not also mental after a fashion, since they all consist of ways to thinking or behaving" (1895/1964:xlix). Thus it is best to think of nonmaterial social facts, at least in part, as mental phenomena, but mental phenomena that are external to, and coercive of, another aspect of the mental process—psychological facts. This confounds Durkheim's differentiation between sociology and psychology somewhat, but it does serve to make the differentiation more realistic and as a result more defensible. Sociology *is* concerned with mental phenomena, but they are usually of a different order from the mental concerns of psychology. Durkheim thus was arguing that sociologists are interested in norms and values, whereas psychologists are concerned with such things as human instincts.

Social facts, then, play a central role in the sociology of Emile Durkheim. A useful way of extracting the most important social facts from his work, and for analyzing his thoughts on the relationships among these phenomena, is to begin with Durkheim's efforts to organize them into *levels* of social reality. He began at the level of material social facts, not because it was the most important level to him, but because its elements often take causal priority in his theorizing. They affect nonmaterial social facts, which are the real focus of his work. (Although we will focus here on both types of social facts, we will have some things to say later about Durkheim's thoughts on the more microscopic aspects of social reality.)

The major levels of social reality (Lukes, 1972:9–10) in Durkheim's work can be depicted as follows:

A. Material Social Facts
1. Society
2. Structural components of society (for example, church and state)
3. Morphological components of society (for example, population distribution, channels of communication, and housing arrangements)
B. Nonmaterial Social Facts
1. Morality
2. Collective conscience
3. Collective representations
4. Social currents

The levels within the two categories are listed in terms of descending order of generality.

It is his focus on macro-level social facts that is one of the reasons why Durkheim played a central role in the development of structural functionalism, which has a similar, macro-level orientation (see Chapter 7 on structural functionalism). More specifically, drawing on biology and using an organismic analogy, Durkheim saw society as composed of "organs" (social facts), or social structures, that had a variety of functions for society. Durkheim urged that we distinguish functions, or the ends served by various structures, from the factors that caused them to come into existence. Durkheim was interested in studying both the causes of social structures and the functions they perform, although he wanted to carefully differentiate between these two topics of study.

We can trace the logic of Durkheim's theory in his analysis of the development of the modern world. This is most clearly shown in one of his most important works, *The Division of Labor in Society* (Durkheim, 1893/1964).

THE DIVISION OF LABOR IN SOCIETY

Durkheim based his analysis in *The Division of Labor in Society* on his conception of two ideal types of society. The more primitive type, characterized by *mechanical solidarity*, has a relatively undifferentiated social structure, with little or no division of labor. The more modern type, characterized by *organic solidarity*, has a much greater and more refined division of labor. To Durkheim the *division of labor in society* is a material social fact that involves the degree to which tasks or responsibilities are specialized. People in primitive societies tend to occupy very general positions in which they perform a wide variety of tasks and handle a large number of responsibilities. In other words, a primitive person tended to be a jack-of-all-trades. In contrast, those who live in more modern societies occupy more specialized positions and have a much narrower range of tasks and responsibilities. For example, being a mother-housewife in primitive societies is a much less specialized position than it is in a modern society. Laundry services, diaper services, home delivery, and labor-saving devices (dishwashers, microwave ovens, Cuisinarts, and so forth) perform a number of tasks that were formerly the responsibility of the mother-housewife.

The changes in the division of labor have had enormous implications for the structure of society, and some of the more important implications are reflected in the differences between the two types of solidarity—mechanical and organic. In addressing the issue of solidarity, Durkheim was interested in what holds society together. A society characterized by mechanical solidarity is unified because all people are generalists. The bond among people is that they are all engaged in similar activities and have similar responsibilities. In contrast, a society characterized by organic solidarity is held together by the differences among people, by the fact that they have different tasks and responsibilities. Because people in modern society perform a relatively narrow range of tasks, they need many other people in order to survive. The primitive family headed by father-hunter and mother-food gatherer is practically self-sufficient, but the modern family, in order to make it through the week, needs the grocer, baker, butcher, auto mechanic, teacher, police officer, and so forth. These people, in turn, need the kinds of services that others provide in order to live in the modern world. Modern society, in Durkheim's view, is thus held together by the specialization of people and their need for the services of many others. Furthermore, Durkheim was concerned not only with the specialization of individuals but also that of groups, structures, and institutions. One final difference between mechanical and organic solidarity is worth mentioning. Because people in societies characterized by mechanical solidarity are more likely to be similar to one another in terms of what they do, there is a greater likelihood of competition among them. In contrast, in societies with organic solidarity differentiation allows people to cooperate more and to all be supported by the same resource base.

Dynamic Density

The division of labor was a material social fact to Durkheim because it is the pattern of interaction in the social world. Another, and closely related, material social fact is the major causal factor in Durkheim's theory of the transition from mechanical to organic solidarity—*dynamic density*. This concept refers to the number of people in a society and the amount of interaction that occurs among them. Neither population increase nor an increase in interaction, when taken separately, is a significant factor in societal change. An increase in numbers of people *and* an increase in the interaction among them (which is dynamic density) lead to the change from mechanical to organic solidarity because together they bring about more competition for scarce resources and a more intense struggle for survival among the various parallel and similar

EMILE DURKHEIM: A Biographical Sketch

Emile Durkheim was born on April 15, 1858, in Epinal, France. He was descended from a long line of rabbis and himself studied to be a rabbi, but by the time he was in his teens, he had rejected his heritage and become an agnostic. From that time on, his lifelong interest in religion was academic rather than theological. He was dissatisfied not only with his religious training but also with his general education and its emphasis on literary and esthetic matters. He longed for schooling in scientific methods and in the moral principles needed to guide social life. He rejected a traditional academic career in philosophy and sought instead to acquire the scientific training needed to contribute to the moral guidance of society. Although he was interested in scientific sociology, there was no field of sociology at that time, so between 1882 and 1887 he taught philosophy in a number of provincial schools in the Paris area.

His appetite for science was whetted further by a trip to Germany, where he was exposed to the scientific psychology being pioneered by Wilhelm Wundt. In the years immediately after his visit to Germany, Durkheim published a good deal, basing his work, in part, on his experiences there. These publications helped him gain a position in the department of philosophy at the University of Bordeaux in 1887. There Durkheim offered the first course in social science in a French university. This was a particularly impressive accomplishment, because only a decade earlier, a furor had erupted in a French university by the mention of Auguste Comte in a student dissertation. Durkheim's main responsibility, however, was the teaching of courses in education to schoolteachers, and his most important course was in the area of moral education. His goal was to communicate a moral system to the educators, who he hoped would then pass it on to young people in an effort to help reverse the moral degeneration he saw around him in French society.

The years that followed were characterized by a series of personal successes for Durkheim. In 1893 he published his French doctoral thesis, *The Division of Labor in Society*, as well as his Latin thesis on Montesquieu. His major methodological statement, *The Rules of Sociological Method,* appeared in 1895, followed (in 1897) by his empirical application of those methods in the study *Suicide.* By 1896 he had become a full professor at Bordeaux. In 1902 he was summoned to the famous French university, the Sorbonne, and in 1906 he was named professor of the science of education, a title that was changed in 1913 to professor of the science of education *and sociology.* The other of his most famous works, *The Elementary Forms of Religious Life,* was published in 1912.

Durkheim is most often thought of today as a political conservative, and his influence within sociology certainly has been a conservative one. But in his time, he was considered a liberal, and this was exemplified by the active public role he played in the defense of Alfred Dreyfus, the Jewish army captain whose court-martial for treason was felt by many to be anti-Semitic.

components of primitive society. Because individuals, groups, families, tribes, and so forth perform virtually identical functions, they are likely to clash over these functions, especially if resources are scarce. The rise of the division of labor allows people and the social structures they create to complement, rather

Durkheim was deeply offended by the Dreyfus affair, particularly its anti-Semitism. But Durkheim did not attribute this anti-Semitism to racism among the French people. Characteristically, he saw it as a symptom of the moral sickness confronting French society as a whole. He said:

> When society undergoes suffering, it feels the need to find someone whom it can hold responsible for its sickness, on whom it can avenge its misfortunes: and those against whom public opinion already discriminates are naturally designated for this role. These are the pariahs who serve as expiatory victims. What confirms me in this interpretation is the way in which the result of Dreyfus's trial was greeted in 1894. There was a surge of joy in the boulevards. People celebrated as a triumph what should have been a cause for public mourning. At least they knew whom to blame for the economic troubles and moral distress in which they lived. The trouble came from the Jews. The charge had been officially proved. By this very fact alone, things already seemed to be getting better and people felt consoled.
>
> (Lukes, 1972:345)

Thus, Durkheim's interest in the Dreyfus affair stemmed from his deep and lifelong interest in morality and the moral crisis confronting modern society.

To Durkheim, the answer to the Dreyfus affair and crises like it lay in ending the moral disorder in society. Because that could not be done quickly or easily, Durkheim suggested more specific actions such as severe repression of those who incite hatred of others and government efforts to show the public how it is being misled. He urged people to "have the courage to proclaim aloud what they think, and to unite together in order to achieve victory in the struggle against public madness" (Lukes, 1972:347).

Durkheim's (1928/1962) interest in socialism is also taken as evidence against the idea that he was a conservative, but his kind of socialism was very different from the kind that interested Marx and his followers. In fact, Durkheim labeled Marxism as a set of "disputable and out-of-date hypotheses" (Lukes, 1972:323). To Durkheim, socialism represented a movement aimed at the moral regeneration of society through scientific morality, and he was not interested in short-term political methods or the economic aspects of socialism. He did not see the proletariat as the salvation of society, and he was greatly opposed to agitation or violence. Socialism for Durkheim was very different from what we usually think of as socialism; it simply represented a system in which the moral principles discovered by scientific sociology were to be applied.

Durkheim, as we will see throughout this book, had a profound influence on the development of sociology, but his influence was not restricted to it. Much of his impact on other fields came through the journal *L'année sociologique,* which he founded in 1898. An intellectual circle arose around the journal with Durkheim at its center. Through it, he and his ideas influenced such fields as anthropology, history, linguistics, and—somewhat ironically, considering his early attacks on the field—psychology.

Durkheim died on November 15, 1917, a celebrated figure in French intellectual circles, but it was not until over twenty years later, with the publication of Talcott Parsons's *The Structure of Social Action* (1937), that his work became a significant influence on American sociology.

than conflict with, one another, and this, in turn, makes peaceful coexistence more likely. Furthermore, the increasing division of labor makes for greater efficiency, with the result that resources increase, and more and more people can survive peacefully.

Although Durkheim was interested in explaining how the division of labor and dynamic density lead to different types of social solidarity, he was primarily interested in the impact of these material changes on, and the nature of, nonmaterial social facts in both mechanically and organically solidified societies. However, because of his image of what a *science* of sociology should be, Durkheim felt that it was impossible to study nonmaterial social facts directly. Direct consideration of nonmaterial social facts was, for him, more philosophical than sociological. In order to study nonmaterial social facts scientifically, the sociologist would have to seek and examine material social facts that reflect the nature of, and changes in, nonmaterial social facts. In *The Division of Labor in Society* it is law, and the differences between law in societies with mechanical solidarity and law in societies with organic solidarity, that plays this role.

Law

Durkheim argued that a society with mechanical solidarity is characterized by *repressive law*. Because people are very similar in this type of society, and because they tend to believe very strongly in a common morality, any offense against their shared value system is likely to be of significance to most individuals. Because most people feel the offense and believe deeply in the common morality, an offender is likely to be severely punished for any action that is considered an offense against the collective moral system. The theft of a pig must lead to the cutting off of the offender's hands; blaspheming against God or gods might well result in the removal of one's tongue. Because people are so involved in the moral system, an offense against it is likely to be met with swift, severe punishment.

In contrast, a society with organic solidarity is characterized by *restitutive law*. Instead of being severely punished for even seemingly minor offenses against the collective morality, individuals in this more modern type of society are likely simply to be asked to comply with the law or to repay—make restitution to—those who have been harmed by their actions. Although some repressive law continues to exist in a society with organic solidarity (for example, the death penalty), restitutive law is more characteristic. There is little or no powerful and coercive common morality; the vast majority of people do not react emotionally to a breach of the law. The monitoring of repressive law is largely in the hands of the masses in a society with mechanical solidarity, but the maintenance of restitutive law is primarily the responsibility of specialized agencies (for example, the police and the courts). This is consistent with the increased division of labor in a society with organic solidarity.

Changes in a material social fact like the law are, in Durkheim's theoretical system, merely reflections of changes in the more crucial elements of his sociology—nonmaterial social facts such as morality, collective conscience, collective representations, social currents, and, most questionably from a modern sociological perspective, the group mind. (All these concepts will be discussed below.)

At the most general and all-inclusive level, Durkheim was a sociologist of morality. Indeed, Ernest Wallwork (1972:182) argued that Durkheim's sociology is merely a by-product of his concern with moral issues. That is, Durkheim's interest in the moral problems of his day led him as a sociologist to devote most of his attention to the moral elements of social life. At its most basic level, Durkheim's great concern was with the declining strength of the common morality in the modern world. In Durkheim's view, people were in danger of a "pathological" loosening of moral bonds. These moral bonds were important to Durkheim, for without them the individual would be enslaved by ever-expanding and insatiable passions. People would be impelled by their passions into a mad search for gratification, but each new gratification would lead only to more and more needs. Durkheim held the seemingly paradoxical view that the individual needs morality and external control in order to be free. This is a curious definition of freedom, but it is the position that Durkheim took.

Anomie

Many of the problems that occupied Durkheim stem from his concern with the decline of the common morality. In the concept of *anomie,* Durkheim best manifested his concern with the problems of a weakened common morality (Hilbert, 1986). Individuals are said to be confronted with anomie when they are not faced with sufficient moral constraint, that is, when they do not have a clear concept of what is and what is not proper and acceptable behavior.

The central "pathology" in modern society was, in Durkheim's view, the *anomic* division of labor. By thinking of anomie as a pathology, Durkheim manifested his belief that the problems of the modern world can be "cured." Durkheim believed that the structural division of labor in modern society is a source of cohesion that compensates for the declining strength of the collective morality. However, the thrust of his argument is that the division of labor cannot entirely make up for the loosening of the common morality, with the result that anomie is a pathology associated with the rise of organic solidarity. Individuals can become isolated and be cut adrift in their highly specialized activities. They can more easily cease to feel a common bond with those who work and live around them. But it is important to remember that this is viewed by Durkheim as an abnormal situation, because only in unusual circumstances does the modern division of labor reduce people to isolated and meaningless tasks and positions. The concept of anomie can be found not only in *The Division of Labor* but also in *Suicide* (Durkheim, 1897/1951) as one of the major types of suicide. Anomic suicide occurs because of the decline in collective morality and the lack of sufficient external regulation of the individual to restrain his or her passions.

Collective Conscience

Durkheim attempted to deal with his interest in common morality in various ways and with different concepts. In his early efforts to deal with this issue, Durkheim developed the idea of the *collective conscience*, which he characterized in *The Division of Labor in Society* in the following way:

> The totality of beliefs and sentiments common to average citizens of the same society forms a determinate system which has its own life; one may call it the *collective* or *common conscience*. . . . It is, thus, an entirely different thing from particular consciences, although it can be realized only through them.
>
> (Durkheim, 1893/1964:79–80)

Several points are worth underscoring in this definition, given our interest in the collective conscience as an example of a nonmaterial social fact. First, it is clear that Durkheim thought of the collective conscience as occurring throughout a given society when he wrote of the "totality" of people's beliefs and sentiments. Second, Durkheim clearly conceived of the collective conscience as being an independent, determinate cultural system. Although he held such views of the collective conscience, Durkheim also wrote of its being "realized" through individual consciousness. (That Durkheim did *not* conceive of the collective conscience as totally independent of individual consciousness will be important when we examine the charge that Durkheim holds a group-mind concept.)

The concept of the collective conscience allows us to return to Durkheim's analysis, in *The Division of Labor*, of material social facts and their relationship to changes in the common morality. The logic of his argument is that the increasing division of labor (brought on by the increasing dynamic density) is causing a diminution of the collective conscience. The collective conscience is of much less significance in a society with organic solidarity than it is in a society with mechanical solidarity. People in modern society are more likely to be held together by the division of labor and the resulting need for the functions performed by others than they are by a shared and powerful collective conscience. Anthony Giddens (1972; see also Pope and Johnson, 1983) performed a useful service by pointing out that the collective conscience in the two types of society can be differentiated on four dimensions—volume, intensity, rigidity, and content. *Volume* refers to the number of people enveloped by the collective conscience; *intensity* to how deeply the individuals feel about it; *rigidity* to how clearly it is defined; and *content* to the form that the collective conscience takes in the two polar types of society. In a society characterized by mechanical solidarity, the collective conscience covers virtually the entire society and all its members; it is believed in with great intensity (as reflected, for one thing, by the use of repressive sanctions when it is violated); it is extremely rigid; and its content is highly religious in character. In a society with organic solidarity, the collective conscience is much more limited in its domain and in the number of people enveloped by it; it is adhered to with much less intensity (as reflected in the substitution of restitutive for repressive laws); it is not very rigid; and its content is best described by the phrase "moral individualism," or the elevation of the importance of the individual to a moral precept.

Collective Representations

The idea of the collective conscience, while useful to Durkheim, clearly is very broad and amorphous. Durkheim's dissatisfaction with the character of the concept of the collective conscience led him to abandon it progressively in his later work in favor of the much more specific concept of collective representations. *Collective representations* may be seen as specific states, or substrata, of the collective conscience (Lukes, 1972). In contemporary terms, we may think of collective representations as the norms and values of specific collectivities such as the family, occupation, state, and educational and religious institutions. The concept of collective representations can be used both broadly and specifically, but the critical point is that it allowed Durkheim to conceptualize nonmaterial social facts in a narrower way than the all-encompassing notion of the collective conscience. Despite their greater specificity, collective representations are *not* reducible to the level of individual consciousness: *"Representations collectives* result from the substratum of associated individuals . . . but they have *sui generis* characteristics" (Durkheim, cited in Lukes, 1972:7). The Latin term *sui generis* means unique. When Durkheim used this term to refer to the structure of collective representations, he was saying that their unique character is not reducible to individual consciousness. This places them squarely within the realm of nonmaterial social facts. They transcend the individual because they do not depend on any particular individual for their existence. They are also independent of individuals in the sense that their temporal span is greater than the lifetime of any individual. Collective representations are a central component of Durkheim's system of nonmaterial social facts.

SUICIDE AND SOCIAL CURRENTS

Durkheim offered an even more specific (and more dynamic) and less crystallized concept that is also a nonmaterial social fact—*social currents.* These were defined by Durkheim as nonmaterial social facts "which have the same objectivity and the same ascendancy over the individual" as the social facts discussed above, but "without such crystallized form" (1895/1964:4). He gave as examples "the great movements of enthusiasm, indignation, and pity in a crowd" (Durkheim, 1895/1964:4). Although social currents are less concrete than other social facts, they are nevertheless social facts, as Durkheim made clear when he said, "They come to each one of us from without and can carry us away in spite of ourselves" (1895/1964:4).

Durkheim explicated the idea of social currents in *The Rules of Sociological Method* (1895/1964), but he used it as his major explanatory variable in an empirical study that became a model for the development of American empirical research (Selvin, 1958). In fact, the research reported in *Suicide* (1897/1951) can be seen as an effort to use the ideas developed in *The Rules* in an empirical study of a specific social phenomenon—suicide. In *Suicide* he demonstrated that social facts, in particular social currents, are external to, and coercive of, the individual. Durkheim chose to study suicide because it is a relatively concrete and specific phenomenon. There were relatively good data available on suicide, and above all it is generally considered to be one of the most private and personal of acts. Durkheim believed that if he could show that sociology had a role to play in explaining such a seemingly individualistic act as suicide, it would be relatively easy to extend sociology's domain to phenomena that are much more readily seen as open to sociological analysis. Finally, Durkheim chose to study suicide because if the intellectual community could be convinced of his case in the study of this phenomenon, then sociology would have a reasonable chance of gaining recognition in the academic world.

As a sociologist, Durkheim was not concerned with studying why any specific individual committed suicide. That was to be left to the psychologist. Instead, Durkheim was interested in explaining differences in suicide *rates,* that is, he was interested in why one group had a higher rate of suicide than another. Durkheim tended to assume that biological, psychological, and social-psychological factors remain essentially constant from one group to another or from one time period to another. If there is variation in suicide rates from one group to another or from one time period to another, Durkheim assumed that the difference would be due to variations in sociological factors, in particular, social currents.

Committed as he was to empirical research, Durkheim was not content simply to dismiss other possible causes of differences in suicide rates; instead he tested them empirically. He began *Suicide* with a series of alternative ideas about the causes of suicide. Among these are individual psychopathology, race, heredity, and climate. Although Durkheim marshaled a wide range of facts to reject each of these as crucial to differences in suicide rates, his clearest argument, and the one that was most consistent with his overall perspective, was on the relevance of racial factors to the differences. One of the reasons that race was rejected is that suicide rates varied among groups *within* the same race. If race were a significant cause of differences in suicide rates, then we would assume that it would have a similar impact on the various subgroups. Another piece of evidence against race as a significant cause of variations in rates is the change in rates for a given race when it moves from one society to another. If race were a relevant social fact, it should have the same effect in different societies. Although Durkheim's argument is not powerful here, and is even weaker on the other factors that he rejected, this does give us a feel for the nature of Durkheim's approach to the problem of empirically dismissing what he considered extraneous factors so that he could get to what he thought of as the most important causal variables.

In addition to rejecting the factors discussed above, Durkheim examined and rejected the imitation theory associated with the early French social psychologist Gabriel Tarde (1843–1904). The theory of imitation argues that people commit suicide (and engage in a wide range of other actions) because they are imitating the actions of others who have committed suicide. This social-psychological approach to sociological thinking is foreign to Durkheim's focus on social facts. As a result, Durkheim took pains to reject it. For example, Durkheim reasoned that if imitation were truly important, we should find that the nations that border on a country with a high suicide rate would themselves have high rates. He looked at the data on the significance of this geographical factor and concluded that no such relationship existed. Durkheim admitted that some individual suicides may be the result of imitation, but it is such a minor factor that it has no significant effect on the overall suicide rate. In the end, Durkheim rejected imitation as a significant factor because of his view that one social fact could only be the cause of another social fact. Because imitation is a social-psychological variable, it cannot, in his system, serve as a significant cause of differences in social suicide rates. As Durkheim put it, "The social suicide-rate can be explained only sociologically" (1897/1951: 299).

To Durkheim, the critical factors in changes in suicide rates were to be found in differences at the level of social facts. Of course, there are two types of social facts—material and nonmaterial. As usual, material social facts occupy the position of causal priority but not of causal primacy. For example, Durkheim looked at the significance of dynamic density for differences in suicide rates but found that its effect is only indirect. But differences in dynamic density (and other material social facts) do have an effect on differences in nonmaterial social facts, and these differences have a direct effect on suicide rates. Durkheim was making two related arguments. On the one hand, he was arguing that different collectivities have different collective consciences and collective representations. These, in turn, produce different social currents, which have differential effects on suicide rates. One way to study suicide is to compare different societies or other types of collectivities. On the other hand, Durkheim was arguing that changes in the collective conscience lead to changes in social currents, which, in turn, lead to changes in suicide rates. This leads to the historical study of changes in suicide rates within a given collectivity. In either case, cross-culturally or historically, the logic of the argument is essentially the same: differences or changes in the collective conscience lead to differences or changes in social currents, and these, in turn, lead to differences or changes in suicide rates. In other words, changes in suicide rates are due to changes in social facts, primarily social currents. Durkheim was quite clear on the crucial role played by social currents in the etiology of suicide:

Each social group has a collective inclination for the act, quite its own, and the source of all individual inclination rather than their result. It is made up of *currents of egoism, altruism or anomy* running through . . . society. . . . These tendencies of the whole social body, by affecting individuals, cause them to commit suicide.

(Durkheim, 1897/1951:299–300; italics added)

The Four Types of Suicide

Durkheim's theory of suicide, and the structure of his sociological reasoning, can be seen more clearly if we examine each of his four types of suicide— egoistic, altruistic, anomic, and fatalistic. Durkheim linked each of the types of suicide to the degree of integration into, or regulation by, society. *Integration* refers to the degree to which collective sentiments are shared. Altruistic suicide is associated with a high degree of integration and egoistic suicide with a low degree of integration. *Regulation* refers to the degree of external constraint on people. Fatalistic suicide is associated with high regulation, anomic suicide with low regulation. Whitney Pope (1976:12–13) offered a very useful summary of the four types of suicide discussed by Durkheim. He did this by interrelating high and low degrees of integration and regulation in the following way:

Integration	Low	$\longrightarrow$	Egoistic suicide
	High	$\longrightarrow$	Altruistic suicide
Regulation	Low	$\longrightarrow$	Anomic suicide
	High	$\longrightarrow$	Fatalistic suicide

Egoistic Suicide   High rates of *egoistic suicide* are likely to be found in those societies, collectivities, or groups in which the individual is not well integrated into the larger social unit. This lack of integration leads to a sense of meaninglessness among individuals. Societies with a strong collective conscience and the protective, enveloping social currents that flow from it are likely to prevent the widespread occurrence of egoistic suicide by, among other things, providing people with a sense of the broader meaning of their lives. When these social currents are weak, individuals are able rather easily to surmount the collective conscience and do as they wish. In large-scale social units with a weak collective conscience, individuals are left to pursue their private interests in whatever way they wish. Such unrestrained egoism is likely to lead to considerable personal dissatisfaction, because all needs cannot be fulfilled, and those that are fulfilled simply lead to the generation of more and more needs and, ultimately, to dissatisfaction—and, for some, to suicide (Breault, 1986). However, strongly integrated families, religious groups, and polities act as agents of a strong collective conscience and discourage suicide. Here is the way Durkheim puts it in terms of religious groups:

> Religion protects man against the desire for self-destruction. . . . What constitutes religion is the existence of a certain number of beliefs and practices common to all the faithful, traditional and thus obligatory. The more numerous and strong these

collective states of mind are, the stronger the integration of the religious community, also the *greater its preservative* value.

(Durkheim, 1897/1951:170; italics added)

The disintegration of society produces distinctive social currents, and these are the principal causes of differences in suicide rates. For example, Durkheim talked of societal disintegration leading to "currents of depression and disillusionment" (1897/1951:214). The moral disintegration of society predisposes the individual to commit suicide, but the currents of depression must also be there to produce differences in rates of egoistic suicide. Interestingly, Durkheim was here reaffirming the importance of social forces, even in the case of egoistic suicide, where the individual might be thought to be free of social constraints. Actors are *never* free of the force of the collectivity: "However individualized a man may be, there is always something collective remaining—the very depression and melancholy resulting from this same exaggerated individualism. He effects communion through sadness when he no longer has anything else with which to achieve it" (Durkheim, 1897/1951:214). The case of egoistic suicide indicates that in even the most individualistic, most private of acts, social facts are the key determinant.

Altruistic Suicide   The second type of suicide discussed by Durkheim is altruistic suicide. Whereas egoistic suicide is more likely to occur when social integration is too weak, *altruistic suicide* is more likely when "social integration is too strong" (Durkheim, 1897/1951:217). The individual is literally forced into committing suicide.

One notorious example of altruistic suicide was the mass suicide of the followers of the Reverend Jim Jones in Jonestown, Guyana. They knowingly took a poisoned drink and in some cases had their children drink it as well. They were clearly committing suicide because they were pushed, either forcefully or gently, into giving their lives for the tightly integrated society of Jones's fanatical followers. More generally, those who commit altruistic suicide do so because they feel that it is their duty to do so.

As was the case with egoistic suicide, the degree of integration (in this case, a high degree) is not the direct cause of altruistic suicide. Rather, different degrees of integration produce different social currents, and these different currents affect suicide rates. As with egoistic suicide, Durkheim saw melancholy social currents as the cause of high rates of altruistic suicide. Whereas higher rates of egoistic suicide stem from "incurable weariness and sad depression," the increased likelihood of altruistic suicide "springs from hope, for it depends on the belief in beautiful perspectives beyond this life" (Durkheim, 1897/1951:225).

Anomic Suicide   The final major form of suicide discussed by Durkheim is *anomic suicide,* which is more likely to occur when the regulative powers of society are disrupted. Such disruptions are likely to leave individuals dissatisfied because there is little control over their passions (see below), which are free to run wild in an insatiable race for gratification. Rates of anomic suicide are likely to rise whether the nature of the disruption is positive (for example, an economic boom) or negative (an economic depression). Either type of disruption renders the collectivity temporarily incapable of exercising its authority over individuals. Such changes put people in new situations in which the old norms no longer apply but new ones have yet to develop. Periods of disruption unleash currents of anomie—moods of rootlessness and normlessness—and these currents lead to an increase in rates of anomic suicide. This is relatively easy to envisage in the case of a depression. The closing of a factory due to an economic depression may lead to the loss of a job, with the result that the individual is cut adrift from the regulative effect that both the company and the job may have had. Being cut off from these structures or others (for example, family, religion, and state) can leave the individual highly vulnerable to the effects of currents of anomie. Somewhat more difficult to imagine is the effect of an economic boom. In this case, it might be argued that sudden success leads individuals away from the traditional structures in which they are embedded. Economic success may lead individuals to quit their jobs, move to a new community, perhaps even find a new spouse. All these changes disrupt the regulative effect of extant structures and leave the individual in boom periods vulnerable to anomic social currents.

The increases in rates of anomic suicide during periods of deregulation of social life are consistent with Durkheim's views on the pernicious effect of individual passions when freed of external constraint. People thus freed will become slaves to their passions and as a result, in Durkheim's view, commit a wide range of destructive acts, including killing themselves in greater numbers than they ordinarily would.

Fatalistic Suicide   There is a little mentioned fourth type of suicide—fatalistic—that Durkheim discussed only in a footnote in *Suicide*. Whereas anomic suicide is more likely to occur in situations in which regulation is too weak, *fatalistic suicide* is more likely to occur when regulation is excessive. Durkheim described those who are more likely to commit fatalistic suicide as "persons with futures pitilessly blocked and passions violently choked by oppressive discipline" (1897/1951:276). The classic example is the slave who takes his own life because of the hopelessness associated with the oppressive regulation of his every action. Too much regulation—oppression—unleashes currents of melancholy that, in turn, cause a rise in the rate of fatalistic suicide.

A Group Mind?

Given the emphasis on norms, values, and culture in contemporary sociology, we have little difficulty accepting Durkheim's interest in nonmaterial social facts. It is true that the concept of social currents does cause us a few problems. Particularly troublesome is the idea of a set of independent social currents "coursing" through the social world as if they are somehow suspended in a social void. This problem has led many to accuse Durkheim of having a group-mind orientation (Catlin, 1964:xxii–xxiii; see also Pope, 1976:192–194). Those who accuse Durkheim of having such a perspective argue that he accorded nonmaterial social facts an autonomous existence, separate from actors. But cultural phenomena cannot float by themselves in a social void, and Durkheim was well aware of this.[1]

As a specific component of the supposed group mind, the notion of social currents can be defended as an unfortunately named, but otherwise now widely accepted, part of the cultural world. In more contemporary terms, social currents can be viewed as sets of meanings that are shared intersubjectively by members of a collectivity. As such, they cannot be found in the mind of any given individual, but they are mentally shared by the set of actors in the collectivity. To take one of Durkheim's examples, a social current of "languorous melancholy" cannot be deduced from any one individual, but it can be derived from the mood of a significant segment of the total population. These collective "moods," or social currents, vary from one collectivity to another, with the result that there is variation in the rates of certain behaviors, including suicide. Similarly, as these collective "moods" change, the rates of suicide also may change (Douglas, 1967:42).

In defense of Durkheim at a more general level, it must be argued that Durkheim had a very modern conception of nonmaterial social facts that encompasses what we now call norms, values, culture, and a variety of shared social-psychological phenomena. Such a conception is not susceptible to the group-mind charge, but its defense is complicated, because in order to lay out a separate domain for sociology, Durkheim often made some highly exaggerated claims about social facts. As we saw earlier in this chapter, Durkheim often talked as if social facts were rigidly separated from psychological facts, and such a separation would be supportive of the group-mind argument. However, in other places Durkheim admitted that this was an artificial dichotomy; in other words, nonmaterial social facts are firmly anchored in the mental processes of individuals (1893/1964:350; see also Lukes, 1972:16).

Durkheim put to rest once and for all the group-mind thesis:

> Either the *collective conscience* floats like a void, a kind of indescribable absolute, or else it is connected to the rest of the world by a substratum upon which, consequently, it is dependent. Moreover, what can this substratum be made up of, if it is not the members of society as they are combined socially?
>
> (Durkheim, cited in Giddens, 1972:159)

It seems that Durkheim, outside of some outrageous arguments made to justify a niche for the fledgling sociology, offered an eminently reasonable position on nonmaterial social facts. Durkheim began with an interest in this level, retained it throughout his career, and, if anything, grew even more

---

[1] Some Durkheimians would argue that Durkheim did offer, in many places, ideas that reflect a belief in something like a group mind.

interested in it in his later years. This increasing concern can best be seen in *The Elementary Forms of Religious Life,* published in 1912.

RELIGION

As we have seen, Durkheim felt the need to focus on material manifestations of nonmaterial social facts (for example, law in *The Division of Labor* and suicide rates in *Suicide*). But in *The Elementary Forms of Religious Life,* Durkheim felt comfortable enough to address nonmaterial social facts, in particular religion, more directly.[2] Religion is, in fact, the ultimate nonmaterial social fact, and an examination of it allowed him to shed new light on this entire aspect of his theoretical system. Religion has what Durkheim calls a "dynamogenic" quality; that is, it has the capacity not only to dominate individuals but also to elevate them above their ordinary abilities and capacities (R. Jones, 1986).

Although the research reported in *The Elementary Forms* is not Durkheim's own, he felt it necessary, given his commitment to empirical science, to embed his thinking on religion in published data. The major sources of his data were studies of a primitive Australian tribe, the Arunta. Durkheim felt it important to study religion within such a primitive setting for several reasons. For one thing, he believed that it is much easier to gain insight into the essential nature of religion in a primitive setting than in more modern society. Religious forms in primitive society could be "shown in all their nudity," and it would require "only the slightest effort to lay them open" (Durkheim, 1912/1965:18). Second, primitive religions' ideological systems are less well developed than those of modern religions, with the result that there is less obfuscation. As Durkheim put it, "That which is accessory or secondary . . . has not yet come to hide the principal elements. All is reduced to that which is indispensable, to that without which there could be no religion" (1912/1965:18). Third, whereas religion in modern society takes diverse forms, in primitive society there is "intellectual and moral conformity" (Durkheim, 1912/1965:18). As a result, religion can be studied in primitive society in its most pristine form. Finally, although Durkheim studied primitive religion, it was not because of his interest in that religious form per se. Rather, he studied it in order "to lead to an understanding of the religious nature of man, that is to say, to show us an essential and permanent aspect of humanity" (Durkheim, 1912/1965:13). More specifically, Durkheim examined primitive religion to shed light on religion in modern society.

Given the uniform and ubiquitous character of religion in primitive societies, we may equate that religion with the collective conscience. That is, religion in primitive society is an all-encompassing collective morality. But as society develops and grows more specialized, religion comes to occupy an increasingly narrow domain. Instead of being the collective conscience in mod-

---

[2] Alexander (1988:11) argues that it is this work that forms the basis of renewed contemporary interest in cultural studies. Collins (1988b:108) sees it as his "most important book."

ern society, religion becomes simply one of a number of collective representations. Although it expresses some collective sentiments, other institutions
(for example, law and science) come to express other aspects of the collective
morality. Although Durkheim recognized that religion per se comes to occupy
an ever narrower domain, he also contended that most, if not all, of the various collective representations of modern society have their origin in the all-
encompassing religion of primitive society.

Sacred and Profane

The ultimate question for Durkheim was the source of modern religion.
Because specialization and the ideological smoke screen make it impossible to
study directly the roots of religion in modern society, Durkheim addressed
the issue in the context of primitive society. The question is: Where does primitive (and modern) religion come from? Operating from his basic methodological position that only one social fact can cause another social fact,
Durkheim concluded that society is the source of all religion. Society (through
individuals) creates religion by defining certain phenomena as sacred and others as profane. Those aspects of social reality that are defined as *sacred*—that
is, that are set apart and deemed forbidden—form the essence of religion. The
rest are defined as *profane*—the everyday, the commonplace, the utilitarian,
the mundane aspects of life. The sacred brings out an attitude of reverence,
respect, mystery, awe, and honor. The respect accorded to certain phenomena
transforms them from the profane to the sacred.

The differentiation between the sacred and the profane, and the elevation
of some aspects of social life to the sacred level, are necessary but not sufficient
conditions for the development of religion. Three other conditions are needed.
First, there must be the development of a set of religious beliefs. These *beliefs*
are "the representations which express the nature of sacred things and the
relations which they sustain, either with each other or with profane things"
(Durkheim, 1912/1965:56). Second, a set of religious *rites* is necessary. These
are "the rules of conduct which prescribe how a man should comport himself
in the presence of these sacred objects" (Durkheim, 1912/1965:56). Finally, a
religion requires a *church*, or a single overarching moral community. The interrelationships among the sacred, beliefs, rites, and church led Durkheim to the
following definition of a religion: *"A religion is a unified system of beliefs and
practices which unite into one single moral community called a Church, all those who
adhere to them"* (1912/1965:62).

Totemism

Durkheim's view that society is the source of religion shaped his examination
of totemism among the Australian Arunta. *Totemism* is a religious system in
which certain things, particularly animals and plants, come to be regarded as
sacred and as emblems of the clan. Durkheim viewed totemism as the sim-

plest, most primitive form of religion. It is paralleled by a similarly primitive form of social organization, the *clan*. If Durkheim could have shown that the clan is the source of totemism, he could have demonstrated his argument that society is at the root of religion. Here is the way that Durkheim made this argument:

> A religion so closely connected to a social system surpassing all others in simplicity may well be regarded as the most elementary religion we can possibly know. If we succeed in discovering the origins of the beliefs which we have just analyzed, we shall very probably discover at the same time the causes leading to the rise of the religious sentiment in humanity.
>
> (Durkheim, 1912/1965:195)

Although a clan may have a large number of totems, Durkheim was not inclined to view these as a series of separate, fragmentary beliefs about specific animals or plants. Instead, he tended to view them as an interrelated set of ideas that give the clan a more or less complete representation of the world. The plant or animal is not the source of totemism; it merely represents that source. The totems are the material representations of the immaterial force that is at their base. And that immaterial force is none other than the now familiar collective conscience of society:

> Totemism is the religion, not of such and such animals or men or images, but of an anonymous and impersonal force, found in each of these beings but not to be confounded with any of them. . . . Individuals die, generations pass and are replaced by others; but this force always remains actual, living and the same. It animates the generations of today as it animated those of yesterday and as it will those of tomorrow.
>
> (Durkheim, 1912/1965:217)

Totemism, and more generally religion, is derived from the collective morality and becomes itself an impersonal force. It is not simply a series of mythical animals, plants, personalities, spirits, or gods.

Collective Effervescence

The collective conscience is the source of religion, but where does the collective conscience itself come from? In Durkheim's view, it comes from only one source—society. In the primitive case examined by Durkheim, this meant that the clan is the ultimate source of religion. Durkheim was quite explicit on this point: "Religious force is nothing other than the collective and anonymous force of the clan" (1912/1965:253). Although we may agree that the clan is the source of totemism, the question remains: How does the clan create totemism? The answer lies in a central but little discussed component of Durkheim's conceptual arsenal—*collective effervescence*.

The notion of collective effervescence is not well spelled out in any of Durkheim's works, including *The Elementary Forms of Religious Life*. He seemed to have in mind, in a general sense, the great moments in history when a collectivity is able to achieve a new and heightened level of collective exaltation that in turn can lead to great changes in the structure of society. The Reformation and the Renaissance would be examples of historical periods when collective effervescence had a marked effect on the structure of society. Durkheim also argued that it is out of collective effervescence that religion arises: "It is in the midst of these effervescent social environments and out of this effervescence itself that the religious idea seems to be born" (1912/1965:250). During periods of collective effervescence, the clan members create totemism.

In sum, totemism is the symbolic representation of the collective conscience, and the collective conscience, in turn, is derived from society. Therefore, society is the source of the collective conscience, religion, the concept of God, and ultimately everything that is sacred (as opposed to profane). In a very real sense, then, we can argue that the sacred (and ultimately God, as something sacred) and society are one and the same. This is fairly clear-cut in primitive society. It remains true today, even though the relationship is greatly obscured by the complexities of modern society.

SOCIAL REFORMISM

We have now worked our way through most of Durkheim's most important types of nonmaterial social facts—morality, collective conscience, collective representations, social currents, and religion. These concepts were at the center of Durkheim's thinking from the beginning of his career. Earlier we touched on the significance of material social facts in Durkheim's work, but it is clear that they were not nearly as important to him as nonmaterial social facts. They occupy the role of either causal priorities to nonmaterial social facts (for example, dynamic density in the *The Division of Labor*) or objective indices of nonmaterial social facts (for example, law in *The Division of Labor*). There is still another significant part that material social facts play in Durkheim's system—as structural solutions to the moral problems of our times.

Durkheim was a social reformer who saw problems in modern society as temporary aberrations and not as inherent difficulties (Fenton, 1984:45). In taking this position, he stood in opposition to both the conservatives and the radicals of his day. Conservatives like Louis de Bonald and Joseph de Maistre saw no hope in modern society and sought instead a return to a more primitive type of existence. Radicals like the Marxists of Durkheim's time agreed that the world could not be reformed, but they hoped that a revolution would bring into existence socialism and communism. In contrast, Durkheim, following up on his analogy between social and biological processes, argued that the problems of the day were "pathologies" that could be "cured" by the "social physician" who recognized the moral nature of the modern world's problems and undertook structural reforms to alleviate them. For example, in *The Division of Labor*, Durkheim talked of three abnormal, or pathological, forms of the division of labor. These are caused by temporary or transient forces and are not inherent in modern society. The pathologies Durkheim described are anomie, inequality in the structure of the work world (the wrong people in the wrong positions), and inadequate organization (incoherence) in the work world.

Durkheim was a reformist, not a radical or a revolutionary. Thus, when he devoted a book to socialism, it was to study it as a social fact, not to outline a revolutionary doctrine (Durkheim, 1928/1962). He was quite explicit about his political position in discussing his interest in the study of social facts:

> Our reasoning is not at all revolutionary. We are even, in a sense, essentially conservative, since we deal with social facts as such, recognize their flexibility, but conceive them as deterministic rather than arbitrary. How much more dangerous is the doctrine which sees in social phenomena only the results of unrestrained manipulation, which can in an instant, by a simple dialectical artifice, be completely upset.
>
> (Durkheim, 1895/1964:xxxviii–xxxix)[3]

More specific to a communist revolution, Durkheim said:

> Let us suppose that by a miracle the whole system of property is entirely transformed overnight and that on the collectivist formula the means of production are taken out of the hands of the individual and made over absolutely to collective ownership. All the problems around us that we are debating today will still persist in their entirety.
>
> (Durkheim, 1957:30)

Occupational Associations

The major reform that Durkheim proposed for social pathologies was the development of occupational associations. In looking at the organizations of his time, Durkheim did not believe that there was a basic conflict of interest among the various types of people found within them—owners, managers, and workers. In this, of course, he was taking a position diametrically opposed to that of Marx, who saw an essential conflict of interest between the owners and the workers. Durkheim believed that such a clash was occurring at that time because the various people involved lacked a common morality and that the lack of morality was traceable to the lack of an integrative structure. He suggested that the structure needed to provide this integrative morality was the occupational association, which would encompass "all the agents of the same industry united and organized into a single group" (Durkheim, 1893/1964:5). Such an organization was deemed to be different from, and superior to, such organizations as labor unions and employer associations, which in Durkheim's view served only to intensify the differences between owners, managers, and workers. Involved in a common organization, people in these categories would recognize their common interests as well as their common

---

[3] Not only was Durkheim treating us to his own conservative politics, but he also was attacking the revolutionary theories of Marx and Marx's followers.

need for an integrative moral system. That moral system, with its derived rules and laws, would serve to counteract the tendency toward atomization in modern society as well as help stop the decline in significance of collective morality.

Cult of the Individual

In the end, structural reform was subordinated in Durkheim's mind to changes in the collective morality. He believed that the essential problems of modern society were moral in nature and that the only real solution lay in reinforcing the strength of the collective morality. Although Durkheim recognized that there was no returning to the powerful collective conscience of societies characterized by mechanical solidarity, he felt that a modern, although weakened, version of it was emerging. He labeled the modern form of the collective conscience the *cult of the individual.* This was a curious concept for Durkheim, because it seems to fuse the seemingly antagonistic forces of morality and individualism. Embedded in this concept is the idea that individualism is becoming the moral system of modern society. Elevated to the status of a moral system, individualism was acceptable to Durkheim. What he continued to oppose was egoism, because this is individualism without a collective base; it is rampant hedonism. Presumably, by following a morality of individualism, the actor would be able to keep his or her passions in check. Ironically, paradoxically, and ultimately a bit unsatisfactorily, Durkheim proposed the cult of the individual as the solution to modern egoism. It appears that Durkheim came to recognize that there was no stemming the tide of individualism in modern society, so rather than continue to fight it, he made the best of a bad situation (judged by his moral principles) by elevating at least some forms of individualism to the level of a moral system. One of the many problems with this view is the virtual impossibility of differentiating in real life between actions based on moral individualism and those based on egoism. However, Durkheim might argue that it is possible to distinguish between people guided by a morality which requires them to give due recognition to the inherent dignity, rights, and freedom of the individual and people who are simply acting to promote their own egotistically defined self-interest.

THE ACTOR IN DURKHEIM'S THOUGHT

The bulk of this chapter is devoted to Durkheim's concern with social facts. However, Durkheim had insights into the microscopic aspects of social reality, and we will deal with some of them here. The reader should keep in mind that much of what Durkheim offered at this level was derived from his overriding interest in social facts and cannot really be separated from it.

Durkheim's often overly zealous arguments for sociology and against psychology have led many to argue that he had little to offer on the human actor and the nature of action (Lukes, 1972:228). Many contend that Durkheim had little to say about individual consciousness (Nisbet, 1974:32; Pope, 1975:368, 374), because he did not feel that it was amenable to scientific analysis. As Robert Nisbet put it:

> We cannot go to internal states of mind. . . . Consciousness, though real enough, will not serve the austere tests of scientific method. If we are to study mere phenomena in an objective fashion, we must substitute for the internal fact of consciousness an external index which symbolizes it and study the former in light of the latter.
>
> (Nisbet, 1974:52; see also Pope, 1976:10–11)

Although there is some truth to this claim, it grossly exaggerates the reality to be found in Durkheim's work. Although Durkheim may have made statements against the study of consciousness, he did deal with it in a variety of places and ways. Nevertheless, it is true that he treated the actor, and the actor's mental processes, as secondary factors, or more commonly as dependent variables to be explained by the independent and focal factors—social facts.

Durkheim was critical of dealing with consciousness, but he demonstrated his awareness of the significance of mental processes and even integrated them directly into his work. Although he made a similar point in several places (for example, Durkheim, 1897/1951:315), the following is Durkheim's clearest statement of his interest in mental processes:

> In general, we hold that sociology has not completely achieved its task so long as it has not penetrated into the mind . . . of the individual in order to relate the institutions it seeks to explain to their psychological conditions. . . . Man is for us less a point of departure than a point of arrival.
>
> (Durkheim, cited in Lukes, 1972:498–499)

It appears that Durkheim focused on "external" facts—suicide rates, laws, and so forth—because they are open to scientific analysis, but he did not deem such a macroscopic focus sufficient in itself. The ultimate goal was to integrate an understanding of mental processes into his theoretical system. This is manifest, for example, in his work on suicide, in which social causes are linked to subjective states. Even though he never quite achieved an adequate integration, he did address the issue of consciousness in several different ways.

Assumptions about Human Nature

We may gain insight into Durkheim's views on consciousness by examining his assumptions about human nature. Despite having made a number of crucial assumptions about human nature, Durkheim denied that he had done so. He argued that he did *not* begin by postulating a certain conception of human nature in order to deduce a sociology from it. Instead, he said that it was from sociology that he sought an increasing understanding of human nature. However, Durkheim may have been less than honest with us, and perhaps even with himself.

Durkheim did in fact identify a number of components of human nature. At a basic level, he accepted the existence of biological drives. But of greater significance to sociology, he acknowledged the importance of social feelings, including "love, affection, sympathetic concern, and associated phenomena" (Wallwork, 1972:28). Durkheim viewed people as naturally social, for "if men were not naturally inclined toward their fellows, the whole fabric of society, its customs and institutions, would never arise" (Wallwork, 1972:29–30). However, these sentiments did not play an active role in his sociology, and he therefore relegated them to psychology. Another of Durkheim's basic assumptions, which received only scant attention from him, is the idea that people are able to think: "Men differ from animals, Durkheim contends, precisely because images and ideas intervene between innate inclinations and behavior" (Wallwork, 1972:30).

Whereas the preceding are of marginal significance to his work, another of Durkheim's assumptions about human nature—one that we have already encountered—may be viewed as the basis of his entire sociology. That assumption is that people are endowed with a variety of egoistic drives that, if unbridled, constitute a threat to themselves as well as to society. To Durkheim, people possess an array of passions. If these passions are unrestrained, they multiply to the point where the individual is enslaved by them. This led Durkheim to his curious (on the surface) definition of *freedom* as external control over passions. People are free when their passions are constrained by external forces, and the most general and most important of these forces is the common morality. It can be argued that Durkheim's entire theoretical edifice, especially his emphasis on collective morality, was erected on this basic assumption about people's passions. As Durkheim put it, "Passion individualizes, yet it also enslaves. Our sensations are essentially individual; yet we are more personal the more we are freed from our senses and able to think and act with concepts" (1912/1965:307–308). This same issue is manifest in the differentiation Durkheim (1914/1973) made between body and soul and the eternal conflict between them. The body represents the passions; the soul stands for civilization's common morality. "They mutually contradict and deny each other" (Durkheim, 1914/1973:152). Clearly, Durkheim wished this conflict to be resolved in the direction of the soul rather than of the body: "It is civilization that has made man what he is; it is what distinguishes him from the animal: man is man only because he is civilized" (1914/1973:149).

For Durkheim, freedom came from without rather than from within. This requires a collective conscience to constrain the passions. "Morality begins with disinterest, with attachment to something other than ourselves" (Durkheim, 1914/1973:151). But freedom, or autonomy, has another sense in Durkheim's work. That is, freedom is also derived from the internalization of a common morality that emphasizes the significance and independence of the individual (Lukes, 1972:115, 131). However, in both senses freedom is a characteristic of society, not of individuals. Here, as elsewhere, we see the degree to which Durkheim emphasized nonmaterial social facts (in this case "moral individualism") over mental processes.

We can also include *individual representations* within Durkheim's assumptions about human nature. Whereas collective representations are created by the interaction of people, individual representations are formed by the interaction of brain cells. Individual representations were relegated to psychology, as were many other aspects of Durkheim's thoughts on consciousness. This is the portion of the mental process that Durkheim was unwilling to explore, and it is on this that he is most vulnerable to attack. George Homans (1969), for example, argued that Durkheim exhibited a very limited conception of psychology by confining it to the study of instincts. The psychology of today goes far beyond the study of instincts and encompasses a number of social phenomena that Durkheim would have seen as part of sociology. Homans concluded that "sociology is surely not a corollary of the kind of psychology Durkheim had in mind" (1969:18). However, it is much harder, if not impossible, in Homans's view, to clearly separate sociology from the psychology of today.

Socialization and Moral Education

Given his views on innate human passions and the need to constrain them by common morality, it should come as no surprise that Durkheim was very much interested in the *internalization* of social morals through education and, more generally, through socialization. Social morality exists primarily at the cultural level, but it is also internalized by the individual. In Durkheim's words, common morality "penetrates us" and "forms part of us" (Lukes, 1972:131).

Durkheim was not primarily concerned with the issue of internalization but rather with how it bore upon the cultural and structural problems of his day (Pope, 1976:195). He did not specify how the common morality was internalized. He was much more concerned with what seemed to be a lessening of the power of this internalization of morality in contemporary society. The essence of the matter for Durkheim was the decline in the degree to which social facts exercise constraint upon consciousness. As Robert Nisbet put it, "Durkheim would never really abandon the idea that the Western society he knew was undergoing a major crisis and that the crisis consisted at bottom in a pathological loosening of moral authority upon the lives of individuals" (1974:192). Durkheim put it this way: "History records no crisis as serious as that in which European societies have been involved for more than a century. Collective discipline in its traditional form has lost its authority" (1973:101). Durkheim's interest in anomie in both *Suicide* and *The Division of Labor in Society* can be seen as a manifestation of this concern.

Much of Durkheim's work on education, and socialization in general, can be seen in light of this concern for moral decay and possible reforms to halt the spread of it. *Education* and *socialization* were defined by Durkheim as the processes by which the individual learns the ways of a given group or society—acquires the physical, intellectual, and, most important to Durkheim, moral tools needed to function in society (Durkheim, 1922/1956:71). Moral education has three important aspects (Wallwork, 1972).

First, its goal is to provide individuals with the *discipline* they need to restrain the passions that threaten to engulf them:

> The totality of moral regulations really forms about each person an imaginary wall, at the foot of which a multitude of human passions simply die without being able to go further. For the same reason—that they are contained—it becomes possible to satisfy them. But if at any point this barrier weakens, human forces—until now restrained—pour tumultuously through the open breach; once loosed, they find no limits where they can or must stop.
>
> (Durkheim, 1973:42)

More specifically, on the education of children, Durkheim says that only through discipline "and by means of it alone are we able to teach the child to rein in his desires, to set limits to his appetites of all kinds, to limit, and through limitation, to define the goals of his activity. This limitation is the condition of happiness and of moral health" (1973:43–44).

Second, individuals are provided with a sense of autonomy, but it is a characteristically atypical kind of autonomy in which "the child understands the reasons why the rules prescribing certain forms of behavior should be 'freely desired,' that is to say, 'willingly accepted' by virtue of 'enlightened assent'" (Wallwork, 1972:127).

Finally, the process of socialization aims at developing a sense of devotion to society and to its moral system. These aspects of moral education are efforts to combat the pathological loosening of the grip of collective morality on the individual in modern society.

At the most general level, Durkheim was concerned with the way in which collective morality constrains people both externally and internally. In one sense, nonmaterial social facts stand outside people and shape their thoughts (and actions). Of course, social facts cannot act on their own but only through their agents. Of greater importance, however, is the degree to which individuals constrain themselves by internalizing social morality. As Durkheim put it, "The collective force is not entirely outside of us; it does not act upon us wholly from without; but rather, since society cannot exist except in and through individual consciousness, this force must also penetrate us and organize itself within us" (1912/1965:240). In addition to making clear the process of internalization, the preceding quotation also shows once again that Durkheim rejected the idea of a group mind, for he stated that collective forces can exist only in individual consciousness. Ernest Wallwork did an excellent job of clarifying the importance of the internalization of morality in Durkheim's system:

A normal mind, Durkheim observes, cannot consider moral maxims without considering them as obligatory. Moral rules have an "imperative character"; they "exercise a sort of ascendancy over the will which feels constrained to conform to them." This constraint is not to be confused with physical force or compulsion; the will is not forced to conform to the norms it entertains even if these norms are enforced by public opinion. Moral "constraint does not consist in an exterior and mechanical pressure; it has a more intimate and psychological character." But this intimate, psychological sense of obligation is, nevertheless, none other than the authority of public opinion which penetrates, like the air we breathe, into the deepest recesses of our being.

(Wallwork, 1972:38)

Durkheim offered a specific example of internal constraint in his study on religion:

If [an individual] acts in a certain way towards the totemic beings, it is not only because the forces resident in them are physically redoubtable, but because he feels himself morally obliged to act thus; he has the feeling that he is obeying an imperative, that he is fulfilling a duty.

(Durkheim, 1912/1965:218)

These concerns with internalization, socialization, and education all can be seen in the context of the constraining effect of collective morality on the actor. Whether the constraint is external or internal, it still comes down to collective morality controlling the thoughts and actions of individuals.

Durkheim's limited thoughts on consciousness led many people to assume that his ideal actor is one who is almost wholly controlled from without—a total conformist. Although there is much to recommend this view—and some modern sociologists in following Durkheim seem to have adopted this position—Durkheim himself did not subscribe to such an extreme view of the actor: "Conformity must not be pushed to the point where it completely subjugates the intellect. Thus it does not follow from a belief in the need for discipline that it must be blind and slavish" (cited in Giddens, 1972:113). Durkheim does see a role for individuals: they are all not simply mirror images of collective ideas; there is individuality. Each of us has unique temperaments, habits, and so forth. "Each of us puts his own mark on them [collective ideas]; and this accounts for the fact that each person has his own particular way of thinking . . . about the rules of common morality" (Durkheim, 1914/1973:161; see also Durkheim 1913–14/1983:91–92). Although Durkheim left open the possibility of individuality, the thrust of his work is in the direction of outlining external constraints on actors and, furthermore, the desirability of such constraint.

Dependent Variables

In Durkheim's works, consciousness most often occupies the position of a dependent variable, determined by various material and especially nonmaterial social facts.

Durkheim viewed sociologically relevant subjective states as the product of social causes. They "are like prolongations . . . inside individuals" . . . of the social causes on which they depend. They may enter sociological explanations as effects, but never as causes. Appeal to subjective states as causal agents, according to Durkheim, threatened the legitimacy of sociology's claim to scientific status by reducing it to psychology.

(Pope, Cohen, and Hazelrigg, 1975:419)

Although we will discuss several such dependent variables, it should be made clear that Durkheim usually dealt with them in only a vague and cursory way. In *Suicide,* for example, Durkheim was quite uncertain about how social currents affect individual consciousness and how changed consciousness, in turn, leads to a heightened likelihood of suicide (Pope, 1976:191). The same criticism applies to every other treatment by Durkheim of consciousness.

In *The Division of Labor,* consciousness was dealt with indirectly, but it is clear that it is a dependent variable. That is, the sense of the argument is that changes at the cultural and societal levels lead to changes in the processes of individual consciousness. In a society with mechanical solidarity, individual consciousness is limited and highly constrained by a powerful collective conscience. In a society with organic solidarity, individual potentialities expand, as does individual freedom. But again, although this sense of consciousness as a dependent variable is there, it was left largely implicit by Durkheim. In *Suicide,* however, the status of consciousness as a dependent variable is much clearer. Schematically, the main independent variable is collective morality, and the ultimate dependent variable is suicide rates, but intervening is another set of dependent variables that can only be mental states. Steven Lukes, in the following statement about "weak points" in the individual, implied the mental level: "The currents impinge from the outside on suicide-prone individuals at their 'weak points'" (1972:214).

Lukes (1972:216–217) went further on this issue and argued that there is a social-psychological theory beneath the "aggressively sociologistic language" found in *Suicide.* One part of that theory is the belief that individuals need to be attached to social goals. Another aspect is that individuals cannot become so committed to such goals that they lose all personal autonomy. Finally, as we have discussed before, there was Durkheim's belief that individuals possess passions and that they can be contented and free only if these passions are restrained from without.

We find in *Suicide* specific conscious states associated with each of the three main types of suicide:

These subjective states, themselves effects of given social conditions, impel the individual to suicide. . . . The egoistic suicide is characterized by a general depression in the form either of melancholic languor or Epicurean indifference. . . . Anomic suicide is accompanied by anger, disappointment, irritation, and exasperated weariness . . . while the altruistic suicide may experience a calm feeling of duty, the mystic's enthusiasm, or peaceful courage.

(Pope, 1976:197)

Durkheim perceived well-defined states of consciousness accompanying each form of suicide. It is clear that these were peripheral interests for him, as he maintained a consistently large-scale focus. Even such an ardent supporter as Nisbet wished that Durkheim had given more attention to individual consciousness: "Admittedly, one might wish that Durkheim had given more attention to the specific mechanisms by which collective representations in society are translated, in distinctly human, often creative ways, into the individual representations that reflect man's relationship to society" (1974:115). Lukes made the same point: "[Durkheim's] exclusive concentration on the society end of the schema, on the impact of social conditions on individuals rather than the way individuals perceive, interpret, and respond to social conditions, led him to leave inexplicit and unexamined the social-psychological assumptions on which his theories rested" (1972:35).

Mental Categories   We can find a specific example of this tendency to accord priority to the level of society in Durkheim and Marcel Mauss's[4] work on the impact of the structure of society on the form of individual thought. Basically, Durkheim (and Mauss) argued that the form society takes affects the form that thought patterns take. Contesting those who believe that mental categories shape the social world, their view was that the social world shapes mental categories: "Far from it being the case . . . that the social relations of men are based on logical relations between things, in reality it is the former which have provided the prototype for the latter" (Durkheim and Mauss, 1903/1963:82). Although specific large-scale structures (for example, family structure and economic and political systems) play a role in shaping logical categories, Durkheim and Mauss devoted most of their attention to the effect of society as a whole:

> Society was not simply a model which classificatory thought followed; it was its own divisions which served as divisions for the system of classification. The first logical categories were social categories; the first classes of things were classes of men. . . . It was because men were grouped, and thought of themselves in the form of groups, that in their ideas they grouped other things, and in the beginning the two modes of grouping were merged to the point of being indistinct.
> (Durkheim and Mauss, 1903/1963:82–83)

Durkheim's emphasis on large-scale phenomena is well illustrated by this discussion of the impact of society on logical categories. However, Durkheim did not analyze the corresponding process—the way in which the operation of mental categories, in turn, shapes the structures of society.

To create a more adequate sociology, Durkheim had to do more with consciousness than treat it as an unexplored dependent variable. An almost total focus on large-scale phenomena leaves out important elements of an adequate sociological model. Lukes made some telling points in his discussion of *Sui-*

---

[4] Marcel Mauss, Durkheim's nephew and a scholar of some note, coauthored the material on mental categories with Durkheim.

cide. He argued, quite rightly, that an adequate explanation of suicide cannot stop with an examination of social currents. In his view, "Explaining suicide— and explaining suicide rates—*must* involve explaining why people commit it" (Lukes, 1972:221; italics added). Durkheim also was wrong in assuming that consciousness is not open to scientific inquiry and explanation. Such inquiry can and must be undertaken if we are to go beyond partial theories of social life. Nothing is solved by simply acknowledging the existence of consciousness and refusing to examine it. Durkheim's commitment to a narrow view of science led him astray, as did his tendency toward making radically sociologistic statements that rule out recourse to consciousness:

> He need only have claimed that "social" facts cannot be wholly explained in terms of "individual" facts; instead he claimed that they can only be explained in terms of social facts. . . . It would have been enough to have claimed that no social phenomenon, indeed few human activities, can either be identified or satisfactorily explained without reference, explicit or implicit, to social factors.
>
> (Lukes, 1972:20)

Durkheim also failed to give consciousness an active role in the social process. People are in general controlled by social forces in his system; they do not actively control those systems. This led Wallwork to contend that "the principal weakness . . . is Durkheim's failure to consider *active* moral judgment" (1972:65; italics added). Durkheim gave too little independence to actors (Pope and Cohen, 1978:1364). Actors can reject some, most, or perhaps even all of the moral principles to which they are exposed. When Durkheim did talk of autonomy, it was in terms of the acceptance of moral norms of autonomy. Individuals seem capable of accepting moral constraint and of controlling themselves only through the internalization of such norms. But as Wallwork pointed out, autonomy has a much more active component: "Autonomy also involves willful exploration, spontaneous initiative, competent mastery, and creative self-actualization. . . . The child must also be encouraged to exercise his own will, initiative, and creativity" (1972:148).

Indeed, research into cognitive processes, in part done by Jean Piaget, who was working in the Durkheimian tradition, indicates that individual creativity is an important component of social life. In summarizing the work of Piaget, Lawrence Kohlberg (who did research on the cognitive elements in moral development), and others, Wallwork said:

> In addition to cultural conditioning, the cognitive activity of the subject is necessary to constitute the experience. Piaget and Kohlberg conclude from their studies that the distinctive phenomenological character of moral experience is always as much a product of the cognitive construction of the subject as it is an accommodation to cultural conditioning by the subject.
>
> (Wallwork, 1972:67)

In other words, a more complete sociology requires a more creative actor and deeper insight into the creative processes.

We have seen that, contrary to the view of many, Durkheim did have a variety of things to say about mental processes. However, the peripheral character of mental processes in his theoretical system makes his insights vague and amorphous. More damning is the fact that the thrust of his work leads to a passive image of the actor, although an active actor is, in this author's view, an essential component of a fully adequate sociological theory.

INDIVIDUAL ACTION AND INTERACTION

Durkheim was weakest in his work on individual action and interaction. Implied in his system are various changes at this level resulting from changes at the level of large-scale social phenomena, but they are not detailed. For example, it seems clear that the nature of action and interaction is quite different in societies with mechanical rather than organic solidarity. The individual in a society with mechanical solidarity is likely to be enraged at a violation of the collective conscience and to act quickly and aggressively toward the violator. In contrast, an individual in a society with organic solidarity is more likely to take a more measured approach, such as calling the police or suing in the courts.[5] Similarly, in *Suicide* the assumption behind the study of changes in suicide rates is that the nature of individual action and interaction changes as a result of alterations in social currents. Suicide rates are used as cumulative measures of changes at the individual level, but the nature of these changes is not explored, at least not in any detail. Similar points could be made about Durkheim's other works, but the critical point is that individual action and interaction are largely unanalyzed in Durkheim's work.

SUMMARY

Emile Durkheim offered a more coherent theory than any of the other classical sociological theorists. He articulated a rather clear theoretical orientation and used it in a variety of specific works. Supporters would say that the clarity of Durkheim's thinking stems from this coherence, whereas detractors might contend that the clarity is the result of the comparative simplicity of his theory. Whatever the case, it is certainly easier to convey the essence of Durkheim's thinking than that of the other classical theorists.

The heart of Durkheim's theory lies in his concept of social fact. Durkheim differentiated between two basic types of social facts—material and nonmaterial. Although they often occupied a place of causal priority in his theorizing, material social facts (for example, division of labor, dynamic density, and law) were not the most important large-scale forces in Durkheim's theoretical system. The most important focus for Durkheim was on nonmaterial social facts. He dealt with a number of them, including collective conscience, collective representations, and social currents.

---

[5] Although in some cases (for example, an assault on one's baby), people in both types of society are likely to react violently. Thus, to some degree, differences between the two societies are dependent on the nature of the crime.

Durkheim's study of suicide is a good illustration of the significance of nonmaterial social facts in his work. In his basic causal model, changes in nonmaterial social facts ultimately cause differences in suicide rates. Durkheim differentiated among four types of suicide—egoistic, altruistic, anomic, and fatalistic—and showed how each is affected by different changes in social currents. The study of suicide was taken by Durkheim and his supporters as evidence that sociology has a legitimate place in the social sciences. After all, it was argued, if sociology could explain so individualistic an act as suicide, then it certainly could be used to explain other, less individual aspects of social life.

Given his focus on nonmaterial social facts and some unfortunate statements made in an effort to define a distinctive domain for sociology, Durkheim is sometimes accused of having a metaphysical, "group-mind" orientation. Despite some seemingly indefensible statements, Durkheim did not believe in a group mind and, in fact, had a very modern conception of culture.

In his later work, Durkheim focused on another aspect of culture, religion. In his analysis of primitive religion, Durkheim sought to show the roots of religion in the social structure of society. It is society that defines certain things as sacred and others as profane. Durkheim demonstrated the social sources of religion in his analysis of primitive totemism and its roots in the social structure of the clan. Furthermore, totemism was seen as a specific form of the collective conscience as manifested in a primitive society. Its source, as well as the source of all collective products, lies in the process of collective effervescence. In the end, Durkheim argued that religion and society are one and the same, two manifestations of the same general process.

Because he identified society with God, and because he deified society, Durkheim did not urge social revolution. Instead, he should be seen as a social reformer interested in improving the functioning of society. Whereas Marx saw irreconcilable differences between capitalists and workers, Durkheim believed that these groups could be united in occupational associations. He urged that these associations be set up to restore some collective morality to the modern world and to cope with some of the curable pathologies of the modern division of labor. But in the end, such narrow, structural reforms could not really cope with the broader cultural problems that plague the modern world. Here Durkheim invested some hope in the curious modern system of collective morality that he labeled the "cult of the individual."

Durkheim had comparatively little to say about micro-level phenomena, but this is not to say he had nothing to offer here. He had useful insights into human nature, socialization, and moral education. But micro-level phenomena are most often treated in his work as dependent variables determined by large-scale changes. Although Durkheim dealt with all major levels of social reality, he focused on the large-scale forces and their causal impact on the individual level.

MAX WEBER

*M*AX Weber (1864–1920) is probably the best-known and most influential figure in sociological theory (R. Collins, 1985; Scaff, 1989; Sica, 1988).[1] Weber was a prolific writer and a complicated thinker, and this, while it contributed to his fame, makes it difficult to summarize his work in a single chapter. Not only do we have to deal with the enormous amount of work produced by Weber, but we also need to consider the even larger body of work produced by his numerous critics and analysts. To make matters even more difficult, Weber is known not only for his general theoretical approach but also for the number of specific ideas that in themselves have generated a considerable amount of analysis and critique. For example, a large part of the work in the sociology of organizations is traceable to his work on bureaucracies. Similarly, his ideas on the relationship between Protestantism and capitalism have been extraordinarily controversial. The bulk, diversity, and complexity of Weber's work make it difficult enough to summarize, but the problem is exacerbated by Weber's inconsistency and his occasional failure to say precisely what he meant. Thus, although Weber's work is provocative and rich in insight, it defies simple summary and analysis.

Weber's work is so varied and subject to so many interpretations that it has influenced a wide array of sociological theories. It certainly had an influ-

---

[1] For a time, his position was threatened by the increase in interest in the work of Karl Marx who was already much better known to those in other fields and to the general public. But with the demise of world communism, Weber's position of preeminence seems secure once again.

ence on structural functionalism, especially through the work of Talcott Parsons. It has also come to be seen as important to the conflict tradition (R. Collins, 1975, 1990) and to critical theory, which was shaped almost as much by Weber's ideas as it was by Marx's orientation, as well as that of Jurgen Habermas, major inheritor of the critical-theory tradition. Symbolic interactionists have been affected by Weber's ideas on *verstehen,* as well as by other of Weber's ideas. Alfred Schutz, whom we will consider in Chapter 10, was powerfully affected by Weber's work on meanings and motives, and he, in turn, played a crucial role in the development of both phenomenology and ethnomethodology. Weber was and is a widely influential theorist.

We begin this chapter with a discussion of Weber's (1903–17/1949) ideas on the methodology of the social sciences, because a clear understanding of these ideas is necessary in dealing with Weber's substantive and theoretical ideas. Weber was opposed to pure abstract theorizing. Instead, his theoretical ideas are embedded in his empirical, usually historical, research. Weber's methodology shaped his research, and the combination of the two lies at the base of his theoretical orientation.

METHODOLOGY

History and Sociology

Weber tended to deemphasize methodological issues, viewing them as "the precondition of fruitful intellectual work" (1903–17/1949:115; see also Marianne Weber, 1975:309). Weber focused on substantive work: "Only by laying bare and solving *substantive problems* can sciences be established and their methods developed. On the other hand, purely epistemological and methodological reflections have never played the crucial role in such developments" (1903–17/1949:116). It is important to examine Weber's methodological orientations, in spite of their secondary role in his work, not only because they help us better understand his substantive sociology, but also because many of them are important in sociological methodology today.

To deal with Weber's methodology, we first must clarify his thinking on the relationship between history and sociology. Even though Weber was a student of, and took his first academic job in, law, his early career was dominated by an interest in history. In fact, his doctoral dissertations were historical studies of the Middle Ages and of Rome. In his later years, however, he identified more and more with sociology. It has been argued that it was in 1909, the year Weber started writing his massive *Economy and Society,* that he began to devote himself fully to sociology (R. Frank, 1976:13).

As Weber moved more in the direction of the relatively new field of sociology, he sought to clarify its relationship to the established field of history. Although Weber felt that each field needed the other, his view was that the task of sociology was to provide a needed "service" to history (Roth, 1976: 307). In Weber's words, sociology performed only a "preliminary, quite mod-

MAX WEBER: A Biographical Sketch

Max Weber was born in Erfurt, Germany, on April 21, 1864, into a decidedly middle-class family. Important differences between his parents had a profound effect upon both his intellectual orientation and his psychological development. His father was a bureaucrat who rose to a relatively important political position. He was clearly a part of the political establishment and as a result eschewed any activity or idealism that would require personal sacrifice or threaten his position within the system. In addition, the senior Weber was a man who enjoyed earthly pleasures, and in this and many other ways he stood in sharp contrast to his wife. Max Weber's mother was a devout Calvinist, a woman who sought to lead an ascetic life largely devoid of the pleasures craved by her husband. Her concerns were more otherworldly; she was disturbed by the imperfections that were signs that she was not destined for salvation. These deep differences between the parents led to marital tension, and both the differences and the tension had an immense impact on Weber.

Because it was impossible to emulate both parents, Weber was presented with a clear choice as a child (Marianne Weber, 1975:62). He first seemed to opt for his father's orientation to life, but later he drew closer to his mother's approach. Whatever the choice, the tension produced by the need to choose between such polar opposites negatively affected Max Weber's psyche.

At age eighteen, Max Weber left home for a short time to attend the Unversity of Heidelberg. Weber had already demonstrated intellectual precocity, but on a social level he entered Heidelberg shy and underdeveloped. However, that quickly changed after he gravitated toward his father's way of life and joined his father's old dueling fraternity. There he developed socially, at least in part because of the huge quantities of beer he consumed with his peers. In addition, he proudly displayed the dueling scars that were the trademarks of such fraternities. Weber not only manifested his identity with his father's way of life in these ways but also chose, at least for the time being, his father's career—the law.

After three terms, Weber left Heidelberg for military service, and in 1884 he returned to Berlin and to his parents' home to take courses at the University of Berlin. He remained there for most of the next eight years as he completed his studies, earned his Ph.D., became a lawyer, and started teaching at the University of Berlin. In the process, his interests shifted more toward his lifelong concerns—economics, history, and sociology. During his eight

est task" (cited in R. Frank, 1976:21). Weber explained the difference between sociology and history: "Sociology seeks to formulate type concepts and generalized uniformities of empirical processes. This distinguishes it from history, which is oriented to the causal analysis and explanation of individual actions, structures, and personalities possessing cultural significance" (1921/1968:19). Despite this seemingly clear-cut differentiation, in his own work Weber was able to combine the two. His sociology was oriented to the development of clear concepts so that he could perform a causal analysis of historical phenomena. Weber defined his ideal procedure as "the sure imputation of individual concrete events occurring in historical reality *to concrete, historically*

years in Berlin, Weber was financially dependent on his father, a circumstance he progressively grew to dislike. At the same time, he moved closer to his mother's values, and his antipathy to his father increased. He adopted an ascetic life and plunged deeply into his work. For example, during one semester as a student, his work habits were described as follows: "He continues the rigid work discipline, regulates his life by the clock, divides the daily routine into exact sections for the various subjects, saves in his way, by feeding himself evenings in his room with a pound of raw chopped beef and four fried eggs" (Mitzman, 1970:48; Marianne Weber, 1975:105). Thus Weber, following his mother, had become ascetic and diligent, a compulsive worker—in contemporary terms a "workaholic."

This compulsion for work led in 1896 to a position as professor of economics at Heidelberg. But in 1897, with Weber's academic career blossoming, his father died following a violent argument between them. Shortly thereafter Weber began to manifest symptoms that were to culminate in a nervous breakdown. Often unable to sleep or to work, Weber spent the next six or seven years in near-total collapse. After a long hiatus, some of his powers began to return in 1903, but it was not until 1904, when he delivered (in the United States) his first lecture in six and one-half years, that Weber was able to begin to return to active academic life. In 1904 and 1905, he published one of his best-known works, *The Protestant Ethic and the Spirit of Capitalism*. In this work, Weber announced the ascendance of his mother's religion on an academic level. Weber devoted much of his time to the study of religion, though he was not personally religious.

Although he continued to be plagued by psychological problems, after 1904 Weber was able to function, indeed to produce some of his most important work. In these years, Weber published his studies of the world's religions in world-historical perspective (for example, China, India, and ancient Judaism). At the time of his death (June 14, 1920), he was working on his most important work, *Economy and Society*. Although this book was published, and subsequently translated into many languages, it was unfinished.

In addition to producing voluminous writings in this period, Weber undertook a number of other activities. He helped found the German Sociological Society in 1910. His home became a center for a wide range of intellectuals, including sociologists such as Georg Simmel and Robert Michels and the philosopher and literary critic Georg Lukács (Scaff, 1989:186–222). In addition, Weber was active politically and wrote essays on the issues of the day.

There was a tension in Weber's life and, more important, in his work, between the bureaucratic mind, as represented by his father, and his mother's religiosity. This unresolved tension permeates Weber's work as it permeated his personal life.

given causes through the study of precise empirical data which have been selected from specific points of view" (1903–17/1949:69). We can think of Weber as a historical sociologist.

Weber's thinking on sociology was profoundly shaped by a series of intellectual debates (*Methodenstreit*) raging in Germany during his time. The most important of these was over the issue of the relationship between history and science. At the poles in this debate were those (the positivists) who thought that history was composed of general (*nomothetic*) laws and those (the subjectivists) who reduced history to idiosyncratic (*idiographic*) actions and events. (The positivists thought that history could be like a natural science; the subjectivists saw the two as radically different.) For example, a nomothetic thinker would generalize about social revolutions, whereas an idiographic analyst would focus on the specific events leading up to the American Revolution. Weber rejected both extremes and in the process developed a distinctive way of dealing with historical sociology. In Weber's view, history is composed of unique empirical events; there can be no generalizations at the empirical level. Sociologists must, therefore, separate the empirical world from the conceptual universe that they construct. The concepts never completely capture the empirical world, but they can be used as heuristic tools for gaining a better understanding of reality. With these concepts, sociologists can develop generalizations, but these generalizations are not history and must not be confused with empirical reality.

Although Weber was clearly in favor of generalizing, he also rejected those historians who sought to reduce history to a simple set of laws: "For the knowledge of historical phenomena in their concreteness, the most general laws, because they are devoid of content, are also the least valuable" (1903–17/1949:80). For example, he rejected one historian (Wilhelm Roscher) who took as his task the search for the laws of the historical evolution of a people and who believed that all peoples went through a typical sequence of stages (Weber, 1903–06/1975). As Weber put it, "The reduction of empirical reality . . . to 'laws' is meaningless" (1903–17/1949:80). In other terms: "A systematic science of culture . . . would be senseless in itself" (Weber, 1903–17/1949:84). This view is reflected in various specific historical studies. For example, in his study of ancient civilizations, Weber admitted that, although in some respects earlier times were precursors of things to come, "the long and continuous history of Mediterranean-European civilization does not show either closed cycles or linear progress. Sometimes phenomena of ancient civilizations have disappeared entirely and then come to light again in an entirely new context" (1896–1906/1976:366).

In rejecting these opposing views of German historical scholarship, Weber fashioned his own perspective, which constituted a fusion of the two orientations. Weber felt that history (that is, historical sociology) was appropriately concerned with both individuality *and* generality. The unification was accomplished through the development and utilization of general concepts (what we later will call "ideal types") in the study of particular individuals, events, or societies. These general concepts are to be used "to identify and define the individuality of each development, the characteristics which made the one conclude in a manner so different from that of the other. Thus done, one can then determine the causes which led to the differences" (Weber, 1896–1906/1976:385). In doing this kind of causal analysis, Weber rejected, at least at a conscious level, the idea of searching for a single causal agent throughout history.[2] He instead used his conceptual arsenal to rank the various factors

---

[2] Ironically, Weber did seem (as we will see later in this chapter) to argue in his substantive work that there was such a causal agent in society—rationalization.

involved in a given historical case in terms of their causal significance (Roth, 1971).

Weber's views on historical sociology were shaped in part by the availability of, and his commitment to the study of, empirical historical data. His was the first generation of scholars to have available reliable data on historical phenomena from many parts of the world (MacCrae, 1974). Weber was more inclined to immerse himself in these historical data than he was to dream up abstract generalizations about the basic thrust of history. Although this led him to some important insights, it also created serious problems in understanding his work; he often got so involved in historical detail that he lost sight of the basic reasons for the historical study. In addition, the sweep of his historical studies encompassed so many epochs and so many societies that he could do little more than make rough generalizations (Roth, 1971). Despite these problems, Weber's commitment to the scientific study of empirical phenomena made him attractive to the developing discipline of sociology in the United States.

In sum, Weber believed that history was composed of an inexhaustible array of specific phenomena. To study these phenomena, it was necessary to develop a variety of concepts designed to be useful for research on the real world. As a general rule, although Weber (as we will see) did not adhere to it strictly and neither do most sociologists and historians, the task of sociology was to develop these concepts, which history was to use in causal analyses of specific historical phenomena. In this way, Weber sought to combine the specific and the general in an effort to develop a science that did justice to the complex nature of social life.

Verstehen

Weber felt that sociologists had an advantage over natural scientists. That advantage resided in the sociologist's ability to *understand* social phenomena, whereas the natural scientist could not gain a similar understanding of the behavior of an atom or a chemical compound. The German word for understanding is *verstehen*. Weber's special use of the term *verstehen* in his historical research is one of his best-known, and most controversial, contributions to the methodology of contemporary sociology. As we clarify what Weber meant by *verstehen*, we will also underscore some of the problems involved in his conceptualization of it. The controversy surrounding the concept of *verstehen*, and some of the problems involved in interpreting what Weber meant, grows out of a general problem with Weber's methodological thoughts. As Thomas Burger (1976; see also Hekman, 1983:26) argued, Weber was neither very sophisticated nor very consistent in his methodological pronouncements. He tended to be careless and imprecise because he felt that he was simply repeating ideas that were well known in his day among German historians. Furthermore, as pointed out above, Weber did not think too highly of methodological reflections.

Weber's thoughts on *verstehen* were relatively common among German historians of his day and were derived from a field known as *hermeneutics* (Mueller-Vollmer, 1985). Hermeneutics was a special approach to the understanding and interpretation of published writings. Its goal was to understand the thinking of the author as well as the basic structure of the text. Weber and others (for example, Wilhelm Dilthey) sought to extend this idea from the understanding of texts to the understanding of social life:

> Once we have realized that the historical method is nothing more or less than the classical method of interpretation applied to overt action instead of to texts, a method aiming at indentifying a human design, a "meaning" behind observable events, we shall have no difficulty in accepting that it can be just as well applied to human interaction as to individual actors. From this point of view all history is interaction, which has to be interpreted in terms of the rival plans of various actors.
> (Lachman, 1971:20)

In other words, Weber sought to use the tools of hermeneutics to understand actors, interaction, and indeed all of human history.[3]

One common misconception about *verstehen* is that it is simply the use of "intuition" by the researcher. Thus many critics see it as a "soft," irrational, subjective research methodology. However, Weber categorically rejected the idea that *verstehen* involved simply intuition, sympathetic participation, or empathy (1903–17/1949). To him, *verstehen* involved doing systematic and rigorous research rather than simply getting a "feeling" for a text or social phenomenon. In other words, for Weber (1921/1968) *verstehen* was a rational procedure of study.

The key question in interpreting Weber's concept of *verstehen* is whether he thought that it was most appropriately applied to the subjective states of individual actors or to the subjective aspects of large-scale units of analysis (for example, culture). We can find aspects of Weber's work that support both alternatives, and there are supporters of both perspectives among Weber's interpreters.

If we look only at Weber's bare position statements, there seems to be overwhelming evidence on the side of the individual-level interpretation of *verstehen* (for example, Weber, 1903–06/1975:125). This interpretation is supported by a number of observers (Burger, 1976; Schutz, 1932/1967; Warriner, 1969).

But a number of people have interpreted *verstehen*, and Weber's statements about it, as a technique aimed at understanding culture. Susan Hekman sees this as the newer interpretation of what Weber meant by focusing on such cultural elements as "intersubjective meanings or socially constituted rules which define the meaning of action within a given society" (1983:46). L. M.

---

[3] Hermeneutics has become a major intellectual concern in recent years, especially in the work of Martin Heidegger, Hans-Georg Gadamer, and Jurgen Habermas (Bleicher, 1980). For a strong argument in favor of using hermeneutics today, see Sica (1986), and for an appreciation of Weber's hermeneutics, see Oliver (1983).

Lachman was particularly clear on this: "The plan elements which interest us are not the millions of individual purposes pursued, but the common elements of norms, institutions, and of the general environment in which all these plans have to be carried out" (1971:21). Along the same lines, W. G. Runciman (1972) and Murray Wax (1967) saw *verstehen* as a tool for learning the culture and the language of a given society. Wax argued not only *for* the large-scale interpretation of *verstehen* but also *against* an individual perspective. Wax used the term *interpersonal intuition* to refer to the individual view. To him, Weber did not intend that we use *verstehen* to understand actors, but rather that we use it to understand the larger culture in which actors exist and which constrains their thoughts and actions.

Finally, some have argued that *verstehen* involves both approaches. P. A. Munch (1975), for example, said that to understand action fully we must (1) identify the sense of the action as intended by the actor and (2) recognize the context in which the action belongs and makes sense.

The multiple interpretations of *verstehen* help us to see why Weber occupies such a central role in sociological theory. The cultural-level interpretation of *verstehen* would be consistent with large-scale theories (for example, structural functionalism), whereas an individual-level view is appropriate for small-scale theories (for example, symbolic interactionism). Munch's compromise position would be acceptable to both sets of theories. Which of these three interpretations is correct? At one level, we can say that it does not really matter. What is important is that there are different interpretations and that they have influenced different theoretical perspectives. On another level, we must come to some conclusion about *verstehen* on the basis of Weber's work. It is in his substantive work, rather than in his programmatic statements about methodology, that we will find the most reliable information on what Weber really meant by *verstehen* and by the other methodological tools that we will encounter. As we will see, Weber's focus on the cultural and social-structural contexts of action leads us to the view that *verstehen* is a tool for macro-level analysis.

Causality

Another aspect of Weber's methodology was his commitment to the study of causality. Weber was inclined to see the study of the causes of social phenomena as being within the domain of history, not sociology. Yet to the degree that history and sociology cannot be clearly separated—and they certainly are not clearly separated in Weber's substantive work—the issue of causality is relevant to sociology. Causality is also important because it is, as we will see, another place in which Weber sought to combine nomothetic and idiographic approaches.

By *causality* Weber (1921/1968) simply meant the probability that an event will be followed or accompanied by another event. It was not, in his view, enough to look for historical constants, repetitions, analogies, and parallels, as many historians are content to do. Instead, the researcher has to look at the reasons for, as well as the meanings of, historical changes (Roth, 1971). Although Weber is most often thought of as having a one-way causal model— in contrast to Marx's dialectical mode of reasoning—in his substantive sociology, he was always attuned to the interrelationships among the economy, society, polity, organization, social stratification, religion, and so forth (Roth, 1968).

Weber was quite clear on the issue of multiple causality in his study of the relationship between Protestantism and the spirit of capitalism. Although he is sometimes interpreted differently, Weber (1904–05/1958) simply argued that the Protestant ethic was *one* the causal factors in the rise of the modern spirit of capitalism. He labeled as "foolish" the idea that Protestantism was the sole cause. Similarly foolish, in Weber's view, was the idea that capitalism could have arisen "only" as a result of the Protestant Reformation; other factors could have led to the same result. Here is the way Weber made his point:

> We shall as far as possible clarify the manner and the general *direction* in which
> . . . the religious movements have influenced the development of material culture.
> Only when this has been determined with reasonable accuracy can the attempt be
> made to estimate to what extent the historical development of modern culture can
> be attributed to those *religious forces and to what extent to others.*
> (Weber, 1904–05/1958:91–92; italics added)

In *The Protestant Ethic and the Spirit of Capitalism,* as well as in most of the rest of his historical work, Weber was interested in the question of causality, but he did not operate with a simple one-way model; he was always attuned to the interrelationships among a number of social factors.

The critical thing to remember about Weber's thinking on causality is his belief that because we can have a special understanding of social life (*verstehen*), the causal knowledge of the social sciences is different from the causal knowledge of the natural sciences. As Weber put it: " 'Meaningfully' interpretable human conduct ('action') is identifiable by reference to 'valuations' and meanings. For this reason, our criteria for *causal* explanation have a unique kind of satisfaction in the 'historical' explanation of such an 'entity' " (1903–06/1975:185). Thus the causal knowledge of the social scientist is different from the causal knowledge of the natural scientist.

Weber's thoughts on causality were intimately related to his efforts to come to grips with the conflict between nomothetic and idiographic knowledge. Those who subscribe to a nomothetic point of view would argue that there is a necessary relationship among social phenomena, whereas the supporters of an idiographic perspective would be inclined to see only random relationships among these entities. As usual, Weber took a middle position, epitomized in his concept of "adequate causality." The notion of *adequate causality* adopts the view that the best we can do in sociology is make probabilistic statements about the relationship between social phenomena; that is, if x occurs, then it is *probable* that y will occur. The goal is to "estimate the *degree* to which a certain effect is "favored" by certain 'conditions' " (Weber, 1903–17/1949:183).

Ideal Types

The ideal type is one of Weber's best-known contributions to contemporary sociology (Hekman, 1983; McKinney, 1966). As we have seen, Weber believed it was the responsibility of sociologists to develop conceptual tools, which could be used later by historians and sociologists. The most important such conceptual tool was the ideal type.

> An ideal type is formed by the one-sided *accentuation* of one or more points of view and by the synthesis of a great many diffuse, discrete, more or less present and occasionally absent *concrete individual* phenomena, which are arranged according to those one-sidedly emphasized viewpoints into a unified *analytical* construct. . . . In its conceptual purity, this mental construct . . . cannot be found empirically anywhere in reality.
>
> (Weber, 1903–17/1949:90)

In spite of this definition, Weber was not totally consistent in the way he used the ideal type. To get a grasp of what the concept means initially, we will have to overlook some of the inconsistencies. At its most basic level, an *ideal type* is a concept constructed by a social scientist, on the basis of his or her interests and theoretical orientation, to capture the essential features of some social phenomenon.

The most important thing about ideal types is that they are heuristic devices; they are to be useful and helpful in doing empirical research and in understanding the social world. As Lachman said, an ideal type is "essentially a measuring rod" (1971:26). Here is the way Weber put it: "Its function is the comparison with empirical reality in order to establish its divergences or similarities, to describe them with the *most unambiguously intelligible concepts*, and to understand and explain them causally" (1903–17/1949:43). Ideal types are heuristic devices to be used in the study of slices of historical reality. For example, social scientists would construct an ideal-typical bureaucracy on the basis of their immersion in historical data. This ideal type can then be compared to actual bureaucracies. The researcher looks for divergences in the real case from the exaggerated ideal type. Next, the social scientist must look for the causes of the deviations. Some typical reasons for these divergences are:

1 Bureaucrats whose actions are motivated by *misinformation*
2 *Strategic errors*, primarily by the bureaucratic leaders
3 *Logical fallacies* undergirding the actions of leaders and followers
4 Decisions made in the bureaucracy on the basis of *emotion*
5 Any *irrationality* in the action of bureaucratic leaders and followers

To take another example, an ideal-typical military battle delineates the principal components of such a battle—opposing armies, opposing strategies, materiel at the disposal of each, disputed land ("no-man's" land), supply and support forces, command centers, and leadership qualities. Actual battles may not have all these elements, and that is one thing a researcher wants to know.

The basic point is that the elements of any particular military battle may be compared with the elements identified in the ideal type.

The elements of an ideal type (such as the components of the ideal-typical military battle) are not to be thrown together arbitrarily; they are combined on the basis of their compatibility. As Hekman puts it, "Ideal types are not the product of the whim or fancy of a social scientist, but are logically constructed concepts" (1983:32).

In Weber's view, the ideal type was to be derived inductively from the real world of social history. Weber did not believe that it was enough to offer a carefully defined set of concepts, especially if they were deductively derived from an abstract theory. The concepts had to be empirically adequate (Roth, 1971). Thus, in order to produce ideal types, researchers had first to immerse themselves in historical reality and then derive the types from that reality.

In line with Weber's efforts to find a middle ground between nomothetic and idiographic knowledge, he argued that ideal types should be neither too general nor too specific. For example, in the case of religion he would reject ideal types of the history of religion in general, but he would also be critical of ideal types of very specific phenomena, such as an individual's religious experience. Rather, ideal types are developed of such intermediate phenomena as Calvinism, Pietism, Methodism, and Baptism (Weber, 1904–05/1958).

Although ideal types are to be derived from the real world, they are not to be mirror images of that world. Rather, they are to be one-sided exaggerations of the essence of what goes on in the real world. In Weber's view, the more exaggerated the ideal type, the more useful it will be for historical research.

The use of the word *ideal* or *utopia* should not be construed to mean that the concept being described is in any sense the best of all possible worlds. As used by Weber, the term meant that the form described in the concept was rarely, if ever, found in the real world. In fact, Weber argued that the ideal type need not be positive or correct; it can just as easily be negative or even morally repugnant (1903–17;1949).

Ideal types should make sense in themselves, the meaning of their components should be compatible, and they should aid us in making sense out of the real world. Although we have come to think of ideal types as describing static entities, Weber believed that they could describe either static or dynamic entities. Thus we can have an ideal type of structure, such as a bureaucracy, or of a social development, such as bureaucratization.

Ideal types also are not developed once and for all. Because society is constantly changing, and the interests of social scientists are as well, it is necessary to develop new typologies to fit the changing reality. This is in line with Weber's view that there can be no timeless concepts in the social sciences (Roth, 1968).

Although we have presented a relatively unambiguous image of the ideal type, there are contradictions in the way Weber defined the concept. In addition, in his own substantive work, Weber used the ideal type in ways that differed from the ways he said it was to be used. As Burger noted, "The ideal types presented in *Economy and Society* are a mixture of definitions, classification, and specific hypotheses seemingly too divergent to be reconcilable with Weber's statements" (1976:118). Although she disagrees with Burger on Weber's inconsistency in defining ideal types, Hekman (1983:38–59) also recognizes that Weber offers several varieties of ideal types:

1 *Historical ideal types.* These relate to phenomena found in some particular historical epoch (for example, the modern capitalistic marketplace).
2 *General sociological ideal types.* These relate to phenomena that cut across a number of historical periods and societies (for example, bureaucracy).
3 *Action ideal types.* These are pure types of action based on the motivations of the actor (for example, affectual action).
4 *Structural ideal types.* These are forms taken by the causes and consequences of social action (for example, traditional domination).

Clearly Weber developed an array of varieties of ideal types, and some of the richness in his work stems from their diversity, although common to them all is their mode of construction.

Values

Modern sociological thinking in America on the role of values in the social sciences has been shaped to a large degree by an interpretation, often simplistic and erroneous, of Weber's notion of *value-free* sociology. A common perception of Weber's view is that social scientists should *not* let their personal values influence their scientific research in any way. As we will see, Weber's work on values is far more complicated and should not be reduced to the simplistic notion that values should be kept out of sociology.

Values and Teaching Weber (1903–17/1949) was most clear about the need for teachers to control their personal values in the classroom. From his point of view, academicians have a perfect right to express their personal values freely in speeches, in the press, and so forth, but the academic lecture hall is different. Weber was opposed to those teachers who preached "their evaluations on ultimate questions 'in the name of science' in governmentally privileged lecture halls in which they are neither controlled, checked by discussion, nor subject to contradiction . . . the lecture hall should be held separate from the arena of public discussion" (1903–17/1949:4). The most important difference between a public speech and an academic lecture lies in the nature of the audience. A crowd watching a public speaker has chosen to be there and can leave at any time. But students, if they want to succeed, have little choice but to listen attentively to their professor's value-laden positions. There is little ambiguity in this aspect of Weber's position on value-freedom. The academician is to express "facts," not personal values, in the classroom. Although teachers may be tempted to insert values because they make a course more interesting, teachers should be wary of employing values, because such values will "weaken the students' taste for sober empirical analysis" (Weber, 1903–17/1949:9). The only question is whether it is realistic to think that professors could eliminate most values from their presentations. Weber could adopt this position because he believed it possible to separate fact and value. However, Marx would disagree, because in his view fact and value were intertwined, dialectically interrelated.

Values and Research   Weber's position on the place of values in social research is far more ambiguous. Weber did believe in the ability to separate fact from value, and this view could be extended to the research world: "Investigator and teacher should keep unconditionally separate the establishment of empirical facts . . . and *his* own personal evaluations, i.e., his evaluation of these facts as satisfactory or unsatisfactory" (1903–17/1949:11). He often differentiated between existential knowledge of what is and normative knowledge of what ought to be (Weber, 1903–17/1949). For example, on the founding of the German Sociological Society, he said: "The Association rejects, in principle and definitely, all propaganda for action-oriented ideas from its midst." Instead, the association was pointed in the direction of the study of "what is, why something is the way it is, for what historical and social reasons" (Roth, 1968:5).

However, several facts point in a different direction and show that despite the above evidence, Weber did not operate with the simplistic view that values should be totally eliminated from social research. While, as we will see, Weber perceived a role for values in a specific aspect of the research process, he thought that they should be kept out of the actual collection of research data. By this Weber meant that we should employ the regular procedures of scientific investigation, such as accurate observation and systematic comparison.

Values are to be restricted to the time before social research begins. They should shape the selection of what we choose to study. Weber's (1903–17/1949:21) ideas on the role of values prior to social research are captured in his concept of *value-relevance.* As with many other of Weber's methodological concepts, value-relevance is derived from the work of the German historicist Heinrich Rickert, for whom it involved "a selection of those parts of empirical reality which for human beings embody one or several of those general cultural values which are held by people in the society in which the scientific observers live" (Burger, 1976:36). In historical research, this would mean that the choice of objects to study would be made on the basis of what is considered important in the particular society in which the researchers live. That is, they choose what to study of the past on the basis of the contemporary value system. In his specific case, Weber wrote of value-relevance from the "standpoint of the interests of the modern European" (1903–17/1949:30). For example, bureaucracy was a very important part of the German society of Weber's time, and he chose, as a result, to study that phenomenon (or the lack of it) in various historical settings.

Thus, to Weber, value judgments are not to be completely withdrawn from scientific discourse. Although Weber was opposed to confusing fact and value, he did not believe that values should be excised from the social sciences: "An *attitude of moral indifference* has no connection with *scientific* 'objectivity' " (1903–17/1949:60). He was prepared to admit that values have a certain place, though he warned researchers to be careful about the role of values: "It should be constantly made clear . . . exactly at which point the scientific investigator becomes silent and the evaluating and acting person begins to speak" (Weber, 1903–17/1949:60). When expressing the value positions, sociological researchers must always keep themselves and their audiences aware of those positions.

There is a gap between what Weber said and what he actually did. Weber was not afraid to express a value judgment, even in the midst of the analysis of historical data. For example, he said that the Roman state suffered from a convulsive sickness of its social body. It can be argued that in Weber's actual work values were not only a basic device for selecting subjects to study but also were involved in the acquisition of meaningful knowledge of the social world.

Most American sociologists regard Weber as an exponent of value-free sociology. The truth is that most American sociologists themselves subscribe to the idea of value-freedom, and they find it useful to invoke Weber's name in support of their position. As we have seen, however, Weber's work is studded with values.

One other aspect of Weber's work on values worth noting is his ideas on the role of the social sciences in helping people make choices among various ultimate value positions. Basically, Weber's view is that there is *no* way of scientifically choosing among alternative value positions. Thus social scientists cannot presume to make such choices for people. "The social sciences, which are strictly empirical sciences, are the least fitted to presume to save the individual the difficulty of making a choice" (Weber, 1903–17/1949:19). The social scientist can derive certain factual conclusions from social research, but this research cannot tell people what they "ought" to do. Empirical research can help people choose an adequate means to an end, but it cannot help them choose that end as opposed to other ends. Weber says, "It can never be the task of an empirical science to provide binding norms and ideals from which directions for immediate practical activity can be derived" (1903–17/1949:52).

SUBSTANTIVE SOCIOLOGY

We turn now to Weber's substantive sociology. We will begin, as did Weber in his monumental *Economy and Society,* at the levels of action and interaction, but we will soon encounter the basic anomaly in Weber's work:[4] despite his seeming commitment to a sociology of small-scale processes, his work is primarily at the large-scale levels of the social world.

[4] Many Weberians would disagree with this portrayal of anomaly in Weber's work.

What Is Sociology?

In discussing what Weber meant by sociology, as well as the inconsistencies between his programmatic statements and his substantive sociology, we should remember that his work on sociology per se came late in his career, long after he had done most of his historical studies. It may well be that the gaps and inconsistencies that appear in his work are traceable to the inherent differences between sociology and history and not simply to differences between his programmatic statements and his substantive work.

In articulating his view on sociology, Weber often took a stance against the large-scale evolutionary sociology, the organicism, that was preeminent in the field at the time. For example, Weber said: "I became one [a sociologist] in order to put an end to collectivist notions. In other words, sociology, too, can only be practiced by proceeding from the action of one or more, few or many, individuals, that means, by employing a strictly 'individualist' method" (Roth, 1976:306). Despite his stated adherence to an "individualist" method, Weber was forced to admit that it is impossible to eliminate totally collective ideas from sociology.[5] But even when he admitted the significance of collective concepts, Weber ultimately reduced them to patterns and regularities of individual action: "For the subjective interpretation of action in sociological work these collectivities must be treated as *solely* the resultants and modes of organization of the particular acts of individual persons, since these alone can be treated as agents in a course of subjectively understandable action" (1921/1968:13). At the individual level, Weber was deeply concerned with meaning, and the way in which it was formed. There seems little doubt that Weber believed in, and intended to undertake, a microsociology. But is that, in fact, what he did? Guenther Roth, one of Weber's foremost interpreters, provides us with an unequivocal answer in his description of the overall thrust of *Economy and Society:* "the first strictly *empirical comparison of social structure* and normative order in *world-historical* depth" (1968:xxvii). Mary Fulbrook directly addresses the discontinuity in Weber's work:

> Weber's overt emphasis on the imporance of [individual] meanings and motives in causal explanation of social action does not correspond adequately with the true mode of explanation involved in his comparative-historical studies of the world religions. Rather, the ultimate level of causal explanation in Weber's substantive writings is that of the social-structural conditions under which certain forms of meaning and motivation can achieve historical efficacy.
>
> (Fulbrook, 1978:71)

Lars Udehn (1981) has cast light on this problem in interpreting Weber's work by distinguishing between Weber's methodology and his substantive concerns and recognizing that there is a conflict or tension between them. In Udehn's view, Weber uses an "individualist and subjectivist methodology" (1981:131). In terms of the latter, Weber is interested in what individuals do

---

[5] In fact, Weber's ideal types *are* collective concepts.

and why they do it (their subjective motives). In the former, Weber is interested in reducing collectivities to the actions of individuals. However, in most
of his substantive sociology (as we will see), Weber focuses on large-scale
structure (such as bureaucracies, capitalism) and is not focally concerned with
what individuals do or why they do it.[6] Such structures are not reduced by
Weber to the actions of individuals, and the actions of those in them are
determined by the structures, not by their motives. There is little doubt that
there is an enormous contradiction in Weber's work, and it will concern us
through much of this chapter.

With this as background, we are now ready for Weber's definition of *sociology:* "Sociology . . . is a *science* concerning itself with the *interpretive understanding* of *social action* and thereby with a *causal* explanation of its course and
consequences" (1921/1968:4). This definition provides a useful bridge between
the preceding section on Weber's methodology and the ensuing discussion of
his substantive work. Among the themes discussed earlier that are mentioned
or implied in this definition are:

Sociology should be a science.
Sociology should be concerned with causality. (Here, apparently, Weber
was combining sociology and history.)
Sociology should utilize interpretive understanding (*verstehen*).

We are now ready for the specific components of Weber's microsociology.

Social Action

Weber's entire sociology, if we accept his words at face value, was based on
his conception of social action (S. Turner, 1983). He differentiated between
action and purely reactive behavior. The concept of behavior is reserved, then
as now (Ritzer, 1975a), to automatic behavior that involves no thought processes. A stimulus is presented and behavior occurs, with little intervening
between stimulus and response. Such behavior was not of interest in Weber's
sociology. He was concerned with action that clearly involved the intervention
of thought processes (and the resulting meaningful action) between the occurrence of a stimulus and the ultimate response. To put it slightly differently,
action was said to occur when individuals attached subjective meanings to
their action. To Weber, the task of sociological analysis involved "the interpretation of action in terms of its subjective meaning" (1921/1968:8). A good,
and more specific, example of Weber's thinking on action is found in his
discussion of *economic action,* which he defined as "a *conscious, primary* orientation to economic consideration . . . for what matters is not the objective
necessity of making economic provision, but the belief that it is necessary"
(1921/1968:64).

In embedding his analysis in mental processes and the resulting meaningful

---

[6] Udehn argues that one exception is Weber's analysis of the behavior of leaders.

action, Weber (1921/1968) was careful to point out that it is erroneous to regard psychology as the foundation of the sociological interpretation of action. Weber seemed to be making essentially the same point made by Durkheim in discussing at least some nonmaterial social facts. That is, sociologists are interested in mental processes, but this is not the same as psychologists' interest in the mind, personality, and so forth.

Although Weber implied that he had a great concern with mental processes, he actually spent little time on them. Hans Gerth and C. Wright Mills called attention to Weber's lack of concern with mental processes: "Weber sees in the concept of personality a much abused notion referring to a profoundly irrational center of creativity, a center before which analytical inquiry comes to a halt" (1958:55). Schutz (1932/1967) was quite correct when he pointed out that although Weber's work on mental processes is suggestive, it is hardly the basis for a systematic microsociology. But it was the suggestiveness of his work that made him relevant to those who developed the theories of individuals and their behavior—symbolic interactionism, phenomenology, and so forth.

In his action theory, Weber's clear intent was to focus on individuals and patterns and regularities of action and not on the collectivity. "Action in the sense of subjectively understandable orientation of behavior exists only as the behavior of one or more *individual* human beings" (Weber, 1921/1968:13). Weber was prepared to admit that for some purposes, we may have to treat collectivities as individuals, "but for the subjective interpretation of action in sociological work these collectivities must be treated as *solely* the resultants and modes of organization of the particular acts of individual persons, since these alone can be treated as agents in a course of subjectively understandable action" (1921/1968:13). It would seem that Weber could hardly be more explicit: the sociology of action is ultimately concerned with individuals, *not* collectivities.

Weber utilized his ideal-type methodology to clarify the meaning of *action* by identifying four basic types of action. Not only is this typology significant for understanding what Weber meant by action, but it is also, in part, the basis for Weber's concern with larger social structures and institutions. Of greatest importance is Weber's differentiation between the two basic types of rational action. The first is *means-ends rationality,* or action that is "determined by expectations as to the behavior of objects in the environment and of other human beings; these expectations are used as 'conditions' or 'means' for the attainment of the actor's own rationally pursued and calculated ends" (Weber, 1921/1968:24). The second is *value rationality,* or action that is "determined by a conscious belief in the value for its own sake of some ethical, aesthetic, religious, or other form of behavior, independently of its prospects for success" (Weber, 1921/1968:24–25). *Affectual* action (which was of little concern to Weber) is determined by the emotional state of the actor. *Traditional* action (which was of far greater concern to Weber) is determined by the actor's habitual and customary ways of behaving.

It should be noted that although Weber differentiated four ideal-typical forms of action, he was well aware that any given action usually involves some combination of all four ideal types of action. In addition, Weber argued that sociologists have a much better chance of understanding action of the more rational variety than they do of understanding action dominated by affect or tradition.

We turn now to Weber's thoughts on social stratification, or his famous ideas on class, status, and party (or power). His analysis of stratification is one of the areas in his work in which Weber does operate, at least at first, as an action theorist.

Class, Status, and Party

One import of this analysis is that Weber refused to reduce stratification to economic factors (or class, in Weber's terms) but saw it as multidimensional. Thus, society is stratified on the bases of economics, status, and power. One implication of this is that people can rank high on one or two of these dimensions of stratification and low on the other (or others). This permits a far more sophisticated analysis of social stratification than is possible when stratification is simply reduced (as it was by some Marxists) to variations in one's economic situation.

Starting with class, Weber adhered to his action orientation by arguing that a class is not a community. Rather, a class is a group of people whose shared situation is a possible, and sometimes frequent, basis for action by the group. Weber contends that a "class situation" exists when three conditions are met:

> (1) A number of people have in common a specific causal component of their life chances, insofar as (2) this component is represented exclusively by economic interests in the possession of goods and opportunities for income, and (3) is represented under the conditions of the commodity or labor markets. This is "class situation."
>
> (Weber, 1921/1968:927)

The concept of "class" refers to any group of people found in the same class situation. Thus a class is *not* a community but merely a group of people in the same economic, or market, situation.

In contrast to class, status does normally refer to communities; status groups are ordinarily communities, albeit rather amorphous ones. "Status situation" is defined by Weber as "every typical component of the life of men that is determined by a specific, positive or negative, social estimation of *honor*" (1921/1968:932). As a general rule, status is associated with a style of life. (Status relates to consumption of goods produced, while class relates to economic production.) Those at the top of the status hierarchy have a different lifestyle than do those at the bottom. Thus, while high-status people may have cocktail parties, low-status people may be more likely to have "beer blasts." Those at the top may wear tuxedos to their social occasions, while those at the bottom may wear jeans. In this case, lifestyle, or status, is related to class situation. But class and status are not necessarily linked to one another: "Money and an entrepreneurial position are not in themselves status qualifications, although they may lead to them; and the lack of property is not in itself a status disqualification, although this may be a reason for it" (Weber, 1921/1968:306). There is a complex set of relationships between class and status, and it is made even more complicated when we add the dimension of party.

While classes exist in the economic order and status groups in the social order, parties can be found in the political order. To Weber parties "are always *structures* struggling for domination" (cited in Gerth and Mills, 1958:195; italics added). Thus parties are the most organized elements of Weber's stratification system. Weber thinks of parties very broadly as including not only those that exist in the state but also those that may exist in a social club. Parties usually, but not always, represent class and/or status groups. Whatever they represent, parties are oriented to the attainment of power.

While Weber remained close to his action approach in his ideas on social stratification, these ideas already indicate a movement in the direction of macro-level communities and structures. In most of his other work, Weber focused on such large-scale units of analysis. Not that Weber lost sight of the action; the actor simply moved from being the focus of his concern to being largely a dependent variable determined by a variety of large-scale forces. For example, as we will see, Weber believed that individual Calvinists are impelled to act in various ways by the norms, values, and beliefs of their religion, but his focus was not on the individual but on the collective forces that impel the actor.

Structures of Authority

Weber's sociological interest in the structures of authority was motivated, at least in part, by his political interests. Weber was no political radical; in fact, he was often called the "bourgeois Marx" to reflect the similarities in the intellectual interests of Marx and Weber as well as their very different political orientations. Although Weber was almost as critical of modern capitalism as Marx, he did not advocate revolution. He wanted to change society gradually, not overthrow it. He had little faith in the ability of the masses to create a "better" society. But Weber also saw little hope in the middle classes, which he felt were dominated by shortsighted, petty bureaucrats. Weber was critical of authoritarian political leaders like Bismarck, who he felt left lower-level political leadership severely weakened. Nevertheless, for Weber the hope—if indeed he had any hope—lay with the great political leaders rather than with the masses or the bureaucrats. Along with his faith in political leaders went his unswerving nationalism. He placed the nation above all else: "The vital interests of the nation stand, of course, above democracy and parliamentarianism" (Weber, 1921/1968:1383). Weber preferred democracy as a political form not because he believed in the masses but because it offered maximum dynamism and the best milieu to generate political leaders (Mommsen, 1974). Weber noted that authority structures exist in every social institution, and his political views were related to his analysis of these structures in all settings. Of course, they were most relevant to his views on the polity.

Weber began his analysis of authority structures in a way that was consistent with his assumptions about the nature of action. He defined *domination* as the "probability that certain specific commands (or all commands) will be obeyed by a given group of persons" (Weber, 1921/1968:212). Domination can have a variety of bases, legitimate as well as illegitimate, but what mainly interested Weber were the legitimate forms of domination, or what he called *authority*. What concerned Weber, and what played a central role in much of his sociology, were the three bases on which authority is made legitimate to followers—the rational, traditional, and charismatic bases. In defining these three bases, Weber remained fairly close to his ideas on individual action, but he rapidly moved to the large-scale structures of authority. Authority legitimized on *rational* grounds rests "on a belief in the legality of enacted rules and the right of those elevated to authority under such rules to issue commands" (Weber, 1921/1968:215). Authority legitimized on *traditional* grounds is based on "an established belief in the sanctity of immemorial traditions and the legitimacy of those exercising authority under them" (Weber, 1921/1968: 215). Finally, authority legitimized by *charisma*[7] rests on the devotion of followers to the exceptional sanctity, heroism, or exemplary character of leaders as well as on the normative order sanctioned by them. All these modes of legitimizing authority clearly imply individual actors, thought processes (beliefs), and actions. But from this point, Weber, in his thinking about authority, did move quite far from an individual action base, as we will see when we discuss the authority structures erected on the basis of these types of legitimacy.

Legal Authority Legal authority can take a variety of structural forms, but the one that interested Weber most was the *bureaucracy*, which he considered "the purest type of exercise of legal authority" (1921/1968:220).

Ideal-Typical Bureaucracy Weber depicted bureaucracies in ideal-typical terms. Although he was well aware of their failings, Weber portrayed bureaucracies in a highly positive way:

> From a purely technical point of view, a bureaucracy is capable of attaining the highest degree of efficiency, and is in this sense formally the most rational known means of exercising authority over human beings. It is superior to any other form in precision, in stability, in the stringency of its discipline, and its reliability. It thus makes possible a particularly high degree of calculability of results for the heads of the organization and for those acting in relation to it. It is finally superior both in

---

[7] The term *charisma* is also used in Weber's work in a variety of other ways and contexts; see Miyahara (1983).

intensive efficiency and in the scope of its operations and is formally capable of application to all kinds of administrative tasks.

(Weber, 1921/1968:223)

Despite his discussion of the positive characteristics of bureaucracies, here and elsewhere in his work, there is a fundamental ambivalence in his attitude toward them. Although he detailed their advantages, he was well aware of their problems. Weber expressed various reservations about bureaucritic organizations. For example, he was cognizant of the "red tape" that often makes dealing with bureaucracies so trying and so difficult. His major fear, however, was that the rationalization that dominates all aspects of bureau-cratic life was a threat to individual liberty. As Weber put it:

> No machinery in the world functions so precisely as this apparatus of men and, moreover, so cheaply. . . . Rational calculation . . . reduces every worker to a cog in this bureaucratic machine and, seeing himself in this light, he will merely ask how to transform himself into a somewhat bigger cog. . . . The passion for bureau-cratization drives us to despair.
>
> (Weber, 1921/1968:liii)

Weber was appalled by the effects of bureaucratization and, more generally, of the rationalization of the world of which bureaucratization is but one com-ponent, but he saw no way out. He described bureaucracies as "escape proof," "practically unshatterable," and among the hardest institutions to destroy once they are established. Along the same lines, he felt that individual bureau-crats could not "squirm out" of the bureaucracy once they were "harnessed" in it. Weber concluded that "the future belongs to bureaucratization" (1921/1968:1401), and time has borne out his prediction.

Weber would say that his depiction of the advantages of bureaucracy is part of his ideal-typical image of the way it operates. The ideal-typical bureaucracy is a purposeful exaggeration of the rational characteristics of bureaucracies. Such an exaggerated model is useful for heuristic purposes and for studies of organizations in the real world, but it is not to be mistaken for a realistic depiction of the way bureaucracies actually operate.

Weber distinguished the ideal-typical bureaucracy from the ideal-typical bureaucrat. He conceived of bureaucracies as structures and of bureaucrats as positions within those structures. He did *not,* as his action orientation might lead us to expect, offer a social psychology of organizations or of the individ-uals who inhabit those bureaucracies (as modern symbolic interactionists, eth-nomethodologists, and phenomenologists might).

The ideal-typical bureaucracy is a type of organization. Its basic units are offices organized in a hierarchical manner with rules, functions, written doc-uments, and means of compulsion. All these are, to varying degrees, large-scale structures that represent the thrust of Weber's thinking. He could, after all, have constructed an ideal-typical bureaucracy that focused on the thoughts and actions of individuals within the bureaucracy. There is a whole school of thought in the study of organizations that focuses precisely on this level rather than on the structures of bureaucracies (see, for example, Blankenship, 1977).

The following are the major characteristics of the ideal-typical bureaucracy:

1 It consists of a continuous organization of official functions (offices) bound by rules.
2 Each office has a specified sphere of competence. The office carries with it a set of obligations to perform various functions, the authority to carry out these functions, and the means of compulsion required to do the job.
3 The offices are organized into a hierarchical system.
4 The offices may carry with them technical qualifications that require that the participants obtain suitable training.
5 The staff that fills these offices does not own the means of production associated with them,[8] staff members are provided with the use of those things that they need to do the job.
6 The incumbent is not allowed to appropriate the position; it always remains part of the organization.
7 Administrative acts, decisions, and rules are formulated and recorded in writing.

A bureaucracy is one of the rational structures that is playing an ever-increasing role in modern society, but one may wonder whether there is any alternative to the bureaucratic structure. Weber's clear and unequivocal answer was that there is no possible alternative: "The needs of mass administration make it today completely indispensable. The choice is only between bureaucracy and dilettantism in the field of administration" (1921/1968:223).

Although we might admit that bureaucracy is an intrinsic part of modern capitalism, we might ask whether a socialist society might be different. Is it possible to create a socialist society without bureaucracies and bureaucrats? Once again, Weber was unequivocal: "When those subject to bureaucratic control seek to escape the influence of existing bureaucratic apparatus, this is normally possible only by creating an organization of their own which is equally subject to the process of bureaucratization" (1921/1968:224). In fact, Weber believed that in the case of socialism we would see an increase, not a decrease, in bureaucratization. If socialism were to achieve a level of efficiency comparable to capitalism, "it would mean a tremendous increase in the importance of professional bureaucrats" (Weber 1921/1968:224). In capitalism, at least the owners are not bureaucrats, but in socialism even the top-level leaders would be bureaucrats. Weber thus believed that even with its problems "capitalism presented the best chances for the preservation of individual freedom and creative leadership in a bureaucratic world" (Mommsen, 1974:xv).

---

[8] Here and elsewhere in his work Weber adopts a Marxian interest in the means of production. This is paralleled by his concern with alienation, not only in the economic sector but throughout social life (science, politics, and so forth).

We are once again at a key theme in Weber's work: his view that there is really no hope for a better world. Socialists can, in Weber's view, only make things worse by expanding the degree of bureaucratization in society. Weber noted: "Not summer's bloom lies ahead of us, but rather a polar night of icy darkness and hardness, no matter which group may triumph externally now" (cited in Gerth and Mills, 1958:128).

A ray of hope in Weber's work—and it is a small one—is that professionals who stand outside the bureaucratic system can control it to some degree. In this category, Weber included professional politicians, scientists, and even capitalists, as well as the supreme heads of the bureaucracies. For example, Weber said that politicians "must be the countervailing force against bureaucratic domination" (1921/1968:1417). His famous essay "Politics as a Vocation" is basically a plea for the development of political leaders with a calling to oppose the rule of bureaucracies and of bureaucrats. Similarly, in "Science as a Vocation" Weber made a plea for professional scientists who can counteract the increasing bureaucratization and rationalization of science. But in the end these appear to be rather feeble hopes. In fact, a good case can be made that these professionals are simply another aspect of the rationalization process and that their development only serves to accelerate that process (Nass, 1986; Ritzer, 1975c; Ritzer and Walczak, 1988).

In Weber's recently translated " 'Churches' and 'Sects' in North America: An Ecclesiastical Socio-Political Sketch" (1906/1985), Colin Loader and Jeffrey Alexander (1985) see a forerunner of Weber's thoughts on the hope provided by an ethic or responsibility in the face of the expansion of bureaucratization. American sects such as the Quakers practice an ethic of responsibility by combining rationality and larger values. Rogers Brubaker defines the *ethic of responsibility* as "the passionate commitment to ultimate values with the dispassionate analysis of alternative means of pursuing them" (1984:108). He contrasts this to the *ethic of conviction*, in which a rational choice of means is foregone and the actor orients "his action to the realization of some absolute value or unconditional demand" (1984:106). The ethic of conviction often involves a withdrawal from the rational world, whereas the ethic of responsibility involves a struggle within that world for greater humanness. The ethic of responsibility provides at least a modicum of hope in the face of the onslaught of rationalization and bureaucratization.

Traditional Authority   In his thinking about traditional authority structures, Weber used his ideal-typical bureaucracy as a methodological tool. His objective was to pinpoint the differences between a traditional authority structure and the ideal-typical bureaucracy.

Whereas legal authority stems from the legitimacy of a rational-legal system, traditional authority is based on a claim by the leaders, and a belief on the part of the followers, that there is virtue in the sanctity of age-old rules and powers. The leader in such a system is not a superior but a personal master. The administrative staff consists not of officials but mainly of personal retainers. In Weber's words, "Personal loyalty, not the official's impersonal duty, determines the relations of the administrative staff to the master" (1921/ 1968:227). Although the bureaucratic staff owes its allegiance and obedience to enacted rules and to the leader, who acts in their name, the staff of the traditional leader obeys because the leader carries the weight of tradition—he or she has been chosen for that position in the traditional manner.

What interested Weber was the staff of the traditional leader and how it measured up to the ideal-typical bureaucratic staff. He concluded that it was lacking on a number of counts. The traditional staff lacks offices with clearly defined spheres of competence that are subject to impersonal rules. It also does not have a rational ordering of relations of superiority and inferiority; it lacks a clear hierarchy. There is no regular system of appointment and promotion on the basis of free contracts. Technical training is not a regular requirement for obtaining a position or an appointment. Appointments do not carry with them fixed salaries paid in money.

Weber used his ideal-type methodology not only to compare traditional to rational-legal authority and to underscore the most salient characteristics of traditional authority but also to analyze historically the different forms of traditional authority. He differenitated between two very early forms of traditional authority. A *gerontocracy* involves rule by elders, whereas *primary patriarchalism* involves leaders who inherit their positions. Both of these forms have a supreme chief but lack an administrative staff. They therefore lack a bureaucracy. A more modern form is *patrimonialism,* which is traditional domination with an administration and a military force that are purely personal instruments of the master. Still more modern is *feudalism,* which limits the discretion of the master through the development of more routinized, even contractual, relationships between leader and subordinate. This, in turn, leads to more stabilized power positions than exist in patrimonialism. All four of these forms may be seen as structural variations of traditional authority, and all of them differ significantly from rational-legal authority.

Weber saw structures of traditional authority, in any form, as barriers to the development of rationality. This is our first encounter with an overriding theme in Weber's work—factors that facilitate or impede the development of (formal) rationality (see below). Over and over we find Weber concerned, as he was here, with the structural factors conducive to rationality in the Western world and the structural and cultural impediments to the development of a similar rationality throughout the rest of the world. In this specific case, Weber argued that the structures and practices of traditional authority constitute a barrier to the rise of rational economic structures—in particular, capitalism— as well as to various other components of a rational society. Even patrimonialism—a more modern form of traditionalism—while permitting the development of certain forms of "primitive" capitalism, does not allow for the rise of the highly rational type of capitalism characteristic of the modern West.

Charismatic Authority   Charisma is a concept that has come to be used very broadly. The news media and the general public are quick to point to a politician, a movie star, or a rock musician as a charismatic individual. By this they most often mean that the person in question is endowed with extraordinary qualities. The concept of charisma plays an important role in the work of Max Weber, but he had a conception of it very different from that held by most laypeople today. Although Weber did not deny that a charismatic leader may have outstanding characteristics, his sense of charisma was more dependent on the group of disciples and the way that they *define* the charismatic leader. To put Weber's position bluntly, if the disciples define a leader as charismatic, then he or she is likely to be a charismatic leader irrespective of whether he or she actually possesses any outstanding traits. A charismatic leader, then, can be someone who is quite ordinary. What is crucial is the process by which such a leader is set apart from ordinary people and treated as if endowed with supernatural, superhuman, or at least exceptional powers or qualities that are not accessible to the ordinary person (Miyahara, 1983).

To Weber, charisma was a revolutionary force, one of the most important revolutionary forces in the social world. Whereas traditional authority clearly is inherently conservative, the rise of a charismatic leader may well pose a threat to that system (as well as to a rational-legal system) and lead to a dramatic change in that system. What distinguishes charisma as a revolutionary force is that it leads to changes in the minds of actors; it causes a "subjective or internal reorientation." Such changes may lead to "a radical alteration of the central attitudes and direction of action with a completely new orientation of all attitudes toward different problems of the world" (Weber, 1921/1968:245). Although Weber was here addressing changes in the thoughts and actions of individuals, such changes are clearly reduced to the status of dependent variables. Weber focused on changes in the structure of authority, that is, the rise of charismatic authority. When such a new authority structure emerges, it is likely to change people's thoughts and actions dramatically.

The other major revolutionary force in Weber's theoretical system, and the one with which he was much more concerned, is (formal) rationality. Whereas charisma is an internal revolutionary force that changes the minds of actors, Weber saw (formal) rationality as an external revolutionary force changing the structures of society first and then ultimately the thoughts and actions of individuals. We will have more to say about rationality as a revolutionary force later, but this closes our discussion of charisma as a revolutionary factor, because Weber had very little to say about it. Weber was interested in the revolutionary character of charisma as well as its structure and the necessity that its basic character be transformed and routinized in order for it to survive as a system of authority.

In his analysis of charisma, Weber began, as he did with traditional authority, with the ideal-typical bureaucracy. He sought to determine to what degree the structure of charismatic authority, with its disciples and staff, differs from the bureaucratic system. Compared to that of the ideal-typical bureaucracy, the staff of the charismatic leader is lacking on virtually all counts. The staff members are not technically trained but are chosen instead for their possession of charismatic qualities or, at least, of qualities similar to those possessed by the charismatic leader. The offices they occupy form no clear hierarchy. Their work does not constitute a career, and there are no promotions, clear appointments, or dismissals. The charismatic leader is free to intervene whenever he or she feels that the staff cannot handle a situation. The organization has no formal rules, no established administrative organs, and no precedents to guide new judgments. In these and other ways, Weber found the staff of the charismatic leader to be "greatly inferior" to the staff in a bureaucratic form of organization.

Weber's interest in the organization behind the charismatic leader and the staff that inhabits it led him to the question of what happens to charismatic authority when the leader dies. After all, a charismatic system is inherently fragile; it would seem to be able to survive only as long as the charismatic leader lives. But is it possible for such an organization to live after the leader dies? The answer to this question is of greatest consequence to the staff members of the charismatic leader, for they are likely to live on after the leader dies. They are also likely to have a vested interest in the continued existence of the organization: if the organization ceases to exist, they are out of work. Thus the challenge for the staff is to create a situation in which charisma in some adulterated form persists even after the leader's death. It is a difficult struggle because, for Weber, charisma is by its nature unstable; it exists in its pure form only as long as the charismatic leader lives.

In order to cope with the departure of the charismatic leader, the staff (as well as the followers) may adopt a variety of strategies to create a more lasting organization. The staff may search out a new charismatic leader, but even if the search is successful, the new leader is unlikely to achieve the same aura as his or her predecessor. A set of rules also may be developed that allows the group to identify future charismatic leaders. But such rules rapidly become tradition, and what was charismatic leadership is on the way toward becoming traditional authority. In any case, the nature of leadership is radically changed as the purely personal character of charisma is eliminated. Still another technique is to allow the charismatic leader to designate his or her successor and thereby to transfer charisma symbolically to the next in line. Again it is questionable whether this is ever very successful or whether it can be successful in the long run. Another strategy is having the staff designate a successor and having its choice accepted by the larger community. The staff could also create ritual tests, with the new charismatic leader being the one who successfully undergoes the tests. However, all these efforts are doomed to failure. In the long run, charisma cannot be routinized; it must be transformed into either traditional or rational-legal authority (or into some sort of institutionalized charisma like the Catholic Church).

Indeed, we find a basic theory of history in Weber's work. If successful, charisma almost immediately moves in the direction of routinization. But once routinized, charisma is en route to becoming either traditional or rational-legal authority. Once it achieves one of those states, the stage is set for the cycle to begin all over again. However, despite a general adherence to a cyclical theory, Weber believed that a basic change has occurred in the modern world and that we are more and more likely to see charisma routinized in the direction of rational-legal authority. Furthermore, he saw rational systems of authority as stronger and as increasingly impervious to charismatic movements. The modern, rationalized world may well mean the death of charisma as a significant revolutionary force. Weber contended that rationality—not charisma—is the most irresistible and important revolutionary force in the modern world.

In this section, we have discussed the three types of authority as ideal types, but Weber was well aware that in the real world, any specific form of authority involves a combination of all three. Thus we can think of Franklin D. Roosevelt as a president of the United States who ruled on all three bases. He was elected president in accord with a series of rational-legal principles. By the time he was elected president for the fourth time, a good part of this rule had traditional elements. Finally, many disciples and followers regarded him as a charismatic leader.

Although we have presented the three forms of authority as parallel structures, in the real world there is constant tension and, sometimes, conflict among them. The charismatic leader is a constant threat to the other forms of authority. Once in power, the charismatic leader must address the threat posed by the other two forms. Even if charismatic authority is successfully routinized, there then arises the problem of maintaining its dynamism and its original revolutionary qualities. Then there is the conflict produced by the constant development of rational-legal authority and the threat it poses to the continued existence of the other forms. If Weber was right, however, we might face a future in which the tension among the three forms of authority is eliminated, a world of the uncontested hegemony of the rational-legal system. This is the "iron cage" of a totally rationalized society that Weber feared so much. If such a society were to materialize, the only hope would lie with isolated charismatic individuals who manage somehow to avoid the coercive power of society. But a small number of isolated individuals hardly represents a significant hope in the face of an increasingly powerful bureaucratic machine.

Rationalization

There has been a growing realization in recent years that rationalization lies at the heart of Weber's substantive sociology (Antonio, 1979; Brubaker, 1984; R. Collins, 1980; Eisen, 1978; Kalberg, 1980, 1990; Levine, 1981a; Ritzer, 1983, forthcoming a; Scaff, 1989; Schluchter, 1981; Sica, 1988). However, it is difficult to extract a clear definition of *rationalization* from Weber's work. In fact, he operated with a number of different definitions of the term, and he often failed to specify which definition he was using in a particular discussion (Brubaker, 1984:1). As we saw earlier, Weber did define *rationality;* indeed, he differentiated between two types—means-ends and value rationality. However, these concepts refer to types of *action*. They are the basis of, but not coterminous with, Weber's larger-scale sense of rationalization. Weber is interested in far more than fragmented action orientations; his main concern is with regularities and patterns of action within civilizations, institutions, organizations, strata, classes, and groups. Donald Levine (1981a) argues that Weber is interested in "objectified" rationality; that is, action that is in accord with some process of external systematization. Stephen Kalberg (1980) performs a useful service by identifying four basic types of ("objective") rationality in Weber's work. (Levine offers a very similar differentiation.) These types of rationality were "the basic heuristic tools [Weber] employed to scrutinize the historical fates of rationalization as sociocultural processes" (Kalberg, 1980:1172).

The first type is *practical rationality*, which is defined by Kalberg as "every way of life that views and judges worldly activity in relation to the individual's purely pragmatic and egoistic interests" (1980:1151). People who practice practical rationality accept given realities and merely calculate the most expedient ways of dealing with the difficulties that they present. This type of rationality arose with the severing of the bonds of primitive magic, and it exists trans-civilizationally and trans-historically; that is, it is not restricted to the modern Occident. This type of rationality stands in opposition to anything that threatens to transcend everyday routine. It leads people to distrust all impractical values, either religious or secular-utopian, as well as the theoretical rationality of the intellectuals, the type of rationality to which we now turn.

Theoretical rationality involves a cognitive effort to master reality through increasingly abstract concepts rather than through action. It involves such abstract cognitive processes as logical deduction, induction, attribution of causality, and the like. This type of rationality was accomplished early in history by sorcerers and ritualistic priests and later by philosophers, judges, and scientists. Unlike practical rationality, theoretical rationality leads the actor to transcend daily realities in a quest to understand the world as a meaningful cosmos. Like practical rationality, it is trans-civilizational and trans-historical. The effect of intellectual rationality on action is limited. In that it involves cognitive processes, it need not affect action taken, and it has the potential to introduce new patterns of action only indirectly.

Substantive rationality (like practical rationality, but *not* theoretical rationality) directly orders action into patterns through clusters of values. Substantive rationality involves a choice of means to ends within the context of a system of values. This means that one value system is no more (substantively) rational than another. Thus, this type of rationality also exists trans-civilizationally and trans-historically, wherever consistent value postulates exist.

Finally, and most important from the author's point of view, is *formal rationality*, which involves means-ends calculation. But whereas in practical rationality this calculation occurs in reference to pragmatic self-interests, in formal rationality it occurs with reference to "universally applied rules, laws, and regulations." As Brubaker puts it, "Common to the rationality of industrial capitalism, formalistic law and bureaucratic administration is its objectified, institutionalized, supra-individual form; in each sphere, rationality is embodied in the social structure and confronts individuals as something external to them" (1984:9). Weber makes this quite clear in the specific case of bureaucratic rationalization:

> Bureaucratic rationalization . . . revolutionizes with *technical means,* in principle, as does every economic reorganization, 'from without': It *first* changes the material and social orders, and *through* them the people, by changing the conditions of adaptation, and perhaps the opportunities for adaptation, through a rational determination of means and ends.
>
> (Weber, 1921/1968:1116)

Although all the other types of rationality are trans-civilizational and epoch-transcending, formal rationality arose *only* in the West with the coming of industrialization. The universally applied rules, laws, and regulations that characterize formal rationality in the West are found particularly in the economic, legal, and scientific institutions, as well as in the bureaucratic form of domination. Thus, we have already encountered formal rationality in our discussion of rational-legal authority and the bureaucracy.

Although Weber had a complex, multifaceted sense of rationalization, he used it most powerfully and meaningfully in his image of the modern Western world, especially in the capitalistic economy (R. Collins, 1980; Weber, 1927/ 1981) and bureaucratic organizations (Cohen, 1981:xxxi; Weber, 1921/1968: 956–1005), as an iron cage (Mitzman, 1970; Tiryakian, 1981) of formally rational structures. Weber described capitalism and bureaucracies as "two great rationalizing forces" (1921/1968:698).[9] In fact, Weber saw capitalism and bureaucracies as being derived from the same basic source (innerworldly asceticism), involving similarly rational and methodical action, reinforcing one another and in the process furthering the rationalization of the Occident.[10] In Weber's (1921/1968:227, 994) view, the only real rival to the bureaucrat in technical expertise and factual knowledge was the capitalist.

However, if we take Weber at his word, it is difficult to argue that he had an overarching theory of rationalization. He rejected the idea of "general evolutionary sequence" (Weber, 1927/1981:34). He was critical of thinkers like Hegel and Marx, who he felt offered general, teleological theories of society. In his own work, he tended to shy away from studies of, or proclamations about, whole societies. Instead, he tended to focus, in turn, on social structures and institutions such as bureaucracy, stratification, law, the city, religion, the polity, and the economy. Lacking a sense of the whole, he was unlikely to

---

[9] In the 1920 introduction to *The Protestant Ethic and the Spirit of Capitalism,* Weber focused on "a specially trained organization of officials" (bureaucracy) in his discussion of rationalization, but he also mentioned capitalism in the same context as "the most fateful force in our modern life."

[10] Of course, these are not completely distinct because large capitalistic enterprises are one of the places in which we find bureaucracies (Weber, 1922–23/1958:299). On the other hand, Weber also sees the possibility that bureaucracies can stand in opposition to, can impede, capitalism.

make global generalizations, especially about future directions. Furthermore, the rationalization process that Weber described in one social structure or institution was usually quite different from the rationalization of another structure or institution. As Weber put it, the process of rationalization assumes "unusually varied forms" (1922–23/1958:293; see also Weber, 1921/1958:30; 1904–05/1958:78), and "the history of rationalism shows a development which by no means follows parallel lines in the various departments of life" (1904–05/1958:77; see also Brubaker, 1984:9; Kalberg, 1980:1147).

This being said, it is clear that Weber does have a deep concern for the overarching effect of the formal rationalization of the economy and bureaucracies on the Western world (Brubaker, 1984). For example, in *Economy and Society,* Weber says:

> This whole process of rationalization in the factory as elsewhere, and especially in the bureaucratic state machine, parallels the centralization of the material implements of organization in the hands of the master. Thus, discipline inexorably takes over ever larger areas as the satisfaction of political and economic needs is increasingly rationalized. This universal phenomenon more and more restricts the importance of charisma and of individually differentiated conduct.
>
> (Weber, 1921/1968:1156)

Formal rationalization will be our main, but certainly not only, concern in this section.

Various efforts have been made to delineate the basic characteristics of formal rationality. In our view, formal rationality may be defined in terms of six basic characteristics (Ritzer, 1983, forthcoming a.) First, formally rational structures and institutions emphasize *calculability,* or those things that can be counted or quantified. Second, there is a focus on *efficiency,* on finding the best means to a given end. Third, there is great concern with ensuring *predictability,* or that things operate in the same way from one time or place to another. Fourth, a formally rational system progressively reduces human technology and ultimately *replaces human technology with nonhuman technology.* Nonhuman technologies (such as computerized systems) are viewed as more calculable, more efficient, and more predictable than human technologies. Fifth, formally rational systems seek to gain *control* over an array of uncertainties, especially the uncertainties posed by human beings who work in, or are served by, them. Finally, rational systems tend to have a series of *irrational consequences* for people involved with them and for the systems themselves, as well as for the larger society (Sica, 1988).

Formal rationality stands in contrast to all the other types of rationality but is especially in conflict with substantive rationality (Brubaker, 1984:4). Kalberg argues that Weber believed that the conflict between these two types of rationality played "a particularly fateful role in the unfolding of rationalization processes in the West" (1980:1157).

In addition to differentiating among the four types of rationality, Kalberg also deals with their capacity to introduce methodical ways of life. Practical rationality lacks this ability because it involves reactions to situations rather than efforts to order them. Theoretical rationality is cognitive and, therefore, has a highly limited ability to suppress practical rationality and seems to be more of an end product than a producer. To Weber, substantive rationality is the *only* type with the "potential to introduce methodical ways of life" (Kalberg, 1980:1165). Thus, in the West, a particular substantive rationality with an emphasis on a methodical way of life—Calvinism—subjugated practical rationality and led to the development of formal rationality.

Weber's fear was that substantive rationality was becoming less significant than the other types of rationality, especially formal rationality, in the West. Thus practitioners of formal rationality, like the bureaucrat and the capitalist, were coming to dominate the West, and one was witnessing a fading away of the type that "embodied Western civilization's highest ideals: the autonomous and free individual whose actions were given continuity by their reference to ultimate values" (Kalberg, 1980:1176).

Although we have emphasized the differences among Weber's four types of rationalization in this section, there are a number of commonalities among them. They all involve mental processes that seek to master reality by banishing particularized perceptions and to order them into comprehensible and meaningful regularities. Thus as we move from institution to institution in the ensuing discussion, we, like Weber, sometimes focus on rationalization in general and, at other times, on the specific types of rationalization.

Economy The most systematic presentation of Weber's thoughts on the rationalization of the economic institution is to be found in his *General Economic History*. Weber's concern is with the development of the rational capitalistic economy in the Occident, which is a specific example of a rational economy defined as a "functional organization oriented to money-prices which originate in the interest-struggles of men in the *market*" (Weber, 1915/1958:331). Although there are the outlines of a general evolutionary trend in *General Economic History*, Weber, as always, is careful to point out that there are various sources of capitalism, alternative routes to it, and a range of results emanating from it. In fact, in the course of rejecting the socialistic theory of evolutionary change, Weber rejects the whole idea of a "general evolutionary sequence" (1927/1981:34).

Weber begins by depicting various irrational and traditional forms such as the household, clan, village, and manorial economies. For example, the lord of the manor in feudalism was described by Weber as being too traditionalistic, "too lacking in initiative to build up a business enterprise in a large scale into which the peasants would have fitted as a labor force" (1927/1981:72). However, by the twelfth and thirteenth centuries in the Occident, feudalism began to break down as the peasants and the land were freed from control by the lord and a money economy was introduced. With this breakdown, the manorial system "showed a strong tendency to develop in a capitalistic direction" (Weber, 1927/1981:79).

At the same time, in the Middle Ages, cities were beginning to develop. Weber focuses on the largely urban development of industry involved in the transformation of raw materials. Especially important to Weber is the development of such industrial production beyond the immediate needs of the house community. Notable here is the rise of free craftsmen in the cities. They developed in the Middle Ages in the Occident because, for one thing, this society had developed greater consumptive needs than any other. In general, there were larger markets, more purchasers, and the peasantry had greater purchasing power. On the other side, forces operated against the major alternative to craftsmen—slaves. Slavery was found to be too unprofitable and too unstable, and it was made increasingly more unstable by the growth of the towns that offered freedom to the slaves.

In the Occident, along with free craftsmen came the development of the *guild,* defined by Weber as "an organization of craft workers specialized in accordance with the type of occupation . . . [with] internal regulation of work and monopolization against outsiders" (1927/1981:136). Freedom of association was also characteristic of the guilds. But although rational in many senses, guilds also had traditional, anticapitalistic aspects. For example, one master was not supposed to have more capital than another, and this requirement was a barrier to the development of large capitalistic organizations.

As the Middle Ages came to a close, the guilds began to disintegrate. This disintegration was crucial because the traditional guilds stood in the way of technological advance. With the dissolution of the guild system came the rise of the domestic system of production, especially the "putting out" system in the textile industry. In such a system, production was decentralized, with much of it taking place within the homes of the workers. Although domestic systems were found throughout the world, it was only in the Occident that the owners controlled the means of production (for example, tools, raw materials) and provided them to the workers in exchange for the right to dispose of the product. Whereas a fully developed domestic system developed in the West, it was impeded in other parts of the world by such barriers as the clan system (China), the caste system (India), traditionalism, and the lack of free workers.

Next, Weber details the development of the workshop (a central work setting without advanced machinery) and then the emergence of the factory in the fourteenth through sixteenth centuries. In Weber's view, the factory did not arise out of craft work or the domestic system, but alongside them. Similarly, the factory was not called into existence by advances in machinery; the two developments were correlated with each other. The factory was characterized by free labor that performed specialized and coordinated activities, ownership of the means of production by the entrepreneur, the fixed capital of the entrepreneur, and the system of accounting that is indispensable to such capitalizaton. Such a factory was, in Weber's view, a capitalistic organization. In addition to the development of the factory, Weber details the rise of other components of a modern capitalistic economy, such as advanced machinery, transportation systems, money, banking, interest, bookkeeping systems, and so on.

What most clearly defines modern rational capitalistic enterprises for Weber is their calculability, which is best represented in their reliance on modern bookkeeping. Isolated calculable enterprises existed in the past in the Occident as well as in other societies. However, an entire society is considered capitalistic only when the everyday requirements of the population are supplied by capitalistic methods and enterprises. Such a society is found only in the Occident and there only since the mid-nineteenth century.

The development of a capitalistic system hinged on a variety of developments within the economy as well as within the larger society. Within the economy, some of the prerequisites included a free market with large and steady demand, a money economy, inexpensive and rational technologies, a free labor force, a disciplined labor force, rational capital-accounting techniques, and the commercialization of economic life involving the use of shares, stocks, and the like. Many of the economic prerequisites were found only in the Occident. Outside the economy, Weber identified a variety of needed developments such as a modern state with "professional administration, specialized officialdom, and law based on the concept of citizenship" (1927/ 1981:313), rational law "made by jurists and rationally interpreted and applied" (1927/1981:313), cities, and modern science and technology. To these Weber adds a factor that will concern us in the next section, "a rational ethic for the conduct of life . . . a religious basis for the ordering of life which consistently followed out must lead to explicit rationalism" (1927/1981:313– 314). Like the economic prerequisites, these noneconomic presuppositions occurred together only in the Occident. The basic point is that a rational economy is dependent upon a variety of noneconomic forces throughout the rest of society in order to develop.

Religion Although we will focus on the rationalization of religion in this section, Weber spent much time analyzing the degree to which early, more primitive religions—and religions in much of the world—acted as impediments to the rise of rationality. Weber noted that "the sacred is the uniquely unalterable" (1921/1968:406). Despite this view, religion in the West did prove to be alterable; it was amenable to rationalization, and it did play a key role in the rationalization of other sectors of society (Kalberg, 1990).

Early religion was composed of a bewildering array of gods, but with rationalization a clear and coherent set of gods (a pantheon) emerged. Early religions had household gods, kin-group gods, local political gods, and occupational and vocational gods. We get the clear feeling that Weber did believe that a cultural force of (theoretical) rationality impelled the emergence of this set of gods: "*Reason* favored the primacy of universal gods; and every consistent crystallization of a pantheon followed systematic *rational* principles" (1921/1968:417). A pantheon of gods was not the only aspect of the rationalization of religion discussed by Weber. He also considered the delimitation of the jurisdiction of gods, monotheism, and the anthropomorphization of gods as part of this development. Although the pressure for rationalization exists in many of the world's religions, in areas outside the Western world, the barriers to rationalization more than counterbalance the pressures for rationalization.

Although Weber had a cultural conception of rationalization, he did not view it simply as a force "out there" that impels people to act. He did not have a group-mind concept. In religion, rationalization is tied to concrete groups of people, in particular to priests. Specifically, the professionally trained priesthood is the carrier and the expediter of rationalization. In this, priests stand in contrast to magicians, who support a more irrational religious system. The greater rationality of the priesthood is traceable to several factors. Members go through a systematic training program, whereas the training of magicians is unsystematic. Also, priests are fairly highly specialized, whereas magicians tend to be unspecialized. Finally, priests possess a systematic set of religious concepts, and this, too, sets them apart from magicians. We can say that priests are both the products and the expediters of the process of rationalization.

The priesthood is not the only group that plays a key role in rationalization. Prophets and a laity are also important in the process. Prophets can be distinguished from priests by their personal calling and their emotional preaching. The key role of the prophet is the mobilization of the laity, because there would be no religion without a group of followers. Weber differentiated between two types of prophets, ethical and exemplary. *Ethical prophets* (Muhammad, Jesus Christ, and the Old Testament Prophets) believe that they have received a commission directly from God and demand obedience from followers as an ethical duty. *Exemplary prophets* (Buddha is a model) demonstrate to others by personal example the way to religious salvation. In either case, successful prophets are able to attract large numbers of followers, and it is this mass, along with the priests, that forms the heart of religion. Prophets are likely at first to attract a personal following, but it is necessary that that group be transformed into a permanent congregation. Once such a laity has been formed, major strides have been made in the direction of the rationalization of religion.

Prophets play a key initial role, but once a congregation is formed, they are no longer needed. In fact, because they are largely irrational, they represent a barrier to that rationalization of religion. A conflict develops between priests and prophets, but it is a conflict that must be won in the long run by the more rational priesthood. In their conflict, the priests are aided by the rationalization proceeding in the rest of society. As the secular world becomes more and more literate and bureaucratized, the task of educating the masses falls increasingly to the priests, whose literacy gives them a tremendous advantage over the prophets. In addition, while the prophets tend to do the preaching, the priests take over the task of day-to-day pastoral care. Although preaching is important during extraordinary times, pastoral care, or the daily religious cultivation of the laity, is an important instrument in the growing power of the priest-hood. It was the church in the Western world that combined a rationalized pastoral character with an ethical religion to form a peculiarly influential and rational form of religion. This rationalized religion proved particularly well suited to winning converts among the urban middle class, and it was there that it played a key role in the rationalization of economic life as well as all other sectors of life.

Law *Law* is defined by Weber not in terms of people's definitions, atti-tudes, and beliefs but rather as a body of norms (Kronman, 1983:12). Addi-tionally, this body of norms is seen as being external to, and coercive of, individuals and their thoughts and actions. The emphasis is not on how peo-ple create law, interpret it, and daily recreate it but on its coercive effect on the individual.

As with his analysis of religion, Weber began his treatment of law with the primitive, which he saw as highly irrational. Primitive law was a rather undif-ferentiated system of norms. For example, no distinction was made between a civil wrong (a tort) and a crime. Thus cases involving differences over a piece of land and homicide were likely to be handled, and offenders punished, in much the same way. In addition, primitive law tended to lack any official machinery. Vengeance dominated reactions to a crime, and law was generally free from procedural formality or rules. Leaders, especially, were virtually unrestrained in what they could do to followers. From this early irrational period, Weber traced a direct line of development to a formalized legal pro-cedure. And as was usual in Weber's thinking, it is only in the West that a rational, systematic theory of law is held to have developed.

Weber traced several stages in the development of a more rational legal system. An early stage involves charismatic legal revelation through law prophets. Then there is the empirical creation and founding of law by hon-orary legal officials. Later there is the imposition of law by secular or theo-cratic powers. Finally, in the most modern case, we have the systematic elaboration of law and professionalized administration of justice by persons who have received their legal training formally and systematically.

In law, as in religion, Weber placed great weight on the process of profes-sionalization: the legal profession is crucial to the rationalization of Western law. There are certainly other factors (for example, the influence of Roman law), but the legal profession was central to his thinking: "Formally elaborated law constituting a complex of maxims consciously applied in decisions has never come into existence without the decisive cooperation of trained spe-cialists" (Weber, 1921/1968:775). Although Weber was aware that there was a series of external pressures—especially from the rationalizing economy—impelling law toward rationalization, his view was that the most important force was the internal factor of the professionalization of the legal profession (1921/1968:776).

Weber differentiated between two types of legal training but saw only one as contributing to the development of rational law. The first is *craft training*, in which apprentices learn from masters, primarily during the actual practice of law. This kind of training produces a formalistic type of law dominated by precedents. The goal is not the creation of a comprehensive, rational system of law but, instead, the production of practically useful precedents for dealing with recurring situations. Because these precedents are tied to specific issues in the real world, a general, rational, and systematic body of law cannot emerge.

In contrast, *academic legal training* laid the groundwork for the rational law of the West. In this system, law is taught in special schools, where the emphasis is placed on legal theory and science—in other words, where legal phenomena are given rational and systematic treatment. The legal concepts produced have the character of abstract norms. Interpretation of these laws occurs in a rigorously formal and logical manner. They are general, in contrast to the specific, precedent-bound laws produced in the case of craft training.

Academic legal training leads to the development of a rational legal system with a number of characteristics, including the following:

1 Every concrete legal decision involves the application of abstract legal propositions to concrete situations.
2 It must be possible in every concrete case to derive the decision logically from abstract legal propositions.
3 Law must tend to be a gapless system of legal propositions or at least be treated as one.
4 The gapless legal system should be applicable to all social actions.

Weber seemed to adopt the view that history has seen law evolve from a cultural system of norms to a more structured system of formal laws. In general, actors are increasingly constrained by a more and more rational legal system. Although this is true, Weber was too good a sociologist to lose sight completely of the independent significance of the actor. For one thing, Weber (1921/1968:754–755) saw actors as crucial in the emergence of, and change in, law. However, the most important aspect of Weber's work in this area—for the purposes of this discussion—is the degree to which law is regarded as part of the general process of rationalization throughout the West.

Polity The rationalization of the political system is intimately linked to the rationalization of law and, ultimately, to the rationalization of all elements of the social system. For example, Weber argued that the more rational the political structure becomes, the more likely it is to eliminate systematically the irrational elements within the law. A rational polity cannot function with an irrational legal system, and vice versa. Weber did not believe that political leaders follow a conscious policy of rationalizing the law; rather, they are impelled in that direction by the demands of their own increasingly rational means of administration. Once again, Weber took the position that actors are being impelled by structural (the state) and cultural (rationalization) forces.

Weber defined the *polity* as "a community whose social action is aimed at subordinating to orderly domination by the participants a territory and the conduct of the persons within it, through readiness to resort to physical force, including normally force of arms" (1921/1968:901). This type of polity has existed neither everywhere nor always. It does not exist as a separate entity where the task of armed defense against enemies is assigned to the household, the neighborhood association, an economic group, and so forth. Although Weber clearly viewed the polity as a social structure, he was more careful to link his thinking here to his individual action orientations. In his view, modern political associations rest on the prestige bestowed upon them by their members.

As was his usual strategy, Weber went back to the primitive case in order to trace the development of polity. He made it clear that violent social action is primordial. However, the monopolization and rational ordering of legitimate violence did not exist in early societies but evolved over the centuries. Not only is rational control over violence lacking in primitive society, but other basic functions of the modern state either are totally absent or are not ordered in a rational manner. Included here would be functions like legislation, police, justice, administration, and the military. The development of the polity in the West involves the progressive differentiation and elaboration of these functions. But the most important step is their subordination under a single, dominant, rationally ordered state.

The City   Weber was also interested in the rise of a distinctively rational city in the West. He defined a *city* as having the following characteristics:

1 It is a relatively closed settlement.
2 It is relatively large.
3 It possesses a marketplace.
4 It has partial political autonomy.

Although many cities in many societies had these characteristics, Western cities developed a peculiarly rational character with, among other things, a rationally organized marketplace and political structure.

Weber looked at various other societies in order to determine why they did not develop the rational form of the city. He concluded that barriers like the traditional community in China and the caste system in India impeded the rise of such a city. But in the West, a number of rationalizing forces coalesced to create the modern city. For example, the development of a city requires a relatively rational economy. But of course the converse is also true: the development of a rational economy requires the modern city.

Art Forms   To give the reader a sense of the breadth of Weber's thinking, we need to say a few words about his work on the rationalization of various art forms. For example, Weber (1921/1958) viewed music in the West as having developed in a peculiarly rational direction. Musical creativity is reduced to routine procedures based on comprehensive principles. Music in the Western world has undergone a "transformation of the process of musical production into a calculable affair operating with known means, effective instruments, and understandable rules" (Weber, 1921/1958:li). Although the process of rationalization engenders tension in all the institutions in which it occurs, that tension is nowhere more noticeable than in music. After all, music is supposed to be an arena of expressive flexibility, but it is being progressively reduced to a rational, and ultimately mathematical, system.

Weber (1904–05/1958) sees a similar development in other art forms. For example, in painting, Weber emphasizes "the rational utilization of lines and spatial perspective—which the Renaissance created for us" (1904–05/1958:15). In architecture, "the rational use of the Gothic vault as a means of distributing pressure and of roofing spaces of all forms, and above all as the constructive principle of great monumental buildings and the foundation of a *style* extending to sculpture and painting, such as that created by our Middle Ages, does not occur elsewhere [in the world]" (Weber, 1904–05/1958:15).

We have now spent a number of pages examining Weber's ideas on rationalization in various aspects of social life. Although nowhere does he explicitly say so, we believe that Weber adopted the view that changes in the cultural level of rationality are leading to changes in the structures as well as in the individual thoughts and actions of the modern world. The rationalization process is not left to float alone above concrete phenomena but is embedded in various social structures and in the thoughts and actions of individuals. To put it slightly differently, the key point is that the cultural system of rationality occupies a position of casual priority in Weber's work. We can illustrate this in still another way by looking at Weber's work on the relationship between religion and economics, more specifically, the relationship between religion and the development, or lack of development, of a capitalist economy.

Religion and the Rise of Capitalism

Weber spent much of his life studying religion—this in spite of, or perhaps because of, his being areligious, or, as he once described himself, "religiously unmusical" (Gerth and Mills, 1958:25). One of his overriding concerns was the relationship among a variety of the world's religions and the development only in the West of a capitalist economic system. It is clear that the vast bulk of this work is done at the structural and cultural levels; the thoughts and actions of Calvinists, Buddhists, Confucians, Jews, Muslims (B. Turner, 1974), and others are held to be affected by changes in social structures and social institutions. Weber was primarily interested in the systems of ideas of the world's religions, in the "spirit" of capitalism, and in rationalization as a modern system of norms and values. He was also very interested in the structures of the world's religions, the various structural components of the societies in which they exist that serve to facilitate or impede rationalization, and the structural aspects of capitalism and the rest of the modern world.

Weber's work on religion and capitalism involved an enormous body of cross-cultural historical research. Freund summarized the complicated interrelationships involved in this research:

1 Economic forces influenced Protestantism.
2 Economic forces influenced religions other than Protestantism (for example, Hinduism, Confucianism, and Taoism).
3 Religious idea systems influence individual thoughts and actions—in particular, economic thoughts and actions.
4 Religious idea systems have been influential throughout the world.
5 Religious idea systems (particlarly Protestantism) have had the unique effect in the West of helping to rationalize the economic sector and virtually every other institution.

(Freund, 1968:213)

To this we can add:

6 Religious idea systems in the non-Western world have encountered overwhelming structural barriers to rationalization.

By according the religious factor great importance, Weber appeared to be simultaneously building on and criticizing his image of Marx's work. Weber, like Marx, operated with a complicated model of the interrelationship of primarily large-scale systems: "Weber's sociology is related to Marx's thought in the common attempt to grasp the interrelations of institutional orders making up a social structure: In Weber's work, military and religious, political and juridical institutional systems are functionally related to the economic order in a variety of ways" (Gerth and Mills, 1958:49). In fact, Weber's affinities with Marx are even greater than are often recognized. Although Weber, especially early in his career, gave primacy to religious ideas, he later came to see that material forces, not idea systems, are of central importance (Kalberg, 1985:61). As Weber said, "Not ideas, but material and ideal interests, directly govern men's conduct. Yet very frequently the 'world images' that have been created by 'ideas' have, like switchmen, determined the tracks along which action has been pushed by the dynamic of interest" (Gerth and Mills, 1958: 280).

In analyzing the relationship between the world's religions and the economy, Weber (1921/1963) developed a typology of the paths of salvation. *Asceticism* is the first broad type of religiosity, and it combines an orientation toward action with the commitment of believers to denying themselves the pleasures of the world. Ascetic religions are divided into two subtypes. *Otherworldly asceticism* involves a set of norms and values that command the followers to work within the secular world but to fight against its temptations. Of greater interest to Weber, because it encompasses Calvinism, was *innerworldly asceticism*. Such a religion does not reject the world; instead, it actively urges its members to work within the world so that they can find salvation, or at least signs of it. The distinctive goal here is the strict, methodical control of the members' patterns of life, thought, and action. Members are urged to reject everything unethical, esthetic, or dependent on their emotional reactions to the secular world. Innerworldly ascetics are motivated to systematize their own conduct.

Whereas both types of ascetisicm involve some type of action and self-denial, *mysticism* involves contemplation, emotion, and inaction. Weber subdivided mysticism in the same way as asceticism. *World-rejecting mysticism* involves total flight from the world. *Innerworldly mysticism* leads to contemplative efforts to understand the meaning of the world, but these efforts are doomed to failure, because the world is viewed as being beyond individual comprehension. In any case, both types of mysticism and world-rejecting asceticism can be seen as idea systems that inhibit the development of capitalism and rationality. In contrast, innerworldly asceticism is the system of norms and values that contributed enormously to the development of these phenomena in the West.

The Protestant Ethic and the Spirit of Capitalism In Max Weber's best-known work, *The Protestant Ethic and the Spririt of Capitalism* (1904–05/1958), he traced the impact of ascetic Protestantism—primarily Calvinism—on the rise of the spirit of capitalism. This work is but a small part of a larger body of scholarship that traces the relationship between religion and modern capitalism throughout much of the world.

Weber, especially later in his work, made it clear that his most general interest was in the rise of the distinctive rationality of the West. Capitalism, with its rational organization of free labor, its open market, and its rational bookkeeping system, is but one component of that developing system. He directly linked it to the parallel development of rationalized science, law, politics, art, architecture, literature, universities, and the polity.

Weber did not directly link the idea system of the Protestant ethic to the structures of the capitalist system; instead, he was content to link the Protestant ethic to another system of ideas, the "spirit of capitalism." In other words, two systems of ideas are directly linked in this work. Although links of the capitalist economic system to the material world are certainly implied and indicated, they were not Weber's primary concern. Thus, *The Protestant Ethic* is not about the rise of modern capitalism but is about the origin of a peculiar spirit that eventually made capitalism possible.

Weber began by examining and rejecting alternative explanations of why capitalism arose in the West in the sixteenth and seventeenth centuries. To those who contended that capitalism arose because the material conditions were right at that time, Weber retorted that material conditions were also ripe at other times and capitalism did not arise. Weber also rejected the psychological theory that the development of capitalism was due simply to the acquisitive instinct. In his view, such an instinct always has existed, yet it did not produce capitalism in other situations.

Evidence for Weber's views on the significance of Protestantism was found in an examination of those countries with mixed religious systems. In looking at these countries, he discovered that the leaders of the economic system—business leaders, owners of capital, high-grade skilled labor, and more advanced technically and commercially trained personnel—were all overwhelmingly Protestant. This was taken to mean that Protestantism was a significant cause in the choice of these occupations and, conversely, that other religions (for example, Roman Catholicism) failed to produce idea systems that impelled individuals into these vocations.

In Weber's view, the spirit of capitalism is not defined simply by economic greed; it is in many ways the exact opposite. It is a moral and ethical system, an ethos, that among other things stresses economic success. In fact, it was the turning of profit making into an ethos that was critical in the West. In other societies, the pursuit of profit was seen as an individual act motivated at least in part by greed. Thus it was viewed by many as morally suspect. However, Protestantism succeeded in turning the pursuit of profit into a moral crusade. It was the backing of the moral system that led to the unprecedented expansion of profit seeking and, ultimately, to the capitalist system. On a theoretical level, by stressing that he was dealing with the relationship between one ethos (Protestantism) and another (the spirit of capitalism), Weber was able to keep his analysis primarily at the level of systems of ideas.

The spirit of capitalism can be seen as a normative system that involves a number of interrelated ideas. For example, its goal is to instill an "attitude which seeks profit rationally and systematically" (Weber, 1904–05/1958:64). In addition, it preaches an avoidance of life's pleasures: "Seest thou a man diligent in business? He shall stand before kings" (Weber, 1904–05/1958:53). Also included in the spirit of capitalism are ideas such as "time is money," "be industrious," "be frugal," "be punctual," "be fair," and "earning money is a legitimate end in itself." Above all, there is the idea that it is people's duty ceaselessly to increase their wealth. This takes the spirit of capitalism out of the realm of individual ambition and into the category of ethical imperative. Although Weber admitted that a type of capitalism (for example, adventurer capitalism) existed in China, India, Babylon, and the classical world and during the Middle Ages, it was different from Western capitalism, primarily because it lacked "this particular ethos" (1904–05/1958:52).

Weber was interested not simply in describing this ethical system but also in explaining its derivations. He thought that Protestantism, particularly Calvinism, was crucial to the rise of the spirit of capitalism. Calvinism is no longer necessary to the continuation of that economic system. In fact, in many senses modern capitalism, given its secularity, stands in opposition to Calvinism and to religion in general. Capitalism today has become a real entity that combines norms, values, market, money, and laws. It has become, in Durkheim's terms, a social fact that is external to, and coercive of, the individual. As Weber put it:

Capitalism is today an immense cosmos into which the individual is born, and which presents itself to him, at least as an individual, as an unalterable order of things in which he must live. It forces the individual, in so far as he is involved in the system of market relationships, to conform to capitalist rules of action.

(Weber, 1904–05/1958:54)

Another crucial point here is that Calvinists did not consciously seek to create a capitalist system. In Weber's view, capitalism was an *unanticipated consequence* of the Protestant ethic. The concept of unanticipated consequences has broad significance in Weber's work, for he believed that what individuals and groups intend by their actions often leads to a set of consequences that are at variance with their intentions. Although Weber did not explain this point, it seems that it is related to his theoretical view that people create social structures but that those structures soon take on a life of their own, over which the creators have little or no control. Because people lack control over them, structures are free to develop in a variety of totally unanticipated directions. Weber's line of thinking led Arthur Mitzman (1970) to argue that Weber created a sociology of reification. Reified social structures are free to move in unanticipated directions, as both Marx and Weber showed in their analyses of capitalism.

Calvinism and the Spirit of Capitalism   Calvinism was the version of Protestantism that interested Weber most. One feature of Calvinism was the idea that only a small number of people are chosen for salvation. In addition, Calvinism entailed the idea of predestination; people were predestined to be either among the saved or among the damned. There was nothing that the individual or the religion as a whole could do to affect that fate. Yet the idea of predestination left people uncertain about whether they were among the saved. To reduce this uncertainty, the Calvinists developed the idea that *signs* could be used as indicators of whether a person was saved. People were urged to work hard, because if they were diligent, they would uncover the signs of salvation, which were to be found in economic success. In sum, the Calvinist was urged to engage in intense, worldly activity and to become a "man of vocation."

However, isolated actions were not enough. Calvinism, as an ethic, required self-control and a systematized style of life that involved an integrated round of activities, particularly business activities. This stood in contrast to the Christian ideal of the Middle Ages, in which individuals simply engaged in isolated acts as the occasion arose in order to atone for particular sins and to increase their chances of salvation. "The God of Calvinism demanded of his believers not single good works, but a life of good works combined into a unified system" (Weber, 1904–05/1958:117). Calvinism produced an ethical system and ultimately a group of people who were nascent capitalists. Calvinism "has the highest ethical appreciation of the sober, middle-class, self-made man" (Weber, 1904–05/1958:163). Weber neatly summarized his own position on Calvinism and its relationship to capitalism as follows:

The religious valuation of restless, continuous, systematic work in a worldly calling, as the highest means of asceticism, and at the same time the surest and most evident proof of rebirth and genuine faith, must have been the most powerful conceivable lever for the expansion of . . . the spirit of capitalism.

(Weber, 1904–05/1958:172)

In addition to its general link to the spirit of capitalism, Calvinism also had some more specific links. First, as already mentioned, capitalists could ruthlessly pursue their economic interests and feel that such pursuit was not merely self-interest but was, in fact, their ethical duty. This not only permitted unprecedented mercilessness in business but also silenced potential critics, who could not simply reduce these actions to self-interest. Second, Calvinism provided the rising capitalist "with sober, conscientious and unusually industrious workmen who clung to their work as to a life purpose willed by god" (Weber, 1904–05/1958:117). With such a work force, the nascent capitalist could raise the level of exploitation to unprecedented heights. Third, it legitimized an unequal stratification system by giving the capitalist the "comforting assurances that the unequal distribution of the goods of this world was a special dispensation of Divine Providence" (Weber, 1904–05/1958:117).

Weber also had reservations about the capitalist system, as he did about all aspects of the rationalized world. For example, he pointed out that capitalism tends to produce "specialists without spirit, sensualists without heart; this nullity imagines that it has attained a level of civilization never before achieved" (Weber, 1904–05/1958:182).

Although in *The Protestant Ethic* Weber focused on the effect of Calvinism on the spirit of capitalism, he was well aware that social and economic conditions have a reciprocal impact on religion. He chose not to deal with such relationships in this book, but he made it clear that his goal was not to substitute a one-sided spiritualist interpretation for the one-sided materialist explanation that he attributed to Marxists.

If Calvinism was the major fact in the rise of capitalism in the West, then the question arises: Why didn't capitalism arise in other societies? In his effort to answer this question, Weber dealt with spiritual and material barriers to the rise of capitalism. Let us look briefly at Weber's analysis of those barriers in two societies—China and India.

Religion and Capitalism in China   One crucial assumption that allowed Weber to make legitimate the comparison between the West and China is that both had the prerequisites for the development of capitalism. In China, there was a tradition of intense acquisitiveness and unscrupulous competition. There was great industry and an enormous capacity for work in the populace. Powerful guilds existed. The population was expanding. And there was a steady growth in precious metals. With these and other material prerequisites, why didn't capitalism arise in China? As has been pointed out before, Weber's general answer was that social, structural, and religious barriers in China prevented the development of capitalism. This is not to say that capitalism was entirely absent in China. There were moneylenders and purveyors who sought high rates of profit. But a market, as well as various other components of a rational capitalistic system, were absent. In Weber's view, the rudimentary capitalism of China "pointed in a direction opposite to the development of rational economic corporate enterprises" (1916/1964:86).

Structural Barriers Weber listed several structural barriers to the rise of capitalism in China. First, there was the structure of the typical Chinese community. It was held together by rigid kinship bonds in the form of sibs. The sibs were ruled by elders, who made them bastions of traditionalism. The sibs were self-contained entities, and there was little dealing with other sibs. This encouraged small, encapsulated land holdings and a household-based, rather than a market, economy. The extensive partitioning of the land prevented major technological developments, because economies of scale were impossible. Agricultural production remained in the hands of peasants, industrial production in the hands of small-scale artisans. Modern cities, which were to become the centers of Western capitalism, were inhibited in their development because the people retained their allegiance to the sibs. Because of the sibs' autonomy, the central government was never able to govern these units effectively or to mold them into a unified whole.

The structure of the Chinese state was a second barrier to the rise of capitalism. The state was largely patrimonial and governed by tradition, prerogative, and favoritism. In Weber's view, a rational and calculable system of administration and law enforcement, which was necessary for industrial development, did not exist. There were very few formal laws covering commerce, there was no central court, and legal formalism was rejected. This irrational type of administrative structure was a barrier to the rise of capitalism, as Weber made clear: "Capital investment in industry is far too sensitive to such irrational rule and too dependent upon the possibility of calculating the steady and rational operation of the state machinery to emerge within an administration of this type" (1916/1964:103). In addition to its general structure, a number of more specific components of the state acted against the development of capitalism. For example, the officials of the bureaucratic administration had vested material interests that made them oppose capitalism. Officials often bought offices primarily to make a profit, and this kind of orientation did not necessarily make for a high degree of efficiency.

A third structural barrier to the rise of capitalism was the nature of the Chinese language. In Weber's view, it militated against rationality by making systematic thought difficult. It remained largely in the realm of the "pictorial" and the "descriptive." Logical thinking was also inhibited because intellectual thought remained largely in the form of parables, and this hardly was the basis for the development of a cumulative body of knowledge.

Although there were other structural barriers to the rise of capitalism (for example, a country without wars or overseas trade), a key factor was the lack of the required "mentality," the lack of the needed idea system. Weber looked at the two dominant systems of religious ideas in China—Confucianism and Taoism—and the characteristics of both that militated against the development of a spirit of capitalism.

Confucianism A central characteristic of Confucian thinking was its emphasis on a literary education as a prerequisite for office and for social status. To acquire a position in the ruling strata, a person had to be a member of the literati. Movement up the hierarchy was based on a system of ideas that tested literary knowledge, not the technical knowledge needed to conduct the office in question. What was valued and tested was whether the individual's mind was steeped in culture and whether it was characterized by ways of thought suitable to a cultured man. In Weber's terms, Confucianism encouraged "a highly bookish literary education." The literati produced by this system came to see the actual work of administration as beneath them, mere tasks to be delegated to subordinates. Instead, the literati aspired to clever puns, euphemisms, and allusions to classical quotations—a purely literary kind of intellectuality. With this kind of orientation, it is easy to see why the literati were unconcerned with the state of the economy or with economic activities. The world view of the Confucians ultimately grew to be the policy of the state. As a result, the Chinese state came to be only minimally involved in rationally influencing the economy and the rest of society. The Confucians maintained their influence by having the constitution decree that only they could serve as officials, and competitiors to Confucians (for example, the bourgeoisie, prophets, and priests) were blocked from serving in the government. In fact, if the emperor dared to deviate from this rule, he was thought to be toying with disaster and his potential downfall.

Many other components of Confucianism militated against capitalism. It was basically an ethic of adjustment to the world and to its order and its conventions. Rather than viewing material success and wealth as a sign of salvation as the Calvinist did, the Confucian simply was led to accept things as they were. In fact, there was no idea of salvation in Confucianism, and this lack of tension between religion and the world also acted to inhibit the rise of capitalism. The snobbish Confucian was urged to reject thrift, because it was something that commoners practiced. It was not regarded as proper for a Confucian gentleman to work, although wealth was prized. Active engagement in a profitable enterprise was regarded as morally dubious and unbecoming to a Confucian's station. The acceptable goal for such a gentleman was a good position, not high profits. The ethic emphasized the abilities of a gentleman rather than the highly specialized skills that could have proved useful to a developing capitalist system. In sum, Weber contended that Confucianism became a relentless canonization of tradition.

Taoism Weber perceived Taoism as a mystical Chinese religion in which the supreme good was deemed to be a psychic state, a state of mind, and not a state of grace to be obtained by conduct in the real world. As a result, Taoists did not operate in a rational way to affect the external world. Taoism was essentially traditional, and one of its basic tenets was "Do not introduce innovations" (Weber, 1916/1964:203). Such an idea system was unlikely to produce any major changes, let alone one as far-reaching as capitalism.

One trait common to Taoism and Confucianism is that neither produced enough tension, or conflict, among the members to motivate them to much innovative action in this world:

> Neither in its official state cult nor in its Taoist aspect could Chinese religiosity produce sufficiently strong motives for a religiously oriented life for the individual such as the Puritan method represents. Both forms of religion lacked even the traces of the Satanic force or evil against which [the] pious Chinese might have struggled for his salvation.
>
> (Weber, 1916/1964:206)

As was true of Confucianism, there was no inherent force in Taoism to impel actors to change the world or, more specifically, to build a capitalist system.

Religion and Capitalism in India For our purposes, a very brief discussion of Weber's (1916–17/1958) thinking on the relationship between religion and captialism in India will suffice. The argument, though not its details, parallels the Chinese case. For example, Weber discussed the structural barriers of the caste system (Gellner, 1982:534). Among other things, the caste system erected overwhelming barriers to social mobility, and it tended to regulate even the most minute aspects of people's lives. The idea system of the Brahmans had a number of components. For example, Brahmans were expected to avoid vulgar occupations and to observe elegance in manners and proprieties in conduct. Indifference to the world's mundane affairs was the crowning idea of Brahman religiosity. The Brahmans also emphasized a highly literary kind of education. Although there certainly were important differences between them, the ethos of the Brahmans, like that of Confucians, presented overwhelming barriers to the rise of capitalism.

The Hindu religion posed similar ideational barriers. Its key idea was reincarnation. To the Hindu, a person is born into the caste that he or she deserves by virtue of behavior in a past life. Through faithful adherence to the ritual of caste, the Hindu gains merit for the next life. Hinduism, unlike Calvinism, was traditional in the sense that salvation was to be achieved by faithfully following the rules; innovation, particularly in the economic sphere, could not lead to a higher caste in the next life. Activity in this world was not important, because the world was seen as a transient abode and an impediment to the spiritual quest. In these and other ways, the idea system associated with Hinduism failed to produce the kind of people who could create a capitalist economic system and, more generally, a rationally ordered society.

SUMMARY

Max Weber has had a more powerful positive impact on a wide range of sociological theories than any other sociological theorist. This influence is traceable to the sophistication, complexity, and sometimes even confusion of Weberian theory. Despite its problems, Weber's work represents a remarkable fusion of historical research and sociological theorizing.

We open this chapter with a discussion of the theoretical roots and methodological orientations of Weberian theory. We see that Weber, over the course of his career, moved progressively toward a fusion of history and sociology, that is, toward the development of a historical sociology. One of his most critical methodological concepts is *verstehen*. Although this is often interpreted as a tool to be used to analyze individual consciousness, in Weber's hands it was more often a scientific tool to analyze structural and institutional constraints on actors. We also discuss other aspects of Weber's methodology, including his propensity to think in terms of causality and to employ ideal types. In addition, we examine his analysis of the relationship between values and sociology.

The heart of Weberian sociology lies in substantive sociology, not in methodological statements. Although Weber based his theories on his thoughts about social action and social relationships, his main interest was the large-scale structures and institutions of society. We deal especially with his analysis of the three structures of authority—legal, traditional, and charismatic. In the context of legal authority, we deal with his famous ideal-typical bureaucracy and show how he used that tool to analyze traditional and charismatic authority. Of particular interest is Weber's work on charisma. Not only did he have a clear sense of it as a structure of authority, but he was also interested in the processes by which such a structure is produced.

Although his work on social structures—such as authority—is important, it is at the cultural level, in his work on the rationalization of the world, that Weber's most important insights lie. Weber articulated the idea that the world is becoming increasingly dominated by norms and values of rationalization. In this context, we discuss Weber's work on the economy, religion, law, the polity, the city, and art forms. Weber argued that rationalization was sweeping across all these institutions in the West, whereas there were major barriers to this process in the rest of the world.

Weber's thoughts on rationalization and various other issues are illustrated in his work on the relationship between religion and capitalism. At one level, this is a series of studies of the relationship between ideas (religious ideas) and the development of the spirit of capitalism and, ultimately, capitalism itself. At another level, it is a study of how the West developed a distinctively rational religious system (Calvinism) that played a key role in the rise of a rational economic system (capitalism). Weber also studied other societies, in which he found religious systems (for example, Confucianism, Taoism, and Hinduism) that inhibit the growth of a rational economic system. It is this kind of majestic sweep over the history of many sectors of the world that helps give Weberian theory its enduring significance.

GEORG SIMMEL

*T*HE impact of the ideas of Georg Simmel (1858–1918) on American sociological theory differs markedly from that of the three theorists discussed in the preceding three chapters of this book. Marx, Durkheim, and Weber, despite their later significance, had relatively little influence on American theory in the early twentieth century. Simmel was much better known to the early American sociologists. In recent years, Simmel has been eclipsed by Marx, Durkheim, and Weber, although he is far more influential today than other classical thinkers such as Comte or Spencer. His influence is apparent in several specific theories, such as conflict theory, symbolic interactionism, exchange theory, and network theory. Moreover, it is possible that we will see an increase in Simmel's impact on sociological theory (Levine, 1985, 1989) as a result of the growing influence of one of his most important works, *The Philosophy of Money* (1907/1978).

PRIMARY CONCERNS

While we will focus on Simmel's contributions to sociological theory, it should be pointed out that he was primarily a philosopher and that most of his publications dealt with philosophical issues (for example, ethics) and other philosophers (for example, Kant).

   With the exception of his contribution to the primarily macroscopic conflict theory (Coser, 1956; Simmel, 1908/1955), Georg Simmel is best known as a microsociologist who played a significant role in the development of small-group research (Caplow, 1968), symbolic interactionism, and exchange theory. All of Simmel's contributions in these areas reflect his belief that sociologists should primarily study social interaction. Robert Nisbet presents this view of Simmel's contribution to sociology:

GEORG SIMMEL: A Biographical Sketch

Georg Simmel was born in the heart of Berlin on March 1, 1858. He studied a wide range of subjects at the University of Berlin. However, his first effort to produce a dissertation was rejected, and one of his professors remarked, "We would do him a great service if we do not encourage him further in this direction" (Frisby, 1984:23). Despite this, Simmel persevered and received his doctorate in philosophy in 1881. He remained at the university in a teaching capacity until 1914, although he occupied a relatively unimportant position as *privatdozent* from 1885 to 1900. In the latter position, Simmel served as an unpaid lecturer whose livelihood was dependent on student fees. Despite his marginality, Simmel did rather well in this position, largely because he was an excellent lecturer and attracted large numbers of (paying) students (Frisby, 1981:17). His style was so popular that even cultured members of Berlin society were drawn to his lectures, which became public events.

Simmel wrote innumerable articles ("The Metropolis and Mental Life") and books (*The Philosophy of Money*). He was well known in German academic circles and even had an international following, especially in the United States, where his work was of great significance in the birth of sociology. Finally, in 1900, Simmel received official recognition, a purely honorary title at the University of Berlin, which did not give him full academic status. Simmel tried to obtain many academic positions, but he failed in spite of the support of such scholars as Max Weber.

One of the reasons for Simmel's failure was that he was a Jew in a nineteenth-century Germany rife with anti-Semitism (Kasler, 1985). Thus, in a report on Simmel written to a

---

It is the *microsociological* character of Simmel's work that may always give him an edge in timeliness over the other pioneers. He did not disdain the small and the intimate elements of human association, nor did he ever lose sight of the primacy of human beings, of concrete individuals, in his analysis of institutions.

(Nisbet, 1959:480)

David Frisby makes a similar point: "The grounding of sociology in some psychological categories may be one reason why Simmel's sociology has proved attractive not merely to the interactionist but also to social psychology" (1984:57). However, it is often forgotten that Simmel's microsociological work on the forms of interaction is embedded in a broader theory of the relations between individuals and the larger society.

Simmel had a much more complicated and sophisticated theory of social reality than he is commonly given credit for in contemporary American sociology. Tom Bottomore and David Frisby (1978) argue that there are four basic levels of concern in Simmel's work. First are his microscopic assumptions about the psychological components of social life. Second, on a slightly larger scale, is his interest in the sociological components of interpersonal relation-

minister of education, Simmel was described as "an Israelite through and through, in his external appearance, in his bearing and in his mode of thought" (Frisby, 1981:25). Another reason was the kind of work that he did. Many of his articles appeared in newspapers and magazines; they were written for a more general audience than simply academic sociologists. In addition, because he did not hold a regular academic appointment, he was forced to earn his living through public lectures. Simmel's audience, both for his writings and his lectures, was more the intellectual public than professional sociologists, and this tended to lead to derisive judgments from fellow professionals. For example, one of his contemporaries damned him because "his influence remained . . . upon the general atmosphere and affected, above all, the higher levels of journalism" (Troeltsch, cited in Frisby, 1981:13). Simmel's personal failures can also be linked to the low esteem that German academicians of the day had for sociology.

In 1914 Simmel finally obtained a regular academic appointment at a minor university (Strasbourg), but he once again felt estranged. On the one hand, he regretted leaving his audience of Berlin intellectuals. Thus his wife wrote to Max Weber's wife: "Georg has taken leave of the auditorium very badly. . . . The students were very affectionate and sympathetic. . . . It was a departure at the full height of life" (Frisby, 1981:29). On the other hand, Simmel did not feel a part of the life of his new university. Thus, he wrote to Mrs. Weber: "There is hardly anything to report from us. We live . . . a cloistered, closed-off, indifferent, desolate external existence. Academic activity is = 0, the people . . . alien and inwardly hostile" (Frisby, 1981:32).

World War I started soon after Simmel's appointment at Strasbourg; lecture halls were turned into military hospitals, and students went off to war. Thus, Simmel remained a marginal figure in German academia until his death in 1918. He never did have a normal academic career. Nevertheless, Simmel attracted a large academic following in his day, and his fame as a scholar has, if anything, grown over the years.

---

ships. Third, and most macroscopic, is his work on the structure of, and changes in, the social and cultural "spirit" of his times. Not only did Simmel operate with this image of a three-tiered social reality, but he adopted the principle of *emergence,* the idea that the higher levels emerge out of the lower levels: "Further development replaces the immediacy of interacting forces with the creation of higher supra-individual formations, which appear as independent representatives of these forces and absorb and mediate the relations between individuals" (1907/1978:174). He also said, "If society is to be an autonomous object of an independent science, then it can only be so through the fact that, out of the sum of the individual elements that constitute it, a new entity emerges; otherwise all problems of social science would only be those of individual psychology" (Frisby, 1984:56–57). Overarching these three tiers is a fourth that involves ultimate metaphysical principles of life. These eternal truths affect all of Simmel's work and, as we will see, lead to his image of the future direction of the world.

This concern with multiple levels of social reality is reflected in Simmel's (1950; originally published in 1918) definition of three separable problem "areas" in sociology. The first he described as "pure" sociology. In this area, psychological variables are combined with forms of interaction. Although Simmel clearly assumed that actors have creative mental abilities, he gave little explicit attention to this aspect of social reality. His most microscopic work is with the *forms* that interaction takes as well as with the *types* of people who engage in interaction. The forms include subordination, superordination, exchange, conflict, and sociability. In his work on types, he differentiated between positions in the interactional structure, such as "competitor" and "coquette," and orientations to the world, such as "miser," "spendthrift," "stranger," and "adventurer." At the intermediate level is Simmel's "general" sociology, dealing with the social and cultural products of human history. Here Simmel manifested his larger-scale interests in the group, the structure and history of societies and cultures. Finally, in Simmel's "philosophical" sociology, he dealt with his views on the basic nature, and inevitable fate, of humankind. Throughout this chapter, we will touch on all these levels and sociologies. We will find that although Simmel sometimes separated the different levels and sociologies, he more often integrated them into a broader totality.

Dialectical Thinking

Simmel's way of dealing with the interrelationships among three basic levels of social reality (leaving out his fourth, metaphysical level) gave his sociology a dialectical character reminiscent of Marx's sociology. A dialectical approach, as we saw earlier, is multicausal and multidirectional, integrates fact and value, rejects the idea that there are hard-and-fast dividing lines between social phenomena, focuses on social relations (B. Turner, 1986), looks not only at the present but also at the past and the future, and is deeply concerned with both conflicts and contradictions.

In spite of the similarities between Marx and Simmel in their use of a dialectical approach, there are important differences between them. Of greatest importance is the fact that they focused on very different aspects of the social world and offered very different images of the future of the world. Instead of Marx's revolutionary optimism, Simmel had a view of the future closer to Weber's image of an "iron cage" from which there is no escape (for more on the intellectual relationship between Simmel and Weber, see Scaff, 1989:121–151).

Simmel manifested his commitment to the dialectic in various ways. For one thing, Simmel's sociology was always concerned with relationships, especially interaction (*association*). Overall he was ever attuned to dualisms, conflicts, and contradictions in whatever realm of the social world he happened to be working on. Donald Levine states that this perspective reflects Simmel's belief that *"the world can best be understood in terms of conflicts and contrasts between opposed categories"* (1971:xxxv). Rather than try to deal with this mode of thinking throughout Simmel's work, let us illustrate it from his work on one of his forms of interaction—*fashion*. Simmel used a similar mode of dialectical thinking in most of his essays on social forms and social types, but this discussion of fashion amply illustrates his method of dealing with these phenomena. We will also deal with the dialectic in Simmel's thoughts on subjective-objective culture and the concepts of "more-life" and "more-than-life."

Fashion   In one of his typically fascinating and dualistic essays, Simmel (1904/1971) illustrated the contradictions in fashion in a variety of ways. On the one hand, fashion is a form of social relationship that allows those who wish to conform to the demands of the group to do so. On the other hand, fashion also provides the norm from which those who wish to be individualistic can deviate. Fashion involves a historical process as well: at the initial stage, everyone accepts what is fashionable; inevitably individuals deviate from this; and finally, in the process of deviation, they may adopt a whole new view of what is in fashion. Fashion is also dialectical in the sense that the success and spread of any given fashion leads to its eventual failure. That is, the distinctiveness of something leads to its being considered fashionable. However, as large numbers of people come to accept it, it ceases to be distinctive and hence it loses its attractiveness. Still another duality involves the role of the leader of a fashion movement. Such a person leads the group, paradoxically, by *following* the fashion better than anyone else, that is, by adopting it more determinedly. Finally, Simmel argued that not only does following what is in fashion involve dualities but so does the effort on the part of some people to be out of fashion. Unfashionable people view those who follow a fashion as being imitators and themselves as mavericks, but Simmel argued that the latter are simply engaging in an inverse form of imitation. Individuals may avoid what is in fashion because they are afraid that they, like their peers, will lose their individuality, but, in Simmel's view, such a fear is hardly a sign of great personal strength and independence. In sum, Simmel noted that in fashion "all . . . leading antithetical tendencies . . . are represented in one way or another" (1904/1971:317).

Simmel's dialectical thinking can be seen at a more general level as well. As we will see throughout this chapter, he was most interested in the conflicts and contradictions that exist between the individual and the larger social and cultural structures that individuals construct. These structures ultimately come to have a life of their own, over which the individual can exert little or no control.

Individual (Subjective) Culture and Objective Culture   People are influenced, and in Simmel's view threatened, by social structures and, more importantly, for Simmel, by their cultural products. Simmel distinguished between individual culture and objective culture. *Objective culture* refers to those things that people produce (art, science, philosophy, and so on). *Individual (subjective) culture* is the capacity of the actor to produce, absorb, and control the elements of objective culture. In an ideal sense, individual culture shapes, and is shaped by, objective culture. The problem is that objective culture comes to have a life of its own. As Simmel put it, "They [the elements of culture] acquire fixed identities, a logic and lawfulness of their own; this new rigidity inevitably places them at a distance from the spiritual dynamic which created them and which makes them independent" (1921/1968:11). The existence of these cultural products creates a contradiction with the actors who created them because it is an example of

> the deep estrangement or animosity which exists between organic and creative processes of the soul and its contents and products: the vibrating, restless life of the creative soul; which develops toward the infinite contrasts with its fixed and ideally unchanging product and its uncanny feedback effect, which arrests and indeed rigidifies this liveliness. Frequently it appears as if creative movement of the soul was dying from its own product.
>
> (Simmel, 1921/1968:42)

As K. Peter Etzkorn said, "In Simmel's dialectic, man is always in danger of being slain by those objects of his own creation which have lost their organic human coefficient" (1968: 2).

More-Life and More-Than-Life   Another area of Simmel's thinking, his philosophical sociology, is an even more general manifestation of his dialectical thinking. In discussing the emergence of social and cultural structures, Simmel took a position very similar to some of Marx's ideas. Marx used the concept of the fetishism of commodities to point up the separation between people and their products. For Marx, this separation reached its apex in capitalism, could be overcome only in the future socialist society, and thus was a specific historical phenomenon. But for Simmel this separation is inherent in the nature of human life. In philosophical terms, there is an inherent and inevitable contradiction between "more-life" and "more-than-life" (Oakes, 1984:6; Weingartner, 1959).

The issue of more-life and more-than-life is central in Simmel's essay, "The Transcendent Character of Life" (1918/1971). As the title suggests, and Simmel makes clear, *"Transcendence is immanent in life"* (1918/1971:361). People possess a doubly transcendent capability. First, because of their restless, creative capacities (more-life), people are able to transcend themselves. Second, this transcendent, creative ability makes it possible for people to constantly produce sets of objects that transcend them. The objective existence of these phenomena (more-than-life) comes to stand in irreconcilable opposition to the creative forces (more-life) that produced the objects in the first place. In other words, social life "creates and sets free from itself something that is not life but 'which has its own significance and follows its own law'" (Weingartner, citing Simmel, 1959:53). Life is found in the unity, and the conflict, between the two. As Simmel concludes, "Life finds its essence, its process, in being more-life and more-than-life" (1918/1971:374).

Thus, because of his metaphysical conceptions, Simmel came to an image of the world far closer to Weber's than to Marx's. Simmel, like Weber, saw the world as becoming an iron cage of objective culture from which people have progressively less chance of escape. We will have more to say about a number of these issues in the following sections, which deal with Simmel's thoughts on the major components of social reality.

INDIVIDUAL CONSCIOUSNESS

At the individual level, Simmel focused on forms of association and paid relatively little attention to the issue of individual consciousness, which was rarely dealt with directly in his work. Still, Simmel clearly operated with a sense that human beings possess creative consciousness. As Frisby put it, the bases of social life to Simmel were "conscious individuals or groups of individuals who interact with one another for a variety of motives, purposes, and interests" (1984:61). This interest in creativity is manifest in Simmel's discussion of the diverse forms of interaction, the ability of actors to create social structures, as well as the disastrous effects those structures have on the creativity of individuals.

All of Simmel's discussions of the forms of interaction imply that actors must be consciously oriented to one another. Thus, for example, interaction in a stratified system requires that superordinates and subordinates orient themselves to each other. The interaction would cease and the stratification system collapse if a process of mutual orientation did not exist. The same is true of all other forms of interaction.

Consciousness plays other roles in Simmel's work. For example, although Simmel believed that social (and cultural) structures come to have a life of their own, he realized that people must conceptualize such structures in order for them to have an effect on the people. Simmel stated that society is not simply "out there" but is also "'my representation'—something dependent on the activity of consciousness" (1908/1959a:339).

Simmel also had a sense of individual conscience and of the fact that the norms and values of society become internalized in individual consciousness. The existence of norms and values both internally and externally

> explains the dual character of the moral command: that on the one hand, it confronts us as an impersonal order to which we simply have to submit, but that, on the other, no external power, but only our most private and internal impulses, imposes it upon us. At any rate, here is one of the cases where the individual, within his own consciousness, repeats the relationships which exist between him, as a total personality, and the group.
>
> (Simmel, 1908/1950a:254)

This very modern conception of internalization is a relatively undeveloped assumption in Simmel's work.

In addition, Simmel had a conception of people's ability to confront themselves mentally, to set themselves apart from their own actions, that is very similar to the views of George Herbert Mead and symbolic interactionists (Simmel, 1918/1971:364; see also Simmel, 1907/1978:64). The actor can take in external stimuli, assess them, try out different courses of action, and then decide what to do. Because of these mental capacities, the actor is not simply enslaved by external forces. But there is a paradox in Simmel's conception of the actor's mental capacities. The mind can keep people from being enslaved by external stimuli, but it also has the capacity to reify social reality, to create the very objects that come to enslave it. As Simmel said, "Our mind has a remarkable ability to think of contents as being independent of the act of thinking" (1907/1978:65). Thus, although their intelligence enables people to avoid being enslaved by the same external stimuli that constrain lower animals, it also creates the structures and institutions that constrain their thoughts and actions.

Although we can find manifestations of Simmel's concern with consciousness in various places in his work, he did very little other than assume its existence. Raymond Aron clearly makes this point: "He [Simmel] must know the laws of behavior . . . of human reaction. But he does not try to discover or to explain what goes on in the mind itself" (1965:5–6).

SOCIAL INTERACTION ("ASSOCIATION")

Georg Simmel is best known in contemporary sociology for his contributions to our understanding of the patterns, or forms, of social interaction. He expressed his interest in this level of social reality in this way:

> We are dealing here with microscopic-molecular processes within human material, so to speak. These processes are the actual occurrences that are concatenated or hypostatized into those macrocosmic, solid units and systems. That people look at one another and are jealous of one another; that they exchange letters or have dinner together; that apart from all tangible interests they strike one another as pleasant or unpleasant; that gratitude for altruistic acts makes for inseparable union; that one asks another to point out a certain street; that people dress and adorn themselves for each other—these are a few casually chosen illustrations from the whole range of relations that play between one person and other. They may be momentary or permanent, conscious or unconscious, ephemeral or of grave consequence, but they incessantly tie men together. At each moment such threads are spun, dropped, taken up again, displaced by others, interwoven with others. These interactions among the atoms of society are accessible only to psychological microscopy.
>
> (Simmel, 1908/1959b:327–328)

Simmel made clear here that one of his primary interests was interaction (association) among conscious actors and that his intent was to look at a wide range of interactions that may seem trivial at some times but crucially important at others. His was not a Durkheimian expression of interest in social facts but a declaration of a smaller-scale focus for sociology.

Because Simmel sometimes took an exaggerated position on the importance of interaction in his sociology, many have lost sight of his insights into the larger-scale aspects of social reality. At times, for example, he equated society with interaction: "Society . . . is only the synthesis or the general term for the totality of these specific interactions. . . . 'Society' is identical with the sum total of these relations" (Simmel, 1907/1978:175). Such statements may be taken as a reaffirmation of his interest in interaction, but, as we will see, in his general and philosophical sociologies, Simmel held a much larger scale conception of society as well as culture.

Interaction: Forms and Types

One of Simmel's dominant concerns was the *form* rather than the *content* of social interaction. This concern stemmed from Simmel's identification with the Kantian tradition in philosophy, in which much is made of the difference between form and content. Simmel's position here, however, was quite simple. From Simmel's point of view, the real world is composed of innumerable events, actions, interactions, and so forth. To cope with this maze of reality (the "contents"), people order it by imposing patterns, or forms, on it. Thus, instead of a bewildering array of specific events, the actor is confronted with a limited number of forms. In Simmel's view, the sociologist's task is to do precisely what the layperson does, that is, impose a limited number of forms on social reality, on interaction in particular, so that it may be better analyzed. This methodology generally involves extracting commonalities that are found in a wide array of specific interactions. For example, the superordination and subordination forms of interaction are found in a wide range of settings, "in the state as well as in a religious community, in a band of conspirators as in an economic association, in art school as in a family" (Simmel, 1908/1959b: 317). Donald Levine, one of Simmel's foremost contemporary analysts, describes Simmel's method of doing formal interactional sociology in this way: "His method is to select some bounded, finite phenomenon from the world of flux; to examine the multiplicity of elements which compose it; and to ascertain the cause of their coherence by disclosing its form. Secondarily, he investigates the origins of this form and its structural implications" (1971: xxxi). More specifically, Levine points out that "forms are the patterns exhibited by the associations" of people (1981b:65).[1]

Simmel's interest in the forms of social interaction has been subjected to various criticisms. For example, he has been accused of imposing order where there is none and of producing a series of unrelated studies that in the end really impose no better order on the complexities of social reality than does the layperson. Some of these criticisms are valid only if we focus on Simmel's concern with forms of interaction, his formal sociology, and ignore the other types of sociology he practiced.

However, there are a number of ways to defend Simmel's approach to

---

[1] In the specific case of interaction, contents are the *"drives, purposes and ideas which lead people to associate* with one another" (Levine, 1981b:65).

formal sociology. First, it is close to reality, as reflected by the innumerable real-life examples employed by Simmel. Second, it does not impose arbitrary and rigid categories on social reality but tries instead to allow the forms to flow from social reality. Third, Simmel's approach does not employ a general theoretical schema into which all aspects of the social world are forced. He thus avoided the reification of a theoretical schema that plagues a theorist like Talcott Parsons. Finally, formal sociology militates against the poorly conceptualized empiricism that is characteristic of much of sociology. Simmel certainly used empirical "data," but they are subordinated to his effort to impose some order on the bewildering world of social reality.

Social Geometry   In Simmel's formal sociology, one sees most clearly his effort to develop a "geometry" of social relations. Two of the geometric coefficients that interested him are numbers and distance (others are position, valence, self-involvement, and symmetry [Levine, 1981b]).

Numbers   Simmel's interest in the impact of numbers of people on the quality of interaction can be seen in his discussion of the difference between a dyad and a triad.

Dyad and triad. For Simmel (1950) there was a crucial difference between the *dyad* (two-person group) and the *triad* (three-person group). The addition of a third person causes a radical and fundamental change. Increasing the membership beyond three has nowhere near the same impact as adding a third member. Unlike all other groups, the dyad does not achieve a meaning beyond the two individuals involved. There is no independent group structure in a dyad; there is nothing more to the group than the two separable individuals. Thus, each member of a dyad retains a high level of individuality. The individual is not lowered to the level of the group. This is not the case in the triad. A triad does have the possibility of obtaining a meaning beyond the individuals involved. There is likely to be more to a triad than the individuals involved. It is likely to develop an independent group structure. As a result, there is a greater threat to the individuality of the members. A triad can have a general leveling effect on the members.

With the addition of a third party to the group, a number of new social roles become possible. For example, the third party can take the role of arbitrator or mediator in disputes within the group. Then the third party can use disputes between the other two for his or her own gain or become an object of competition between the other two parties. The third member also can intentionally foster conflict between the other two parties in order to gain superiority (divide and rule). A stratification system and an authority structure then can emerge. The movement from dyad to triad is essential to the development of social structures that can become separate from, and dominant over, individuals. Such a possibility does not exist in a dyad.

The process that is begun in the transition from a dyad to a triad continues as larger and larger groups and, ultimately, societies emerge. In these large social structures, the individual, increasingly separated from the structure of society, grows more and more alone, isolated, and segmented. This results finally in a dialectical relationship between individuals and social structures: "According to Simmel, the socialized individual always remains in a dual relation toward society: he is incorporated within it and yet stands against it. . . . The individual is determined, yet determining; acted upon, yet self-actuating" (Coser, 1965:11). The contradiction here is that "society allows the emergence of individuality and autonomy, but it also impedes it" (Coser, 1965:11).

Group size. At a more general level, there is Simmel's (1908/1871a) ambivalent attitude toward the impact of group *size.* On the one hand, he took the position that the increase in the size of a group or society increases individual freedom. A small group or society is likely to control the individual completely. However, in a larger society, the individual is likely to be involved in a number of groups, each of which controls only a small portion of his or her total personality. In other words, *"Individuality in being and action generally increases to the degree that the social circle encompassing the individual expands"* (Simmel, 1908/1971a:252). However, Simmel took the view that large societies create a set of problems that ultimately threaten individual freedom. For example, he saw the masses as likely to be dominated by one idea, the simplest idea. The physical proximity of a mass makes people suggestible and more likely to follow simplistic ideas, to engage in mindless, emotional actions.

Perhaps most important, in terms of Simmel's interest in forms of interaction, is that increasing size and differentiation tend to loosen the bonds between individuals and leave in their place much more distant, impersonal, and segmental relationships. Paradoxically, the large group that frees the individual simultaneously threatens that individuality. Also paradoxical is Simmel's belief that one way for individuals to cope with the threat of the mass society is to immerse themselves in small groups such as the family.

Distance   Another of Simmel's concerns in social geometry was *distance.* Levine offers a good summation of Simmel's views on the role of distance in social relationships: *"The properties of forms and the meanings of things are a function of the relative distances between individuals and other individuals or things."* (1971:xxxiv). This concern with distance is manifest in various places in Simmel's work. We will discuss it in two different contexts—in Simmel's massive *The Philosophy of Money* and in one of his cleverest essays, "The Stranger."

In *The Philosophy of Money* (1907/1978), Simmel enunciated some general principles about value—and about what makes things valuable—that served as the basis for his analysis of money. Because we deal with this work in detail later in this chapter, we discuss this issue only briefly here. The essential point is that the value of something is determined by its distance from the actor. It is not valuable if it is either too close and too easy to obtain or too distant and too difficult to obtain. Objects that are attainable, but only with great effort, are the most valuable.

Distance also plays a central role in Simmel's "The Stranger" (1908/1971b), an essay on a type of actor who is neither too close nor too far. If he (or she) were too close, he would no longer be a stranger, but if he were too far, he would cease to have any contact with the group. The interaction that the stranger engages in with the group members involves a combination of closeness and distance. The peculiar distance of the stranger from the group allows him to have a series of unusual interaction patterns with the members. For example, the stranger can be more objective in his relationships with the group members. Because he is a stranger, other group members feel more comfortable expressing confidences to him. In these and other ways, a pattern of coordination and consistent interaction emerges between the stranger and the other group members. The stranger becomes an organic member of the group. But Simmel not only considered the stranger a social type; he considered strangeness a form of social interaction. A degree of strangeness, involving a combination of nearness and remoteness, enters into all social relationships, even the most intimate. Thus we can examine a wide range of specific interactions in order to discover the degree of strangeness found in each.

Although geometric dimensions enter a number of Simmel's types and forms, there is much more to them than simply geometry. The types and forms are constructs that Simmel used to gain a greater understanding of a wide range of interaction patterns.

Social Types We have already encountered one of Simmel's types, the stranger; others include the miser, the spendthrift, the adventurer, and the nobleman. To illustrate his mode of thinking in this area, we will focus on one of his types, the poor.

The Poor As is typical of types in Simmel's work, the *poor* were defined in terms of social relationships, as being aided by other people or at least having the right to that aid. Here Simmel quite clearly did not hold the view that *poverty* is defined by a quantity, or rather a lack of quantity, of money.

Although Simmel focused on the poor in terms of characteristic relationships and interaction patterns, he also used the occasion of his essay "The Poor" (1908/1971c) to develop a wide range of interesting insights into the poor and poverty. It was characteristic of Simmel to offer a profusion of insights in every essay. Indeed, this is one of his great claims to fame. For example, Simmel argued that a reciprocal set of rights and obligations defines the relationship between the needy and the givers. The needy have the right to receive aid, and this right makes receiving aid less painful. Conversely, the giver has the obligation to give to the needy. Simmel also took the functionalist position that aid to the poor by society helps to support the system. Society requires aid to the poor "so that the poor will not become active and dangerous enemies of society, so as to make their reduced energies more productive, and so as to prevent the degeneration of their progeny" (Simmel, 1908/1971c:154). Thus aid to the poor is for the sake of society, not so much for the poor per se. The state plays a key role here, and, as Simmel saw it, the treatment of the poor grows increasingly impersonal as the mechanism for giving aid becomes more bureaucratized.

Simmel also had a relativistic view of poverty. That is, the poor are not simply those who stand at the bottom of society. From his point of view, poverty is found in *all* social strata. This concept foreshadowed the later socio- logical concept of *relative deprivation*. If people who are members of the upper classes have less than their peers, then they are likely to feel poor in compar- ison to them. Therefore, government programs aimed at eradicating poverty can never succeed. Even if those at the bottom are elevated, many people throughout the stratification system will still feel poor in comparison to their peers.

Social Forms   As with social types, Simmel looked at a wide range of social forms, including exchange, conflict, prostitution, and sociability. We can illustrate Simmel's (1908/1971d) work on social forms through his discussion of domination, that is, superordination and subordination.

Superordination and Subordination   Superordination and subordination have a reciprocal relationship. The leader does not want to determine com- pletely the thoughts and actions of others. Rather, the leader expects the sub- ordinate to react either positively or negatively. Neither this nor any other form of interaction can exist without mutual relationships. Even in the most oppressive form of domination, subordinates have at least some degree of personal freedom.

To most people, superordination involves an effort to eliminate completely the independence of subordinates, but Simmel argued that a social relation- ship would cease to exist if this were the case.

Simmel asserted that one can be subordinated to an individual, a group, or an objective force. Leadership by a single individual generally leads to a tightly knit group either in support of or in opposition to the leader. Even when opposition arises in such a group, discord can be resolved more easily when the parties stand under the same higher power. Subordination under a plurality can have very uneven effects. On the one hand, the objectivity of rule by a plurality may make for greater unity in the group than the more arbitrary rule of an individual. On the other hand, hostility is likely to be engendered among subordinates if they do not get the personal attention of a leader.

Simmel found subordination under an objective principle to be most offen- sive, perhaps because human relationships and social interactions are elimi- nated. People feel they are determined by an impersonal law that they have no ability to affect. Simmel saw subordination to an individual as freer and more spontaneous: "Subordination under a person has an element of freedom and dignity in comparison with which all obedience to laws has something mechanical and passive" (1908/1971d:115). Even worse is subordination to objects (for example, icons), which Simmel found a "humiliatingly harsh and unconditional kind of subordination" (1908/1971d:115). Because the individ- ual is dominated by a thing, "he himself psychologically sinks to the category of mere thing" (Simmel, 1908/1971d:117).

Again, Simmel dealt with a wide range of forms of interaction throughout his work, and this discussion of domination is simply meant to illustrate the kinds of work done by Simmel in this area.

Recently, Guy Oakes (1984) linked Simmel's discussion of forms to his basic problematic, the growing gap between objective and subjective culture. He begins with the position that in "Simmel's view, the discovery of objectivity—the independence of things from the condition of their subjective or psychological genesis—was the greatest achievement in the cultural history of the West" (Oakes, 1984:3). One of the ways that Simmel addresses this objectivity is in his discussion of forms, but although such formalization and objectification are necessary and desirable, they can come to be quite undesirable:

> On the one hand, forms are necessary conditions for the expression and the realization of the energies and interests of life. On the other hand, these forms become increasingly detached and remote from life. When this happens, a conflict develops between the process of life and the configurations in which it is expressed. Ultimately, this conflict threatens to nullify the relationship between life and form, and thus to destroy the conditions under which the process of life can be realized in autonomous structures.
>
> (Oakes, 1984:4)

SOCIAL STRUCTURES

Simmel said relatively little directly about the large-scale structures of society. In fact, at times, given his focus on patterns of interaction, he denied the existence of that level of social reality. A good example of this is found in his effort to define *society*, where he rejected the realist position exemplified by Emile Durkheim that society is a real, material entity. Lewis Coser notes, "He did not see society as a thing or an organism" (1965:5). Simmel was also uncomfortable with the nominalist conception that society is nothing more than a collection of isolated individuals. He adopted an intermediate position, conceiving of society as a set of interactions (Spykman, 1925/1966:88). "*Society* is merely the name for a number of individuals connected by 'interaction'" (Simmel, cited in Coser, 1965:5).

Although Simmel enunciated this interactionist position, in much of his work he operated as a realist, as if society were a real material structure. There is, then, a basic contradiction in Simmel's work on the social-structural level. Simmel noted, "Society transcends the individual and lives its own life which follows its own laws. It, too, confronts the individual with a historical, imperative firmness" (1908/1950a:258). Coser catches the essence of this aspect of Simmel's thought: "The larger superindividual structures—the state, the clan, the family, the city, or the trade union—turn out to be but crystallizations of this interaction, even though they may attain autonomy and permanency and confront the individual as if they were alien powers" (1965:5). Rudolph Heberle makes essentially the same point: "One can scarcely escape the impression that Simmel views society as an interplay of structural factors, in which the human beings appear as passive objects rather than as live and willing actors" (1965:117).

The resolution of this paradox lies in the difference between Simmel's formal sociology, in which he tended to adhere to an interactionist view of society, and his historical and philosophical sociologies, in which he was much more inclined to see society as an independent, coercive social structure. In the latter sociologies, he saw society as part of the broader process of the development of objective culture, which worried him. Although objective culture is best seen as part of the cultural realm, Simmel included the growth of large-scale social structures as part of this process. That Simmel related the growth of social structures to the spread of objective culture is clear in this statement: "The increasing objectification of our culture, whose phenomena consist more and more of impersonal elements and less and less absorb the subjective totality of the individual . . . also involves sociological structures" (1908/1950b:318). In addition to clarifying the relationship between society and objective culture, this leads to Simmel's thoughts on the cultural level of social reality.

OBJECTIVE CULTURE

One of the main focuses of Simmel's historical and philosophical sociology is the cultural level of social reality, or what he called the "objective culture." In Simmel's view, people produce culture, but because of their ability to reify social reality, the cultural world and the social world come to have lives of their own, lives that come increasingly to dominate the actors who created, and daily re-create, them. "The cultural objects become more and more linked to each other in a self-contained world which has increasingly fewer contacts with the [individual] subjective psyche and its desires and sensibilities" (Coser, 1965:22). Although people always retain the capacity to create and re-create culture, the long-term trend of history is for culture to exert a more and more coercive force on the actor.

> The preponderance of objective over [individual] subjective culture that developed during the nineteenth century . . . this discrepancy seems to widen steadily. Every day and from all sides, the wealth of objective culture increases, but the individual mind can enrich the forms and content of its own development only by distancing itself still further from that culture and developing its own at a much slower pace.
> (Simmel, 1907/1978:449)

In various places in his work, Simmel identified a number of components of the objective culture, for example:

- Tools
- Means of transport
- Products of science
- Technology

- Arts
- Language
- Intellectual sphere
- Conventional wisdom
- Religious dogma
- Philosophical systems
- Legal systems
- Moral codes
- Ideals (for example, the "fatherland")

These and many others constitute the objective cultural level in Simmel's work.

The objective culture grows and expands in various ways. First, its absolute size grows with increasing modernization. This can be seen most obviously in the case of scientific knowledge, which is expanding exponentially, although this is just as true of most other aspects of the cultural realm. Second, the number of different components of the cultural realm also grows. Finally, and perhaps most important, the various elements of the cultural world become more and more intertwined in an ever more powerful, self-contained world that is increasingly beyond the control of the actors (Oakes, 1984:12). Simmel was not only interested in describing the growth of objective culture but also greatly disturbed by it: "Simmel was impressed—if not depressed—by the bewildering number and variety of human products which in the contemporary world surround and unceasingly impinge upon the individual" (Weingartner, 1959:33).

What worried Simmel most was the threat to individual culture posed by the growth of objective culture. Simmel's personal sympathies were with a world dominated by individual culture, but he saw the possibility of such a world as more and more unlikely. It is this that Simmel described as the "tragedy of culture." (We will comment on this in detail in the discussion of *The Philosophy of Money*.) Simmel's specific analysis of the growth of objective culture over individual subjective culture is simply one example of a general principle that dominates all of life: "The total value of something increases to the same extent as the value of its individual parts declines" (1907/1978:199).

We can relate Simmel's general argument about objective culture to his more basic analysis of forms of interaction. In one of his best-known essays, "The Metropolis and Mental Life" (1903/1971), Simmel analyzed the forms of interaction that take place in the modern city. He saw the modern metropolis as the "genuine arena" of the growth of objective culture and the decline of individual culture. It is the scene of the predominance of the money economy, and money, as Simmel often made clear, has a profound effect on the nature of human relationships. The widespread use of money leads to an emphasis on calculability and rationality in all spheres of life. Thus genuine human relationships decline, and social relationships tend to be dominated by a blasé and reserved attitude. Whereas the small town was characterized by greater feeling and emotionality, the modern city is characterized by a shallow intellectuality that matches the calculability needed by a money economy. The city is also the center of the division of labor, and as we have seen, specialization plays a central role in the production of an ever-expanding objective culture, with a corresponding decline in individual culture. The city is a "frightful leveler," in which virtually everyone is reduced to emphasizing unfeeling calculability. It is more and more difficult to maintain individuality in the face of the expansion of objective culture.

It should be pointed out that in his essay on the city (as well as in many other places in his work) Simmel also discussed the liberating effect of this modern development. For example, he emphasized the fact that people are freer in the modern city than in the tight social confines of the small town. We will have more to say about Simmel's thoughts on the liberating impact of modernity at the close of the following section, devoted to Simmel's book *The Philosophy of Money.*

Before we get to that work, it is necessary to indicate that one of the many ironies of Simmel's influence on the development of sociology is that his micro-analytic work is used, but its broader implications are almost totally ignored. Take the example of Simmel's work on exchange relationships. He saw exchange as the "purest and most developed kind" of interaction (Simmel, 1907/1978:82). Although all forms of interaction involve some sacrifice, it occurs most clearly in exchange relationships. Simmel thought of all social exchanges as involving "profit and loss." Such an orientation was crucial to Simmel's microsociological work and specifically to the development of his largely micro-oriented exchange theory. However, the fact is that his thoughts on exchange are also expressed in his broader work on money. To Simmel, money is the purest form of exchange. In contrast to a barter economy, where the cycle ends when one object has been exchanged for another, an economy based on money allows for an endless series of exchanges. This possibility is crucial for Simmel because it provides the basis for the widespread development of social structures and objective culture. Consequently, money as a form of exchange represented for Simmel one of the root causes of the alienation of people in a modern reified social structure.

In his treatment of the city and exchange, one can see the elegance of Simmel's thinking as he related small-scale sociological forms of exchange to the development of modern society in its totality. Although this link can be found in his specific essays, it is clearest in *The Philosophy of Money.*

THE PHILOSOPHY OF MONEY

The Philosophy of Money (1907/1978) illustrates well the breadth and sophistication of Simmel's thinking. It demonstrates conclusively that Simmel deserves at least as much recognition for his general theory as for his essays on microsociology, many of which can be seen as specific manifestations of his general theory.

Although the title makes it clear that Simmel's focus is money, his interest in that phenomenon is embedded in a set of his broader theoretical and philosophical concerns. For example, as we have already seen, Simmel was interested in the broad issue of value, and money can be seen as simply a specific form of value. At another level, Simmel was interested not in money per se but in its impact on such a wide range of phenomena as the "inner world" of actors and the objective culture as a whole. At still another level, he treated money as a specific phenomenon linked with a variety of other components of life, including "exchange, ownership, greed, extravagance, cynicism, individual freedom, the style of life, culture, the value of the personality, etc." (Kracauer, cited in Bottomore and Frisby, 1978:7). Finally, and most generally, Simmel saw money as a specific component of life capable of helping us to understand the totality of life. As Tom Bottomore and David Frisby put it, Simmel sought no less than to extract "the totality of the spirit of the age from his analysis of money" (1978:7).

The Philosophy of Money has much in common with the work of Karl Marx. Like Marx, Simmel focused on capitalism and the problems created by a money economy. Despite this, the differences are overwhelming. For example, Simmel saw the economic problems of his time as simply a specific manifestation of a more general cultural problem, the alienation of objective from subjective culture. To Marx these problems are specific to capitalism, but to Simmel they are part of a universal tragedy—the increasing powerlessness of the individual in the face of the growth of objective culture. Whereas Marx's analysis is historically specific, Simmel's analysis seeks to extract timeless truths from the flux of human history. As Frisby says, "In his *The Philosophy of Money* . . . [w]hat is missing . . . is a historical sociology of money relationships" (1984:58). This difference in their analyses is related to a crucial political difference between Simmel and Marx. Because Marx saw economic problems as time-bound, the product of capitalist society, he believed that eventually they could be solved. Simmel, however, saw the basic problems as inherent in human life and held out no hope for future improvement. In fact, Simmel believed that socialism, instead of improving the situation, would heighten the kinds of problems discussed in *The Philosophy of Money*. Despite some substantive similarities to Marxian theory, Simmel's thought is far closer to that of Weber and his "iron cage" in terms of his image of both the modern world and its future.

The Philosophy of Money begins with a discussion of the general forms of money and value. Later the discussion moves to the impact of money on the "inner world" of actors and on culture in general. Because the argument is so complex, we can merely highlight it here.

One of Simmel's initial concerns in the work, as we discussed briefly earlier, is the relationship between money and value. In general, he argued that people create value by making objects, separating themselves from them, and then seeking to overcome the "distance, obstacles, difficulties" (Simmel, 1907/1978:66). The greater the difficulty of obtaining an object, the greater its value.

However, difficulty of attainment has a "lower and an upper limit" (Simmel, 1907/1978:72). The general principle is that the value of things comes from the ability of people to distance themselves properly from objects. Things that are too close, too easily obtained, are not very valuable. Some exertion is needed for something to be considered valuable. Conversely, things that are too far, too difficult, or nearly impossible to obtain are also not very valuable. Things that defy most, if not all, of our efforts to obtain them cease to be valuable to us. Those things that are most valuable are neither too distant nor too close. Among the factors involved in the distance of an object from an actor are the time it takes to obtain it, its scarcity, the difficulties involved in acquiring it, and the need to give up other things in order to acquire it. People try to place themselves at a proper distance from objects, which must be attainable, but not too easily.

In this general context of value, Simmel discussed money. In the economic realm, money serves both to create distance from objects and to provide the means to overcome it. The money value attached to objects in a modern economy places them at a distance from us; we cannot obtain them without money of our own. The difficulty in obtaining the money and therefore the objects makes them valuable to us. At the same time, once we obtain enough money, we are able to overcome the distance between ourselves and the objects. Money thus performs the interesting function of creating distance between people and objects and then providing the means to overcome that distance.

In the process of creating value, money also provides the basis for the development of the market, the modern economy, and ultimately modern (capitalistic) society. Money provides the means whereby these entities acquire a life of their own that is external to, and coercive of, the actor. This stands in contrast to earlier societies in which barter or trade could not lead to the reified world that is the distinctive product of a money economy. Money permits this development in various ways. For example, Simmel argued that money allows for "long-range calculations, large-scale enterprises and long-term credits" (1907/1978:125). Later, Simmel said that "money has . . . developed . . . the most objective practices, the most logical, purely mathematical norms, the absolute freedom from everything personal" (1907/1978:128). He saw this process of reification as but part of the more general process whereby the mind embodies and symbolizes itself in objects. These embodiments, these symbolic structures, become reified and come to exert a controlling force on actors.

Not only does money help to create a reified social world, but it also contributes to the increasing rationalization of that social world (B. Turner, 1986). This is another of the concerns that Simmel shared with Weber. A money economy fosters an emphasis on quantitative rather than qualitative factors. Simmel stated:

> It would be easy to multiply the examples that illustrate the growing preponderance of the category of quantity over that of quality, or more precisely the tendency to

dissolve quality into quantity, to remove the elements more and more from quality, to grant them only specific forms of motion and to interpret everything that is specifically, individually, and qualitatively determined as the more or less, the bigger or smaller, the wider or narrower, the more or less frequent of those colourless elements and awarenesses that are only accessible to numerical determination—even though this tendency may never absolutely attain its goal by mortal means. . . .

Thus, one of the major tendencies of life—the reduction of quality to quantity— achieves its highest and uniquely perfect representation in money. Here, too, money is the pinnacle of a cultural historical series of developments which unambiguously determines its direction.

(Simmel, 1907/1978:278–280)

Less obviously, money contributes to rationalization by increasing the importance of intellectuality in the modern world (B. Turner, 1986). On the one hand, the development of a money economy presupposes a significant expansion of mental processes. As an example, Simmel pointed to the complicated mental processes that are required by such money transactions as covering bank notes with cash reserves. On the other hand, a money economy contributes to a considerable change in the norms and values of society; it aids in the "fundamental reorientation of culture towards intellectuality" (Simmel, 1907/1978:152). In part because of a money economy, intellect has come to be considered the most valuable of our mental energies.

Simmel saw the significance of the individual declining as money transactions become an increasingly important part of society and as reified structures expand. This is part of his general argument on the decline of individual subjective culture in the face of the expansion of objective culture (the "tragedy of culture"):

The rapid circulation of money induces habits of spending and acquisition; it makes a specific quantity of money psychologically less significant and valuable, while money in general becomes increasingly important because money matters now affect the individual more vitally than they do in a less agitated style of life. We are confronted here with a very common phenomenon; namely, that the total value of something increases to the same extent as the value of its individual parts declines. For example, the size and significance of a social group often becomes greater the less highly the lives and interests of its individual members are valued; the objective culture, the diversity and liveliness of its content attain their highest point through a division of labour that often condemns the individual representative and participant in this culture to a monotonous specialization, narrowness, and stunted growth. The whole becomes more perfect and harmonious, the less the individual is a harmonious being.

(Simmel, 1907/1978:199)

In some senses, it may be difficult to see how money can take on the central role that it does in modern society. On the surface, it appears that money is simply a means to a variety of ends or, in Simmel's words, "the purest form of the tool" (1907/1978:210). However, money has come to be the most extreme example of a means that has become an end in itself:

Never has an object that owes its value exclusively to its quality as a means, to its convertibility into more definite values, so thoroughly and unreservedly developed into a psychological value absolute, into a completely engrossing final purpose governing our practical consciousness. This ultimate craving for money must increase to the extent that money takes on the quality of a pure means. For this implies that the range of objects made available to money grows continuously, that things submit more and more defencelessly to the power of money, that money itself becomes more and more lacking in quality yet thereby at the same time becomes powerful in relation to the quality of things.

(Simmel, 1907/1978:232)

A society in which money becomes an end in itself, indeed the ultimate end, has a number of negative effects on individuals, two of the most interesting of which are the increase in cynicism and in a blasé attitude. Cynicism is induced when both the highest and lowest aspects of social life are for sale, reduced to a common denominator—money. Thus we can "buy" beauty or truth or intelligence almost as easily as we can buy cornflakes or underarm deodorant. This leveling of everything to a common denominator leads to the cynical attitude that everything has its price, that anything can be bought or sold on the market. A money economy also induces a blasé attitude, "all things as being of an equally dull and grey hue, as not worth getting excited about" (Simmel, 1907/1978:256). The blasé person has lost completely the ability to make value differentiations among the ultimate objects of purchase. Put slightly differently, money is the absolute enemy of esthetics, reducing everything to formlessness, to purely quantitative phenomena.

Another negative effect of a money economy is the increasingly impersonal relations among people. Instead of dealing with individuals with their own personalities, we are increasingly likely to deal solely with positions—the delivery person, the baker, and so forth—regardless of who occupies those positions. In the modern division of labor characteristic of a money economy, we have the paradoxical situation that while we grow more dependent on other positions for our survival, we know less about the people who occupy those positions. The specific individual who fills a given position becomes progressively insignificant. Personalities tend to disappear behind positions that demand only a small part of them. Because so little is demanded of them, many individuals can fill the same position equally well. People thus become interchangeable parts.

Related to this is the impact of the money economy on individual freedom. A money economy leads to an increase in individual enslavement. The individual in the modern world becomes atomized and isolated. No longer embedded within a group, the individual stands alone in the face of an ever-expanding and increasingly coercive objective culture. The individual in the modern world is thus enslaved by a massive objective culture.

Another impact of the money economy is the reduction of all human values to dollar terms, "the tendency to reduce the value of man to a monetary expression" (Simmel, 1907/1978:356). For example, Simmel offers the case in primitive society of atonement for a murder by a money payment. But his best example is the exchange of sex for money. The expansion of prostitution is traceable in part to the growth of the money economy.

Some of Simmel's most interesting insights lie in his thoughts on the impact of money on people's styles of life. For example, a society dominated by a money economy tends to reduce everything to a string of causal connections that can be comprehended intellectually, not emotionally. Related to this is what Simmel called the "calculating character" of life in the modern world. The specific form of intellectuality that is peculiarly suited to a money economy is a mathematical mode of thinking. This, in turn, is related to the tendency to emphasize quantitative rather than qualitative factors in the social world. Simmel concluded that "the lives of many people are absorbed by such evaluating, weighing, calculating, and reducing of qualitative values to quantitatives ones" (1907/1978:444).

The key to Simmel's discussion of money's impact on style of life is in the growth of objective culture at the expense of individual culture. The gap between the two grows larger at an accelerating rate:

> This discrepancy seems to widen steadily. Every day and from all sides, the wealth of objective culture increases, but the individual mind can enrich the forms and contents of its own development only by distancing itself still further from that culture and developing its own at a much slower pace.
>
> (Simmel, 1907/1978:449)

The major cause of this increasing disparity is the increasing division of labor in modern society (Oakes, 1984:19). Increased specialization leads to an improved ability to create the various components of the cultural world. But at the same time, the highly specialized individual loses a sense of the total culture and loses the ability to control it. As objective culture grows, individual culture atrophies. One of the examples of this is that language in its totality has clearly expanded enormously, yet the linguistic abilities of given individuals seem to be declining. Similarly, with the growth of technology and machinery, the abilities of the individual worker and the skills required have declined dramatically. Finally, although there has been an enormous expansion of the intellectual sphere, fewer and fewer individuals seem to deserve the label "intellectual." Highly specialized individuals are confronted with an increasingly closed and interconnected world of products over which they have little or no control. A mechanical world devoid of spirituality comes to dominate individuals, and their lifestyles are affected in various ways. Acts of production come to be meaningless exercises in which individuals do not see their roles in the overall process or in the production of the final product. Relationships among people are highly specialized and impersonal. Consumption becomes little more than a devouring of one meaningless product after another.

The massive expansion of objective culture has had a dramatic effect upon the rhythm of life. In general, the unevenness that was characteristic of earlier epochs has been leveled and replaced in modern society by a much more consistent pattern of living. Examples of this leveling of modern culture abound:

In times past, food consumption was cyclical and often very uncertain. What foods were consumed and when they were available depended on the harvest. Today, with improved methods of preservation and transportation, we can consume virtually any food at any time. Furthermore, the ability to preserve and store huge quantities of food has helped to offset disruptions caused by bad harvests, natural catastrophes, and so forth.

In communication the infrequent and unpredictable mail coach has been replaced by the telegraph, telephone, daily mail service, and fax machines, which make communication available at all times.

In an earlier time, night and day gave life a natural rhythm. Now, with artificial lighting, the natural rhythm has been greatly altered. Many activities formerly restricted to daylight hours can now be performed at night as well.

Intellectual stimulation, which was formerly restricted to an occasional conversation or a rare book, is now available at all times because of the ready availability of books and magazines. In this realm, as in all the others, the situation has grown even more pronounced since Simmel's time. With radio, television, video tape recorders, and home computers, the availability and possibilities of intellectual stimulation have grown far beyond anything Simmel could have imagined.

There are positive elements to all this, of course. For example, people have much more freedom because they are less restricted by the natural rhythm of life. In spite of the human gains, problems arise because all these developments are at the level of objective culture and are integral parts of the process by which objective culture grows and further impoverishes individual culture.

In the end, money has come to be the symbol of, and a major factor in, the development of a relativistic mode of existence. Money allows us to reduce the most disparate phenomena to numbers of dollars, and this allows them to be compared to each other. In other words, money allows us to relativize *everything*. Our relativistic way of life stands in contrast to earlier methods of living in which people believed in a number of eternal verities. A money economy destroys such eternal truths. The gains to people in terms of increased freedom from absolute ideas are far outweighed by the costs. The alienation endemic to the expanding objective culture of a modern money economy is a far greater threat to people, in Simmel's eyes, than the evils of absolutism. Perhaps Simmel would not wish us to return to an earlier, simpler time, but he certainly would warn us to be wary of the seductive dangers associated with the growth of a money economy and objective culture in the modern world.

While we have focused most of our attention on the negative effects of the modern money economy, it also has its liberating aspects (Levine, 1981b). First, it allows us to deal with many more people in a much-expanded marketplace. Second, our obligations to one another are highly limited (to specific services or products) rather than all-encompassing. Third, the money economy allows people to find gratifications that were unavailable in earlier economic systems. Fourth, people have greater freedom in such an environment to develop their individuality to a fuller extent. Fifth, people are better able to maintain and protect their subjective center, since they are involved only in very limited relationships. Sixth, the separation of the worker from the means of production, as Simmel points out, allows the individual some freedom from those productive forces. Finally, money helps people grow increasingly free of the constraints of their social groups. For example, in a barter economy people are largely controlled by their groups, but in the modern economic world such constraints are loosened, with the result that people are freer to make their own economic deals. However, while Simmel is careful to point out a variety of liberating effects of the money economy, and modernity in general, in our view the heart of his work lies in his discussion of the problems associated with modernity, especially the "tragedy of culture."

SECRECY: A CASE STUDY IN SIMMEL'S SOCIOLOGY

While *The Philosophy of Money* demonstrates that Simmel has a theoretical scope that rivals that of Marx, Weber, and Durkheim, it remains an atypical example of his work. Thus, in this closing section we return to a more characteristic type of Simmelian scholarship, his work on a specific form of interaction—secrecy. *Secrecy* is defined as the condition in which one person has the intention of hiding something while the other is seeking to reveal that which is being hidden. In this discussion, we are not only interested in outlining Simmel's many insightful ideas on secrecy but also in bringing together under one heading many of the sociological ideas raised through this chapter.

Simmel begins with the basic fact that people must know some things about other people in order to interact with them. For instance, we must know with whom we are dealing (for example, a friend, a relative, a shopkeeper). We may come to know a great deal about other people, but we can never know them absolutely. That is, we can never know all the thoughts, moods, and so on of other people. However, we do form some sort of unitary conception of other people out of the bits and pieces that we know about them; we form a fairly coherent mental picture of the people with whom we interact. Simmel sees a dialectical relationship between interaction (being) and the mental picture we have of others (conceiving): "Our relationships thus develop upon the basis of reciprocal knowledge, and this knowledge upon the basis of actual relations. Both are inextricably interwoven" (1906/1950:309).

In all aspects of our lives we acquire not only truth but also ignorance and error. However, it is in the interaction with other people that ignorance and error acquire a distinctive character. This relates to the inner lives of the people with whom we interact. People, in contrast to any other object of knowledge, have the capacity to *intentionally* reveal the truth about themselves *or* to lie and conceal such information.

The fact is that even if people wanted to reveal all (and they almost always do not), they could not do so because so much information "would drive everybody into the insane asylum" (Simmel, 1906/1950:312). Thus, people must select the things that they report to others. From the point of view of Simmel's concern with quantitative issues, we report only "fragments" of our inner lives to others. Furthermore, we choose which fragments to reveal and which to conceal. Thus, in all interaction, we reveal only a part of ourselves, and which part we opt to show depends on how we select and arrange the fragments we choose to reveal.

This brings us to the *lie*, a form of interaction in which the liar *intentionally* hides the truth from others. In the lie, it is not just that others are left with an erroneous conception but also that the error is traceable to the fact that the liar intended that the others be deceived.

Simmel discusses the lie in terms of social geometry, specifically his ideas on distance. For example, in Simmel's view, we can better accept and come to terms with the lies of those who are distant from us. Thus, we have little difficulty learning that the politicians who habituate Washington, D.C., frequently lie to us. In contrast, "If the persons closest to us lie, life becomes unbearable" (Simmel, 1906/1950:313). The lie of a spouse, lover, or child has a far more devastating impact on us than the lie of a government official whom we know only through the television screen.

More generally, in terms of the issue of distance, it is the case that all everyday communication combines elements known to both parties with facts known to only one or the other. It is the existence of the latter that leads to "distanceness" in all social relationships. Indeed, Simmel argues that social relationships require *both* elements that are known to the interactants and those that are unknown to one party or the other. In other words, even the most intimate relationships require both nearness and distance, reciprocal knowledge and mutual concealment. Thus, secrecy is an integral part of all social relationships, although a relationship may be destroyed if the secret becomes known to the person from whom it was being kept.

Secrecy is linked to the size of society. In small groups, it is difficult to develop secrets; "Everybody is too close to everybody else and his circumstances, and frequency and intimacy of contact involve too many temptations to revelation" (Simmel, 1906/1950:335). Furthermore, in small groups, secrets are not even needed because everyone is much like everyone else. In large groups, in contrast, secrets can more easily develop and are much more needed because there are important differences among people.

On the issue of size, at the most macroscopic level, we should note that secrecy not only is a form of interaction (which, as we have seen, affects many other forms) but also can come to characterize a group in its entirety. Unlike the secret possessed by a single individual, the secret in a *secret society* is shared by all members and determines the reciprocal relations among them.

As with the individual case, however, the secret of the secret society cannot be hidden forever. In such a society there is a constant tension caused by the fact that the secret can be uncovered, or revealed, and thus the entire basis for the existence of the secret society can be eliminated.

Simmel examines various forms of social relationships from the point of view of reciprocal knowledge and secrecy. For example, we all are involved in a range of interest groups in which we interact with other people on a very limited basis, and the total personalities of these people are irrelevant to our specific concerns. Thus, in the university the student is concerned with what the professor says and does in the classroom and not in all aspects of the professor's life and personality. Linking this to his ideas on the larger society, Simmel argues that the increasing objectification of culture brings with it more and more limited-interest groups and the kinds of relationships associated with them. Such relationships require less and less of the subjective totality of the individual (individual culture) than do associations in premodern societies.

In the impersonal relationships characteristic of modern objectified society, *confidence,* as a form of interaction, becomes increasingly important. To Simmel "Confidence is intermediate between knowledge and ignorance about a man" (1906/1950:318). In premodern societies people are much more likely to know a great deal about the people they deal with. But in the modern world we do not, and cannot, have a great deal of knowledge about most of the people with whom we have associations. Thus, students do not know a great deal about their professors (and vice versa), but they must have the confidence that their professors will show up at the appointed times and talk about what they are supposed to discuss.

Another form of social relationship is *acquaintanceship.* We know our acquaintances, but we do not have intimate knowledge of them: "One knows of the other only what he is toward the outside, either in the purely social-representative sense, or in the sense of that which he shows us" (Simmel, 1906/1950:320). Thus, there is far more secretiveness among acquaintances than there is among intimates.

Under the heading of "acquaintanceship," Simmel discusses another form of association—*discretion.* We are discrete with our acquaintances, staying "away from the knowledge of all the other does not expressly reveal to us. It does not refer to anything particular which we are not permitted to know, but to a quite general reserve in regard to the total personality" (Simmel, 1906/1950:321). In spite of being discrete, we often come to know more about other people than they reveal to us voluntarily. More specifically, we often come to learn things that others would prefer we do not know. Simmel offers a very Freudian example of how we learn such things: "To the man with the psychologically fine ear, people innumerable times betray their most secret thoughts and qualities, not only *although,* but often *because,* they anxiously try to guard them" (1906/1950:323–324). In fact, Simmel argues that human interaction is dependent on both discretion *and* the fact that we often come to know more than we are supposed to know.

Turning to another form of association, *friendship,* Simmel contradicts the assumption that friendship is based on total intimacy, full reciprocal knowledge. This lack of full intimacy is especially true of friendships in modern, differentiated society: "Modern man, possibly, has too much to hide to sustain a friendship in the ancient sense" (Simmel, 1906/1950:326). Thus, we have a series of differentiated friendships based on such things as common intellectual pursuits, religion, and shared experiences. There is a very limited kind of intimacy in such friendships and thus a good deal of secrecy. However, in spite of these limitations, friendship still involves some intimacy:

> But the relation which is thus restricted and surrounded by discretions, may yet stem from the center of the total personality. It may yet be reached by the sap of the ultimate roots of the personality, even though it feeds only part of the person's periphery. In its idea, it involves the same affective depth and the same readiness for sacrifice, which less differentiated epochs and persons connect only with a common *total* sphere of life, for which reservations and discretion constitute no problem.
>
> (Simmel, 1906/1950:326)

Then there is what is usually thought of as the most intimate, least secret form of association—*marriage.* Simmel argues that there is a temptation in marriage to reveal all to the partner, to have no secrets. However, in his view, this would be a mistake. For one thing, all social relationships require "a certain proportion of truth and error," and thus it would be impossible to remove all error from a social relationship (Simmel, 1906/1950:329). More specifically, complete self-revelation (assuming such a thing is even possible) would make a marriage matter-of-fact and remove all possibility of the unexpected. Finally, most of us have limited internal resources, and every revelation reduces the (secret) treasures that we have to offer to others. Only those few with a great storehouse of personal accomplishments can afford numerous revelations to a marriage partner. All others are left denuded (and uninteresting) by excessive self-revelation.

Next, Simmel turns to an analysis of the functions, the positive consequences, of secrecy. Simmel sees the secret as "one of man's greatest achievements . . . the secret produces an immense enlargement of life: numerous contents of life cannot even emerge in the presence of full publicity. The secret offers, so to speak, the possibility of a second world alongside the manifest world" (1906/1950:330). More specifically in terms of its functionality, the secret, especially if it is shared by a number of people, makes for a strong "we feeling" among those who know the secret. High status is also associated with the secret; there is something mysterious about superordinate positions and superior achievements.

Human interaction in general is shaped by secrecy and its logical opposite, *betrayal.* The secret is always accompanied dialectically by the possibility that it can be discovered. Betrayal can come from two sources. Externally, another person can discover our secret, while internally there is always the possibility that we will reveal our secret to others. "The secret puts a barrier between men but, at the same time, it creates the tempting challenge to break through it, by gossip or confession. . . . Out of the counterplay of these two interests, in concealing and revealing, spring nuances and fates of human interaction that permeate it in its entirety" (Simmel, 1906/1950:334).

Simmel links his ideas on the lie to his views on the larger society of the modern world. To Simmel, the modern world is much more dependent on honesty than earlier societies. For example, the modern economy is increasingly a credit economy, and credit is dependent on the fact that people will repay what they promise. For another, in modern science, researchers are dependent on the results of many other studies that they cannot examine in minute detail. Those studies are produced by innumerable other scientists who the researchers are unlikely to know personally. Thus, the modern scientist is dependent on the honesty of all other scientists. Simmel concludes: "Under modern conditions, the lie, therefore, becomes something much more devastating than it was earlier, something which questions the very foundations of our life" (1906/1950:313).

More generally, Simmel connects secrecy to his thoughts on the social structure of modern society. On the one hand, a highly differentiated society permits and requires a high degree of secrecy. On the other hand, and dialectically, the secret serves to intensify such differentiation.

Simmel associates the secret with the modern money economy; money makes possible a level of secrecy that was unattainable previously. First, money's "compressibility" makes it possible to make others rich by simply slipping them checks without anyone else noticing the act. Second, the abstractness and qualityless character of money makes it possible to hide "transactions, acquisitions, and changes in ownership" that could not be hidden if more tangible objects were exchanged (Simmel, 1906/1950:335). Third, money can be invested in very distant things, thereby making the transaction invisible to those in the immediate environment.

Simmel also sees that in the modern world public matters, such as those relating to politics, have tended to lose their secrecy and inaccessibility. In contrast, private affairs are much more secret than they are in premodern societies. Here Simmel ties his thoughts on secrecy to those on the modern city by arguing that "modern life has developed, in the midst of metropolitan crowdedness, a technique for making and keeping private matters secret" (Simmel, 1906/1950:337). Overall, "What is public becomes even more public, and what is private becomes even more private" (Simmel, 1906/1950:337).

Thus, in this section we have seen how Simmel's work on secrecy illustrates many aspects of his theoretical orientation.

SUMMARY

The work of Georg Simmel has been influential in American sociological theory for many years. The focus of this influence seems to be shifting from microsociology to a general sociological theory. Simmel's microsociology is embedded in a broad dialectical theory that interrelates the cultural and individual levels. We identify four basic levels of concern in Simmel's work: psychological, interactional, structural and institutional, and the ultimate metaphysics of life.

Simmel operated with a dialectical orientation, although it is not as well articulated as that of Karl Marx. We illustrate Simmel's dialectical concerns in various ways. We deal with the way they are manifested in forms of interaction—specifically, fashion. Simmel was also interested in the conflicts between the individual and social structures, but his greatest concern was those conflicts that develop between individual culture and objective culture. He perceived a general process whereby objective culture expands and individual culture becomes increasingly impoverished in the face of this development. Simmel saw this conflict, in turn, as part of a broader philosophical conflict between more-life and more-than-life.

The bulk of this chapter is devoted to Simmel's thoughts on each of the four levels of social reality. Although he has many useful assumptions about consciousness, he did comparatively little with them. He had much more to offer on forms of interaction and types of interactants. In this formal sociology, we see Simmel's great interest in social geometry, for example, numbers of people. In this context, we examine Simmel's work on the crucial transition from a dyad to a triad. With the addition of one person, we move from a dyad to a triad and with it the possibility of the development of large-scale structures that can become separate from, and dominant over, individuals. This creates the possibility of conflict and contradiction between the individual and the larger society. In his social geometry, Simmel was also concerned with the issue of distance, as in, for example, his essay on the "stranger," including "strangeness" in social life. Simmel's interest in social types is illustrated in a discussion of the poor, and his thoughts on social forms are illustrated in a discussion of domination, that is, superordination and subordination.

At the macro level, Simmel had comparatively little to say about social structures. In fact, at times he seemed to manifest a disturbing tendency to reduce social structures to little more than interaction patterns. Simmel's real interest at the macro level was objective culture. He was interested in both the expansion of this culture and its destructive effects on individuals. This general concern is manifest in a variety of his specific essays, for example, those on the city and exchange.

In *The Philosophy of Money* Simmel's discussion progressed from money to value to the problems of modern society and, ultimately, to the problems of life in general. Finally, we discussed Simmel's work on secrecy in order to illustrate the full range of his theoretical ideas. The discussion of Simmel's work on money, as well as his ideas on secrecy, demonstrates that he has a far more elegant and sophisticated theoretical orientation than he is usually given credit for by those who are familiar with only his thoughts on micro-level phenomena.

PART TWO

SOCIOLOGICAL THEORY: THE MAJOR SCHOOLS

CHAPTER 6

A HISTORICAL SKETCH OF SOCIOLOGICAL THEORY: THE LATER YEARS

*I*N Chapter 1 we discussed the development of sociological theory, largely in nineteenth-century Europe. In this chapter, we focus on late nineteenth- and twentieth-century developments, with particular attention to developments in the United States. Figure 6.1 shows the important intellectual influences on this development as well as the major theories and theorists.

EARLY AMERICAN SOCIOLOGICAL THEORY

It is difficult to give a precise date for the founding of sociology in the United States. There was a course in social problems taught at Oberlin as early as

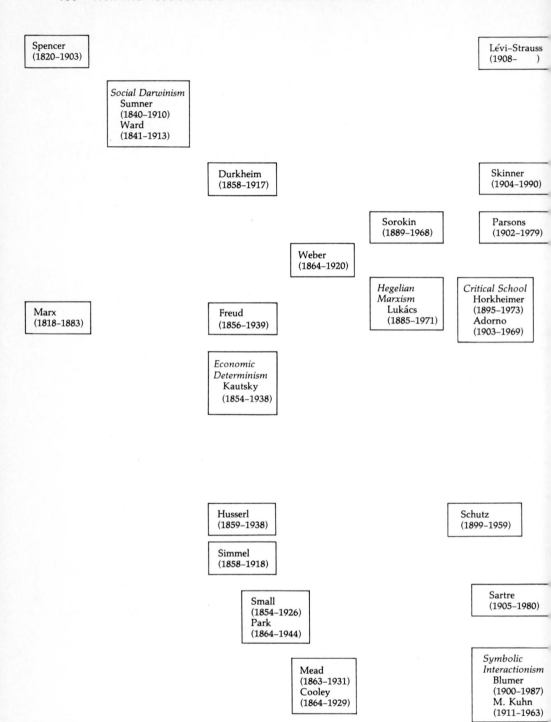

FIGURE 6.1   Sociological Theory: The Later Years

Structuralism			

Poststructuralism
Foucault
(1926–1984)

Network Theory

Exchange Theory
Blau
(1918–   )
Emerson
(1925–1982)

Homans
(1910–1989)

Structural Functionalism
Merton
(1910–   )

Neofunctionalism
Alexander
(1947–   )

Radical Sociology
Mills
(1916–1962)

Conflict Theory
Dahrendorf
(1929–   )

Structural Marxism
Althusser
(1918–1990)

Feminist
Sociological Theory

Economic Marxism
Sweezy
(1910–   )
Braverman
(1920–1976)

Habermas
(1929–   )

Micro–Macro and
Agency–Structure
Integration Theory

Metatheorizing
in Sociology

Historical Marxism
Wallerstein
(1930–   )

Synthetic
Theory

Phenomenological
Sociology
Berger
(1929–   )
Luckmann
(1927–   )

Ethnomethodology
Garfinkel
(1929–   )

Existential Sociology

Goffman
(1922–1982)

1858; Comte's term *sociology* was used by George Fitzhugh in 1854; and William Graham Sumner taught social science courses at Yale beginning in 1873. During the 1880s, courses specifically bearing the title "Sociology" began to appear. The first department with *sociology* in its title was founded at the University of Kansas in 1889. In 1892, Albion Small moved to the University of Chicago and set up the new department of sociology. The Chicago department became the first important center of American sociology in general and of sociological theory in particular (Matthews, 1977).

The Politics of Early American Sociology

A major study of the politics of early American sociological theory (Schwendinger and Schwendinger, 1974) argued that the early sociologists are best described as political liberals and not, as was true of most early European theorists, as conservatives. The liberalism characteristic of early American sociology had basically two elements. First, it operated with a belief in the freedom and welfare of the individual. In this, it was far more influenced by Spencer's orientation than by Comte's more collective position. Second, many sociologists associated with this orientation adopted an evolutionary view of social progress (W. Fine, 1979). However, they split over how best to bring about this progress. Some argued that steps should be taken by the government to aid social reform, while others pushed a laissez-faire doctrine, arguing that the various components of society should be left to solve their own problems.

Liberalism, taken to its extreme, comes very close to conservatism. The belief in social progress—in reform or a laissez-faire doctrine—and the belief in the importance of the individual both lead to positions supportive of the system as a whole. The overriding belief is that the social system works or can be reformed to work. There is little criticism of the system as a whole; in the American case this means, in particular, that there is little questioning of capitalism. Instead of imminent class struggle, the early sociologists saw a future of class harmony and class cooperation. Ultimately this meant that early American sociological theory helped to rationalize exploitation, domestic and international imperialism, and social inequality (Schwendinger and Schwendinger, 1974). In the end, the political liberalism of the early sociologists had enormously conservative implications.

Social Change, Intellectual Currents, and Early American Sociology

In their analyses of the founding of American sociological theory, Roscoe Hinkle (1980) and Ellsworth Fuhrman (1980) outline several basic contexts from which that body of theory emerged. Of utmost importance are the social changes that occurred in American society after the Civil War (Bramson, 1961). In Chapter 1, we discussed an array of factors involved in the development of European sociological theory; several of these factors (such as industrialization and urbanization) were also intimately involved in the development of theory in America. In Fuhrman's view, the early American sociologists saw the positive possibilities of industrialization, but they were also well aware of its dangers. Although these early sociologists were attracted to the ideas about dealing with the dangers of industrialization generated by the labor movement and socialist groups, they were not in favor of radically overhauling society.

Arthur Vidich and Stanford Lyman (1985) have recently made a strong case for the influence of Christianity, especially Protestantism, on the founding of American sociology. In their view, American sociologists retained the Prostestant interest in saving the world and merely substituted one language (science) for another (religion). They argue: "From 1854, when the first works in sociology appeared in the United States, until the outbreak of World War I, sociology was a moral and intellectual reponse to the problems of American life and thought, institutions, and creeds" (Vidich and Lyman, 1985:1). Sociologists sought to define, study, and help solve these social problems. While the clergyman worked within religion to help improve it and people's lot within it, the sociologist did the same within society. Given their religious roots, and the religious parallels, the vast majority of sociologists did not challenge the basic legitimacy of society.

Another major factor in the founding of American sociology discussed by both Hinkle and Fuhrman is the simultaneous emergence in America, in the late 1800s, of both academic professions (including sociology) and the modern university system. In Europe, in contrast, the university system was already well established *before* the emergence of sociology. Although sociology had a difficult time becoming established in Europe, it found the going easier in the more fluid setting of the new American university system.

Still another factor was the impact of established European theory on American sociological theory. European theorists largely created sociological theory, and the Americans were able to rely on this groundwork. The Europeans most important to the Americans were Spencer and Comte. Simmel was of some importance in the early years, but the influence of Durkheim, Weber, and Marx was not to have a dramatic effect for a number of years. As an illustration of the impact of early European theory on American sociology, the history of the ideas of Herbert Spencer is interesting and informative.

Herbert Spencer's Influence on Sociology   Why were Spencer's ideas so much more influential in the early years of American sociology than those of Comte, Durkheim, Marx, and Weber? Hofstadter (1959) offered several explanations. To take the easiest first, Spencer wrote in English, while the others did not. In addition, Spencer did not write very technically, thereby making his work broadly accessible. Indeed, some have argued that the lack of technicality is traceable to Spencer's *not* being a very sophisticated scholar. But there are other, more important reasons for Spencer's broad appeal. He offered a scientific orientation that was attractive to an audience becoming enamored of science and its technological products. He offered a comprehensive theory that seemed to deal with the entire sweep of human history. The breadth of his ideas, as well as the voluminous work he produced, allowed his theory to be many different things to many different people. Finally, and perhaps most important, his theory was soothing and reassuring to a society undergoing the wrenching process of industrialization—society was, according to Spencer, steadily moving in the direction of greater and greater progress.

Spencer's most famous American disciple was William Graham Sumner, who accepted and expanded upon many of Spencer's Social Darwinist ideas. Spencer also influenced other early American sociologists, among them Lester Ward, Charles Horton Cooley, E. A. Ross, and Robert Park.

But by the 1930s, Spencer was in eclipse in the intellectual world in general, as well as in sociology. His Social Darwinist, laissez-faire ideas seemed ridiculous in the light of massive social problems, a world war, and a major economic depression. In 1937 Talcott Parsons announced Spencer's intellectual death for sociology when he echoed historian Crane Brinton's words of a few years earlier, "Who now reads Spencer?" Today Spencer is of little more than historical interest, but his ideas *were* important in shaping early American sociological theory. Let us look briefly at the work of two American theorists who were influenced, at least in part, by Spencer's work.

William Graham Sumner (1840–1910)   It is convenient to start a discussion of early American sociological theorists with William Graham Sumner, because he was the person who taught the first course in the United States that could be called sociology. Sumner contended that he had begun teaching sociology "years before any such attempt was made at any other university in the world" (Curtis, 1981:63).

Sumner was the major exponent of Social Darwinism in the United States, although he appeared to change his view late in life (N. Smith, 1979). The following exchange between Sumner and one of his students illustrates his "liberal" views on the need for individual freedom and his position against government interference:

> "Professor, don't you believe in any government aid to industries?"
>   "No! It's root, hog, or die."
>   "Yes, but hasn't the hog got a right to root?"
>   "There are no rights. The world owes nobody a living."
>   "You believe then, Professor, in only one system, the contract-competitive system?"
>   "That's the only sound economic system. All others are fallacies."
>   "Well, suppose some professor of political economy came along and took your job away from you. Wouldn't you be sore?"
>   "Any other professor is welcome to try. If he gets my job, it is my fault. My business is to teach the subject so well that no one can take the job away from me."
>
> (Phelps, cited in Hofstadter, 1959:54)

Sumner basically adopted a survival-of-the-fittest approach to the social world. Like Spencer, he saw people struggling against their environment, and the fittest were those who would be successful. Thus Sumner was a supporter of human aggressiveness and competitiveness. Those who succeeded deserved it, and those who did not succeed deserved to fail. Again like Spencer, Sumner was opposed to efforts, especially government efforts, to aid those who had failed. In his view such intervention operated against the natural selection that, among people as among lower animals, allowed the fit to survive and the unfit to perish. As Sumner put it, "If we do not like the survival of the fittest, we have only one possible alternative, and that is survival of the unfittest" (Curtis, 1981:84). This theoretical system fit in well with the development of capitalism because it provided theoretical legitimacy for the existence of great differences in wealth and power.

Sumner is of little more than historical interest for two main reasons. First, his orientation and Social Darwinism in general have come to be regarded as little more than a crude legitimation of competitive capitalism and the status quo. Second, he failed to build a solid enough base at Yale to build a school of sociology with many disciples. That kind of success was to occur some years later at the University of Chicago (Heyl and Heyl, 1976). In spite of success in his time, "Sumner is remembered by few today" (Curtis, 1981:146).

Lester F. Ward (1841–1913) Another sociologist of note in his time but of little lasting significance is Lester Ward. He had an unusual career in that he spent most of it as a paleontologist working for the federal government. During that time, Ward read Spencer and Comte and developed a strong interest in sociology. He published a number of works in the late 1800s and early 1900s in which he expounded his sociological theory. As a result of the notoriety that this work achieved, Ward was elected the first president of the American Sociological Society in 1906. It was only then that he took his first academic position, at Brown University, a position that he held until his death.

Ward, like Sumner, was influenced by the ideas of Herbert Spencer. He accepted the idea that people had evolved from lower forms to their present status. He believed that early society was characterized by its simplicity and its moral poverty, whereas modern society was more complex, happier, and offered greater freedom. One task of sociology, *pure sociology*, was to study the basic laws of social change and social structure. But Ward was not content simply to have sociology study social life. He believed that sociology should have a practical side; there should also be an *applied sociology*. This involved the conscious use of scientific knowledge to attain a better society. Thus, Ward was not an extreme Social Darwinist; he believed in the need for and importance of social reform.

Although of historical significance, Sumner and Ward have not been of long-term significance to sociological theory. We turn now, however, to some theorists, especially Mead, and to a school, the Chicago school, that came to dominate sociology in America. The Chicago school was unusual in the history of sociology in that it was one of the few (the Durkheimian school in Paris was another) "collective intellectual enterprises of an intergrated kind" in the history of sociology (Bulmer, 1984:1). The tradition begun at the University of Chicago is of continuing importance to sociology and its theoretical (and empirical) status.

The Chicago School[1]

The department of sociology at the University of Chicago was founded in 1892 by Albion Small. Small's intellectual work is of less contemporary significance than the key role he played in the institutionalization of sociology in the United States (Faris, 1970; Matthews, 1977). He was instrumental in creating a department at Chicago that was to become the center of the discipline in the United States for many years. Small collaborated on the first textbook in sociology in 1894. In 1895 he founded the *American Journal of Sociology*, a journal that to this day is a dominant force in the discipline. In 1905, Small cofounded the American Sociological Society, *the* major professional association of American sociologists to this date (Rhoades, 1981). (The embarrassment caused by the initials of the American Sociological Society, A.S.S., led to a name change in 1959 to the American Sociological Association—A.S.A.)

Early Chicago Sociology   The early Chicago department had several distinctive characteristics. For one thing, it had a strong connection with religion (Vidich and Lyman, 1985). Some members were ministers themselves, and others were sons of ministers. Small, for example, believed that "the ultimate goal of sociology must be essentially Christian" (Matthews, 1977:95). This opinion led to a view that sociology must be interested in social reform, and this was combined with a belief that sociology should be scientific.[2] Scientific sociology with an objective of social amelioration was to be practiced in the burgeoning city of Chicago, which was beset by the positive *and* negative effects of urbanization and industrialization.

We might note here the contributions of one of the earliest members of the Chicago sociology department, W. I. Thomas (1863–1947). In 1895, Thomas became a fellow at the Chicago department, where he wrote his dissertation in 1896. Thomas's lasting significance was in his emphasis on the need to do scientific research on sociological issues (Lodge, 1986). Although he championed this position for many years, its major statement came in 1918 with the publication of *The Polish Peasant in Europe and America*, which he coauthored with Florian Znaniecki. Martin Bulmer sees it as a "landmark" study because it moved sociology away from "abstract theory and library research and toward the study of the empirical world utilizing a theoretical framework"

---

[1] See Bulmer (1985) for a discussion of what defines a school and why we can speak of the "Chicago school." Tiryakian (1979, 1986) also deals with schools in general, and the Chicago school in particular, and emphasizes the role played by charismatic leaders as well as methodological innovations. See also Amsterdamska (1985).

[2] As we will see, however, the Chicago school's conception of science was to become too "soft," at least in the eyes of the positivists who later came to dominate sociology.

(1984:45). Norbert Wiley sees *The Polish Peasant* as crucial to the founding of sociology in the sense of "clarifying the unique intellectual space into which this discipline alone could see and explore" (1986:20). The book was the product of eight years of research in both Europe and the United States and was primarily a study of social disorganization among Polish migrants. The data were of little lasting importance. However, the methodology was significant. It involved a variety of data sources, including autobiographical material, paid writings, family letters, newspaper files, public documents, and institutional letters.

Although *The Polish Peasant* was primarily a macrosociological study of social institutions, over the course of his career, Thomas gravitated toward a microscopic, social-psychological orientation. He is best known for his social-psychological statement: "If men define situations as real, they are real in their consequences" (Thomas and Thomas, 1928:572). The emphasis was on the importance of what people think and how this affects what they do. This microscopic, social-psychological focus stood in contrast to the macroscopic, social-structural and -cultural perspectives of such European scholars as Marx, Weber, and Durkheim. It was to become one of the defining characteristics of Chicago's theoretical product—symbolic interactionism (Rock, 1979:5).

Another figure of significance at Chicago was Robert Park (1864–1944). Park had come to Chicago as a part-time instructor in 1914 and quickly worked his way into a central role in the department. As was true of Small, Park's long-term significance was not simply in his intellectual contributions. His importance for the development of sociology lay in several areas. First, he became the dominant figure in the Chicago department, which, in turn, dominated sociology into the 1930s. Second, Park had studied in Europe and was instrumental in bringing Continental thinkers to the attention of Chicago sociologists. Of particular theoretical importance, Park had taken courses with Simmel, and Simmel's ideas, particularly his focus on action and interaction, were instrumental in the development of the Chicago school's theoretical orientation (Rock, 1979:36–48). Third, prior to becoming a sociologist, Park had been a reporter, and this experience gave him a sense of the importance of urban problems and of the need to go out into the field to collect data through personal observation. Out of this emerged the Chicago school's substantive interest in urban ecology. Fourth, Park played a key role in guiding graduate students and helping develop "a cumulative program of graduate research" (Bulmer, 1984:13). Finally, in 1921, Park and Ernest W. Burgess published the first truly important sociology textbook, *An Introduction to the Science of Sociology*. It was to be an influential book for many years and was particularly notable for its commitments to science, to research, and to the study of a wide range of social phenomena.

Beginning in the late 1920s and early 1930s, Park began to spend less and less time in Chicago. Finally, his lifelong interest in race relations (he had been secretary to Booker T. Washington before becoming a sociologist) led him to take a position at Fisk University (a black university) in 1934. Although the

ROBERT PARK: A Biographical Sketch

Robert Park did not follow the typical career route of an academic sociologist—college, graduate school, professorship. Instead, he led a varied career before he became a sociologist late in life. Despite his late start, Park had a profound effect on sociology in general and on theory in particular. Park's varied experiences gave him an unusual orientation to life, and this view helped to shape the Chicago school, symbolic interactionism, and, ultimately, a good portion of sociology.

Park was born in Harveyville, Pennsylvania, on February 14, 1864 (Matthews, 1977). As a student at the University of Michigan, he was exposed to a number of great thinkers, such as John Dewey. Although he was excited by ideas, Park felt a strong need to work in the real world. As Park said, "I made up my mind to go in for experience for its own sake, to gather into my soul . . . 'all the joys and sorrows of the world' " (1927/1973:253). Upon graduation, he began a career as a journalist, which gave him this real-world opportunity. He particularly liked to explore ("hunting down gambling houses and opium dens" [Park, 1927/1973:254]). He wrote about city life in vivid detail. He would go into the field, observe and analyze, and finally write up his observations. In fact, he was already doing essentially the kind of research ("scientific reporting") that came to be one of the hallmarks of Chicago sociology—that is, urban ethnology using participant observation techniques.

Although the accurate description of social life remained one of his passions, Park grew dissatisfied with newspaper work, because it did not fulfill his familial or, more important, his intellectual needs. Furthermore, it did not seem to contribute to the improvement of the world, and Park had a deep interest in social reform. In 1898, at age thirty-four, Park left newspaper work and enrolled in the philosophy department at Harvard. He remained there for a year

decline of the Chicago department was not caused solely or even chiefly by Park's departure, its status began to wane in the 1930s. But before we can deal with the decline of Chicago sociology and the rise of other departments and theories, we need to return to the early days of the school and the two figures whose work was to be of the most lasting theoretical significance— Charles Horton Cooley and, most important, George Herbert Mead.

Charles Horton Cooley (1864–1929)   The association of Cooley with the Chicago school is interesting in that he spent his career at the University of Michigan, not the University of Chicago. But Cooley's theoretical perspective was in line with the theory of symbolic interactionism that was to become Chicago's most important product.

Cooley received his Ph.D. from the University of Michigan in 1894. He had developed a strong interest in sociology, but there was as yet no department of sociology at Michigan. As a result, the questions for his Ph.D. examination came from Columbia University, where sociology had been taught since 1889 under the leadership of Franklin Giddings. Cooley began his teaching career but then decided to move to Germany, at that time the heart of the world's intellectual life. In Berlin he encountered Georg Simmel, whose work was to have a profound influence on Park's sociology. In fact, Simmel's lectures were the *only* formal sociological training that Park received. As Park said, "I got most of my knowledge about society and human nature from my own observations" (1927/1973:257). In 1904, Park completed his doctoral dissertation at the University of Heidelberg. Characteristically, he was dissatisfied with his dissertation: "All I had to show was that little book and I was ashamed of it" (Matthews, 1977: 57). He refused a summer teaching job at the University of Chicago and turned away from academe as he had earlier turned away from newspaper work.

His need to contribute to social betterment led him to become secretary and chief publicity officer for the Congo Reform Association, which was set up to help alleviate the brutality and exploitation then taking place in the Belgian Congo. During this period, he met Booker T. Washington, and he was attracted to the cause of improving the lot of black Americans. He became Washington's secretary and played a key role in the activities of the Tuskegee Institute. In 1912 he met W. I. Thomas, the Chicago sociologist, who was lecturing at Tuskegee. Thomas invited him to give a course on "the Negro in America" to a small group of graduate students at Chicago, and Park did so in 1914. It was successful, and he gave it again the next year to an audience twice as large. At this time, he joined the American Sociological Society, and only a decade later he became its president. Park gradually worked his way into a full-time appointment at Chicago, although he did not get a full professorship until 1923, when he was fifty-nine years old. Over the approximately two decades that he was affiliated with the University of Chicago, he played a key role in shaping the intellectual orientation of the sociology department.

Park remained peripatetic even after his retirement from Chicago in the early 1930s. He taught courses and oversaw research at Fisk University until he was nearly eighty years old. He traveled extensively. He died on February 7, 1944, one week before his eightieth birthday.

at Michigan in 1892 before completion of his doctorate, and he remained there throughout his career.

Although Cooley had a wide range of views, he is mainly remembered today for his insights into the social-psychological aspects of social life. His work in this area is in line with that of George Herbert Mead, although Mead was to have a deeper and more lasting effect on sociology than Cooley. Cooley had an interest in consciousness, but he refused (as did Mead) to separate consciousness from the social context. This is best exemplified by a concept of his that survives to this day—the *looking-glass self.* By this concept, Cooley understood that people possess consciousness and that it is shaped in continuing social interaction.

A second basic concept that illustrates Cooley's social-psychological interests, and which is also of continuing interest and importance, is that of the primary group. *Primary groups* are intimate, face-to-face groups that play a key role in linking the actor to the larger society. Especially crucial are the primary groups of the young—mainly the family and the peer group. Within these groups, the individual grows into a social being. It is basically within the primary group that the looking-glass self emerges and that the ego-centered child learns to take others into account and, thereby, to become a contributing member of society.

Both Cooley and Mead rejected a *behavioristic* view of human beings, the view that people blindly and unconsciously respond to external stimuli. On the positive side, they believed that people had consciousness, a self, and that it was the responsibility of the sociologist to study this aspect of social reality. Cooley urged sociologists to try to put themselves in the place of the actors they were studying, to use the method of *sympathetic introspection*, in order to analyze consciousness. By analyzing what they as actors might do in various circumstances, sociologists could understand the meanings and motives that are at the base of social behavior. The method of sympathetic introspection seemed to many to be very unscientific. In this area, among others, Mead's work represents an advance over Cooley's. Nevertheless, there is a great deal of similarity in the interests of the two men, not the least of which is their shared view that sociology should focus on such social-psychological phenomena as consciousness, action, and interaction.

George Herbert Mead **(1863–1931)**   *The* most important thinker associated with the Chicago school and symbolic interactionism was not a sociologist but a philosopher, George Herbert Mead.[3] Mead started teaching philosophy at the University of Chicago in 1894, and he taught there until his death in 1931. He is something of a paradox, given his central importance in the history of sociological theory, both because he taught philosophy, not sociology, and because he published comparatively little during his lifetime. The paradox is, in part, resolved by two facts. First, Mead taught courses in social psychology in the philosophy department, and they were taken by many graduate students in sociology. His ideas had a profound effect on a number of them. These students combined Mead's ideas with those they were getting in the sociology department from people like Park and Thomas. Although there was no theory known as symbolic interactionism at the time, it was created by students out of these various inputs. Thus Mead had a deep, personal impact on the people who were later to develop symbolic interactionism. Second, these students put together their notes on Mead's courses and published a posthumous volume under his name. The work, *Mind, Self and Society* (Mead, 1934/1962), moved his ideas from the realm of oral to that of written tradition. Widely read to this day, this volume forms the main intellectual pillar of symbolic interactionism.

We deal with Mead's ideas in Chapter 9, but it is necessary at this point to underscore a few points in order to situate him historically. Mead's ideas need to be seen in the context of psychological behaviorism. Mead was quite impressed with this orientation and accepted many of its tenets. He adopted

---

[3] For a dissenting view on this, see Lewis and Smith (1980).

its focus on the actor and his behavior. He regarded as sensible the behavior-ists' concern with the rewards and costs involved in the behaviors of the actors. What troubled Mead was that behaviorism did not seem to go far enough. That is, it excluded consciousness from serious consideration, arguing that it was not amenable to scientific study. Mead vehemently disagreed and sought to extend the principles of behaviorism to an analysis of the "mind." In so doing, Mead enunciated a focus similar to that of Cooley. But whereas Cooley's position seemed unscientific, Mead promised a more scientific con-ception of consciousness by extending the highly scientific principles and methods of psychological behaviorism.

Mead offered American sociology a social-psychological theory that stood in stark contrast to the primarily societal theories offered by most of the major European theorists—Marx, Weber, Durkheim, Comte, and Spencer. The only exception was Simmel. Thus symbolic interactionism was developed, in large part, out of Simmel's interest in action and interaction and Mead's interest in consciousness. However, such a focus led to a weakness in Mead's work, as well as in symbolic interactionism in general, at the societal and cultural levels.

The Waning of Chicago Sociology   Chicago sociology reached its peak in the 1920s, but by the 1930s, with the death of Mead and the departure of Park, the department began to lose its position of central importance in American sociology. Fred Matthews (1977; see also Bulmer, 1984) pinpoints several rea-sons for the decline of Chicago sociology, two of which seem of utmost impor-tance.

First, the discipline had grown increasingly preoccupied with being scien-tific—that is, using sophisticated methods and employing statistical analysis. However, the Chicago school was viewed as emphasizing descriptive, eth-nographic studies, often focusing on their subjects' personal orientations (in Thomas's terms, their "definitions of the situation"). Park came progressively to despise statistics (he called it "parlor magic") because it seemed to prohibit the analysis of subjectivity, of the idiosyncratic, and of the peculiar. The fact that important work in quantitative methods was done at Chicago (Bulmer, 1984:151–189) tended to be ignored in the face of its overwhelming association with qualitative methods. Second, more and more individuals outside of Chi-cago grew increasingly resentful of Chicago's dominance of both the American Sociological Society and the *American Journal of Sociology.* The Eastern Socio-logical Society was founded in 1930, and eastern sociologists became more vocal about the dominance of the Midwest in general and Chicago in partic-ular (Wiley, 1979:63). By 1935, the revolt against Chicago led to a non-Chicago secretary of the association and the establishment of a new official journal, the *American Sociological Review* (Lengermann, 1979). According to Wiley, "the Chicago school had fallen like a mighty oak" (1979:63). This signaled the growth of other power centers, most notably Harvard and the Ivy League in general. Symbolic interactionism was largely an indeterminate, oral tradition and as such eventually lost ground to more explicit and codified theoretical systems like the structural functionalism associated with the Ivy League (Rock, 1979:12).

SOCIOLOGICAL THEORY TO MID-CENTURY

The Rise of Harvard, the Ivy League, and Structural Functionalism

We can trace the rise of sociology at Harvard from the arrival of Pitirim Sorokin in 1930. When Sorokin arrived at Harvard, there was no sociology department, but by the end of his first year one had been organized, and he had been appointed its head. Although Sorokin was a sociological theorist, and he continued to publish into the 1960s, his work is surprisingly little cited today. His theorizing has not stood the test of time very well. Sorokin's long-term significance may well have been in the creation of the Harvard sociology department and the hiring of Talcott Parsons (who had been an instructor of economics at Harvard) for the position of instructor of sociology. Parsons became *the* dominant figure in American sociology for introducing European theorists to an American audience, for his own sociological theories, and for his many students who themselves became major sociological theorists.

Pitirim Sorokin (1889–1968)   Sorokin wrote an enormous amount and developed a theory that, if anything, surpassed Parsons's in scope and complexity. The most complete statement of this theory is contained in the four-volume *Social and Cultural Dynamics* published between 1937 and 1941. In it, Sorokin drew on a wide range of empirical data to develop a general theory of social and cultural change. In contrast to those who sought to develop evolutionary theories of social change, Sorokin developed a cyclical theory. He saw societies as oscillating among three different types of mentalities—sensate, ideational, and idealistic. Societies dominated by *sensatism* emphasize the role of the senses in comprehending reality; those dominated by a more transcendental and highly religious way of understanding reality are *ideational;* and *idealistic* societies are transitional types balancing sensatism and religiosity.

The motor of social change is to be found in the internal logic of each of these sytems. That is, they are pressed internally to extend their mode of thinking to its logical extreme. Thus a sensate society ultimately becomes so sensual that it provides the groundwork for its own demise. As sensatism reaches its logical end point, people turn to ideational systems as a refuge. But once such a system has gained ascendancy, it too is pushed to its end point, with the result that society becomes excessively religious. The stage is then set for the rise of an idealistic culture and, ultimately, for the cycle to repeat itself. Sorokin not only developed an elaborate theory of social change, but he also marshaled detailed evidence from art, philosophy, politics, and so forth to support his theory. It was clearly an impressive accomplishment.

There is much more to Sorokin's theorizing, but this introduction should give the reader a feeling for the breadth of his work. It is difficult to explain why Sorokin has fallen out of favor in sociological theory. Perhaps it is the result of one of the things that Sorokin loved to attack, and in fact wrote a book about, *Fads and Foibles in Modern Sociology and Related Sciences* (1956). It may be that Sorokin will be rediscovered by a future generation of sociological theorists. At the moment, his work remains outside the mainstream of modern sociological theorizing.

Talcott Parsons (1902–1979)   Although he published some early essays, Parsons's major contribution in the early years was in his influence on graduate students who themselves were to become notable sociological theorists. The most famous was Robert Merton, who received his Ph.D. in 1936 and soon became a major theorist and the heart of Parsonsian-style theorizing at Columbia University. In the same year (1936), Kingsley Davis received his Ph.D., and he, along with Wilbert Moore (who received his Harvard degree in 1940), wrote one of the central works in structural-functional theory, the theory that was to become the major product of Parsons and the Parsonsians. But Parsons's influence was not restricted to the 1930s. Remarkably, he produced graduate students of great influence well into the 1960s.

The pivotal year for Parsons and for American sociological theory was 1937, the year in which he published *The Structure of Social Action.* This book was of significance to sociological theory in America for four main reasons. First, it served to introduce grand European theorizing to a large American audience. The bulk of the book was devoted to Durkheim, Weber, and Pareto. His interpretations of these theorists shaped their images in American sociology for many years.

Second, Parsons devoted almost no attention to Marx, although he emphasized the work of Durkheim and Weber and even Pareto. As a result, Marxian theory was to continue to be largely excluded from legitimate sociology.

Third, *The Structure of Social Action* made the case for sociological theorizing as a legitimate and significant sociological activity. The theorizing that has taken place in the United States since then owes a deep debt to Parsons's work.

Finally, Parsons argued for specific sociological theories that were to have a profound influence on sociology. At first, Parsons was thought of, and thought of himself, as an action theorist. He seemed to focus on actors and their thoughts and actions. But by the close of his 1937 work and increasingly in his later work Parsons sounded more like a structural-functional theorist focusing on large-scale social and cultural systems. Although Parsons argued that there was no contradiction between these theories, he became best known as a structural functionalist, and he was the primary exponent of this theory, which gained dominance within sociology and maintained that position until

PITIRIM A. SOROKIN: A Biographical Sketch

Pitirim Sorokin was born in a remote village in Russia on January 21, 1889. In his teenage years, and while a seminary student, Sorokin was arrested for revolutionary activities and spent four months in prison. Eventually, Sorokin made his way to St. Petersburg University and interspersed diligent studies, teaching responsibilities, and revolutionary activities that once again landed him in prison briefly. Sorokin's dissertation was scheduled to be defended in March 1917, but before his examination could take place, the Russian Revolution was under way. Sorokin was not able to earn his doctorate until 1922. Active in the revolution, but opposed to the Bolsheviks, Sorokin took a position in Kerensky's provisional government. But when the Bolsheviks emerged victorious, Sorokin once again found himself in prison, this time at the hands of the Bolsheviks. Eventually, under direct orders from Lenin, Sorokin was freed and allowed to return to the university and pick up where he had left off. However, his work was censored, and he was harassed by the secret police. Sorokin finally was allowed to leave Russia, and, after a stay in Czechoslovakia, he arrived in the United States in October 1923.

At first, Sorokin gave lectures at various universities but eventually obtained a position at the University of Minnesota. He soon became a full professor. Sorokin already had published several books in Russia, and he continued to turn them out at a prodigious rate in the United States. Of his productivity at Minnesota, Sorokin said, "I knew it exceeded the lifetime productivity of the average sociologist" (1963:224). Books such as *Social Mobility* and *Contemporary Sociological Theories* gave him a national reputation, and by 1929 he was offered (and accepted) the first chair at Harvard University in sociology. The position was placed in the department of economics because there was not yet a sociology department at Harvard.

Soon after his arrival at Harvard, a separate department of sociology was created, and Sorokin was named as its first chairman. In that position, Sorokin helped build the most important sociology department in the United States. During this period, Sorokin also completed what would become his best-known work, *Social and Cultural Dynamics* (1937–1941).

Pitirim Sorokin has been described as "the Peck's bad boy and devil's advocate of American sociology" (Williams, 1980b:100). Blessed with an enormous ego, Sorokin seemed critical of almost everyone and everything. As a result, Sorokin and his work were the subject

recent years. Parsons's theoretical strength, and that of structural functionalism, lay in delineating the relationships among large-scale social structures and institutions (see Chapter 7).

Parsons's major statements on his structural-functional theory came in the early 1950s in several works, most notably *The Social System* (1951). In that work and others, Parsons tended to concentrate on the structures of society and their relationship to each other. These structures were seen as mutually supportive and tending toward a dynamic equilibrium. The emphasis was on how order was maintained among the various elements of society. Change was seen as an orderly process, and Parsons (1966, 1971) ultimately came to

of much critical analysis. All of this is clear in an excerpt from a letter he wrote to the editor of the *American Journal of Sociology:*

> The strongly disparaging character of the reviews is a good omen for my books because of a high correlation between the damning of my books . . . and their subsequent career. The more strongly they have been damned (and practically all my books were damned by your reviewers), the more significant and successful were my damned works.
>
> (Sorokin, 1963:229)

One of Sorokin's more interesting and long-running feuds was with Talcott Parsons. Parsons had been appointed at Harvard as an instructor of sociology when Sorokin was chairman of the department. Under Sorokin's leadership, Parsons made very slow career progress at Harvard. Eventually, however, he emerged as the dominant sociologist at Harvard and in the United States. The conflict between Sorokin and Parsons was heightened by the extensive overlap between their theories. Despite the similarities, Parsons's work attracted a far wider and far more enduring audience than did Sorokin's. As the years went by, Sorokin developed a rather interesting attitude toward Parsons's work, which was reflected in several of his books. On the one hand, he was inclined to criticize Parsons for stealing many of his best ideas. On the other hand, he was severely critical of Parsonsian theory. Another tension in their relationship was over graduate students. One of the great achievements of the early Harvard department was its ability to attract talented graduate students like Robert Merton. Although these students were influenced by the ideas of both men, Parsons's influence proved more enduring than Sorokin's. Parsons replaced Sorokin as chairman of the sociology department and transformed it into the Department of Social Relations. Of that, Sorokin said:

> So I am not responsible for whatever has happened to the department since, either for its merging with abnormal and social psychology and cultural anthropology to form a "Department of Social Relations," or for the drowning of sociology in an eclectic mass of the odds and ends of these disciplines. . . . The Department of Social Relations . . . has hardly produced as many distinguished sociologists as the Department of Sociology did . . . under my chairmanship.
>
> (Sorokin, 1963:251)

Sorokin was eventually isolated in the Harvard department, relegated to a "desolate looking" office, and reduced to putting a mimeographed statement under the doors of departmental offices claiming that Parsons had stolen his ideas (Coser, 1977:490).

Sorokin died on February 11, 1968.

adopt a neoevolutionary view of social change. Parsons was concerned not only with the social system per se but also with its relationship to the other *action systems,* especially the cultural and personality systems. But his basic view on intersystemic relations was essentially the same as his view of intrasystemic relations, that is, that they were defined by cohesion, consensus, and order. In other words, the various *social structures* performed a variety of positive *functions* for each other.

It is clear, then, why Parsons came to be defined primarily as a *structural functionalist.* As his fame grew, so did the strength of structural-functional theory in the United States. His work lay at the core of this theory, but his students and disciples also concentrated on extending both the theory and its dominance in the United States.

Although Parsons played a number of important and positive roles in the history of sociological theory in the United States, his work also had a number of negative consequences. First, he offered interpretations of European theorists that seemed to reflect his own theoretical orientation more than theirs. Many American sociologists were initially exposed to erroneous interpretations of the European masters. Second, as was pointed out above, early in his career Parsons largely ignored Marx, with the result that Marx's ideas continued for many years on the periphery of sociology. Third, his own theory as it developed over the years had a number of serious weaknesses. However, Parsons's preeminence in American sociology served for many years to mute or overwhelm the critics. Not until much later did the weaknesses of Parsons's theory, and more generally of structural functionalism, receive a full airing.

But we are getting too far ahead of the story, and we need to return to the early 1930s and other developments at Harvard. We can gain a good deal of insight into the development of the Harvard department by looking at it through an account of its other major figure—George Homans.

George Homans (1910–1989)   A wealthy Bostonian, George Homans received his bachelor's degree from Harvard in 1932 (Homans, 1962, 1984). As a result of the Great Depression, he was unemployed but certainly not penniless. In the fall of 1932, L. J. Henderson, a physiologist, was offering a course in the theories of Vilfredo Pareto, and Homans was invited to attend and accepted. (Parsons also attended the Pareto seminars.) Homans's description of why he was drawn to and taken with Pareto says much about why American sociological theory was so highly conservative, so anti-Marxist:

> I took to Pareto because he made clear to me what I was already prepared to believe. I do not know all the reasons why I was ready for him, but I can give one. Someone has said that much modern sociology is an effort to answer the arguments of the revolutionaries. As a Republican Bostonian who had not rejected his comparatively wealthy family, I felt during the thirties that I was under personal attack, above all from the Marxists. I was ready to believe Pareto because he provided me with a defense.
>
> (Homans, 1962:4)

Homans's exposure to Pareto led to a book, *An Introduction to Pareto* (coauthored with Charles Curtis), published in 1934. The publication of this book made Homans a sociologist even though Pareto's work was virtually the only sociology he had read up to that point.

In 1934 Homans was named a junior fellow at Harvard, a program started to avoid the problems associated with the Ph.D. program. In fact, Homans never did earn a Ph.D. even though he became one of the major sociological figures of his day. Homans was a junior fellow until 1939, and in those years he absorbed more and more sociology. In 1939 Homans was affiliated with the sociology department, but the connection was broken by the war.

By the time Homans had returned from the war, the Department of Social Relations had been founded by Parsons at Harvard, and Homans joined it. Although Homans respected some aspects of Parsons's work, he was highly critical of his style of theorizing. A long-run exchange began between the two men that later manifested itself publicly in the pages of many books and journals. Basically, Homans argued that Parsons's theory was not a theory at all but rather a vast system of intellectual categories into which most aspects of the social world fit. Further, Homans believed that theory should be built from the ground up on the basis of careful observations of the social world. Parsons's theory, however, started on the general theoretical level and worked its way down to the empirical level.

In his own work, Homans amassed a large number of empirical observations over the years, but it was only in the 1950s that he hit upon a satisfactory theoretical approach with which to analyze these data. That theory was psychological behaviorism, as it was best expressed in the ideas of his colleague at Harvard, the psychologist B. F. Skinner. On the basis of this perspective, Homans developed his exchange theory. We will pick up the story of this theoretical development later in the chapter. The crucial point here is that Harvard and its major theoretical product, structural functionalism, became preeminent in sociology in the late 1930s, replacing the Chicago school and symbolic interactionism.

The Chicago School in Decline

We left the Chicago department in the mid-1930s on the wane with the death of Mead, the departure of Park, the revolt of eastern sociologists, and the founding of the *American Sociological Review*. But the Chicago school did not disappear. Into the early 1950s it continued to be an important force in sociology. Important Ph.D.s were still produced there, such as Anselm Strauss and Arnold Rose. Major figures remained at Chicago, such as Everett Hughes (Faught, 1980), who was of central importance to the development of the sociology of occupations.

However, the central figure in the Chicago department in this era was Herbert Blumer (1900–1987) (*Symbolic Interaction*, 1988). He was a major exponent of the theoretical approach developed at Chicago out of the work of Mead, Cooley, Simmel, Park, Thomas, and others. In fact, it was Blumer who coined the phrase *symbolic interactionism* in 1937. Blumer played a key role in keeping this tradition alive through his teaching at Chicago. He also wrote a number of essays that were instrumental in keeping symbolic interactionism vital into the 1950s. Blumer was also important because of the organizational positions he held in sociology. From 1930 to 1935, he was the secretary-treasurer of the American Sociological Society, and in 1956 he became its president. More important, he held institutional positions that affected the nature of what was published in sociology. Between 1941 and 1952, he was editor of the *American Journal of Sociology* and was instrumental in keeping it one of the major outlets for work in the Chicago tradition in general and symbolic interactionism in particular.

While the East Coast universities were coming under the sway of structural functionalism, the Midwest remained (and to this day remains) a stronghold of symbolic interactionism. In the 1940s, major symbolic interactionists fanned out across the Midwest—Arnold Rose was at Minnesota, Robert Habenstein at Missouri, Gregory Stone at Michigan State, and, most important, Manford Kuhn (1911–1963) at Iowa.

There developed a split between Blumer at Chicago and Kuhn at Iowa; in fact, people began to talk of the differences between the Chicago and the Iowa schools of symbolic interactionism. Basically, the split occurred over the issue of science and methodology. Kuhn accepted the symbolic-interactionist focus on actors and their thoughts and actions, but he argued that they should be studied more scientifically—for example, by using questionnaires. Blumer was in favor of "softer" methods such as sympathetic introspection and participant observation.

Despite this flurry of activity, the Chicago school was in decline, especially given the movement of Blumer in 1952 from Chicago to the University of California at Berkeley. The University of Chicago continued to have a strong sociology department, of course, but it had less and less in common with the Chicago tradition. Although the Chicago school was moribund, symbolic interactionism still had vitality with its major exponents being dispersed across the country.

Developments in Marxian Theory

From the early 1900s to the 1930s, Marxian theory had continued to develop largely independently of mainstream sociological theory. At least partially, the exception to this was the emergence of the critical, or Frankfurt, school out of the earlier Hegelian Marxism.

The idea of a Frankfurt school for the development of Marxian theory was the product of Felix J. Weil. The Institute of Social Research was officially founded in Frankfurt, Germany, on February 3, 1923 (Bottomore, 1984; Jay, 1973, 1986). Over the years, a number of the most famous thinkers in Marxian theory were associated with the critical school—Max Horkheimer, Theodor Adorno, Erich Fromm, Herbert Marcuse, and, more recently, Jurgen Habermas.

The institute functioned in Germany until 1934, but by then things were growing increasingly uncomfortable under the Nazi regime. The Nazis had little use for the Marxian ideas that dominated the institute, and their hostility was heightened because many of those associated with the institute were Jewish. In 1934 Horkheimer, as head of the institute, came to New York to discuss its status with the president of Columbia University. Much to Horkheimer's surprise, he was invited to affiliate the institute with the university, and he was even offered a building on campus. And so *a* center of Marxian theory moved to *the* center of the capitalist world. The institute stayed there until the end of the war, but after the war, pressure mounted to return it to Germany. In 1949, Horkheimer did return to Germany, and he brought the institute with him. Although the institute itself moved to Germany, many of the figures associated with it took independent career directions.

It is important to underscore a few of the most important aspects of critical theory. In its early years, those associated with the institute tended to be fairly traditional Marxists devoting a good portion of their attention to the economic domain. But around 1930, a major change took place as this group of thinkers began to shift its attention from the economy to the cultural system, which it came to see as the major force in modern capitalist society. This was consistent with, but an extension of, the position taken earlier by Hegelian Marxists like Georg Lukács. To help them understand the cultural domain, the critical theorists were attracted to the work of Max Weber (Greisman and Ritzer, 1981). The effort to combine Marx with Weber gave the critical school some of its distinctive orientations and served to make it more legitimate in later years to sociologists who began to grow interested in Marxian theory.

A second major step taken by at least some members of the critical school was to employ the rigorous social-scientific techniques developed by American sociologists to research issues of interest to Marxists. This, like the adoption of Weberian theory, made the critical school more acceptable to mainstream sociologists.

Third, critical theorists made an effort to integrate individually oriented Freudian theory with the societal- and cultural-level insights of Marx and Weber. This seemed to many sociologists to represent a more inclusive theory than that offered by either Marx or Weber alone. If nothing else, the effort to combine such disparate theories proved stimulating to sociologists and many other intellectuals.

The critical school has done much useful work since the 1920s, and a significant amount of it is of relevance to sociologists. However, the critical school had to await the late 1960s before it was "discovered" by large numbers of American theorists.

SOCIOLOGICAL THEORY FROM MID-CENTURY

Structural Functionalism: Peak and Decline

The 1940s and 1950s were paradoxically the years of greatest dominance and the beginnings of the decline of structural functionalism. In these years, Parsons produced his major statements that clearly reflected his shift from action theory to structural functionalism. Parsons's students had fanned out across the country and occupied dominant positions in many of the major sociology departments (for example, Columbia and Cornell). These students were producing works of their own that were widely recognized contributions to structural-functional theory. For example, in 1945 Kingsley Davis and Wilbert

Moore published an essay analyzing social stratification from a structural-functional perspective. It was one of the clearest statements ever made of the structural-functional view. In it, they argued that stratification was a structure that was functionally necessary for the existence of society. In other words, in ideological terms they came down on the side of inequality.

In 1949 Merton (1949/1968) published an essay that became *the* program statement of structural functionalism. In it, Merton carefully sought to delineate the essential elements of the theory and to extend it in some new directions. He made it clear that structural functionalism should deal not only with positive functions but also with negative consequences (dysfunctions). Moreover, it should focus on the net balance of functions and dysfunctions or whether a structure is overall more functional or more dysfunctional.

However, just as it was gaining theoretical hegemony, structural functionalism came under attack, and the attacks mounted until they reached a crescendo in the 1960s and 1970s. The Davis-Moore structural-functional theory of stratification was attacked from the start, and the criticisms persist to this day. Beyond that, a series of more general criticisms received even wider recognition in the discipline. There was an attack by C. Wright Mills on Parsons in 1959, and other major criticisms were mounted by David Lockwood (1956), Alvin Gouldner (1959/1967, 1970), and Irving Horowitz (1962/1967). In the 1950s, these attacks were seen as little more than "guerrilla raids," but as sociology moved into the 1960s, the dominance of structural functionalism was clearly in jeopardy.[4]

George Huaco (1986) linked the rise and decline of structural functionalism to the position of American society in the world order. As America rose to world dominance after 1945, structural functionalism achieved hegemony within sociology. Structural functionalism supported America's dominant position in the world in two ways. First, the structural-functional view that "every pattern has consequences which contribute to the preservation and survival of the larger system" was "nothing less than a celebration of the United States and its world hegemony" (Huaco, 1986:52). Second, the structural-functional emphasis on equilibrium (the best social change is no change) meshed well with the interests of the United States, then "the wealthiest and most powerful empire in the world." The decline of U.S. world dominance in the 1970s coincided with structural functionalism's loss of its preeminent position in sociological theory.

Radical Sociology in America: C. Wright Mills

As we have seen, although Marxian theory was largely ignored or reviled by mainstream American sociologists, there were exceptions, the most notable of which is C. Wright Mills (1916–1962). Although Mills's own lasting theoretical

---

[4]In spite of this, Patricia Wilner (1985) reports a continuing focus on "consensus" articles in the *American Sociological Review* between 1936 and 1982. However, it should be added that although structural functionalism is sometimes called consensus theory, a focus on consensus does *not* mean that one is necessarily using structural-functional theory.

C. WRIGHT MILLS: A Biographical Sketch

C. Wright Mills was born on August 28, 1916, in Waco, Texas. He came from a conventional middle-class background; his father was an insurance broker and his mother a housewife. He attended the University of Texas and by 1939 had obtained both a bachelor's and a master's degree. He was quite an unusual student who, by the time he left Texas, already had published articles in the two major sociology journals. Mills did his doctoral work at, and received a Ph.D. from, the University of Wisconsin (Scimecca, 1977). He took his first job at the University of Maryland but spent the bulk of his career, from 1945 until his death, at Columbia University.

Mills was a man in a hurry (Horowitz, 1983). By the time he died at forty-five from his fourth heart attack, Mills had made a number of important contributions to sociology.

One of the most striking things about C. Wright Mills was his combativeness; he seemed to be constantly at war. He had a tumultuous personal life, characterized by many affairs, three marriages, and a child from each marriage. He had an equally tumultuous professional life. He seemed to have fought with and against everyone and everything. As a graduate student at Wisconsin, he took on a number of his professors. Later, in one of his early essays, he engaged in a thinly disguised critique of the ex-chairman of the Wisconsin department. He called the senior theorist at Wisconsin, Howard Becker, a "real fool" (Horowitz, 1983). He eventually came into conflict with his coauthor, Hans Gerth, who called Mills "an excellent operator, whippersnapper, promising young man on the make, and Texas cowboy á la ride and shoot" (Horowitz, 1983:72). As a professor at Columbia, Mills was isolated and estranged from his colleagues. Said one of his Columbia colleagues:

> There was no estrangement between Wright and me. We began estranged. Indeed, at the memorial services or meeting that was organized at Columbia University at his death, I seemed to be the only person who could not say: 'I used to be his friend, but we became somewhat distant.' It was rather the reverse.
>
> (cited in Horowitz, 1983:83)

Mills was an outsider and he knew it: "I am an outlander, not only regionally, but down deep and for good" (Horowitz, 1983:84). In *The Sociological Imagination* (1959), Mills not only challenged the dominant theorist of his day, Talcott Parsons, but also the dominant methodologist, Paul Lazarsfeld, who also happened to be a colleague at Columbia.

Mills, of course, was not only at odds with people; he was also at odds with American society and challenged it on a variety of fronts. But perhaps most telling is the fact that when Mills visited the Soviet Union and was honored as a major critic of American society, he took the occasion to attack the censorship in the Soviet Union with a toast to an early Soviet leader who had been purged and murdered by the Stalinists: "to the day when the complete works of Leon Trotsky are published in the Soviet Union!" (Tilman, 1984:8)

C. Wright Mills died in Nyack, New York, on March 20, 1962.

contributions are few, he is notable for his almost single-handed effort to keep a Marxian tradition alive in sociological theory. Modern Marxian sociologists have far outstripped Mills in theoretical sophistication, but they owe him a deep debt nonetheless for the personal and professional activities that helped set the stage for their own work (Alt, 1985–1986). Mills was not a Marxist, and he did not read Marx until the mid-1950s. Even then he was restricted to the few available English translations, because he could not read German. As Mills had published most of his major works by then, his work was not informed by a very sophisticated Marxian theory.

Mills published two major works that reflected his radical politics as well as his weaknesses in Marxian theory. The first was *White Collar* (1951), an acid critique of the status of a growing occupational category, white-collar workers. The second was *The Power Elite* (1956), a book that sought to show how America was dominated by a small group of businessmen, politicians, and military leaders. Sandwiched in between was his most theoretically sophisticated work, *Character and Social Structure* (1953), coauthored with Hans Gerth. Ironically, considering Mills's major role in the history of Marxian sociological theory, this book was stronger in Weberian and Freudian theory than Marxian theory. Despite this, the book is a major theoretical contribution, though it is not widely read today—possibly because it did not seem to fit well with Mills's best-known radical works. In fact, it was heavily influenced by Hans Gerth, who had a keen interest in Weberian theory.

In the 1950s, Mills's interest moved more in the direction of Marxism and in the problems of the Third World. This interest resulted in a book on the communist revolution in Cuba, *Listen, Yankee: The Revolution in Cuba* (1960) and *The Marxists* (1962). Mills's radicalism put him on the periphery of American sociology. He was the object of much criticism, and he, in turn, became a severe critic of sociology. The critical attitude culminated in *The Sociological Imagination* (1959). Of particular note is Mills's severe criticism of Talcott Parsons and his practice of grand theory. In fact, many sociologists were more familiar with Mills's critique than they were with the details of Parsons's work.

Mills died in 1962, an outcast in sociology. However, before the decade was out, both radical sociology and Marxian theory were to begin to make important inroads into the discipline.

The Development of Conflict Theory

Another precursor to a true union of Marxism and sociological theory was the development of a conflict-theory alternative to structural functionalism. As we have just seen, structural functionalism had no sooner gained leadership in sociological theory than it came under increasing attack. The attack was multifaceted: structural functionalism was accused of such things as being politically conservative, unable to deal with social change because of its focus on static structures, and incapable of adequately analyzing social conflict.

One of the results of this criticism was an effort on the part of a number of sociologists to overcome the problems of structural functionalism by integrating a concern for structure with an interest in conflict. This work constituted the development of *conflict theory* as an alternative to structural-functional theory. Unfortunately, it often seemed little more than a mirror image of structural functionalism with little intellectual integrity of its own.

The first effort of note was Lewis Coser's (1956) book on the functions of social conflict. This work clearly tried to deal with social conflict from within the framework of a structural-functional view of the world. Although it is useful to look at the functions of conflict, there is much more to the study of conflict than an analysis of its positive functions.

Other people sought to reconcile the differences between structural functionalism and conflict theory (Coleman, 1971; Himes, 1966; van den Berghe, 1963). Although these efforts had some utility, the authors were generally guilty of papering over the major differences between the two theoretical alternatives (A. Frank, 1966/1974).

The biggest problem with most of conflict theory was that it lacked what it needed most—a sound basis in Marxian theory. After all, Marxian theory was well developed outside of sociology and should have provided a base on which to develop a sophisticated sociological theory of conflict. The one exception here is the work of Ralf Dahrendorf (born 1929).

Dahrendorf is a European scholar who is well versed in Marxian theory. He sought to embed his conflict theory in the Marxian tradition. However, in the end his conflict theory looked more like a mirror image of structural functionalism than a Marxian theory of conflict. Dahrendorf's major work, *Class and Class Conflict in Industrial Society* (1959), was the most influential piece in conflict theory, but that was largely because it sounded so much like structural functionalism that it was palatable to mainstream sociologists. That is, Dahrendorf operated at the same level of analysis as the structural functionalists (structures and institutions) and looked at many of the same issues. (In other words, structural functionalism and conflict theory are part of the same paradigm; see Appendix.) He recognized that although aspects of the social system could fit together rather neatly, there also could be considerable conflict and tension among them.

In the end, conflict theory should be seen as little more than a transitional development in the history of sociological theory. It failed because it did not go far enough in the direction of Marxian theory. It was still too early in the 1950s and 1960s for American sociology to accept a full-fledged Marxian approach. But conflict theory was helpful in setting the stage for the beginning of that acceptance by the late 1960s.

We should note the contribution to conflict theory by Randall Collins (1975, 1990). On the one hand, Collins's effort suffers from the same weakness as the other works in the conflict tradition: it is relatively impoverished in terms of Marxian theory. However, Collins did point up another weakness in the conflict tradition, and he attempted to overcome it. The problem is that conflict theory generally focuses on social structures; it has little or nothing to say about actors and their thoughts and actions. Collins, schooled in the phenomenological-ethnomethodological tradition (see below), attempted to move conflict theory in this direction.

The Birth of Exchange Theory

Another important theoretical development begun in the 1950s was the rise of exchange theory. The major figure in this development is George Homans, a sociologist whom we left earlier just as he was being drawn to B. F. Skinner's psychological behaviorism. Skinner's behaviorism is the major source of Homans's, and sociology's, exchange theory.

Dissatisfied with Parsons's deductive strategy of developing theory, Homans was casting about for a workable alternative for handling sociological theory inductively. Further, Homans wanted to stay away from the cultural and structural foci of Parsonian theory and wanted to concentrate instead on people and their behavior. With this in mind, Homans turned to the work of his colleague at Harvard, B. F. Skinner. At first, Homans did not see how Skinner's propositions, developed to help explain the behavior of pigeons, might be useful for understanding human social behavior. But as Homans looked further at data from sociological studies of small groups and anthropological studies of primitive societies, he began to see that Skinner's behaviorism was applicable and that it provided a theoretical alternative to Parsonian-style structural functionalism. This led to an article entitled "Social Behavior as Exchange" in 1958 and in 1961 to a full-scale, book-length statement of Homans's theoretical position, *Social Behavior: Its Elementary Forms.* These works represented the birth of exchange theory as an important perspective in sociology. Since then exchange theory has attracted a good deal of attention, both positive and negative.

Homans's basic view was that the heart of sociology lies in the study of individual behavior and interaction. He was little interested in consciousness or in the various kinds of large-scale structures and institutions that were of concern to most sociologists. His main interest was rather in the reinforcement patterns, the history of rewards and costs, that lead people to do what they do. Basically, Homans argued that people continue to do what they have found to be rewarding in the past. Conversely, they cease doing what has proved to be costly in the past. In order to understand behavior, we need to understand an individual's history of rewards and costs. Thus, the focus of sociology should not be on consciousness or on social structures and institutions but on patterns of reinforcement.

As its name suggests, exchange theory is concerned not only with individual behavior but also with interaction between people involving an exchange of rewards and costs. The premise is that interactions are likely to continue when there is an exchange of rewards. Conversely, interactions that are costly to one or both parties are much less likely to continue.

Another major statement in exchange theory is Peter Blau's *Exchange and Power in Social Life,* published in 1964. Blau basically adopted Homans's perspective, but there was an important difference. Whereas Homans was content to deal mainly with elementary forms of social behavior, Blau wanted to integrate this with exchange at the structural and cultural levels, beginning with exchanges among actors, but quickly moving on to the larger structures that emerge out of this exchange. He ended by dealing with exchanges among large-scale structures. This is very different from the exchange theory envisioned by Homans. In some senses, it represents a return to the kind of Parsonsian-style theorizing that Homans found so objectionable. Nevertheless, the effort to deal with both small- and large-scale exchange in an integrated way proved a useful theoretical step.

While he was eclipsed for many years by Homans and Blau, Richard Emerson (1981) has recently emerged as a central figure in exchange theory. He is particularly noted for his effort to develop a more integrated macro-micro approach to exchange theory. In sum, exchange theory has now developed into a significant strand of sociological theory, and it continues to attract new adherents and to take new directions (Cook, O'Brien, and Kollock, 1990; see also below).

Dramaturgical Analysis: The Work of Erving Goffman

Erving Goffman (1922–1982) is often thought of as the last major thinker associated with the original Chicago school. He received his Ph.D. from Chicago in 1953, one year after Herbert Blumer (who had been Goffman's teacher) had left Chicago for Berkeley. Soon after, Goffman joined Blumer at Berkeley, where they were able to develop something of a center of symbolic interactionism. However, it never became anything like Chicago had been. Blumer was past his organizational prime, and Goffman did not become a focus of graduate-student work. After 1952 the fortunes of symbolic interactionism declined, although it continues to be a prominent sociological theory.

In spite of the decline of symbolic interactionism in general, Goffman carved out a strong and distinctive place for himself in contemporary sociological theory. Between the 1950s and the 1970s, Goffman published a series of books and essays that gave birth to dramaturgical analysis as a variant of symbolic interactionism. Although Goffman shifted his attention in his later years, he remained best known for his *dramaturgical theory.*

Goffman's best-known statement of dramaturgical theory, *Presentation of Self in Everyday Life,* was published in 1959. (Over the next fifteen years Goffman published several books and a number of essays that expanded upon his dramaturgical view of the world.) To put it simply, Goffman saw much in common between theatrical performances and the kinds of "acts" we all put on in our day-to-day actions and interactions. Interaction is seen as very fragile, maintained by social performances. Poor performances or disruptions are seen as great threats to social interaction just as they are to theatrical performances.

Goffman went quite far in his analogy between the stage and social interaction. In all social interaction there is a *front region,* which is the parallel of the stage front in a theatrical performance. Actors on the stage and in social life are both seen as being interested in appearances, wearing costumes, and using props. Furthermore, in both there is a *back region,* a place to which the actors can retire to prepare themselves for their performance. Backstage, or offstage in theater terms, the actors can shed their roles and be themselves.

Dramaturgical analysis is clearly consistent with its symbolic-interactionist roots. It has a focus on actors, action, and interaction. Working in the same arena as traditional symbolic interactionism, Goffman found a brilliant metaphor in the theater to shed new light on small-scale social processes.

Goffman's work is widely read today and acknowledged for its originality and its profusion of insights (R. Collins, 1986b; Ditton, 1980). Although he is viewed as an important theorist, not everyone accepts that view. There are several reasons for this. First, he is seen as having been interested in rather esoteric topics rather than the truly essential aspects of social life. Second, he was a micro theorist in an era in which the great rewards have gone to macro theorists. As Randall Collins says, "The more we look at this [Goffman's] work . . . the more he emerges as the leading figure in the microsociology of our times" (1981c:6). Third, he attracted few students who were able to build theoretically upon his insights; indeed, some believe that it is impossible to build upon Goffman's work. It is seen as little more than a series of idiosyncratic bursts of brilliant insight. Finally, little theoretical work has been done by others in the dramaturgical tradition (one exception is Lyman and Scott [1970].)

The one area in which Goffman's work has proved fruitful is in empirical research utilizing his dramaturgical approach. In recent years a number of works employing his dramaturgical approach have appeared, including Snow, Zurcher, and Peters's (1984) study of victory celebrations of crowds at football games as dramaturgical performances, Haas and Shaffir's (1982) dramaturgical analysis of the medical profession, Zurcher's (1985) look at war games, and Kitahara's (1986) study of the dramaturgical devices used by Commodore Perry to open Japan to the West.

It is difficult to predict the future of dramaturgical analysis, although it has been dimmed because Goffman himself later moved in structural directions in his work.

The Development of the "Creative" Sociologies

The 1960s and 1970s witnessed a boom (Ritzer, 1985) in several theoretical perspectives that Monica Morris (1977) lumped together under the heading of "creative" sociology. Included under this heading are phenomenological sociology, ethnomethodology, and existential sociology.

Phenomenological Sociology and the Work of Alfred Schutz (1899–1959)   The philosophy of phenomenology, with its focus on consciousness, has a long history, but the effort to develop a sociological variant of phenomenology can be traced to the publication of Alfred Schutz's *The Phenomenology of the Social World* in Germany in 1932. However, it was not translated into English until 1967, with the result that it has only recently had a dramatic effect on American sociological theory. Schutz arrived in the United States in 1939 after fleeing the Nazis in Austria. Shortly after, he took a position at the New School for Social Research in New York, from which he was able to influence the development of phenomenological, and later ethnomethodological, sociology in the United States.

As we will see in Chapter 10, Schutz took the phenomenological philosophy of Edmund Husserl, which was aimed inward toward an understanding of the transcendental ego, and turned it outward toward a concern for intersubjectivity. Schutz was focally concerned with the way in which people grasp the consciousness of others while they live within their own stream of consciousness. Schutz also used intersubjectivity in a larger sense to mean a concern with the social world, especially the social nature of knowledge.

Much of Schutz's work focuses on an aspect of the social world called the *life-world*, or the world of everyday life. This is an intersubjective world in which people both create social reality and are constrained by the preexisting social and cultural structures created by our predecessors. While much of the life-world is shared, there are also private (biographically articulated) aspects of that world. Within the life-world, Schutz differentiated between intimate face-to-face relationships ("we-relations") and distant and impersonal relationships ("they-relations"). While face-to-face relations are of great importance in the life-world, it is far easier for the sociologist to study more impersonal relations scientifically. Although Schutz turned away from consciousness and to the intersubjective life-world, he did offer insights into consciousness, especially in his thoughts on meaning and people's motives.

Overall, Schutz was concerned with the dialectical relationship between the way people construct social reality and the obdurate social and cultural reality that they inherit from those who preceded them in the social world.

The mid-1960s were crucial in the development of phenomenological sociology. Not only was Alfred Schutz's major work translated and his collected essays published, but Peter Berger and Thomas Luckmann collaborated to publish a book, *The Social Construction of Reality* (1967), that became one of the most widely read theory books of the time. It made at least two important contributions. First, it constituted an introduction to Schutz's ideas that was written in such a way as to make it available to a large American audience. Second, it presented an effort to integrate Schutz's ideas with those of mainstream sociology. Since 1967 phenomenology has grown in popularity in sociology.

Ethnomethodology   Although we will see that there are important differences between them, this theoretical perspective is, in the eyes of many people, hard to distinguish from phenomenology. Indeed, the creator of this perspective, Harold Garfinkel, was a student of Alfred Schutz at the New School. Garfinkel had an interesting intellectual background. He was a student of Parsons in the late 1940s and fused Parsons's orientation with that of Schutz, whom he was exposed to a few years later. After he received his Ph.D. from

Harvard in 1952, Garfinkel arrived in 1954 (Sharrock and Anderson, 1986) at the University of California at Los Angeles (Heritage, 1984), and it was there that ethnomethodology was developed by Garfinkel and his graduate students. Geographically, ethnomethodology was the first distinctive theoretical product of the West Coast, and it has remained centered there to this day (although there is now a large group of British ethnomethodologists). In part, this is a result of the desire of the ethnomethodologists to remain together, but it is at least equally the result of opposition to this perspective by most mainstream sociologists.

Garfinkel became the focal point for a group of students and faculty members at UCLA interested in his approach. A series of seminars was held at UCLA beginning in the early 1950s. Over the years a number of major ethnomethodologists emerged from this milieu.

Ethnomethodology began to receive a wide national audience with the publication in 1967 of Garfinkel's *Studies in Ethnomethodology*. Although written in a difficult and obscure style, the book elicited a lot of interest. Coming at the same time as the translation of Schutz's *The Phenomenology of the Social World* and the publication of Berger and Luckmann's *The Social Construction of Reality*, it seemed to indicate that "subjective" or "creative" sociology was coming of age.

Basically, *ethnomethodology* is the study of "the body of common-sense knowledge and the range of procedures and considerations [the methods] by means of which the ordinary members of society make sense of, find their way about in, and act on the circumstances in which they find themselves" (Heritage, 1984:4). Writers in this tradition are heavily tilted in the direction of the study of everyday life at the individual level. While phenomenological sociologists tend to focus on what people think, ethnomethodologists are more concerned with what people actually do. Thus, ethnomethodologists devote a lot of attention to the detailed study of conversations. Such micro-level concerns stand in stark contrast to the interest of many mainstream sociologists in such large-scale objective phenomena as bureaucracies, capitalism, the division of labor, and the social system. Ethnomethodologists might be interested in these structures as contexts of everyday life; they are not interested in such structures as phenomena in themselves.

Although the works of ethnomethodologists had links to earlier sociological perspectives such as symbolic interactionism and dramaturgical analysis, there was clearly something threatening here to the mainstream sociologists who were still in control of the discipline. In fact, both phenomenology and, more important, ethnomethodology have been subjected to some brutal attacks by mainstream sociologists. Here are two examples. The first is from a review of Garfinkel's *Studies in Ethnomethodology* by James Coleman:

> Garfinkel simply fails to generate any insights at all from the approach. . . .
>
> Perhaps the program would be more fertile in the hands of someone more carefully observant but it is strangely sterile here. . . .

. . . this chapter appears to be not only an ethnomethodological disaster in itself but also evidence of the more general inadequacies of ethnomethodology. . . .
. . . this chapter is another major disaster, combining the rigidities of the most mathematically enraptured technicians with the technical confusions and errors of the soft clinician and without the insights or the technical competence of the creative and trained sociologist.
Once again, Garfinkel elaborates very greatly points which are so commonplace that they would appear banal if stated in straightforward English. As it is, there is an extraordinarily high ratio of reading time to information transfer, so that the banality is not directly apparent upon a casual reading.

(Coleman, 1968:126–130)

The second example is Lewis Coser's 1975 presidential address to the American Sociological Association. Coser saw few redeeming qualities in ethnomethodology and subjected it to a savage attack, engaging in a great deal of name-calling, labeling ethnomethodology "trivial," "a massive cop-out," "an orgy of subjectivism," and a "self-indulgent enterprise." The bitterness of these and other attacks is an indication of the success of both ethnomethodology and phenomenology and the degree to which they represent a threat to the establishment in sociology.

Existential Sociology   Of the three creative sociologies, existential sociology is the least important, at least at the moment. It shares with the other approaches an interest in actors and their thoughts and actions. *Existential sociology* focuses on the complexities of individual life and on the ways actors attempt to deal with those complexities. It has a particular interest in individual feelings, sentiments, and the self. Although it shares a number of intellectual roots with phenomenology and ethnomethodology, existential sociology also tries to separate itself from them (see Fontana, 1980, 1984). It sees itself as more involved in the real world than either of the other creative sociologies. It also has a number of distinctive sources, such as the work of Jean-Paul Sartre (Craib, 1976). Although existential sociology has made some headway in the discipline (for example, Douglas and Johnson, 1977; Hayim, 1980; Kotarba and Fontana, 1984; Manning, 1973; Tiryakian, 1965), it remains on the periphery. But when its influence is combined with that of ethnomethodology and phenomenology, we can see that the creative sociologies are making inroads in sociology despite substantial opposition from many sociologists.

In the last few pages, we have dealt with an array of micro theories— exchange theory, phenomenological sociology, ethnomethodology, and existential sociology. Although the last three theories share a sense of a thoughtful and creative actor, such a view is not held by exchange theorists. Nevertheless, all four theories have a micro orientation to actors and their actions and behavior. In the 1970s, such theories grew in strength in sociology and threatened to replace more macro-oriented theories (such as structural functionalism, conflict theory, neo-Marxian theories) as the dominant theories in sociology (Knorr-Cetina, 1981a; Ritzer, 1985).

Systems Theory

One of the more interesting developments in sociology was the meteoric rise and equally meteoric fall of systems theory. Systems theory more or less burst on the scene in the 1960s, culminating in the publication of Walter Buckley's *Sociology and Modern Systems Theory* in 1967. Systems theory is derived from the hard sciences, where both organic and mechanical entities are viewed in systems terms. *Systems theory* views society as a huge system composed of a number of interrelated parts. It is necessary to examine the relationship among the parts as well as the relationship between the system and other social systems. Concern is also focused on the inputs into the social system, the way the inputs are processed by society, and the outputs that are produced.

Systems theory seemed quite attractive to sociologists in the 1960s. Structural functionalism was under attack, and systems theory seemed a likely successor. After all, Parsons had entitled his 1951 book *The Social System* and had talked in terms that were close to systems theory. Furthermore, systems theory, with its roots in the hard sciences, was very attractive to sociologists interested in furthering scientific sociology. But systems theory was a bright prospect that never blossomed. Little was done with it either theoretically or empirically. Only eleven years after Buckley's book was published, Robert Lilienfeld (1978) published a blistering attack on systems theory for its failures, its scientific pretensions, and its implicit conservative ideology. In recent years systems theory has enjoyed a modest rebirth in the work of Archer (1988) and Bailey (1990).

The Ascendancy of Marxian Sociology

The late 1960s also were the point at which Marxian theory finally began to make significant inroads into American sociological theory (Jay, 1984). There are a number of reasons for this. First, the dominant theory (structural functionalism) was under attack for a number of things, including being too conservative. Second, Mills's radical sociology and conflict theory, although not representing sophisticated Marxian theory, had laid the groundwork for an American theory that was true to the Marxian tradition. Third, the 1960s was the era of black protests, the reawakening of the women's movement, the student movement, and the anti–Vietnam War movement. Many of the young sociologists trained in this atmosphere were attracted to radical ideas. At first, this interest was manifest in what was called in those days "radical sociology" (Colfax and Roach, 1971). This was useful as far as it went, but like Mills's work, it was rather weak on the details of Marxian theory.

It is hard to single out one work as essential to the development of Marxian sociology in America, but one that did play an important role was Henri

Lefebvre's *The Sociology of Marx* (1968). It was important for its essential argument, which was that although Marx was not a sociologist, there was a sociology in Marx. Since that time an increasing number of sociologists have turned to Marx's original work, as well as that of many Marxists, for insights that would be useful in the development of a Marxian sociology. At first this simply meant that American theorists were finally reading Marx seriously, but we now see many significant pieces of Marxian scholarship by American sociologists.

American theorists have been particularly attracted to the work of the critical school, especially because of its fusion of Marxian and Weberian theory. Many of the works have been translated into English, and a number of American scholars have made careers for themselves by writing books about the critical school for an American audience (for example, Jay, 1973, 1986).

Along with an increase in interest has come institutional support for such an orientation. Several journals devote considerable attention to Marxian sociological theory, including *Theory and Society, Telos,* and *Marxist Studies.* A section on Marxist sociology was created in the American Sociological Association in 1977. Not only is the first generation of critical theorists now well known in America, but second-generation thinkers, especially Jurgen Habermas, have received wide recognition.

Of greatest importance is the development of significant pieces of American sociology done from a Marxian point of view. One very significant strand is a group of sociologists doing historical sociology from a Marxian perspective (for example, Skocpol, 1979; Wallerstein, 1974, 1980, 1989). Another is a group analyzing the economic realm from a sociological perspective (for example, Baran and Sweezy, 1966; Braverman, 1974; Burawoy, 1979). Still others are doing fairly traditional empirical sociology, but work that is informed by a strong sense of Marxian theory (Kohn, 1976, for example).

The Challenge of Feminist Theory

Beginning in the late 1970s, precisely at the moment that Marxian sociology gained significant acceptance from American sociologists, a new theoretical outsider issued a challenge to established sociological theories—and even to Marxian sociology itself. This latest brand of radical social thought is contemporary feminist theory.

In Western societies, one can trace the record of critical feminist writings back almost 400 years (Donovan, 1985; Rossi, 1974; Spender, 1982) and there has been an organized political movement by and for women for more than 150 years (Banner, 1984; Carden, 1974; Chafetz and Dworkin, 1986; Deckard, 1979; Giddings, 1984; Kandal, 1988; O'Neill, 1971; Ryan, 1990). In America in 1920, that movement finally won the right for women to vote, fifty-five years after that right had been constitutionally extended to black men. Exhausted and to a degree satiated by victory, the American women's movement over the next thirty years weakened in both size and vigor, only to spring back to life, fully reawakened, in the 1960s. Three factors helped create this new wave of feminist activism: the general climate of critical thinking that characterized the period; the anger of women activists who flocked to the antiwar, civil rights, and student movements only to encounter the sexist attitudes of the liberal and radical men in those movements (Densimore, 1973; Evans, 1980; Morgan, 1970; Shreve, 1989; Snitow, et al., 1983); and women's experience of prejudice and discrimination as they moved in ever larger numbers into wage work and higher education (Bookman and Morgen, 1988; Garland, 1988; Lengermann and Wallace, 1985; MacKinnon, 1979). For these reasons, particularly the last, the women's movement in this new second phase continued to expand during the 1970s and into the 1980s, even though the activism of many other 1960s movements faded. Moreover during these years activism by and for women became an international phenomenon.

A major feature of this international women's movement has been an explosively growing new literature on women that makes visible all aspects of women's hitherto unconsidered lives and experiences. This literature, which is popularly referred to as *women's studies* or the *new scholarship on women*, is the work of an international and interdisciplinary community of writers, located both within and outside universities and writing for both the general public and specialized academic audiences. In what must be one of the more impressive examples of sustained intellectual work in recent times, feminist scholars have launched a probing, multifaceted critique that makes visible the complexity of the system that subordinates women.

Feminist theory is the theoretical strand running through this literature: sometimes implicit in writings on such substantive issues as work (Daniels, 1988; Kanter, 1977; Rollins, 1985) or rape (Sanday, 1990; Scully, 1990) or popular culture (Radway, 1984); sometimes centrally and explicitly presented, as in the analyses of motherhood by Adrienne Rich (1976), Nancy Chodorow (1978), and Jessica Benjamin (1988); and as the new scholarship on women has achieved critical mass, with increasing frequency the sole, systematic effort of a piece of writing. Of this recent spate of wholly theoretical writing, certain statements have been particularly salient to sociology because they are directed to sociologists by people well versed in sociological theory (Chafetz, 1984; P. Collins, 1990; Cook and Fonow, 1986; Hartsock, 1983; Lengermann and Niebrugge-Brantley, 1990; Smith, 1979, 1987, 1990a; Stacey and Thorne, 1986; Wallace, 1989). Journals that bring feminist theory to the attention of sociologists include *Signs, Feminist Studies, Sociological Inquiry*, and *Gender and Society*, as does the professional association Sociologists for Women in Society (S.W.S.) and the National Women's Studies Association (NWSA).

Feminist theory looks at the world from the vantage point of a hitherto unrecognized and invisible minority, women, with an eye to discovering the significant but unacknowledged ways in which the activities of that minority help to create our world. This viewpoint dramatically reworks our understanding of social life. From this base, feminist theorists have begun to challenge sociological theory.

Those issuing this challenge argue that sociologists have persistently refused to incorporate the insights of the new scholarship on women into their discipline's understanding of the social world. Instead, feminist sociologists have been segregated from the mainstream, and feminism's comprehensive theory of social organization has been reduced to a single research variable, sex, and a simple social role pattern, gender (Farnham, 1987; Smith, 1990b; Stacey and Thorne, 1985; Wallace, 1989; Yeatman, 1987). To date these charges seem valid. Reasons for sociology's avoidance of feminist theory may include deep antifeminist prejudices, suspicion of the scientific credentials of a theory so closely associated with political activism, and caution born of half recognition of the profoundly radical implications of feminist theory for sociological theory and method. Yet it should also be remembered that it took some time for Marxian theory to "arrive" in sociology and that a significant body of explicitly theoretical feminist writings is a very recent event in academic life. These writings have begun, however, to assume a critical mass. They offer an exciting new and important theory of social life. And those whose experiences and perceptions make them a receptive audience for this theory—women in general and both women and men affected by feminism in particular—are an important constituency in the sociological community. For all these reasons, implications of feminist theory are moving increasingly into the mainstream of the discipline.

Structuralism and Poststructuralism

One development that we have said little about up to this point is the increase in interest in *structuralism* (Lemert, 1990). Usually traced to France (and often called *French structuralism* [Clark and Clark, 1982; Kurzweil, 1980]), structuralism has now become an international phenomenon. Although its roots lie outside sociology, structuralism clearly has made its way into sociology. The problem is that structuralism in sociology still is so undeveloped that it is difficult to define it with any precision. The problem is exacerbated by structuralism's more or less simultaneous development in a number of fields; it is difficult to find one single coherent statement of structuralism. Indeed, there are significant differences among the various branches of structuralism.

We can get a preliminary feeling for structuralism by delineating the basic differences that exist among those who support a structuralist perspective. There are those who focus on what they call the "deep structures of the mind." It is their view that these unconscious structures lead people to think and act as they do. The work of the psychoanalyst Sigmund Freud might be seen as an example of this orientation. Then there are structuralists who focus on the invisible larger structures of society and see them as determinants of the actions of people as well as of society in general. Marx is sometimes thought of as someone who practiced such a brand of structuralism, with his focus on the unseen economic structure of capitalist society. Still another group sees structures as the models they construct of the social world. Finally, a number of structuralists are concerned with the dialectical relationship between individuals and social structures. They see a link between the structures of the mind and the structures of society. The anthropologist Claude Lévi-Strauss is most often associated with this view.

The problem with structural sociology at the moment is that it remains largely a melange of ideas derived from various fields, including linguistics (Saussure), anthropology (Lévi-Strauss), psychology (Freud, Lacan), and Marxism (Althusser). Until these ideas are put together in a coherent fashion, structuralism will remain marginal to sociology. However, the developments in related fields have been so significant and so attractive to those in sociology that a structural theory in sociology is likely to attract more attention in coming years.

As structuralism grows within sociology, outside of sociology a movement is developing beyond the early premises of structuralism: *poststructuralism* (Lemert, 1990). The major representative of poststructuralism is Michel Foucault. In his early work, Foucault focused on structures, but he later moved beyond structures to focus on power and the linkage between knowledge and power. More generally, poststructuralists accept the importance of structure but go beyond it to encompass a wide range of other concerns.

SOCIOLOGICAL THEORY IN THE 1990s

While many of the developments discussed in the preceding pages are still important in the 1990s, in this section we will deal with four broad movements that promise to be of utmost importance in this decade, as well as decades to come—the interest in micro-macro integration, agency-structure integration, theoretical syntheses, and metatheorizing in sociology.

Micro-Macro Integration

A good deal of the most recent work in American sociological theory has been concerned with the linkage between micro and macro theories and levels of analysis. In fact, I have argued (Ritzer, 1990a) that micro-macro linkage emerged as the central problematic in American sociological theory in the 1980s and it continues to be of focal concern in the 1990s.

There are a number of recent examples of efforts to link micro-macro levels of analysis and/or theories. In my own work (Ritzer, 1979; 1981a), I have sought to develop an integrated sociological paradigm that integrates micro and macro levels in both their objective and subjective forms. Thus, in my view, there are four major levels of social analysis that must be dealt with in an integrated manner—macro-subjectivity, macro-objectivity, micro-subjectivity, and micro-objectivity. Jeffrey Alexander (1982–83) has created a "multi-dimensional sociology" which deals, at least in part, with a model of levels of analysis that closely resembles the model developed by Ritzer. Alexander (1987) develops his model based on the problem of order, which is seen as having individual (micro) and collective (macro) levels, and the problem of action, which is viewed as possessing materialist (objective) and idealist (subjective) levels. Out of these two continuua, Alexander develops four major levels of analysis—collective-idealist, collective-materialist, individual-idealist, individual-materialist. While the overall model developed by Alexander is strikingly similar to Ritzer's, Alexander accords priority to the collective-idealist level, while Ritzer insists that we be concerned with the dialectical relationship among all levels. Still another kindred approach is developed by Norbert Wiley (1988) who also delineates four very similar major levels of analysis—self or individual, interaction, social structure, and culture. However, while both Ritzer and Alexander focus on both objective and subjective levels, Wiley's are purely subjective. James Coleman (1986) has concentrated on the micro-to-macro problem, while Allen Liska (1990) has extended Coleman's approach to deal with the macro-to-micro problem as well. Coleman (1990) has recently extended his micro-to-macro model and developed a much more elaborate theory of the micro-macro relationship based on a rational choice approach derived from economics.

There are many other efforts at micro-macro integration (see Chapter 14). There is much work to be done on this issue, and it promises to be a significant area of concern in American sociological theory for some time to come.

Agency-Structure Integration

Paralleling the growth in interest in the United States in micro-macro integration, has been a concern in Europe for agency-structure integration. Just as I saw the micro-macro issue as the central problem in American theory, Margaret Archer (1988) sees the agency-structure topic as the basic concern in European social theory. While there are many similarities between the micro-macro and agency-structure literatures, there are also substantial differences between them. For example, while agents are usually micro-level actors, collectivities like labor unions can also be agents. And while structures are usually macro-level phenomena, we also find structures at the micro-level. Thus, we must be careful in equating these two bodies of work and much care needs to be taken in trying to interrelate them.

There are four major efforts underway in contemporary European social theory that can be included under the heading of agency-structure integration. The first is Anthony Giddens's (1984) structuration theory. The key to Giddens's approach is that he sees agency and structure as a "duality." That is, they cannot be separated from one another: agency is implicated in structure and structure is involved in agency. Giddens refuses to see structure as simply constraining (as, for example, does Durkheim), but sees structure as both constraining *and* enabling. Margaret Archer (1982) rejects the idea that agency and structure can be viewed as a duality, but rather sees them as a dualism. That is, agency and structure can and should be separated. In distinguishing them, we become better able to analyze their relationship to one another.

Archer (1988) is also notable for extending the structure-agency literature to a concern for the relationship between culture and agency.

While both Giddens and Archer are British, the third major contemporary figure involved in the agency-structure literature is Pierre Bourdieu (1977) from France. In Bourdieu's work, the agency-structure issue translates into a concern for the relationship between habitus and field. Habitus is an internalized mental, or cognitive, structure, through which people deal with the social world. The habitus both produces, and is produced by, the society. The field is a network of relations among objective positions. The structure of the field serves to constrain agents, be they individuals or collectivities. Overall, Bourdieu is concerned with the relationship between habitus and field. While the field conditions the habitus, the habitus constitutes the field. Thus, there is a dialectical relationship between habitus and field.

The final major theorist of the agency-structure linkage is the German, Jurgen Habermas. We have already mentioned Habermas as a significant contemporary contributor to critical theory. In his more recent work, Habermas (1987) has dealt with the agency-structure issue under the heading of "the colonization of the life-world." The life-world is a micro-world where people interact and communicate. The system has its roots in the life-world, but it ultimately comes to develop its own structural characteristics. As these structures grow in independence and power, they come to exert more and more control over the life-world. In the modern world, the system has come to "colonize" the life-world, that is, to exert control over it.

As we will see in Chapter 15, there is much more to agency-structure integration than the work of Giddens, Archer, Bourdieu and Habermas. However, they are the major representatives of this contemporary genre of sociological theory.

Theoretical Syntheses

The movements toward micro-macro and agency-structure integration began in the 1980s and both continue to be strong in the 1990s. They set the stage for the broader movement toward theoretical syntheses which began at about the beginning of the 1990s. What is involved here is a wide-ranging effort to synthesize two or more different theories (for example, structural functionalism and symbolic interactionism). Such efforts have always occurred in the history of sociological theory. However, there are two distinctive aspects of the new synthetic work in sociological theory. First, it is very widespread and not restricted to isolated attempts at synthesis. Secondly, the goal is generally a relatively narrow synthesis of theoretical ideas, and not the development of a grand synthetic theory that overarches all of sociological theory.

These synthetic works are occurring within and among many of the theories discussed in this chapter as well as in and among some theories we have yet to mention.

Within structural functionalism, we have seen the rise of neofunctionalism

(Alexander, 1985; Alexander and Colomy, 1985; Alexander and Colomy, 1990; Colomy, 1990a). Neofunctionalism seeks to overcome many of the limitations of structural functionalism by integrating into it ideas derived from a wide range of other theories. Alexander and Colomy see this as a dramatic reconstruction of structural functionalism so that a new name, neofunctionalism, is required to differentiate this new theoretical approach from its ancestor.

Symbolic interactionism is undergoing a dramatic transformation as it has, in Fine's terms, "cobbled a new theory from the shards of other theoretical approaches" (1990:136–137). Thus symbolic interactionists are borrowing ideas from phenomenological sociology, feminist theory, and exchange theory, among others. In addition, major figures in the history of symbolic interactionism such as Mead and Blumer are being redefined as being more synthetic and integrative theorists.

Exchange theory has long had integrative and synthetic works like Blau's *Exchange and Power in Social Life* (1964). In recent years increasing attention is being devoted to the work of Richard Emerson (1972a; 1972b) and that of his disciples, especially Karen Cook (1987a). Emerson began with the principles of behaviorism, but ultimately sought to relate them to social structure and social exchange relationships. More recently, Cook, O'Brien and Kollock (1990) have come to define exchange theory in inherently integrative terms and to synthesize it with ideas derived from other theories such as symbolic interactionism and network theory.

A relatively new, and inherently synthetic development in sociological theory is the rise of postmodernist social theory (Baudrillard, 1983; Harvey, 1989; Lyotard, 1984; Kellner, 1990a, 1990b). This theory is premised on the idea that we have moved in recent years from a modern to a postmodern society. While modern society was highly rational and rigid, postmodern society is viewed as more irrational and more flexible. A new, postmodernist theory has arisen to analyze this new type of society. Postmodernist theory is inherently integrative drawing upon ideas from a wide range of disciplines—philosophy, cultural theory, and social theory, among others. Moreover, postmodernists reject the idea of the development of a single grand overarching theory, or as they call it, a "metadiscourse." Rather, postmodernists argue for far narrower and specific synthetic efforts of the kind being undertaken in sociological theory in the 1990s.

Post-Marxist theory encompasses three synthetic theoretical developments. The first is analytic Marxism which involves the efforts to bring "state-of-the-art" methods of analytical philosophy and social science to bear on traditional Marxian concerns. Thus, for example, a number of theorists (Roemer, 1986c; Elster, 1985) are using the ideas of rational choice theory to analyze Marxian issues. Others (for example, Wright, 1985) are employing mainstream sociological methods to analyze such issues as class. The second is a set of postmodern Marxists (for example, Laclau and Mouffe, 1985; Jameson, 1984; Harvey, 1989) who are borrowing ideas from postmodernist theory and synthesizing them with aspects of traditional Marxian theory. Finally, there is the work of Bowles and Gintis (1987) which seeks to integrate Marxian and liberal theory.

Many other synthetic efforts will be discussed in Chapters 16 and 17.

Metatheorizing in Sociology

Metatheorizing may be defined very broadly as the systematic study of the underlying structure of sociological theory (Ritzer, 1990c, 1990d, forthcoming b, forthcoming c). It may be distinguished from theorizing even though most theorists have done metatheorizing and most metatheorists have also theorized. While metatheorists take theory as their subject of study, theorists think about the social world. There has been a considerable increase in metatheoretical work (Fuhrman and Snizek, 1990), and there is every sign that such work will continue to grow in the future.

Metatheoretical work has been part of sociology since the inception of the field. Most of the early theorists did metatheoretical studies of their intellectual ancestors. Particularly notable are Marx's studies of Hegel, the Young Hegelians, the political economists, and the utopian socialists. Parsons's *The Structure of Social Action* (1937, 1949) is described by him as an "empirical" study of the work of his theoretical ancestors. In the 1950s Paul Furfey (1953/1965) offered the first, albeit significantly flawed, systematic effort to define metatheoretical work. Alvin Gouldner's attempt in *The Coming Crisis of Western Sociology* (1970) to define a sociology of sociological theory is an important, although also flawed, precursor to contemporary metatheorizing. A specific set of works (Friedrichs, 1970; Ritzer 1975a), based on Thomas Kuhn's (1962, 1970) concept of a paradigm, also played a key role in the development of metatheoretical work in sociology.

Metatheorizing in sociology is coming of age in the 1990s (see Appendix) and it promises to play a central role in clarifying extant sociological theories as well as in helping in the development of new integrative and synthetic theories.

SUMMARY

This chapter picks up where Chapter 1 left off and deals with the history of sociological theory since the beginning of the twentieth century. We begin with the early history of American sociological theory, which was characterized by its liberalism, by its interest in Social Darwinism, and consequently by the influence of Herbert Spencer. In this context, the work of the two early sociological theorists, Sumner and Ward, is discussed. However, they did not leave a lasting imprint on American sociological theory. In contrast, the Chicago school, as embodied in the work of people like Small, Park, Thomas, Cooley, and, especially Mead, did leave a strong mark on sociological theory, especially on symbolic interactionism.

While the Chicago school was still predominant, a different form of sociological theory began to develop at Harvard. Pitirim Sorokin played a key role in the founding of sociology at Harvard, but it was Talcott Parsons who was to lead Harvard to a position of preeminence in American theory, replacing Chicago's symbolic interactionism. Parsons was important not only for legitimizing "grand theory" in the United States and for introducing European theorists to an American audience but also for his role in the development of action theory and, more important, structural functionalism. In the 1940s and 1950s, structural functionalism was furthered by the disintegration of the Chicago school that began in the 1930s and was largely complete by the 1950s.

The major development in Marxian theory in the early years of the twentieth century was the creation of the Frankfurt, or critical, school. This Hegelianized form of Marxism also showed the influence of sociologists like Weber and of the psychoanalyst Sigmund Freud. Marxism did not gain a widespread following among sociologists in the early part of the century.

Structural functionalism's dominance within American theory in mid-century was rather short-lived. Although traceable to a much earlier date, phenomenological sociology, especially the work of Alfred Schutz, began to attract significant attention in the 1960s. Marxian theory was still largely excluded from American theory, but C. Wright Mills kept a radical tradition alive in America in the 1940s and 1950s. Mills also was one of the leaders of the attacks on structural functionalism, attacks that mounted in intensity in the 1950s and 1960s. In light of some of these attacks, a conflict-theory alternative to structural functionalism emerged in this period. Although influenced by Marxian theory, conflict theory suffered from an inadequate integration of Marxism. Still another alternative born in the 1950s was exchange theory, and it continues to attract a small but steady number of followers. Although symbolic interactionism was in eclipse, the work of Erving Goffman on dramaturgical analysis in this period kept it from being moribund.

Important developments took place in the "creative sociologies" in the 1960s and 1970s. Phenomenological sociology, ethnomethodology, and existential sociology continue to attract a great deal of attention in sociology. At the same time, Marxian sociology came into its own, and its several varieties continue to cause a great deal of excitement in sociological theory. While creative sociology and Marxian theory have been on the rise, systems theory gained popularity in the 1960s only to encounter a dramatic drop in popularity in the 1970s. Among the most important recent developments in sociological theory are feminist theory, structuralism, and poststructuralism.

Four developments are most striking about sociological theory in the 1980s and 1990s. First, is the rise in interest in the United States in the micro-macro link. Second, is the parallel increase in attention in Europe to the relationship between agency and structure. Third, there is the growth, especially in the 1990s, of a wide range of synthetic efforts. Finally, there is the increase in interest in metatheoretical work, or the systematic study of sociological theory.

CHAPTER 7

STRUCTURAL FUNCTIONALISM AND THE CONFLICT-THEORY ALTERNATIVE

CONSENSUS AND CONFLICT
STRUCTURAL FUNCTIONALISM
  Historical Roots
  The Functional Theory of Stratification and Its Critics
  The Functional Prerequisites of a Society
  Talcott Parsons's Structural Functionalism
  Robert Merton's Structural Functionalism
  The Major Criticisms
THE CONFLICT-THEORY ALTERNATIVE
  The Work of Ralf Dahrendorf
  The Major Criticisms
  Efforts to Reconcile Structural Functionalism and Conflict Theory
  Toward a More Marxian Conflict Theory

*T*HE first part of this chapter focuses on structural functionalism, which was for many years *the* dominant sociological theory. However, in the last two decades structural functionalism has declined in importance and, in at least some senses, has receded into the (recent) history of sociological theory. Thus, Colomy (1990a) now describes structural functionalism as a theoretical "tradition." Its main importance today is its role in the history of sociological theory and its contribution to the formation of "one of sociology's most significant contemporary developments"—neofunctionalism (Colomy, 1990b: xlvii). We will discuss neofunctionalism in Part Three of this book, where we deal with the most recent, synthetic developments in sociological theory.

A similar argument can be made about conflict theory, which will be the focus of the second part of this chapter. We will discuss traditional conflict theory there, while in Part Three we will focus on some of the newer, more integrative work in conflict theory.

This chapter begins with a discussion of some of structural functionalism's basic principles and historical roots. Then we discuss three major examples of classic structural functionalism—the functional theory of stratification, the functional prerequisites of society, and, most important, Talcott Parsons's structural-functional theory. Next, we analyze Robert Merton's efforts to deal with some of the problems in classic structural functionalism and to develop a more adequate theoretical perspective. We then turn to the major criticisms of structural functionalism, critiques that helped lead to the loss of its dominant position in sociological theory.

In the second part of the chapter, we discuss conflict theory, especially the work of Ralf Dahrendorf, as an alternative to structural functionalism. We also deal with the major criticisms of conflict theory, the most important of which is that it is not true to its Marxian roots.

CONSENSUS AND CONFLICT

Before turning to the specifics of structural functionalism and conflict theory, we need, following Thomas Bernard (1983), to place these theories in the broader context of the debate between consensus theories (one of which is structural functionalism) and conflict theories (one of which is the sociological conflict theory to be discussed in this chapter). *Consensus theories* see shared norms and values as fundamental to society, focus on social order based on tacit agreements, and view social change as occurring in a slow and orderly fashion. In contrast, *conflict theories* emphasize the dominance of some social groups by others, see social order as based on manipulation and control by dominant groups, and view social change as occurring rapidly and in a disorderly fashion as subordinate groups overthrow dominant groups.

Although these criteria broadly define the essential differences between the sociological theories of structural functionalism and conflict theory, Bernard's view is that the disagreement is far broader and has "been a recurring debate that has taken a variety of different forms throughout the history of Western thought" (1983:6). Bernard traced the debate back to ancient Greece and the differences between Plato (consensus) and Aristotle (conflict). He traced the debate through the history of philosophy, through (the conflict thinker is listed first) Augustine and Aquinas, Machiavelli and Hobbes, and Locke and Rousseau. Later, in sociology the debate was joined by (again, conflict theorist listed first) Marx and Comte, Simmel and Durkheim, and Dahrendorf and Parsons. We already have examined the ideas of the first two pairs of sociologists (although, as we have seen, their work is far broader than is implied by the label of "conflict" or "consensus" theorist); in this chapter we examine Dahrendorf's conflict theory and Parsons's consensus theory, among others.

Bernard differentiates among four types of consensus and conflict theories, but we focus on only two of them, *sociological consensus* (Parsons, Merton) and *sociological conflict* (Dahrendorf) in this chapter. A third type, *radical conflict theory*, has been touched on in the chapter on Marx and will be discussed further in the chapter on neo-Marxian theories. Bernard's final type, *conservative consensus theory*, will not be discussed because it "is not widely held among modern sociologists" (1983:201).

Although we emphasize the differences between structural functionalism and conflict theory, we should not forget that there are important similarities between them. In fact, Bernard argues that "the areas of agreement among them are more extensive than the areas of disagreement" (1983:214). For example, they are both macro-level theories focally concerned with large-scale social structures and social institutions. In George Ritzer's (1980) terms, both theories exist within the same sociological ("social facts") paradigm (see the Appendix).

Before turning to a more specific discussion of structural functionalism, we need to reflect on the consensus-conflict distinction from the vantage point of the 1990s. First, it tended to oversimplify the realities of structural function-alism and conflict theory, as well as the distinctions between them. Many conflict theorists were interested in order and what held society together, and it was not unusual for structural functionalists to be interested in tension, change, and forces that were leading to disintegration in society. Second, the consensus-conflict distinction was more useful in the 1960s, when efforts were being made to rigidly distinguish between these theories and then to make the case for one or the other. Third, with the general movement in sociological theory toward integration and synthesis, and with significant work in neo-functionalism and conflict theory now being oriented in this direction, a con-sensus-conflict distinction is even less accurate today than it was in the past.

STRUCTURAL FUNCTIONALISM

Robert Nisbet argued that structural functionalism was "without any doubt, the single most significant body of theory in the social sciences in the present century" (cited in Turner and Maryanski, 1979:xi). Kingsley Davis (1959) took the position that structural functionalism was, for all intents and purposes, synonymous with sociology. Alvin Gouldner (1970) implicitly took a similar position when he attacked Western sociology largely through a critical anal-ysis of the structural-functional theories of Talcott Parsons.

Despite its undoubted hegemony in the two decades after World War II, structural functionalism has declined in importance as a sociological theory. Even Wilbert Moore, a man who was intimately associated with this theory, argued that it had "become an embarrassment in contemporary theoretical sociology" (1978:321). Two observers even stated: "Thus, functionalism as an explanatory theory is, we feel, 'dead' and continued efforts to use function-alism as a theoretical explanation should be abandoned in favor of more prom-ising theoretical perspectives" (Turner and Maryanski, 1979:141).[1] Nicholas Demerath and Richard Peterson (1967) took a more positive view, arguing that structural functionalism is not a passing fad. However, they admitted that it is likely to evolve into another sociological theory, just as this theory itself evolved out of the earlier organicism (see the following section). The rise of neofunctionalism (see Chapter 16) seems to support Demerath and Peter-

---

[1] Despite this statement, Jonathan Turner and Alexandra Maryanski (1979) are willing to argue that functionalism can continue to be useful as a method.

son's position rather than the more negative perspective of Turner and Maryanski.

In structural functionalism, the terms *structural* and *functional* need not be used in conjunction, although they are typically conjoined. We could study the structures of society without being concerned with their functions (or consequences) for other structures. Similarly, we could examine the functions of a variety of social processes that may not take a structural form. Still, the concern for both elements characterizes structural functionalism.

Mark Abrahamson (1978) argued that structural functionalism is not monolithic. He identified three varieties of structural functionalism. The first is *individualistic functionalism.* Here the focus is on the needs of actors and the various large-scale structures (for example, social institutions, cultural values) that emerge as functional responses to these needs. The anthropologist Bronislaw Malinowski was a major proponent of this perspective. The second is *interpersonal functionalism,* and the exemplar was another anthropologist, A. B. Radcliffe-Brown. Here the focus is on social relationships, particularly the mechanisms to accommodate strains that exist in such relationships. The third variety, *societal functionalism,* is the dominant approach among sociological structural functionalists (Sztompka, 1974), and as such will be the focus of this chapter. The primary concern of societal functionalism is the large-scale social structures and institutions of society, their interrelationships, and their constraining effects on actors.

Historical Roots

Three classic sociologists were the most important influences on contemporary structural functionalism: Auguste Comte, Herbert Spencer, and Emile Durkheim (Turner and Maryanski, 1979).

Comte had a normative conception of the "good" society, which led to an interest in what any given social phenomenon contributes to that society. He also had a sense of equilibrium within societies. However, his theory of *organicism*—the tendency to see analogies between societies and biological organisms—was his most influential concept. He viewed social systems as organic systems that functioned in much the same way as biological organisms. Thus, whereas biology was to study the individual organism, sociology was to study the social organism. Among the specific analogies that Comte saw between biological and social organisms were those of cells on the biological level to families in the social world, of tissues to social classes and castes, and of the organs of the body to cities and communities in the social world.

The English sociologist Herbert Spencer also adopted organicism, but in his sociology it coexisted uncomfortably with a utilitarian philosophy. Thus although his organicism led him to look at social wholes and the contributions of parts to the whole, his utilitarianism led him to focus on self-seeking actors. Despite the intellectual problem this presented, Spencer's organicism was influential in the development of structural functionalism.

Spencer saw various similarities between social and individual organisms. First, both social and individual organisms grow and develop, whereas inorganic matter does not. Second, in both, an increase in size tends to lead to increasing complexity and differentiation. Third, progressive differentiation of structures in both tends to be accompanied by progressive differentiation in function. Fourth, the parts of both organisms are mutually interdependent. Thus a change in one is likely to lead to changes in the other parts. Finally, each of the parts of both social and individual entities can be seen as an organism in itself.

Spencer had a number of other insights that were influential in the development of structural functionalism. His concern with the "needs" of the social organism was picked up by later structural functionalists, who, among other things, translated it into the idea that societies "need" various things in order to survive. Spencer also developed a law of social evolution, which influenced the development of later structural-functional theories of evolution, such as those associated with Durkheim and Parsons. Perhaps of greatest importance was Spencer's use of the terms *structure* and *function* as well as his differentiation between them. He tended to speak of the functions that various structures had for the society as a whole.

Although both Comte and Spencer are important in their own right, their greatest impact on structural functionalism came through their effect on the thinking of Durkheim. Most generally, Durkheim's interest in social facts reflected an interest in the parts of the social organism and their interrelationships as well as their impact on the society as a whole. In terms of structural functionalism, Durkheim had much to say about structures, functions, and their relationship to the needs of society. Perhaps of greatest importance was his separation of the concepts of social cause and social function. The study of social causes is concerned with why a given structure exists as well as why it takes a certain form. In contrast, the study of social functions is concerned with the needs of the larger system met by a given structure. Durkheim's emphasis on morality and cultural factors (for example, in his ideas on the collective conscience and collective representations) had a profound effect on Parsons, who came, as we will see, to a similar position. Finally, Durkheim's emphasis on the strains in modern society, especially anomie, and how they were dealt with had an important impact on structural functionalism, especially the work of Robert Merton (see below).[2]

Modern structural functionalism operates on the basis of several assumptions derived from the ideas of these three classic sociologists. Structural functionalists, especially the societal functionalists, are likely to take a macroscopic approach to the study of social phenomena. They focus on the social system

---

[2] In addition to the figures discussed above, Weber also influenced Parsons (and other structural functionalists), although the impact was far greater on Parsons's action theory than on his structural functionalism.

as a whole as well as on the impact of the various parts (especially social structures and social institutions) on it.

They tend to see the components of the system as contributing positively to its continued operation (Abrahamson, 1978).[3] In addition, structural functionalism is concerned with the relationship of one part of the system to another (Davis, 1959). The parts of the system, as well as the system as a whole, are seen as existing in a state of equilibrium, so that changes in one part lead to changes in other parts. Changes in parts may balance each other so that there is no change in the system as a whole; if they do not, the entire system probably changes. Thus although structural functionalism adopts an equilibrium perspective, it is not necessarily a static point of view. In this equilibrium of the social system, those changes that do occur are seen as doing so in an orderly, not a revolutionary, way.

Let us now discuss some more concrete examples of structural functionalism.

The Functional Theory of Stratification and Its Critics

The functional theory of stratification as articulated by Kingsley Davis and Wilbert Moore (1945) is perhaps the best-known single piece of work in structural-functional theory. Davis and Moore made it clear that they regarded social stratification as both universal and necessary. They argued that no society is ever unstratified, or totally classless. Stratification is, in their view, a *functional* necessity. All societies need such a system, and this need brings into existence a system of stratification.[4] They also viewed a stratification system as a structure, pointing out that stratification refers not to the individuals in the stratification system but rather to a system of *positions*. They focused on how certain positions come to carry with them different degrees of prestige and not on how individuals come to occupy certain positions.

Given this focus, the major functional issue is how a society motivates and places people in their "proper" positions in the stratification system. This is reducible to two problems. First, how does a society instill in the "proper" individuals the desire to fill certain positions? Second, once people are in the right positions, how does society then instill in them the desire to fulfill the requirements of those positions?

The problem of proper social placement in society arises from three basic reasons. First, some positions are more pleasant to occupy than others. Second,

---

[3] As we will see, some structural functionalists (especially Merton) did deal with strains and negative effects (dysfunctions).

[4] This is an example of a teleological argument. We will have occasion to discuss this issue later in the chapter, but for now we can define a *teleological argument* as one that sees the social world as having purposes, or goals, which bring needed structures or events into being. In this case society "needs" stratification, so it brings such a system into existence.

some positions are more important to the survival of society than others. Third, social positions require different abilities and talents.

Although these issues apply to all social positions, Davis and Moore were concerned with the functionally more important positions in society. The positions that rank high within the stratification system are presumed to be those that are *less* pleasant to occupy but *more* important to the survival of society and that require the greatest ability and talent. In addition, society must attach sufficient rewards to these positions so that enough people will seek to occupy them and the individuals who do come to occupy them will work diligently. The converse was implied by Davis and Moore but not discussed. That is, low-ranking positions in the stratification system are presumed to be *more* pleasant and *less* important and to require less ability and talent. Also, society has less need to be sure that individuals occupy these positions and perform their duties with diligence.

Davis and Moore did not argue that a society consciously develops a stratification system in order to be sure that the high-level positions are filled, and filled adequately. Rather, they made it clear that stratification is an "unconsciously evolved device." However, it is a device that every society does, and *must*, develop if it is to survive.

In order to be sure that people occupy the higher-ranking positions, society must, in Davis and Moore's view, provide these individuals with various rewards, including great prestige, high salary, and sufficient leisure. For example, to ensure enough doctors for our society, we need to offer them these and other rewards. Davis and Moore implied that we could not expect people to undertake the "burdensome" and "expensive" process of medical education if we did not offer such rewards. The implication seems to be that people at the top must receive the rewards that they do. If they did not, those positions would remain understaffed or unfilled and society would crumble.

The structural-functional theory of stratification has been subject to much criticism since its publication in 1945 (see Tumin, 1953, for the first important criticism; Huaco, 1966, for a good summary of the main criticisms to that date).

One basic criticism is that the functional theory of stratification simply perpetuates the privileged position of those people who already have power, prestige, and money. It does this by arguing that such people deserve their rewards; indeed they need to be offered such rewards for the good of society.

The functional theory also can be criticized for assuming that simply because a stratified social structure has existed in the past, it must continue to exist in the future. It is possible that future societies can be organized in other, nonstratified ways.

In addition, it has been argued that the idea of functional positions varying in their importance to society is difficult to support. Are garbage collectors really any less important to the survival of society than advertising executives? Despite the lower pay and prestige of the garbage collectors, they actually may be *more* important to the survival of the society. Even in cases where it could be said that one position serves a more important function for society, the greater rewards do not necessarily accrue to the more important position. Nurses may be much more important to society than movie stars, but nurses have far less power, prestige, and income than movie stars.

Is there really a scarcity of people capable of filling high-level positions? In fact, many people are prevented from obtaining the training they need to achieve prestigious positions, even though they have the ability. In the medical profession, for example, there is a persistent effort to limit the number of practicing doctors. In general, many able people never get a chance to show that they can handle high-ranking positions even though there is a clear need for them and their contributions. The fact is that those in high-ranking positions have a vested interest in keeping their numbers small and their power and income high.

Finally, it can be argued that we do not have to offer people power, prestige, and income to get them to want to occupy high-level positions. People can be equally motivated by the satisfaction of doing a job well or by the opportunity to be of service to others.

The Functional Prerequisites of a Society

One of the major concerns of structural functionalists is an analysis of the things—the structures, and particularly the functions—that a social system needs in order to survive. We shall examine the major example of this kind of analysis by D. F. Aberle and his associates (1950/1967). Later in this chapter, we will discuss a more general effort by Parsons to define the four functional prerequisites of any action system—adaptation, goal attainment, integration, and pattern maintenance.

Aberle and his colleagues discuss the basic conditions that, were they to cease to exist, would cause the termination of society. The first factor deals with the population characteristics of the society. The extinction, or the dispersion, of its population clearly would threaten the existence of society. This would occur if society lost enough of its population to make its various structures inoperative. Second, an apathetic population would be a threat to society. Although this is a question of degree, because some segments of a society always manifest at least some apathy, at some point the population could become so apathetic that various components of society would cease to operate, and ultimately the entire society would disintegrate. Third, a war of "all against all" within the population would threaten society's existence. A high level of internal conflict within society would require the intervention of various social control agents who would use force to contain the conflict. Structural functionalists believe that a society cannot operate for any length of time on the basis of force. As Aberle and his colleagues put it, "A society based solely on force is a contradiction in terms" (1950/1967:322). To structural functionalists, society is held together by the consensus of its members; to them, a society held together by force is no society at all. Finally, a society could be terminated by absorption into another society through annexation, conquest, and so forth.

The reverse side of this discussion of functional prerequisites includes the characteristics that a society must have in order to survive. For one thing, a society must have an adequate method of dealing with its environment. Of the two aspects of the environment that can be differentiated, the first is the ecology. A society must be able to extract from the environment what it needs to survive (food, fuel, raw materials, and so forth) without destroying the sources. We are all painfully aware of this problem in an era of environmental pollution, energy shortages, and starvation in many areas of the world. The second aspect of the environment is the other social systems with which a society must be able to cope. This involves, among other things, trade, cultural exchanges, adequate communication, and adequate military defense in the event of intersocietal hostilities.

A society also must have an adequate method for sexual recruitment. Heterosexual relationships have to be patterned in such a way that men and women have adequate opportunities to interact. Beyond that, both sexes must be endowed with the motivation needed for a rate of reproduction sufficient to maintain the society. On the average, a couple must produce something above two children. Furthermore, the society needs to be sure that there is a sufficient number of people and that they have diverse enough interests and skills to allow the society to function.

A society also must have sufficient differentiation of roles, as well as a way of assigning people to those roles. In all societies certain activities must be performed and roles must be constructed so that they can be performed. The most important form of role differentiation is social stratification. As we have seen, one of the basic tenets of structural functionalism is that societies must be stratified to survive. Stratification is seen as performing various functions, such as ensuring that people are willing to take on the responsibilities of high-status positions, ensuring the stability of the social system, and so forth.

An adequate communication system is also viewed as a functional requirement of any social system. Its elements include language and channels of communication. Clearly, society itself would be impossible if people were not able to interact and communicate. However, when structural functionalists discuss society's communication system, they also mean the shared symbolic systems that people learn during the socialization process and that make communication possible. Shared symbolic systems make possible a cultural value system. It is the cultural system that is crucial to the structural-functional view of society and how it is held together. The common value pattern is a bulwark against the possibility of continual conflict within society.

Not only must there be a shared cultural system, but structural functionalists also talk of the need for a shared system of values at the individual level. People must look at the world in essentially the same way. This allows them to predict, with a high degree of accuracy, what others will think and do. These mutual cognitive orientations perform various functions. Of perhaps greatest importance, they make social situations stable, meaningful, and predictable. In short, a stable society, which is of enormous importance to structural functionalists, is made possible by the fact that actors operate with shared orientations. Such shared orientations also allow people to account in similar ways for those things that they cannot control or predict; they enable them to sustain their involvement in, and commitment to, social situations.

Structural functionalists also argue that society needs a shared, articulated set of goals. If people were pursuing many unrelated goals, the resulting chaos would make society impossible. Shared goals, such as marital happiness, the success of children, and occupational achievement, help to give a high level of cohesion to society.

Society requires some method of regulating the means to achieve these goals, and the normative system performs this function. Without the normative regulation of means, society would be afflicted by chaos, anomie, and apathy. If occupational success could be obtained by *any* means possible, there would be, according to the structural functionalists, societal disorder.

A society also must regulate affective expression, because unbridled emotions would be another source of chaos. Some emotions are clearly necessary; for example, love and family loyalty are necessary to ensure an adequate population. Although it may be difficult for anyone to define precisely the line between necessary and dangerous levels of emotion, to the structural functionalists it is clear that at some level emotionalism is a threat to the social system.

Implied in many of the preceding points is the idea that society requires the socialization of new members in order to survive. People must learn many things, including their place in the stratification system, the common value system, shared cognitive orientations, acceptable goals, norms defining proper means to these goals, and regulations on affective states. If actors have not learned and internalized such things, society is viewed as impossible by the structural functionalist.

Finally, society requires effective control over disruptive forms of behavior. Ideally, if the socialization process has led actors to internalize all the proper values, then they conform of their own volition. To the structural functionalists, society runs best when there is no need for external control of actors. However, when external control proves necessary, various social control agents are brought to bear. These range from the raised eyebrow of a friend to the billy club of the police officer or, in extreme cases, the bayonet of the soldier.

Talcott Parsons's Structural Functionalism

Over the course of his life, Talcott Parsons did a great deal of theoretical work. There are important differences between his early work and his later work. In this section, we deal with his later, structural-functional theorizing. (For a

TALCOTT PARSONS: A Biographical Sketch

Talcott Parsons was born in 1902 in Colorado Springs, Colorado. He came from a religious and intellectual background; his father was a Congregational minister, a professor, and ultimately president of a small college. Parsons got an undergraduate degree from Amherst College in 1924 and set out to do graduate work at the London School of Economics. In the next year, he moved on to Heidelberg, Germany. Max Weber had spent a large portion of his career at Heidelberg, and although he had died five years before Parsons arrived, Weber's influence survived and his widow continued to hold meetings in her home, meetings that Parsons attended. Parsons was greatly affected by Weber's work and ultimately wrote his doctoral thesis at Heidelberg dealing, in part, with Weber's work.

Parsons became an instructor at Harvard in 1927, and although he switched departments several times, Parsons remained at Harvard until his death in 1979. His career progress was not rapid; he did not obtain a tenured position until 1939. Two years previously, he had published *The Structure of Social Action,* a book that not only introduced major sociological theorists like Weber to large numbers of sociologists but also laid the groundwork for Parsons's own developing theory.

After that, Parsons made rapid academic progress. He was made chairman of the Harvard sociology department in 1944 and two years later set up and chaired the innovative Department of Social Relations, which included not only sociologists but a variety of other social scientists. By 1949 he had been elected president of the American Sociological Association. In the 1950s and into the 1960s, with the publication of such books as *The Social System* (1951), Parsons became the dominant figure in American sociology.

However, by the late 1960s, Parsons came under attack from the emerging radical wing of American sociology. Parsons was seen as being a political conservative, and his theory was seen as highly conservative and little more than an elaborate categorization scheme. But in the 1980s, there was a resurgence in interest in Parsonian theory not only in the United States but around the world (Alexander, 1982–83; Buxton, 1985; Camic, 1990; Holton and Turner, 1986; Sciulli and Gerstein, 1985). Holton and Turner have perhaps gone the farthest, arguing that "Parsons' work . . . represents a more powerful contribution to sociological theory than that of Marx, Weber, Durkheim or any of their contemporary followers"

more complete discussion of Parsons's work, see Ritzer, 1992). We begin this discussion of Parsons's structural functionalism with the four functional imperatives for all "action" systems, his famous AGIL scheme. After this discussion of the four functions, we will turn to an analysis of Parsons's ideas on structures and systems.

AGIL   A *function* is "a complex of activities directed towards meeting a need or needs of the system" (Rocher, 1975:40). Using this definition, Parsons believes that there are four functional imperatives that are necessary for (char-

(1986:13). Furthermore, Parsons's ideas are influencing not only conservative thinkers but neo-Marxian theorists as well, especially Jurgen Habermas.

Upon his death, a number of his former students, themselves sociologists of considerable note, reflected on Parsonsian theory as well as on the man behind the theory. In their musings, these sociologists offered some interesting insights into Parsons and his work. The few glimpses of Parsons reproduced here do not add up to a coherent picture, but they do offer some provocative glimpses of the man and his work.

Robert Merton was one of his students when Parsons was just beginning his teaching career at Harvard. Merton, who became a noted theorist in his own right, makes it clear that graduate students did not come to Harvard in those years to study with Parsons but rather with Pitirim Sorokin, the senior member of the department, who was to become Parsons's archenemy:

> Of the very first generation of graduate students coming to Harvard . . . precisely none came to study with Talcott. They could scarcely have done so for the simplest of reasons: in 1931, he had no public identity whatever as a sociologist.
> Although we students came to study with the renowned Sorokin, a subset of us stayed to work with the unknown Parsons.
>
> (Merton, 1980:69)

Merton's reflections on Parsons's first course in theory are interesting too, especially because the material provided the basis for one of the most influential theory books in history:

> Long before Talcott Parsons became one of the Grand Old Men of world sociology, he was for an early few of us its Grand Young Man. This began with his first course in theory. . . . [It] would provide him with the core of his masterwork, *The Structure of Social Action* which . . . did not appear in print until five years after its first oral publication.
>
> (Merton, 1980:69–70)

Although all would not share Merton's positive evaluation of Parsons, they would acknowledge the following:

> The death of Talcott Parsons marks the end of an era in sociology. When [a new era] does begin . . . it will surely be fortified by the great tradition of sociological thought which he has left to us.
>
> (Merton, 1980:71)

acteristic of) all systems—(A) adaptation, (G) goal attainment, (I) integration, and (L) latency, or pattern maintenance (AGIL). In order to survive, a system must perform these four functions:

1. *Adaptation:* A system must cope with external situational exigencies. It must adapt to its environment and adapt the environment to its needs.
2. *Goal attainment:* A system must define and achieve its primary goals.
3. *Integration:* A system must regulate the interrelationship of its component parts. It also must manage the relationship among the other three functional imperatives (A, G, L).

4. *Latency* (*pattern maintenance*): A system must furnish, maintain, and renew both the motivation of individuals and the cultural patterns that create and sustain the motivation.

Parsons designed the AGIL scheme to be used at *all* levels in his theoretical system. We will illustrate how Parsons uses AGIL in the discussion below on the four action systems.

The *biological organism* is the action system that handles the adaptation function by adjusting to and transforming the external world. The *personality system* performs the goal-attainment function by defining system goals and mobilizing resources to attain them. The *social system* copes with the integration function by controlling its component parts. Finally, the *cultural system* performs the latency function by providing actors with the norms and values that motivate them for action. Figure 7.1 summarizes the structure of the action system in terms of the AGIL schema.

The Action System   We are now ready to discuss the overall shape of Parsons's action system, which is, in many ways, a system of levels of social analysis (see the Appendix). Figure 7.2 is an outline of the major levels in Parsons's schema.

It is obvious that Parsons had a clear notion of "levels" of social analysis as well as their interrelationship. The hierarchical arrangement is clear, and the levels are integrated in Parsons's system in two ways. First, each of the lower levels provides the conditions, the energy, needed for the higher levels. Second, the higher levels control those below them in the hierarchy.

In terms of the environments of the action system, the lowest level, the physical and organic environment, involves the nonsymbolic aspects of the human body, its anatomy and physiology. The highest level, ultimate reality, has, as Jackson Toby suggests "a metaphysical flavor," but Toby also argues that Parsons "is not referring to the supernatural so much as to the universal tendency for societies to address symbolically the uncertainties, concerns, and tragedies of human existence that challenge the meaningfulness of social organization" (1977:3).

The heart of Parsons's work is found in his four action systems. In the assumptions that Parsons made regarding his action systems we encounter the problem of order that was his overwhelming concern and that has become a major source of criticism of his work (Schwanenberg, 1971). The Hobbesian

L
Cultural System	Social System
Behavioral Organism	Personality System

I

A   G

FIGURE 7.1   Structure of the General Action System

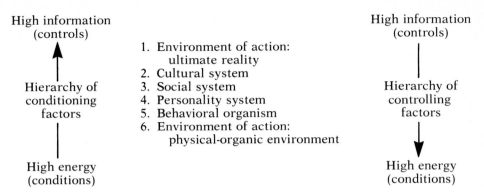

High information
(controls)

Hierarchy of
conditioning
factors

High energy
(conditions)

1. Environment of action:
   ultimate reality
2. Cultural system
3. Social system
4. Personality system
5. Behavioral organism
6. Environment of action:
   physical-organic environment

High information
(controls)

Hierarchy of
controlling
factors

High energy
(conditions)

FIGURE 7.2   Parsons's Action Schema

problem of order—what prevents a social war of all against all—was not answered to Parsons's (1937) satisfaction by the earlier philosophers. Parsons found his answer to the problem of order in structural functionalism, which operates in his view with the following set of assumptions:

1. Systems have the property of order and interdependence of parts.
2. Systems tend toward self-maintaining order, or equilibrium.
3. The system may be static or involved in an ordered process of change.
4. The nature of one part of the system has an impact on the form that the other parts could take.
5. Systems maintain boundaries with their environments.
6. Allocation and integration are two fundamental processes necessary for a given state of equilibrium of a system.
7. Systems tend toward self-maintenance involving the maintenance of boundaries and of the relationships of parts to the whole, control of environmental variations, and control of tendencies to change the system from within.

These assumptions led Parsons to make the analysis of the *ordered* structure of society his first priority. In so doing, he did little with the issue of social change, at least until later in his career:

> We feel that it is uneconomical to describe changes in systems of variables before the variables themselves have been isolated and described; therefore, we have chosen to begin by studying particular combinations of variables and to move toward description of how these combinations change only when a firm foundation for such has been laid.
>
> (Parsons and Shils, 1951:6)

Parsons was so heavily criticized for his static orientation that he devoted more and more attention to change; in fact, as we will see, he eventually focused on the evolution of societies. However, in the view of most observers, even his work on social change tended to be highly static and structured.

In reading about the four action systems, the reader should keep in mind that they do not exist in the real world but are, rather, analytical tools for analyzing the real world.

Social System   Parsons's conception of the social system begins at the micro level with interaction between ego and alter ego, defined as the most elementary form of the social system. He spent little time analyzing this level, although he did argue that features of this interaction system are present in the more complex forms taken by the social system. Parsons defined a *social system* thus:

> A social system consists in a plurality of individual actors *interacting* with each other in a situation which has at least a physical or environmental aspect, actors who are motivated in terms of a tendency to the "optimization of gratification" and whose relation to their situations, including each other, is defined and mediated in terms of a system of culturally structured and shared symbols.
>
> (Parsons, 1951:5–6)

This definition seeks to define a social system in terms of many of the key concepts in Parsons's work—actors, interaction, environment, optimization of gratification, and culture.

Despite his commitment to viewing the social system as a system of interaction, Parsons did not take interaction as his fundamental unit in the study of the social system. Rather, he used the *status-role* complex as the basic unit of the system. This is neither an aspect of actors nor an aspect of interaction, but rather a *structural* component of the social system. *Status* refers to a structural position within the social system, and *role* is what the actor does in such a position, seen in the context of its functional significance for the larger system. The actor is viewed not in terms of thoughts and actions but instead (at least in terms of position in the social system) as nothing more than a bundle of statuses and roles.

In his analysis of the social system, Parsons was interested primarily in its structural components. In addition to a concern with the status-role, Parsons (1966:11) was interested in such large-scale components of social systems as collectivities, norms, and values. In his analysis of the social system, however, Parsons was not simply a structuralist but also a functionalist. He thus delineated a number of the functional prerequisites of a social system. First, social systems must be structured so that they operate compatibly with other systems. Second, to survive, the social system must have the requisite support from other systems. Third, the system must meet a significant proportion of the needs of its actors. Fourth, the system must elicit adequate participation from its members. Fifth, it must have at least a minimum of control over potentially disruptive behavior. Sixth, if conflict becomes sufficiently disruptive, it must be controlled. Finally, a social system requires a language in order to survive.

It is clear in Parsons's discussion of the functional prerequisites of the social system that his focus was large-scale systems and their relationship to one another (societal functionalism). Even when he talked about actors, it was from the point of view of the system. Also, the discussion reflects Parsons's concern with the maintenance of order within the social system.

However, Parsons did not completely ignore the issue of the relationship between actors and social structures in his discussion of the social system. In fact, he called the integration of value patterns and need-dispositions "the fundamental dynamic theorem of sociology" (Parsons, 1951:42). Given his central concern with the social system, of key importance in this integration are the processes of internalization and socialization. That is, Parsons was interested in the ways that the norms and values of a system are transferred to the actors within the system. In a successful socialization process these norms and values are internalized; that is, they become part of the actors' "consciences." As a result, in pursuing their own interests, the actors are in fact serving the interests of the system as a whole. As Parsons put it, "The combination of value-orientation patterns which is acquired [by the actor in socialization] *must in a very important degree be a function of the fundamental role structure and dominant values of the social system*" (1951:227).

In general, Parsons assumed that actors usually are passive recipients in the socialization process.[5] Children learn not only how to act but also the norms and values, the morality, of society. Socialization is conceptualized as a conservative process in which need-dispositions (which are themselves largely molded by society) bind children to the social system, and it provides the means by which the need-dispositions can be satisfied. There is little or no room for creativity; the need for gratification ties children to the system as it exists. Parsons sees socialization as a lifelong experience. Because the norms and values inculcated in childhood tend to be very general, they do not prepare children for the various specific situations that they encounter in adulthood. Thus socialization must be supplemented throughout the life cycle with a series of more specific socializing experiences. Despite this need later in life, the norms and values learned in childhood tend to be stable and, with a little gentle reinforcement, tend to remain in force throughout life.

Despite the conformity induced by lifelong socialization, there is a wide range of individual variation in the system. The question is: Why is this normally not a major problem for the social system, given its need for order? For one thing, a number of social control mechanisms can be employed to induce conformity. However, as far as Parsons was concerned, social control is strictly a second line of defense. A system runs best when social control is used only sparingly. For another thing, the system must be able to tolerate some variation, some deviance. A flexible social system is stronger than a brittle one that accepts no deviation. Finally, the social system should provide a wide range

---

[5] This is a controversial interpretation of Parsons's work with which many disagree. François Bourricaud, for example, talks of "the dialectics of socialization" (1981:108) in Parsons's work and not of passive recipients of socialization.

of role opportunities that allow different personalities to express themselves without threatening the integrity of the system.

Socialization and social control are the main mechanisms that allow the social system to maintain its equilibrium. Modest amounts of individuality and deviance are accommodated, but more extreme forms must be met by reequilibrating mechanisms. Thus social order is built into the structure of Parsons's social system:

> Without deliberate planning on anyone's part there have developed in our type of social system, and correspondingly in others, mechanisms which, within limits, are capable of forestalling and reversing the deep-lying tendencies for deviance to get into the vicious circle phase which puts it beyond the control of ordinary approval-disapproval and reward-punishment sanctions.
>
> (Parsons, 1951:319).

Again, Parsons's main interest was the system as a whole rather than the actor in the system—how the system controls the actor, not how the actor creates and maintains the system. This reflects Parsons's commitment on this issue to a structural-functional orientation.

Although the idea of a social system encompasses all types of collectivities, one specific and particularly important social system is *society*, "a relatively self-sufficient collectivity the members of which are able to satisfy all their individual and collective needs and to live entirely within its framework" (Rocher, 1975:60). As a structural functionalist, Parsons distinguished among four structures, or subsystems, in society in terms of the functions (AGIL) they perform (see Figure 7.3). The *economy* is the subsystem that performs the function for society of adapting to the environment through labor, production, allocation. Through such work, the economy adapts the environment to society's needs, and it helps society adapt to these external realities. The *polity* (or political system) performs the function of goal attainment by pursuing societal objectives and mobilizing actors and resources to that end. The *fiduciary system* (for example, in the schools, the family) handles the latency function by transmitting culture (norms and values) to actors and allowing it to be internalized by them. Finally, the integration function is performed by the *societal community* (for example, the law), which coordinates the various components of society (Parsons and Platt, 1973).

As important as the structures of the social system were to Parsons, the cultural system was more important. In fact, as we saw earlier, the cultural

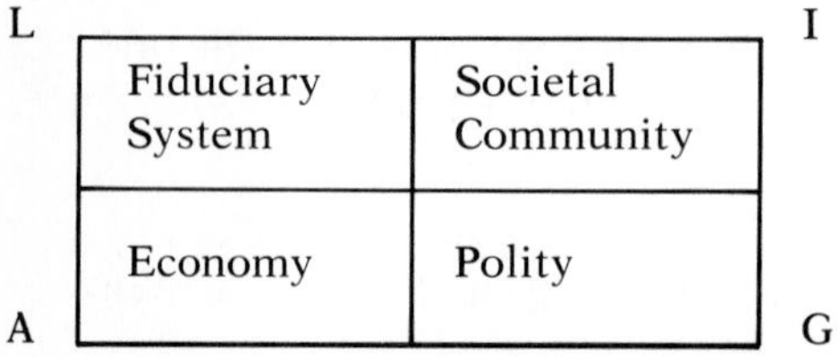

L   I

Fiduciary System	Societal Community
Economy	Polity

A   G

FIGURE 7.3   Society, Its Subsystems, and the Functional Imperatives

system stood at the top of his action system, and Parsons (1966) labeled himself a "cultural determinist."

Cultural System   Parsons conceived of culture as the major force binding the various elements of the social world, or, in his terms, the action system. It mediates interaction among actors and integrates the personality and the social systems. Culture has the peculiar capacity to become, at least in part, a component of the other systems. Thus in the social system culture is embodied in norms and values, and in the personality system it is internalized by the actor. But the cultural system is not simply a part of other systems; it also has a separate existence in the form of the social stock of knowledge, symbols, and ideas. These aspects of the cultural system are available to the social and personality systems, but they do not become part of them (Morse, 1961:105; Parsons and Shils, 1951:6).

Parsons defined the cultural system, as he did his other systems, in terms of its relationship to the other action systems. Thus *culture* is seen as a patterned, ordered system of symbols that are objects of orientation to actors, internalized aspects of the personality system, and institutionalized patterns (Parsons, 1990) in the social system. Because it is largely symbolic and subjective, culture is readily transmitted from one system to another. This allows it to move from one social system to another through diffusion and from one personality system to another through learning and socialization. However, the symbolic (subjective) character of culture also gives it another characteristic, the ability to control Parsons's other action systems. This is one of the reasons that Parsons came to view himself as a cultural determinist.

However, if the cultural system is preeminent in Parsonsian theory, then that leads us to question whether he offers a genuinely integrative theory. As pointed out in the Appendix, a truly integrative theory gives rough equivalency to all major levels of analysis. Cultural determinism, indeed any kind of determinism, is highly suspect from the point of view of an integrated sociology. (For a more integrated conception of Parsons's work, see Camic, 1990.) This problem is exacerbated when we look at the personality system and see how weakly it is developed in Parsons's work.

Personality System   The personality system is controlled not only by the cultural system but also by the social system. That is not to say that Parsons did not accord some independence to the personality system:

> My view will be that, while the main content of the structure of the personality is derived from social systems and culture through socialization, the personality becomes an independent system through its relations to its own organism and through the uniqueness of its own life experience; it is not a mere epiphenomenon.
> (Parsons, 1970a:82)

We get the feeling here that Parsons is protesting too much. If the personality system is not an epiphenomenon, it is certainly reduced to secondary or dependent status in his theoretical system.

The *personality* is defined as the organized system of orientation and motivation of action of the individual actor. The basic component of the personality is the "need-disposition." Parsons and Shils defined *need-dispositions* as the "most significant units of motivation of action" (1951:113). They differentiated need-dispositions from drives, which are innate tendencies—"physiological energy that makes action possible" (Parsons and Shils, 1951:111). In other words, drives are better seen as part of the biological organism. Need-dispositions are then defined as "these same tendencies when they are not innate but acquired through the process of action itself" (Parsons and Shils, 1951:111). In other words, need-dispositions are drives that are shaped by the social setting.

Need-dispositions impel actors to accept or reject objects presented in the environment or to seek out new objects if the ones that are available do not adequately satisfy need-dispositions. Parsons differentiated among three basic types of need-dispositions. The first type impels actors to seek love, approval, and so forth from their social relationships. The second type includes internalized values that lead actors to observe various cultural standards. Finally, there are the role expectations that lead actors to give and get appropriate responses.

This gives a very passive image of actors. They seem to be either impelled by drives, dominated by the culture, or, more usually, shaped by a combination of drives and culture (that is, by need-dispositions). A passive personality system is clearly a weak link in an integrated theory, and Parsons seemed to be aware of it. On various occasions, he tried to endow the personality with some creativity. For example, he said: "We do not mean . . . to imply that a person's values are entirely 'internalized culture' or mere adherence to rules and laws. The person makes creative modifications as he internalizes culture; but the novel aspect is not the culture aspect" (Parsons and Shils, 1951:72). Despite claims such as these, the dominant impression that emerges from Parsons's work is one of a passive personality system.

Parsons's emphasis on need-dispositions creates other problems. Because it leaves out so many other important aspects of personality, his system becomes a largely impoverished one. Alfred Baldwin, a psychologist, makes precisely this point:

> It seems fair to say that Parsons fails in his theory to provide the personality with a reasonable set of properties or mechanisms aside from need-dispositions, and gets himself into trouble by not endowing the personality with enough characteristics and enough different kinds of mechanisms for it to be able to function.
>
> (Baldwin, 1961:186)

Baldwin makes another telling point about Parsons's personality system, arguing that even when Parsons analyzed the personality system, he was really not focally interested in it: "Even when he is writing chapters on personality structure, Parsons spends many more pages talking about social systems than he does about personality" (1961:180). This is reflected in the various ways that Parsons linked the personality to the social system. First, actors must learn to see themselves in a way that fits with the place they occupy in society (Parsons and Shils, 1951:147). Second, role expectations are attached to each of the roles occupied by individual actors. Then there is the learning of self-discipline, internalization of value orientations, identification, and so forth. All these forces point toward the integration of the personality system with the social system, which Parsons emphasized. However, he also pointed out the possible malintegration, which is a problem for the system that needs to be overcome.

Another aspect of Parsons's work reflects the passivity of the personality system. This is his interest in internalization as the personality system's side of the socialization process. Parsons (1970a:2) derived this interest from Durkheim's work on internalization as well as from Freud's work, primarily that on the superego. In emphasizing internalization and the superego, Parsons once again manifested his conception of the personality system as passive and externally controlled.

Although Parsons was willing to talk about the subjective aspects of personality in his early work, he progressively abandoned that perspective. In so doing, he limited the insights into the personality system he could offer. Parsons at one point stated clearly that he was shifting his attention away from the internal meanings that the actions of people may have: "The organization of observational data in terms of the theory of action is quite possible and fruitful in modified behavioristic terms, and such formulation avoids many of the difficult questions of introspection or empathy" (Parsons and Shils, 1951: 64).

Behavioral Organism   Though he included the behavioral organism as one of the four action systems, Parsons had very little to say about it. It is included because it is the source of energy for the rest of the systems. Although it is based on genetic constitution, its organization is affected by the processes of conditioning and learning that occur during the individual's life.[6] The biological organism is clearly a residual system in Parsons's work, but at the minimum Parsons is to be lauded for including it as a part of his sociology, if for no other reason than that he anticipated the interest in sociobiology by at least some sociologists.

Change and Dynamism in Parsonsian Theory
Evolutionary Theory   Parson's work with such conceptual tools as the four action systems and the functional imperatives led to the accusation that he offered a structural theory that was unable to deal with social change. Parsons had long been sensitive to this charge, arguing that although a study of change was necessary, it must be preceded by a study of structure. But by the 1960s

---

[6] Because of this social element, in his later work Parsons dropped the word *organism* and labeled this the "behavioral system" (1975:104).

he could resist the attacks no longer and made another major shift in his work, this time to the study of social change,[7] particularly the study of social evolution (Parsons, 1977b:50).

Parsons's (1966) general orientation to the study of social change was shaped by biology. To deal with this process, Parsons developed what he called "a paradigm of evolutionary change."

The first component of that paradigm is the process of *differentiation*. Parsons assumed that any society is composed of a series of subsystems that differ in terms of both their *structure* and their *functional* significance for the larger society. As society evolves, new subsystems are differentiated. This is not enough, however; they also must be more adaptive than earlier subsystems. This led Parsons to the essential aspect of his evolutionary paradigm, the idea of *adaptive upgrading*. Parsons described this process:

> If differentiation is to yield a balanced, more evolved system, each newly differentiated substructure . . . must have increased adaptive capacity for performing its *primary* function, as compared to the performance of *that* function in the previous, more diffuse structure. . . . We may call this process the *adaptive upgrading* aspect of the evolutionary change cycle.
>
> (Parsons, 1966:22)

This is a highly positive model of social change. It assumes that as society evolves, it grows generally better able to cope with its problems. In contrast, in Marxian theory social change leads to the eventual destruction of capitalist society. For this reason, among others, Parsons is often thought of as a very conservative sociological theorist. In addition, while he did deal with change, he tended to focus on the positive aspects of social change in the modern world rather than on its dark side.

Next, Parsons argued that the process of differentiation leads to a new set of problems of *integration* for society. As subsystems proliferate, the society is confronted with new problems in coordinating the operations of these units.

A society undergoing evolution must move from a system of ascription to one of achievement. A wider array of skills and abilities is needed to handle the more diffuse subsystems. The generalized abilities of people must be freed from their ascriptive bonds so that they can be utilized by society. Most generally, this means that groups formerly excluded from contributing to the system must be freed for inclusion as full members of the society.

Finally, the *value* system of the society as a whole must undergo change as social structures and functions grow increasingly differentiated. However, since the new system is more diverse, it is harder for the value system to encompass it. Thus a more differentiated society requires a value system that is "couched at a higher level of generality in order to legitimize the wider variety of goals and functions of its subunits" (Parsons, 1966:23). However,

---

[7] To be fair, Parsons had done some earlier work on social change, but it did not become a paramount concern, and his contributions were minimal, until the 1960s (see Parsons, 1942, 1947; see also Alexander, 1981; Baum and Lechner, 1981).

this process of generalization of values often does not proceed smoothly as it meets resistance from groups committed to their own narrow value systems.

Evolution proceeds through a variety of cycles, but no general process affects all societies equally. Some societies may foster evolution, whereas others may "be so beset with internal conflicts or other handicaps" that they impede the process of evolution, or they may even "deteriorate" (Parsons, 1966:23). What most interested Parsons were those societies in which developmental "breakthroughs" occur, since he believed that once they occur, the process of evolution would follow his general evolutionary model.

Although Parsons conceived of evolution as occurring in stages, he was careful to avoid a unilinear evolutionary theory: "We do not conceive societal evolution to be either a continuous or a simple linear process, but we can distinguish between broad levels of advancement without overlooking the considerable variability found in each" (1966:26). Making it clear that he was simplifying matters, Parsons distinguished three broad evolutionary stages— primitive, intermediate, and modern. Characteristically, he differentiated among these stages primarily on the basis of cultural dimensions. The crucial development in the transition from primitive to intermediate is the development of language, primarily written language. The key development in the shift from intermediate to modern is "the institutionalized codes of normative order," or law (Parsons, 1966:26).

Parsons next proceeded to analyze a series of specific societies in the context of the evolution from primitive to modern society. One particular point is worth underscoring here: Parsons turned to evolutionary theory, at least in part, because he was accused of being unable to deal with social change. However, his analysis of evolution is *not* in terms of process; rather, it is an attempt to "order structural types and relate them sequentially" (Parsons, 1966:111). This is comparative *structural* analysis, not really a study of the processes of social change. Thus, even when he was supposed to be looking at change, Parsons remained committed to the study of structures and functions.

Generalized Media of Interchange   One of the ways in which Parsons introduces some dynamism, some fluidity (Alexander, 1983:115) into his theoretical system is through his ideas on the generalized media of interchange within and among the four action systems (especially within the social system) discussed above. The model for the generalized media of interchange is money, which operates as such a medium within the economy. But instead of focusing on material phenomena such as money, Parsons focuses on *symbolic* media of exchange. Even when Parsons does discuss money as a medium of interchange within the social system, he focuses on its symbolic rather than its material qualities. In addition to money, and more clearly symbolic, are other generalized media of interchange—political power, influence, and value commitments. Parsons makes it quite clear why he is focusing on symbolic media of interchange: "The introduction of a theory of media into the kind of structural perspective I have in mind goes far, it seems to me, to refute the frequent allegations that this type of structural analysis is inherently plagued with a static bias, which makes it impossible to do justice to dynamic problems" (1975:98–99).

Symbolic media of interchange have the capacity, like money, to be created and to circulate in the larger society. Thus, within the social system, those in the political system are able to create political power. More importantly, they can expend that power, thereby allowing it to circulate freely in, and have influence over, the social system. Through such an expenditure of power, leaders presumably strengthen the political system as well as the society as a whole. More generally, it is the generalized media that circulate between the four action systems and within the structures of each of those systems. It is their existence and movement that gives dynamism to Parsons's largely structural analyses.

As Alexander (1983:115) points out, generalized media of interchange lend dynamism to Parsons's theory in another sense. They allow for the existence of "media entrepreneurs" (for example, politicians) who do not simply accept the system of exchange as it is. That is, they can be creative and resourceful and in this way alter not only the quantity of the generalized media but also the manner and direction in which the media flow.

Robert Merton's Structural Functionalism

While Talcott Parsons is the most important structural-functional theorist, his student Robert Merton authored some of *the* most important statements on structural functionalism in sociology (1949/1968). Merton criticized some of the more extreme and indefensible aspects of structural functionalism. But equally important, his new conceptual insights helped to give structural functionalism a continuing usefulness.

A Structural-Functional Model   Merton criticized what he saw as the three basic postulates of functional analysis. The first is the postulate of the functional unity of society. This postulate holds that all standardized social and cultural beliefs and practices are functional for society as a whole as well as for individuals in society. This view implies that the various parts of a social system must show a high level of integration. However, Merton maintained that although it may be true of small, primitive societies, the generalization cannot be extended to larger, more complex societies.

Universal functionalism is the second postulate. That is, it is argued that *all* standardized social and cultural forms and structures have positive functions. Merton argued that this contradicts what we find in the real world. It is clear that not every structure, custom, idea, belief, and so forth has positive functions. For example, rabid nationalism can be highly dysfunctional in a world of proliferating nuclear arms.

Third is the postulate of indispensability. The argument here is that all standardized aspects of society not only have positive functions but also represent indispensable parts of the working whole. This postulate leads to the idea that all structures and functions are functionally necessary for society. No other structures and functions could work quite as well as those that are currently found within society. Merton's criticism, following Parsons, was that we must at least be willing to admit that there are various structural and functional alternatives to be found within society.

Merton's position was that all these functional postulates rely on nonempirical assertions based on abstract, theoretical systems. At a minimum, it is the responsibility of the sociologist to examine each empirically. Merton's belief that empirical tests, not theoretical assertions, are crucial to functional analysis led him to develop his "paradigm" of functional analysis as a guide to the integration of theory and research.

Merton made it clear from the outset that structural-functional analysis focuses on groups, organizations, societies, and cultures. He stated that any object that can be subjected to structural-functional analysis must "represent a standardized (that is, patterned and repetitive) item" (Merton, 1949/ 1968:104). He had in mind such things as "social roles, institutional patterns, social processes, cultural patterns, culturally patterned emotions, social norms, group organization, social structure, devices for social control, etc." (Merton, 1949/1968:104).

Early structural functionalists tended to focus almost entirely on the *functions* of one social structure or institution for another. However, in Merton's view, early analysts tended to confuse the subjective motives of individuals with the functions of structures or institutions. The focus of the structural functionalist should be on social functions rather than on individual motives. *Functions*, according to Merton, are defined as "those observed consequences which make for the adaptation or adjustment of a given system" (1949/ 1968:105). However, there is a clear ideological bias when one focuses only on adaptation or adjustment, for they are always positive consequences. It is important to note that one social fact can have negative consequences for another social fact. To rectify this serious omission in early structural functionalism, Merton developed the idea of a *dysfunction.* Just as structures or institutions could contribute to the maintenance of other parts of the social system, they also could have negative consequences for them. Slavery in the southern United States, for example, clearly had positive consequences for white southerners, such as supplying cheap labor, support for the cotton economy, and social status. It also had dysfunctions, such as making southerners overly dependent on an agrarian economy and therefore unprepared for industrialization. The lingering disparity between the North and the South in industrialization can be traced, at least in part, to the dysfunctions of the institution of slavery in the South.

Merton also posited the idea of *nonfunctions*, which he defined as consequences that are simply irrelevant to the system under consideration. Included here might be social forms that are "survivals" from earlier historical times. Although they may have had positive or negative consequences in the past, they have no significant effect on contemporary society. One example, although a few might disagree, is the Women's Christian Temperance Movement.

To help answer the question of whether positive functions outweigh dysfunctions, or vice versa, Merton developed the concept of *net balance*. However, we never can simply add up positive functions and dysfunctions and objectively determine which outweighs the other, because the issues are so complex and based on so much subjective judgment that they cannot easily be calculated and weighed. The usefulness of Merton's concept comes from the way it orients the sociologist to the question of relative significance. To return to the example of slavery, the question becomes whether, on balance, slavery was more functional or dysfunctional to the South. Still, this question is too broad and obscures a number of issues (for example, that slavery was functional for groups like white slaveholders).

To cope with problems like these, Merton added the idea that there must be *levels of functional analysis*. Functionalists had generally restricted themselves to analysis of the society as a whole, but Merton made it clear that analysis also could be done on an organization, institution, or group. Returning to the issue of the functions of slavery for the South, it would be necessary to differentiate several levels of analysis and ask about the functions and dysfunctions of slavery for black families, white families, black political organizations, white political organizations, and so forth. In terms of net balance, slavery was probably more functional for certain social units and more dysfunctional for other social units. Addressing the issue at these more specific levels helps in analyzing the functionality of slavery for the South as a whole.

Merton also introduced the concepts of *manifest* and *latent* functions. These two terms have also been important additions to functional analysis.[8] In simple terms, *manifest functions* are those that are intended, whereas *latent functions* are unintended. The manifest function of slavery, for example, was to increase the economic productivity of the South, but it had the latent function of providing a vast underclass that served to increase the social status of southern whites, both rich and poor. This idea is related to another of Merton's concepts—*unanticipated consequences*. Actions have both intended and unintended consequences. Although everyone is aware of the intended consequences, it requires sociological analysis to uncover the unintended consequences; indeed, to some this is the very essence of sociology. Peter Berger (1963) has called this "debunking," or looking beyond stated intentions to real effects.

---

[8] Colin Campbell (1982) has criticized Merton's distinction between manifest and latent functions. Among other things, he points out that Merton is vague about these terms and uses them in various ways (for example, as intended versus actual consequences and as surface meanings versus underlying realities). More important, he feels that Merton (like Parsons) never adequately integrated action theory and structural functionalism. The result is that we have an uncomfortable mixture of the intentionality ("manifest") of action theory and the structural consequences ("functions") of structural functionalism. Due to these and other confusions, Campbell believes, Merton's distinction between manifest and latent functions is little used in contemporary sociology.

Merton made it clear that unanticipated consequences and latent functions are not the same. A latent function is one type of unanticipated consequence, one that is functional for the designated system. But there are two other types of unanticipated consequences: "those that are dysfunctional for a designated system, and these comprise the latent dysfunctions," and "those which are irrelevant to the system which they affect neither functionally or dysfunctionally . . . non-functional consequences" (Merton, 1949/1968:105).

As further clarification of functional theory, Merton pointed out that a structure may be dysfunctional for the system as a whole and yet may continue to exist. One might make a good case that discrimination against blacks, females, and other minority groups is dysfunctional for American society, yet it continues to exist because it is functional for a part of the social system; for example, discrimination against females is generally functional for males. However, these forms of discrimination are not without some dysfunctions, even for the group for which they are functional. Males do suffer from their discrimination against females; similarly, whites are hurt by their discriminatory behavior toward blacks. One could argue that these forms of discrimination adversely affect those who discriminate by keeping vast numbers of people underproductive and by increasing the likelihood of social conflict.

Merton contended that not all structures are indispensable to the workings of the social system. Some parts of our social system *can* be eliminated. This helps functional theory overcome another of its conservative biases. By recognizing that some structures are expendable, functionalism opens the way for meaningful social change. Our society, for example, could continue to exist (and even be improved) by the elimination of discrimination against various minority groups.

Merton's clarifications are of great utility to sociologists (for example, Gans, 1972) who wish to perform structural-functional analyses.

Social Structure and Anomie   Before leaving this section, we must devote some attention to one of the best-known contributions to structural functionalism, indeed all of sociology, Merton's (1968) analysis of the relationship between culture, structure, and anomie. Merton defines *culture* as "that organized set of *normative values* governing behavior which is common to members of a designated society or group" and *social structure* as "that organized set of *social relationships* in which members of the society or group are variously implicated" (1968:216; italics added). Anomie occurs "when there is an acute disjunction between the cultural norms and goals and the socially structured capacities of members of the group to act in accord with them" (Merton, 1968:216). That is, because of their position in the social structure of society, some people are unable to act in accord with normative values. The culture calls for some type of behavior that is prevented from occurring by the social structure.

For example, in American society, the culture places great emphasis on material success. However, the position of many people within the social

ROBERT K. MERTON: An Autobiographical Sketch*

It is easy enough to identify the principal teachers, both close at hand and at a distance, who taught me most. During my graduate studies, they were: P. A. Sorokin, who oriented me more widely to European social thought and with whom, unlike some other students of the time, I never broke although I could not follow him in the directions of inquiry he began to pursue in the late 1930s; the then quite young Talcott Parsons, engaged in thinking through the ideas which first culminated in his magisterial *Structure of Social Action*; the biochemist and sometime sociologist L. J. Henderson, who taught me something about the disciplined investigation of what is first entertained as an interesting idea; the economic historian E. F. Gay, who taught me about the workings of economic development as reconstructible from archival sources; and, quite consequentially, the then dean of the history of science, George Sarton, who allowed me to work under his guidance for several years in his famed (not to say, hallowed) workshop in the Widener Library of Harvard. Beyond these teachers with whom I studied directly, I learned most from two sociologists: Emile Durkheim, above all others, and Georg Simmel, who could teach me only through the powerful works they left behind, and from that sociologically sensitive humanist, Gilbert Murray. During the latter period of my life, I learned most from my colleague, Paul F. Lazarsfeld, who probably had no idea of how much he taught me during our uncountable conversations and collaborations during more than a third of a century.

Looking back over my work through the years, I find more of a pattern in it than I had supposed was there. For almost from the beginning of my own work, after those apprenticeship years as a graduate student, I was determined to follow my intellectual interests as they evolved rather than pursue a predetermined lifelong plan. I chose to adopt the practice of my master-at-a-distance, Durkheim, rather than the practice of my master-at-close-range, Sarton. Durkheim repeatedly changed the subjects he chose to investigate. Starting with his study of the social division of labor, he examined methods of sociological inquiry and then turned successively to the seemingly unrelated subjects of suicide, religion, moral education, and socialism, all the while developing a theoretical orientation which, to his mind, could be effectively developed by attending to such varied aspects of life in society. Sarton had proceeded quite the other way: in his earliest years as a scholar, he had worked out a program of research in the history of science that was to culminate in his monumental five-volume *Introduction [sic] to the History of Science* (which carried the story through to the close of the fourteenth century!).

The first of these patterns seemed more suitable for me. I wanted and still want to advance sociological theories of social structure and cultural change that will help us understand how social institutions and the character of life in society come to be as they are.

structure prevents them from achieving such success. If one is born into the lower socioeconomic classes and as a result is able to acquire, at best, a high school degree, then one's chances of achieving economic success in the generally accepted way (for example, through succeeding in the conventional work world) are slim or nonexistent. Under such circumstances (and they are

That concern with theoretical sociology has led me to avoid the kind of subject specialization that has become (and, in my opinion, has for the most part rightly become) the order of the day in sociology, as in other evolving disciplines. For my purposes, study of a variety of sociological subjects was essential.

In that variety, only one special field—the sociology of science—has persistently engaged my interest. During the 1930s, I devoted myself almost entirely to the social contexts of science and technology, especially in seventeenth-century England, and focused on the unanticipated consequences of purposive social action. As my theoretical interests broadened, I turned, during the 1940s and afterward, to studies of the social sources of nonconforming and deviant behavior, of the workings of bureaucracy, mass persuasion, and communication in modern complex society, and to the role of the intellectual, both within bureaucracies and outside them. In the 1950s, I centered on developing a sociological theory of basic units of social structure: the role-set and status-set and the role models people select not only for emulation but also as a source of values adopted as a basis for self-appraisal (this latter being "the theory of reference groups"). I also undertook, with George Reader and Patricia Kendall, the first large-scale sociological study of medical education, aiming to find out how, all apart from explicit plan, different kinds of physicians are socialized in the same schools of medicine, this being linked with the distinctive character of professions as a type of occupational activity. In the 1960s and 1970s, I returned to an intensive study of the social structure of science and its interaction with cognitive structure, these two decades being the time in which the sociology of science finally came of age, with what's past being only prologue. Throughout these studies, my primary orientation was toward the connections between sociological theory, methods of inquiry, and substantive empirical research.

I group these developing interests by decades only for convenience. Of course, they did not neatly come and go in accord with such conventional divisions of the calendar. Nor did all of them go, after the first period of intensive work on them. I am at work on a volume centered on the unanticipated consequences of purposive social action, thus following up a paper first published almost half a century ago and intermittently developed since. Another volume in the stocks, entitled *The Self-Fulfilling Prophecy,* follows out in a half-dozen spheres of social life the workings of this pattern as first noted in my paper by the same title, a mere third of a century ago. And should time, patience, and capacity allow, there remains the summation of work on the analysis of social structure, with special reference to status-sets, role-sets, and structural contexts on the structural side, and manifest and latent functions, dysfunctions, functional alternatives, and social mechanisms on the functional side.

Mortality being the rule and painfully slow composition being my practice, there seems small point in looking beyond this series of works in progress.

widespread in contemporary American society) anomie can be said to exist, and as a result, there is a tendency toward deviant behavior. In this context, deviance often takes the form of alternative, unacceptable and sometimes illegal means of achieving economic success. Thus, becoming a drug dealer or a prostitute in order to achieve economic success is an example of deviance generated by the disjunction between cultural values and social-structural means of attaining those values. This is one way in which the structural functionalist would seek to explain crime and deviance.

Thus, in this example of structural functionalism, Merton is looking at social (and cultural) structures, but he is not focally concerned with the functions of those structures. Rather, consistent with his functional paradigm, he is mainly concerned with dysfunctions, in this case anomie. More specifically, as we have seen, Merton links anomie with deviance and thereby is arguing that disjunctions between culture and structure have the dysfunctional consequence of leading to deviance within society.

The Major Criticisms

No single sociological theory in the history of the discipline has been the focus of as much interest as structural functionalism. From the late 1930s to early 1960s, it was virtually unchallenged as the dominant sociological theory in the United States. By the 1960s, however, criticisms of the theory had increased dramatically and ultimately became more prevalent than praise. Mark Abrahamson depicted this situation quite vividly: "Thus, metaphorically, functionalism has ambled along like a giant elephant, ignoring the stings of gnats, even as the swarm of attackers takes its toll" (1978:37).

Let us look at some of these major criticisms. We will deal first with the major *substantive* criticisms of structural functionalism and then focus on the *logical and methodological* problems associated with the theory.

Substantive Criticisms   One major criticism is that structural functionalism does not deal adequately with history—that it is inherently ahistorical. In fact, structural functionalism was developed, at least in part, in reaction to the historical evolutionary approach of certain anthropologists. Many of the early anthropologists were seen as describing the various stages in the evolution of a given society or society in general. Frequently, depictions of the early stages were highly speculative. Furthermore, the later stages were often little more than idealizations of the society in which the anthropologist lived. Early structural functionalists were seeking to overcome the speculative character and ethnocentric biases of these works. In its early years in particular, structural functionalism went too far in its criticism of evolutionary theory and came to focus on either contemporary or abstract societies. However, structural functionalism need not be ahistorical (Turner and Maryanski, 1979). Although practitioners have tended to operate as if it were ahistorical, nothing in the theory prevents them from dealing with historical issues. In fact, Parsons's (1966, 1971) work on social change, as we have seen, reflects the ability of structural functionalists to deal with change if they so wish.

Structural functionalists also are attacked for being unable to deal effectively with the *process* of social change (Abrahamson, 1978; P. Cohen, 1968; Mills, 1959; Turner and Maryanski, 1979). Whereas the preceding criticism deals with the seeming inability of structural functionalism to deal with the past, this one is concerned with the parallel incapacity of the approach to deal with the contemporary process of social change. Structural functionalism is far more likely to deal with static structures than with change processes. Percy Cohen (1968) sees the problem as lying in structural-functional theory, in which all the elements of a society are seen as reinforcing one another as well as the system as a whole. This makes it difficult to see how these elements can also contribute to change. While Cohen sees the problem as inherent in the theory, Turner and Maryanski believe, again, that the problem lies with the practitioners and not the theory.

In the view of Turner and Maryanski, structural functionalists frequently do not address the issue of change, and even when they do, it is in developmental rather than revolutionary terms. However, according to them, there is no reason why structural functionalists could not deal with social change. Whether the problem lies in the theory or in the theorists, the fact remains that the main contributions of structural functionalists lie in the study of static, not changing, social structures.[9]

Perhaps the most often voiced criticism of structural functionalism is that it is unable to deal effectively with conflict (Abrahamson, 1978; P. Cohen, 1968; Gouldner, 1970; Horowitz, 1962/1967; Mills, 1959; Turner and Maryanski, 1979).[10] This criticism takes a variety of forms. Alvin Gouldner argues that Parsons, as the main representative of structural functionalism, tended to overemphasize harmonious relationships. Irving Louis Horowitz contends that structural functionalists tend to see conflict as necessarily destructive and as occurring outside the framework of society. Most generally, Abrahamson argues that structural functionalism exaggerates societal consensus, stability, and integration and, conversely, tends to disregard conflict, disorder, and change. The issue once again is whether this is inherent in the theory or in the way that practitioners have interpreted and used it (P. Cohen, 1968; Turner and Maryanski, 1979). Whatever one's position, it is clear that structural functionalism has had little to offer on the issue of social conflict.

The overall criticisms that structural functionalism is unable to deal with history, change, and conflict have led many (for example, P. Cohen, 1968; Gouldner, 1970) to argue that structural functionalism has a conservative bias. As Gouldner vividly puts it in his criticism of Parsons's structural functionalism: "Parsons persistently sees the partly filled glass of water as half *full* rather than half *empty*" (1970:290). One who sees a glass as half full is emphasizing the positive aspects of a situation, whereas one who sees it as half empty is focusing on the negative side. To put this in social terms, a conservative structural functionalist would emphasize the economic advantages of living in our society rather than its disadvantages.

---

[9] However, there are some important works on social change by structural functionalists (C. Johnson, 1966; Smelser, 1959, 1962).

[10] Again, there are important exceptions—see Coser (1956, 1967), Goode (1960), and Merton (1975).

It may indeed be true that there is a conservative bias in structural functionalism that is attributable not only to what it ignores (change, history, conflict) but also to what it chooses to focus on. For one thing, structural functionalists have tended to focus on culture, norms, and values (P. Cohen, 1968; Mills, 1959; Lockwood, 1956). David Lockwood (1956), for example, is critical of Parsons for his preoccupation with the normative order of society. More generally, Percy Cohen (1968) argues that structural functionalists focus on normative elements, although this is not inherent in the theory. Crucial to structural functionalism's focus on cultural and societal factors and what leads to the theory's conservative orientation is a passive sense of the individual actor. People are seen as constrained by cultural and social forces. Structural functionalists (for example, Parsons) lack a dynamic, creative sense of the actor. As Gouldner says, to emphasize his criticism of structural functionalism, "Human beings are as much engaged in using social systems as in being used by them" (1970:220).

Related to their cultural focus is the tendency of structural functionalists to mistake the legitimizations employed by elites in society for social reality (Gouldner, 1970; Horowitz, 1962/1967; Mills, 1959). The normative system is interpreted as reflective of the society as a whole, when it may in fact be better viewed as an ideological system promulgated by, and existing for, the elite members of society. Horowitz enunciates this position quite explicitly: "Consensus theory . . . tends to become a metaphysical representation of the dominant ideological matrix" (1962/1967:270).

These substantive criticisms point in two basic directions. First, it seems clear that structural functionalism has a rather narrow focus that prevents it from addressing a number of important issues and aspects of the social world. Second, its focus tends to give it a very conservative flavor; as it was often practiced and still is, to some degree, structural functionalism operates in support of the status quo and dominant elites (Huaco, 1986).

Methodological and Logical Criticisms One of the often expressed criticisms (see, for example, Abrahamson, 1978; Mills, 1959) is that structural functionalism is basically vague, unclear, and ambiguous. For example: What exactly is a structure? A function? A social system? How are parts of social systems related to each other as well as to the larger social system? Part of the ambiguity is traceable to the level on which structural functionalists choose to work. They deal with abstract social systems instead of real societies. In much of Parsons's work, no "real" society is discussed. Similarly, the discussion of functional prerequisites by Aberle and his colleagues (1950/1967) is not concretely tied to a real society but occurs at a very high level of abstraction.

A related criticism is that, although no one grand scheme ever can be used to analyze all societies throughout history (Mills, 1959), structural functionalists have been motivated by the belief that there is a single theory or at least a set of conceptual categories that could be used to do this. The belief in the existence of such a grand theory lies at the base of much of Parsons's work, the functional prerequisites of Aberle and his colleagues (1950/1967), and the Davis-Moore (1945) theory of stratification. Many critics regard this grand theory as an illusion, believing that the best sociology can hope for is more historically specific, "middle-range" (Merton, 1968) theories.

Among the other specific methodological criticisms is the issue of whether there exist adequate methods to study the questions of concern to structural functionalists. Percy Cohen (1968), for instance, wonders what tools can be used to study the contribution of one part of a system to the system as a whole. Another methodological criticism is that structural functionalism makes comparative analysis difficult. If the assumption is that part of a system makes sense only in the context of the social system in which it exists, how can we compare it with a similar part in another system? Cohen asks, for example: If the English family makes sense only in the context of English society, how can we compare it to the French family?

Teleology and Tautology   Percy Cohen (1968) and Turner and Maryanski (1979) see teleology and tautology as the two most important logical problems confronting structural functionalism. Some tend to see teleology as an inherent problem (Abrahamson, 1978; P. Cohen, 1968), but the author believes that Turner and Maryanski (1979) are correct when they argue that the problem with structural functionalism is not teleology per se, but *illegitimate* teleology. In this context, *teleology* is defined as the view that society (or other social structures) has purposes or goals. In order to achieve these goals, society creates, or causes to be created, specific social structures and social institutions. Turner and Maryanski do not see this view as necessarily illegitimate; in fact, they argue that social theory *should* take into account the teleological relationship between society and its component parts.

The problem, to Turner and Maryanski, is the extension of teleology to unacceptable lengths. An illegitimate teleology is one that implies "that purpose or end states guide human affairs when such is not the case" (Turner and Maryanski, 1979:118). For example, it is illegitimate to assume that because society needs procreation and socialization it will create the family institution. A variety of alternative structures could meet these needs; society does not "need" to create the family. The structural functionalist must define and document the various ways in which the goals do, in fact, lead to the creation of specific substructures. It also would be useful to be able to show why other substructures could not meet the same needs. A legitimate teleology would be able to define and demonstrate *empirically* and *theoretically* the links between society's goals and the various substructures that exist within society. An illegitimate teleology would be satisfied with a blind assertion that a link between a societal end and a specific substructure must exist. Turner and Maryanski admit that functionalism is often guilty of presenting illegitimate teleologies: "We can conclude that functional explanations often become illegitimate teleologies—a fact which seriously hampers functionalism's utility for understanding patterns of human organization" (1979:124).

The other major criticism of the logic of structural functionalism is that it is tautological. A tautological argument is one in which the conclusion merely makes explicit what is implicit in the premise or is simply a restatement of the premise. In structural functionalism, this circular reasoning often takes the form of defining the whole in terms of its parts and then defining the parts in terms of the whole. Thus, it would be argued that a social system is defined by the relationship among its component parts and that the component parts of the system are defined by their place in the larger social system. Because each is defined in terms of the other, neither the social system nor its parts are in fact defined at all. We really learn nothing about either the system or its parts. Structural functionalism has been particularly prone to tautologies, although there is some question about whether this propensity is inherent in the theory or simply characteristic of the way most structural functionalists have used, or misused, the theory.

THE CONFLICT-THEORY ALTERNATIVE

A premise of this chapter is that conflict theory can be seen as a development that took place, at least in part, in reaction to structural functionalism and as a result of many of the criticisms discussed earlier. However, it should be noted that conflict theory has various other roots, such as Marxian theory and Simmel's work on social conflict. In the 1950s and 1960s, conflict theory provided an alternative to structural functionalism, but it has been superseded in recent years by a variety of neo-Marxian theories (see Chapter 8). Indeed, one of the major contributions of conflict theory was the way it laid the groundwork for theories more faithful to Marx's work, theories that came to attract a wide audience in sociology. The basic problem with conflict theory is that it never succeeded in divorcing itself sufficiently from its structural-functional roots. It was more a kind of structural functionalism turned on its head than a truly critical theory of society.

The Work of Ralf Dahrendorf

Conflict theorists, like functionalists, are oriented toward the study of social structures and institutions. In the main, this theory is little more than a series of contentions that are often the direct opposites of functionalist positions. This is best exemplified by the work of Ralf Dahrendorf (1958, 1959), in which the tenets of conflict and functional theory are juxtaposed. To the functionalists, society is static or, at best, in a state of moving equilibrium, but to Dahrendorf and the conflict theorists every society at every point is subject to processes of change. Where functionalism emphasizes the orderliness of society, conflict theorists see dissension and conflict at every point in the social system. Functionalists (or at least early functionalists) argue that every element in society contributes to stability; the exponents of conflict theory see many societal elements contributing to disintegration and change.

Functionalists tend to see society as being held together informally by norms, values, and a common morality. Conflict theorists see whatever order there is in society as stemming from the coercion of some members by those at the top. Where functionalists focus on the cohesion created by shared societal values, conflict theorists emphasize the role of power in maintaining order in society.

Dahrendorf (1959, 1968) is the major exponent of the position that society has two faces (conflict and consensus) and that sociological theory therefore should be divided into two parts, conflict theory and consensus theory. Consensus theorists should examine value integration in society, and conflict theorists should examine conflicts of interest and the coercion that holds society together in the face of these stresses. He recognized that society could not exist without both conflict and consensus, which are prerequisites for each other. Thus, we cannot have conflict unless there is some prior consensus. For example, French housewives are highly unlikely to conflict with Chilean chess players because there is no contact between them, no prior integration to serve as a basis for a conflict. Conversely, conflict can lead to consensus and integration. An example is the alliance between the United States and Japan that has developed since World War II.

Despite the interrelationship between the processes of consensus and conflict, Dahrendorf was not optimistic about developing a single sociological theory encompassing both processes: "It seems at least conceivable that unification of theory is not feasible at a point which has puzzled thinkers ever since the beginning of Western philosophy" (1959:164). Eschewing a singular theory, Dahrendorf set out to construct a conflict theory of society.[11]

Dahrendorf began with, and was heavily influenced by, structural functionalism. He noted that to the functionalist, the social system is held together by voluntary cooperation or general consensus or both. However, to the conflict (or coercion) theorist, society is held together by "enforced constraint." This means that some positions in society are delegated power and authority over others. This fact of social life led Dahrendorf to his central thesis that the differential distribution of authority "invariably becomes the determining factor of systematic social conflicts" (1959:165).

Authority   Dahrendorf concentrated on the larger social structures.[12] Central to his thesis is the idea that various positions within society have different amounts of authority. Authority does not reside in individuals but in positions. Dahrendorf was interested not only in the structure of these positions but also in the conflict among them: "The *structural* origin of such conflicts must be sought in the arrangement of social roles endowed with expectations

---

[11] Dahrendorf called conflict and coercion "the ugly face of society" (1959:164). We can ponder whether a person who regards them as "ugly" can develop an adequate theory of conflict and coercion.

[12] In his other work, Dahrendorf (1968) continued to focus on social facts (for example, positions and roles), but he also manifested a concern for the dangers of reification endemic to such an approach.

of domination or subjection" (1959:165; italics added). The first task of conflict analysis, to Dahrendorf, was to identify various authority roles within society. In addition to making the case for the study of large-scale structures like authority roles, Dahrendorf was opposed to those who focus on the individual level. For example, he was critical of those who focus on the psychological or behavioral characteristics of the individuals who occupy such positions. He went so far as to say that those who adopted such an approach were not sociologists.

The authority attached to positions is the key element in Dahrendorf's analysis. Authority always implies both superordination and subordination. Those who occupy positions of authority are expected to control subordinates; that is, they dominate because of the expectations of those who surround them, not because of their own psychological characteristics. These expectations, like authority, are attached to positions, not people. Authority is not a generalized social phenomenon; those who are subject to control, as well as permissible spheres of control, are specified in society. Finally, because authority is legitimate, sanctions can be brought to bear against those who do not comply.

Authority is not a constant as far as Dahrendorf was concerned. This is traceable to the fact that authority resides in positions and not persons. Thus, a person in authority in one setting does not necessarily hold a position of authority in another setting. Similarly, a person in a subordinate position in one group may be in a superordinate position in another. This follows from Dahrendorf's argument that society is composed of a number of units that he called *imperatively coordinated associations*. These may be seen as associations of people controlled by a hierarchy of authority positions. In that society contains many such associations, an individual can occupy a position of authority in one and a subordinate position in another.

Authority within each association is dichotomous; thus two, and only two, conflict groups can be formed within any association. Those in positions of authority and those in positions of subordination hold certain interests that are "contradictory in substance and direction." Here we encounter another key term in Dahrendorf's theory of conflict—*interests*. Groups on top and at the bottom are defined by common interests. Dahrendorf continued to be firm in his thinking that even these interests, which sound so psychological, are basically large-scale phenomena:

> For purposes of the sociological analysis of conflict groups and group conflicts, it is necessary to assume certain *structurally generated* orientations of the actions of incumbents of defined *positions*. By analogy to conscious ("subjective") orientations of action, it appears justifiable to describe these as interests. . . . The assumption of "objective" interests associated with social positions has *no psychological implications* or ramifications; it belongs to the level of sociological analysis proper.
>
> (Dahrendorf, 1959:175; italics added)

Within every association, those in dominant positions seek to maintain the status quo while those in subordinate positions seek change. A conflict of interest within any association is at least latent at all times, which means that the legitimacy of authority is *always* precarious. This conflict of interest need not be conscious in order for superordinates or subordinates to act. The interests of superordinates and subordinates are objective in the sense that they are reflected in the expectations (roles) attached to positions. Individuals do not have to internalize these expectations or even be conscious of them in order to act in accord with them. If they occupy given positions, then they will behave in the expected manner. Individuals are "adjusted" or "adapted" to their roles when they contribute to conflict between superordinates and subordinates. Dahrendorf called these unconscious role expectations *latent interests*. *Manifest interests* are latent interests that have become conscious. Dahrendorf saw the analysis of the connection between latent and manifest interests as a major task of conflict theory. Nevertheless, actors need not be conscious of their interests in order to act in accord with them.

Next Dahrendorf distinguished three broad types of groups. The first is the *quasi-group*, or "aggregates of incumbents of positions with identical role interests" (Dahrendorf, 1959:180). These are the recruiting grounds for the second type of group—the *interest group*. Dahrendorf described the two groups:

> Common modes of behavior are characteristic of *interest groups* recruited from larger quasi-groups. Interest groups are groups in the strict sense of the sociological term; and they are the real agents of group conflict. They have a structure, a form of organization, a program or goal, and a personnel of members.
>
> (Dahrendorf, 1959:180)

Out of all the many interest groups emerge *conflict groups*, or those that actually engage in group conflict.

Dahrendorf felt that the concepts of latent and manifest interests, of quasi-groups, interest groups, and conflict groups, were basic to an explanation of social conflict. Under *ideal* conditions no other variables would be needed. However, because conditions are never ideal, many different factors do intervene in the process. Dahrendorf mentioned technical conditions such as adequate personnel, political conditions such as the overall political climate, and social conditions such as the existence of communication links. The way people are recruited into the quasi-group was another social condition important to Dahrendorf. He felt that if the recruitment is random and determined by chance, then an interest group, and ultimately a conflict group, is unlikely to emerge. In contrast to Marx, Dahrendorf did not feel that the *lumpenproletariat*[13] would ultimately form a conflict group, because people are recruited to it by chance. However, when recruitment to quasi-groups is structurally determined, these groups provide fertile recruiting grounds for interest groups and, in some cases, conflict groups.

The final aspect of Dahrendorf's conflict theory is the relationship of conflict to change. Here Dahrendorf recognized the importance of Lewis Coser's work

---

[13] This is Marx's term for the mass of people at the bottom of the economic system, those who stand below even the proletariat.

(see below), which focused on the functions of conflict in maintaining the status quo. Dahrendorf felt, however, that the conservative function of conflict is only one part of social reality; conflict also leads to change and development.

Briefly, Dahrendorf argued that once conflict groups emerge, they engage in actions that lead to changes in social structure. When the conflict is intense, the changes that occur are radical. When it is accompanied by violence, structural change will be sudden. Whatever the nature of conflict, sociologists must be attuned to the relationship between conflict and change as well as that between conflict and the status quo.

The Major Criticisms

Conflict theory has been criticized on a variety of grounds. For example, it has been attacked for ignoring order and stability, whereas structural functionalism has been criticized for ignoring conflict and change. Conflict theory has also been criticized for being ideologically radical, whereas functionalism was criticized for its conservative ideology. In comparison to structural functionalism, conflict theory is rather underdeveloped. It is not nearly as sophisticated as functionalism, perhaps because it is a more derivative theory.

Dahrendorf's conflict theory has been subjected to a number of critical analyses (for example, Hazelrigg, 1972; J. Turner, 1973; Weingart, 1969), including some critical reflections by Dahrendorf (1968) himself. First, Dahrendorf's model is not so clear a reflection of Marxian ideas as he claimed. In fact, it constitutes an inadequate translation of Marxian theory into sociology (see below). Second, as has been noted, conflict theory has more in common with structural functionalism than with Marxian theory. Dahrendorf's emphasis on such things as systems (imperatively coordinated associations), positions, and roles links him directly to structural functionalism. As a result, his theory suffers from many of the same inadequacies as structural functionalism. For example, conflict seems to emerge mysteriously from legitimate systems (just as it does in structural functionalism). Further, conflict theory seems to suffer from many of the same conceptual and logical problems (for example, vague concepts, tautologies) as structural functionalism. Finally, like structural functionalism, it is almost wholly a macroscopic theory and as a result has little to offer to our understanding of individual thought and action.

Both functionalism and Dahrendorf's conflict theory are inadequate, because each is itself useful for explaining only a *portion* of social life. Sociology must be able to explain order as well as conflict, structure as well as change. This last fact has motivated several efforts to reconcile conflict and functional theory. Although none has been totally satisfactory, these efforts suggest at least some agreement among sociologists that what is needed is a theory explaining *both* consensus and dissension. Still, not all theorists seek to reconcile these conflicting perspectives. Dahrendorf, for example, saw them as alternative perspectives to be used situationally. According to Dahrendorf, when we are interested in conflict we should use conflict theory; when we wish to examine order, we should take a functional perspective. This seems an unsatisfactory position, because there is a strong need for a theoretical perspective that enables us to deal with conflict and order *simultaneously*.

Jonathan Turner (1975, 1982) has sought to reformulate conflict theory. Turner pointed to three major problems in conflict theories like that of Dahrendorf. First, there is a lack of a clear definition of conflict that delimits both what it is and what it is not. Second, conflict theory remains vague, largely because there is a failure to specify the level of analysis on which one is working: "Typically, just what units are in conflict is left vague—whether they be individuals, groups, organizations, classes, nations, communities, and the like" (J. Turner, 1982:178). Third, there is the implicit functionalism in conflict theory, which leads it away from its Marxian roots.

Turner focused on "conflict as a process of events leading to overt interaction of varying degrees of violence among at least two parties" (1982:183). He developed a nine-stage process leading to overt conflict. Although it appears at first glance to be a one-way causal model, Turner was careful to specify a number of feedback loops, or dialectical relations, among the stages. The nine-stage process looks like this:

1 The social system is composed of a number of interdependent units.
2 There is an unequal distribution of scarce and valued resources among these units.
3 Those units not receiving a proportionate share of the resources begin to question the legitimacy of the system. (Turner noted that this questioning is most likely to take place when people feel their aspirations for upward mobility are blocked, when there are insufficient channels for redressing grievances, and when people are deprived of rewards in a variety of sectors.)
4 Deprived people become aware that it is in their interests to alter the system of resource allocation.
5 Those who are deprived become emotionally aroused.
6 There are periodic, albeit often disorganized, outbursts of frustration.
7 Those involved in the conflict grow increasingly intense about it and more emotionally involved in it.
8 Increased efforts are made to organize the deprived groups involved in the conflict.
9 Finally, open conflict of varying degrees of violence breaks out between the deprived and the privileged. The degree of violence is affected by such things as the ability of the conflicting parties to define their true interests and the degree to which the system has mechanisms for handling, regularizing, and controlling conflict.

Turner has done a useful job of filling in conflict theory, especially in beginning to delineate some of the conflict relations between actors and social structures. However, Turner's work, like that of many other conflict theorists, remains embedded within the structural-functional tradition. As a result, he has failed to reflect the many insights into the nature of social conflict found within the various branches of neo-Marxian theory.

Efforts to Reconcile Structural Functionalism and Conflict Theory

Pierre van den Berghe (1963) has made the major effort to reconcile structural functionalism and conflict theory. He noted several points that the two approaches have in common. First, both perspectives are *holistic*; that is, they look at societies as interrelated parts and are concerned with the interrelationship among the parts. Second, the theorists focus on the variables in their own theory while ignoring variables of concern to the other perspective. They should recognize, however, that conflict can contribute to integration and, conversely, that integration can be a cause of conflict. Third, van den Berghe noted that the two theories share an evolutionary view of social change—the view that society is moving forward and upward. A conflict theorist is likely to see society as advancing irrevocably toward a utopian society. A functionalist such as Parsons sees it as becoming increasingly differentiated and ever better able to cope with its environment. Finally, van den Berghe saw both as basically equilibrium theories. Functional theory emphasizes societal equilibrium. In conflict theory, relational processes lead inevitably to a new state of equilibrium in some future stage. Van den Berghe's work demonstrates points in common between the two theories but does not reconcile them; many outstanding differences remain.

The work of Lewis Coser (1956) and Joseph Himes (1966) focused on the functions of social conflict. These basically functional treatments of conflict do move toward integrating conflict and structural-functional theory. Although their concern was the equilibrating effect of conflict, what is needed is parallel work discussing the disequilibrating effects of order. Certain kinds of order or too much order can lead to disequilibrium in the social system; for example, totalitarian rulers, despite their emphasis on order, can destroy the stability of society. However, because little work has been done on the way that order produces change, we focus below on the functions of social conflict.

The early seminal work on the functions of social conflict was done by Georg Simmel, but it has been expanded by Coser, who argued that conflict may serve to solidify a loosely structured group. In a society that seems to be disintegrating, conflict with another society may restore the integrative core. The cohesiveness of Israeli Jews might be attributed, at least in part, to the long-standing conflict with the Arab nations in the Middle East. The end of the conflict might well exacerbate underlying strains in Israeli society. Conflict as an agent for solidifying a society is an idea that has long been recognized by propagandists, who may construct an enemy where none exists or seek to fan antagonisms toward an inactive opponent.

Conflict with one group may serve to produce cohesion by leading to a series of alliances with other groups. For example, conflict with the Arabs has led to an alliance between the United States and Israel. A lessening of the Israeli-Arab conflict might weaken the bonds between Israel and the United States.

Within a society, conflict can bring some ordinarily isolated individuals into an active role. The protests over the Vietnam War motivated many young people to take vigorous roles in American political life for the first time. With the end of that conflict, a more apathetic spirit emerged again among American youth.

Conflict also serves a communication function. Prior to conflict, groups may be unsure of their adversary's position, but as a result of conflict, positions and boundaries between groups often become clarified. Individuals therefore are better able to decide on a proper course of action in relation to their adversary. Conflict also allows the parties to get a better idea of their relative strengths and may well increase the possibility of rapprochement, or peaceful accommodation.

From a theoretical perspective, it is possible to wed functional and conflict theory by looking at the functions of social conflict. Still, it must be recognized that conflict also has dysfunctions.

Himes (1966), like Coser, was interested in the functions of conflict, although he focused specifically on the functions of racial conflict. Himes discussed what he considered to be *rational* group action by American blacks. He was concerned with deliberate collective behavior designed to achieve predetermined social goals. Such behavior involves a conscious attack on overtly defined social abuses. Examples include legal redress (to achieve voting rights, educational opportunities, and public accommodations), political action (such as voting and lobbying), and nonviolent mass action. The kind of conflict with which Himes was concerned involves peaceful work within the system; his analysis excludes acts of violence, such as riots and lynchings.

Although Himes ignored violent collective conflict, we could just as easily perform a functional analysis of these forms as of peaceful conflict. The riots of the late 1960s clearly had functions for American blacks. They demonstrated blacks' power and the weakness of the white power structure, although they certainly had dysfunctions (in the form of white backlash).

As Himes saw it, racial conflict has structural, communications, solidarity, and identity functions. *Structurally,* conflict can change the power balance between blacks and the dominant white majority, increasing the power of blacks so that whites will meet with them to discuss issues of mutual importance. Racial conflict can perform *communications* functions such as increasing attention to racial matters, increasing coverage of racial matters by the mass media, allowing uninformed people to get new information, and changing the content of interracial communication. Racial conflict can put an end to the old "etiquette of race relations," bringing a greater likelihood of open dialogue over substantive issues. Racial conflict may increase *solidarity,* because it may help unify blacks and establish a relationship between the races. Even if this relationship is based only on conflict, ultimately it may form the basis for a more peaceful and long-lasting relationship. The *identity* functions of racial conflict include giving blacks a greater sense of who they are and clarifying group boundaries. Perhaps the most important identity function is the sense black participants can get of their identity as Americans fighting for the basic principle of freedom.

Each of these conflict theories is concerned with integrating, or at least relating, structural functionalism and conflict theory. Virtually all the efforts have remained at the large-scale societal level.[14]

Toward a More Marxian Conflict Theory

As a transition to the next chapter on Marxian theories, we now offer André Gunder Frank's (1966/1974) criticisms of van den Berghe's efforts to reconcile conflict theory and structural functionalism. Of greatest importance is Frank's contention that conflict theory is an inadequate Marxian theory. Thus, whereas van den Berghe may be able to reconcile conflict theory as it stands with structural functionalism, he would find it much more difficult to reconcile the two if conflict theory were true to Marxian theory.

Frank refuted, point by point, van den Berghe's argument on the reconciliation of conflict and structural-functional theory. Van den Berghe's first point was that both theories take a holistic approach to the social world. Frank admitted that there is at least some correspondence here. He also noted a number of crucial differences. For one thing, Frank argued that true Marxists do tend to focus on the whole, whereas structural functionalists, despite a supposedly similar focus, spend most of their time on parts of social systems. Frank was correct here, but at least some varieties of truer neo-Marxian theory also have tended to focus on one component (for example, the economy, the culture) of the social whole. Frank's second refutation of van den Berghe's first point was more telling. He argued that Marxian thinkers, given their commitment to materialism, look at real social wholes, whereas structural functionalists (and some conflict theorists) tend to look at abstract wholes. Parsons's concept of a social system is an excellent example of the latter point.

Still on the issue of holism, Frank argued that structural functionalists and true Marxian thinkers ask very different questions when they study social totalities. For one thing, the former tend to take the existing social system for granted and do not question its legitimacy. Marxian scholars, however, question existing society (whether it be capitalist, socialist, or communist) and subject it to intense scrutiny and criticism. They are oriented toward the development of some future society, not a deification of the contemporary one. In addition, there is a substantive difference here between the two approaches. True Marxists focus on the social totality and view knowledge of it as helpful in understanding its various parts. But even when structural

---

[14] In Chapter 16 we will discuss Randall Collins's (1975, 1990) effort to relate large- and small-scale concerns under the heading "conflict theory."

functionalism focuses on the whole of society, its ultimate goal is to understand the parts, especially specific social institutions.

Finally, because structural functionalists work on abstract systems, they can focus on any totality they wish. In that Marxian thinkers are committed to naturalism, the totality they choose to study is constrained by the real social world. The world, not an abstract theoretical system, determines what they study. Furthermore, the dialectician is oriented to changing the social whole, not just studying it, as is the case with structural functionalists.

Van den Berghe's second point was that each school ignores the variables of concern to the other. Thus structural functionalists are urged by van den Berghe to learn about conflict from conflict theorists, and, conversely, conflict theorists can learn about consensus from structural functionalists. Frank criticized this position in several ways. First, he argued that it slights both perspectives, because both Marxian theory and structural functionalism have had things to say about *both* conflict and consensus. Second, Frank contended that when the structural functionalists do try to integrate Marxian ideas, they distort them beyond all recognition. Third, even when structural functionalists are interested in conflict, it is only a very limited concern. For instance, they might be willing to look at the functions of social conflict but not to examine such issues as social disintegration and social revolution.

According to Frank, structural functionalism has a limited ability to integrate the issues of conflict and consensus. However, he felt that these issues could be integrated with Marxian theory. Marxian theory can cover a wide range of kinds and degrees of conflict, including disintegrative conflict. More important, given its commitment to the dialectic, Marxian theory is particularly well suited to deal with the integration of cohesion and conflict.

Van den Berghe's third point was that the two theories share an interest in evolutionary change, but Frank noted three important differences. First, structural functionalists are likely to look solely at change within the system, whereas dialecticians are more likely to be interested in the change of the entire system and its social structure. Second, the two schools have different priorities in the study of change. To structural functionalists, structure is the source of change; to dialecticians, change is the source of structure. Finally, for the functionalist, change is an abstract process, whereas for Marxists it is a dialectical process within real societies.

Finally, van den Berghe argued that both approaches were basically equilibrium theories. This is clearly true of structural functionalism, but it does not adequately describe Marxian theory. It ignores, above all, the Marxian sense of disequilibrium, of negations, within the society. To the Marxist, society contains within it the seeds of its own transformation and revolution. Marxists may have a sense of equilibrium, but they have an even stronger image of disequilibrium and change.

In sum, Frank argued that van den Berghe was not true to Marxian theory in his delineation of conflict theory and its integration with structural functionalism. Although conflict theory has some Marxian elements, it is not a true heir of Marx's original theory. In the next chapter, we turn to those theories that are more legitimate heirs.

SUMMARY

Not too many years ago, structural functionalism was *the* dominant theory in sociology. Conflict theory was its major challenger and was the likely alternative to replace it in that position. However, dramatic changes have taken place in recent years. Both theories have been the subject of intense criticism, whereas a series of alternative theories (to be discussed throughout the rest of this book) developed that have attracted ever greater interest and ever larger followings. Structural functionalism and conflict theory are still significant, but they must take their place alongside a number of important theories in sociology. Furthermore, like all traditional theories, they are being overtaken by the theoretical developments to be discussed in Part Three of this book.

Although several varieties of structural functionalism exist, our focus here is on societal functionalism and its large-scale focus, its concern with the interrelationships at the societal level and with the constraining effects of social structures and institutions on actors. Societal structural functionalism has its roots in the work of Comte, Spencer, and Durkheim and their interest in organicism, societal needs, and, more pointedly, structures and functions. On the basis of this work, structural functionalists developed a series of large-scale concerns in social systems, subsystems, relationships among subsystems and systems, equilibrium, and orderly change.

We examine four works by structural functionalists (Davis and Moore, Aberle et al., Parsons, and Merton). Davis and Moore, in one of the best-known and most criticized pieces in the history of sociology, examined social stratification as a social system and the various positive functions it performs. Aberle and his colleagues, in a more general essay, were concerned with the various structures and functions that they believed a society must have in order to survive. Among others, a society must have sufficient population, means to deal with its environment, methods of sexual recruitment, role differentiation and the means to assign people to different roles, communications systems, shared cognitive orientations, shared goals, methods of regulating means to those goals, methods of regulating affectivity, adequate socialization, and effective social control.

We also discuss in some detail Talcott Parsons's structural-functional theory and his ideas on the four functional imperatives of all action systems—adaptation, goal attainment, integration, and latency (AGIL). We also analyze his structural-functional approach to the four action systems—the social system, cultural system, personality system, and behavioral organism. Finally, we deal with his structural-functional approach to dynamism and social change—his evolutionary theory and his ideas on the generalized media of interchange.

Merton's effort to develop a "paradigm" for functional analysis is the most important single piece in modern structural functionalism. Merton began by criticizing some of the more naive positions of structural functionalism. He then sought to develop a more adequate model of structural-functional analysis. On one point Merton agreed with his predecessors—the need to focus on large-scale social phenomena. But, Merton argued, in addition to focusing on positive functions, structural functionalism should be concerned with dysfunctions and even nonfunctions. Given these additions, Merton urged that analysts concern themselves with the net balance of functions and dysfunctions. Further, he argued, in performing structural-functional analysis, we must move away from global analyses and specify the *levels* on which we are working. Merton also added the idea that structural functionalists should be concerned not only with manifest (intended) but also with latent (unintended) functions. This section concludes with a discussion of Merton's application of his functional paradigm to the issue of the relationship between social structure and culture and anomie and deviance.

Next, we discuss the numerous criticisms of structural functionalism that have succeeded in damaging its credibility and popularity. We discuss the criticisms that structural functionalism is ahistorical, unable to deal with conflict and change, highly conservative, preoccupied with societal constraints on actors, accepting of elite legitimations, teleological, and tautological.

The second part of this chapter is devoted to the major alternative to structural functionalism in the 1950s and 1960s—conflict theory. The best-known work in this tradition is by Ralf Dahrendorf, who, although he consciously tried to follow the Marxian tradition, is best seen as having inverted structural functionalism. Dahrendorf looked at change rather than equilibrium, conflict rather than order, how the parts of society contribute to change rather than stability, and conflict and coercion rather than normative constraint. Dahrendorf offered a large-scale theory of conflict that parallels the structural functionalist's large-scale theory of order. His focus on authority, positions, imperatively coordinated associations, interests, quasi-groups, interest groups, and conflict groups reflects this orientation. Dahrendorf's theory suffers from some of the same problems as structural functionalism; in addition, it represents a rather impoverished effort to incorporate Marxian theory. Dahrendorf also can be criticized for being satisfied with alternative theories of order and conflict rather than seeking a theoretical integration of the two.

This last criticism leads us to several pieces of work aimed at reconciling conflict theory and structural functionalism. Van den Berghe discussed several general points that the two theories have in common, and Coser and Himes analyzed the functions of social conflict. Although all these efforts offer some insights, they have serious weaknesses, especially in the tendency to concentrate almost exclusively on large-scale phenomena.

We close this chapter with Frank's criticism of van den Berghe's effort to integrate conflict and structural-functional theory. Frank's central point is that conflict theory is an inadequate reflection of insights from Marxian theory. With this in mind, we turn in Chapter 8 to a discussion of a number of the efforts to develop a more adequate Marxian sociological theory.

VARIETIES OF NEO-MARXIAN SOCIOLOGICAL THEORY

*I*N Chapter 7 we discussed the emergence of conflict theory as a reaction to some of the problems of structural functionalism. A central point made in that chapter was that although conflict theory purported to be within the Marxian tradition, it was actually a rather poor version of Marxian theory. In this chapter we will deal with a variety of sociological theories that are better reflections of Marx's ideas. As we will note, Marx's influence has been far from uniform. Because Marx's theory is encyclopedic, a variety of different theorists all can claim to be working within the guidelines set down in his original work. In fact, although each claims to be the true inheritor of Marx's theory, there are many irreconcilable differences among them.

We have taken care to focus on the sociological elements of the Marxian theories we discuss. To paraphrase Henri Lefebvre's (1968) comment about

Marx, there is a sociological theory in neo-Marxism, but not all neo-Marxism is sociological theory.

Our goal is to survey the wide variety of work being done in neo-Marxian sociological theory. First, we provide a brief statement on the economic determinists. Their work is not directly related to sociology, but it does represent the position that many neo-Marxian sociologists reacted against in developing their own orientation. Second, we deal with some early Hegelian Marxists, in particular Georg Lukács and Antonio Gramsci. Their significance lies in their effort to integrate subjective concerns with traditional Marxian interests in objective, material structures. Third, we discuss the critical, or Frankfurt, school, which turned these early Hegelian criticisms into a full-scale revision of Marxian theory. In connection with this, we comment on those who sought to extend traditional Marxian interests to individual-level phenomena. We devote special attention to the ideas of a contemporary critical theorist, Jurgen Habermas. Fourth, we discuss structural Marxism, which constitutes a reaction against the Hegelian revisionists and a return to what these theorists call Marx's "real" concern with unconscious structures. Fifth, we discuss some of the work in institutional neo-Marxian economics that is relevant to sociology. Sixth, we touch on work being done in historically oriented Marxism (for example, Wallerstein, 1974, 1980, 1989).

In addition to the neo-Marxian theories discussed in this chapter, a number of "post-Marxist" theories will be covered in Chapter 17. Included among these post-Marxist theories are analytical Marxism, postmodern Marxism, as well as the ideas of Samuel Bowles and Herbert Gintis (1987) on democracy and capitalism. These post-Marxist theories are seen as going far beyond the traditional boundaries of Marxian theory, and some observers even argue that they should no longer be considered part of Marxian theory.

ECONOMIC DETERMINISM

In a number of places in his work, Marx sounded like an economic determinist; that is, he seemed to consider the economic system of paramount importance and to argue that it determined all other sectors of society—politics, religion, idea systems, and so forth. Although Marx did see the economic sector as preeminent, at least in capitalist society, as a dialectician he could not have taken a deterministic position because the dialectic is characterized by the notion that there is continual feedback and mutual interaction among the various sectors of society. Politics, religion, and so on cannot be reduced to epiphenomena determined by the economy, because they affect the economy just as they are affected by it. Despite the nature of the dialectic, Marx still is being interpreted as an economic determinist. Although some aspects of Marx's work would lead to this conclusion, adopting it means ignoring the overall dialectical thrust of his theory.

Agger (1978) argued that economic determinism reached its peak as an interpretation of Marxian theory during the period of the Second Communist

International, between 1889 and 1914. This historical period is often seen as the apex of early market capitalism, and its booms and busts led to many predictions about its imminent demise. Those Marxists who believed in economic determinism saw the breakdown of capitalism as inevitable. In their view, Marxism was capable of producing a scientific theory of this breakdown (as well as other aspects of capitalist society) with the predictive reliability of the physical and natural sciences. All an analyst had to do was examine the structures of capitalism, especially the economic structures. Built into these structures was a series of processes that would inevitably bring down capitalism, so it was up to the economic determinist to discover how these processes worked.

Friedrich Engels, Marx's collaborator and benefactor, led the way in this interpretation of Marxian theory, as did such people as Karl Kautsky and Eduard Bernstein. Kautsky, for example, discussed the inevitable decline of capitalism as

> unavoidable in the sense that the inventors improve technic and the capitalists in their desire for profit revolutionize the whole economic life, as it is also inevitable that the workers aim for shorter hours of labor and higher wages, that they organize themselves, that they fight the capitalist class and its state, as it is inevitable that they aim for the conquest of political power and the overthrow of capitalist rule. Socialism is inevitable because the class struggle and the victory of the proletariat is inevitable.
>
> (Kautsky, cited in Agger, 1978:94)

The imagery here is of actors impelled by the structures of capitalism into a series of actions.

It was this imagery that led to the major criticism of scientifically oriented economic determinism—that it was untrue to the dialectical thrust of Marx's theory. Specifically, the theory seemed to short-circuit the dialectic by making individual thought and action insignificant. The economic structures of capitalism that determined individual thought and action were the crucial element. This interpretation also led to political quietism and therefore was inconsistent with Marx's thinking. Why should individuals act if the capitalist system was going to crumble under its own structural contradictions? Clearly, given Marx's desire to integrate theory and practice, a perspective that omits action and even reduces it to insignificance would not be in the tradition of his thinking.

HEGELIAN MARXISM

As a result of the criticisms just discussed, economic determinism began to fade in importance, and a number of theorists developed other varieties of Marxian theory. One group of Marxists returned to the Hegelian roots of Marx's theory in search of a subjective orientation to complement the strength of the early Marxists at the objective, material level. The early Hegelian Marxists sought to restore the dialectic between the subjective and the objective aspects of social life. Their interest in subjective factors laid the basis for the later development of critical theory, which came to focus almost exclusively on subjective factors. A number of thinkers could be taken as illustrative of Hegelian Marxism (for example, Karl Korsch), but we will focus on the work of one who has gained great prominence, George Lukács, especially his book *History and Class Consciousness* (1922/1968). We also give brief attention to the ideas of Antonio Gramsci.

Georg Lukács

The attention of Marxian scholars of the early twentieth century was limited mainly to Marx's later, largely economic works, such as *Capital* (1867/1967). The early work, especially *The Economic and Philosophic Manuscripts of 1844* (1932/1964), which was more heavily influenced by Hegelian subjectivism, was largely unknown to Marxian thinkers. The rediscovery of the *Manuscripts* and their publication in 1932 was a major turning point. However, by the 1920s, Lukács already had written his major work, in which he emphasized the subjective side of Marxian theory. As Martin Jay puts it, "*History and Class Consciousness* anticipated in several fundamental ways the philosophical implications of Marx's *1844 Manuscripts*, whose publication it antedated by almost a decade" (1984:102).

Lukács major contribution to Marxian theory lies in his work on two major ideas—reification and class consciousness. Lukács made it clear from the beginning that he was not totally rejecting the work of the economic Marxists on reification, but simply seeking to broaden and extend their ideas. Lukács commenced with the Marxian concept of commodities, which he characterized as "the central, structural problem of capitalist society" (1922/1968:83). A *commodity* is at base a relation among people that, they come to believe, takes on the character of a thing and develops an objective form. People in their interaction with nature in capitalist society produce various products, or commodities (for example, bread, automobiles, motion pictures). However, people tend to lose sight of the fact that they produce these commodities and give them their value. Value comes to be seen as produced by a market that is independent of the actors. The *fetishism of commodities* is the process by which commodities and the market for them are granted independent objective existence by the actors in capitalist society. Marx's concept of the fetishism of commodities was the basis for Lukács's concept of reification.

The crucial difference between the fetishism of commodities and reification is in the extensiveness of the two concepts. Whereas the former is restricted to the economic institution, the latter is applied by Lukács to all society—the state, the law, *and* the economic sector. The same dynamic applies in all sectors of capitalist society: people come to believe that social structures have a life of their own, and as a result they do come to have an objective character. Lukács delineated this process:

Man in capitalist society confronts a reality "made" by himself (as a class) which appears to him to be a natural phenomenon alien to himself; he is wholly at the mercy of its "laws"; his activity is confined to the exploitation of the inexorable fulfillment of certain individual laws for his own (egoistic) interests. But even while "acting" he remains, in the nature of the case, the object and not the subject of events.

(Lukács, 1922/1968:135)

In developing his ideas on reification, Lukács integrated insights from Weber and Simmel. However, because reification was embedded in Marxian theory, it was seen as a problem limited to capitalism and not, as it was to Weber and Simmel, the inevitable fate of humankind.

The second major contribution of Lukács was his work on *class consciousness*, which refers to the belief systems shared by those who occupy the same class position within society. Lukács made it clear that class consciousness is neither the sum nor the average of individual consciousnesses; rather, it is a property of a group of people who share a similar place in the productive system. This view leads to a focus on the class consciousness of the bourgeoisie and especially of the proletariat. In Lukács's work, there is a clear link between objective economic position, class consciousness, and the "real, psychological thoughts of men about their lives" (1922/1968:51).

The concept of class consciousness necessarily implies, at least in capitalism, the prior state of *false consciousness*. That is, classes in capitalism generally do not have a clear sense of their true class interests. For example, until the revolutionary stage, members of the proletariat do not fully realize the nature and extent of their exploitation in capitalism. The falsity of class consciousness is derived from the class's position within the economic structure of society: "Class consciousness implies a class-conditioned *unconsciousness* of one's own socio-historical and economic condition. . . . The 'falseness,' the illusion implicit in this situation, is in no sense arbitrary" (Lukács, 1922/1968:52). Most social classes throughout history have been unable to overcome false consciousness and thereby achieve class consciousness. The structural position of the proletariat within capitalism, however, gives it the peculiar ability to achieve class consciousness.

The ability to achieve class consciousness is peculiar to capitalist societies. In precapitalist societies, a variety of factors prevented the development of class consciousness. For one thing, the state, independent of the economy, affected social strata; for another, status (prestige) consciousness tended to mask class (economic) consciousness. As a result, Lukács concluded, "There is therefore no possible position within such a society from which the economic basis of all social relations could be made conscious" (1922/1968:57). In contrast, the economic base of capitalism is clearer and simpler. People may not be conscious of its effects, but they are at least unconsciously aware of them. As a result, "class consciousness arrived at the point where *it could become conscious*" (Lukács, 1922/1968:59). At this stage, society turns into an ideological battleground in which those who seek to conceal the class character of society are pitted against those who seek to expose it.

Lukács compared the various classes in capitalism on the issue of class consciousness. He argued that the petty bourgeoisie and the peasants cannot develop class consciousness because of the ambiguity of their structural position within capitalism. Because these two classes represent vestiges of society in the feudal era, they are not able to develop a clear sense of the nature of capitalism. The bourgeoisie can develop class consciousness, but at best it understands the development of capitalism as something external, subject to objective laws, that it can experience only passively.

The proletariat has the capacity to develop true class consciousness, and as it does, the bourgeoisie is thrown on the defensive. Lukács refused to see the proletariat as simply driven by external forces but viewed it instead as an active creator of its own fate. In the confrontation between the bourgeoisie and the proletariat, the former class has all the intellectual and organizational weapons, whereas all the latter has, at least at first, is the ability to see society for what it is. As the battle proceeds, the proletariat moves from being a "class in itself," that is, a structurally created entity, to a "class for itself," a class conscious of its position and its mission. In other words, "the class struggle must be raised from the level of economic necessity to the level of conscious aim and effective class consciousness" (Lukács, 1922/1968:76). When the struggle reaches this point, the proletariat is capable of the action that can overthrow the capitalist system.

Lukács had a rich sociological theory, although it is embedded in Marxian terms. He was concerned with the dialectical relationship among the structures (primarily economic) of capitalism, the idea systems (especially class consciousness), individual thought, and, ultimately, individual action. His theoretical perspective provides an important bridge between the economic determinists and more modern Marxists.

Antonio Gramsci

The Italian Marxist Antonio Gramsci, although offering a less rich theoretical perspective than Lukács, also played a key role in the transition from economic determinism to more modern Marxian positions (Salamini, 1981). Gramsci was critical of Marxists who are "deterministic, fatalistic and mechanistic" (1971:336). In fact, he wrote an essay entitled "The Revolution against 'Capital'" (Gramsci, 1917/1977) in which he celebrated "the resurrection of political will against the economic determinism of those who reduced Marxism to the historical laws of Marx's best-known work [*Capital*]" (Jay, 1984:155). Although he recognized that there were historical regularities, he rejected the idea of automatic or inevitable historical developments. Thus, the masses had to act in order to bring about a social revolution. But to act, the masses had to become conscious of their situation and the nature of the system in which they lived. Thus, although Gramsci recognized the importance of structural factors, especially the economy, he did not believe that these structural factors led the masses to revolt. The masses needed to develop a revolutionary ideology, but they could not do so on their own. Gramsci operated with a rather elitist conception in which ideas were generated by intellectuals and then extended to the masses and put into practice by them. The masses could not generate such ideas, and they could experience them, once in existence, only on faith. The masses could not become self-conscious on their own; they needed the help of social elites. However, once the masses had been influenced by these ideas, they would take the actions that lead to social revolution. Gramsci, like Lukács, focused on collective ideas rather than on social structures like the economy, and both operated within traditional Marxian theory.

Gramsci's central concept, and one that reflects his Hegelianism, is hegemony (for a contemporary use of the concept of hegemony, see the discussion of the work of Laclau and Mouffe in Chapter 17). According to Gramsci, "the essential ingredient of the most modern philosophy of praxis [the linking of thought and action] is the historical-philosophical concept of 'hegemony' " (1932/1975:235). *Hegemony* is defined by Gramsci as cultural leadership exercised by the ruling class. He contrasts hegemony to coercion that is "exercised by legislative or executive powers, or expressed through police intervention" (Gramsci, 1932/1975:235). Economic Marxists tended to emphasize the economy and the coercive aspects of state domination. In contrast, Gramsci emphasized " 'hegemony' and cultural leadership" (1932/1975:235). In an analysis of capitalism, Gramsci wanted to know how some intellectuals, working on behalf of the capitalists, achieved cultural leadership and the assent of the masses.

Not only does the concept of hegemony help us to understand domination within capitalism, but it also serves to orient Gramsci's thoughts on revolution. That is, through revolution, it is not enough to gain control of the economy and the state apparatus; it is also necessary to gain cultural leadership over the rest of society. It is here that Gramsci sees a key role for communist intellectuals and the communist party.

We turn now to critical theory, which grew out of the work of Hegelian Marxists like Lukács and Gramsci, and which has moved even further from the traditional Marxian roots of economic determinism.

CRITICAL THEORY

Critical theory is the product of a group of German neo-Marxists who were dissatisfied with the state of Marxian theory, particularly its tendency toward economic determinism. The school was officially founded in Frankfurt, Germany, on February 23, 1923, although a number of its members had been active prior to that time. With the coming to power of the Nazis in the 1930s, many of the major figures emigrated to the United States and continued their work at an institute affiliated with Columbia University in New York City.

Following World War II, some of the critical theorists returned to Germany; others remained in the United States (Bottomore, 1984; G. Friedman, 1981; Held, 1980; Jay, 1973, 1986; Slater, 1977). Today critical theory has spread beyond the confines of the Frankfurt school (*Telos*, 1989–90). Critical theory was and is today largely a European orientation, although its influence in American sociology has grown (van den Berg, 1980).

The Major Critiques

Critical theory is composed largely of criticisms of various aspects of social and intellectual life. It takes its inspiration from Marx's work, which was first shaped by a critical analysis of philosophical ideas and later by critiques of the nature of the capitalist system. The critical school constitutes a critique both of society and of various systems of knowledge (Farganis, 1975). Much of the work is in the form of critiques, but its ultimate goal is to reveal more accurately the nature of society (Bleich, 1977). First we focus on the major criticisms offered by the school, all of which manifest a preference for oppositional thinking and for unveiling and debunking various aspects of social reality (Connerton, 1976).

Criticisms of Marxian Theory Critical theory is a variant of Marxian theory that takes as its starting point a critique of Marxian theories. The critical theorists are most disturbed by the economic determinists, the mechanistic, or mechanical, Marxists (Antonio, 1981; Schroyer, 1973; Sewart, 1978). Some (for example, Habermas, 1971) criticize the determinism implicit in parts of Marx's original work, but most focus their criticisms on the neo-Marxists, primarily because they had interpreted Marx's work too mechanistically. The critical theorists do not say that economic determinists were wrong in focusing on the economic realm but that they should have been concerned with other aspects of social life as well. As we will see, the critical school seeks to rectify this imbalance by focusing its attention on the cultural realm (Schroyer, 1973:33). In addition to attacking other Marxian theories, the critical school also critiqued societies, like the Soviet Union, built, ostensibly, on Marxian theory (Marcuse, 1958).

Criticisms of Positivism Critical theorists also focus on the philosophical underpinnings of scientific inquiry, especially positivism (Bottomore, 1984). The criticism of positivism is related, at least in part, to the criticism of economic determinism, because some of those who were determinists accepted part or all of the positivistic theory of knowledge. Positivism is depicted as standing for various things (Schroyer, 1970; Sewart, 1978). Positivism accepts the idea that a single scientific method is applicable to all fields of study. It takes the physical sciences as the standard of certainty and exactness for all disciplines. Positivists believe that knowledge is inherently neutral. They feel that they can keep human values out of their work. This, in turn, leads to the view that science is not in the position of advocating any specific form of social action. (See Chapter 1 for a further discussion of positivism.)

Positivism is opposed by the critical school on various grounds (Sewart, 1978). For one thing, positivism tends to reify the social world and see it as a natural process. The critical theorists prefer to focus on human activity as well as on the ways in which such activity affects larger social structures. In short, positivism loses sight of the actors (Habermas, 1971), reducing them to passive entities determined by "natural forces." Given their belief in the distinctiveness of the actor, the critical theorists would not accept the idea that the general laws of science can be applied without question to human action. Positivism is assailed for being content to judge the adequacy of means toward given ends and for not making a similar judgment about ends. This leads to the view that positivism is inherently conservative, incapable of challenging the existing system. As Martin Jay says of it, "The result was the absolutizing of 'facts' and the reification of the existing order" (1973:62). Positivism leads the actor and the social scientist to passivity. Few Marxists of any type would support a perspective that does not relate theory and practice. Despite these criticisms of positivism, some Marxists (for example, some structuralists, analytic Marxists) espouse positivism, and Marx himself was often guilty of being overly positivistic (Habermas, 1971).

Criticisms of Sociology The critical school also has taken on sociology as a target (Frankfurt Institute for Social Research, 1973). It is attacked for its "scientism," that is, for making the scientific method an end in itself. In addition, sociology is accused of accepting the status quo. The critical school maintains that sociology does not seriously criticize society, nor does it seek to transcend the contemporary social structure. Sociology, the critical school contends, has surrendered its obligation to help people oppressed by contemporary society.

In addition to such political criticisms, the critical school also has a related substantive criticism. That is, it is critical of sociologists' tendency to reduce everything human to social variables. When sociologists focus on society as a whole rather than on individuals in society, they ignore the interaction of the individual and society. Although most sociological perspectives are *not* guilty of ignoring this interaction, this view is a cornerstone of the critical school's attacks on sociologists. Because they ignore the individual, sociologists are seen as being unable to say anything meaningful about political changes that could lead to a "just and humane society" (Frankfurt Institute for Social Research, 1973:46). As Zoltan Tar put it, sociology becomes "an integral part of the existing society instead of being a means of critique and a ferment of renewal" (1977:x).

Critique of Modern Society Most of the critical school's work is aimed at a critique of modern society and a variety of its components. Whereas much of early Marxian theory aimed specifically at the economy, the critical school has shifted its orientation to the cultural level in light of what it considers the realities of modern capitalist society. That is, the locus of domination in the modern world had shifted from the economy to the cultural realm. Still, the critical school retains its interest in domination,[1] although in the modern world it is likely to be domination by cultural rather than economic elements. The critical school thus seeks to focus on the cultural repression of the individual in modern society.

The critical thinkers have been shaped not only by Marxian theory but also by Weberian theory, as reflected in their focus on rationality as the dominant development within the modern world. As Trent Schroyer (1970) made clear, the view of the critical school is that in modern society the repression produced by rationality has replaced economic exploitation as the dominant social problem. The critical school clearly has adopted Weber's differentiation between *formal rationality* and *substantive rationality*, or what the critical theorists think of as *reason*. To the critical theorists, formal rationality is concerned unreflectively with the question of the most effective means for achieving any given purpose (Tar, 1977). This is viewed as "technocratic thinking," in which the objective is to serve the forces of domination, not to emancipate people from domination. The goal is simply to find the most efficient means to whatever ends are defined as important by those in power. Technocratic thinking is contrasted to reason, which is, in the minds of critical theorists, the hope for society. Reason involves the assessment of means in terms of the ultimate human values of justice, peace, and happiness. Critical theorists identified Nazism in general, and its concentration camps more specifically, as examples of formal rationality in mortal combat with reason. Thus, as George Friedman puts it, "Auschwitz was a rational place, but it was not a reasonable one" (1981:15).

Despite the seeming rationality of modern life, the critical school views the modern world as rife with irrationality. This can be labeled the "irrationality of rationality," or more specifically the irrationality of formal rationality. As Herbert Marcuse saw it, although it appears to be the embodiment of rationality, "this society is irrational as a whole" (1964:ix; see also Farganis, 1975). It is irrational that the rational world is destructive of individuals and their needs and abilities; that peace is maintained through a constant threat of war; and that despite the existence of sufficient means, people remain impoverished, repressed, exploited, and unable to fulfill themselves.

The critical school focuses primarily on one form of formal rationality—modern technology. Marcuse (1964), for example, was a severe critic of modern technology. He saw technology in modern society as leading to totalitarianism. In fact, he viewed it as leading to new, more effective, and even more "pleasant" methods of external control over individuals. The prime example is the use of television to socialize and pacify the population (other examples

---

[1] This is made abundantly clear by Trent Schroyer (1973), who entitles his book on the critical school *The Critique of Domination*.

are mass sports and sex). He rejected the idea that technology is neutral in the modern world and saw it instead as a means to dominate people. It is effective because it is made to seem neutral when it is in fact enslaving. It serves to suppress individuality. The actor's inner freedom has been "invaded and whittled down" by modern technology. The result is what Marcuse called "one-dimensional society," in which individuals lose the ability to think critically and negatively about society. Marcuse did not see technology per se as the enemy, but rather technology as it is employed in modern capitalist society: "Technology, no matter how 'pure,' sustains and streamlines the continuum of domination. This fatal link can be cut only by a revolution which makes technology and technique subservient to the needs and goals of free men" (1969:56). Marcuse retained Marx's original view that technology is not inherently a problem and that it can be used to develop a "better" society.

Critique of Culture According to Friedman, "the Frankfurt School focused its most intense attention on the cultural realm" (1981:136). The critical theorists level significant criticisms at what they call the "culture industry," the rationalized, bureaucratized structures (for example, the television networks) that control modern culture. Interest in the culture industry reflects their concern with the Marxian concept of "superstructure" rather than with the economic base. The *culture industry*, producing what is conventionally called "mass culture," is defined as the "administered . . . nonspontaneous, reified, phony culture rather than the real thing" (Jay, 1973:216). Two things worry the critical thinkers most about this industry. First, they are concerned about its falseness. They think of it as a prepackaged set of ideas mass-produced and disseminated to the masses by the media. Second, the critical theorists are disturbed by its pacifying, repressive, and stupefying effect on people (Friedman, 1981; Tar, 1977:83).

In a recent book, Douglas Kellner (1990c) self-consciously does a critical theory of television. While he embeds his work in the cultural concerns of the Frankfurt school, Kellner draws on other Marxian traditions to present a more rounded conception of the television industry. He critiques the critical school because it "neglects detailed analysis of the political economy of the media, conceptualizing mass culture merely as an instrument of capitalist ideology" (Kellner, 1990c:14). Thus, in addition to looking at television as part of the culture industry, Kellner connects it to both corporate capitalism and the political system. Furthermore, Kellner does not see television as monolithic or as controlled by coherent corporate forces, but rather as a "highly conflictual mass medium in which competing economic, political, social and cultural forces intersect" (1990c:14). Thus, while working within the tradition of critical theory, Kellner rejects the view that capitalism is a totally administered world. Nevertheless, Kellner sees television as a threat to democracy, individuality, and freedom and offers suggestions (for example, more democratic accountability, greater citizen access and participation, greater diversity on television) to deal with the threat. Thus, Kellner goes beyond a mere critique to offer proposals for dealing with the dangers posed by television.

The critical school is also interested in and critical of what it calls the "knowledge industry," which refers to entities concerned with knowledge production (for example, universities and research institutes) that have become autonomous structures in our society. Their autonomy has allowed them to extend themselves beyond their original mandate (Schroyer, 1970). They have become oppressive structures interested in expanding their influence throughout society.

Marx's critical analysis of capitalism led him to have hope for the future, but many critical theorists have come to a position of despair and hopelessness. They see the problems of the modern world not as specific to capitalism but as endemic to a rationalized world, including socialist societies. They see the future, in Weberian terms, as an "iron cage" of increasingly rational structures from which hope for escape lessens all the time.

Much of critical theory (like the bulk of Marx's original formulation) is in the form of critical analyses. Even though the critical theorists also have a number of positive interests, one of the basic criticisms made of critical theory is that it offers more criticisms than it does positive contributions. This incessant negativity galls many, and for this reason they feel that critical theory has little to offer sociological theory.

The Major Contributions

Subjectivity   The great contribution of the critical school has been its effort to reorient Marxian theory in a subjective direction. Although this constitutes a critique of Marx's materialism and his dogged focus on economic structures, it also represents a strong contribution to our understanding of the subjective elements of social life. The subjective contributions of the critical school are at both the individual and the cultural levels.

The Hegelian roots of Marxian theory are the major source of interest in subjectivity. Many of the critical thinkers see themselves as returning to those roots, as expressed in Marx's early works, especially *The Economic and Philosophic Manuscripts of 1844* (1932/1964). In this, they are following up on the work of the early twentieth-century Marxian revisionists, such as Karl Korsch and Georg Lukács, who sought not to focus on subjectivity but simply to integrate such an interest with the traditional Marxian concern with objective structures (Agger, 1978). Korsch and Lukács did not seek a fundamental restructuring of Marxian theory, although the later critical theorists do have this broader and more ambitious objective.

We begin with the critical school's interest in culture. As pointed out above, the critical school has shifted to a concern with the cultural "superstructure" rather than with the economic "base." One factor motivating this shift is that the critical school feels that Marxists have overemphasized economic structures and that this has served to overwhelm their interest in the other aspects of social reality, especially the culture. In addition to this factor, a series of external changes in the society point to such a shift (Agger, 1978). In particular, the prosperity of the post–World War II period *seems* to have led to a disappearance of internal economic contradictions in general and class conflict in particular. False consciousness *seems* to be nearly universal as all social classes, including the working class, appear to be beneficiaries and ardent supporters of the capitalist system. To this might be added the realization that the Soviet Union, despite its socialist economy, is at least as oppressive, even in this era of *perestroika,* as capitalist society. Because the two societies have different economies, the critical thinkers have had to look elsewhere for the major source of oppression. What they looked toward initially was culture.

To the previously discussed aspects of the Frankfurt school's concerns— rationality, the culture industry, and the knowledge industry—can be added an additional set of concerns, the most notable of which is an interest in ideology. By *ideology* they mean the idea systems, often false and obfuscating, produced by societal elites. All these specific aspects of the superstructure and the critical school's orientation to them can be subsumed under the heading "critique of domination" (Agger, 1978; Schroyer, 1973). This interest in domination was at first stimulated by fascism in the 1930s and 1940s, but it has shifted to a concern with domination in capitalist society. The modern world has reached a stage of unsurpassed domination of individuals. In fact, the control is so complete that it no longer requires deliberate actions on the part of the leaders. The control pervades all aspects of the cultural world and, more important, is internalized in the actor. In effect, actors have come to dominate themselves in the name of the larger social structure. Domination has reached such a complete stage that it no longer appears to be domination at all. Because domination is no longer perceived as personally damaging and alienating, it often seems as if the world is the way it is supposed to be. It is no longer clear to actors what the world *ought* to be like. This buttresses the pessimism of the critical thinkers, who no longer can see how rational analysis can help alter the situation.

One of the critical school's concerns at the cultural level is with what Habermas (1975) called *legitimations.* These can be defined as systems of ideas generated by the political system, and theoretically by any other system, to support the existence of the system. They are designed to "mystify" the political system, to make it unclear exactly what is happening.

In addition to such cultural interests, the critical school is also concerned with actors and their consciousness and what happens to them in the modern world. The consciousness of the masses came to be controlled by external forces (such as the culture industry). As a result, the masses failed to develop a revolutionary consciousness. Unfortunately, the critical theorists, like most Marxists and most sociologists, often fail to differentiate clearly between individual consciousness and culture, nor do they specify the many links between them. In much of their work, they move freely back and forth between con-sciousness and culture with little or no sense that they are changing levels.

Of great importance here is the effort by critical theorists, most notably Marcuse (1969), to integrate Freud's insights at the level of consciousness (and unconsciousness) into the critical theorists' interpretation of the culture. Fried-man (1981) argues that critical theorists derive three things from Freud's work: (1) a psychological structure to work with in their theories; (2) a sense of psychopathology that allows them to understand both the negative impact of modern society and the failure to develop revolutionary consciousness; and (3) the possibilities of psychic liberation. One of the benefits of this interest in individual consciousness is that it offers a useful corrective to the pessimism of the critical school and its focus on cultural constraints. Although people are controlled, imbued with false needs, and anesthetized, in Freudian terms they are also endowed with a libido (broadly conceived as sexual energy), which provides the basic source of energy for creative action oriented toward the overthrow of the major forms of domination.

Dialectics   The second main positive focus of critical theory is an interest in dialectics (for a critique of this idea from a Marxian viewpoint, see Chapter 17) in general, as well as in a variety of its specific manifestations. At the most general level, a dialectical approach means a focus on the social *totality*.[2] Paul Connerton gave a good sense of the critical approach to the social totality: "No partial aspect of social life and no isolated phenomenon may be compre-hended unless it is related to the historical whole, to the social structure con-ceived as a global entity" (1976:12). This involves a rejection of a focus on any *specific* aspect of social life, especially the economic system, outside of its broader context. This approach also means a concern with the interrelation of the various levels of social reality—most important, individual consciousness, the cultural superstructure, and the economic structure. Dialectics also carries with it a methodological prescription: One component of social life cannot be studied in isolation from the rest.

This idea has both diachronic and synchronic components. A *synchronic* view leads us to be concerned with the interrelationship of components of society within a contemporary totality. A *diachronic* view carries with it a con-cern for the historical roots of today's society as well as for where it might be going in the future (Bauman, 1976). The domination of people by social and cultural structures—the "one-dimensional" society, to use Marcuse's phrase—is the result of a specific historical development and is not a universal char-acteristic of humankind. This historical perspective counteracts the common-sense view that emerges in capitalism that the system is a natural and inevi-table phenomenon. In the view of the critical theorists (and other Marxists), people have come to see society as "second nature"; it is "perceived by com-

---

[2] Jay (1984) sees "totality" as the heart of Marxian theory in general, not just of critical theory. On the other hand, this idea is rejected by postmodern Marxists (see Chapter 17).

mon-sensical wisdom as an alien, uncompromising, demanding and high-handed power—exactly like non-human nature. To abide by the rules of reason, to behave rationally, to achieve success, to be free, man now had to accommodate himself to the 'second nature' " (Bauman, 1976:6).

The critical theorists also are oriented to thinking about the future, but following Marx's original lead, they refuse to be utopian; rather, they focus on criticizing and changing contemporary society. However, instead of directing their attention to society's economic structure as Marx had done, they concentrate on its cultural superstructure. Their dialectical approach commits them to work in the real world. On one level, this means that they are not satisfied with seeking truth in scientific laboratories. The ultimate test of their ideas is the degree to which they are accepted and used in practice. This process they call *authentication*, which occurs when the people who have been the victims of distorted communication take up the ideas of critical theory and use them to free themselves from that system (Bauman, 1976:104). This leads to another aspect of the concerns of the critical thinkers—the *liberation* of humankind (Marcuse, 1964:222).

In more abstract terms, critical thinkers can be said to be preoccupied with the interplay and relationship between theory and practice. The view of the Frankfurt school was that the two have been severed in capitalist society (Schroyer, 1973:28). That is, theorizing is done by one group, which is delegated, or more likely takes, that right, whereas practice is relegated to another, less powerful group. In many cases, the theorist's work is uninformed by what went on in the real world, leading to an impoverished and largely irrelevant body of Marxian and sociological theory. The point is to unify theory and practice so as to restore the relationship between them. Theory thus would be informed by practice, whereas practice would be shaped by theory. In the process, both theory and practice would be enriched.

Despite this avowed goal, most of critical theory has failed abysmally to integrate theory and practice. In fact, one of the most often voiced criticisms of critical theory is that it is written in such a way as to be totally inaccessible to the mass of people. Furthermore, in its commitment to studying culture and superstructure, it addresses a number of very esoteric topics and has little to say about the pragmatic, day-to-day concerns of most people.

One of the best-known dialectical concerns of the critical school is that of Jurgen Habermas (1970, 1971). His interest in the relationship between knowledge and human interests is an example of a broader dialectical concern with the relationship between subjective and objective factors. But he has been careful to point out that subjective and objective factors cannot be dealt with in isolation from one another. To Habermas, knowledge systems exist at the objective level whereas human interests are more subjective phenomena.

Habermas differentiated among three knowledge systems and their corresponding interests. The interests that lie behind and guide each system of knowledge are generally unknown to laypeople, and it is the task of the critical theorists to uncover them. The first type of knowledge is *analytic science,* or *classical positivistic scientific systems.* In Habermas's view, the underlying interest of such a knowledge system is technical control, which can be applied to the environment, other societies, or people within society. In Habermas's view, analytic science lends itself quite easily to enhancing oppressive control. The second type of knowledge system is *humanistic knowledge,* and its interest is in *understanding* the world. It operates from the general view that understanding our past generally helps us to understand what is transpiring today. It has a practical interest in mutual and self-understanding. It is neither oppressive nor liberating. The third type is *critical knowledge,* which Habermas, and the Frankfurt school in general, espoused. The interest attached to this type of knowledge is *human emancipation.* It was hoped that the critical knowledge generated by Habermas and others would raise the self-consciousness of the masses (through mechanisms articulated by the Freudians) and lead to a social movement that would result in the hoped-for emancipation.

Criticisms of Critical Theory

A number of criticisms have been leveled at critical theory (Bottomore, 1984). First, critical theory has been accused of being largely ahistorical, of examining a variety of events (for example, Nazism in the 1930s, anti-Semitism in the 1940s, student revolts in the 1960s) without paying much attention to their historical and comparative contexts. This is a damning criticism of any Marxian theory, which should be inherently historical and comparative. Second, the critical school, as we have seen already, generally has ignored the economy. Finally, and relatedly, critical theorists have tended to argue that the working class has disappeared as a revolutionary force, a position decidedly in opposition to traditional Marxian analysis.

Criticisms such as these have led such traditional Marxists as Bottomore to conclude, "The Frankfurt School, in its original form, and as a school of Marxism or sociology, is dead" (1984:76). Similar sentiments have been expressed by Greisman, who labels critical theory "the paradigm that failed" (1986:273). If it is dead as a distinctive school, it is because many of its basic ideas have found their way into Marxism, neo-Marxian sociology, and even mainstream sociology. Thus, as Bottomore himself concludes in the case of Habermas, the critical school has undergone a rapproachment with Marxism and sociology, and "at the same time some of the distinctive ideas of the Frankfurt School are conserved and developed" (1984:76).

Although critical theory *may* be on the decline, Jurgen Habermas and his theories are very much alive. Although we have touched on a few of his thoughts earlier in this chapter, we close this section on critical theory with a more detailed look at his ideas (still more of his thinking will be covered in Chapter 15).

The Ideas of Jurgen Habermas

A good place to begin a discussion of Habermas's ideas is with his views on Karl Marx's theories. As Habermas makes clear, his goal over the years has been "to develop a theoretical program that I understand as a reconstruction of historical materialism" (1979:95). Habermas takes Marx's starting point (human potential, species-being, "sensuous human activity") as his own. However, Habermas (1971) argues that Marx failed to distinguish between two analytically distinct components of species-being—work (or labor, purposive-rational action) and social (or symbolic) interaction (or communicative action). In Habermas's view, Marx tended to ignore the latter and to reduce it to work. As Habermas put it, the problem in Marx's work is the *"reduction of the self-generative act of the human species* to labor" (1971:42). Thus, Habermas says: "I take as my starting point the fundamental distinction between *work* and *interaction*" (1970:91). Throughout his writings, Habermas looks at his distinction, although he is most prone to use the terms *purposive-rational action* (work) and *communicative action* (interaction).

Under the heading "purposive-rational action," Habermas distinguishes between instrumental action and strategic action. Both involve the calculated pursuit of self-interest. *Instrumental action* is concerned with a single actor rationally calculating the best means to a given goal. *Strategic action* involves two or more individuals coordinating purposive-rational action in the pursuit of a goal. The objective of *both* instrumental and strategic action is instrumental mastery.

Habermas is most interested in *communicative action*, in which

> the actions of the agents involved are coordinated not through egocentric calculations of success but through acts of *reaching understanding*. In communicative action participants are not primarily oriented to their own successes; they pursue their individual goals under the condition that they can *harmonize* their plans of action on the basis of *common situation definitions*.
>
> (Habermas, 1984:286; italics added)

Whereas the end of purposive-rational action is to achieve a goal, the objective of communicative action is to achieve communicative understanding.

Clearly, there is an important speech component in communicative action. However, such action is broader than that encompassing "speech acts or equivalent nonverbal expressions" (Habermas, 1984:278).

Habermas's key point of departure from Marx is to argue that communicative action, *not* purposive-rational action (work), is the most distinctive and most pervasive human phenomenon. It (not work) is the foundation of all sociocultural life as well as all the human sciences. Whereas Marx was led to focus on work, Habermas is led to focus on communication.

Not only did Marx focus on work, but he took free and creative work (species-being) as his baseline for critically analyzing work in various historical epochs, especially capitalism. Habermas, too, adopts a baseline, but in the realm of communicative rather than purposive-rational action. Habermas's baseline is undistorted communication, communication without compulsion. With this baseline, Habermas is able to critically analyze distorted communication. Habermas is concerned with those social structures that distort communication, just as Marx examined the structural sources of the distortion of work. Although they have different baselines, both Habermas and Marx *have* baselines, and these permit them to escape relativism and render judgments about various historical phenomena. Habermas is critical of those theorists, especially Weber and previous critical theorists, for their lack of such a baseline and their lapse into relativism.

There is still another parallel between Marx and Habermas and their baselines. For both, these baselines represent not only their analytical starting points but also their political objectives. That is, whereas for Marx the goal was a communist society in which undistorted work (species-being) would exist for the first time, for Habermas the political goal is a society of undistorted communication (communicative action). In terms of immediate goals, Marx seeks the elimination of (capitalist) barriers to undistorted work, and Habermas is interested in the elimination of barriers to free communication.

Here Habermas (1973), like other critical theorists, draws on Freud and sees many parallels between what psychoanalysts do at the individual level and what he thinks needs to be done at the societal level. Habermas sees psychoanalysis as a theory of distorted communication and as preoccupied with allowing individuals to communicate in an undistorted way. The psychoanalyst seeks to find the sources of distortions in individual communication, that is, repressed blocks to communication. Through reflection, the psychoanalyst attempts to help the individual overcome these blocks. Similarly, through *therapeutic critique,* "a form of argumentation that serves to clarify systematic self-deception" (Habermas, 1984:21), the critical theorist (and the communist party [Habermas, 1973]) attempts to aid people in general to overcome social barriers to undistorted communication. There is, then, an analogy (many critics think an illegitimate analogy) between psychoanalysis and critical theory. The psychoanalyst aids the patient in much the same way that the social critic helps oppressed groups in society.

As for Marx, the basis of Habermas's ideal future society exists in the contemporary world. That is, for Marx elements of species-being are found in work in capitalist society. For Habermas, elements of undistorted communication are to be found in every act of contemporary communication.

This brings us to the central issue of rationalization in Habermas's work. Here Habermas is influenced not only by Marx's work but by Weber's as well. In his work on rationalization, Habermas's distinction between purposive-rational and communicative action remains centrally important. Most prior work, in Habermas's view, has focused on the rationalization of purposive-rational action, which has led to a growth of productive forces and an increase in technological control over life (Habermas, 1970). This form of rationalization, as it was to Weber and Marx, is a major, perhaps *the* major, problem in the modern world. However, the problem is rationalization of purposive-rational action, *not* rationalization in general. In fact, for Habermas, the solution to the problem of the rationalization of purposive-rational action lies in the rationalization of communicative action. The rationalization of communicative action leads to communication free from domination, free and open communication. Rationalization here involves emancipation, *"removing restrictions on communication"* (Habermas, 1970:118; see also Habermas, 1979). This is where Habermas's previously mentioned work on *legitimations* and, more generally, *ideology* fits in. That is, these are two of the main causes of distorted communication, causes that must be eliminated if we are to have free and open communication.

At the level of social norms, such rationalization would involve decreases in normative repressiveness and rigidity leading to increases in individual flexibility and reflectivity. The development of this new, less restrictive or nonrestrictive normative system lies at the heart of Habermas's theory of social evolution. Instead of a new productive system, rationalization for Habermas (1979) leads to a new, less distorting normative system. Although he regards it as a misunderstanding of his position, many have accused Habermas of cutting his Marxian roots in this shift from the material to the normative level.

The end point of this evolution for Habermas is a rational society. *Rationality* here means removal of the barriers that distort communication, but more generally it means a communication system in which ideas are openly presented and defended against criticism; unconstrained agreement develops during argumentation. To understand this better, we need more details of Habermas's communication theory.

Habermas distinguishes between the previously discussed communicative action and discourse. Whereas communicative action occurs in everyday life, *discourse* is

> that form of communication that is removed from contexts of experience and action and whose structure assures us: that the bracketed validity claims of assertions, recommendations, or warnings are the exclusive object of discussion; that participants, themes, and contributions are not restricted except with reference to the goal of testing the validity claims in questions; that no force except that of the better argument is exercised; and that all motives except that of the cooperative search for truth are excluded.
>
> (Habermas, 1975:107–108)

In the theoretical world of discourse, but also hidden and underlying the world of communicative actions, is the "ideal speech situation," in which force or power does not determine which arguments win out; instead the better argument emerges victorious. The weight of evidence and argumentation determine what is considered to be valid or true. The arguments that emerge from such a discourse (and that the participants agree on) are true. Thus Habermas adopts a consensus theory of truth (rather than a copy [or "reality"] theory of truth). This truth is part of all communication, and its full expression is the goal of Habermas's evolution theory. As Thomas McCarthy says, "The idea of truth points ultimately to a form of interaction that is free from all distorting influences. The 'good and true life' that is the goal of critical theory is inherent in the notion of truth; it is anticipated in every act of speech" (1982:308).

Consensus arises theoretically in discourse (and pretheoretically in communicative action) when four types of validity claims are raised and recognized by interactants. First, the speaker's utterances are seen as understandable, comprehensible. Second, the propositions offered by the speaker are true; that is, the speaker is offering reliable knowledge. Third, the speaker is being truthful (veracious) in offering the propositions; the speaker is reliable. Fourth, it is right and proper for the speaker to utter such propositions; he or she has the right to do so. Consensus arises when all these validity claims are raised and accepted; it breaks down when one or more are questioned (for example, questioning the right of the speaker to utter certain propositions). Returning to an earlier point, there are forces in the modern world that distort this process, prevent the emergence of a consensus, and would have to be overcome for Habermas's ideal society to come about.

Thus, within the tradition of critical theory, Habermas has developed a powerful variant of his own. Although it remains broadly within the critical theory and, more generally, Marxian traditions, it has a number of quite distinctive elements. Furthermore, the theory continues to develop, and in his recent work Habermas (1984, 1987) has moved in some interesting new directions, directions that take his theory even further from critical and Marxian theory. We discuss these recent developments in Habermas's theory in Chapter 15 of this book.

STRUCTURAL MARXISM

Structural Marxism is usually associated with a group of French thinkers (for example, Louis Althusser, Nicos Poulantzas, and Maurice Godelier) and thus is sometimes called "French structuralism." However, because this approach has many followers outside of France, we refer to this school as structural Marxism.

As the name suggests, *structural Marxism* represents the fusion of two schools—Marxism and structuralism. Structuralism is devoted to the analysis of the hidden, underlying structures of social life. Later we will see that structuralism encompasses a wide array of complicated ideas. In Chapter 13, in addition to a detailed discussion of structuralism, we will include a discussion of the relationship between structuralism in general and structural Marxism in particular. We will see that although the two orientations have a number of things in common, there are important differences between them. Our concern here is with the kind of Marxism that structural Marxism represents; in Chapter 13 we will deal with it as a kind of structuralism.

Criticisms of Other Marxian Theories

A good way to approach structural Marxism is to discuss its criticisms of other Marxian theories. In general, structural Marxists see themselves as being truest to Marx's work, especially his later work. In addition to questioning the purity of other Marxian theorists, structural Marxists make a number of more specific attacks (Burris, 1979).

First, structural Marxists criticize the tendency of many Marxists to emphasize empirical data in their analyses. In the view of such structural Marxists as Godelier (1972a), the truly important realities of capitalist life are to be found in its underlying structure and not in the observable facts that often obscure the true nature of that structure.

Second, structural Marxists reject the tendency of many Marxists toward historical research, because historicism is also seen as focusing on empirical data and neglecting the underlying structure. In addition, they reject historicism because of their belief that the primary task of Marxism is the study of contemporary structure. Only after we understand the basic structure of the contemporary world can we begin to grasp historical processes. Interestingly, this is reminiscent of the position taken by a major critic of Marxian theory, Talcott Parsons, who also argued that a study of structure was a prerequisite to a theory of history and social change.

Third, structural Marxists sharply criticize the reductionistic economic determinism that is characteristic of some Marxian theories. Although the structural Marxists see the importance of the economy and even see it as determinant "in the last instance," they also accord significance to other sectors of the social world, especially the political and ideological structures. Poulantzas, for example, rejected the idea that the state merely reflects the economy; it can be seen as possessing "relative autonomy." More specifically, he took issue with those determinists who argue that economic development would follow whatever type of state exists. In other words, he criticized those who argued that it makes no difference whether we have fascism or democracy. Poulantzas concluded, "Here, as elsewhere, the forms that bourgeois domination assumes are far from a matter of indifference" (1976:21).

Poulantzas singled out for criticism the passive position of those Marxian theorists who argued that fascism somehow would crumble as a result of its own internal economic contradictions and that thus there was no need to take any action against fascist societies. Poulantzas also criticized those who argued that imperialism is simply an economic phenomenon. To him, it is a much more complex process, involving political, ideological, and economic aspects. Although Poulantzas (and other structural Marxists) recognized the importance of the economy, he also contended that at any given moment other social structures may come to occupy a dominant position.

Finally, the structural Marxists criticize the tendency of a large number of other Marxists (especially critical theorists) to subjectivize and humanize the field. As Jay puts it, structural Marxists "disdainfully rejected the humanist, subjectivist concept of Marxism" (1984:388). To the structuralists, the focus should be on the objective structures of society—economy, polity, ideology—and not the human actors within those structures. Thus the structuralists reject a humanistic interpretation of Marx's theory; the effort to resurrect Marx's historical concerns; a focus on Marx's more humanistic works (for example, the *1844 Manuscripts*); the emphasis on the Hegelian roots of Marxian theory; and a focus on voluntaristic actors, feelings, interpersonal relations, or even conscious efforts at self-organization (Appelbaum, 1979). For example, instead of seeing social classes as composed of voluntaristic actors, structuralists see them as "objectively antagonistic relations" (Burris, 1979:14). Althusser depicted the emphasis on structures and the fact that actors are determined by those structures:

> The structure of the relations of production determines the *places* and *functions* occupied and adopted by the agents of production, who are never anything more than the occupants of these places, insofar as they are the "supports" . . . of the functions. The true "subjects" (in the sense of constitutive subjects of the process) are therefore not these occupants or functionaries . . . but the *relations* of *production* (and political and ideological social relations).
>
> (Althusser, cited in Burris, 1979:8)

In sum, in rejecting humanistic Marxism, the structuralists clearly have enunciated an interest in the structures of capitalist society. Let us now state the premises of structural Marxism in more positive terms.

Tenets of Structural Marxism

Structural Marxists are oriented to the study of the hidden, underlying structures of capitalist society. Although their basic concern is not "real" structures, they do believe that there are real structures in the world that constrain or determine what actors think and do. Structural Marxists accept the importance of the economy but also look at various other structures. Furthermore, although they accept the idea of the economy as determinant in the last instance, they do not simply reduce other structures to reflections of it. In fact, not only do structural Marxists accept the importance of the polity and ideology, but they also see them as possessing "relative autonomy." These structures may follow rather independent paths of development and may at any given time come to be the dominant forces in society.

Whatever structures they focus on, to structural Marxists actors simply fill positions in those structures; that is, they are seen as largely constrained by those structures. Despite the passive implications of such a viewpoint, as practicing Marxists the structuralists are disinclined to conclude that people should simply sit and wait for the ultimate breakdown of the structural system. As Poulantzas said, "If we confine ourselves to waiting, we will not get the 'great day' at all, but rather the tanks in the small hours of the morning" (1976:133).

The idea of a breakdown of the structures of society implies another major concern of structural Marxists—the contradictions within the system. Their tendency is to focus on contradictions among structures rather than on the contradictions that confront the actor.

Structural Marxists emphasize theoretical rather than empirical research.

Clearly, because the structures are invisible, the presumption is that they can be ascertained only theoretically; thus no amount of empirical research can uncover them.

In part for the same reason, structural Marxists focus on *contemporary* society. They put little credence in historical data or research. They believe that the priority should be the study of static structures rather than historical processes; history can be known only when we have a good grasp of contemporary structure.

Reanalyzing Marx: The Work of Louis Althusser

The work of Louis Althusser is defined largely by the nature of his focus on Marx's work. Althusser's view was that most Marxists had not interpreted Marx's ideas properly; indeed, he felt that they had done great violence to them. He sought to deal with this problem by developing what he believed to be a "correct" reading of Marx's work. Althusser's work is best examined in the context of the debate surrounding Marx's work.

One issue in the debate is whether Marx took a consistent intellectual position throughout his life (Veltmeyer, 1978). This is related to the issue of whether Marx is a structural and deterministic, or a humanistic and dialectical, thinker. Those Marxists who see Marx as a structuralist focus on his later works, particularly *Capital* (1867/1967). Others point to what they see as a more humanistic perspective in the essential continuity between *Capital* and *The Economic and Philosophic Manuscripts of 1844* (1932/1964). In fact, there is ample evidence in Marx's work to support either interpretation.[3]

Althusser deals with the debate about the "two Marxes," or "what distinguishes the object of *Capital* . . . from the object . . . of the *1844 Manuscripts*" (Althusser and Balibar, 1970:14). To Althusser, the *1844 Manuscripts* were written while Marx was still heavily influenced by Hegel, philosophy, humanism, and a concern for the devastating effect of the alienating conditions of capitalism on the individual. As far as Althusser was concerned, such concerns were unscientific and needed to be overcome in order to develop scientific materialism (P. Anderson, 1976). The philosophical, humanistic, and historical bases of Marx's early work led him to center on an active, creative, and free actor. Such imagery was, in Perry Anderson's view, anathema to Althusser: "The archetypical delusion was men's belief that they were in any way free in their volition, when in fact they were permanently governed by *laws* of which they were *unconscious*" (1976:65; italics added). Althusser believed that

---

[3] Among those who see continuity in Marx's work are Mészáros (1970), Ollman (1976), and Wallimann (1981), and those who support the discontinuity thesis include McMurty (1978) and Gandy (1979). An interesting middle-ground position is developed by Barbalet, who argues that although there is continuity in Marx's use of essential concepts, and although the early works do provide the foundation for the later ones, the same concepts "are understood through different theoretical frameworks at different stages of his development" (1983:2).

NICOS POULANTZAS: A Biographical Sketch

Born in Athens, Greece, on September 21, 1936, Nicos Poulantzas became "the single most important and influential Marxist theorist of the state and politics in the postwar period" (Jessop, 1985:5). His father was a professor and a leading figure in Greek society. A precocious student, Poulantzas became fluent in French at an early age and received his baccalaureate in 1953 at age seventeen. He then entered the school of law at Athens University and completed his law degree by 1957. Although he took a law degree, it was not so much because he was interested in law as because it allowed him to study philosophy and the social sciences. Although somewhat active in left-wing politics during this period, Poulantzas had not yet become a Marxist. After three years in the Greek navy, Poulantzas was admitted to the bar, but he never actually practiced law. Instead, he went abroad to do graduate work and soon found his way to Paris.

Poulantzas arrived at the Sorbonne in 1960, obtained a coveted teaching assistantship, and taught law there until 1964. He completed his doctoral dissertation in that year, and in the interim had become active in French intellectual life, developing close ties with people like Jean-Paul Sartre and Simone de Beauvoir. He married a young novelist, Annie Leclerc, in 1966, and they had a daughter in 1970.

In the 1960s and 1970s, Poulantzas grew more involved in Marxist thought and political activity. He remained in France, and his ideas were shaped by French intellectual life, but he also retained ties with Greece. He wrote about issues relevant to ongoing events in Greece and became a card-carrying member of the Greek communist party. But as Jessop says, "He tended to react to Greek events with French eyes" (1985:13).

In the late 1960s, Poulantzas's writings began to attract international attention. He also began teaching sociology at an experimental French university. He published actively in the 1960s and 1970s and was involved in both both French and Greek political life. Poulantzas committed suicide on October 3, 1979. Since that time his work has attracted world attention and is regarded as one of the most significant neo-Marxist perspectives.

He was disinclined to think of structures as unified totalities but saw them rather as composed of a number of substructures. His best-known idea here is that of *fractions* of social classes (Poulantzas, 1975:23). In other words, a social class is not a unified totality but is rather composed of various subunits (Poulantzas, 1976:92). Similarly, within political and ideological structures he spoke of subunits, this time called *categories* and "defined principally by their place in the political and ideological relations. Examples of categories include the state bureaucracy, defined by its relation to the state apparatuses, and the intellectuals, defined by their role in elaborating and deploying ideology" (Poulantzas, 1975:23). He also differentiated among the various subunits within the state (*apparatuses*), whose main function is maintaining social cohesion politically and ideologically. These include repressive state apparatuses like the army and prisons, as well as ideological state apparatuses such as education and culture (Poulantzas, 1975:24–25). Thus Poulantzas had a much more complicated image of the structures of capitalism and its numerous substructures than did many of his peers.

Poulantzas took great care in these structural differentiations, because he saw each of the substructures as having relatively autonomous social consequences. Furthermore, each has at least the potential to play a central role in society (Poulantzas, 1973, 1975).

Poulantzas's thinking on contradictions was shaped by his pluralistic image of the structures of capitalist society. Like other structural Marxists, Poulantzas did not restrict himself to the analysis of economic contradictions but was interested in, among other things, the contradictions among the economy, the polity, and ideology. Poulantzas, however, went much further and examined the contradictions among the various fractions, categories, and apparatuses within each of the three basic structural units. For example, Poulantzas argued "that every bourgeois state is riven by contradictions between its various apparatuses and branches (and not just between political parties), as the organizational bases of one or other fraction and component of the power bloc" (1976:103–104).

Poulantzas's main theoretical focus, and that of most structural Marxists, was on the interrelationship of the three major components of capitalist society. For example, he linked the state and ideology by arguing that the *state* can never exercise its function of domination, in the long run, by repression alone; this must always be accompanied by *ideological* domination (Poulantzas, 1976).

Poulantzas also linked ideology to the economy. The most important role of ideology, expressed through the socialization process, is training people to occupy various positions and occupations within the economic sector. Although he saw socialization as important, he was careful to point out that a capitalist society not only must produce (socialize) people to fill positions but also must continually produce the positions for these people to fill. To underscore his structuralist orientation, Poulantzas stated clearly that the primary significance lies with structural positions and not with actors and their socialization:

> While it is true that the agents themselves must be reproduced—"trained" and "subjected"—in order to occupy certain places, it is equally true that the distribution of agents does not depend on their own choices or aspirations but on the reproduction of these places themselves. This is because the principal aspect of class determination is that of their places, and not that of the agents that occupy these places.
>
> (Poulantzas, 1975:29)

Although he recognized the importance of socialization, Poulantzas (1975:34) carefully differentiated his position from that taken by many sociologists in which ideological factors are given much greater significance than he thought due them.

In terms of links between the state and the economy, Poulantzas argued that in the stage of monopoly capitalism the state acquires a decisive importance. This follows logically from his more general position that "there was *never* a stage in capitalism in which the state did not play an important economic role" (Poulantzas, 1974:220; italics added).

At the most general level, Poulantzas was likely to look at the interrelationship of *all three* of the basic structures of capitalism. For example, he noted that imperialism "is not a phenomenon which can be reduced to economic developments alone. . . . Imperialism is a phenomenon with economic, political, and ideological implications" (Poulantzas, 1974:22). This is another way of saying that Poulantzas rejected the simplistic economic determinism of many Marxists. To Poulantzas the superstructure that is made of "juridico-political and ideological forms . . . intervenes decisively in the production process" (1974:41). Such a pluralistic notion led Poulantzas, like Althusser, to the notion of the uneven development of the capitalist system. This, in turn, gave Poulantzas's work a dialectic at the structural level that kept it, like the work of Althusser, from being totally deterministic.

We conclude this discussion of Poulantzas's orientation with mention of his work on social classes. As a structuralist, Poulantzas argued, according to Andor Skotnes, that "social classes are *structurally determined*; they exist objectively, independent of the will and 'consciousness' of class members" (1979:35). However, classes are not determined totally by economic structures (Poulantzas, 1974) but also by political and ideological factors. Poulantzas made a great effort to avoid that perpetual problem of structuralists, a static view of social classes. He argued that social classes are determined only in the continuing process of class struggle, which is itself broken down into economic, political, and ideological struggles. Classes are formed out of the confluence of these ongoing struggles.

Poulantzas was careful to differentiate between such a general analysis of social classes and class positions at any given historical juncture. At any particular point in history, classes or fractions of classes may take up positions not in accord with their general structural position. A labor aristocracy, for example, may identify with the bourgeoisie, or members of the middle class may take positions aligned with those of the proletariat. But these are temporary historical developments not in line with the general structure of class struggle. Thus deviations are possible within the broad sweep of history. This is another area of flexibility and dialectical process within Poulantzas's structural Marxism.

Critical Reactions to Structural Marxism

Structural Marxism has come under attack by other Marxists. First, it has been critiqued for being ahistorical. E. P. Thompson argued that "Althusser's structuralism is a structuralism of *stasis,* departing from Marx's own historical method" (1978:197). Val Burris argued that structural Marxists had misrepresented historically specific structures as "universal principles of social organization" (1979:16). Second, structural Marxists were attacked for their blind support of scientism (Appelbaum, 1979:26). Third, structural Marxism was seen as elitist, with only communist party scientists and officials able to understand the truth about the social world. Fourth, structural Marxists were attacked for losing sight of the actor and consciousness. Fifth, they have been criticized for giving inadequate attention to empirical research (Miliband, 1972:256). Sixth, the structural Marxists have been assailed for their determinism.

Interestingly, structural Marxism has come to be associated in the minds of some critics with the sociological theories that most Marxists find anathema—structural functionalism and conflict theory (Appelbaum, 1979:27–28). Even as sympathetic a critic as Jessop critiques the "implicit functionalism" (1985:111) of some aspects of Poulantzas's work. Along these same lines, Nancy DiTomaso (1982) has seen strong similarities in the work of Althusser and Parsons.

Structural Marxism is one of the most controversial developments in neo-Marxian theory. It involves pointed criticism of other varieties of Marxian theory and is itself subject to much criticism by Marxists of other theoretical persuasions.

NEO-MARXIAN ECONOMIC SOCIOLOGY

As we have seen throughout this chapter, many neo-Marxists (for example, critical theorists, structural Marxists) have made relatively few comments on the economic institution, at least in part as a reaction against the excesses of the economic determinists. However, these reactions have themselves set in motion a series of counterreactions. In this section we will deal with the work of some of those Marxists who have returned to a focus on the economic realm. Their work does not simply repeat early Marxian theory; it constitutes an effort to adapt Marxian theory to the realities of modern capitalist society.

There is, of course, a vast literature dealing with economic issues from a Marxian point of view. Much of this is relevant only to the field of economics, but some of it also has been influential in sociology. We will deal with two bodies of work in this section. The first focuses on the broad issue of capital and labor. The second comprises the narrower, and more contemporary, work on the transition from Fordism to post-Fordism.

Capital and Labor

Monopoly Capital   Marx's original insights into economic structures and processes were based on his analysis of the capitalism of his time—what we can think of as competitive capitalism. Capitalist industries were comparatively small, with the result that no one industry, or small group of industries, could gain complete and uncontested control over a market. Much of Marx's economic work was based on the premise, accurate for his time, that capitalism was a competitive system. To be sure, Marx foresaw the possibility of future monopolies, but he commented only briefly on them. Many later Marxian theorists continued to operate as if capitalism remained much as it had been in Marx's time.

It is in this context that we must examine the work of Baran and Sweezy (1966). They began with a criticism of Marxian social science for repeating familiar formulations and for failing to explain important recent developments in capitalistic society. They accused Marxian theory of stagnating because it continued to rest on the assumption of a competitive economy. A modern Marxian theory must, in their view, recognize that competitive capitalism has been largely replaced by monopoly capitalism.

A central issue for Baran and Sweezy was a delineation of the nature of monopoly capitalism. *Monopoly capitalism* means that one, or a few, capitalists control a given sector of the economy. Clearly, there is far less competition in monopoly capitalism than in competitive capitalism. In competitive capitalism, organizations competed on a price basis; that is, capitalists tried to sell more goods by offering lower prices. In monopolistic capitalism, firms no longer have to compete in this way because one or a few firms control a market; competition shifts to the sales domain. Advertising, packaging, and other methods of appealing to potential consumers are the main areas of competition.

The movement from price to sales competition is part of another process characteristic of monopoly capitalism—*progressive rationalization*. Price competition comes to be seen as highly irrational. That is, from the monopoly capitalist's point of view, offering lower and lower prices can lead only to chaos in the marketplace, to say nothing of lower profits and perhaps even bankruptcy. Sales competition, in contrast, is not a cutthroat system; in fact, it even provides work for the advertising industry. Furthermore, prices can be kept high, with the costs of the sales and promotion simply added to the price. Thus sales competition is also far less risky than price competition.

Another crucial aspect of monopoly capitalism is the rise of the giant corporation, with a few large corporations controlling most sectors of the economy. In competitive capitalism, the organization was controlled almost single-handedly by an entrepreneur. The modern corporation is owned by a large number of stockholders, but a few large stockholders own most of the stock. Although stockholders "own" the corporation, managers exercise the actual day-to-day control. The managers are crucial in monopoly capitalism, whereas the entrepreneurs were central in competitive capitalism. Managers have considerable power, which they seek to maintain. They even seek financial independence for their firms by trying, as much as possible, to generate whatever funds they need internally rather than relying on external sources of funding.

Baran and Sweezy commented extensively on the central position of the corporate manager in modern capitalist society. Managers are viewed as a highly rational group oriented to maximizing the profits of the organization. Therefore they are not inclined to take the risks that were characteristic of the early entrepreneurs. They have a longer time perspective than the entrepreneur. Whereas the early capitalist was interested in maximizing profits in the short run, modern managers are aware that such efforts may well lead to chaotic price competition that might adversely affect the long-term profitability of the firm. The manager will thus forgo *some* profits in the short run to maximize long-term profitability.

(The central issue in monopoly capitalism is the ability of the system to generate and use economic surplus.) *Economic surplus* is defined as the difference between the value of what a society produces and the costs of producing it. Because of their concern with the surplus issue, Baran and Sweezy moved away from Marx's interest in the exploitation of labor and stressed instead the links between the economy and other social institutions, in particular in the absorption of economic surplus by these other institutions.

Modern capitalistic managers are victims of their own success. On the one hand, they are able to set prices arbitrarily because of their monopolistic position in the economy. On the other hand, they seek to cut costs within the organization, particularly the costs associated with blue-collar work. The ability to set high prices and to cut costs leads to the rising level of economic surplus.

The issue that then confronts the capitalist is what to do with the surplus. One possibility is to consume it—to pay managers huge salaries and stockholders huge dividends that are turned into yachts, Rolls-Royces, jewelry, and caviar. This *is* done to some extent, but the surplus is so huge that elites could never consume even a small part of it. In any case, conspicuous consumption was more characteristic of the early entrepreneurs than of the modern manager and stockholder.

A second alternative is to invest the surplus in such things as improved technology and foreign ventures. This seemingly reasonable action, which is taken by managers to some extent, has the major drawback that such investments, if made wisely, generate even more surplus. This only exacerbates the problem of using economic surplus.

Increasing sales effort also may absorb some of the surplus. Modern capitalists can stimulate the demand for their products by advertising; by creating and expanding the markets for their products; and by such devices as model changes, planned obsolescence, and readily available consumer credit. However, this alternative also has problems. First, it cannot absorb enough surplus. Second, it is likely to stimulate even further expansion of the corporation, which, in turn, leads to still greater levels of surplus.

According to Baran and Sweezy, the only choice remaining is *waste*. The surplus needs to be squandered, and there are two ways of so doing. The first is nonmilitary government spending through keeping millions of workers in government jobs and supporting myriad governmental programs. The second is military spending, including the military's vast payroll and its budget of billions of dollars for expensive hardware that rapidly becomes obsolete.

Baran and Sweezy's position has several weaknesses. For one thing, it seems as if there is really *no good way* of getting rid of surplus, and perhaps that is the view Baran and Sweezy wish communicated. It leaves us with the clear impression that this is an irresolvable contradiction within capitalism. Virtually all the capitalists' expenditures lead to greater demand and ultimately to greater surpluses. Government and military employees spend their money on more goods; as some military equipment is consumed (for example, in the 1991 war with Iraq), there is a demand for new and better equipment.

Another criticism that can be leveled at Baran and Sweezy is that they overemphasize the rationality of managers. Herbert Simon (1957), for example, would argue that managers are more interested in finding (and are only able to find) minimally satisfactory solutions than they are in finding the most rational and most profitable solutions. Another issue is whether managers are, in fact, the pivotal figures in modern capitalism. Many would argue that the large stockholders really control the capitalistic system.

In sum, Baran and Sweezy accepted the traditional economic focus of Marxian theory and then moved it in a new and important direction. In particular, they shifted the focus from the labor process to economic structures of modern capitalistic society. We turn now to Braverman, who was influenced by the work of Baran and Sweezy but sought to return to the traditional Marxian interest in the labor process.

Labor and Monopoly Capital   Harry Braverman (1974) considered the labor process and the exploitation of the worker to be the heart of Marxian theory. Although his emphasis is different from that of Baran and Sweezy, he saw his work as tied closely to theirs (Braverman, 1974). The title of his book, *Labor and Monopoly Capital,* reflects his main focus, and its subtitle, *The Degradation of Work in the Twentieth Century,* shows his interest in adapting Marx's perspective of the realities of work in the twentieth century.

Braverman intended not only to update Marx's interest in manual workers but also to examine what has happened to white-collar and service workers. Marx paid little attention to these two groups, but since his time they have become major occupational categories that need to be subjected to serious scrutiny. In relation to Baran and Sweezy's work, it could be said that one of the major developments in monopoly capitalism has been the relative decline in blue-collar workers and the simultaneous increases in white-collar and service workers to staff the large organizations characteristic of monopoly capitalism.

Braverman's analysis begins with a point reminiscent of Marx's orientation. Braverman made it quite clear that his criticisms of the contemporary work world do not reflect a yearning for an era now past. He said that he was not romanticizing the old-time crafts and "the outworn conditions of now archaic modes of labor" (Braverman, 1974:6). Also like Marx, Braverman was a critic not of science and technology per se but simply of the way that they are used in capitalism "as weapons of domination in the creation, perpetuation and deepening of a gulf between classes in society" (1974:6). In the employ of the capitalist, science and technology have been used systematically to rob work of its craft heritage without providing anything to take its place. Braverman believed that in different (that is, socialist) hands, science and technology could be used differently to produce

> an age that has not yet come into being, in which, for the worker, the craft satisfaction that arises from conscious and purposeful mastery of the labor process will be combined with the marvel of science and the ingenuity of engineering, an age in which everyone will be able to benefit, in some degree, from this combination.
> (Braverman, 1974:7)

Toward the goal of extending Marx's analysis of blue-collar workers to white-collar and service workers, Braverman argued that the concept "working class" does not describe a specific group of people or occupations but is rather an expression of a process of buying and selling labor power. In terms of that process, Braverman argued that in modern capitalism virtually no one owns the means of production; therefore the many, including most white-collar and service workers, are forced to sell their labor power to the few who do. In his view, capitalist control and exploitation, as well as the derivative processes of mechanization and rationalization, are being extended to white-collar and service occupations, although their impact is not yet as great as it has been on blue-collar occupations.

Braverman based his analysis on Marx's anthropology, specifically his concept of human potential (species-being). Braverman argued that all forms of life need to sustain themselves in their natural environment; that is, they need to appropriate nature for their own use. Work is the process by which nature is altered in order to enhance its usefulness. In that sense, animals work, too, but what is distinctive about humans is their consciousness. People have a set of mental capacities that other animals lack. Human work is thus characterized by a unity of conception (thought) and execution (action). This unity can be dissolved, and capitalism is a crucial stage in the destruction of the unity of thought and execution in the working world.

A key ingredient in this breakdown in capitalism is the sale and purchase of labor power. Capitalists can purchase certain kinds of labor power and not others. For instance, they can purchase manual labor and insist that mental labor be kept out of the process. Although the opposite can also occur, it is less likely. As a result, capitalism is characterized by an increasing number of manual workers and fewer and fewer mental workers. This seems to contradict the statistics, which reflect a massive growth in white-collar, presumably mental, occupations. However, as we will see, Braverman believed that many white-collar occupations are being *proletarianized,* made indistinguishable in many ways from manual work.

Managerial Control   Braverman recognized economic exploitation, which was Marx's focus, but concentrated on the issue of *control*. He asked the question: How do the capitalists control the labor power that they employ? One answer is that they exercise such control through managers. In fact, Braverman defined *management* as *"a labor process conducted for the purpose of control within the corporation"* (1974:267).

Braverman concentrated on the more impersonal means employed by managers to control workers. One of his central concerns was the utilization of specialization to control workers. Here he carefully differentiated between the division of labor in society as a whole and specialization of work within the organization. All known societies have had a division of labor (for example, between men and women, farmers and artisans, and so forth), but the specialization of work within the organization is a special development of capitalism, although it appears in existing socialist societies as well. Braverman believed that the division of labor at the societal level may enhance the individual, whereas specialization in the workplace has the disastrous effect of subdividing human capabilities: "The subdivision of the individual, when carried on without regard to human capabilities and needs, is a crime against the person and against humanity" (1974:73).

Specialization in the workplace involves the continual division and subdivision of tasks or operations into minute and highly specialized activities, each of which is then likely to be assigned to a *different* worker. This constitutes the creation of what Braverman calls "detail workers." Out of the range of abilities any individual possesses, capitalists select a small number that the worker is to use on the job. As Braverman put it, the capitalist first breaks down the work process and then "dismembers the worker as well" (1974:78) by requiring the worker to use only a small proportion of his or her skills and abilities. In Braverman's terms, the worker "never voluntarily converts himself into a lifelong detail worker. This is the contribution of the capitalist" (1974:78).

Why does the capitalist do this? First, it increases the control of management. It is easier to control a worker doing a specified task than it is one employing a wide range of skills. Second, it increases productivity. That is, a group of workers performing highly specialized tasks can produce more than the same number of craftspeople, each of whom has all the skills and performs all the production activities. For instance, workers on an automobile assembly line produce more cars than would a corresponding number of skilled craftspeople, each of whom produces his or her own car. Third, specialization allows the capitalist to pay the least for the labor power needed. Instead of highly paid, skilled craftspeople, the capitalist can employ lower-paid, unskilled workers. Following the logic of capitalism, employers seek progressively to cheapen the labor of workers, which results in a virtually undifferentiated mass of what Braverman called "simple labor."

Specialization is not a sufficient means of control for capitalists and the managers in their employ. Another important means is scientific technique, including such efforts as scientific management, which is an attempt to apply science to the control of labor on the behalf of management. To Braverman, scientific management is the science of "how best to control alienated labor" (1974:90). Scientific management is found in a series of stages aimed at the control of labor—gathering many workers in one workshop, dictating the length of the workday, supervising workers directly to ensure diligence, enforcing rules against distractions (for example, talking), and setting minimum acceptable production levels. Overall scientific management contributed to control by *"the dictation to the worker of the precise manner in which work is to be performed"* (Braverman, 1974:90). For example, Braverman discussed F. W. Taylor's early work on the shoveling of coal, which led him to develop rules about the kind of shovel to use, the way to stand, the angle at which the shovel should enter the coal pile, and how much coal to pick up in each motion. In other words, Taylor developed methods that ensured almost total control over the labor process. Workers were to be left with as few independent decisions as possible; thus, a separation of the mental and manual was accomplished. Management used its monopoly over work-related knowledge to control each step of the labor process. In the end, the work itself was left without any meaningful skill, content, or knowledge. Craftsmanship was utterly destroyed.

Braverman also saw machinery as a means of control over workers. Modern machinery comes into existence "when the tool and/or the work are given a fixed motion path by the structure of the machine itself" (Braverman, 1974:188). The skill is built into the machine rather than left for the worker to acquire. Instead of controlling the work process, workers come to be controlled by the machine. Furthermore, it is far easier for management to control machines than workers.

Braverman argued that through such mechanisms as the specialization of work, scientific management, and machines, management has been able to extend its control over its manual workers. Although this is a useful insight, especially the emphasis on control, Braverman's distinctive contribution has been his effort to extend this kind of analysis to sectors of the labor force that were not analyzed in Marx's original analysis of the labor process. Braverman argued that white-collar and service workers are now being subjected to the same processes of control that were used on manual workers in the last century.

One of Braverman's examples is white-collar clerical workers. At one time such workers were considered to be a group distinguished from manual workers by such things as their dress, skills, training, and career prospects (Lockwood, 1956). However, today both groups are being subjected to the same means of control. Thus it has become more difficult to differentiate between the factory and the modern factorylike office, as the workers in the latter are progressively proletarianized. For one thing, the work of the clerical worker has grown more and more specialized. This means, among other things, that the mental and manual aspects of office work have been separated. Office managers, engineers, and technicians now perform the mental work, whereas the "line" clerical workers do little more than manual tasks such as typing, filing, and keypunching. As a result, the level of skills needed for these jobs has been lowered, and the jobs require little or no special training.

Scientific management also is now seen as invading the office. Clerical tasks have been scientifically studied, and as a result of that research, they have been simplified, routinized, and standardized. Finally, mechanization is beginning to make significant inroads into the office, primarily through the computer and computer-related equipment.

By applying these mechanisms to clerical work, managers find it much easier to control such workers. It is unlikely that such control mechanisms are as strong and effective in the office as in the factory; still, the trend is toward the development of the white-collar "factory."[4]

Several obvious criticisms can be leveled at Braverman. For one thing, he has probably overestimated the degree of similarity between manual and clerical work. For another, his preoccupation with control has led him to devote relatively little attention to the dynamics of economic exploitation in capitalism. Nonetheless, he has enriched our understanding of the labor process in modern capitalist society.

Other Work on Labor and Capital   Although Braverman recognized economic exploitation, which was Marx's focus, he concentrated, as we have seen, on the issue of managerial *control* over workers. The issue of control is even more central to Richard Edwards in his book, *Contested Terrain: The Transformation of the Workplace in the Twentieth Century* (1979). To Edwards control lies at the heart of the twentieth-century transformation of the workplace. Following Marx, Edwards sees the workplace, both past and present, as an arena of class conflict, in his terms a "contested terrain." Within this arena, dramatic changes have taken place in the way in which those at the top control those at the bottom. During nineteenth-century competitive capitalism, "simple" control was used, in which "bosses exercised power personally, intervening in the labor process often to exhort workers, bully and threaten them, reward good performance, hire and fire on the spot, favor loyal employees, and generally act as despots, benevolent or otherwise" (Edwards, 1979:19). Although this system of control continues in many small businesses, it has proven too crude for modern, large-scale organizations. In such organizations, simple control has tended to be replaced by impersonal and more sophisticated technical and bureaucratic control. Modern workers can be controlled by the technologies with which they work. The classic example of this is the automobile assembly line, in which the workers' actions are determined by the incessant demands of the line. Another example is the modern computer, which can keep careful track of how much work an employee does and how many mistakes he or she makes. Modern workers also are controlled by the impersonal rules of bureaucracies rather than the personal control of supervisors. Capi-

---

[4] It is important to note that Braverman's book was written before the boom in computer technology in the office, especially the now-widespread use of the word processor. It may be that such technology, requiring greater skill and training than older office technologies, will serve to increase worker autonomy (Zuboff, 1988).

talism is constantly changing and with it the means by which workers are controlled.

Also of note is Michael Burawoy's *Manufacturing Consent: Changes in the Labor Process under Monopoly Capital* (1979). Burawoy is interested in the question of why workers in a capitalist system work so hard. He rejects Marx's explanation that such hard work is a result of coercion. The advent of labor unions and other changes have largely eliminated the arbitrary power of management. "Coercion alone could no longer explain what workers did once they arrived on the shop floor" (Burawoy, 1979:xii). To Burawoy, workers, at least in part, consent to work hard in the capitalist system, and at least part of that consent is produced in the workplace.

We can illustrate Burawoy's approach with one aspect of his research, the games that workers play on the job and, more generally, the informal practices that they develop. Most analysts see these as workers' efforts to reduce alienation and other job-related discontent. In addition, they usually have been seen as social mechanisms that workers develop to oppose management. In contrast, Burawoy concludes that these games "are usually neither independent nor in opposition to management" (1979:80). In fact, "Management, at least at the lower levels, actually participates not only in the organization of the game but in the enforcement of its rules" (1979:80). Rather than challenging management, the organization or, ultimately, the capitalist system, these games actually support them. For one thing, playing the game creates consent among the workers about the rules on which the game is based and, more generally, about the system of social relations (owner-manager-worker) that defines the rules of the game. For another, because managers and workers both are involved in the game, the system of antagonistic social relations to which the game was supposed to respond is obscured.

Burawoy argues that such methods of generating active cooperation and consent are far more effective in getting workers to cooperate in the pursuit of profit than coercion (such as firing those who do not cooperate). In the end, Burawoy believes that games and other informal practices are all methods of getting workers to accept the system and of eliciting their contributions to ever higher profits.

One other work worth noting is Dan Clawson's *Bureaucracy and the Labor Process* (1980), in which he examines the bureaucratization and technological advance of American industry between 1860 and 1920. His main thesis is that the degradation of work during this period was (and is) *not* inevitable. That is, this problem was not inherent in bureaucracy and technology but in the way that they were employed in capitalist society. In Clawson's view, therefore, we can have efficiency, abundance, *and* satisfying human work. Work was degraded because capitalists used bureaucracies and technologies to control laborers and the labor process. Clawson takes as his objective and the objective of socialism the "reorganization of the labor process, so that it becomes the most important arena for people to freely develop their human capacities rather than an area where people are mutilated and degraded" (1980:260).

In sum, the works of Baran and Sweezy, Braverman, Edwards, Burawoy, and Clawson represent a return to the traditional Marxian focus on the economic sector. At a theoretical level, they are valuable for reinstilling interest in the economic factor as well as refining and making more contemporary our understanding of this dimension. In addition, they have been important sources of sociological thinking and research into various aspects of work and industry.

Fordism and Post-Fordism

One of the most recent concerns of economically oriented Marxists is the issue of whether we have witnessed, or are witnessing, a transition from "Fordism" to "post-Fordism." This is related to the broader issue of whether we have undergone a transition from a modern to a postmodern society. We will discuss this larger issue in general, as well as the way in which it is addressed by contemporary Marxian theorists, in Chapter 17. While the reader may want to look ahead to the relevant sections of Chapter 17, this discussion can be read and understood without doing so. In general, *Fordism* is associated with the modern era, while *post-Fordism* is linked to the more recent, postmodern epoch. (The Marxian interest in Fordism is not new; Gramsci [1971] published an essay on it in 1931.)

Fordism, of course, refers to the ideas, principles, and systems spawned by Henry Ford. Ford is generally credited with the development of the modern mass-production system, primarily through the creation of the automobile assembly line. The following characteristics may be associated with Fordism:

• The mass production of homogeneous products.
• The use of inflexible technologies such as the assembly line.
• The adoption of standardized work routines (Taylorism).
• Increases in productivity derived from "economies of scale as well as the deskilling, intensification and homogenization of labor" (Clarke, 1990:73).
• The resulting rise of the mass worker and bureaucratized unions.
• The negotiation by the unions of uniform wages tied to increases in profits and productivity.
• The growth of a market for the homogenized products of mass-production industries and the resulting homogenization of consumption patterns.
• A rise in wages, due to unionization, leading to a growing demand for the increasing supply of mass-produced products.
• A market for products that is governed by Keynesian macroeconomic policies, and a market for labor that is handled by collective bargaining overseen by the state.
• Mass educational institutions providing the mass workers required by industry (Clarke, 1990:73).

While Fordism grew throughout the twentieth century, especially in the United States, it reached its peak and began to decline in the 1970s, especially after the oil crisis of 1973 and the subsequent decline of the American automobile industry and rise of its Japanese counterpart. As a result, it is argued that we are witnessing the decline of Fordism and the rise of post-Fordism, characterized by the following:

• A decline of interest in mass products is accompanied by a growth of interest in more specialized products, especially those high in style and quality.
• More specialized products requiring shorter production runs, resulting in smaller and more productive systems.
• More flexible production is made profitable by the advent of new technologies.
• This requires that workers, in turn, have more diverse skills and better training, more responsibility and greater autonomy.
• Production must be controlled through more flexible systems.
• Huge, inflexible bureaucracies need to be altered dramatically in order to operate more flexibly.
• Bureaucratized unions (and political parties) no longer adequately represent the interests of the new, highly differentiated labor force.
• Decentralized collective bargaining replaces centralized negotiations.
• The workers become more differentiated as people and require more differentiated commodities, lifestyles, and cultural outlets.
• The centralized welfare state can no longer meet the needs (for example, health, welfare, education) of a diverse population, and differentiated, more flexible institutions are required (Clarke, 1990:73–74).

If one needed to sum up the shift from Fordism to post-Fordism, it would be described as the transition from homogeneity to heterogeneity. There are two general issues involved here. First, has a transition from Fordism to post-Fordism actually occurred (Pelaez and Holloway, 1990)? Second, does post-Fordism hold out the hope of solving the problems associated with Fordism?

First, of course, there has been *no* clear historical break between Fordism and post-Fordism (S. Hall, 1988). Even if we are willing to acknowledge that elements of post-Fordism have emerged in the modern world, it is equally clear that elements of Fordism persist and show no signs of disappearing. For example, something we might call "McDonaldism," a phenomenon that has many things in common with Fordism, is growing at an astounding pace in contemporary society. On the basis of the model of the fast-food restaurant, more and more sectors of society are coming to utilize the principles of McDonaldism (Ritzer, forthcoming a). McDonaldism shares many characteristics with Fordism—homogeneous products, rigid technologies, standardized work routines, deskilling, homogenization of labor (and customer), the mass worker, homogenization of consumption, and so on. Thus, Fordism is alive and well in the modern world, although it has been transmogrified into McDonaldism. Furthermore, classic Fordism—for example, in the form of the assembly line—remains a significant presence in the American economy.

Second, even if we accept the idea that post-Fordism is with us, does it represent a solution to the problems of modern capitalist society? Some neo-Marxists (and many supporters of the capitalist system [Womack et al., 1990]) hold out great hope for it: "Post-Fordism is mainly an expression of hope that future capitalist development will be the salvation of social democracy" (Clarke, 1990:75). However, this is merely a hope, and in any case, there is already evidence that post-Fordism may not be the nirvana hoped for by some observers.

The Japanese model is widely believed to be the basis of post-Fordism. However, research on Japanese industry (Satoshi, 1982) and on American industries utilizing Japanese management techniques (Parker and Slaughter, 1990) indicates that there are great problems with these systems and that they may even serve to *heighten* the level of exploitation of the worker. Parker and Slaughter label the Japanese system as it is employed in the United States (and it is probably worse in Japan) "management by stress": "The goal is to stretch the system like a rubber band on the point of breaking" (1990:33). Among other things, work is speeded up even further than on the traditional American assembly lines, putting enormous strain on the workers, who need to labor heroically just to keep up with the line. More generally, Levidow describes the new, post-Fordist workers as "relentlessly pressurized to increase their productivity, often in return for lower real wages—be they factory workers, homeworkers in the rag trade, privatized service workers or even polytechnic lecturers" (1990:59). Thus, it may well be that rather than representing a solution to the problems of capitalism, post-Fordism may simply be merely a new, more insidious phase of the heightening of the exploitation of workers by capitalists.

HISTORICALLY ORIENTED MARXISM

Structural Marxism makes the case *for* ahistorical and *against* historical analyses, but many Marxists are oriented toward historical research. In adopting this orientation, they argue that they are being true to the Marxian concern for historicity. The most notable of Marx's historical researches was his study of precapitalist economic formations (1857–58/1964). There is a good deal of subsequent historical work from a Marxian perspective (for example, Amin, 1977; Dobb, 1964; Hobsbawm, 1965). In this section, we deal with two pieces of work that reflect a historical orientation—Immanuel Wallerstein's *The Modern World-System* (1974, 1980, 1989) and Theda Skocpol's *States and Social Revolutions* (1979). Although these are not typical of Marxian historical research in all respects, they are among the most influential in contemporary sociology.

The Modern World-System

Wallerstein chose a unit of analysis unlike those used by most Marxian think-ers. He did not look at workers, classes, or even states, because he found most of these too narrow for his purposes. Instead, he looked at a broad economic entity with a division of labor that is not circumscribed by political or cultural boundaries. He found that unit in his concept of the *world-system,* which is a largely self-contained social system with a set of boundaries and a definable life span; that is, it does not last forever. It is composed internally of a variety of social structures and member groups. However, Wallerstein was not inclined to define the system in terms of a consensus that holds it together. Rather, he saw the system as held together by a variety of forces that are in inherent tension. These forces always have the potential for tearing the system apart.

The world-system is a very abstract concept, and in fact Wallerstein offered it only at the end of his first book, after he had discussed all the historical detail needed for its formulation. Wallerstein argued that thus far we have had only two types of world-systems. One was the world empire, of which ancient Rome is an example. The other is the modern capitalist world-econ-omy. A world empire is based on political (and military) domination, whereas a capitalist world-economy relies on economic domination. A capitalist world-economy is seen as more stable than a world empire for several reasons. For one thing, it has a broader base, because it encompasses many states. For another, it has a built-in process of economic stabilization. The separate polit-ical entities within the capitalist world-economy absorb whatever losses occur, while economic gain is distributed to private hands. Wallerstein foresaw the *possibility* of still a third world-system, a *socialist world government.* Whereas the capitalist world-economy separates the political from the economic sector, a socialist world-economy would reintegrate them.

To orient the reader for the historical discussion to follow, we now intro-duce the concepts developed by Wallerstein that describe the geographical division of labor in the world-system of greatest concern to him—the capitalist world-economy—the core, the periphery, and the semiperiphery. In general, the *core* geographical area dominates the world-economy and exploits the rest of the system. The *periphery* consists of those areas that provide raw materials to the core and are heavily exploited by it. The *semiperiphery* is a residual category that encompasses a set of regions somewhere between the exploiting and the exploited. The key point here is that to Wallerstein the international division of exploitation is defined not by state borders but by the economic division of labor in the world.

In the first volume on the world-system, Wallerstein (1974) dealt with the origin of the world-system roughly between the years 1450 and 1640. The significance of this development was the shift from political (and thus mili-tary) to economic dominance. Wallerstein saw economics as a far more effi-cient and less primitive means of domination than politics. Political structures are very cumbersome, whereas economic exploitation "makes it possible to

IMMANUEL WALLERSTEIN: A Biographical Sketch

Although he achieved recognition in the 1960s as an expert on Africa, Immanuel Wallerstein's most important contribution to sociology is his 1974 book, *The Modern World-System.* That book was an instant success. It has received worldwide recognition and has been translated into ten languages and Braille.

Born on September 28, 1930, Wallerstein received all his degrees from Columbia University, including a doctorate in 1959. He next assumed a position on the faculty at Columbia; after many years there, and a five-year stint at McGill University in Montreal, Wallerstein became, in 1976, distinguished professor of sociology at the State University of New York at Binghamton.

Wallerstein was awarded the prestigious Sorokin Award for the first volume of *The Modern World-System* in 1975. Since that time, he has continued to work on the topic and has produced a number of articles as well as two additional volumes, in which he takes his analysis of the world-system up to the 1840s. We can anticipate more work from Wallerstein on this issue in the coming years. He is in the process of producing a body of work that will attract attention for years to come.

In fact, in many ways the attention it has already attracted and will continue to attract is more important than the body of work itself. The concept of the world-system has become the focus of thought and research in sociology, an accomplishment to which few scholars can lay claim. Many of the sociologists now doing research and theorizing about the world-system are critical of Wallerstein in one way or another, but they all clearly recognize the important role he played in the genesis of their ideas.

Although the concept of the world-system is an important contribution, at least as significant has been the role Wallerstein played in the revival of theoretically informed historical research. The most important work in the early years of sociology, by people like Marx, Weber, and Durkheim, was largely of this variety. However, in more recent years, most sociologists have turned away from doing this kind of research and toward using such ahistorical methods as questionnaires and interviews. These methods are quicker and easier to use than historical methods, and the data produced are easier to analyze with a computer. Use of such methods tends to require a narrow range of technical knowledge rather than a wide range of historically oriented knowledge. Furthermore, theory plays a comparatively minor role in research utilizing questionnaires and interviews. Wallerstein has been in the forefront of those involved in a revival of interest in historical research with a strong theoretical base.

increase the flow of the surplus from the lower strata to the upper strata, from the periphery to the center, from the majority to the minority" (Wallerstein, 1974:15). In the modern era, capitalism provided a basis for the growth and development of a world-economy; this has been accomplished without the aid of a unified political structure. Capitalism can be seen as an economic alternative to political domination. It is better able to produce economic surpluses than the more primitive techniques employed in political exploitation.

Wallerstein argued that three things were necessary for the rise of the capitalist world-economy out of the "ruins" of feudalism: geographical expansion through exploration and colonization, development of different methods of labor control for zones (for example, core, periphery) of the world-economy, and development of strong states that were to become the core states of the emerging capitalist world-economy. Let us look at each of these in turn.

Geographical Expansion Wallerstein argued that geographical expansion by nations is a prerequisite for the other two stages. Portugal took the lead in overseas exploration, and other European nations followed. Wallerstein was wary of talking about specific countries or about Europe in general terms. He preferred to see overseas expansion as caused by a group of people acting in their immediate interests. Elite groups, such as nobles, needed overseas expansion for various reasons. For one thing, they were confronted with a nascent class war brought on by the crumbling of the feudal economy. The slave trade provided them with a tractable labor force on which to build the capitalist economy. The expansion also provided them with various commodities needed to develop it—gold bullion, food, and raw materials of various types.

A Worldwide Division of Labor Once the world had undergone geographical expansion, it was prepared for the next stage, the development of a worldwide division of labor. In the sixteenth century, capitalism replaced statism as the major mode of dominating the world, but capitalism did not develop uniformly around the world. In fact, Wallerstein argued, the solidarity of the capitalist system was ultimately based on its unequal development. Given his Marxian orientation, Wallerstein did not think of this as a consensual equilibrium but rather as one that was laden with conflict from the beginning. Different parts of the capitalist world-system came to specialize in specific functions—breeding labor power, growing food, providing raw materials, and organizing industry. Furthermore, different areas came to specialize in producing particular types of workers. For example, Africa produced slaves; western and southern Europe had many peasant tenant-farmers; western Europe was also the center of wage workers, the ruling classes, and other skilled and supervisory personnel.

More generally, each of the three parts of the international division of labor tended to differ in terms of mode of labor control. The core had free labor; the periphery was characterized by forced labor; and the semiperiphery was the heart of sharecropping. In fact, Wallerstein argued that the key to capitalism lies in a core dominated by a free labor market for skilled workers and a coercive labor market for less skilled workers in peripheral areas. Such a combination is the essence of capitalism. If a free labor market should develop throughout the world, we would have socialism.

Some regions of the world begin with small initial advantages, which are used as the basis for developing greater advantages later on. The core area in the sixteenth century, primarily western Europe, rapidly extended its advantages as towns flourished, industries developed, and merchants became important. It also moved to extend its domain by developing a wider variety of activities. At the same time, each of its activities became more specialized in order to produce more efficiently. In contrast, the periphery stagnated and moved more toward what Wallerstein called a "monoculture," or an undifferentiated, single-focus society.

Development of Core States The third stage of the development of the world-system involved the political sector and how various economic groups used state structures to protect and advance their interests. Absolute monarchies arose in western Europe at about the same time as capitalism developed. From the sixteenth to the eighteenth centuries, the states were the central economic actors in Europe, although the center later shifted to economic enterprises. The strong states in the core areas played a key role in the development of capitalism and ultimately provided the economic base for their own demise. The European states strengthened themselves in the sixteenth century by, among other things, developing and enlarging bureaucratic systems and creating a monopoly of force in society, primarily by developing armies and legitimizing their activities so that they were assured of internal stability. Whereas the states of the core zone developed strong political systems, the periphery developed correspondingly weak states.

In the second volume, Wallerstein (1980) picked up the story of the consolidation of the world-economy between 1600 and 1750. This was not a period of a significant expansion of the European world-economy, but there were a number of significant changes within that system. For example, Wallerstein discussed the rise and subsequent decline in the core of the Netherlands. Later, he analyzed the conflict between two core states, England and France, as well as the ultimate victory of England. In the periphery, Wallerstein detailed, among other things, the cyclical fortunes of Hispanic America. In the semiperiphery we witness, among other things, the decline of Spain and the rise of Sweden. Wallerstein continued his historical analysis from a Marxian viewpoint of the various roles played by different societies within the division of labor of the world-economy. Although Wallerstein paid close attention to political and social factors, his main focus remained the role of economic factors in world history.

In his most recent work, Wallerstein (1989) brings his historical analysis up to the 1840s. Wallerstein looks at three great developments during the period from 1730 to the 1840s—the Industrial Revolution (primarily in England), the French Revolution, and the independence of the once-European colonies in America. In his view, none of these were fundamental challenges to the world capitalist system; instead, they represented its "further consolidation and entrenchment" (Wallerstein, 1989:256).

Wallerstein continues the story of the struggle between England and France for dominance of the core. Whereas the world-economy had been stagnant during the prior period of analysis, it was now expanding, and Great Britain was able to industrialize more rapidly and come to dominate large-scale industries. This occurred in spite of the fact that in the eighteenth century France had dominated in the industrial realm. The French Revolution played an important role in the development of the world capitalist system, especially by helping to bring the lingering cultural vestiges of feudalism to an end and by bringing the cultural-ideological system into line with economic and political realities. However, it served to inhibit the industrial development of France, as did the ensuing Napoleonic rules and wars. By the end of this period, "Britain was finally truly hegemonic in the world-system" (Wallerstein, 1989:122).

The period between 1750 and 1850 was marked by the incorporation of vast new zones (the subcontinent of India, the Ottoman and Russian empires, and west Africa) into the periphery of the world-economy. These zones had been part of what Wallerstein calls the "external area" of the world-system and thus had been linked to, but not in, that system. *External zones* are those which the capitalist world-economy wanted goods from but which were able to resist the importation of manufactured goods in return from the core nations. As a result of the incorporation of these external zones, countries adjacent to the once-external nations were also drawn into the world-system. Thus, the incorporation of India contributed to China's becoming part of the periphery. By the end of the nineteenth century and the beginning of the twentieth, the pace of incorporation quickened, and "the entire globe, even those regions that had never been part even of the external area of the capitalist world-economy were pulled inside" (Wallerstein, 1989:129).

The pressure for incorporation into the world-economy never comes from the nations being incorporated but "rather from the need of the world-economy to expand its boundaries, a need which was itself the outcome of pressures internal to the world-economy" (Wallerstein, 1989:129). Furthermore, the process of incorporation is not an abrupt process but one which occurs gradually.

Reflecting his Marxian focus on economics, Wallerstein (1989:170) argues that becoming part of the world-economy "necessarily" means that the political structures of the involved nations must become part of the interstate system. Thus, states in incorporated zones must either transform themselves into part of that interstate political system, be replaced by new political forms willing to accept this role, or be taken over by states that already are part of that political system. The states that emerge at the end of the process of incorporation must not only be part of the interstate system but also be strong enough to protect their economies from external interference. However, they must not be too strong; that is, they must not become powerful enough to be able to refuse to act in accord with the dictates of the capitalist world-economy.

Finally, Wallerstein examines the decolonization of the Americas between 1750 and 1850. That is, he details the fact that the Americas freed themselves from the control of Great Britain, France, Spain, and Portugal. This decolonization, especially in the United States, was, of course, to have great conse-quences for later developments in the world capitalist system.

Marxists have criticized the world-system perspective for its failure to ade-quately emphasize relations between social classes (Bergesen, 1984). From their point of view, Wallerstein focuses on the wrong issue. To them the key is not the core-periphery international division of labor, but rather class rela-tionships *within* given societies. Bergesen seeks to reconcile these positions by arguing that there are strengths and weaknesses on both sides. His middle-ground position is that core-periphery relations are not only unequal exchange relations but also global *class* relations. His key point is that core-periphery relations *are* important, not only as exchange relations, as Wallerstein argues, but also, and more important, as power-dependence relationships, that is, class relationships.

States and Social Revolutions

Another example of Marxian-influenced historical research is Theda Skocpol's *States and Social Revolutions* (1979). Although she shared some intellectual roots with Wallerstein, she had a much different orientation. Skocpol recognized the importance of Wallerstein's work and of the world-system, but she argued that it is not necessary to "accept arguments that national economic devel-opments are actually determined by the overall structure and market dynam-ics of a 'world capitalist system' " (1979:70). In fact, she accused Wallerstein of being "economically reductionistic." Similarly, Skocpol accorded Marx the central position in her theoretical roots, even though she was also critical of him: "Marxism failed to foresee or adequately explain the autonomous power, for good or ill, of states as administrative and coercive machineries embedded in a militarized international states system" (1979:292). Skocpol thus made it clear that although she was working within the Marxian tradition, she intended to stress political rather than economic factors.

In a historical-comparative study that focused on social revolutions in France (1787–1800), Russia (1917–1921), and China (1911–1949), Skocpol con-centrated on the similarities among these revolutions. However, she was also attuned to crucial differences. Her objective was to develop explanations of social revolutions that were both historically grounded and generalizable. For comparative purposes, Skocpol also looked at nations (Japan, Prussia, Eng-land) where revolutions did not take place.

The focus of Skocpol's research was *social revolutions*, which she defined as "rapid, basic transformations of a society's state and class structures; and they are accompanied and in part carried through by class-based revolts from above" (1979:4). Despite this objective, she returned over and over again to economic (class-based) considerations.

In that our focus is on theory, the general principles that stand behind her work are our concern here. First, she intended to adopt what she called a "structural, nonvoluntaristic perspective." Second, she considered it important to single out the international and world-historical contexts for particular examination. Third, her objective was to focus on the *state* as at least a potentially autonomous unit. We shall consider each of these principles separately.

Skocpol began by setting her approach apart from what she called "voluntaristic images" of how revolutions occur (1979:14). Most observers, in her view, see revolutions as deliberate efforts by leaders, followers, or both. She saw this tendency in Marx's work itself, but it was exaggerated by those who followed in his tradition. This is manifest in the Marxian focus on such factors as class consciousness and the party organization. However, Skocpol rejected this position outright: "No successful social revolution has ever been 'made' by a mass-mobilizing, avowedly revolutionary movement" (1979:17).

In rejecting a voluntaristic image of social revolutions, Skocpol rejected a focus on both the thoughts and motives of actors and the large-scale idea systems, such as ideology and class consciousness. Skocpol's focus on the structural level *may* be right, but that does not mean that the other levels are insignificant.

In Skocpol's view revolutions are not made; they happen. This includes both causes and outcomes of revolutions. We need to focus on the structural factors that cause revolutions. As she pointedly put it, "A structural perspective . . . is essential for the analysis of social revolutions" (Skocpol, 1979:18).

Skocpol recognized the importance of intranational factors, but she underscored the importance of transnational, or international, factors: "Transnational relations have contributed to the emergence of all social revolutionary crises and have invariably helped to shape revolutionary struggles and outcomes" (1979:18). However, she set herself apart from Wallerstein, who had adopted a similar perspective. He focused on international *economic* relations, whereas her intention was to focus on international *political* factors. Although not denying the importance of international economic variables, Skocpol looked to what she called the "international system of competing states." However, she did recognize the interplay between the two factors: "Throughout modern history, it [the international states system] represents an analytically autonomous level of transnational realism—interdependent in its structure and dynamics with world capitalism, but not reducible to it" (Skocpol, 1979:2).

Skocpol differentiated between two aspects of transnational relations in time—the structural relationships between states in the contemporary period and relationships between states over time. For example, actors in a later revolution are affected by the successes and failures of actors in an earlier revolution. Breakthroughs such as the Industrial Revolution create a series of new opportunities and necessities between one social revolution and the other.

Within the structural realm, Skocpol singled out the state for special attention. She said that the state is "a structure with a logic and interests of its own not necessarily equivalent to, or fused with, the interests of the dominant class in society or the full set of member groups in the polity" (Skocpol, 1979:27).

She argued that there is a need for an explanation of social revolutions that is more state-centered than economic-centered. Political factors are not epi-phenomena but rather have direct effects on social revolutions. Skocpol here adopted the structural Marxian position on the potential autonomy of the state. However, she was careful to point out that the degree to which the state is autonomous, free from class control, varies from one setting to another.

Skocpol closed her theoretical introduction with a clear statement of her perspective:

> We shall analyze the causes and processes of social revolutions from a nonvolun-tarist, structural perspective, attending to international and world-historical, as well as intranational structures and processes. And an important theoretical concomitant will be to move states—understood as potentially autonomous organizations located at the interface of class structures and international situations—to the very center of attention.
>
> (Skocpol, 1979:33)

Skocpol found the roots of the French, Russian, and Chinese revolutions in the political crises that existed in what she termed their "old-regime states." Crises developed when those states were unable to meet the challenges of evolving international relations. The states faced not only international prob-lems but intranational conflicts among social classes, especially between the landed aristocracy and the peasantry. Unable to cope with these pressures, the old-regime autocratic states broke down.

These crises made the situation ripe for revolution, but a revolution would not have occurred unless the sociopolitical structures were conducive to it. Because these were primarily agrarian societies, the peasants rather than the urban workers were crucial to the revolution. Skocpol said, "Peasant revolts have been the crucial insurrectionary ingredient in virtually all (that is, suc-cessful) social revolutions to date" (1979:112–113).

In this explanation of peasant revolts, Skocpol rejected extant theories that focus on ideology as well as theories focusing on relative deprivation of actors. Instead, her view was that the key factors in peasant rebellions are structural and situational. One such factor is the degree of solidarity of the peasant communities. Another is the degree of freedom of the peasants from the direct day-to-day supervision and control of landlords and their agents. Finally, the relaxation of the state's coercive sanctions against peasants is likely to be con-ducive to revolutionary activity. The susceptibility of the old-regime states to international pressures and the existence of such structures in the agrarian sector were, in Skocpol's view, the "sufficient" causes of the revolutions in France in 1789, Russia in 1917, and China in 1911.

Such structural factors were significant not only in the genesis of social revolutions but also in their outcomes. That is, the outcomes of these revo-lutions were "fundamental and enduring structural transformations" in the societies in question (Skocpol, 1979:161). There are important variations in the cases she studied, but there are also these important similarities: First, the agrarian class relationships were dramatically transformed. Second, the autocratic and proto-bureaucratic regimes of the old states were replaced by bureaucratic, professionalized states able to manage masses of people. Third, the prerevolutionary landed upper classes lost exclusive privileges.

In her discussion of structural outcomes of revolutions, Skocpol attacked those who emphasize ideological factors. She refused to see the leaders of social revolutions as merely the representatives of social classes and their actions as simple reflections of the ideologies of those classes. Rather, she wanted to focus on what revolutionary leaders *do*—struggle for state power. She took their activities more seriously than the ideological pressures on them. Furthermore, the results of their activities are determined not by ideologies but by structural exigencies: "Revolutionary crises are *not* total breakpoints in history that suddenly make anything at all possible if only it is envisaged by willful revolutionaries" (Skocpol, 1979:171). We need to look at real structural forces and constraints and not people's ideas about them.

SUMMARY

In this chapter we examine a wide range of approaches that can be categorized as neo-Marxian sociological theories. All of them take Marx's work as their point of departure, but they often go in very different directions. Although these diverse developments give neo-Marxian theory considerable vitality, they also create at least some unnecessary and largely dysfunctional differentiation and controversy. Thus one task for the modern Marxian sociological theorist is integrating this broad array of theories while recognizing the value of various specific pieces of work.

The first neo-Marxian theory historically, but the least important at present, especially to the sociologically oriented thinker, is economic determinism. It was against this limited view of Marxian theory that other varieties developed. Hegelian Marxism, especially in the work of Georg Lukács, was one such reaction. This approach sought to overcome the limitations in economic determinism by returning to the subjective, Hegelian roots of Marxian theory. Hegelian Marxism is also of little contemporary relevance; its significance lies largely in its impact on later neo-Marxian theories.

The critical school, which was the inheritor of the tradition of Hegelian Marxism, *is* of contemporary importance to sociology. The great contributions of the critical theorists (Marcuse, Habermas, and so forth) are the insights offered into culture, consciousness, and their interrelationships. These theorists have enhanced our understanding of such cultural phenomena as instrumental rationality, the "culture industry," the "knowledge industry," communicative action, domination, and legitimations. To this they add a concern with consciousness, primarily in the form of an integration of Freudian theory in their work. However, critical theory has gone too far in its efforts to compensate for the limitations of economic determinism; it needs to reintegrate a concern for economics, indeed, for large-scale social forces in general.

Another neo-Marxian approach is structural Marxism. Whereas the critical school emphasizes subjective factors, the structural Marxists focus primarily on structural factors. Structural Marxists like Althusser and Poulantzas also take economic determinism as their starting point. This leads them toward such structures as the state and ideology, which are seen as having "relative autonomy" vis-à-vis the economy. Nevertheless, the economy is still seen as *the* most important structural factor. The structural Marxists not only reject the limitations of economic determinism at the structural level but are also highly critical of the subjectivity of the critical school and Hegelian Marxism. They regard these developments as dangerous, antiscientific trends in Marxian theory. Although the structural Marxists are highly critical of other branches of Marxian theory, they themselves have been the subject of a series of strong attacks from both within and without Marxian theory.

Next we offer discussions of two lines of work in neo-Marxian economic sociology. The first deals with the relationship between capital and labor, especially in the works of Baran and Sweezy and Braverman. The second is concerned with the transition from Fordism to post-Fordism. Both sets of work represent efforts to return to some of the traditional economic concerns of Marxian sociology. This work is significant for its effort to update Marxian economic sociology by taking into account the emerging realities of contemporary capitalist society.

The chapter closes with two examples of neo-Marxian historical scholarship: Wallerstein, who analyzes economics and world systems, and Skocpol, who focuses on politics and social revolution.

We will discuss other aspects of neo-Marxian theory in later chapters of this book. For example, in Chapter 13, we will discuss structural Marxism again and under the heading of "poststructuralism," we will analyze the work of Michel Foucault, whose work is derived in part from a Marxian tradition and has come to represent a challenge to that tradition. In Chapter 15, some of the recent ideas of Jurgen Habermas will be analyzed. Finally, and most importantly, in Chapter 17 we will discuss some of the most recent book in the Marxian tradition—post-Marxist theory.

Overall, despite the moribund state of communist societies, neo-Marxian theory continues to be lively, controversial, and sometimes confused. It is likely to continue to attract the attention of large numbers of social theorists.

SYMBOLIC INTERACTIONISM

*L*IKE other major sociological theories, symbolic interactionism presents an extremely broad perspective. The theories of George Herbert Mead and, to a lesser extent, Charles Horton Cooley and W. I. Thomas provided its initial core, but a variety of different perspectives developed in the ensuing years. Traditional symbolic interactionism is represented by the ideas of Herbert Blumer; other varieties include Manford Kuhn's more "scientific" approach, Erving Goffman's dramaturgical approach, and perhaps even ethnomethodology and phenomenology.[1] The last two theories are conceived of as separate ori-

---

[1] This was manifest in a plenary session of the meetings of the Society of Symbolic Interaction, over a decade ago, at which the theme was varieties of symbolic interactionism and the speakers included representatives of phenomenology and ethnomethodology.

entations and will be dealt with in Chapter 10. Here we discuss the core of symbolic-interaction theory, as represented primarily in the works of Mead and Blumer, although some of the other approaches also receive attention.

THE MAJOR HISTORICAL ROOTS

We begin our discussion of symbolic interactionism with Mead,[2] who actually taught philosophy, not sociology, at the University of Chicago from 1894 to 1931 (Faris, 1970). However, many graduate students in sociology took his courses. Those students were later instrumental in Mead's "oral tradition" of symbolic interactionism (M. Kuhn, 1964) being turned into a written one, since their notes from Mead's classes were used as the basis for his seminal work, *Mind, Self and Society: From the Standpoint of a Social Behaviorist* (Mead, 1934/ 1962). The two most significant intellectual roots of Mead's work in particular, and of symbolic interactionism in general, are the philosophy of pragmatism and psychological behaviorism (Joas, 1985; Rock, 1979).[3]

Pragmatism

Pragmatism is a wide-ranging philosophical position, from which we can identify several aspects that influenced Mead's developing sociological orientation (Charon, 1985). First, to pragmatists true reality does not exist "out there" in the real world; it "is actively created as we act in and toward the world" (Hewitt, 1984:8; see also Shalin, 1986). Second, people remember and base their knowledge of the world on what has proven useful to them. They are likely to alter what no longer "works." Third, people define the social and physical "objects" that they encounter in the world according to their use for them. Finally, if we want to understand actors, we must base that understanding on what they actually do in the world. Three points are critical for symbolic interactionism: (1) a focus on the interaction between the actor and the world; (2) a view of both the actor and the world as dynamic processes and not static structures; and (3) the great importance attributed to the actor's ability to interpret the social world.

The last point is most pronounced in the work of the philosophical pragmatist John Dewey. Dewey did not conceive of the mind as a thing or a structure but rather as a thinking process that involves a series of stages. These stages include defining objects in the social world, outlining possible modes of conduct, imagining the consequences of alternative courses of action, eliminating unlikely possibilities, and finally selecting the optimal mode of action

---

[2] The entire fall 1981 issue of *Symbolic Interaction* was devoted to Mead; see also Fisher and Strauss (1979). Notable recent work on Mead includes Collins (1989b) and Luscher (1990).
[3] Another important input was the theories of Georg Simmel, especially his ideas on interaction (see Chapter 5).

(Stryker, 1980). This focus on the thinking process was enormously influential in the development of symbolic interactionism.

In fact, David Lewis and Richard Smith argue the Dewey (along with William James) was more influential in the development of symbolic interactionism than Mead. They go so far as to say that "Mead's work was peripheral to the mainstream of early Chicago sociology" (Lewis and Smith, 1980:xix).[4] In making this argument, they distinguish between two branches of pragmatism—"philosophical realism" (associated with Mead) and "nominalist pragmatism" (associated with Dewey and James). In their view, symbolic interactionism was more influenced by the nominalist approach and even inconsistent with philosophical realism. The nominalist position is that although macro-level phenomena exist, they do not have "independent and determining effects upon the consciousness of and behavior of individuals" (Lewis and Smith, 1980:24). More positively, this view "conceives of the individuals themselves as existentially free agents who accept, reject, modify, or otherwise 'define' the community's norms, roles, beliefs, and so forth, according to their own personal interests and plans of the moment" (Lewis and Smith, 1980:24). In contrast, to social realists the emphasis is on society and how it constitutes and controls individual mental processes. Rather than being free agents, actors and their cognitions and behaviors are controlled by the larger community.[5]

Given this distinction, Mead fits better into the realist camp and therefore did not mesh well with the nominalist direction taken by symbolic interactionism. The key figure in the latter development is Herbert Blumer, who, while claiming to operate with a Meadian approach, was in fact himself better thought of as a nominalist. The issue of the differences between Mead and Blumer is important; we encounter it later in this chapter in a discussion of methodology. Theoretically, Lewis and Smith catch the essence of their differences:

> Blumer . . . moved completely toward psychical interactionism. . . . Unlike the Meadian social behaviorist, the psychical interactionist holds that the meanings of symbols are not universal and objective; rather meanings are individual and subjective in that they are "attached" to the symbols by the receiver according to however he or she chooses to "interpret" them.
>
> (Lewis and Smith, 1980:172)

Behaviorism

Buttressing the Lewis and Smith interpretation of Mead is the fact that he was also influenced by psychological behaviorism (J. Baldwin, 1986, 1988a, 1988b), a perspective which also led him in a realist and an empirical direction. In fact, Mead called his basic concern *social behaviorism* to differentiate it from the *radical behaviorism* of John B. Watson (who was one of Mead's students).

---

[4] For a review symposium on this work, see *Symbolic Interaction* (1983).
[5] For a criticism of the distinctions made here, see Miller (1982b, 1985).

Radical behaviorists of Watson's persuasion (K. Buckley, 1989) were concerned with the *observable* behaviors of individuals. Their focus was on the stimuli that elicted the responses, or behaviors, in question. They either denied or were disinclined to attribute much importance to the covert mental process that occurred between the time that a stimulus was applied and a response emitted. Mead recognized the importance of observable behavior, but he also felt that there were *covert* aspects of behavior that the radical behaviorists had ignored. But because he accepted the empiricism that was basic to behaviorism, Mead did not simply want to philosophize about these covert phenomena. Rather, he sought to extend the empirical science of behaviorism to them—that is, to what goes on between stimulus and response. Bernard Meltzer summarized Mead's position:

> For Mead, the unit of study is "the act," which comprises both overt and covert aspects of human action. Within the act, all the separated categories of the traditional, orthodox psychologies find a place. Attention, perception, imagination, reasoning, emotion, and so forth, are seen as parts of the act . . . the act, then encompasses the total process involved in human activity.
>
> (Meltzer, 1964/1978:23)

Mead and the radical behaviorists also differed in their views on the relationship between human and animal behavior. Whereas radical behaviorists tended to see no difference between humans and animals, Mead argued that there was a significant, qualitative difference. The key to this difference was seen as the human possession of mental capacities that allowed people to use language between stimulus and response in order to decide how to respond.

Mead simultaneously demonstrated his debt to Watsonian behaviorism and dissociated himself from it. Mead made this clear when he said, on the one hand, that "we shall approach this latter field [social psychology] from a behavioristic point of view." On the other hand, Mead criticized Watson's position when he said, "The behaviorism which we shall make use of is *more adequate* than that of which Watson makes use" (1934/1962:2; italics added).

Charles Morris, in his introduction to *Mind, Self and Society,* enumerated three basic differences between Mead and Watson. First, Mead considered Watson's exclusive focus on behavior too simplistic. In effect, he accused Watson of wrenching behavior out of its broader social context. Mead wanted to deal with behavior as a small part of the broader social world.

Second, Mead accused Watson of an unwillingness to extend behaviorism into mental processes. Watson had no sense of the actor's consciousness and mental processes, as Mead made vividly clear: "John B. Watson's attitude was that of the Queen in *Alice in Wonderland*—'Off with their heads!'—there were no such things. There was no . . . consciousness" (1934/1962:2–3). Mead contrasted his perspective with Watson's: "It is behavioristic, but unlike Watsonian behaviorism it recognizes the parts of the act which do not come to external observation" (1934/1962:8). More concretely, Mead saw his mission as extending the principles of Watsonian behaviorism to include mental processes.

Finally, because Watson rejected the mind, Mead saw him as having a passive image of the actor as puppet. Mead, on the other hand, subscribed to a much more dynamic and creative image of the actor, and it was this that made him attractive to later symbolic interactionists.

Pragmatism and behaviorism, especially in the theories of Dewey and Mead, were transmitted to many graduate students at the University of Chicago, primarily in the 1920s. These students, among them Herbert Blumer, established symbolic interactionism. Of course, other important theorists influenced these students, the most important of whom was Georg Simmel (Chapter 5). Simmel's interest in forms of action and interaction was both compatible with and an extension of Meadian theory. There were, of course, many other influences on the development of symbolic interaction, but pragmatism, radical behaviorism, and Simmelian theory are far and away the most important.

Between Reductionism and Sociologism

Blumer coined the term *symbolic interactionism* in 1937 and wrote several essays that were instrumental in its development. Whereas Mead sought to differentiate the nascent symbolic interactionism from behaviorism, Blumer saw symbolic interactionism as embattled on two fronts. First was the reductionist behaviorism that had worried Mead. To this was added the serious threat from larger-scale sociologistic theories, especially structural functionalism. To Blumer, behaviorism and structural functionalism both tended to focus on factors (for example, external stimuli and norms) that cause human behavior. As far as Blumer was concerned, both ignored the crucial process by which actors endow the forces acting upon them and their own behaviors with meaning (Morrione, 1988).

To Blumer, behaviorists, with their emphasis on the impact of external stimuli on individual behavior, were clearly psychological reductionists. In addition to behaviorism, several other types of psychological reductionism troubled Blumer. For example, he criticized those who seek to explain human action by relying on conventional notions of the concept of "attitude" (Blumer, 1955/1969:94). In his view, most of those who use the concept think of an attitude as an "already organized tendency" within the actor; they tend to think of actions as being impelled by attitudes. In Blumer's view, this is very mechanistic thinking; what is important is not the attitude as an internalized tendency "but the defining process through which the actor comes to forge his act" (Blumer, 1955/1969:97). Blumer also singled out for criticism those who focus on conscious and unconscious motives. He was particularly irked by their view that actors are impelled by independent, mentalistic impulses over which they are supposed to have no control. Freudian theory, which sees actors as impelled by such forces as the id or libido, is an example of the kind of psychological theory to which Blumer was opposed. In short, Blumer was opposed to any psychological theory that ignores the process by which actors construct meaning—the fact that actors have selves and relate to themselves. Blumer's general criticisms were similar to Mead's, but he extended them beyond behaviorism to include other forms of psychological reductionism as well.

Blumer also was opposed to sociologistic theories (especially structural functionalism) that view individual behavior as determined by large-scale external forces. In this category Blumer included theories that focus on such social-structural and -cultural factors as " 'social system,' 'social structure,' 'culture,' 'status position,' 'social role,' 'custom,' 'institution,' 'collective representation,' 'social situation,' 'social norm,' and 'values' " (Blumer, 1962/1969:83). Both sociologistic theories and psychological theories ignore the importance of meaning and the social construction of reality. Blumer summarized his criticisms of both psychological and sociologistic theories in this way:

> In both such typical psychological and sociological explanations the meanings of things for the human beings who are acting are either bypassed or swallowed up in the factors used to account for their behavior. If one declares that the given kinds of behavior are the result of the particular factors regarded as producing them, there is no need to concern oneself with the meaning of the things towards which human beings act.
>
> (Blumer, 1969b:3)

With this background of symbolic interactionism, we are ready to discuss its basic principles. First, however, we examine the ideas of George H. Mead, the most important thinker in the founding of symbolic interactionism, and his most important work, *Mind, Self and Society*. Lest we think Mead's work is merely of historical interest, in a major recent work on symbolic interactionism, Robert Perinbanayagam sees him "as a genius of the first rank" and says that his own book, *Signifying Acts*, "proves after all a study of Mead's views" (1985:xiii).

THE IDEAS OF GEORGE HERBERT MEAD

As we have seen, Mead was heavily influenced by pragmatism and behaviorism and sought a middle ground between reductionism and sociologism. In this section we go into considerable depth on the ideas associated with this most important theorist.

The Priority of the Social

In his review of Mead's best-known work, *Mind, Self and Society*, Ellsworth Faris argued that "not mind and then society; but society first and then minds arising with that society . . . would probably have been [Mead's] preference" (cited in Miller, 1982a:2). Faris's inversion of the title of this book reflects the

GEORGE HERBERT MEAD: A Biographical Sketch

Most of the important theorists discussed throughout this book achieved their greatest recognition in their lifetimes for their published work. George Herbert Mead, however, was at least as important, at least during his lifetime, for his teaching as for his writing. His words had a powerful impact on many people who were to become important sociologists in the twentieth century. As one of his students said, "Conversation was his best medium; writing was a poor second" (T. V. Smith, 1931:369). Let us have another of his students, himself a well-known sociologist— Leonard Cottrell—describe what Mead was like as a teacher:

For me, the course with Professor Mead was a unique and unforgettable experience. . . . Professor Mead was a large, amiable-looking man who wore a magnificent mustache and a Vandyke beard. He characteristically had a benign, rather shy smile matched with a twinkle in his eyes as if he were enjoying a secret joke he was playing on the audience. . . .

As he lectured—always without notes—Professor Mead would manipulate the piece of chalk and watch it intently. . . . When he made a particularly subtle point in his lecture he would glance up and throw a shy, almost apologetic smile over our heads—never looking directly at anyone. His lecture flowed and we soon learned that questions or comments from the class were not welcome. Indeed, when someone was bold enough to raise a question there was a murmur of disapproval from the students. They objected to any interruption of the golden flow. . . .

His expectations of students were modest. He never gave exams. The main task for each of us students was to write as learned a paper as one could. These Professor Mead read with great care, and what he thought of your paper was your grade in the course. One might suppose that students would read materials for the paper rather than attend his lectures but that was not the case. Students always came. They couldn't get enough of Mead.

(Cottrell, 1980:49–50)

Over the years, many of Mead's sociological ideas came to be published, especially in *Mind, Self and Society*. This book and others of Mead's works have had a powerful influence on contemporary sociology.

Born in South Hadley, Massachusetts, on February 27, 1863, Mead was trained mainly in philosophy and its application to social psychology. He received a bachelor's degree from Oberlin College (where his father was a professor) in 1883, and after a few years as a secondary-school teacher, surveyor for railroad companies, and private tutor, Mead began graduate study at Harvard in 1887. After a few years of study at Harvard, as well as at the Universities of Leipzig and Berlin, Mead was offered an instructorship at the University of Michigan in 1891. It is interesting to note that Mead *never* received any graduate degrees. In 1894, at the invitation of John Dewey, he moved to the University of Chicago and remained there for the rest of his life. In addition to his teaching and his scholarly activities, Mead was active politically, especially in the reform movement in Chicago (Joas, 1985).

George Herbert Mead died on April 26, 1931.

widely acknowledged fact, recognized by Mead himself, that society, or more broadly the social, is accorded priority in Mead's analysis.

In Mead's view, traditional social psychology began with the psychology of the individual in an effort to explain social experience; in contrast, Mead always gives priority to the social world in understanding social experience. Mead explains his focus in this way:

> We are not, in social psychology, building up the behavior of the social group in terms of the behavior of separate individuals composing it; rather, we are *starting out with a given social whole* of complex group activity, into which we analyze (as elements) the behavior of each of the separate individuals composing it. . . . We attempt, that is, to explain the conduct of the social group, rather than to account for the organized conduct of the social group in terms of the conduct of the separate individuals belonging to it. For social psychology, the *whole* (*society*) *is prior to the part* (*the individual*), not the part to the whole; and the part is explained in terms of the whole, not the whole in terms of the part or parts.
>
> (Mead, 1934/1962:7; italics added)

To Mead, the social whole precedes the individual mind both logically and temporally. A thinking, self-conscious individual is, as we will see later, logically impossible in Mead's theory without a prior social group. The social group comes first, and it leads to the development of self-conscious mental states.

The Act

Mead considers the act to be the most "primitive unit" in his theory (1982: 27). It is not in itself an emergent phenomenon but is rather the base of all emergence. In other words, the act is the base from which all other aspects of Mead's analysis emerge. In analyzing the act, Mead comes closest to the behaviorist's approach and focuses on stimulus and response. However, even here the stimulus does not elicit an automatic, unthinking response from the human actor. As Mead says, "We conceive of the stimulus as an occasion or opportunity for the act, not as a compulsion or a mandate" (1982:28).

Mead (1938/1972) identified four basic and interrelated stages in the act; the four stages represent an organic whole (in other words, they are dialectically interrelated). Both lower animals and humans act, and Mead is interested in the similarities, and especially the differences, between the two. The first stage is that of the *impulse*, which involves an "immediate sensuous stimulation" and the actor's reaction to the stimulation, the need to do something about it. Hunger is a good example of an impulse. The actor (both nonhuman and human) may respond immediately and unthinkingly to the impulse, but more likely the human actor will think about the appropriate response (for example, eat now or later). In thinking about a response, the person will consider not only the immediate situation but also past experiences and anticipated future results of the act.

We have focused above on an impulse, hunger, that can be traced to the individual, but such impulses also involve the environment. Hunger may come from an inner state of the actor or may be elicited by the presence of food in the environment, or, most likely, it may arise from some combination of the two. Furthermore, the hungry person must find a way of satisfying the impulse in an environment in which food may not be immediately available or plentiful. This impulse, like all others, may be related to a problem in the environment (that is, the lack of immediately available food), a problem that must be overcome by the actor. Indeed, while an impulse like hunger may come largely from the individual (although even here hunger can be induced by an external stimulus, and there are also social definitions of when it is appropriate to be hungry), it is usually related to the existence of a problem in the environment (for example, the lack of food). To take another example, the approach of a dangerous wild animal may be an impulse to a person to act. Overall, the impulse, like all other elements of Mead's theory, involves both the actor and the environment.

The second stage of the act is *perception,* in which the actor searches for, and reacts to, stimuli that relate to the impulse, in this case hunger as well as the various means available to satisfy it. People have the capacity to sense or perceive stimuli through hearing, smell, taste, and so on. Perception involves both incoming stimuli as well as the mental images they create. People do not simply respond immediately to external stimuli but rather think about, and assess, them through mental imagery. People are not simply subject to external stimulation; they also actively select characteristics of a stimulus and choose among sets of stimuli. That is, a stimulus may have several dimensions, and the actor is able to select among them. Furthermore, people are usually confronted with many different stimuli, and they have the capacity to choose which to attend to and which to ignore. Mead refuses to separate people from the objects that they perceive. It is the act of perceiving an object that makes it an object to a person; perception and object cannot be separated from (are dialectically related to) one another.

Third is the stage of *manipulation.* Once the impulse has been manifest and the object has been perceived, the next step is manipulating the object or, more generally, taking action with regard to it. In addition to their mental advantages, people have another advantage over lower animals. People have hands (with opposable thumbs) that allow them to manipulate objects far more subtly than can lower animals. The manipulation phase constitutes, for Mead, an important temporary pause in the process so that a response is not manifest immediately. A hungry human being sees a mushroom, but before eating it, he or she is likely to pick it up first, examine it, and perhaps check in a guidebook to see whether that particular variety is edible. The lower animal, on the other hand, is likely to eat the mushroom without handling and examining it (and certainly without reading about it). The pause afforded by handling the object allows humans to contemplate various responses. In thinking about whether to eat the mushroom, both the past and the future are involved. People may think about past experiences in which they ate certain mushrooms that made them ill, and they may think about the future sickness, or even death, that might accompany eating a poisonous mushroom. The manipulation of the mushroom becomes a kind of experimental method in which the actor mentally tries out various hypotheses about what would happen if the mushroom is consumed.

On the basis of these deliberations, the actor may decide to eat the mushroom (or not), and this constitutes the last phase of the act, *consummation*, or more generally the taking of action which satisfies the original impulse. Both humans and lower animals may consume the mushroom, but the human is less likely to eat a bad mushroom because of his or her ability to manipulate the mushroom and to think (and read) about the implications of eating it. The lower animal must rely on a trial-and-error method, and this is a less efficient technique than the capacity of humans to think through their actions. Trial and error in this situation is quite dangerous; as a result, it seems likely that lower animals are more prone to die from consuming poison mushrooms than are humans.

While, for ease of discussion, the four stages of the act have been separated from one another in sequential order, the fact is that Mead sees a dialectical relationship among the four stages. John Baldwin expresses this idea in the following way: "Although the four parts of the act sometimes *appear* to be linked in linear order, they actually interpenetrate to form one organic process: Facets of each part are present at all times from the beginning of the act to the end, such that each part affects the other" (1986:55–56). Thus, the later stages of the act may lead to the emergence of earlier stages. For example, the manipulation of food may lead the individual to the impulse of hunger and the perception that one is hungry and that food is available to satisfy the need.

Gestures

While the act involves only one person, the *social act* involves two or more persons. The *gesture* is in Mead's view the basic mechanism in the social act and in the social process more generally. As he defines them, "Gestures are movements of the first organism which act as specific stimuli calling forth the (socially) appropriate responses of the second organism" (Mead, 1934/1962: 14; see also Mead, 1959:187). Both lower animals and humans are capable of gestures in the sense that the action of one individual mindlessly and automatically elicits a reaction by another individual. The following is Mead's famous example of a dog fight in terms of gestures:

> The act of each dog becomes the stimulus to the other dog for his response. . . . The very fact that the dog is ready to attack another becomes a stimulus to the other dog to change his own position or his own attitude. He has no sooner done this than the change of attitude in the second dog in turn causes the first dog to change his attitude.
>
> (Mead, 1934/1962:42–43)

Mead labels what is taking place in this situation a "conversation of gestures." One dog's gesture automatically elicits a gesture from the second; there are no thought processes taking place on the part of the dogs.

Humans sometimes engage in mindless conversations of gestures. Mead gives as examples many of the actions and reactions that take place in boxing and fencing matches, where one combatant adjusts "instinctively" to the actions of the second. Mead labels such unconscious actions "nonsignificant" gestures; what distinguishes humans is their ability to employ "significant" gestures, or those that require thought on the part of the actor before a reaction takes place.

The vocal gesture is particularly important in the development of significant gestures. However, not all vocal gestures are significant. The bark of one dog to another is not significant; even some human vocal gestures (for example, a mindless grunt) may not be significant. However, it is the development of vocal gestures, especially in the form of language, which is the most important factor in making possible the distinctive development of human life: "The specialization of the human animal within this field of the gesture has been responsible, ultimately, for the origin and growth of present human society and knowledge, with all the control over nature and over the human environment which science makes possible" (Mead, 1934/1962:14).

The above development is related to a distinctive characteristic of the vocal gesture. When we make a physical gesture, such as a facial grimace, we cannot see what we ourselves are doing (unless we happen to be looking in the mirror). On the other hand, when we utter a vocal gesture, we hear ourselves just as others do. One result of this is that the vocal gesture can affect the speaker in much the same way that it affects the listeners. Another is that we are far better able to stop ourselves in vocal gestures than we are able to do in physical gestures. In other words, we have far better control over vocal gestures than physical ones. This ability to control oneself and one's reactions is critical, as we will see, to the other distinctive capabilities of humans. More generally, "It has been the vocal gesture that has preeminently provided the medium of social organization in human society" (Mead, 1959:188).

Significant Symbols

A significant symbol is a kind of gesture, one of which only humans are capable. Gestures become *significant symbols* when they arouse in the individual making them the same kind of response (it need not be identical) as they are supposed to elicit from those to whom the gestures are addressed. Only when we have significant symbols can we truly have communication; communication in the full sense of the term is not possible among ants, bees, and so on. Physical gestures can be significant symbols, but as we have seen, they are not ideally suited to this because people cannot easily see or hear their own physical gestures. Thus, it is vocal utterances that are most likely to become significant symbols, although not all vocalizations are such symbols. The set of vocal gestures that is most likely to become significant symbols is *language:* "a symbol which answers to a meaning in that experience of the first individual and which also calls out the meaning in the second individual.

Where the gesture reaches that situation it has become what we call 'language.' It is now a significant symbol and it signifies a certain meaning" (Mead, 1934/1962:46). In a conversation of gestures, only the gestures themselves are communicated. However, with language the gestures as well as their meanings are communicated.

One of the things that language, or significant symbols more generally, does is call out the same response in the individual as it does in others. The word *dog* or *cat* elicits the same mental image in the person uttering the word as it does in those to whom it is addressed. Another effect of language is that it stimulates the person speaking as it does others. The person yelling "fire" in a crowded theater is at least as motivated to leave the theater as are those to whom the shout is addressed. Thus, significant symbols allow people to be the stimulators of their own actions.

Adopting his pragmatist orientation, Mead also looks at the "functions" of gestures, in general, and significant symbols, in particular. The function of the gesture "is to make adjustment possible among the individuals implicated in any given social act with reference to the object or objects with which that act is concerned" (Mead, 1934/1962:46). Thus, an involuntary facial grimace may be made in order to prevent a child from going too close to the edge of a precipice and thereby prevent him or her from being in a potentially dangerous situation. While the nonsignificant gesture works, the

> significant symbol affords far greater facilities for such adjustment and readjustment than does the nonsignificant gesture, because it calls out in the individual making it the same attitude toward it . . . and enables him to adjust his subsequent behavior to theirs in the light of that attitude. In short, the conscious or significant conversation of gestures is a much more adequate and effective mechanism of mutual adjustment within the social act . . . than is the unconscious or nonsignificant conversation of gestures.
>
> (Mead, 1934/1962:46)

From a pragmatic point of view, a significant symbol works better in the social world than a nonsignificant gesture. In other words, in communicating our displeasure to others, an angry verbal rebuke works far better than contorted body language. The individual manifesting displeasure is not usually conscious of body language and therefore is unlikely to be able to consciously adjust later actions in light of how the other person reacts to the body language. On the other hand, a speaker is conscious of uttering an angry rebuke and reacts to it in much the same way (and at about the same time) as the person to whom it is aimed reacts. Thus, the speaker can think about how the other person might react and can prepare his or her reaction to that reaction.

Of crucial importance in Mead's theory is another function of significant symbols, and that is that they make the mind, mental processes, and so on possible. It is only through significant symbols, especially language, that human *thinking* is possible (lower animals cannot think, in Mead's terms). Mead defines *thinking* as "simply an internalized or implicit conversation of the individual with himself by means of such gestures" (1934/1962:47). Even more strongly, Mead argues: "Thinking is the same as talking to other people" (1982:155). In other words, thinking involves talking to oneself. Thus, we can see clearly here how Mead defines thinking in behaviorist terms. Conversations involve behavior (talking), and that behavior also occurs within the individual; when it does, thinking is taking place. This is not a mentalistic definition of thinking; it is decidedly behavioristic.

Significant symbols also make possible *symbolic interaction*. That is, people can interact with one another not just through gestures but also through significant symbols. This, of course, makes a world of difference and makes possible much more complex interaction patterns and forms of social organization than would be possible through gestures alone.

The significant symbol obviously plays a central role in Mead's thinking. In fact, Miller accords the significant symbol *the* central role in Mead's theory: "Mead's most profound insight consists in understanding that the significant symbol, the language symbol, consists of a gesture whose meaning is had by both the one who makes the gesture and the other to whom it is addressed. He spent most of his intellectual life unraveling the implications of this insight" (1982a:10–11).

Mental Processes and the Mind

Mead uses a number of similar-sounding concepts when discussing mental *processes,* and it is important to sort them out. Before we do, the point should be made that Mead is always inclined to think in terms of processes rather than structures or contents. In fact, Mead is often labeled a "process philosopher" (Cronk, 1987; Miller, 1982a).

One term that sounds like it belongs under the heading of "mental processes" but actually does not in Mead's thinking is *intelligence.*[6] Mead defines *intelligence* most broadly as the mutual adjustment of the acts of organisms. By this definition, lower animals clearly have "intelligence" because in a conversation of gestures they adapt to one another. Similarly, humans can adapt to one another through the use of nonsignificant symbols (for example, involuntary grimaces). However, what distinguishes humans is that they can also exhibit intelligence, or mutual adaptation, through the use of significant symbols. Thus, a bloodhound has intelligence, but the intelligence of the detective is distinguished from that of the bloodhound by the capacity to use significant symbols.

Mead argues that animals have "unreasoning intelligence." In contrast, humans have "reason," which Mead defines in a characteristically behavioristic manner: "When you are reasoning you are indicating to yourself the characters that call out certain responses—and that is all you are doing"

---

[6] Although, as we will see later, Mead uses this term inconsistently; it is sometimes used to include mental processes.

(1934/1962:93). In other words, individuals are carrying on conversations with themselves.

What is crucial to the reflective intelligence of humans is their ability to temporarily inhibit action, to delay their reactions to a stimulus (Mead, 1959:84). In the case of lower animals, a stimulus leads immediately and inevitably to a reaction; lower animals lack the capacity to temporarily inhibit their reactions. As Mead puts it, "Delayed reaction is necessary to intelligent[7] conduct. The organization, implicit testing, and final selection . . . would be impossible if his overt responses or reactions could not in such situations be delayed" (1934/1962:99). There are three components here. First, humans, because of their ability to delay reactions, are able to organize in their own minds the array of possible responses to a situation. Humans possess in their minds the alternative ways of completing a social act in which they are involved. Second, people are able to test out mentally, again through an internal conversation with themselves, the various courses of action. In contrast, lower animals lack this capacity and therefore must try out reactions in the real world in trial-and-error fashion. The ability to try out responses mentally, as we saw in the case of the poison mushroom, is much more effective than the trial-and-error method. There is no social cost involved in mentally trying out a poorly adapted response. However, when a lower animal actually uses such a response in the real world (for example, when a dog approaches a poisonous snake), the results can be costly, even disastrous. Finally, humans are able to pick out one stimulus among a set of stimuli rather than simply reacting to the first or strongest stimulus. In addition, humans can select among a range of alternative actions, whereas lower animals simply act. As Mead says:

> It is the entrance of the alternative possibilities of future response into the determination of present conduct in any given environmental situation, and their operation, through the mechanism of the central nervous system, as part of the factors or conditions determining present behavior, which *decisively* contrasts intelligent conduct or behavior with reflex, instinctive, and habitual conduct or behavior-delayed reaction with immediate reaction.
>
> (Mead, 1934/1962:98; italics added)

The ability to choose among a range of actions makes it probable that the choices of humans are likely to be better adapted to the situation than the immediate and mindless reactions of lower animals. As Mead contends, "Intelligence is largely a matter of selectivity" (1934/1962:99).

Mead also discusses *consciousness*, which he sees as having two distinguishable meanings (1938/1972:75). The first is that to which the actor alone has access, that which is entirely subjective. Mead is less interested in this sense of consciousness than the second, which basically involves reflective intelligence. Thus, Mead is less interested in the way in which we experience imme-

---

[7] Here is one place where Mead is using *intelligence* in a different sense than the way he employed it in the above discussion.

diate pain or pleasure than he is in the way in which we think about the social world.

Consciousness is to be explained or accounted for within the social process. That is, in contrast to most analysts, Mead believes that consciousness is *not* lodged in the brain: "Consciousness is functional not substantive; and in either of the main senses of the term it must be located in the objective world rather than in the brain—it belongs to, or is a characteristic of, the environment in which we find ourselves. What is located, what does take place, in the brain, however, is the physiological process whereby we lose and regain consciousness" (1934/1962:112).

In a similar manner, Mead refuses to position *mental images* in the brain but sees them as social phenomena:

> What we term 'mental images' . . . can exist in their relation to the organism without being lodged in a substantial consciousness. The mental image is a memory image. Such images which, as symbols, play so large a part in thinking, belong to the environment. The passage we read is made up from memory images, and the people we see about us we see very largely by the help of memory images. . . . We can proceed with *a behavioristic treatment* without having the difficulties in which Watson found himself in dealing with mental images.
>
> (Mead, 1934/1962:332; italics added)

Meaning is yet another related concept that Mead addresses behavioristically. Characteristically, Mead rejects the idea that meaning lies in consciousness: "Awareness or consciousness is not necessary to the presence of meaning in the process of social experience" (1934/1962:77). Similarly, Mead rejects the idea that meaning is a "psychical" phenomenon or an "idea." Rather, *meaning* lies squarely within the social act: "Meaning arises and lies within the field of the relation between the gesture of a given human organism and the subsequent behavior of this organism as indicated to another human organism by that gesture. If that gesture does so indicate to another organism the subsequent (or resultant) behavior of the given organism, then it has meaning" (Mead, 1934/1962:75–76). It is the adjustive response of the second organism that gives meaning to the gesture of the first organism. The meaning of a gesture can be seen as the "ability to predict the behavior that is likely to occur next" (J. Baldwin, 1986:72).

While meaning is to be found in behavior, it becomes conscious when meaning is associated with symbols. However, while meaning can become conscious among humans, it is present in the social act *prior* to the emergence of consciousness and the awareness of meaning. Thus, in these terms, lower animals (and humans) can engage in meaningful behavior even though they are not aware of the meaning.

Like consciousness, the *mind,* which is defined by Mead as a process and not a thing, as an inner conversation with one's self, is not found within the individual; it is not intracranial but is a social phenomenon. It arises and develops within the social process and is an integral part of that process. Thus, the social process precedes the mind; it is not, as many believe, a product of the mind. Thus, the mind, too, is defined functionally rather than substantively. Given these similarities to ideas like consciousness, is there anything distinctive about the mind? We have already seen that humans have the peculiar capacity to call out in themselves the response they are seeking to elicit from others. A distinctive characteristic of the mind is the ability of the individual "to call out in himself not simply a single response of the other but the response, so to speak, of the community as a whole. That is what gives to an individual what we term 'mind.' To do anything now means a certain organized response; and if one has in himself that response, he has what we term 'mind' " (Mead, 1934/1962:267). Thus, the mind can be distinguished from other like-sounding concepts in Mead's work by its ability to respond to the overall community and put forth an organized response.

Mead also looks at the mind in another, pragmatic way. That is, the mind involves thought processes oriented toward problem solving. The real world is rife with problems, and it is the function of the mind to try to solve those problems and permit people to operate more effectively in the world.

Self

Much of Mead's thinking in general, and especially on the mind, involves his ideas on the critically important concept of the "self." Up to this point we have avoided this concept, but it is now necessary to discuss it in order to get a fuller flavor of Mead's thinking.

The *self* is basically the ability to take oneself as an object; the self has the peculiar ability to be both subject and object. As is true of all Mead's major concepts, the self presupposes a social process: communication among humans. Lower animals do not have selves, nor do human infants at birth. The self arises with development and through social activity and social relationships. To Mead, it is impossible to imagine a self arising in the absence of social experiences. However, once a self has developed, it is possible for it to continue to exist without social contact. Thus, Robinson Crusoe developed a self while he was in civilization, and he continued to have it when he was living alone on what he thought for awhile was a deserted island. In other words, he continued to have the ability to take himself as an object. Once it is developed, people usually, but not always, manifest a self. For example, the self is not involved in habitual actions or in immediate physiological experiences of pleasure or pain.

The self is dialectically related to the mind. That is, on the one hand, Mead argues that the body is not a self and becomes a self only when a mind has developed. On the other hand, the self, and its reflexiveness, is essential to the development of the mind. Of course, it is impossible to separate mind and self, because the self is a mental process. However, even though we may think of it as a mental process, the self—like all other mental processes in Mead's theoretical system—is a social process. In his discussion of the self, as we saw above in regard to all other mental phenomena, Mead resists the idea of lodging it in consciousness and instead embeds it in social experience and social processes. In this way, Mead seeks to give a behavioristic sense of the self: "But it is where one does respond to that which he addresses to another and where that response of his own becomes a part of his conduct, where he not only hears himself but responds to himself, talks and replies to himself as truly as the other person replies to him, that we have *behavior* in which the individuals become objects to themselves" (1934/1962:139; italics added). The self, then, is simply another aspect of the overall social process of which the individual is a part.

The general mechanism for the development of the self is reflexivity, or the ability to put ourselves unconsciously into others' places and to act as they act. As a result of this, people are able to examine themselves as others would examine them. As Mead says:

> It is by means of reflexiveness—the turning-back of the experience of the individual upon himself—that the whole social process is thus brought into the experience of the individuals involved in it; it is by such means, which enable the individual to take the attitude of the other toward himself, that the individual is able consciously to adjust himself to that process, and to modify the resultant process in any given social act in terms of his adjustment to it.
>
> (Mead, 1934/1962:134)

The self also allows people to take part in their conversations with others. That is, one is aware of what one is saying and as a result is able to monitor what is being said and to determine what is going to be said next.

In order to have selves, individuals must be able to get "outside themselves" so that they can evaluate themselves, so that they can become objects to themselves. To do this, people basically put themselves in the same experiential field as they put everyone else. The fact is that everyone is an important part of that experiential situation, and people must take themselves into account if they are to be able to act rationally in a given situation. Having done this, they seek to examine themselves impersonally, objectively and without emotion.

However, people cannot experience themselves directly. They can do so only indirectly by putting themselves in the position of others and viewing themselves from that standpoint. People can do this either by putting themselves in the position of other particular individuals or by looking at themselves from the viewpoint of the social group as a whole. As Mead puts it, most generally, "It is only by taking the roles of others that we have been able to come back to ourselves" (1959:184–185). We will have more to say shortly about this important distinction between putting ourselves in the place of a specific individual or putting ourselves in the position of a collectivity.

Mead is very interested in the genesis of the self. He sees the conversation of gestures as the background for the self, but it does not involve a self, since in such a conversation the people are not taking themselves as objects. Mead traces the genesis of the self through two stages in childhood development. The first is the *play stage,* and it is during this stage that children learn to take the attitude of particular others to themselves. While lower animals also play, only human beings "play at being someone else" (Aboulafia, 1986:9). Mead gives the example of a child playing (American) "Indian": "This means that the child has a certain set of stimuli which call out in itself the responses they would call out in others, and which answer to an Indian" (Mead, 1934/1962: 150). As a result of such play, the child learns to become both subject and object and begins to become able to build a self. However, it is a limited self because the child is only capable of taking the role of distinct and separate others. Children may play at being "mommy" and "daddy" and in the process develop the ability to evaluate themselves as their parents, and other specific individuals, do. However, they lack a more general and organized sense of themselves.

It is the next stage, the *game stage,* that is required if the person is to develop a self in the full sense of the term. While in the play stage the child takes the role of discrete others, in the game stage the child must take the role of everyone else involved in the game. Furthermore, these different roles must have a definite relationship to one another. In illustrating the game stage, Mead gives his famous example of a baseball (or, as he calls it, "ball nine") game:

> But in a game where a number of individuals are involved, then the child taking one role must be ready to take the role of everyone else. If he gets in a ball nine he must have the responses of each position involved in his own position. He must know what everyone else is going to do in order to carry out his own play. He has to take all of these roles. They do not all have to be present in consciousness at the same time, but at some moments he has to have three or four individuals present in his own attitude, such as the one who is going to throw the ball, the one who is going to catch it, and so on. These responses must be, in some degree, present in his own make-up. In the game, then, there is a set of responses of such others so organized that the attitude of one calls out the appropriate attitudes of the other.
>
> (Mead, 1934/1962:151)

In the play stage, children are not organized wholes because they play at a series of discrete roles. As a result, in Mead's view they lack definite personalities. However, in the game stage,[8] such organization begins and a definite personality starts to emerge. Children begin to become able to function in organized groups and, most importantly, to determine what they will do within a specific group.

The game stage yields one of Mead's (1959:87) best-known concepts, the *generalized other.* The generalized other is the attitude of the entire community or, in the example of the baseball game, the attitude of the entire team. The ability to take the role of the generalized other is essential to the self: "Only in so far as he takes the attitudes of the organized social group to which he

---

[8] While Mead discusses games, it is clear, as Aboulafia (1986:198) points out, that he means any system of organized responses (for example, the family).

belongs toward the organized, co-operative social activity or set of such activities in which that group is engaged, does he develop a complete self" (Mead, 1934/1962:155). It is also crucial that people be able to evaluate themselves from the point of view of the generalized other and not merely from the viewpoint of discrete others. Taking the role of the generalized other, rather than that of discrete others, allows for the possibility of abstract thinking and objectivity (Mead, 1959:190). Here is the way Mead describes the full development of the self:

> So the self reaches its full development by organizing these individual attitudes of others into the organized social or group attitudes, and by thus becoming an individual reflection of the general systematic pattern of social or group behavior in which it and others are involved—a pattern which enters as a whole into the individual's experience in terms of these organized group attitudes which, through the mechanism of the central nervous system, he takes toward himself, just as he takes the individual attitudes of others.
>
> (Mead, 1934/1962:158)

In other words, to have a self, one must be a member of a community and be directed by the attitudes common to the community. While play requires only pieces of selves, the game requires a coherent self.

Not only is taking the role of the generalized other essential to the self, but it is also crucial for the development of organized group activities. A group requires that individuals direct their activities in accord with the attitudes of the generalized other. The generalized other also represents Mead's familiar propensity to give priority to the social, since it is through the generalized other that the group influences the behavior of individuals.

Mead also looks at the self from a pragmatic point of view. At the individual level, the self allows the individual to be a more efficient member of the larger society. Because of the self, people are more likely to do what is expected of them in a given situation. Since people often try to live up to group expectations, they are more likely to avoid the inefficiencies that come from failing to do what the group expects. Furthermore, the self allows for greater coordination in society as a whole. Because individuals can be counted on to do what is expected of them, the group can operate more effectively.

The preceding, as well as the overall discussion of the self, might lead us to believe that Mead's actors are little more than conformists and that there is little individuality, since everyone is busy conforming to the expectations of the generalized other. But Mead is clear that each self is different from all others. Selves share a common structure, but each self receives unique biographical articulation. In addition, it is clear that there is not simply one grand generalized other but that there are many generalized others in society, because there are many groups in society. People, therefore, have multiple generalized others and, as a result, multiple selves. Each person's unique set of selves makes him or her different from everyone else. Furthermore, people need not accept the community as it is; they can reform things and seek to make them better. We are able to change the community because of our capacity to think. But Mead is forced to put this issue of individual creativity in familiar, behavioristic terms: "The only way in which we can react against the disapproval of the entire community is by setting up a higher sort of community which in a certain sense out-votes the one we find . . . he may stand out by himself over against it. But to do that he has to comprehend the voices of the past and of the future. That is the only way the self can get a voice which is more than the voice of the community" (1934/1962:167–168). In other words, to stand up to the generalized other, the individual must construct a still larger generalized other, composed not only from the present but also from the past and the future, and then respond to it.

Mead identifies two aspects, or phases, of the self, which he labels the "I" and the "me." As Mead puts it, "The self is essentially a social process going on with these two distinguishable phases" (1934/1962:178). It is important to bear in mind that the "I" and "me" are processes within the larger process of the self; they are not "things." The "I" is the immediate response of an individual to others. It is the incalculable, unpredictable, and creative aspect of the self. People do not know in advance what the action of the "I" will be: "But what that response will be he does not know and nobody else knows. Perhaps he will make a brilliant play or an error. The response to that situation as it appears in his immediate experience is uncertain" (Mead, 1934/1962:175). We are never totally aware of the "I," and through it we surprise ourselves with our actions. We know the "I" only after the act has been carried out. Thus, we know the "I" only in our memories. Mead lays great stress on the "I" for four reasons. First, it is a key source of novelty in the social process. Second, Mead believes that it is in the "I" that our most important values are located. Third, the "I" constitutes something that we all seek—the realization of the self. It is the "I" that permits us to develop a "definite personality." Finally, Mead sees an evolutionary process in history in which people in primitive societies are dominated more by "me" while in modern societies there is a greater component of "I."

The "I" gives Mead's theoretical system some much-needed dynamism and creativity. Without it, Mead's actors would be totally dominated by external and internal controls. With it, Mead is able to deal with the changes brought about not only by the great figures in history (for example, Einstein) but also by individuals on a day-to-day basis. It is the "I" that makes these changes possible. Since every personality is a mix of "I" and "me," the great historical figures are seen as having a larger proportion of "I" than most others. But in day-to-day situations, anyone's "I" may assert itself and lead to change in the social situation. Uniqueness is also brought into Mead's system through the biographical articulation of each individual's "I" and "me." That is, the specific exigencies of each person's life give him or her a unique mix of "I" and "me."

The "I" reacts against the "me," which is the "organized set of attitudes of others which one himself assumes" (Mead, 1934/1962:175). In other words, the "me" is the adoption of the "generalized other." In contrast to the "I," people are conscious of the "me"; the "me" involves conscious responsibility. As Mead says, "The 'me' is a conventional, habitual individual" (1934/1962:197). Conformists are dominated by "me," although everyone—whatever his or her degree of conformity—has, and must have, substantial "me." It is through the "me" that society dominates the individual. Indeed, Mead defines the idea of *social control* as the dominance of the expression of the "me" over the expression of the "I." Later in *Mind, Self and Society*, Mead elaborates on his ideas on social control:

> Social control, as operating in terms of self-criticism, exerts itself so intimately and extensively over individual behavior or conduct, serving to integrate the individual and his actions with reference to the organized social process of experience and behavior in which he is implicated. . . . Social control over individual behavior or conduct operates by virtue of the social origin and basis of such [self-] criticism. That is to say, self-criticism is essentially social criticism, and behavior controlled socially. Hence social control, so far from tending to crush out the human individual or to obliterate his self-conscious individuality, is, on the contrary, actually consti-tutive of and inextricably associated with that individuality.
>
> (Mead, 1934/1962:255)

Mead also looks at the "I" and "me" in pragmatic terms. The "me" allows the individual to live comfortably in the social world, while the "I" makes the change of society possible. Society gets enough conformity to allow it to function, and it gets a steady infusion of new developments to prevent it from stagnating. The "I" and the "me" are thus part of the whole social process and allow both individuals and society to function more effectively.

SOCIETY

At the most general level, Mead uses the term *society* to mean the ongoing social process that precedes both the mind and the self. Given its importance in shaping the mind and self, society is clearly of central importance to Mead. At another level, society to Mead represents the organized set of responses that are taken over by the individual in the form of the "me." Thus, in this sense individuals carry society around with them, and it is this that allows them, through self-criticism, to control themselves. Mead also deals with the evolution of society. But Mead has relatively little to say explicitly about soci-ety, in spite of its centrality in his theoretical system. His most important contributions lie in his thoughts on mind and self. Even John Baldwin, who sees a much more societal (macro) component in Mead's thinking, is forced to admit: "The macro components of Mead's theoretical system are not as well developed as the micro" (1986:123).

At a more specific societal level Mead does have a number of things to say about social *institutions*. Mead broadly defines an *institution* as the "common

response in the community"or "the life habits of the community" (1934/
1962:261, 264; see also Mead, 1936:376). More specifically he says that "the
whole community acts toward the individual under certain circumstances in
an identical way . . . there is an identical response on the part of the whole
community under these conditions. We call that the formation of the institution" (Mead, 1934/1962:167). We carry this organized set of attitudes around
with us, and they serve to control our actions, largely through the "me."

Education is the process by which the common habits of the community
(the institution) are "internalized" in the actor. This is an essential process,
since, in Mead's view, people neither have selves nor are genuine members
of the community until they can respond to themselves as the larger community does. To do so, people must have internalized the common attitudes
of the community.

But again Mead is careful to point out that institutions need not destroy
individuality or stifle creativity. Mead recognizes that there are "oppressive,
stereotyped, and ultra-conservative social institutions—like the church—
which by their more or less rigid and inflexible unprogressiveness crush or
blot out individuality" (1934/1962:262). However, he is quick to add: "There
is no necessary or inevitable reason why social institutions should be oppressive or rigidly conservative, or why they should not rather be, as many are,
flexible and progressive, fostering individuality rather than discouraging it"
(Mead, 1934/1962:262). To Mead, institutions should define what people
ought to do only in a very broad and general sense and should allow plenty
of room for individuality and creativity. Mead here demonstrates a very modern conception of social institutions as both constraining individuals *and* enabling them to be creative individuals (see Giddens, 1984).

What Mead lacks in his analysis of society in general, and institutions in
particular,[9] is a true macro sense of them in the way that theorists like Marx,
Weber, and Durkheim dealt with this level of analysis. This is true in spite of
the fact that Mead does have a notion of *emergence* in the sense that the whole
is seen as more than the sum of its parts. More specifically, "Emergence
involves a reorganization, but the reorganization brings in something that was
not there before. The first time oxygen and hydrogen come together, water
appears. Now water is a combination of hydrogen and oxygen, but water was
not there before in the separate elements" (Mead, 1934/1962:198). However,
Mead is much more prone to apply the idea of emergence to consciousness
than to apply it to the larger society. That is, mind and self are seen as emergent from the social process. Moreover, Mead is inclined to use the term *emergence* merely to mean the coming into existence of something new or novel
(Miller, 1973:41).

---

[9] There are at least two places where Mead offers a more macro sense of society. At one point
he defines *social institutions* as "organized forms of group or social activity" (Mead, 1934/
1962:261). Earlier, in an argument reminiscent of Comte, he offers a view of the family as the
fundamental unit within society and as the base of such larger units as the clan and state.

SYMBOLIC INTERACTIONISM: THE BASIC PRINCIPLES

The heart of this chapter is our discussion of the basic principles of symbolic interaction theory. Although we try to characterize the theory in general terms, this is not easy to do for, as Paul Rock says, it has a "deliberately constructed vagueness" and a "resistance to systematisation" (1979:18–19). There are significant differences within symbolic interactionism, some of which are discussed as we proceed. We also address a number of the criticisms of symbolic interactionism.

A number of symbolic interactionists (Blumer, 1969a; Manis and Meltzer, 1978; Rose, 1962) have tried to enumerate the basic principles of the theory. These principles include the following:

1. Human beings, unlike lower animals, are endowed with the capacity for thought.
2. The capacity for thought is shaped by social interaction.
3. In social interaction people learn the meanings and the symbols that allow them to exercise their distinctively human capacity for thought.
4. Meanings and symbols allow people to carry on distinctively human action and interaction.
5. People are able to modify or alter the meanings and symbols that they use in action and interaction on the basis of their interpretation of the situation.
6. People are able to make these modifications and alterations because, in part, of their ability to interact with themselves, which allows them to examine possible courses of action, assess their relative advantages and disadvantages, and then choose one.
7. The intertwined patterns of action and interaction make up groups and societies.

Capacity for Thought

The crucial assumption that human beings possess the ability to think differentiates symbolic interactionism from its behaviorist roots. This assumption also provides the basis for the entire theoretical orientation of symbolic interactionism. Bernard Meltzer, James Petras, and Larry Reynolds stated that the assumption of the human capacity for thought is one of the major contributions of early symbolic interactionists, such as James, Dewey, Thomas, Cooley, and of course Mead: "Individuals in human society were not seen as units that are motivated by external or internal forces beyond their control, or within the confines of a more or less fixed structure. Rather, they were viewed as reflective or interacting units which comprise the societal entity" (1975:42). The ability to think enables people to act reflectively rather than just behave unreflectively. People must often construct and guide what they do, rather than just release it.

The ability to think is embedded in the mind, but the symbolic interactionists have a somewhat unusual conception of the mind. They distinguish it from the physiological brain. People must have brains in order to develop minds, but a brain does not inevitably produce a mind, as is clear in the case of lower animals (Troyer, 1946). Also, symbolic interactionists do not conceive of the mind as a thing, a physical structure, but rather as a continuing process. It is a process that is itself part of the larger process of stimulus and response. The mind is related to virtually every other aspect of symbolic interactionism, including socialization, meanings, symbols, the self, interaction, and even society.

Thinking and Interaction

People possess only a general capacity for thought. This capacity must be shaped and refined in the process of social interaction. Such a view leads the symbolic interactionist to focus on a specific form of social interaction—*socialization*. The human ability to think is developed early in childhood socialization and is refined during adult socialization. Symbolic interactionists have a view of the socialization process that is different from that of most other sociologists. To symbolic interactionists, conventional sociologists are likely to see socialization as simply a process by which people learn the things that they need to survive in society (for instance, culture, role expectations). To the symbolic interactionists, socialization is a more dynamic process that allows people to develop the ability to think, to develop in distinctively human ways. Furthermore, socialization is not simply a one-way process in which the actor receives information, but is a dynamic process in which the actor shapes and adapts the information to his or her own needs (Manis and Meltzer, 1978:6).

Symbolic interactionists are, of course, interested not simply in socialization but in interaction in general, which is of "vital importance in its own right" (Blumer, 1969b:8). *Interaction* is the process in which the ability to think is both developed and expressed. All types of interaction, not just interaction during socialization, refine our ability to think. Beyond that, thinking shapes the interaction process. In most interaction, actors must take account of others and decide if and how to fit their activities to others. However, not all interaction involves thinking. The differentiation made by Blumer (following Mead) between two basic forms of social interaction is relevant here. The first, nonsymbolic interaction—Mead's conversation of gestures—does not involve thinking. The second, symbolic interaction, does require mental processes.

The importance of thinking to symbolic interactionists is reflected in their views on *objects*. Blumer differentiates among three types of objects: *physical objects*, such as a chair or a tree; *social objects*, such as a student or a mother; and *abstract objects*, such as an idea or a moral principle. Objects are seen simply as things "out there" in the real world; what is of greatest significance is the way that they are defined by actors. This leads to the relativistic view that different objects have different meanings for different individuals: "A tree will be a different object to a botanist, a lumberman, a poet, and a home gardener" (Blumer, 1969b:11).

Individuals learn the meanings of objects during the socialization process. Most of us learn a common set of meanings, but in many cases, as with the tree mentioned above, we have different definitions of the same objects. Although this can be taken to an extreme, symbolic interactionists need not deny the existence of objects in the real world. All they need do is point out the crucial nature of the definition of those objects as well as the possibility that actors may have different definitions of the same object. As Herbert Blumer said: "The nature of an object . . . consists of the meaning that it has for the person for whom it is an object" (1969b:11).

Learning Meanings and Symbols

Symbolic interactionists, following Mead, tend to accord causal significance to social interaction. Thus, meaning does not stem from mental processes but from the process of interaction. This focus derives from Mead's pragmatism: he focused on human action and interaction, not isolated mental processes. Symbolic interactionists have in general continued in this direction. Among other things, the central concern is not how people mentally create meanings and symbols but how they learn them during interaction in general and socialization in particular.

People learn symbols as well as meanings in social interaction. Whereas people respond to signs unthinkingly, they respond to symbols in a thoughtful manner. Signs stand for themselves (for example, the gestures of angry dogs or water to a person dying of thirst). "*Symbols are social objects used to represent* (or 'stand in for,' 'take the place of') whatever people agree they shall represent" (Charon, 1985:39). Not all social objects stand for other things, but those that do are symbols. Words, physical artifacts, and physical actions (for example, the word *boat,* a cross or a Star of David, and a clenched fist) all can be symbols. People often use symbols to communicate something about themselves: they drive Rolls-Royces, for instance, to communicate a certain style of life.

Symbolic interactionists conceive of language as a vast system of symbols. Words are symbols, because they are used to stand for things. Words make all other symbols possible. Acts, objects, and other words exist and have meaning only because they have been and can be described through the use of words.

Symbols are crucial in allowing people to act in distinctively human ways. Because of the symbol, the human being "does not respond passively to a reality that imposes itself but actively creates and re-creates the world acted in" (Charon, 1985:62). In addition to this general utility, symbols in general and language in particular have a number of specific functions for the actor (Charon, 1985).

First, symbols allow people to deal with the material and social world by allowing them to name, categorize, and remember the objects that they encounter there. In this way, people are able to order a world that otherwise would be confusing. Language allows people to name, categorize, and especially remember much more efficiently than they could with other kinds of symbols, such as pictorial images.

Second, symbols improve people's ability to perceive the environment. Instead of being flooded by a mass of indistinguishable stimuli, the actor can be alerted to some parts of the environment rather than others.

Third, symbols improve the ability to think. Although a set of pictorial symbols would allow a limited ability to think, language greatly expands this ability. Thinking, in these terms, can be conceived of as symbolic interaction with one's self.

Fourth, symbols greatly increase the ability to solve various problems. Lower animals must use trial and error, but human beings can think through symbolically a variety of alternative actions before actually taking one. This reduces the chance of making costly mistakes.

Fifth, the use of symbols allows actors to transcend time, space, and even their own persons. Through the use of symbols, actors can imagine what it was like to live in the past or might be like to live in the future. In addition, actors can transcend their own persons symbolically and imagine what the world is like from another person's point of view. This is the well-known symbolic-interactionist concept of *taking the role of the other* (Miller, 1981).

Sixth, symbols allow us to imagine a metaphysical reality, such as heaven or hell. Seventh, and most generally, symbols allow people to avoid being enslaved by their environment. They can be active rather than passive—that is, self-directed in what they do.

Action and Interaction

Symbolic interactionists' primary concern is with the impact of meanings and symbols on human action and interaction. Here it is useful to employ Mead's differentiation between covert and overt behavior. *Covert behavior* is the thinking process, involving symbols and meanings. *Overt behavior* is the actual behavior performed by an actor. Some overt behavior does not involve covert behavior (habitual behavior or mindless responses to external stimuli). However, most human action involves both kinds. Covert behavior is of greatest concern to symbolic interactionists, whereas overt behavior is of greater concern to exchange theorists or to traditional behaviorists in general.

Meanings and symbols give human social action (which involves a single actor) and social interaction (which involves two or more actors engaged in mutual social action) distinctive characteristics. Social action is that in which the individuals are "acting with others in mind" (Charon, 1985:130). In other words, in undertaking an action, people simultaneously try to gauge its impact on the other actors involved. Although they often engage in mindless, habitual behavior, people have the capacity to engage in social action.

In the process of social interaction, people symbolically communicate meanings to the others involved. The others interpret those symbols and orient their responding action on the basis of their interpretation. In other words, in social interaction, actors engage in a process of mutual influence.

Making Choices

Partly because of the ability to handle meanings and symbols, people, unlike lower animals, can make choices in the actions in which they engage. People need not accept the meanings and symbols that are imposed on them from without. On the basis of their own interpretation of the situation, "humans are capable of forming new meanings and new lines of meaning" (Manis and Meltzer, 1978:7).

W. I. Thomas was instrumental in underscoring this creative capacity in his concept of *definition of the situation*: "If men define situations as real, they are real in their consequences" (Thomas and Thomas, 1928:572). Thomas knew that most of our definitions of situations have been provided for us by society. In fact, he emphasized this, pointing especially to the family and the community as sources of our social definitions. However, Thomas's position is distinctive for his emphasis on the possibility of "spontaneous" individual definitions of situations, which allow people to alter and modify meanings and symbols.

We also can say that to the symbolic interactionist, actors have at least some autonomy. They are not simply constrained or determined; they are capable of making unique and independent choices. Furthermore, they are able to develop a life that has a uniqueness and a style of its own (Perinbanayagam, 1985:53).

This ability of actors to make a difference is reflected in an essay by Gary Fine and Sherryl Kleinman (1983) in which they look at the phenomenon of a "social network." Instead of viewing a social network as an unconscious and/or constraining social structure, Fine and Kleinman see a network as a set of social relationships that people endow with meaning and which are used by people for personal and/or collective purposes.

The Self

The self is a concept of enormous importance to symbolic interactionists. In fact, Rock argues that the self "constitutes the very hub of the interactionists' intellectual scheme. All other sociological processes and events revolve around that hub, taking from it their analytic meaning and organization" (1979:102). In attempting to understand this concept beyond its initial Meadian formulation, we must first understand the idea of the *looking-glass self* developed by Charles Horton Cooley. Cooley defined this concept as

a somewhat definite imagination of how one's self—that is, any idea he appropri-
ates—appears in a particular mind, and the kind of self-feeling one has is determined by the attitude toward this attributed to that other mind. . . . So in
imagination we perceive in another's mind some thought of our appearance, manners, aims, deeds, character, friends, and so on, and are variously affected by it.

(Cooley, 1902/1964:169)

By the looking-glass self Cooley meant the capacity to see ourselves as we
see any other social object. The idea of a looking-glass self can be broken down
into three components. First, we imagine how we appear to others. Second,
we imagine what their judgment of that appearance must be. Third, we
develop some self-feeling, such as pride or mortification, as a result of our
imagining others' judgments.

Cooley's concept of the looking-glass self and Mead's concept of the self
were important in the development of the modern symbolic-interactionist conception of the self. Blumer defined the *self* in extremely simple terms: "Nothing
esoteric is meant by this expression [self]. It means merely that a human being
can be an object of his own action . . . he acts toward himself and guides
himself in his actions toward others on the basis of the kind of object he is to
himself" (1969b:12). The self is a process, not a thing (Perinbanayagam, 1985).
As Blumer made clear, the self helps allow human beings to act rather than
simply respond to external stimuli:

The process [interpretation] has two distinct steps. First, the actor indicates to himself the things toward which he is acting; he has to point out in himself the things
that have meaning. . . . This interaction with himself is something other than an
interplay of psychological elements; it is an instance of the person engaging in a
process of communicating with himself. . . . Second, by virtue of this process of
communicating with himself, interpretation becomes a matter of handling meanings.
The actor selects, checks, suspends, regroups, and transforms the meanings in the
light of the situation in which he is placed and the direction of his action.

(Blumer, 1969b:5)

Although this underscores the part played by the self in the process of choosing how to act, Blumer has really not gone much beyond the early formulations of Cooley and Mead. However, other modern thinkers and researchers
have refined the concept of the self.

Although symbolic interactionists have made important contributions to
our understanding of the self (for example, Ralph Turner, 1968), the best-
known recent work on this topic has been done by a sociologist not usually
associated with this theory, Morris Rosenberg (1979). Although not a symbolic
interactionist, Rosenberg has been heavily influenced by people like Mead and
Cooley. His thoughts on the self generally are compatible with and extend the
symbolic-interactionist orientation to this concept.

Rosenberg began by making it clear that his main interest was in the self-
concept and not the self. The self is a more general concept, being both a
subject and an object. The self-concept is the self as an object. Rosenberg

defines the *self-concept* as *"the totality of the individual's thoughts and feelings having reference to himself as an object"* (1979:7). Thus the self-concept is only a part of the self and an even smaller part of the total personality, but it is endowed with unusual significance, because it "is an important object to everyone, usually the most important object in the world" (Rosenberg, 1979:24). In addition to their importance, beliefs about the self are distinctive in a number of ways. For example, they are the only attitudes that are reflexive—that is, the individual is both subject and object. The self-concept is the result of certain incommunicable information; it reflects the individual's unique body of information and point of view about himself or herself. Although attitudes toward the self have much in common with other attitudes, there are unique attitudes toward the self, especially pride and shame. Accuracy and verifiability are much more important in attitudes toward the self than in attitudes toward bowling or tuna fish. In spite of its importance, the accuracy of self-attitudes "is difficult to ascertain because of low verifiability" (Rosenberg, 1979:33).

Rosenberg differentiated among the content, the structure, the dimensions, and the boundaries of the self-concept. In terms of *content,* Rosenberg distinguished social identities from dispositions. *Social identities* are the "groups, statuses or categories" to which an individual "is socially recognized as belonging" (Rosenberg, 1979:10). Examples include being recognized as a Democrat, middle-aged, black, or male. An individual sees himself or herself not only in terms of such categories but also as possessing certain tendencies to respond, certain *dispositions.* A person who sees himself or herself as brave or introverted or liberal is likely to have his or her actions affected by such dispositions. In addition to discussing the content of the self-concept, Rosenberg also discussed its structure. The *structure* of the self is the relationship among an individual's various social identities and dispositions. *Dimensions* refers to the attitudes and feelings one has about one's self. Self-attitudes, like all other attitudes, vary on a variety of dimensions, including "content, direction, intensity, salience, consistency, stability, clarity, accuracy and verifiability" (Rosenberg, 1979:23). Finally, Rosenberg discussed the *boundaries* of the self-concept, especially the ego-extensions to which it is applied. These are objects outside the actor that lead him or her to feel pride and shame: "pride in my shiny new automobile, shame at my unfashionable clothes, pride in an honor bestowed, shame or embarrassment at the defeat of my school team" (Rosenberg, 1979:35).

Rosenberg also distinguished among the extant self, the desired self, and the presenting self. The *extant self* is our picture of what we are like; the *desired self* is a picture of what we would like to be like; and the *presenting self* is the way we present ourselves in a given situation.

Rosenberg underscored the point that the self-concept involves a set of motivations, a set of desired goals for the actors. Two motives stand out above all others. First is *self-esteem,* or "the wish to think well of one's self" (Rosenberg, 1979:53). Second is *self-consistency,* or "the wish to protect the self-concept against change or to maintain one's self-picture" (Rosenberg, 1979:53). Rosenberg has done extensive empirical research on self-esteem and is widely recognized for this research. However, his conceptual analysis of the self-concept is an important contribution to the key idea of symbolic interactionism.

The Work of Erving Goffman   Another important work on the self is *Presentation of Self in Everyday Life* (1959) by Erving Goffman, one of the most exciting modern symbolic interactionists. Goffman's conception of the self is deeply indebted to Mead's ideas, in particular his discussion of the tension between *I*, the spontaneous self, and *me*, social constraints within the self. This is mirrored in Goffman's work on what he called the "crucial discrepancy between our all-too-human selves and our socialized selves" (1959:56). The tension is due to the difference between what people expect us to do and what we may want to do spontaneously. We are confronted with the demand to do what is expected of us; moreover, we are not supposed to waver. As Goffman put it, "We must not be subject to ups and downs" (1959:56). In order to maintain a stable self-image, people perform for their social audiences. As a result of this interest in performance, Goffman focused on *dramaturgy,* or a view of social life as a series of dramatic performances akin to those performed on the stage.

Dramaturgy   Goffman's sense of the self was shaped by his dramaturgical approach. To Goffman (as to Mead and most other symbolic interactionists), the self is

> not an organic thing that has a specific location. . . . In analyzing the self then we are drawn from its possessor, from the person who will profit or lose most by it, for he and his body merely provide the peg on which something of collaborative manufacture will be hung for a time. . . . The means of producing and maintaining selves do not reside inside the peg.
>
> (Goffman, 1959:252–253)

He perceived the self not as a possession of the actor but rather as the product of the dramatic interaction between actor and audience. The self "is a dramatic effect arising . . . from a scene that is presented" (Goffman, 1959:253). Because the self is a product of dramatic interaction, it is vulnerable to disruption during the performance. Goffman's dramaturgy is concerned with the processes by which such disturbances are prevented or dealt with. Although the bulk of his discussion focuses on these dramaturgical contingencies, Goffman pointed out that most performances are successful. The result is that in ordinary circumstances a firm self is accorded to performers, and it "appears" to emanate from the performer.

Goffman assumed that when individuals interact, they want to present a certain sense of self that will be accepted by others. However, even as they present that self, actors are aware that members of the audience can disturb their performance. For that reason actors are attuned to the need to control the audience, especially those elements of it that might be disruptive. The actors hope that the sense of self that they present to the audience will be strong enough for the audience to define the actors as the actors want. The actors also hope that this will cause the audience to act voluntarily as the actors want them to. Goffman characterized this central interest as "impression management." It involves techniques actors use to maintain certain impressions in the face of problems they are likely to encounter, and methods they use to cope with these problems.

Following this theatrical analogy, Goffman spoke of a front stage. The *front* is that part of the performance that generally functions in rather fixed and general ways to define the situation for those who observe the performance. Within the front stage, Goffman further differentiated between the setting and the personal front. The *setting* refers to the physical scene that ordinarily must be there if the actors are to perform. Without it, the actors usually cannot perform. For example, a surgeon generally requires an operating room, a taxi driver a cab, and an ice skater ice. The *personal front* consists of those items of expressive equipment that the audience identifies with the performers and expects them to carry with them into the setting. A surgeon, for instance, is expected to dress in a medical gown, have certain instruments, and so on.

Goffman then subdivided the personal front into appearance and manner. *Appearance* includes those items that tell us the performer's social status (for instance, the surgeon's medical gown). *Manner* tells the audience what sort of role the performer expects to play in the situation (for example, the use of physical mannerisms, demeanor). A brusque manner and a meek manner indicate quite different kinds of performances. In general, we expect appearance and manner to be consistent.

Although Goffman approached the front and other aspects of his system as a symbolic interactionist, he did discuss their structural character. For example, he argued that fronts tend to become institutionalized so that "collective representations" arise about what is to go on in a certain front. Very often when actors take on established roles they find particular fronts already established for such performances. The result, Goffman argued, is that fronts tend to be selected, not created. This conveys a much more structural image than we would receive from most symbolic interactionists.

Despite such a structural view, Goffman's most interesting insights lie in the domain of interaction. He argued that because people generally[10] try to present an idealized picture of themselves in their front-stage performances, inevitably they feel that they must hide things in their performances. First, actors may want to conceal secret pleasures (for instance, drinking alcohol) engaged in prior to the performance or in past lives (for instance, as drug addicts) that are incompatible with their performance. Second, actors may want to conceal errors that have been made in the preparation of the performance as well as steps that have been taken to correct these errors. For example, a taxi driver may seek to hide the fact that he started in the wrong direc-

---

[10] But not always—see Ungar (1984) on self-mockery as a way of presenting the self.

ERVING GOFFMAN: A Biographical Sketch

Erving Goffman died in 1982 at the peak of his fame. He had long been regarded as a "cult" figure in sociological theory. This status was achieved in spite of the fact that he had been professor in the prestigious sociology department at the University of California, Berkeley, and later held an endowed chair at the Ivy League's University of Pennsylvania.

By the 1980s he had emerged as a centrally important theorist. In fact, he had been elected president of the American Sociological Association in the year he died but was unable to give his presidential address because of advanced illness. Given Goffman's maverick status, Randall Collins says of his address: "Everyone wondered what he would do for his Presidential address: a straight, traditional presentation seemed unthinkable for Goffman with his reputation as an iconoclast . . . we got a far more dramatic message: Presidential address cancelled, Goffman dying. It was an appropriately Goffmanian way to go out" (1986b:112).

Goffman was born in Alberta, Canada, on June 11, 1922 (S. Williams, 1986). He did his graduate work at the University of Chicago and is usually thought of as a member of the Chicago school and a symbolic interactionist. (But it is hard to squeeze his work into a single category, and so we also deal with his later, more structural work in Chapter 13.) In creating his theoretical perspective, Goffman drew on many sources and created a distinctive orientation.

Collins (1986b; Williams, 1986) links Goffman more to social anthropology than to symbolic interactionism. As an undergraduate at the University of Toronto, Goffman had studied with an anthropologist, and at Chicago "his main contacts were not with Symbolic Interactionists, but with W. Lloyd Warner [an anthropologist]" (Collins, 1986b:109). In Collins's view, an examination of the citations in Goffman's early work indicates that he was influenced by social anthropologists and rarely cited symbolic interactionists, and when he did, it was to be critical of them. However, Goffman was influenced by the descriptive studies produced at Chicago and integrated their outlook with that of social anthropology to produce his distinctive perspective. Thus, whereas a symbolic interactionist would look at how people create or negotiate their self-image, Goffman was concerned with how "society . . . forces people to present a certain image of themselves . . . because it forces us to switch back and forth between many complicated roles, is also making us always somewhat untruthful, inconsistent, and dishonorable" (Collins, 1986a:107)

Despite the distinctiveness of his perspective, Goffman had a powerful influence on symbolic interactionism. In addition, it could be argued that he had a hand in shaping another "creative sociology," ethnomethodology. In fact, Collins sees Goffman as a key figure in the formation of not only ethnomethodology, but conversation analysis as well: "It was Goffman who pioneered the close empirical study of everyday life, although he had done it with his bare eyes, before the days of tape recorders and video recorders" (1986b:111). (See Chapter 10 for a discussion of the relationship between ethnomethodology and conversation analysis.) In fact, a number of important ethnomethodologists (Sacks, Schegloff) studied with Goffman at Berkeley and not with the founder of ethnomethodology, Harold Garfinkel.

Given their influence on symbolic interactionism, structuralism, and ethnomethodology, Goffman's theories are likely to be influential for a long time.

tion. Third, actors may find it necessary to show only end products and to conceal the process involved in producing them. For example, professors may spend several hours preparing a lecture, but they may want to act as if they have always known the material. Fourth, it may be necessary for actors to conceal from the audience that "dirty work" was involved in the making of the end products. Dirty work may include tasks that "were physically unclean, semi-legal, cruel, and degrading in other ways" (Goffman, 1959:44). Fifth, in giving a certain performance, actors may have to let other standards slide. Finally, actors probably find it necessary to hide any insults, humiliations, or deals made so that the performance could go on. Generally, actors have a vested interest in hiding all such facts from their audience.

Another aspect of dramaturgy in the front stage is that actors often try to convey the impression that they are closer to the audience than they actually are. For example, actors may try to foster the impression that the performance in which they are engaged at the moment is their only performance or at least their most important one. To do this, actors have to be sure that their audiences are segregated so that the falsity of the performance is not discovered. Even if it is discovered, Goffman argued, the audiences themselves may try to cope with the falsity, so as not to shatter their idealized image of the actor. This reveals the interactional character of performances. A successful performance depends on the involvement of all the parties. Another example of this kind of impression management is an actor's attempt to convey the idea that there is something unique about this performance as well as his or her relationship to the audience. The audience, too, wants to feel that it is the recipient of a unique performance.

Actors try to make sure that all the parts of any performance blend together. In some cases, a single discordant aspect can disrupt a performance. However, performances vary in the amount of consistency required. A slip by a priest on a sacred occasion would be terribly disruptive, but if a taxi driver made one wrong turn, it would not be likely to damage the overall performance greatly.

Another technique employed by performers is *mystification*. Actors often tend to mystify their performance by restricting the contact between themselves and the audience. By generating "social distance" between themselves and the audience, they try to create a sense of awe in the audience. This, in turn, keeps the audience from questioning the performance. Again Goffman pointed out that the audience is involved in this process and often itself seeks to maintain the credibility of the performance by keeping its distance from the performer.

This leads us to Goffman's interest in teams. To Goffman, as a symbolic interactionist, a focus on individual actors obscured important facts about interaction. Goffman's basic unit of analysis was thus not the individual but the team. A *team* is any set of individuals who cooperate in staging a single routine. Thus the preceding discussion of the relationship between the performer and audience is really about teams.[11] Each member is reliant on the others, because all can disrupt the performance and all are aware that they are putting on an act. Goffman concluded that a team is a kind of "secret society."

Goffman also discussed a *back stage* where facts suppressed in the front or various kinds of informal actions may appear. A back stage is usually adjacent to the front stage, but it is also cut off from it. Performers can reliably expect no members of their front audience to appear in the back. Furthermore, they engage in various types of impression management to make sure of this. A performance is likely to become difficult when actors are unable to prevent the audience from entering the back stage. There is also a third, residual domain, the *outside*, which is neither front nor back.

No area is *always* one of these three domains. Also, a given area can occupy all three domains at different times. A professor's office is front stage when a student visits, back stage when the student leaves, and outside when the professor is at a university basketball game.

Impression Management Goffman closed *Presentation of Self in Everyday Life* with some additional thoughts on the art of impression management. In general, *impression management* is oriented to guarding against a series of unexpected actions, such as unintended gestures, inopportune intrusions, and faux pas, as well as intended actions, such as making a scene. Goffman was interested in the various methods of dealing with such problems. First, there is a set of methods involving actions aimed at producing dramaturgical loyalty by, for example, fostering high in-group loyalty, preventing team members from identifying with the audience, and changing audiences periodically so that they do not become too knowledgeable about the performers. Second, Goffman suggested various forms of dramaturgical discipline, such as having the presence of mind to avoid slips, maintaining self-control, and managing the facial expressions and verbal tone of one's performance. Third, he identified various types of dramaturgical circumspection, such as determining in advance how a performance should go, planning for emergencies, selecting loyal teammates, selecting good audiences, being involved in small teams where dissension is less likely, making only brief appearances, preventing audience access to private information, and settling on a complete agenda to prevent unforeseen occurrences.

The audience also has a stake in successful impression management by the actor or team of actors. The audience often acts to save the show through such devices as giving great interest and attention to it, avoiding emotional outbursts, not noticing slips, and giving special consideration to a neophyte performer.

---

[11] A performer and the audience are one kind of team, but Goffman also talked of a group of performers as one team and the audience as another. Interestingly, Goffman argued that a team can also be a single individual. His logic, following classic symbolic interactionism, was that an individual can be his or her own audience—can *imagine* an audience to be present.

Albas and Albas (1988) used the idea of impression management in a study of the efforts of university students to manage impressions after having their examinations returned and receiving their grades. Albas and Albas differentiated among three types of students—"Aces" (those who received high grades), "Middle of the Roaders" (average grades), and "Bombers" (poor grades). The focus of the study was on the Aces and the Bombers and the fact that the Aces are inclined to develop strategies that allow them to reveal their (high) grades to others without appearing to be immodest while the Bombers are oriented toward strategies that help them conceal their (low) grades.

Albas and Albas discovered a number of strategies used by Aces to reveal their grades. For example, while the norm of modesty prevents students from overtly expressing their joy at obtaining a high score, they often employ a strategy of "repressed bubbling," in which their satisfaction is made to appear as though it were seeping out against their will. While this strategy is sometimes consciously employed by students, it more often seems to occur in spite of the students' wishes. A more overt dramaturgical manipulation takes place when students "accidentally" allow others to see their high grades. Still another overt dramaturgical strategy involves asking others how they did on the exam, with the expectation that they will respond by asking the Ace student how he or she did on the exam, thereby allowing that student to reveal the high grade.

Just as Aces seek through dramaturgical devices to reveal their grades, Bombers usually try to conceal their grades, and they use an array of strategies to help them achieve that end. For example, anticipating a poor grade, a Bomber may not attend the class in which the exam is to be returned or may leave the class at the first possible moment after the exam has been returned. Others may actually lie about their grades by adding points to the total, or they may simply make it abundantly clear that they do not wish to discuss grades. A Bomber may express "role distance" (see below) from his or her grade by appearing nonchalant and unconcerned about the return of the exam and the grade that appears on it. Such nonchalance makes it unclear how the student did on the exam.

Goffman followed up his work in *Presentation of Self in Everyday Life* with a series of fascinating and important books and essays (for instance, Goffman, 1961, 1963a, 1963b, 1967, 1971, 1972, 1974). We close this discussion with just a few illustrations of his distinctive mode of thought.

In "Role Distance" (1961) Goffman was interested in the degree to which an individual embraces a given role. In his view, because of the large number of roles, few people get completely involved in any given role. *Role distance* deals with the degree to which individuals separate themselves from the roles that they are in. For example, if older children ride on a merry-go-round, they are likely to be aware that they are really too old to enjoy such an experience. One way of coping with this is to demonstrate distance from the role by doing it in a careless, lackadaisical way of performing seemingly dangerous acts while on the merry-go-round. In performing such acts, the older children are really explaining to the audience that they are not as immersed in the activity as small children might be or that if they are, it is because of the special things they are doing.

One of Goffman's key insights is that role distance is a function of one's social status. High-status people often manifest role distance for reasons other than those of people in low-status positions. For example, a high-status surgeon may manifest role distance in the operating room to relieve the tension of the operating team. People in low-status positions usually manifest more defensiveness in exhibiting role distance. For instance, people who clean toilets may do so in a lackadaisical and uninterested manner. They may be trying to tell their audience that they are too good for such work.

One of Goffman's most interesting books is *Stigma* (1963b). Goffman was interested in the gap between what a person ought to be, *"virtual social identity,"* and what a person actually is, *"actual social identity."* Anyone who has a gap between these two identities is stigmatized. The book focuses on the dramaturgical interaction between stigmatized people and normals. The nature of that interaction depends on which of the two types of stigma an individual is troubled by. In the case of *discredited* stigma, the actor assumes that the differences are known by the audience members or are evident to them (for example, a paraplegic or someone who has lost a limb). A *discreditable* stigma is one in which the differences are neither known by audience members nor perceivable by them (for example, a person who has had a colostomy or a homosexual passing as straight). For someone with a discredited stigma, the basic dramaturgical problem is managing the tension produced by the fact that people know of the problem. For someone with a discreditable stigma, the dramaturgical problem is managing information so that the problem remains unknown to the audience.

Most of the text of *Stigma* is devoted to people with obvious, often grotesque stigmas (for instance, the loss of a nose). However, as the book unfolds, the reader realizes that Goffman is really saying that we are all stigmatized at some time or other, or in one setting or other. His examples include the Jew "passing" in a predominantly Christian community, the fat person in a group of people of normal weight, and the individual who has lied about his past and must be constantly sure that the audience does not learn of this.

At this point mention of the more recent directions and changes in Goffman's mode of thinking is called for. In *Frame Analysis* (1974), Goffman moved away from his classic symbolic-interactionist roots and toward the study of the small-scale structures of social life. Although he still felt that people define situations in the sense meant by W. I. Thomas, he now thought that such definitions were less important: "Defining situations as real certainly has consequences, but these may contribute very marginally to the events in progress" (Goffman, 1974:1). Furthermore, even when people define situations, they do not ordinarily create those definitions. Action is defined more by mechanical adherence to rules than through an active, creative, and negotiated process. Goffman enunciated his goal: "to try to isolate some of the basic frameworks of understanding available in our society for making sense out of events and to analyze the special vulnerabilities to which these frames of reference are subject" (1974:10).

Goffman's primary interest became the small-scale structures that govern the thoughts and actions of actors. In the view of some, this was a shift in emphasis and a movement away from classic symbolic interactionism. In fact, George Gonos said that "Goffman's work stands opposed to the central tenets and most basic assumptions of symbolic interactionism" (1977:855). Gonos argued that Goffman's work, especially *Frame Analysis,* is better seen as structuralism than symbolic interactionism.

However, a number of observers have made the point that there may not have been much of a shift after all (Collins, 1986b; Perinbanayagam, 1985). For example, Perinbanayagam describes Goffman's dramaturgy as "an examination of the *instruments* and *techniques* of communication that actors use" (1985:66). It can be argued that Goffman always had a dual concern with structuring *and* structures. (As Perinbanayagam says, "Structure is both noun and verb" [1985:75].) Thus, in contrast to Gonos, Perinbanayagam concludes that frame analysis and symbolic interactionism are "interdependent" perspectives in Goffman's work (1985:75). (We will discuss this issue further in Chapter 13.)

Although Goffman may or may not have changed his perspective, his earlier work on dramaturgy has been most influential. For example, David Snow, Louis Zurcher, and Robert Peters (1984) have recently looked at the victory celebrations of crowds at a football game as dramaturgical performances; Jack Haas and William Shaffir (1982) have looked at the medical profession from a dramaturgical viewpoint; Zurcher (1985) has examined the dramaturgy of war games; and Michio Kitahara (1986) looked back at the dramaturgical devices (showing rank, deploying ships, brandishing weapons) used by Commodore Perry to open Japan to the West between 1853 and 1854.

Groups and Societies

Symbolic interactionism was concerned with the interrelationships of individual thought and action, and this gave it a distinctive perspective on society's large-scale structures.

Blumer on Large-Scale Social Structures   Symbolic interactionists are generally highly critical of the tendency of other sociologists to focus on macro structures. As Rock says, "Interactionism discards most macrosociological thought as an unsure and overambitious metaphysics . . . not accessible to intelligent examination" (1979:238). Dmitri Shalin points to "interactionist criticism aimed at the classical view of social order as external, atemporal, determinate at any given moment and resistant to change" (1986:14). Rock also says, "Whilst it [symbolic interactionism] does not wholly shun the idea of social structure, its stress upon activity and process relegates structural metaphors to a most minor place" (1979:50).

Blumer is in the forefront of those who are critical of this "sociological determinism [in which] the social action of people is treated as an outward flow or expression of forces playing on them rather than as acts which are built up by people through their interpretation of the situations in which they are placed" (1962/1969:84). This focus on the constraining effects of large-scale social structures leads traditional sociologists to a set of assumptions about the actor and action different from those held by symbolic interactionists. Instead of seeing actors as those who actively define their situations, traditional sociologists tend to reduce actors to "mindless robots on the societal or aggregate level" (Manis and Meltzer, 1978:7). In an effort to stay away from determinism and a robotlike view of actors, symbolic interactionists take a very different view of large-scale social structures, a view that is ably presented by Blumer.[12]

To Blumer, society is not made up of macro structures. The essence of society is to be found in actors and action: "Human society is to be seen as consisting of acting people, and the life of the society is to be seen as consisting of their actions" (Blumer, 1962/1969:85). Human society is action; group life is a "complex of ongoing activity." However, society is not made up of an array of isolated acts. There is collective action as well, which involves "individuals fitting their lines of action to one another . . . participants making indications to one another, not merely each to himself" (Blumer, 1969b:16). This gives rise to what Mead called the *social act* and Blumer, *joint action.*

Blumer accepted the idea of emergence, that large-scale structures emerge from microprocesses (Morrione, 1988). According to Maines, "The key to understanding Blumer's treatment of large-scale organizations rests on his conception of joint action" (1988:46). A joint action is not simply the sum total of individual acts—it comes to have a character of its own. A joint action thus is not external to or coercive of actors and their actions; rather, it is created by actors and their actions. The study of joint action is, in Blumer's view, the domain of the sociologist.

From this discussion one gets the sense that the joint act is almost totally flexible—that is, that society can become almost anything that the actors want it to be. However, Blumer was not prepared to go as far as that. He argued that each instance of joint action must be formed anew, but he did recognize that joint action is likely to have a "well-established and repetitive form" (Blumer, 1969b:17). Not only does most joint action recur in patterns, but Blumer was also willing to admit that such action is guided by systems of preestablished meanings, such as culture and social order.

It would appear that Blumer admitted that there are large-scale structures and that they are important. Here Blumer followed Mead (1934/1962), who

---

[12] Although they recognize that Blumer does take this view, Wood and Wardell (1983) argue that Mead did *not* have an "astructural bias." See also Joas (1981).

admitted that such structures are very important. Despite this, such structures have an extremely limited role in symbolic interactionism.[13] For one thing, Blumer most often argued that large-scale structures are little more than "frameworks" within which the really important aspects of social life, action and interaction, take place (1962/1969:87). Large-scale structures do set the conditions and set limitations on human action, but they do not determine it. In his view, people do not act within the context of such structures as society; rather, they act in situations. Large-scale structures are important in that they shape the situations in which individuals act and supply to actors the fixed set of symbols that enable them to act.

Even when Blumer discussed such preestablished patterns, he hastened to make it clear that "areas of unprescribed conduct are just as natural, indigenous, and recurrent in human group life as those areas covered by preestablished and faithfully followed prescriptions of joint action" (1969b:18). Not only are there many unprescribed areas, but even in prescribed areas joint action has to be consistently created and re-created. Actors are guided by generally accepted meanings in this creation and re-creation, but they are not determined by them. They may accept them as is, but they also can make minor and even major alterations in them. In Blumer's words, "It is the social process in group life that creates and upholds the rules, not the rules that create and uphold group life" (1969b:19).

Clearly, Blumer was not inclined to accord culture independent and coercive status in his theoretical system. Nor was he about to accord this status to the extended connections of group life, or what is generally called "social structure," for example, the division of labor. "A network or an institution does not function automatically because of some inner dynamics or system requirements; it functions because people at different points do something, and what they do is a result of how they define the situation in which they are called on to act" (Blumer, 1969b:19).

METHODOLOGICAL PRINCIPLES

In addition to its theoretical principles, symbolic interactionism also encompasses a set of methodological postulates.

Blumer on Methods

Blumer had great respect for the difficulties involved in studying the action and interaction that take place in the real world. He often spoke of the "obdurate character" of the real world. Sociologists must engage in constant efforts to develop ways of studying it. Scientific models are to be developed and

---

[13] In Chapter 16, we will discuss some more recent perspectives in symbolic interactionism which accord a greater role to large-scale structures and which argue, more specifically, that Blumer adopted such a position (Blumer, 1990; Maines, 1989a, 1989b; Maines and Morrione, 1990).

tested in and against the real world and are useful only if they help us understand that world (D. Wellman, 1988).

Blumer was a severe critic of what he considered the tendency toward mindless scientism in sociology (Shibutani, 1988). He did not reject the use of quantitative methods, though he clearly saw them as far less valuable than most conventional sociologists consider them. Many methods may prove useful in understanding the real world (Maines, 1989b). Similarly, Blumer (1956/ 1969) was critical of the tendency to reduce the complexity of social life to scientific variables. The simplistic correlation of variables tends to ignore the interpretive process that is so central to social life. Blumer criticized abstract theoretical schema for much the same reason: "primarily an interpretation which orders the world into its mold, not a studious cultivation of empirical facts to see if the theory fits" (1954/1969:141).

Blumer also was critical of most sociological concepts that serve as prescriptions for what sociologists should see in the real world. Such concepts do enormous violence to the reality of that world. Instead of advocating traditional concepts, Blumer supported the use of "sensitizing concepts" (1954/ 1969:148), which simply suggest what to look for and where to look and which do less violence to the real world. Finally, Blumer urged the use of *sympathetic introspection* to study social life. In other words, in their research, symbolic interactionists must put themselves in the places of the actors whom they are studying in order to understand the situation from their point of view. This leads to a preference for "soft" rather than "hard" methods in symbolic interactionism. However, Blumer did not believe that this preference reflects the scientific immaturity of sociology; rather, it indicates the distinctive subject matter of the field.[14]

Blumer was not the only spokesperson for symbolic interactionism on methodological issues (or any other issue, for that matter). We can get a sense of at least one of the schisms in symbolic interactionism by discussing the methodological differences between Blumer, a leading spokesperson for the Chicago school, and Manford Kuhn, the major representative of the Iowa school of symbolic interactionism (Couch, Saxton, and Katovich, 1986a, 1986b).

Blumer versus Kuhn on Methods   The most basic differences between Blumer and Kuhn are methodological (Meltzer, Petras, and Reynolds, 1975). Blumer, as we have seen, argued for a distinctive methodology for studying human behavior, a methodology that is nongeneralizing. Manford Kuhn (1964), in contrast, stressed the unity of the scientific method; all scientific fields, including sociology, should aim toward generalization and laws. Although Blumer and Kuhn agreed on at least one essential subject matter of symbolic interactionism—"what goes on 'inside the heads' of humans"

---

[14] See Maines for a discussion of a view of Blumer offering a "harder" conception of science involving "formal theorizing, definitive concepts, empirical research, testing of hypotheses and propositions, and cumulative scientific knowledge" (1989a:394).

(Meltzer, Petras, and Reynolds, 1975:57)—they disagreed on how it should be studied.

Blumer was inclined to use sympathetic introspection in order to get inside the actors' world and view it as they do. Sociologists should use their intuition in order to take the point of view of the actors whom they are studying, even going so far as using the same categories as they do. Kuhn was interested in the same empirical phenomena, but he urged sociologists to reject nonscientific techniques and instead use overt behavioral indices of what goes on in actors' heads. For instance, the answers of respondents to a series of questions should be the data for the symbolic interactionist to work with, not the "unreliable" and "unscientific" intuition of the sociologist.

In addition, Blumer accepted less formal sensitizing concepts and rejected the use of more scientific operational concepts to define the real world. Kuhn preferred the traditional scientific methods of using researchable variables and operational definitions. For example, Kuhn operationalized the concept of the self, which can be so elusive in traditional symbolic interactionism, as the answer to the question "Who am I?" The responses that people gave to this simple question were viewed as the empirical manifestations of the self. Also, Blumer was inclined to attack sociological variables as mechanistic tools, but Kuhn accepted and used them. Whereas Blumer saw large elements of unpredictability in human action, Kuhn held that action was socially determined and hence could be studied scientifically in the search for antecedent causes of action. Finally, Blumer was inclined to think in terms of continuing processes, whereas Kuhn tended to think in more static terms, which are also more amenable to scientific study.

Blumer's Interpretation of Mead   The debate between supporters of Blumer and supporters of Kuhn continues, but Blumer's orientation is still the dominant position within symbolic interactionism. However, questions recently have been raised about whether Blumer was being as true to his Meadian roots as he claimed (Lewis and Smith, 1980; Warshay and Warshay, 1986).[15] Clark McPhail and Cynthia Rexroat (1979) argued that there are marked differences between the methodological orientations of Mead and Blumer. Because of the influence of behaviorism, Mead was much more oriented to "hard" science than was Blumer and may, in fact, have been closer to Kuhn than Blumer. As McPhail and Rexroat expressed their position, "Mead's emphasis on systematic observation and experimental investigation is quite different from Blumer's naturalistic methodology. . . . Naturalistic inquiry neither complements nor extends Mead's methodological perspective, nor is Blumer's framework suited to the investigation and development of Mead's theoretical ideas" (1979:449).

Blumer (1980) responded heatedly to the charges made by McPhail and

---

[15] On the ambiguities in Mead's work, especially *Mind, Self and Society,* and the impossibility of arriving at a single interpretation, see Fine and Kleinman (1986).

Rexroat. He argued that they "seriously misrepresented" his views on social reality and naturalistic study, as well as Mead's views on social behavior and scientific method. McPhail and Rexroat (1980) responded that Blumer in his reply failed to specify his criteria for arguing that they misinterpreted him and that he failed to use systematic evidence in support of his position. Blumer was accused of often failing to cite the relevant passages in Mead's work in his counterargument. McPhail and Rexroat argued that in many cases Blumer "simply asserts that *his* interpretation of Mead is *the* correct one" (1980:420). In the end, we have Blumer proclaiming his interpretation of Mead to be the correct one and McPhail and Rexroat taking the opposite position. Although this debate is of current interest, the historical fact is that it was Blumer's interpretation of Mead's position, not Mead's methodological position itself, that became the dominant orientation in symbolic interactionism.

The key issue in the debate between Blumer and McPhail and Rexroat is the "hard" versus "soft" science issue. In Blumer's view, McPhail and Rexroat are interested in fostering a "hard" science image of Meadian theory:

> I discern underneath the McPhail-Rexroat discussion what they really have in mind in alleging ontological and methodological differences between Mead and me. Their fundamental intention is to justify and promote a special mode of scientific inquiry that relies on controlled experiments. But they also regard themselves as followers of George Herbert Mead. They are, thus, forced to interpret Mead in such a way as to support their methodological orientation. They seek to do this in two ways. First, they try to interpret Mead's thought on "scientific method" in such a way as to uphold their methodological preference. Second, they endeavor to depict Mead's "social behaviorism" in such a manner as to fit their experimental or near-experimental commitment.
>
> (Blumer, 1980:414–415)

In McPhail and Rexroat's response to Blumer, they argued that Mead favored *both* experimental and nonexperimental methods. Whether or not Mead did, McPhail and Rexroat clearly favored more of a "hard" science, experimental approach to symbolic interaction than did Blumer. The issue is whether complex forms of social behavior are amenable to experimental study. Blumer felt that they are not, whereas McPhail and Rexroat felt that they are. Here, at least in part, is a more recent version of the debate between Blumer and Kuhn.

CRITICISMS

Having analyzed the ideas of symbolic interactionism, particularly those of the Chicago school of Mead, Blumer, and Goffman, we will now enumerate some of the major criticisms of this perspective.

The first criticism is that the mainstream of symbolic interactionism has too readily given up on conventional scientific techniques. Eugene Weinstein and Judith Tanur expressed this point well: "Just because the contents of consciousness are qualitative, does not mean that their exterior expression cannot be coded, classified even counted" (1976:105). Science and subjectivism are *not* mutually exclusive.

Second, Manford Kuhn (1964), William Kolb (1944), Bernard Meltzer, James Petras, and Larry Reynolds (1975), and many others have criticized the vagueness of essential Meadian concepts such as mind, self, I, and me. Most generally, Kuhn (1964) spoke of the ambiguities and contradictions in Mead's theory. Beyond Meadian theory, they have criticized many of the basic symbolic-interactionist concepts for being confused and imprecise and therefore incapable of providing a firm basis for theory and research. Because these concepts are imprecise, it is difficult, if not impossible, to operationalize them; the result is that testable propositions cannot be generated (Stryker, 1980).

The third criticism of symbolic interactionism is that larger structures are downplayed or ignored. Somewhat less predictable is the fourth criticism, that symbolic interactionism is not sufficiently microscopic, that it ignores the importance of such factors as the unconscious and emotions (Meltzer, Petras, and Reynolds, 1975; Stryker, 1980). Similarly, symbolic interactionism has been criticized for ignoring such psychological factors as needs, motives, intentions, and aspirations. In their effort to deny that there are immutable forces impelling the actor to act, symbolic interactionists have focused instead on meanings, symbols, action, and interaction. They ignore psychological factors that might impel the actor, which parallels their neglect of the larger societal constraints on the actor. In both cases, symbolic interactionists are accused of making a "fetish" out of everyday life (Meltzer, Petras, and Reynolds, 1975: 85). This, in turn, leads to a marked overemphasis on the immediate situation and an "obsessive concern with the transient, episodic, and fleeting" (Meltzer, Petras, and Reynolds, 1975:85).

The major criticism of symbolic interactionism has been of its tendency to downplay or ignore large-scale social structures. This has been expressed in various ways. For example, Weinstein and Tanur argued that symbolic interactionism ignores the connectedness of outcomes to each other: *"It is the aggregated outcomes that form the linkages among episodes of interaction that are the concern of sociology qua sociology. . . .* The concept of social structure is necessary to deal with the incredible density and complexity of relations through which episodes of interaction are interconnected" (1976:106). Sheldon Stryker argued that the micro focus of symbolic interactionism serves "to minimize or deny the facts of social structure and the impact of the macro-organizational features of society on behavior" (1980:146). Meltzer, Petras, and Reynolds were inclined to see this weakness at the structural level as one of the two main problems with symbolic interactionism:

> Of all the presumed difficulties of the symbolic interactionist paradigm, then, two stand forth as the most crucial: (1) limited consideration of human emotions, and (2) unconcern with social structure. In effect, the first of these shortcomings implies that symbolic interaction is not psychological enough, while the second implies that symbolic interaction is not sociological enough.
>
> (Meltzer, Petras, and Reynolds, 1975:120)

SUMMARY

This chapter begins with a brief discussion of the roots of symbolic interactionism in philosophical pragmatism (the work of John Dewey) and psychological behaviorism (the work of John B. Watson). Out of the confluence of pragmatism, behaviorism, and other influences, such as Simmelian sociology, symbolic interactionism developed at the University of Chicago in the 1920s.

The symbolic interactionism that developed stood in contrast to the psychological reductionism of behaviorism and the structural determinism of more macro-oriented sociological theories, such as structural functionalism. Its distinctive orientation was toward the mental capacities of actors and their relationship to action and interaction. All this was conceived in terms of process; there was a disinclination to see the actor impelled by either internal psychological states or large-scale structural forces.

The single most important theory in symbolic interactionism is that of George Herbert Mead. Substantively, Mead's theory accorded primacy and priority to the social world. That is, it is out of the social world that consciousness, the mind, the self, and so on emerge. The most basic unit in his social theory is the act, which includes four dialectically related stages—impulse, perception, manipulation, and consummation. A *social* act involves two or more persons, and the basic mechanism of the social act is the gesture. While lower animals and humans are capable of having a conversation of gestures, only humans can communicate the conscious meaning of their gestures. Humans are peculiarly able to create vocal gestures, and this leads to the distinctive human ability to develop and use significant symbols. Significant symbols lead to the development of language and the distinctive capacity of humans to communicate, in the full sense of the term, with one another. Significant symbols also make possible thinking as well as symbolic interaction.

Mead looks at an array of mental processes as part of the larger social process, including reflective intelligence, consciousness, mental images, meaning, and, most generally, the mind. Humans have the distinctive capacity to carry on an inner conversation with themselves. All the mental processes are not, in Mead's view, lodged in the brain but rather in the social process.

The self is the ability to take oneself as an object. Again, the self arises within the social process. The general mechanism of the self is the ability of people to put themselves in the place of others, to act as they act and to see themselves as others see them. Mead traces the genesis of the self through the play and game stages of childhood. Especially important in the latter stage is the emergence of the generalized other. The ability to view oneself from the point of view of the community is essential to the emergence of the self as well as of organized group activities. The self also has two phases—the "I," which is the unpredictable and creative aspect of the self, and the "me," which is the organized set of attitudes of others assumed by the actor. Social control is manifest through the "me," while the "I" is the source of innovation in society.

Mead has relatively little to say about society, which is most generally seen by him as the ongoing social processes that precede mind and self. Mead largely lacks a macro sense of society. Institutions are defined as little more than collective habits.

Symbolic interactionism may be summarized by the following basic principles:

1 Human beings, unlike lower animals, are endowed with a capacity for thought.
2 The capacity for thought is shaped by social interaction.
3 In social interaction, people learn the meanings and the symbols that allow them to exercise their distinctively human capacity for thought.
4 Meanings and symbols allow people to carry on distinctively human action and interaction.
5 People are able to modify or alter the meanings and symbols that they use in action and interaction on the basis of their interpretation of the situation.
6 People are able to make these modifications and alterations because, in part, of their ability of interact with themselves, which allows them to examine possible courses of action, assess their relative advantages and disadvantages, and then choose one.
7 The intertwined patterns of action and interaction make up groups and societies.

In the context of these general principles, we seek to clarify the nature of the work of several important thinkers in the symbolic-interactionist tradition, including Charles Horton Cooley, Herbert Blumer, Morris Rosenberg, and, most important, Erving Goffman. We present in detail Goffman's dramaturgical analysis of the self and his related works on role distance and stigma. However, we also note that Goffman's recent work has exaggerated a tendency in his earlier work and moved further in the direction of a structuralist analysis.

Although we are not interested in methodology per se in this book, several of the methodological principles of symbolic interactionism are discussed, because they help us gain a greater understanding of this theoretical orientation. Especially important here is the debate between Blumer, representing the "soft," intuition-guided Chicago school orientation to symbolic interactionism, and Manford Kuhn, representing the more "hard science" approach characteristic of the Iowa school. Although this debate continues, the Chicago approach has predominated within symbolic interactionism.

We close with a discussion of a number of the criticisms of symbolic interactionism, in particular its weaknesses at the level of large-scale phenomena.

CHAPTER 10

PHENOMENOLOGICAL SOCIOLOGY AND ETHNOMETHODOLOGY

*P*HENOMENOLOGICAL sociology and ethnomethodology, like symbolic interactionism, focus on the everyday world, although in a manner that, as we will see, differs from the approaches of Mead, Blumer, and Goffman. Although phenomenological sociology is the far older tradition, and even though it was a key source of ethnomethodology, it has been far outstripped in recent years by the boom in interest in ethnomethodology around the world. However, given its strong philosophical and theoretical roots, it would not be surprising to see a resurgence of interest in phenomenology.

Phenomenological sociology and ethnomethodology have often been discussed together. George Ritzer (1975a, 1975b) saw them as two theoretical components of the "social definition paradigm"; Monica Morris (1977) viewed them as two varieties of what she called "creative sociology"; Jack Douglas (1980) and Andrew Weigert (1981) included them under the heading "sociologies of everyday life"; and Richard Hilbert (1986) saw them as varieties of "social constructionism."[1] While there are important similarities between them, there are also strong differences that persuade us to deal with the two theories separately in this chapter.

---

[1] These are not the only theories discussed under these headings. Symbolic interactionism, which we have already discussed at length in Chapter 9, is also included under these rubrics (as is existential sociology; see Chapter 13).

SIMILARITIES AND DIFFERENCES

Contemporary practitioners of both phenomenological sociology and ethno-methodology trace their intellectual roots to the philosophical work of Edmund Husserl (1859–1938). Many of his ideas are the inspiration for a number of contemporary aspects of phenomenological sociology. More important, they were the major inspiration for the work of Alfred Schutz. Schutz took Husserl's philosophy and transformed it into a sociology, and it is that orientation that influenced both phenomenological sociology and ethnomethodology. Contemporary phenomenological sociology is traceable directly to the work of Schutz. In ethnomethodology, Husserl's influence is less direct. Harold Garfinkel, the founder of ethnomethodology, studied with Schutz, and it is Garfinkel's (and his supporters') adaptation of Schutz's ideas that is a major basis of ethnomethodology.

The two theories have several important similarities. Both focus on how people actively produce and sustain the meaning of situations. They are also interested in the way people's actions constitute situations. Furthermore, phenomenological sociology and ethnomethodology both focus on everyday life, that is, on the mundane and commonplace activities of people throughout society. Meaning, production of the social situation, and a focus on everyday life are not the only substantive elements the two theories have in common, but they illustrate their overlapping concerns.

In spite of these and other similarities, many adherents of both theories seem to agree that there are differences between the two and that it is best to keep them separate. For example, James Heap and Phillip Roth (1973) argued that ethnomethodology involves a combination of phenomenology and elements of sociology that has produced a unique and independent domain of study. Similarly, Don Zimmerman contended that despite their common intellectual heritage, the two theories are not equivalent: "Strictly speaking, the term 'phenomenological' is inappropriate as a blanket characterization of the working tools, methods and problems of ethnomethodology, if for no other reason than that it blurs the distinction between heritage and intellectual content" (1978:8). Although phenomenology, both philosophical and sociological, has influenced ethnomethodology, ethnomethodology also has been shaped by linguistics, anthropology, and even mainstream sociology. Ethnomethodology has blended phenomenology with these other sources to produce a theoretical orientation that is not reducible to phenomenology (Sharrock and Anderson, 1986).

One key difference between the two theories is methodology. In general, because of Schutz's influence, much of the early work in phenomenological sociology was conceptual and theoretical (Freeman, 1980). For a time, phenomenological sociology spawned comparatively little empirical research—that is, few experiments, surveys, or observational studies. Some saw this as inherent in phenomenological sociology, but others discerned it as a stage in the development of the theory. There has been a modest increase in research in phenomenological sociology (Psathas, 1989), much of it influenced by the social constructionism of Berger and Luckmann (1967) (see below), who, in turn, had been inspired by Schutz's ideas. Psathas (1973) is one who believes that phenomenological sociologists will come to do much more empirical research in the future.

In contrast, ethnomethodology from its very beginnings, and to this day, has been highly empirical and has produced infinitely more empirical studies than theoretical or philosophical treatises. Indeed, the heart of ethnomethodology lies in these research studies and the theoretical lessons to be derived from them. Examples include studies of telephone conversations, newspaper reports, courtroom procedures, political speeches, and even walking. In these studies, ethnomethodologists have generally used methods not too different from those used in mainstream sociological research. Most generally, ethnomethodologists have come to use a wide range of methods—intensive and extensive fieldwork involving direct observation, participant observation, documentary analysis, and so on. They have also developed some distinctive methodologies. One of the earliest and best known (although it is rarely used today) is the so-called *breaching experiments* (see below) developed by Garfinkel as a way of demonstrating basic ethnomethodological principles. The basic procedure is for the researcher to enter a social setting, violate (or breach) the rules that govern it, and then study how people deal with the breach. Among other things, the ethnomethodologist hopes to study the way people construct, or reconstruct, social reality. Another rather distinctive methodology is detailed analysis of audiotapes and videotapes. Ethnomethodologists are very interested in conversational analysis, and they have used audiotapes and videotapes to good advantage. Tape recordings are essential in conversational analysis because the minute details of people's speaking practices cannot be captured in any other way. The study of such details requires the repeated examination of actual speaking practices in order to identify and analyze such phenomena as the way people take turns in conversations (see below). Furthermore, since in speaking people are accomplishing social actions, tape recordings provide the possibility of discovering how such actions are organized, their systematic features, and their regularities. Videotapes have proven particularly useful in analyses of such behaviors as walking, face-to-face communication, and interaction in various settings.

Robert Freeman (1980) saw these methodological differences as derived from more fundamental differences in the substantive focuses of the two theories. Phenomenological sociologists have a great concern for consciousness. Ethnomethodologists, following in the phenomenological tradition, accept the fundamental importance of consciousness in social life. However, given their roots in traditional sociology, they tend to focus on more empirically observable social activities.

One of the most difficult problems in the history of all sociology has been how to study subjectivities and the activities of consciousness empirically. Like other theorists, phenomenologists have not been able to solve this problem adequately. As a result, their best work lies in their efforts to philosophize, theorize, or reflect on the operation of consciousness and meaning construction. When phenomenologists have done "research," they have historically relied on studies of themselves and their own experiences. Thus, Schutz (1976b, 1976c) wrote essays on the "stranger" and the "homecomer" on the basis of his own experiences. More recently, some phenomenologists have developed systematic methods for the analysis of other people's subjective experiences as reported to an interviewer. Direct access to subjectivity, although not possible, is gained through careful listening and by providing the subject with the opportunity to respond to open-ended questions. By accepting such reports uncritically, the phenomenologically oriented researcher tries to understand what the other person experiences. Analysis is then directed toward trying to explicate the structures of such experiences in order to discern their common or underlying features. Such studies show that although direct access to the consciousness or subjective experiences of others is not possible, it is possible to understand their nature and content through the expressions and reports of others.

While the focus on subjectivity has caused phenomenologists great difficulty when it comes to empirical research, ethnomethodologists have had few such problems because of their concentration on more objective phenomena. Specifically, the ethnomethodologists' focus on observable activities, stemming from conscious processes, means that they can rely much more on traditional sociological research methods.

Accentuating the differences, Mary Rogers argues "that ethnomethodology is *not* significantly phenomenological in its conceptualizations and methods" (1983:117). She argues that ethnomethodology makes little use of phenomenological terminology and generally ignores post-Schutzian phenomenologists and, most important, that "ethnomethodologists make rare reference to and adopt no clear position on human consciousness" (Rogers, 1983:117). Here, Rogers paraphrases one of Garfinkel's well-known statements: "Nothing in actor heads concerns ethnomethodology; there are only brains" (1983:119). In other words, observers are unable to study thoughts, ideas, beliefs, assumptions, and so on that take place inside the head; they can find such subjective phenomena only as they are manifested in what people actually say and do. All that is empirically observable are people's actions, including what they say. But that is enough to the ethnomethodologist, because that is all that is available to anyone. By examining actions, ethnomethodologists can reveal how social life is produced and organized in an ongoing manner. But critics like Rogers argue that there is more to be done with the body of consciousness than has been accomplished by the ethnomethodologists. Not only does phenomenology have much to offer here, but it also has much more to say about macroscopic phenomena because "ethnomethodology excludes explicit attention to institutions, collectivities, the social stock of knowledge, and other macro-level social realities" (Rogers, 1983:130). In other words, in Rogers's view, ethnomethodology is neither as microscopic (not dealing with consciousness) nor as macroscopic (not dealing with culture and social institutions) as phenomenology.

While there are certainly important differences between phenomenological sociology and ethnomethodology, strong similarities remain. Perhaps the best conclusion on this issue is offered by Maynard and Clayman (forthcoming), who argue that a "phenomenological sensibility" is manifest in ethnomethodological studies.

PHENOMENOLOGICAL SOCIOLOGY

As we have seen, the strength of phenomenological sociology lies in its theoretical work, and the major theorist associated with this approach is Alfred Schutz. Thus, we devote the bulk of this section to his work, although we will also deal with a major theoretical effort derived in large part from Schutz's perspective, Peter Berger and Thomas Luckmann's *The Social Construction of Reality*.

The Theories of Alfred Schutz

Intersubjectivity   Most broadly, Schutz's phenomenological sociology focuses on intersubjectivity. The study of intersubjectivity seeks to answer questions such as these: How do we know other minds? Other selves? How is reciprocity of perspectives possible? How is mutual understanding and communication possible?

An intersubjective world is not a private world; it is common to all. It exists "because we live in it as men among other men, bound to them through common influence and work, understanding others and being understood by them" (Schutz, 1973:10). Intersubjectivity exists in the "vivid present" in which we speak and listen to each other. We share the same time and space with others. "This simultaneity is the essence of intersubjectivity, for it means that *I grasp the subjectivity of the alter ego at the same time as I live in my own stream of consciousness.* . . . And this grasp in simultaneity of the other as well as his reciprocal grasp of me makes possible *our* being in the world together" (Natanson, 1973a:xxxii–xxxiii; italics added).

The italicized portion of the last quotation gets to the essence of Schutz's thinking on intersubjectivity. Schultz was not interested in the physical interaction of people but in the way they grasp each other's consciousness, the manner in which they relate to one another intersubjectively.

Thus, while phenomenological philosophers focused primarily on consciousness, Schutz turned phenomenology outward to a concern for the intersubjective, social world. (While this is an important difference, we should not lose sight of the fact that both focused on subjectivity, phenomenological philosophers within the realm of consciousness and Schutz in the social world.)

Typifications and Recipes   People develop and use *typifications* (first-order constructs) in the social world. In any given situation in the world of everyday

ALFRED SCHUTZ: A Biographical Sketch

Alfred Schutz was not widely known during his lifetime, and only in recent years has his work attracted the attention of large numbers of sociologists. Although his obscurity was in part a result of his intellectual orientation—his then highly unusual interest in phenomenology—a more important cause was his very unusual career as a sociologist.

Born in Vienna, Austria, in 1899, Schutz received his academic training at the University of Vienna (Wagner, 1983). Soon after completing his law examination, he embarked on a lifelong career in banking. Although rewarding economically, banking did not satisfy his need for deeper meaning in his life. Schutz found that meaning in his work on phenomenological sociology. He was not an academician in the 1920s, but many of his friends were, and he participated in a number of informal lecture and discussion circles (Prendergast, 1986). Schutz was drawn to Weberian theory, especially Weber's work on action and the ideal type. Although impressed with Weber's work, Schutz sought to overcome its weaknesses by integrating ideas from the philosophers Edmund Husserl and Henri Bergson. According to Christopher Prendergast (1986), Schutz was motivated to provide the Austrian School of Economics with a scientific, subjective theory of action. These influences led to the publication by Schutz in 1932 of what was to become a very important book in sociology, *The Phenomenology of the Social World*. It was not translated into English until 1967, so that a wide appreciation of Schutz's work in the United States was delayed thirty-five years.

As World War II approached, Schutz emigrated, with an intervening period in Paris, to the United States, where for many years he divided his time between serving as legal counsel to a number of banks and writing about and teaching phenomenological sociology. Simultaneously with his work in banking, Schutz began teaching courses in 1943 at the New School for Social Research in New York City. As Richard Grathoff points out, the result was

life an action is determined "by means of a type constituted in earlier experiences" (Schutz and Luckmann, 1973:229). Typifications ignore individual, unique features and focus on only generic and homogeneous characteristics.

While we routinely typify others, it is also possible for people to engage in self-typification. "Man typifies to a certain extent his own situation within the social world and the various relations he has to his fellow-men and cultural objects" (Schutz, 1976a:233).

Typification takes many forms. When we label something (for example, a man, a dog), we are engaging in typification. More generally, any time we are using language, we are typifying; indeed Schutz calls language "the typifying medium *par excellence*" (1973:75). Language can be thought of as a "treasure house" of typologies that we use to make sense of the social world.

The linking of typifications to language makes it clear that typifications exist in the larger society and that people acquire and store typifications throughout the socialization process, indeed throughout their lives. The typol-

that "the social theorist for whom scientific thought and everyday life defined two rather distinct and separate realms of experience upheld a similar division in his personal life" (1978:112). Not until 1956 did Schutz give up his dual career and concentrate entirely on teaching and writing phenomenological sociology. Because of his interest in phenomenology, his dual career, and his teaching at the then avant-garde New School, Schutz remained on the periphery of sociology during his lifetime. Nevertheless, Schutz's work and his influence on students (for example, Peter Berger, Thomas Luckmann, Harold Garfinkel) moved him to the center of sociological theory.

Another factor in Schutz's marginal position in sociological theory was that his theory seemed highly abstract and irrelevant to the mundane social world. Although Schutz did separate theory from reality, he did not feel that his work was irrelevant to the world in which he lived. To put it in terms of his phenomenology, he saw a relationship between the everyday construction of reality and the pregiven historical and cultural world. To think otherwise is to think that the man who fled National Socialism (Nazism) regarded his academic work as irrelevant. The following quotation from one of his letters indicates that although Schutz was not optimistic, he was not prepared to accept the irrelevance of his theorizing and, more generally, the social construction of reality to the world as a whole:

> You are still optimist enough to believe that phenomenology may save itself among the ruins of this world—as the *philosophica aera perennis?* I do not believe so. More likely the African natives must prepare themselves for the ideas of national socialism. This shall not prevent us from dying the way we have lived; and we must try, therefore, to build . . . order into *our* world, which we must find lacking in—our *world.* The whole conflict is hidden in this shift of emphasis.
>
> (Schutz, cited in Grathoff, 1978:130)

In short, although the ability of people to affect the larger society is restricted by such phenomena as Nazism, they must continue to strive to build a social and cultural reality that is *not* beyond their reach and control.

Alfred Schutz died in 1959.

ogies that we use are largely socially derived and socially approved. They have stood the test of time and have come to be institutionalized as traditional and habitual tools for dealing with social life. While the individual may create some typifications, most of them are preconstituted and derived from the larger society.

Schutz sometimes talks of *recipes* when he discusses typifications, and he often uses the terms synonymously. Recipes, like typifications, "serve as techniques for understanding or at least controlling aspects of . . . experience" (Natanson, 1973a:xxix). Recipes, however, tend to deal with situations, while typifications refer more to people. People use recipes to handle the myriad routine situations that they encounter each day. Thus, when someone greets us with the recipe "How are you?" we respond with the recipe "Fine, and you?" Continuing the cooking analogy, Schutz argues that we function with "cook-book knowledge . . . recipes . . . to deal with the routine matters of daily life. . . . Most of our daily activities from rising to going to bed are of this kind. They are performed by following recipes reduced to cultural habits of unquestioned platitudes" (1976a:73–74). Even when we encounter unusual or problematic situations, we first try to use our recipes. Only when it is abundantly clear that our recipes won't work do we abandon them and seek to create, to work out mentally, new ways of dealing with situations.

Schutz and Luckmann (1973:231) outline conditions under which situations become problematic and people must create new ways of dealing with them (new recipes or typifications). If there is no recipe available to handle a novel situation, or if a recipe does not allow one to handle the situation it is supposed to deal with, a new one must be created. In other words, when the stock of knowledge currently available is inadequate, the person must add to it by creating new recipes (or typifications).

Because of the recurrent existence of problematic situations, people cannot rely totally on recipes and typifications. They must be adaptive enough to deal with unforeseen circumstances. People need "practical intelligence" in order to deal with unpredictable situations by assessing alternative courses of action and devising new ways of handling situations.

The Life-World The *life-world* (or *Lebenswelt*) is Schutz's term (derived from Husserl) for the world in which intersubjectivity and the use of typifications and recipes take place. Schutz uses many terms to communicate his sense of this world, including "common-sense world," "world of everyday life," "everyday working world," "mundane reality," "the paramount reality of common-sense life," and so on (Natanson, 1973a:xxv). It is in this world that people operate in the "natural attitude"; that is, they take the world for granted and do not doubt its reality or existence until a problematic situation arises.

Schutz defines six basic characteristics of the life-world. First, it is characterized by a special tension of consciousness, which Schutz labels "wide-awakeness" (1973:213), in which the actor gives "full attention to life and its requirements." Second, the actor suspends doubt in the existence of this world. Third, it is in the life-world that people engage in working; that is, they engage in "action in the outer world, based upon a project and characterized by the intention to bring about the projected state of affairs by bodily movement" (Schutz, 1973:212). It is work that lies at the heart of the life-world:

> The core region of the life-world is the world of working. . . . Specifically, it is a sphere of activities directed upon objects, animals, and persons "within our actual reach." Typically, operations in it follow "tested recipes of action": it is "my world of routine activities." . . . Such working is planful physical acting upon tangible objects in order to shape and use them for tangible purposes.
>
> (Wagner, 1983:290)

Fourth, there is a specific form of experiencing one's self in which the working self is experienced as the total self. Fifth, the life-world is characterized by a specific form of sociality involving the "common intersubjective world of communication and social action" (Schutz, 1973:230). Finally, in the life-world there is a specific time perspective that involves the intersection of the person's own flow of time and the flow of time in the larger society. By contrast, in dreams or fantasies the person's flow of time is usually out of touch with the flow of time in the larger society. That is, one may fantasize, for example, about life in the Middle Ages while one is living in the twentieth century.

While Schutz writes often as if there is only one life-world, the fact is that each of us has our own life-world, although there are many common elements in all of them. Thus others belong to our life-world and we belong to the life-worlds of many others.

The life-world is an intersubjective world, but it is one which existed long before our birth; it was created by our predecessors. It (particularly typifications and recipes, but also social institutions and so on) is given to us to experience and to interpret. Thus in experiencing the life-world, we are experiencing an obdurate world that constrains what we do. However, we are not simply dominated by the preexisting structure of the life-world.

> We have to dominate it and we have to change it in order to realize the purposes which we pursue within it among our fellow-men . . . these objects offer resistance to our acts which we have either to overcome or to which we have to yield . . . a pragmatic motive governs our natural attitude toward the world of everyday life. World, in this sense, is something that we have to modify by our actions or that modifies our actions.
>
> (Schutz, 1973:209)

It is here that we begin to get a sense of Schutz's thinking as dialectical, with actors and structures mutually affecting one another. Wagner takes such a dialectical position when he argues that Schutz's ideas on the life-world blend individual experience "not only with those of social interaction and therefore with the life worlds of others but also with the socially pregiven interpretive schemes and prescriptions [typifications and recipes] for practical conduct" (1983:289).

This dialectic is even clearer in Schutz's thinking about the cultural world. On the one hand, it is clear that the cultural world was created by people in the past as well as in the present, since it "originates in and has been instituted by human actions, our own and our fellow-men's, contemporaries and predecessors. All cultural objects—tools, symbols, language systems, works of art, social institutions, etc.—point back by their very origin and meaning to the activities of human subjects" (Schutz, 1973:329). On the other hand, this cultural world is external and coercive of actors: "I find myself in my everyday life within a world not of my own making . . . I was born into a preorganized social world which will survive me, a world shared from the outset with fellow-men who are organized in groups" (Schutz, 1973:329).

In his analysis of the life-world, Schutz was mainly concerned with the shared social stock of knowledge that leads to more or less habitual action. We have already discussed *knowledge of typifications and recipes*, which is a major component of the stock of knowledge. Schutz views such knowledge as the most variable element in our stock of knowledge because in a problematic situation we are able to come up with innovative ways of handling the situation. Less likely to become problematic are the other two aspects of our stock of knowledge. *Knowledge of skills* (for example, how to walk) is the most basic form of knowledge in that it rarely becomes problematic (an exception in the case of walking would be temporary paralysis) and thus is accorded a high degree of certainty. *Useful knowledge* (for example, driving a car or playing the piano) is a definite solution to a situation that was once problematic. Useful knowledge is more problematic (for example, needing to think about one's driving in an emergency situation) than knowledge of skills, but it is not as likely to become problematic as are recipes and typifications.

Private Components of Knowledge   Schutz also was aware that all the elements of the cultural realm can and often do vary from individual to individual because personal experience differs. The stock of knowledge is "biographically articulated":

> That means that I "know" more or less adequately that it is the "result" of prior situations. And further, I "know" that this, my situation, is in that respect absolutely "unique." Indeed, the stock of knowledge, through which I determine the present situation, has its "unique" biographical articulation. This refers not only to the content, the "meaning" of all the prior experiences sedimented in it, in situations. It refers also to the intensity, . . . duration, and sequence of these experiences. This circumstance is of singular importance, since it really constitutes the individual stock of knowledge.
>
> (Schutz and Luckmann, 1973:111–112)

Thus, according to Schutz, the stock of knowledge always has a private component. However, even this unique and private component of the stock of knowledge is not solely of the actor's own making: "It must be stressed . . . that sequence, experiential depth and nearness, and even the duration of experiences and the acquisition of knowledge, are socially objectivated and determined. In other words, there are social categories of biographical articulation" (Schutz and Luckmann, 1973:113).

Because of their source in individual biography, private stocks of knowledge are not part of the life-world. Because they are biographical in nature, Schutz did not feel that the unique and private components of knowledge are amenable to scientific study. They are, in Schutz's view, nonetheless important components of the everyday life of actual actors.

Realms of Social Reality   Schutz identified four distinct realms of social reality. Each is an abstraction of the social world and is distinguished by its degree of immediacy (the degree to which situations are within reach of the actor) and determinability (the degree to which they can be controlled by the actor). The four realms are *umwelt,* the realm of directly experienced social reality; *mitwelt,* the realm of indirectly experienced social reality; *folgewelt,* the realm of successors; and *vorwelt,* the realm of predecessors. The realms of successors and predecessors *(folgewelt* and *vorwelt)* were of peripheral interest to Schutz. However, we shall deal with them briefly because the contrast between them illustrates some of the characteristics of Schutz's major focus— the *umwelt* and the *mitwelt.*

Folgewelt and Vorwelt The future *(folgewelt)* is a purely residual category in Schutz's work (in contrast to Marx's, for example, where it plays a crucial role in his dialectic). It is a totally free and completely indeterminant world. It can be anticipated by the social scientist only in a very general way and cannot be depicted in any great detail. One could not place great stock in the ideal types and models of the future constructed by the social scientist. Thus, there is little that Schutz's phenomenological sociology has to offer to the conventional scientist seeking to understand or predict the future.[2]

The past *(vorwelt),* on the other hand, is somewhat more amenable to analysis by the social scientist. The action of those who lived in the past is totally determined; there is no element of freedom, because the causes of their actions, the actions themselves, and their outcomes have already occurred. Despite its determinacy, the study of predecessors presents difficulties for a subjective sociology. It is difficult to interpret the actions of people who lived in an earlier time because we would probably have to use contemporary categories of thought in the historical glance back rather than the categories that prevailed at the time. The interpretation of contemporaries is likely to be more accurate because sociologists share interpretive categories with those whose action they seek to understand. Thus, although a subjective sociology of the past is possible, the probability of misinterpretation is great.

The essential point here is that the objective for Schutz was to develop a sociology based on the interpretations of the social world made by the actors being studied. It is difficult to know the interpretations of predecessors and impossible to understand those of successors. However, it is possible to understand contemporaries *(mitwelt)* and the interpretations of those with whom we are in immediate face-to-face contact *(umwelt).*

Umwelt and We Relations *We relations* are defined by a relatively high degree of intimacy, which is determined by the extent to which the actors are acquainted with one another's personal biographies. The pure we relation is a face-to-face relationship "in which the partners are aware of each other and sympathetically participate in each other's lives for however short a time" (Schutz, 1932/1967:164). The we relation encompasses the consciousness of the participants as well as the patterns of face-to-face interaction. The we relation is characterized by a "thou orientation," which "is the universal form in which the other is experienced 'in person' " (Schutz and Luckmann, 1973:62). In other words, we relations are highly personal and immediate.

The immediacy of interaction has two implications for social relations. First,

[2] We can study what contemporaries *expect* of the future, but we cannot study the future itself.

in a we relation, there are abundant indicators of the other's subjective experience. Immediacy allows each actor to enter into the consciousness of the other. Second, when entering any social relation, an individual has only typical knowledge of the other. However, in the continuing process of a face-to-face interaction, typifications of the other are tested, revised, reenacted and modified. That is, interaction with others necessarily modifies typologies.

Schutz not only offered a number of insights into we relations per se but also linked these relationships to cultural phenomena in the real world. For example, in we relations actors learn the typifications and recipes that allow them to survive socially. People not only learn typifications and recipes in we relations but use them there as well—trying them out, altering them when they prove ineffective or inappropriate.

Schutz was aware that there is considerable give and take among actors in we relations. People try out different courses of action on other people. They may quickly abandon those that elicit hostile reactions and continue to use those that are accepted. People also may find themselves in situations where recipes do not work at all, and they must create appropriate and workable sets of actions. In other words, in we relations people constantly adjust their actions with regard to those with whom they interact.

People also adjust their conceptions of others. They enter a given relationship with certain assumptions about what the other actors are thinking. In general, people assume that the thinking of others is of the same order as their own. Sometimes this is confirmed by what they find, but in other circumstances the facial expressions, the movements, the words, and the actions of others are inconsistent with people's sense of what others are thinking. People then must revise their view of others' thought processes and then adjust their responses on the basis of this new image of what others are thinking. This is an indirect process, because people cannot actually know what others are thinking. Thus they may tentatively change their actions in the hope that this will elicit responses consistent with what they now think is going on in others' minds. People may be forced to revise their conception of others' thought processes and their actions a number of times before they are able to understand why others are acting in a particular way. It is even conceivable that in some instances people cannot make an adequate number of adjustments, with the result that they are likely to flee the particular interaction, completely confused. In such a case, they may seek more comfortable situations where familiar recipes can be applied.

Even within we relations in everyday life most action is guided by recipes. People do not *usually* reflect on what they do or on what others do. However, when they encounter problems, inappropriate thoughts and actions, they must abandon their recipes and reflect on what is going on to create an appropriate response. This is psychologically costly, because people prefer to act and interact in accord with recipes.

While it is difficult to analyze the *umwelt* scientifically, it is far easier to study the *mitwelt* in this manner. However, although it may be easier to study the *mitwelt*, such study is not likely to be as rewarding as a study of the *umwelt* because of the latter's key role in the creation of typifications and recipes and its central role in the social lives of people in the life-world.

Mitwelt and They Relations The *mitwelt* is that aspect of the social world in which people deal only with types of people or with larger social structures rather than with actual actors. People do fill these types and these structures, but in this world of "contemporaries," these people are not experienced directly. Because actors are dealing with types rather than with actual people, their knowledge of people is not subject to constant revision on the basis of face-to-face interaction. This relatively constant knowledge of general types of subjective experience can be studied scientifically and can shed light on the general process by which people deal with the social world. A number of specific levels of the *mitwelt* will be discussed below.

While in the *umwelt* people coexist in the same time and space, in the *mitwelt* spatial distances make it impossible to interact on a face-to-face basis. If the spatial situation changes and the people draw closer to each other, then face-to-face interaction becomes possible, but if it occurs, we have returned to the *umwelt*. People who were once in our *umwelt* may draw away from us and ultimately, because of spatial distances, become part of the *mitwelt*. Thus, there is a gradual transition from *umwelt* to *mitwelt* as people grow apart from one another. Here is the way Schutz describes this gradual transition:

> Now we are face-to-face, saying good-bye, shaking hands; now he is walking away. Now he calls back to me; now I see him waving to me; now he has disappeared around the corner. It is impossible to say at which precise moment the face-to-face situation ended and my partner became a mere contemporary of whom I have knowledge (he has, probably, arrived home) but no direct experience.
>
> (Schutz, 1976a:37)

Similarly, there are no clear dividing lines among the various levels of the *mitwelt* discussed below.

The *mitwelt* is a stratified world with levels arranged by degree of anonymity. The more anonymous the level, the more people's relationships are amenable to scientific study. Some of the major levels within the *mitwelt*, beginning with the least anonymous, are:

1 Those whom actors encountered face-to-face in the past and could meet again. Actors are likely to have fairly current knowledge of them because they have been met before and could be met again. Although there is a relatively low level of anonymity here, such a relationship does not involve ongoing face-to-face interaction. If these people were to be met personally at a later date, this relationship would become part of the *umwelt* and no longer be part of the *mitwelt*.

2 Those once encountered not by us but by people with whom we deal. Because this level is based on second-hand knowledge of others, it involves more anonymity than the level of relationships with people we

have encountered in the past. If we were ever to meet people at this level, the relationship would become part of the *umwelt*.

3 Those whom we are on the way to meet. As long as we have not yet met them, we relate to them as types, but once we actually meet them, the situation again becomes part of the *umwelt*.

4 Those whom we know not as concrete individuals but simply as positions and roles. For example, we know that there are people who sort our mail or process our checks, but although we have attitudes about them as types, we never encounter them personally.

5 Collectivities whose function we may know without knowing any of the individuals who exist within them. For example, we know about the Senate, but few people actually know any of the individuals in it, although we do have the possibility of meeting those people.

6 Collectivities that are so anonymous that we have little chance of ever encountering people in them. For most people, the Mafia would be an example of such a collectivity.

7 Objective structures of meaning that have been created by contemporaries with whom actors do not have and have not had face-to-face interaction. The rules of English grammar would be an example of such a structure of meaning.

8 Physical artifacts that have been produced by a person we have not met and whom we are not likely to meet. For example, people would have a highly anonymous relationship with a museum painting.

As we move further into the *mitwelt* relationships, they become more impersonal and anonymous. People do not have face-to-face interaction with others and thus cannot know what goes on in others' minds. Their knowledge is therefore restricted to "general types of subjective experience" (Schutz, 1932/1967:181).

They relations, which are found in the *mitwelt,* are characterized by interaction with impersonal contemporaries (for example, the unseen postal employee who sorts our mail) rather than consociates (for example, a personal friend). In they relations, the thoughts and actions of people are dominated by anonymous typifications and recipes.

In the "pure" they relation, the typical schemes of knowledge used to define other actors are not available for modification. Because we do not interact with actual people but with impersonal contemporaries, information that varies from our typifications is not provided to us. In other words, new experiences are not constituted in they relations. Cultural typifications determine action, and they cannot be altered by the thoughts and actions of actors in a they relationship. Thus, whereas we relations are subject to negotiation, they relations are not. In spite of the distinction between we and they relations, the typifications used in they relations have their historical roots in we relations: "The first and originally objective solution of a problem was still largely dependent on the subjective relevance awareness of the individual" (Schutz and Luckmann, 1973:225). However, these solutions ultimately become more typified and anonymous—in short, more and more a part of the cultural realm.

Consciousness   While phenomenological philosophers had focused on consciousness, Schutz, as we have seen, turned away from consciousness and toward the direction of intersubjectivity, the life-world, and we and they relations. Thus consciousness is not of focal concern to Schutz; rather, it constitutes the point to departure for his science of intersubjectivity.

Schutz believed that in the everyday world, as long as things are running smoothly in accord with recipes, consciousness is relatively unimportant and actors pay little attention to what is going on in their minds as well as in the minds of others. Similarly, Schutz (1932/1967:190) believed that in the science of phenomenological sociology one could ignore individual consciousness. In fact, because Schutz found the mind impervious to scientific study, and because he wanted to focus on intersubjectivity, he admitted in his own work that he was going to abandon the traditional phenomenological focus on mental processes (1932/1967:97). We thus have the seemingly paradoxical situation of a sociologist who is the field's most famous phenomenologist abandoning the approach for which phenomenology is best known. However, the paradox is resolved when we realize that Schutz does carry on the traditional phenomenological concern with subjectivity. Instead of focusing on individual subjectivity, Schutz focuses, as we have seen throughout this section, on *intersubjectivity.*

Despite Schutz's avowed focus on intersubjectivity, he offered many insights into consciousness. In fact, Schutz argued that the base of all his sociological concerns lay in the "processes of meaning establishment and understanding occurring within individuals, processes of interpretation of the behavior of other people and processes of self-interpretation" (1932/1967:11).

The philosophical basis of Schutz's image of the social world, albeit a basis that is, for him, not amenable to scientific study, is deep consciousness (durée), in which is found the processes of meaning establishment, understanding, interpretation, and self-interpretation. A phenomenological sociology must be based on "the way meaning is constituted in the individual experience of the solitary Ego. In so doing we shall track meaning to its very point of origin in the inner time consciousness in the duration of the ego as it lives through its experience" (Schutz, 1932/1967:13). This is the domain that was of central concern to Schutz's philosophical predecessors, Henri Bergson and Edmund Husserl. They were interested in philosophizing about what went on in the mind, but a central question to Schutz was how to turn this interest into a scientific sociological concern.

Schutz was drawn to the work of Max Weber, particularly that part of Weber's work concerned with social action, because it reflected, he thought, both an interest in consciousness and a concern for a scientific sociology. As we saw in Chapter 4, the interest in individual action was only a minor and secondary concern for Weber, who was more concerned with the impact of social structures on action than with the bases of action in consciousness. According to Prendergast, Schutz had "no apparent interest in Weber's theory of bureaucracy, sociology of religion, political sociology, or general economic history" (1986:15). Schutz, therefore, was concerned with only a small and peripheral portion of Weber's sociology. But even in that, Weber was a less-than-satisfying model for Schutz but not for the reasons implied above. To Schutz, the problem with Weber's work was that there were inadequacies in his conception of consciousness. Weber failed to distinguish among types of meanings, and he failed to distinguish meanings from motives. In clarifying what Weber failed to do, Schutz told us much about his own conception of consciousness.

Meanings and Motives   Schutz argued that we must distinguish meanings from motives. In the process, he differentiated between two subtypes of both meanings and motives. Although he did not always succeed in keeping them neatly separated, for Schutz *meanings* concern how actors determine what aspects of the social world are important to them, whereas *motives* involve the reasons that actors do what they do. One type of meaning is the *subjective* meaning context. That is, through our own independent mental construction of reality, we define certain components of reality as meaningful. However, although this process is important in the everyday life-world, Schutz did not see it as amenable to scientific study because it is too idiosyncratic.

Of concern to scientific sociology is the second type of meaning, the *objective* meaning context, the sets of meanings that exist in the culture as a whole and that are the shared possession of the collectivity of actors. In that these sets of meanings are shared rather than idiosyncratic, they are as accessible to sociologists as to anyone else. In that they have an objective existence, they can be studied scientifically by the sociologist, and they were one of Schutz's main concerns. Schutz was critical of Weber for failing to differentiate between subjective and objective meaning and for failing to make it clear that objective meaning contexts can be most easily scrutinized in scientific sociology.

Schutz also differentiated between two types of motives—"in-order-to" and "because" motives. Both involve reasons for an individual's actions, but only because motives are accessible to both the person acting and the sociologist. *In-order-to motives* are the reasons that an actor undertakes certain actions; actions are undertaken to bring about some future objective or occurrence. They exist only when action is taking place. In-order-to motives are "subjective." They are part of deep consciousness, the ongoing stream of consciousness, and as such are inaccessible to both the actor and the scientific observer. In-order-to motives can be grasped only retrospectively by the actor, after the action is completed and the objective is (or is not) achieved. Sociology is little concerned with in-order-to motives because they are difficult to study scientifically. But sociology can study *because motives,* or retrospective glances at the past factors (for example, personal background, individual psyche, environment) that caused individuals to behave as they did. Since because motives are "objective," they can be studied retrospectively using scientific methods. Since the actions have already occurred, the reasons for them are accessible to both the actor and the social scientist. However, neither other actors nor social scientists can know others' motives, even because motives, fully. Both actors and scientists must be satisfied with being able to deal with typical motives.

In spite of their greater accessibility to the social scientist, Schutz was little more inclined to study because motives than in-order-to motives. They represented a return to a concern for consciousness, while Schutz, as we have seen many times, was interested in moving on to the intersubjective world. However, Schutz believed that all social interaction was founded on a reciprocity of motives: "The actor's in-order-to motives will become because-motives of his partner and vice versa" (1976a:12).

Schutz embeds his most basic sociological concepts in consciousness. *Action,* for example, is "conduct self-consciously projected by the actor" (Natanson, 1973a:xxxiv), "conduct devised by the actor in advance" (Schutz, 1973:19). More explicitly, Natanson argues. "The crucial feature of action in every case is its purposive and projective character. Action has its source in the *consciousness* of the actor" (1973a:xxxiv; italics added). *Social action* is "action which involves the attitudes and actions of others and is oriented to them in its course" (Schutz, 1976a:13).

One other point should be made about Schutz's thoughts on consciousness. Schutz sees within consciousness a fundamental human anxiety that lies at the base of his intersubjective world:

> I know that I shall die and I fear to die. This basic experience we suggest calling the *fundamental anxiety.* It is the primordial anticipation from which all the others originate. From the fundamental anxiety spring the many interrelated systems of hopes and fears, of wants and satisfactions, of chances and risks which incite man within the natural attitude to attempt the mastery of the world; to overcome obstacles, to draft projects and to realize them.
>
> (Schutz, 1973:228)

The Social Construction of Reality

Peter Berger and Thomas Luckmann's book *The Social Construction of Reality* (1967) seeks to extend the concerns of phenomenological sociology to social structures and institutions. Furthermore, the authors sought to integrate the individual and societal levels. We will be concerned not only with what they have done but with how successful they have been in achieving their objectives.

Berger and Luckmann's work is one of the most widely read and influential books in contemporary sociology. One of its main attractions is that it translated Alfred Schutz's sometimes arcane phenomenology into the terms of mainstream sociological theory. Berger and Luckmann also attempted to go beyond Schutz's work, to buttress it with Mead's social psychology and to complement both Schutz's and Mead's work with the work of Marx and Durkheim on society and culture. They attempted to integrate Weber's work on social action with Durkheim's thoughts on social facts as external realities. In relating these thinkers to one another, Berger and Luckmann made it quite clear that they wanted to deal in an integrated fashion with "the dual character of society in terms of objective facticity *and* subjective meaning" (1967:18). Even more explicit is this statement, which seems to give the essence of an approach to social reality that integrates a concern with large- and small-scale phenomena: *"Society is a human product. Society is an objective reality. Man is a social product"* (Berger and Luckmann, 1967:61). In other words, people are the products of the very society that they create.

The book's subtitle, *A Treatise in the Sociology of Knowledge,* provides the key to their analysis. Their view of the sociology of knowledge is unusual. To them, it is concerned with the social construction of reality. In articulating this view, their goal was to move the sociology of knowledge away from the study of intellectual history and to the everyday construction of reality, the process of everyday knowledge production in which we all engage. However, despite their intent to deal with both large- and small-scale phenomena, and their commitment to deal with the work of people such as Marx and Durkheim, they said little about objectivity, especially large-scale social structures, even though the longest chapter in their book is titled "Society as Objective Reality."

Everyday Life   Berger and Luckmann began their analysis at the individual level with the reality of everyday life, the common-sense world. Here Berger and Luckmann relied almost exclusively on the work of Alfred Schutz.

Berger and Luckmann were particularly interested in people's phenomenological tendency to view subjective processes as objective realities. In their view, people tend to apprehend everyday life as an ordered reality; that is, social reality seems to the actor to be independent of the actor's apprehension of it. It appears already objectified, and it seems to impose itself on the actor. Crucial to this tendency toward objectification is language, which "continuously provides [people] with the necessary objectifications and posits the order within which these make sense and within which everyday life has meaning for [people]" (Berger and Luckmann, 1967:23). We take the reality of everyday life for granted; although we could question it, we suspend that ability in order to live comfortably within it. The thrust of Berger and Luckmann's discussion was a view of the social world as the cultural product of conscious processes.

Berger and Luckmann's discussion of face-to-face interaction is welcome, although it adds little to Schutz's work. In their description of face-to-face interactions, which, following Schutz, they called *we relationships,* Berger and Luckmann emphasized that such relationships involve an immediate interchange of meanings. In we relationships, there is much less typification than in they relationships (which involve anonymous others). In other words, instead of relating to people on the basis of culturally defined recipes, in we relationships people relate to each other in more personalized ways. Because we relationships are less dominated by typifications, there is more latitude for negotiations among the actors. As we move away from immediate, face-to-face relationships to relationships with people with whom we are less intimate or even strangers, there is more likelihood of typification and less of inter-personal negotiation. In other words, our relationships with others in the they relationship grow progressively more impersonal and stereotypic. The impor-tance of typifications (and recipes) to Berger and Luckmann is illustrated by their definition of social structures, a definition clearly not in line with an objective view of such structures. They define *social structures* as "the sum total of these typifications and of the recurrent patterns of interaction estab-lished by means of them" (Berger and Luckmann, 1967:33).

As with many phenomenologists, language is very important to Berger and Luckmann, especially as it relates to the typification process. Berger and Luck-mann viewed language as a specific form of the process of "signification," a subtype of objectification distinguished by its explicit purpose of standing for a wide range of subjective meanings. Language is a system of vocal symbols, the most important symbol system in society. The reason for its importance is that language can be detached from the here and now, from face-to-face interaction, and can communicate meanings that are not immediate expres-sions of subjectivity. Language also allows us to deal with things that we never have experienced and perhaps never will experience ourselves. It also can help us accumulate meanings and knowledge that can then be passed on to future generations. In these and other ways, language is, in Berger and Luckmann's system, the most important social structure: "I encounter language as a fac-ticity external to myself and it is coercive on me" (1967:38). Here they self-consciously took a Durkheimian position on language as an external and coer-cive social fact. However, this is an exception to their general tendency to pay little attention to social structures, or the objective components of society.

Objective Components of Society   Despite their perspective on language, Berger and Luckmann are weakest on the objective components of society. For example, they defined social structure as nothing more that recurrent patterns of action. In their chapter "Society as an Objective Reality," they were inter-ested primarily in the process by which that world, such as it is, is produced and how a *sense* of its objectivity is created. They carefully reminded readers that this sense as well as whatever objective reality there "really" is out there, is produced by people.

Institutionalization   Beneath this process by which a sense of social reality is constructed lies the fact that people must externalize; that is, they must produce what they need to survive. In the process of externalizing, people are prone to develop habitualized patterns of acting and interacting in recurrent situations. Life would be impossible without habits. It would be very difficult to decide the proper action in every new situation.

Habitualized actions set the stage for the development of institutionalization. This occurs when people develop typifications of what others are likely to do in a given situation. Berger and Luckmann defined an *institution* as a kind of reciprocal process of typification. This microscopic conception of an institution is quite different from most sociological conceptions of institutions. Although to Berger and Luckmann institutions are not large-scale phenomena, they are nonetheless external and coercive. Berger and Luckman argued that institutions "*control* human conduct by setting up predefined patterns of conduct" (1967:55)

The stream of history allows these institutions to acquire objectivity. However, when Berger and Luckmann considered these institutions, they were inclined to think of them subjectively also:

> This means that the institutions that now have been crystallized . . . are *experienced* as existing over and beyond the individuals who "happen to" embody them at the moment. In other words, the institutions are now *experienced* as possessing a reality of their own, a reality that confronts the individual as an external and coercive fact.
> (Berger and Luckmann, 1967:58; italics added)

By emphasizing the *experience* of institutions, rather than their external reality, Berger and Luckmann made their subjective biases quite clear, even when they were supposedly dealing with external realities.

Children perceive the institutional world as an objective reality; that is, it was there before they were born and it will be there after they die. As individuals mature, they apprehend their biographies as episodes within the objective history of society.

The various institutions within society tend to "hang together," but in Berger and Luckmann's view this is due not to their objective qualities but to the tendency of people to perceive them in that way. In other words, what is crucial is the knowledge that people have of society. Thus sociology should focus on how people reconstruct their knowledge of social reality, not only in the historical production of the world but also in the continuing creation of that world on a day-to-day basis.

Roles Berger and Luckmann's definition of *roles* is typical of their sense of objective social reality. To them, roles are typifications of what can be expected of actors in given social situations. Roles are not to be confused with objective positions, as they tend to be in the work of many others. The role was particularly important to Berger and Luckmann because it constitutes a mediation or link between the large- and small-scale worlds. In Berger and Luckmann's hands, it served to mediate *only* between culture and consciousness: "The analysis of role is of particular importance to the sociology of knowledge because it reveals the mediations between the macroscopic *universe* *of meaning* objectivated in a society and the ways in which these universes are *subjectively* real to individuals" (1967:79; italics added).

Reification   Reification, as we saw in Chapter 2 on Marx, is a particularly important tool for dealing in an integrated way with the social world, but Berger and Luckmann limited its utility by the way they used it. They defined *reification* solely as a subjective phenomenon: "The apprehension of human phenomena as if they were things, that is, in nonhuman or possibly supra-human terms" (Berger and Luckmann, 1967:89). Reification is the tendency to *perceive* human products as if they were something else, "such as facts of nature, results of cosmic laws, or manifestations of divine will" (Berger and Luckmann, 1967:89). In other words, people simply lose sight of the dialectical relationship between them and their products. People can objectify social phenomena without reifying them; that is, they can produce objects and view the world in objective terms without forgetting that people produce them. However, Berger and Luckmann gave absolutely no sense of the other aspect of reification—that is, the degree to which society, as a result of the subjective processes they describe, objectively comes to acquire a life of its own.

Legitimations   Also telling, in terms of their tendency to ignore objective structures in the sense that that term is ordinarily used in sociology, was Berger and Luckmann's extensive treatment of *legitimations,* or the explanations and justifications of the institutional system. Again, instead of dealing with the objective structures themselves, Berger and Luckmann focused on the knowledge that is used to support their existence: "Legitimation 'explains' the institutional order by ascribing cognitive validity to its objectivated meaning. Legitimation justifies the institutional order by giving a normative dignity to its practical imperatives" (1967:83). The focus is not on the structures being legitimated but on the means by which they are legitimated.

Criticisms   Berger and Luckmann's chapter on society as objective reality really dealt with subjective phenomena. In their next chapter, on society as a subjective reality, Berger and Luckmann discussed the socialization process, the process by which cultural phenomena are communicated to and internalized in consciousness. This chapter added little beyond elementary knowledge about socialization.

Berger and Luckmann provided an almost purely subjective characterization of the social world. However, this may not be a fair criticism, because their stated intention was to present a sociology of knowledge. Furthermore, near the end of their work Berger and Luckmann admitted the need for a structural sociology to complement their subjective orientation (1967:186). Still, they are vulnerable to criticism because they promised more than simply a subjective sociology, including integrating Freud, Mead, and Weber on social action with Marx and Durkheim on social structures—and they did not deliver. More important was what they promised in their pivotal statement:

"Society is a human product. Society is an objective reality. Man is a social product" (Berger and Luckmann, 1967:61). They failed to produce any sense of society as an objective reality; as a result, their entire dialectic loses much of its significance. In Marx's hands a similar discussion is much more powerful, because of his strong sense of the obdurate structures of the social world and the difficulties involved in overcoming these structures. Berger and Luckmann were right to state that they needed Marx's sociology, but unfortunately they did not follow through on this.

In spite of the harsh criticism aimed at Berger and Luckmann in this section, they are to be praised for the effort to extend phenomenology beyond its traditional focus on consciousness. Their failure to deal satisfactorily with social structures despite their avowed desire to do so, does not mean that phenomenological sociology *cannot* integrate a concern with social structure into its approach, but it does mean that it will be difficult. Phenomenological sociology *may* be able to deal with larger-scale social structures, but that remains to be demonstrated. Its strengths continue to lie in the understanding of consciousness and its relationship to action and interaction and in the study of culture and its constraining effects on actors.

ETHNOMETHODOLOGY

Given its Greek roots, the term *ethnomethodology* literally means the methods that people use on a daily basis to accomplish their everyday lives. To put it slightly differently, the social world is seen as an ongoing practical accomplishment. People are viewed as rational, but they use "practical reasoning" in accomplishing their everyday lives. The emphasis in ethnomethodology is on what people *do,* whereas in phenomenological sociology it is on what people think.

Defining Ethnomethodology

However, while ethnomethodologists focus on action, it is action that implies and involves a thoughtful actor; ethnomethodology does not deny the existence of mental processes.[3] Ethnomethodologists are critical of some varieties of sociological theory (for example, structural functionalism and structural Marxism) that treat the actor as a "judgmental dope." While ethnomethodologists refuse to treat actors as judgmental dopes, they do not believe that people are "almost endlessly reflexive, self-conscious and calculative" (Heritage, 1984:118). Rather, following Schutz, they recognize that most often action is routine and relatively unreflective.

Given these introductory comments, we repeat the definition of *ethnomethodology* offered in Chapter 6: the study of "the body of commonsense knowl-

---

[3] However, as we will see at the end of this section, some critics feel that ethnomethodology is losing sight of the thoughtful actor.

edge and the range of procedures and considerations by means of which the ordinary members of society make sense of, find their way about in, and act on the circumstances in which they find themselves" (Heritage, 1984:4).

We can get a better understanding of ethnomethodology by examining a recent effort by Garfinkel (1988:103) to define *ethnomethodology*. First, like Durkheim, Garfinkel considers "social facts" to be the fundamental sociological phenomenon. However, Garfinkel's social facts are very different from Durkheim's social facts. For Durkheim, social facts are external to and coercive over individuals. Those who adopt such a focus tend to see actors as constrained or determined by social structures and institutions and able to exercise little or no independent judgment. In my terms (see the Appendix) Durkheim's social facts are macro-objective phenomena, while Garfinkel's social facts are micro-objective. That is, Garfinkel, like Durkheim, sees social facts as objective phenomena, but unlike Durkheim, Garfinkel sees them as existing at the micro level. Along these lines, Heritage sees ethnomethodology as focusing on "the molecular and submolecular levels of social structure" (1984:311). To put it another way, ethnomethodology is concerned with the organization of everyday life, or as Garfinkel calls it, "immortal, ordinary society" (1988:104). Pollner describes this as "the extraordinary organization of the ordinary" (1987:xvii). To use more of Garfinkel's definition, such organization is "locally, endogenously produced" and it is "naturally organized."

In Maynard and Clayman's (forthcoming) view, Garfinkel has sought a new way to get at the traditional concerns of sociology—the objective reality of social facts. But instead of conceiving of social facts as external and coercive, Garfinkel sees them as the result of the concerted work of people going about their everyday lives. In focusing on this concerted work, Garfinkel is not focally interested in the cognitive processes necessary for this to occur but rather in peoples' "procedures," "methods," or "practices." To pick up still more of Garfinkel's definition, social order is an "ongoing, practical achievement."

Various aspects of Garfinkel's definition are oriented to the view that the use of these practical procedures is universal and inescapable—that is, they are "everywhere, always, only, exactly and entirely members' work, with no time out, and with no possibility of evasion, hiding out, passing, postponement, or buy-outs" (1988:103). People cannot avoid using ethnomethods in their everyday lives.

Finally, Garfinkel sees these ethnomethods as "reflexively accountable." To understand this, we need to deal with two key concepts in ethnomethodology—reflexivity and accounts. By *reflexivity*, the ethnomethodologists mean the process in which we all engage to create social reality through our thoughts and actions. However, we are rarely aware of this process, usually because we conceal it from ourselves. When we say hello to someone and the person responds similarly, we are not conscious of the reflexive work being done by both parties. But when the other person scowls and walks away without returning the greeting, we become aware that we were trying to create a certain reality with our actions and that we failed. We may then attempt to reaffirm the world of greetings as we know it by trying to explain away the individual's inappropriate response ("He didn't hear me" or "She wasn't feeling well").

Order in society stems, at least in part, from people's reflexivity. That is, the ethnomethodologist rejects the idea that order comes from mere conformity to norms. Rather, it is the actors' awareness of their options, as well as their ability to anticipate how others are going to react to what they say and do, that helps make for order in the everyday world.

Accounts are the ways in which actors do such things as describe, criticize, and idealize specific situations (Bittner, 1973). *Accounting* is the process by which people offer accounts in order to make sense of the world. Ethnomethodologists devote a lot of attention to analyzing people's accounts as well as the ways in which accounts are offered and accepted (or rejected) by others. This is one of the reasons that ethnomethodologists are preoccupied with analyzing conversations. To take an example, when a student explains to her professor why she failed to take an examination, she is offering an account. The student is trying to make sense out of an event for her professor. Ethnomethodologists are interested in the nature of that account but more generally in the *accounting practices* (Sharrock and Anderson, 1986) by which the student offers the account and the professor accepts or rejects it. In analyzing accounts, ethnomethodologists adopt a stance of "ethnomethodological indifference." That is, they do not judge the nature of the accounts but rather analyze them in terms of how they are used in practical action. They are concerned with the accounts as well as the methods needed by both speaker and listener to proffer, understand, and accept or reject accounts.

Extending the idea of accounts, ethnomethodologists take great pains to point out that sociologists, like everyone else, offer accounts. Thus, reports of sociological studies can be seen as accounts and analyzed in the same way that all other accounts can be studied. This serves to disenchant the work of sociologists, indeed all scientists. A good deal of sociology (indeed all sciences) involves common-sense interpretations. Ethnomethodologists can study the accounts of the sociologist in the same way that they can study the accounts of the layperson. Thus, the everyday practices of sociologists and all scientists come under the scrutiny of the ethnomethodologist.

Returning now to Garfinkel's idea that everyday methods are *reflexively accountable,* we can get a better understanding of what he means. People are able to reflect on the things that they do and as a result are able to offer accounts of those actions to others. It is joint reflexivity, as well as the offer and acceptance of accounts, that helps to explain why the everyday world is orderly.

While we are in the process of defining key terms, a few others need to be outlined here in order to enable the student to better understand ethnomethodology.

Indexicality is a concept derived from linguistics, where it describes the fact that sentences have different meanings in different contexts. " 'It's raining' has different meanings: on the day of a long awaited picnic, at the end of a drought, when the rivers are already overflowing their banks, or when one is driving and the temperature is near freezing" (Handel, 1982:41). Extending this idea, ethnomethodologists adopt the view that all accounts—in fact, all expressions and practical actions—must be interpreted within their particular context. This means that ethnomethodologists must not impose their view of reality on actors. Instead, they must try to put themselves in the actor's place in order to understand what is being said and done.

Both laypersons and sociologists use the *documentary method,* which involves an effort to identify "an *underlying pattern* behind a series of appearances such that each appearance is seen as referring to, an expression of, or a document of, the underlying pattern" (Wilson, 1970:68; italics added; see also Heritage, 1984:84). Neither the layperson nor the sociologist can be content with the analysis of isolated events; both need to uncover the underlying pattern of which the event is part. The documentary method allows laypeople to better understand what is happening and to better orient their actions. In interacting with others, we trust that they are interpreting what we say and do as part of the same documentary pattern that we are relying on. If our trust is misplaced, and this is not the case, then interaction will break down. To the sociologist, the documentary method permits a deeper understanding of what is transpiring in the social world.

In order to carry out their everyday lives, people must employ the *etcetera principle.* According to this principle, all situations involve incomplete aspects that must be filled in by the participants in order to allow the situation to continue. Despite being confronted with all sorts of gaps and ambiguities, we carry on our social lives. In order to do so, we allow unclear situations and information to pass unquestioned, on the assumption that they will be clarified later on. If we were to seek total clarity at every moment, social life would be impossible. As action proceeds, either the needed information is forthcoming or we actively seek it in order to allow us to clarify, and get a better grasp on, what is transpiring. It is because people accept the etcetera principle, and are willing to proceed in the face of ambiguity in the hopes that things will become clearer, that social life is possible.

Finally, ethnomethodologists place great importance on *natural language.* This is the system of practices that allows people to speak, hear, and witness the objective production and display of social life. Natural language is not the linguistic elements that we use to communicate with one another but rather the nonlinguistic elements of interpersonal communication. It involves such things as the need to take turns in conversations and to cope with disruptions in a conversation. Ultimately, it involves a concern with the basic structure of speaker-listener interaction. As we will soon see, this is a major concern of a branch of ethnomethodology known as *conversation analysis.*

The Diversification of Ethnomethodology

Ethnomethodology was "invented" by Garfinkel beginning in the late 1940s, but it was first systematized with the publication of his *Studies in Ethnomethodology* in 1967. Over the years, ethnomethodology has grown enormously and expanded in a number of different directions. This led Don Zimmerman to conclude in 1978 that by that time there already was no longer one ethnomethodology but several varieties. As Zimmerman put it, ethnomethodology now "encompasses a number of more or less distinct and sometimes incompatible lines of inquiry" (1978:6). A decade later, Paul Atkinson (1988) underscored the lack of coherence in ethnomethodology and argued further that at least some ethnomethodologists had strayed too far from the underlying premises of the approach. Thus, while it is a very vibrant type of sociological theory, ethnomethodology has experienced some increasing "growing pains" in recent years. It is safe to say that ethnomethodology, its diversity, and its problems are likely to proliferate in coming years. After all, the subject matter of ethnomethodology is the infinite variety of everyday life. As a result, there will be many more studies, more diversification, and further "growing pains."

Maynard and Clayman (forthcoming) describe a number of varieties of work in ethnomethodology, but two stand out from our point of view.[4] The first type is ethnomethodological *studies of institutional settings*. Early ethnomethodological studies carried on by Garfinkel and his associates (which are discussed briefly below under "Breaching Experiments") took place in casual, noninstitutionalized settings like the home. Later, there was a move toward studying everyday practices in a wide variety of institutional settings—courtrooms, medical clinics, and police departments. The goal of such studies is an understanding of the way people in these settings perform their official tasks and, in the process, constitute the institution in which the tasks take place.

Conventional sociological studies of such institutional settings focus on their structure, formal rules, and official procedures to explain what people do within them. To the ethnomethodologists, such external constraints are inadequate for explaining what really goes on in these institutions. People are not determined by these external forces; rather, they use them to accomplish their tasks and to create the institution in which they exist. People employ their practical procedures not only to make their daily lives but also to manufacture the institutions' products. For example, the crime rates compiled by the police department are not merely the result of officials' following clearly defined rules in their production. Rather, officials utilize a range of common-sense procedures to decide, for example, whether victims should be classified

---

[4] Another body of ethnomethodological work deals with the *study of work*, particularly in scientific fields like mathematics, astronomy, biology, and optics (for example, Lynch, 1985). In common with the rest of ethnomethodology, studies in this area concentrate on the common-sense procedures, the practical reasoning employed by scientists even in some of the greatest discoveries in the history of mathematics and science. The focus is on the work that scientists do as well as the conversations in which they engage. The ethnomethodologist is concerned with the "workbench practices" employed by scientists on a day-to-day basis.

as homicides. Thus, such rates are based on the interpretive work of professionals, and we need to be careful in interpreting official statistics.

The second, and most important, variety of ethnomethodology is *conversation analysis*. The goal of conversation analysis is "the detailed understanding of the fundamental structures of conversational interaction" (Zimmerman, 1988:429). *Conversation* is defined in terms that are in line with the basic elements of the ethnomethodological perspective: "Conversation is an *interactional activity* exhibiting *stable, orderly* properties that are the analyzable *achievements* of the conversants" (Zimmerman, 1988:406; italics added). While there are rules and procedures for conversations, they do not determine what is said but rather are used to "accomplish" a conversation. The focus of conversational analysis is the constraints on what is said that are internal to the conversation itself and not external forces that constrain talk. Conversations are seen as internally, sequentially ordered.

Zimmerman details five basic working principles of conversation analysis. First, conversation analysis requires the collection and analysis of highly detailed data on conversations. This data includes not only words but also "the hesitations, cut-offs, restarts, silences, breathing noises, throat clearings, sniffles, laughter and laughterlike noises, prosody, and the like, not to mention the "nonverbal" behaviors available on video records that are usually closely integrated with the stream of activity captured on the audiotape" (Zimmerman, 1988:413). All these things are part of most conversations, and they are seen as methodic devices in the making of a conversation by the actors involved.

Second, even the finest detail of a conversation must be presumed to be an orderly accomplishment. Such minute aspects of a conversation are not ordered just by the ethnomethodologist; they are first "ordered by the methodical activities of the social actors themselves" (Zimmerman, 1988:415).

Third, interaction in general and conversation in particular have stable, orderly properties that are the achievements of the actors involved. In looking at conversations, ethnomethodologists treat them as if they were autonomous, separable from the cognitive processes of the actors as well as the larger context in which they take place.

Fourth, "the fundamental framework of conversation is sequential organization" (Zimmerman, 1988:422). Finally, and relatedly, "the course of conversational interaction is managed on a turn-by-turn or local basis" (Zimmerman, 1988:423). Here Zimmerman invokes Heritage's (1984) distinction between "context-shaped" and "context-renewing" conversation. Conversations are context-shaped in the sense that what is said at any given moment is shaped by the preceding sequential context of the conversation. Conversations are context-shaping in that what is being said in the present turn becomes part of the context for future turns.

Methodologically, conversation analysts are led to study conversations in naturally occurring situations, often using audiotape or videotape. This method allows information to flow from the everyday world rather than being imposed on it by the researcher. The researcher can examine and reexamine an actual conversation in minute detail instead of relying on his or her notes. This technique also allows the researcher to do highly detailed analyses of conversations.

Conversation analysis is based on the assumption that conversations are the bedrock of other forms of interpersonal relations. They are the most pervasive form of interaction, and a conversation "consists of the fullest matrix of socially organized communicative practices and procedures" (Heritage and Atkinson, 1984:13).

We have tried to give some general sense of ethnomethodology in the preceding pages. However, the fact is that the heart of ethnomethodology lies not in its theoretical statements but in its empirical studies. What we know theoretically is derived from those studies. Thus, we turn now to a series of those studies in the hope that this will give the reader a better feel for ethnomethodology.

Examples of Ethnomethodology

Breaching Experiments   We begin with some of the early research in ethnomethodology that gained for it much early notoriety. While the early methods are rarely, if ever, used today, they tell us a good deal about ethnomethodological research.

In breaching experiments social reality is violated in order to shed light on the methods by which people construct social reality. The assumption behind this research is not only that the methodical production of social life occurs all the time but also that the participants are unaware that they are engaging in such actions. The objective of the breaching experiment is to disrupt normal procedures so that the process by which the everyday world is constructed or reconstructed can be observed and studied. In his work, Garfinkel (1967) offered a number of examples of breaching experiments, most of which were undertaken by his students in casual settings to illustrate the basic principles of ethnomethodology. Let us give one example to illustrate the procedure.

Garfinkel asked his students to spend between fifteen minutes and an hour in their homes imagining that they were boarders and then acting on the basis of that assumption. "They were instructed to conduct themselves in a circumspect and polite fashion. They were to avoid getting personal, to use formal address, to speak only when spoken to" (Garfinkel, 1967:47). In the vast majority of cases, family members were dumbfounded by such behavior: "Reports were filled with accounts of astonishment, bewilderment, shock, anxiety, embarrassment, and anger, and with charges by various family members that the student was mean, inconsiderate, selfish, nasty, or impolite" (Garfinkel, 1967:47). These reactions indicate how important it is that people act in accord with the common-sense assumptions about how they are supposed to behave.

What most interested Garfinkel was how the family members sought in common-sense ways to cope with such a breach. They demanded explanations from the students for their behavior. In their questions, they often implied an explanation of the aberrant behavior:

> "Did you get fired?"
> "Are you sick?"
> "Are you out of your mind or are you just stupid?"
>
> (Garfinkel, 1967:47)

Family members also sought to explain the behaviors to themselves in terms of previously understood motives. For example, a student was thought to be behaving oddly because she was working too hard or had had a fight with her fiancé. Such explanations are important to participants—the other family members, in this case—because the explanations help them feel that under normal circumstances interaction would occur as it always had.

If the student did not acknowledge the validity of such explanations, family members were likely to withdraw and to seek to isolate, denounce, or retaliate against the culprit. Deep emotions were aroused because the effort to restore order through explanation was rejected by the student. The other family members felt that more intense statements and actions were necessary to restore the equilibrium:

> "Don't bother with him, he's in one of his moods again."
> "Why must you always create friction in our family harmony?"
> "I don't want any more of *that* out of *you* and if you can't treat your mother decently you'd better move out!"
>
> Garfinkel, 1967:48)

In the end, the students explained the experiment to their families, and in most situations harmony was restored. However, in some instances hard feelings lingered.

Breaching experiments are undertaken to illustrate the way people order their everyday lives. These experiments also reveal the fragility of social reality and the common-sense ways in which people seek to understand and to heal breaches. It is assumed that the way people handle these breaches tells us much about how they handle their everyday lives (Handel, 1982). Although these experiments seem innocent enough, they often lead to highly emotional reactions. These extreme reactions reflect how important it is to people to engage in routine, common-sense activities. The reactions to breaches are sometimes so extreme that Hugh Mehan and Houston Wood have cautioned about their use: *"Interested persons are strongly advised not to undertake any new breaching studies"* (1975:113).

Accomplishing Gender   It seems incontrovertible that one's gender—male or female—is biologically based. People are seen as simply manifesting the behaviors that are an outgrowth of their biological makeup. People are not usually thought of as *accomplishing* their gender. In contrast, sexiness is clearly an accomplishment; people need to speak and act in certain ways in order to be seen as sexy. However, it is generally assumed that one does not have to do or say *anything* to be seen as a man or a woman. Ethnomethodology has investigated the issue of gender, with some very unusual results.

The ethnomethodological view is traceable to one of Harold Garfinkel's (1967) now classic demonstrations of the utility of this orientation. In the 1950s, Garfinkel met a person named Agnes, who seemed unquestionably a woman. Not only did she have the figure of a woman, but it was virtually a "perfect" figure with an ideal set of measurements. She also had a pretty face, a good complexion, no facial hair, and plucked eyebrows—and she wore lipstick. This was clearly a woman, or was it? Garfinkel discovered that Agnes had not always appeared to be a woman. In fact, at the time he met her, Agnes was trying to convince officials that she needed an operation to remove her male genitalia and create a vagina.

Agnes was defined as a male at birth. In fact, she was by all accounts a boy until she was sixteen years of age. At that age, sensing something was awry, Agnes ran away from home and started to dress like a girl. She soon discovered that dressing like a woman was not enough; she had to *learn to act* like a woman if she was to be accepted as one. She did learn the accepted practices and as a result came to be defined, and to define herself, as a woman. The more general point here is that we are not simply born men or women; we all also learn and routinely use the commonplace practices that define us as men or women. It is only in doing this that we come to be, in a sociological sense, a man or a woman.

"Doing" Walking Few of us ever give more than a passing thought to the common-sense knowledge and procedures involved in the act of walking, let alone subject it to serious sociological analysis, but that is precisely what A. Lincoln Ryave and James N. Schenkein (1974) did. Their concern was not simply with walking but with "doing" walking. Although we all possess routine, methodical practices for walking, we must actually use those routines to "do" walking. Furthermore, we must do it in concert with the other people who walk with, by, or toward us; in other words, walking is the concerted accomplishment of members of the community. Ryave and Schenkein examined walking not just to understand this specific act but to understand a wide range of such phenomena: "In treating this commonplace phenomenon as the problematic achievement of members, we hope to build towards a greater understanding of social phenomena as on-going situated accomplishments" (1974:265).

Their basic resource in this study was a series of videotapes of people walking. Their central concern was the ways in which people navigate and avoid collisions. For successful walking to occur, the parties must not only *recognize* what they are doing but also *produce* the appropriate walking strategy. This is a striking example of how, using ethnomethodology, sociologists can take a mundane situation and demonstrate its problematic character.

Let us take the issue of how walking together is accomplished. To walk together, people have to produce a collective pattern. For example, they must maintain a certain proximity to each other. If one participant gets too far ahead or behind, that person engages in "repair work" in order to restore walking together. The individual may hurry up, slow down, or explain (at the time or later on) why she was out of step. If the participant refuses to engage in repair work and continues out of step, it becomes a serious threat to the reality of walking together.

The act of walking together also makes possible a set of walking-together activities: "For example, such activities as conversing, being available for conversation, touching, laughing, offering of offerables such as cigarettes or sweets, parting, and so on, are made relevant, and expectable, by the sheer fact of walking together" (Ryave and Schenkein, 1974:272).

Ryave and Schenkein also viewed the phenomenon of walking alone as a social accomplishment. For example, how does the lone walker avoid the appearance of walking together when he or she passes another walker on the street? Ryave and Schenkein's videotapes indicate that the individual manipulates direction, pace, and body attitude so that the moment of copresence is only fleeting. Similarly, it takes work to avoid engaging in violations while walking. For example, an individual could easily seem to be "following" someone in the street. The manner of one's approach could appear to be a threat to others. To avoid such violations or appearances of violations, walkers not only must be conscious that these acts are possible but also must be ready and able to take actions that would prevent their occurrence.

Telephone Conversations: Identification and Recognition   In this example and several that follow, we turn to conversation analysis. The goal is to look at the taken-for-granted ways in which conversation is organized. Conversation analysts are concerned with the relationship among utterances rather than the relationship between speakers and hearers (Sharrock and Anderson, 1986:68).

Emanuel A. Schegloff (1979) viewed his examination of the way in which telephone conversations are opened as part of a larger effort to understand the orderly character of social interaction:

> The work in which my colleagues and I have been engaged is concerned with the *organization of social interaction*. We bring to the materials with which we work— audio and videotapes of *naturally occurring* interaction, and transcripts of those tapes—an interest in *detecting* and *describing* the *orderly* phenomena of which conversation and interaction are composed, and an interest in depicting the *systematic organizations* by reference to which those phenomena are produced.
>
> (Schegloff, 1979:24, italics added)

The interest of Schegloff and his colleagues extended to various orderly phenomena within interaction, such as the organization of turn taking in conversations and the ways in which people seek to repair breaches in normal conversational procedure. Beyond this, they were interested in the overall structure of a conversation, including openings, closings, and regularly recurring internal sequences.

In this context Schegloff looked at the opening of a phone conversation, which he defined as "a place where the type of conversation being opened can be proffered, displayed, accepted, rejected, modified—in short, incipiently constituted by the parties to it" (1979:25). Although the talk one hears on the phone is no different from that in face-to-face conversations, the participants lack visual contact. Schegloff focused on one element of phone conversations not found in face-to-face conversations, the sequence by which the parties who have no visual contact identify and recognize each other.

In his research, Schegloff drew on data from 450 telephone openings. He found that telephone openings are often quite straightforward and standardized:

A. Hello?
B. Shar'n?
A. Hi!

Or:

A. Hello.
B. Hello, Charlie?
A. Oh, hi.

(Schegloff, 1979:52)

But some openings "look and sound idiosyncratic—almost virtuoso performances" (Schegloff, 1979:68):

A. Hello.
B. Hello Margie?
A. Yes.
B. hhh We do painting, antiquing,
A. is that right.
B. eh, hh—hhh
A. hnh, hnh, hnh
B. nhh, hnh, hnh! hh
A. hh
B. keep people's pa'r tools
A. y(hhh)! hnh, hnh
B. I'm sorry about that—that—I din' see that.

(adapted from Schegloff, 1979:68)

Although these may be different from the usual openings, they are not without their organization. They are "engendered by a systemic sequential organization adapted and fitted by the parties to some particular circumstances" (Schegloff, 1979:68). For example, the preceding conversation is almost incomprehensible until we understand that B is calling to apologize for keeping some borrowed power tools too long. B makes a joke out of it by building it into a list (painting, antiquing), and it is only at the end when both are laughing that the apology comes.

Schegloff's conclusion was that even where cases are very idiosyncratic, they are to be examined for their organizational pattern:

> Particular cases can, therefore, be examined for their local, interactional, biographical, ethnographic, or other idiosyncratic interest. The same materials can be inspected so as to extract from their local particularities the formal organization into which their particularities are infused. For students of interaction, the organizations through which the work of social life gets accomplished occupy the center of attention.
>
> (Schegloff, 1979:71)

Initiating Laughter   Gail Jefferson (1979; see also Jefferson, 1984) looked at the question of how one knows when to laugh in the course of a conversation. The lay view is that laughter is a totally free event in the course of a conversation or interaction. However, Jefferson found that several basic structural characteristics of an utterance are designed to induce the other party to laugh. The first is the placement, by the speaker, of a laugh at the end of his utterance:

> Dan.   I thought that was pretty out of sight. Did you hear me say you're a
> junkie . . . heh, heh
> Dolly.   heh, heh, heh.
>
> (adapted from Jefferson, 1979:80)

The second device reported by Jefferson is within-speech laughter—for example, in mid-sentence:

> A.   You know I didn't . . . you know
> B.   Hell, *you* know I'm on ret (haha);
> A.   ehh, yeh, ha ha.
>
> (adapted from Jefferson, 1979:83)

Jefferson concluded from these examples that the occurrence of laughter is more organized than we realize:

> It appears, then, that the order of alternative responses to a candidate laughable is not organized as freely as one might suppose; i.e., the issue is not that *something* should occur, laughter *or* whatever else, but that *laughter* should occur, on a volunteer basis *or* by invitation.
>
> (Jefferson, 1979:83)

But Jefferson was interested not only in the decision to laugh but also in the declining of an invitation to laugh. She found that silence after an invitation is not enough, that a clear signal is required indicating refusal of the invitation. If, for example, someone refuses to laugh, a strategy would be to commence, just after the onset of the speaker's laugh, a serious pursuit of the topic.

More recently, Glenn (1989) has examined the initiation of shared laughter in a multiparty conversation. While Jefferson focused on two-person interaction, the existence of a number of people makes the issue of laughter more complex. Glenn argues that whereas in two-party interactions the speaker ordinarily laughs first, in multiparty interactions someone other than the speaker usually provides the first laugh. In a two-party interaction, the speaker is virtually forced to laugh at his or her own material because of the fact that there is only one other person present who can perform that function. However, in a multiparty interaction, the fact that there are many other people who can laugh first means that the speaker can better afford the risk of not taking the initiative of being the first to laugh.

Generating Applause   Derived from a body of work developed by J. Maxwell Atkinson (1984a, 1984b), John Heritage and David Greatbatch (1986) have studied the rhetoric of British political speeches and uncovered basic devices by which speakers generate applause from their audiences. They argue that applause is generated by "statements that are verbally constructed (a) to *emphasize* and thus highlight their contents against a surrounding background of speech materials and (b) to *project a clear completion point* for the message in question" (Heritage and Greatbatch, 1986:116). Emphasis tells the audience that applause is appropriate, and advance notice of a clear completion point allows the audience to begin applauding more or less in unison. In their analysis of British political speeches, Heritage and Greatbatch uncovered seven basic rhetorical devices:

1 *Contrast:*   For example, a politician might argue: "Too much is spent on war . . . too little is spent on peace." Such a statement generates applause because, for emphasis, the same point is made first in negative and then in positive terms. The audience is also able to anticipate when to applaud by matching the unfolding of the second half of the statement with the already completed first half.
2 *List:*   A list of political issues, especially the often used three-part list, provides emphasis as well as a completion point that can be anticipated by the audience.
3 *Puzzle solution:*   Here the politician first poses a puzzle for the audience and then offers a solution. This double presentation of the issue provides emphasis, and the audience can anticipate the completion of the statement at the end of the solution.
4 *Headline—punch line:*   Here the politician proposes to make a statement and then makes it.
5 *Combination:*   This involves use of two or more of the devices just listed.
6 *Position-taking:*   This involves an initial description of a state of affairs that the speaker would be expected to feel strongly about. However, at first it is presented nonevaluatively. Only at the end does the speaker offer his or her own position.

7 *Pursuit:* This occurs when an audience fails to respond to a particular message. The speaker may actively pursue applause by, for example, restating the central point.

In the political party conferences studied by Heritage and Greatbatch, these seven devices accounted for slightly more than two-thirds of the total applause. Of the seven, the *contrast* (accounting for almost a quarter of applause events) was by far the most commonly applauded format. In addition to these devices, the speaker's manner of delivering the message ("intonation, timing, and gesture") also is important (Heritage and Greatbatch, 1986:143). Finally, Heritage and Greatbatch note that the seven devices are not restricted to political speech making, but also are found in advertising slogans, newspaper editorials, scientific texts, and so forth. In fact, they conclude that these devices have their roots and are found in everyday, natural, conversational interaction. The implication is that we all use these devices daily to generate positive reactions from those with whom we interact.

The Interactive Emergence of Sentences and Stories   Charles Goodwin (1979) challenged the traditional linguistic assumption that sentences can be examined in isolation from the process of interaction in which they occur. His view was that "sentences emerge with conversation" (Goodwin, 1979:97). The fact is that the "speaker can reconstruct the meaning of his sentence *as he is producing it* in order to maintain its appropriateness to its recipient of the moment" (Goodwin, 1979:98; italics added).

Goodwin's essential point was that speakers pay acute attention to listeners as they are speaking. As the listeners react verbally, facially, or with body language, the speaker adjusts the sentence as it is emerging on the basis of these reactions. The reactions allow the speaker to decide whether his or her point is being made, and if not, to alter the structure of the sentence. In a rather complicated conversation that he analyzed, Goodwin described some of the alterations that took place in a particular sentence sequence:

> In the course of its production the unfolding meaning of John's sentence is reconstructed twice, a new segment is added to it, and another is deleted prior to its production but replaced with a different segment. The sentence eventually produced emerges as the product of a dynamic process of interaction between speaker and hearer as they mutually constructed the turn of talk.
>
> (Goodwin, 1979:112)

In other words, sentences are the products of collaborative processes.

More recently, Mandelbaum (1989) has examined the interactive emergence of stories. Her key point is that the audience is not passive, as is conventionally assumed, but rather can be seen as the "co-author" of the story. Paralleling Goodwin's analysis of the interactive emergence of sentences, Mandelbaum shows that the audience members have resources that allow them to work with the author to alter a story while the storytelling is in process. The audience participates by allowing the suspension of turn-by-turn talk so that the storyteller may dominate the conversation. The audience members also help the story along by displaying their understanding through the use of such expressions as "uh huh" and "mm hm." The audience may also "repair" some problem in the story, thereby permitting it to proceed more smoothly. Most importantly, for the purposes of this section, the audience may intervene in the story and cause it to move off in a new direction. Thus, in a very real sense, stories, like sentences and conversations in general, are interactional products.

Formulations   Heritage and Watson (1979) were interested in the general issue of orderliness within conversations. They placed this issue within the general context of ethnomethodological concerns:

> A central focus of ethnomethodological work is the analysis of the practical socio-logical reasoning through which social activity is rendered accountable and orderly. Assumed by this concern is the notion that all scenic features of social interaction [for example, biographies, events, personalities, locations] are occasioned and established as a concerted practical accomplishment, in and through which the parties display for one another their competence in the practical management of social order. As analysts, our interest is to explicate, in respect of naturally occurring occasions of use, the methods by which such orderliness can be displayed, managed, and recognized by members.
>
> (Heritage and Watson, 1979:123–124)

Their specific concern was the issue of when conversational order itself becomes a topic of conversation for the participants. Specifically, they looked at *formulations,* which they defined as a part of a conversation used to describe that conversation. In particular, their concern was a specific type of formulation, one in which an actor seeks to "characterize states of affairs already described or negotiated (in whole or in part) in the preceding talk" (Heritage and Watson, 1979:126).

The conversations that Heritage and Watson used are too lengthy to include here, but the following gives a sense of what they meant by formulations:

A.   I was so depressed that . . .
B.   Yes
A.   . . . that I climbed on the railing of the bridge
B.   *You were prepared to commit suicide because* . . .
A.   Yes, I am so overweight.

In this example, in saying that *A* was prepared to commit suicide, *B* is formulating what *A* was trying to say in his previous two statements.

Such formulations illustrate the practical management of conversations. A formulation is a part of a conversation in which the objective "is manifestly and specifically to exhibit participants' understanding" (Heritage and Watson, 1979:129). A formulation is one example of how members demonstrate their understanding of what is occurring.

Integration of Talk and Nonvocal Activities   Conversation analysts have focused on talk and other ethnomethodologists on nonvocal activities. Some researchers are using videotapes and films to analyze the integration of vocal and nonvocal activities. Goodwin (1984), for example, examined a videotape of a dinner party involving two couples. One issue in the relationship between vocal and nonvocal activities is the body posture of a person (Ann) who tells a story at the party:

> Ann clasps her hands together, places both elbows on the table, and leans forward while gazing toward her addressed recipient, Beth. With this posture the speaker displays full orientation toward her addressed recipient, complete engagement in telling her story, and lack of involvement in any activities other than conversation. The posture appears to . . . constitute a visual display that a telling is in progress.
> (Goodwin, 1984:228)

More generally, Goodwin concludes, "Ann's telling is thus made visible not only in her talk but also in the way in which she organizes her body and activities during the telling" (1984:229).

Another nonvocal activity examined by Goodwin is the gaze, which he relates to talk:

> When a speaker gazes at a recipient that recipient should be gazing at him. When speakers gaze at nongazing recipients, and thus locate violations of the rule, they frequently produce phrasal breaks such as restarts and pauses, in their talk. These phrasal breaks both orient to the event as a violation by locating the talk in progress at that point as impaired in some fashion and provide a remedy by functioning as requests for the gaze of the hearer. Thus just after phrasal breaks nongazing recipients frequently begin to move their gaze to the speaker.
> (Goodwin, 1984:230)

Body posture and gaze are only two of many nonvocal activities that are intimately related to vocal activities.

Some Ethnomethodological Studies of Institutions   As pointed out earlier in this chapter, a number of ethnomethodologists have grown interested in the study of conversation and interaction in various social institutions. In this section we will examine a few examples of this kind of work.

Some ethnomethodologists have turned their attention to the work world. For example, Button (1987) has looked at the job interview. Not surprisingly, he sees the interview as a sequential, turn-taking conversation and as the "situated practical accomplishment of the parties to that setting" (Button, 1987:160). One issue addressed in this study involves the things that interviewers can do, after an answer has been given, to move on to something else, thereby preventing the interviewee from returning to, and perhaps correcting, his or her answer. First, the interviewer may indicate that the interview as a whole is over. Second, the interviewer may ask another question that moves the discussion off in a different direction. Third, the interviewer may assess the answer given in such a way that the interviewee is precluded from returning to it.

Button wonders what it is that makes a job interview an interview? He argues that it is not the sign on the door or the gathering together of people. Rather, it is "what those people do, and how they structure and organize their interactions with one another, that achieves for some social settings its characterizability as an interview. This integrally involves the way in which the participants organize their speech exchange with one another" (Button, 1987:170). Thus it is the nature of the interaction, of the conversation, that defines a job interview.

Anderson, Hughes, and Sharrock (1987) have examined the nature of negotiations among business executives. One of their findings about such negotiations is how reasonable, detached, and impersonal they are:

> Everything is carried out in a considered, measured, reasonable way. No personal animus is involved or intended in their maneuverings. It is simply what they do; part of their working day. . . . Animosities, disagreements and disputes are always contained, in hand, controlled. If a deal cannot be made this time, so be it.
>
> (Anderson, Hughes, and Sharrock, 1987:155)

This kind of interaction tells us a great deal about the business world.

Interestingly, Anderson, Hughes, and Sharrock go on to argue that what takes place in the business world is no different from what takes place in everyday life. In most of our social relationships we behave the way the business executives described above behaved. "Business life does not take place in a sealed compartment, set off from the rest of social life. It is continuous with and interwoven with it" (Anderson, Hughes, and Sharrock, 1987:155).

Whalen and Zimmerman (1987) have examined telephone calls to emergency communications centers. The context of such calls leads to a reduction of the opening of telephone conversations. In normal telephone conversations we usually find summons-answer, identification-recognition, greeting, and "howareyou" sequences. In emergency calls, however, the opening sequences are reduced and recognitions, greetings, and "howareyous" are routinely absent.

Another interesting aspect of emergency phone calls is that certain opening events that would be ignored in a normal conversation are treated quite seriously:

> . . . those situations in which caller hangs up after dispatcher answers, or there is silence on the line or sounds such as dogs barking, arguing and screaming in the background, or a smoke alarm ringing. Despite the lack of direct conversational engagement on the line, dispatchers initially treat these events as possible indicators of a need for assistance, and thus as functional or *virtual* requests.
>
> (Whalen and Zimmerman, 1987:178)

The peculiar nature of the emergency telephone conversation leads to these and other adaptations to the structure of the normal conversation.

In a related study, Whalen, Zimmerman, and Whalen (1988) looked at a specific emergency telephone conversation that failed, leading to the delayed dispatch of an ambulance and the death of a woman. While the media tended to blame the dispatcher for this incident, Whalen, Zimmerman, and Whalen trace the problem to the nature of the specific emergency phone conversation:

> Our investigation revealed that the participants had rather different understandings of what was happening and different expectations of what was supposed to happen in this conversation. Over the course of the interaction the talk of both caller and nurse-dispatcher (and her supervisor) operated to extend and deepen this misalignment. This misalignment contributed in a fundamental way to a dispute that contaminated and transformed the participants' activity.
>
> (Whalen, Zimmerman, and Whalen, 1988:358)

Thus, it was the nature of the specific conversation, not the abilities of the dispatcher, that "caused" the mishap.

Institutional studies are proliferating rapidly. Other examples include Clayman's (1988) effort to demonstrate the techniques that television news interviewers use to appear objective and Marlaire and Maynard's (1990) study of standardized tests (for example, IQ tests) as interactional phenomena. The possibilities here are endless as conversation analysts and ethnomethodologists study interaction in order to shed light on the nature of interaction as well as on a wide range of institutions in which the interactions take place.

Criticisms of Traditional Sociology

Ethnomethodologists criticize traditional sociologists for imposing *their* sense of social reality on the social world (Mehan and Wood, 1975). They believe that sociology has not been attentive enough or true enough to the everyday world that should be its ultimate source of knowledge (Sharrock and Anderson, 1986). Enamored of their own view of the social world, sociologists have tended not to share the same social reality as those they study. As Mehan and Wood put it, "In attempting to do a social *science*, sociology has become alienated from the social" (1975:63).

Within this general orientation, Mehan and Wood (see also Sharrock and Anderson, 1986) leveled a number of specific criticisms at sociology. The concepts used by sociologists are said to distort the social world, to destroy its ebb and flow. Further distortion is caused by sociology's reliance on scientific techniques and statistical analyses of data. Statistics simply do not usually do justice to the elegance and sophistication of the real world. The coding techniques used by sociologists, when they translate human behavior into their preconceived categories, distort the social world. Furthermore, the seeming simplicity of the codes conceals the complicated and distorting work involved in turning aspects of the social world into the sociologist's preconceived categories. Sociologists are also seen as tending to accept unquestioningly a respondent's description of a phenomenon rather than looking at the phenomenon itself. Thus, a description of a social setting is taken to *be* that setting rather than one conception of that setting. Finally, Mehan and Wood argued that sociologists are prone to offer abstractions of the social world that are increasingly removed from the reality of everyday life.

Taking a slightly different approach, Don Zimmerman and Melvin Pollner (1970) argued that conventional sociology has suffered from a confusion of *topic* and *resource*. That is, the everyday social world is a resource for the favorite topics of sociology, but it is rarely a topic in its own right. This can be illustrated in a variety of ways. For example, Roy Turner (1970; see also Sharrock and Anderson, 1986) argued that sociologists usually look at everyday speech not as a topic in itself but as a resource with which to study hidden realities such as norms, values, attitudes, and so on. However, instead of being a resource, everyday speech can be seen as one of the ways in which the business of social life is carried on—a topic in itself. Matthew Speier (1970) argued that when sociologists look at childhood socialization, they look not at the processes themselves but at a series of abstract "stages" generalized from those processes. Speier argued that *"socialization is the acquisition of interactional competencies"* (1970:189). Thus, the ethnomethodologist must look at the way these competencies are acquired and used in the everyday reality of the real world.

Another analysis of childhood socialization, by Robert W. Mackay (1974), is even more useful as a critique of traditional sociology and the confusion of topic and resource. Mackay contrasted the "normative" approach of traditional sociology with the interpretive approach of ethnomethodology. The normative approach is seen as arguing that socialization is merely a series of stages in which "complete" adults teach "incomplete" children the ways of society. Mackay viewed this as a "gloss" that ignores the reality that socialization involves an interaction between children and adults. Children are not passive, incomplete receptacles; rather, they are active participants in the socialization process, because they have the ability to reason, invent, and acquire knowledge. Socialization is a two-sided process. Mackay believed that the ethnomethodological orientation "restores the interaction between adults and children based on interpretive competencies as the phenomenon of study" (1974:183).

Don Zimmerman and Melvin Pollner (1970) cited other examples of the confusion of topic and resource. For example, they argued that sociologists normally explain action in bureaucracies by the rules, norms, and values of the organization. However, had they looked at organizations as topics, they would have seen that actors often simply make it *appear* through their actions that those actions can be explained by the rules. It is not the rules but the actors' *use* of the rules that should be the topic of sociological research. Zimmerman and Pollner then cited the example of a code of behavior among prison convicts. Whereas traditional sociology would look at the ways in which actors are constrained by a convict code, ethnomethodologists would examine how the convicts use the code as an explanatory and persuasive device. Don Zimmerman and Lawrence Wieder offered the following generalization on the confusion of topic and resource:

> The ethnomethodologist is *not* concerned with providing casual explanations of observably regular, patterned, repetitive actions by some kind of analysis of the actor's point of view. He *is* concerned with how members of society go about the task of *seeing, describing,* and *explaining* order in the world in which they live.
>
> (Zimmerman and Wieder, 1970:289)

Social order is not a reality in itself to the ethnomethodologist but an accomplishment of social actors.

Stresses and Strains in Ethnomethodology

While ethnomethodology has made enormous strides in sociology and has demonstrated, especially in the area of conversation analysis, some capacity to cumulate knowledge of the world of everyday life, there are some problems worth noting.

First, while ethnomethodology is far more accepted today than it was a decade ago, it is still regarded with considerable suspicion by many sociologists. They view it as focusing on trivial matters and ignoring the crucially important issues confronting society today. The ethnomethodologists' response is that they *are* dealing with the crucial issues because it is everyday life that matters most. Paul Atkinson sums up the situation: "Ethnomethodology continues to be greeted with mixtures of incomprehension and hostility in some quarters, but it is unquestionably a force to be reckoned with when it comes to the theory, methods, and empirical conduct of sociological inquiry" (1988:442).

Second, there is a strain in ethnomethodology in the micro direction. That is, there are those (for example, P. Atkinson, 1988) who believe that ethnomethodology has lost sight of its phenomenological roots and its concern for conscious, cognitive processes (exceptions are Cicourel [1974] and Coulter [1983, 1989], although the latter is inclined to embed cognition within the everyday world). Instead of focusing on such conscious processes, ethnomethodologists, especially conversation analysts, have come to focus on the "structural properties of the talk itself" (P. Atkinson, 1988:449). Ignored in the process are motives and the internal motivations for action. In Atkinson's view, ethnomethodology has grown "unduly restricted" and come to be "behaviorist and empiricist" (1988:441). In moving in this direction, ethnomethodology is seen as having gone back on some of its basic principles, including its desire not to treat the actor as a judgmental dope:

> Garfinkel's early inspiration was to reject the judgmental dope image in order to focus attention on the skillful and artful, methodical work put into the production of social order. In the intervening years, however, some versions of ethnomethodology have returned to the judgmental dope as their model actor. Intentionality and meaning have been all but eliminated.
>
> (P. Atkinson, 1988:449)

Finally, there is a strain in ethnomethodology in the macro direction. While ethnomethodology obviously focuses on micro-level phenomena, some ethnomethodologists have worried about how they can be linked with a concern for larger social structures. Zimmerman, for example, some years ago viewed cross-fertilization with macrosociology as "an open question, and an intriguing possibility" (1978:12). More recently, Pollner has urged that ethnomethodology "return to sociology to understand those [taken for granted] practices in their larger social context . . . mundane reason in terms of structural and historical processes. Mundane reason, it is suggested is not simply the product of local work of mundane reasoners, for it is also shaped by longer term and larger scale dynamics" (1987:xvi). Some such cross-fertilization has been undertaken by people like Giddens (1984), who has integrated ethnomethodological ideas into his structuration theory, and Chua (1977), who has analyzed the relationship between ethnomethodology and Marxian theory. More generally, Boden (1990a) has outlined what ethnomethodology has to offer to the issue of the relationship between structure and agency. She argues that the findings of ethnomethodological studies are relevant not only to micro structures but to macro structures as well. There is some hope that the institutional studies being undertaken by ethnomethodologists will shed light on the macro structure and its relationship to micro-level phenomena.

SUMMARY

This chapter is devoted to two related sociological theories—phenomenological sociology and ethnomethodology. Phenomenological sociology, especially the ideas of Alfred Schutz, played a key role in the development of ethnomethodology. But ethnomethodology had other intellectual inputs, with the result that while there are some similarities between the two theories, there are also some important differences between them.

The first part of the chapter is devoted to phenomenological sociology, and the bulk of that section focuses on the theory of Alfred Schutz. Schutz was focally concerned with intersubjectivity, or the way in which people grasp the consciousness of others while they live within their own streams of consciousness. Much of Schutz's work focuses on the life-world, or the world of everyday life. This is an intersubjective world in which people both create social reality and are constrained by the preexisting social and cultural structures created by their predecessors. While much of the life-world is shared, there are also private (biographically articulated) aspects of that world.

Typifications (and recipes) are central to people in the everyday world. Typifications are usually socially derived and socially approved and allow people to function on a daily basis. It is only in problematic situations that people (reluctantly) abandon their typifications (and recipes) and create new ways of dealing with the social world.

There are four realms of the social world—the future (*folgewelt*), the past (*vorwelt*), the present world of consociates with whom we have face-to-face contact (*umwelt*), and the present world of contemporaries whom we know only as types (*mitwelt*). Typifications (and recipes) are created in the *umwelt*. Intimate we relations are found in the *umwelt*, and typified they relations characterize the *mitwelt*.

Although Schutz had turned away from consciousness, he did offer insights into it, especially in his thoughts on meaning and motives.

Schutz offers a theory which is concerned with the dialectical relationship between the way people construct social reality and the already present, obdurate cultural reality that others have constructed and are continuing to construct. People are influenced by these realities, but they are also capable of "making sense" of, interpreting, and even reconstructing the cultural world.

The section on phenomenology concludes with a discussion of Berger and Luckmann's *The Social Construction of Reality*. While heavily indebted to Schutz's theory, this work was also affected by a number of other theoretical inputs. The heart of this work lies in its contention that people create society and that society comes to be an objective reality which, in turn, creates people. While a highly promising effort, *The Social Construction of Reality* is limited by its single-minded commitment to subjective processes.

The second half of the chapter is devoted to a discussion of ethnomethodology. While phenomenologists tend to focus on what people think, ethnomethodology is primarily concerned with what people do. The ethnomethodologist is mainly interested in the practices through which people handle their everyday lives. A number of the most basic ethnomethodological concepts are introduced, including reflexivity, accounts and accounting practices, indexicality, the documentary method, the etcetera principle, and natural language. Two major types of ethnomethodology—studies of institutional settings and conversation analysis—are introduced.

The essence of ethnomethodology is to be found in its research studies. A number of such studies are discussed, beginning with Garfinkel's early breaching experiments and his study of Agnes. The rest of the section is devoted primarily to specific conversation studies as well as to studies of institutional settings. The section concludes with a discussion of some of ethnomethodology's criticisms of mainstream sociology as well as a brief look at a number of the stresses and strains that exist in contemporary ethnomethodology.

EXCHANGE THEORY AND BEHAVIORAL SOCIOLOGY

*E*XCHANGE theory and behavioral sociology are atypical sociological theories. What makes them unique is that their roots lie in theories which exist outside of sociology and which have a micro-social orientation. The major source of these theories is psychology, specifically the behaviorism of B. F. Skinner. It is this influence, and the way it shaped these two theories, that will be our primary concern in this chapter. Behaviorism is the common thread that unites exchange theory and behavioral sociology and allows us to deal with them together in this chapter.

While behavioral sociology remains pure in terms of the influence of psychological behaviorism, exchange theory has another source that has grown in importance in recent years.[1] That second foundation is economics, especially rational choice theory (Cook O'Brien, and Kollock 1990; Heath, 1976). While we will not focus on the impact of rational choice theory in this chapter, we will discuss how George Homans, the leading exchange theorist, integrated that theory into his largely behavioristic approach.

We will have much more to say about rational choice theory and its rela-

---

[1] There are also a number of sociologists who focus on behavior and exchange without accepting much, if anything, of behaviorism or rational choice theory. Alvin Gouldner's (1960) classic essay on reciprocity and William Goode's (1960) work on role strain illustrate this type of exchange theory. This version of exchange theory emphasizes the reciprocal nature of social relationships and how power and prestige grow out of imbalances in reciprocity (Goode, 1978).

tionship to exchange theory in Chapter 17. In that context we will also discuss a number of other aspects of, and developments in, exchange theory, including its roots in anthropology and its ties to recent work in network theory (Cook, O'Brien, and Kollock, 1990; Ekeh, 1974). Thus, exchange theory is far more diverse theoretically than is reflected in the presentation in this chapter. Furthermore, much of the recent work in exchange theory is much more synthetic and integrative than the largely microscopic exchange theory discussed in this chapter (Uehara, 1990). Especially important in this context is the work of Richard Emerson (1981) and Karen Cook (Cook and Emerson, 1978; Cook et al., 1983; Cook, O'Brien, and Kollock, 1990), and their ideas will also concern us in Chapter 17.

Thus, our focus here is on comparatively "pure" behavioral sociology and exchange theory (as reflected in Homans's [1958, 1961] early work). These theories fit nicely into the author's sense of sociology's multiple paradigms (Ritzer, 1975a, 1975b, 1980; see also the Appendix). In fact, all the chapters in Part Two of this book are shaped, at least in part, by my sense of sociology's multiple paradigms as well as the place of various theories within them. We can take this opportunity to discuss briefly the multiple paradigms and their relationship to the theories discussed up to this point in the book.

In the author's view, sociology is composed of three major paradigms—the social-facts, social-definition, and social-behavior paradigms. Each paradigm has four major components, but of importance to us at the moment are only the paradigms' images of the subject matter of sociology and the theories each encompasses. The *social-facts paradigm* takes as the subject matter of sociology large-scale social structures and institutions and their coercive effect on actors and their thoughts and actions. Structural functionalism, conflict theory, and several varieties of neo-Marxian theory are associated with the social-facts paradigm. The *social-definition paradigm* accepts as the primary concern of sociology actors, the ways in which they construct social reality, and the action that results from such construction. Thus actors, to the social definitionist, are relatively free and creative, whereas to the social factist they are largely determined by large-scale structures and institutions. Symbolic interactionists, phenomenologists, ethnomethodologists, and at least some neo-Marxists operate within this paradigm. Finally, there is the *social-behavior paradigm*, in which the subject matter of sociology is individual behavior and the reinforcers and punishers that affect it. The theories we are about to discuss, behavioral sociology and exchange theory, are encompassed by this paradigm.

This multiple-paradigm schema plays a key role in this chapter. First, it attunes us to the main concerns of the two theories—antecedents to behavior, behavior, reinforcement, and punishment. Second, it alerts us to the fact that the theorists associated with this paradigm are not primarily concerned with, and some even reject an interest in, large-scale structures and institutions as well as the social construction of reality and social action. Third, although many associated with this paradigm have adopted a dogmatic position on what it should and should not concern itself with, some others have sought to integrate the traditional concerns of social behaviorism with those of social factism and social definitionism. Throughout this chapter we try to sort out the complex interrelationship between social behaviorism and the other sociological paradigms.

Given the preeminent place of B. F. Skinner and his behaviorism in exchange theory, we begin this chapter with his general orientation. Next, we discuss behavioral sociology, because it represents the most pristine translation of Skinner's ideas into sociological principles. Finally, we turn to exchange theory, particularly as it is represented in the work of George Homans and Peter Blau. We discuss Blau's exchange theory here, rather than in Part Three, on synthetic theories, because of limitations in his integrative approach, which seeks to move from the micro to the macro levels. As Uehara points out: "Although Blau . . . introduced the group into the exchange equation, his was still essentially a dyadic analysis in which the group is conceived as a single, albeit collective, actor" (1990:525). In spite of its limitations, Blau's work did anticipate the more integrative exchange theory that will be discussed later in the book.

SKINNER AND BEHAVIORISM

Behaviorism has a long history in the social sciences and in particular in psychology. However, modern behaviorism in all the social sciences and in particular in sociology can be traced to the work of B. F. Skinner. Skinner's work, although steadfastly devoted to the principles of behaviorism, has covered a broad spectrum, including scientific tracts (Skinner, 1938), a utopian novel (Skinner, 1948), polemical and political essays (Skinner, 1971), practical applications of behaviorism (Skinner, 1968), and autobiographical works (Skinner, 1983). His scientific, utopian, political, and practical works all have played a role in the development of a sociological version of behaviorism.

First, let us examine Skinner's analysis of other sociological theories. He regarded them as rather nonscientific, mystical enterprises. He felt this way about the macro theories associated with the social-facts paradigm, such as structural functionalism and conflict theory, as well as the micro theories associated with the social-definition paradigm, such as symbolic interactionism, ethnomethodology, and phenomenology. He saw these theories as constructing mystical entities that distract the sociologist from the only concrete entities of scientific study—antecedents of behavior, behavior, and the consequences that make that behavior more or less likely to occur (Molm, 1981). Take, for example, Skinner's criticism of the concept of *culture,* often defined by a typical social factist as "traditional (i.e., historically derived and selected) ideas and especially their attached values" (1971:121). He argued that this definition has created unnecessarily mystical elements such as "ideas" and "values." Scientists do not see ideas and values when they look at society. Instead, they see "how people live, how they raise their children, how they gather or cultivate food, what kinds of dwellings they live in, what they wear, what games they play, how they treat each other, how they govern themselves, and so on" (Skinner, 1971:121). The culture of a community is composed of behaviors. To understand behaviors we do not need concepts such as *ideas* and *values*; instead, we need to understand such things as rewards and costs.

Skinner leveled his strongest criticisms at the theories of social definitionism. One of Skinner's major goals in *Beyond Freedom and Dignity* (1971) was to eliminate the idea that he labels "autonomous man" from the social sciences—indeed, from the world. The idea of an autonomous man is an integral part of the social-definition paradigm and an attack on it thus means an attack on the social definitionists. Skinner, speaking for social behaviorism, did not want to reconcile his differences with the social definitionists. In fact, he was interested in destroying the theories associated with the social-definition paradigm.

What is this notion of an autonomous man that Skinner sought to eliminate? People, in this view, have an inner core (which cannot be analyzed scientifically) from which their actions emanate. This inner core enables them to initiate, originate, and create. This active, creative, voluntaristic view of people is clearly in line with the social-definitionist position, and Skinner's effort to attack this idea is, indirectly, an effort to oppose the theories of social definitionism.

To Skinner, the idea that people have an inner, autonomous core is a mystical, metaphysical position of the kind that must be eliminated from the social sciences: "Autonomous man serves to explain only the things we are not yet able to explain in other ways. His existence depends on our ignorance, and he naturally loses status as we come to know more about behavior" (1971:12). Behavior, as well as the conditions that produce behavior, primarily other behaviors, are the primary subject matter to Skinner. He believed we should not focus primarily on such concepts as "feelings"; we should mainly focus on the examination (and control) of behavior and the contingencies that affect it.[2] Linda Molm amplified this point by arguing that Skinner was concerned with what he called "private events," or "events that take place inside an individual and that are not directly observable by others" (1981:161). In this category, he included thoughts, feelings, and perceptions. However, Skinner was willing to accept a concern with such internal states only under two conditions. First, they cannot be independent, or mediating, variables but can occupy only the role of dependent variables in a behaviorist's schema. In other words, they cannot be explanatory variables, only variables to be explained by other factors. Second, they must be observable in some way. The self-reports of actors (as well as their behaviors) count as observable phenomena.

---

[2] A number of behaviorists are willing to include such things as cognition, emotion, and the "mind" in their domain. For example, Arthur Staats (1976) made the case for including the mind in behaviorism. John Baldwin and Janice Baldwin (1978) argued that behaviorists, indeed all sociologists, should use both traditional scientific techniques and the *verstehen* methodology to understand a variety of social phenomena, including subjectivity and meaning.

Such a limited, scientific view of mental states is not likely to be acceptable to those who adopt the social-definition paradigm.

Skinner and social behaviorists in general are interested in the relationship between individuals and their environment (Molm, 1981), which is composed of a variety of social and nonsocial objects. The social behaviorist argues that the principles that govern the relationship between an individual and a social object are the same as those that govern the relationship between an individual and a nonsocial object.[3] Don Bushell and Robert Burgess defined the subject matter of behaviorists as "the behavior of individuals that operates on the environment in such a way as to produce some consequence or change in it which, in turn, modifies subsequent performances of that behavior" (1969:27). Thus they focus on the "functional relationship" between behavior and changes in the environment of the actor. This means that a child tossing a stone into a river is an object of study to the behaviorist in exactly the same way as are a mother scolding a child, a teacher instructing a class, or a business executive meeting a board of directors.

Social behaviorists are interested in an interaction process, but the process is conceptualized very differently from the way it is in the theories of the social definitionists. Actors, to the social definitionist, are dynamic, creative forces in the interaction process (Perinbanayagam, 1981). They do not simply respond to stimuli but interpret them and act on the basis of their definitions of them. The social behaviorist, in contrast, allows the individual far less "free will." To the behaviorist, "Thinking is the behavior of the brain. Most brain activity is not conscious" (Baldwin and Baldwin, 1986:264). Thus, whereas to the social definitionist the actor is busy consciously constructing social reality, to the social behaviorist he or she is unconsciously responding to stimuli. The individual's response is determined by the nature of the external stimuli. The image is of a much more mechanical[4] person than that conceived by the social definitionists.[5]

The image of actors in social-factist theories (for example, structural functionalism) is almost as mechanistic as in the social-behaviorist paradigm. The social factist sees the individual as determined by external norms, values, structures, and the like. The major difference between social factism and social behaviorism lies in the source of control over the individual. To the social factist, large-scale structures and institutions control the individual. Social behaviorists are concerned with the relationship between individuals and the antecedents and consequences that make a behavior more or less likely to occur.[6]

---

[3] This is one of the places in which Molm disagreed with more traditional social behaviorists, such as Homans. She took pains to differentiate between the orientations of behavioral psychologists and behavioral sociologists.

[4] Behaviorists reject the accusation that they have a mechanical image of people by arguing that they are interested in human creativity as long as it is studied scientifically.

[5] This is still another point on which Molm disagreed.

[6] To be fair, the antecedents may come from, and the consequences have an impact on, both small-scale and large-scale structures.

BEHAVIORAL SOCIOLOGY

Behavioral sociology (or as Baldwin and Baldwin [1986] call it, "behavior science") represents an effort to apply the principles of psychological behaviorism to sociological questions. The behavioral sociologist is concerned with the relationship between the effects of an actor's behavior on the environment and their impact on the actor's later behavior. This is basic to *operant conditioning*, or the learning process by which "behavior is modified by its consequences" (Baldwin and Baldwin, 1986:6). To put this in another way, an actor emits some behavior. One might almost think of this, at least initially in the infant as a random behavior. The environment in which the behavior exists, be it social or physical, is affected by the behavior and in turn "acts" back in various ways. That reaction—positive, negative, or neutral—affects the actor's later behavior. If the reaction has been rewarding to the actor, the same behavior is likely to be emitted in the future in similar situations. If the reaction has been painful or punishing, the behavior is less likely to occur in the future. The behavioral sociologist is interested in the relationship between the *history* of environmental reactions or consequences and the nature of present behavior. The behavioral sociologist is saying that the past consequences of a given behavior govern its present state. By knowing what elicited a certain behavior in the past, we can predict whether an actor will produce the same behavior in the present situation.

Basic Concepts

A key concept in behavioral sociology is *reinforcement*, which may be defined as a reward. Nothing inherent in an object makes it a reward. Reinforcers cannot be defined on a priori grounds apart from their effects on behavior. Thus a "reward" that does not affect the actor is not a reinforcer. Food might generally be considered a reward in our society, but if a given individual is not hungry, food will not serve as a reinforcer. One crucial determinant of whether a given reward will, in fact, serve as as reinforcer is the actors' level of deprivation. If actors have been deprived of food, for example, they will be hungry and food will act as a reinforcer. But if they have just eaten, their level of deprivation will be minimal and food will not be an effective reinforcer. This is an example of physiological deprivation. If we deny people food, sex, water, or air, these things serve as potent reinforcers. If, however, the people's physiological needs are well met, these things will not be useful reinforcers. Reinforcers can also be learned. For example, some people learn to love rock music and others classical music. Thus, there can be major differences in the things people find rewarding. Once we learn to need things, they serve as reinforcers when we are deprived of them.

Reinforcers are defined by their ability to strengthen (that is, reinforce) behavior. For example, being able to hear good music reinforces turning on the stereo system. Reinforcers may be either positive or negative (Baldwin and Baldwin, 1986). Positive reinforcement occurs when behavior is followed by pleasurable rewards, "which thereby increase the probability of behavior occurring in the future" (Bushell and Burgess, 1969:28–29). In this situation the actor is rewarded; for example, the salesperson knocks on a door and makes a sale. Behavioral theorists would view the sale as a positive reinforcement *if* the salesperson then knocks on more doors in the hopes of repeating the success. Baldwin and Baldwin conclude: *"People usually enjoy learning via positive reinforcement because it increases the good effects and pleasurable experiences in their lives"* (1986:15). Negative reinforcement also increases the likelihood of a behavior's occurring in the future, but it takes the form of removing something aversive from the environment. Turning off a noisy radio, for example, may improve a person's ability to write or read. In the future, a person's ability to write or read may improve when the radio is turned off.

In considering reinforcers, *punishment* must also be taken into account: "A consequence which decreases the frequency of the response that precedes it is a *punisher*" (Bushell and Burgess, 1969:29; see also Baldwin and Baldwin, 1986:25). For example, a criticism or even the mere threat of a criticism may prevent someone from repeating a given act. However, a punishment to one person may be a reward to another. A person who loves to argue, for instance, may find criticisms rewarding and may say things in order to elicit them. Thus, in order to determine whether something will be a reward or a punishment, we must know the individual's personal history as well as his or her physiological properties.

Punishments, like reinforcers, can be either positive or negative. Whereas reinforcers strengthen behavior, punishments reduce the frequency of a response. A positive punishment occurs when the onset of an aversive stimulus suppresses behavior. Reprimanding a child every time he or she runs into the street is an example of positive punishment. Punishment takes a negative form when behavior is suppressed because a reward is lost or removed. This is labeled *response cost,* or loss of reinforcers. If we remove or threaten to remove privileges enjoyed by a child because he or she won't do household chores, we are employing a negative form of punishment. Don Bushell and Robert Burgess argued that response cost "is the mainstay of control procedures in social organizations" (1969:30). Rather than give rewards or implement positive punishments, most social organizations prefer to remove, or threaten to remove, rewards people are already enjoying.

As pointed out earlier, the behavioral sociologist is concerned primarily with the relationship between actors and their environment. The reinforcement-punishment relationship between actors and their environment occurs in patterns, some of which are naturally determined (for example, by food deprivation) and some of which are socially determined. In the simplest pattern, reinforcement follows each and every act. This pattern of continuously reinforced behavior is most likely to be found in childhood, when, for example, a child's cry is immediately followed by attention from parents. This pattern is less likely to occur in adulthood. Adult reinforcement is much more likely to be intermittent, with reinforcement occurring at an uneven pace. Traveling salespeople do not expect every knock on a door to produce a sale;

but knocks on doors do lead to some sales, which keep salespeople on the job. If they were never rewarded with a sale, their sales behavior would be *extinguished*, and they would cease functioning as salespeople. Interestingly, continuously reinforced behavior is more easily extinguished than intermittently rewarded behavior. Salespeople become accustomed to intermittent reward, and a good deal of time passes after the last sale before they realize that they may not be rewarded again. Thus extinguishing their sales behavior takes a long time. If they had been rewarded continuously and the rewards suddenly stopped, they might continue working for only a short time. They would cease their activities far more quickly than they would had they been rewarded intermittently.

Reinforcement is far more complex than simply doing something and receiving the desired (or undesired) reaction. Many conditions in the environment determine the probability for reinforcement of a given act. Some conditions make the response likely, whereas others make it less likely. These conditions are things that have in the past been associated with a reinforcement or a punishment. If, for example, the person doing the reinforcing has always worn some sort of uniform, that uniform may elicit a given response even when it is worn by someone else. Similarly, if a classroom has always been associated with punishment, a response to punishment will be elicited even if the student is transferred to a rewarding classroom situation. This is the process by which originally neutral stimuli—for example, the uniform— become *secondary*, or *conditioned, reinforcers*. Once transformed, a neutral stimulus can become a positive reinforcer. Because reinforcement rarely occurs in a vacuum, a number of secondary reinforcers inevitably become associated with the original one. By this process the number of reinforcers mushrooms.

Although many reinforcers are specific to a given situation, some are *generalized reinforcers*. These are defined by Bushell and Burgess as reinforcers that

> have great power and importance in social analyses because they retain their effectiveness in the absence of any specific deprivation. The term "generalized" refers to the fact that these stimuli stand for, represent, or provide access to a wide range of other reinforcers, both unconditioned and conditioned, which may differ from time to time and from person to person.
>
> (Bushell and Burgess, 1969:38).

Money and status are two good examples of generalized reinforcers. They can be used to acquire many other desirable things. Because generalized reinforcers represent a number of other different things, they become more and more reinforcing in themselves. The behavioral sociologist sees the individual as difficult to satiate in terms of such generalized reinforcers. Large amounts of money or status are not likely to dull the desire for more.

Behavior Modification

When a given response is reinforced, a number of other responses similar to the one being rewarded are almost inevitably reinforced at the same time.

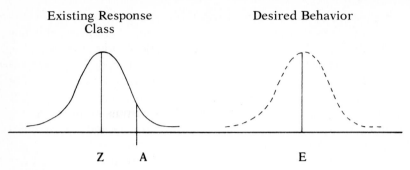

FIGURE 11.1   Behavior Modification: Existing and Desired Behaviors

This fact allows the behavioral sociologist to speak of *systematic shaping of behavior,* or *behavior modification.* Here is the way that John Baldwin and Janice Baldwin define this phenomenon: *"Systematic shaping involves changing behavior in steps of successive approximation toward a preestablished final performance. At each step, reinforcement is given for behavior that best approximates the final performance"* (1986:159). Figure 11.1 illustrates this process.

If a person is already capable of behavior Z, that behavior can be modified to gradually reach behavior E. Because we possess a given reward, we are able to elicit behavior Z from an individual. In eliciting this behavior, we also elicit a number of similar behaviors, including A. Suppose that the behavior we really want to elicit is E. How do we get our subject to respond with behavior E? We begin by rewarding A, which is already in our range of elicited responses. By repeatedly eliciting A, we move the center of the curve beyond A and bring behaviors closer to E, the desired behavior, within our range. Ultimately, we elicit behavior E. The process is illustrated in Figure 11.2.

The process of behavior modification has been adapted to therapeutic situations. Behavior modification is seen as a six-step process:

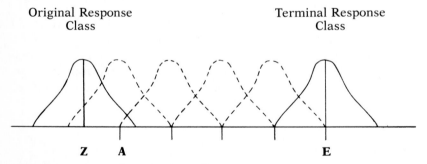

FIGURE 11.2   Behavior Modification: Eliciting the Desired Behavior

1 Therapists must identify the specific final behaviors that they want to elicit.
2 They must determine the nature of the existing response class of the subject, that is, the range of behaviors currently being elicited and how close this is to the desired behavior.
3 Therapists must construct a favorable training site. "This means eliminating distracting stimuli, the possibility of conflicting or incompatible behavior, and providing stimuli which are discriminative for the desired response" (Bushell and Burgess, 1969:43).
4 Therapists must establish motivation in the subject by acquiring an effective reinforcer. Although specific reinforcers can be used, general reinforcers such as money, social attention, and social status are most often used.
5 Therapists must begin the shaping process by "differential reinforcement of responses that are successively closer to the terminal state" (Bushell and Burgess, 1969:43–44).
6 Finally, when the modification has "taken," therapists should apply the reinforcers more intermittently. The reinforcement should eventually come less from an artificial device and more from the natural world.

The applications of behavioral sociology—for example, to behavior modification—set it apart from other sociological theories, including exchange theory. Although there are instances such as the human relations school of industrial sociology, which seeks to manipulate group processes in order to increase the productivity of workers, behavioral sociology has far more of an applied, practical character than any other sociological theory (Baldwin and Baldwin, 1986).

The above discussion emphasizes planned, intentional behavior modification. In fact, however, most behavior modification occurs unintentionally. That is, people on a daily basis engage in actions that modify the behavior of others.

EXCHANGE THEORY

Exchange theory constitutes an effort to take the principles of behaviorism, fuse them with other ideas, and apply them to the concerns of sociologists. Although exchange theory can be traced back many years (Knox, 1963), it underwent a boom in the 1950s and 1960s in the work of George Homans (Beniger and Savory, 1981). Homans's exchange theory can be viewed, at least in part, as a reaction to the social-facts paradigm and its sociological theories, especially structural functionalism.

Homans and Durkheim

Homans (1969) confronted the structural functionalists by directly attacking the work of Emile Durkheim on three points: the issue of emergence, his view of psychology, and his method of explanation. Homans recognized Durkheim's view that during interaction new phenomena emerge. He felt that such a view is acceptable to social behaviorists. However, how do we explain what emerges from interaction? Homans took the position that no new propositions, beyond those already applying to simple individual behavior, are needed. He said, "All the usual examples of emergent social phenomena can readily be shown to follow from psychological propositions" (Homans, 1969:14). Thus, Durkheim thought that emergent forms could be explained only by sociology, whereas Homans felt they could be explained by psychological principles.

Homans pointed out correctly that because Durkheim wrote in the late nineteenth century, the psychology that he knew was primitive. Psychology in Durkheim's day focused primarily on instinctive forms of behavior and assumed that human nature was the same in all individuals. Thus Durkheim was right to disentangle sociology from the psychology of his day. "Sociology is surely not a corollary of the kind of psychology Durkheim had in mind" (Homans, 1969:18). However, contemporary psychology is far more sophisticated and complex than the psychology of Durkheim's time; that Durkheim was able to separate psychology from sociology does not mean that the same feat can be accomplished today.

Finally, Homans attacked Durkheim for his method of explanation. Homans argued that Durkheim considered something explained if we were able to find its cause or causes. Specifically, a social fact is explained when we can find the social facts that cause it. Homans admitted that social facts are often the cause of other social facts, but such a finding does not in his view constitute an explanation. To Homans, what needs to be explained is the *relationship* between cause and effect, why one social fact causes another social fact. Homans thought that explanation was inevitably psychological. (It should be noted that when Homans used the term *psychological* he meant *behavioral*, "the behavior of men as men," as he put it.) Homans's explanation of a particular historical cause and effect is instructive:

> The price rise of the sixteenth century, which I take to be a social fact, was certainly a determining cause of the enclosure movement among English landlords. But were we to construct an explanation why this particular cause has this particular effect, we should have to say that the price rise presented English landlords both with great opportunities for monetary gain and great risks of monetary loss, that enclosure tended to increase the gain and avoid the loss, that the landlords found monetary gain rewarding (which is a state of individual consciousness, if you like), and finally, that men are likely to take actions whose results they find rewarding—which, as I cannot repeat too often, is a general psychological proposition.
>
> (Homans, 1969:19)

Thus individual responses (behavior) always intervene between social facts. Homans argued that social facts lead to individual responses, which in turn lead to new social facts. However, the essential factor is the behavior, not the social fact.

Homans and Lévi-Strauss

Homans reacted not only against Durkheim but also against those who followed in the Durkheimian tradition. Peter P. Ekeh (1974) has argued that Homans's orientation was shaped directly as a reaction against the work of neo-Durkheimian anthropologist Claude Lévi-Strauss (Homans and Schneider, 1955). In fact, what Homans reacted against was Lévi-Strauss's neo-Durkheimian version of exchange theory. (We encounter a very different aspect of Lévi-Strauss's theory in Chapter 13.) We learn a good deal about Homans's exchange theory by examining his reaction to Lévi-Strauss's orientation to the same theoretical perspective.

Ekeh's basic position was that exchange theory emerged out of two "nonmarriageable" traditions. On the one hand, Lévi-Strauss (1949) developed his view of exchange theory, at least in part, in the French collectivist tradition, of which Durkheim was the major exponent. On the other, Homans was the inheritor of the British individualistic tradition, of which Herbert Spencer was a major spokesman. With such different orientations, it is not surprising that Lévi-Strauss and Homans came to have such different images of exchange theory. In Ekeh's view, Lévi-Strauss developed his orientation first, and Homans shaped his own ideas in reaction to the collectivist thrust of Lévi-Strauss's work.

In his dispute with Lévi-Strauss, Homans believed that he was doing battle with a newer version of Durkheimian theory, with its focus on collectivities and its tendency to view the individual as nonessential. Homans saw Durkheim's work (and therefore Lévi-Strauss's) as an assault on "one of the unstated assumptions of the western intellectual tradition, the notion that the nature of individuals determined finally the nature of society" (1962:8). Homans said of Durkheimian functionalism, with its focus on the functions of social facts for society as a whole: "I was suspicious of it from the beginning without learning why. It had been a splinter under my skin that has taken me a long time to get out" (1962:23). And Homans did get the "splinter" of functionalism out, in large part in this critique of Lévi-Strauss's neo-Durkheimian exchange theory: "His reading of Lévi-Strauss . . . was the last straw that broke his patience with functionalism of the Durkheimian type" (Ekeh, 1974:88).

Durkheim saw the actor as constrained by social facts, especially the collective conscience, but Lévi-Strauss went further, because he believed in a collective *un*conscious, which is buried deep in humanity and is unknown to the actors themselves. This was, from Homans's point of view, even more constraining, pernicious, and mystifying than Durkheim's ideas of collective conscience and social facts. As Ekeh put it, "In Lévi-Strauss' work the individual is accorded less of a place in social processes than in Durkheim's sociology" (1974:42). With this general background, we now turn to a brief outline of Lévi-Strauss's exchange theory and, more important, Homans's critical reaction to it.

According to Ekeh, Lévi-Strauss erected his exchange theory on two basic

GEORGE CASPAR HOMANS: An Autobiographical Sketch

How I became a sociologist, which was largely a matter of accident, I have described in other publications. [For a full autobiography, see Homans, 1984.] My sustained work in sociology began with my association, beginning in 1933, with Professors Lawrence Henderson and Elton Mayo at the Harvard Business School. Henderson, a bio-chemist, was studying the physiological characteristics of industrial work, Mayo, a psychologist, the human factors. Mayo was then and later the director of the famous researches at the Hawthorne Plant of the Western Electric Company in Chicago.

I took part in a course of readings and discussions under Mayo's direction. Among other books, Mayo asked his students to read several books by prominent social an-thropologists, particularly Malinowski, Radcliffe-Brown, and Firth. Mayo wanted us to read these books so that we should understand how in aboriginal, in contrast to modern, societies social rituals supported productive work.

I became interested in them for a wholly different reason. In those days the cultural anthropologists were intellectually dominant, and friends of mine in this group, such as Clyde Kluckhohn, insisted that every culture was unique. Instead I began to perceive from my reading that certain institutions of aboriginal societies repeated themselves in places so far separated in time and space that the societies could not have borrowed them from one another. Cultures were not unique and, what was more, their similarities could only be explained on the assumption that human nature was the same the world over. Members of the human species working in similar circumstances had independently created the similar institutions. This was not a popular view at the time. I am not sure it is now.

By this time I had also been exposed to a number of concrete or "field" studies of small human groups both modern and aboriginal. When I was called to active duty in the Navy in World War II, I reflected on this material during long watches at sea. Quite suddenly, I conceived that a number of these studies might be described in concepts common to them all. In a few days I had sketched out such a conceptual scheme.

Back at Harvard with a tenured position after the war, I began working on a book, later entitled *The Human Group*, which was intended to apply my conceptual scheme to the

assumptions. First, he believed that social exchange is a distinctively human process of which lower animals are incapable. By implication, one cannot learn about human exchange from the behavior of nonhuman animals. Humans are capable of culturally directed action, whereas lower animals can respond only naturally. Similarly, Lévi-Strauss saw actors as capable of creative, dynamic action, whereas animals behave in a static way. Homans's reaction to this was that there is no clear distinction between humans and lower animals. Thus he rejected all Lévi-Strauss's ideas about the distinctiveness of human behavior.

Second, Lévi-Strauss rejected the idea that human exchange can be explained in terms of individual self-interest. He did not deny that such self-interest may be involved, but he argued that it is not sufficient to sustain social relationships based on exchange. Lévi-Strauss argued that social exchange is

studies in question. In the course of this work it occurred to me that a conceptual scheme was useful only as the starting point of a science. What was next required were propositions relating the concepts to one another. In *The Human Group,* I stated a number of such propositions, which seemed to hold good for the groups I had chosen.

I had long known Professor Talcott Parsons and was now closely associated with him in the Department of Social Relations. The sociological profession looked upon him as its leading theorist. I decided that what he called theories were only conceptual schemes, and that a theory was not a theory unless it contained at least a few propositions. I became confident that this view was correct by reading several books on the philosophy of science.

Nor was it enough that a theory should contain propositions. A theory of a phenomenon was an explanation of it. Explanation consisted in showing that one or more propositions of a low order of generality followed in logic from more general propositions applied to what were variously called given or boundary conditions or parameters. I stated my position on this issue in my little book *The Nature of Social Science* (1967).

I then asked myself what general propositions I could use in this way to explain the empirical propositions I had stated in *The Human Group* and other propositions brought to my attention by later reading of field and experimental studies in social psychology. The general propositions would have to meet only one condition: in accordance with my original insight, they should apply to individual human beings as members of a species.

Such propositions were already at hand—luckily, for I could not have invented them for myself. They were the propositions of behavioral psychology as stated by my old friend B. F. Skinner and others. They held good of persons both when acting alone in the physical environment and when in interaction with other persons. In the two editions of my book *Social Behavior* (1961 and revised in 1974), I used these propositions to try to explain how, under appropriate given conditions, relatively enduring social structures could arise from, and be maintained by, the actions of individuals, who need not have intended to create the structures. This I conceive to be the central intellectual problem of sociology.

Once the structures have been created, they have further effects on the behavior of persons who take part in them or come into contact with them. But these further effects are explained by the same propositions as those used to explain the creation and maintenance of the structures in the first place. The structures only provide new given conditions to which the propositions are to be applied. My sociology remains fundamentally individualistic and not collectivistic.

[George Homans died in 1989.]

sustained by supraindividual forces, by collective forces, by cultural forces. This human exchange is seen by Lévi-Strauss as symbolic rather than self-interested.

Society plays a variety of roles in the exchange process. Where there is scarcity, society must intervene to provide rules of appropriate conduct in order to forestall destructive human conduct. In some situations a social exchange is justified in terms of social expectations rather than the benefits the exchange brings those involved. This is done in order to inhibit the development of disruptive negative feelings. For example, people had a wedding reception because it is the custom rather than because they want to benefit from the gifts received. Finally, customs may develop in which one feels obliged to reciprocate another's action not by repaying him or her but by rewarding a third party. For example, instead of repaying parents for all they have done, children may instead pass similar benefits on to their own children. In general, Lévi-Strauss saw a *moral system of exchange* rather than the operation of individual self-interest.

Homans, of course, rejected all this. He focused largely on two-party exchanges rather than on the more extended societal forms of exchange implied in the last example of parent and child. Homans also rejected the emphasis on a moral system, arguing instead that the basis of human exchange lies in self-interest based on a combination of economic and psychological needs.

Homans and Structural Functionalism

In addition to these specific attacks on Durkheim and Lévi-Strauss, Homans attacked the structural-functionalist explanation of *institutions*, which he defined as "relatively persistent patterns of social behavior to whose maintenance the actions of many men contribute" (1969:6). He argued that four types of explanation have been used in analyzing institutions; the two he rejected are associated with structural functionalism.

The first type of explanation is *structural*; it argues that a "particular institution exists because of its relation to other institutions in a social system" (1969:6). For Homans, the assertion that certain institutions are correlated with others does not explain them. The second type of explanation, which is *functional*, contends that "the institution exists because the society could not survive or remain in equilibrium without it" (Homans, 1969:6). This is a vulgarized form of functional explanation that ignores the modern work on the subject, such as that of Robert Merton (1949/1968). Having set up the functional explanation as a straw man, Homans then attacked it:

> The trouble with functional explanations in sociology is not a matter of principle but of practice. From the characteristic general proposition of functionalism we can draw the conclusion in logic that a society failing to survive did *not* possess institutions of type *x*—whatever *x* may be. Now there are societies—a very few—that have not survived in any sense of the word. For some of these societies we have accounts of the social organization before their disappearance, and it turns out that they did not possess institutions of type *x*. If these societies failed to survive, it was not for lack of social institutions, unless resistance to measles and alcohol be a social institution. That is, there is inadequate evidence so far for the truth of the general propositions of functionalism—and after all truth does make a difference. It is conceivable that the difficulties will be overcome, that better statements of the conditions for the survival or equilibrium of any society may be devised, from which nothing but true conclusions will be drawn. But in spite of endless efforts nothing of the sort is in sight. Whatever its status in principle, functional explanation in sociology is in practice a failure.
>
> (Homans, 1969:9)

Had Homans taken on Merton's functional paradigm, rather than a vulgarized form of functionalism that no contemporary functionalist would support, we could take Homans more seriously. Having taken on only easy targets, Homans could cavalierly conclude that structural explanation is no explanation at all and that functional explanation is unsatisfactory, since it leads to both true and false conclusions.

Homans (1969) used the label *historical* for the third type of explanation of institutions. Here the institution is seen as the end product of a historical process. Interestingly, he saw historical explanation as basically *psychological* explication, his fourth type of explanation. He saw institutional change as ubiquitous and its study as central to sociology. When we perform a historical analysis correctly, we must conclude that the explanation of this change lies at the psychological level:

> All human institutions are products of processes of historical change. In fact, most institutions are continually changing. When we have enough factual information, which we often do not, even to begin explaining historical change, and when we try to supply the major premises of our unstated deductive systems, we find that there are certain premises we absolutely cannot avoid using, and that these premises are not propositions about the interrelations of institutions, as in structural explanation, or propositions about the conditions for the survival of societies, as in functional explanation, but . . . propositions about the behavior of men as men. . . . That is, they are psychological propositions: in their major premises history and psychology are one.
>
> (Homans, 1969:11)

In sum, Homans argued that institutional change must be explained by sociologists and that any explanation of change will be psychological at its base. Homans illustrated this with the example of the introduction of power-driven machinery into the English textile industry in the eighteenth century. He argued that this event was of great sociological importance, because it was one of the first steps in the Industrial Revolution that led to many of our present-day institutions. His starting point was the growth in English cotton exports in the eighteenth century:

> [This] led to an increased demand on the part of the industrial entrepreneurs for supplies of cotton thread, a demand that was not fully met by the existing labor force, spinning thread by hand on spinning wheels, so that the wages of spinners began to rise, threatening to raise the price of cloth and thus check the expansion of trade.
>
> (Homans, 1969:10)

To prevent this rise in wages, costs, and prices and the reduction in trade, entrepreneurs in the textile industry, who already knew of power-driven machines in other industries, developed machines driven by waterpower or steam that could spin several threads at a time. Driven by the pursuit of higher profits, many tried to develop such machines, and some succeeded.

Homans argued that this process can be reduced to a deductive system that would explain why entrepreneurs took the actions they did. This deductive system, based upon psychological principles, takes the following form:

1 Men are likely to take actions that they perceive are, in the circumstances, likely to achieve rewarding results.
2 The entrepreneurs were men.
3 As entrepreneurs, they were likely to find results in the form of increasing profits rewarding (Homans, 1969).

Starting with his basic assumption about the psychological nature of human beings, Homans argued that he had explained the coming of power-driven machines to the eighteenth-century English textile industry. By using this example, Homans concluded that historical change can be explained only by psychological principles. Homans drummed structural functionalism out of sociology and argued that the only true sociology is based on psychological principles. However, Homans was more than simply polemical; he tried to develop a theory based on psychological principles.

Homans's Basic Propositions

Although some of Homans's propositions deal with at least two interacting individuals, he was careful to point out that his propositions are based on psychological principles. According to Homans, they are psychological for two reasons. First, "they are usually stated and empirically tested by persons who call themselves psychologists" (Homans, 1967:39–40). Second, and more important, they are psychological because of the level at which they deal with the individual in society: "They are propositions about the behavior of individual human beings, rather than propositions about groups or societies as such; and *the behavior of men, as men,* is generally considered the province of psychology" (Homans, 1967:40; italics added). As a result of this position, Homans admitted to being "what has been called—and it is a horrid phrase—a psychological reductionist" (1974:12). Reductionism, to Homans is "the process of showing how the propositions of one named science [in this case, sociology] follow in logic from the more general propositions of another named science [in this case, psychology]" (1984:338).

Although Homans made the case for psychological principles, he did not think of individuals as isolated. He recognized that people are social and spend a considerable portion of their time interacting with other people. He attempted to explain social behavior with psychological principles: "What the position [Homans's] does assume is that the general propositions of psychology, which are propositions about the effects on human behavior of the results thereof, do not change when the results come from other men rather than from the physical environment" (Homans, 1967:59). Homans did not deny the Durkheimian position that something new emerges from interaction. Instead, he argued that those emergent properties can be explained by psychological principles; there is no need for new sociological propositions to explain social facts. He used the basic sociological concept of a norm to illustrate this:

> The great example of a social fact is a social norm, and the norms of the groups to which they belong certainly constrain towards conformity the behavior of many

individuals. The question is not that of the existence of constraint, but of its explanation. . . . The norm does not constrain automatically: individuals conform, when
they do so, because they perceive it is to their net advantage to conform, and it is
psychology that deals with the effect on behavior of perceived advantage.

(Homans, 1967:60)

In numerous publications Homans detailed a program to, in his words,
"bring men back in[to]" sociology, but he also tried to develop a theory that
focuses on psychology, people, and the "elementary forms of social life." That
theory has come to be called *exchange theory*. According to Homans, it "envis-
ages social *behavior* as an exchange of activity, tangible or intangible, and more
or less rewarding or costly, between at least two persons" (1961:13; italics
added).

In the example discussed above, Homans sought to explain the development of power-driven machinery in the textile industry and thereby the Industrial Revolution through the psychological principle that people are likely to
act in such a way as to increase their rewards. More generally, in his version
of exchange theory, he sought to explain elementary social behavior in terms
of rewards and costs. He was motivated in part by the work of the social
factists, in particular the structural-functional theories of his acknowledged
"colleague and friend," Talcott Parsons. He argued that such theories "possess
every virtue except that of explaining anything" (Homans, 1961:10). To
Homans, the structural functionalists did little more than create conceptual
categories and schemes. Homans admitted that a scientific sociology needs
such categories, but sociology "also needs a set of general propositions about
the relations among the categories, for without such propositions explanation
is impossible. No explanation without propositions!" (1974:10). Homans,
therefore, set for himself the task of developing those propositions that focus
on the psychological level; these form the groundwork of exchange theory.

In *Social Behavior: Its Elementary Forms* (1961, 1974),[7] Homans acknowledged
that his exchange theory is derived from both behavioral psychology and elementary economics. In fact, Homans (1984) regrets that his theory was labeled
"exchange theory" because he sees it as a behavioral psychology applied to
specific situations. Homans began with a discussion of the exemplar of the
behaviorist paradigm, B. F. Skinner, in particular of Skinner's study of
pigeons:[8]

Suppose, then, that a fresh or naive pigeon is in its cage in the laboratory. One of
the items in its inborn repertory of behavior which it uses to explore its environment
is the peck. As the pigeon wanders around the cage pecking away, it happens to
hit a round red target, at which point the waiting psychologists or, it may be, an
automatic machine feeds it grain. The evidence is that the probability of the pigeon's

---

[7] In the following discussion we move back and forth between the two editions of Homans's
book. We do not restrict ourselves to the revised edition because many aspects of the first edition
more clearly reflect Homans's position. In the preface to the revised edition, he said that although
it is a thorough revision, he had not "altered the substance of the underlying argument" (Homans,
1974:v). Thus we feel safe in dealing simultaneously with both volumes.

[8] Skinner also studied other species, including humans.

emitting the behavior again—the probability, that is, of its not just pecking but pecking on the target—has increased. In Skinner's language the pigeon's behavior in pecking the target is an *operant;* the operant has been *reinforced;* grain is the *reinforcer;* and the pigeon has undergone *operant conditioning.* Should we prefer our language to be ordinary English, we may say that the pigeon has learned to peck the target by being rewarded for doing so.

(Homans, 1961:18)

Skinner was interested in this instance in pigeons; Homans's concern was humans. According to Homans, Skinner's pigeons are not engaged in a true exchange relationship with the psychologist. The pigeon is engaged in a one-sided exchange relationship, whereas human exchanges are at least two-sided. The pigeon is being reinforced by the grain, but the psychologist is not truly being reinforced by the pecks of the pigeon. The pigeon is carrying on the same sort of relationship with the psychologist as it would with the physical environment. Because there is no reciprocity, Homans defined this as *individual behavior.* Homans seemed to relegate the study of this sort of behavior to the psychologist, whereas he urged the sociologist to study social behavior "where the activity of each of at least two animals reinforces (or punishes) the activity of the other, and where accordingly each influences the other" (1961:30). However, it is significant that, according to Homans, *no new propositions* are needed to explain social behavior as opposed to individual behavior. The laws of individual behavior as developed by Skinner in his study of pigeons explain social behavior as long as we take into account the complications of mutual reinforcement. Homans admitted that he might ultimately have to go beyond the principles derived by Skinner, but only reluctantly.

In his theoretical work, Homans restricted himself to everyday social interaction. It is clear, however, that he believed that a sociology built on his principles would ultimately be able to explain all social behavior. Here is the case Homans used to exemplify the kind of exchange relationship he was interested in:

> Suppose that two men are doing paperwork jobs in an office. According to the office rules, each should do his job by himself, or, if he needs help, he should consult the supervisor. One of the men, whom we shall call Person, is not skillful at the work and would get it done better and faster if he got help from time to time. In spite of the rules he is reluctant to go to the supervisor, for to confess his incompetence might hurt his chances for promotion. Instead he seeks out the other man, whom we shall call Other for short, and asks him for help. Other is more experienced at the work than is Person; he can do his work well and quickly and be left with time to spare, and he has reason to suppose that the supervisor will not go out of his way to look for a breach of rules. Other gives Person help and in return Person gives Other thanks and expressions of approval. The two men have exchanged help and approval.

(Homans, 1961:31–32)

Although Homans would ultimately deal with more complex social behavior, initially he aimed his exchange theory at this level. Focusing on this sort of situation, and basing his ideas on Skinner's findings, Homans developed several propositions. These are the basis of his exchange theory of social behavior.

The Success Proposition

> For all actions taken by persons, the more often a particular action of a person is rewarded, the more likely the person is to perform that action.
>
> (Homans, 1974:16)

In terms of Homans's Person-Other example in an office situation, this proposition means that a person is more likely to ask others for advice if he or she has been rewarded in the past with useful advice. Furthermore, the more often a person received useful advice in the past, the more often he or she will request more advice. Similarly, the other person will be more willing to give advice and give it more frequently if he or she often has been rewarded with approval in the past. Generally, behavior in accord with the success proposition involves three stages: first, a person's action; next, a rewarded result; and finally, a repetition of the original action or at minimum one similar in at least some respects.

Homans specified a number of things about the success proposition. First, although it is generally true that increasingly frequent rewards lead to increasingly frequent actions, this cannot go on indefinitely. At some point individuals simply cannot act that way as frequently. Second, the shorter the interval between behavior and reward, the more likely a person is to repeat the behavior. Conversely, long intervals between behavior and reward lower the likelihood of repeat behavior. Finally, it was Homans's view that intermittent rewards are more likely to elicit repeat behavior than regular rewards. Regular rewards lead to boredom and satiation, whereas rewards at irregular intervals (as in gambling) are very likely to elicit repeat behaviors.

The Stimulus Proposition

> If in the past the occurrence of a particular stimulus, or set of stimuli, has been the occasion on which a person's action has been rewarded, then the more similar the present stimuli are to the past ones, the more likely the person is to perform the action, or some similar action.
>
> (Homans, 1974:23)

Again we look at Homans's office example: If, in the past, Person and Other found the giving and getting of advice rewarding, then they are likely to engage in similar actions in similar situations in the future. Homans offered an even more down to earth example: "A fisherman who has cast his line into a dark pool and has caught a fish becomes more apt to fish in dark pools again" (1974:23).

Homans was interested in the process of *generalization*, that is, the tendency to extend behavior to similar circumstances. In the fishing example, one aspect of generalization would be to move from fishing in dark pools to fishing in any pool with any degree of shadiness. Similarly, success in catching fish is likely to lead from one kind of fishing to another (for instance, freshwater to saltwater) or even from fishing to hunting. However, the process of *discrimination* is also of importance. That is, the actor may fish only under the specific circumstances that proved successful in the past. For one thing, if the conditions under which success occurred were too complicated, then similar conditions may not stimulate behavior. If the crucial stimulus occurs too long before behavior is required, then it may not actually stimulate that behavior. An actor can become oversensitized to stimuli, especially if they are very valuable to the actor. In fact, the actor could respond to irrelevant stimuli, at least until the situation is corrected by repeated failures. All this is affected by the individual's alertness or attentiveness to stimuli.

The Value Proposition

The more valuable to a person is the result of his action, the more likely he is to perform the action.

(Homans, 1974:25)

In the office example, if the rewards each offers to the other are considered valuable, then the actors are more likely to perform the desired behaviors than if the rewards are not valuable. At this point, Homans introduced the concepts of rewards and punishments. Rewards are actions with positive values; an increase in rewards is more likely to elicit the desired behavior. Punishments are actions with negative values; an increase in punishment means that the actor is less likely to manifest undesired behaviors. Homans found punishments to be an inefficient means of getting people to change their behavior, because people may react in undesirable ways to the punishment. It is preferable simply not to reward undesirable behavior; then such behavior eventually becomes extinguished. Rewards are clearly to be preferred, but they may be in short supply. Homans did make it clear that his is not simply a hedonistic theory; rewards can be either materialistic (for example, money) or altruistic (helping others).

The Deprivation-Satiation Proposition

The more often in the recent past a person has received a particular reward, the less valuable any further unit of that reward becomes for him.

(Homans, 1974:29)

In the office, Person and Other may reward each other so often for giving and getting advice that the rewards cease to be valuable to each other. Time is crucial here; people are less likely to become satiated if particular rewards are stretched over a long period of time.

At this point, Homans defined two other critical concepts: cost and profit. The *cost* of any behavior is defined as the rewards lost in forgoing alternative lines of action. *Profit* in social exchange is seen as the greater number of rewards gained over costs incurred. The latter led Homans to recast the deprivation-satiation proposition as "the greater the profit a person receives as a result of his action, the more likely he is to perform the action" (1974:31).

The Aggression-Approval Propositions

Proposition A: When a person's action does not receive the reward he expected, or receives punishment he did not expect, he will be angry; he becomes more likely to perform aggressive behavior, and the results of such behavior become more valuable to him.

(Homans, 1974:37)

In the office case, if Person does not get the advice he or she expected and Other does not receive the praise he or she anticipated, then both are likely to be angry.[9] We are surprised to find the concepts of frustration and anger in Homans's work, because they would seem to refer to mental states. In fact, Homans admitted as much: "When a person does not get what he expected, he is said to be frustrated. A purist in behaviorism would not refer to the expectation at all, because the word seems to refer . . . to a state of mind" (1974:31). Homans went on to argue that frustration of such expectations need *not* refer "only" to an internal state. It can also refer to "wholly external events," observable not just by Person but also by outsiders.

Proposition A on aggression-approval refers only to negative emotions, whereas Proposition B deals with more positive emotions:

Proposition B: When a person's action receives the reward he expected, especially a greater reward than he expected, or does not receive punishment he expected, he will be pleased; he becomes more likely to perform approving behavior, and the results of such behavior become more valuable to him.

(Homans, 1974:39)

For example, in the office, when Person gets the advice that he or she expects and Other gets the praise that he or she expects, both are pleased and more likely to get or give advice. Advice and praise become more valuable to each.

---

[9] Although Homans still called this the "law of distributive justice" in the revised later edition, he developed the concept more extensively in the first edition. *Distributive justice* refers to whether the rewards and costs are distributed fairly among the individuals involved. In fact, Homans originally stated it as a proposition: "The more to a man's disadvantage the rule of distributive justice fails of realization, the more likely he is to display the emotional behavior we call anger" (1961:75).

The Rationality Proposition

In choosing between alternative actions, a person will choose that one for which, as perceived by him at the time, the value, V, of the result, multiplied by the probability, p, of getting the result, is the greater.

(Homans, 1974:43)

While the earlier propositions rely heavily on behaviorism, the rationality proposition demonstrates most clearly the influence of the economist's rational choice theory on Homans's approach. In economic terms, actors who act in accord with the rationality proposition are maximizing their utilities.

Basically, people examine and make calculations about the various alternative actions open to them. They compare the amount of rewards associated with each course of action. They also calculate the likelihood that they will actually receive the rewards. Highly valued rewards will be devalued if the actors think it unlikely that they will obtain them. On the other hand, lesser-valued rewards will be enhanced if they are seen as highly attainable. Thus, there is an interaction between the value of the reward and the likelihood of attainment. The most desirable rewards are those that are *both* very valuable *and* highly attainable. The least desirable rewards are those that are not very valuable and are unlikely to be attained.

Homans relates the rationality proposition to the success, stimulus, and value propositions. The rationality proposition tells us that whether or not people will perform an action depends on their perceptions of the probability of success. But what determines this perception? Homans argues that perceptions of whether chances of success are high or low are shaped by past successes and the similarity of the present situation to past successful situations. The rationality proposition also does not tell us why an actor values one reward more than another; for this we need the value proposition. In these ways, Homans links his rationality principle to his more behavioristic propositions.

In the end, Homans's theory can be condensed to a view of the actor as a rational profit seeker. However, Homans's theory was weak on mental states and large-scale structures. For example, on consciousness Homans admitted the need for a "more fully developed psychology" (1974:45).

Despite such weaknesses, Homans remained a behaviorist who worked resolutely at the level of individual behavior. He argued that large-scale structures can be understood if we adequately understand elementary social behavior. He contended that exchange processes are "identical" at the individual and societal levels, although he granted that at the societal level, "the way the fundamental processes are combined is more complex" (Homans, 1974:358).

Homans's exchange theory called forth strong criticism in sociology (see, for example, Abrahamsson, 1970; Ekeh, 1974; Mitchell, 1978; Molm, 1981). We focus on the two crucial weaknesses in Homans's theory as well as criticisms of them by other sociologists. The key problems are Homans's failure to deal with mental processes and his unwillingness to deal adequately with the cultural and social levels.

Criticisms of Homans's Theory of Consciousness

A major criticism of Homans's theory is its failure to do an adequate analysis of consciousness. Bengt Abrahamsson, for example, argued that Homans tends to focus on overt behaviors and ignore the inner experiences of the actors: "Knowing the *experience* of individuals and their perceptions of rewards of certain acts is often of great importance for understanding and predicting their behavior" (1970:283). Jack N. Mitchell also was critical of Homans's reductionism and his failure to deal with the dynamics of consciousness: "Any theory that purports to explain or 'get to' the nature of man's social behavior cannot assume explicitly or tacitly that interaction is merely the working out of the rationality of needs, biological or psychological—or of economic processes. What is lacking . . . is a sense of . . . uncertainty, problematics and negotiation" (1978:81). To overcome the limitations of exchange theory in the analysis of consciousness, Mitchell argued for the incorporation into exchange theory of insights from the work of social definitionists such as Goffman and Garfinkel.

Criticisms of Homans's Theory of Society and Culture

Ekeh (1974), for example, criticized Homans for focusing solely on two-person, or dyadic, exchange and for downplaying more large-scale patterns of exchange. Ekeh was also critical of Homans for ignoring the norms and values that symbolically shape exchange relations. However, the criticism of Talcott Parsons, from a social-factist point of view, best illustrates the problems in Homans's work at the societal level.

Parsons versus Homans Parsons pinpointed two basic differences between himself and Homans. First, he contended that Homans tended to "slur" the difference between the behavior of people and that of lower animals. Parsons, however, saw a very clear dividing line. To Parsons, the principles used to explain human behavior are qualitatively different from those used to explain animal behavior. Parsons objected to Homans's derivation of human exchange principles from Skinner's study of pigeons.

Parsons's second objection is even more crucial: "The most general formulations applicable to men as men (which *I* would call principles of *action*, rather than psychological) do *not* suffice to explain . . . the complex subsystems of action" (1964:216). In other words, psychological principles do not, indeed cannot, explain social facts. Homans had been unable to show how psychological principles apply at the societal level. As Parsons said, "Homans is under obligation to show how his principles can account for the principal structural features of large scale social systems" (1964:216). He concluded that even if Homans were to try to do this, he would inevitably fail, because social facts are variables capable of explaining, and being explained, without reference to Homans's psychological principles:

> The alternative to this [Homans's] emphasis is to see acting units as part of organized systems, which have properties other than those attributed to . . . the . . . interaction between "men as men." They have languages, cultural values, legal systems, various kinds of institutional norms and generalized media. Concrete behavior is not a function simply of elementary properties, but of the kinds of systems, their various structures and the processes taking place within them. From this point of view it is quite legitimate to be concerned with the organization of complex systems . . . long before their properties can be derived from elementary principles.
>
> (Parsons, 1964:219)

In reply to Parsons, Homans maintained that the key issue concerns explanations of the structures and institutions of complex societies: "Here is the nub of the matter. Parsons thinks psychological propositions do not suffice to explain them; I think they do" (1971:375). Homans recognized that social facts emerge out of interaction, but he thought that they could be explained by psychological principles. Conversely, Parsons thought that only social facts could explain social facts.

Homans replied to the attack by Parsons and others with a counterattack aimed at social factists:

> Let them therefore specify what properties of social behavior they consider to be emergent and show, by constructing the appropriate deductive systems, how they propose to explain them without making use of psychological propositions. I guarantee to show either that the explanations fail to explain or that they in fact use psychological propositions, in however disguised a form.
>
> (Homans, 1971:376)

What has occurred between Homans and Parsons is a series of charges and countercharges, with each party claiming that the other's theory has little explanatory power. Replying to Parsons's statements that he is under an obligation to show how his principles can explain the structural features of large-scale societies, Homans said: "I am under no more obligation than Parsons is under himself, who has not shown how his principles can explain the existence of these principal structural features. Indeed, it is not at all clear what his principles *are*" (1971:376). We are left with an unresolved argument in which Parsons says that Homans has not explained structure and Homans says that Parsons has not explained structure. However, the dialogue does clarify once again the battle lines between the social-facts and social-behavior paradigms in general and between structural functionalism and exchange theory in particular.

Blau's Integrated Exchange Theory

Whereas Homans and Parsons can manage nothing better than a simple declaration of the boundaries that separate them, Peter Blau (1964) went a good deal further in his effort to develop an exchange theory that combines social behaviorism and social factism. (We encounter a very different form of Blau's theorizing in Chapter 13.) Blau's goal was "an understanding of social structure on the basis of an analysis of the social processes that govern the relations between individuals and groups. The basic question . . . is how social life becomes organized into increasingly complex structures of associations among men" (1964:2). Blau's intention, as stated here, was to go beyond Homans's concern with elementary forms of social life and into an analysis of complex structures. Homans was content to work at the behavioral level, but Blau viewed such work only as a means to a larger end: "The main sociological purpose of studying processes of face-to-face interaction is to lay the foundation for an understanding of the social structures that evolve and the emergent social forces that characterize their development" (1964:13).[10]

Blau focused on the process of exchange, which, in his view, directs much of human behavior and underlies relationships among individuals as well as among groups. In effect, Blau envisioned a four-stage sequence leading from interpersonal exchange to social structure to social change:

Step 1: Personal exchange transactions between people give rise to . . .
Step 2: Differentiation of status and power, which leads to . . .
Step 3: Legitimization and organization, which sow the seeds of . . .
Step 4: Opposition and change.

On the individual level, Blau and Homans were interested in similar processes. However, Blau's concept of social exchange is limited to actions that are contingent, that depend on rewarding reactions from others—actions that cease when expected reactions are not forthcoming. People are attracted to each other for a variety of reasons that induce them to establish social associations. Once initial ties are forged, the rewards that they provide to each other serve to maintain and enhance the bonds. The opposite situation is also possible: with insufficient rewards, an association will weaken or break. Rewards that are exchanged can be either intrinsic (for instance, love, affection, respect) or extrinsic (for instance, money, physical labor). The parties cannot always reward each other equally; when there is inequality in the exchange, a difference of power will emerge within an association.

When one party needs something from another but has nothing comparable to offer in return, four alternatives are available. First, people can force other people to help them. Second, they can find another source to obtain what they need. Third, they can attempt to get along without what they need from the

---

[10] It is interesting to note that Blau (1987b) no longer accepts the idea of building macro theory on a micro base.

others. Finally, and most important, they can subordinate themselves to the others, thereby giving the others "generalized credit" in their relationship; the others then can draw on this credit when they want them to do something. (This latter alternative is, of course, the essential characteristic of power.)

Up to this point, Blau's position is similar to Homans's position, but Blau extended his theory to the level of social facts. He noted, for example, that we cannot analyze processes of social interaction apart from the social structure that surrounds them. Social structure emerges from social interaction, but once this occurs, social structures have a separate existence that affects the process of interaction.

Social interaction exists first within social groups. People are attracted to a group when they feel that the relationships offer more rewards than those in other groups. Because they are attracted to the group, they want to be accepted. To be accepted, they must offer group members rewards. This involves impressing the group members by showing the members that associating with the new people will be rewarding. The relationship with the group members will be solidified when the newcomers have impressed the group—when members have received the rewards they expected. Newcomers' efforts to impress group members generally lead to group cohesion, but competition and, ultimately, social differentiation can occur when too many people actively seek to impress each other with their abilities to reward.

The paradox here is that although group members with the ability to impress can be attractive associates, their impressive characteristics also can arouse fears of dependence in other group members and cause them to acknowledge their attraction only reluctantly. In the early stages of group formation, competition for social recognition among group members actually acts as a screening test for potential leaders of the group. Those best able to reward are most likely to end up in leadership positions. Those group members with less ability to reward want to continue to receive the rewards offered by the potential leaders, and this usually more than compensates for their fears of becoming dependent on them. Ultimately, those individuals with the greater ability to reward emerge as leaders, and the group is differentiated.

The inevitable differentiation of the group into leaders and followers creates a renewed need for integration. Once they have acknowledged the leader's status, followers have an even greater need for integration. Earlier, followers flaunted their most impressive qualities. Now, to achieve integration with fellow followers, they display their weaknesses. This is, in effect, a public declaration that they no longer want to be leaders. This self-deprecation leads to sympathy and social acceptance from the other also-rans. The leader (or leaders) also engages in some self-deprecation at this point, in order to improve overall group integration. By admitting that subordinates are superior in some areas, the leader reduces the pain associated with subordination and demonstrates that he or she does not seek control over every area of group life. These types of forces serve to reintegrate the group despite its new, differentiated status.

All this is reminiscent of Homans's discussion of exchange theory. Blau, however, moved to the societal level and differentiated between two types of social organization. Exchange theorists and behavioral sociologists also recognize this emergence, but there is, as we will see, a basic difference between Blau and "purer" social behaviorists on this issue. The first type, in which Blau recognized the emergent properties of social groups, emerges from the processes of exchange and competition discussed above. The second type of social organization is not emergent but is explicitly established to achieve specified objectives—for example, manufacturing goods that can be sold for a profit, participating in bowling tournaments, engaging in collective bargaining, and winning political victories. In discussing these two types of organization, Blau clearly moved beyond the "elementary forms of social behavior" that are typically of interest to social behaviorists.

In addition to being concerned with these organizations, Blau was interested in the subgroups within them. For example, he argued that leadership and opposition groups are found in both types of organization. In the first type, these two groups emerge out of the process of interaction. In the second, leadership and opposition groups are built into the structure of the organization. In either case, differentiation between the groups is inevitable, and this lays the groundwork for opposition and conflict within the organization between leaders and followers.

Having moved beyond Homans's elementary forms of behavior and into complex social structures, Blau knew that he must adapt exchange theory to the societal level. Blau recognized the essential difference between small groups and large collectivities, whereas Homans minimized this difference in his effort to explain all social behavior in terms of basic psychological principles.

> The complex social structures that characterize large collectives differ fundamentally from the simpler structures of small groups. A structure of social relations develops in a small group in the course of social interaction among its members. Since there is no direct social interaction among most members of a large community or entire society, some other mechanism must mediate the structure of social relations among them.
>
> (Blau, 1964:253)

This statement requires scrutiny. On the one hand, Blau clearly ruled out social behaviorism as an adequate paradigm for dealing with complex social structures. On the other, he ruled out the social-definitionist paradigm, because he argued that social interaction and the social definitions that accompany it do not occur directly in a large-scale organization. Thus, starting from the social-behavior paradigm, Blau aligned himself with the social-facts paradigm in dealing with more complex social structures.

For Blau, the mechanisms that mediate among the complex social structures are the norms and values (the value consensus) that exist within society:

Commonly agreed upon values and norms serve as media of social life and as mediating links for social transactions. They make indirect social exchange possible, and they govern the processes of social integration and differentiation in complex social structures as well as the development of social organization and reorganization in them.

(Blau, 1964:255)

Other mechanisms mediate among social structures, but Blau focused upon value consensus. Looking first at social norms, Blau argued that they substitute indirect exchange for direct exchange. One member conforms to the group norm and receives approval for that conformity and implicit approval for the fact that conformity contributes to the group's maintenance and stability. In other words, the group or collectivity engages in an exchange relationship with the individual. This is in contrast to Homans's simpler notion, which focused on interpersonal exchange. Blau offered a number of examples of collectivity-individual exchanges replacing individual-individual exchanges:

Staff officials do not assist line officials in their work in exchange for rewards received from them, but furnishing this assistance is the official obligation of staff members, and in return for discharging these obligations they receive financial rewards from the company.

Organized philanthropy provides another example of indirect social exchange. In contrast to the old-fashioned lady bountiful who brought her baskets to the poor and received their gratitude and appreciation, there is no direct contact and no exchange between individual donors and recipients in contemporary organized charity. Wealthy businessmen and members of the upper class make philanthropic contributions to conform with the normative expectations that prevail in their social class and to earn the social approval of their peers, not in order to earn the gratitude of the individuals who benefit from their charity.

(Blau, 1964:260)

The concept of norm in Blau's formulation moves Blau to the level of exchange between individual and collectivity, but the concept of values moves him to the largest-scale societal level and to the analysis of the relationship *among collectivities.* Blau said:

Common values of various types can be conceived of as media of social transactions that expand the compass of social interaction and the structure of social relations through social space and time. Consensus on social values serves as the basis for extending the range of social transactions beyond the limits of direct social contacts and for perpetuating social structures beyond the life span of human beings. Value standards can be considered media of social life in two senses of the term; the value context is the medium that molds the form of social relationships; and common values are the mediating links for social associations and transactions on a broad scale.

(Blau, 1964:263–264)

In Blau's view, there are four basic types of values, each of which performs different functions. First are *particularistic* values, which are the media of integration and solidarity. These values serve to unite the members of a group around such things as patriotism, or the good of the school, or the company. These are seen as similar at the collective level to sentiments of personal attraction that unite individuals on a face-to-face basis. However, they extend integrative bonds beyond mere personal attraction. Particularistic values also differentiate the in-group from the out-group, thereby enhancing their unifying function.

The second type of values is *universalistic* values. These are standards by which the relative worth of the various things that can be exchanged is assessed. The existence of these standards allows for the possibility of indirect exchange. An individual may make a contribution to a segment of a community, and universalistic values allow the community to assess the value of the contribution and to reward the individual in an appropriate manner (for example, by higher social status).

The values that *legitimate authority* are the third type. The value system that accords some people (for example, bosses, presidents) more power than others extends the scope of organized social control. This is related to the fourth type of value—values of *opposition*. Opposition (or revolutionary) values allow for the spread of a feeling for a need for change far beyond that possible merely by personal contact among those who oppose the established order. These values (for example, socialism and anarchism in a capitalist society) legitimate opposition to those whose power is legitimated by authority values.

Blau's four types of values have carried us far from Homans's version of exchange theory. The individual and individual behavior, paramount for Homans, have almost disappeared in Blau's conception. Taking the place of the individual are a wide variety of *social facts.* For example, Blau discussed groups, organizations, collectivities, societies, norms, and values. Blau's analysis is concerned with what holds large-scale social units together and what tears them apart, clearly traditional concerns of the social factist.

Although Blau argued that he was simply extending exchange theory to the societal level, in so doing he twisted exchange theory beyond recognition. He was even forced to admit that processes at the societal level are fundamentally different from those at the individual level. In his effort to extend exchange theory, Blau managed only to transform it into another theory congruent with the social-facts paradigm. Blau seemed to recognize that exchange theory is primarily concerned with face-to-face relations. As a result, it needs to be complemented by other theoretical orientations that focus mainly on macro structures. Blau (1987b) has now come to recognize this, and his most recent work (see Chapter 13) focuses on macro-level, structural phenomena.

CRITICISMS OF BEHAVIORAL THEORIES AND REBUTTALS

Given their roots outside of sociology, behavioral sociology and exchange theory have often been singled out for critique. A good example of a general rejection of these theories is the following:

> Many scientists exhibit a tremendous talent, even a joy, in finding some human behavior which can be explained in a nonhuman way by reference either to an animal model or to a completely mechanical model. . . . When the history of current social science is written, it will be largely a story of treating social science as if it were something else, or trying to get away from the human properties of human beings, and of the strange faith of scientists who can measure exactly stimulus and response to reinforcement.
>
> (Back, 1970:1100)

A useful summary of the specific criticisms of behavioral theories, as well as the rebuttals to those critiques, can be found in an essay by Linda Molm (1981). Molm's basic position is that social behaviorism is a legitimate form of sociology, one that is not as different from other sociological approaches as many believe. Molm blamed both behaviorists and their opponents for a distorted view of this perspective: "In attempting to establish the behavioral perspective as a distinctive approach, behavioral sociologists tended to emphasize their differences from other sociologists and these differences were sometimes distorted, in the course of debate, into wide gulfs" (1981:153). She concluded that the differences from other sociological theories "are based more on misunderstanding than on fact" (1981:154). It is in the context of this view of the misunderstandings surrounding sociological behaviorism that Molm looked at the three basic criticisms of it.

The first criticism is that social behaviorism is reductionistic, because it focuses on individual behavior. This, in her view, is certainly not true of macro behaviorists (such as Blau), but further she felt that it is not even true of micro-behavioral sociologists. Although she agreed that behavioral psychologists are reductionistic, she argued that behavioral sociologists are not. Behavioral psychologists "study how a single subject's behavior is affected by *individual* or independent contingencies: relationships in which the individual's reinforcers are contingent solely on his own behavior" (Molm, 1981:154). Behavioral sociologists, in contrast, "study how two or more subjects' behaviors are jointly affected by mutual *social* contingencies: relationships in which each person's reinforcers are at least partially contingent on the behaviors of one or more other persons" (Molm, 1981:154).

Whereas Homans and other purists focus on how one individual's behavior is affected by another person's behavior, many behavioral sociologists "are asking how the *relationship* between persons' *behaviors* is affected by the *relationship* between their *behaviors and rewards*" (Molm, 1981:155). Social behaviorists are not reductionistic because they look at the "*structural relationships* between persons, and thus they are clearly within the domain of sociology. They are not characteristics of individuals or aggregations of individual characteristics; they are truly *relational* variables" (Molm, 1981:155).

In fact, Molm went further and argued that social behaviorism is actually less reductionistic than other sociological theories:

> The behavioral sociologists' study of dyadic or group behavior stands in sharp contrast to most of contemporary social psychology and much of structural sociology,

in which the individual is the unit of analysis, and aggregated, nonrelational variables are studied. At the same time, it should be evident that behavioral sociologists who study social contingencies *are* studying structural variables, albeit micro structures.

(Molm, 1981:156)

Molm certainly is correct in saying that much of the rest of sociology is reductionistic when it conducts empirical research (Akers, 1981; McPhail, 1981), but this does not constitute a solid defense against behaviorism's reductionism. Robert Perinbanayagam made this point when he argued that Molm's position "hardly meets the criticism: the charge of reductionism is applied when the key explanatory variables do not take into account the emergent properties of interactions, exchanges, groups, and even situations" (1981:168). Even in Cook's (1987a) volume on exchange theory, which is self-consciously aimed at moving to the macro levels, J. Turner (1987) concludes: "The chapters in this volume are decidedly micro in tone."

The second criticism of behavioral sociology is that it leaves many things unexplained, especially norms and values. On the one hand, Molm argued that behaviorists (Stolte, 1987) have done no worse on this score than other sociologists. On the other hand, she argued that they do have a theory of the formation of norms and values, albeit in this author's view a very questionable theory, extending individual behavioristic principles to large-scale units: "To understand the formation of norms, we must examine the learning history of the group, institution, or culture under consideration, just as we would examine the learning history of an individual to understand individual behavior" (Molm, 1981:158).

The third criticism of social behaviorism is that it operates with a mechanical and unfeeling conception of the actor. Molm counters this claim by arguing that operant behaviors "are not automatically elicited by any prior stimulus; they simply occur—they are emitted by the organism, not *elicited* by a stimulus" (1981:160). But this is hardly an active, creative image of the actor, as Perinbanayagam pointed out: "Such claims, far from meeting the criticism of mechanism, merely confirm it. They neatly capture the behaviorist image of a human as a passive, machinelike entity, incapable of volition and originality, that 'emits' behaviors" (1981:166). In other words, Molm's image of the actor has nothing to say about *"constructing a social act"* (Perinbanayagam, 1981:166).

Overall, the basic criticisms of behavioral theories are that the theories are neither sufficiently microscopic nor adequately macroscopic. In Chapter 17 we will deal with recent work in exchange theory which attempts to deal with these critiques by developing a more integrative sociological theory.

SUMMARY

In this chapter we discuss behavioral sociology and exchange theory as well as their roots in psychological behaviorism. We trace exchange theory back to its source in the work of behavioral psychologist B. F. Skinner. Skinner rejected the tenets of theories associated with social definitionism (for instance, symbolic interactionism, phenomenology, ethnomethodology) *and* social factism (for instance, structural functionalism and conflict theory).

Behavioral sociologists adopt a microscopic focus. Their concern is with the relationship between the history of environmental consequences and the nature of present behavior. In short, individuals are seen as likely to repeat behaviors that in the past have been rewarding, but not those that proved costly. In this context, we discuss a number of the concepts of central importance to the behavioral sociologist—positive and negative reinforcers, positive and negative punishments, response cost, generalized reinforcers, and behavior modification.

Next we examine exchange theory, the major representative of behaviorism in sociology. The most important spokesperson for exchange theory is George Homans, who was heavily and directly influenced by the work of B. F. Skinner. Homans criticized the macro-level explanations of social behavior of such people as Durkheim, Parsons, and Lévi-Strauss. Instead, he sought to explain social behavior in terms of psychological principles—that is, behaviorism. He believed that psychological principles can be used to explain not only individual behavior but also social structures *and* social change. The heart of Homans's theory lies in the following basic propositions: (1) the success proposition; (2) the stimulus proposition; (3) the value proposition; (4) the deprivation-satiation proposition; (5) the aggression-approval propositions; and (6) the rationality proposition.

Given its orientation to individual behavior, Homans's theory has been criticized by social factists for ignoring large-scale structures and by social definitionists for ignoring mental processes. The debate between Parsons and Homans can be seen in terms of the differences between the social-factist and the social-behaviorist orientations. Although such a dialogue is important, even more significant was the effort by Peter Blau to extend exchange theory from the individual to the societal level. Blau outlined the four-stage sequence leading from interpersonal exchange to social structure to social change. Blau's work, although commendable, transforms exchange theory at the societal level so that it is no longer identifiable as a behavioristic orientation.

In addition to being criticized for its weaknesses at the societal level, exchange theory has been criticized for its inattention to mental processes.

The chapter closes with Molm's discussion of, and rebuttals to, the major criticisms of behavioral theories in general.

CHAPTER 12

CONTEMPORARY FEMINIST THEORY

Patricia Madoo Lengermann
The George Washington University

Jill Niebrugge-Brantley
Northern Virginia Community College

*F*EMINIST theory is that part of the new scholarship on women that implicitly or formally presents a generalized, wide-ranging system of ideas about the basic features of social life and of human experience as these can be understood from a woman-centered perspective. Feminist theory is woman-centered in three ways. First, its major "object" for investigation, the starting point of all its investigation, is the situation (or the situations) and experiences of women in society. Second, it treats women as the central "subjects" in the investigative process; that is, it seeks to see the world from the distinctive vantage point (or vantage points) of women in the social world. Third, feminist theory is critical and activist on behalf of women, seeking to produce a better world for women—and thus, it argues, for humankind.

Feminist theory, however, differs from most sociological theories in a number of ways. First, it is the work of an interdisciplinary community, which includes not only sociologists but also scholars from other disciplines, such as anthropology, biology, economics, history, law, literature, philosophy, political science, psychology, and theology; people best recognized as creative writers; people who see themselves primarily as political activists; spokespersons for women of color; and writers from various European or Third World intellectual communities.[1] Second, feminist sociologists, like other feminist theorists, orient their efforts only in part to extending their discipline of origin. Much more central to all feminist scholarship is the development of a critical understanding of society intended to change the social world in directions deemed more just and humane. Third, most sociologists have been particularly hesitant to incorporate feminist theory into their sociological work, in part because that theory seems so new and radical, in part because so many of its creators are not sociologists, and in part because of suspicions about the scientific credentials of a scholarly undertaking so closely linked to political activism. Fourth, feminist theory is not anchored in any one of the three paradigms that have long patterned sociology's orientation to its subject matter— the social-facts paradigm, the social-definition paradigm, and the social-behavior paradigm (see the Appendix). This is because feminist theory has gone a long way toward effectively integrating, and thus transcending, the microsocial vs. macro-social debate, which is one of the major causes of this paradigmatic division (see Chapter 14). This transcendence of the macro versus micro issue may make it difficult for sociologists based in one of the discipline's long-standing theories to work out their relation to feminist theory. Yet at the same time, this transcendence is one of the most exciting implications of feminist theory for those working on the frontiers of contemporary sociological theory (Ritzer, 1990e). We will expand on this aspect of feminist theory in the final section of this chapter.

In the remainder of the chapter we describe the basic theoretical questions addressed by feminist theorists; look briefly at the history of feminist thought, particularly within sociology; and then examine in more detail the varieties of feminist theory that have become visible over the course of this history. In the chapter's main section, we discuss major themes in contemporary feminist sociological theory.

THE BASIC THEORETICAL QUESTIONS

The impetus for contemporary feminist theory is a deceptively simple question:*"And what about the women?"* In other words, where are the women in any situation being investigated? If they are not present, why? If they are present, what exactly are they doing? How do they experience the situation? What do they contribute to it? What does it mean to them?

---

[1] This chapter, however, draws primarily on the English-language contribution to this international effort.

The consequences of trying to answer feminism's basic question—"And what about the women?"—have been revolutionary. Dramatically, the contemporary scholarly community discovered that what it had assumed to be the universe of experience was really a particularistic account of male actors and male experience. The recognition of a whole new set of actors called for a reworking of our understanding and patterning of every social situation. Women, feminists exulted, could lay claim to "half the firmament." And indeed, the effect was rather like discovering, through the lens of a new telescope, a multitude of hitherto undetected stars in the universe, a fundamentally new configuration for each constellation.

Twenty years of posing this question have produced some generalizable conclusions. Women are present in most social situations. Where they are not, it is not because they lack ability or interest but because there have been deliberate efforts to exclude them. Where they are present, women have played roles very different from the popular conception of them (as, for example, passive wives and mothers). Indeed, both as wives and as mothers and in a series of other roles, women have, along with men, actively created the situations being studied. Yet though women are actively present in most social situations, scholars and social actors themselves have been blind to their presence. Moreover, women's roles in most social situations, although essential, have not been identical to those of the men in those situations. Overall, their roles have been different from, less privileged than, and subordinate to those of men. Their invisibility is only one indicator of this inequality.

As the women's movement has expanded, the circle of feminists exploring issues raised by feminism's basic question has become larger and more inclusive. A consequence of this has been close scrutiny of the monolithic sameness implied in the phrase *the women* and a deepening awareness of the theoretical significance of differences among women—in class, race, age, affectional preference, religion, ethnicity, and global location. In answering the question "And what about the women?" feminists now know not only that women are invisibly and unequally present in social situations, and that they are in roles significant but different from those of the visible and privileged men, but that the particularities of invisibility, inequality, and role are profoundly affected by a woman's social location, that is, by her class, race, age, affectional preference, religion, ethnicity, and global location.

All this leads us to feminism's second basic question: *"Why then is all this as it is?"* As the first question calls for a description of the social world, this second question requires that one develop an explanation of that world. Description and explanation of the social world are two faces of any sociological theory. Feminism's attempts to answer its two central questions have therefore produced a theory of universal importance for sociology.[2]

How general is this theory? Some might argue that because the questions

---

[2] The third question for all feminists is *"How can we change and improve the world?"* Within sociology only the theories of Marx and neo-Marxism share this intense interest in change. We include descriptions of feminist programs for change in later sections of this chapter.

are particular to the situation of a "minority group," women, the theory that is produced will also be particular and restricted in scope, equivalent to sociology's theories of deviance, or small-group processes. But in fact feminism's two basic questions have produced a theory of social life universal in its applicability. The appropriate parallels to feminist theory are not theories of small groups or deviance, each of which is created when sociologists turn their attention away from the "whole picture" and to the details of a feature of that picture. Rather, the appropriate parallel is to one of Marx's epistemological accomplishments. Marx helped social scientists discover that the knowledge people had of society, what they assumed to be an absolute and universal statement about reality, in fact reflected the experience of those who economically and politically ruled the social world. Marxian theory effectively demonstrated that one could also view the world from the vantage point of the world's workers, those who, though economically and politically subordinate, were nevertheless indispensable producers of our world. This new vantage point relativized ruling-class knowledge and, in allowing us to juxtapose that knowledge with knowledge gained from taking the workers' perspective, vastly expanded our ability to analyze social reality. A century after Marx's death we are assimilating the implications of this discovery.

Feminism's two theoretical questions similarly produce a revolutionary switch in our understanding of the world. These questions, too, lead us to discover that what we have taken as universal and absolute knowledge of the world is, in fact, knowledge derived from the experiences of a powerful section of society, men as "masters." That knowledge is relativized if we rediscover the world from the vantage point of a hitherto invisible, unacknowledged "underside": women, who in subordinated but indispensable "serving" roles have worked to sustain and re-create the society that we live in. This discovery raises questions about everything that we have thought we knew about society. This discovery and its implications constitute the essence of contemporary feminist theory's significance for sociological theory.

THE MAJOR HISTORICAL ROOTS

To understand the significance of the present convergence between feminist theory and sociology, we need to look at two past strands of intellectual work. First is the tradition of feminist writings, which has formed part of the Western record of social protest for over 300 years, a tradition that lays the foundation for contemporary feminist theory and that formed part of the environment within which sociology itself took shape. Second is the deeply ambivalent position, from the 1840s to the 1960s, taken by sociologists on the issue of gender inequality.

Feminism: 1600–1960

In one sense, there always has been a feminist perspective. Wherever women are subordinated, and they have been subordinated almost always and everywhere, they seem to have recognized and protested that situation in some form (Chafetz and Dworkin, 1986). In the Western world, the formal dating of feminism begins with the *published* works of protest. With one or two exceptions, these first appeared in the 1630s and continued for about another 150 years as a thin but persistent trickle. Then, in the two centuries from 1780 to the present, feminist writing increasingly becomes a significant collective effort, growing in both the number of its participants and the scope of its critique. (Fuller descriptions of the ideas of these earlier feminists are to be found in Cott, 1977; Donovan, 1985; Lougee, 1976; Martin, 1972; A. Rossi, 1974; Showalter, 1971; Spender, 1982, 1983, 1989.)

The record of feminism, however, is not one of steady, uninterrupted development. Women are after all a relatively powerless and subordinated group in Western societies—a "minority."[3] Feminist protest of this minority status always threatens, and therefore is opposed by, the more powerful and dominant "majority"—men. The opportunities for public feminist protest expand and contract as societies swing between moments of liberationist change and receptivity on the one hand and periods of greater conservatism and repression on the other. The high points in the record of feminist activity and writing occur in the liberationist "moments" of modern Western history: a first flurry of productivity in the 1780s and 1790s; a far more organized, focused effort in the 1850s; massive mobilization for suffrage in the early twentieth century; and in the 1960s and 1970s, the modern, broad-based, multifaceted movement discussed in Chapter 6. In the intervals between those periods, feminism becomes far less visible, essentially because dominant groups deliberately try to repress it (Spender, 1982, 1989).

Yet throughout all this, women created feminist theories (Table 12.1 lists a few of the most significant of these works). Each is a distinctive product, a particular patterning of critical ideas shaped by the writer's historical context, milieu, personality, and biography. Yet amidst all this diversity three broad types of theory are discernible: one orientation that focuses on gender differences, another that focuses on gender inequality, and a third that focuses on gender oppression. These orientations, at least in their contemporary articulation, are more fully described in the next section of this chapter. With all its diversity, this body of theory was consistently critical of existing social arrangements and focused on such essential sociological variables as social inequality, social change, power, interests and beliefs, and the social institutions of family, law, politics, work, religion, and education.

Sociology and Feminism: 1840–1960

Sociology took shape first as a perspective between 1840 and 1860, during one high point in feminist protest, and then as an organized professional undertaking between 1890 and 1920, during another expansionary feminist

---

[3] The terms *minority* and *majority* describe the relative power of groups rather than their relative size.

TABLE 12-1
SELECTED INFLUENCES IN THE FEMINIST INTELLECTUAL TRADITION IN THE ENGLISH-SPEAKING WORLD PRIOR TO 1960*

Date	Event	Historical context— Liberationist movement	Development in sociology
1650	**Anne Bradstreet** (1612–1672), *The Tenth Muse Lately Sprung Up in America*	Puritan revolution in England and America	
1670	**Aphra Behn** (1640–1680), *The Forced Marriage*	Restoration in England (period of loosening social norms)	
1694	**Mary Astell** (1668–1731), *A Serious Proposal for the Ladies*	The Glorious Revolution in England	
1770s–1780s	**Abigail Adams** (1744–1818) and **Mercy Otis Warren** (1728–1814), letters to each other and Abigail's to husband John (American statesman who will be second President)	American Revolution	
1790	**Judith Sargent Murray** (1751–1820), "On the Equality of the Sexes"	American Revolution and subsequent debates on Constitution and Bill of Rights	
1792	**Mary Wollstonecraft** (1759–1797), *A Vindication of the Rights of Women*	Effects of American and French revolutions in Britain	
1837	**Harriet Martineau** (1802–1876), "The Political Nonexistence of Women" in *Society in America*	Rise of middle-class reformism	
1838	**Sarah Grimké** (1792–1873), *Letters on the Equality of the Sexes*	Worldwide antislavery movement	
1845	**Margaret Fuller** (1810–1850), *Women in the Nineteenth Century*	Romanticism, abolitionism, nationalism	
1848	**Lucretia Mott** (1793–1880), **Elizabeth Cady Stanton** (1815–1902), **Lucy Stone** (1818–1893), **Susan B. Anthony** (1820–1906), Seneca Falls Convention (first women's rights meeting in America)	Antislavery movement	1848 Marx (1818–1883) and Engels (1820–1895), *The Communist Manifesto*
1860	**Elizabeth Blackwell** (1821–1910) and **Emily Blackwell** (1826–1911), *Medicine as a Profession for Women*	Antislavery movement	1851 Spencer (1820–1903), *Social Statics*
1869	**John Stuart Mill** (1806–1873) with **Harriet Taylor** (1807–1858), *The Subjection of Women*	Middle-class reformism	1867 Marx, *Capital*

Development in sociology (additional):
1830– Comte (1798–1857),
1842 *The Positive Philosophy*

Year	Person / Work	Theme
1881	**E. C. Stanton, S. B. Anthony, and Matilda Joslyn Gage** (1826–1898), *History of Woman Suffrage*	Stirrings of Progressivism and revisionist Social Darwinism
1883	**Olive Schreiner** (1855–1920), *The Story of an African Farm*	Working-class political movements
1884	**Friedrich Engels** (1820–1895), *Origins of the Family*	Working-class political movements
1896	**Ida Wells Barnett** (1862–1931) and **Mary Church Terrell** (1863–1954), National Association of Colored Women	Populism
1898	**Ida H. Harper** (1851–1931), *The Life and Work of Susan B. Anthony*	Progressivism
1898	**E. C. Stanton**, *The Woman's Bible*	Populism, progressivism
1899	**Charlotte Perkins Gilman** (1860–1935), *Women and Economics*	Socialism
1910	**Jane Addams** (1860–1935), *Twenty Years at Hull House*	Progressivism
1911	**Sylvia Pankhurst** (1882–1960), *The Suffragette*	Nationalism and socialism in Europe
1913	**Christabel Pankhurst** (1880–1956), *The Great Scourge and How to End It*	Nationalism and socialism in Europe
1917	**Margaret Sanger** (1879–1966), *Family Limitation*	Progressivism
1918	British women over 30 granted suffrage	Suffrage movement and working-class political struggles
1920	American women win suffrage	Suffrage movement and last gasp of Progressivism

1880–1918	Simmel (1858–1918), essays
1893–1897	Durkheim (1858–1917), *The Division of Labor, The Rules of Sociological Method, Suicide*
1904–1905	Weber (1864–1920), *The Protestant Ethic*
1918	Thomas (1863–1947) and Znaniecki (1882–1958), *The Polish Peasant*
1920	Weber, *Economy and Society* (incomplete at death)
1921	Park (1864–1944) and Burgess (1886–1966), *Introduction to the Science of Sociology*

TABLE 12-1 (Continued)
SELECTED INFLUENCES IN THE FEMINIST INTELLECTUAL TRADITION IN THE ENGLISH-SPEAKING WORLD PRIOR TO 1960*

Date	Event	Historical context—Liberationist movement	Development in sociology
1926	**Suzanne LaFollette** (1882–1941), *Concerning Women*	Progressivism, suffrage movement	1893– Mead (1863–1931), 1931 lectures that will become *Mind, Self and Society*
1931	**Virginia Woolf** (1882–1941), *A Room of One's Own*	Socialism, cultural post-Victorianism	
1933	**Eleanor Roosevelt** (1884–1963), *It's Up to the Women*	New Deal	
1935	**Margaret Mead** (1901–1978), *Sex and Temperament in Three Primitive Societies*	Pacifism (from World War I), cultural relativism of social-science training	1937 Parsons (1902–1979), *The Structure of Social Action*
1938	**V. Woolf**, *Three Guineas*	Socialism, cultural post-Victorianism	
1946	**Mary Ritter Beard** (1876–1958), *Women as a Force in History*	Reactionism against totalitarianism, fascism	
			1951 Parsons, *The Social System*
1957	**Simone de Beauvoir** (1908–1985), *The Second Sex*	Existentialism	
1959	**Betty Friedan** (b. 1921), *The Feminine Mystique*	Civil rights movement	1959 Mills (1916–1962), *The Sociological Imagination*

* Major sources for this overview of the tradition are A. Rossi (1974) and Spender (1983).

phase. How did the early sociologists respond to this intellectual tradition?

Current research on gender issues in the history of sociology suggests a three-part answer to the question (Deegan, 1988; Fitzpatrick, 1990; Kandal, 1988; Oakes, 1984a; R. Rosenberg, 1982). First, between 1840 and 1960, sociology emerged as a perspective and then as an organized and professional academic discipline against a backdrop of gender politics, which over time pushed the "founding mothers" of the discipline to the periphery of the profession, annexed or discounted their ideas, and wrote them out of sociology's public record of its history. Second, feminist concerns filtered into sociology only on the margins of the field, in the work of marginal male theorists or of marginalized women theorists. Third, the men who assumed centrality in the profession—from Spencer, through Weber and Durkheim, to Parsons—made basically conservative responses to the feminist arguments going on around them, making issues of gender an inconsequential topic in the sociology they developed and typically responding in a conventional rather than a critical way on those rare occasions when issues of gender difference and inequality were addressed in their work.

Data supporting our first generalization are most extensive on the issue of gender politics in the development of American sociology. Because of the research of scholars like Deegan (1988), Fitzpatrick (1990), and R. Rosenberg (1982), we are now aware of a large number of women who made significant and sometimes absolutely foundational contributions to American sociology: Edith Abbot, Sophonisba Breckenridge, Katherine Davis, Frances Keller, Virginia Robinson, Jessie Taft, Marion Talbot, and, above all, Jane Addams of Hull House. In the European formulations of sociology we can now dimly perceive the role of such thinkers and writers as Harriet Martineau, Clothilde de Vaux, Gertrud Simmel, and Marianne Weber (Kandal, 1988). The fact that these women, and possibly many others, who helped to create sociology have vanished from the discipline's record of its history is in part the result of institutionalized sexism in higher education (over this entire period no woman achieved senior academic standing in any sociology department except in the "women's colleges"). Even more dramatically, the invisibility of these women is due to conscious acts of exclusion by male sociologists who, over a hundred-year period, worked to create a male-dominated discipline and then to produce an account of that discipline which made the centrality of men within it appear to be the result of natural rather than political processes. The results of these actions are easy to see. As a quick glance back over the earlier chapters of this text will show, sociology has a well-known list of "founding fathers," both from the classic period between 1840 and 1935 and from the period of the major modern theorists that extends from 1935 to about 1965. But no text on the history of this period identifies a single "founding mother."

Our second generalization is that until 1960, feminist ideas were introduced into sociology only on the margins of the discipline. For example, such ideas came from various male theorists who were marginal to professional sociology, even though their ideas were subsequently influential on sociology. Thinkers like Simmel (Oakes, 1984a), W. I. Thomas (R. Rosenberg, 1982), and

Marx and Engels can be included in this group. This generalization also holds for the earliest formally trained women social scientists, who tried to deal with the issue of gender relations only to find that their research and arguments were relegated to the margins of the field because they were women.

Finally, the more centrally situated men in the profession essentially were resistant to feminism. The major works of these theorists, the statements that have fundamentally shaped the sociological perspective, give almost no attention to gender as a social arrangement, and on those rare occasions when women's lives are discussed, as in Durkheim's analysis of suicide, the approach is wholly conventional and uncritical.

The best example of this conventionality perhaps is to be found in the theories of Talcott Parsons (see Chapter 7). Central to Parsons's entire theory[4] is the assertion that the institution of the family is an indispensable prerequisite for social stability. As the primary socializing agent for children, the family is essential to that internalization of social control on which any society's stability ultimately depends. Moreover, as the primary focus in the emotional life of adults, the family is a formidable agent of external social control and a vital outlet for those adult tensions that might otherwise erupt into public life.

Parsons argues that for the family to function effectively, there must be a sexual division of labor in which adult males and females play very different roles. Men who tie the family unit into the wider social system must be "instrumental" in orientation, manifesting qualities of drive, ambition, and self-control. Women, whose task is the internal functioning of the family, supportive of both children and adult males, must be "expressive," that is, gentle, nurturant, loving, and emotionally open. If men and women become too similar in family function and orientation, competition between them will disrupt family life, weakening the family's vital role in upholding social stability (Parsons, 1954c:79). As is self-evident, this sociology of sex roles is essentially, if perhaps unintentionally, antifeminist in orientation and is perhaps the most dramatic instance of mainstream sociology's lack of involvement, down to the 1960s, with feminism.

VARIETIES OF CONTEMPORARY FEMINIST THEORY

Contemporary feminist theory forms the literature base for the development of any feminist sociological theory, such as the one discussed in the next major section of this chapter. Thus we present here an overview of feminist theory, that system of general ideas designed to describe and explain social life and human experience from a woman-centered vantage point. Our goal in this review is to present the themes that feminist theory offers for the construction of a feminist sociological theory.

Contemporary feminist scholars have produced a rapidly growing, extraor-

[4] The description of Parsons's gender theories in this and the next paragraph is a restatement of an argument presented in Lengermann and Wallace (1985:11–12).

dinarily rich, and highly diverse collection of theoretical writings, a demonstration of effective intellectualism that Jessie Bernard (forthcoming) labeled "the feminist enlightenment." The range and continuous expansion of this literature makes trying to map it challenging, rewarding, and sometimes a little confusing. The "map" of feminist theory presented here is *one* construct, or ideal type, for patterning this complex body of intellectual work.[5]

Our typology of feminist theory is based on the two basic questions (discussed above) that unite all these theories: the descriptive question, *What about the women?* and the explanatory question, *Why is this situation as it is?* The pattern of response to the descriptive question generates the main categories for our classification (see Table 12.2). Essentially we see three answers to the question "What about the women?" The first answer is that women's location in, and experience of, most situations is *different* from that of the men in that situation. Investigation then focuses on the details of that difference. A second answer is that women's location in most situations is not only different from but less privileged than or *unequal* to that of men. The focus of the ensuing description then is on the nature of that inequality. A third answer is that women's situation also has to be understood in terms of a direct power relationship between men and women. Women are *oppressed,* that is, restrained, subordinated, molded, and used and abused by men. Descriptions then focus on the quality of the oppression. Each of the various types of feminist theory can be classified as a theory of *difference,* or of *inequality,* or of *oppression.*

In our discussion we make distinctions within these basic categories—difference, inequality, and oppression—in terms of their differing answers to the second or explanatory question, "Why is this as it is?" (The various types of answers are summarized in Table 12.2.)

This classificatory method has an important function: it allows us to pattern not only the general body of contemporary feminist theory but also the expanding literature, particularly the theoretical literature on gender that has developed within sociology since the 1960s. The burgeoning of this literature reflects not only the reactivation of visible feminist protest in the society but also the unparalleled movement of women into higher education, as undergraduates, graduates, and faculty, between 1960 and the present (Lengermann and Wallace, 1985; Vetter et al., 1982). Feminist questions have by this latter means been injected directly into the university-based, academic discourse of professional sociology. But as sociologists have turned their efforts to an exploration of gender issues, they have typically used some portion of the existing body of sociological theory as a point of departure for what is called

---

[5] Several other classificatory systems already exist, for example, those developed by Chafetz (1988); Glennon (1979); Jaggar (1983); Jaggar and Rothenberg (1984); Lengermann and Wallace (1985); Snitow et al. (1983); and Sokoloff (1980). Readers might turn to these for balance or amplification of the ideal type presented here. In combination, these efforts have generated a long list of types of feminist theory, including black feminism, conservatism, expressionism, instrumentalism, lesbian feminism, liberalism, Marxism, polarism, psychoanalytic feminism, radicalism, separatism, socialism, and synthesis. Our own typology attempts to include most of these theories, though not always as identified by these specific labels.

TABLE 12.2
OVERVIEW OF VARIETIES OF FEMINIST THEORY*

Basic varieties of feminist theory—answers to the descriptive question, "What about the women?"	Distinctions within theories—answers to the explanatory question, "Why is women's situation as it is?"
Theories of difference	
Women's location in, and experience of, most situations is different from that of men in the situation.	Biosocial explanations of difference Institutional explanations of difference Social-psychological explanations of difference
Theories of inequality	

Women's location in most situations is not only different from but less privileged than or *unequal* to that of men.	Liberal feminist explanations of inequality
	Marxian explanations of inequality
	  Marx and Engels's explanations
	  Contemporary Marxian explanations

Theories of oppression	
Women are *oppressed,* not just different from or unequal to, but actively restrained, subordinated, molded, and used and abused by men.	Psychoanalytic explanations of oppression Radical feminist explanations of oppression Socialist feminist explanations of oppression Third-wave feminist explanations of oppression

   * The left column categorizes varieties of feminist theory by their answer to the basic question, "What about the women?" The right column presents distinctions within these categories in terms of the basic explanatory question, "Why is women's situation as it is?"

in the discipline the *sociology of gender.* Although the term *gender* is often used euphemistically in sociology for "women," the sociology of gender is, more precisely, the study of socially constructed male and female roles, relations, and identities—a somewhat different subject from feminism's focus on women. This focus on the interrelationship of men and women is not equivalent to a feminist theory. As we have said before, feminist theory seeks to present a woman-centered patterning of human experience. As we shall show later, a feminist sociology can describe the social world from a woman-centered standpoint. Overall the sociology of gender simply treats gender as one variable among many within social relations and structures. Nevertheless, some sociologists who begin from a sociology-of-gender standpoint have produced works of significance for feminist theory (and many sociologists are directly involved in producing feminist theory).

   The remainder of this section explores the feminist theories of difference, of inequality, and of oppression, describing in each case the general features of the approach, some key lines of variation within it, and its recommendations for change. Two notes of caution are, however, important. First, many theorists' work resists neat categorization. One must either talk about their main theoretical emphasis or distinguish among various of their theoretical statements. Second, this is a selective review. Given the volume of recent feminist and sociological writings on women's situation, comprehensiveness is beyond the scope of this chapter.

Theories of Gender Differences

Although a focus on gender differences is a minority position in contemporary feminism, some influential contributions to modern feminist theory do take this approach (Bernikow, 1980; Gilligan, 1982; Kessler and McKenna, 1978; J. Miller, 1976; Ruddick, 1980; Snitow, 1979). There also have been research documents (Hite, 1976; Masters and Johnson, 1966) with findings on male-female differences that have deeply affected contemporary feminist thinking. In addition, a great deal of the recent sociological literature on gender has gender difference as its topic. Included here are theoretical works anchored in an essentially institutional, quasi-functionalist view of society (J. Bernard, 1982), biosocial writings (A. Rossi, 1977, 1983), symbolic-interactionist statements (Best, 1983; Lever, 1978), phenomenological works (Berger and Kellner, 1964), and ethnomethodological statements (Garfinkel, 1967). Indeed if we add to this basic core of theoretical statements the vast empirical literature by sociologists that now factors in "sex" or "gender" as a key independent variable, the focus on gender differences may be the dominant one in sociology (Huber, 1976; Stacey and Thorne, 1985).

The central theme in the contemporary literature on gender differences is that women's inner psychic life is, in its overall configuration, different from that of men. In their basic values and interests (Ruddick, 1980), their mode of making value judgments (Gilligan, 1982), their construction of achievement motives (Kaufman and Richardson, 1982), their literary creativity (Gilbert and Gubar, 1979), their sexual fantasies (Hite, 1976; Radway, 1984; Snitow et. al. 1983), their sense of identity (Laws and Schwartz, 1977), and their general processes of consciousness and selfhood (Kasper, 1986; J. Miller, 1976), women bring a different vision and a different voice to the construction of social reality. A second theme is that the overall configuration of women's relationships and life experiences is distinctive. Women relate differently than men to their biological offspring (A. Rossi, 1977, 1983); boys and girls have distinctively different styles of play (Best, 1983; Lever, 1978); adult women relate to each other (Bernikow, 1980) and to the women subjects they study as scholars (Ascher et al., 1984) in unique ways. Indeed the overall life experience of females from infancy to old age is fundamentally different from that of men (J. Bernard, 1981). In combination, this literature on differences in consciousness and life experience presents one unique answer to the question "What about the women?"

Raising the second question, "Why?" identifies the key lines of variation

within this overall focus on gender differences. Explanations of the psychological and relational differences between women and men are essentially of
three types: biological, institutional, and, broadly construed, social psychological.

Biological Explanations of Gender Differences   Biological explanations
have been the standby of conservative thinking on gender differences. Freud
traced the different personality structures of men and women to their different
genitals and to cognitive and emotional processes that begin when children
discover these physiological differences. Contemporary sociobiologists Lionel
Tiger and Robin Fox (1971) write of variable "biogrammars" laid down in
early hominid evolution that lead women to bond emotionally with their
infants and men to bond practically with other men. But the biological argument also has been used in writings much more sympathetic to feminism.
Masters and Johnson's exploration of the anatomy of female sexuality has
given feminist theorists basic facts for rethinking the whole question of the
social patterning of sexuality, and Alice Rossi (1977; 1983) has given serious
attention to the biological foundations of gender-specific behavior. Rossi has
linked the different biological functions of males and females to different patterns of hormonally determined development over the life cycle and this, in
turn, to sex-specific variation in such traits as sensitivity to light and sound
and to differences in left and right brain connections. These differences, she
feels, feed into the different play patterns in childhood noted by Carol Gilligan
(1982), Janet Lever (1978), and Raphaela Best (1983); the well-known female
"math anxiety"; and also the apparent fact that women are more predisposed
to care for infants in a nurturing way than are men. Rossi's feminism leads
her to argue for sociocultural arrangements that make it possible for each
gender to compensate, through social learning, for biologically "given" disadvantages, but as a biosociologist she also argues for rational acknowledg-
ment of the implications of biological research.

Institutional Explanations of Gender Differences   Institutional explanations of gender differences often also lay great stress on women's distinctive
functions in bearing and caring for infants. This responsibility for mothering
is seen as a major determinant of the broader sexual division of labor that
links women in general to the functions of wife, mother, and household
worker, to the private sphere of the home and family, and thus to a lifelong
series of events and experiences very different from those of men. In this
setting, women develop distinctive interpretations of achievement, distinctive
interests and values, characteristic but necessary skills for openness in relationships, "caring attention to others," and particular networks of support
with the other women (mothers, daughters, sisters, cowives, friends) who
inhabit their separate sphere. Although some of the institutional theorists of
difference accept the sexual division of labor as socially necessary (Berger and
Berger, 1983), others are aware that the separate spheres for women and men

may be embedded within broader patterns of gender inequality (J. Bernard, 1981; M. Johnson, 1989; Kelly-Godol, 1983) or even of oppression (Ruddick, 1980). The writings cited in this section, however, focus primarily on gender difference and its institutional roots.

Social-Psychological Theories of Gender   Social-psychological explanations of gender differences are of two types: phenomenological and post-structuralist theories on the one hand and socialization theories on the other. Phenomenological and poststructuralist theories (Butler, 1990; Cixous and Clement, 1986; Flax, 1990; Garfinkel, 1967; Goffman, 1977; Kessler and McKenna, 1978; Laws and Schwartz, 1977; Moi, 1986; Stanton, 1985) focus on the pervasive patterning of our culture, language, and everyday reality by concepts derived from male experience and by the simple dichotomous categories or "typifications" of maleness and femaleness. They emphasize the interactional and conceptual work we all do to maintain these typifications and the ways in which this collective work determines, through definition, the distinctive spheres and psychological profiles of women and men. The problem of language as an essentially male province has been discussed by many theorists, including Dorothy E. Smith and Audre Lorde (discussed below), but it has been the particular focus of a group of French feminists—Hélène Cixous, Luce Irigaray, Julia Kristeva. These thinkers, trained in a rigorous philosophic tradition, have taken as a starting point an idea central to French psychoanalysis, that is, that all presently existing languages are phallocentric—anchored in and reflective of the experiences and conceptualizations of dominant males—and that this relation between language and maleness is structured by the child's discovery of both language and identity through learning the patronymics of its society. Beginning with this idea, and accepting it, they have posed in the most dramatic form in feminism the question: How then can women ever give voice to their experience?

Socialization theory (see Stockard and Johnson, 1980; Walum-Richardson, 1981, for selected bibliographies) complements institutional analyses by exploring the social learning experiences that mold people in general but particularly young children for the separate roles and institutional spheres of maleness and femaleness.

Except for conservative, nonfeminist theorists who argue simply for the inevitability of difference and therefore for the need to yield to its demands, the recommendations about women's situation that flow from these theories of gender difference center on the need for *respect*. Theorists of difference typically demand that women's distinctive ways of being be recognized not as departures from the normal but as viable alternatives to male modes and that public knowledge, academic scholarship, and the very patterning of social life adjust to take serious account of female ways of being. Indeed at the most militantly feminist end of the continuum of this theoretical approach, we find a centuries-old claim of feminism: that when a major infusion of women's ways becomes part of public life, the world will be a safer, more humane place for all of us.

Theories of Gender Inequality

Four themes characterize the theories of gender inequality. First, men and women are not only differently situated in society but also unequally situated. Specifically, women get less of the material resources, social status, power, and opportunities for self-actualization than the men who share their social location—be it a location based on class, race, occupation, ethnicity, religion, education, nationality, or any other socially significant factor. Second, this inequality results from the organization of society, not from any significant biological or personality differences between women and men. The third theme of all inequality theory is that although individual human beings may vary somewhat from each other in their profile of potentials and traits, no significant pattern of natural variation distinguishes the sexes. Instead, all human beings are characterized by a deep need for freedom to seek self-actualization and by a fundamental malleability that leads them to adapt to the constraints or opportunities of the situations in which they find themselves. To say that there is gender inequality, then, is to claim that women are situationally less empowered than men to realize the need they share with men for self-actualization. Fourth, inequality theories all assume that both women and men will respond fairly easily and naturally to more egalitarian social structures and situations. They affirm, in other words, that it is possible to change the situation. In this, theorists of gender inequality contrast with the theorists of gender difference, who present a picture of social life in which gender differences are, whatever their cause, durable, deeply penetrative of personality, and only partially reversible.

Explanations of gender inequality vary around this common core of interpretation. Two major variants of contemporary feminist theory that focus on and try to explain gender inequality are reviewed here: liberal feminism and Marxian feminism.

Liberal Feminism   Within contemporary feminist theory, liberal feminism is a minority position (Bird, 1979; Epstein, 1988; Friedan, 1963, 1981; Janeway, 1981; Lippman-Blumen, 1984; Trebilcot, 1973). Yet at the same time, liberal feminism is the most widely diffused approach within the contemporary women's movement in America: it undergirds much popular writing on careers for women, equal parenting, and the need for gender-free schooling for young children; it guides many of the policies initiated by the movement (Gelb and Paley, 1982; Tinker, 1983) and is embodied in the programmatic statement of the most powerful of women's organizations, the National Organization for Women (NOW). An easy complementarity between liberal feminism and the mainstream of American political beliefs helps to make understandable the popularity of this variant on feminist theory.

Liberal feminism's explanation of gender inequality begins where theories of gender differences leave off: with an identification of the sexual division of labor, the existence of separate public and private spheres of social activity, men's primary location in the former and women's in the latter, and the systematic socialization of children so that they can move into the adult roles and spheres appropriate to their gender. In contrast to theorists of difference, however, liberal feminists see nothing of particular value about the private sphere, except perhaps that it permits emotional openness. Instead, the private sphere consists of the endless round of demanding, mindless, unpaid, and undervalued tasks associated with housework, child care, and the emotional, practical, and sexual servicing of adult men. The true rewards of social life— money, power, status, freedom, opportunities for growth and self-worth—are to be found in the public sphere. The system that restricts women's access to that sphere, burdens them with private-sphere responsibilities, isolates them in individual households, and excuses their mates from any sharing of private-sphere drudgeries is the system that produces gender inequality.

When asked to identify the key forces in this system, liberal feminists point to *sexism,* an ideology similar to racism, which consists partly of prejudices and discriminatory practices against women and partly of taken-for-granted beliefs about the "natural" differences between women and men that suit them to their different social destinies. Because of sexism, females are, from childhood on, limited and maimed, so that they can move into their adult roles and in those roles "dwindle" from full humanness into the mindless, dependent, subconsciously depressed beings created by the constraints and requirements of their gender-specified roles.

The description of women dwindling from full humanness is taken from Jessie Bernard's *The Future of Marriage* (1982). Bernard is a sociologist who has been writing about the issue of gender since the 1940s, long before it was perceived as a significant topic by sociologists. *The Future of Marriage* is perhaps her best-known book on this topic. In the dispassionate voice of mainstream, institutionally oriented, empirically anchored sociology, Bernard presents sociologists with a novel and devastating portrait of the institution of marriage. Marriage is at one and the same time a cultural system of beliefs and ideals, an institutional arrangement of roles and norms, and a complex of interactional experiences for individual women and men. Culturally, marriage is idealized as the destiny and source of fulfillment for women; a mixed blessing of domesticity, responsibility, and constraint for men; and for American society as a whole an essentially egalitarian association between husband and wife. Institutionally, marriage empowers the role of husband with authority and with the freedom, indeed, the obligation, to move beyond the domestic setting; it meshes the idea of male authority with sexual prowess and male power; and it mandates that wives be compliant, dependent, self-emptying, and essentially centered on the activities and chores of the isolated domestic household. Experientially then there are two marriages in any institutional marriage: the man's marriage, in which he holds to the belief of being con-

JESSIE BERNARD: A Biographical Sketch

Jessie Bernard's life and work have been characterized by an extraordinary capacity for growth and outgrowth: she has constantly moved beyond herself into new intellectual territory.* She has described this process in "My Four Revolutions: An Autobiographical Account of the American Sociological Association" (1973). In this article and in her current work, Bernard treats her last revolution as a movement toward contemporary feminism or toward what she will eventually name as "the feminist enlightenment" (forthcoming). By tracing Bernard's movement to participation in the feminist enlightenment, we can see much of the history of women's participation in twentieth-century American sociology.

Bernard was born Jessie Ravitch on June 8, 1903, in Minneapolis. Her first significant outgrowth was to move from her Jewish immigrant family to the University of Minnesota at the age of seventeen. At the university not only did she go outside that first immigrant milieu but, more significantly, she herself became connected with the attempts to establish sociology as a fully recognized profession within American academia. She studied with Sorokin, who would go on to establish the sociology department at Harvard, and with L. L. Bernard, who would be instrumental in founding the *American Sociological Review*. Jessie Ravitch served as Bernard's research assistant for four years and married him in 1925. Her study with Bernard gave her a grounding in a positivistic approach to sociology as science that left its mark on all her later work in her ability to draw successfully on quantitative research to do what would increasingly become qualitative and critical analysis.

Bernard moved with her husband as he held a variety of academic appointments. She earned her Ph.D. in sociology at Washington University in St. Louis in 1935. By the mid-1940s, the Bernards were at Pennsylvania State University, and Jessie was in the midst of her outgrowth of positivism.

Jessie Bernard's movement away from positivism came in response to the events of World War II. The Nazi holocaust destroyed her faith in the capacity of science to know and produce a just world—it also made her reexamine her own Jewish immigrant roots. These experiences increased Bernard's sensitivity to the social contextuality of all knowledge, although she would move slowly toward this feminist position.

Coinciding with the beginnings of this break with positivism, in the mid-1940s, Bernard began to establish her own independent academic position at Penn State. Her husband died in 1951, but Jessie remained at Penn State until about 1960, teaching, writing, and raising her three children. During the early sixties she commuted between Washington, D.C., and Penn State and finally moved out of academic life to devote herself full-time to writing and research. Her home base since the mid-sixties has been Washington, D.C., although she

strained and burdened, while experiencing what the norms dictate—authority, independence, and a right to domestic, emotional, and sexual service by the wife; and the wife's marriage, in which she affirms the cultural belief of fulfillment, while experiencing normatively mandated powerlessness and dependence, an obligation to provide domestic, emotional, and sexual services, and a gradual "dwindling away" of the independent young person she

remains professor emeritus at Penn State. Thus, the two decades following World War II constituted yet another period of growth and outgrowth for Bernard, one in which she established a professional identity independent at first of her husband and then of the conventional trappings of the university and began an increasingly public rejection of sociology as positivistic science.

But the most dramatic period of growth and outgrowth has been from 1964 to the present. This fact is significant both in terms of the quality and quantity of Bernard's productivity and also for what it says in itself about the career patterns of women's lives. During this period, Bernard has published twelve books and offered innumerable articles and presentations, establishing herself as one of the leading interpreters of the sociology of gender. Her movement to leadership has been marked by this same pattern of growth and outgrowth. Thus, she has declined traditional leadership roles, such as the presidency of the ASA, in favor of time for research, writing, and increasing involvement with the women's movement. She has also rethought her own early writings on family and gender, moving increasingly toward a feminist interpretation.

Bernard's interest in women's lives illustrates her ability to rethink core concerns within new intellectual contexts. She has been studying and writing about women's lives since the late 1930s. Her major works include *American Family Behavior* (1942), *Marriage and Family among Negroes* (1956), *Remarriage: A Study of Marriage* (1957), *Academic Women* (1964), *The Sex Game: Communication between the Sexes* (1968), *Women and the Public Interest: An Essay on Policy and Protest* (1971), *The Future of Motherhood* (1974), *Women, Wives, Mothers: Values and Options* (1975), *The Female World* (1980), *The Future of Marriage* (1982), *The Female World in a Global Perspective* (1987), and *The Feminist Enlightenment* (forthcoming).

These works are characterized by four essential qualities. One, Bernard is consistently able to bring macro-level data to bear in reaching conclusions about microinteraction and subjective experience. Two, she increasingly recognizes the importance of subjective experience in the establishment of macro-social structures. Three, an obvious outgrowth of two, she increasingly emphasizes the social contextuality of knowledge and the methodological necessity of studying the lives of invisible groups in and of themselves, not merely in comparison to the dominant patriarchally determined type. Four, she has moved from a framing of her curiosity about women's lives within the traditional context of the sociology of the family through a framing that focuses on women within the sociology of gender to a framing that is critical and feminist.

Bernard has garnered numerous honors in her career and has had perhaps the highest honor of having several awards named after her—awards designed, as Lipman-Blumen says, to mark "those who, like Jessie Bernard herself, have contributed intellectually, professionally, and humanely to the world of scholarship and feminism" (1979:55).

*This biographical sketch is heavily indebted to Lippman-Blumen (1979) and J. Bernard (1973).

was before marriage. The results of all this are to be found in the data that measure human stress: *married* women, whatever their claims to fulfillment, and *unmarried* men, whatever their claims to freedom, rank high on all stress indicators, including heart palpitations, dizziness, headaches, fainting, nightmares, insomnia, and fear of nervous breakdown; *unmarried* women, whatever their sense of social stigma, and *married* men rank low on all the stress indicators. Marriage then is good for men and bad for women and will cease to be so unequal in its impact only when couples feel free enough from the prevailing institutional constraints to negotiate the kind of marriage that best suits their individual needs and personalities.

To liberal feminists, American society, anchored in its constitutionally given institutions and rights, permits more individual freedom and equality than most other societies. Even here, however, equal opportunity is limited by both racism and sexism. These belief systems are functionless carryovers from earlier times, supported by little more than tradition, convention, and unsubstantiated prejudice. Sexism, like racism, forces men and women into rigid characterological molds, denies the community the full range of talents available in the population, diminishes women, and poses a constant denial of our most cherished cultural values of individual worth and freedom. Because of all this, liberal feminists maintain, contemporary American society must be changed to eliminate sexism, and they believe that most people can be educated to see the reasonableness of the feminist critique.

Liberal feminists propose the following strategies for eliminating gender inequality: mobilization to use existing political and legal channels for change; equal economic opportunities; changes in family, school, and mass-media messages so that people no longer are socialized into rigidly compartmentalized sex roles; and attempts by all individuals to challenge sexism where they encounter it in daily life. For liberal feminists, the ideal gender arrangement is one in which each individual chooses the lifestyle most suitable to her or him and has that choice accepted and respected, be it for housewife or househusband, unmarried careerist or part of a dual-income family, childless or with children, heterosexual or homosexual. Liberal feminists see this ideal as one that enhances the practice of freedom and equality, central cultural ideals in America. Liberal feminism then is consistent with the dominant American ethos in its basic acceptance of America's institutions and culture, its reformist orientation, and its appeal to the values of individualism, choice, freedom, and equality of opportunity.

Marxian Feminism   Marxism presents one of the best-known and intellectually most elaborate theories of social oppression. Beginning with Marx and Engels and continuing through the whole body of neo-Marxian literature, this perspective develops the theory of social class oppression, focusing on the domination of workers in the interests of the ruling class and on the pervasiveness of class domination, oppression, and conflict in patterning both intranational and international social relations. Marxian feminism brings together Marxian class analysis and feminist social protest. Yet this amalgam produces not an intensified theory of oppression but rather a more muted statement of inequality, that is, of gender inequality.[6] The foundation of this theory was laid by Marx and Engels.

---

[6] This theory has been elaborated in recent times by Benston (1970); James and Costa (1973); Kuhn and Wolpe (1978); Juliet Mitchell (1975); Reed (1970); Rowbotham (1973); Vogel (1984); and Zaretsky (1976).

Marx and Engels   The major concern of Marx and Engels was social class oppression, but they frequently turned their attention to gender oppression. Their most famous exploration of this issue is presented in *The Origins of the Family, Private Property and the State,* written and published by Engels in 1884 from extensive notes made by Marx in the years immediately preceding Marx's death in 1883 (Barrett, 1985). The major arguments of this book are:

1 Woman's subordination results not from her biology, which is presumably immutable, but from social arrangements that have a clear and traceable history, arrangements that presumably may be changed. (This claim alone, taken in the context of nineteenth-century beliefs about women, makes *The Origins* a feminist text.)

2 The relational basis for women's subordination lies in the family, an institution aptly named from the Latin word for servant, because the family as it exists in complex societies is overwhelmingly a system of dominant and subordinate roles. Key features of the family in Western societies are that it centers on a mating pair and its offspring, typically located within a single household; it is patrilineal, with descent and property passing through the male line, patriarchal, with authority invested in the male household head, and monogamous at least in the enforcement of the rule that the wife have sexual relations only with her husband. The double standard allows men far greater sexual freedom. Within such an institution, particularly when, as in the middle-class family, the woman has no job outside the house and no economic independence, women are in fact the chattels or possessions of their husbands.

3 Society legitimizes this family system by claiming that such a structure is the fundamental institution in all societies. This is in fact a false claim, as much anthropological and archaeological evidence shows. For much of human prehistory there were no family structures of this type. Instead, people were linked in extensive kin networks—the *gens,* large-scale associations among people sharing blood ties. Moreover these ties were traced through the female line because one's direct link to one's mother was far more easily demonstrable than one's ties to one's father—the *gens* was, in other words, matrilineal. It was also matriarchal, with significant power resting in the hands of women, who, in those primitive hunting-and-gathering economies, had an independent and crucial economic function as the gatherers, crafters, storers, and distributors of essential materials. This power was exercised in collective and cooperative communal living arrangements, commodity use, child rearing, and decision making and through the free and unencumbered choice of love and sexual partners by both women and men. This type of society, which Marx and Engels describe elsewhere as primitive communism, is associated in *The Origins* with a free and empowered social status for women.

4 The factors that destroyed this type of social system, producing what Engels calls "the world historic defeat of the female sex" (Engels, 1884/ 1970:87) are economic, specifically the replacement of hunting and gath-

ering by herding, horticulture, and farming economies. With this change emerged *property,* the idea and reality of some group members' claiming as their own the essential resources for economic production. It was men who asserted this claim, as their mobility, strength, and monopoly over certain tools gave them economic ascendency. With these changes men also, as property owners, developed enforceable needs both for a compliant labor force—be it of slaves, captives, women-wives, or children— and for heirs who would serve as a means of preserving and passing on property. Thus emerged the first *familia,* a master and his slave-servants, wife-servants, children-servants, a unit in which the master fiercely defended his claim to sole sexual access to his wives and thus to certainty about his heirs. And the sons, too, would support this system of sexual control, because on it would rest their property claims.

5 Since then, the exploitation of labor has developed into increasingly complex structures of domination, most particularly class relations; the political order was created to safeguard all these systems of domination; and the family itself has evolved along with the historic transformations of economic and property systems into an embedded and dependent institution, reflecting all the more massive injustices of the political economy and consistently enforcing the subordination of women. Only with the destruction of property rights in the coming communist revolution will women attain freedom of social, political, economic, and personal action.

The Origins has been challenged by anthropologists and archaeologists on questions of evidence and by feminists for failing in various ways to grasp the full complexity of women's oppression. But in making the claim at all that women are oppressed, in analyzing how this oppression is sustained by the family, an institution regarded as almost sacred by powerful sectors of society, and in tracing the ramifications of this subordination for women's economic and sexual status, *The Origins* presents a powerful sociological theory of gender inequality, one that contrasts dramatically with Parsons's mainstream sociological theory.

Contemporary Marxian Feminism Contemporary Marxian feminists embed gender relations within what they consider to be the more fundamental structure of the class system and particularly within the structure of the contemporary capitalist class system. From this theoretical vantage point, the quality of each individual's life experiences is a reflection first of his or her class position and only second of his or her gender. Women of markedly different class backgrounds have fewer life experiences in common than women of any particular class have with the men of their class. For example, in both their class-determined experiences and their interests, upper-class, wealthy women are antagonistic to blue-collar or poor welfare women but share many experiences and interests with upper-class, wealthy men. Given this starting point, Marxian feminists acknowledge that *within* any class, women are less advantaged than men in their access to material goods, power, status, and possibilities for self-actualization. The causes of this inequality lie in the organization of capitalism itself.

The embeddedness of gender inequality within the class system is most simply and starkly visible within the dominant class of contemporary capitalism, the bourgeoisie. Bourgeois men own the productive and organizational resources of industrial production, commercialized agriculture, and national and international trade. Women of the bourgeois class are not propertied but are themselves property, the wives and possessions of bourgeois men, men who understand at the deepest level the art of possession. Bourgeois women are attractive and distinctive commodities in an ongoing process of exchange between men (G. Rubin, 1975) and often are a means of sealing property alliances among men. Bourgeois women produce and train sons who will inherit their fathers' socioeconomic resources. Bourgeois women also provide emotional, social, and sexual services for the men in their class. For all this, they are rewarded with an appropriately luxurious lifestyle. Bourgeois women are, to use Rosa Luxemburg's phrase, "the parasite of a parasite" (1971:220; quoted in MacKinnon, 1982:7).

Gender inequality in the wage-earning classes also is functional for capitalism and therefore is perpetuated by capitalists. Women as wage earners are, because of their lower social status, more poorly paid and, because of their sense of wage-sector marginality, difficult to unionize. Thus they serve as an unresisting source of profit for the ruling classes. Moreover, women's marginality to the wage sector makes them an important part of the reserve labor force that, as a pool of alternative workers, acts as a threat to and a brake on unionized male wage demands. As housewives, wives, and mothers, women unwittingly further support the process of bourgeois profit making as consumers of goods and services for the household and as unpaid care givers who subsidize and disguise the real costs of reproducing and maintaining the work force (Gardiner, 1979). Finally, but for Marxians least significantly, the wage earner's wife provides her spouse with a minuscule experience of personal power, compensation for his actual powerlessness in society. She is, in other words, "the slave of a slave" (MacKinnon, 1982:8).

Women, then, are unequal to men not because of any basic and direct conflict of interest between the genders but because of the working out of class oppression, with its attendant factors of property inequality, exploited labor, and alienation. The fact that within any class women are less advantaged than men, rather than vice versa, seems in Marxian feminism to have no immediate structural cause. Rather, as in liberal feminism, this fact results from a historic carryover from the collapse of primitive communism that Engels described. Consequently, the solution for gender inequality is the destruction of class oppression. This destruction will come through revolutionary action by a united wage-earning class, including both women and men. Any direct mobilization of women against men is counterrevolutionary, because it divides the potentially revolutionary working class. A working-class revolution that destroys the class system by making all economic assets the assets of the entire community also will free society from the by-product of class exploitation, gender inequality.

Theories of Gender Oppression

All theories of gender oppression describe women's situation as the consequence of a direct power relationship between men and women in which men, who have fundamental and concrete interests in controlling, using, subjugating, and oppressing women, effectively implement those interests. Women's situation, then, for theorists of gender oppression, is centrally that of being used, controlled, subjugated, and oppressed by men. This pattern of oppression is incorporated in the deepest and most pervasive ways into society's organization, a basic structure of domination most commonly called *patriarchy*. Patriarchy is not the unintended and secondary consequence of some other set of factors—be it biology or socialization or sex roles or the class system. It is a primary power structure sustained by strong and deliberate intention. Indeed, to most theorists of oppression, gender differences and gender inequality are by-products of patriarchy.

Whereas most earlier feminist theorists focused on issues of gender inequality, a hallmark of contemporary feminist theory is the breadth and intensity of its concern with oppression (Jaggar, 1983). It is probably fair to say that a majority of contemporary feminist theorists are oppression theorists and certainly that the richest and most innovative theoretical developments within contemporary feminism have been the work of this cluster of theorists. Theoretical works on gender oppression constitute the cutting edge, the dynamic and expanding frontier of contemporary feminist theory. In contrast, although, as we shall see, a few sociologists have made important contributions to this literature, sociologists who deal with gender issues are not, as a community, strongly attracted to theories of oppression. It is probably this divergence of theoretical orientation to women's situation, with sociologists favoring theories of difference and inequality and feminist theorists favoring theories of oppression, that explains the ongoing disagreement between the two communities about whether sociological theory has taken any serious account of the implications of issues raised by feminist scholarship.

We turn now to four major variants of feminist theory, all of which focus on oppression but each of which is distinctive in its explanation of oppression. These theories are psychoanalytic feminism, radical feminism, socialist feminism, and third-wave feminism.

Psychoanalytic Feminist Theory   Contemporary psychoanalytical feminists attempt to explain patriarchy by using the theories of Freud and his intellectual heirs (al-Hibri, 1981; Chodorow, 1978; Dinnerstein, 1976; Kittay, 1984). These theories, broadly speaking, map and emphasize the emotional dynamics of personality, emotions often deeply buried in the subconscious or unconscious areas of the psyche; they also highlight the importance of infancy and early childhood in the patterning of these emotions. In attempting to use Freud's theories, however, feminists have to undertake a fundamental reworking of his conclusions. For Freud himself was notoriously patriarchal. He acknowledged gender differences and gender inequality but not gender oppression. Women to him were second-class human beings whose basic psychic nature fit them only for a lesser life than that experienced by men. Feminist theorists, therefore, have had to follow through on directions implicit in Freud's theories while rejecting his gender-specific conclusions.

Psychoanalytical feminists operate with a particular model of patriarchy. Like all oppression theorists, they see patriarchy as a system in which men subjugate women, a universal system, pervasive in its social organization, durable over time and space, and triumphantly maintained in the face of occasional challenge. Distinctive to psychoanalytic feminism, however, is the view that this system is one that all men, in their individual daily actions, work continuously and energetically to create and sustain. Women resist only occasionally but are to be discovered far more often either acquiescing in or actively working for their own subordination. The puzzle that psychoanalytical feminists set out to solve is why men bring everywhere enormous, unremitting energy to the task of sustaining patriarchy and why there is an absence of countervailing energy on the part of women.

In searching for an explanation to this puzzle, these theorists give short shrift to the argument that a cognitive calculus of practical benefits is sufficient for male support for patriarchy. Cognitive mobilization does not seem a sufficient source for the intense energy that men invest in patriarchy, especially because, in light of the human capacity to debate and second-guess, men may not always and everywhere be certain that patriarchy is of unqualified value to them. Moreover, an argument anchored in the cognitive pursuit of self-interest would suggest that women would as energetically mobilize against patriarchy. Instead, these theorists look to those aspects of the psyche so effectively mapped by the Freudians: the zone of human emotions, of half-recognized or unrecognized desires and fears, and of neurosis and pathology. Here one finds a clinically proven source of extraordinary energy and debilitation, one springing from psychic structures so deep that they cannot be recognized or monitored by individual consciousness. In searching for the energic underpinnings of patriarchy, psychoanalytical feminists have identified two possible explanations for male domination of women: the fear of death and the socioemotional environment in which the personality of the young child takes form.

Fear of death, of the ceasing of one's individuality, is viewed in psychoanalytic theory as one of those existential issues that everyone, everywhere, must on occasion confront and as one that causes everyone, in that confrontation, to experience terror. Feminist theorists who develop this theme argue that women, because of their intimate and protracted involvement with bearing and rearing new life, are typically far less oppressed than men by the realization of their own mortality (al-Hibri, 1981; Dinnerstein, 1976). Men, however, respond with deep dread to the prospect of their individual extinction and adopt a series of defenses, all of which lead to their domination of women. Men are driven to produce things that will outlast them—art and architecture, wealth and weapons, science and religion. All these then become resources by which men can dominate women (and each other). Men also are driven—partly by envy of women's reproductive role, partly by their own passionate desire for immortality through offspring—to seek to control the reproductive process itself. They claim ownership of women, seek to control women's bodies, and lay claim through norms of legitimacy and paternity to the products of those bodies, children. Finally, driven by fear, men seek to separate themselves from everything that reminds them of their own mortal bodies: birth, nature, sexuality, their human bodies and natural functions, and women, whose association with so many of these makes them the symbol of them all. All of these aspects of existence must be denied, repressed, and controlled as men seek constantly to separate from, deny, and repress their own mortality. And women, who symbolize all these forbidden topics, also must be treated as Other: feared, avoided, controlled.

The second theme in psychoanalytic feminism centers on two facets of early childhood development: one, the assumption that human beings grow into mature people by learning to balance a never-resolved tension between the desire for freedom of action—*individuation*—and the desire for confirmation by another—*recognition;* and two, the observable fact that in all societies infants and children experience their earliest and most crucial development in a close, uninterrupted, intimate relationship with a woman, their mother or mother substitute (Benjamin, 1985, 1988; Chodorow, 1978, 1990; Dinnerstein, 1976). As infants and young children, for considerable periods lacking even language as a tool for understanding experience, individuals experience their earliest phases of personality development as an ongoing turbulence of primitive emotions: fear, love, hate, pleasure, rage, loss, desire. The emotional consequences of these early experiences stay with people always as potent but often unconscious "feeling memories." Central to that experiential residue is a cluster of deeply ambivalent feelings for the woman/mother/caregiver: need, dependence, love, possessiveness, but also fear and rage over her ability to thwart one's will. Children's relationship to the father/man is much more occasional, secondary, and emotionally uncluttered. From this beginning, the male child, growing up in a culture that positively values maleness and devalues femaleness and increasingly aware of his own male identity, attempts to achieve an awkwardly rapid separation of identity from the woman/mother. This culturally induced separation is not only partial but also destructive in its consequences. In adulthood the emotional carryover from early childhood toward women—need, love, hate, possessiveness—energizes the man's quest for a woman of his own who meets his emotional needs and yet is dependent on and controlled by him—that is, he has an urge to dominate and finds mutual recognition difficult. The female child, bearing the same feelings toward the woman/mother, discovers her own female identity in a culture that devalues women. She grows up with deeply mixed positive and negative feelings about herself and about the woman/mother and in that ambivalence dissipates much of her potential for mobilized resistance to her social subordination. She seeks to resolve her emotional carryover in adulthood by emphasizing her capacities for according recognition—often submissively with males in acts of sexual attraction and mutually with females in acts of kinship maintenance and friendship. And rather than seeking mother substitutes, she re-creates the early infant-woman relationship by becoming a mother.

Psychoanalytical feminist theorists have successfully extended their explanations beyond individual personality to culture—or, at least, to Western culture. The emphases in Western science on a distinct separation between "man" and "nature," on "man" as the "dominator" of "nature," and on a "scientific method" derived from these attitudes and promising "objective" truth have been challenged and reinterpreted as the projection by the overindividuated male ego of its own desire for domination and its own fear of intersubjective recognition (Jaggar and Bordo, 1989; Keller, 1985). This critique has been carried not only into social science but into the more sacrosanct regions of "objective" natural science. What has been presented as sound method—objectivity, distance, control, absence of affect—is now interpreted as a working out of the gendered personality. Motifs in popular culture—such as the repeated positioning in both plot and image of the male as dominant over the female—are interpreted by psychoanalytical theorists as a sign of a breakdown in the requisite tensions between a need for individuation and a need for recognition (Benjamin, 1985, 1988). When this breakdown reaches, in a culture or personality, severe enough proportions, two pathologies result—the overindividuated dominator, who "recognizes" the other only through acts of control, and the underindividuated subordinate, who relinquishes independent action to find identity only as a mirror of the dominator.

Psychoanalytical feminists, then, explain women's oppression in terms of men's deep emotional need to control women, a drive arising from near-universal male neuroses centering on the fear of death and on ambivalence toward the mothers who reared them. Women either lack these neuroses or are subject to complementary neuroses, but in either case they are left psychically without an equivalent source of energy to resist domination. Much clinical psychiatric evidence supports the argument that these neuroses are in fact widespread, at least in Western societies. But these theories, in drawing a straight line from universal human emotions to universal female oppression, fail to explore the intermediate social arrangements that link emotion to oppression and fail to suggest possible lines of variation in either emotions, social arrangements, or oppression. Moreover, and partly because of these omissions, psychoanalytic feminist theory suggests very few strategies for change, except perhaps that we restructure our childbearing practices and begin some massive psychocultural reworking of our orientation toward death. These theories thus give us some provocative insights into and deepened understanding of the roots of gender oppression, but they require a great deal more elaboration of both sociological factors and change strategies. Both of these tasks are taken up more fully by three other variants of oppression theory: radical feminism, socialist feminism, and third-wave feminism.

Radical Feminism Central to radical feminism is an intense positive valuation of women and, as part of this, deep grief and rage over their oppression.[7] Radical feminists affirm woman's special worth in defiance of a universal system that devalues her; they rage at woman's oppression by presenting a detailed and shocking catalogue of the offenses committed against her worldwide. In this passionate mixture of love and rage, radical feminists resemble the more militant mode of racial and ethnic groups, the "black is beautiful" claims of black Americans or the detailed "witnessing" of oppression by Jews. As we explore radical feminists' appeal for and on behalf of women, we also can see quite clearly their position on social organization, gender oppression, and strategies for change.

Radical feminists see all society as characterized by oppression. Every institution is a system by which some people dominate others, and in society's most basic structures, in the associational patterns between broad groups or categories of people, one perceives a continuous pattern of domination and submission—between classes; castes; racial, ethnic, and religious groups; age and gender categories. Of all these systems of domination and subordination, the most fundamental structure of oppression is gender, the system of patriarchy. Not only was patriarchy, as Engels described, historically the first structure of domination and submission, but it continues as the most pervasive and enduring system of inequality, the basic societal model of domination. Through participation in patriarchy men learn how to hold other human beings in contempt, to see them as nonhuman, and to control them. Within patriarchy men see and women learn what subordination looks like. Patriarchy creates guilt and repression, sadism and masochism, manipulation and deception, all of which drive men and women to other forms of tyranny. Patriarchy, to radical feminists, is the least noticed and yet the most significant structure of social inequality.

Central to this analysis is the image of patriarchy as violence practiced by men and by male-dominated organizations against women. Violence may not always take the form of overt physical cruelty. It can be hidden in more complex practices of exploitation and control: in standards of fashion and beauty; in tyrannical ideals of motherhood, monogamy, chastity, and heterosexuality; in sexual harassment in the workplace; in the practices of gynecology, obstetrics, and psychotherapy; in unpaid household drudgery and underpaid wage work. Violence exists whenever one group controls in its own interests the life chances, environments, actions, and perceptions of another group, as men do women.

But the theme of violence as overt physical cruelty lies at the heart of radical feminism's linking of patriarchy to violence: rape, sexual abuse, sexual slavery

---

[7] This section is adapted from Lengermann and Wallace (1985:141–144).

in enforced prostitution, spouse abuse, incest, sexual molestation of children, hysterectomies and other excessively radical forms of surgery, and the explicit sadism in pornography are all linked to the historic and cross-cultural practices of witch burning, the stoning to death of adulteresses, the persecution of lesbians, female infanticide, Chinese foot-binding, the forced suicides of Hindu widows, and the savage practice of clitorectomy. Through the radical lens, we are given an image of women mutilated and bleeding as the visual representation of what patriarchy does.

Patriarchy exists as a near-universal social form ultimately because men can muster the most basic power resource, physical force, to establish control. Once patriarchy is in place, the other power resources—economic, ideological, legal, and emotional—also can be marshaled to sustain it. But physical violence always remains its last line of defense, and in both interpersonal and intergroup relations, that violence repeatedly is used to protect patriarchy from women's individual and collective resistance.

Men create and maintain patriarchy not only because they have the resources to do so but because they have real interests in making women serve as compliant tools. Women are, for one thing, a uniquely effective means of satisfying male sexual desire. Their bodies are, further, essential to the production of children, who satisfy both practical and, as psychoanalysts have shown, neurotic needs for men. Women are a useful labor force, as the Marxians have noted. They also can be ornamental signs of male status and power. As carefully controlled companions to both the child and the adult male, they are pleasant partners, sources of emotional support, and useful foils who reinforce, over and over again, the males' sense of their own central social significance. These useful functions mean that men everywhere seek to keep women compliant. But differing social circumstances give different rank orders to these functions and therefore lead to cross-cultural variations in the patterning of patriarchy. Radical feminists, unlike psychoanalytical feminists, give us both an explanation of universal gender oppression *and* a model for understanding cross-cultural variations in this oppression.

How is patriarchy to be defeated? Radicals hold that this defeat must begin with a basic reworking of women's consciousness so that each woman recognizes her own value and strength; rejects patriarchal pressures to see herself as weak, dependent, and second-class; and works in unity with other women, regardless of differences among them, to establish a broad-based sisterhood of trust, support, appreciation, and mutual defense. With this sisterhood in place, two strategies suggest themselves: a critical confrontation with any facet of patriarchal domination whenever it is encountered; and a degree of separatism as women withdraw into women-run businesses, households, communities, centers of artistic creativity, and love relationships.

How does one evaluate radical feminism? Emotionally each of us will respond to it in light of our own degree of personal radicalism, some seeing it as excessively critical and others as entirely convincing. But in attempting a theoretical evaluation, one should note that radical feminism incorporates

DOROTHY E. SMITH: An Autobiographical Sketch

Dorothy E. Smith explains that her sociological theory derives from her life experiences as a woman, particularly as a woman moving between two worlds—the male-dominated academic sphere and the essentially female-centered life of the single parent. Remembering herself at Berkeley in the early 1960s studying for a doctorate in sociology and single parenting, Smith reflects that her life seems to have been framed by what she sees as "not so much as a career as a series of contingencies, of accidents" (1979:151). This theme of contingency is one of many personal experiences that have led Smith to challenge sociological orthodoxy such as the image of the voluntary actor working through role conflicts.

Whether they occurred by accident or design, the following events appear to the outsider as significant stages in Smith's development. She was born in 1926 in Great Britain; she earned her bachelor's degree in sociology from the University of London in 1955 and her Ph.D. in sociology from the University of California at Berkeley in 1963. During this same period, she had "the experience of marriage, of immigration [to Canada] closely following marriage, of the arrival of children, of the departure of a husband rather early one morning, of the jobs that became available" (Smith, 1979:151). Of these events, Smith stresses, they "were moments in which I had in fact little choice and certainly little foreknowledge." The jobs that became available included research sociologist at Berkeley; lecturer in sociology at Berkeley; lecturer in sociology at the University of Essex, Colchester, England; associate professor and then professor in the department of sociology at the University of British Columbia; and since 1977, professor of sociology in education at the Ontario Institute for Studies in Education, Toronto.

Smith has written on a fairly wide variety of topics, all connected by a concern with "bifurcation," sometimes as a central theme and sometimes as a motif. Smith sees the experience of bifurcation manifesting itself in the separation between social-scientific description and people's lived experience, between women's lived experience and the patriarchal ideal types they are given for describing that experience, between the micro-world

arguments made by both Marxian and psychoanalytical feminists about the reasons for women's subordination and yet moves beyond those theories. It is the broadest of the variants of feminism that we have thus far encountered. Radical feminists, moreover, have done significant research to support their thesis that patriarchy ultimately rests on the practice of violence against women (Barry, 1979; Bunch, 1987; Dworkin, 1987; 1989; Frye, 1983; Griffin, 1978, 1981; Millet, 1970; Rich, 1976, 1980). They have a reasonable though perhaps incomplete program for change. They have been faulted in their exclusive focus on patriarchy. This focus seems to simplify the realities of social organization and social inequality and thus to approach the issues of ameliorative change somewhat unrealistically. The third group of gender oppression theories, socialist feminism, sets out explicitly to address this criticism of radical feminism's unidimensional concern with patriarchy.

and the macro-world structures that dictate micro experience, and, especially, between the micro world of the oppressed and the micro world of the dominants whose actions create the macro structures of oppression. The concretization of these themes can be seen in a selective review of the titles of some of Smith's works: "The Statistics on Women and Mental Illness: How Not to Read Them" (1975), "What It Might Mean to Do a Canadian Sociology: The Everyday World as Problematic" (1976), "K is Mentally Ill: The Anatomy of a Factual Account" (1978), "Where There Is Oppression, There Is Resistance" (1979), "Women, Class and Family" (1981)—and, above all, her most important contribution to feminist sociology, "A Sociology for Women" (1979). In 1987 Smith produced her most extensive and integrated treatment of these themes in what has become a landmark in feminist sociology, *The Everyday World as Problematic.* She followed this with *The Conceptual Practices of Power* (1990a) and *Texts, Facts and Femininity* (1990b).

What Smith is producing for feminist sociologists, and indeed for all sociologists interested in the theoretical frontiers of the profession, is a sociology that integrates neo-Marxian concerns with the structures of domination and phenomenological insights into the variety of subjective and micro-interactional worlds. Smith sees these various everyday life-worlds as being commonly shaped by macro structures which are themselves shaped by the historical specifics of economic demand. What Smith wishes to avoid, in developing this line of reasoning, is a vision of the world in which the oppressors are consistently interpreted as individual actors making rational decisions on the basis of self-interest. What Smith sees is that self-interest itself is structurally situated, and what she calls for sociologists to focus on is always the ultimate structure producing the outcome at hand. But she believes that this structure can become known only by beginning with the outcome at hand, that is, by exploring the everyday worlds of situated individuals. Smith is concerned that much social science serves to obfuscate rather than clarify the structures that produce these worlds because much social science begins with an assumption that the structures are already known and can be known separately from the everyday life-worlds.

Sociologists working out of a feminist perspective are currently turning increasingly to Smith for a systematic framing of their major concerns. The implications of Smith's work for sociological theory form the basis for much of this chapter.

Socialist Feminism   Socialist feminism is a highly diverse cluster of theoretical writings unified more by a theoretical agenda and less by substantive theoretical conclusions (Eisenstein, 1979; Hartman, 1979; Hartsock, 1983; MacKinnon, 1982, 1989; Ruddick, 1980; Smith, 1974, 1975, 1978, 1979, 1987, 1989, 1990a, 1990b). Three goals guide all socialist feminism: theoretical synthesis (see Chapter 17), a combination of theoretical breadth and precision, and an explicit and adequate method for social analysis and social change.

Socialist feminists have set themselves the formal project of achieving both a synthesis of and a theoretical step beyond extant feminist theories. More specifically, socialist feminists seek to bring together what they perceive as the two broadest and most valuable feminist traditions: Marxian and radical feminist thought.

Out of this project of synthesis have flowed two distinctive subvarieties of socialist feminism. The first focuses exclusively on women's oppression and on understanding it in a way that brings together knowledge (from Marxism) of class oppression and (from radical feminism) of gender oppression. Through this theoretical intersection, these theorists seek to map the commonalities and variations in women's experiences of subordination. The term most frequently used by these theorists for the system they describe is *capitalist patriarchy* (Eisenstein, 1979; Hartman, 1979).

The second variant of socialist feminism sets out to describe and explain all forms of social oppression, using knowledge of class and gender hierarchies as a base from which to explore systems of oppression centering not only on class and gender but also on race, ethnicity, age, sexual preference, and location within the global hierarchy of nations. The term most frequently used by these theorists for the system they describe is *domination* (Frye, 1983; Lorde, 1984; D. Smith, 1979). Women remain central to this theoretical approach in two ways. First, as with all feminism, the oppression of women remains a primary topic for analysis. The theorists of domination can map even more elaborately than those of capitalist patriarchy the variations and permutations in that oppression. Second, women's location and experience of the world serve as the essential vantage point on domination in all its forms. Ultimately, though, these theorists are concerned with all experiences of oppression, either by women or by men. They even explore how some women, themselves oppressed, may yet actively participate in the oppression of other women, as, for example, white women in American society who oppress black women. Indeed, one strategy of all socialist feminists is to confront the prejudices and oppressive practices *within* the community of women itself (Frye, 1983; Lorde, 1984).

Both the focus on capitalist patriarchy and that on domination are linked to a commitment, either explicit or implicit, to historical materialism as an analytical strategy (Jaggar, 1983). *Historical materialism,* a basic principle in Marxian social theory, refers to the position that the material conditions of human life, inclusive of the activities and relationships that produce those conditions, are the key factors that pattern human experience, personality, ideas, and social arrangements; that those conditions change over time because of dynamics imminent within them; and that history is a record of the changes in the material conditions of a group's life and of the correlative changes in experiences, personality, ideas, and social arrangements. Historical materialists hold that any effort at social analysis must trace in historically concrete detail the specifics of the group's material conditions and the links between those conditions and the experiences, personalities, events, ideas, and social arrangements characteristic of the group. In linking historical materialism to their focus on domination,[8] socialist feminists attempt to realize their goal of

---

[8] From here on, we use the term *domination* to refer to the central concerns of both variants of socialist feminism. Both groups are in fact concerned with hierarchy, broadly conceived, rather than with any particular system of hierarchy.

a theory that probes the broadest of human social arrangements, domination, and yet remains firmly committed to precise, historically concrete analyses of the material and social arrangements that frame particular situations of domination.

The historical materialism that is a hallmark of socialist feminism shows clearly the school's indebtedness to Marxian thought. But in their use of this principle, socialist feminists move beyond the Marxians in three crucial ways: their redefinition of material conditions, their reevaluation of the significance of ideology, and their focus on domination. First, they broaden the meaning of the *material conditions* of human life. Marxians typically mean by this idea the economic dynamics of society, particularly the ways in which goods of a variety of types are created for and exchanged in the market. In the various exploitative arrangements here, which make some wealthy and others poor, they locate the roots of class inequality and class conflict. Socialist feminist analysis includes economic dynamics and also, more broadly, other conditions that create and sustain human life: the human body, its sexuality and involvement in procreation and child rearing; home maintenance, with its unpaid, invisible round of domestic tasks; emotional sustenance; and the production of knowledge itself. In *all* these life-sustaining activities, exploitative arrangements profit some and impoverish others. Full comprehension of all these basic arrangements of life production and exploitation is the essential foundation for a theory of domination.

This redefinition of the concept of material conditions transforms the Marxian assumption that human beings are producers of goods into a theme of human beings as creators and sustainers of all human life. This shift brings us to the second point of difference between Marxian historical materialism and historical materialism as it is developed in socialist feminism, namely, the latter perspective's emphasis on what some Marxians might call, dismissively, *mental or ideational phenomena:* consciousness, motivation, ideas, social definitions of the situation, knowledge, ideology, the will to act in one's interests or acquiesce to the interests of others.[9] To socialist feminists all these factors deeply affect human personality, human action, and the structures of domination that are realized through that action. Moreover, these aspects of human subjectivity are produced by social structures that are inextricably intertwined with, and as elaborate and powerful as, those that produce economic goods. Within all these structures, too, exploitative arrangements enrich and empower some while impoverishing and immobilizing others. Analysis of the processes that pattern human subjectivity is vital to a theory of domination, and that analysis also can be honed to precision by applying the principles of historical materialism.

The third difference between socialist feminists and Marxians is that the object of analysis for socialist feminists is not primarily class inequality but

---

[9] Admittedly some neo-Marxians, notably the critical theorists, have also reevaluated the explanatory significance of ideology (see Chapter 8).

the complex intertwining of a wide range of social inequalities. Socialist feminism develops a portrait of social organization in which the public structures of economy, polity, and ideology interact with the intimate, private processes of human reproduction, domesticity, sexuality, and subjectivity to sustain a *multifaceted system of domination,* the workings of which are discernible both as enduring and impersonal social patterns and in the more varied subtleties of interpersonal relationships. To analyze this system, socialist feminists shuttle between a mapping of large-scale systems of domination and a situationally specific, detailed exploration of the mundane daily experiences of oppressed people. Their strategy for change rests in this process of discovery, in which they attempt to involve the oppressed groups that they study and through which they hope that both individuals and groups, in large and small ways, will learn to act in pursuit of their collective emancipation.

An important criticism of socialist feminism, and indeed of all the varieties of feminism described so far, is that despite their emancipatory claims they tend to be located in the assumptions and aspirations of white, middle-class, North Atlantic women. There is a growing concern within feminist theory over the practical and theoretical problematic posed by the exploitation of women of one class, race, ethnic group, and global position by women of another. This problematic is the focus of the theorists discussed in the following section.

Third-Wave Feminism   The term *third-wave feminism* refers to critical and theoretical statements, formulated within the women's movement primarily in the 1980s, that build on the theme of *difference.* Third-wave feminism looks critically at the tendency of work done in the 1960s and 1970s to use a generalized, monolithic concept of "woman" as a generic category in stratification and focuses instead on the factual and theoretical implications of differences among women. The differences considered are those that result from an unequal distribution of socially produced goods and services on the basis of position in the global system, class, race, ethnicity, and affectional preference as these interact with gender stratification. Perhaps the most significant bloc of writings within this particular new development in feminism is that being generated by women of color. This section focuses on the North American contribution to these writings (Allen, 1989; Anzaldua, 1990; Aptheker, 1989; P. Collins, 1990; Giddings, 1984; Hooks, 1984, 1989; Lorde, 1984; Moraga and Anzaldua, 1981; Rollins, 1985; Walker, 1983, 1988, 1989).

The writings of North American women of color who are helping to elaborate third-wave feminism are all distinguished by the fact that they aim their critical effort not only against sexual ideology and the unequal status of women but more broadly at all systems of domination—sexist, racist, classist, heterosexist, and imperialist—and at the particular false consciousness that has let middle-class white heterosexual women use the term *woman* as a monolithic category in opposing male domination while ignoring their own acts of domination toward women who do not share their class, race, and affectional preference. Central to this perspective are five themes. First, truth about social relations is best discovered through the vantage point of oppressed peoples (both women and men), whose accounts must therefore be uncovered. Second, a particularly revealing knowledge of the social relations of domination is that of North American women of color who find themselves intimately linked to those who control and exploit them in situations of domestic employment, poorly paid service work, and sexual, emotional, and reproductive work, both paid and unpaid. Women of color find themselves closely linked to those who oppress them as women, as people of color, and as poor people and have the experience of "the stranger within" the circles of domination (P. Collins, 1990). Third, exploring the vantage point of women of color reveals a global and intricately interwoven system of class, race, and gender oppression. Fourth, the oppressive system produces pathological attitudes, actions, and personalities within the ranks of both the oppressor and the oppressed. Examples of these pathologies within circles of the oppressed include the conflict between affluent women and poor women, the conflict between white and nonwhite women, and the violence of men toward women in minority communities. Fifth, resistance to both oppression and pathology is located first in the unquenchable need of human beings for full, individuated self-actualization and second, and dialectically, by membership in one's particular community of oppressed people, whose culture, nurturance, and survival strategies are essential to the well-being of its individual members.

Recent theoretical statements by women of color expand and enrich feminism's exploration of the structures of oppression, its explanation of these structures, and its program for amelioration. We raise three notes of caution. First, theoretically, if one starts with an assumption of difference, or distinctiveness, as *the* quality that deserves theoretical exploration in one's work on women, where logically does one stop? How can one justify generalizations about African-American women, Third World women, or lesbian women? Second, a corollary to this is that the very phrase "women of color" in its way derives from a so-called white definition of the world—white women and men do have color despite their ideology that places them beyond the color boundary. Finally, there is the practical consideration: Is there not a risk to effective coalitions against oppression posed by the particular claims to entitlements by various subcommunities of women?

Nevertheless, despite the many varieties of contemporary feminist theory, there is a consistent concern with the basic sociological question of how and why social organization takes the form it does in any particular society at any particular time. We will see the significance of feminist theory for a sociological theory of social organization in the next section.

A FEMINIST SOCIOLOGICAL THEORY

One of the principles of intellectual practice raised by feminism, and which we take as a starting point for a feminist *sociological* theory, is that there can be no disinterested observers. For example, even sociologists observe social organization from a social position of relative social advantage. Therefore, we should identify our position as feminists. According to the descriptions we have set forth, we are oppression theorists who fall somewhere between radical and socialist theory.[10] From that perspective, we identify four distinctive features of a feminist sociology:

1 A distinctive sociology of knowledge
2 A distinctive model of the organization of society at the macro-social level
3 An exploration of the relational situation of women that alters the traditional sociological understanding of micro interaction
4 A revision of sociology's model of subjectivity

A Feminist Sociology of Knowledge

Feminist sociological theory turns on a distinctive sociology of knowledge, that branch of sociology which studies how knowledge is itself a product of social relations. Feminist theory's sociology of knowledge is rooted in an epistemology that is at the core of feminist thought because it is fundamental to women's life experiences.

Feminist sociology of knowledge sees everything that people label "knowledge of the world" as having four characteristics: (1) It is always discovered from the vantage point of an embodied actor situated in a social structure; (2) it is, thus, always partial and interested, never total and objective; (3) it varies from person to person because of differences in embodiment and social situation; (4) it is always affected by power relations—whether it is discovered from the vantage point of the dominant or the subordinate. Thus, in beginning any study from a feminist sociological perspective, the feminist theorist would argue, one must take knowledge as the key *problematic*, the issue that is yet to be determined, that frames further inquiry. For feminist sociological theory, the framing tasks for any inquiry are (1) to identify and describe the complexity of the actor's social situation as a "vantage point" on reality; (2) to establish the standards by which the sociologist working with admittedly partial accounts can lay claim to producing any knowledge, to knowing anything at the end of the study, and (3) to analyze how power relations become manifest in knowledge claims. Above all, the unpardonable error from the standpoint of feminist epistemology is to perform, speak, or write in the stance of "the god eye" (Haraway, 1988), that is, to act as though you were a disembodied, distant, omniscient observer, outside and above but all-knowing about your research subject. (In the most common example of "the god eye," obser-

---

[10] The fullest sense of our intellectual position may be suggested by acknowledging our intellectual debt at both the theoretical and empirical levels to Dorothy Smith's pioneering woman-centered sociology (Smith, 1979, 1987, 1990a, 1990b). Other major feminist sources of this effort are J. Bernard (1982); Chodorow (1978, 1990); P. Collins (1990); Gilligan (1982); Haraway (1988); Harding and Hintikka (1983); Harding (1987); Hartsock (1983); Heilbrun (1988); Jaggar and Bordo (1989); Lorde (1984); MacKinnon (1989); Rich (1976, 1979); L. Rubin (1976, 1979, 1985); Ruddick (1980), and Stacey and Thorne (1985).

vations made by an embodied person are rewritten from "I learned" to "Research shows.")

The first task is to identify the social actors who construct their knowledge on the foundations of their situated experiences and interests. Feminists, starting where Marx left off, identified three crucial groups—owner, workers, *and* women—whose life circumstances and relations with each other are only in part patterned by economic factors. Then, as feminists have explored the differences among women, they have discovered a multiplicity of differently situated groups of people. In tracing the relationships among all these groups, feminists have moved beyond a class model of domination to a vision of a complex system of unequally empowered groups relating through shifting arrangements of coalition and opposition. Further, feminists have realized that actors are embodied people whose social vantage point shifts over time and by issue; thus, there is no abstract locus for knowledge—no "Third World woman" or "disinterested biologist" or "religious mystic." There are people for whom these labels may signify part of their identity, but the total human is someone infinitely more complex—because embodied—than such terms imply.

The second task is to explain on what basis one can, as a sociologist, make any truth claims if the foregoing is an accurate account, that is, if knowledge is discovered by social actors whose positions must be unstable if only because of the fact of human mortality alone. Feminist sociological theorists try not to collapse into a relativism in which one account cancels out another (see D. Smith, 1990a, for a good example of how to avoid this). Instead, they provide several bases for asserting knowledge. One is asserting the validity of what Haraway terms (1988) "webbed accounts," that is, accounts woven together by reporting all the actors' versions of an experience and describing the situations from which the actors came to create these versions. This approach, pursued in various ways in feminist empirical studies, demands that both reader and researcher hold in mind, and work with, a complex understanding of knowledge. It concretizes the complexity of the ideal of recognizing vantage points. A corollary to this approach is one in which the researcher identifies her or his partiality (in all meanings of that word) and takes responsibility for asserting knowledge gained from a particular location. In a third approach, the feminist researcher takes as a primary task the analysis of how things work to produce what is called *knowledge*. She or he looks at the processes by which an account becomes "fact," that is, becomes accepted by a majority of people as the way that an event occurred. She or he may offer a webbed account of what "actually" occurred and a procedural account of how the event becomes fact. In all this, the researcher is drawn to an analysis of power relations and of her or his complicity as a social scientist transforming accounts into facts in sustaining these relations.

The third epistemological task is to analyze the relations between knowledge and power because what finally happens to any actor's account of any event depends on the actor's location within a social system in which power determines placement and placement, power. This conception of the relation between knowledge and power provides the philosophic basis for feminists' insistent valuation of the viewpoints of less privileged groups, for a major factor in privilege is that the viewpoints of favorably situated actors become "the viewpoints of the society" (an expansion of Marx's dictum, "The ruling ideas of any age are the ideas of its ruling class"). This awareness presses feminists constantly to call attention not only to the "women's" view of a situation but to the views among differing groups of women and, by extension, to the views of people whose placement by race, age, affectional preference, or global location makes them less privileged.

Feminist studies show how institutionalized forms—and here we mean *form* as in *text*—can be used to present a ruling elite's definition of an event. A presidential commission report, a hospital admission form, and a social worker's case analysis are all patterned by dominants as ways of presenting the facts about their own and subordinates' lives. A critical element of feminist sociological inquiry involves describing and analyzing the construction of facts, seeing whose accounts (the oral narrative versus the police report, for instance) are allowed to emerge from the social process as fact.

As we have said, all this stems finally from women's daily experiences. Women's social situation traditionally has made them, on the one hand, balancers of a variety of views and, on the other hand, parties who have seen their own views discounted or distorted by male power. They are, in the first instance, expected—in their roles as wives, mothers, and daughters and in the larger, slightly less gender-prescribed world of economic, educational, religious, and political production—to serve as moderators who ensure that all positions receive a "fair" hearing. But if they reflect at all, they are also aware of how many times, in the second instance, they and other disempowered persons—children, the elderly, the poor, racial minorities, and women as women—are not allowed to have their participation in discourse taken seriously (Heilbrun, 1988:18). Women thus find knowledge not by accepting unilateral claims to truth but by balancing and weighing the accounts of reality presented to them by a variety of others.

The Macro-Social Order

In this and the sections that follow we operate within the established sociological conventions of vocabulary and conceptualization by organizing our presentation around such phrases as *macro social, micro social,* and *subjectivity.* Certainly one can extract much from feminist theory that relates to one or other of these established sociological concepts—although, as we shall see, much of what is extracted poses a fundamental critique of existing sociological assertions about these topics. But the critique goes even deeper. Feminist theory is in the process of articulating a new conceptual vocabulary for sociology which moves outside and away from the old bifurcation of macro social versus micro social/subjective, making that vision of social reality obsolete. For this reason, although in the interest of effective communication we use the old mileposts—macro, micro, subjective—as a point of entry into feminist theory, we turn in the final part of this section to the new concepts, with which feminist sociologists are beginning to move beyond the older model of social reality.

Feminist sociology's view of the macro-social order emphasizes the impact of both social structure (or macro-objective productions) and ideology (or macro subjectivity) on actors' perceptions of social reality.

Feminist sociology begins by expanding the Marxian concept of economic production into a much more general concept of social production, that is, the production of all human social life. Along with the production of commodities for the market, social production for feminists also includes arrangements like the organization of housework, which produce outside of the market or money economy the essential commodities and services of the household; arrangements like the social organization of sexuality, which pattern and satisfy human desire and human emotional needs for acceptance, approval, love, and self-esteem; arrangements such as the state and religion, which create the rules and laws of a community; and arrangements like politics, mass media, and academic discourse, which establish institutionalized, public definitions of the situation.

Thus framed and expanded, the Marxian model of intergroup relations remains visible in feminist theory's model of social organization. Each of the various types of social production is based on an arrangement by which some actors, controlling the resources crucial to that activity, act as dominants, or "masters," who dictate and profit from the circumstances of production. Within each productive sector, productivity rests on the work of subordinates, or "servants," whose energies create the world ordered into being by their masters and whose exploitation denies them the rewards and satisfactions produced by their work. Through feminist theory, we see, more vividly than through Marxian theory, the intimate association between masters and servants that lies at the heart of *all* production and the indispensability of the servant's work in creating and sustaining everything necessary to human social life. Social production occurs through a multidimensional structure of domination and exploitation that organizes class, gender, race, sex, power, and knowledge into overlapping hierarchies of intimately associated masters and workers.

Turning to another aspect of the macro order, feminist research shows that women and other nondominants do not experience social life as a movement among compartmentalized roles, as structural functionalists assert. Instead, they are involved in a balancing of rules, a merging of role-associated interests and orientations, and, through this merging, in a weaving together of social institutions. This is true of the working mother as well as working women in "typically female" job categories like secretary or nurse. It is also true when women link the activities of housewife and economic consumer or of mother of school-age children and spouse of wage-sector participant. Moreover, in the classic double bind or "no-win situation" which marks women's experience of subordination, this blending and balancing is expected of women while used as a basis of invidious comparisons between women's role behavior and "typical" or compartmentalized role performance. Thus it is said disparagingly that women "bring outside concerns into the office," "let their emotions affect their performance," and "cannot keep the fact that they are women out of the situation."

The feminist model of stratification in social production offers a direct critique of the structural-functionalist vision of a society composed of a system of separate institutions and distinct through interrelated roles. Feminist theory claims that this image is not generalizable but that instead it depicts the experiences and vantage points of a particular situated group—white, male, upper class, and adult. Indeed, one indicator of this group's control over the situations of production may be that its members can achieve this kind of purposive compartmentalization in *their* role behavior, a condition that serves to reproduce their control over situations. But feminist sociology stresses that this condition depends on the subordinate services of actors who cannot compartmentalize their lives and actions. Indeed, were these subordinate actors to similarly compartmentalize, the whole system of production in complex industrialized societies would collapse. In contrast to the structural-functional model, the feminist model emphasizes that the role-merging experience of women may be generalizable to the experience of many other subordinate "servant" groups whose work produces the fine-grained texture of daily life. The understandings that such subordinated groups have of the organization of social life may be very different from the understanding depicted in structural-functionalist theory; even their identification of key institutional spheres may differ. Yet their vantage point springs from situations necessary to society as it is presently organized and from work that makes possible the masters' secure sense of an institutionally compartmentalized world.

Further, feminism emphasizes the centrality of ideological domination to the structure of social domination. Ideology is an intricate web of beliefs about reality and social life that is institutionalized as public knowledge and disseminated throughout society so effectively that it becomes taken-for-granted knowledge for all social groups. Thus what feminists see as "public knowledge of social reality" is not an overarching culture, a consensually created social product, but a reflection of the interests and experiences of society's dominants and one crucial index of their power in society. What distinguishes this view from most Marxian views is that for feminists ideological control is *the* basic process in domination, and the hierarchical control of discourse and knowledge is the key element in societal domination.

Central to feminist concerns about the macro-social order, of course, is the macro-structural patterning of gender inequality. Ideology plays a crucial role in the maintenance of this societal vector of dominance and subordination. Gender inequality is reproduced by a system of institutionalized knowledge that reflects the interests and experiences of men. Among other things, this gender ideology identifies men as the bearers of sociocultural authority and allocates to the male role the right to dominate and to the female role the obligation to serve in all dimensions of social production. Gender ideology also systematically flattens and distorts women's productive activities by (1) trivializing some of them, for example, housework; (2) idealizing to the point of unrecognizability other activities, for example, mothering; and (3) making invisible yet other crucial work, for example, women's multiple and vital contributions to the production of marketplace commodities. These ideological processes may be generalizable to the macro-structural production of all social subordination.

The Micro-Social Order

At the micro-interactional level, feminist sociology (like some microsociological perspectives) focuses on how individuals take account of each other as they pursue objective projects or subjectively shared meanings. Feminist sociology differs in five important ways from social definitionism and social behaviorism, both of which focus on the micro-interactional order. A review of these five differences reveals important aspects of the feminist model of the micro order.

Responsive Action versus Purposeful Action   Most mainstream microsociology presents a model of purposive human beings setting their own goals and pursuing these in linear courses of action in which they (individually or collectively) strive to link means to ends. In contrast, feminist research shows, first, that women's lives have a quality of incidentalness, as women find themselves caught up in agendas that shift and change with the vagaries of marriage, husbands' courses of action, children's unpredictable impact on life plans, divorce, widowhood, and the precariousness of most women's wage-sector occupations. Second, in their daily activities, women find themselves not so much pursuing goals in linear sequences but responding continuously to the needs and demands of others. This theme has been developed from Chodorow's (1978) analysis of the emotional and relational symbiosis between mothers and daughters, through Lever's (1978) and Gilligan's (1982) descriptions of intensely relational female play groups, to analyses of women in their typical occupations as teachers, nurses, secretaries, receptionists, and office helpers and accounts of women in their roles as wives, mothers, and community and kin coordinators. In calling women's activities "responsive," we are not describing them as passively reactive. Instead, we are drawing a picture of beings who are oriented not so much to their own goals as to the tasks of monitoring, coordinating, facilitating, and moderating the wishes, actions, and demands of others. In place of microsociology's conventional model of purposeful actors, then, feminist research presents a model of actors who are in their daily lives responsively located at the center of a web of others' actions and who in the long term find themselves located in one or another of these situations by forces that they can neither predict nor control.

Intermittent Interaction versus Continuous Interaction   Microsociology's typical picture of social life shows purposive actors who are almost continuously in face-to-face interactions in which they orient to each other and in which they assume that all the other actors in the situation are fundamentally like them. Feminist theory describes a world in which women experience highly variable interactions that seldom assume all the interactive qualities of that model. For long periods of each day, adult women located in households work in isolation from face-to-face interactions and orient to others only subjectively and responsively rather than purposively. In other settings, particularly in low-status office, factory, or service jobs, women find themselves working at structurally patterned routines in proximity to, but not in interaction with, each other. In many of their most significant interactive situations, they find themselves relating to other beings whom they do not assume to be fundamentally like themselves: children so young that they must be treated as less than self and adult men whom they know to be fundamentally different from them in personality, experience of life, and social situation—their existential "other" (de Beauvoir, 1957). Only when they come together in spontaneous and open association with other adult women does their interactive experience meet assumptions built into the conventional microsociological model of typical interaction. Feminist theory then raises these questions: Whose experiences of interaction provide sociology with its model of prototypical interaction? What, from the standpoint of women, constitutes prototypical interaction? Feminists answer these questions by claiming, first, that the experience of dominant men is mirrored in sociology's basic model of interaction and, second, that women's relationship to these men is, at least in its frequency and practical consequences, women's crucial and prototypical interaction. Feminists' exploration of male-female interactions takes us further into the feminist model of micro interaction.

The Assumption of Inequality versus the Assumption of Equality   Conventional micro-social theory assumes that the pressures in interactive situations toward collaboration and meaning construction are so great that actors, bracketing considerations of the macro structure, orient toward each other on an assumption of equality. Feminist research on interactions between women and men flatly contradicts this, showing that these social interactions are pervasively patterned by influences from their macro-structural context. In their daily activities, women are affected by the fact that they are structurally subordinate to the men with whom they interact in casual associations, courtship, marriage, family, and wage work. Any interpersonal equality or dominance that women as individuals may achieve is effectively offset, within the interactive process itself, by these structural patterns—of which the most pervasive is the institution of gender. The macro-structural patterning of gender inequality is intricately woven through the interactions between women and men and affects not only its broad division of labor, in who sets and who implements projects, but also its processual details, which repeatedly show the enactment of authority and deference in seating and seating-standing arrangements, forms of address and conversation, eye contact, and the control of space and time.

Stratified Meanings versus Common Meanings Conventional microsociology either brackets the issue of meaning (the social behaviorists) or assumes that the activities and relationships that occur in situated interactions become the basis and focus of collaborative meaning construction (the social definitionists). Actors, seeing each other in activity and interaction, form shared understandings through communication and ultimately a common vantage point on their experiences. Feminists argue that this assumption must be drastically qualified by the fact that micro interactions are embedded in and permeated by the macro structure. Women's everyday actions and relationships occur against a backdrop of public or institutionalized understanding of everyday experience, that is, as we have said, a macrostructural layer of ideology that flattens and distorts the reality by trivializing, idealizing, or making invisible women's activity and experience. This ideology patterns the meanings assigned to activities in interaction. Men (dominants) in interaction with women are more likely to assign to women's activity meanings drawn from the macro structure of gender ideology than either to enter the situation with an attitude of open inquiry or to draw on any other macro-level typing for interpreting women's activity. Women, immersed in the same ideological interpretation of their experiences, stand at a point of dialectical tension, balancing this ideology against the actuality of their lives. A great diversity of meanings develops out of this tension.

As everything that has been said so far indicates, social definitionists assume that actors, relating and communicating intimately and over long periods of time, create a common vantage point or system of shared understanding. Feminists research on what may be the most intimate, long-term, male-female association, marriage, shows that, for all the reasons reported above, marriage partners remain strangers to each other and inhabit separate worlds of meaning. Moreover, Dorothy Smith (1979) argues convincingly that this "stranger-ness" may be a variable in which the dominant man, in the interests of effective control, is more a stranger to women's meanings than women as subordinates can afford to be to the dominant's meanings.

Constraint versus Choice in Meaning-Creating Locations A profoundly democratic ethos shapes both social-definitionist and social-behaviorist descriptions of interaction. Conventional models consistently imply that people have considerable equality of opportunity and freedom of choice in moving in and out of interactional settings. Feminist research shows that the interactions in which women are most free to create with others meanings that depict their life experiences are those which occur when they are in relationship and communication with similarly situated women. Moreover, these associations can be deeply attractive to women because of the practical, emotional, and meaning-affirming support that they provide. Women, however, are not freely empowered to locate in these settings. Law, interactional domination, and ideology restrict and demean this associational choice so that, insidiously, even women become suspicious of its attractions. Under these circumstances, the association becomes not a free and open choice but a subterranean, circumscribed, and publicly invisible arena for relationship and meaning.

What does all this add up to in a feminist sociology of the micro order? First, it suggests not that the conventional models are wholly inaccurate but that they are only partial models. But if we return to our starting point, that truth lies at the intersection of vantage points, then a partial model must have elements of distortion—especially when that partial model is allowed to stand unchallenged. The conventional model of interaction may depict how equals in the macro-structural, power-conferring categories create a vantage point. It may also depict how, from the vantage point of structural dominance, one experiences interaction with both equals and subordinates. And it may well suggest a strain or tendency in all interactional arrangements. But, and second, when structural unequals interact, there are many other qualities to their association than those suggested by the conventional models. Indeed, these other features suggest another model that better captures the realities of the subordinate's experience; incidentalness of project, responsiveness of action, movement in and out of very different interaction experiences, continuous enactment of power differentials, activities whose meanings are invisible or obscured, estrangement from the meanings of others involved in the interaction, and restricted access to those settings where meaningfulness is most likely to be a genuinely shared experience. Third, we need to ask whether this latter model is not generalizable to the experience of all subordinates and whether sociologists must not plot the reality of the micro-interactional order at the dialectical intersection of all these models of interpersonal association.

Subjectivity

One of the most striking features of feminist sociology is its insistence on a third level of social activity—the subjective. Most sociological theories subsume this level under micro-social action (micro subjectivity) or as "culture" or "ideology" at the macro level (macro subjectivity) (see Chapter 14; Appendix). Feminist sociology, however, insists that the actor's individual interpretation of goals and relationships must be looked at as a distinct level. This insistence, like so much of feminist sociology, grows out of the study of women's lives and seems applicable to the lives of subordinates in general. Women (and perhaps other subordinates) are particularly aware of the distinctiveness of their subjective experience precisely because, as we have indicated, their own experience so often runs counter to prevailing cultural and micro-interactionally established definitions.

When sociologists do look at the subjective level of experience, usually as part of the micro-social order, they focus on four major issues: role taking and knowledge of the other; the process of the internalization of community norms; the nature of the self as social actor; and the nature of the consciousness of everyday life. This section explores the feminist thesis on each of these issues.

The Issue of Role Taking and the Sense of Other   The conventional sociological model of subjectivity (as presented to us in the theories of Mead [see Chapter 9] and Schutz [see Chapter 10]) assumes that in the course of role taking, the social actor learns to see the self through the eyes of others deemed more or less the same as the actor. But feminist sociology shows that women are socialized to see themselves through the eyes of men. Even when significant others are women, they have been so socialized that they too take the male view of self and of other women. Women's experience of learning to role-take is shaped by the fact that they must, in a way men need not, learn to take the role of the genuine *other*, not just a social other who is taken to be much like oneself. The other for women is the male and is alien. The other for men is, first and foremost, men who are to some degree like them in a quality that the culture considers of transcendent importance: gender.

The Internationalization of Community Norms   Role taking usually is seen as culminating in the internalization of community norms via the social actor's learning to take the role of "the generalized other," a construct that the actor mentally creates out of the amalgam of macro- and micro-level experiences that form her or his social life. The use of the singular *other* indicates that microsociologists usually envision this imagined generalized other as a cohesive, coherent, singular expression of expectations. But feminists argue, first, that in a male-dominated patriarchal culture, the generalized other represents a set of male-dominated community norms that force the woman to picture herself as "less than" or "unequal to" men. To the degree that a woman succeeds in formulating a sense of generalized other that accurately reflects the dominant perceptions of the community, she may have in a sense damaged her own possibilities for self-esteem and self-exploration.

Second, the insights of feminism call into question the very existence of a unified generalized other for the majority of people—indeed, perhaps for all people. The central point with which we began this section is that the truth of a given social situation lies in the intersection of vantage points. Presumably any of these vantage points could constitute a generalized other by which a person might view herself or himself as an object and judge her or his performance. Only with the awareness of how a multiplicity of others affect an individual's sense of self can we begin to capture the potential complexity of having or being a self. The subordinate, in particular, does not have the luxury or the illusion of the existence of a single standardized other (unless the subordinate has been so oppressed as to have surrendered all powers of separate reflection).

The Nature of the Self as a Social Actor   Microsociologists describe the social actor as picturing the everyday world as something to be mastered according to one's particular interests. Feminist sociologists argue that women may find themselves so overwhelmingly limited by their status as women that the idea of projecting their own plans onto the world becomes meaningless in all but theory. Further, women may not experience the life-world as something to be mastered according to their own particular interests. They may be socialized to experience that life-world as a place in which one balances a variety of actors' interests. Indeed, Gilligan (1982) has been at pains to assure women that one mark of maturity is an ability to have and protect one's own interests as a way of protecting oneself for others. Women may not have the same experience of control of particular spheres of space, free from outside interference. They find themselves still in search of "a room of one's own." Similarly, their sense of time rarely can follow the simple pattern of first things first because they have as a life project the balancing of the interests and projects of others. Thus women may experience planning and actions as acts of concern for a variety of interests, their own and others, and as acts, above all, of cooperation and not mastery.

This idea ties in with the idea discussed earlier of women's role experience as one of "role merging." In combination, these ideas suggest the need for renaming role *conflict* as role *balancing* (to stay within the confines of the present language). Then the ability to role-balance, one of women's and other subordinates' primary abilities and experiences of space and time, would come to be explored as a positive social value. Compartmentalization then might be seen as a sign of the "less than" functional personality.

Consciousness of Everyday Life   Feminist sociologists have critically evaluated the thesis of a unified consciousness of everyday life that traditional microsociologists usually assume. Feminist sociologists stress that for women the most pervasive feature of the cognitive style of everyday life is that of a bifurcated consciousness. Women experience what Dorothy Smith (1979) has called "a line of fault" between their own personal, lived, and reflected-on experience and the established types available in the social stock of knowledge to describe that experience. Everyday life itself thus divides into two realities for subordinates: the reality of actual, lived, reflected-on experience and the reality of social types. Often aware of the way that their own experience differs from that of the culturally dominant males with whom they interact, women are less trusting of the ease of shared subjectivity. And as biological and social beings whose activities are not perfectly regulated by patriarchal standard time, they are more aware of the demarcation between time as lived experience and time as a social mandate. A feminist sociology of subjectivity perhaps would begin here: How do people survive when their own experience does not fit the established social typifications of that experience? We know already that some do so by avoiding acts of sustained reflection; some do so by cultivating their own series of personal types to make sense of their experience; some do so by seeking community with others who share this bifurcated reality; some do so by denying the validity of their own experience. But survive they do.

What we have generalized here for women's subjectivity may be true for the subjectivity of all subordinates. One, their experience of role taking is complicated by their intense awareness that they must learn the expectations of an other who by virtue of differences in power is alien. Two, they must relate not to a generalized other but to many generalized others, many subcultures, both the subculture of the powerful and the various subcultures of the less empowered and the disempowered. Three, they do not experience themselves as purposive social actors who can chart their own course through life—although they may be constantly told that they can do so, especially within the American ethos. And finally, and most pervasively, they live daily with a bifurcated consciousness, a sense of the line of fault between their own lived experiences and what the dominant culture tells them is the social reality.

A MICRO-MACRO SYNTHESIS

The picture of social organization that emerges in feminist sociological theory is highly integrative. It combines economic activity with other forms of human social production (child rearing, emotional sustenance, knowledge, home maintenance, sexuality, and so on); it sees material production as elaborately linked with ideological production; it describes the interpenetration of apparently autonomous social institutions and apparently voluntary individual actions and relations; it connects structure to interaction and consciousness. Recently, in the effort to devise a vocabulary for talking about these various and simultaneous realities at once, socialist feminists, particularly in the work of Dorothy Smith, have introduced the concepts of "relations of ruling," "generalized, anonymous, impersonal texts," and "local actualities of lived experience" (D. Smith, 1987, 1990a, 1990b). *Relations of ruling* refers to the complex, nonmonolithic but intricately connected social activities that attempt to control human social production. Human social production must by its material nature occur at some moment in the *local actualities of lived experience*—that is, the places where some actual person sits while writing or reading a book (or plants food or produces clothing). The relations of ruling in late capitalist patriarchy manifest themselves through *texts* that are characterized by their essential *anonymity, generality, and authority.* These texts are designed to pattern and translate real-life, specific, individualized experience into a language form acceptable to the relations of ruling. This criteria of "acceptability" is met when the text imposes the dominants' definition on the situation. The texts may range from contracts to police reports to official boards-of-inquiry statements to school certificates to medical records. Everywhere they alter the material reality—reinterpreting what has occurred, determining what will be possible. Thus, in seeking to interact with the relations of ruling, even at a fairly local level, a given individual (such as a student applying for a summer job in a restaurant owned by a family friend) finds that she or he must fill out some texts (tax information cards, for instance) which have been established not by the face-to-face employer but by part of the apparatus of ruling. These texts continuously create intersections between the relations of ruling and the local actualities of lived experience. It is important to observe that this intersection works both ways: at some series of moments in historic time, embodied actors, situated in absolutely individual locations, sit at desks or computer workstations or conference tables generating the forms that will become part of the apparatus of ruling.

All three aspects of social life—relations of ruling, local actualities of lived experience, and texts—are widespread, enduring, constant features of the organization of social life and of domination. All at the same time can and must be studied as the actions, relationships, and work of embodied human beings. Each dimension has its distinctive internal dynamic—the drive for control in the relations of ruling, the drive for production and communication in the local actualities, the drive toward objectivity and the claim of facticity in the generalized texts. Each dimension is determining of and yet is determined by the others. Through this lens the micro-versus-macro split becomes irrelevant. The elements of structure and interaction are fused. Domination and production as defined by feminists become the problematic, and their manifestations involve and thus absorb the age-old sociological distinctions of the macro-social, micro-social, and subjective aspects of social reality. In this, feminist theory is in accord with much of the work discussed in Part 3 of this book on micro-macro and agency structure integration and theoretical synthesis.

SUMMARY

Feminist sociological theory grows out of feminist theory in general, that branch of the new scholarship on women that seeks to provide a system of ideas about human life that features woman as object and subject, doer and knower.

Feminism has a history as long as women's subordination—and women have been subordinated almost always and everywhere. From 1630 to about 1780 feminist writing survives as a thin but persistent trickle of protest. From the 1780s to the present, feminist writing becomes a growing tide of critical work involving increasing participants and areas of critique. But this growth has not been steady, precisely because women as minority or oppressed members of society always have found their protests subject to suppression by male interests and patriarchal power. Generally, feminist theory, at least from the 1780s, has paralleled the swings between reform and retrenchment in Western social movements.

Feminist theory also has paralleled the growth of sociology itself. But feminist theory has remained on the margin of sociology, ignored by the central male formulators of the discipline until 1960. Feminist concerns have been addressed by female and male sociologists who were on the margins of the profession when they wrote (for instance, Marx and Engels). The central figures in the discipline have largely ignored feminist concerns and knowledge, and when they have looked at gender issues, they have been conventional and uncritical in their treatment (as, for instance, in the work of Talcott Parsons).

The feminist questions so rich in possibility for sociological theory today have been kept alive in the body of feminist theory formulated between 1960 and the present. This body of ideas can be classified according to the two basic questions of feminist scholarship: *And what about the women?* and *Why is women's situation as it is?* The answers to the first question provide our major categories of varieties of feminist theory. In our system, there have been three main descriptions of women's social situation: (1) It is different from men's; (2) it is unequal to men's; (3) it is that of an oppressed group and the oppressors are men or the male-constructed patriarchal social system.

Within each of these broad categories—difference, inequality, and oppression—there are further variations based on the answers to the question of why women's situation is as it is. Theorists who see women's situation as essentially different from men's explain that difference in three basic ways: biosocial conditioning, institutional socialization, and social-psychological interfacing. Theorists who emphasize inequality explanations account for women's positions in terms of *liberal feminism's* view of unequal opportunity structures and *Marxian* accounts of women's position as part of a complex class-system of exploitation in which women exploit and are exploited partly in terms of gender and partly in terms of class position. Some theorists who emphasize oppression explain that oppression in terms of *psychoanalytic* theories that see males as having an innate need to subjugate women in order to achieve deep psychological goals. Others offer a *radical feminist* answer that sees the root of patriarchal oppression in males' greater ability and willingness to use brute force to subjugate others. Still others offer a *socialist feminist* analysis that attempts to synthesize various forms and theories of oppression, using terms such as *capitalist patriarchy* and *domination* to describe the multifaceted system of oppression based on arrangements of production, class, age, ethnicity, sexual preference, and global position, as well as gender—a system oppressing all women and most men. And most recently, *third wave feminists* focus on the implications these differences—class, age, ethnicity, sexual preference, and global position—for relations among women at both the micro and macro levels.

Feminist theory offers a basis for a revision of standard sociological theories of social organization. The feminist sociological theory that we present as an exemplar of what feminist theory can offer to general sociological theory may be summarized in terms of six main propositions, which draw on and synthesize the varieties of feminist theory. First, the practice of sociological theory must be based in a sociology of knowledge that recognizes the knower as embodied and socially located, the partiality of all knowledge, and the function of power in effecting what becomes knowledge.

Second, macro-social structures are based in processes controlled by dominants acting in their own interests and executed by subordinates whose work is made largely invisible and undervalued even to themselves by the social ideology. Thus even the understanding of what constitutes production is distorted. Focusing on women's position can give particular insights into these macro structures of subordination because women, whatever their class position, are primary doers of invisible work: housework, childbearing and rearing, emotional and sexual service, and coordinating activities (such as waiting, adjusting, being interrupted) in wage-sector work.

Third, micro-interactional processes in society make real these dominant-subordinate power arrangements and the nonacknowledgment or distortion of the subordinates' contribution. Thus, women find their contributions to social production either disregarded, as in housework or wage-sector coordinating activities, or idealized beyond any recognition of actual experience, as in mothering.

Fourth, these conditions create in women's subjectivity a constant "line of fault" that they must navigate. This line of fault separates the patriarchal ideology and women's reflected-on experience of the actuality of their roles in producing social life at the macro and micro levels. Women navigate this line of fault in various ways—by repression, by acquiescence, by rebellion, and by attempts at micro and macro organization for reform.

Fifth, what has been said for women may be applicable to all subordinate people in some parallel, although not identical, form.

Sixth, one must question the use of any categories developed by an essentially male-dominated discipline, and most particularly the divisions between micro- and macro-sociologies. Current feminist conceptualizations of the social order have transcended this classic sociological dichotomy, using concepts like "relations of ruling," "local actualities of lived experience," and "generalized texts." The closing question of feminist sociological theory raises for everyone this issue: Can we stay within the established disciplinary categories for describing and explaining the world, or must we create new concepts if we are to describe and explain the world as viewed by its subordinate, disadvantaged, and often invisible members?

STRUCTURAL SOCIOLOGICAL THEORIES

*I*N this chapter we discuss an array of theories that can be dealt with under the heading "structural sociological theories." Although, as we will see, there are important differences in the ways in which these theories conceive of structure, they are unified in their concern with, or opposition to, this phenomenon. Most share an interest in structure with structural functionalism (see Chapter 7), but they look at structures directly, unburdened by the need to deal also with the functions of those structures.

We begin with a broad intellectual movement known as "structuralism." This is largely French in character and can be traced in sociology to Durkheim's later work (see Chapter 3). In this chapter we will discuss its roots in linguistics as well as its major statement in the work of Claude Lévi-Strauss, who, although an anthropologist, has been enormously influential in a number of fields, including sociology. We then discuss, once again, structural Marxism, but this time as a form of structuralism rather than as a form of neo-Marxian theory (see Chapter 8). We then turn to a recent movement, poststructuralism, especially the work of the major thinker associated with that approach, Michel Foucault. Next, we look at existential sociology and systems theory, largely because their theoretical orientations stand in contrast to, and as critiques of, structuralism and post-structuralism. Finally, we deal with some specifically sociological variants of structuralism—Erving Goffman's structural approach (as distinct from his symbolic interactionism—see (Chapter 9), Peter Blau's structural theory (in contrast to his more integrative exchange theory—see Chapter 11), and network theory.

STRUCTURALISM

Although we have already looked at it several times in this book, it is now time to discuss structuralism systematically. What, exactly, is structuralism? We can define *structuralism,* most generally, as the search for the "universal and invariant laws of humanity that are operative at all levels of human life —at the most primitive and at the most advanced" (Ekeh, 1982:128).

Roots in Linguistics

Structuralism emerged from diverse developments in various fields. The source of modern structuralism and its strongest bastion to this day is linguistics. The work of Ferdinand de Saussure (1857–1913) stands out in the development of structural linguistics and, ultimately, structuralism in various other fields (Culler, 1976). Of particular interest to us is Saussure's differentiation between *langue* and *parole,* which was to have enormous significance. *Langue* is the formal, grammatical system of language. It is a system of phonic elements whose relationships are governed, Saussure and his followers believed, by determinate laws. Much of linguistics since Saussure's time has been oriented to the discovery of those laws. The existence of *langue* makes *parole* possible. *Parole* is actual speech, the way that speakers use language to express themselves. Although Saussure recognized the significance of people's use of language in subjective and often idiosyncratic ways, he believed that that cannot be the concern of the scientifically oriented linguist. Such a linguist must look at *langue,* the formal system of language, not at the subjective ways in which it is used by actors.

The concern for structure has been extended beyond language to the study of all sign systems. This focus on the structure of sign systems has been labeled "semiotics" and has attracted many followers (Hawkes, 1977). *Semiotics* is broader than structural linguistics, because it encompasses not only language but also other sign and symbol systems, such as facial expressions, body language, literary texts, indeed all forms of communication.

Many of the fields to which structuralism has been extended are concerned in one way or another with communication. These include Marxism, psychiatry, the plastic arts, musical theater, literary criticism, philosophy, and—most important for the development of a structural sociology—anthropology, especially in the work of Claude Lévi-Strauss (Ehrmann, 1970; I. Rossi, 1982). Although there are a number of similarities in the use of structuralism in these various fields, there are also a number of important differences. Structuralism is far from a unified perspective.

Anthropological Structuralism: Claude Lévi-Strauss

The most important work in structuralism, as far as sociology is concerned, has been done in anthropology by Claude Lévi-Strauss (Kurzweil calls Lévi-Strauss "the father of structuralism" [1980:13]). Over the years he has produced an enormous body of complex work that has dramatically altered the field of anthropology—and other fields as well. Structuralists in sociology have been influenced strongly by Lévi-Strauss's work.

One of the reasons for the complexity of Lévi-Strauss's work is that various types of structures are to be found in it. The first type consists of the large-scale structures and institutions of the social world, but he took pains to deny that structures of this kind are really structures. Although these are structural realities to most anthropologists and sociologists, to Lévi-Strauss they serve to conceal the real underlying structures of society. This leads to the second, and more important, type of structure in Lévi-Strauss's work, the model that the social scientist constructs to get at the underlying structure of society. But there is a third, and most important, type of structure to Lévi-Strauss, and that is the structure of the human mind (Leach, 1974). The models of the social world that social scientists construct take similar form in diverse societies because human products around the world have the same basic source, the human mind. *It is the structure of the mind that is the ultimate structure in Lévi-Strauss's work.*

At one level, Lévi-Strauss can be seen as simply extending Saussure's work on language to anthropological issues—for example, to myths in primitive societies. However, Lévi-Strauss went further and applied structuralism more broadly to all forms of communication. His major innovation was to reconceptualize a wide array of social phenomena (for instance, kinship systems) as systems of communication and thereby make them amenable to structural analysis (Burris, 1979). The exchange of spouses, for example, can be analyzed in the same way as the exchange of words. Both are social exchanges that can be studied through the use of structural anthropology.

We can illustrate Lévi-Strauss's (1967) thinking with the example of the similarities between linguistic systems and kinship systems. First, terms used to describe kinship, like phonemes in language, are basic units of analysis to the structuralist. Second, neither the kinship terms nor phonemes have meaning in themselves. Instead, both acquire meaning only when they are integral parts of a larger system. The overall structure of the system gives each of the component parts meaning. Third, Lévi-Strauss admitted that there is empirical variation from setting to setting in both phonemic and kinship systems, but even these variations can be traced to the operation of general, although implicit, laws. Finally, and ultimately in terms of Lévi-Strauss's sense of structure, both phonemic systems and kinship systems are the products of the structures of the mind. However, they are not the products of a conscious process. Instead, they are the products of the unconscious, logical structure of the mind. These systems, as well as the logical structure of the mind from which they are derived, operate on the basis of general laws.

Lévi-Strauss subjected anthropological data to structural analysis in much the same way that Saussure analyzed linguistic data. In contrast, most anthropologists and sociologists, for that matter, are likely to accept the subjective reports of respondents. To Lévi-Strauss, such reports are simply the basic resources out of which to construct the underlying structures. In his analyses of primitive societies, Lévi-Strauss was interested in uncovering the underlying structure of myths and kinship systems, indeed of the entire society.

Although Lévi-Strauss devoted his attention to primitive societies, he believed that all societies, including modern ones, have a similar underlying structure. He focused on primitive societies because there is less distortion and it is easier to discover the structure. In modern societies, a number of conscious models, or normative systems, have been developed to conceal the structural reality. Lévi-Strauss did not totally denigrate the importance of such models. These normative systems, including their biases and distortions, are important products of people in a society. However, these systems are not of primary importance, because "cultural norms are not of themselves structures" (Lévi-Strauss, 1967:274).

Most anthropologists study what people say and do, but Lévi-Strauss was more concerned with their human products (I. Rossi, 1974b). He was concerned with the objective structure of these products, not their subjective meanings or their origins in subjective processes. In looking at various human products—myths, kinship systems, and others— Lévi-Strauss was interested in their interrelationships. The charting of such interrelationships is *the* structure or at least a structure. Because a structure is created by the observer, different observers can construct different structures. Two important points need to be underscored here. First, structures are the creations of observers. Second, the structures that are created do not exist in the real world. As Lévi-Strauss put it, "The term 'social structure' has nothing to do with empirical reality but with models which are built up after it" (1967:271).

Lévi-Strauss was not interested in merely charting the structure of a simple primitive society. Rather, his concern was in comparing a wide array of available data on a number of such societies. He hoped that such comparative analyses would yield an underlying structure common to all societies. Although he searched for such structure, Lévi-Strauss did not adopt the dogmatic point of view that structures are the same for all places and for all times. Contrary to the view of most observers, there is flexibility in his system.

Lévi-Strauss rejected the traditional orientations of anthropologists. For example, he rejected the idea that myths can be explained either by their narrative content or by their functions for society. Instead, the meaning of myths must be sought at the unconscious structural level. Lévi-Strauss's methodology for the analysis of myths can be broken down into a series of steps. First, he would examine a number of variants of a particular myth. Second, he would isolate in these variants the basic thematic elements. Third, he would chart the complex patterns in which thematic elements within each variant are interwoven. Fourth, he would construct "a table of possible permutations between these terms" (Lévi-Strauss, 1963:16). Fifth, the table itself would become the structure, "the general object of analysis which, at this level only, can yield necessary connections, the empirical phenomenon considered at the beginning being only one possible combination among others" (Lévi-Strauss, 1963:16). Finally, such a table, or structure, would allow the analyst not only to understand the myth in general but also to hypothesize about the meaning of a particular myth within a particular society.

On the surface, it would appear that Lévi-Strauss's structures are the same as Durkheim's social facts; both seem to have a life of their own that is external to, and coercive of, the actor. However, Lévi-Strauss did not operate at the societal level, at the level of social facts. Lévi-Strauss was influenced by Durkheim's later work on primitive classification rather than his earlier work on social facts. Lévi-Strauss's actors are constrained, but not by social facts. People, in his view, are constrained by the structures of the mind.

Perhaps, then, it was Sigmund Freud, not Durkheim, who was closest to Lévi-Strauss in orientation and a major influence on his work. It would appear that Lévi-Strauss accepted the view of Freudian psychiatry that actors are determined by unconscious forces. Although Lévi-Strauss was interested in the unconscious, there is a crucial difference between Lévi-Strauss and Freud on this issue (I. Rossi, 1974a). Freud conceived of the unconscious largely in terms of its hidden emotional content; actors are seen as impelled by emotions that are unknown to them at a conscious level. However, Lévi-Strauss was clearly not interested in the emotional aspects of the unconscious; his focus in the unconscious was "the permanent and logical structures of the mind" (I. Rossi, 1974a:19). Lévi-Strauss's actors are constrained not by unconscious emotions but by the unconscious, logical structures of their minds. Here is one way in which Lévi-Strauss expressed his interest in the unconscious:

> If, as we believe to be the case, the unconscious activity of the mind consists in imposing forms upon content, and, if these forms are fundamentally the same for all minds—ancient or modern, primitive or civilized . . . then it is necessary and sufficient to grasp the unconscious structure underlying each institution and each custom in order to obtain a principle of interpretation valid for other institutions and other customs, provided, of course, that the analysis is carried far enough.
>
> (Lévi-Strauss, 1967:21–22)

Lévi-Strauss's view, of course, led to a problem common in the social sciences: that the mind is not accessible to immediate observation (Scheffler, 1970). This caused Lévi-Strauss to focus on the human products discussed above and their interrelationships. Here his interest was not in those products in themselves but in what they can tell us about the logical structure of the mind. Thus his studies of the structure of the primitive world in general and kinship and mythical systems in particular are not ends in themselves but rather means to help him understand basic mental structures.

In his search for the basic structures of the mind, it would seem that Lévi-Strauss undertook a project resembling those of at least some phenomenologists. However, Lévi-Strauss, like most structuralists, had a deep distaste for phenomenology (and existentialism; see below). In his view, phenomenologists seek to place human, subjective consciousness at the center of the social sciences. To structuralists, consciousness is not amenable to scientific analysis. Whereas phenomenologists are seen as engaged in an effort to humanize the social sciences, structuralists almost self-consciously seek to *dehumanize* those fields. They want to remove people from the center of the social sciences and substitute various structures, such as the logical structure of the mind, language, various components of society, or society in general. Charles Lemert (1979), for example, was pleased to see that the social sciences are witnessing the approach of the demise of people as the heart of their fields. In the view of most structuralists, a focus on people, especially on their subjective processes, retards, if not prevents, the development of social *science*. To engage in a science, the focus must shift from people to some sort of objective structure.

Lévi-Strauss's orientation and interest in mental structures would suggest that he was engaged in an enterprise similar to that undertaken by the philosopher Immanuel Kant. Although there are some similarities, there is also a crucial difference between them. As a philosopher, Kant sought to uncover the basic mental categories through introspection or philosophizing or both. As a social *scientist*, Lévi-Strauss rejected such methods and sought instead to examine empirically the structures of the social world, in order to shed light on mental structures.

Thus, although it seems that Lévi-Strauss was doing work resembling that of a number of other thinkers, a closer examination indicates important differences between Lévi-Strauss and all of them. Indeed, this is a measure of Lévi-Strauss's distinctive and important contribution to the social sciences.

Somewhat harshly, Kurzweil concludes, "Structuralism as originally conceived by Lévi-Strauss is dead. The universal mental structures have not emerged, albeit no one any longer searches for them" (1980:10). Nevertheless, she recognizes that Lévi-Strauss laid the groundwork for other types of structuralism as well as poststructuralism.

Structural Marxism

In addition to the anthropological structuralism of Lévi-Strauss, another important variant of structuralism is the French structural Marxism which we discussed in Chapter 8.

In this section, we focus on what is distinctive about French structural Marxism, differentiating it from other varieties of structuralism, particularly that of Lévi-Strauss. First, however, we will look at the similarities between structuralism in general and structural Marxism (Glucksmann, 1974)—in other words, the reasons that the work of Althusser, Poulantzas, and others *is* structuralism.

Although we have presented the case that modern structuralism began with Saussure's work in linguistics, there are those who argue that it started with the work of Karl Marx: "When Marx assumes that structure is not to be confused with visible relations and explains their hidden logic, he inaugurates the modern structuralist tradition" (Godelier, 1972b:336). Although structural Marxism and structuralism in general are both interested in "structures," each field conceptualizes structure differently.

At least some structural Marxists share with structuralists an interest in the study of structure as a prerequisite to the study of history. As Maurice Godelier said, "The study of the internal functioning of a structure must precede and illuminate the study of its genesis and evolution" (1972b:343). In another work, Godelier said, "The inner *logic* of these systems must be analyzed *before* their *origin* is analyzed" (1972a:xxi). Another view shared by structuralists and structural Marxists is that structuralism should be concerned with the structures, or systems, that are formed out of the interplay of social relations. Both schools see structures as real (albeit invisible), although they differ markedly on the nature of the structure that they consider real. For Lévi-Strauss the real structure is the model, whereas for structural Marxists it is the underlying structure of society.

Perhaps most important, both structuralism and structural Marxism reject empiricism and accept a concern for underlying invisible structures. Godelier argued: "What both structuralists and Marxists reject are the empiricist definitions of what constitutes a social structure" (1972a:xviii). Godelier also made this statement:

> For Marx as for Lévi-Strauss a structure is *not* a reality that is *directly* visible, and so directly observable, but a *level of reality* that exists *beyond* the visible relations between men, and the functioning of which constitutes the underlying logic of the system, the subjacent order by which the apparent order is to be explained.
>
> (Godelier, 1972a:xix)

Godelier went even further and argued that such a pursuit defines all science: "What is visible is a *reality* concealing *another,* deeper reality, which is hidden and the discovery of which is the very purpose of scientific cognition" (1972a:xxiv).

Despite the similarities between structural Marxism and structuralism, in general there are major differences between structuralism (Marxian and non-Marxian) and at least the main thrust of Marxian theory. First, the two schools use different modes of logic. Marxists generally adopt dialectical reasoning, whereas structuralists are more inclined to employ analytic reason. Structuralists expound on the need to do synchronic studies; Marxists are more likely to see the need for diachronic analyses. Humanistic Marxists are likely to focus on the human subject, but structuralists (Marxian and non-Marxian) see such a concern as nonscientific (Burris, 1979). Marxists believe that theory can help in social change. The argument of the structuralists is that—given the universality of certain structures and the inclination of people, especially in modern society, to mystify the social world—the chance of meaningful political change is small (Glucksmann, 1974).

Perhaps the ultimate difference between structuralism in general and Marxism in general lies in their levels of analysis. In Val Burris's (1979) terms, the difference is between materialism and psychological reductionism. Marxists tend to focus on the structures of society (economic, political, ideological), whereas structuralists are concerned with the "deep structures" of the mind. Thus Marx and most Marxists are concerned with the underlying logic of the large-scale structures of capitalist society. Although structuralists may deal with large-scale structures, they usually do so not as an end in itself but only as a means of understanding the ultimate subject, the structure of the mind. Some structuralists are interested in the societal level and some Marxists in structures of the mind, but there is a basic difference in focus.

In this light, it is interesting to underscore a point made by Godelier. As a French structural Marxist trained in Lévi-Strauss's structuralism, Godelier was in a good position to analyze the relationship between French structural Marxism and structuralism. Although he recognized some overlap and some differences, Godelier argued for an integration of the two, so that their strengths would be fused and their weaknesses overcome. For example, in discussing the weaknesses in Lévi-Strauss's work, Godelier stated:

> What is lacking is analysis of the precise functions of these forms of thought, of the circulation of these forms of ideology with other levels of social reality, and of the conditions of their transformation. . . . To go further than a structural morphology means, therefore, trying to account for the forms, functions, modes of articulation and conditions of transformation of the social structures within the concrete societies studied by the historian and the anthropologist. It is precisely in order to accomplish this complex task, which presupposes a combination of several theoretical methods, that Marx's hypothesis of the determination, in the last analysis, of the forms and the evolution of societies by the conditions of production and reproduction of their material life is needed as the central hypothesis.
>
> (Godelier, 1972a:xli)

Godelier's main sympathies seem to lie with Marxism. However, true integration would require serious attention to the strengths and weaknesses of both orientations.

Barriers to Acceptance

French structuralism has far to go to achieve widespread acceptance in sociology (Lemert, 1990). There are some almost insurmountable barriers it must overcome. As David Goddard (1976) so well understood, structuralism not only has little to offer to traditional sociological concerns but also constitutes a deep threat to those interests. For example, structuralists are generally little

interested in such traditional small-scale sociological topics as creative consciousness, actors, action, behavior, and interaction. The actor and various
individual-level processes are difficult to find in structuralism. Moreover,
structuralism, except for French structural Marxism, seems almost totally inap-
plicable to the traditional large-scale concerns of sociologists:

> To put it bluntly, if there were laws of structural organization in large-scale, het-
> erogeneous societies—laws relating to significant phenomena such as class, bureauc-
> racy, power, change, development, solidarity, and the varied interrelations between
> these phenomena—structural analysis could not provide the requisite assumptions,
> methods or theories which would lead to the discovery of such laws.
>
> (Goddard, 1976:126)

To Goddard and many others, structuralism represents a frontal assault on
many of the basic premises of sociology. In fact, Goddard saw dire consequences should sociology adopt a structural paradigm, because such an
approach would "compromise absolutely what is perhaps its own fundamental premise . . . that ideas and symbols are formed in their material context
of given social milieux . . . the idea of a sociological materialism which inau-
gurated sociology as a special discipline would have to be completely abandoned" (1976:132). Given such harsh attacks, it will be difficult for French
structuralism to achieve general acceptance in sociology.

POSTSTRUCTURALISM

Structuralism has been largely a French phenomenon that includes Durkheim
(in his later work), Saussure, Lévi-Strauss, structural Marxists like Althusser
and Godelier, and others, especially Jean Piaget. Nevertheless, by the 1980s
structuralism had peaked, and Kurzweil argued that "in Paris, the structuralist
age is nearly over" (1980:2). However, structuralism did not disappear; it was
superseded by what has been termed *poststructuralism* (or *neostructuralism*)
(Giddens, 1987; G. Rose, 1984; Wuthnow et al., 1984). Lemert (1990) traces the
beginning of poststructuralism to a 1966 speech by Jacques Derrida, one of
the leading thinkers associated with this approach, in which he proclaimed
that structuralism was in transition and that a new poststructuralist age was
dawning. The origin of structuralism can be traced, in part, to its effort to
distance itself from subjectivistic perspectives like existentialism (see below)
and articulate, in contrast, an objectivistic orientation. Poststructuralism
involves an effort to extend structuralism by, among other things, including
within it a range of theoretical perspectives.

Poststructuralism involves not only a theoretical change but also a transformation in the social world. While structuralism was locked into a focus on
the modern world, poststructuralism takes as its subject postmodern society.
Indeed, many of the leading poststructuralists are also associated with the
intellectual movement known as *postmodernism* (see Chapter 17). Lemert
argues that the birth of postmodernism can be traced, at least symbolically, to

> The death of modernist architecture at 3:32 P.M., July 15, 1972—the moment at which the Pruitt-Igoe housing project in St. Louis was destroyed. . . . This massive housing project in St. Louis represented modernist architecture's arrogant belief that by building the biggest and best public housing planners and architects could eradicate poverty and human misery. To have recognized, and destroyed the symbol of that idea was to admit the failure of modernist architecture, and by implication modernity itself.
>
> (Lemert, 1990:233; following Jencks, 1977)

In a sense, postmodernism represents an assault on structure, in this case an architectural structure.

One issue that unifies structuralism, poststructuralism, and postmodernism is a concern for language (Giddens, 1987). This is derived, in part, from their roots in linguistics, particularly the ideas of Saussure. Involved in a focus on language is an implied attack on positivism because, as Lyotard says, "scientific knowledge is a form of discourse" (1984:3). If science is merely one of many forms of talk, then it has no privileged status. Supporters of these approaches seek to replace positivism with a new approach to the social world that is based on language. They are one in their belief "that language is now necessarily the central consideration in all attempts to know, act, and live" (Lemert, 1990:234). The social world is seen as a series of texts that need to be interpreted largely in relation to other texts. But if the world is nothing more than a series of texts that can be interpreted only in relation to one another, then it is no longer possible, as positivists and modernists attempted, "to view the world as internally and necessarily coherent" (Lemert, 1990:236).

What does it mean for sociology to see the world as a series of texts? Lemert (1990) makes four points here. First, theory is a form of discourse that produces texts. Second, the empirical reality that theory deals with is other texts (interviews, census data, videotapes). Third, the meaning of empirical texts depends on their being read from the point of view of theoretical texts. Finally, a study of empirical texts leads to greater understanding than other kinds of empirical analyses.

This leads to another key aspect of poststructuralism (and postmodernism)—its view of social totality. While positivists seek a grand organizing principle that unifies the world, poststructuralists argue that it is not some unity that marks the world but rather that it is difference that lies at the heart of the world. The goal becomes the study of the differences rather than the search for unity. Politically, this leads poststructuralists to take the side of those minority groups (for example, blacks, women) that are different from the majority group.

Another concern of poststructuralism (shared with structuralism) is the decentering of the subject. This involves rejection of a focus on the actor, the consciousness of the actor, subjectivity, and, more generally, humanism (all of which are foci of existential sociology; see below). In terms of the focus on texts, this means that the poststructuralist concentrates on the internal structure of the text. The author of the text is regarded as more or less irrelevant. It is not the intentions of the author that matter, but rather the "internal play of signifiers" (Giddens, 1987:207). More generally, this means that we should focus on the structure of society and not the role of actors in constructing that society.

We will have more to say about these issues in Chapter 17 where we will discuss postmodernism in greater detail. Our focus in the remainder of this section is on the work of the major thinker associated with poststructuralism, Michel Foucault (1926–1984).

The Ideas of Michel Foucault

Although the influence of Foucault's work extends far beyond the borders of sociology, there is clearly a sociology or maybe several sociologies in it (Smart, 1985). It is a wide-ranging body of work encompassing methodological concerns (Foucault, 1966, 1969) as well as specific empirical studies of madness and the asylum (Foucault, 1965), medicine and the birth of clinical practice (Foucault, 1975), crime and the carceral system (Foucault, 1979), and sex and social control over sexuality (Foucault, 1980, 1985). It is a body of work that is relevant not only to sociological theory but also to a variety of subfields within sociology. In addition to being wide-ranging, Foucault's work is also dense and subject to multiple interpretations. Further complicating matters is the fact that Foucault is purposely elusive: "Do not ask who I am and do not ask me to remain the same" (1969:17). In fact, Foucault did not remain the same; his work showed important shifts over the course of his career.

Foucault's work also shows a variety of theoretical inputs (Smart, 1985). This variety makes Foucault's work provocative and difficult to handle. Furthermore, the ideas are not simply adopted from other thinkers but transformed as they are integrated into Foucault's unusual theoretical orientation. Thus, Weber's theory of rationalization has an impact, but to Foucault it is found only in certain "key sites," and it is not an "iron cage;" there is always resistance. Marxian ideas (Smart, 1983) are found in Foucault's work, but Foucault does not restrict himself to the economy; he focuses on a range of institutions. He is more interested in the "micro-politics of power" than in the traditional Marxian concern with power at the societal level. He practices hermeneutics in order to better understand the social phenomena of concern to him. Moreover, Foucault has no sense of some deep, ultimate truth; there are simply ever more layers to be peeled away. There is a phenomenological influence, but Foucault rejects the idea of an autonomous, meaning-giving subject. There is a strong element of structuralism but no formal rule-governed model of behavior. Finally, and perhaps most importantly, Foucault adopts Nietzsche's interest in the relationship between power and knowledge, but that link is analyzed much more sociologically by Foucault. This multitude of theoretical inputs is one of the reasons that Foucault is thought of as a poststructuralist. As we will soon see, structuralism had a strong influence on Foucault's early work but tended to recede in importance in the later, more poststructuralist, work.

Foucault clearly is a theorist to be reckoned with, and his work is likely to continue to attract interest and attention. In this relatively brief section, we can do little more than give the reader a sense of his ideas by first looking at his conceptual work and then turning to some of his specific studies.

In his early work on methodology, Foucault (1966) is doing an "archaeology of knowledge." His objects of study are bodies of knowledge, ideas, modes of discourse. He contrasts his archaeology of knowledge to history and the history of ideas, both of which he regards as being too rational and as seeing too much continuity in the history of knowledge. Alan Sheridan contends that Foucault's archaeology of knowledge involves a search for "a set of rules of formation that determine the conditions of possibility of all that can be said within the particular discourse at any given time" (1980:48). Here, clearly, we see the influence of structuralism. This influence is also manifest in Foucault's desire to study discursive events, spoken and written statements. He is particularly interested in early statements in the history of a field. He wants to uncover the basic conditions that make discourse possible. The unity of these statements, the way that they come to form a science or a discipline, does not come from the subject, but rather from basic discursive rules and practices. More specifically, Foucault was interested in the basic discursive practices that formed the base of scientific discourse, particularly in the human sciences. This highly structural approach in Foucault's early work was later abandoned for a poststructuralist orientation because it was silent on the issue of power as well as on the link between knowledge and power.

Foucault's (1969) later orientation is best caught by the phrase "genealogy of power." Here he borrows heavily from Nietzsche, who is thought of as a philosopher of power. Foucault is concerned with how people govern themselves and others through the production of knowledge. Among other things, he sees knowledge generating power by constituting people as subjects and then governing the subjects with the knowledge. He is critical of the hierarchization of knowledge. Because the highest-ranking forms of knowledge (the sciences) have the greatest power, they are singled out for the most severe critique. Foucault is interested in techniques, the technologies that are derived from knowledge (especially scientific knowledge), and how they are used by various institutions to exert power over people. Although he sees links between knowledge and power, Foucault does not see a conspiracy by elite members of society. Such a conspiracy would imply conscious actors, whereas Foucault is more inclined to see structural relationships, especially between knowledge and power. Looking over the sweep of history, Foucault does not see progress from primitive brutishness to more modern humaneness based on more sophisticated knowledge systems. Instead, Foucault sees history lurching from one system of domination (based on knowledge) to another. Although this is a generally bleak image, on the positive side Foucault believes that knowledge-power is always contested; there is always ongoing resistance to it. Foucault looks at historical examples, but he is primarily interested in the modern world. As he puts it, he is "writing the history of the present" (Foucault, 1979:31).

With this background, let us look at some of Foucault's specific, substantive works. In *Madness and Civilization* (1965), Foucault is doing an archaeology of knowledge, specifically of psychiatry. He begins with the Renaissance, when madness and reason were not separated. However, between 1650 and 1800 (the classical period), distance between them is established, and, ultimately, reason comes to subjugate madness. In other words, he is describing "a broken dialogue" between reason and madness (Foucault, 1965:x). Foucault describes the end result:

> Here reason reigned in the pure state, in a triumph arranged for it in advance over a frenzied unreason. Madness was thus torn from that imaginary freedom which still allowed it to flourish on the Renaissance horizon. Not so long ago, it had floundered about in broad daylight: in *King Lear*, in *Don Quixote*. But in less than a half-century, it had been sequestered and, in the fortress of confinement, bound to Reason, to the rules of morality and to their monotonous nights.
>
> (Foucault, 1965:64)

There is a clear Weberian, iron-cage imagery here—the "monotonous nights" to be spent by the "mad" (the irrational) in the iron cage constructed by those with reason (rationality).

The scientific psychology of the nineteenth century eventually arose out of the separation of the mad from the sane in the eighteenth century (psychiatry is labeled a "monologue of reason about madness" [Foucault, 1965:xi]). At first, medicine was in charge of the physical and moral treatment of the mad, but later scientific psychological medicine took over the moral treatment. "A purely psychological medicine was made possible only when madness was alienated in guilt" (Foucault, 1965:182–183). Later, Foucault says, "What we call psychiatric practice is a certain moral tactic contemporary with the end of the eighteenth century, preserved in the rights of asylum life, and overlaid by the myths of positivism" (1965:276). Thus, for Foucault psychology (and psychiatry) is a moral enterprise, not a scientific endeavor, aimed against the mad, who are progressively unable to protect themselves from this "help." He sees the mad as being sentenced by so-called scientific advancement to a "gigantic moral imprisonment."

Needless to say, Foucault here rejects the idea that over the years we have seen scientific, medical, and humanitarian advances in the treatment of the mad. What he sees, instead, are increases in the ability of the sane and their agents (physicians, psychologists, psychiatrists) to oppress and repress the mad, who, we should not forget, had been on equal footing with the sane in the seventeenth century. The most recent development is that now the mad are less judged by these external agents; "madness is ceaselessly called upon to judge itself" (Foucault, 1965:265). In many senses such internalized control is the most repressive form of control. Clearly, Foucault's archaeology of knowledge leads him to very different conclusions from those of traditional historians about the history and current status of the mad and their relationship to the sane (and their agents). In addition, he is looking at the roots of the human sciences (especially psychology and psychiatry) in the distinction between the mad and the sane and the exertion of moral control over the mad. This is part of his more general thesis about the role of the human sciences in the moral control of people.

As for Foucault's structuralism in this early work, he argues that madness occurs at two "levels," and at "a deeper level madness is a form of discourse" (1965:96). Specifically, madness, at least in the classical age, is not mental or physical changes; instead, "delirious language is the ultimate truth of madness" (Foucault, 1965:97). But there is an even broader structuralism operating in this early work: "Let classical culture formulate, *in its general structure*, the experience it had of madness, an experience which crops up with the same meanings, in the identical order of its inner logic, in both the order of speculation and in the order of institutions, in *both discourse and decree*, in both word and watchword—wherever, in fact, a signifying element can assume for us the value of a language" (Foucault, 1965:116; italics added).

Foucault continues to use a structuralist method in *The Birth of the Clinic*, in which he focuses on medical discourse and its underlying structure: "What counts in the things said by men is not so much what they may have thought or the extent to which these things represent their thoughts, as *that which systematizes them from the outset*, thus making them thereafter endlessly accessible to new discourses and open to the task of transforming them" (1975:xiv; italics added).

In *Madness and Civilization*, medicine was an important precursor of the human sciences, and that is an even more central theme in *The Birth of the Clinic*. (As Foucault said, "The science of man . . . was medically . . . based" [1975:36].) Prior to the nineteenth century, medicine was a classificatory science, and the focus was on a clearly ordered system of diseases. But in the nineteenth century, medicine came to focus on diseases as they existed in individuals and the larger society (epidemics). Medicine came to be extended to healthy people (preventive care), and it adopted a normative posture distinguishing between healthy and unhealthy and, later, normal and pathological states. Medicine had become, again, a forerunner of the human sciences that were to adopt this normal-pathological stance toward people.

As yet, however, there was no clinical structure in medicine. The key was the development of the clinic where patients were observed in bed. Here Foucault uses a key term, the *gaze*, in this case a "gaze that was at the same time knowledge" (1975:81). In other words, knowledge was derived from what physicians could see in contrast to what they read in books. As a structuralist, Foucault saw the gaze as a kind of language, "a language without words" (1975:68), and he was interested in the deep structure of that "language." The ability to see and touch (especially in autopsies) sick (or dead) people was a crucial change and an important source of knowledge. Foucault says of the autopsy, "The living night is dissipated in the brightness of death" (1975:146). Foucault sees the anatomo-clinical gaze as the "great break" in Western medicine. Thus, there was not an evolution of knowledge, but an epistemic change. Doctors were no longer playing the same game; it was a different game with different rules. *The* game was that people (patients) had become the object of scientific knowledge and practice (instead of the disease as an entity). In terms of his structuralist orientation, what had changed was the nature of discourse—names of diseases, groupings, field of objects, and so forth (Foucault, 1975:54).

Once again, medicine takes on for Foucault the role of forerunner to the human sciences. "It is understandable, then, that medicine should have had such importance in the constitution of the sciences of man—an importance that is not only methodological, but ontological, in that it concerns man's becoming an object of positive knowledge" (Foucault, 1975:197). Specifically on the medical autopsy, Foucault says, "Death left its old tragic heaven and became the lyrical core of man: his invisible truth, his visible secret" (1975:172). In fact, for Foucault the broader change is the individual as subject and object of his own knowledge, and the change in medicine is but one "of the more visible witnesses to these changes in the fundamental structures of experience" (1975:199).

Many of the same themes appear in *Discipline and Punish* (Foucault, 1979), but now we see more of the genealogy of power and much less on structuralism, discourse, and the like. Here "power and knowledge directly imply one another" (Foucault, 1979:27). Foucault here is concerned with the period between 1757 and the 1830s, a period during which the torture of prisoners was replaced by control over them by prison rules. (Characteristically, Foucault sees this change developing in an irregular way; it does not evolve rationally.) The general view is that this represented a humanization of the treatment of criminals; it had grown more kind, less painful, and less cruel. The reality, from Foucault's point of view, was that punishment had grown more rationalized ("the executioner [in the guillotine] need be no more than a meticulous watchman" [1979:13]) and in many ways impinged more on prisoners. The early torture of prisoners may have made for good public displays, but it was "a bad economy of power" because it tended to incite unrest among the viewers of the spectacle (Foucault, 1979:79). The link between knowledge and power was clear in the case of torture; with the development of rules, that link became far less clear. The new system of rules was "more regular, more effective, more constant, and more detailed in its effects; in short, which increase its effects while diminishing its economic cost" (Foucault, 1979:80–81). The new system was not designed to be more humane, but "to punish better . . . to insert the power to punish more deeply into the social body" (Foucault, 1979:82). In contrast to torture, this new technology of the power to punish occurred earlier in the deviance process, was more numerous, more bureaucratized, more efficient, more impersonal, more invariable, more sober, and involved the surveillance not just of criminals but of the entire society.

This new technology, a technology of disciplinary power, was based on the military model. It did not involve a single overarching power system, but rather a system of micro powers. Foucault describes a "micro-physics of power" with "innumerable points of confrontation" (1979:26–27). He identifies three instruments of disciplinary power. First is *hierarchical observation,* or the ability of officials to oversee all they control with a single *gaze.* Second is the ability to make *normalizing judgments* and to punish those who violate the norms. Thus, one might be negatively judged and punished on the dimensions of time (for being late), activity (for being inattentive), and behavior (for being impolite). Third is the use of *examination* to observe subjects and to make normalizing judgments about people. The third instrument of disciplinary power involves the other two.

Foucault does not simply take a negative view toward the growth of the disciplinary society; he sees that it has positive consequences as well. For example, he sees discipline as functioning well within the military and industrial factories. However, Foucault communicates a genuine fear of the spread of discipline, especially as it moves into the state-police network for which the entire society becomes a field of perception and an object of discipline.

Foucault does not see discipline sweeping uniformly through society. Instead, he sees it "swarming" through society and affecting bits and pieces of society as it goes. Eventually, however, most major institutions are affected. Foucault asks rhetorically, "Is it surprising that prisons resemble factories, schools, barracks, hospitals, which all resemble prisons?" (1979:228). In the end, Foucault sees the development of a carceral system in which discipline is transported "from the penal institution to the entire social body" (1979:298). Although there is an iron-cage image here, as usual Foucault sees the operation of forces in opposition to the carceral system; there is an ongoing structural dialectic in Foucault's work.

Although Foucault's greater emphasis on power in *Discipline and Punish* is evident in the discussion to this point, he is also concerned in this work with his usual theme of the emergence of the human sciences. The transition from torture to prison rules constituted a switch from punishment of the body to punishment of the soul or the will. This, in turn, brought with it considerations of normality and morality. Prison officials and the police came to judge the normality and morality of the prisoner. Eventually, this ability to judge was extended to other "small-scale judges" such as psychiatrists and educators. Out of this emerged new bodies of scientific penal knowledge, and these served as the base of the modern "scientifico-legal complex." The new mode of subjugation was that people were defined as the object of knowledge, of scientific discourse. The key point is that the modern human sciences have their roots here. Here is how Foucault bitterly depicts the roots of the human sciences in the disciplines: "These sciences, which have so delighted our "humanity' for over a century, have their technical matrix in the petty, malicious minutiae of the disciplines and their investigations" (1979:226).

One other point about *Discipline and Punish* is worth mentioning. Foucault is interested in the way that knowledge gives birth to technologies that exert power. In this context, he deals with the Panopticon. A *Panopticon* is a structure that allows officials the possibility of complete observation of criminals. In fact, officials need not always be present; the mere existence of the structure (and the possibility that officials might be there) constrains criminals. The Panopticon might take the form of a tower in the center of a circular prison from which guards could see into all cells. The Panopticon is a tremendous source of power for prison officials because it gives them the possibility of total surveillance. More important, its power is enhanced because the prisoners come to control themselves; they stop themselves from doing various things because they fear that they *might* be seen by the guards. There is a clear link here among knowledge, technology, and power. Furthermore, Foucault returns to his concern for the human sciences, for he sees the Panopticon as a kind of laboratory for the gathering of information about people. It was the forerunner of the social-scientific laboratory and other social-science techniques for gathering information about people. At still another level, Foucault sees the Panopticon as the base of "a whole type of society" (1979:216), the disciplinary society.[1]

Finally, we can look at the first volume of *The History of Sexuality* (Foucault, 1980). Again, the emphasis here is on the genealogy of power. To Foucault sexuality is "an especially dense transfer point for relations of power" (1980:103). He sees his goal as being to "define the regime of power-knowledge-pleasure that *sustains* the discourse on human sexuality in our part of the world" (Foucault, 1980:11). He examines the way that sex is put into discourse and the way that power permeates that discourse.

Foucault takes issue with the conventional view that Victorianism had led to the repression of sexuality in general and of sexual discourse in particular. In fact, he argues the exact opposite position—that Victorianism led to an explosion in discourses on sexuality. As a result of Victorianism, there was more analysis, stocktaking, classification, specification, and quantitative/causal study of sexuality. Said Foucault, "People will ask themselves why we were so bent on ending the rule of silence regarding what was the noisiest of our preoccupations" (1980:158). This was especially the case in schools, where instead of repression of sexuality, "the question of sex was a constant preoccupation" (1980:27). Here is the way that Foucault sums up the Victorian hypothesis and his alternative view:

> We must therefore abandon the hypothesis that modern industrial societies ushered in an age of increased sexual repression. We have not only witnessed a visible explosion of unorthodox sexualities . . . never have there existed more centers of

---

[1] For an interesting use of this idea, see Zuboff (1988), who views the computer as a modern Panopticon that gives superiors virtually unlimited surveillance over subordinates.

power; never more attention manifested and verbalized . . . never more sites where the intensity of pleasures and the persistency of power catch hold, only to spread elsewhere.

(Foucault, 1980:49)

Once again, Foucault accords a special place to medicine and its discourses on sexuality. Whereas to most, medicine is oriented to the scientific analysis of sexuality, Foucault sees more morality than science in the concerns of medicine. (In fact, Foucault is characteristically hard on medicine, seeing the aim of its discourse "not to state the truth, but to prevent its very emergence" [1980:55].) Also involved in the morality of sexuality is religion, especially Western Christianity, the confession, and the need for the subject to tell the truth about sexuality. All this is related to the human sciences and their interest in gaining knowledge of the subject. Just as people confessed to their priests, they also confessed to their doctors, their psychiatrists, and their sociologists. The confession, especially the sexual confession, came to be cloaked in scientific terms.

In the West, "the project of the science of the subject has gravitated, in evernarrowing circles, around the question of sex" (Foucault, 1980:70). Questions aimed at ascertaining who we are have come to be increasingly directed to sex. Foucault sums this all up: "Sex, the explanation of everything" (1980:78).

Instead of focusing on the repression of sexuality, Foucault argues that the scientific study of sex should focus on the relationship between sex and power. Again, that power does not reside in one central source; it exists in a variety of micro settings. Furthermore, as is always the case with Foucault, there is resistance to the imposition of power over sex. Power and the resistance to power are everywhere.

Prior to the eighteenth century, society sought control over death, but beginning in that century the focus shifted to control over life, especially sex. Power over life (and sex) took two forms. First, there was the "anatomo-politics of the human body," in which the goal was to discipline the human body (and its sexuality). Second, there was the "bio-politics of population," in which the object was to control and regulate population growth, health, life expectancy, and so forth. In both cases, society came to see "life as a political object" (Foucault, 1980:145). Sex was central in both cases: "Sex was a means of access both to the life of the body and the life of the species" (Foucault, 1980:146). In the modern West, sex has become more important than the soul (and we know how important that is in Foucault's work) and almost as important as life itself. Through knowledge of sexuality, society is coming to exercise more power over life itself. Yet despite this increase in control, Foucault holds out the hope of emancipation:

It is the agency of sex that we must break away from, if we aim—through a tactical reversal of the various mechanisms of sexuality—to counter the grips of power with the claims of bodies, pleasures, and knowledges, in their multiplicity and their possibility of resistance. The rallying point for the counterattack against the deployment of sexuality ought not to be sex-desire, but bodies and pleasures.

(Foucault, 1980:157)

Foucault's work, as well as ongoing work in poststructuralism in general, offers an exciting new set of inputs into mainstream sociological theory.

ANTISTRUCTURALISM

Now that we have analyzed structuralism and poststructuralism, it would be useful to discuss two theoretical perspectives—existential sociology and systems theory—that in many ways can be described as antistructuralist. The basic character of these antistructuralist theories will give us a sense of some of the weaknesses in structuralism. Existential sociology represents the kind of subjectivistic and humanistic perspective that was rejected by structuralism and poststructuralism. Systems theory offers a processual rather than a structural view of the social world.

Existential Sociology

Existential sociology is "the study of human experience in the world . . . in all its forms" (Douglas and Johnson, 1977: vii; for a similar definition, see Fontana, 1984). It is oriented to the study of the way that people live, feel, think, and act. It accords special importance to feelings and emotions as well as the "problematic and situated nature of meaningful experience" (Douglas and Johnson, 1977: xiii). In accepting such a view, existential sociology rejects any monocausal (for example, structural) view of human life. To the existential sociologist, "Man is varied, changeable, uncertain, conflictful, and partially free to choose what he will do and what he will become, because he must be so to exist in a world that is varied, changeable, uncertain, and conflictful" (Douglas, 1977:14). This underscores a dominant theme in existential sociology: people are both free *and* constrained.

This idea as well as many other aspects of existential sociology derive from the work of Jean-Paul Sartre, the French novelist and philosopher. Of particular interest to sociologists was Sartre's effort to relate individual freedom and societal constraints. Sartre sought to fuse his early phenomenological interests and his later Marxian concerns into a dialectical whole. In Ian Craib's (1976) view, Sartre's thought underwent evolution. In his early work, Sartre focused on the individual level, especially on individual freedom. At that point he adhered to the view that people are not subject to or determined by any social laws. In other words, man "cannot justify his actions by reference to anything outside himself" (Craib, 1976:4). However, later in his career, Sartre became more intrigued by Marxian theory and as a result shifted his focus to the "*free* individual situated in a *massive and oppressive social structure* which limits and alienates his activities" (Craib, 1976:9; italics added). Sartre did not simply shift to a societal level of concern but sought to combine it with his earlier interest in the actor. Craib concluded that later in his career, Sartre succeeded in unifying large- and small-scale theory.

In her analysis of Sartre's work, Gila Hayim (1980) sees continuity between his early and his late work. In *Being and Nothingness,* published in 1943, Sartre focuses more on the free individual and takes the view that "existence is defined by and through one's acts. . . . *One is what one does"* (Hayim, 1980: 3). At the same time, Sartre attacks the structuralist view of "objective structures as completely deterministic of behavior" (Hayim, 1980:5). For Sartre and existentialists in general, actors have the capacity to go beyond the present, to move toward the future. For Sartre, then, people are free; they are responsible for everything that they do; they have no excuses. In some senses, this is a tremendous source of anguish to people, these "staggering responsibilities of freedom" (Hayim, 1980:17). In other senses, this is a source of optimism to people—their fates are in their hands. In the *Critique of Dialectical Reason,* published in 1963, Sartre devotes more attention to social structures, but even here he emphasizes the "human prerogative for transcendence—the surpassing of the given" (Hayim, 1980:16). In this, Sartre is critical of various Marxists (structural Marxists) who overemphasize the role and place of social structure. "Dogmatic Marxists have, by Sartre's view, eliminated the humanistic component of Marx's original idea" (Hayim, 1980:72). As an existentialist, Sartre *always* retained this humanism.

A good illustration of existential sociology was offered by Andrea Fontana, who drew it from George Orwell's short story "Shooting an Elephant":

> As soon as I saw the elephant I knew with perfect certainty that I ought not to shoot him. . . . I decided that I would watch him for a little while to make sure that he did not turn savage again, and then go home. . . .
>
> But at that moment I glanced round at the crowd that had followed me. It was an immense crowd. . . . They were watching me. . . . They did not like me, but with the magical rifle in my hands I was momentarily worth watching. And suddenly I realized that I should have to shoot the elephant after all. The people expected it of me and I had got to do it; I could feel their two thousand wills pressing me forward, irresistibly.
>
> (Fontana, 1980:172)

This vignette illustrates several basic components of existential thought. First, the focus is on the actor, in this case the hunter, and his thoughts and actions. Second, there is the situated and problematic character of social life. Left to his own devices, the hunter would not have shot the elephant. However, he found himself in a situation in which he was led to change his course of action. Third, there is the social setting, the crowd, which "forced" the hunter to shoot the elephant. Finally, there is Sartre's theme of "bad faith." The hunter did not have to shoot the elephant, as he claimed. He could have said no to the pressure. This illustrates the political theme of existentialism. Despite the existence of external pressures, one can always say no. The Nazi concentration camp officer is practicing bad faith when he says that he was just carrying out orders; he could have said no.

Existential sociology has a deep commitment to the naturalistic study of actors and their thoughts, feelings, and actions. Within this general arena, it emphasizes several phenomena. For one thing, existential sociologists (for instance, Kotarba, 1979; Manning, 1973) have a strong interest in feelings, sentiments, and the like, in stark contrast to the propensity of most sociologists, who emphasize the rational aspects of human existence (a notable exception being Kemper 1978a, 1978b, 1981). Joseph A. Kotarba made clear precisely how important the study of feelings is to the existential sociologist: "Underlying all the work, however, is an emphasis on and a deep commitment to understanding how feelings form the foundations of our lives, as well as the intricate social realities we construct" (1979:350). In other words, our understanding, not only of people but of their social products as well, is made possible by the study of human feelings.

Another crucial concern of the existential sociologist is the *self* (Kotarba and Fontana, 1984), or the "individual's total experience of being." According to Kotarba, "The existential self refers to an individual's unique experience of being within the context of contemporary social conditions, an experience most notably marked by an incessant sense of becoming and an active participation in social change" (1984:225). The self, to the existentialist, cannot be separated from the physical body in which it is found. The relationship between the mental and physical dimensions of life is deemed important and worthy of study (Kotarba, 1977). Furthermore, the self is viewed not as a static structure but as a process, something constantly in a state of becoming (Johnson and Ferraro, 1984). That is, the self is creative and spontaneous, strongly affected by its immediate situation. In this definition, the self is always seen as at least partially problematic and situational.

It is the interest among existentialists in thoughts, feelings, actions, and the self that structuralists rejected. They wanted to decenter social thought and move away from the human actor and toward the direction of concern for structure. Existential sociology helps us understand the origins of structuralism. In addition, it represents a challenge to it in that structuralists are unable to deal adequately with the concerns of the existentialist.

Systems Theory

Systems theory is the product of a variety of scientific ideas imported into sociology from other fields, including cybernetics, information theory, operations research, and economic systems theory (Lilienfeld, 1978). These ideas were then remolded to apply to social life. In *Sociology and Modern Systems Theory* (1967), Walter Buckley answered the question of what sociology has to gain from systems theory (see also Bailey, 1990).

First, because systems theory is derived from the hard sciences and because it is, at least in the eyes of its proponents, applicable to *all* behavioral and social sciences, it promises a common vocabulary to unify them. Second, systems theory is multileveled and can be applied equally well to the largest-scale and the smallest-scale, to the most objective and the most subjective, aspects of the social world. Third, systems theory is interested in the varied relationships of the many aspects of the social world and thus operates against piecemeal analyses of the social world. The argument of systems theory is that the intricate relationship of parts cannot be treated out of the context of the whole. Systems theorists reject the idea that society or other large-scale components of society should be treated as unified social facts. Instead, the focus is on relationships or processes at various levels within the social system. Buckley described the focus:

> The kind of system we are interested in may be described generally as a complex of elements or components directly or indirectly related in a causal network, such that each component is related to at least some others in a more or less stable way within any particular period of time.
>
> (Buckley, 1967:41)

Richard A. Ball offers a clear conception of the relational orientation of systems theory, or what he calls General Systems Theory (GST):

> GST begins with a processual conception of reality as consisting fundamentally of relationships among relationships, as illustrated in the concept of "gravity" as used in modern physics. The term "gravity" does not describe an entity at all. There is no such "thing" as gravity. It is a *set of relationships.* To think of these relationships as entities is to fall into reification. . . . The GST approach demands that sociologists develop the logic of relationships and conceptualize social reality in relational terms.
>
> (Ball, 1978:66)

Fourth, the systems approach tends to see all aspects of sociocultural system in process terms, especially as networks of information and communication. Fifth, and perhaps most important, systems theory is inherently integrative. Buckley, in his definition of the perspective, saw it involving the integration of large-scale objective structures, symbol systems, action and interaction, and "consciousness and self-awareness." Ball also accepted the idea of integration of levels: "The individual and society are treated equally, not as separate entities but as mutually constitutive fields, related through various 'feedback' processes" (1978:68). In fact, systems theory is so attuned to integration that Buckley criticized the tendency of other sociologists to make analytical distinctions among levels:

> We note the tendency in much of sociology to insist on what is called an "analytical distinction" between "personality" (presumably intracranial), symbol systems (culture), and matrices of social relations (social systems), though the actual work of the proponents of the distinctions shows it to be misleading or often untenable in practice.
>
> (Buckley, 1967:101)

(Buckley was somewhat unfair here, because he did much the same thing throughout his own work. Making analytical distinctions is apparently acceptable to systems theorists as long as one is making such distinctions in order to make better sense out of the interrelationships among the various aspects of social life.) Finally, systems theory tends to see the social world in dynamic terms, with an overriding concern for "sociocultural emergence and dynamics in general" (Buckley, 1967:39).

Buckley discussed the relationship among sociocultural systems, mechanical systems, and organic systems. Buckley focused on delineating the essential differences among these systems. On a number of dimensions a continuum runs from the mechanical systems to organic systems to sociocultural systems—going from least to most complexity of the parts, from least to most instability of the parts, and from lowest to highest degree to which the parts are attributable to the system as a whole.

On other dimensions, the systems differ qualitatively rather than simply quantitatively. In mechanical systems, the interrelationships of the parts are based on transfers of energy. In organic systems, the interrelationships of the parts are based more on exchange of information than on energy. In sociocultural systems, the interrelationships are based even more on information exchange.

The three types of systems also differ in the degree to which they are open or closed—that is, in the degree of interchange with aspects of the larger environment. A more open system is better able to respond selectively to a greater range and detail of the endless variety of the environment. In these terms, mechanical systems tend to be closed; organic systems more open; and sociocultural systems the most open of the three. The degree of openness of a system is related to two crucial concepts in systems theory: *entropy,* or the tendency of systems to run down; and *negentropy,* or the tendency of systems to elaborate structures (Bailey, 1990). Closed systems tend to be entropic, whereas open systems tend to be negentropic. Sociocultural systems also tend to have more tension built into them than the other two. Finally, sociocultural systems can be purposive and goal-seeking because they receive feedback from the environment that allows them to keep moving toward their goals.

Feedback is an essential aspect of the cybernetic approach that systems theorists take to the social system. This is in contrast to the equilibrium approach, which is characteristic of many sociologists (for instance, Parsons) who purportedly operate from a systems approach. Using feedback enables cybernetic systems theorists to deal with friction, growth, evolution, and sudden changes. The openness of a social system to its environment and the impact of environmental factors on the system are important concerns to these systems theorists.

A variety of internal processes also affect social systems. Two other concepts are critical here. *Morphostasis* refers to those processes that help the system maintain itself, whereas *morphogenesis* refers to those processes that help the system change, grow more elaborate. Social systems develop more and more complex "mediating systems" that intervene between external forces and the action of the system. Some of these mediating systems help the system to maintain itself, and others help it to change. These mediating systems grow more and more independent, autonomous, and determinative of the actions of the system. In other words, these mediating systems permit the social system to grow less dependent on the environment.

These complex mediating systems perform a variety of functions in the social system. For example, they allow the system to adjust itself temporarily to external conditions. They can direct the system from harsh to more congenial environments. They can also allow the system to reorganize its parts in order to deal with the environment more effectively.

Buckley (1976) moved from a discussion of general principles to the specifics of the social world to show the applicability of systems theory. He began at the individual level, where he was very impressed by Mead's work, in which consciousness and action are interrelated. In fact, Buckley recast the Meadian problematic in systems-theory terms. Action begins with a *signal* from the environment, which is transmitted to the actor. However, the transmission may be complicated by *noise* in the environment. When it gets through, the signal provides the actor with *information.* On the basis of this information, the actor is allowed to *select* a response. The key here is the actor's possession of a mediating mechanism—self-consciousness. Buckley discussed self-consciousness in the terminology of systems theory:

> In the language of cybernetics, such self-consciousness is a mechanism of internal feedback of the system's own states which may be mapped or compared with other information from the situation and from memory, permitting a selection from a repertoire of actions in a goal-directed manner that takes one's own self and behavior implicitly into account.
>
> (Buckley, 1967:100)

To Mead and the symbolic interactionists and systems theorists, consciousness is not separated from action and interaction but rather is an integral part of both.

Despite his views that consciousness and interaction are interrelated and that levels should not be separated, Buckley did move from consciousness to the interactional domain. Patterns of interaction—namely, imitation and response—clearly fit into a systemic view of the world. More important, Buckley tied the interpersonal realm directly to the personality system; indeed, he saw the two as mutually determinative. Finally, Buckley turned to the large-scale organization of society, especially roles and institutions, which he saw in systemic terms and as related to, if not indistinguishable from, the other levels of social reality.

Buckley concluded by discussing some of the general principles of systems theory as they apply to the sociocultural domain. First, the systems theorist accepts the idea that tension is a normal, ever-present, and necessary reality of the social system. Second, there is a focus on the nature and sources of variety in the social system. The emphasis on both tension and variety makes the systems perspective a dynamic one. Third, there is a concern for the selection process at both the individual and the interpersonal levels, whereby the various alternatives open to the system are sorted and sifted. This lends further dynamism. Fourth, the interpersonal level is seen as the basis of the development of larger structures. The transactional processes of exchange, negotiation, and bargaining are the processes out of which emerge relatively stable social and cultural structures. Finally, despite the inherent dynamism of the systems approach, there is a recognition of the processes of perpetuation and transmission. As Buckley put it, "Out of the continuous transactions emerge some relatively stable accommodations and adjustments" (1967:160).

An interesting note: There are a number of rather striking similarities between systems theory and the dialectical approach, even though they are derived from extremely different sources (one scientific, the other philosophical) and have very different vocabularies (Ball, 1978). Similarities between them include a focus on relations, process, creativity, and tension.

Having examined some of the basic premises of systems theory, we need to return to the issue of its antistructuralism. What is it about systems theory that leads us to think of it as antistructuralist? First, systems theory is multilevel and integrative, whereas structuralism tends to be reductionistic. That is, structuralism tends to accord primacy either to the micro structures of the mind or to the underlying macro structures of society. Second, systems theory's rejection of a piecemeal analysis of the world, and its focus on interrelationships, implies a critique of structuralism's tendency to focus on either micro or macro structures. Third, and perhaps of greatest importance, is systems theory's processual and dynamic character, which stands in contrast to structuralism's tendency to do static analyses of the social world. Looking at structuralism through the lessons of systems theory allows us to critique structuralism for being reductionistic, nonrelational, and static.

SOCIOLOGICAL VARIANTS

Structuralism holds a number of attractions for sociologists, especially those oriented to the development of a science of sociology (Goddard, 1976). For example, it is a highly abstract system of thought that allows a good deal of analytical rigor. It promises the possibility of formal modeling as well as the use of sophisticated statistical and mathematical techniques. It also seems to offer a transhistorical perspective on social life. Above all, it offers a perspective with great scope capable of dealing with everything from the structure of the mind to the structure of society to the structure of the natural world.

For these reasons and others, at least some sociologists have gravitated toward a structural orientation in recent years. For example, some ethnomethodologists, most notably Aaron Cicourel, have sought to employ a structuralist orientation. Cicourel argued that ethnomethodologists should be interested in actors' basic interpretive procedures, which he sees as being "like deep structure grammatical rules" (1974:27). Interestingly, Cicourel saw these deep structures in a nondeterministic way, that is, as generating *innovative* responses to social situations.

Erving Goffman's Structuralism

The work of Erving Goffman, especially his later works, including *Frame Analysis* (1974), also illustrates a drift toward structuralism. George Gonos argued that Goffman's work constitutes "an American variant of contemporary structuralism" (1977:854). Goffman looked beyond and behind everyday situations in a search for the structures that invisibly govern them. These are " 'schemata of interpretation' that enable individuals 'to locate, perceive, identify, and label' occurrences within their life space and the world at large. By rendering events or occurrences meaningful, frames function to organize experience and guide action, whether individual or collective" (Snow, 1986:464). Goffman labeled these invisible structures *frames*. Although situations may vary in their particularities, the frames retain stable rules of operation. Gonos provided other structural characteristics of frames:

> From Goffman's analyses of particular framed activities, we can derive certain principal characteristics of frames. A frame is not conceived as a loose, somewhat accidental amalgamation of elements put together over a short time-span. Rather, it is constituted of a set number of essential components, having a definite arrangement and stable relations. These components are not gathered from here and there, as are the elements of a situation, but are always found together as a system. The standard components cohere and are complete. . . . Other less essential elements are present in any empirical instance and lend some of their character to the whole. . . . In all this, frames are very close in conception to "structures."
>
> (Gonos, 1977:860)

To George Gonos (1980), frames are largely rules or laws that fix interaction. The rules are usually unconscious and ordinarily nonnegotiable. Among the rules identified by Gonos are those that define "how signs are to be 'interpreted,' how outward indications are to be related to 'selves,' and what 'experience' will accompany activity" (1980:160). Gonos concludes, "Goffman's problematic thus promotes the study not of observable interaction of 'everyday life' as such, but its eternal structure and ideology; not of situations, but of their frames" (1980:160). Goffman seems to be offering a conception of structures of interaction that promises the possibility of integration with Lévi-Strauss's mental structures and the French structural Marxists' large-scale structures.

While Goffman's structural approach bears some resemblance to French structuralism, there are several other sociological approaches which, although they can be described as structural, have little in common with French structuralism. We will deal with two examples here—structural theory, especially that of Peter Blau, and network theory.

Structural Theory

One of the more interesting developments in sociological theory has been the rebirth of interest in structural theory—that is, a return to the roots of sociology in Emile Durkheim's concept of social facts. This rebirth has been led by many of the leaders of sociology's "old guard," including such people as Robert Merton, Lewis Coser, William Goode, Seymour Martin Lipset, and, most important, Peter Blau. Having witnessed their traditional orientations under attack from the various sides, they felt the need to reiterate their focus on large-scale structures.

The politics of this revival are interesting and tell us a good deal about structural theory. Lewis Coser (1975a) was particularly upset that many of his colleagues in sociology seemed to have succumbed to "a veritable orgy of subjectivism" in adopting such small-scale theories as phenomenology and ethnomethodology. He argued that the study of large-scale structures is the "cornerstone" of sociology. Sociologists are urged not to give in to the subjectivists but rather to return to the work of Durkheim, as well as to that of Simmel and Marx, which teaches "us that individual striving is not sufficient to free us from the grip of societal constraints" (Coser, 1975b:210). The ultimate focus of sociology should be on the "stubborn facticity of structural arrangements" (Coser, 1975b:210).

It is not that Coser wanted to focus exclusively on large-scale structures but rather that he wanted to treat them as the ultimate determinants of the other aspects of social reality. His basic model is that social structures impinge on social processes (for instance, social conflict), which in turn affect individual behavior.

The other major "enemy" of the structuralists is the group of sociologists who have focused on the cultural level, on the normative systems of society (Goode, 1975).[2] One of those whom William J. Goode had in mind here must have been Parsons, with his brand of cultural determinism. Goode suggested that, instead of focusing on such normative or cultural forces, we focus on such structural phenomena as communication systems, authority systems, paths of travel, and the physical layout of housing. Peter Blau (1975a) extended this list by including the following large-scale structures: class structure, structural change, division of labor, associations that structure social relations, status sets and role sets, structural roots of deviance and rebellion, and the interrelationship among the environment, population, and social structure. In addition to this enumeration, he offered a definition: "Social structure refers to the patterns discernible in social life, the regularities observed, the configurations detected" (Blau, 1975a:3). Blau also defined the antithesis of social structure: "chaos, formlessness, idiosyncratic human behavior that exhibits no regularities and hence is unstructured" (citing Homans, 1975a:3).

Robert K. Merton (1975) clearly supported a large-scale structural approach.

---

[2] Interestingly, Lipset (1975), supposedly operating from a structural perspective, focused on the normative system. He was clearly out of step with the rest of this group.

He recognized that it is not the answer to all sociological problems but is the best we have. Characteristically, Merton wanted structural work to focus on the link between societal and individual levels, although he stated that it is social structure that structures individual alternatives. In discussing deviance, for instance, Merton argued that social structure generates different rates of deviant behavior. However, Merton was generally inclined to take a more balanced approach to the relationship between societal and individual levels. He argued that each new cohort not only enters a social structure that it never created, and by which it is constrained, but also proceeds to modify that structure. Structures are changeable and, more important, cannot exhaustively explain all of social life.

Not surprisingly, some Marxists, such as Tom Bottomore (1975), were attracted to structural sociology. In fact, Bottomore (citing Macdonald) offered a good description of the structural realities that attract the interest of Marxists:

> I remember once walking in the street and suddenly really *seeing* the big heavy buildings in their obstinate actuality and realizing I simply couldn't imagine all this recalcitrant matter transformed by socialism. How would the street *look* when the workers took it over, how would, how could revolution transfigure the miles and miles of stubborn stone?
>
> (Bottomore, 1975:159)

Bottomore did not see all social structures as rocklike; however, he was unwilling to go to the other extreme and see them as a ceaseless and formless flux of events.

As a Marxist, Bottomore was interested in developing a conception of large-scale structures, but one that allows for conflict and change. In his view, we must describe these structures but in such a way that we do not neglect "the flow of historical action by individuals and social groups which sustains, re-creates, revises, or destructs this order" (Bottomore, 1975:160). What preoccupied Bottomore were the sources of variation in social structures. The first source of variation is the circulation of membership. The new people who enter are never totally socialized into the group so that they construct new subgroups, alter their roles, and so on. Second, the growth in knowledge and the resulting expansion of science and technology lead to continual structural change. Third, the progressive processes of social differentiation lead to changes in social structure. New positions and roles lead to new ideas, mental orientations, social definitions, and social interests. Finally, there is the possibility of change within structures themselves and in their impact on culture and consciousness.

Peter Blau's Structural Theory   The work of Peter Blau (1975b, 1977a, 1977b; Blau and Merton, 1981) is the most important representation of this "reborn" structuralism. Blau offered a rather extreme version of this structural orientation. For one thing, he clearly defined the *task of sociology* in structural terms: "The most distinctive task of sociology is the structural analysis of various forms of differentiation, their interrelations, the conditions producing them and changes in them and their implications for social relations" (Blau, 1977a, 6–7). In this definition, Blau pointedly eliminated cultural- and individual-level variables from sociology. On the cultural issue, Blau stated, "I am a structural determinist, who believes that the structures of objective social positions among which people are distributed exert more fundamental influences on social life than do cultural values and norms" (1977a:x). Blau wanted to look at social structures, but without the cultural and functional connotations of structural functionalism. Furthermore, he was going to ignore the individual levels. From his point of view, the parts of society are groups or classes of people, not actors and their thoughts and actions. "The focus is on structures of differentiated positions and their influences on the relations of human beings, not on the intensive analysis of the sociopsychological processes involved in human relations" (Blau, 1977a:4). Blau recognized the importance of such factors but stated that he would not deal with them. This means that there is an inherent limitation in his approach: "To be sure, these theorems are deterministic only for groups, not for individuals, for whom they are only probabilistic" (Blau, 1977a:7).

Blau also found it necessary to differentiate himself from Lévi-Strauss's brand of structuralism. He examined Lévi-Strauss's claim that in his system the concept of social structure has nothing to do with empirical reality, but rather with theoretical models built about this reality. Blau took the opposite position, arguing that the social structures with which he was concerned were *real social phenomena*. Furthermore, while Lévi-Strauss saw structures as invisible, Blau argued that they are "observable aspects of social life, not theories about it" (1977a:2).

Blau also defined *social structure:* "population distributions among social positions along various lines—positions that affect people's role relations and social interaction" (1975b:221). There are two key elements of this definition: positions and population. Social positions define social structures. They are, in turn, defined by the various parameters implicit in the social distinctions that people make in their social interaction. Examples of these parameters include age, sex, race, and socioeconomic status. Blau contended that his basic thesis "is that the study of the various forms of differentiation among people, their interrelations, the conditions producing them, and their implications is *the* distinctive task of sociology" (1975b:222).

As implied above, Blau was interested in both the differentiation and interrelationship of social positions. In terms of interrelationships, Blau saw two factors linking social positions: first, the various social associations among people; second, the process of social mobility, which he defined very broadly as *all* movements of people between social positions.

In discussing differentiation, Blau outlined two major types of structural parameters. The first type is *nominal* parameters, which serve to differentiate a population without ranking the different subsets. Each subset has a distinct boundary. Among the nominal parameters that Blau discussed are sex and race. The second type is *graduated* structural parameters, which serve to differentiate people on status dimensions. The differences are stated in terms of gradations, and there are no clear dividing lines between subsets (for example, income and wealth).

Based on his differentiation between parameters, Blau presented two types of social positions, each of which is distinguished by a given structural parameter. A *group* is determined on the basis of nominal parameters, whereas a *status* is determined on the basis of graduated parameters.

Building on parameters and social positions, Blau developed two generic forms of differentiation. The first is *heterogeneity*, which involves the distribution of a population among various groups in terms of nominal parameters. The second is *inequality*, which is determined by status distributions in terms of graduated parameters. We see reflected here Blau's values: there is too much inequality in society, and there can never be too much heterogeneity.

Blau explained in great detail what he meant by parameters of social structure. He did this by explaining what his structural theory does or does not concern itself with. For example, he would not be interested in the ethnic backgrounds of individual actors, but he would be interested in the ethnic heterogeneity of a population. He would not be interested in occupational performance but would be interested in the division of labor. In short, Blau was interested in large-scale structural factors and not in small-scale behavioral and attitudinal factors.

To illustrate his approach, Blau identified several problem areas that would be the focus of structural analyses. One is the issue of social *differentiation and integration.* Unlike Lipset and Parsons, Blau did not believe that such factors as culture, values, and norms produce social integration. Instead, the degree of structural differentiation produces integration among groups and individuals. Blau's parameters, especially nominal parameters, determine the degree of integration. In general, integration occurs when a segment of the population has a high degree of similarity in parameters such as age, sex, race, occupation, and neighborhood. A great deal of heterogeneity tends to produce barriers to social integration. At some point, however, when heterogeneity is too great, the barriers tend to break down. With enough differentiation, people prefer out-group associates to no associates at all. In fact, in modern society numerous nominal parameters produce multiform heterogeneity, which means that virtually everyone belongs to a multitude of groups and has multiple roles. Such a structure *"compels* people to have associates outside their own groups" (Blau, 1975b:233; italics added). This is the most characteristic form of macrostructural sociology—social structures determining individual action.

Blau (1980) published a "fable" in which he tried to illustrate his theory. He described a fictional spaceship, carrying, among others, two sociologists, that lands on a planet called Stellar 8R. There they encounter "Aytars," or living creatures that Blau described as being "more like people than like protozoa" (1980:777). The Aytars, who live in small villages on an island, are all alike except for two things. First, they come in two colors, blue and green (a *nominal* parameter). Second, they vary in height from 10 to 30 inches (a *graduated* parameter). There were no differentiations in sex or in age, for although time elapsed, it did not change Aytars.

Although the people varied only in these two characteristics, the "research sociologists" found that the villages that the Aytars lived in varied along five dimensions. First, the villages varied in population size from many to comparatively few Aytars. Second, the ratio of blue to green Aytars varied among the villages; some villages were disproportionately blue, others disproportionately green. Third, the villages differed in the average height of the Aytars. Some villages had comparatively tall populations; others had populations that were smaller on the average. Fourth, the differences in height led to inequality in some villages where the population was not homogeneous. "Since size was the only quantitative difference among Aytars, large ones could dominate small ones; they could simply roll over them" (Blau, 1980:777). Fifth, the villages varied in the extent to which size and color were related. Some villages were dominated numerically by tall green Aytars, others by short blue ones. In sum, although the population differed on only two characteristics, these differences led to major differences in the structure of the villages in which they lived.

Blau's sociologists then discovered that there were other islands on Stellar 8R and that there were more villages on each of these islands. The individuals were the same—that is, varying only in height and color—but these villages could be differentiated along eight dimensions. The first five dimensions were the same as those that differentiated the Aytars on the first island. Sixth, although the ratio of blue to green Aytars on two or more islands might be the same, it could be the result of very different ratios within the villages on each island. Thus, a one-to-one ratio could be the result of a one-to-one ratio within most villages, or it could be the result of great variations between villages that tended to cancel each other out. Seventh, Blau made the same point about height. That is, the average height on an island could come about because all or most villages on the island were similar in height, or it could result from the canceling out of some villages dominated by tall Aytars by others dominated by small Aytars. Eighth, the same issue was raised about the relationship between color and size. Again, there could be a similar correlation in most villages, or some villages might be peopled mostly by taller greens and others by smaller blues. Thus, although the demographic characteristics of two islands might be the same, the ecological structures of the villages on the two islands could be very different. Blau's biggest interest was the effect of such ecological (that is, structural) differences on social relationships. As Blau said, "The composition and ecological structure of villages and islands influence the social relations of Aytars independent of their psychological preferences" (1980:780).

Blau began with the assumption that in general people prefer to associate with others like themselves. However, Blau's hypothetical scientists discov-

PETER M. BLAU: A Biographical Sketch

Peter Blau was born in Vienna, Austria, on February 7, 1918. He emigrated to the United States in 1939 and became a United States citizen in 1943. In 1942 he received his bachelor's degree from the relatively little known Elmhurst College in Elmhurst, Illinois. His schooling was interrupted by World War II, and he served in the United States Army and was awarded the Bronze Star. After the war, he returned to school and completed his education, receiving his Ph.D. from Columbia University in 1952.

Blau first received wide recognition in sociology for his contributions to the study of formal organizations. His empirical studies of organizations as well as his textbooks on formal organizations are still widely cited in that subfield, and he continues to be a regular contributor to it. He is also noted for a book he coauthored with Otis Dudley Duncan, *The American Occupational Structure,* which won the prestigious Sorokin Award from the American Sociological Association in 1968. That work constitutes a very important contribution to the sociological study of social stratification.

Although he is well known for a range of work, what interests us here is Blau's contribution to sociological theory. What is distinctive about it, as reflected in the way in which it has been treated in this book, is that Blau has made important contributions to two distinct theoretical orientations. As we saw in Chapter 11, his 1964 book *Exchange and Power in Social Life* is a major component of contemporary exchange theory. Blau's chief contribution there was to take the primarily small-scale exchange theory and try to apply it to larger-scale issues. Although it has some notable weaknesses, it constitutes an important effort to theoretically integrate large- and small-scale sociological issues. More recently, Blau has been in the forefront of structural theory. During his term as president of the American Sociological Association (1973–1974), he made this the theme of the annual meeting of the association. Since then he has published a number of books and articles designed to clarify and to extend structural theory.

ered that Aytars of different size and color were sometimes found in each other's company. In their "survey," they uncovered some representative comments: "At least we have the same color, and there is nobody my size around here." "Sure, my friend is green, but to me size is more important than color" (Blau, 1980:780). Blau argued that the chance of one Aytar having out-group friends is the product of several structural realities. For example, if one's own kind is a small minority in a village, one is more likely to have out-group friends. If one exists within small groups, then the chances of out-group friendships are increased because one will have fewer people with similar characteristics to choose from. Finally, the intersection of parameters tends to inhibit out-group choices. That is, if size and color are substantially related (if, for example, green Aytars are also likely to be short), the intersection of these two factors tends to cause the factors to reinforce each other and make in-group choices even more likely.

Structural theory includes some old sociological ideas (as, for example, from Simmel and Durkheim) cast in a new form. It remains to be seen how far structural theory can go in sociology, with its exclusive focus on the large-scale structural level of social reality. Although that strict focus might appear to limit its explanatory power, compared to some of the more integrative sociological theories, structural theory appeals to some very basic propensities of sociologists. It will probably prove attractive especially to those sociologists who reject subjective or small-scale factors as primary concerns of sociology.

Blau's theory has led to a number of empirical studies (Blau, Beeker, and Fitzpatrick, 1984; Blau, Blum, and Schwartz, 1982; Blum, 1984). To take one example, Terry Blum tested two hypotheses derived from Blau's theory: "(1) Ethnic heterogeneity fosters interethnic interactions despite the prevalence of in-group preferences" (2) religious heterogeneity encourages interreligious interactions despite the prevalence of in-group preferences" (1985:513). Blum's results support Blau's theory and its most general point that "macrosocial structure exerts constraints on interpersonal interaction by providing or limiting opportunities for such interactions" (1985:520–521).

Network Theory

Another structural approach in modern sociology is network theory. Although it is a type of structuralism, it is less tied to the kinds of external developments discussed earlier and more indigenous to sociology. Thus, although network theorists are interested in "deep structures," the structures are closer to traditional sociological social structures than, for example, to Lévi-Strauss's interest in mental structures. Also in accord with the theory's link to mainstream sociology, network theorists are little interested in philosophizing about structures and much more interested in methodological, even mathematical, rigor and the empirical study of various kinds of networks.

Network analysts take pains to differentiate their approach from what Ronald Burt calls "atomistic" and "normative" sociological approaches (Burt, 1982; see also Granovetter, 1985). Atomistic sociological orientations focus on actors making decisions in isolation from other actors. More generally, they focus on the "personal attributes" of actors (Wellman, 1983). Atomistic approaches are rejected because they are too microscopic and ignore links among actors. As Barry Wellman puts it, "Accounting for individual motives is a job better left to psychologists" (1983:163). This, of course, constitutes a rejection of a number of sociological theories that are in one way or another deeply concerned with motives—symbolic interactionism, phenomenological sociology, existential sociology, Weberian theory, Schutzian theory, and others.

In the view of network theorists, normative approaches focus on culture and the socialization process through which norms and values are internalized in actors. In the normative orientation, what holds people together are sets of shared ideas. Network theorists reject such a view and argue that one should focus on the objective pattern of ties linking the members of society. Here is how Wellman articulates this view:

> Network analysts want to study regularities in how people and collectivities behave rather than regularities in beliefs about how they ought to behave. Hence network analysts try to avoid normative explanations of social behavior. They dismiss as non-structural any explanation that treats social process as the sum of individual actors' personal attributes and internalized norms.
>
> (Wellman, 1983:162)

In this, network theorists reject a large part of structural functionalism, Parsonian cultural determinism, Durkheimian emphasis on the collective conscience, Simmelian interest in objective and subjective culture, the critical theorist's interest in culture, and so on.

Having made clear what it is not, network theory then clarifies its major concern—the objective pattern of ties linking the members (individual and collective) of society. Let us look at how Wellman articulates this focus:

> Network analysts start with the simple, but powerful, notion that the primary business of sociologists is to study social structure. . . . The most direct way to study a social structure is to analyze the pattern of ties linking its members. Network analysts search for *deep* structures—regular network patterns beneath the often complex surface of social systems. . . . Actors and their behavior are seen as constrained by these structures. Thus, the focus is not on voluntaristic actors, but on structural constraint.
>
> (Wellman, 1983:156–157)

One distinctive aspect of network theory is that it focuses on a wide range of micro to macro structures. That is, to network theory the actors may be people (Wellman and Wortley, 1990), but they also may be groups, corporations (Baker, 1990; Clawson, Neustadtl, and Bearden, 1986; Mizruchi and Koenig, 1986), and societies. Links occur at the large-scale, social-structural level as well as at more microscopic levels. Mark Granovetter describes such micro-level links as action "embedded" in "the concrete personal relations and structures (or 'networks') of such relations" (1985:490). Basic to any of these links is the idea that any "actor" (individual or collective) may have differential access to valued resources (wealth, power, information). The result is that structured systems tend to be stratified, with some components dependent on others.

One key aspect of network analysis is that it tends to move sociologists away from the study of social groups and social categories and toward the study of ties among and between actors that are not "sufficiently bounded and densely knit to be termed groups" (Wellman, 1983:169). A good example of this is Granovetter's (1973, 1983) work on "the strength of weak ties." Granovetter differentiates between "strong ties," for example, links between people and their close friends, and "weak ties," for example, links between people and mere acquaintances. Sociologists have tended to focus on people with strong ties or social groups. They have tended to regard strong ties as crucial, whereas weak ties have been thought of as being of trivial sociological impor-tance. Granovetter's contribution is to make it clear that weak ties can be very important. For example, weak ties between two actors can serve as a bridge between two groups with strong internal ties. Without such a weak tie, the two groups might be totally isolated. This, in turn, could lead to a more frag-mented social system. An individual lacking in weak ties would find himself or herself isolated in a tightly knit group and lack information about what is going on in other groups as well as in the larger society. Weak ties therefore prevent isolation and allow for individuals to be better integrated into the larger society. Although Granovetter emphasizes the importance of weak ties, he hastens to make it clear "that strong ties can also have value" (1983:209). For example, people with strong ties have greater motivation to help one another and are more readily available to one another.

Network theory is relatively new and undeveloped. As Burt says, "There is currently a loose federation of approaches referenced as network analysis" (1982:20). But it is growing, as evidenced by the number of papers and books being published from a network perspective and the fact that there is now a journal *(Social Networks)* devoted to it. Although it may be a loose conglom-eration of work, network theory does seem to rest on a coherent set of prin-ciples (Wellman, 1983).

First, ties among actors usually are symmetrical in both content and inten-sity. Actors supply each other with different things, and they do so with greater or lesser intensity. Second, the ties among individuals must be ana-lyzed within the context of the structure of larger networks. Third, the struc-turing of social ties leads to various kinds of nonrandom networks. On the one hand, networks are transitive: if there is a tie between *A* and *B* and *B* and *C*, there is likely to be a tie between *A* and *C*. The result is that there is more likely to be a network involving *A*, *B*, and *C*. On the other hand, there are limits to how many links can exist and how intense they can be. The result is that there are also likely to develop network clusters with distinct boundaries separating one cluster from another. Fourth, the existence of clusters leads to the fact that there can be cross-linkages between clusters as well as between individuals. Fifth, there are asymmetric ties among elements in a system, with the result that scarce resources are differentially distributed. Finally, the un-equal distribution of scarce resources leads to both collaboration and compe-tition. Some groups band together to acquire scarce resources collaboratively, whereas others compete and conflict over resources. This gives network theory a dynamic quality (Rosenthal et al., 1985), with the structure of the system changing with shifting patterns of coalition and conflict.

We can close this section on network theory with a discussion of a recent study that demonstrates its distinctive theoretical orientation. Mizruchi (1990) is interested in the issue of the cohesion of corporations and its relationship to power. He argues that historically *cohesion* has been defined in two different ways. The first, or subjective view, is that "cohesion is a function of group members' feelings of identification with the group, in particular their feeling that their individual interests are bound up with the interests of the group" (Mizruchi, 1990:21). The emphasis here is on the normative system, and cohesion is produced either by the internalization of the normative system or by group pressure. The second, or objective view, is that "solidarity can be viewed as an objective, observable process independent of the sentiments of individuals" (Mizruchi, 1990:22). Needless to say, given his alignment with network theory, Mizruchi comes down on the side of the objective approach to cohesion.

Mizruchi sees similarity of behavior as a result of not only cohesion but also what he calls *structural equivalence:* "Structurally equivalent actors are those with identical relations with other actors in the social structure" (1990: 25). Thus, structural equivalence exists among, say, corporations, even though there may be no communication among them. They behave in the same way because they stand in the same relationship to some other entity in the social structure. Mizruchi concludes that structural equivalence plays at least as strong a role as cohesion in explaining similarity of behavior. Mizruchi accords great importance to structural equivalence, which, after all, implies a network of social relations.

SUMMARY

In this chapter we examine a number of structural sociological theories. First, we discuss structuralism, which is largely French in character. Under this heading we deal with the roots of structuralism in linguistics, especially Saussure's distinction between *langue* and *parole*. Considerable attention is devoted to the anthropological structuralism in the theories of Lévi-Strauss. Although he uses structures in several different ways, of greatest importance is his emphasis on the structure of the mind. We turn then to a discussion of structural Marxism. Structural Marxists are concerned with the underlying, large-scale structures of society—political, ideological, and especially economic. They look at macro structures, whereas Lévi-Strauss is mainly concerned with the micro structures of the mind. While the ideas of French structuralism are important, they must overcome major barriers if they are to be more broadly accepted in mainstream sociology.

Structuralism, itself, has recently been largely supplanted by poststructuralism. Poststructuralism is defined by a movement away from a single-minded concern with structure and the utilization of a variety of theoretical inputs. Our major concern here is the theories of the leading poststructuralist, Michel Foucault. While his early work tended to focus on structures, his later work examined a wider array of social phenomena. Furthermore, his work progressively showed the influence of an increasingly wide range of theoretical inputs. Foucault offers a rich and diverse body of work that will be influential in sociology for many years to come. We also discuss antistructuralism, especially in the form of existential sociology and systems theory. Existential sociology's concern with the actor, consciousness, and humanism was rejected by the structuralists. However, it points out the weakness of structuralism in dealing with the agent. Systems theory's integrative, relational, and processional character points out basic weaknesses in structuralism and stands in stark contrast to it.

Finally, we discuss three sociological variants of a structural approach to the social world. First, we examine Goffman's structuralism, especially his frame analysis, which shows strong similarities to French structuralism. Second, there is a discussion of structural theory, primarily that of Peter Blau. Sociological structural theory rejects outright structuralism's interest in invisible structures. Whereas structuralism imported ideas from other fields, structural theory returns to sociology's early Durkheimian roots in the study of material social facts. Third, there is a discussion of network theory. This theory is oriented to analyzing underlying social structures, but it is closely tied to mainstream sociology, and much of it is embedded in highly sophisticated empirical studies of social networks throughout the social world.

PART THREE

THREE

RECENT DEVELOPMENTS IN SOCIOLOGICAL THEORY: INTEGRATION AND SYNTHESES

MICRO-MACRO INTEGRATION

*I*N this chapter, as well as the next three, we deal with three of the most important developments in recent sociological theory. Our concern in this chapter is with a dramatic development which occurred largely in the United States in the 1980s and which continues to this day. That development is the growth in interest in the issue of the *micro-macro linkage*. In the following chapter we will deal with a parallel development in European sociological theory—the rise in interest in the *relationship between agency and structure*. As we will see, there are important similarities *and* crucial differences between the American micro-macro literature and the European work on agency and structure. Finally, in Chapters 16 and 17 we will deal with the most recent development in sociological theory in the 1990s—the remarkably wide and deep interest in *theoretical syntheses* of all types. In fact, the micro-macro and agency-structure literatures can, themselves, be seen as synthetic developments and as precursors of the broader interest in theoretical syntheses of all types.

MICRO-MACRO EXTREMISM

Until recently, *one* of the major divisions in twentieth-century American sociological theory has been the conflict between extreme *microscopic* and *macroscopic*[1] theories (and theorists) and, perhaps more importantly, between

---

[1] While the use of the terms *micro* and *macro* might suggest that we are dealing with a dichotomy, we are always aware of the fact that there is a *continuum* ranging from the micro to the macro end.

those who have *interpreted* sociological theories in this way (Archer, 1982). Such extreme theories and interpretations of theories have tended to heighten the image of a great chasm between micro and macro theories and, more generally, of conflict and disorder (Gouldner, 1970; Wardell and Turner, 1986a; Wiley, 1985) in sociological theory.

Although it is possible to interpret (and many have) the classic sociological theorists discussed in Part One of this book (Marx, Weber, Durkheim, Simmel) as either micro or macro extremists, the most defensible perspective, or at least the one that will orient this chapter, is that they were most generally concerned with the micro-macro linkage. Marx can be seen as being interested in the coercive and alienating effect of capitalist society on individual workers (and capitalists). Weber may be viewed as being focally concerned with the plight of the individual within the iron cage of a formally rational society. Simmel was primarily interested in the relationship between objective (macro) and subjective (or individual, micro) culture. Even Durkheim was concerned with the effect of macro-level social facts on individuals and individual behavior (for example, suicide). If we accept these characterizations of the classic sociological theorists, then it appears that much of the last half-century of American sociological theory has involved a loss of concern for this linkage and the dominance of micro and macro extremists—that is, the preeminence of theorists and theories that accord overwhelming power and significance to either the micro or the macro level. Thus, the theories discussed in Part Two of this book tended toward micro or macro extremism. On the macro-extreme side were structural functionalism, conflict theory, some varieties of neo-Marxian theory (especially economic determinism and structural Marxism), and most forms of structuralism. On the micro-extreme end were symbolic interactionism, phenomenology, ethnomethodology, existential sociology, behavioral sociology, and exchange theory.

Among the most notable of the twentieth-century macro extremists are the later Parsons (1966) and his "cultural determinism";[2] Dahrendorf's (1959) conflict theory, with its focus on imperatively coordinated associations; and Peter Blau's macrostructuralism, epitomized by his proud announcement, "I am a structural determinist" (1977a:x). Macro-structural extremism comes from other sources as well (Rubinstein, 1986), including network theorists like White, Boorman, and Breiger (1976), ecologists like Duncan and Schnore (1959), and structuralists like Mayhew (1980). Few are more extreme than Mayhew, who says such things as, "In structural sociology the unit of analysis is always the social network, *never the individual*" (1980:349).

On the micro-extreme side we can point to a good portion of symbolic interactionism and the work of Blumer (1969a), who often seemed to have

---

[2] Even as sympathetic an observer as Jeffrey Alexander (1987:296) admits Parsons's "own collectivist bias;" see also Coleman (1986:1310). However, while Parson's greatest influence was in collectivistic theory, it is also possible to find within his work a strong micro-macro integrative theory.

structural functionalism in mind as he positioned symbolic interactionism as a sociological theory seemingly single-mindedly concerned with micro-level phenomena (see Chapter 16 for a very different interpretation of Blumer's perspective). An even clearer case of micro extremism is exchange theory and George Homans (1974), who sought an alternative to structural functionalism and found it in the extreme micro orientation of Skinnerian behaviorism. Then there is ethnomethodology and its concern for the everyday practices of actors. Garfinkel (1967) was put off by the macro foci of structural functionalism and its tendency to turn actors into "judgmental dopes."

THE MOVEMENT TOWARD MICRO-MACRO INTEGRATION

While micro-macro extremism has characterized much of twentieth-century sociological theory, it has been possible, mainly in the 1980s, to discern a movement, largely in American sociology, away from micro-macro extremism and toward a broad consensus that *the* focus, instead, should be on *the integration (or synthesis, linkage) of micro and macro theories and/or levels of social analysis.* This represents quite a change from the 1970s, when Kemeny argued: "So little attention is given to this distinction that the terms 'micro' and 'macro' are not commonly even indexed in sociological works" (1976:731). It could be argued that at least in this sense American sociological theorists have rediscovered the theoretical project of the early masters.

While developments in the 1980s were particularly dramatic, isolated earlier works directly addressed the micro-macro linkage. For example, in the mid-1960s Helmut Wagner (1964) dealt with the relationship between small-scale and large-scale theories. At the end of the decade Walter Wallace (1969) examined the micro-macro continuum, but it occupied a secondary role in his analysis and was included as merely one of the "complications" of his basic taxonomy of sociological theory. In the mid-1970s Kemeny (1976) called for greater attention to the micro-macro distinction as well as to the ways in which micro and macro relate to one another.

However, it was in the 1980s that we witnessed a flowering of work on the micro-macro linkage issue. Collins argued that work on this topic "promises to be a significant area of theoretical advance for some time to come" (1986a:1350). In their introduction to a two-volume set of books, one devoted to macro theory (Eisenstadt and Helle, 1985a) and the other to micro theory (Helle and Eisenstadt, 1985), Eisenstadt and Helle concluded that "the confrontation between micro- and macro-theory belong[s] to the past" (1985b:3). Similarly, Münch and Smelser, in their conclusion to the anthology *The Micro-Macro Link* (Alexander et al., 1987), asserted: "Those who have argued polemically that one level is more fundamental than the other . . . must be regarded as in error. Virtually every contributor to this volume has correctly insisted on the mutual interrelations between micro and macro levels" (1987:385).

On the other hand, even though they were seeking to overcome it, these integrative efforts in the 1980s were shaped and distorted by the history of twentieth-century micro-macro extremism. Most sociologists working toward integration came at it from bases in either extreme micro or extreme macro theories, and these bases often served as straitjackets that limited integrative efforts. Although this is a serious problem, there are now some signs that it is being overcome.

Among the works stemming from the micro-theoretical end, there are Hechter's (1983a, 1983b; see also Wippler and Lindenberg, 1987) and Coleman's (1990) efforts, based on rational choice theory; Collins's (1981a; 1987a; 1987b) attempt, which focuses on "interactional ritual chains"; efforts (for example, by Kurzweil, 1987; Smelser, 1987) to build toward the macro level from a Freudian base; Schegloff's (1987) work, building on an ethnomethodological–conversational-analysis base, as well as similar work by Knorr-Cetina (1981a) and Cicourel (1981); and Emerson's (1981) integrative work, stemming from an exchange-theory orientation. Coming more from the macro-theoretical end are, for example, Alexander's (1982–83, 1987) multidimensional approach, stemming from a structural-functional base; Bailey's (1990) social-entropy theory, derived from systems theory; and Burt's (1982) integrative effort, rooted in macro-oriented network theory. Thus, efforts came from both micro and macro directions and from a variety of theoretical positions within and between each. In general, whether they started with a micro or a macro base, or with an integrative orientation, many sociological theorists seemed to be converging in their efforts to develop an integrated theory.

From the vantage point of the 1990s, there is now enough work on the micro-macro linkage to begin to take stock of this body of work. In the process, we will introduce the reader to some of the major examples of this kind of theoretical work.

There are two major strands of work on micro-macro integration. Some theorists focus on integrating micro and macro *theories*, while others are concerned with developing a theory that deals with the linkage between micro and macro *levels* (Alford and Friedland, 1985; Edel, 1959) of social analysis. Earlier in this chapter, for example, we quoted Eisenstadt and Helle (1985b: 3), who concluded that the confrontation between micro and macro *theories* was behind us, while Münch and Smelser (1987:385) came to a similar conclusion about the need to choose between emphasizing either micro or macro *levels*. There are important differences between trying to integrate macro (for example, structural-functionalism) and micro (for example, symbolic-interactionism) theories and attempting to develop a theory that can deal with the relationship between macro (for example, social-structure) and micro (for example, personality) levels of social analysis.

Among those who define the task, at least in part, as a problem of integrating theories are Burt (1982), Fararo and Skvoretz (1986), Hechter (1983a), Hindess (1986), and Smelser (1987). On the other side, those who define the task primarily in terms of developing a theory that focuses on integrating micro and macro levels of analysis include Alexander (1982–83, 1985), Coleman (1986, 1987), Collins (1981a), Liska (1990), Ritzer (1979, 1981a), and Wiley

(1988). Gerstein offers a good example of the latter approach when he distinguishes between the two basic levels of analysis and then argues for the need "to create theoretical concepts that translate or map variables at the individual level into variables characterizing social systems, and vice versa" (1987:86).

In addition, there are substantial differences within the groups working toward theoretical integration and integration of levels of social analysis. Among those seeking to integrate macro and micro theories, there are important differences depending on which specific theories are being integrated. For example, Hindess (1986) sought to avoid the extremes of "theoretical humanism" and "structuralism;" Hechter (1983a) pitted rational choice theory against normative and structural theories; Burt (1982) tried to bridge the schism between atomistic and normative orientations; Fararo and Skvoretz (1986) endeavored to integrate structural theory and expectation-states theory; and Smelser (1987) sought to synthesize psychoanalytic and sociological perspectives.

There are similar differences among the theorists seeking to deal with the relationship between micro and macro levels of social analysis. For example, are they seeking to integrate micro and macro structures, micro and macro processes, or more specific aspects of the micro and macro levels of social analysis? More specifically, differences in levels are reflected in Alexander's (1982:65) multidimensional sociology, involving an "alternation of freedom and constraint" in both action and order and, particularly, in the interrelationship among individual-instrumental, individual-normative, collective-instrumental, and collective-normative levels (Alexander, 1985); Ritzer's (1981a) integrated paradigm, focusing on the dialectical interrelationship of macro objectivity and subjectivity and micro objectivity and subjectivity; Wiley's (1988) concern with the relationship among self (or individual), interaction, social structure, and culture; Collins's (1981a) focus on "interaction ritual chains"; and Coleman's (1986) interest in the micro-to-macro relationship.

The task of empirical integration is made even more difficult because there are great differences among sociologists in terms of what they define as the micro and macro levels (Münch and Smelser, 1987). Depending on who is offering the definition, the micro level can range from psychological phenomena to individuals to interaction patterns among individuals. The macro level ranges from positions to populations to society and its structures to world systems. Thus, seemingly similar views about integrating micro and macro levels are, in fact, quite dissimilar because they are integrating very different social phenomena. As a basic requisite, theorists working with the terms *micro* and *macro* should clearly define what they mean by each.

Furthermore, even though like-sounding terms may be used by sociologists at the micro level (psychological characteristics, action, behavior, practices, intentional agent, micro objectivity and subjectivity, interaction, life-world, etc.) and at the macro level (structural context, system, population, positions, macro objectivity and subjectivity, structural properties of social systems, society, culture), there are in fact often substantial differences among these phenomena. For example, at the micro level, those who see behavior as produced by rewards and costs tend to have a very different sense of the social world than those who are concerned with action produced by intentional agents. Similarly, there are substantial differences between those who work at the macro level with population structures and those who focus on culture. Thus, sociologists need to do more than just carefully define their terms; they also need to spell out the theoretical implications of the kinds of terms they use at both levels.

Further complicating matters is the existence of another point of view among those who use the terms *micro* and *macro;* namely, the claim that the *micro-macro* terms are not descriptions of empirical realities but rather are analytic concepts that can be used to analyze any empirical reality. Alexander (and neo-Parsonsians in general) is a strong advocate of this position: "There can be no empirical referents for micro or macro as such. They are analytical contrasts, suggesting emergent levels within empirical units themselves. . . . The terms 'micro' and 'macro' are completely relativistic. What is macro at one level will be micro at another" (1987:290–291). While it is certainly useful to employ the terms *micro* and *macro* analytically, the fact is that most sociologists use these terms empirically. Therefore, although *micro* and *macro* can be used both empirically and analytically, sociologists must clearly define how they are using the terms.

Given this general introduction, we turn now to some examples of micro-macro integration. The examples that follow all focus on integrating micro-macro levels of social analysis. We will reserve discussion of efforts to integrate micro and macro theories until Chapters 16 and 17 where we will include it as part of a more general discussion of theoretical syntheses.

EXAMPLES OF MICRO-MACRO INTEGRATION

George Ritzer: Integrated Sociological Paradigm

This section begins with my own effort (Ritzer, 1979, 1981a) because it predates the other works to be discussed in this section and it anticipates the wide-scale development of interest in micro-macro integration that occurred in the 1980s. The discussion here will be relatively brief, since the integrated sociological paradigm is also discussed in the Appendix. It is summarized there because it represents the metatheoretical schema that serves to orient and organize this book. In this section the focus is on what the integrated paradigm has to say about the micro-macro linkage issue.

It should be noted that Ritzer's thinking on the integrated paradigm in general, and more specifically on micro-macro linkage, was shaped by the work of a number of predecessors, especially that of Edel (1959) and Georges Gurvitch (1964; see also Bosserman, 1968). Gurvitch operates with the belief

Horizontal, Micro-Macro Levels

Vertical, "Depth" Levels	Forms of Sociality	Groupings	Social Class	Social Structure	Global Structures
1) Ecological					→
2) Organizations					→
3) Social Patterns					→
4) Unorganized Collective Behavior					→
5) Social Roles					→
6) Collective Attitudes					→
7) Social Symbols					→
8) Creative Collective Behavior					→
9) Collective Ideas and Values					→
10) The Collective Mind					

FIGURE 14.1   Intersection of Gurvitch's Horizontal and Vertical Levels of Social Reality

that the social world can be studied in terms of "horizontal," or micro-macro, levels. Gurvitch thinks in terms of the following five levels, presented in ascending order from micro to macro: forms of sociality, groupings, social class, social structure, and global structures. To complement this, Gurvitch also offers ten "vertical," or "depth," levels, beginning with the most objective social phenomena (for example, ecological factors, organizations) and ending with the most subjective social phenomena (collective ideas and values, the collective mind). To create the major levels of social analysis, Gurvitch cross-cuts his horizontal and vertical dimensions in order to produce no less than fifty levels of social analysis. Figure 14.1 offers a summary of Gurvitch's image of the social world.

While highly promising and attractive, Gurvitch's model offers an overly complex view of the social world in general and the micro-macro relationship in particular. Ritzer's work on the integrated sociological paradigm was motivated, in part, by the need to build upon Gurvitch's insights but to produce a more parsimonious model. It begins with the micro-macro continuum (Gurvitch's horizontal levels), ranging from individual thought and action to world systems (see the Appendix, Figure A.1). To this is added an objective-subjective continuum (Gurvitch's vertical levels), ranging from material phenomena like individual action and bureaucratic structures to nonmaterial phenomena like consciousness and norms and values (see the Appendix, Figure A.2). Like Gurvitch, Ritzer crosscuts these two continua, but in this case they yield a far more manageable four, rather than fifty, levels of social analysis. Figure 14.2 offers a depiction of Ritzer's major levels of social analysis.[3]

---

[3] I am reproducing this model here as well as in the Appendix because of the fact that some instructors may regard the Appendix as optional and not assign it to students.

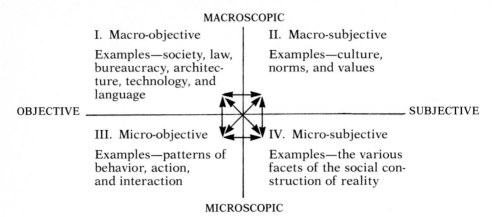

FIGURE 14.2   Ritzer's Major Levels of Social Analysis*
* Note that this is a "snapshot" in time. It is embedded in an ongoing historical process.

In terms of the micro-macro issue, Ritzer's view is that it cannot be dealt with apart from the objective-subjective continuum. All micro and macro social phenomena are also either objective or subjective. This leads to the conclusion that there are four major levels of social analysis *and* that sociologists must focus on their dialectical interrelationship. The macro-objective level involves large-scale material realities like society, bureaucracy, and technology. The macro-subjective level encompasses large-scale nonmaterial phenomena like norms and values. At the micro levels, micro objectivity involves small-scale objective entities such as patterns of action and interaction, whereas micro subjectivity is concerned with the small-scale mental processes by which people construct social reality. Each of these four levels is important in itself, but of utmost importance is the dialectical relationship among and between them. This image of the social world, employing only four major levels, is clearly far more parsimonious than the model offered by Gurvitch.

Jeffrey Alexander: Multidimensional Sociology

Jeffrey Alexander has offered what he calls a "new 'theoretical logic' for sociology" (1982:xv). That new logic affects "sociological thought at every level of the intellectual continuum" (Alexander, 1982:65). In this spirit, Alexander offers what he terms a *multidimensional sociology*. While *multidimensionality* has several meanings in his work, the most relevant here is Alexander's multidimensional sense of levels of social analysis.

We can begin with what Alexander (following Parsons) terms the *problem of order*. Alexander suggests that the micro-macro continuum ("an 'individual' or 'collective' level of analysis" [1982:93]) is involved in the way order is created in society. At the macro end of the continuum, order is externally created and is collectivist in nature; that is, order is produced by collective

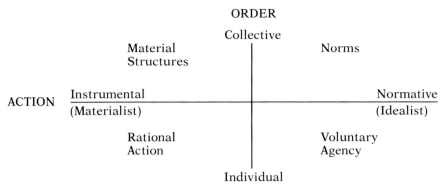

ORDER

FIGURE 14.3   Alexander's Integrative Model

phenomena. At the micro end, order is derived from internalized forces and is individualistic in nature; that is, order stems from individual negotiation.

To the problem of order is added, in a classic Parsonsian position, the *problem of action*. Action involves a materialist-idealist continuum which parallels the objective-subjective continuum employed in Ritzer's integrated sociological paradigm. At the material end, action is described as instrumental, rational, and conditional. At the nonmaterial pole, action is normative, nonrational, and affective. When we crosscut Alexander's order and action continua, we come up with four levels of social analysis that strongly resemble the four levels employed by Ritzer (see Figure 14.3).

Although the terminology is slightly different, there are few if any differences between the models offered by Alexander and Ritzer. The major difference lies in the way the two authors relate the four levels. While Ritzer wants to focus on the dialectical relationship among all four levels, Alexander seeks to grant priority to one of the levels.

Alexander believes that according privilege to the micro levels is "a theoretical mistake" (1987:295). He is highly critical of all theories such as symbolic interactionism that begin at the individual-normative level with nonrational voluntary agency and build toward the macro levels. From his point of view, the problem with these theories is that while maintaining notions of individual freedom and voluntarism, they are unable to deal with the unique (*sui generis*) character of collective phenomena. Alexander is also critical of theories such as exchange theory that start at the individual-instrumental level and move toward macro-level structures like the economy. Such theories are also unable to handle adequately macro-level phenomena. Thus, Alexander is critical of all theories that have their origins at the micro levels and seek to explain macro-level phenomena from that base.

At the macro level, Alexander is critical of collective-instrumental theories (for example economic and structural determinism) that emphasize coercive order and eliminate individual freedom. Basically, the problem is that such theories do not allow for individual agency.

While he expressed an interest in focusing on the relationships among all four of his levels, Alexander's sympathies (not surprisingly, given his Parsonsian and structural-functionalist roots) lay with the collective-normative level and theories that begin at that level. As he put it, "The hope for combining collective order and individual voluntarism lies with the normative, rather than the rationalist tradition" (Alexander, 1982:108). Central to this belief is his view that such an orientation is preferable because the sources of order are internalized (in the conscience) rather than externalized, as is the case with the collective-instrumental orientation. This allows for *both* order and voluntary agency.

Overall, Alexander argues that any individual, or micro, perspective is to be rejected because it ends with "randomness and complete unpredictability" rather than order (1985:27). Thus, "the general framework for social theory can be derived *only* from a collectivist perspective" (1985:28; italics added). And between the two collectivist perspectives, Alexander subscribes to the collective-normative position.

Thus, to Alexander social theorists must choose either a collectivist (macro) or individualist (micro) perspective. If they choose a collectivist position, they can incorporate only a "relatively small" element of individual negotiation. If, however, they choose an individualist theory, they are doomed to the "individualist dilemma" of trying to sneak into theory supraindividual phenomena to deal with the randomness inherent in their theory. This dilemma can be resolved only "if the formal adherence to individualism is abandoned" (Alexander, 1985:27).

Thus, while Alexander employs four levels of analysis that closely resemble those utilized by Ritzer, there is an important difference in the two models. Alexander accords priority to collective-normative theories and to a focus on norms in social life. Ritzer refuses to accord priority to any level and argues for the need to examine the dialectical relationship among and between all four levels. Alexander ends up giving inordinate significance to macro (subjective) phenomena, and, as a result, his contribution to the development of a theory of micro-macro integration is highly limited. In a later work, Alexander said, "I believe theorists falsely generalize from a single variable to the immediate reconstruction of the whole" (1987:314). It can be argued that Alexander is one of these theorists, since he seeks to falsely generalize from the collective-normative level to the rest of the social world.

While not directly addressing Alexander's work, Giddens (1984) came to the similar conclusion that *all* work derived from the Parsonsian distinction between action and order inevitably ends up weak at the micro levels, especially on "the knowledgeability of social actors, as constitutive in part of social practices. I [Giddens] do not think that *any* standpoint which is heavily indebted to Parsons can cope satisfactorily with this issue at the very core of social theory" (1984:xxxvii).

However, it should be noted that Alexander has shown some signs of moving toward a more truly integrative perspective, one that defines *micro* and *macro* in terms of one another. Here is the way he expresses this perspective: "The collective environments of action simultaneously inspire and confine it. If I have conceptualized action correctly, these environments will be seen as its products; if I can conceptualize the environments correctly, action will be seen as their end result" (Alexander, 1987:303). It appears that Alexander is moving toward a more complex, dialectical sense of the micro-macro nexus, one that is more similar to Ritzer's integrated sociological paradigm.

Norbert Wiley: Levels of Analysis

More recently, Norbert Wiley (1988) has offered a model of micro-macro relationships that closely resembles the models offered by Ritzer and Alexander. What is distinctive about Wiley's approach is that it is purely subjective, whereas the approaches of Ritzer and Alexander involve both subjectivity *and* objectivity. Wiley makes clear his subjectivity by arguing that his starting point for the delineation of the levels is their relationship to the subject. The following are Wiley's four major levels of analysis, as well as the parallel level (in parentheses) within Ritzer's work: self or individual (micro-subjective), interaction (micro-objective), social structure (macro-objective), culture (macro-subjective). While Ritzer's (and Alexander's) four levels bear a striking resemblance to Wiley's levels, it is clear that objective reality is neglected by Wiley. In other words, in Wiley's work the levels of interaction and social structure, like the others, are defined subjectively.

Wiley's analysis begins with the micro-level self, or individual. Alexander, as we have seen, would clearly have trouble with such a point of origin. The view here is that it does not matter where one begins as long as one ultimately deals with the dialectical relationship among all levels of analysis. However, Wiley offers a highly limited conception of the micro-subjective level. Specifically, he gives undue importance to the self and therefore ignores a number of other important components of the micro-subjective level—mind, consciousness, the social construction of reality, and so on. To put it another way, the self, as any social psychologist would recognize, far from exhausts the micro-subjective level.

Similarly, his concern with interaction, or the micro-objective level, is also limited. Much more goes on at this level than mere interaction. At the minimum, we must include action (including a conscious antecedent) and behavior (lacking such an antecedent) at this level. These clearly belong here because they are micro-level phenomena that cannot be included, at least totally, in Wiley's other, intrasubjective micro-level category. Furthermore, while interaction, action, and behavior may have a subjective component, they also have an objective existence; all three of them can come to be institutionalized in repetitive patterns. In Ritzer's work, the subjective aspects of these processes are dealt with at the micro-subjective level, and the objective aspects come under the heading "micro objectivity." In any case, we must deal with *both* their subjective and objective moments.

Wiley's conception of social structure and Ritzer's sense of macro objectivity are closer than their micro analyses, even though Wiley continues his pattern by approaching this level from a subjective point of view. He writes of the "generic self" at this level, but he clearly implies the existence of macro-objective structures when he describes the generic self "as filler of roles and follower of rules" (Wiley, 1988:258). While Wiley emphasizes the subjective generic self here, Ritzer would place greatest importance on the objective structures (society, the world system) that create the rules and the roles filled by the self.

There are few important differences between Wiley's cultural level and Ritzer's macro subjectivity. This is because both are discussed in large-scale, subjective terms. The only quarrel here is that Wiley's thoughts on "pure meaning" at this level are too general and could profit from greater specificity and some discussion of such well-known sociological concepts as norms and values.

Wiley and Ritzer are similar not only in terms of their conceptualizations of the four major levels of social analysis but also in terms of their sense of the relationships among levels. Wiley talks of a continuing process of "emergence" that links lower to higher levels and of a process of "feedback" (also presumably continuous), which flows from higher to lower levels. Similarly, Ritzer is concerned with the dialectical (that is, the ongoing, multidirectional) relationship among all levels of social analysis. While Ritzer's sense of the dialectical relationship among levels of social analysis may be seen as vaguer and more general than Wiley's emergence-feedback specification, there are many more kinds of relationships among and between levels of social analysis than Wiley suggests. A wide array of familiar sociological concepts (for example, externalization, objectification, socialization, internalization, social control) concern themselves with various aspects of the dialectical relationship between micro and macro levels.

While the micro-macro perspectives offered by Wiley and Alexander have both been summarized and critiqued from the point of view of Ritzer's integrated paradigm, the overriding point is that all three perspectives offer virtually identical models of the major levels of social analysis. This is particularly striking since the three theorists come at this issue from very different theoretical viewpoints—Ritzer's dialectical approach; Alexander's multidimensional, neofunctionalist orientation; and Wiley's subjective viewpoint. We turn now to some very different approaches to the micro-macro linkage issue.

James Coleman: Micro-to-Macro Model and *Foundations of Social Theory*

In his early thinking on this issue, James Coleman (1986, 1987) expressed an interest in the micro-macro relationship. (We will deal with Coleman's [1990] later and far more elaborate rational choice theory below.) However, Coleman

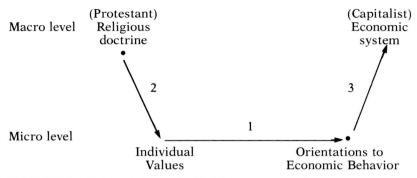

FIGURE 14.4   Coleman's Integrative Model

focuses on the "micro-to-macro" problem and downplays the significance of the "macro-to-micro" issue. Thus, from the point of view of the far more balanced micro-macro approaches offered by Ritzer, Alexander, and Wiley, Coleman's orientation to this issue is highly limited. A fully adequate approach to this problem must deal with *both* the micro-to-macro and the macro-to-micro problems.

Coleman begins by offering a partially adequate model of the micro-macro relationship. In doing so, he uses Weber's Protestant ethic thesis (see Chapter 4) as an illustration. As shown in Figure 14.4, this model deals with *both* the macro-to-micro issue (arrow 2) and the micro-to-macro question (arrow 3); it also deals with the micro-to-micro relationship (arrow 1). While promising, this model is posed in causal terms, with arrows flowing in only one direction. A more adequate model would be dialectical, with all arrows pointing in both directions; that is, it would allow for feedback among all levels of analysis. However, the major weakness in Coleman's approach is that he wants to focus only on arrow 3, the micro-to-macro relationship. While this is important, it is no more important than the macro-to-micro relationship. A fully adequate micro-macro model must deal with *both* of these relationships.

Allen Liska (1990) has recently sought to cope with the weaknesses in Coleman's approach by dealing with both the micro-to-macro and the macro-to-micro problems. Liska's model, like Coleman's, uses Weber's Protestant ethic thesis as an example (See Figure 14.5).

This model has two advantages over Coleman's approach. First, of course, is Liska's willingness to deal with the macro-to-micro linkage. Second is the detailing of a relationship (arrow *a*) between the two macro-level phenomena. However, Liska, like Coleman, utilizes one-way causal arrows, thereby losing sight of the dialectical relationship among all these factors.

Liska employs a well-known scheme for dealing with macro phenomena as well as the micro-macro linkage. That scheme involves three basic ways of describing macrophenomena. The first is *aggregation,* or the summation of individual properties in order to yield a group property. Thus, one could describe a group in terms of such things as its mean income or its suicide rate. The

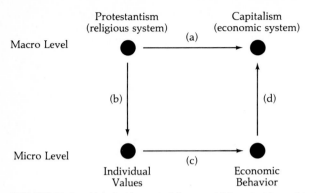

FIGURE 14.5   Liska's Macro-to-Micro and Micro-to-Macro Model

second is *structural,* and it involves relationships between individuals within a group; examples are relationships involving power or communication. Finally, there are *global* phenomena, which involve what are usually thought of as emergent properties, such as law and language.

In terms of the micro-macro linkage, Liska details the difficulties involved in using structural or global factors. These are qualitatively different from the characteristics of individual action, and it is difficult to know how they emerge out of the micro level. Sociologists use the idea of emergence to deal with them, but they know very little about how emergence actually works. Thus, Liska emphasizes the importance of aggregation as a micro-to-macro linkage. In this case, it is relatively clear how individual properties combine to yield group properties. Thus, for example, "Individual suicides can be aggregated, or 'combined,' over some social unit and expressed as a rate of that unit" (Liska, 1990:292). While aggregation may not be the most interesting way to move from the micro to the macro level, it has the advantage of being clear and less mystical than structural or global approaches.

Turning to the macro-to-micro issue, Liska argues for the importance of contextual variables as causes of micro-level phenomena. Here Liska includes aggregates, structural relations, and global properties as contexts of individual phenomena. He argues that sociologists have too frequently relied on micro-level factors when working on the individual level. By using macro-level, contextual factors, microsociologists would be moving in the direction of a greater understanding of the macro-to-micro linkage.

Liska's work comes down to a plea to sociologists who focus on either the macro or the micro level. Those who focus on the macro level have tended to ignore aggregation because it sounds too individualistic and does not have the emergent qualities of global or structural factors. Those who focus on the micro level have tended to use micro-level factors and to ignore contextual factors. Liska concludes that macro theorists should do more with aggregation and micro theorists more with contextual factors.

Foundations of Social Theory   More recently, James Coleman (1990) has greatly extended his theory by drawing upon the economists' rational choice theory in his book, *Foundations of Social Theory* (see also Friedman and Hechter, 1988, 1990). In this work, Coleman argues that sociology should focus on social systems, but that such macro phenomena must be explained by factors internal to them, prototypically individuals. He favors working at this level for several reasons, including the fact that data are usually gathered at the individual level and then aggregated or composed to yield the system level. Among the other reasons for favoring a focus on the individual level is that this is where "interventions" are ordinarily made to create social changes. As we will see, central to Coleman's perspective is the idea that social theory is not merely an academic exercise but that it should affect the social world through such "interventions."

Given his focus on the individual, Coleman recognizes that he is a methodological individualist, although he sees his particular perspective as a "special variant" of that orientation. It is special in the sense that it accepts the idea of emergence as well as the fact that while it focuses on factors internal to the system, those factors are not necessarily individual actions and orientations. That is, micro-level phenomena other than individuals can be the focus of his analysis.

Coleman's rational choice orientation is clear in his basic idea that "persons act purposively toward a goal, with the goal (and thus the actions) shaped by values or preferences" (1990:13). But Coleman (1990:14) then goes on to argue that for most theoretical purposes, he will need a more precise conceptualization of the rational actor derived from economics, one that sees the actors choosing those actions that will maximize utility, or the satisfaction of their needs and wants.

There are two key elements in his theory—actors and resources. Resources are those things over which actors have control and in which they have some interest. Given these two elements, Coleman details how their interaction leads to the system level:

> A minimal basis for a social system of action is two actors, each having control over resources of interest to the other. It is each one's interest in resources under the other's control that leads the two, as purposive actors, to engage in actions that involve each other . . . a system of action. . . . It is this structure, together with the fact that the actors are purposive, each having the goal of maximizing the realization of his interests, that gives the interdependence, or systemic character, to their actions.
>
> (Coleman, 1990:29)

Although he has faith in rational choice theory, Coleman does not believe that this perspective, at least as yet, has all the answers. But it is clear that he believes that it can move in that direction, since he argues that the "success of a social theory based on rationality lies in successively diminishing that domain of social activity that cannot be accounted for by the theory" (Coleman, 1990:18).

Coleman recognizes that in the real world people do not always behave rationally, but he feels that this makes little difference in his theory: "My implicit assumption is that the theoretical predictions made here will be substantively the same whether the actors act precisely according to rationality as commonly conceived or deviate in the ways that have been observed" (1990:506).

Given his orientation to individual rational action, it follows that Coleman's focus in terms of the micro-macro issue is the micro-to-macro linkage, or how the combination of individual actions brings about the behavior of the system. While he accords priority to this issue, Coleman is here also interested in the macro-to-micro linkage, or how the system constrains the orientations of actors. Finally, he evinces an interest in the micro-micro aspect of the relationship, or the impact of individual actions on other individual actions.

In spite of this seeming balance, there are at least three major weaknesses in Coleman's approach. First, he accords overwhelming priority to the micro-to-macro issue, thereby giving short shrift to the other relationships. Second, he ignores the macro-macro issue. Finally, his causal arrows go in only one direction; in other words, he ignores the dialectical relationship among and between micro and macro phenomena.

Utilizing his rational choice approach, Coleman explains a series of macro-level phenomena. His basic position is that theorists need to keep their conceptions of the actor constant and generate from those concentrations various images of macro-level phenomena. In this way, differences in macro phenomena can be traced to different structures of relations at the macro level and not to variations at the micro level.

A key step in the micro-to-macro movement is the granting of the authority and rights possessed by one individual to another. This tends to lead to the subordination of one actor to another. More importantly, it creates the most basic macro phenomenon—an acting unit consisting of two people rather than two independent actors. The resulting structure functions independently of the actors. Instead of maximizing his or her own interests, in this instance an actor seeks to realize the interests of another actor, or of the independent collective unit. Not only is this a different social reality, but it is one that "has special deficiencies and generates special problems" (Coleman, 1990:145). Given his applied orientation, Coleman is interested in the diagnosis and solution of these problems.

One example of Coleman's approach to dealing with macro phenomena is the case of collective behavior. He chooses to deal with collective behavior because its often disorderly and unstable character is thought to be hard to analyze from a rational choice perspective. But Coleman's view is that rational choice theory can explain all types of macro phenomena, not just those that are orderly and stable. What is involved in moving from the rational actor to "the wild and turbulent systemic functioning called collective behavior is a simple (and rational) transfer of control over one's actions to another actor . . . made unilaterally, not as part of an exchange" (Coleman, 1990:198).

Why do people unilaterally transfer control over their actions to others? The answer, from a rational choice perspective, is that they are doing so in an attempt to maximize their utility. Normally, individual maximization involves a balancing of control among several actors, and this produces equilibrium within society. However, in the case of collective behavior, because there is a unilateral transfer of control, individual maximization does not necessarily lead to system equilibrium. Instead, there is the disequilibrium characteristic of collective behavior.

Another macro-level phenomenon that comes under Coleman's scrutiny is norms. While most sociologists take norms as given and invoke them to explain individual behavior, they do not explain why and how norms come into existence. Coleman wonders how, in a group of rational actors, norms can emerge and be maintained. Coleman argues that norms are initiated and maintained by some people who see benefits resulting from the observation of norms and harm stemming from the violation of those norms. People are willing to give up some control over their own behavior, but in the process they gain some control (through norms) over the behavior of others. Coleman summarizes his position on norms:

> The central element of this explanation . . . is the giving up of partial rights of control over one's own action and the receiving of partial rights of control over the actions of others, that is, the emergence of a norm. The end result is that control . . . which was held by each alone, becomes widely distributed over the whole set of actors, who exercise that control.
>
> (Coleman, 1990:292)

Once again, people are seen as maximizing their utility by partially surrendering rights of control over themselves and gaining partial control over others. Because the transfer of control is not unilateral, there is equilibrium in the case of norms.

But there are also circumstances in which norms act to the advantage of some people and the disadvantage of others. In some cases, actors surrender the right to control their own actions to those who initiate and maintain the norms. Such norms become effective when a consensus emerges that some people have the right to control (through norms) the actions of other people. Furthermore, the effectiveness of norms depends on the ability to enforce that consensus. It is consensus and enforcement that prevent the kind of disequilibrium characteristic of collective behavior.

Coleman recognizes that norms become interrelated, but he sees such a macro issue as beyond the scope of his work on the foundations of social systems. On the other hand, he is willing to take on the micro issue of the internalization of norms. He recognizes that in discussing internalization he is entering "waters that are treacherous for a theory grounded in rational choice" (Coleman, 1990:292). He sees the internalization of norms as the establishment of an internal sanctioning system; people sanction themselves when they violate a norm. Coleman looks at this in terms of the idea of one actor or set of actors endeavoring to control others by having norms internalized in them. Thus, it is in the interests of one set of actors to have another set internalize norms and be controlled by them. He feels that this is rational "when such attempts can be effective at reasonable cost" (Coleman, 1990:294).

Coleman looks at norms from the point of view of the three key elements of his theory—micro to macro, purposive action at the micro level, and macro to micro. Norms are macro-level phenomena that come into existence on the basis of micro-level purposive action. Once in existence, norms, through sanctions or the threat of sanctions, affect the actions of individuals. Certain actions may be encouraged, while others are discouraged.

With the case of norms, Coleman has moved to the macro level, and he continues his analysis at this level in a discussion of the corporate actor. Within such a collectivity, actors may not act in terms of their self-interest but must act in the interest of the collectivity.

There are various rules and mechanisms for moving from individual choice to collective (social) choice. The simplest is the case of voting and the procedures for tabulating the individual votes and coming up with a collective decision. This is the micro-to-macro dimension, while such things as the slate of candidates proposed by the collectivity involves the macro-to-micro linkage.

Coleman argues that both corporate actors and human actors have purposes. Furthermore, within a corporate structure such as an organization human actors may pursue purposes of their own that are at variance with corporate purposes. This helps us understand the sources of revolts against corporate authority. The micro-to-macro linkage here involves the ways in which people divest authority from the corporate structure and vest legitimacy in those engaged in the revolt. But there is also a macro-to-micro linkage in that certain macro-level conditions lead people to such acts of divestment and investment.

As a rational choice theorist, Coleman starts with the individual and with the idea that all rights and resources exist at this level. It is the interests of individuals that determine the course of events. However, this is untrue, especially in modern society, where "a large fraction of rights and resources, and therefore sovereignty, may reside in corporate actors" (Coleman, 1990:531). In the modern world corporate actors have taken on increasing importance. The corporate actor may act to the benefit or the harm of the individual. How are we to judge the corporate actor in this regard? Coleman contends that "only by starting conceptually from a point where all sovereignty rests with individual persons is it possible to see just how well their ultimate interests are realized by any existing social system. The postulate that individual persons are sovereign provides a way in which sociologists may evaluate the functioning of social systems" (1990:531–532).

The key social change to Coleman has been the emergence of corporate actors to complement "natural person" actors. Both may be considered actors because they have "control over resources and events, interests in resources and events, and the capability of taking actions to realize those interests through that control" (Coleman, 1990:542). Of course, there have always been corporate actors, but the old ones like the family are steadily being replaced by new, purposively constructed, freestanding corporate actors. The existence of these new corporate actors raises the issue of how to ensure their social responsibility. Coleman suggests that we can do this by instituting internal reforms or by changing the external structure such as the laws affecting such corporate actors or the agencies that regulate them.

Coleman differentiates between primordial structures based on the family, such as neighborhoods and religious groups, and purposive structures, such as economic organizations and the government. He sees a progressive "unbundling" of the activities that were once tied together within the family. The primordial structures are "unraveling" as their functions are being dispersed and being taken over by a range of corporate actors. Coleman is concerned about this unraveling as well as about the fact that we are now forced to deal with positions in purposive structures rather than with the people who populated primordial structures. He thus concludes that the goal of his work is "providing the foundation for constructing a viable social structure, as the primordial structure on which persons have depended vanishes" (Coleman, 1990:652).

Coleman is critical of most of social theory for adopting a view that he labels *homo sociologicus*. This perspective emphasizes the socialization process and the close fit between the individual and society. Therefore, *homo sociologicus* is unable to deal with the freedom of individuals to act as they will in spite of the constraints placed upon them. Furthermore, this perspective lacks the ability to evaluate the actions of the social system. In contrast, *homo economicus*, in Coleman's view, possesses all these capacities. In addition, Coleman attacks traditional social theory for doing little more than chanting old theoretical mantras and for being irrelevant to the changes taking place in society and incapable of helping us know where society is headed. Sociological theory (as well as sociological research) must have a purpose, a role in the functioning of society. Coleman is in favor of social theory that is interested not just in knowledge for the sake of knowledge but also in "a search for knowledge for the reconstruction of society" (1990:651).

Coleman's views on social theory are closely linked to his views on the changing nature of society. The passing of primordial structures and their replacement by purposive structures has left a series of voids that have not been filled adequately by the new social organizations. Social theory, and the social sciences more generally, are made necessary by the need to reconstruct a new society. The goal is not to destroy purposive structures but rather to realize the opportunities and avoid the problems of such structures. The new society requires a new social science. The linkages among institutional areas have changed, and as a result the social sciences must be willing to cut across traditional disciplinary boundaries.

Coleman's work is but part of a strong movement in sociology in the direction of economics and its rational choice theory. While there are those like Coleman who adopt such a position wholeheartedly, there are others like Etzioni (1988) who adopt a compromise position, one that Etzioni labels "socio-economics." Still others like Hirsch, Michaels, and Friedman (1987) are critical of the efforts by sociologists to use economists' rational choice theory. It is likely that rational choice theory will continue to attract adherents in sociology. However, its prospects seem limited by the fact that it takes as its starting point a model of the actor *(homo economicus)* that most sociologists rejected in an effort to develop a more "realistic" model of the less rational actor driven by norms, values, and beliefs.

Randall Collins: The Micro Foundations of Macrosociology

In an essay entitled "On the Microfoundations of Macrosociology," Randall Collins (1981a; see also 1981b) has offered a highly reductionistic orientation toward the micro-macro link question (for a critique, see Ritzer, 1985). In fact, despite the inherently integrative title of his essay, Collins labels his approach "radical microsociology." Collins's focus, the focus of radical microsociology, is what he calls "interaction ritual chains," or bundles of "individual chains of interactional experience, crisscrossing each other in space as they flow along in time" (1981a:998). In focusing on interaction ritual chains, Collins seeks to avoid what he considers to be even more reductionistic concerns with individual behavior and consciousness. Collins raises the level of analysis to interaction, chains of interaction, and the "marketplace" for such interaction. Collins thus rejects the extreme micro levels of thought and action (behavior) and is critical of the theories (such as phenomenology and exchange theory) that focus on these levels.

Collins also seeks to distance himself from macro theories and their concerns with macro-level phenomena. For example, he is critical of structural functionalists and their concern with macro-objective (structure) and macro-subjective (norms) phenomena. In fact, he goes so far as to say that "the terminology of norms ought to be dropped from sociological theory" (Collins, 1981a:991). He has a similarly negative attitude toward concepts associated with conflict theory, arguing, for example, that there are no "inherent objective" entities like property or authority; there are only "varying senses that people feel at particular places and times of how strong these enforcing coalitions are" (Collins, 1981a:997). His point is that only people do anything; structures, organizations, classes, and societies "never *do* anything. Any causal explanation must ultimately come down to the actions of real individuals" (Collins, 1975:12).

Collins seeks to show how "all macrophenomena" can be translated "into combinations of micro events" (1981a:985). Specifically, he argues that social structures may be translated empirically into "patterns of repetitive micro interaction" (Collins, 1981a:985).

Thus, in the end, Collins does *not* seek an integrated approach but the predominance of micro theory and micro-level phenomena (for a similar critique, see Giddens, 1984). As Collins puts it, "The effort coherently to reconstitute macro sociology upon radically empirical micro foundations is the crucial step toward a more successful sociological science" (1981b:82).

We can contrast Collins's orientation to that of Karin Knorr-Cetina (1981a), who articulated her position in the introduction to a volume in which one of Collins's essays on radical microsociology appeared. Although she too accords great importance to the interactional domain, Knorr-Cetina grants a greater role to both consciousness and macro-level phenomena in her work. Although Knorr-Cetina, like Collins, makes the case for a radical reconstruction of macro theory on a microsociological base, she is also willing to consider the much less radical course of simply integrating microsociological results into macro-social theory. In addition, she seems to take the position that the ultimate goal of microsociological research is a better understanding of the larger society, its structure, and institutions:

> I . . . believe in the seeming paradox that it is through micro-social approaches that we will learn most about the macro order, for it is these approaches which through their unashamed empiricism afford us a glimpse of the reality about which we speak. Certainly, we will not get a grasp of whatever is the whole of the matter by a microscopic recording of face-to-face interaction. However, it may be enough to begin with if we—for the first time—hear the macro order tick.
>
> (Knorr-Cetina, 1981a:41–42)

Thus, it seems clear that Knorr-Cetina takes a far more balanced position on the relationship between the macro and micro levels than does Collins.

An even more integrative position is taken by the other editor of the volume mentioned above, Aaron Cicourel (1981). He argues, "Neither micro nor macro structures are self-contained levels of analysis; they *interact* with each other at all times despite the convenience and sometimes the dubious luxury of only examining one or the other level of analysis" (Cicourel, 1981:54). There is an implied criticism of Collins here, but Cicourel adopts another position that can be seen as a more direct critique of the kind of position adopted by Collins: "The issue is not simply one of dismissing one level of analysis or another, but showing how they must be integrated if we are not to be convinced about one level to the exclusion of the other by conveniently ignoring competing frameworks for research and theory" (1981:76). To his credit, Cicourel understands not only the importance of linking macro and micro levels but also the fact that that link needs to take place ontologically, theoretically, and methodologically.

Collins continued to subscribe to his micro-reductionistic position for some time. For example, in a later work Collins argued: "Macrostructure consists

RANDALL COLLINS: An Autobiographical Sketch

I started becoming a sociologist at an early age. My father was working for military intelligence at the end of World War II and then joined the State Department as a foreign service officer. One of my earliest memories is of arriving in Berlin to join him in the summer of 1945. My sisters and I couldn't play in the park because there was live ammunition everywhere, and one day Russian soldiers came into our backyard to dig up a corpse. This gave me a sense that conflict is important and violence always possible.

My father's subsequent tours of duty took us to the Soviet Union, back to Germany (then under American military occupation), to Spain and South America. In between foreign assignments we would live in the States, so I went back and forth between being an ordinary American kid and being a privileged foreign visitor. I think this resulted in a certain amount of detachment in viewing social relationships. As I got older the diplomatic life looked less dramatic and more like an endless round of formal etiquette in which people never talked about the important politics going on; the split between backstage secrecy and front-stage ceremonial made me ready to appreciate Erving Goffman.

When I was too old to accompany my parents abroad, I was sent to a prep school in New England. This taught me another great sociological reality: the existence of stratification. Many of the other students came from families in the Social Register, and it began to dawn on me that my father was not in the same social class as the ambassadors and undersecretaries of state whose children I sometimes met.

I went on to Harvard, where I changed my major half a dozen times. I studied literature and tried being a playwright and novelist. I went from mathematics to philosophy; I read Freud and planned to become a psychiatrist. I finally majored in social relations, which covered sociology, social psychology, and anthropology. Taking courses from Talcott Parsons settled me onto a path. He covered virtually everything, from the micro to the macro

of nothing more than large numbers of microencounters, repeated (or sometimes changing over time and across space)" (1987b:195). He concluded, unashamedly: "This may sound as if I am giving a great deal of prominence to the micro. That is true" (Collins, 1987b:195). However, it is worth noting that just one year later Collins (1988a) was willing to give the macro-level greater significance. This led to a more balanced conception of the micro-macro relationship: "The micro-macro translation shows that everything macro is composed out of micro. Conversely, anything micro is part of the composition of macro; it exists in a macro context . . . it is possible to pursue the micro-macro connection fruitfully in either direction" (Collins, 1988a:244). The latter contention implies a more dialectical approach to the micro-macro relationship. Yet Collins (1988a:244), like Coleman, subscribes to the view that the "big challenge" in sociology is showing "how micro affects macro." Thus,

and across the range of world history. What I got from him was not so much his own theory but rather the ideal of what sociology could do. He also provided me with some important pieces of cultural capital: that Weber was less concerned with the Protestant Ethic than he was with comparing the dynamics of all the world religions and that Durkheim asked the key question when he tried to uncover the precontractual basis of social order.

I thought I wanted to become a psychologist and went to Stanford, but a year of implanting electrodes in rats' brains convinced me that sociology was a better place to study human beings. I switched universities and arrived in Berkeley in the summer of 1964, just in time to join the civil-rights movement. By the time the free-speech movement emerged on campus in the fall, we were veterans of sit-ins, and being arrested for another cause felt emotionally energizing when one could do it in solidarity with hundreds of others. I was analyzing the sociology of conflict at the same time that we were experiencing it. As the Vietnam War and the racial conflicts at home escalated, the opposition movement began to repudiate its non-violent principles; many of us became disillusioned and turned to the cultural lifestyle of the hippie dropouts. If you didn't lose your sociological consciousness, it could be illuminating. I studied Erving Goffman along with Herbert Blumer (both of them Berkeley professors at the time) and began to see how all aspects of society—conflict, stratification, and all the rest—are constructed out of the interaction rituals of our everyday lives.

I never set out to be a professor, but by now I have taught in many universities. I tried to put everything together into one book, *Conflict Sociology* (1975), but it turned out I had to write another, *The Credential Society* (1979), to explain the inflationary status system in which we are all enmeshed. Taking my own analysis seriously, I quit the academic world and for a while made a living by writing a novel and textbooks. Eventually, attracted by some interesting colleagues, I got back into teaching. Our field is learning some tremendous things, from a new picture of world history down through the micro details of social emotions. One of the most important influences for me is my second wife, Judith McConnell. She organized women lawyers to break down discriminatory barriers in the legal profession, and now I am learning from her about the backstage politics of the higher judiciary. In sociology and in society, there is plenty yet to be done.

while Collins has shown some growth in his micro-macro theory, it continues to be a highly limited approach.

Interactor Theory

In a recent essay, Joseph Berger, Dana P. Eyre, and Morris Zelditch, Jr. (1989) have proposed what they call "interactor theory." The theory focuses on actors and their interrelationships. Actors can be individuals, but they also can be collectivities like organizations or even nation-states. This means that interactor theory can be applied at either the micro or the macro level of analysis. It is sufficiently abstract and general—that is, it has a sufficiently broad sense of the actor—that it can be applied at both ends of the continuum. Berger et al. contrast their abstract interactor theory to "concrete" theories (for example, symbolic interactionism, conflict theory) that can be applied to only one level of analysis.

There are a number of interactor theories in sociology "that describe the mechanisms or processes by which actors act in relation to other actors in situations of action" (Berger, Eyre, and Zelditch, 1989:21). The basic unit of analysis in interactor theory is the "actor-in-situation." The situation is "a specific set of conditions that can generate, define, and determine the course of a process" (Berger, Eyre, and Zelditch, 1989:21). The focus on an actor in a situation indicates that interactor theory is a "process theory." The process in question is often animated by some kind of problematic situation. The resulting process is defined by three elements. First, there are the conditions of action, such as the ecological situation or the amount of available information. Second, there is the social framework of the process—the structural and/or cultural context in which the process occurs. Third, the process takes place within the context of the things (for example, local knowledge) that are the products of past interaction between the specific actors in question.

The actors in interactor theory are seen as having *agency*, here defined as "the capacity to control some of the variation in its [actors'] own actions" (Berger, Eyre, and Zelditch, 1989:23). The particular nature of agency may vary from one theory to another, but all interactor theories have a sense of agency. While agency is obviously a property of individuals, in interactor theory it can also be a property of collectivities. In interactor theory actors need not have intentionality or awareness. Actors need not even be aware of the pattern of relations in which they are enmeshed. However, all interactor theories involve a number of actors, the actors form systems, and the systems may be described in terms of the relationships among actors.

Interactor theory focuses on a range of processes, including "how activating conditions, the social framework, and products of past interaction are transformed into definitions of particular actors in particular situations; it requires that they explain the nature, conditions, and consequences of particular processes of action; and it requires that they explain how the outcomes of such processes are transformed into elements of the history and social framework of subsequent interaction" (Berger, Eyre, and Zelditch, 1989:24). These processes are governed by "states," or "situationally specific, stable, relational structures" (Berger, Eyre, and Zelditch, 1989:24). However, there is a dialectical process here, as not only do states determine behavior but behavior affects the nature of the state. In other words, interactor theories imply both agency and structure.

Since it is a product of American sociology, interactor theory is framed as a micro-macro theory. However, as should be clear from the preceding discussion and the terminology employed in it, interactor theory has more in common with the agency-structure theories to be discussed in Chapter 15. While it would have been enriched by insights from the work on agency and structure, the creators of interactor theory demonstrate no familiarity with the European literature.

The key point for our purposes is that Berger et al. believe that interactor theory is sufficiently abstract that it can be applied anywhere on the micro-macro continuum of levels of social analysis.

SOME PROMISING NEW DIRECTIONS

As we have seen, perhaps the most troubling issue now facing advances in our understanding of the micro-macro linkage is the fact that major tensions have already surfaced among those oriented to the development of an integrated approach. Given the fact that most people working on this issue have been shaped by the history of micro-macro extremism in sociology, some integrationists are tugging in a micro direction (for example, Collins) while others are pulling the other way (for example, Alexander). Thus they threaten to undermine the nascent effort at integration and to repeat *within* the integrative approach the largely unnecessary tension between micro and macro orientations that has dominated American sociological theory in the twentieth century. In this section we will look at some of the ways of avoiding this problem.

One less than wholly satisfactory solution is for macro-oriented theorists to focus on micro-level issues and micro-oriented theorists to work at the macro level. Two good examples of this are Alexander's (1987) focus (coming from macro-level neofunctionalism) on such micro-level processes as typification, strategization, and invention and Fine's (1988) effort to delineate (from a micro-level, symbolic-interactionist perspective) the "obdurate reality" of the built environment, institutional linkages, tradition, and beliefs in organizational primacy. It is highly beneficial to the development of an integrated micro-macro approach for theorists to focus on the empirical realities that are on the opposite end of the continuum from their theoretical orientations. The major problem is the tendency for theorists to allow their theoretical biases to affect their work at the other end of the social continuum.

More promising are efforts at integrating micro and macro theories by those who are not apparently predisposed to one or the other (for example, Hindess, 1986; Fararo and Skvoretz, 1986). While this lack of commitment (Mitroff, 1974) may make such works more evenhanded, the works may suffer if the theorists lack intimate knowledge of, and devotion to, the theoretical perspectives they are working with.

Another possibility would involve starting at neither the micro nor the macro level but, rather, somewhere in the middle of the social continuum, on what has been termed the "meso level" in the study of formal organizations (Hage, 1980). There are problems involved in meso-level perspectives as manifest in the sociology of formal organizations. If one focuses at the meso level (say, formal organizations), can one adequately get at, and deal with, macro-level phenomena? At the same time, it can also be asked whether such a meso-level focus allows one to be sufficiently microscopic. Meso-level analyses have yet to demonstrate the ability to be satisfactorily integrative.

Still another promising direction involves focusing on ongoing relationships between the micro and macro levels. Münch and Smelser (1987) have offered some useful beginnings here, but since their ideas are drawn from work influenced by micro-macro extremism, their analysis shows again how easily we can move in either an extreme micro or an extreme macro direction. The useful part of their essay involves a discussion of the linkages betwen micro and macro; the focus is on relationships rather than the micro or macro extreme. Among these relationships they discuss aggregation; externalization; creating, sustaining, and reproducing the macro; conformity; internalization; and limit setting. A focus on these relational processes helps us move away from micro-macro extremism, and it is inherently integrative. However, Münch and Smelser divide these processes into micro-to-macro and macro-to-micro categories, thereby tending, once again, to reflect the strain toward micro-macro extremism.

A much more promising alternative is to reject a focus on *any* level (micro, meso, macro) of analysis and adopt instead an inherently integrative, a dialectical, approach. Despite the earlier criticisms of Alexander's collectivistic bias, there are signs in his recent work of the development of such an inherently integrative position, one that defines *macro* and *micro* in terms of one another. More generally, Ritzer's integrated paradigm does not focus on any single level of social analysis but is interested in the dialectical relationships among and between all levels.

MICRO-MACRO INTEGRATION: WORK TO BE DONE

While the various forms of micro and macro extremism are far from dead, and even highly likely to enjoy periodic resurgences, it is safe to say that an integrative micro-macro approach is now well established in American sociology and is likely to remain an attractive alternative into the foreseeable future. In fact, it is likely to attract more adherents in the future because it is being advanced by some of the best young theorists in the field, because it is stemming from a wide variety of theoretical directions, because it represents a rediscovery of an orientation that lay at the base of the work of the discipline's classic theorists, and because it is a vast and complex area that offers many challenges to sociological theorists.

A decade ago Kemeny argued, "What is first needed is increasing awareness of the problem of scope so that positions are not taken unwittingly and implicitly" (1976:747). Given recent developments, it is doubtful that present and future sociologists will be able to operate without a sense of the issue of scope in their work. In other words, it is now unlikely that sociologists will ignore scale or unwittingly take a position on this issue. All in all, the basic point is that micro-macro integration is emerging as the central problematic in American sociological theory.

In spite of this emerging consensus, there is much to be done. First, much of the work that sociologists have to do on the micro-macro linkage involves specifying in much greater detail the nature of what is, at the moment, only a very general orientation. Many of those working on this general issue are, in fact, focusing on very different things. They have different senses of what they mean by micro phenomena, macro phenomena, and the linkages between them. Careful definitions are required, and theorists need to address conceptual differences between their own work on this issue and that of others. In the same realm, much more work is needed of the type undertaken by Markovsky (1987) in specifying the conditions that affect the relative significance of micro- and macro-level phenomena.

Second, while there is obviously a great need to continue to extend work on the micro-macro linkage, sociologists must also do additional work *within* the micro and macro domains. That is, there is a continuing need for sociologists to focus their attention on micro or macro issues, thereby extending knowledge of those domains. The emergence of a central micro-macro problematic does not preclude work on a given level. Even the keenest advocates of a focus on micro-macro linkages do not see it as becoming the sole focus of sociology. In fact, advances in sociological knowledge of the micro and macro levels can serve to enrich work on micro-macro integration.

Third, while there is a need for further work within the micro and macro domains, social theorists must be sure that the still-immature effort at micro-macro integration is not overwhelmed by reinvigorated supporters of micro and/or macro extremism. While there is an increasing focus on micro-macro integration, there are, at the same time, some very powerful theoretical forces pulling sociology away from this central problem and toward micro or macro extremism. In other words, concomitant with the emergence of a theoretical consensus are the existence and emergence of theoretical perspectives that are threatening that consensus before it is even solidified. In this category are extreme micro-oriented theories that deny or downplay the existence and significance of macro-level phenomena as well as extreme macro-level theories that deny or minimize the role of micro-level phenomena.

There are also some very powerful sociologists overtly arguing *against* the possibility of micro-macro integration. One such voice is that of Peter Blau, who, by his own admission, has changed his mind on this issue since the publication of his (Blau, 1964) integrative effort within exchange theory (see Chapter 11):

An important issue in constructing macrosociological theory is the linkage with microsociological theory. One approach is to start with microsociological principles and use these as the foundation for building macrosociological theory. The alternative approach rests on the assumption that different perspectives and conceptual frameworks are necessary for micro and macro theories, primarily because the major terms of macrosociological theories refer to emergent properties of population structures and have no equivalent in microsociological analysis. *I have come to the conclusion that the second approach is the only viable one, at least at this stage of sociological development.*

(Blau, 1987b:87; italics added)

Thus, while we have made the case for a growing consensus in sociology on micro-macro integration, it is clear that such an orientation is far from universal and has some very powerful opponents.

Fourth, perhaps a greater danger lies in the extremists *within* the group working on micro-macro integration. They threaten to tear apart this intellectual movement before it has a chance to develop fully. Sociological theorists must be wary of re-creating extremism within the micro-macro camp.

Fifth, there is a great need for sociologists to clarify the relationship between efforts aimed at integrating micro and macro theories and those aimed at developing a theory that deals with the integration of micro and macro levels of social analysis. Sociological thinking on this relationship is most likely to be advanced by more work that seeks to bring together theoretical and empirical efforts.

Sixth, social theorists need to do additional work on the relationship between the micro-macro continuum and the various other continua (for example, the methodological individualism-holism continuum) that have been used to analyze the social world. Particularly promising are those efforts at integrating the micro-macro and objective-subjective continua.

Seventh, this highly abstract metatheoretical work needs to be translated into terms and approaches that are accessible to those interested in concrete empirical and theoretical questions. In other words, it needs to be transformed into ideas, concepts, tools, theories, and methods that can be used by sociologists in their professional activities.

Finally, there is a need for more methodologists and empirical researchers to address the micro-macro issue, which to this time has been largely dominated by theorists. Some welcome signs in this area are Bailey's (1987) work on micro-macro methods, Markovsky's (1987) experimental efforts, and Marini's (1988:45) criticism of gender researchers for studying macro-level phenomena using micro-level data.

In the 1990s it is likely that there will be a subtle, yet crucially important, shift in the work on micro-macro integration. Up to this point, given the micro and macro extremism of much of twentieth-century sociology, those who have dealt with the issue have come at it from either the micro or the macro end of the continuum. As micro-macro linkage becomes widely accepted as a (the) central theoretical problem, the focus will shift to more inherently integrative orientations. Among the promising directions are the works that integrate micro and macro theories without being predisposed to either; the focus on the micro level from a macro-theoretical orientation (and vice versa); the work at the meso level; the interest in the ongoing relationships between micro and macro; and, most promising of all, the work that defines micro and macro in terms of one another, thereby focusing on an ongoing dialectic. These types of work, especially the latter, promise to move work on micro-macro integration to a new level, a level in which the emphasis will be on *integration* or *synthesis* rather than on the micro or macro pole of the social continuum. This is in line with, but more specific than, the view expressed by Alexander and

Giesen, who argue for the need for "establishing a radically different starting point" in order to make "a genuinely inclusive micro-macro link" (1987:37). Since virtually all extant theories are primarily either micro or macro perspectives, such a shift in emphasis will lead to the need for the creation of new theories (or new combinations of several extant theories) primarily attuned to such integrative concerns. Most generally, we are likely to move away from a concern for micro and macro levels and/or theories and toward more synthetic existential interests and theoretical efforts.

SUMMARY

The focus in this chapter is the major development in American sociological theory in the 1980s—the rise in interest in micro-macro integration. This represents a return to the concerns of the early giants of sociological theory and a movement away from the theoretical extremism, either micro or macro, that characterized much of twentieth-century American sociological theory. While little attention was given to the micro-macro issue prior to the 1980s, during that decade interest in the topic exploded. The works came from both the micro and the macro extremes as well as various points in between these two extremes. Some of this work focused on integrating micro and macro theories, while the rest was concerned with the linkage between micro and macro levels of social analysis. In addition to this basic difference, there are also important differences among those working on integrating theories and levels.

The heart of the chapter is a discussion of several major examples of work integrating micro and macro levels of social analysis. Three works, those by Ritzer, Alexander, and Wiley, develop very similar micro-macro models of the social world. While there are important differences among these works, their similar images of the social world reflect considerable consensus among those seeking to link micro and macro levels of social analysis.

A much more limited example is offered by Coleman, who focuses on the micro-to-macro linkage. This work is criticized for its failure to also deal with the macro-to-micro linkage as well as for its lack of a dialectical image of the social world. Liska's work is discussed in this context because of its effort to overcome the limitations of Coleman's micro-to-macro focus and to deal, as well, with the macro-to-micro issue. Liska emphasizes the importance of aggregation and contextual factors in dealing with the micro-macro linkage. We then discuss at some length Coleman's much more elaborate integrative theory, which is based on a rational choice approach. Collins's effort at micro-macro integration is discussed and criticized for its micro reductionism—its tendency to reduce macro phenomena to micro phenomena. The final example is Berger et al.'s interactor theory, which focuses on the relationship between micro and/or macro actors. Berger et al.'s interactor theory is abstract and therefore applicable to both micro and macro levels.

A variety of promising new directions in work on micro-macro integration are discussed. One such approach involves micro theorists working on macro issues and macro theorists dealing with micro topics. More promising is work on the linkage issue by those who are not predisposed to one level or the other. Also with potential are works that start at the meso level and work outward to the micro and macro levels. Then there are efforts to focus on the ongoing relationships between micro and macro. Of greatest promise are those works that focus on the dialectical relationships among all levels of social analysis.

The chapter closes with a discussion of a wide variety of things that remain to be done by social theorists interested in the micro-macro relationship.

AGENCY-STRUCTURE INTEGRATION

INTRODUCTION

AS was pointed out in the last chapter, paralleling the growth in interest in American sociological theory in the micro-macro issue has been an increase in interest among European theorists in the relationship between agency and structure. For example, Margaret Archer has contended that "the problem of structure and agency has rightly come to be seen as the basic issue in modern social theory" (1988:ix). In fact, she argues that dealing with this linkage (as well as a series of other linkages implied by it) has become the "acid test" of a general social theory and the "central problem" in theory (Archer, 1988:x). Earlier, Dawe went even further than Archer: *"Here, then, is the problematic around which the entire history of sociological analysis could be written: the problematic of human agency"* (1978:379). Implied in Dawe's concern with agency is also an interest in social structure as well as the constant tension between them.[1]

Thus, many observers on both sides of the Atlantic have noted the emergence of what appears to be a new consensus. Not only are there apparent agreements within the United States and Europe, but the surface similarities between the micro-macro and agency-structure terminologies and orientations seem to imply the possibility of an international consensus in social theory.

[1] In fact, agency is often used in such a way as to include a concern for structure (Abrams, 1982:xiii).

All this harmony would seem to be good news to social theory, which has long been characterized by bitter differences and an inability to communicate across theoretical boundaries. Unfortunately, in spite of the use of like-sounding terms, the consensus that has emerged in the United States is somewhat different from the European consensus. Furthermore, there are substantial differences *within* the literatures of Europe and the United States. Thus the apparent consensus seems quite superficial and is largely negated by differences between, and within, contemporary social theory in the United States and Europe.

A concern for the agency-structure linkage lies at the core of the work of a number of theorists who write in the European tradition, such as Giddens's (1979, 1982, 1984) structuration theory; Archer's (1982) interest in morphogenesis, as well as her (Archer, 1988) later concern for the linkage between culture and agency; Bourdieu's (1977, 1984) habitus and field; Habermas's (1984, 1987) effort to integrate life-world and system; Burns's (1986; Burns and Flam, 1986) social rule-system theory; Lukes's (1977; see also Layder, 1985) power and structure; Abrams's (1982) historical structuring; Touraine's (1977) self-production of society; and Crozier and Friedberg's (1980) game-theory approach. Before we go much further, we need to define the ways in which the terms *agency* and *structure* are used and compare them to the micro-macro terminology.

At a superficial level the micro-macro and agency-structure issues sound similar, and they are often treated as if they resemble one another greatly. I have tended to treat those works that deal with agency and structure as part of the concern for micro-macro linkage (Ritzer, 1990a). Similarly, Archer (1988) argues that the agency-structure issue connotes a concern for the micro-macro relationship (as well as voluntarism-determinism and subjectivism-objectivism). Such positions seem justified since there appears, after all, to be a fairly close association between the micro level and the agent and the macro level and structure. There is, that is, *if* we are thinking of individual human agents (micro) and large-scale social structure (macro). However, there are other ways to think of both agency-structure and micro-macro issues that make the significant differences between these two conceptualizations quite clear.

While *agency* generally refers to micro-level, individual human actors, it can also refer to (macro) collectivities that act. For example, Burns sees human agents as including "individuals as well as organized groups, organizations and nations" (1986:9). Touraine focuses on social classes as actors. If we accept such collectivities as agents, then we cannot equate agency and micro-level phenomena. In addition, while *structure* usually refers to large-scale social structures, it can also refer to micro structures such as those involved in human interaction. Giddens's definition of *systems* (which is closer to the usual meaning of structure than his own concept of structure) implies both types of structures, since it involves "reproduced relations between actors or collectivities" (1979:66). Thus both agency and structure can refer to either micro-level or macro-level phenomena or to both.

Turning to the micro-macro distinction, *micro* often refers to the kind of conscious, creative actor of concern to many agency theorists, but it can also refer to a more mindless "behaver" of interest to behaviorists, exchange theorists, and rational choice theorists. Similarly, the term *macro* can refer not only to large-scale social structures but also to the cultures of collectivities. Thus micro may or may not refer to "agents" and macro may or may not refer to "structures."

When we look closely at the micro-macro and agency-structure schemas, we find that there are substantial differences between them. Since American theorists tend to focus on the micro-macro linkage (Berger, Eyre, and Zelditch, 1989, are one exception) and Europeans on the relationship between agency and structure, there are substantial differences between the consensuses in the United States and Europe.

Before going further with this general discussion of the agency-structure literature, as well as its relationship to the micro-macro literature, let us take a more detailed look at several major examples of work in this genre. Such a discussion will give us a better feel for the general nature of work on agency and structure.

MAJOR EXAMPLES OF AGENCY-STRUCTURE INTEGRATION

Anthony Giddens: Structuration Theory

One of the best-known and most articulated efforts to integrate agency and structure is Anthony Giddens's structuration theory (I. Cohen, 1989; Held and Thompson, 1989). Giddens (1976:8) began "introducing" this theory in the 1970s, but it appeared in its most fully developed form in his book *The Constitution of Society* (1984), which is subtitled *Outline of the Theory of Agency*. In this work, Giddens goes so far as to say, "Every research investigation in the social sciences or history is involved in relating action [often used synonymously with *agency*] to structure . . . there is no sense in which structure 'determines' action or vice versa" (1984:219).

While he is not a Marxist, there is a powerful Marxian influence in Giddens's work, and he even sees *The Constitution of Society* as an extended reflection on Marx's inherently integrative dictum: "Men make history, but they do not make it just as they please; they do not make it under circumstances chosen by themselves, but under circumstances directly encountered, given, and transmitted from the past" (1869/1963:15).[2]

Marx's theory is but one of many theoretical inputs into structuration theory. At one time or another, Giddens has analyzed and critiqued most major theoretical orientations and derived a range of useful ideas from many of them. Structuration theory is extraordinarily eclectic.

---

[2] I agree with according Marx such a central place in structuration theory and, more generally, in theories that integrate agency and structure. As I concluded in my own metatheoretical work, Marx's work is the best "exemplar for an integrated sociological paradigm" (Ritzer, 1981a:232).

Giddens surveys a wide range of theories that begin with either the individual/agent (for example, symbolic interactionism) or the society/structure (for example, structural functionalism) and rejects both of these polar alternatives. Rather, Giddens argues that we must begin with "recurrent social practices" (1989:252). Giving slightly more detail, he argues: "The basic domain of the study of the social sciences, according to the theory of structuration, is neither the experience of the individual actor, nor the existence of any form of social totality, but social practices ordered across time and space" (Giddens, 1984:2).

At its core Giddens's structuration theory, with its focus on social practices, is a theory of the relationship between agency and structure. According to Bernstein, "the very heart of the theory of structuration" is "intended to illuminate the duality and dialectical interplay of agency and structure" (1989:23). Thus, agency and structure cannot be conceived of apart from one another; they are two sides of the same coin. In Giddens's terms, they are a duality (in the next section we will discuss Archer's critique of this orientation). All social action involves structure, and all structure involves social action. Agency and structure are inextricably interwoven in ongoing human activity or practice.

As pointed out above, Giddens's analytical starting point is human practices, but he insists that they be seen as recursive. That is, activities are "not brought into being by social actors but continually recreated by them via the very means whereby they express themselves as actors. In and through their activities agents produce the conditions that make these activities possible (Giddens, 1984:2). Thus, activities are not produced by consciousness, by the social construction of reality, nor are they produced by social structure. Rather, in expressing themselves as actors, people are engaging in practice, and it is through that practice that both consciousness and structure are produced. Focusing on the recursive character of structure, Held and Thompson argue that "structure is reproduced in and through the succession of situated practices which are organized by it" (1989:7). The same thing can be said about consciousness. Giddens is concerned with consciousness, or reflexivity. However, in being reflexive, the human actor is not merely self-conscious but is also engaged in the monitoring of the ongoing flow of activities and structural conditions. This leads Bernstein to argue that "agency itself is reflexively and recursively implicated in social structures" (1989:23). Most generally, it can be argued that Giddens is concerned with the dialectical process in which practice, structure, and consciousness are produced. Thus, Giddens deals with the agency-structure issue in a historical, processual, and dynamic way.

Not only are social actors reflexive, but so are the social researchers who are studying them. This leads Giddens to his well-known ideas on the "double hermeneutic." Both social actors and sociologists use language. Actors use language to account for what they do, and sociologists, in turn, use language to account for the actions of social actors. Thus, we need to be concerned with the relationship between lay and scientific language. We particularly need to be aware of the fact that the social scientist's understanding of the social world may have an impact on the misunderstandings of the actors being studied. In that way, social researchers can alter the world they are studying and thus lead to distorted findings and conclusions.

Let us discuss some of the major components of Giddens's structuration theory, starting with his thoughts on agents, who, as we have seen, continuously monitor their own thoughts and activities as well as their physical and social contexts. Actors are capable of rationalization, which in Giddens's work means the development of routines that enable them to efficiently deal with their social lives. Actors also have motivations to act, and these motivations involve the wants and desires that prompt action. Thus, while rationalization and reflexivity are continuously involved in action, motivations are more appropriately thought of as potentials for action. Motivations provide overall plans for action, but most of our action, in Giddens's view, is not directly motivated. While such action is not motivated, and our motivations are generally unconscious, motivations play a significant role in human conduct.

Also within the realm of consciousness, Giddens makes a (permeable) distinction between discursive and practical consciousness. *Discursive consciousness* entails the ability to put things into words. *Practical consciousness* involves that which is simply done by actors without their being able to express what they are doing in words. It is the latter type of consciousness that is particularly important to structuration theory, reflecting a primary interest in what is done rather than what is said.

Given this focus on practical consciousness, we make a smooth transition from agents to agency, the things that agents actually *do*. "Agency concerns events of which an individual is a perpetrator. . . . Whatever happened would not have happened if that individual had not intervened" (Giddens, 1984:9). Thus, Giddens gives great (his critics say too much) weight to the importance of agency. Giddens takes great pains to separate agency from intentions because he wants to make the point that actions often end up being different from what was intended; in other words, intentional acts often have unintended consequences. The idea of unintended consequences plays a great role in Giddens's theory and is especially important in getting us from agency to the social system level.

Consistent with his emphasis on agency, Giddens accords the agent great power. In other words, Giddens's agents have the ability to make a difference in the social world. Even more strongly, agents make no sense without power; that is, an actor ceases to be an agent if he or she loses the capacity to make a difference. Giddens certainly recognizes that there are constraints on actors, but this does not mean that actors have no choices and make no difference. To Giddens, power is logically prior to subjectivity because action involves power, or the ability to transform the situation. Thus, Giddens's structuration theory accords power to the actor and action and is in opposition to theories that are disinclined to such an orientation and instead grant great importance either to the intent of the actor (phenomenology) or to the external structure (structural functionalism).

The conceptual core of structuration theory lies in the ideas of structure, system, and duality of structure. *Structure* is defined as "the structuring properties [*rules and resources*] . . . the properties which make it possible for discernibly similar social practices to exist across varying spans of time and space and which lend them systemic form" (Giddens, 1984:17). Structure is made possible by the existence of rules and resources. Structures themselves do not exist in time and space. Rather, social phenomena have the capacity to become structured. Giddens contends that "structure only exists in and through the activities of human agents" (1989:256). Thus, Giddens offers a very unusual definition of *structure* that does not follow the Durkheimian pattern of viewing structures as external to and coercive over actors. He takes pains to avoid the impression that structure is "outside" or "external" to human action. "In my usage, structure is what gives form and shape to social life, but it is not *itself* that form and shape" (Giddens, 1989:256). As Held and Thompson put it, structure to Giddens is not a framework "like the girders of a building or the skeleton of a body" (1989:4).

Giddens does not deny the fact that structure can be constraining on action, but he feels that sociologists have exaggerated the importance of this constraint. Furthermore, they have failed to emphasize the fact that structure "is *always* both constraining *and* enabling" (Giddens, 1984:25, 163; italics added). Structures often allow agents to do things they would not otherwise be able to do. While Giddens deemphasizes structural constraint, he does recognize that actors can lose control over the "structured properties of social systems" as they stretch away in time and space. However, he is careful to avoid Weberian iron-cage imagery and notes that such a loss of control is *not* inevitable.

The conventional sociological sense of structure is closer to Giddens's concept of social system (Thompson, 1989:60). Giddens defines *social systems* as reproduced social practices, or "reproduced relations between actors or collectivities organized as regular social practices" (1984:17, 25). Thus, the idea of social system is derived from Giddens's focal concern with practice. Social systems do *not* have structures, but they do exhibit structural properties. Structures do not themselves exist in time and space, but they do become manifested in social systems in the form of reproduced practices. While some social systems may be the product of intentional action, Giddens places greater emphasis on the fact that such systems are often the unanticipated consequences of human action. These unanticipated consequences may become unrecognized conditions of action and feed back into it. These conditions may elude efforts to bring them under control, but nevertheless actors continue in their efforts to exert such control.

Thus structures are "instantiated" in social systems. In addition, they are also manifest in "memory traces orienting the conduct of knowledgeable human agents" (Giddens, 1984:17). As a result, rules and resources manifest themselves at both the macro level of social systems and the micro level of human consciousness.

We are now ready for the concept of *structuration*, which is premised on the idea that "[t]he constitution of agents and structures are not two indepen-dently given sets of phenomena, a dualism, but represent a duality . . . the structural properties of social systems are both medium and outcome of the practices they recursively organize," or "the moment of the production of action is also one of reproduction in the contexts of the day-to-day enactment of social life" (Giddens, 1984:25, 26). It is clear that structuration involves the dialectical relationship between structure and agency. Structure and agency are a duality; neither can exist without the other.

As has already been indicated above, *time* and *space* are crucial variables in Giddens's theory. Both depend on whether other people are present tempo-rally or spatially. The primordial condition is face-to-face interaction, in which others are present at the same time and in the same space. However, social systems extend in time and space, so others may no longer be present. Such distancing in terms of time and space is made increasingly possible in the modern world by new forms of communication and transportation. Gregory (1989) argues that Giddens devotes more attention to time than to space. Underscoring the importance of space, Saunders contends that "any sociolog-ical analysis of *why* and *how* things happen will need to take account of *where* (and when) they happen" (1989:218). The central sociological issue of social order depends on how well social systems are integrated over time and across space. One of Giddens's most widely recognized achievements in social theory is his effort to bring the issues of time and space to the fore.

We end this section by bringing Giddens's very abstract structuration the-ory closer to reality by discussing the research program that can be derived from it. First, instead of focusing on human societies, structuration theory would concentrate on "the orderings of institutions across time and space" (Giddens, 1989:300). (Institutions are viewed by Giddens as clusters of prac-tices, and he identifies four of them—symbolic orders, political institutions, economic institutions, and law.) Second, there would be a focal concern for changes in institutions over time and space. Third, researchers would need to be sensitive to the ways in which the leaders of various institutions intrude on and alter social patterns. Fourth, structurationists would need to monitor, and be sensitive to, the impact of their findings on the social world. Most generally, Giddens is deeply concerned with the "shattering impact of modernity" (1989:301), and the structurationist should be concerned with the study of this pressing social problem.

There is a great deal more to structuration theory than can be presented here; Giddens goes into great detail about the elements of the theory outlined above and discusses many others as well. Along the way he analyzes, inte-grates, and/or critiques a wide range of theoretical ideas. More recently, he is devoting increasing attention to utilizing his theory to critically analyze the modern world (Giddens, 1990). Unlike many others, Giddens has gone beyond a program statement for agency-structure integration; he has given a detailed analysis of its various elements and, more important, has focused on the nature of the interrelationship. What is most satisfying about Giddens's approach is the fact that his key concern, structuration, is defined in inherently integrative terms. The constitutions of agents and structures are not independent of one another; the properties of social systems are seen as both medium and outcome of the practices of actors, and those system properties recursively organize the practices of actors.

Margaret Archer: Culture and Agency

Margaret Archer (1988) has recently moved the agency-structure literature in a new direction by focusing on the linkage between agency and culture. In fact, this approach is derived from an earlier work by Archer (1982) in which she critiqued Giddens's structuration theory and sought to articulate a systems-theory (see Chapter 13) alternative to it. We begin with this earlier work because it provides a backdrop for her later theory of culture and agency.

Archer's focus is on *morphogenesis;* stemming from systems theory, this is the process by which complex interchanges lead not only to changes in the structure of the system but also to an end product—structural elaboration. (While morphogenesis implies change, *morphostasis* is the opposite, an absence of change.) This implies that there are emergent properties that are separable from the actions and interactions that produced them. Once structures have emerged, they react upon and alter action and interaction. The morphogenetic perspective looks at this over time, seeing endless sequences and cycles of structural change, alterations in action and interaction, and structural elaboration.

One key difference between Giddens and Archer is Giddens's case for dualities as opposed to Archer's critique of Giddens's devotion to dualities and her case for the utility of using (analytic) dualisms for analyzing the social world. In her view, structure (and culture) and agency are analytically distinct, although they are intertwined in social life. She clearly has Giddens in mind when she argues that "too many have concluded too quickly that the task is therefore how to look at both faces of the same medallion at once. . . . [This] foregoes the possibility of examining the interplay between them over time. . . . Any form of conceptualization which prevents examination of this interplay should therefore be resisted" (Archer, 1988:xii). Archer's main fear is that thinking in terms of dualities of "parts" and "people" will mean that "their influences upon one another cannot be unravelled" (1988:xiv).

In our view, both dualities and dualisms have a role to play in analyzing the social world. In some cases it may be useful to separate structure and action, or micro and macro, in order to look at the way in which they relate to one another. In other cases, it may help to look at structure and action and micro and macro as dualities that are inseparable. In fact, it may well be that the degree to which the social world is characterized by dualities or dualisms is an empirical question. That is, in one case the social setting might better be analyzed using dualities, while in another case it might be better to use dualisms. Similar points could also be made about different moments in time. We should be able to study and measure the degree of dualities and dualisms in any social setting at any given time.

A second major critique of Giddens is that his structuration theory does not seem to have any end result. There is just an endless cycle of agency and structure without any direction. In contrast, Archer's morphogenetic approach leads in the direction of structural elaboration. There are many other critiques of Giddens from the perspective of Archer's morphogenetic approach, but the key point for us here is that morphogenesis is the background for, and plays a key role in, culture-agency theory.

Archer begins with the premise that the problem of structure and agency has "overshadowed" the issue of culture and agency. She sees, as do most sociologists, a distinction between the two. However, the distinction is a conceptual one, since structure and culture are obviously intertwined in the real world. While structure is the realm of material phenomena and interests, culture involves nonmaterial phenomena and ideas. Not only are structure and culture substantively different, but they are also relatively autonomous. Thus, in Archer's view, structure and culture must be dealt with as relatively autonomous, not "clamped together in a conceptual vice" (1988:ix). However, in spite of a revival of "cultural sociology" (Lamont and Wuthnow, 1990), cultural analysis lags far behind structural analysis. (Archer describes "cultural analysis as a poor relation" [1988:xii]; she says that, as a result, there has been little discussion of the relationship between culture and agency.)

Within morphogenetic theory, the focus in the realm of structure is on how structural conditioning affects social interaction and on how this, in turn, leads to structural elaboration. The parallel concern within the cultural domain is on how cultural conditioning affects sociocultural interaction and, again, on how this leads to cultural elaboration. In both cases, time is accorded a central place in morphogenetic theory. Cultural conditioning refers to the parts, or components, of the cultural system. Sociocultural interaction deals with the relationships between cultural agents. The relationship between cultural conditioning and sociocultural interaction is, then, a variant of the (cultural) structure-agency issue.

Archer begins with the cultural system "because any Socio-Cultural action, wherever it is situated historically takes place in the context of innumerable interrelated theories, beliefs and ideas which had developed prior to it, and, as will be seen, exert a conditional influence on it" (1988:xix). The sociocultural system logically predates sociocultural action and interaction and affects, and is affected by, such action. Finally, cultural elaboration comes after sociocultural action and interaction and the changes induced in them by alterations in the sociocultural system. Archer is interested in explaining not only cultural elaboration in general but also its specific manifestations. Here is the way Archer summarizes her temporal, dialectical approach to the relationship among the three "stages": "Thus Cultural Elaboration is the future which is forged in the present, hammered out of past inheritance by current innovation" (1988:xxiv).

There is also a conflict-and-order dimension to Archer's theorizing. The parts of the cultural system may be either contradictory or complementary. This helps determine whether agents will engage in orderly or conflictual relationships with one another. These relationships, in turn, will aid in determining whether cultural relationships are stable or changing.

In terms of agency, Archer is concerned with specifying the ways in which the cultural system impinges on sociocultural action. In addition, she is interested in the effect of social relationships on agents. Then there is the issue of the ways in which agents respond to, and react upon, the cultural system. Archer expresses her focal concern with the culture-agency nexus in the following manner: "Our prime interest in the Cultural System lies precisely in its two-fold relationship with human agency; that is with its effects upon us . . . and our effects on it" (1988:143). Agents have the ability to either reinforce or resist the influence of the cultural system.

While Archer is making the case for the study of the relationship between culture and agency under the broad heading "morphogenesis," her ultimate objective is a unified analysis of the relationship between structure, culture, and agency. In such future analyses, one will need to get at the reciprocal impact of structure and culture as well as the relative impact of both on agency.

Archer sees culture as being on a par with the social system and as being analyzable using a similar, systems-theory perspective. She distinguishes her approach to culture from three other general orientations. The first is downward conflation, or the idea that culture is a macro phenomenon that acts on actors behind their backs. The second is upward conflation, or the view that one group imposes its world view on others. Finally, there is central conflation, which Archer associates with Giddens's approach. This is part of her critique of Giddens's thinking in terms of dualities, and here it refers to his refusal to analyze separately the cultural system and the sociocultural level. As Archer puts her preferred position, "Culture is the product of human agency but at the same time any form of social interaction is embedded in it" (1988:77–78).

Four general positions lie at the base of Archer's theory. First, the cultural system is made up of components that have a logical relationship to one another. Second, the cultural system has a causal impact on the sociocultural system. Third, there is a causal relationship among the individuals and groups that exist at the sociocultural level. Finally, changes at the sociocultural level lead to elaboration of the cultural system.

Clearly, Archer has barely scratched the surface of an analysis of the relationship between culture and agency. More needs to be done in exploring this realm as well as in integrating structural and cultural analyses from a morphogenetic perspective.

Pierre Bourdieu: Habitus and Field

A perspective on agency and structure that is comparable to that of Giddens in many ways, and similarly ambitious, is Pierre Bourdieu's theory, which focuses on the dialectical relationship between *habitus* and *field*. Before defining these two terms and discussing their relationship, we need to offer the theoretical backdrop for Bourdieu's perspective.

Bourdieu's (1984:483) theory is animated by the desire to overcome what he considers to be the false opposition between objectivism and subjectivism. As Bourdieu puts it, "the most steadfast (and, in my eyes, the most important) intention guiding my work has been to overcome" the opposition between objectivism and subjectivism (1989:15). He places Durkheim and his study of social facts (see Chapter 3) and the structuralism of Saussure, Lévi-Strauss, and the structural Marxists (see Chapter 13) within the objectivist camp. These perspectives are critiqued for focusing on objective structures and ignoring the process of social construction by which actors perceive, think about, and construct these structures and then proceed to act on that basis. Objectivists ignore agency and the agent, whereas Bourdieu favors a position that is structuralist without losing sight of the agent. Schutz's phenomenology, Blumer's symbolic interactionism, and Garfinkel's ethnomethodology are thought of as examples of subjectivism, focusing on the way agents think about, account for, or represent the social world while ignoring the objective structures in which those processes exist. Bourdieu sees these theories as concentrating on agency and ignoring structure. Instead, Bourdieu focuses on the dialectical relationship between objective structures and subjective phenomena:

> On the one hand, the objective structures . . . form the basis for . . . representations and constitute the structural constraints that bear upon interactions: but, on the other hand, these representations must also be taken into consideration particularly if one wants to account for the daily struggles, individual and collective, which purport to transform or to preserve these structures.
>
> (Bourdieu, 1989:15)

To sidestep the objectivist-subjectivist dilemma, Bourdieu (1977:3) focuses on *practice*, which he sees as the outcome of the dialectical relationship between structure and agency. Practices are not objectively determined, nor are they the product of free will. (Another reason for Bourdieu's focus on practice is that such a concern avoids the often irrelevant intellectualism that he associates with objectivism and subjectivism.)

Reflecting his interest in the dialectic between structure and the way people construct social reality, Bourdieu labels his own orientation "constructivist structuralism" (or "structuralist constructivism"). He subscribes, at least in part, to a structuralist perspective, but it is one that is different from the structuralism of Saussure and Lévi-Strauss (as well as the structural Marxists). While they, in turn, focused on structures in language and culture, Bourdieu argues that structures also exist in the social world itself. Bourdieu sees "objective structures [as] independent of the consciousness and will of agents, which are capable of guiding and constraining their practices or their representations" (1989:14). He simultaneously adopts a constructivist position which allows him to deal with the genesis of schemes of perception, thought, and action as well as of social structures.

While Bourdieu seeks to bridge structuralism and constructivism, and he succeeds to some degree, there is a bias in his work in the direction of structuralism. It is for this reason that he (along with Foucault and others—see Chapter 13) is thought of as a poststructuralist. There is more continuity in his work with structuralism than there is with constructivism. Unlike the approach of most others (for example, phenomenologists, symbolic interactionists), Bourdieu's constructivism ignores subjectivity and intentionality. He does think it important to include within his sociology the way people, on the basis of their position in social space, perceive and construct the social world. However, the perception and construction that takes place in the social world is both animated and constrained by structures. We can describe what he is interested in as the relationship "between social structures and mental structures" (Bourdieu, 1984:471). Thus, the so-called creative sociologies would all be uncomfortable with Bourdieu's perspective and would see it as little more than a more fully adequate structuralism. Yet there is a dynamic actor in Bourdieu's theory, an actor capable of *"intentionless invention* of regulated improvisation" (1977:79). The heart of Bourdieu's work, and of his effort to bridge subjectivism and objectivism, lies in his concepts of habitus and field, as well as their dialectical relationship to one another. While habitus exist in the minds of actors, fields exist outside their minds. We will examine these two concepts in some detail over the next few pages.

Habitus   We begin with the concept for which Bourdieu is most famous—habitus.[3] *Habitus* are the "mental, or cognitive structures" through which people deal with the social world. People are endowed with a series of internalized schemes through which they perceive, understand, appreciate, and evaluate the social world. It is through such schemes that people both produce their practices and perceive and evaluate them. Dialectically, habitus are "the product of the internalization of the structures" of the social world (Bourdieu, 1989:18). In fact, we can think of habitus as "internalized, 'embodied' social structures" (Bourdieu, 1984:468). They reflect objective divisions in the class structure, such as age groups, genders, and social classes. A habitus is acquired as a result of long-term occupation of a position within the social world. Thus, habitus varies depending on the nature of one's position in that world; not everyone has the same habitus. However, those who occupy the same position within the social world tend to have similar habitus. The habitus allows people to make sense out of the social world, but the existence of a

---

[3] This idea was not created by Bourdieu but is, rather, a traditional philosophical idea that he resuscitated (Wacquant, 1989).

multitude of habitus means that the social world and its structures do not impose themselves uniformly on all actors.

The habitus available at any given time have been created over the course of collective history: "The habitus, the product of history, produces individual and collective practices, and hence history, in accordance with the schemes engendered by history" (Bourdieu, 1977:82). The habitus manifested in any given individual is acquired over the course of individual history and is a function of the particular point in social history in which it occurs.

The habitus both produces and is produced by the social world. On the one hand, habitus is a "structuring structure"; that is, it is a structure that structures the social world. On the other hand, it is a "structured structure"; that is, it is a structure which is structured by the social world. Another way in which this is described by Bourdieu is as the *"dialectic of the internalization of externality and the externalization of internality"* (1977:72).

It is practice that mediates between habitus and the social world. On the one hand, it is through practice that the habitus is created; on the other, it is as a result of practice that the social world is created. Bourdieu expresses the mediating function of practice when he defines the habitus as "the system of structured and structuring dispositions which is constituted by practice and constantly aimed at practical . . . functions" (cited in Wacquant, 1989:42; see also Bourdieu, 1977:72). While practice tends to shape habitus, habitus, in turn, serves to both unify and generate practice.

While habitus is an internalized structure that constrains thought and choice of action, it does *not* determine them. It is this lack of determinism that is one of the main things that distinguishes Bourdieu's position from that of mainstream structuralists. The habitus merely "suggests" what people should think and what they should choose to do. People engage in a conscious deliberation of options, although this reflects the operation of the habitus. The habitus provides the principles by which people make choices and choose the strategies that they will employ in the social world.

The habitus functions "below the level of consciousness and language, beyond the reach of introspective scrutiny and control by the will" (Bourdieu, 1984:466). While we are not conscious of habitus and its operation, it manifests itself in our most practical activities, such as the way we eat, walk, talk, and even blow our noses. While the habitus operates as a structure, people do not simply respond mechanically to it or to external structures that are operating on them. Thus, in Bourdieu's approach we avoid the extremes of unpredictable novelty and total determinism.

Field We turn now to the "field," which Bourdieu thinks of relationally rather than structurally. The *field* is a network of relations among the objective positions within it. These relations exist apart from individual consciousness and will. They are *not* interactions or intersubjective ties among individuals. The occupants of positions may be either agents or institutions, and they are constrained by the structure of the field. There are a number of fields in the social world (for example, artistic, religious, economic), all with their own specific logics and all generating among actors a belief about the things that are at stake in a field.

Bourdieu sees the field as an arena of struggle. It is the structure of the field that both "undergirds and guides the strategies whereby the occupants of these positions seek, individually or collectively to safeguard or improve their position, and to impose the principle of hierarchization most favorable to their own products" (Bourdieu, cited in Wacquant, 1989:40). The field is a type of competitive marketplace in which various kinds of capital (economic, cultural, social, symbolic) are employed and deployed. The positions of various agents in the field are determined by the amount and relative weight of the capital they possess. Bourdieu even uses military imagery to describe the field, calling it an arena of "strategic emplacements, fortresses to be defended and captured in a field of struggles" (1984:244).

In underscoring the importance of *both* habitus and field, Bourdieu is rejecting the split between methodological individualists and methodological holists and adopting a position that has recently been termed "methodological relationism" (Ritzer and Gindoff, forthcoming). That is, Bourdieu is focally concerned with the *relationship* between habitus and field. He sees this as operating in two main ways. On the one hand, the field *conditions* the habitus; on the other, the habitus *constitutes* the field as something that is meaningful, that has sense and value, and that is worth the investment of energy.

Applying Habitus and Field Bourdieu does not simply seek to develop an abstract theoretical system but he also relates it to a series of empirical concerns and thereby avoids the trap of pure intellectualism. We will illustrate the application of his theoretical approach in his empirical study, *Distinction,* which examines the aesthetic preferences of different groups throughout society. In this work, Bourdieu is attempting, among other things, to demonstrate that culture can be a legitimate object of scientific study. He is attempting to reintegrate culture in the sense of "high culture" (for example, preferences for classical music) with the anthropological sense of culture, which looks at all its forms, both high and low. More specifically, in this work Bourdieu is linking taste for refined objects with taste for the most basic food flavors.

Because of structural invariants, especially field and habitus, the cultural preferences of the various groups within society (especially classes and fractions of classes) constitute coherent systems. Bourdieu is focally concerned with variations in aesthetic "taste," the acquired disposition to differentiate among the various cultural objects of aesthetic enjoyment and to appreciate them differentially. Taste is also practice that serves, among other things, to give an individual, as well as others, a sense of his or her place in the social order. Taste serves to unify those with similar preferences *and* to differentiate them from those with different tastes. That is, through the practical applications and implications of taste, people classify objects and thereby, in the process, classify themselves. We are able to categorize people by the tastes they manifest, for example, by their preferences for different types of music or movies. These practices, like all others, need to be seen in the context of all mutual relationships, that is, within the totality. Thus, seemingly isolated tastes for art or movies are related to preferences in food, sports, or hairstyles.

Two interrelated fields are involved in Bourdieu's study of taste—class relationships (especially within fractions of the dominant class) and cultural relationships. He sees these fields as a series of positions in which a variety of "games" are undertaken. The actions taken by the agents (individual or collective) who occupy specific positions are governed by the structure of the field, the nature of the positions, and the interests associated with them. However, it is also a game that involves self-positioning and use of a wide range of strategies to allow one to excel at the game. Taste is an opportunity to both experience and assert one's position within the field. But the field of social class has a profound effect on one's ability to play this game; those in the higher classes are far better able to have their tastes accepted and to oppose the tastes of those in the lower classes. Thus, the world of cultural works is related to the hierarchical world of social class and is itself both hierarchical and hierarchizing.

Needless to say, Bourdieu also links taste to his other major concept, habitus. Tastes are shaped far more by these deep-rooted and long-standing dispositions than they are by surface opinions and verbalizations. Peoples' preferences for even such mundane aspects of culture as clothing, furniture, or cooking are shaped by the habitus. And it is these dispositions "that forge the unconscious unity of a class" (Bourdieu, 1984:77). Bourdieu puts this more colorfully later: "Taste is a matchmaker . . . through which a habitus confirms its affinity with other habitus" (1984:243). Dialectically, of course, it is the structure of the class that shapes the habitus.

While both field and habitus are important to Bourdieu, it is their dialectical relationship that is of utmost importance and significance; field and habitus mutually define one another:

> The dispositions constituting the cultivated *habitus* are only formed, only function and are only valid in a *field,* in the relationship with a field . . . which is itself a 'field of possible forces,' a 'dynamic' situation in which forces are only manifested in their relationship with certain dispositions. This is why the same practices may receive opposite meanings and values in different fields, in different configurations, or in opposing sectors of the same field.
>
> (Bourdieu, 1984:94; italics added)

Or, as Bourdieu puts it, in more general terms: "There is a strong correlation between social positions and the dispositions of the agents who occupy them" (1984:110). It is out of the relationship between habitus and field that practices, cultural practices in particular, are established.

Bourdieu sees culture as a kind of economy, or marketplace. In this marketplace people utilize cultural rather than economic capital. This capital is largely a result of peoples' social class origin and their educational experience.

In the marketplace, people accrue more or less capital and either expend it to improve their position or lose it, thereby causing their position within the economy to deteriorate.

People pursue distinction in a range of cultural fields—the beverages they drink (Perrier or cola), the automobiles they drive (Mercedes Benz or Ford Escort), the newspapers they read (*The New York Times* or *USA Today*), or the resorts they visit (The French Riviera or Disney World). Relationships of distinction are objectively inscribed in these products and reactivated each time they are appropriated. In Bourdieu's view, "The total field of these fields offers well-nighly inexhaustible possibilities for the pursuit of distinction" (1984: 227). The appropriation of certain cultural goods (for example, a Mercedes Benz) yields "profit," while that of others (an Escort) yields no gain, or even a "loss."

There is a dialectic between the nature of the cultural products and tastes. Changes in cultural goods lead to alterations in taste, but changes in taste are also likely to result in transformations in cultural products. The structure of the field not only conditions the desires of the consumers of cultural goods but also structures what the producers create in order to satisfy those demands.

Changes in taste (and Bourdieu sees all fields temporally) result from the struggle between opposing forces in both the cultural (the supporters of old versus new fashions, for example) and the class (the dominant versus the dominated fractions within the dominant class) arenas. However, the heart of the struggle lies within the class system, and the cultural struggle between, for example, artists and intellectuals is a reflection of the interminable struggle between the different fractions of the dominant class to define culture, indeed the entire social world. It is oppositions within the class structure that condition oppositions in taste and in habitus. While Bourdieu gives great importance to social class, he refuses to reduce it to merely economic matters or to the relations of production but sees class as defined by habitus as well.

Bourdieu offers a distinctive theory of the relationship between agency and structure within the context of a concern for the dialectical relationship between habitus and field. It is also distinguished by its focus on practice (in the above case, aesthetic practices) and its refusal to engage in arid intellectualism. In that sense it represents a return to the Marxian concern for the relationship between theory and practice.

Jurgen Habermas: Colonization of the Life-World

We have discussed Habermas's earlier ideas in Chapter 8, on neo-Marxian theory, under the heading "critical theory." While, as we will see, Habermas's perspective can still be thought of, at least in part, as being a neo-Marxian orientation, it has broadened considerably and is increasingly difficult to contain within that, or any other, theoretical category. Habermas's theory has grown and become more diverse as he has addressed, and incorporated, the ideas of a wide number of sociological theorists, most recently and most notably those of George Herbert Mead, Talcott Parsons, Alfred Schutz, and Emile Durkheim. In spite of the difficulties involved in categorizing Habermas's innovative theoretical perspective, we will discuss his most recent ideas, which can be broadly thought of as the "colonization of the lifeworld," under the heading "agency-structure issue." It is, at least in part, in his thoughts on the life-world that Habermas deals with agency. Structure is dealt with primarily in Habermas's ideas on the social system, which, as we will see, is the force that is colonizing the life-world. What does Habermas mean by life-world, system, and colonization? We address these phenomena and their interrelationship, as well as other key ideas in Habermas's most recent theorizing, in this section.

Before we get to these concepts, it should be made clear that Habermas's major focus continues to be on communicative action. Free and open communication remains both his theoretical baseline and his political objective. It also has the methodological function, much like Weber's ideal types, of allowing him to analyze variations from the model: "The construction of an unlimited and undistorted discourse can serve at most as a foil for setting off more glaringly the rather ambiguous developmental tendencies in modern society" (Habermas, 1987:107). Indeed, his focal interest in the colonization of the life-world is the ways in which that process is adversely affecting free communication.

He also retains an interest in the Weberian process of rationalization, but here it lies in the issue of the differential rationalization of life-world and system and the impact of this difference on the colonization of the former by the latter. In Weberian terms, the *system* is the domain of formal rationality, while the *life-world* is the site of substantive rationality. The *colonization of the life-world*, therefore, involves a restatement of the Weberian thesis that in the modern world, formal rationality is triumphing over substantive rationality and coming to dominate areas that were formally defined by substantive rationality. Thus, while Habermas's theory has taken some interesting new turns, it retains its theoretical roots, especially in its Marxian and Weberian orientations.

The Life-World This concept, of course, is derived from phenomenological sociology in general and, more specifically, the theories of Alfred Schutz (see Chapter 10). But Habermas also interprets the ideas of George Herbert Mead as contributing to insights about the life-world. To Habermas, the life-world represents an internal perspective (while, as we will see, the system represents an external viewpoint): "Society is conceived from the perspective of the acting subject" (1987:117).

Habermas views the life-world and communicative action as "complementary" concepts. More specifically, communicative action can be seen as occurring within the life-world:

> The lifeworld is, so to speak, the transcendental site where speaker and hearer meet, where they reciprocally raise claims that their utterances fit the world . . . and

where they can criticize and confirm those validity claims, settle their disagreements, and arrive at agreements.

Habermas, 1987:126)

The life-world is a "context-forming background of processes of reaching understanding" through communicative action (Habermas, 1987:204). It involves a wide range of unspoken presuppositions about mutual understanding that must exist and be mutually understood for communication to take place.

Habermas is concerned with the rationalization of the life-world, which involves, for one thing, increasingly rational communication in the life-world. He believes that the more rational the life-world becomes, the more likely it is that interaction will be controlled by "rationally motivated mutual understanding." Such understanding, or a rational method of achieving consensus, is based ultimately on the authority of the better argument.

Habermas sees the rationalization of the life-world as involving the progressive differentiation of its various elements. The life-world is composed of culture, society, and personality (note the influence of Parsons and his action systems). Each of these refers to interpretive patterns, or background assumptions, about culture and its effect on action, appropriate patterns of social relations (society), and what people are like (personality) and how they are supposed to behave. Engaging in communicative action and achieving understanding in terms of each of these themes leads to the reproduction of the life-world through the reinforcement of culture, the integration of society, and the formation of personality. While these components are closely intertwined in archaic societies, the rationalization of the life-world involves the "growing differentiation between culture, society and personality" (Habermas, 1987:288).

System While the life-world represents the viewpoint of acting subjects on society, system involves an external perspective that views society "from the observer's perspective of someone not involved" (Habermas, 1987:117). In analyzing systems, we are attuned to the interconnection of actions, as well as the functional significance of actions and their contributions to the maintenance of the system. Each of the major components of the life-world (culture, society, personality) has corresponding elements in the system. Cultural reproduction, social integration, and personality formation take place at the system level.

The system has its roots in the life-world, but ultimately it comes to develop its own structural characteristics. Examples of such structures include the family, the judiciary, the state, and the economy. As these structures evolve, they grow more and more distant from the life-world. As in the life-world, rationalization at the system level involves progressive differentiation and greater complexity. These structures also grow more self-sufficient. As they grow in power, they exercise more and more steering capacity over the life-world. They come to have less and less to do with the process of achieving consensus and, in fact, limit the occurrence of that process in the life-world. In other words, these rational structures, instead of enhancing the capacity to communicate and reach understanding, threaten those processes through the exertion of external control over them.

Social Integration and System Integration   Given the preceding discussion of life-world and system, Habermas concludes: *"The fundamental problem of social theory is how to connect in a satisfactory way the two conceptual strategies indicated by the notions of 'system' and 'lifeworld' "* (1987:151; italics added). Habermas labels those two conceptual strategies "social integration" and "system integration."

The perspective of *social integration* focuses on the life-world and the ways in which the action system is integrated through either normatively guaranteed or communicatively achieved consensus. Theorists who believe that society is integrated through social integration begin with communicative action and see society *as* the life-world. They adopt the internal perspective of the group members, and they employ a hermeneutic approach in order to be able to relate their understanding to that of the members of the life-world. The ongoing reproduction of society is seen as a result of the actions undertaken by members of the life-world to maintain its symbolic structures. It is also seen only from their perspective. Thus, what is lost in this hermeneutic approach is the outsider's viewpoint as well as a sense of the reproductive processes that are occurring at the system level.

The perspective of *system integration* is focally concerned with the system and the way in which it is integrated through external control over individual decisions that are not subjectively coordinated. Those who adopt this perspective see society as a self-regulating system. They adopt the external perspective of the observer, but this prohibits them from really getting at the structural patterns that can be understood only hermeneutically from the internal perspective of members of the life-world.

Thus, Habermas concludes that while each of these two broad perspectives has something to offer, both have serious limitations. On the basis of his critique of social and system integration, Habermas offers his alternative, which seeks to integrate these two theoretical orientations in which he sees

> society as a system that has to fulfill conditions for the maintenance of sociocultural lifeworlds. The formula-societies are *systematically stabilized* complexes of action of *socially integrated* groups. . . . [I] stand for the heuristic proposal that we view society as an entity that, in the course of social evolution, gets differentiated *both* as a *system* and a *lifeworld*.
>
> (Habermas, 1987:151–152; italics added)

Having argued that he is interested in *both* system and life-world, Habermas makes it clear at the end of the above quotation that he is also concerned with the evolution of the two. While both evolve in the direction of increasing rationalization, that rationalization takes different forms in life-world and system, and that differentiation is the basis of the colonization of the life-world.

Colonization   Crucial to the understanding of the idea of colonization is the fact that Habermas sees society as being composed of *both* life-world and system. Furthermore, while both concepts were closely intertwined in earlier history, today there is an increasing divergence between them; they have become "uncoupled." While both have undergone the process of rationalization, that process has taken different forms in the two settings. Although Habermas sees a dialectical relationship between system and life-world (they both limit and open up new possibilities for one another), his main concern is with the way in which system in the modern world has come to control the life-world. In other words, he is interested in the breakdown of the dialectic between system and life-world and the growing power of the former over the latter.

Habermas contrasts the increasing rationality of system and life-world. The rationalization of the life-world involves growth in the rationality of communicative action. Furthermore, action that is oriented toward achieving mutual understanding is increasingly freed from normative constraint and relies more and more on everyday language. In other words, social integration is achieved more and more through the processes of consensus formation in language.

But the result of this is the fact that the demands on language grow and come to overwhelm its capacities. Delinguistified media (especially money and power)—having become differentiated in, and emanating from, the system—come to fill the void and replace, to at least some degree, everyday language. Instead of language coordinating action, it is money and power that perform that function. More generally, the increasingly complex system "unleashes system imperatives that burst the capacity of the lifeworld they instrumentalize" (Habermas, 1987:155). Thus, Habermas writes of the "violence" exercised over the life-world by the system through the ways in which it restricts communication. This violence, in turn, produces "pathologies" within the life-world. Habermas embeds this development within a view of the history of the world:

> The far-reaching uncoupling of system and lifeworld was a necessary condition for the transition from the stratified class societies of European feudalism to the economic class societies of the early modern period; but the capitalist pattern of modernization is marked by a *deformation*, a reification of the symbolic structures of the lifeworld under the imperatives of subsystems differentiated out via money and power and rendered self-sufficient.
>
> (Habermas, 1987:283; italics added)

It might be noted that by linking the deformities to capitalism, Habermas continues, at least in this sense, to operate within a neo-Marxian framework. However, when he looks at the modern world, Habermas is forced to abandon a Marxian approach, since he concludes that the deformation of the life-world is "no longer localizable in any class-specific ways" (1987:333). Given this limitation, and in line with his roots in critical theory, Habermas demonstrates that his work is also strongly influenced by Weberian theory. In fact, he argues that the distinction between life-world and system, and the ultimate colonization of the life-world, allows us to see in a new light the Weberian thesis "of a modernity at variance with itself" (Habermas, 1987:299). In Weber, this was found primarily in the conflict between substantive and formal rationality and the triumph in the West of the latter over the former. To Habermas, the rationalization of the system comes to triumph over the rationalization of the life-world, with the result that the life-world comes to be colonized by the system.

Habermas adds specificity to his thoughts on colonization by arguing that the main forces in the process are "formally organized domains of action" at the system level, such as the economy and the state. In traditional Marxian terms, Habermas sees modern society as subject to recurrent systemic crises. In seeking to deal with these crises, institutions like the state and the economy undertake actions that adversely affect the life-world, leading to pathologies and crises within it. Basically, the life-world comes to be denuded by these systems, and communicative action comes to be less and less directed to the achievement of consensus. Communication becomes increasingly rigidified, impoverished, and fragmented, and the life-world itself seems poised on the brink of dissolution. This assault on the life-world worries Habermas greatly, given his concern for the communicative action that takes place within it. However, no matter how extensive the colonization by the system, the life-world is "never completely husked away" (Habermas, 1987:311).

If the essential problem in the modern world is the uncoupling of system and life-world and the domination of the life-world by the system, then the solutions are clear-cut. On the one hand, life-world and system need to be recoupled. On the other, the dialectic between system and life-world needs to be reinstated so that, instead of the latter being deformed by the former, the two become mutually enriching and enhancing. While the two were intertwined in primitive society, the rationalization process that has occurred in both system and life-world makes it possible that the future recoupling will produce a level of system, life-world, and their interrelationship unprecedented in human history.

Thus, once again, Habermas is back to his Marxian roots. Marx, of course, did not look back in history for the ideal state but saw it in the future in the form of communism and the full flowering of species-being. Habermas, too, does not look back to archaic societies where nonrationalized system and life-world were more unified but looks to a future state involving the far more satisfactory unification of rationalized system and life-world.

Habermas also reinterprets the Marxian theory of basic struggles within society. Marx, of course, emphasized the conflict between proletariat and capitalist and traced it to the exploitative character of the capitalist system. Habermas focuses not on exploitation but on colonization and sees many of the struggles of recent decades in this light. That is, he sees social movements such as those oriented to greater equality, increased self-realization, the preservation of the environment, and peace "as reactions to system assaults on the lifeworld. Despite the diversity of interests and political projects of these heterogeneous groups, they have resisted the colonization of the lifeworld" (Seidman, 1989:25). The hope for the future clearly lies in resistance to the encroachments on the life-world and in the creation of a world in which system and life-world are in harmony and serve to mutually enrich one another to a historically unprecedented degree.

MAJOR DIFFERENCES IN THE AGENCY-STRUCTURE LITERATURE

As is the case with work on micro-macro integration in the United States, there are significant differences among Europeans working on the agency-structure issue. For example, there is considerable disagreement in the literature on the nature of the agent. Most of those working within this realm tend to treat the agent as an individual actor (for example, Giddens, Bourdieu), but Touraine's "actionalist sociology" treats collectivities such as social classes as agents. In fact, Touraine defines *agency* as "an organization directly implementing one or more elements of the system of historical action and therefore intervening directly in the relations of social domination" (1971:459). A third, middle-ground position on this issue is taken by Burns and Flam (see also Crozier and Friedberg, 1980), who regard either individuals or collectivities as agents. This lack of agreement on the nature of the agent is a source of substantial differences in the agency-structure literature.

There is considerable disagreement even among those who focus on the individual actor as agent. For example, Bourdieu's agent, dominated by habitus, seems far more mechanical than Giddens's (or Habermas's) agent. Bourdieu's habitus involves "systems of durable, transposable *dispositions*, structuring structures, that is, as principles of the generation and structuring of practices and representations" (1977:72). The habitus is a source of strategies "without being the product of a genuine strategic intention" (Bourdieu, 1977:73). It is neither subjectivistic nor objectivistic but combines elements of both. It clearly rejects the idea of an actor with "the free and wilful power to constitute" (Bourdieu, 1977:73). Giddens's agents may not have intentionality and free will either, but they have much more willful power than Bourdieu's. Where Bourdieu's agents seem to be dominated by their habitus, by internal ("structuring") structures, the agents in Giddens's work are the perpetrators of action. They have at least some choice, at least the possibility of acting differently than they do. They have power, and they make a difference in their worlds (see also Lukes, 1977). Most importantly, they constitute (and are constituted by) structures. In contrast, in Bourdieu's work, a sometimes seemingly disembodied habitus is involved in a dialectic with the external world.[4]

---

[4] Although I am emphasizing the differences between Giddens and Bourdieu on agency, Giddens (1979:217) sees at least some similarities between the two perspectives.

Similarly, there are marked disagreements among agency-structure theorists on precisely what they mean by structure.[5] Some adopt a specific structure as central, such as the organization in the work of Crozier and Friedberg and Touraine's relations of social domination as found in political institutions and organizations; others (for example, Burns, 1986:13) focus on an array of social structures, such as bureaucracy, the polity, the economy, and religion. Giddens offers a very idiosyncratic definition of *structure* ("recursively organized sets of rules and resources" [1984:25]) that is at odds with virtually every other definition of *structure* in the literature (Layder, 1985). However, his definition of *systems* as reproduced social practices is very close to what many sociologists mean by structure. In addition to the differences among those working with structure, differences exist between these theorists and others. Archer, as we have seen, excoriates Giddens (and implicitly all the others) for focusing on structure to the exclusion of culture.

The attempts at agency-structure linkage flow from a variety of very different theoretical directions. For example, within social theory Giddens seems to be animated by functionalism and structuralism versus phenomenology, existentialism, and ethnomethodology and, more generally, by new linguistic structuralism, semiotics, and hermeneutics (Archer, 1982), while Archer is mainly influenced by systems theory, especially that of Walter Buckley. One result of this is that Giddens's agents tend to be active and creative people ("corporeal beings" with selves) involved in a continual flow of conduct, while Archer's are often reduced to systems, particularly the sociocultural system. In France, Crozier develops his orientation primarily on the basis of organizational and game theory, while Bourdieu seeks to find a satisfactory alternative to subjectivism and objectivism within anthropological theory. Habermas seeks to synthesize ideas derived from Marx, Weber, critical theorists, Durkheim, Mead, Schutz, and Parsons. Among the reasons for the substantial differences in the work on agency and structure are basic differences in theoretical roots.

As with the strain toward the micro or macro direction in micro-macro efforts in the United States, there is a strain toward either the agency or the structural direction in Europe. Certainly Bourdieu is strongly pulling in the direction of structure, while Giddens has a more powerful sense of agency than most other theorists of this genre (Layder, 1985:131). In spite of the existence of pulls in the directions of agency and structure, what is distinctive about the European work on agency and structure, as compared to American micro-macro work, is a much stronger sense of the need to refuse to separate the two and to deal with them dialectically (for example, Giddens, Bourdieu, Habermas). In the American micro-macro literature, one parallel to the European efforts to deal with agency and structure dialectically is Ritzer's attempt to deal dialectically with the integration of the micro-macro and objective-subjective continua.

[5] I am focusing here mainly on Europeans who deal with social structure and not those who see structure as hidden, underlying elements of culture.

AGENCY-STRUCTURE AND MICRO-MACRO LINKAGES

Basic Similarities

The most general similarity in the work in the United States and that in Europe is the shared desire for integration and synthesis. Beyond this, there has been a tendency for both Americans and Europeans to be animated in their thinking by their aversion to the excesses of extant dominant theories. Both Americans and Europeans have attacked the macro determinism of structural functionalism. A similar aversion exists to the excesses of structuralism, although the feeling is stronger in Europe, where structuralism made far greater inroads than it did in the United States. In Europe structural functionalism and structuralism are seen as emphasizing structure and giving agency little or no importance (see, for example, Giddens, 1979:50). In America they are seen as focusing on the macro level and giving little attention to micro-level phenomena.

Similarly, theorists on both sides of the ocean have been wary of the excesses of micro/agency theories such as symbolic interactionism, ethnomethodology, and existentialism and phenomenology. The shared concern here is that these theories have little to say about the macro/structural level, with the result that actors are accorded far too much voluntarism. For example, Giddens argues: "Symbolic interactionism has placed most emphasis upon regarding social life as an active accomplishment of purposive, knowledgeable actors . . . the subsequent evolution of this tradition . . . has not successfully developed modes of institutional analysis" (1979:50). Similarly, as we saw in Chapter 14, Alexander believes that according privilege to the micro level is "a theoretical mistake" (1987:295).

Fundamental Differences

The most general differences between the American micro-macro literature and the European work on agency and structure has been discussed above in terms of the major terminological differences between agency-structure and micro-macro work. These, however, do not exhaust the differences between the two literatures.

Of great interest in this section is Giddens (1984:139) case "against" the micro-macro dualism. Giddens' (1984:141) seems to be opposed to setting micro and macro off in opposition to one another, to fostering "the micro/macro distinction." He is opposed to the "phoney war" between microsociology and macrosociology as well as the "unhappy division of labour [that] tends to come into being between them" (Giddens, 1984:139). More specifically, Giddens critiques Collins for his overemphasis on the micro level and the corresponding weakness of his approach at the macro level (a view which is shared by some American theorists [for example, Porpora, 1989; Ritzer, 1985]). However, Giddens's opposition is to the micro-macro dualism; it would appear that he would be less opposed to those who treat the relationship as a duality.

One of the central differences between American and European theorists is their images of the actor. What is distinctive about American theory is the much greater influence of behaviorism as well as of exchange theory, derived, in part, from a behavioristic perspective. The strength of these perspectives, even among theorists who do not accept or support them, has tended to give American theorists a more ambivalent attitude toward the actor. The actor is sometimes seen as actively involved in creating the social world, but there is also a recognition that actors sometimes behave in a mindless fashion in accord with histories of rewards and costs. Thus, American theorists share the interest of (some) Europeans in conscious, creative action, but it is limited by a recognition of the importance of mindless behavior. To put it simply, behavior (as opposed to action) has played a greater role in American social theory than it has in European theory. This tendency to see the actor as behaving mindlessly is being enhanced now by the growing interest in rational choice theory in American sociology. The image here is of an actor more or less automatically choosing the most efficient means to ends.[6] The influence of rational choice theory in the United States promises to drive an even greater wedge between European and American conceptions of action and agency.

At the macro/structure level, Europeans have been inclined to focus on social structure. In cases where there has not been a single-minded focus on it, social structure has not been adequately differentiated from culture. (Indeed, this is the motivation behind Archer's [1988] recent work.) On the other hand, there has been a much greater tendency in the United States to deal with *both* structure and culture in efforts aimed at micro-macro integration. For example, in my own work, I differentiated macro objectivity (mainly social structure) and macro subjectivity (mainly culture) and sought to deal with their dialectical interrelationship with micro objectivity and micro subjectivity (Ritzer, 1981a).

Another difference in the macro/structure issue stems from differences in theoretical influence in the United States and Europe. In the United States, the main influence on thinking on the macro/structure issue has been structural functionalism. The nature of that theory has led American theorists to focus on both large-scale social structures *and* culture. Structural functionalism clearly had an interest in social structures, but it ultimately accorded priority to the cultural system. In Europe, the main influence has been structuralism, which has a much more wide-ranging sense of structures, extending all the way from micro structures of the mind to macro structures of society. Culture has been of far less importance to structuralists than to structural functionalists.

If we ignore for the moment the far greater impact of behaviorism,

---

[6] DeVille (1989) sees such an actor as robotlike.

exchange theory, and rational choice theory in the United States, theoretical differences in the micro/agency issue seem to have been much less consequential than those at the macro/structural level. Existentialism and phenomenology (as well as Freudian theory) have had the greatest influence in Europe, while in the United States the key influences have stemmed from symbolic interactionism and exchange theory. However, differences in the impact of these theories on thoughts on the micro/agency issue in the United States and Europe seem to have been negligible. Furthermore, the micro/agency theories seem to be more widely read and utilized on both sides of the Atlantic than the macro/structural theories. For example, ethnomethodology seems to have had an almost equally strong impact on both sides of the Atlantic.

Another key difference between the two literatures is the fact that the micro-macro issue is subsumable under the broader issue of levels of analysis (Edel, 1959; Ritzer, 1981a, 1989b; Wiley, 1988) while the concern for agency and structure is not. We can clearly think of the micro-macro linkage in terms of some sort of vertical hierarchy, with micro-level phenomena on the bottom, macro-level phenomena at the top, and meso-level entities in between. However, the micro-macro continuum is not coterminous with levels of analysis, since other factors (for example, objectivity, subjectivity—see Ritzer, 1981a; Wiley, 1988), not merely micro-macro concerns, are involved in the levels issue. On the other side, the agency-structure linkage seems to have no clear connection to the levels-of-analysis issue, since both agency and structure can be found at any level of social analysis.

The agency-structure issue is much more firmly embedded in a historical, dynamic framework than is the micro-macro issue. This characteristic is clearest in the work of Giddens, Habermas, and Archer, but it is manifest throughout the literature on agency and structure. In contrast, theorists who deal with micro-macro issues are more likely to depict them in static, hierarchical, ahistorical terms. Nevertheless, at least some of those who choose to depict the micro-macro relationship rather statically make it clear that they understand the dynamic character of the relationship: "The study of levels of social reality and their interrelationship is inherently a *dynamic* rather than a static approach to the social world. . . . A dynamic and historical orientation to the study of levels of the social world can be seen as integral parts of a more general *dialectical* approach" (Ritzer, 1981a:208; see also Wiley, 1988:260).

Finally, we must mention that morality is a central issue to agency-structure theorists but is largely ignored in the micro-macro literature. This may be traced, in part, to differences in theoretical roots and reference groups. Agency-structure theory has much more powerful roots in, and a stronger orientation to, philosophy, including its great concern with moral issues. In contrast, micro-macro theory is largely indigenous to sociology and oriented to the hard sciences as a reference group—areas where moral issues are of far less concern than they are in philosophy. The result is that a sense of moral concern, even moral outrage, is far more palpable in the agency-structure than the micro-macro literature.

EXPLAINING AMERICAN-EUROPEAN DIFFERENCES

American concern with the micro-macro issue, or at least the use of that terminology to describe their interest, is of fairly recent vintage. As we saw in Chapter 14, although there were some earlier efforts, in 1976 Kemeny detected almost no explicit interest in the micro-macro issue. Where did this micro-macro terminology come from? Internally, it can be traced to the long-standing and well-known theoretical split in the United States between macro (for example, structural functionalism and conflict theory) and micro (for example, symbolic interactionism and exchange theory) theories. Externally, its attraction can be tied to the utilization of micro and macro terminology in the hard sciences as well as in economics. Within the social sciences, economics tends to be a model for sociology, and its differentiation between microeconomics and macroeconomics proved alluring to many sociologists. The success of these fields made many things about them (their scientific orientation, their terminology) attractive to American sociologists, who wanted to emulate them in as many ways as possible.

In contrast, European sociology has not had the long and strong tradition of micro and macro theories that has existed in the United States. Especially lacking has been strong micro-theoretical tradition, and this has tended to obscure the significance of the micro-macro dichotomy.[7] Furthermore, European social theorists have generally been less enamored of the hard sciences and economics than American theorists have been, and therefore they are much less likely to take them as their models.

European theorists tend to be much more interested in philosophy than are American theorists, and there is a long tradition of interest in philosophy in human agency. European theorists have built on the philosophy of agency and added the structural dimension to it. Bernstein (1971) traces a concern for agency (a term that he uses interchangeably with *praxis* and *action* [for example, "agents or human actors"]) back to ancient Greece in general, and the philosophy of Aristotle in particular. More contemporaneously, he identifies four strands of thought in which agency is central. The first is Marx (and Marxism), with his systematic theory of praxis. Second is analytic philosophy, in which action has become the focal point in recent years. Linking Marxism's interest in praxis and analytic philosophy's interest in action, Bernstein argues that "the meanings of *'praxis'* and action are very close" (1971:xii), and presumably the two are closely tied to agency. The third theoretical strand is pragmatism: "The image of man that emerges from the pragmatic point of

---

[7] But far from completely, as is shown, for example, in the efforts of the critical theorists to integrate Freudian and Marxian theories.

view is man as a craftsman, as an active manipulator advancing new hypotheses, actively testing them, always open to ongoing criticism, and reconstructing himself and his environment. Practice and activity informed by reason and intelligence become central to their vision of man in the universe" (Bernstein, 1971:313). Finally, there is phenomenology, especially the primarily European existentialism, in which "the central issue again turns out to be the nature of human action" (Bernstein, 1971:xiii). Bernstein concludes: "The investigation of the nature, status, and significance of *praxis* and action has become the dominant concern of the most influential philosophic movements that have emerged since Hegel" (1971:xiii).

It is clear that European social theorists are much more steeped in Marxism, analytic philosophy, and existentialism than are American theorists. The one exception would seem to be pragmatism, which is primarily an American philosophy and which has influenced some American social theorists (especially symbolic interactionists). However, most other American theorists are probably less knowledgeable about pragmatism than their European counterparts are. Thus, overall the philosophies of agency have clearly played a far greater role in the development of European than American social theory.

However, Bernstein's equation of agency with praxis and action creates problems for us. If we accept the equation of these terms, then there would seem to be little difference among contemporary European theories of agency and structure, Marxian theories of praxis and the structure of capitalist society, and American theories (for example, those of Parsons and Alexander) of action and structure. It seems clear, however, that contemporary Europeans accord far more importance to agents than some Marxists and many Americans give to actors. The tendency in the work on agency and structure among contemporary European theorists is to refuse to think about structure without agency or agency without structure. In other words, a world without agents is inconceivable. In contrast, some Marxists (especially structural Marxists) have been able to conceive of a capitalist world without meaningful actors. Some American "action theorists" (especially Parsons) developed theories in which social structure and culture achieved preeminence and the actor and action were reduced to comparative insignificance. Thus, there is more to the issue than the similarities in the terms *agency, praxis,* and *action.* What distinguishes the current work among European theorists is an unwillingness to submerge the agent under the weight of social structure (and culture).

This leads to the point that the real issue is not agency and structure per se but the relative weight of agency and structure. Contemporary European theorists are willing to give a rough equivalency to the power and significance of agency and structure, or are unwilling to disentangle them. Many Marxists and mainstream American theorists have tended to give structure primacy over action and praxis. Other American theorists (and some Marxists) have tended to give action primacy over structure. In this sense, virtually all theorists would seem to be concerned with the agency-structure linkage. This seems to be the position adopted by Dawe (1978), who differentiates between the sociology of social action and the sociology of social system but sees both as sociologies of social action (and presumably social structure). However, to argue in this way is to lose sight of the significance of contemporary European work on agency and structure. What is distinctive about much of this work is its dedication to taking *both* agency and structure seriously. This is also one of its main contributions in comparison to the philosophy of agency, which has little to offer to our understanding of social structure.

While we can be sympathetic to the theoretical ideas being developed in Europe today, we cannot always assume that agency and structure are of equivalent importance.[8] The degree of their equivalency is a historical question. In some epochs structure may gain the ascendancy over agency. (This was Marx's view of the situation in capitalist society.) In other epochs the agent may play a greater role, and the significance of structure would be reduced. In still others, there may be a rough equivalence of the two. One cannot posit a single agency-structure relationship for all history. One of the pressing needs in the agency-structure literature is to begin to specify the relative weight of agency and structure in different historical epochs. Furthermore, there are clearly contemporaneous differences in the relative weight of agency and structure in various societies around the world. All these crucial differences are lost if we talk only in very general terms about agency and structure.

SUMMARY

This chapter deals with the largely European literature on the agency-structure linkage. This literature has a number of similarities to the American work on micro-macro integration, but there are also a number of substantial differences between the literatures.

While a large number of contemporary European theorists are dealing with the agency-structure relationship, the bulk of this chapter is devoted to the work of four major examples of this type of theorizing. The first is Giddens's structuration theory. The core of Giddens's theory is his refusal to treat agents and structures apart from one another; they are seen as being mutually constitutive. Next is Archer's theory of the culture-agency relationship. Archer is critical of Giddens's refusal to separate agent and structure for analytic purposes. More generally, she is critical of agency-structure theorists for ignoring culture, and she seeks to rectify this by dealing with the agency-culture relationship. We then turn to Bourdieu's theory, which focuses primarily on the relationship between habitus and field. Finally, we analyze Habermas's recent ideas on life-world and system and the colonization of the life-world by the system.

---

[8] The ensuing discussion assumes that we are dealing with a dualism rather than a duality. Since a Giddens-like duality assumes that agency and structure cannot be separated, it would be hard to assess their relative significance under that condition.

Following a discussion of these specific agency-structure works, we return to a more general discussion of this literature. We begin with a discussion of major differences in this literature, including differing views on the nature of the agent and structure. Another source of difference is the varying theoretical traditions on which these works are based. Some of these works strain in the direction of agency, while others pull in the direction of structure.

The next issue is the similarities between the agency-structure and micro-macro literatures. Both literatures share an interest in integration and are wary of the excesses of micro/agency and macro/structural theories. There are, however, far more differences than similarities between these literatures. There are differences in their images of the actor, the ways in which structure is conceived, the theories from which their ideas are derived, the degree to which they may be subsumed under the idea of levels of analysis, the extent to which they are embedded in a historical, dynamic framework, and the degree to which they are concerned with moral issues.

Finally, we deal with some of the reasons for the differences between the American and European literatures. The American micro-macro theorists have been heavily influenced by fields like economics, with a long history of concern for micro-macro issues. The European theorists have been greatly affected by the philosophical literature on agency. The chapter concludes with the point that the ultimate question is the relative weight of agency and structure in different cultural and historical settings.

SYNTHESES IN SOCIOLOGICAL THEORY—I

As is clear throughout Part Two of this book, sociological theory, at least until the 1980s, was characterized by theoretical extremism of one kind or another as well as by the destructive political conflicts that often went hand in hand with such extremism. The developments that took place during the 1980s were very different from those of any previous epoch, as a wide range of theorists moved away from theoretical extremism and began to grapple with micro-macro and agency-structure integration. This is not to say that there were no efforts at integration and synthesis prior to these periods. In fact, sociology has always had such attempts, and we will deal with some of these efforts in this chapter and the next. However, these early integrative works were clearly in the minority and were swamped by theoretical extremism.

Micro-macro and agency-structure integration appears to have been the pioneering movement that paved the way for a broad array of synthetic efforts. (We use the term *integration* when discussing micro-macro and agency-structure linkage, while *synthesis* is used to describe the effort to link various theories.) Integrative efforts set the stage for the much broader, dramatic change to be discussed in this and the next chapter—the emergence of a wide range of efforts at theoretical synthesis (Alexander and Colomy, 1990a; Fararo, 1989; Ritzer, 1990a, 1990b; Smelser, 1988). It is clear that sociological theory finally shows strong signs of moving away from decades of destructive political conflict among extremist theories of one stripe or another.

Once theorists had a sense of the advantages of synthesis from the work on micro-macro and agency-structure integration, the floodgates seemed to open and synthetic efforts began to flow from and in all directions. In some cases these attempts were direct results of efforts at micro-macro and agency-

597

structure integration as sociologists sought to synthesize a wide range of theories. In addition, once the movement toward theoretical synthesis began, a variety of other efforts at theoretical synthesis emerged. Thus, in the case of micro-macro integration, we now see not only micro-to-macro and macro-to-micro attempts at integration but also micro-to-micro (for example, symbolic interactionism and ethnomethodology [Boden, 1990b]) and macro-to-macro efforts (for example, conflict theory and structural functionalism [Alexander and Colomy, 1990a]) as well. And the movement toward synthesis does not stop with various micro-macro and agency-structure possibilities, since there now also seems to be a new openness to ideas from an array of other disciplines and nations, especially in such growth areas of sociological theory as feminist theory and postmodernism (See Chapter 17).

By the 1980s theorists had grown weary of the micro-macro and agency-structure splits, but as we move into the 1990s a more general dissatisfaction with the straitjacket of *any* theoretical label or concern with *any* specific aspect of social reality has emerged. The old, reified labels that have dominated sociological theory for many decades ("structural functionalism," "symbolic interactionism") seem increasingly less meaningful and important. As Alexander and Colomy put it: "The old debates have become stale and dry. We are in the midst of a sea change in sociological theory. Alignments are dissolving; new configurations are being born" (1990a:56). As a younger generation of sociological theorists takes center stage, older theoretical (for example, structural functionalism vs. symbolic interactionism) and conceptual (for example, agency-structure) boundaries and divisions are breaking down; some younger theorists are even taking an active role in trying to shatter those borders. Contemporary supporters are much less interested in defending traditional interpretations of theories and far more interested in reaching out to other theoretical traditions in an effort to develop new, more synthetic theories. In addition, more recent theories are less likely to focus on a single aspect of social analysis and more apt to be interested in the interrelationship of multiple domains. Instead of viewing theories and theoretical domains solely as important bases of operation, many sociological theorists are now coming to see that they can be blinders that are more often hindrances than aids in dealing with the social world. In contrast, in the past there was a strong need on the part of sociologists to identify with and to defend a particular theoretical perspective (and/or domain). The only thing that varied much in the past was the theory with which sociologists identified.

It was this reality that led to a call on my part (Ritzer, 1979, 1981a; see also Chapter 14 and the Appendix) for a more integrated sociological paradigm. While such a paradigm did not emerge immediately, and in fact has not emerged to this day, developments in the 1980s and the beginning of the 1990s auger well for the possibility of the development of such a paradigm (Ritzer, forthcoming b). The efforts at micro-macro and agency-structure linkage in the 1980s were just the beginning of this movement. It is the more general movement toward theoretical synthesis at virtually every theoretical juncture that shows real promise as the base for the development of an integrated sociological paradigm. It may not occur immediately, it may not add up to a new paradigm, and it may not be called an "integrated paradigm," but there are powerful developments afoot that indicate a major transformation of sociological theory in particular and sociology in general.

There is in these synthetic efforts the potential for a dramatic alteration of the landscape of sociological theory. For the last half decade sociology has been dominated by the theoretical schools delineated in Part Two as well as the ubiquitous conflict among them. It is possible that the movement toward integration and synthesis indicates that those theories are receding into history and will be replaced by newer, more synthetic perspectives. This is not to say that those theoretical schools are in imminent danger of demise. The commitments to them run too deep for them to disappear overnight. But it is to say that we may be witnessing the beginning of a trend that will see those theories increasingly become part of the history of sociology. The theoretical developments discussed in the previous two chapters, as well as in this one and the next, may be giving us a glimpse of the sociological theories of the future.

The main type of synthesis to be discussed in this chapter and the one to follow is the integration of various theories. Along the way, there will also be some discussion of the effort within theories or integrated sets of theories to deal with various domains of analysis. Rather than focusing on a given domain, more and more theories are examining the interrelationships among multiple domains.

While there is great interest in syntheses of all types, there seems to be a recognition that earlier efforts to create a single, overarching synthetic theory were misguided. Thus, the new move toward syntheses is very different from past efforts at creating a massive, overarching synthetic perspective. Examples of the latter are the grand theories of Karl Marx and Talcott Parsons. In fact, as we will see, a number of recent intellectual developments (for example, postmodernism, post-Marxism) involve an attack on the very idea of such a grand synthesis (Antonio, 1990; Kellner, 1990a; Lemert, 1990). Those now working toward theoretical syntheses see such overarching efforts as misguided and are working on much narrower synthetic attempts. These may not be as dramatic as efforts like those of Marx or Parsons, but they are likely to be more fruitful and productive. These theorists are working at integrating the "nuts and bolts" of specific theories, and it is these highly detailed efforts that are likely to be very useful to sociologists. Thus, we can think of the "new syntheses" rather than a "new synthesis." *This move toward theoretical syntheses is the overriding theme of the two concluding chapters of this book and of sociological theory in the 1990s.*

This new movement might take its marching orders from the comments of Robert Merton at the Thomas and Znaniecki conference on sociological theory:

> Pessimism results from the growing pains of a rapidly differentiating discipline in which the differentiation has multiplied so fast that we haven't the human resources

JEFFREY C. ALEXANDER: An Autobiographical Sketch

Since my earliest days as an intellectual I have been pre-occupied with the problems of social action and social order and with the possibilities of developing approaches to these problems that avoid the extremes of one-dimensional thought. I have always been convinced that tense dichotomies, while vital as ideological currents in a democratic society, can be overcome in the theoretical realm.

My theoretical concerns first took form during the late 1960s and early 1970s, when I participated in the student protest movements as an undergraduate at Harvard College and as a graduate student at University of California, Berkeley. New Left Marxism represented a sophisticated effort to overcome the economism of vulgar Marxism, as it tried to reinsert the actor into history. Because it described how material structures are interpenetrated with culture, personality, and everyday life, New Left Marxism—which for better or worse we largely taught ourselves—provided my first important training in the path to theoretical synthesis which has marked my intellectual career.

In the early 1970s, I became dissatisfied with New Left Marxism, in part for political and empirical reasons. The New Left's turn toward sectarianism and violence frightened and depressed me, whereas the Watergate crisis demonstrated America's capacity for self-criticism. I decided that capitalist democratic societies provided opportunities for inclusion, pluralism, and reform that could not be envisioned even within the New Left version of Marxian thought.

Yet there were also more abstract theoretical reasons for leaving the Marxian approach to synthesis behind. As I more fully engaged classical and contemporary theory, I realized that this synthesis was achieved more by hyphenating—psychoanalytic-Marxism, cultural-Marxism, phenomenological-Marxism—than by opening up the central categories of action and order. In fact, the neo-Marxist categories of consciousness, action, community, and culture were black boxes. This recognition led me to the traditions which supplied the theoretical resources upon which New Left Marxism had drawn. I was fortunate in this graduate student effort to be guided by Robert Bellah and Neil Smelser, whose ideas about culture, social structure, and sociological theory made an indelible impression upon me and continue to be intellectual resources today.

In *Theoretical Logic in Sociology* (1982–1983), I published the results of this effort. The idea for this multivolume work began germinating in 1972, after an extraordinary encounter with Talcott Parsons's masterpiece, *The Structure of Social Action,* allowed me to see my problems with Marxism in a new way. Later, under the supervision of Bellah, Smelser, and

to develop each sphere of inquiry in sufficient degree. The sociological enterprise requires a sense of tolerance rather than of battle, consolidating a mutual awareness of various theoretical orientations with a reasonable confidence that their mutual theoretical connections will be progressively defined.

(Merton, 1986:61)

Merton's confidence in the fact that sociology will see more theoretical synthesis was borne out by developments in the 1980s and especially those occurring at the present time in sociological theory.

Leo Lowenthal, I worked through classical and contemporary theory with this new framework in mind.

My ambition in *Theoretical Logic* was to show that Durkheim and Weber supplied extensive theories of the culture that Marx had neglected and that Weber actually developed the first real sociological synthesis. I concluded, however, that Durkheim ultimately moved in an idealistic direction and that Weber developed a mechanistic view of modern society. I suggested that Parsons's work should be seen as a masterly modern effort at synthesis rather than as theory in the functionalist mode. Yet Parsons, too, failed to pursue synthesis in a truly determined way, allowing his theory to become overly formal and normatively based.

In my work over the last decade I have tried to re-create the framework for synthesis which I take to be the unfulfilled promise of earlier work. In *Twenty Lectures: Sociological Theory since World War II* (1987), I argued that the divisions in post-Parsonsian sociology—between conflict and order theories, micro and macro approaches, structural and cultural views—were not fruitful. These groupings obscured basic social processes, like the continuing play of order and conflict and the dichotomized dimensions of society, that are always intertwined.

My response to this dead end has been to return to the original concerns of Parsons (Alexander, 1985b; Alexander and Colomy, 1990a) and to the earlier classics (Alexander, 1988).

Yet, in trying to push theory into a new, "post-Parsonsian" phase, I have also tried to go beyond classical and modern theory. My encounters with the powerful group of phenomenologists in my home department at UCLA, particularly those with Harold Garfinkel, were an important stimulus. In "Action and Its Environments" (1987), which I still regard as my most important piece of theoretical work, I laid out the framework for a new articulation of the micro-macro link.

I have also concentrated on developing a new cultural theory. An early reading of Clifford Geertz convinced me that traditional social-science approaches to culture are too limited. Since that time, my approach has been powerfully affected by semiotics, hermeneutics, and poststructuralist thought. Incorporating theories from outside of sociology, I have tried to theorize the manifold ways in which social structure is permeated by symbolic codes and meanings (see Alexander, 1988).

I believe this movement toward theoretical synthesis is being pushed forward by events in the world at large. In the postcommunist world, it seems important to develop models that help us understand our complex and inclusive, yet very fragile, democracies. I am presently at work on a theory of democracy that emphasizes the communal dimension which I call "civil society." I am also publishing a collection of essays which I have written criticizing the growing relativism in the human studies. I would like to believe, despite a great deal of evidence to the contrary, that progress is possible not only in society but in sociology as well. It is only through a multidimensional and synthetic view of society that such progress can be achieved.

Although the emphasis here is on the emergence of the movement toward theoretical syntheses on the threshold of the 1990s, it would be wrong, as was pointed out above, to conclude that synthetic efforts did not occur in the past. Indeed, every epoch in the history of sociological theory has had its share of such efforts. However, in previous eras they were much more likely to be isolated and aberrant cases swamped in a sea of extremism. Furthermore, they were likely to be met by hostile reactions from the supporters of one or the other of the theories that was the object of integration. A good example of this, to be discussed in detail later, was Peter Singlemann's (1972) essay, which sought to integrate exchange theory and symbolic interactionism. His effort did not go anywhere, in part because it was an isolated attempt and in part because it was met by hostile reactions from diehard supporters of exchange theory (Abbott, Brown, and Crosbie, 1973). What distinguishes the new set of synthetic developments is that they are widespread and are forming a coherent whole which appears to be coming to define the entire period. Hostile reactions to these efforts can be anticipated, but they are likely to be met by more effective responses from the wide variety of theorists interested in synthesis.

In spite of the promising synthetic developments, the same caution is in order here as was offered earlier in this book. The forces of theoretical extremism are alive and well in sociology (for example, Blau, 1987b) and stand ready to snuff out the movement toward syntheses with a renewed burst of theoretical extremism. Given the long history of theoretical extremism, and the relatively brief fling with integration and syntheses, sociologists interested in the latter directions, in spite of their growing numbers and influence, cannot afford to grow complacent.

Given this background, we turn to a discussion of synthetic work within and between most of the major theories discussed in Part Two of this book. While some early synthetic work will be discussed in many sections, the main concern will be with recent efforts at theoretical synthesis.

NEOFUNCTIONALISM

Much of the work taking place in structural functionalism today can be included under the heading "neofunctionalism." Under a barrage of criticisms, outlined in Chapter 7, structural functionalism declined in significance from the mid-1960s to the present day. However, by the mid-1980s, a major effort was under way to revive the theory under the heading "neofunctionalism." The term *neofunctionalism* was used to indicate continuity with structural functionalism but also to demonstrate that an effort was being made to extend structural functionalism and overcome its major difficulties. Jeffrey Alexander and Paul Colomy define *neofunctionalism* as "a self-critical strand of functional theory that seeks to broaden functionalism's intellectual scope while retaining its theoretical core" (1985:11). Thus, it seems clear that Alexander and Colomy see structural functionalism as overly narrow and that their goal is the creation of a more synthetic theory, which they prefer to label "neofunctionalism."[1]

Before we turn to a brief discussion of neofunctionalism, it should be noted that while structural functionalism in general, and Talcott Parsons's theories

---

[1] Turner and Maryanski (1988a) have challenged neofunctionalism by arguing that it is not really functional in its orientation, since it has abandoned many of the basic tenets of structural functionalism.

in particular, did become extremist, there was a strong synthetic core in the theory from its beginnings. On the one hand, throughout his intellectual life Parsons sought to integrate a wide range of theoretical inputs. On the other, he was interested in the interrelationship of the major domains of the social world, most notably the cultural, social, and personality systems. However, in the end, Parsons adopted a narrow structural-functionalist orientation and came to see the cultural system as determining the other systems. Thus, Parsons abandoned his synthetic orientation, and neofunctionalism can be viewed as an effort to recapture such an orientation.

Alexander (1985:10) has enumerated the problems associated with structural functionalism that neofunctionalism will need to surmount, including "anti-individualism," "antagonism to change," "conservatism," "idealism," and an "anti-empirical bias." Efforts are being made to overcome these problems programmatically (Alexander, 1985) and at more specific theoretical levels, for example Colomy's (1986; Alexander and Colomy, 1990b) attempt to refine differentiation theory.

Despite his enthusiasm for neofunctionalism, in the mid-1980s Alexander was forced to conclude that "neofunctionalism is a tendency rather than a developed theory" (1985:16). More recently, Colomy (1990b) has sought to consolidate the general theoretical position of neofunctionalism and to detail its contributions to cultural, political, and feminist sociology, as well as to the study of social change, the professions, and inequality. Only five years after Alexander's confession of the weakness of neofunctionalism, Colomy sees it as having made enormous strides:

> In the ensuing five years that tendency has crystallized into a self-conscious intellectual movement. It has generated significant advances at the level of general theory and played a leading part in pushing sociological metatheory in a synthetic direction . . . neofunctionalism is delivering on its promissory notes. Today, neofunctionalism is more than a promise; it has become a field of intense theoretical discourse and growing empirical investigation.
>
> (Colomy, 1990b: xxx)

While there is no question that neofunctionalism has made some strides in recent years, it is doubtful that it is quite as far advanced as Colomy would have us believe.

While it still may not be a developed theory, Alexander (1985; see also Colomy, 1990b) has outlined some of the basic orientations of neofunctionalism. First, neofunctionalism operates with a descriptive model of society that sees it as composed of elements which, in interaction with one another, form a pattern. This pattern allows the system to be differentiated from its environment. Parts of the system are "symbiotically connected," and their interaction is not determined by some overarching force. Thus, neofunctionalism rejects any monocausal determinism and is open-ended and pluralistic.

Second, Alexander argues that neofunctionalism devotes roughly equal attention to action and order. It thus avoids the tendency of structural functionalism to focus almost exclusively on the macro-level sources of order in social structures and culture and to give attention to more micro-level action patterns. Neofunctionalism also purports to have a broad sense of action, including not only rational but also expressive action.

Third, neofunctionalism retains the structural-functional interest in integration, *not* as an accomplished fact but rather as a social *possibility!* It recognizes that deviance and social control are realities within social systems. There is concern for equilibrium within neofunctionalism, but it is broader than the structural-functional concern encompassing both moving and partial equilibrium. There is a disinclination to see social systems as characterized by static equilibrium. *Equilibrium,* broadly defined, is seen as a reference point for functional analysis but not as descriptive of the lives of individuals in actual social systems.

Fourth, neofunctionalism accepts the traditional Parsonsian emphasis on personality, culture, and social system. In addition to being vital to social structure, the interpenetration of these systems also produces tension that is an ongoing source of both change and control.

Fifth, neofunctionalism focuses on social change in the processes of differentiation within the social, cultural, and personality systems. Thus, change is not productive of conformity and harmony but rather "individuation and institutional strains" (Alexander, 1985:10).

Finally, Alexander argues that neofunctionalism "implies the commitment to the independence of conceptualization and theorizing from other levels of sociological analysis" (1985:10).

Whereas Alexander has tried to delineate neofunctionalism in general, programmatic terms, Colomy (1986) has dealt more specifically with a revised structural-functional theory of change. He argues that the structural-functional theory of change ("differentiation theory") derived from Parsonsian theory has three basic weaknesses. First, it is highly abstract and lacks empirical and historical specificity. Second, it does not devote enough attention to concrete groups and social processes or to power and conflict. Third, it overemphasizes the integration produced by structural change.

As a result of these criticisms, the structural-functional theory of change has undergone several revisions. First, the original master trend (progressive differentiation) has been supplemented with an analysis of patterned deviations from that trend. For example, in addition to differentiation, societies have experienced *de-differentiation,* or "a type of structural change that rejects societal complexity and moves toward less differentiated levels of social organization" (Colomy, 1986:143). Such de-differentiation is likely to occur as a result of discontent with modernization. Also important is "unequal development" across various institutional spheres as well as "uneven differentiation" within a single institution. *Uneven differentiation* "refers to the varying rate and degree of differentiation of a single institution. . . . Uneven differentiation suggests, then, that the master trend of change proceeds at an uneven rate and degree across the distinct regions of a society" (Colomy, 1990c:122).

Second, revisionists have pushed differentiation theory toward more concern for how concrete groups affect change as well as how change is affected by such factors as power, conflict, and contingency (Colomy, 1990d). Various specific groups have been identified as instigators of change in the direction of greater differentiation as have groups that have stood in opposition to such change. This leads to a focus on the conflict between groups over the process of differentiation and the forms that a resolution of that conflict might take. Great historical and empirical detail is presented in these studies on the contending groups involved in the process of differentiation. This work also moves away from an overemphasis on integration and toward, in Parsonsian terms, "much more sustained attention to the potential contradictions and strains associated with differentiation between and within cultural, social, and personality systems" (Colomy, 1986:149). These efforts are, in Colomy's view, leading to a more comprehensive explanatory framework for analyzing differentiation.

Third, early differentiation theory focused on greater efficiency and reintegration as the main effects of the process of differentiation, but more recent work has outlined a much wider array of possible outcomes.

It might be argued that although the theory of differentiation has been widened, it also has lost its distinctive flavor with its newfound focus on conflict and competition. So much has been borrowed from other intellectual traditions that one wonders whether the kind of approach outlined above can, or should, be labeled "structural functionalism" or even "neofunctionalism."

Returning to neofunctionalism in general, Alexander and Colomy (1990a) have staked out a very ambitious claim for it. They do not see neofunctionalism as, in their terms, a mere modest "elaboration," or "revision," of structural functionalism but rather as a much more dramatic "reconstruction" of it in which differences with the founder (Parsons) are clearly acknowledged and explicit openings are made to other theorists and theories.[2] Efforts are made to integrate into neofunctionalism insights from the masters, such as Marx's work on material structures and Durkheim's on symbolism. In an attempt to overcome the idealist bias of Parsonsian structural functionalism, especially its emphasis on macro-subjective phenomena like culture, openings are urged to more materialist approaches. The structural-functional tendency to emphasize order is countered by a call for rapprochement with theories of social change. Most importantly, to compensate for the macro-level biases of traditional structural functionalism, efforts are made to integrate ideas from exchange theory, symbolic interactionism, pragmatism, phenomenology, and so on. In other words, and consistent with the basic theme of this chapter, Alexander and Colomy are endeavoring to synthesize structural functionalism with a number of other theoretical traditions. Such reconstruction can both

---

[2] This seems to be in accord, at least partially, with Turner and Maryanski's (1988a) claim that neofunctionalism has little in common with structural functionalism.

revive structural functionalism and provide the base for the development of a new theoretical tradition.

Alexander and Colomy recognize an important difference between neo-functionalism and structural functionalism:

> Earlier functional research was guided by . . . envisioning a single, all embracing conceptual scheme that tied areas of specialized research into a tightly wrought package. What neofunctionalist empirical work points to, by contrast, is a loosely organized package, one organized around a general logic and possessing a number of rather autonomous "proliferations" and "variations" at different levels and in different empirical domains.
>
> (Alexander and Colomy, 1990a:52)

The thoughts of Alexander and Colomy indicate that we are moving away from the Parsonsian tendency to see structural functionalism as a grand over-arching theory. Instead, they are offering a more limited, a more synthetic, but still a holistic theory.

CONFLICT THEORY

The major figure in the effort to develop a more synthetic and integrative conflict theory has been Randall Collins. In this section we will discuss an early (Collins, 1975) effort to develop a more integrative conflict theory as well as his more recent (Collins, 1990) ideas on such a theory.

Collins's *Conflict Sociology* (1975) was highly integrative because it moved in a much more micro-oriented direction than the macro-conflict theory of Dahrendorf and others. Collins himself says of his early work, "My own main contribution to conflict theory . . . was to add a micro level to these macro-level theories. I especially tried to show that stratification and organization are grounded in the interactions of everyday life" (1990:72). Later, "My own contributions to conflict theory came by way of building on the empirical[3] contributions of Goffman, Garfinkel, Sacks and Schegloff" (Collins, 1990:72–73). These theorists, of course, are associated with micro-level symbolic inter-actionism and ethnomethodology.

Collins (1975) made it clear from the beginning that his focus on conflict would not be ideological—that is, he did not begin with the political view that conflict is either good or bad. Rather, he claimed, he chose conflict as a focus on the realistic ground that conflict is a—perhaps *the*—central process in social life.

Unlike others who started, and stayed, at the societal level, Collins approached conflict from an individual point of view since his theoretical roots lie in phenomenology and ethnomethodology. Despite his preference for individual-level and small-scale theories, Collins was aware that "sociology

---

[3] Collins also stresses the point that conflict theory, more than other sociological theories, has been open to the integration of the findings of empirical research.

cannot be successful on the microlevel alone" (1975:11); conflict theory cannot do without the societal level of analysis. However, whereas most conflict theorists believed that social structures are external to, and coercive of, the actor, Collins saw social structures as inseparable from the actors who construct them and whose interaction patterns are their essence. Collins was inclined to see social structures as interaction patterns rather than external and coercive entities. In addition, whereas most conflict theorists saw the actor as constrained by external forces, Collins viewed the actor as constantly creating and re-creating social organization.

Collins saw Marxian theory as the "starting point" for conflict theory, but it is, in his view, laden with problems. For one thing, he saw it (like structural functionalism) as heavily ideological, which he wanted to avoid. For another, he tended to see Marx's orientation as reducible to an analysis of the economic domain, although this is an unwarranted criticism of Marx's theory. Actually, although Collins invoked Marx frequently, his conflict theory shows relatively little Marxian influence. It is far more influenced by Weber, Durkheim, and above all phenomenology and ethnomethodology.

Collins chose to focus on social stratification because it is an institution that touches so many features of life, including "wealth, politics, careers, families, clubs, communities, lifestyles" (1975:49). In Collins's view, the great theories of stratification are "failures." In this category he placed both the Marxian and the structural-functional theories. He criticized Marxian theory, for example, as "a monocausal explanation for a multicausal world" (Collins, 1975:49). He viewed Weber's theory as little more than an "antisystem" with which to view the features of the two great theories. Weber's work was of some use to Collins, but "the efforts of phenomenological sociology to ground all concepts in the observables of every life" (Collins, 1975:53) were the most important to him because his major focus in the study of social stratification was small-scale, not large-scale. In his view, social stratification, like all other social structures, is reducible to people in everyday life encountering each other in patterned ways.

Despite his ultimate commitment to a microsociology of stratification, Collins began (even though he had some reservations about them) with the large-scale theories of Marx and Weber as underpinnings for his own work. He started with Marxian principles, arguing that they, "with certain modifications, provide the basis for a conflict theory of stratification" (Collins, 1975:58).

First, Collins contended that it was Marx's view that the material conditions involved in earning a living in modern society are the major determinants of a person's lifestyle. The basis of earning a living for Marx is a person's relationship to private property. Those who own or control property are able to earn their livings in a much more satisfactory way than those who do not and who must sell their labor time to gain access to the means of production.

Second, from a Marxian perspective, material conditions affect not only how individuals earn a living but also the nature of social groups in the different social classes. The dominant social class is better able to develop more coherent social groups, tied together by intricate communication networks, than is the subordinate social class.

Finally, Collins argued that Marx also pointed out the vast differences among the social classes in their access to, and control over, the cultural system. That is, the upper social classes are able to develop highly articulated symbol and ideological systems, systems that they are often able to impose on the lower social classes. The lower social classes have less developed symbol systems, many of which are likely to have been imposed on them by those in power.

Collins viewed Weber as working within and developing further Marx's theory of stratification. For one thing, Weber was said to have recognized the existence of different forms of conflict that lead to a multifaceted stratification system (for example, class, status, and power). For another, Weber developed the theory of organizations to a high degree, which Collins saw as still another arena of conflict of interest. Weber was also important to Collins for his emphasis on the state as the agency that controls the means of violence, which shifted attention from conflict over the economy (means of production) to conflict over the state. Finally, Weber was recognized by Collins for his understanding of the social arena of emotional products, in particularly religion. Conflict clearly can occur in this arena, and these emotional products, like other products, can be used as weapons in social conflict.

With this background, Collins turned to his own conflict approach to stratification, which has more in common with phenomenological and ethnomethodological theories than with Marxian or Weberian theory. Collins opened with several assumptions. People are seen as inherently sociable but also as particularly conflict-prone in their social relations. Conflict is likely to occur in social relations because "violent coercion" can always be used by one person or many people in an interaction setting. Collins believed that people seek to maximize their "subjective status" and that their ability to do this depends on their resources as well as the resources of those with whom they are dealing. He saw people as self-interested; thus, clashes are possible because sets of interests may be inherently antagonistic.

This conflict approach to stratification can be reduced to three basic principles. First, Collins believed that people live in self-constructed subjective worlds. Second, other people may have the power to affect, or even control, an individual's subjective experience. Third, other people frequently try to control the individual, who opposes them. The result is likely to be interpersonal conflict.

On the basis of this, Collins developed five principles of conflict analysis that he applied to social stratification, although he believed that they could be applied to any area of social life. First, Collins believed that conflict theory must focus on real life rather than abstract formulations. This seems to reflect a preference for a Marxian-style material analysis over the abstraction of structural functionalism. Collins urged us to think of people as animals whose actions, motivated by self-interest, can be seen as maneuvers to obtain various advantages so that they can achieve satisfaction and avoid dissatisfaction. However, unlike exchange and rational choice theorists, Collins did not see people as wholly rational. He recognized that they are vulnerable to emotional appeals in their efforts to find satisfaction.

Second, Collins believed that a conflict theory of stratification must examine the material arrangements that affect interaction. Although the actors are likely to be affected by such material factors as "the physical places, the modes of communication, the supply of weapons, devices for staging one's public impression, tools, goods" (Collins, 1975:60), not all actors are affected in the same way. A major variable is the resources that the different actors possess. Actors with considerable material resources can resist or even modify these material constraints, whereas those with fewer resources are more likely to have their thoughts and actions determined by their material setting.

Third, Collins argued that in a situation of inequality, those groups that control resources are likely to try to exploit those that lack resources. He was careful to point out that this need not involve conscious calculation on the part of those who gain from the situation; rather, they are merely pursuing what they perceive to be their best interests. In the process they may be taking advantage of those who lack resources.

Fourth, Collins wanted the conflict theorist to look at such cultural phenomena as beliefs and ideals from the point of view of interests, resources, and power. It is likely that those groups with resources and, therefore, power can impose their idea systems on the entire society; those without resources have an idea system imposed on them.

Finally, Collins made a firm commitment to the scientific study of stratification and every other aspect of the social world. This led him to prescribe several things. Sociologists should not simply theorize about stratification but should study it empirically, if possible in a comparative way. Hypotheses should be formulated and tested empirically through comparative studies. Last, the sociologist should look for the causes of social phenomena, particularly the multiple causes of any form of social behavior.

This kind of scientific commitment led Collins to develop a wide array of propositions about the relationship between conflict and various specific aspects of social life. We can present only a few here, but they should allow readers to get a feel for Collins's type of conflict sociology.

> **1.0** Experiences of giving and taking orders are the main determinants of individual outlooks and behaviors.
> **1.1** The more one gives orders, the more he is proud, self-assured, formal, and identifies with organizational ideals in whose name he justifies the orders.
> **1.2** The more one takes orders, the more he is subservient, fatalistic, alienated from organizational ideals, externally conforming, distrustful of others, concerned with extrinsic rewards, and amoral.
>
> (Collins, 1975:73–74)

Among other things, these propositions all reflect Collins's commitment to the *scientific study* of the small-scale social manifestations of social conflicts.

Collins was not content to deal with conflict within the stratification system but sought to extend it to various other social domains. For example, he extended his analysis of stratification to relationships between the sexes as well as among age groups. He took the view that the family is an arena of sexual conflict, in which males have been the victors, with the result that women are dominated by men and subject to various kinds of unequal treatment. Similarly, he saw the relationship between age groups—in particular, between young and old—as one of conflict. This contrasts with the view of structural functionalists, who saw harmonious socialization and internalization in this relationship. Collins looked at the resources possessed by the various age groups. Adults have a variety of resources, including experience, size, strength, and the ability to satisfy the physical needs of the young. In contrast, one of the few resources young children have is physical attractiveness. This means that young children are likely to be dominated by adults. However, as children mature, they acquire more resources and are better able to resist, with the result of increasing social conflict between the generations.

Collins also looked at formal organizations from a conflict perspective. He saw them as networks of interpersonal influences and also as the arenas in which conflicting interests are played out. In short, "Organizations are arenas for struggle" (Collins, 1975:295). Collins again couched his argument in propositional form. For example, he argued that "coercion leads to strong efforts to avoid being coerced" (Collins, 1975:298). In contrast, he felt that the offering of rewards is a preferable strategy: "Control by material rewards leads to compliance to the extent that rewards are directly linked to the desired behavior" (Collins, 1975:299). These propositions and others all point to Collins's commitment to a scientific, largely micro-oriented study of conflict.

In sum, Collins is, like Dahrendorf (see Chapter 7), not a true exponent of Marxian conflict theory, although for different reasons. Although he used Marx as a starting point, Weber, Durkheim, and particularly ethnomethodology were much more important influences on his work. Collins's small-scale orientation is a helpful beginning toward the development of a more integrated conflict theory. However, despite his stated intentions of integrating large- and small-scale theory, he did not accomplish the task fully.

In his later work, Collins takes the general view that conflict theory is preferable to most other theories because of its willingness to be synthetic: "Conflict theory . . . engages freely in what may be called intellectual piracy: it is quite willing to incorporate . . . elements . . . of micro-sociologies" (1990:72). While little overt conflict theorizing was done between 1975 and 1990, Collins believes that conflict theory, in spite of the appearances, had not been moribund for a decade and a half but had been developing quietly under a variety of different guises in a number of areas within sociology.

For one thing, Collins believes that conflict theory has become the dominant perspective within a number of subareas in sociology. Although he does not go into it in detail, one example of what he has in mind is the emergence of the "power approach" as the dominant orientation in the sociological study of the professions (Ritzer and Walczak, 1986). An integrative effort worth doing, but only implied by Collins, would be a review of the array of specific conflict perspectives that have developed within various subareas in sociology, with the objective of putting this disparate body of work together, combining it with extant conflict theory, and thereby greatly enhancing the broader conflict theory of society.

Collins himself seeks integration in two other directions. For one thing, he sees a conflict approach as lying at the heart of much historical-comparative research, especially the work of Michael Mann (1986). Thus, conflict theory stands to be enriched by the integration of a wide range of insights that can be derived from historical-comparative research. Furthermore, Collins sees Mann as utilizing a kind of network theory, and this leads to an interest in synthesizing Mann's approach with mainstream work in network theory. More generally, there is the possibility of integrating network and conflict theory. In fact, as we will see, network theory plays a prominent role in contemporary efforts at synthesis, since there are those from other theoretical perspectives, especially exchange theory, who see possibilities of integration with it. Curiously, Collins does not address the possibility of integration with his own theory of interaction ritual chains (see Chapter 14). This is surprising, since that theory's micro-level insights would mesh well with the traditional macro-level concerns of conflict theory. Perhaps Collins did not suggest such an integration because his own variety of conflict theory is itself highly microscopic and already encompasses interaction ritual chains.

More generally, Collins defines conflict theory in such a sweeping way that it seems open to insights from all theories and seems capable of covering all levels of social reality. Specifically, Collins seeks to differentiate between narrow *theories of conflict* (for example, those of Simmel and Coser) and *conflict theory*, which he defines as "a theory about the organization of society, the behavior of people and groups, it explains why structures take the forms that they do . . . and how and what kinds of changes occur. . . . Conflict theory is a general approach to the entire field of sociology" (1990:70). Thus, Collins is after more than a series of specific syntheses; he is interested in pushing conflict theory in the direction of a more holistic perspective. While such holistic perspectives are welcome as an antidote to excessive pluralism, one must be wary of the theoretical imperialism implied by this and the similar tone that pervades Collins's essay.

NEO-MARXIAN THEORY

Marxian theory has always had an integrative and synthetic thrust. Marx sought to deal with the full range of social phenomena, especially the dialectical relationship between the micro-level agent in the form of the individual proletarian and the macro-level structure of capitalist society. In addition, Marx sought to synthesize a wide range of theories (for example, Hegelian, neo-Hegelian, utopian socialism, political economy) in his own theory of capitalist society. For its part, there are so many different varieties of neo-Marxian theory that virtually all theories and all domains of the social world have been integrated into them at one time or another. Just to take one example, Jurgen Habermas, as we saw in Chapters 8 and 15, has dealt with the full range of social phenomena and integrated into his own theories the insights of a wide array of social theorists. Nevertheless, there are strands of neo-Marxian theory (for example, economic determinism, structural Marxism) that are limited in scope and draw on a very narrow range of theoretical ideas.

Moreover, much of Marxian and neo-Marxian theory has been oriented to the development of a grand synthesis rather than the narrow syntheses that characterize sociological theory in the 1990s. For many years neo-Marxian theory was dominated by a "grand theory," one of Marx's totalistic perspectives, his materialist emancipatory modernism (Antonio, 1990). In this, Marx offered a grand view of society as moving toward its teleological end (communism), impelled by the collective subject, the proletariat. For a time, this view shaped (and distorted) Marxian theory, but later an array of neo-Marxian theorists sought in a variety of ways to distance themselves from this grand narrative. In some cases, however, they merely replaced Marx's materialist emancipatory modernism with other equally problematic grand narratives. More recently, an array of neo-Marxian theories have emerged. While they have served to overcome the excesses of Marx's materialist emancipatory modernism, they threaten to offer an excessively pluralistic image of society. Efforts to deal with this excessive pluralism would involve syntheses of a variety of these neo-Marxian theories.

This development of an array of theoretical syntheses, while quite promising, threatens to cause us to lose sight of any possibility of holistic thinking. This would be unfortunate because the fact that it may be impossible to develop a grand theory does not mean that all forms of holistic thinking are useless and undesirable. There is a need for holistic thinking that does not imply that it offers the ultimate answer to all theoretical issues. Thus, Antonio suggests that neo-Marxists build on Marx's "historical holism" rather than his emancipatory modernism. Historical holism is a global theory of capitalism without the excesses (for example, claims to provide all answers to all questions, teleology) of materialist emancipatory modernism. Importantly, Antonio argues that this new holistic perspective not only would integrate ideas from an array of neo-Marxist perspectives but should also involve "theoretical infusions from non-Marxist approaches" (for example, Habermas's use of Weberian and pragmatist ideas) which will "presage a richer historical holism" (1990:109). Similarly, while supporting the postmodernist (see below) attack on grand theory, in his own ideas on "techno-capitalism," Kellner (1990a) seeks to develop a holistic approach that rescues viable aspects of Marxian theory and synthesizes them with the ideas of the postmodernists (see Chapter 17). In this sense Kellner, like Antonio, comes down on the side of the need for a new holistic perspective and, at the same time, accepts the need for a wide range of synthetic efforts. Overall, while we are discussing throughout this chapter the rush toward an array of syntheses, it would be disastrous to lose all traces of holistic theory in sociology.

We will have much more to say about the issue of syntheses in Marxian theory at the end of the next chapter, where we discuss a variety of post-Marxist theories.

SYMBOLIC INTERACTIONISM

It may have been out of self-defense, but symbolic interactionism, as it evolved primarily under the stewardship of Herbert Blumer, moved in a decidedly micro direction. This stood in contrast to at least the implications of the more integrative title of George Herbert Mead's *Mind, Self and Society.* However, symbolic interactionism has entered a new, "post-Blumerian" age (Fine, 1990). On one front, there are efforts to reconstruct Blumerian theory and argue that it always had an interest in macro-level phenomena (see below, as well as the special issue of *Symbolic Interaction* [1988], devoted to Herbert Blumer). More importantly, there are ongoing efforts to synthesize symbolic interactionism with ideas derived from a number of other theories. This "new" symbolic interactionism has, in Fine's terms, "cobbled a new theory from the shards of other theoretical approaches" (1990:136–137). The new symbolic interactionists

> are almost promiscuous in their willingness to thrash in any theoretical bedding they can find: there are Durkheimian . . . Simmelian . . . Weberian . . . Marxist . . . postmodernist . . . phenomenological . . . radical feminist . . . semiotic . . . and behaviorist interactionists.
>
> (Fine, 1990:120)

Symbolic interactionism now combines indigenous insights with those from other micro theories like exchange theory, ethnomethodology and conversation analysis, and phenomenology. More surprising is the integration of ideas from macro theories (for example, structural functionalism) as well as of the ideas of macro theorists like Parsons, Durkheim, Simmel, Weber, and Marx. Symbolic interactionists are also endeavoring to integrate insights from post-structuralism, postmodernism, and radical feminism. Post-Blumerian symbolic interactionism is becoming a much more synthetic perspective than it was in Blumer's heyday.

Redefining Mead and Blumer

In addition to ongoing synthetic work in symbolic interactionism there is an effort to redefine the major thinkers associated with it, especially Mead and Blumer, as having more integrative orientations than is usually thought to be the case.

As we saw in Chapter 9, despite his lack of interest in macro-level phenomena, there is much in Mead's ideas on mind, self, and society that suggests an integrated sociological theory. In this context, it is useful to look at John Baldwin's (1986) analysis of Mead. Baldwin notes the fragmentation of the social sciences in general, and sociological theory in particular, and argues that such fragmentation is serving to prevent the development of a general "unifying" sociological theory and, more generally, a science of the social world. He makes the case for the need for such a theory and for Meadian theory as a model for that theory:

> Perhaps it is time for us to try to organize our fragmented discipline around a theory that has the potential to unify the field. Because Mead succeeded more than most social theorists have at creating a nondualistic theory that unifies data on mind and body, micro and macro society, along with other related factors, his work deserves attention as a possible foundation for building a unified social science.
>
> (Baldwin, 1986:156)

While Baldwin is proposing the kind of grand synthesis that is being rejected in this chapter, we can welcome his effort to see a more integrative approach in Meadian theory.

Baldwin makes the case for Mead on several grounds. First, he argues that Mead's theoretical system covers the full range of social phenomena from micro to macro levels—"physiology, social psychology, language, cognition, behavior, society, social change and ecology" (Baldwin, 1986:156). Along these lines, Baldwin offers a model of Mead's theoretical orientation, as shown in Figure 16.1.

Second, Baldwin argues that not only does Mead have an integrated, micro-macro, sense of the social world but he also offers "a flexible system for interweaving contributions from all schools of contemporary social science (1986:156). Thus, Mead's theory provides a base not only for micro-macro

FIGURE 16.1   An Overview of the Components of Mead's Theoretical System

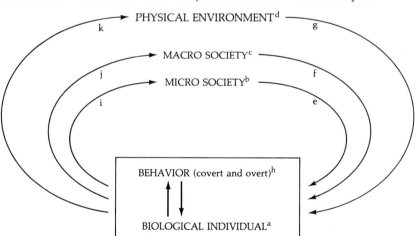

integration but for theoretical synthesis as well. Finally, Baldwin contends that Mead's "commitment to scientific methods helps ensure that data and theories on all components of the social system can be integrated in a balanced manner, with their relative importance established in an empirically defensible manner" (1986:156).

As we turn to the effort to redefine Herbert Blumer's theoretical approach, it should be recalled that in Chapter 9 we depicted him as offering a very limited conception of macro and objective phenomena. Recently, however, several symbolic interactionists have sought to demonstrate that Blumer had a stronger sense of macro structures and objectivity and that this, along with the obvious strength of his theory at the micro levels and on subjectivity, gives his theory an integrative orientation (Maines, 1989a, 1989b; Maines and Morrione, 1990; Morrione, 1988).

Maines (1989a) has attacked three "myths" associated with Blumer's theory—that it is unscientific, subjectivistic, and astructural. It is the latter two myths that concern us here because they go to the heart of creating a more integrated conception of Blumer's ideas. That is, if Blumer can be shown to offer a more objectivist position to supplement his clear interest in subjectivity *and* a macro sense to complement his obvious micro orientation, he could then be seen as offering a fully integrated sociological theory. Indeed, such a micro-macro, objective-subjective conception would be in full accord with my sense of an integrated sociological paradigm.

On the issue of subjectivity, Maines argues that Blumer is merely adopting a position that is in line with contemporary thinking on human agency (see Chapter 15). Agency implies a concern with *both* the subjective manner in which people construct social reality and the resulting objective action, interaction, and their patterns. Furthermore, Maines sees Blumer adopting the position of some, but *not* all, agency theorists that collective entities such as "organizations, institutions, social movements, social classes, nations, interest groups, or races" act and are characterized by subjective processes (1989a:389).

In fleshing out Blumer's thoughts on macro-level phenomena, Maines discusses three implications of Blumer's conception of joint action (see Chapter 9). First, joint action involves social organization, since action occurs in recurrent patterns. Second, actions tend to be interconnected; that is, they tend to be institutionalized. Finally, social action has continuity; that is, it has history. A concern with organization, institutionalization, and history would clearly associate Blumer with a macro orientation, and Maines proceeds to demonstrate Blumer's macro concerns in a series of substantive areas (for example, race relations and industrialization).

More recently, Maines and Morrione have posthumously published Blumer's book entitled *Industrialization as an Agent of Social Change*. The book was originally written in the early 1960s, but it was never published because Blumer was not satisfied with it. The publication of this book points to Blumer's macro and objectivistic side. The industrialization process clearly occurs at the macro level, and it involves such objective structures as production systems based on mechanization, procurement, and distribution systems and a service structure (Maines and Morrione, 1990:xviii). Blumer may not be fully satisfactory as an integrative theorist, but recent interpretations of his work demonstrate that his thinking is more in line with contemporary developments than is often believed. It is the need to reinterpret Blumer (and Mead) in this way that demonstrates the power of the movement toward integrative and synthetic sociological theory.

As we pointed out in the beginning of this chapter, the move within symbolic interactionism toward integration and synthesis is not new, although it is now far broader in scope and far more institutionalized than it was in the past. In this context, it is instructive to look at Peter Singelmann's effort, mentioned earlier in this chapter, to synthesize symbolic interactionism and exchange theory and to examine the hostile reaction that it engendered. We will also look at Sheldon Stryker's (1980) early effort to move symbolic interactionism in a more integrative direction. Stryker's work can be seen as anticipating much of the later integrative work (and interpretations) in symbolic interactionism discussed above.

Integrating Symbolic Interactionism and Exchange Theory

Peter Singelmann's (1972) effort to integrate the main concepts of symbolic interaction and exchange theory began with Mead's categories of mind, self, and society.

Mind Singelmann stated that to the symbolic interactionist, the concept of mind "reflects the human capacity to *conceive* what the organism *perceives*, define situations, evaluate phenomena, convert gestures into symbols, and exhibit pragmatic and goal-directed behavior" (1972:416). According to Singelmann, the actor is an active agent to both the symbolic interactionist and the exchange theorist. He argued that the symbolic-interactionist concept of the mind has been "explicitly recognized" by exchange theorists. As evidence that such a concept of mind exists among exchange theorists, he cited discussions by exchange theorists of such things as individuals' awareness of alternatives, aspirations, and expectations. He also detected evidence of mental processes in Homans's concept of distributive justice. One must subjectively evalute different rewards in order to determine whether the law of distributive justice has been violated.

On the basis of this kind of analysis, Singelmann concluded, "Current exchange theory has thus gone beyond the purely 'behavioristic' approach of many reinforcement theories by recognizing, more or less explicitly, that the human mind mediates the relationships between stimuli and behavioral responses" (1972:417). Thus, a reward is not a reward in itself but must be *defined* as a reward to operate as a reinforcer. In Singelmann's view, this process of definition brings exchange theory in line with the symbolic interactionist position.

Most behaviorists would agree with Singelmann that there is nothing inherent in an object that makes it a reward. A reward may be defined as a reinforcer if it in fact affects behavior. However, Singelmann aside, behaviorists, though aware of the process of social definition, are not concerned with it. They are concerned only with the behavioral manifestations of the definition process, not the process itself.

Self   Singelmann pointed out that symbolic interactionists are concerned with the idea of self both in the sense used by Mead, "as process in which actors reflect on themselves as objects" (1972:417), and in the sense of the self-concept held by actors. Singelmann suggested that at some level exchange theorists understand that an individual has a self and a self-concept and that these ideas are perfectly appropriate to exchange theory. For exchange relationships to develop and persist, each party must be able to take the role of the other as well as the generalized other, in order to determine what rewards they should offer and what rewards they are likely to receive. Although this is a useful insight, many exchange theorists are not likely to find it relevant to their concerns. They are not concerned with the process by which individuals decide what rewards they will offer but only with the exchange relationship itself. Pure exchange theorists would want to know about behavior and not about such concepts as self, generalized other, and taking the role of the other. These are for a philosopher to dabble in, not something of concern to the "scientist" who identifies with the behaviorist paradigm. Thus, for example, Skinner defined the *self* as simply "a repertoire of behavior" (1971:189), a definition very different from that of symbolic interactionists.

Society   Singelmann argued that both symbolic interactionists and exchange theorists focus on the micro-social level in analyzing social structure. In addition, he saw two other points of convergence. First, he argued that symbolic interactionists focus on how people fit their interaction patterns together, whereas Homans is concerned with the stabilization of relationships on the basis of the most profitable exchanges. Both imply a constant construction and reconstruction of interaction patterns. Second, Singelmann argued that "exchange may be conceptualized as symbolic interaction" (1972:419), meaning that exchange entails a communication of symbols. This is a clue to Singelmann's implicit argument that exchange theory can be subsumed under symbolic interactionism. Exchange theory is transformed into something very different by Singelmann, but symbolic interactionism remains unscathed.

Interestingly, Singelmann is weakest on the societal level of integration, which reflects his orientation toward symbolic interactionism. To him society seems to be little more than patterned interaction and symbols. The real strength of Singelmann's analysis is in his discussion of mind and self and how the insights of symbolic interactionism and exchange theory are mutually reinforcing on those issues. In his conclusion, Singelmann attempted a theoretical synthesis involving four basic points:

1 In exchange, actors construct normative and existential definitions of themselves, others, actions, goals, and assessments of "fairness."
2 These definitions are not only subjectively constructed but to a large extent socially shared and thus constitute a constraint external to the individual actors.
3 In exchange, the hedonistic strivings of actors are limited and qualified by the nature of the subjective and socially shared definitions of the objective world which includes the self and others.
4 In exchange, actors will change their behaviors or definitions when:
   a changes in the objective world render existing behaviors and definitions problematic,
   b changes in some of their subjective definitions render other definitions or existing objective conditions and behaviors problematic.

(Singelmann, 1972:422)

While Singelmann is seeking reconciliation, the amount of attention devoted to social definitions in the preceding list indicates that his real sympathies lie with symbolic interactionism.

Reflective of Singelmann's biases as well as the extremist times in which his essay was written, Singelmann's integrative effort met with a frosty reaction. For example, Abbott, Brown, and Crosbie (1973) argued that exchange theory and symbolic interactionism have entirely different premises and that efforts to integrate them are futile. They felt that such an effort would only serve to destroy the integrity of both perspectives. As supporters of exchange theory, they were particularly upset by what they considered to be Singelmann's distortion of exchange theory. They were resistant to what they saw as Singelmann's effort to destroy a pure exchange-theory perspective in the pursuit of theoretical synthesis.

Toward a More Integrative Symbolic Interactionism

We close this section with a discussion of the work of Sheldon Stryker (1980) and his effort to develop a symbolic interactionism that is able to deal more adequately with macro-level social phenomena. (For an argument against such a project, see Rock, 1979.)

Stryker enunciated an integrative goal for symbolic interactionism: "A satisfactory theoretical framework must bridge social structure and person, must be able to move from the level of the person to that of large-scale social structure and back again. . . . There must exist a conceptual framework facilitating movement across the levels of organization and person" (1980:53). (Perinbanayagam articulated a similar goal for symbolic interactionism: "the existence of structure *and* meaning, self *and* others, the dialectic of being and emergence, leading to a dialectical interactionism" [1985:xv].) Stryker embedded his orientation in Meadian symbolic interactionism but sought to extend it to the societal level, primarily through the use of role theory:

This version begins with Mead, but goes beyond Mead to introduce role theoretic concepts and principles, in order to adequately deal with the reciprocal impact of social person and social structure. The nexus in this reciprocal impact is interaction.

> It is in the context of the social process—the ongoing patterns of interaction joining individual actors—that social structure operates to constrain the conceptions of self, the definitions of the situation, and the behavioral opportunities and repertoires that bound and guide the interaction that takes place.
>
> (Stryker, 1980:52)

Stryker developed his orientation in terms of eight general principles:

1 Human action is dependent on a named and classified world in which the names and classifications have meaning for actors. People learn through interaction with others how to classify the world as well as how they are expected to behave toward it.

2 Among the most important things that people learn are the symbols used to designate social *positions*. A critical point here is that Stryker conceived of positions in structural terms: "the relatively stable, morphological components of social structure" (Stryker, 1980:54). Stryker also accorded *roles* central importance, conceiving of them as the shared behavioral expectations attached to social positions.

3 Stryker also recognized the importance of larger social structures, although he was inclined, like other symbolic interactionists, to conceive of them in terms of organized patterns of behavior. In addition, his discussion treated social structure as simply the "framework" within which people act. Within these structures, people name one another, that is, recognize one another as occupants of positions. In so doing, people evoke reciprocal expectations of what each is expected to do.

4 Furthermore, in acting in this context, people not only name each other but also name themselves; that is, they apply positional designations to themselves. These self-designations become part of the self, internalized expectations with regard to their own behavior.

5 When interacting, people define the situation by applying names to it, to other participants, to themselves, and to particular features of the situation. These definitions are then used by the actors to organize their behavior.

6 Social behavior is not determined by social meanings, although it is constrained by them. Stryker is a strong believer in the idea of *role making*. People do not simply take roles; rather, they take an active, creative orientation to their roles.

7 Social structures also serve to limit the degree to which roles are "made" rather than just "taken." Some structures permit more creativity than others.

8 The possibilities of role making make various social changes possible. Changes can occur in social definitions—in names, symbols, and classifications—and in the possibilities for interaction. The cumulative effect of these changes can be alterations in the larger social structures.

Although Stryker offered a useful beginning toward a more adequate symbolic interactionism, his work has a number of limitations. The most notable is that he said little about larger social structures per se. Stryker saw the need to integrate these larger structures in his work, but he recognized that a "full-fledged development of how such incorporation could proceed is beyond the scope of the present work" (1980:69). Stryker saw only a limited future role for large-scale structural variables in symbolic interactionism. He hoped ultimately to incorporate such structural factors as class, status, and power as variables constraining interaction, but he was disinclined to see symbolic interactionism deal with the interrelationships among these structural variables. Presumably, this kind of issue is to be left to other theories that focus more on large-scale social phenomena.

Thus, symbolic interactionism, like most other sociological theories, was not without its early efforts at synthesis (Singelmann) and integration (Stryker).

PHENOMENOLOGY AND ETHNOMETHODOLOGY

Phenomenological sociology, especially in the perspectives of Schutz and Berger and Luckmann, is inherently integrative and synthetic. Schutz sought to analyze the relationship between micro subjectivity and macro subjectivity. Berger and Luckmann's integrative perspective is reflected in their dialectical model of the relationship between people and society. However, what limits both approaches is that they operate purely within the realm of subjectivity and have little to offer on micro and macro objectivity. Also worth noting is the synthetic attempt by Berger and Luckmann to draw on a wide array of theoretical perspectives. However, that synthesis is limited to a utilization of purely subjective ideas and ignores the contributions of those theories to our understanding of objectivity.

Even ethnomethodology, one of the most determinedly micro-extremist perspectives in sociological theory, has shown some signs of openness to synthesis and integration. For example, ethnomethodology seems to be expanding into domains that appear more in line with mainstream sociology. A good example is Heritage and Greatbatch's (1986) analysis of British political speeches and the methods used to generate applause from audiences. The typology of devices developed by them seems little different from the kinds of typologies employed by various other types of sociological theorists.

However, ethnomethodology remains embattled and insecure and thus, in some ways, seems to run counter to the trend toward theoretical synthesis. Seemingly rejecting the idea of synthesis, Garfinkel sees ethnomethodology as an "incommensurably alternate sociology" (1988:108). Boden (1990a) finds it necessary to make a strong, albeit somewhat self-conscious, case *for* ethnomethodology and conversation analysis. It is certainly true, as Boden suggests, that ethnomethodology has widened and deepened its support in sociology. However, one wonders whether it, or any sociological theory for that matter, is, as Boden contends, "here to stay." In any case, such an argument contradicts the basic theme of this chapter (and the next), which is that theoretical boundaries are weakening and new synthetic perspectives are emerging. It may be that ethnomethodology is still too new and too insecure to consider an erosion of its boundaries.

Nevertheless, much of Boden's (1990a) essay deals with synthetic efforts *within* ethnomethodology, especially in terms of dealing with such integrative issues as the relationship between agency and structure, the embeddedness of action, and fleeting events within the course of history. Boden also deals with the extent to which an array of European and American theorists have begun to integrate ethnomethodology and conversation analysis into their orientations. Unfortunately, what is lacking is a discussion of the degree to which ethnomethodologists are integrating the ideas of other sociological theories into their perspective. Ethnomethodologists seem quite willing to have other theorists integrate ethnomethodological perspectives, but they seem far less eager to reciprocate.

Boden (1990b) has also contributed to the slight movement within ethnomethodology toward synthesis in her discussion of its linkages to symbolic interactionism. Conversation analysis is, as we saw in Chapter 10, focally concerned with talk. As Boden puts it, "Talk is the stuff, the very sinew, of social interaction. The mundane of momentous talk of people in their everyday work is what conversation analysis studies." (1990b:244). While symbolic interactionists are interested in talk, their main concern is with action and interaction. Boden (1990b:244) provides the linkage here by defining *talk* as "language-in-action" and arguing that "it is here, as thought becomes action through language, that conversation analysis meets symbolic interaction (and vice versa)." She goes further to note that the social world needs "to be studied in situ, and the combined creative forces of symbolic interaction and conversation analysis can expose just that momentary yet recurrent and patterned quality of the world" (Boden, 1990b:246).

To further solidify the linkage between symbolic interactionism and conversation analysis, Boden suggests a redefinition of conversation analysis. She argues that the term *conversation analysis* is, in fact, too narrow because researchers are interested, as we saw in Chapter 10, in far more than the exchange of words. She suggests, instead, that such work be called "interactional analysis" because researchers are interested in "everything in the interaction, from a quiet in-breath to the entire spatial and temporal organization of the scene" (Boden, 1990b:248). By using the term *interactional analysis* to describe the interest in both verbal and nonverbal phenomena, Boden clearly aligns conversation analysis with symbolic interactionism.

As we saw in Chapter 9, Mead was interested in mental processes but saw them as forms of action and interaction. This is part of Mead's effort to extend behaviorism into the mind. Boden contends that "the symbolic interaction that is *thought*, in Mead's sense, becomes quite concretely available, both for analysis and further theorizing, through the fine-grained activities of talk in interaction" (1990b:253). Thus, in studying talk, conversation analysts (and symbolic interactionists) are shedding light on mental processes. Similarly, Boden seeks to link conversation analysis with Blumer's interest in "joint action." Her point here is that conversation is joint action not just in the sense that it is negotiated locally but also in the sense that "talk and tasks are mutually elaborative in a turn-by-turn manner" (Boden, 1990b:255).

In her conclusion, Boden offers some broad linkages between conversation analysis and symbolic interactionism: "Symbolic interactionists and conversation analysts travel together more broadly along a route that examines the intertwining of meaning, shared symbols, joint action, and social order" (1990b:265). Furthermore, she explicitly links the two theories to the integrative concerns discussed in the previous chapter: "Thus, at the larger intersection of *agency and structure*, sociologists generally may expect to find both symbolic interactionists and conversation analysts" (Boden, 1990b:265; italics added).

Boden's effort to tie the relationship between conversation analysis and symbolic interactionism to agency and structure brings us to Hilbert's (1990) work on the relationship between ethnomethodology and the micro-macro order. Hilbert rejects the conventional idea that ethnomethodology is a microsociology, but it is not, in his view, to be seen as a macrosociology either. Rather, Hilbert argues that ethnomethodology "transcends" the micro-macro issue because it is concerned "with social practices which are the methods of producing *both* microstructure and macrostructure as well as any presumed 'linkage' between these two" (1990:794).

Hilbert, somewhat erroneously (see Chapter 14), reduces the micro-macro linkage issue to a set of structural concerns. That is, it involves a focus on micro structures, macro structures, and the linkage between them. In Hilbert's view, ethnomethodologists are "indifferent" to structures *at any level*. Instead of being concerned with either micro or macro structures, ethnomethodologists are interested in the practices, the "ethnomethods," "the artful production," of structure in general. That is, ethnomethodologists are interested in the "methods of producing, maintaining, sustaining, and reproducing social structure by and for the membership, whether oriented to large scale institutional (macro) structure or smaller, more intimate (micro) structure" (Hilbert, 1990:799).

Hilbert offers what he calls the "radical thesis" of ethnomethodology, which serves to transcend the issue of micro-macro linkage:

> The empirical phenomena that conversation analysts witness but which members cannot possible know about, and . . . the structural phenomena that members orient to and take for granted but which nevertheless are nonempirical and unavailable for social science are (in a subtle way) . . . *the same phenomena.*
>
> (Hilbert, 1990:801)

In other words, to the ethnomethodologist there is no distinction to be made between micro and macro structures because they are simultaneously generated. However, neither ethnomethodologists nor any other sociological theorists have offered the ultimate solution to the micro-macro issue. Hilbert's effort is marred by his reduction of this issue to a concern for the linkage of micro and macro *structures.* As we saw in Chapter 14, there is far more to this issue than such a linkage. Nevertheless, the ethnomethodologists do offer an interesting, indeed radical, approach to this question, dissolving it and arguing that the micro and the macro are the same thing! It is certainly the case that one way to deal with the micro-macro issue is to refuse to separate the two levels, seeing them instead as part of the same general process.

SUMMARY

This chapter is devoted to a discussion of the movement toward theoretical syntheses in neofunctionalism, conflict theory, neo-Marxian theory, symbolic interactionism, and phenomenology and ethnomethodology. In the next chapter we pick up the discussion with theoretical syntheses in exchange theory, network theory, rational choice theory, feminist sociological theory, postmodernism, and post-Marxist theory.

SYNTHESES IN SOCIOLOGICAL THEORY—II

*I*N this chapter, we conclude the discussion of theoretical syntheses in contemporary sociological theory.

EXCHANGE THEORY

Exchange theory had some notable early efforts at the development of a more integrative theoretical orientation (see Chapter 11 for a discussion of Blau's integrative exchange theory). In this section we discuss the ideas of Richard Emerson, as well as those of his disciples, especially Karen Cook.

Toward a More Integrative Exchange Theory: Emerson and Cook

In two essays published in 1972, Richard Emerson developed the basis of an integrative exchange theory. The first essay (Emerson, 1972a) dealt with the "psychological basis for social exchange," while the second (Emerson, 1972b) turned to the macrolevel and "exchange relations and network structures." In a later essay, Emerson made the micro-macro linkage issue explicit: "I am attempting to extend exchange theory and research from *micro* to more *macro* levels of analysis through the study of *exchange network structures*" (cited in Cook, 1987b:212). Karen Cook agrees with the importance of exchange networks for linking micro and macro: "The use of the notion, exchange networks, allows for the development of theory that bridges the conceptual gap between isolated individuals or dyads and larger aggregates or collections of individuals (e.g., formal groups or associations, organizations, neighborhoods, political parties, etc.)" (1987b:219).[1]

Both Emerson and Cook accept and begin with the basic, micro-level premises of exchange theory. Emerson, for example, says, "The exchange approach takes as its first focus of attention the benefits people obtain from, and contribute to, the process of social interaction" (1981:31). More specifically, Emerson accepts behavioristic, operant-conditioning principles as his starting point. Emerson (1981:33) outlines three core assumptions of exchange theory:

1 People for whom events are beneficial tend to act "rationally" so that such events occur.
2 People eventually become satiated with behavioral events so that such events come to be of diminishing utility.
3 The benefits that people obtain through social processes are dependent on the benefits that they are able to provide in exchange. This gives exchange theory "its focus [on] the flow of *benefits through social interaction.*"

All this is quite familiar and has been extensively covered in Chapter 11. However, Emerson begins to point behavioristically oriented exchange theory in a different direction at the close of his first, micro-oriented 1972 essay: "Our main purpose in this chapter is to incorporate operant principles into a framework which can handle more complex situations than operant psychology confronts" (1972a:48).

This theme opens the second 1972 essay: "The purpose of this essay is to begin construction of a theory of social exchange in which *social structure* is taken as the dependent variable" (Emerson, 1972b:58). Whereas in the first 1972 essay Emerson was concerned with a single actor involved in an exchange relation with his or her environment (for example, a person fishing in a lake), in the second essay Emerson turns to social-exchange relationships as well as to exchange networks.

The actors in Emerson's macro-level exchange theory can be either individuals or collectivities. Emerson is concerned with the exchange relationship among actors. An *exchange network* has the following components (Cook et al., 1983:277):

1 There is a set of either individual or collective actors.
2 Valued resources are distributed among the actors.
3 There is a set of exchange opportunities among all actors in the network.
4 Exchange relations, or exchange opportunities, exist among the actors.
5 Exchange relations are connected to one another in a single network structure.

In sum: "An 'exchange network' is a specific social structure formed by two or more connected exchange relations between actors" (Cook et al., 1983:277).

---

[1] Emerson and Cook (as well as Blau) are not the only ones to develop integrative exchange theories. See also Uehara (1990) and Willer, Markovsky, and Patton (1989).

The nature (and intensity) of the connection between exchange *relations* is of great importance and is critical to linking exchange between two actors (dyadic exchange) to more macro-level phenomena (Yamagishi, Gillmore, and Cook, 1988:835). The connection between two or more dyadic relations is "positive" if exchange in one relation is contingent on exchange in the other relation. The connection is "negative" if exchange in one is contingent on nonexchange in the other. (There also may be mixed, that is, both positive and negative, connections [Cook and Gillmore, 1984].) In both positive and negative (as well as mixed) connections, what is crucial is the contingent relationship between dyadic exchanges. Thus, we may say that two dyadic-exchange relations, *A-B* and *A-C*, form a minimal network (*A-B-C*) when exchange in one is contingent on exchange (or nonexchange) in the other. It is *not* enough for *A, B,* and *C* to have a common membership for an exchange network to develop; there must be a contingent relationship between exchanges in *A-B* and *B-C*. Thus a macro-level network theory is not sufficient in itself; also required is the more micro-level exchange-theory principles.

In a 1983 study, Cook et al. sought to analyze the relationship between exchange and network approaches in terms of the issues of power and dependence. Emerson originally defined *power* as "the level of potential *cost* which one actor can induce another to 'accept,' " while *dependence* involves "the level of potential cost an actor will accept within a relation" (1972b:64). This leads to Emerson's power-dependency theory, which Yamagishi et al. summarize in the following way: "The power of one party over another in an exchange relation is an inverse function of his or her dependence on the other party" (1988:837). Unequal power and dependency lead to imbalances in relationships, but over time these move toward a more balanced power-dependency relationship.

In explaining power dependence, network-structural theory looks at things such as structural centrality, while exchange theory focuses on the dyadic relation between actors. The Cook et al. research (1983) tends to find support for the importance of the exchange relationship and points up weaknesses in the network-structural approach. However, Cook et al. (1983:298) are well aware of the micro biases of exchange theory and the need to integrate it with, to raise it to, the macroscopic level.

In order to move away from the dyadic approach of exchange theory and toward a focus on the power of a position within a structure, Cook and Emerson argue that the determination of the power of a position is based on the amount of dependence of the entire structure on that position. Such system-wide dependence will, in their view, be a function of *both* the structural centrality of the position and the nature of power-dependence relationships. They argue that they are adopting a " 'vulnerability' approach to the problem of raising power-dependence theory from a dyadic to a more macrostructural level of analysis" (Cook et al., 1983:301). Vulnerability involves the network-wide dependence on a particular structural position. Cook et al. conclude:

It is clear that the integration of structural network principles with exchange net-work theory provides useful insights into the dynamics of power in networks of connected exchange relations. . . . This theoretical formulation offers an explicit procedure for linking actors' exchange behavior to network properties . . . and suggests mechanisms which may yield "possible transformations" of these net-works as a result of power dynamics or changes in the nature of the exchange connections.

(Cook et al., 1983:303)

Yamagishi, Gillmore, and Cook (1988) go further in linking exchange theory and network theory. They argue that power (and dependence) are central to exchange theory but that power cannot be studied meaningfully in the dyad. Rather, power "is fundamentally a social structural phenomenon" (Yamagishi et al., 1988:834). They are able to generate predictions about the distribution of power in all three types of exchange networks—positive, negative, and mixed—and support their predictions with experiments and computer simu-lations. Fully adequate analysis must involve the traditional exchange-theory concerns with processes within exchange relations as well as the traditional network concern with the linkages between exchange relations.

Most recently, Cook, O'Brien, and Kollock (1990) define *exchange theory* in inherently integrative terms as being concerned with exchanges at various levels of analysis, including those among interconnected individuals, corpo-rations, and nation-stages. They identify two strands of work in the history of exchange—one at the micro level, focusing on social behavior as exchange, and the other at the more macro level, viewing social structure as exchange. They see the strength of exchange theory in micro-macro integration since "it includes within a single theoretical framework propositions that apply to indi-vidual actors as well as to the macro-level (or systemic level) and it attempts to formulate explicitly the consequences of changes at one level for other levels of analysis" (Cook, O'Brien, and Kollock, 1990:175).

Cook, O'Brien, and Kollock identify three contemporary trends, all of which point toward a more integrative exchange theory. The first is the increasing use of field research focusing on more macroscopic issues, which can comple-ment the traditional use of the laboratory experiment to study microscopic issues. Second, they note the shift, discussed above, in substantive work away from a focus on dyads and toward larger networks of exchange. Third, and most important, is the ongoing effort, also discussed above, to synthesize exchange theory and structural sociologies, especially network theory. (We will say more about network theory shortly.)

Along the way, Cook, O'Brien, and Kollock discuss the gains to be made from integrating insights from a variety of other micro theories. Decision the-ory offers "a better understanding of the way actors make choices relevant to transactions" (Cook, O'Brien, and Kollock, 1990:168). More generally, cogni-tive science (which includes cognitive anthropology and artificial intelligence) sheds "more light on the way in which actors perceive, process, and retrieve information" (Cook, O'Brien, and Kollock, 1990:168). Symbolic interactionism offers knowledge about how actors signal their intentions to one another, and this is important in the development of trust and commitment in exchange relationships. Most generally, they see their synthetic version of exchange theory as being well equipped to deal with the centrally important issue of the agency-structure relationship. In their view, "Exchange theory is one of a limited number of theoretical orientations in the social sciences that explicitly conceptualize purposeful actors in relation to structures" (Cook, O'Brien, and Kollock, 1990:172).

While there is much of merit in the integrative objectives of the Emerson-Cook variant of exchange theory, the weakness of their effort on the micro-subjective level should be mentioned. Note, for example, this conclusion to one of their studies: "Power is a function of position in the network, even when the position occupants are ignorant of the actual network structure and their own position in it" (Cook et al., 1983:281). While structure may act behind the backs of actors, it remains the case that the integrative exchange theory has little to say about conscious processes.

NETWORK THEORY

As indicated several times in this chapter, network theory shows great promise from the point of view of theoretical synthesis. The focus of network theory is on social structure, the pattern of ties linking individual (Granovetter, 1973, 1983, 1985; Wellman and Wortley, 1990) and collective (Baker, 1990; Clawson, Neustadtl, and Bearden, 1986; Mizruchi and Koenig, 1986) members of society. While these may be seen as deep structures, that is, structures that lie below the surface (Wellman, 1983), they are closer to sociology's traditional sense of social structure than to the structures of concern to, for example, French structuralists (see Chapter 13). It is its closeness to the traditional sense of social structure that makes network theory an attractive target for those interested in synthesis. Furthermore, since the networks can be either micro (among individual actors) or macro (among collective actors), both historically micro (for example, exchange) and macro (for example, conflict) theories can seek integration with it. Furthermore, this interest in both micro and macro networks makes network theory, at least in some senses, inherently integrative.

Of prime interest, as mentioned above, are the emerging ties between network theory and exchange theory (and, as we have noted, between network theory and conflict theory). Network theory appears to offer exchange theory a highly compatible macro theory that complements exchange theory's basic micro orientation, derived from behaviorism as well as rational choice theory. For example, network theorists, like exchange theorists, are little interested in individual motives. The network theorists' interest in objective ties meshes nicely with the exchange theorists' interest in objective patterns of behavior. To put it in negative terms, network theory would not fit as well with the sociological theories that are primarily interested in consciousness (symbolic interactionism, phenomenology, existentialism). On the other side, exchange theory would not tie in as well with the (macro) subjectivistic orientation of other macro theories such as structural functionalism and critical theory. Network theory also allows exchange theorists to see the dyads of traditional concern to them as being embedded in larger networks or relationships. This means that exchange theorists can examine the effects of interpersonal exchange transactions on larger networks and conversely the effects of those networks on exchange transactions. However, Cook, O'Brien, and Kollock, like others (for example, McMahon, 1984), are wary of the dangers associated with moving a traditionally micro-level theory in a macro direction:

> While exchange network theory has much promise, there are potential pitfalls in any attempt to extend a well-developed micro-level framework to apply to more macro-levels. Exchange theory will need a more explicit specification of the processes at the macro-level it seeks to explain and some vision of the nature of these macro-level processes in relation to other existing structures and events (e.g. an explicit acknowledgement of the historical, political, and institutional context in which events of interest are likely to occur.)
>
> (Cook, O'Brien, and Kollock, 1990:174–175)

While there are various ongoing efforts to utilize network theory in an attempt to develop more integrative and synthetic theories, there are also efforts within network theory to develop such an orientation.

Ronald Burt (1982) has been in the forefront of network theorists who have sought to develop an integrated approach instead of another form of structural determinism. Burt begins by articulating a schism within action theory between the "atomistic" and "normative" orientations. The atomistic orientation "assumes that alternative actions are evaluated independently by separate actors so that evaluations are made without reference to other actors," whereas the "normative perspective is defined by separate actors within a system having interdependent interests as social norms generated by actors socializing one another" (Burt, 1982:5).

Burt develops a perspective that "circumvents the schism between atomistic and normative action," one that "is less a synthesis of the existing two perspectives on action than it is a third view intellectually bridging the two views" (1982:8). Although he admittedly borrows from the other two perspectives, Burt develops what he calls a *structural perspective* that differs from the other two "in the criterion for the postulate of marginal evaluation. The criterion assumed by the proposed structural perspective is an actor's status/role-set as generated by the division of labor. An actor evaluates the utility of alternative actions partly in regard to his personal conditions and partly in regard to the conditions of others" (1982:8). He sees his approach as a logical extension of the atomistic approach and an "empirically accurate restriction" on normative theory.

Figure 17.1 depicts Burt's structural theory of action. Burt describes the premise of a structural theory of action as "actors are purposive under social structural constraints" (1982:9). In his view:

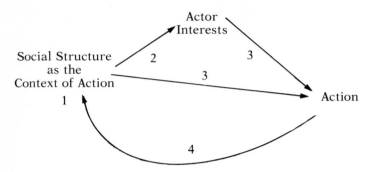

FIGURE 17.1 Ronald Burt's Integrative Model

Actors find themselves in a social structure. That social structure defines their social similarities, which in turn pattern their perceptions of the advantages to be had by taking each of several alternative actions. At the same time, social structure differentially constrains actors in their ability to take actions. Actions eventually taken are therefore a joint function of actors pursuing their interests to the limit of their ability where both interests and ability are patterned by social structure. Finally, actions taken under social structural constraint can modify social structure itself, and these modifications have the potential to create new constraints to be faced by actors within the structure.

(Burt, 1982:9)

RATIONAL CHOICE THEORY

Rational choice theory is very interesting from the point of view of theoretical synthesis. On the one hand, this is one of the most micro-extremist theories in sociology. This work is unified in its methodological individualism and seeks to base sociological theory on a philosophical anthropology (homo economicus) of rational, maximizing, self-interested actors making the correct, most efficient choices of means to ends on the basis of information available to them. It was just such a philosophical anthropology that was rejected by many of the early sociological theorists who sought to develop a more realistic, that is, less rational, view of the actor as driven by such things as beliefs. Furthermore, the micro extremism of rational choice theory was rejected by many who moved in the direction of developing more macro-oriented theories. However, in recent years, the success of economics has urged some sociologists back to the micro model of the rational actor with the promise of clean, simple, and elegant theories.

We have already discussed (see Chapter 14) in some detail Coleman's recent, more integrative rational choice theory. Friedman and Hechter (1988, 1990) are also exponents of a more integrative and synthetic rational choice theory. They recognize some of the limitations of rational choice theory, and, among other things, they urge extending the model on the micro level on such issues as the rationality of individual actors and its internal limits and the origin of preferences within actors. In other words, they are pushing for more integration on the micro levels and at least some movement toward such micro theories as symbolic interactionism and ethnomethodology. In addition, they are pressing for more integration with such macro-level concerns as how to aggregate from individual actions to macro-social outcomes and how rational egoists produce institutions. Friedman and Hechter are urging a fuller sense of the actor and greater concern with various facets of the micro-macro linkage. In emphasizing this linkage, Friedman and Hechter are pursuing a more synthetic type of rational choice theory than is usually found in the literature: "Why, then, prefer rational choice? Perhaps the most compelling reason is that it is explicitly concerned with linking micro and macro levels of analysis rather than asserting the analytical supremacy of one or the other" (1988:212). This is clearly a very different image of rational choice theory than the micro extremism that we usually associate with it.

While much of the above deals with the integration of extant, usually American, sociological theories, there is also another kind of synthesis taking place in sociological theory. This is the integration into American theory of ideas and theories drawn from other disciplines and/or nations.[2] A few examples of this are examined below.

FEMINIST SOCIOLOGICAL THEORY

As was pointed out in Chapter 12, feminist sociological theory is inherently synthetic, since it has been formed out of the intersection of three broad inputs—theories of gender differences, including biological, institutional, and social-psychological theories of gender; theories of gender inequality, including liberal feminism and Marxian feminism; and theories of gender oppression, including psychoanalytic, radical feminist and socialist feminist theories. Some of these idea systems are indigenous to sociology, while others feed into sociology from a variety of external sources. The confluence of these internal and external forces is leading to the development of a distinctive feminist sociological theory. Although that theory is still in its early, formative stages, it seems clear that such a theory (or theories) will undergo expansion and consolidation in the coming years.

In addition to the integration of feminist theory into sociological theory in the next few years (Alexander and Colomy and the neofunctionalists, Fine and the symbolic interactionists, and others are welcoming it), other areas of future development are pointed out by Lengermann and Niebrugge-Brantley

---

[2] Again, there is nothing new about this; sociological theory has always been open to such things. This work is notable here because it is now just a part of a much broader integrative movement.

(1990). While they urge a focus on subjective and micro-social situations, they are also conscious of the need to link these to macro-level phenomena. They describe the "dialectic tension between the need to respect the individual and the equally compelling need to generalize" (Lengermann and Niebrugge-Brantley, 1990:330). In addition, they discuss the requirement that feminist sociologists continue to critically analyze sociology's penchant for dualistic rhetoric (for example, male-female and micro-macro terminology) and attempt to develop more integrated conceptions of the social world.

POSTMODERNISM

We turn now to a discussion of the relationship between the move toward theoretical syntheses in sociology and one of the most important multidisciplinary intellectual developments in recent years—postmodernism (D. Harvey, 1989; Kellner 1988, 1990a), particularly as it is manifest in the works of such thinkers as Jean Baudrillard (1983; see also Bogard, 1990), Jean-François Lyotard (1984), and Fredric Jameson (1984; see also Kellner, 1990b).

In this section we will touch on only a small part of postmodern thinking, that part which is related to our concern with theoretical syntheses. In the next section we will deal with the impact of postmodern theory on post-Marxist thinking. There are still other aspects of postmodern thinking that are relevant to contemporary sociological theory, but a full discussion of all the implications of postmodernism is far beyond the scope of these closing sections. For one thing, postmodernism is not a coherent theory. As Kellner argues, "There is nothing like a unified 'postmodern social theory,'" but rather there is a "plurality of different postmodern theories and positions" (1990a:257). More strongly, Callinicos says, "The producers of this discourse . . . offered definitions which were mutually inconsistent, internally contradictory and/or hopelessly vague" (1990:2). For another, postmodern theory is manifest in a wide range of fields such as art, architecture, literature, film, philosophy, cultural theory, social theory, and so on. For still another, postmodern social theory is linked to the development of a postmodern society and there is even less agreement about what constitutes a postmodern society than there is about what is postmodern social theory.

It is clear that postmodern society represents a break from, or a rupture within, modern society; postmodernity follows modernity. However, it is unclear whether there is a radical disjuncture between modernity and postmodernity or whether postmodern society gradually emerges from modernity and is difficult, if not impossible, to distinguish from it at the edges. There is no agreement on what postmodern society looks like, but to offer one example, here is the way Lyotard describes it:

> Eclecticism . . . of contemporary general culture: one listens to reggae, watches a western, eats McDonald's food for lunch and local cuisine for dinner, wears Paris

perfume in Tokyo and "retro" clothes in Hong Kong; knowledge is a matter for TV games. It is easy to find a public for eclectic works. By becoming kitsch, art panders to the confusion which reigns in the "taste" of the patrons. Artists, gallery owners, critics, and public wallow together in the "anything goes," and the epoch is one of slackening.

(Lyotard, 1984:76)

This is but one, admittedly obscure, but clearly highly critical, image of post-modern society. There are many other such views, as well as perspectives that totally reject the idea of a new, postmodern society:

Now I reject all this. I do not believe that we live in "New Times," in a "postin-dustrial and postmodern age" fundamentally different from the capitalist mode of production globally dominant for the last two centuries.

(Callinicos, 1990:4)

Had we the time and space, we could try to sort out the various images of postmodern society and the array of theories about that society. While there are long lists of characteristics that differentiate modernism from postmod-ernism, modernism is generally thought of as highly rational and rigid, while postmodernism is seen as more irrational and more flexible. However, we will not be concerned with the nature of modernism and postmodernism in this section (although it was of some concern in Chapter 8 in the discussion of Fordism and post-Fordism). What is relevant is the fact that postmodernism adopts a series of positions that bear on the movement toward syntheses within sociological theory. It is that set of ideas that we examine in this section. Most relevant to this discussion are the ideas of Jean-François Lyotard, who focuses much of his attention not on postmodern society but on postmodern knowledge.

Lyotard (1984:xxiii) begins by identifying modern (scientific) knowledge with the kind of single grand synthesis (or "metadiscourse") that we have associated with the work of theorists like Marx and Parsons. The kinds of grand narratives he associates with modern science include "the dialectics of Spirit, the hermeneutics of meaning, the emancipation of the rational or work-ing subject, or the creation of wealth" (Lyotard, 1984:xxiii).

If modern knowledge is identified in Lyotard's view with metanarratives, then postmodern knowledge involves a rejection of such grand narratives. As Lyotard puts it: "Simplifying to the extreme, I define *postmodern* as incredulity to metanarratives" (1984:xxiv). More strongly, he argues: "Let us wage war on totality . . . let us activate the differences" (Lyotard, 1984:82). In fact, post-modernism becomes a celebration of a range of different theoretical perspec-tives: "Postmodern knowledge is not simply a tool of authorities; it refines our sensitivity to differences and reinforces our ability to tolerate the incom-mensurable" (Lyotard, 1984:xxv). In these terms, sociology has moved beyond the modern period, into the postmodern period, in its search for a range of more specific syntheses. In the view of Fraser and Nicholson, Lyotard prefers "smallish, localized narrative[s]" to the metanarratives, or the grand narratives, of modernity (1988:89). The new syntheses discussed throughout this chapter and the last may be seen as examples of such "smallish," "localized" sociological narratives.

While Lyotard rejects the grand narrative in general, Baudrillard rejects the idea of a grand narrative in sociology. For one thing, Baudrillard rejects the whole idea of the social. For another, this leads to a rejection of the metanarrative of sociology that is associated with modernity:

> . . . the great organizing principle, the grand narrative of the Social which found its support and justification in ideas on the rational contract, civil society, progress, power, production—that all this may have pointed to something that once existed, but exists no longer. The age of the perspective of the social (coinciding rightly with that ill-defined period known as modernity) . . . is over.
>
> (Bogard, 1990:10)

Thus, postmodernism stands for the rejection of metanarratives in general and of grand narratives within sociology in particular.

Another aspect of postmodernism relevant to this discussion is its tendency to "subvert" and "explode" boundaries between disciplines and subdisciplines and to create a multidisciplinary, multidimensional perspective that synthesizes ideas from a range of fields (for example, philosophy, political economy, cultural theory, history, anthropology, and sociology) and perspectives within a given discipline. Postmodernism proclaims the end of an era in social and intellectual life and the beginning of the search for "new paradigms, new politics, and new theories" (Kellner, 1990a:276). In Kellner's view, such new theories will involve new concatenations of Marxism, critical theory, feminism, postmodern social theory, and other currents of critical social theory to solve the theoretical and political problems confronting us today. From the narrower perspective of sociology, this takes the form of efforts to develop new synthetic theories from ideas drawn from a wide range of theoretical sources.

Still another aspect of postmodernism is its tendency to regard various theories as texts, as the rhetorical constructions of theorists (Brown, 1990b). This view of theories as rhetorical constructs serves to subvert the authority of theories and to assault their privileged status. This leads to a view of science in general, and sociology in particular, as "a conversation of scholar/rhetors" (Brown, 1990b:189). In such a demystified conversation, theorists are free to borrow ideas from one another in an effort to create the range of new synthetic theories discussed throughout this chapter and the last.

In sum, postmodernism stands for four things that are highly relevant to the move toward the new syntheses within sociology. First, there is the rejection of the earlier search for a single, grand synthetic theory. Second, there is the acceptance of a range of narrower synthetic efforts. Third, there is the explosion of boundaries between disciplines and the idea that the new syntheses can draw upon ideas from a range of different disciplines. Fourth, there is the demystification of theoretical rhetoric, allowing sociologists to borrow freely from one another in the creation of synthetic theories.

One other point about postmodernism should be noted. Weinstein and Weinstein (1990) have explicitly linked postmodernism to the subject of the appendix of this book—metatheorizing in sociology (see also Ritzer, 1991a). Briefly, metatheorizing involves the systematic study of sociological theory. Metatheorizing has a number of things in common with postmodernism and, to some extent, can be seen as a postmodernist development within sociological theory. The basic works in postmodernism predate the recent surge of interest in metatheorizing, and thus it would appear that they played a role in that development. However, overt references to postmodernism and its linkage to metatheorizing are of fairly recent vintage. Thus, it seems more likely that the same conditions that made postmodernism attractive to sociological theorists have also helped lead to the growth of metatheorizing.

Metatheorizing, like postmodernism, demystifies and relativizes all theoretical approaches. Metatheorizing is not focally concerned with analyzing what sociological theory ought to be but rather with studying and gaining a deeper understanding of what it is in all its branches, varieties, and manifestations. To some metatheorists such increased understanding is an end in itself, while to others it is a means to the creation of a new theory or an overarching theoretical perspective.

A good portion of what metatheorizing is about can be gleaned from the postmodernist term "deconstruction." As deconstructionists, metatheorists often reread and reanalyze theorists, sociological theories, paradigms, and so on. These are all treated as "texts" that need to be reinterpreted using contemporary perspectives and tools (Harvey, 1989). The object of such deconstruction is often a better understanding of the entity being reanalyzed. Deconstruction can also be undertaken for the ultimately more constructive purpose of putting together diverse sets of ideas drawn from various perspectives in order to form a new theory. Another orientation shared by metatheorists and postmodernists is a critical attitude toward grand narratives, metanarratives, or totalizations.[3] It has become clear that none of the sociological metanarratives is adequate in itself, let alone fully adequate to analyze society as a whole. Rather than being caught in the battle among faulty grand narratives, metatheorists have turned their attention to a study of the narratives, the reasons for their faults, and the ways in which the faults can be overcome in new, more delimited synthetic efforts (Antonio, 1990; Antonio and Kellner, forthcoming).

These new synthetic efforts are also in line with, although not explicitly derived from, the postmodern notion that the boundaries between extant theories need to be subverted or exploded. Most of the contemporary theoretical

---

[3] Even the overarching perspectives produced by metatheorists tend to be limited and provisional (for example, Ritzer, 1981a).

syntheses discussed in this chapter are derived from careful metatheoretical analyses of one or more extant theories and are oriented to the production of new theoretical syntheses that draw upon an array of sociological theories.

In these and many other ways, postmodernism is highly relevant not only to developments in sociological theory but also to those in metatheorizing in sociology. We will have more to say about postmodernism in the following section, on post-Marxist theory, and about metatheorizing in the Appendix.

POST-MARXIST THEORY

The 1980s and early 1990s have brought dramatic changes to neo-Marxian theory (Grossberg and Nelson, 1988; Jay, 1988). The most recent varieties of neo-Marxian theory are rejecting many of the basic premises of Marx's original theory as well as those of the neo-Marxian theories discussed in Chapter 8. Hence these new approaches have come to be thought of as post-Marxist theories (Wright, 1987). While they reject the basic elements of Marxian theory, there are still sufficient affinities with it for them to be considered part of neo-Marxian theory. Post-Marxist theories are discussed here because they often involve the synthesis of Marxian theories with other theories, ideas, methods, and so on. How can we account for these dramatic changes in neo-Marxian theory? Two sets of factors are involved, one external to theory and involving changes in the social world and the other internal to theory itself (P. Anderson, 1984; Ritzer, 1991a).

First, and external to Marxian theory, is the end of the Cold War (at least for the moment) (Halliday, 1990) and the collapse of world communism. The Soviet Union is undergoing *perestroika* (restructuring) and moving away from a socialist, state-run economy and toward a market economy resembling, at least in part, a capitalist economy (Piccone, 1990; Zaslavsky, 1988). The Soviet Union has also relinquished control over Eastern Europe, and many of the countries there are shifting, often even more rapidly than the Soviet Union, in the direction of a capitalist-style economy (Kaldor, 1990). China, following the violent response to the insurrection at Tiananmen Square, seems bankrupt as a model for the rest of the world even though it clings to communism. Cuba appears isolated, awaiting only the death or overthrow of Fidel Castro to move in the direction of *perestroika* and capitalism. Thus, the failure of communism on a worldwide scale made it necessary for Marxists to reconsider and reconstruct their theories (Burawoy, 1990).

These changes in the world were related to a second set of changes, internal to theory itself, the series of intellectual changes that, in turn, affected neo-Marxian theory (P. Anderson, 1990a, 1990b). New theoretical currents such as poststructuralism (see Chapter 13) and postmodernism (see above) had a profound impact on neo-Marxian theory. In addition, a movement known as *analytical Marxism* gained ground, and it was premised on the belief that Marxian theories needed to employ the same methods as any other scientific enterprise. This led to reinterpretations of Marx in more conventional intellectual terms, efforts to apply rational choice theory to Marxian issues, and attempts to study Marxian topics utilizing the methods and techniques of positivistic science.

Thus, a combination of social and intellectual changes has dramatically altered the landscape of neo-Marxian theory in the 1990s. While the theories discussed throughout Chapter 8 remain important, much of the energy in neo-Marxian theory today is focused on the theories to be discussed in this section.

Analytical Marxism

Perry Anderson (1984) contends that the center of Marxian theory has shifted away from Germany and Latin Europe (especially France and Italy), and this is nowhere clearer than in the school known as analytical Marxism, or what Callinicos calls "Anglo Marxism" (1989:3). Here is the way one of the leaders of analytical Marxism, John Roemer, 1986a:1) defines it:

> During the past decade, what now appears as a new species in social theory has been forming: analytically sophisticated Marxism. Its practitioners are largely inspired by Marxian questions, which they pursue with contemporary tools of logic, mathematics and model building. Their methodological posture is conventional. These writers are, self-consciously, products of both the Marxian and neo-Marxian traditions.
>
> (Roemer, 1986a:1)

Thus, analytical Marxists bring mainstream, "state-of-the-art" methods of analytical philosophy and social science to bear on traditional Marxian issues. Analytical Marxism is discussed in this chapter because it "explicitly proposes to synthesize *non-Marxist* methods and Marxist theory" (Weldes, 1989:371).

Analytical Marxism adopts a nondogmatic approach to Marx's theory. It does not blindly and unthinkingly support Marx's theory, it does not deny historical facts in order to support Marx's theory, nor does it totally reject Marx's theory as fundamentally wrong. Rather, it views Marx's theory as a form of nineteenth-century social science with great power and with a valid core but also with substantial weaknesses. Marx's theory should be drawn upon, but it requires the utilization of methods and techniques developed in the late twentieth century. It rejects the idea that there is a distinctive Marxian methodology and criticizes those who think that such a methodology exists and is valid:

> I do not think there is a specific form of Marxist logic or explanation. Too often, obscurantism protects itself behind a yoga of special terms and privileged logic. The yoga of Marxism is "dialectics." Dialectical logic is based on several propositions which may have a certain inductive appeal, but are far from being rules of inference: that things turn into their opposites, and quantity turns into quality. In Marxian social science, dialectics is often used to justify a lazy kind of teleological reasoning. Developments occur because they must in order for history to be played out as it was intended.
>
> (Roemer, 1986b:191)

Similarly, Elster says: "There is no specifically Marxist form of analysis . . . there is no commitment to any specific method of analysis, beyond those that characterize good social science generally" (1986:220). Along the same lines, analytical Marxists reject the idea that fact and value cannot be separated, that they are dialectically related. They seek, following the canons of mainstream philosophic and social-scientific thinking, to separate fact and value and to deal with facts dispassionately through theoretical, conceptual, and empirical analysis.

One might ask why analytical Marxism should be called Marxist. Roemer in reply to this question, says "I am not sure that it should" (1986a:2). However, he does offer several reasons why we can consider it a (neo-) Marxian theory. First, it deals with traditional Marxian topics like exploitation and class. Second, it continues to regard socialism as preferable to capitalism. Third, it seeks to understand and explain the problems associated with capitalism. However, while it is Marxist in these senses, it also "borrows willingly and easily from other viewpoints" (Roemer, 1986a:7). Again, analytical Marxism is very much in line with the move toward theoretical syntheses discussed throughout this chapter and Chapter 16.

Three varieties of analytical Marxism will be discussed, at least briefly, in this section. First, we will discuss the effort to reanalyze Marx's work by utilizing mainstream intellectual tools. Second, we will deal with rational choice and game-theoretic Marxism. Finally, we will touch on empirical research from a Marxian perspective that utilizes state-of-the-art methodological tools.

Reanalyzing Marx As pointed out above, analytical Marxists reject the use of such idiosyncratic concepts as the dialectic and seek instead to analyze Marx (as well as the social world) using concepts that are part of the broader intellectual tradition. The major example of this, and one of the key documents in analytical Marxism, is G. A. Cohen's *Karl Marx's Theory of History: A Defence* (1978). Instead of interpreting Marx as an exotic dialectician, Cohen argues that he employs the much more prosaic functional form of explanation in his work. He offers the following examples of functional explanation in Marx's work:

- "Relations of production *correspond* to productive forces.
- The legal and political superstructure *rises on* real foundation.
- The social, political, and intellectual process *is conditioned by* the mode of production of material life.
- Consciousness is determined by social being."

(Cohen, 1978/1986:221)

In each of the above, the second concept *explains* the first concept. The nature of the explanation is functional, in Cohen's view, because "the character of what is explained is determined by its effect on what explains it" (1978/1986:221). Thus, in the case of the last example, the character of consciousness is explained by its effect on (Becker, 1988:870), more specifically its propensity to sustain, social being. More generally, social phenomena are explained in terms of their consequences for other social phenomena. It is Cohen's view that Marx practices functional thinking in the above examples, and throughout his work, because he seeks to explain social and economic phenomena in this manner. Thus, Marx is not a dialectician; he is a functional thinker. In adopting such a perspective, Cohen is reinterpreting Marx using mainstream philosophic ideas *and* viewing Marx as part of that mainstream.

Cohen takes pains to differentiate functional thinking from the sociological variety of (structural) functional*ism* discussed in Chapter 7. Cohen sees (structural) functionalism as composed of three theses. First, all elements of the social world are interconnected. Second, all components of society reinforce one another as well as the society as a whole. Third, each aspect of society is as it is because of its contribution to the larger society. These theses are objectionable to Marxists for a variety of reasons, especially because of their conservatism. However, the functional explanations mentioned previously can be employed by Marxists without their accepting any of the tenets of functionalism. Thus, functional explanation is not necessarily conservative; indeed it can be quite revolutionary.

Rational Choice Marxism   Many analytical Marxists have drawn on neoclassical economics, especially rational choice theory and game theory (see Chapter 14 for a discussion of the use of rational choice theory in mainstream sociological theory). Roemer argues that "Marxian analysis requires microfoundations," especially rational choice and game theory as well as "the arsenal of modelling techniques developed by neoclassical economics" (1986b:192). In drawing on such approaches, Marxian theory is giving up its pretentions of being different and is utilizing approaches widely used throughout the social sciences. But while neo-Marxian theory can and should draw upon neoclassical economics, it remains different from the latter. For example, it retains an interest in collective action for changing society and accepts the idea that capitalism is an unjust system.

Jon Elster (1982, 1986) is a major proponent, along with John Roemer, of analytical Marxism. Elster believes that neo-Marxian theory has been impeded by its adoption of the kind of functional theorizing discussed by Cohen. He also believes that Marxian theory ought to be making greater use of game theory, a variant of rational choice theory. Game theory, like other types of rational choice theory, assumes that actors are rational and that they seek to maximize their gains. Although it recognizes structural constraints, it does not suggest that they completely determine actors' choices. What is distinctive about game theory as a type of rational choice theory is that it permits the analyst to go beyond the rational choices of a single actor and to deal with the interdependence of the decisions and actions of a number of actors. Elster (1982) identifies three interdependencies among actors involved in a game. First, the reward for each actor depends on the choices made by all actors. Second, the reward for each actor depends on the reward for all. Finally, the choice made by each actor depends on the choices made by all. The analysis of "games" (such as the famous "prisoner's dilemma" game, in which actors end up worse off if they follow their own self-interests than if they sacrifice those interests) helps explain the strategies of the various actors and the emergence of such collectivities as social class. Thus, rational choice Marxism searches for the micro-foundations of Marxist theory, although the rational actor of this theory is very different from critical theory's actor (see Chapter 8), who is largely derived from Freudian theory.

Elster's rational choice orientation is also manifest in *Making Sense of Marx* (1985). In that book Elster argues that Marx's basic method for explaining social phenomena was a concern for the unintended consequences of human action. To Elster, and in contrast to most other Marxists, who see Marx as a "methodological holist" concerned with macro structures, Marx practiced "methodological individualism," or "the doctrine that all social phenomena—their structure and their change—are in principle explicable in ways that only involve individuals—their properties, their goals, their beliefs and their actions" (1985:5). To Elster, Marx *was* concerned with actors, their goals, their intentions, and their rational choices. Elster uses such a rational choice perspective to critique the orientation of the structural Marxists: "Capitalist entrepreneurs are *agents* in the genuinely active sense. They cannot be reduced to mere place-holders in the capitalist system of production" (1985:13). Rational choice Marxism focuses on these rational agents (capitalist and proletariat) and their interrelationships.

Empirically Oriented Marxism The leading figure associated with the importation and application of rigorous methods to the empirical study of Marxian concepts is Erik Olin Wright (1985). Wright explicitly associates himself with analytical Marxism in general and the work of John Roemer in particular. Wright's work involves three basic components: first, the clarification of basic Marxian concepts such as class; second, empirical studies of those concepts; third, the development of a more coherent theory based on those concepts (especially class).

In his book, *Classes* (1985), Wright seeks to answer the question posed by Marx, but never answered by him: "What constitutes class?" He makes it clear that his answer will be true to Marx's original theoretical agenda. However, it will not be the same as the answer Marx might have offered, because since Marx's day there has been over 100 years of both theoretical work and history. Thus, we are more sophisticated theoretically, *and* times have changed. As a result, Wright, like the other analytical Marxists, starts with Marx but does not accept his position as dogma or try to divine how he might have defined *class*. Because of Marx and the theoretical work done since his time, contemporary Marxists are in a better position to come up with such definitions. In any case, we live in very different times, and Marx's definition, even if we could divine it, might well not be appropriate for modern society.

Since this is a book on theory, we need not go into detail about Wright's research or that of any of the other empirically oriented Marxists. However, it would be useful to say something about his best-known conceptual contribution—the idea of "contradictory locations within class relations" (Wright, 1985:43). His basic premise is that a given position need not, as is commonly assumed, be located within a given class; it may be in more than one class simultaneously. Thus, a position may be simultaneously proletarian and bourgeois. For example, managers are bourgeois in the sense that they supervise subordinates, but they are also proletarian in that they are supervised by others. The idea of contradictory class locations is derived through careful conceptual analysis and then is studied empirically.

While, as we have seen, analytical Marxists consider themselves to be Marxists, there are those (for example, Callinicos, 1989) who wonder whether their attraction to mainstream concepts and methods makes this designation meaningless. In response, Elster asserts: "Most of the views that *I* hold to be true and important, I can trace back to Marx" (1985:531).

Postmodern Marxian Theory

Marxian theory has been profoundly affected by theoretical developments in structuralism and poststructuralism (P. Anderson, 1984:33; see also Chapter 13) and, of particular interest here, postmodernism (see above).

A major representative work of postmodern Marxism is Ernesto Laclau and Chantal Mouffe's *Hegemony and Socialist Strategy* (1985). In Ellen Wood's view, this work, accepting the focus on linguistics, texts, and discourse in postmodernism, detaches ideology from its material base and ultimately dissolves "the social altogether into ideology or 'discourse' " (1986:47). As we saw in Chapter 8, the concept of hegemony, which is of central importance to Laclau and Mouffe, was developed by Gramsci to focus on cultural leadership rather than the coercive effect of state domination. This, of course, leads us away from the traditional Marxian concern with the material world and in the direction of ideas and discourse. As Wood puts it, "In short, the Laclau-Mouffe argument is that there *are* no such things as material interests but only discursively constructed *ideas* about them" (1986:61).

In addition to substituting ideas for material interests, Laclau and Mouffe also displace the proletariat from its privileged position at the center of Marxian theory. As Wood argues, Laclau and Mouffe are part of a movement involved in the "declassing of the socialist project" (1986:4). Laclau and Mouffe put the issue of class in subjective, discursive terms. The social world is characterized by diverse positions and antagonisms. As a result, it is impossible to come up with the kind of "unified discourse" that Marx envisioned surrounding the proletariat. The universal discourse of the proletariat "has been replaced by a polyphony of voices, each of which constructs its own irreducible discursive identity" (Laclau and Mouffe, 1985:191). Thus, instead of focusing on the single discourse of the proletariat, Marxian theorists are urged to focus on a multitude of diverse discourses emanating from a wide range of dispossessed voices, such as those of women, blacks, ecologists, immigrants, consumers, and the like. Marxian theory has, as a result, been *decentered* and *detotalized* because it no longer focuses only on the proletariat and no longer sees the problems of the proletariat as *the* problem in society.

Having rejected a focus on material factors and a focal concern for the proletariat, Laclau and Mouffe proceed to reject, as the goal of Marxian theory, communism involving the emancipation of the proletariat. Alternatively, they propose a system labeled "radical democracy." Instead of focusing, as the political right does, on individual democratic rights, they propose to "create a new hegemony, which will be the outcome of the articulation of the greatest number of democratic struggles" (Mouffe, 1988:41). What is needed in this new hegemony is a "hegemony of democratic values, and this requires a multiplication of democratic practices, institutionalizing them into even more diverse social relations" (Mouffe, 1988:41). Radical democracy seeks to bring together under a broad umbrella a wide range of democratic struggles—antiracist, antisexist, anticapitalist, antiexploitation of nature (Eder, 1990), and many others. Thus, this is a "radical and plural democracy" (Laclau, 1990:27). The struggle of one group must not be waged at the expense of the others; all democratic struggles must be seen as equivalent struggles. Thus, it is necessary to bring these struggles together by modifying their identity so that the groups see themselves as part of the larger struggle for radical democracy. As Laclau and Mouffe argue:

> The alternative of the Left should consist of locating itself fully in the field of the democratic revolution and expanding the chains of equivalents between different struggles against oppression. *The task of the Left therefore cannot be to renounce liberal-democratic ideology, but on the contrary, to deepen and expand it in the direction of a radical and plural democracy. . . .* It is not in the abandonment of the democratic terrain but, on the contrary, in the extension of the field of democratic struggles to the whole of civil society and the state, that the possibility resides for a hegemonic strategy of the Left.
>
> (Laclau and Mouffe, 1985:176)

While radical democracy retains the objective of the abolition of capitalism, it recognizes that such abolition will not eliminate the other inequalities within society. Dealing with all social inequalities requires a far broader movement than that anticipated by traditional Marxists.

As we saw in the preceding section of this chapter, postmodernism can be, and has been, disassociated from capitalism. Furthermore, theorists like Laclau and Mouffe have strayed quite far from traditional Marxian concerns and goals. However, other post-Marxists have adopted postmodern ideas while remaining closer to the customary concerns of Marxian theory. For example, Jameson (1984) sees postmodernism as the "cultural logic of late capitalism." Jameson locates the break between modernism and postmodernism (although he is clear that there are no clear dividing lines between the two phenomena and the two epochs) in the 1950s or early 1960s. A "spent and exhausted" modernism gave way to postmodernism (Jameson, 1984:53). While postmodernism is located in, and discussed in terms of, various cultural forms such as architecture, painting, and movies, it is linked to contemporary multinational capitalism. These new cultural forms reflect, and are financed by, elements of capitalist society through foundations and the direct support of business.

Following Marx, Jameson refuses simply to criticize postmodernism and its various cultural manifestations. He argues that Marx urges us to think about capitalism in a way "that would be capable of grasping the demonstrably baleful features of capitalism along with its extraordinary and liberating dynamism simultaneously . . . that capitalism is at one and the same time the best thing that has ever happened to the human race, and the worst" (Jameson, 1984:86). Similarly, in terms of postmodernism, Jameson prods us "to make at least some effort to think of cultural evolution of late capitalism dialectically, as catastrophe and progress all together" (1984:86).

Jameson sees postmodernism as the third great expansion of capitalism. Previously, the world witnessed the growth of national markets and then an imperialist system. Each had its own cultural elements, but both were primarily economic in character. Postmodernism represents an "internationalization of a radically new type" (Jameson, 1984:88). That new internationalization is primarily cultural in nature. To Jameson the contemporary world is characterized by an "explosion" of culture, "a prodigious expansion of culture throughout the social realm, to the point at which everything in our social life—from economic value and state power to practices and to the very structure of the psyche itself—can be said to have become 'cultural' " (1984:87). As a Marxist, Jameson urges that we seek to understand this new postmodern world so that we can act in, and struggle against, it as individuals and collectivities. (In spite of such a call, more orthodox Marxists regard Jameson as "apolitical" [B. Anderson, 1987–88].)

Thus, while many postmodernists have abandoned Marxian theory, Jameson clings to it as a basic, underlying framework. In an interview with Jameson, Stuart Hall describes him as having "an absolutely unquestioned faith in the logic of classical marxism" (Hall and Jameson, 1990:31). Jameson contends that he holds to

> the absolute conviction that this is still capitalism in the classic sense. Postmodernism has this odd double standard where you're convinced that capitalism has triumphed: there's the market on the one hand and everybody's better off and everybody plays their different music, but on the other hand we're also equally convinced that there's incredible misery in these societies, they're getting worse rather than better, . . . the new global wealth and the new global immiseration are true simultaneously. . . . I'm convinced that this new postmodern global form of capitalism will now have a new class logic about it. . . . I still find myself committed to the marxist logic."
>
> (Hall and Jameson, 1990:31)

But while Jameson remains committed to Marxian theory, he is certainly integrating into it ideas drawn from postmodernist thinking.

Another Marxian foray into postmodernist theory is David Harvey's *The Condition of Postmodernity* (1989). While Harvey sees much of merit in postmodern thinking, he sees serious weaknesses in it from a Marxian viewpoint. Postmodernist theory is accused of overemphasizing the problems of the modern world and of underemphasizing its material achievements. Most importantly, it seems to accept postmodernity and its associated problems rather than suggesting ways of overcoming these difficulties: "The rhetoric of postmodernism is dangerous for it avoids confronting the realities of political economy and the circumstances of global power" (Harvey, 1989:117). What postmodernist theory needs to confront is the source of its ideas—the political and economic transformation of late twentieth-century capitalism.

Central to the political economic system is control over markets and the labor process (these two arenas involve the issue of *accumulation* in capitalism). While the postwar period between 1945 and 1973 was characterized by an inflexible process of accumulation, since 1973 we have moved to a more flexible process. Harvey associates the earlier period with Fordism (as well as Keynesian economics) and the later period with post-Fordism, but we need not discuss these issues here, since they have been covered in Chapter 8. While Fordism is inflexible, Harvey sees post-Fordism as associated with flexible accumulation resting "on flexibility with respect to labour processes, labour markets, products, and patterns of consumption. It is characterized by the emergence of entirely new sectors of production, new ways of providing financial services, new markets, and, above all, greatly intensified rates of commercial, technological, and organizational innovation" (1989:147).

While Harvey sees great changes, and argues that it is these changes that lie at the base of postmodern thinking, he believes that there are many *continuities* between the Fordist and post-Fordist eras. His major conclusion is that while "there has certainly been a sea-change in the surface appearance of capitalism since 1973 . . . the underlying logic of capitalist accumulation and its crisis tendencies remain the same" (Harvey, 1989:189). Thus, Harvey adopts a viewpoint that resembles, at least in the latter respect, that of Jameson.

Central to Harvey's approach is the idea of time-space compression. He believes that modernism served to compress both time and space and that that process has accelerated in the postmodern era, leading to "an intense phase of time-space compression that has a disorienting and disruptive impact upon political-economic practices, the balance of class power, as well as upon cultural and social life" (Harvey, 1989:284). But this is *not* essentially different from earlier epochs in capitalism: "We have, in short, witnessed another fierce round in that process of annihilation of space through time that has always lain at the center of capitalism's dynamic" (Harvey, 1989:293). To give an example of the annihilation of space through time, cheeses once available only in France are now widely sold throughout the United States because of rapid, low-cost transportation. Or, in the 1991 war with Iraq, television transported us instantaneously from air raids in Baghdad to "scud" attacks on Tel Aviv to military briefings in Riyadh.

Thus, to Harvey, postmodernism is *not* discontinuous with modernism; they are reflections of the same underlying capitalist dynamic.[4] Both modernism and postmodernism, Fordism and post-Fordism, coexist in today's world. The emphasis on Fordism and post-Fordism will "vary from time to time and place to place, depending on which configuration is profitable and which is not" (Harvey, 1989:344). Such a viewpoint serves to bring the issue of postmodernity under the umbrella of neo-Marxian theory, although it is, in turn, modified by developments in postmodern thinking.

Finally, Harvey discerns changes and cracks in postmodernity, indicating that we may already be moving into a new era, an era that neo-Marxian theory must be prepared to theorize, perhaps by integrating still other idea systems.

Other Post-Marxist Theories

While all the theories discussed thus far in this section can be considered post-Marxist, there is a range of post-Marxist works that cannot be included in the preceding categories. An example of such post-Marxist thinking is *Democracy and Capitalism* by Samuel Bowles and Herbert Gintis (1987). This work draws upon both Marxism and liberalism—hence it is inherently synthetic—but finds both of them wanting. Since Bowles and Gintis are interested in the creation of a democratic society, they find limited guidelines in these two "isms." Liberalism focuses on liberty, not democracy, while Marxism is concerned with classlessness, not democracy. In terms of a related interest in power, liberalism is limited to a concern for state power while Marxism focuses on class power. In contrast, for Bowles and Gintis, power is heterogeneous and not reducible to a single source or structure. Thus, power can be analyzed in all spheres of life (for example, in the patriarchal family) and not just in the state or the economy. Therefore, it is necessary to democratize not simply the economy but "the entire ensemble of social relationships that make up society" (Bowles and Gintis, 1987:91).

The heart of Bowles and Gintis's theory lies in the relationship between structure and action (see Chapter 15 for more efforts to integrate these phenomena). In their view, power involves both structure and action. While action is controlled by structure, action, either individual or collective, has the capacity to change structure. Structures exist in various sites throughout society, and they constrain social action which, in turn, alters structure. Each of these sites is seen as a kind of "game" in which the rules (structure) and the players (actors) are continually transforming one another. However, these games (which overlap one another) are asymmetrical, so one group of players has an advantage over other groups. As a result, domination and power are of central importance in these games.

Turning to the issue of action, Bowles and Gintis find the Marxian model

---

[4] Bauman (1990) contends that capitalism and socialism were simply mirror images of modernity.

wanting (as is liberalism on this issue). Marxists adopt an *"expressive conception of action,* that is, the notion that individual behavior is an expression of collective membership. According to the expressive theory of action, individuals behave according to their class, gender, national, ethnic, and other social positions" (Bowles and Gintis, 1987:146). Lacking in such an approach is a notion of individual choice and individual action. In its place (as well as that of the limited sense of choice and action in liberalism), Bowles and Gintis offer the notion of "becoming by acting," which involves the idea "that individuals constitute themselves in important part through their joint projects" (1987:150).

Following the general linguistic turn in social theory, Bowles and Gintis focus on the importance of "discourses" and the struggle over them in the formation of collective actors: "A democratic social movement depends upon political discourse as its synthesizing force. Like guns and money, discourse is a social force with a character of its own" (1987:155). Their objective is to help create a new, postliberal, post-Marxian democratic discourse. And that discourse, it is hoped, will lead to a postliberal, radical democracy. At the center of such a society is a democratically accountable economy, educational system, family structure, neighborhood, and so on. The emphasis on democratic accountability, the focus on a wide range of institutions, and the effort to draw on both Marxism and liberalism renders this a form of post-Marxist theory.

Before closing this section, it should be noted that many Marxian theorists are unhappy with these post-Marxist developments (for example, Burawoy, 1990; Wood, 1986). Burawoy, for example, attacks the analytical Marxists for eliminating the issue of history and for making a fetish of clarity and rigor. Weldes critiques analytical Marxism for allowing itself to be colonized by mainstream economics, adopting a purely "technical, problem-solving approach," becoming increasingly academic and less political, and growing more conservative (1989:354). Wood picks up on the political issue and critiques analytical Marxism (as well as postmodern Marxism) for its political quietism and its "cynical defeatism, where every radical programme of change is doomed to failure" (1989:88). Even supporters of one branch of analytical Marxism, the rigorous empirical study of Marxian ideas, have been critical of their brethren in rational choice theory who, mistakenly in their view, adopt a position of methodological individualism (Levine, Sober and Wright, 1987). The work of Laclau and Mouffe has come under particularly heavy attack. For example, Allen Hunter criticizes them for their overall commitment to idealism and, more specifically, for situating "themselves at the extreme end of discourse analysis, viewing *everything* as discourse" (1988:892). Similarly, Geras (1987) attacks Laclau and Mouffe for their idealism, but he also sees them as profligate, dissolute, illogical, and obscurantist. The tenor of Laclau and Mouffe's reply to Geras is caught by its title "Post-Marxism without Apologies" (1987). Burawoy attacks Laclau and Mouffe (and Bowles and Gintis) for getting "lost in the web of history where everything is important and explanation is therefore impossible" (1990:790). In contrast, Burawoy believes that Marxism remains useful in understanding capitalism's dynamics and contradictions. Thus, with the demise of communism and the ascendancy of worldwide capitalism, "Marxism will . . . , once more, come into its own" (Burawoy, 1990:792).

It is likely that post-Marxism will continue to be highly controversial both in Marxist intellectual circles and in the larger intellectual community.

CONCLUSION

It is abundantly clear that many sociological theories are now borrowing heavily from one another and cutting across multiple levels of social analysis, with the result that the traditionally clear borders between theories are growing increasingly blurred and porous. How this will sort out is not yet clear. It may be that in the near term we will see a dramatically different, less differentiated, more synthetic theoretical landscape in sociology. Or it may be that old theoretical allegiances will be revived, thereby maintaining the separate and warring fiefdoms that have characterized sociological theory for the last several decades. Many observers (for example, Cook, O'Brien, and Kollock, 1990; Lamont and Wuthnow, 1990) worry explicitly about a renewal of such fiefdoms and the interminable political infighting that inevitably accompanies them. One indicator of this possibility is Garfinkel's (1988) contention that ethnomethodology is an "incommensurably alternate sociology." This, coupled with the absence of much indication of a willingness of the part of ethnomethodology to adopt the ideas of other theories, indicates a high probability of continued conflict between ethnomethodology and other theoretical perspectives. While we need to continue to be concerned about this problem, the diverse body of work pointing in a synthetic (and integrative) direction allows us to luxuriate for the moment in the glow of the new movement toward syntheses within sociological theory.

While it is tempting to end on such an uplifting note, instead let us turn the basic thrust of this chapter and the last on its head and argue that what these syntheses are really succeeding in doing is turning strong theoretical perspectives, ones that have demonstrated their usefulness over long periods of time, into the equivalent of theoretical "mush." If all sociological theories are seeking syntheses with one another, might we not end up with a series of flabby theories that are weak and useless? Take the example of Collins's definition of *conflict theory*, discussed in Chapter 16, as a theory of the organization of society and the behavior of people and groups in society. Defined in this way as a general approach to the entire domain of sociology, it is unclear precisely what conflict theory has to offer to sociology. It is certainly no longer a theory of conflict, which Collins takes pains to differentiate from conflict theory. If all theories are intent on moving in this direction, then what are we left with?

One answer could be one grand integrative theory. Certainly, the neofunc-tionalists, symbolic interactionists, exchange theorists, and others discussed in this chapter and the last would be quite comfortable with the umbrella defi-nition offered by Collins. But this flies in the face of the movement away from the production of grand, overarching theories. Instead, what may be evolving, possibly for the first time, is a sense of sociology's common ground (perhaps, in paradigmatic terms, a common image of the subject matter of sociology). It has often been lamented that, unlike many other established fields, sociology lacks an agreed-upon domain. The development of such a common base would be a most welcome outcome of theoretical syntheses.

However, it is not likely that we are in the process of evolving one grand, commonly agreed-upon sociological theory. The reason is that in order to achieve such agreement, the theory would need to be so general, vague, and amorphous that it could hardly be called "a theory" and would be virtually useless. Returning to my argument about an integrated sociological paradigm (which bears strong similarities with the movement toward theoretical syn-theses described here), my view was that the integrated paradigm would not replace extant paradigms but rather supplement their extremist perspectives with a more integrative one. If we are in the process of developing an inte-grated sociological theory (or theories), it should supplement *not* replace extant theories. This means that extant theories will need to retain their dis-tinctive "teeth" (while searching for the integrative core). Thus, for example, a conflict theorist should be concerned about Collins's eagerness to surrender a theory of conflict. After all, whatever conflict theory has achieved has been based on its theory of conflict.

It is interesting to note in this context that there is an undercurrent of uneas-iness running through this body of work on theoretical syntheses. For exam-ple, Collins (1990) talks of intellectual "piracy" and Fine (1990) of symbolic interactionism's "promiscuity." In addition, Cook, O'Brien, and Kollock (1990) address the "pitfalls" of syntheses within exchange theory. Although these works are not explicit on this, it may be that there is an underlying concern about the costs of excessive synthesis.

A natural damper on this movement toward excessive synthesis is that in spite of the fact that sociologists from many different theoretical perspectives are espousing integration, those same sociologists are likely to reject the spe-cific efforts stemming from other theories. For example, Friedman and Hechter (1988) anticipate hostility to rational choice theory's synthetic efforts from two sources. For one thing, they believe that what they call interpretive approaches (for example, phenomenology, hermeneutics) will be hostile to these efforts because they are based on rational choice theory's positivistic orientation. They also believe that all structuralists (for example, Durkheimians, Marxists, network theorists) will "object on principle to *any* approach that is based on methodological individualism" (Friedman and Hechter, 1988:212). If Fried-man and Hechter are right about the synthetic efforts of rational choice theory, and their argument is extended to theoretical syntheses from all theoretical directions, then it is unlikely that the efforts toward theoretical syntheses will grow too excessive.

On the other hand, there is a delicate balance here. While traditional theoretical allegiances can serve to prevent excessive synthesis, they can also, as was the case with the movement toward micro-macro integration in the 1980s, lead to a repetition of theoretical extremism within the synthetic movement. In other words, we will end up little better off than we were during the decades of theoretical extremism. Thus, a more realistic, albeit less inspiring, conclusion to this chapter and to this book is that we are moving into a particularly interesting and important era in the history of sociological theory. Great gains can be made, but there are great dangers as well. Theorists will need to walk a very fine line as they strive toward greater integration and synthesis without gutting their theories or setting the stage for a renewed period of theoretical extremism. Whatever the gains to be made and dangers to be avoided, this is a particularly interesting and exciting period for the student interested in sociological theory.

APPENDIX

SOCIOLOGICAL METATHEORIZING AND A METATHEORETICAL SCHEMA FOR ANALYZING SOCIOLOGICAL THEORY

*I*N Chapter 6 we saw that one of the most recent developments in sociological theory is the boom in interest in sociological metatheorizing. While theorists take the social world as their subject matter, metatheorists engage in *the systematic study of the underlying structure of sociological theory*. Among our goals in this Appendix is a look at the explosion of interest in metatheorizing in sociology and the basic parameters of this approach. Furthermore, the entire structure of this book rests on a specific set of metatheoretical perspectives developed by the author (Ritzer, 1975a, 1981a). Because the primary objective of the text has been to present sociological theory, it was decided to make this organizing schema as unobtrusive as possible. Thus, all chapters, as well as the book as a whole, can be read without knowledge of the organizing schema that undergirds them. However, some students may be interested in that schema, either early in their reading of the book or after they have finished it. Thus, another objective of this Appendix is to present the metatheoretical ideas that inform the text, but before we can do that, we need to present an overview of metatheorizing in sociology.

METATHEORIZING IN SOCIOLOGY

We start by making it clear that sociologists are not the only ones to do meta-analysis, that is, to reflexively study their own discipline. Others who do such work include philosophers (Radnitzky, 1973), psychologists (Gergen, 1973, 1986; Schmidt et al., 1984), political scientists (Connolly, 1973), a number of other social scientists (various essays in Fiske and Shweder, 1986), and historians (White, 1973). Some of their efforts are quite similar to at least some types of meta-analysis in sociology, while others differ considerably from the types of work done in sociology. The key point is that the study of one's own discipline is not the exclusive province of the sociologist.

Beyond the fact that meta-analysis is found in other fields, it is also the case that various kinds of sociologists, not just metatheorists, do such analysis. We can group the various types of meta-analysis in sociology under the heading "metasociology," which we can define as the reflexive study of the underlying structure of sociology in general, as well as of its various components— substantive areas (for example, Hall's [1983] overview of occupational sociology), concepts (Rubenstein's [1986] analysis of the concept of "structure"), methods (*metamethods*; for example, Brewer and Hunter's [1988] and Noblit and Hare's [1988] efforts to synthesize sociological methods), data (*meta-data-analysis*;[1] for example, Fendrich, 1984; Hunter, Schmidt, and Jackson, 1982; Polit and Falbo, 1987; Wolf, 1986) and theories. It is the latter, *metatheorizing*, that will concern us in this Appendix.

What distinguishes work in this area is not so much the process of metatheorizing (or systematically studying theories, which all metatheorists share) but rather the nature of the end products. There are three varieties of metatheorizing, largely defined by differences in their end products (Ritzer, 1990d, 1991). The first type, *metatheorizing as a means of attaining a deeper understanding of theory* (M_U), involves the study of theory in order to produce a better, more profound understanding of extant theory (Ritzer, 1988).[2] M_U is concerned, more specifically, with the study of theories, theorists, and communities of theorists, as well as the larger intellectual and social contexts of theories and theorists. The second type, *metatheorizing as a prelude to theory development* (M_P), entails the study of extant theory in order to produce new sociological theory. (It is this second type of metatheorizing in which the classical theorists were most likely to engage.) There is also a third type, *metatheorizing as a source of perspectives that overarch sociological theory* (M_O), in which the study of theory is oriented toward the goal of producing a perspective, one could say *a metatheory*, that overarches some part or all of sociological theory. (As we will see, it is this type of metatheorizing that provided the framework used in constructing this book.) Given these definitions, let us examine each type of metatheorizing in greater detail.

---

[1] I have labeled this (somewhat awkwardly) "meta-data-analysis" in order to differentiate it from the more generic meta-analysis. In meta-data-analysis the goal is to seek ways of cumulating research results across research studies. In his introduction to Wolf's *Meta-Analysis,* Niemi defines *meta-analysis* as "the application of statistical procedures to collections of empirical findings from individual studies for the purpose of integrating, synthesizing, and making sense of them" (Wolf, 1986:5).

[2] While in my earlier work (Ritzer, 1987, 1988) I tended to equate this type with all of metatheorizing, I now see it as only one of three major types. I also prefer now to discuss metatheorizing as the generic process rather than metatheory, which is, as we shall see, only one of three possible end products of metatheorizing.

The first type of metatheorizing, M_U, is composed of four basic subtypes, all of which involve the formal or informal study of sociological theory to attain a deeper understanding of it. The first subtype focuses on intellectual or cognitive issues that are internal to sociology. Included here are attempts to identify major cognitive paradigms (Ritzer, 1975a, 1975b; see also the discussion below) and "schools of thought" (Sorokin, 1928), more dynamic views of the underlying structure of sociological theory (Harvey, 1982, 1987; Wiley, 1979) and the development of general metatheoretical tools with which to analyze existing sociological theories and to develop new theories (Alexander et al., 1987; Edel, 1959; Gouldner, 1970; Ritzer, 1989b, 1990a; Wiley, 1988). The second subtype (internal-social) also looks within sociology, but it focuses on social rather than cognitive factors. The main approach here emphasizes the communal aspects of various sociological theories and includes efforts to identify the major "schools" in the history of sociology (Bulmer, 1984, 1985; Tiryakian, 1979, 1986), the more formal, network approach to the study of the ties among groups of sociologists (Mullins, 1973, 1983), as well as studies of theorists themselves that examine their institutional affiliations, their career patterns, their positions within the field of sociology, and so on (Gouldner, 1970). The third variant (external-intellectual) turns to other academic disciplines for ideas, tools, concepts, and theories that can be used in the analysis of sociological theory (for example, Brown, 1987, 1990a). Finally, the external-social approach shifts to a more macro-level to look at the larger society (national setting, sociocultural setting, etc.) and the nature of its impact on sociological theorizing (for example, Vidich and Lyman, 1985).

Most metatheorizing in sociology is not M_U; rather, it is the second type, metatheorizing as a prelude to the development of sociological theory (M_P). Most important classical and contemporary theorists developed their theories, at least in part, on the basis of a careful study of, and reaction to, the work of other theorists. Among the most important examples are Marx's theory of capitalism (see Chapter 2), developed out of a systematic engagement with Hegelian philosophy as well as other ideas such as political economy and utopian socialism; Parsons's action theory (see Chapter 7), developed out of a systematic study of the work of Durkheim, Weber, Pareto, and Marshall; Alexander's (1982–83) multidimensional, neofunctional theory, based on a detailed study of the work of Marx, Weber, Durkheim, and Parsons; and Habermas's (1987) communication theory, based on his examination of the work of various critical theorists as well as that of Marx, Weber, Parsons, Mead, and Durkheim. Let us look in more detail at M_P as it was practiced by two theorists discussed in this book—Marx and Parsons.

In *Economic and Philosophic Manuscripts of 1844*, Marx (1932/1964) develops his theoretical perspective on the basis of a detailed and careful analysis and critique of the works of political economists like Adam Smith, Jean-Baptiste Say, David Ricardo, and James Mill; philosophers like G. W. F. Hegel, the Young Hegelians (for example, Bruno Bauer), and Ludwig Feuerbach; utopian socialists like Etienne Cabet, Robert Owen, Charles Fourier, and Pierre Proudhon; and a variety of other major and minor intellectual schools and figures. It seems safe to say that in almost its entirety the *Manuscripts of 1844* is a metatheoretical treatise in which Marx develops his own ideas out of an engagement with a variety of idea systems.

What of Marx's other works? Are they more empirical? Less metatheoretical? In his preface to *The German Ideology* (Marx and Engels, 1845–46/1970), C. J. Arthur describes that work as comprised mainly of "detailed line by line polemics against the writings of some of their [Marx and Engels's] contemporaries" (1970:1). In fact, Marx himself describes *The German Ideology* as an effort "to set forth together our conception as opposed to the ideological one of German philosophy, in fact to settle accounts with our former philosophical conscience. The intention was carried out in the form of a critique of post-Hegelian philosophy" (1859/1970:22). *The Holy Family* (Marx and Engels, 1845/1956) is, above all, an extended critique of Bruno Bauer, the Young Hegelians, and their propensity toward speculative "critical criticism."[3] In their foreword, Marx and Engels make it clear that this kind of metatheoretical work is a prelude to their coming theorizing: "We therefore give this polemic as a preliminary to the independent works in which we . . . shall present our positive view" (1845/1956:16). In the *Grundrisse* Marx (1857–58/1974) chooses as his metatheoretical antagonists the political economist David Ricardo and the French socialist Pierre Proudhon (Nicolaus, 1974). Throughout the *Grundrisse* Marx is struggling to solve an array of theoretical problems, in part through a critique of the theories and theorists mentioned above and in part through an application of ideas derived from Hegel. In describing the introduction to the *Grundrisse*, Nicolaus says that it "reflects in its every line the struggle of Marx against Hegel, Ricardo and Proudhon. From it, Marx carried off the most important objective of all, namely the basic principles of writing history dialectically" (1974:42). *A Contribution to the Critique of Political Economy* (Marx, 1859/1970) is, as the title suggests, an effort to build a distinctive economic approach on the basis of a critique of the works of the political economists.

Even *Capital* (1867/1967)—which is admittedly one of Marx's most empirical works, since he deals more directly with the reality of the capitalist work world through the use of government statistics and reports—is informed by Marx's earlier metatheoretical work and contains some metatheorizing of its own. In fact, the subtitle, *A Critique of Political Economy*, makes the metatheoretical roots absolutely clear. However, Marx is freer in *Capital* to be much more "positive," that is, to construct his own distinctive theoretical orientation. This freedom is traceable, in part, to his having done much of the metatheoretical groundwork in earlier works. Furthermore, most of the new metatheoretical work is relegated to the so-called fourth volume of *Capital*, published under the title *Theories of Surplus Value* (Marx, 1862–63/1963, 1862–63/1968). *Theories* is composed of many extracts from the work of the major

---

[3] In fact, the book is subtitled *Against Bruno Bauer and Co.*

political economists (for example, Smith, Ricardo) as well as critical analysis of them by Marx. In sum, it is safe to say that Marx was, largely, a meta-theorist, perhaps the *most* metatheoretical of all classical sociological theorists.

Talcott Parsons's *The Structure of Social Action* (1937) may be the purest example (except, perhaps, for the work of the neo-Parsonian, Jeffrey Alexander) of M_P. Most of *The Structure of Social Action* is devoted to a serious study of the work of Alfred Marshall, Vilfredo Pareto, Emile Durkheim, and Max Weber.[4] And Parsons uses that metatheoretical work to begin to lay out his own action theory. The roots of Parsons's work lie not in the empirical world but in what, in his view, were the convergent ideas of the theorists mentioned above.

In fact, Parsons was explicit about his M_P approach. He sees *The Structure of Social Action* as an "*empirical* monograph" and states that the phenomena under scrutiny "happen to be the theories that certain writers have held about other phenomena . . . the theories that have been discussed [are] just as much a question of fact as any other, to be verified by the same method, that of observation. The facts in this case have reference to the published works of these writers" (1949:697). But Parsons is not content simply to analyze extant theories; his study "has also done some explicit theorizing on its own account" (1949:697). In the preface to the second edition of *The Structure of Social Action* Parsons makes a similar point in reflecting on the work over a decade after its publication: "This was a convenient vehicle for the clarification of problems and concepts, of implications and interrelations. It was a means of taking stock of the theoretical resources at our disposal. . . . The clarification gained from this stocktaking has opened up possibilities for further theoretical development of sufficient scope so that its impetus is as yet by no means exhausted" (1949:B).

Only two years after the publication of the second edition of *The Structure of Social Action,* Parsons and Shils (with the assistance of Olds) make the metatheoretical roots of the revised theory of action perfectly clear. In *Toward a General Theory of Action* (1951) they state in the very first footnote, which follows the first four words of text:

> The present exposition of the theory of action represents in one major respect a revision and extension of the position stated in Parsons, *The Structure of Social Action* . . . particularly in the light of psychoanalytic theory, of developments in behavior psychology, and of developments in the anthropological analysis of culture.
>
> (Parsons and Shils, 1951:53)

Between the 1937 publication of *The Structure of Social Action* and the early 1950s' works on the theory of action, Parsons amended and changed his theoretical orientation. It *may* be that those changes were the result of changes in the social world, but it is *certainly* the case that Parsons's theoretical ideas changed as he metatheoretically engaged the ideas of a variety of theorists

---

[4] It also involves studies of a variety of philosophical traditions—for example, utilitarianism, positivism, empiricism.

over the years, including the psychiatrist Sigmund Freud,[5] the anthropologist Franz Boas,[6] the behaviorist Edward Tolman, and so on. Above all, Parsons elaborated his theory on the basis of a metatheoretical reanalysis of his own work as well as of the criticisms of that work. Thus, for example, late in his life Parsons (1966, 1971) shifted to evolutionary theory on the basis of his own analysis of the shortcomings of his earlier work as pointed out by the critics.[7] Parsons makes this clear in one of his earlier works on change:

> I should address myself to the problem of social change. I am very happy to do this, both because of the intrinsic importance of the subject and because its place in my own work has been the subject of considerable concern, even controversy. Furthermore, I have been devoting more explicit attention to this field recently than before, and some of the things I have to say are, I think, new.

While we have singled out Marx and Parsons for detailed discussion, the fact is that virtually all classical and contemporary theorists were metatheorists, and, more specifically, they practiced M_P.

There are a number of examples of the third type of metatheorizing, M_O. They include Wallace's (1988) "disciplinary matrix," Ritzer's (1979, 1981a) "integrated sociological paradigm" (see below), Furfey's (1953/1965) positivistic metasociology, Gross's (1961) "neodialectical" metasociology, Alexander's (1982) "general theoretical logic for sociology" and Lehman's (1988) presuppositions and models of the state (derived from Alexander).

Wallace's and Ritzer's works fit best into the category of M_O because their transcendent perspectives are derived from a careful study of sociological theory. In contrast, the works of Furfey and Gross posit their overarching orientations as preceding and informing sociological theory. Finally, the works of Alexander and Lehman represent mixed types. Their adoption of a multidisciplinary approach precedes the study of theory, while their focus on action and order is derived more from an M_O approach. In spite of these differences, all six works produce overarching theoretical perspectives.

The three varieties of metatheory are ideal types. In actual cases there is often considerable overlap in the objectives of metatheoretical works. Nevertheless, those who do one type of metatheorizing tend to be less interested in achieving the objectives of the other two types. Of course, there are sociologists who at one time or another have done all three types of metatheorizing.

---

[5] In fact, in the preface to the second edition of *The Structure of Social Action*, Parsons discusses the need to do a "full-dress analysis of Freud's theoretical development seen in the context of the 'theory of social action' " (1949).

[6] However, Parsons does not see Boas as being "of comparable *theoretical* stature" to Freud, Durkheim, or the other major thinkers analyzed by him (1949).

[7] In terms of his metatheoretical work, I have not even mentioned Parsons's forays into M_U in his frequent essays on the general state of sociological theory, such as "The Prospects of Sociological Theory" (1954a) and "The Present Position and Prospects of Systematic Theory in Sociology" (1954b). Also worth mentioning is Parsons's role as the initial editor of the original *American Sociologist*, which was founded as a major outlet for metasociological work.

For example, Alexander (1982–1983) creates overarching perspectives (M_O) in the first volume of *Theoretical Logic in Sociology*, uses them in the next three volumes to achieve a better understanding (M_U) of the classic theorists, and more recently has sought to help create neofunctionalism (M_P) as a theoretical successor to structural functionalism (Alexander and Colomy, 1990).

The Gains From Metatheorizing

Metatheorizing provides three absolutely essential aids to sociological theory. First, M_U offers systematic methods of understanding, evaluating, criticizing, and improving extant theories. Second, M_P is one of several important bases for creating new theory. Third, through M_O, theorists (as well as practitioners and researchers) are provided with useful overarching theoretical perspectives. Let us look at each of the three functions in turn.

It is the distinctive responsibility of metatheorizing (M_U) to deepen the level of understanding of all sociological theories. While many sociologists read theory, often very casually, metatheorists systematically study theory and do detailed (often comparative) studies of an array of sociological theories. Metatheorists have at their disposal an arsenal of tools that allows them to uncover many things about sociological theory that would not be visible to the more casual student of theory. Beyond facilitating deeper comprehension of theory, systematic metatheorizing allows them to more adequately evaluate and critically analyze extant theories. Finally, and perhaps most importantly, metatheorists are better able to uncover ways of improving specific theories as well as theory in general.

The use of M_U tools allow metatheorists to uncover interesting, important, and sometimes surprising things about theories and theorists. For example, M_U tools used in comparative analyses show that sociological theory has moved through four major periods over the last four decades (Ritzer, forthcoming b). The paradigm concept allows us to describe the 1960s as multiparadigmatic, with theoretical divisions and conflicts among and within paradigms (Ritzer, 1975a, 1975b). The micro-macro distinction pointed to both the rise of microsociological theories in the 1970s (Ritzer, 1985) and the theoretical efforts at micro-macro synthesis in the 1980s (Ritzer, 1990a). The latter observations have led to the identification of the emergence of a much wider array of synthetic efforts as we enter the 1990s (Ritzer, 1990b).

These analyses, taken together, do *not* constitute a history of recent sociological theory, but they do represent a metatheoretical analysis of that history. They are not offered as an alternative to a history of sociological theory. Indeed, the combination of metatheoretical and more straightforward historical analyses would greatly increase our level of understanding of theory.

Not only does M_U improve the understanding of sociological theory, but it allows metatheorists to systematically evaluate and criticize theories. For example, the micro-macro conceptualization used in a critical examination (Ritzer, 1985) of Randall Collins's (1981a, 1981b) work on interaction ritual chains indicated that the work erred on the side of micro reductionism. Collins's (1988) later work has tried to rectify this imbalance by giving greater importance to macro phenomena.

M_U analyses not only permit metatheorists to better understand and evaluate theories but also can directly help to improve sociological theories. For example, the metatheoretical analysis of the current movement toward theoretical syntheses suggests that sociological theory would be enhanced if *some* supporters of virtually all sociological theories were to move away from narrow adherence to a specific theory or level of analysis. (However, this is not meant to imply that all theorists should move toward synthesis. There is utility in narrower theoretical perspectives.) The model might be, for example, structural functionalism, which is being enhanced as thinkers (Alexander and Colomy, 1990) seek to integrate insights from a range of other theoretical perspectives (for example, conflict theory, ethnomethodology). At the same time, the traditional focus of structural functionalism on macro-level phenomena (social structure, culture) is being extended to include greater interest in micro-level phenomena. This two-pronged extension is transforming structural functionalism into neofunctionalism and greatly enhancing its scope and power. Out of this development we may see either the triumph of a more integrative neofunctionalism or a bifurcation in which structural functionalism remains committed to a macro-level focus and neofunctionalism becomes a distinctive, integrative perspective. Similar kinds of things are occurring at the frontiers of many other theoretical perspectives (for example, symbolic interactionism [Fine, 1990]).

The second major contribution of metatheorizing is the creation of new theory. While this is the distinctive goal of M_P, theory creation also results from M_U. The dividing line between an enhanced theory and a new theory is often quite indistinct. For example, we have argued that Alexander, in part through M_U analysis, has embarked on an effort to enhance structural functionalism. However, there are those (for example, Turner and Maryanski, 1988) who see so many differences between traditional structural functionalism and neofunctionalism that the latter might be considered a new theory.

It is also the case that M_O works can lead to the creation of new theory. Such overarching perspectives as positivism, antipositivism, and postpositivism have helped generate a wide range of theories over the years. Theories like structural functionalism and exchange theory have clear roots in positivism, while many varieties of neo-Marxian theory and phenomenology are more rooted in antipositivistic overarching perspectives. Postpositivism may be seen at the base of postmodernism, poststructuralism, and perhaps even neofunctionalism.

New theory creation is *the* function of M_P. Methatheoretical reflection on the work of other theorists has been, continues to be, and should be an important source of new theory. One of the most important functions of metatheorizing, especially M_P, for the discipline of sociology is the production of a steady and continuing supply of new theory.

The third major function of metatheorizing is the production of overarching theoretical perspectives. While this is the distinctive role of M_O, it is possible for M_U and M_P to function in similar ways. For example, M_U work (Ritzer, 1975a) on the paradigmatic structure of sociology led to the generation of a transcendent orientation, the integrated sociological paradigm (Ritzer, 1981a). M_O, however, is specifically directed toward the generation of overarching perspectives. In an era characterized by a focus on narrow syntheses of theories and levels of analysis (as desirable as such work is), it is important that at least some sociologists produce such transcendent perspectives (see Antonio, 1990; Kellner, 1990). These overarching perspectives are essential in preventing us from losing sight of the field's parameters.

The Critics of Metatheorizing

Until the mid-1980s, the most visible aspects of metatheorizing may have been the criticisms, often quite severe, that were leveled at it (R. Collins, 1986a; Skocpol, 1986; J. Turner, 1985, 1986; for a review and analysis of these critiques, see Ritzer, 1988). This a rare event in academic history—the appearance of highly visible and influential critiques *before* the overt emergence of the field being attacked. What this meant, of course, is that the field, at least in an inchoate state, actually was there all the time. Much metatheoretical work had been done under a wide range of other headings—"sociology of sociology," "sociology of science," "sociology of knowledge," "history of sociology"— and, most notably, as an integral part of sociological theory. In fact, most of the criticisms have been made by closet metatheoreticians (for example, R. Collins, Skocpol, J. Turner) who may not have had a clear conception of what they were criticizing. Let us look at the three major critiques of sociological metatheorizing.

Jonathan Turner is critical of metatheory largely on pragmatic grounds because, in his view, it "often gets bogged down in weighty philosophical matters and immobilizes theory building . . . meta-theory often stymies as much as stimulates theoretical activity because it embroils theorists in inherently unresolvable and always debatable controversies" (1986:10; see also J. Turner 1985). Later, Turner describes metatheory as "interesting but counterproductive" and contends that those who propound it "never get around to developing theory" (1986:26).

In a review of a book (Alford and Friedland, 1985) on political sociology, Theda Skocpol (1986) makes it clear that in her view what is good and useful in that subfield is substantive theory and research. She describes the Alford and Friedland work, pejoratively, as "five hundred pages of nothing but metatheory" (Skocpol, 1986:10). She attacks the authors for "pigeonholing" the work of political sociologists, for arguing for the need for an integrated theory that draws from every pigeonhole but never specifies what it is about, for arguing that different types of approaches fit best at different levels of analysis, and for ignoring the fact that the best work in political sociology has dealt with the interrelations among such levels. She hopes that Alford and Friedland will return to substantive work in political sociology, but in the meantime "may the good lord protect other political sociologists from wandering into the dead end of metatheory" (Skocpol, 1986:11–12). The use of the phrase "dead end" in this sentence, as well as in the title of her review, implies clearly that Skocpol sees *no* productive role for metatheory within sociology.

Perhaps the most interesting critique of metatheory comes from Randall Collins (1986a). At first, Collins associates metatheory with mindless antipositivism. However, he quickly moves to a much broader critique:

> It is not surprising to me that metatheory does not go anywhere; it is basically a reflexive specialty, capable about making comments on other fields but dependent on intellectual life elsewhere that it can formalize and ideologize . . or critique. That is why so much of the intellectual work of today consists of commentaries on works of the past rather than constructions that are creative in their own right.
>
> (R. Collins, 1986a:1343)

In spite of his critique of metatheory, Collins proceeds to do what he condemns: he undertakes a metatheoretical analysis of a variety of works of the (recent) past.

Rather than having the desired effect of retarding the development of metatheorizing in sociology, critiques like those above have had the opposite effect, galvanizing metatheorists and leading to a flowering of metatheoretical work.

The Current Explosion of Interest in Metatheorizing

By the idea of a boom in metatheorizing we simply mean that there is a great increase in the quantity of work that is *explicitly* and *self-consciously* metatheoretical. The most objective evidence comes from a study by Fuhrman and Snizek (1990) of publications over the last decade which indicates strong and growing interest in metatheorizing in sociology. A very large number of the references in their paper are to recently published, or soon-to-be-published, works. Many other metatheoretical works have appeared in the brief time since that study was completed (for example, Berger, Wagner, and Zelditch, 1989; J. Turner, 1989a). This growth is notable in the journal *Sociological Theory*, which has devoted increasing space to essays that are explicitly metatheoretical (for example, Fararo, 1989; Levine, 1989; Ritzer, 1988). In addition, a number of recent (and forthcoming books) have also been overtly metatheoretical (Fiske and Shweder, 1986; Osterberg, 1988; Ritzer, 1991; J. Turner, 1989b) and many, perhaps even most, other books in sociological theory are implicitly metatheoretical. In March 1990, *Sociological Forum* devoted a special mini-issue to metatheorizing in sociology (Ritzer, 1990c), and in 1992 Sage will publish a book devoted to studies in metatheorizing (Ritzer, forthcoming c). Beyond this is a whole, and seemingly expanding, range of works that have dealt with more specific metatheoretical issues such as the micro-macro linkage (Alexander et al., 1987; R. Collins, 1981a, 1981b, 1988; Ritzer, 1990a), the relationship between agency and structure (Archer, 1982, 1988; Bernstein, 1971; Giddens, 1984), and levels of social analysis (Ritzer, 1989; Wiley, 1988, 1989). Although it is possible that all this represents a peak in metatheorizing in sociology, there are many reasons to believe that it more likely represents the takeoff point for a wide variety, and an increasing number, of explicitly metatheoretical works in sociology.

Given this overview, it is now time to turn to the specific metatheoretical approach that undergirds this book. As will become clear, it involves a combination of M_U and M_O. We begin with a brief review of the work of Thomas Kuhn, and then we examine my (M_U) analysis of sociology's multiple paradigms. Finally, we review the metatheoretical tool—the integrated sociological paradigm (M_O)—that is the source of the levels of analysis used to analyze sociological theories throughout this book.

THE IDEAS OF THOMAS KUHN

In 1962 the philosopher of science Thomas Kuhn published a rather slim volume entitled *The Structure of Scientific Revolutions*. Because this work grew out of philosophy, it appeared fated to a marginal status within sociology. This seemed especially likely because it focused on the hard sciences (physics, for example) and had little directly to say about the social sciences. However, the theses of the book proved extremely interesting to people in a wide range of fields (for example, Hollinger, 1980, in history; Searle, 1972, in linguistics; Stanfield, 1974, in economics), and to none was it more important than to sociologists. In 1970 Robert Friedrichs published the first important work from a Kuhnian perspective, *A Sociology of Sociology*. Since then there has been a steady stream of work from this perspective (Eckberg and Hill, 1979; Effrat, 1972; Eisenstadt and Curelaru, 1976; Falk and Zhao, 1990a, 1990b; Friedrichs, 1972a; Greisman, 1986; Lodahl and Gordon, 1972; Phillips, 1973, 1975; Quadagno, 1979; Ritzer, 1975a, 1975b, 1981b; Rosenberg, 1989; Snizek, 1976; Snizek et al., 1979). There is little doubt that Kuhnian theory is an important variety of M_U, but what exactly is Kuhn's approach?

One of Kuhn's goals in *The Structure of Scientific Revolutions* was to challenge commonly held assumptions about the way in which science changes. In the view of most laypeople and many scientists, science advances in a cumulative manner, with each advance building inexorably on all that preceded it. Science has achieved its present state through slow and steady increments of knowledge. It will advance to even greater heights in the future. This conception of science was enunciated by the physicist Sir Isaac Newton, who said, "If I have seen further, it is because I stood on the shoulders of giants." But Kuhn regarded this conception of cumulative scientific development as a myth and sought to debunk it.

Kuhn acknowledged that accumulation plays some role in the advance of science, but the truly major changes come about as a result of revolutions. Kuhn offered a theory of how major changes in science occur. He saw a science at any given time as dominated by a specific *paradigm* (defined for the moment as a fundamental image of the science's subject matter). *Normal science* is a period of accumulation of knowledge in which scientists work to expand the reigning paradigm. Such scientific work inevitably spawns *anomalies,* or findings that cannot be explained by the reigning paradigm. A *crisis* stage occurs if these anomalies mount, and this crisis may ultimately end in a scientific revolution. The reigning paradigm is overthrown as a new one takes its place at the center of the science. A new dominant paradigm is born, and the stage is set for the cycle to repeat itself. Kuhn's theory can be depicted diagrammatically:

Paradigm I ⟶ Normal Science ⟶ Anomalies ⟶
Crisis ⟶ Revolution ⟶ Paradigm II

It is during periods of revolution that the truly great changes in science take place. This view clearly places Kuhn at odds with most conceptions of scientific development.

The key concept in Kuhn's approach, as well as in this Appendix, is the paradigm. Unfortunately, Kuhn is vague on what he means by a paradigm. According to Margaret Masterman (1970), he used it in at least twenty-one different ways. But we will employ a definition of *paradigm* that we feel is true to the sense and spirit of his early work.

A paradigm serves to differentiate one scientific community from another. It can be used to differentiate physics from chemistry or sociology from psychology. These fields have different paradigms. It can also be used to differentiate between different historical stages in the development of a science. The paradigm that dominated physics in the nineteenth century is different from the one that dominated it in the early twentieth century. There is a third usage of the paradigm concept, and it is the one that is most useful to us here. Paradigms can differentiate among cognitive groupings *within* the same science. Contemporary psychoanalysis, for example, is differentiated into Freudian, Jungian, and Horneyian paradigms (among others)—that is, there are *multiple paradigms* in psychoanalysis—and the same is true of sociology and of most other fields.

We can now offer a definition of *paradigm* that we feel is true to the sense of Kuhn's original work:

> A paradigm is a fundamental image of the subject matter within a science. It serves to define what should be studied, what questions should be asked, how they should be asked, and what rules should be followed in interpreting the answers obtained. The paradigm is the broadest unit of consensus within a science and serves to differentiate one scientific community (*or subcommunity*) from another. It subsumes, defines, and interrelates the exemplars, *theories* [italics added], and methods and instruments that exist within it.
>
> (Ritzer, 1975a:7)

With this definition we can begin to see the relationship between paradigms and theories. *Theories are only part of larger paradigms.* To put it another way,

GEORGE RITZER: Autobiography as a Metatheoretical Tool

Biographical and autobiographical work is useful in help-ing us understand the work of sociological theorists, and of sociologists generally. The historian of science, Thomas Hankins explains it this way:

> [A] fully integrated biography of a scientist which includes not only his personality, but also his scientific work and the intel-lectual and social context of his times, [is] . . . still the best way to get at many of the problems that beset the writing of history of science . . . science is created by individuals, and however much it may be driven by forces outside, these forces work through the scientist himself. Biography is the literary lens through which we can best view this process.
>
> (Hankins, 1979:14)

What Hankins asserts about scientists generally informs my orientation to the biographies of sociological theorists, including myself. This autobiographical snippet is designed to sug-gest at least a few ways in which biography can be a useful tool for metatheoretical analysis.

While I have taught in sociology departments for over twenty years, and have written a great deal about and in sociology, my B.A. (City College of New York, 1962) is in psychology, my M.B.A. (University of Michigan, 1964) is in personnel administration, and my Ph.D. (Cor-nell University, 1968) is in industrial and labor relations. This lack of background in sociology has led to the lifelong study of sociological theory, an endeavor I have come to label "meta-theorizing." It has also, at least in one sense, aided my attempt to understand sociological theory. Because I had not been trained in a particular "school," I came to the study of sociological theory with few prior conceptions and biases. Rather, I was a student of all "schools of thought;" they were all equal grist for my theoretical mill.

Perhaps because I have always been unable to handle conflict, in my work I am often seeking to resolve conflict and reconcile competing perspectives and orientations. In my dissertation, later published as a book (Ritzer and Trice, 1969), I was concerned with the ways in which personnel managers resolve role conflict. For many years, I have been inter-ested in the techniques used by workers to cope with conflict on the job. This issue was central to my text on the sociology of occupations (Ritzer and Walczak, 1986). More impor-tantly, conflict resolution goes to the heart of the work on metatheory that has concerned me for almost two decades.

My first metatheoretical work, *Sociology: A Multiple Paradigm Science* (1975a), sought not only to lay out sociology's separable, and often conflicting, paradigms but also to make

a paradigm may encompass two or more *theories,* as well as different *images* of the subject matter, *methods* (and instruments), and *exemplars* (specific pieces of scientific work that stand as a model for all of those who follow). An objec-tive of this Appendix will be to identify the basic paradigms in sociology.

SOCIOLOGY: A MULTIPLE-PARADIGM SCIENCE

The idea that sociology is a multiple-paradigm science has received some empirical support (Lodahl and Gordon, 1972), but most of the analyses of the paradigmatic status of sociology have been conceptual.

the case for paradigm linking, leaping, bridging, and integrating. Uncomfortable with paradigmatic conflict, I wanted to see more harmony and integration in sociology. That led to the publication of *Toward an Integrated Sociological Paradigm* (1981a), in which I more fully developed my sense of an integrated paradigm. In recent years, the interest in resolving theoretical conflict has led me to focus on micro-macro (1990a) and agency-structure (forthcoming a) integration as well as the larger issue of theoretical syntheses (1990b). As I see it, there is considerable evidence that sociological theory is moving away from decades of theoretical extremism and conflict and toward greater theoretical integration and harmony. But, given my personality, what would one expect me to see?

My interest in metatheoretical work is explained by my desire to understand theory better and to resolve conflict within sociological theory. In *Metatheorizing in Sociology* (1991), I have, in effect, raised my own need to know more about sociological theory to the level of a need for the discipline as a whole. Metatheorizing is, after all, simply the systematic study of sociological theory. I believe that we need to do more of this in order to understand theory better, produce new theory, and produce new overarching theoretical perspectives (or metatheories). Metatheoretical study is also oriented to clarifying contentious issues, resolving disputes, and allowing for greater integration and synthesis. In addition, metatheoretical work, from my point of view, is so remote from the real world that the conflict found there is relatively painless and easily managed.

Another personality characteristic, my sense of myself as a highly rational person, informs my theoretical work. My starting point was Weber's theory of rationalization, and I have dealt with the relationship between rationalization and professionalization (see Ritzer, 1975b; Ritzer and Walczak, 1988). In a paper on "McDonaldization" (1983), I argued that while the bureaucracy was the paradigm case of formal rationalization in Weber's day, in modern society that model is the fast-food restaurant. I have recently come back to that issue in *Big Mac Attack: The McDonaldization of Society* (forthcoming a). One of my ongoing projects deals with the failure of the American automobile industry and the success of its Japanese counterpart. My thesis is that the American failure is traceable to its exclusive reliance on formal rationality, while the Japanese success is linked to its hyperrationality, involving the utilization of all four Weberian types of rationality—formal, substantive, intellectual, and practical.

Source: Adapted from George Ritzer, "I Never Metatheory I Didn't Like," *Mid-American Review of Sociology,* 15:21–32, 1991.

In the earliest systematic application of Kuhnian ideas to sociology, Robert Friedrichs (1970) presented two different images of the paradigmatic status of sociology, but both affirmed the idea that sociology was a multiple-paradigm science. At one level, Friedrichs argued that despite greater consensus in the past, sociology is split largely between a *system* paradigm (emphasizing societal integration and consensus) and a *conflict* paradigm (emphasizing societal disintegration and coercion), with a wide array of other perspectives as potential paradigms. These paradigms are based on the fundamental images of the subject matter of sociology, but Friedrichs thinks of them as being of secondary importance to two other paradigms that focus on sociologists' images of themselves as scientific agents. These are the *prophetic* and the *priestly* paradigms. Whereas prophetic sociologists perceive themselves as agents of social change, priestly sociologists conceive of themselves as "value-free" scientists. The crucial point for our purposes is that, whether Friedrichs looks at images of the subject matter or images of the sociologists themselves, he concludes that sociology is a multiple-paradigm science.

Andrew Effrat (1972) clearly aligned himself with those who see sociology as a multiple-paradigm science, although he mistook more specific theories for paradigms. Effrat ended up with a cumbersome list of paradigms, including Marxian, Freudian, Durkheimian, Weberian, phenomenological, ethnomethodological, symbolic interactionist, and exchange theory. As we will see, all these are best viewed as theoretical components of sociology's multiple paradigms, but Effrat was on the right track in his multiparadigmatic image of sociology.

S. N. Eisenstadt and M. Curelaru (1976) differentiated among discrete, closed-system, and open-system paradigms. They framed their paradigms in terms of the historical development of the field. The earliest is the *discrete paradigm,* in which the focus was on separate concrete entities such as ecological properties, size of groups, or racial and psychological characteristics. Given this image of the world as a set of isolated units, those who operated within this paradigm had difficulty dealing with such relational issues as emergence, innovation, and creativity. This early and primitive paradigm left only a small mark on the development of sociology and persists today in only isolated domains. It was replaced, historically, by the *closed-system model,* whose supporters saw society as composed of separate but interrelated elements. Those who operated within this paradigm tended to see one element as dominant over the others. In Eisenstadt and Curelaru's view (but not this author's), Marx was operating within this paradigm with his emphasis on the economic sector. This paradigm was replaced, in turn, by the *open-system model,* which focuses on the "internal systemic dynamics, interconnections, and continuous feedback processes among the components of the social order" (Eisenstadt and Curelaru, 1976:92). Although the evolution of these paradigms follows "no simple, natural, chronological trend," and there is "considerable temporal and operative overlapping of the several approaches, there is in Eisenstadt and Curelaru's view a long-term trend toward the open-system paradigm.

Charles Lemert argued that rather than being composed of multiple paradigms, sociology is unified in its *homocentrism,* "the peculiarly nineteenth-century idea which holds that *man* is the measure of all things" (1979:13). Although it is true that sociology is person-centered, it is questionable whether this is really evidence that sociology is unified. One equally plausible conclusion is that there are multiple paradigms in sociology and that the sources of their differences are their varied interpretations *of* humankind. In the author's view, the ideas of homocentrism and multiple paradigms are not mutually exclusive.

Lemert concluded that in spite of their homocentrism, there are important paradigmatic differences among the various modes of sociological discourse. He differentiated among them on a linguistic basis. The first is *lexical sociology*, which is primarily technical in orientation. Second is *semantical sociology*, which focuses on the interpretation of meaning that only people (not animals) are capable of producing. Finally, there is *syntactical sociology*, which is much more political in its orientation to sociology. Thus, for Lemert, there *are* multiple paradigms, at least in contemporary sociology.

Major Sociological Paradigms

Although all the preceding perspectives have some degree of utility, it is my own earlier work on the paradigmatic status of sociology (Ritzer, 1975a, 1975b, 1980) that provides the basis for the metatheoretical perspective that has guided the analysis of sociological theory throughout this book. Like most of those discussed above, I conceive of sociology as a multiple-paradigm science. In my view, there are *three* paradigms that dominate sociology, with several others having the potential to achieve paradigmatic status. I label the three paradigms the *social-facts, social-definition,* and *social-behavior* paradigms. Each paradigm is analyzed in terms of the four components of a paradigm outlined in the definition discussed earlier.

The Social-Facts Paradigm

1 *Exemplar:* The model for social factists is the work of Emile Durkheim, particularly *The Rules of Sociological Method* and *Suicide.*
2 *Image of the subject matter:* Social factists focus on what Durkheim termed social facts, or large-scale social structures and institutions. Those who subscribe to the social-facts paradigm focus not only on these phenomena but on their effect on individual thought and action.
3 *Methods:* Social factists are more likely than those who subscribe to the other paradigms to use the interview-questionnaire[8] and historical-comparative methods.
4 *Theories:* The social-facts paradigm encompasses a number of theoretical perspectives. *Structural-functional* theorists tend to see social facts as neatly interrelated and order as maintained by general consensus. *Conflict* theorists tend to emphasize disorder among social facts as well as the notion that order is maintained by coercive forces in society. Although structural functionalism and conflict theory are the dominant theories in this paradigm, there are others, including *systems* theory.

The Social-Definition Paradigm

1 *Exemplar:* To social definitionists, the unifying model is Max Weber's work on social action.

---

[8] William Snizek (1976) has shown that the interview-questionnaire is dominant in *all* paradigms.

2 *Image of the subject matter:* Weber's work helped lead to an interest among social definitionists in the way actors define their social situations and the effect of these definitions on ensuing action and interaction.

3 *Methods:* Social definitionists, although they are most likely to use the interview-questionnaire method, are more likely to use the observation method than those in any other paradigm. In other words, observation is the distinctive methodology of social definitionists.

4 *Theories:* There are a wide number of theories that can be included within social definitionism: *action theory, symbolic interactionism, phenomenology, ethnomethodology,* and *existentialism.*

The Social-Behavior Paradigm

1 *Exemplar:* The model for sociologists who accept the social-behavior paradigm is the work of the psychologist B. F. Skinner.

2 *Image of the subject matter:* The subject matter of sociology to social behaviorists is the unthinking *behavior* of individuals. Of particular interest are the rewards that elicit desirable behaviors and the punishments that inhibit undesirable behaviors.

3 *Methods:* The distinctive method of social behaviorism is the experiment.

4 *Theories:* Two theoretical approaches in sociology can be included under the heading "social behaviorism." The first is *behavioral sociology,* which is very close to pure psychological behaviorism, and the second, and much more important, is *exchange theory.*[9]

TOWARD A MORE INTEGRATED SOCIOLOGICAL PARADIGM

In addition to detailing the nature of sociology's multiple paradigms, I also sought in my earlier work to make the case for more paradigmatic integration in sociology. Although there is reason for extant paradigms to continue to exist, there is also a need for a more integrated paradigm. Extant paradigms tend to be one-sided, focusing on specific levels of social analysis while paying little or no attention to the others. This is reflected in the social factists' concern with macro structures; the social definitionists' concern with action, interaction, and the social construction of reality; and the social behaviorists' concern with behavior. It is this kind of one-sidedness that has led to what I perceive to be a growing interest in a more integrated approach among a wide range of sociologists (Ritzer, forthcoming b). (This is but part of what I see as a growing interest in integration within and even among many social sciences; see especially Mitroff and Kilmann, 1978.) For example, Robert Merton, representing social factism, saw it and social definitionism as mutually enriching, as "opposed to one another in about the same sense as ham is opposed to

[9] Analyses of Ritzer's paradigm schema include Eckberg and Hill (1979), Friedheim (1979), Harper, Sylvester, and Walczak (1980), Snizek (1976), and Staats (1976).

eggs: they are perceptively different but mutually enriching" (1975:30). Among social definitionists, Hugh Mehan and Houston Wood argue that one theoretical component of social definitionism (ethnomethodology) accepts at least one basic tenet of social factism, "the reality of an external and constraining world" (1975:180). Among social behaviorists, Arthur Staats (1976) seeks to integrate creative mental processes (a key element of social definitionism) with traditional behaviorism. Calls for a more integrated paradigm are clearly important, but what is necessary is an effort to delineate what such a paradigm might look like.

The key to an integrated paradigm is the notion of *levels* of social analysis (Ritzer, 1979, 1981a). As the reader is well aware, *the social world is not really divided into levels.* In fact, social reality is best viewed as an enormous variety of social phenomena that are involved in continuing interaction and change. Individuals, groups, families, bureaucracies, the polity, and numerous other highly diverse social phenomena represent the bewildering array of phenomena that make up the social world. It is extremely difficult to get a handle on such a large number of wide-ranging and mutually interpenetrating social phenomena. Some sort of conceptual schema is clearly needed, and sociologists have developed a number of such schema in an effort to deal with the social world. The idea of levels of social analysis employed here should be seen as but one of a large number of such schema that can be, and have been, used for purposes of dealing with the complexities of the social world.

Levels of Social Analysis: A Review of the Literature

Although the idea of levels is implicit in much of sociology, it has received relatively little explicit attention. In concentrating on levels here, we are doing little more than making explicit what has been implicit in sociology.

The close of this Appendix will offer a conceptualization of the major levels of social analysis. To understand adequately that conceptualization, some preliminary differentiations must be made. As will be seen, two continua of social reality are useful in developing the major levels of the social world. The first is the *microscopic-macroscopic* continuum. Thinking of the social world as being made up of a series of entities ranging from those large in scale to those small in scale is relatively easy, because it is so familiar. Most people in their day-to-day lives conceive of the social world in these terms. In the academic world, a number of thinkers have worked with a micro-macro continuum (including Alexander et al., 1987; Blalock and Wilken, 1979; Bosserman, 1968; Edel, 1959; Gurvitch, 1964; Johnson, 1981; Korenbaum, 1964; Ritzer, 1990a; Wagner, 1964). For laypeople and academics alike, the continuum is based on the simple idea that social phenomena vary greatly in size. At the macro end of the continuum are such large-scale social phenomena as groups of societies (for example, the capitalist and socialist world systems), societies, and cultures. At the micro end are individual actors and their thoughts and actions. In between are a wide range of groups, collectivities, social classes, and organizations. We have little difficulty recognizing these distinctions and thinking of the world in micro-macro terms. There are no clear dividing lines between the micro social units and the macro units. Instead, there is a continuum ranging from the micro to the macro ends.

The second continuum is the *objective-subjective* dimension of social analysis. At each end of the micro-macro continuum we can differentiate between objective and subjective components. At the micro, or individual, level, there are the subjective mental processes of an actor and the objective patterns of action and interaction in which he or she engages. *Subjective* here refers to something that occurs solely in the realm of ideas, whereas *objective* relates to real, material events. This same differentiation is also found at the macro end of the continuum. A society is made up of both objective structures, such as governments, bureaucracies, and laws, and subjective phenomena, such as norms and values. The objective-subjective continuum is more complicated than the micro-macro continuum, and it is even, as we will see, more complicated than is implied in this introduction. To try to clarify matters and to work toward greater complexity, let us look at a concrete example as well as at the work of a number of sociologists on the objective-subjective continuum.

Consider the purchase of a new automobile. At the micro-subjective level, we would focus on the attitudes and orientations of the individual buyer that influence the kind of car to be purchased. But—and this is the key distinction between the micro-subjective and micro-objective levels of analysis—the buyer may desire (subjective state) a sports car and actually buy (objective act) an economy compact. Some sociologists are interested in subjective mental states, others in objective acts. In many cases it is useful and important to understand the interplay between these two micro levels.

The macro level also has subjective and objective dimensions. For many years most Americans shared a set of preferences for larger and ever more powerful cars. This was a subjective set of attitudes shared by a large number of people. Then a series of objective changes at the societal level had an impact on these shared attitudes. OPEC was formed, oil deliveries to the United States were curtailed, and the government played a more active role in oil-related matters. These and other macro-structural changes led to changes in the shared preferences of large numbers of people. Almost overnight many people came to prize small, fuel-efficient automobiles. This change, in turn, led to a massive alteration in the structure of the American automobile companies. Also affected were the thoughts and actions of many individual Americans. Thus, the purchase of a car, as well as most other mundane and extraordinary activities, involves the complex interaction of the micro-macro and objective-subjective components of social life.

Now let us turn to the work of several sociologists on the objective-subjective continuum. As we saw in Chapters 1 and 2, an important influence on Karl Marx was German idealism, particularly the work of G. W. F. Hegel. The Hegelian dialectic was a subjective process taking place within the realm of ideas. Although affected by this view, Marx and, before him, the Young Hegelians, were dissatisfied with the dialectic because it was not rooted in the objective, material world. Marx, building on the work of Ludwig Feuerbach and others, sought to extend the dialectic to the material world. On the one hand, this meant that he was concerned with real, sentient actors rather than idea systems. On the other hand, he came to focus on the objective structures of capitalist society, primarily the economic structure. Marx became increasingly interested in the real material structures of capitalism and the contradictions that exist among and within them. This is not to say that Marx lost sight of subjective ideas; in fact, notions of false and class consciousness play a key role in his work. It is the materialism-idealism split, as manifest in the work of Marx and others, that is one of the major philosophical roots of the objective-subjective continuum in modern sociology.

We can also find this continuum, although in a different form, in the work of Emile Durkheim (Chapter 3). In his classic work on methodology, Durkheim differentiated between material (objective) and nonmaterial (subjective) social facts. In *Suicide,* Durkheim said, "The social fact is sometimes materialized as to become an element of the external world" (1897/1951:313). He discussed architecture and law as two examples of material (objective) social facts. However, most of Durkheim's work emphasizes nonmaterial (subjective) social facts:

> Of course it is true that not all social consciousness achieves such externalization and materialization. Not all aesthetic spirit of a nation is embodied in the works it inspires; not all morality is formulated in clear precepts. The greater part is diffused. There is a large collective life which is at liberty; all sorts of currents come, go, circulate everywhere, cross and mingle in a thousand different ways, and just because they are constantly mobile are never crystallized in an objective form. Today a breath of sadness and discouragement descends on society: tomorrow, one of joyous confidence will uplift all hearts.
>
> (Durkheim, 1897/1951:315)

These social currents do not have material existence; they can exist only within the consciousness of individuals and between them. In *Suicide,* Durkheim concentrated on examples of this kind of social fact. He related differences in suicide rates to differences in social currents. For example, where there are strong currents of anomie (normlessness), we find high rates of anomic suicide. Social currents such as anomie, egoism, and altruism clearly do not have a material existence, although they may have a material effect by causing differences in suicide rates. Instead, they are intersubjective phenomena that can exist only in the consciousness of people.

Peter Blau (1960) has been in the forefront of those employing an objective-subjective continuum. His differentiation between institutions (subjective entities) and social structures (objective entities) is of this genre. He defined *subjective institutions* as "the common values and norms embodied in a culture or subculture" (Blau, 1960:178). Conversely, there are *social structures* that are "the networks of social relations in which processes of social interaction become organized and through which social positions of individuals and subgroups become differentiated" (Blau, 1960:178).

It can be argued that the objective-subjective continuum plays a crucial role in the thought of people like Marx, Durkheim, Blau, and many others. But there is a rather interesting problem in their use of the continuum: they employ it almost exclusively at the macroscopic level. However, it also can be applied at the microscopic level. Before giving an example of this, we need to underscore the point that we must deal not only with the microscopic-macrosopic and objective-subjective continua *but also with the interaction between them.*

One example of the use of the objective-subjective continuum at the microscopic level is an empirical study by Mary and Robert Jackman (1973) of what they called "objective and subjective social status." Their micro-subjective concern was "the individual's perception of his own position in the status hierarchy" (Jackman and Jackman, 1973:569). Micro subjectivity in this study involved the feelings, the perceptions, and the mental aspects of the actors' positions in the stratification system. These are related to various components of the micro-objective realm that include the actor's socioeconomic status, social contacts, amount of capital owned, ethnic group membership, or status as a breadwinner or a union member. Instead of dealing with actors' feelings, these dimensions involve the more objective characteristics of the individuals—the patterns of action and interaction in which they actually engage.

At a more general level, the microscopic aspect of the objective-subjective continuum is manifest in both the social-definition and social-behavior paradigms, as well as in the differences between them. Although both tend to focus on the micro-objective patterns of action and interaction, they split on the micro-subjective dimension. All the theoretical components of the social-definition paradigm (for example, symbolic interactionism, ethnomethodology, and phenomenology) share an interest in micro-subjectivity—the feelings and thoughts of actors. However, the social behaviorists reject the idea that it is necessary to study the micro-subjective components of social life. This is exemplified by B. F. Skinner's (1971) attack on what he called the idea of "autonomous man." To Skinner, we imply that people are autonomous when we attribute to them such ideas as feeling, minding, freedom, and dignity. People are held to possess some sort of inner core from which their actions emanate. They are able to initiate, originate, and create because of this inner core of micro-subjectivity. To Skinner, the idea that people have an inner, autonomous core is a mystical, metaphysical position of the kind that must be eliminated from the social sciences: "Autonomous man serves to explain only the things we are not yet able to explain in other ways. His existence depends on our ignorance, and he naturally loses status as we come to know more about behavior" (1971:12). Although we need to reject this kind of political diatribe, the key point is this: the microscopic level has *both* a subjective and an objective dimension.

Levels of Social Analysis: A Model

The most important thinker on the issue of levels of social reality was the French sociologist Georges Gurvitch. While he did not use the same terms,

Gurvitch (1964) had a sense of *both* micro-macro and objective-subjective continua. Even more important, he had a profound sense of how these two continua are related. To his credit, he also steadfastly refused to treat the two continua and their interrelationships as static tools but used them to underscore the dynamic quality of social life. But Gurvitch has one major difficulty: his analytical schema is extremely complex and cumbersome (see Chapter 14). The social world is very complicated, and in order to get a handle on it, we need relatively simple models.

The simple model we are seeking is formed out of the intersection of the two continua of levels of social reality discussed in the last several pages. The first, the microscopic-macroscopic continuum, can be depicted as in Figure A.1.

The objective-subjective continuum presents greater problems, yet it is no less important than the micro-macro continuum. In general, an objective social phenomenon has a real, material existence. We can think of the following, among others, as objective social phenomena; actors, action, interaction, bureaucratic structures, law, and the state apparatus. It is possible to see, touch, or chart all these objective phenomena. However, there are social phenomena that exist *solely* in the realm of ideas; they have no material existence. These are sociological phenomena such as mental processes, the social construction of reality (Berger and Luckmann, 1967), norms, values, and many elements of culture. The problem with the objective-subjective continuum is that there are many phenomena in the middle that have *both* objective and subjective elements. The family, for example, has a real material existence as well as a series of subjective mutual understandings, norms, and values. Similarly, the polity is composed of objective laws and bureaucratic structures as well as subjective political norms and values. In fact, it is probably true that the vast majority are mixed types of social phenomena representing some combination of objective and subjective elements. Thus it is best to think of the objective-subjective continuum as two polar types with a series of variously mixed types in the middle. Some of these types may have more objective than subjective characteristics, while others may have the reverse combination. Figure A.2 shows the objective-subjective continuum.

FIGURE A.1 The Microscopic-Macroscopic Continuum, with identification of Some Key Points on the Continuum

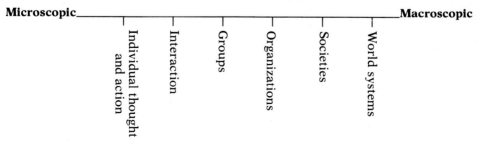

Objective ―――――――――――――――――――――――――――――――――――― Subjective

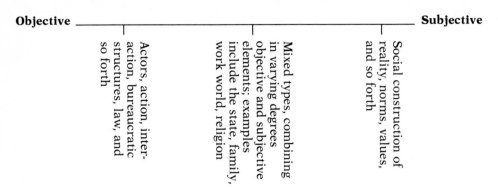

FIGURE A.2   The Objective-Subjective Continuum, with Identification of Some Mixed Types

Although these continua are interesting in themselves, the interrelationship of the two continua concerns us here. Figure A.3 is a schematic representation of the intersection of these two continua and the four major levels of social analysis derived from it.

The contention here is that an integrated sociological paradigm must deal with the four basic levels of social analysis identified in the figure and their interrelationships (for similar models, see Alexander, 1985; Wiley, 1988). It must deal with macroscopic objective entities like bureaucracy, macro-subjective realities like values, micro-objective phenomena like patterns of interaction, and micro-subjective facts like the process of reality construction. We must remember that in the real world, all these gradually blend into the others as part of the larger social continuum, but we have made some artificial and rather arbitrary differentiations in order to be able to deal with social reality. These four levels of social analysis are posited for heuristic purposes and are not meant to be accurate depictions of the social world. An obvious question

FIGURE A.3   Major Levels of Social Analysis

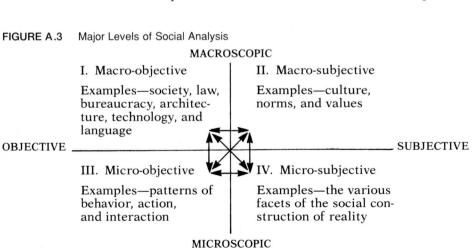

LEVELS OF SOCIAL REALITY   SOCIOLOGICAL PARADIGMS

Macro-subjective

Macro-objective

Micro-subjective

Micro-objective

Social Facts	
Social Definition	Integrated Sociological Paradigm
Social Behavior	

FIGURE A.4   Levels of Social Analysis and the Major Sociological Paradigms

is how these four levels relate to the three paradigms discussed earlier as well as to the integrated paradigm. Figure A.4 relates the four levels to the three paradigms.

The social-facts paradigm focuses primarily on the macro-objective and macro-subjective levels. The social-definition paradigm is largely concerned with the micro-subjective world and that part of the micro-objective world that depends on mental processes (action). The social-behavior paradigm deals with that part of the micro-objective world that does not involve the minding process (behavior). Whereas the three extant paradigms cut across the levels of social reality horizontally, an integrated paradigm cuts across vertically. This depiction makes it clear why the integrated paradigm does not supersede the others. Although each of the three existing paradigms deals with a given level or levels in great detail, the integrated paradigm deals with all levels but does not examine any given level in anything like the degree of intensity of the other paradigms. Thus the choice of a paradigm depends on the kind of question being asked. Not all sociological issues require an integrated approach, but it is certain that at least some do.

What has been outlined in the preceding pages is a model for the image of the subject matter of an integrated sociological paradigm. This sketch will need to be detailed more sharply in future years. But that is another task (see Ritzer, 1981a). The goal of this discussion is not the development of a new sociological paradigm but the delineation of an overarching metatheoretical schema (M_O) that allows us to analyze sociological theory in a coherent fashion. The model developed in Figure A.3 forms the basis for this analysis.

Sociological theory is analyzed using the four levels of social analysis depicted in Figure A.3. This figure provides us with a metatheoretical tool that can be used in the comparative analysis of sociological theories. It enables us to analyze the concerns of a theory and how they relate to the concerns of every other sociological theory.

One thing to be avoided at all costs is the simple identification of a theory or a theorist with specific levels of social analysis. Although it is true, given the preceding description of the current paradigmatic status of sociology, that sociological theorists who adhere to a given paradigm tend to focus on a given level or levels of social analysis, it often does them an injustice simply to equate the breadth of their work with one or more levels. For example, Karl Marx is often thought of as focusing on macro-objective structures—in particular, on the economic structures of capitalism. But the use of the multiple levels of social analysis schema allows us to see that Marx had rich insights regarding all levels of social reality and their interrelationships. Similarly, symbolic interactionism is generally considered a perspective that deals with micro subjectivity and micro objectivity, but it is not devoid of insights into the macroscopic levels of social analysis (Maines, 1977).

It is also important for the reader to remember that the use of levels of social analysis to analyze a theory tends to break up the wholeness, the integrity, and the internal consistency of the theory. Although the levels are useful for understanding a theory and comparing it to others, one must take pains to deal with the interrelationship among levels and with the totality of a theory.

In sum, the metatheoretical schema outlined in Figure A.3, the development of which was traced in this Appendix, provides the basis for the analysis of the various sociological theories discussed in this book.

REFERENCES

Abbott, Carroll, Brown, Charles R., and Crosbie, Paul V.
1973   "Exchange as Symbolic Interaction: For What?" *American Sociological Review* 38:504–506.

Aberle, D. F., et al.
1950/1967   "The Functional Prerequisites of a Society." In N. Demerath and R. Peterson (eds.), *System, Change and Conflict*. New York: Free Press: 317–331.

Aboulafia, Mitchell
1986   *The Mediating Self: Mead, Sartre, and Self-Determination*. New Haven: Yale University Press.

Abrahamson, Mark
1978   *Functionalism*. Englewood Cliffs, N.J.: Prentice-Hall.

Abrahamsson, Bengt
1970   "Homans on Exchange." *American Journal of Sociology* 76:273–285.

Abrams, Philip
1968   *The Origins of British Sociology: 1834–1914*. Chicago: University of Chicago Press.
1982   *Historical Sociology*. Ithaca, N.Y.: Cornell University Press.

Abrams, Philip, Deem, Rosemary, Finch, Janet, and Rock, Paul
1981   *Practice and Progress: British Sociology 1950–1980*. London: Allen and Unwin.

Agger, Ben (ed.)
1978   *Western Marxism: An Introduction*. Santa Monica, Calif.: Goodyear.

Akers, Ronald
1981   "Reflections of a Social Behaviorist on Behavioral Sociology." *American Sociologist* 16:177–180.

Albas, Daniel, and Albas, Cheryl
1988   "Aces and Bombers: The Post-Exam Impression Management Strategies of Students." *Symbolic Interaction* 11:289–302.

Alexander, Jeffrey C.
1981   "Revolution, Reaction, and Reform: The Change Theory of Parsons's Middle Period." *Sociological Inquiry* 51:267–280.
1982   *Theoretical Logic in Sociology. Positivism, Presuppositions, and Current Controversies. Vol. 1*, Berkeley: University of California Press.
1982–1983   *Theoretical Logic in Sociology*. 4 vols. Berkeley: University of California Press.
1983   *Theoretical Logic in Sociology. Vol. 4, The Modern Reconstruction of Classical Thought: Talcott Parsons*. Berkeley: University of California Press.
1984   "The Parsons Revival in German Sociology." In R. Collins (ed.), *Sociological Theory—1984*. San Francisco: Jossey-Bass: 394–412.
1985   "The 'Individualist Dilemma' in Phenomenology and Interactionism." In S. N. Eisenstadt and H. J. Helle (eds.), *Macro-Sociological Theory*, Vol. 1. London: Sage: 25–51.
1987   "Action and Its Environments." In J. Alexander et al. (eds.), *The Micro-Macro Link*. Berkeley: University of California Press: 289–318.

Alexander, Jeffrey C. (ed.)
1985b   *Neofunctionalism*. Beverly Hills, Calif.: Sage.

1988   *Durkheimian Sociology: Cultural Studies.* Cambridge: Cambridge
              University Press.

Alexander, Jeffrey C., et al. (eds.)
1987   *The Micro-Macro Link.* Berkeley: University of California Press.

Alexander, Jeffrey C., and Colomy, Paul
1985   "Toward Neo-Functionalism." *Sociological Theory* 3:11–23.
1990a   "Neofunctionalism: Reconstructing a Theoretical Tradition." In G.
              Ritzer (ed.), *Frontiers of Social Theory: The New Syntheses.* New York:
              Columbia University Press: 33–67.

Alexander, Jeffrey C., and Colomy, Paul (eds.)
1990b   *Differentiation Theory and Social Change: Comparative and Historical
              Perspectives.* New York: Columbia University Press.

Alexander, Jeffrey C., and Giesen, Bernhard
1987   "From Reduction to Linkage: The Long View of the Micro-Macro
              Link." In J. Alexander et al. (eds.), *The Micro-Macro Link.* Berkeley:
              University of California Press: 1–42.

Alford, Robert R., and Friedland, Roger
1985   *Powers of Theory: Capitalism, the State, and Democracy.* Cambridge:
              Cambridge University Press.

al-Hibri, Azizah
1981   "Reproduction, Mothering and the Origins of Patriarchy." In J.
              Trebilcot (ed.), *Mothering: Essays in Feminist Theory.* Totowa, N.J.:
              Rowman and Allanheld: 81–93.

Allen, Paula Gunn (ed.)
1989   *Spider Woman's Granddaughters: Traditional Tales and Contemporary
              Writing by Native American Women.* Boston: Beacon Press.

Alt, John
1985–1986   "Reclaiming C. Wright Mills." *Telos* 66:6–43.

Althusser, Louis
1969   *For Marx.* Harmondsworth, Eng.: Penguin.
1977   *Politics and History.* London: NLB.

Althusser, Louis, and Balibar, Etienne (eds.)
1970   *Reading Capital.* New York: Pantheon.

Amin, Samir
1977   *Unequal Development: An Essay on the Social Formations of Peripheral
              Capitalism.* New York: Monthly Review Press.

Amsterdamska, Olga
1985   "Institutions and Schools of Thought." *American Journal of Sociology*
              91:332–358.

Anderson, Brom
1987–1988   "The Gospel According to Jameson." *Telos* 74:116–125.

Anderson, Perry
1976   *Considerations on Western Marxism.* London: NLB.
1984   *In the Tracks of Historical Materialism.* Chicago: University of Chicago
              Press.
1990a   "A Culture in Contraflow—I."*New Left Review* 180:41–78.
1990b   "A Culture in Contraflow—II." *New Left Review* 182:85–137.

Anderson, R. J., Hughes, J. A., and Sharrock, W. W.
1987   "Executive Problem Finding: Some Material and Initial Observations."
            Social Psychology Quarterly 50:143–159.
Antonio, Robert J.
1979   "Domination and Production in Bureaucracy." *American Sociological
            Review* 44:895–912.
1981   "Immanent Critique as the Core of Critical Theory: Its Origins and
            Development in Hegel, Marx and Contemporary Thought." *British
            Journal of Sociology* 32:330–345.
1985   "Values, History and Science: The Metatheoretic Foundations of the
            Weber-Marx Dialogues." In R. J. Antonio and R. M. Glassman (eds.), *A
            Weber-Marx Dialogue*. Lawrence: University Press of Kansas: 20–43.
1990   "The Decline of the Grand Narrative of Emancipatory Modernity:
            Crisis or Renewal in Neo-Marxian Theory?" In G. Ritzer (ed.), *Frontiers
            of Social Theory: The New Syntheses*. New York: Columbia University
            Press: 88–116.
Antonio, Robert J., and Glassman, Ronald M. (eds.)
1985   *A Weber-Marx Dialogue*. Lawrence: University Press of Kansas.
Antonio, Robert J., and Kellner, Douglas
forthcoming "Metatheorizing Historical Rupture: Classical Theory and Modernity."
            In G. Ritzer (ed.), *Sociological Metatheorizing: Coming of Age*. Beverly
            Hills, Calif.: Sage.
Anzaldua, Catona (ed.)
1990   *Making Face, Making Soul/Hacienda Caras: Creative and Critical Perspectives
            by Women of Color*. San Francisco: Aunt Lute Foundation Books.
Appelbaum, Richard
1979   "Born-Again Functionalism? A Reconsideration of Althusser's
            Structuralism." *Insurgent Sociologist* 9:18–33.
Aptheker, Bettina
1989   *Tapestries of Life: Women's Work, Women's Consciousness and the Meaning
            of Daily Experience*. Amherst: University of Massachusetts Press.
Archer, Margaret S.
1982   "Morphogenesis versus Structuration: On Combining Structure and
            Action." *British Journal of Sociology* 33:455–483.
1985   "Structuration versus Morphogenesis." In S. N. Eisenstadt and H. J.
            Helle (eds.), *Macro-Sociological Theory*. London: Sage: 58–88.
1988   *Culture and Agency: The Place of Culture in Social Theory*. Cambridge:
            Cambridge University Press.
Aron, Raymond
1965   *Main Currents in Sociological Thought*, Vol. 1. New York: Basic Books.
Arthur, C. J.
1970   "Editor's Introduction." In K. Marx and F. Engels. *The German Ideology*,
            Part 1. New York: International Publishers: 4–34.
Ascher, Carol, de Salvo, Louise, and Ruddick, Sara
1984   *Between Women*. Boston: Beacon Press.
Atkinson, J. Maxwell
1984a   *Our Masters' Voices: The Language and Body Language of Politics*. New
            York: Methuen.
1984b   "Public Speaking and Audience Responses: Some Techniques for

Inviting Applause." In J. M. Atkinson and J. Heritage (eds.), *Structures of Social Action*. Cambridge: Cambridge University Press: 370–409.

Atkinson, Paul
1988   "Ethnomethodology: A Critical Review." *Annual Review of Sociology* 14:441–465.

Avineri, Shlomo
1968   *The Social and Political Thought of Karl Marx*. London: Cambridge University Press.

Back, Kurt
1970   Review of Robert Burgess and Don Bushell, *Behavioral Sociology*. *American Sociological Review* 35:1098–1100.

Bailey, Kenneth D.
1987   "Globals, Mutables and Immutables: An Alternative Approach to Micro/Macro Analysis." Paper presented at the meetings of the American Sociological Association, Chicago, Illinois.
1990   *Social Entropy Theory*. Albany: State University of New York Press.

Baker, Wayne E.
1990   "Market Networks and Corporate Behavior." *American Journal of Sociology* 96:589–625.

Baldwin, Alfred
1961   "The Parsonian Theory of Personality." In M. Black (ed.), *The Social Theories of Talcott Parsons*. Englewood Cliffs, N.J.: Prentice-Hall: 153–190.

Baldwin, John C.
1986   *George Herbert Mead: A Unifying Theory for Sociology*. Newbury Park, Calif.: Sage.
1988a   "Mead and Skinner: Agency and Determinism." *Behaviorism* 16:109–127.
1988b   "Mead's Solution to the Problem of Agency." *Sociological Inquiry* 58:139–162.

Baldwin, John D., and Baldwin, Janice I.
1978   "Behaviorism on Verstehen and Erklären." *American Sociological Review* 43:335–347.
1986   *Behavior Principles in Everyday Life*. 2nd ed. Englewood Cliffs, N.J.: Prentice-Hall.

Ball, Richard A.
1978   "Sociology and General Systems Theory." *American Sociologist* 13:65–72.
1979   "The Dialectical Method: Its Application to Social Theory." *Social Forces* 57:785–798.

Banner, Lois
1984   *Women in Modern America: A Brief History*. New York: Harcourt Brace Jovanovich.

Baran, Paul, and Sweezy, Paul M.
1966   *Monopoly Capital: An Essay on the American Economic and Social Order*. New York: Monthly Review Press.

Barbalet, J. M.
1983   *Marx's Construction of Social Theory*. London: Routledge and Kegan Paul.

Barrett, Michele
1985   "Introduction." In F. Engels, *Origins of the Family, Private Property and the State*. New York: Penguin.

Barry, Kathleen
1979   *Female Sexual Slavery*. Englewood Cliffs, N.J.: Prentice-Hall.
Baudrillard, Jean
1983   *Simulations*. New York: Semiotext.
Baum, Rainer C., and Lechner, Frank J.
1981   "National Socialism: Toward an Action-Theoretical Perspective."
            Sociological Inquiry 51:281–308.
Bauman, Zygmunt
1976   *Towards a Critical Sociology: An Essay on Commonsense and Emancipation*.
            London: Routledge and Kegan Paul.
1990   "From Pillars to Post." *Marxism Today* February: 20–25.
Becker, Uwe
1988   "From Social Scientific Functionalism to Open Functional Logic." *Theory
            and Society* 17:865–883.
Bender, Frederick (ed.)
1970   *Karl Marx: The Essential Writings*. New York: Harper.
Beniger, James R., and Savory, Laina
1981   "Social Exchange: Diffusion of a Pardigm." *American Sociologist* 16:240–
            250.
Benjamin, Jessica
1985   "The Bonds of Love: Rational Violence and Erotic Domination." In H.
            Eisenstein and A. Jardine (eds.), *The Future of Difference*. New
            Brunswick, N.J.: Rutgers University Press: 41–70.
1988   *The Bonds of Love: Psychoanalysis, Feminism, and the Problem of
            Domination*. New York: Pantheon.
Benston, Margaret
1970   *The Political Economy of Women's Liberation*. New York: Monthly Review
            Press Reprint.
Benton, Ted
1984   *The Rise and Fall of Structural Marxism: Althusser and His Influence*. New
            York: St. Martin's.
Berger, Brigette, and Berger, Peter
1983   *The War over the Family: Capturing the Middle Ground*. Garden City, N.Y.:
            Anchor.
Berger, Joseph, Eyre, Dana P., and Zelditch Jr., Morris
1989   "Theoretical Structures and the Micro/Macro Problem." In J. Berger,
            M. Zelditch, Jr., and B. Anderson (eds.), *Sociological Theories in Progress:
            New Formulations*. Newbury Park, Calif.: Sage: 11–32.
Berger, Joseph, Wagner, David G., and Zelditch Jr., Morris
1989   "Theory Growth, Social Processes and Metatheory." In J. Turner (ed.),
            Theory Building in Sociology: Assessing Theoretical Cumulation. Newbury
            Park, Calif.: Sage: 19–42.
Berger, Peter
1963   *Invitation to Sociology*. New York: Doubleday.
Berger, Peter, and Kellner, Hansfried
1964   "Marriage and the Social Construction of Reality." In P. Dreitzel (ed.),
            Recent Sociology, No. 2, Patterns of Communicative Behavior. New York:
            Macmillan.

Berger, Peter, and Luckmann, Thomas
1967   *The Social Construction of Reality.* Garden City, N.Y.: Anchor.
Bergeson, Albert
1984   "The Critique of World-System Theory: Class Relations or Division of
            Labor?" In R. Collins (ed.), *Sociological Theory—1984.* San Francisco:
            Jossey-Bass: 365–372.
Berki, R. N.
1983   *Insight and Vision: The Problem of Communism in Marx's Thought.*
            London: J. M. Dent and Sons.
Bernard, Jessie
1971   *Women and the Public Interest.* Chicago: Aldine.
1973   "My Four Revolutions: An Autobiographical Account of the American
            Sociological Association." *American Journal of Sociology,* 78:773–792.
1981   *The Female World.* New York: Free Press.
1982   *The Future of Marriage.* 2nd ed. New Haven: Yale University Press.
forthcoming *The Feminist Enlightenment.*
Bernard, Thomas
1983   *The Consensus-Conflict Debate: Form and Content in Sociological Theories.*
            New York: Columbia University Press.
Bernikow, Louise (ed.)
1974   *The World Split Open: Four Centuries of Women Poets in England and
            America, 1552–1950.* New York: Vintage.
1980   *Among Women.* New York: Harper.
Bernstein, Richard J.
1971   *Praxis and Action: Contemporary Philosophies of Human Activity.*
            Philadelphia: University of Pennsylvania Press.
1989   "Social Theory as Critique." In D. Held and J. B. Thompson (eds.),
            Social Theory of Modern Societies: Anthony Giddens and His Critics.
            Cambridge: Cambridge University Press: 19–33.
Besnard, Philippe
1983a   "The 'Année Sociologique' Team." In P. Besnard (ed.), *The Sociological
            Domain.* Cambridge: Cambridge University Press: 11–39.
Besnard, Philippe (ed.)
1983b   *The Sociological Domain.* Cambridge: Cambridge University Press.
Best, Raphaela
1983   *We've All Got Scars: What Boys and Girls Learn in Elementary School.*
            Bloomington: University of Indiana Press.
Bierstedt, Robert
1963   "The Common Sense World of Alfred Schutz." *Social Research* 30:116–
            121.
1981   *American Sociological Theory: A Critical History.* New York: Academic
            Press.
Bird, Caroline
1979   *The Two Paycheck Family.* New York: Rawson, Wade.
Bittner, Egon
1973   "Objectivity and Realism in Sociology." In G. Psathas (ed.),
            Phenomenological Sociology: Issues and Applications. New York: Wiley:
            109–125.
Blalock, Hubert, and Wilken, Paul
1979   *Intergroup Processes: A Micro-Macro Perspective.* New York: Free Press.

Blankenship, Ralph L. (ed.)
1977   *Colleagues in Organization: The Social Construction of Professional Work.*
              New York: Wiley.

Blau, Peter
1960   "Structural Effects." *American Sociological Review* 25:178–193.
1964   *Exchange and Power in Social Life.* New York: Wiley.
1975a   Introduction, "Parallels and Contrasts in Structural Inquiries." In P.
              Blau (ed.), *Approaches to the Study of Social Structure.* New York: Free
              Press: 1–20.
1975b   "Parameters of Social Structure." In P. Blau (ed.), *Approaches to the
              Study of Social Structure.* New York: Free Press: 220–253.
1977a   *Inequality and Heterogeneity: A Primitive Theory of Social Structure.* New
              York: Free Press.
1977b   "A Macrosociological Theory of Social Structure." *American Sociological
              Review* 83:26–54.
1980   "A Fable about Social Structure." *Social Forces* 58:777–788.
1987a   "Contrasting Theoretical Perspectives." In J. Alexander et al. (eds.), *The
              Micro-Macro Link.* Berkeley: University of California Press: 71–85.
1987b   "Microprocess and Macrostructure." In K. Cook (ed.), *Social Exchange
              Theory.* Beverly Hills, Calif.: Sage: 83–100.

Blau, Peter, and Merton, Robert K. (eds.)
1981   *Continuities in Structural Inquiry.* Beverly Hills, Calif.: Sage.

Blau, Peter, Beeker, Caroline, and Fitzpatrick, Kevin
1984   "Crosscutting Social Circles and Intermarriage." *Social Forces* 62:585–
              606.

Blau, Peter, Blum, Terry C., and Schwartz, Joseph E.
1982   "Heterogeneity and Intermarriage." *American Sociological Review* 47:45–
              61.

Bleich, Harold
1977   *The Philosophy of Herbert Marcuse.* Washington, D.C.: University Press of
              America.

Bleicher, Josef
1980   *Contemporary Hermeneutics: Hermeneutics as Method, Philosophy and
              Critique.* London: Routledge and Kegan Paul.

Blum, Terry C.
1984   "Racial Inequality and Salience: An Examination of Blau's Theory of
              Social Structure." *Social Forces* 62:607–617.
1985   "Structural Constraints on Interpersonal Relations: A Test of Blau's
              Macrosociological Theory." *American Journal of Sociology* 91:511–
              521.

Blumer, Herbert
1954/1969   "What Is Wrong with Social Theory?" In H. Blumer, *Symbolic
              Interaction:* 140–152.
1955/1969   "Attitudes and the Social Act." In H. Blumer, *Symbolic Interaction:* 90–
              100.
1956/1969   "Sociological Analysis and the 'Variable.'" In H. Blumer, *Symbolic
              Interaction:* 127–139.
1962/1969   "Society as Symbolic Interaction." In H. Blumer, *Symbolic Interaction:*
              78–89.

1969a	*Symbolic Interaction: Perspective and Method.* Englewood Cliffs, N.J.: Prentice-Hall.
1969b	"The Methodological Position of Symbolic Interactionism." In H. Blumer, *Symbolic Interaction:* 1–60.
1974	"Comments on 'Parsons as a Symbolic Interactionist.'" *Sociological Inquiry* 45:59–62.
1980	Comment: "Mead and Blumer: The Convergent Methodological Perspectives of Social Behaviorism and Symbolic Interactionism." *American Sociological Review* 45:409–419.
1990	*Industrialization as an Agent of Social Change: A Critical Analysis.* New York: Aldine de Gruyter.

Boden, Deirdre

1990a	"The World as It Happens: Ethnomethodology and Conversation Analysis." In G. Ritzer (ed.), *Frontiers of Social Theory: The New Syntheses.* New York: Columbia University Press: 185–213.
1990b	"People Are Talking: Conversation Analysis and Symbolic Interaction." in H. S. Becker and M. McCall (eds.), *Symbolic Interactionism and Cultural Studies.* Chicago: University of Chicago Press: 244–273.

Bogard, William

1990	"Closing Down the Social: Baudrillard's Challenge to Contemporary Sociology." *Sociological Theory* 8:1–15.

Bookman, Ann, and Morgen, Sandra (eds.)

1988	*Women and the Politics of Empowerment.* Philadelphia: Temple University Press.

Bosserman, Phillip

1968	*Dialectical Sociology: An Analysis of the Sociology of Georges Gurvitch.* Boston: Porter Sargent.

Bottomore, Tom

1975	"Structure and History." In P. Blau (ed.), *Approaches to the Study of Social Structure.* New York: Free Press: 159–171.
1983	"Sociology." In D. McLellan (ed.), *Marx: The First 100 Years.* New York: St. Martin's.
1984	*The Frankfurt School.* Chichester, Eng.: Ellis Horwood.

Bottomore, Tom, and Frisby, David (eds.)

1978	Introduction to the translation of Georg Simmel, *The Philosophy of Money* (orig. 1907). London: Routledge and Kegan Paul: 1–49.

Bourdieu, Pierre

1977	*Outline of a Theory of Practice.* London: Cambridge University Press.
1984	*Distinction: A Social Critique of the Judgment of Taste.* Cambridge: Harvard University Press.
1989	"Social Space and Symbolic Power." *Sociological Theory* 7:14–25.

Bourricaud, François

1981	*The Sociology of Talcott Parsons.* Chicago: University of Chicago Press.

Bowles, Samuel, and Gintis, Herbert

1987	*Democracy and Capitalism: Property, Community, and the Contradictions of Modern Social Thought.* New York: Basic Books.

Bramson, Leon

1961	*The Political Context of Sociology.* Princeton, NJ.: Princeton University Press.

Braverman, Harry
1974   *Labor and Monopoly Capital: The Degradation of Work in the Twentieth Century.* New York: Monthly Review Press.
Breault, K. D.
1986   "Suicide in America: A Test of Durkheim's Theory of Religion, 1933–1980." *American Journal of Sociology* 92:628–656.
Brewer, John, and Hunter, Albert
1989   *Multimethod Research: A Synthesis of Styles.* Newbury Park, Calif.: Sage.
Brown, Richard
1987   *Society as Text: Essays on Rhetoric, Reason and Reality.* Chicago: University of Chicago Press.
1990a   "Social Science and the Poetics of Public Truth." *Sociological Forum* 5: 55–74.
1990b   "Rhetoric, Textuality, and the Postmodern Turn in Sociological Theory." *Sociological Theory* 8:188–197.
Brubaker, Rogers
1984   *The Limits of Rationality: An Essay on the Social and Moral Thought of Max Weber.* London: Allen and Unwin.
Bryant, Christopher G. A.
1985   *Positivism in Social Theory and Research.* New York: St. Martin's.
Buckley, Kerry W.
1989   *Mechanical Man: John Broadus Watson and the Beginnings of Behaviorism.* New York: Guilford Press.
Buckley, Walter
1967   *Sociology and Modern Systems Theory.* Englewood Cliffs, N.J.: Prentice-Hall.
Bulmer, Martin
1984   *The Chicago School of Sociology: Institutionalization, Diversity, and the Rise of Sociological Research.* Chicago: University of Chicago Press.
1985   "The Chicago School of Sociology: What Made It a "School'?" *History of Sociology: An International Review* 5:62–77.
Bunch, Charlotte
1987   *Passionate Politics: Feminist Theory in Action.* New York: St. Martin's.
Burawoy, Michael
1979   *Manufacturing Consent: Changes in the Labor Process under Monopoly Capitalism.* Chicago: University of Chicago Press.
1990   "Marxism as Science: Historical Challenges and Theoretical Growth." *American Sociological Review* 55:775–793.
Burger, Thomas
1976   *Max Weber's Theory of Concept Formation: History, Laws and Ideal Types.* Durham, N.C.: Duke University Press.
Burns, Tom R.
1986   "Actors, Transactions, and Social Structure: An Introduction to Social Rule System Theory." In U. Himmelstrand (ed.), *Sociology: The Aftermath of Crisis.* London: Sage: 8–37.
Burns, Tom R., and Flam, Helena
1986   *The Shaping of Social Organization: Social Rule System Theory with Applications.* Beverly Hills, Calif.: Sage.

Burris, Val
1979   "Introduction." In "The Structuralist Influence in Marxist Theory and
              Research." *Insurgent Sociologist* 9:4–17.
Burt, Ronald
1982   *Toward a Structural Theory of Action: Network Models of Social Structure,*
              Perception, and Action. New York: Academic Press.
Bushell, Don, and Burgess, Robert
1969   "Some Basic Principles of Behavior." In R. Burgess and D. Bushell
              (eds.), *Behavioral Sociology.* New York: Columbia University Press: 27–
              48.
Butler, Judith
1990   *Gender Trouble: Feminism and the Subversion of Identity.* New York:
              Routledge.
Buttel, Frederick H. (ed.)
1990   Symposium: Evolution and Social Change. *Sociological Forum* 5:153–212.
Button, Graham
1987   "Answers as Interactional Products: Two Sequential Practices Used in
              Interviews." *Social Psychology Quarterly* 50:160–171.
Buxton, William
1985   *Talcott Parsons and the Capitalist Nation-State: Political Sociology as a*
              Strategic Vocation. Toronto: University of Toronto Press.
Callinicos, Alex
1989   "Introduction: Analytical Marxism." In Alex Callinicos (ed.), *Marxist*
              Theory. Oxford: Oxford University Press, 1989: 1–16.
1990   *Against Postmodernism: A Marxist Critique.* New York: St. Martin's.
Camic, Charles
1989   "*Structure* after 50 Years: The Anatomy of a Charter." *American Journal*
              of Sociology 95:38–107.
1990   "An Historical Prologue." *American Sociological Review* 55:313–319.
Campbell, Colin
1982   "A Dubious Distinction? An Inquiry into the Value and Use of
              Merton's Concepts of Manifest and Latent Function." *American*
              Sociological Review 47:29–44.
Caplow, Theodore
1968   *Two against One: Coalition in Triads.* Englewood Cliffs, N.J.: Prentice-
              Hall.
Carden, Maren Lockwood
1974   *The New Feminist Movement.* New York: Russell Sage Foundation.
Carver, Terrell
1983   *Marx and Engels: The Intellectual Relationship.* Bloomington: Indiana
              University Press.
Carveth, Donald
1982   "Sociology and Psychoanalysis: The Hobbesian Problem Revisited."
              Canadian Journal of Sociology 7:201–229.
Catlin, George E. G.
1964   "Introduction." In E. Durkheim, *The Rules of Sociological Method.* New
              York: Free Press: xi–xxxvi.
Chafetz, Janet Saltzman
1984   *Sex and Advantage.* Totowa, N.J.: Rowman and Allanheld.

1988   *Feminist Sociology: An Overview of Contemporary Theories.* Itasca, Ill.: Peacock.

Chafetz, Janet Saltzman, and Dworkin, Anthony Gary
1986   *Female Revolt: Women's Movements in World and Historical Perspectives.* Totowa, N.J.: Rowman and Allanheld.

Charon, Joel
1985   *Symbolic Interaction: An Introduction, an Interpretation, an Integration.* 2nd ed. Englewood Cliffs, N.J.: Prentice-Hall.
1989   *Symbolic Interaction: An Introduction, an Interpretation, an Integration.* 3rd ed. Englewood Cliffs, N.J.: Prentice-Hall.

Chitnis, Anand C.
1976   *The Scottish Enlightenment: A Social History.* Totowa, N.J.: Rowman and Littlefield.

Chodorow, Nancy
1978   *The Reproduction of Mothering: Psychoanalysis and the Sociology of Gender.* Berkeley: University of California Press.
1990   *Feminism and Psychoanalytic Theory.* New Haven: Yale University Press.

Chua, Beng-Huat
1977   "Delineating a Marxist Interest in Ethnomethodology." *American Sociologist* 12:24–32.

Cicourel, Aaron
1974   *Cognitive Sociology: Language and Meaning in Social Interaction.* New York: Free Press.
1981   "Notes on the Integration of Micro- and Macro-Levels of Analysis." In K. Knorr-Cetina and A. Cicourel (eds.), *Advances in Social Theory and Methodology.* New York: Methuen: 51–79.

Cixous, Helene, and Clement, Catherine (eds.)
1986   *The Newly Born Woman.* Minneapolis: University of Minnesota Press.

Clark, Priscilla P., and Clark, Terry Nichols
1982   "The Structural Sources of French Structuralism." In I. Rossi (ed.), *Structural Sociology.* New York: Columbia University Press: 22–46.

Clarke, Simon
1990   "The Crisis of Fordism or the Crisis of Social Democracy?" *Telos* 83:71–98.

Clawson, Dan
1980   *Bureaucracy and the Labor Process: The Transformation of U.S. Industry, 1860–1920.* New York: Monthly Review Press.

Clawson, Dan, Neustadtl, Alan, and Bearden, James
1986   "The Logic of Business Unity: Corporate Contributions to the 1980 Congressional Elections." *American Sociological Review* 51:797–811.

Clayman, Steven E.
1988   "Displaying Neutrality in Television News Interviews." *Social Problems* 35:474–492.

Cohen, G. A.
1978   *Karl Marx's Theory of History: A Defence.* Princeton, N.J.: Princeton University Press.
1978/1986   "Marxism and Functional Explanation." In J. Roemer (ed.), *Analytical Marxism.* Cambridge: Cambridge University Press: 221–234.

Cohen, Ira
1981   "Introduction to the Transaction Edition." In M. Weber, *General Economic History*. New Brunswick, N.J.: Transaction Books: xv–lxxxiii.
1989   *Structuration Theory*. London: Macmillan.
Cohen, Percy
1968   *Modern Social Theory*. New York: Basic Books.
Coleman, James
1968   Review of Harold Garfinkel, *Studies in Ethnomethodology*. *American Sociological Review* 33:126–130.
1971   "Community Disorganization and Conflict." In R. Merton and R. Nisbet (eds.), *Contemporary Social Problems*. 3rd ed. New York: Harcourt Brace Jovanovich: 657–708.
1986   "Social Theory, Social Research, and a Theory of Action." *American Journal of Sociology* 91:1309–1335.
1987   "Microfoundations and Macrosocial Behavior." In J. Alexander et al. (eds.), *The Micro-Macro Link*. Berkeley: University of California Press: 153–173.
1990   *Foundations of Social Theory*. Cambridge: Belknap Press of Harvard University Press.
Colfax, J. David, and Roach, Jack L.
1971   *Radical Sociology*. New York: Basic Books.
Collins, Patricia Hill
1990   *Black Feminist Thought: Knowledge, Consciousness and Empowerment*. Boston: Unwin Hyman.
Collins, Randall
1975   *Conflict Sociology: Toward an Explanatory Science*. New York: Academic Press.
1979   *The Credential Society*. New York: Academic Press.
1980   "Weber's Last Theory of Capitalism: A Systematization." *American Sociological Review* 45:925–942.
1981a   "On the Microfoundations of Macrosociology." *American Journal of Sociology* 86:984–1014.
1981b   "Micro-Translation as Theory-Building Strategy." In K. Knorr-Cetina and A. Cicourel (eds.), *Advances in Social Theory and Methodology*. New York: Methuen: 81–108.
1981c   "Introduction." In R. Collins (ed.), *Sociology since Midcentury: Essays in Theory Cumulation*. New York: Academic Press: 1–9.
1985   *Weberian Sociological Theory*. Cambridge: Cambridge University Press.
1986a   "Is 1980s Sociology in the Doldrums?" *American Journal of Sociology* 91:1336–1355.
1986b   "The Passing of Intellectual Generations: Reflections on the Death of Erving Goffman." *Sociological Theory* 4:106–113.
1987a   "Interaction Ritual Chains, Power and Property: The Micro-Macro Connection as an Empirically Based Theoretical Problem." In J. Alexander et al. (eds.), *The Micro-Macro Link*. Berkeley: University of California: 193–206.
1987b   "A Micro-Macro Theory of Intellectual Creativity: The Case of German Idealistic Philosophy." *Sociological Theory* 5:47–69.
1988a   "The Micro Contribution to Macro Sociology." *Sociological Theory* 6:242–253.

1988b   "The Durkheimian Tradition in Conflict Sociology." In J. Alexander (ed.), *Durkheimian Sociology: Cultural Studies.* Cambridge: Cambridge University Press: 107–128.

1989a   "Sociology: Proscience or Antiscience?" *American Sociological Review* 54:124–139.

1989b   "Toward a Neo-Meadian Sociology of Mind." *Symbolic Interaction* 12:1–32.

1990   "Conflict Theory and the Advance of Macro-Historical Sociology." In G. Ritzer (ed.), *Frontiers of Social Theory: The New Syntheses.* New York: Columbia University Press: 68–87.

Colomy, Paul

1986   "Recent Developments in the Functionalist Approach to Change." *Sociological Focus* 19:139–158.

1990a   "Introduction: The Functionalist Tradition." In P. Colomy (ed.), *Functionalist Sociology.* Brookfield, Vt.: Elgar Publishing: xiii–ixi.

1990b   "Introduction: The Neofunctionalist Movement." In P. Colomy (ed.), *Neofunctionalist Sociology.* Brookfield, Vt.: Elgar Publishing: xi–xii.

1990c   "Uneven Differentiation and Incomplete Institutionalization: Political Change and Continuity in the Early American Nation." In J. C. Alexander and P. Colomy (eds.), *Differentiation Theory and Social Change: Comparative and Historical Perspectives.* New York: Columbia University Press: 119–162.

1990d   "Strategic Groups and Political Differentiation in the Antebellum United States." In J. C. Alexander and P. Colomy (eds.), *Differentiation Theory and Social Change: Comparative and Historical Perspectives.* New York: Columbia University Press: 222–264.

Comte, Auguste

1830–1842/   *The Positive Philosophy.* New York: AMS Press.
1974

1851–1854/   *System of Positive Philosophy.* 4 vols. New York: Burt Franklin.
1976

Connerton, Paul (ed.)

1976   *Critical Sociology.* Harmondsworth, Eng.: Penguin.

Connolly, William E.

1973   "Theoretical Self-Consciousness." *Polity* 6:5–35.

Cook, Judith, and Fonow, Mary Margaret

1986   "Knowledge and Women's Interests: Issues of Epistemology and Methodology in Feminist Sociological Research." *Sociological Inquiry* 56: 2–29.

Cook, Karen S.

1987b   "Emerson's Contributions to Social Exchange Theory." In K. S. Cook (ed.), *Social Exchange Theory:* Beverly Hills, Calif.: Sage: 209–222.

Cook, Karen S. (ed.)

1987a   *Social Exchange Theory.* Beverly Hills, Calif.: Sage.

Cook, Karen S., and Emerson, Richard M.

1978   "Power, Equity, Commitment in Exchange Networks." *American Sociological Review* 43:721–739.

Cook, Karen S., Emerson, Richard M., Gillmore, Mary B., and Yamagishi, Toshio

1983   "The Distribution of Power in Exchange Networks: Theory and Experimental Results." *American Journal of Sociology* 89:275–305.

Cook, Karen S., and Gillmore, Mary R.
1984   "Power, Dependence, and Coalitions." *Advances in Group Processes* 1:27–58.

Cook, Karen S., O'Brien, Jodi, and Kollock, Peter
1990   "Exchange Theory: A Blueprint for Structure and Process." In G. Ritzer (ed.), *Frontiers of Social Theory: The New Syntheses.* New York: Columbia University Press: 158–181.

Cooley, Charles H.
1902/1964   *Human Nature and the Social Order.* New York: Scribner's.

Coser, Lewis
1956   *The Functions of Social Conflict.* New York: Free Press.
1967   *Continuities in the Study of Social Conflict.* New York: Free Press.
1975a   Presidential Address: "Two Methods in Search of a Substance." *American Sociological Review* 40:691–700.
1975b   "Structure and Conflict." In P. Blau (ed.), *Approaches to the Study of Social Structure.* New York: Free Press: 210–219.
1977   *Masters of Sociological Thought.* 2nd ed. New York: Harcourt Brace Jovanovich.

Coser, Lewis (ed.)
1965   *Georg Simmel.* Englewood Cliffs, N.J.: Prentice-Hall.

Cott, Nancy F.
1977   *The Bonds of Womanhood: Women's Sphere in New England, 1780–1835.* New Haven: Yale University Press.

Cottrell, Leonard S., Jr.
1980   "George Herbert Mead: The Legacy of Social Behaviorism." In R. K. Merton and M. W. Riley (eds.), *Sociological Traditions from Generation to Generation: Glimpses of the American Experience.* Norwood, N.J.: Ablex.

Couch, C. J., Saxton, S. L., and Katovich, M. A.
1986a   *Studies in Symbolic Interaction: The Iowa School,* Part A. Greenwich, Conn.: JAI Press.
1986b   *Studies in Symbolic Interaction: The Iowa School,* Part B. Greenwich, Conn.: JAI Press.

Coulter, Jeff
1983   *Rethinking Cognitive Theory.* New York: St. Martin's.
1989   *Mind in Action.* Atlantic Highlands, N.J.: Humanities Press.

Craib, Ian
1976   *Existentialism and Sociology: A Study of Jean-Paul Sartre.* Cambridge: Cambridge University Press.

Cronk, George
1987   *The Philosophical Anthropology of George Herbert Mead.* New York: Peter Lang.

Crozier, Michel, and Friedberg, Erhard
1980   *Actors and Systems: The Politics of Collective Action.* Chicago: University of Chicago Press.

Culler, Jonathan
1976   *Ferdinand de Saussure.* Harmondsworth, Eng.: Penguin.

Curtis, Bruce
1981   *William Graham Sumner.* Boston: Twayne.

Dahrendorf, Ralf
1958   "Out of Utopia: Toward a Reorientation of Sociological Analysis."
            American Journal of Sociology 64:115–127.
1959   *Class and Class Conflict in Industrial Society*. Stanford, Calif.: Stanford
            University Press.
1968   *Essays in the Theory of Society*. Stanford, Calif.: Stanford University Press.
Daniels, Arlene Kaplan
1988   *Invisible Careers: Women Civic Leaders from the Volunteer World*. Chicago:
            University of Chicago Press.
Davis, Kingsley
1959   "The Myth of Functional Analysis as a Special Method in Sociology
            and Anthropology." *American Sociological Review* 24:757–772.
Davis, Kingsley, and Moore, Wilbert
1945   "Some Principles of Stratification." *American Sociological Review* 10:242–
            249.
Dawe, Alan
1978   "Theories of Social Action." In T. Bottomore and R. Nisbet (eds.), *A
            History of Sociological Analysis*. New York: Basic Books: 362–417.
de Beauvoir, Simone
1957   *The Second Sex*. New York: Vintage.
Deckard, Barbara Sinclair
1979   *The Women's Movement: Political, Socioeconomic and Psychological Issues*.
            New York: Harper & Row.
Deegan, Mary Jo
1988   *Jane Addams and the Men of the Chicago School, 1892–1918*. New
            Brunswick, N.J.: Rutgers University Press.
Demerath, Nicholas, and Peterson, Richard (eds.)
1967   *System, Change and Conflict*. New York: Free Press.
Densmore, Dana
1973   "Independence from the Sexual Revolution." In A. Koedt et al. (eds.),
            Radical Feminism. New York: Quadrangle: 107–118.
DeVille, Phillippe
1989   "Human Agency and Social Structure in Economic Theory: The General
            Equilibrium Theory and Beyond." Paper presented at the conference on
            "Social Theory and Human Agency," Swedish Collegium for Advanced
            Study in the Social Sciences, Uppsala, Sweden, Sept. 29–Oct. 1.
Dinnerstein, Dorothy
1976   *The Mermaid and the Minotaur*. New York: Harper & Row.
DiTomaso, Nancy
1982   " 'Sociological Reductionism' from Parsons to Althusser: Linking Action
            and Structure in Social Theory." *American Sociological Review* 47:14–28.
Ditton, Jason (ed.)
1980   *The View from Goffman*. New York: St. Martin's.
Dobb, Maurice
1964   *Studies in the Development of Capitalism*. Rev. ed. New York:
            International Publishers.
Donovan, Josephine
1985   *Feminist Theory: The Intellectual Traditions of American Feminism*. New
            York: Ungar.

Douglas, Jack
1967   *The Social Meanings of Suicide.* Princeton, N.J.: Princeton University
     Press.
1977   "Existential Sociology." In J. D. Douglas et al. (eds.), *Existential*
     Sociology. Cambridge: Cambridge University Press: 3–73.
1980   "Introduction to the Sociologies of Everyday Life." In J. Douglas et al.
     (eds.), *Introduction to the Sociologies of Everyday Life.* Boston: Allyn and
     Bacon: 1–19.

Douglas, Jack, and Johnson, John
1977   "Introduction." In J. Douglas et al. (eds.), *Existential Sociology.*
     Cambridge: Cambridge University Press: vii–xv.

Duncan, O. D., and Schnore, L. F.
1959   "Cultural, Behavioral and Ecological Perspectives in the Study of Social
     Organization." *American Journal of Sociology* 65:132–146.

Durkheim, Emile
1893/1960 *Montesquieu and Rousseau: Forerunners of Sociology.* Ann Arbor:
     University of Michigan Press.
1893/1964 *The Division of Labor in Society.* New York: Free Press
1895/1964 *The Rules of Sociological Method.* New York: Free Press.
1897/1951 *Suicide.* New York: Free Press.
1900/1973 "Sociology in France in the Nineteenth Century." In R. Bellah (ed.),
     Emile Durkheim: On Morality and Society. Chicago: University of Chicago
     Press: 3–32.
1912/1965 *The Elementary Forms of Religious Life.* New York: Free Press.
1913–1914/ *Pragmatism and Sociology.* Cambridge: Cambridge University Press.
1983
1914/1973 "The Dualism of Human Nature and Its Social Condition." In R. Bellah
     (ed.), *Emile Durkheim: On Morality and Society.* Chicago: University of
     Chicago Press: 149–163.
1922/1956 *Education and Sociology.* New York: Free Press.
1928/1962 *Socialism.* New York: Collier Books.
1957   *Professional Ethics and Civil Morals.* London: Routledge and Kegan Paul.
1973   *Moral Education: A Study in the Theory and Application of the Sociology of*
     Education. New York: Free Press.

Durkheim, Emile, and Mauss, Marcel
1903/1963 *Primitive Classification.* Chicago: University of Chicago Press.

Dworkin, Andrea
1976   *Our Blood: Prophecies and Discourses on Sexual Politics.* New York:
     Perigee Books.
1987   *Intercourse.* New York: Free Press.
1989   *Letters from the War Zone: Writings 1976–1987.* New York: Dutton.

Eckberg, Douglas Lee, and Hill, Lester
1979   "The Paradigm Concept and Sociology: A Critical Review." *American*
     Sociological Review 44:925–937

Edel, Abraham
1959   "The Concept of Levels in Social Theory." In L. Gross (ed.), *Symposium*
     on Sociological Theory. Evanston, Ill.: Row Peterson: 167–195.

Eder, Klaus
1990   "The Rise of Counter-Culture Movements against Modernity: Nature as
              a New Field of Class Struggle." *Theory, Culture and Society* 7:21–47.
Edwards, Richard
1979   *Contested Terrain: The Transformation of the Workplace in the Twentieth
              Century.* New York: Basic Books.
Effrat, Andrew
1972   "Power to the Paradigms: An Editorial Introduction." *Sociological
              Inquiry* 42:3–33.
Ehrmann, Jacques
1970   "Introduction." In J. Ehrmann (ed.), *Structuralism.* Garden City, N.Y.:
              Anchor: vii–xi.
Eisen, Arnold
1978   "The Meanings and Confusions of Weberian 'Rationality.' " *British
              Journal of Sociology* 29:57–70.
Eisenstadt, S. N.
1973   *Tradition, Change and Modernity.* New York: Wiley.
Eisenstadt, S. N., with Curelaru, M.
1976   *The Form of Sociology: Paradigms and Crises.* New York: Wiley.
Eisenstadt, S. N., and Helle, H. J. (eds.)
1985a   *Macro-Sociological Theory: Perspectives on Sociological Theory,* Vol. 1.
              London: Sage.
1985b   "General Introduction to Perspectives on Sociological Theory." In S. N.
              Eisenstadt and H. J. Helle (eds.), *Macro-Sociological Theory.* London:
              Sage: 1–3.
Eisenstein, Zillah
1979   *Capitalist Patriarchy and the Case for Socialist Feminism.* New York:
              Monthly Review Press.
Ekeh, Peter P.
1974   *Social Exchange Theory: The Two Traditions.* Cambridge: Harvard
              University Press.
1982   "Structuralism, the Principle of Elementarism, and the Theory of
              Civilization." In I. Rossi (ed.), *Structural Sociology.* New York: Columbia
              University Press: 122–148.
Elster, Jon
1982   "Marxism, Functionalism and Game Theory: The Case for
              Methodological Individualism." *Theory and Society* 11:453–482.
1985   *Making Sense of Marx.* Cambridge: Cambridge University Press.
1986   "Further Thoughts on Marxism, Functionalism, and Game Theory." In
              J. Roemer (ed.), *Analytical Marxism.* Cambridge: Cambridge University
              Press: 202–220.
Emerson, Richard M.
1972a   "Exchange Theory, Part I: A Psychological Basis for Social Exchange."
              In J. Berger, M. Zelditch, Jr., and B. Anderson (eds.), *Sociological Theories
              in Progress,* Vol. 2. Boston: Houghton Mifflin: 38–57.
1972b   "Exchange Theory, Part II: Exchange Relations and Networks." In J.
              Berger, M. Zelditch, Jr., and B. Anderson (eds.), *Sociological Theories in
              Progress,* Vol. 2. Boston: Houghton Mifflin: 58–87.
1976   "Social Exchange Theory." In A. Inkeles, J. Coleman, and N. Smelser

(eds.), *Annual Review of Sociology*, Vol. 2. Palo Alto: Annual Reviews: 335–362.

1981   "Social Exchange Theory." In M. Rosenberg and R. H. Turner (eds.), *Social Psychology: Sociological Perspectives*. New York: Basic Books: 30–65.

Engels, Friedrich
1884/1970   *The Origins of the Family, Private Property and the State*. New York: International Publishers.
1890/1972   "Letter to Joseph Bloch." In R. C. Tucker (ed.), *The Marx-Engels Reader*. New York: Norton: 640–642.

Epstein, Cynthia Fuchs
1988   *Deceptive Distinctions: Sex, Gender, and the Social Order*. New Haven: Yale University Press.

Etzioni, Amitai
1988   *The Moral Dimension: Toward a New Economics*. New York: Free Press.

Etzkorn, K. Peter (ed.)
1968   *Georg Simmel: The Conflict in Modern Culture and Other Essays*. New York: Teachers College, Columbia University.

Evans, Sara
1980   *Personal Politics: The Roots of the Women's Liberation Movement in the Civil Rights Movement and the New Left*. New York: Vintage.

Faghirzadeh, Saleh
1982   *Sociology of Sociology: In Search of . . . Ibn-Khaldun's Sociology Then and Now*. Teheran: Soroush Press.

Faia, Michael A.
1986   *Dynamic Functionalism: Strategy and Tactics*. Cambridge: Cambridge University Press.

Falk, William, and Zhao, Shanyang
1990a   "Paradigms, Theories and Methods in Contemporary Rural Sociology: A Partial Replication." *Rural Sociology* 54:587–600.
1990b   "Paradigms, Theories and Methods Revisited: We Respond to Our Critics." *Rural Sociology* 55:112–122.

Fararo, Thomas J.
1989   "The Spirit of Unification in Sociological Theory." *Sociological Theory* 7:175–190.

Fararo, Thomas J., and Skvoretz, John
1986   "E-State Structuralism: A Theoretical Method." *American Sociological Review* 51:591–602.

Farganis, James
1975   "A Preface to Critical Theory." *Theory and Society* 2:483–508.

Faris, R. E. L.
1970   *Chicago Sociology: 1920–1932*. Chicago: University of Chicago Press.

Farnham, C. (ed.)
1987   *The Impact of Feminist Research on the Academy*. Bloomington: Indiana University Press.

Faught, Jim
1980   "Presuppositions of the Chicago School in the Work of Everett Hughes." *American Sociologist* 15:72–82.

Fendrich, Michael
1984   "Wives' Employment and Husbands' Distress: A Meta-analysis and a Replication." *Journal of Marriage and the Family* 46:871–879.
Fenton, Steve
1984   *Durkheim and Modern Sociology*. Cambridge: Cambridge University Press.
Fine, Gary Alan
1988   "On the Macrofoundations of Microsociology: Meaning, Order, and Comparative Context." Paper presented at the meetings of the American Sociological Association, Atlanta, Georgia.
1990   "Symbolic Interactionism in the Post-Blumerian Age." In G. Ritzer (ed.), *Frontiers of Social Theory: The New Syntheses*. New York: Columbia University Press: 117–157.
Fine, Gary Alan, and Kleinman, Sherryl
1983   "Network and Meaning: An Interactionist Approach to Social Structure." *Symbolic Interaction* 6:97–110.
1986   "Interpreting the Sociological Classics: Can There Be a 'True' Meaning of Mead?" *Symbolic Interaction* 9:129–146.
Fine, William F.
1979   *Progressive Evolutionism and American Sociology, 1890–1920*. UMI Research Press (*n.p.*).
Fischer, Norman
1984   "Hegelian Marxism and Ethics." *Canadian Journal of Political and Social Theory* 8:112–138.
Fisher, Berenice, and Strauss, Anselm
1979   "George Herbert Mead and the Chicago Tradition of Sociology—Parts 1 and 2." *Symbolic Interaction* 2,1:9–25; 2,2:9–19.
Fiske, Donald W., and Shweder, Richard A. (eds.)
1986   *Metatheory in Social Science: Pluralisms and Subjectivities*. Chicago: University of Chicago Press.
Fitzpatrick, Ellen
1990   *Endless Crusade: Women Social Scientists and Progressive Reform*. New York: Oxford University Press.
Flax, Jane
1990   *Thinking Fragments: Psychoanalysis, Feminism and Postmodernism in the Contemporary West*. Berkeley: University of California Press.
Fontana, Andrea
1980   "Toward a Complex Universe: Existential Sociology." In J. D. Douglas et al. (eds.), *Introduction to the Sociologies of Everyday Life*. Boston: Allyn and Bacon: 155–181.
1984   "Introduction: Existential Sociology and the Self." In J. Kotarba and A. Fontana (eds.), *The Existential Self in Society*. Chicago: University of Chicago Press: 3–17.
Foucault, Michel
1965   *Madness and Civilization: A History of Insanity in the Age of Reason*. New York: Vintage.
1966   *The Order of Things: An Archaeology of the Human Sciences*. New York: Vintage.

1969	*The Archaeology of Knowledge and the Discourse on Language.* New York: Harper Colophon.
1975	*The Birth of the Clinic: An Archaeology of Medical Perception.* New York: Vintage.
1979	*Discipline and Punish: The Birth of the Prison.* New York: Vintage.
1980	*The History of Sexuality. Vol. 1, An Introduction.* New York: Vintage.
1985	*The Use of Pleasure. The History of Sexuality. Vol. 2.* New York: Pantheon.

Frank, André Gunder
1966/1974   "Functionalism and Dialectics." In R. S. Denisoff, O. Callahan, and M. H. Levine (eds.), *Theories and Paradigms in Contemporary Sociology.* Itasca, Ill.: Peacock: 342–352.

Frank, R. I.
1976   Translator's introduction to Max Weber, *The Agrarian Sociology of Ancient Civilizations.* London: NLB: 7–33.

Frankfurt Institute for Social Research
1973   *Aspects of Sociology.* London: Heinemann.

Fraser, Nancy, and Nicholson, Linda
1988   "Social Criticism without Philosophy: An Encounter between Feminism and Postmodernism." In A. Ross (ed.), *Universal Abandon: The Politics of Postmodernism.* Minneapolis: University of Minnesota Press: 83–104.

Freeman, C. Robert
1980   "Phenomenological Sociology and Ethnomethodology." In J. D. Douglas et al. (eds.), *Introduction to the Sociologies of Everyday Life.* Boston: Allyn and Bacon: 113–154.

Freund, Julian
1968   *The Sociology of Max Weber.* New York: Vintage.

Friedan, Betty
1963   *The Feminine Mystique.* New York: Dell.
1981   *The Second Stage.* New York: Summit.

Friedheim, Elizabeth
1979   "An Empirical Comparison of Rizer's Paradigms and Similar Metatheories: A Research Note." *Social Forces* 58:59–66.

Friedman, Debra, and Hechter, Michael
1988   "The Contribution of Rational Choice Theory to Macrosociological Research." *Sociological Theory* 6:201–218.
1990   "The Comparative Advantages of Rational Choice Theory." In G. Ritzer (ed.), *Frontiers of Social Theory: The New Syntheses.* New York: Columbia University Press: 214–229.

Friedman, George
1981   *The Political Philosophy of the Frankfurt School.* Ithaca, N.Y.: Cornell University Press.

Friedrichs, Robert
1970   *A Sociology of Sociology.* New York: Free Press.
1972a   "Dialectical Sociology: Toward a Resolution of Current 'Crises' in Western Sociology." *British Journal of Sociology* 13:263–274.
1972b   "Dialectical Sociology: An Exemplar for the 1970's." *Social Forces* 50:447–455.

Frisby, David
1981   *Sociological Impressionism: A Reassessment of Georg Simmel's Social Theory.*
            London: Heinemann.
1984   *Georg Simmel.* Chichester, Eng.: Ellis Horwood.
Frye, Marilyn
1983   *The Politics of Reality: Essays in Feminist Theory.* Trumansburg, New
            York: Crossings Press.
Fuhrman, Ellsworth R.
1980   *The Sociology of Knowledge in America: 1883–1915.* Charlottesville:
            University Press of Virginia.
Fuhrman, Ellsworth R., and Snizek, William
1990   "Neither Proscience nor Antiscience: Metasociology as Dialogue."
            Sociological Forum 5:17–31.
Fullbrook, Mary
1978   "Max Weber's 'Interpretive Sociology.' " *British Journal of Sociology* 29:
            71–82.
Furfey, Paul
1953/1965   *The Scope and Method of Sociology: A Metasociological Treatise.* New York:
            Cooper Square Publishers.
Gandy, D. Ross
1979   *Marx and History: From Primitive Society to the Communist Future.* Austin:
            University of Texas Press.
Gans, Herbert
1972   "The Positive Functions of Poverty." *American Journal of Sociology* 78:
            275–289.
Gardiner, Jean
1979   "Women's Domestic Labor." In Zillah Eisenstein (ed.), *Capitalist
            Patriarchy and the Case for Socialist Feminism.* New York and London:
            Monthly Review Press.
Garfinkel, Harold
1963   "A Conception of and Experiment with 'Trust' as a Condition of
            Concerted Stable Actions." In O. J. Harvey (ed.), *Motivations and Social
            Interaction.* New York: Ronald Press.
1967   *Studies in Ethnomethodology.* Englewood Cliffs, N.J.: Prentice-Hall.
1974   "The Origins of the Term 'Ethnomethodology.' " In R. Turner (ed.),
            Ethnomethodology. Harmondsworth, Eng.: Penguin: 15–18.
1988   "Evidence for Locally Produced, Naturally Accountable Phenomena of
            Order, Logic, Reason, Meaning, Method, etc. in and as of the Essential
            Quiddity of Immortal Ordinary Society, (I of IV): An Announcement of
            Studies." *Sociological Theory* 6:103–109.
Garland, Anne Witte
1988   *Women Activists: Challenging the Abuse of Power.* New York: Feminist
            Press.
Gelb, Joyce, and Paley, Marian Lief
1982   *Women and Public Policies.* Princeton, N.J.: Princeton University Press.
Gellner, David
1982   "Max Weber, Capitalism and the Religion of India." *Sociology* 16:526–
            543.

Geras, Norman
1987   "Post-Marxism?" *New Left Review* 163:40–82.
Gergen, Kenneth J.
1973   "Social Psychology as History." *Journal of Personality and Social
            Psychology* 26:309–320.
1986   "Correspondence versus Autonomy in the Language of Understanding
            Human Action." In D. W. Fiske and R. A. Shweder (eds.), *Metatheory in
            Social Science: Pluralisms and Subjectivities*. Chicago: University of
            Chicago Press: 136–162.
Gerstein, Dean
1987   "To Unpack Micro and Macro: Link Small with Large and Part with
            Whole." In J. Alexander et al. (eds.), *The Micro-Macro Link*. Berkeley:
            University of California Press: 86–111.
Gerth, Hans, and Mills, C. Wright
1953   *Character and Social Structure*. New York: Harcourt, Brace and World.
Gerth, Hans, and Mills, C. Wright (eds.)
1958   *From Max Weber*. New York: Oxford University Press.
Giddens, Anthony
1972   "Introduction: Durkheim's Writings in Sociology and Social
            Philosophy." In A. Giddens (ed.), *Emile Durkheim: Selected Writings*.
            Cambridge: Cambridge University Press: 1–50.
1976   *New Rules of Sociological Method: A Positive Critique of Interpretive
            Sociologies*. New York: Basic Books.
1979   *Central Problems in Social Theory: Action, Structure and Contradiction in
            Social Analysis*. Berkeley: University of California Press.
1981   *The Contemporary Critique of Historical Materialism*. Berkeley: University
            of California Press.
1982   *Profiles and Critiques in Social Theory*. Berkeley: University of California
            Press.
1984   *The Constitution of Society: Outline of the Theory of Structuration*. Berkeley:
            University of California Press.
1987   "Structuralism, Post-structuralism and the Production of Culture." In A.
            Giddens and J. H. Turner (eds.), *Social Theory Today*. Stanford, Calif.:
            Stanford University Press: 195–223.
1989   "A Reply to My Critics." In D. Held and J. B. Thompson (eds.), *Social
            Theory of Modern Societies: Anthony Giddens and His Critics*. Cambridge:
            Cambridge University Press: 249–301.
1990   *The Consequences of Modernity*. Stanford: Stanford University Press.
Giddings, Paula
1984   *When and Where I Enter: The Impact of Black Women on Race and Sex in
            America*. New York: William Morrow.
Gilbert, Sandra M., and Gubar, Susan
1979   *The Madwoman in the Attic: The Woman Writer and the Nineteenth-Century
            Literary Imagination*. New Haven: Yale University Press.
Gilligan, Carol
1982   *In a Different Voice: Psychological Theory and Women's Development*.
            Cambridge: Harvard University Press.
Glenn, Phillip J.
1989   "Initiating Shared Laughter in Multi-Party Conversations." *Western
            Journal of Speech Communications* 53:127–149.

Glennon, Lynda M.
1979   *Women and Dualism.* New York: Longman.
Gluckman, Max
1959   *Custom and Conflict in Africa.* Glencoe, Ill.: Free Press.
Glucksmann, Miriam
1974   *Structural Analysis in Contemporary Social Thought: A Comparison of the Theories of Claude Lévi-Strauss and Louis Althusser.* London: Routledge and Kegan Paul.
Goddard, David
1976   "On Structuralism and Sociology." *American Sociologist* 11:123–133.
Godelier, Maurice
1972a   *Rationality and Irrationality in Economics.* London: NLB.
1972b   "Structure and Contradiction in *Capital.*" In R. Blackburn (ed.), *Readings in Critical Social Theory.* London: Fontana: 334–368.
Goffman, Erving
1959   *Presentation of Self in Everyday Life.* Garden City, N.Y.: Anchor.
1961   *Encounters: Two Studies in the Sociology of Interaction.* Indianapolis: Bobbs-Merrill.
1963a   *Behavior in Public Places: Notes on the Social Organization of Gatherings.* Glencoe, Ill.: Free Press.
1963b   *Stigma: Notes on the Management of Spoiled Identity.* Englewood Cliffs., N.J.: Prentice-Hall.
1967   *Interaction Ritual: Essays on Face-to-Face Behavior.* Garden City, N.Y.: Anchor.
1971   *Relations in Public: Microstudies of the Public Order.* New York: Basic Books.
1972   *Strategic Interaction.* New York: Ballantine.
1974   *Frame Analysis: An Essay on the Organization of Experience.* New York: Harper Colophon.
1977   "The Arrangement between the Sexes." *Theory and Society* 40:301–331.
Gonos, George
1977   " 'Situation' versus 'Frame': The 'Interactionst' and the 'Structuralist' Analyses of Everyday Life." *American Sociological Review* 42:854–867.
1980   "The Class Position of Goffman's Sociology: Social Origins of an American Structuralism." In J. Ditton (ed.), *The View from Goffman.* New York: St. Martin's: 134–169.
Goode, William J.
1960   "A Theory of Role Strain." *American Sociological Review* 25:483–496.
1975   "Homans' and Merton's Structural Approach." In P. Blau (ed.), *Approaches to the Study of Social Structure.* New York: Free Press: 66–75.
1978   *The Celebration of Heroes: Prestige as a Social Control System.* Berkeley: University of California Press.
Goodwin, Charles
1979   "The Interactive Construction of a Sentence in Natural Conversation." In G. Psathas (ed.), *Everyday Language: Studies in Ethnomethodology.* New York: Irvington: 97–121.
1984   "Notes on Story Structure and the Organization of Participation." In J. M. Atkinson and J. Heritage (eds.), *Structures of Social Action.* Cambridge: Cambridge University Press: 225–246.

Gould, Carol
1978   *Marx's Social Ontology: Individuality and Community in Marx's Theory of Social Reality.* Cambridge: MIT Press.
Gouldner, Alvin
1958   "Introduction." In E. Durkheim, *Socialism and Saint-Simon.* Yellow Springs, Ohio: Antioch Press.
1959/1967   "Reciprocity and Autonomy in Functional Theory." In N. Demerath and R. Peterson (eds.), *System, Change and Conflict.* New York: Free Press: 141–169.
1960   "The Norm of Reciprocity." *American Sociological Review* 25:161–178.
1970   *The Coming Crisis of Western Sociology.* New York: Basic Books.
Gramsci, Antonio
1917/1977   "The Revolution against 'Capital.'" In Q. Hoare (ed.), *Antonio Gramsci: Selections from Political Writings (1910–1920).* New York: International Publishers: 34–37.
1932/1975   *Letters from Prison: Antonio Gramsci.* Lynne Lawner (ed.). New York: Harper Colophon.
1971   *Selections from the Prison Notebooks.* New York: International Publishers.
Granovetter, Mark
1973   "The Strength of Weak Ties." *American Journal of Sociology* 78:1360–1380.
1983   "The Strength of Weak Ties: A Network Theory Revisited." In R. Collins (ed.), *Sociological Theory—1983.* San Francisco: Jossey-Bass: 201–233.
1985   "Economic Action and Social Structure: The Problem of Embeddedness." *American Journal of Sociology* 91:481–510.
Grathoff, Richard (ed.)
1978   *The Theory of Social Action: The Correspondence of Alfred Schutz and Telcott Parsons.* Bloomington: Indiana University Press.
Gregory, Derek
1989   "Presences and Absences: Time-Space Relations and Structuration Theory." In D. Held and J. B. Thompson (eds.), *Social Theory of Modern Societies: Anthony Giddens and His Critics.* Cambridge: Cambridge University Press: 185–214.
Greisman, Harvey C.
1986   "The Paradigm That Failed." In R. C. Monk (ed.), *Structures of Knowing.* Lanham, Md.: University Press of America: 273–291.
Greisman, Harvey C., and Ritzer, George
1981   "Max Weber, Critical Theory and the Administered World." *Qualitative Sociology* 4:34–55.
Griffin, Susan
1978   *Women and Nature: The Roaring within Her.* New York: Harper & Row.
1979   *Rape, the Power of Consciousness.* New York: Harper & Row.
1981   *Pornography as Silence: Culture's Revenge against Nature.* New York: Harper & Row.
Gross, Llewellyn
1961   "Preface to a Metatheoretical Framework for Sociology." *American Journal of Sociology* 67:125–136.
Grossberg, Lawrence, and Nelson, Cary
1988   "Introduction: The Territory of Marxism." In C. Nelsen and L. Grossberg (eds.), *Marxism and the Interpretation of Culture.* Urbana: University of Illinois Press: 1–13.

Gurney, Patrick J.
1981   "Historical Origins of Ideological Denial: The Case of Marx in
            American Sociology." *American Sociologist* 16:196–201.
Gurvitch, Georges
1964   *The Spectrum of Social Time.* Dordrecht, Neth.: D. Reidel.
Haas, Jack, and Shaffir, William
1982   "Taking on the Role of Doctor: A Dramaturgic Analysis of
            Professionalization." *Symbolic Interaction* 5:187–203.
Habermas, Jurgen
1970   *Toward a Rational Society.* Boston: Beacon Press.
1971   *Knowledge and Human Interests.* Boston: Beacon Press.
1973   *Theory and Practice.* Boston: Beacon Press.
1975   *Legitimation Crisis.* Boston: Beacon Press.
1979   *Communication and the Evolution of Society.* Boston: Beacon Press.
1984   *The Theory of Communicative Action. Vol. 1, Reason and the Rationalization
            of Society.* Boston: Beacon Press.
1987   *The Theory of Communicative Action. Vol. 2, Lifeworld and System: A
            Critique of Functionalist Reason.* Boston: Beacon Press.
Hage, Jerald
1980   *Theories of Organization.* New York: Wiley.
Haines, Valerie
1988   "Is Spencer's Theory an Evolutionary Theory? *American Journal of
            Sociology* 93:1200–1223.
Halfpenny, Peter
1982   *Positivism and Sociology: Explaining Social Life.* London: Allen and
            Unwin.
Hall, Richard
1983   "Theoretical Trends in the Sociology of Occupations." *Sociological
            Quarterly* 24:5–23.
Hall, Stuart
1988   "Brave New World." *Marxism Today* October: 24–29.
Hall, Stuart, and Jameson, Fredric
1990   "Clinging to the Wreckage: A Conversation." *Marxism Today*
            September: 28–31.
Halliday, Fred
1990   "The Ends of the Cold War." *New Left Review* 180:5–23.
Handel, Warren
1982   *Ethnomethodology: How People Make Sense.* Englewood Cliffs, N.J.:
            Prentice-Hall.
Hankin, Thomas L.
1979   "In Defense of Biography: The Use of Biography in the History of
            Science." *History of Science* 17:1–16.
Haraway, Donna
1988   "Situated Knowledge: The Science Question in Feminism and the
            Privilege of Partial Perspective." *Feminist Studies* 14:575–600.
Harding, Sandra (ed.)
1987   *Feminism and Methodology.* Bloomington: Indiana University Press.
Harding, Sandra, and Hintikka, Merrill B. (eds.)
1983   *Discovering Reality: Feminist Perspectives on Epistemology, Metaphysics,
            Methodology and Philosophy of Science.* Boston: Reidel.

Harper, Diane Blake, Sylvester, Joan, and Walczak, David
1980   "An Empirical Comparison of Ritzer's Paradigms and Similar
        Metatheories: Comment on Friedheim." *Social Forces* 59:513–517.
Hartman, Heidi
1979   "Capitalism, Patriarchy and Job Segregation by Sex." In Z. Eisenstein
        (ed.), *Capitalist Patriarchy and the Case for Socialist Feminism*. New York:
        Monthly Review Press: 206–247.
Hartsock, Nancy
1983   *Money, Sex and Power: Towards a Feminist Historical Materialism*. New
        York: Longman.
Harvey, David
1989   *The Condition of Postmodernity: An Enquiry into the Origins of Cultural
        Change*. Oxford: Blackwell.
Harvey, Lee
1982   "The Use and Abuse of Kuhnian Paradigms in the Sociology of
        Knowledge." *British Journal of Sociology* 16:85–101.
1987   "The Nature of 'Schools' in the Sociology of Knowledge: The Case of
        the 'Chicago School.' " *Sociological Review* 35:245–278.
Hawkes, Terence
1977   *Structuralism and Semiotics*. London: Methuen.
Hawthorn, Geoffrey
1976   *Enlightenment and Despair*. Cambridge: Cambridge University Press.
Hayim, Gila
1980   *The Existential Sociology of Jean-Paul Sartre*. Amherst: University of
        Massachusetts Press.
Hazelrigg, Lawrence
1972   "Class, Property and Authority: Dahrendorf's Critique of Marx's
        Theory of Class." *Social Forces* 50:473–487.
Heap, James L., and Roth, Phillip A.
1973   "On Phenomenological Sociology." *American Sociological Review* 38:354–
        367.
Heath, Anthony
1976   *Rational Choice and Social Exchange: A Critique of Exchange Theory*.
        Cambridge: Cambridge University Press.
Heberle, Rudolph
1965   "Simmel's Methods." In L. Coser (ed.), *Georg Simmel*. Englewood Cliffs,
        N.J.: Prentice-Hall: 116–121.
Hechter, Michael
1983a   "Introduction." In M. Hechter (ed.), *The Microfoundations of
        Macrosociology*. Philadelphia: Temple University Press: 3–15.
1983b   "A Theory of Group Solidarity." In Michael Hechter (ed.), *The
        Microfoundations of Macrosociology*. Philadelphia: Temple University
        Press: 16–57.
1987   *Principles of Group Solidarity*. Berkeley: University of California Press.
Hegel, G. W. F.
1807/1967   *The Phenomenology of Mind*. New York: Harper Colophon.
1821/1967   *The Philosophy of Right*. Oxford: Clarendon Press.
Heilbrun, Carolyn
1988   *Writing a Woman's Life*. New York: Norton.

Hekman, Susan
1983   *Weber, the Ideal Type, and Contemporary Social Theory.* Notre Dame, Ind.:
            University of Notre Dame Press.
Held, David
1980   *Introduction to Critical Theory: Horkheimer to Habermas.* Berkeley:
            University of California Press.
Held, David and Thompson, John B.
1989   "Editors' Introduction." In D. Held and J. B. Thompson (eds.), *Social
            Theory of Modern Societies: Anthony Giddens and His Critics.* Cambridge:
            Cambridge University Press: 1–18.
Helle, H. J., and Eisenstadt, S. N. (eds.)
1985   *Micro-Sociological Theory: Perspectives on Sociological Theory,* Vol. 2.
            London: Sage.
Heller, Agnes
1976   *The Theory of Need in Marx.* New York: St. Martin's.
Heritage, John
1984   *Garfinkel and Ethnomethodology.* Cambridge: Polity Press.
Heritage, John, and Atkinson, J. Maxwell
1984   "Introduction." In J. M. Atkinson and J. Heritage (eds.), *Structures of
            Social Action.* Cambridge: Cambridge University Press: 1–15.
Heritage, John, and Greatbatch, David
1986   "Generating Applause: A Study of Rhetoric and Response in Party
            Political Conferences." *American Journal of Sociology* 92:110–157.
Heritage, John, and Watson, D. R.
1979   "Formulations as Conversational Objects." In G. Psathas (ed.), *Everyday
            Language: Studies in Ethnomethodology.* New York: Irvington: 187–
            201.
Hewitt, John P.
1984   *Self and Society: A Symbolic Interactionist Social Psychology.* 3rd ed.
            Boston: Allyn and Bacon.
Heyl, John D., and Heyl, Barbara S.
1976   "The Sumner-Porter Controversy at Yale: Pre-Paradigmatic Sociology
            and Institutional Crisis." *Sociological Inquiry* 46:41–49.
Hilbert, Richard A.
1986   "Anomie and Moral Regulation of Reality: The Durkheimian Tradition
            in Modern Relief." *Sociological Theory* 4:1–19.
1990   "Ethnomethodology and the Micro-Macro Order." *American Sociological
            Review* 55:794–808.
Himes, Joseph
1966   "The Functions of Racial Conflict." *Social Forces* 45:1–10.
Hindess, Barry
1986   "Actors and Social Relations." In M. L. Wardell and S. Turner (eds.),
            Sociological Theory in Transition. Boston: Allen and Unwin: 113–126.
1988   *Choice, Rationality, and Social Theory.* London: Unwin Hyman.
Hinkle, Roscoe
1980   *Founding Theory of American Sociology: 1881–1915.* London: Routledge
            and Kegan Paul.
Hinkle, Roscoe, and Hinkle, Gisela
1954   *The Development of American Sociology.* New York: Random House.

Hirsch, Paul, Michaels, Stuart, and Friedman, Ray
1987   " 'Dirty Hands' versus 'Clean Models': Is Sociology in Danger of Being Seduced by Economics?" *Theory and Society* 16:317–336.
Hite, Shere
1976   *The Hite Report: A Nationwide Study of Female Sexuality.* New York: Dell.
Hobsbawm, Eric J.
1965   *Primitive Rebels.* New York: Norton.
Hofstadter, Richard
1959   *Social Darwinism in American Thought.* New York: Braziller.
Hollinger, David
1980   "T. S. Kuhn's Theory of Science and Its Implications for History." In G. Gutting (ed.), *Paradigms and Revolutions.* Notre Dame, Ind.: Notre Dame University Press: 195–222.
Holton, Robert J., and Turner, Bryan S.
1986   *Talcott Parsons on Economy and Society.* London: Routledge and Kegan Paul.
Homans, George C.
1958   "Social Behavior as Exchange." *American Journal of Sociology* 63:597–606.
1961   *Social Behavior: Its Elementary Forms.* New York: Harcourt, Brace and World.
1962   *Sentiments and Activities.* New York: Free Press.
1967   *The Nature of Social Science.* New York: Harcourt, Brace and World.
1969   "The Sociological Relevance of Behaviorism." In R. Burgess and D. Bushell (eds.), *Behavioral Sociology.* New York: Columbia University Press: 1–24.
1971   "Commentary." In H. Turk and R. Simpson (eds.), *Institutions and Social Exchange.* Indianapolis: Bobbs-Merrill: 363–374.
1974   *Social Behavior: Its Elementary Forms.* Rev. ed. New York: Harcourt Brace Jovanovich.
1984   *Coming to My Senses: The Autobiography of a Sociologist.* New Brunswick, N.J.: Transaction Books.
Homans, George C., and Schneider, David M.
1955   *Marriage, Authority and Final Causes: A Study of Unilateral Cross-Cousin Marriage.* New York: Free Press.
Hook, Sidney
1965   "Pareto's Sociological System." In J. H. Meisel (ed.), *Pareto and Mosca.* Englewood Cliffs, N.J.:Prentice-Hall: 57–61.
Hooks, Bell
1984   *Feminist Theory: From Margin to Center.* Boston: South End Press.
1989   *Talking Back: Thinking Feminist, Thinking Black.* Boston: South End Press.
Horowitz, Irving L.
1962/1967   "Consensus, Conflict, and Cooperation." In N. Demerath and R. Peterson (eds.), *System, Change and Conflict.* New York: Free Press: 265–279.
1983   *C. Wright Mills: An American Utopian.* New York: Free Press.
Huaco, George
1966   "The Functionalist Theory of Stratification: Two Decades of Controversy." *Inquiry* 9:215–240.
1986   "Ideology and General Theory: The Case of Sociological Functionalism." *Comparative Studies in Society and History* 28:34–54.

Huber, Joan
1976   "Sociology." *Signs: Journal of Women in Culture and Society* 1, part 1:685–697.
Hunter, Allen
1988   "Post-Marxism and the New Social Movements." *Theory and Society* 17: 885–900.
Hunter, J. E., Schmidt, F. L., and Jackson, G. B.
1982   *Metaanalysis: Cumulating Research Findings across Studies.* Beverly Hills, Calif.: Sage.
Husserl, Edmund
1931   *Ideas.* London: Allen and Unwin.
Israel, Joachim
1971   *Alienation: From Marx to Modern Sociology.* Boston: Allyn and Bacon.
Jackman, Mary R., and Jackman, Robert W.
1973   "An Interpretation of the Relation between Objective and Subjective Social Status." *American Sociological Review* 38:569–582.
Jaggar, Alison M.
1983   *Feminist Politics and Human Nature.* Totowa, N.J.: Rowman and Allanheld.
Jaggar, Alison M., and Bordo, Susan (eds.)
1989   *Gender/Body/Knowledge: Feminist Reconstructions of Being and Knowing.* New Brunswick, N.J.: Rutgers University Press.
Jaggar, Alison M., and Rothenberg, Paula (eds.)
1984   *Feminist Frameworks.* 2nd ed. New York: McGraw-Hill.
James, Selma, and Costa, Mariarosa Dallacosa
1973   *The Power of Women and the Subversion of Community.* Bristol: Falling Wall Press.
Jameson, Fredric
1984   "Postmodernism, or the Cultural Logic of Late Capitalism." *New Left Review* 146:53–93.
Janeway, Elizabeth
1981   *Powers of the Weak.* New York: Morrow Quill.
Jay Martin
1973   *The Dialectical Imagination.* Boston: Little, Brown.
1984   *Marxism and Totality: The Adventures of a Concept from Lukacs to Habermas.* Berkeley: University of California Press.
1986   *Permanent Exiles: Essays on the Intellectual Migration from Germany to America.* New York: Columbia University Press.
1988   *Fin-de-Siecle Socialism and Other Essays.* New York: Routledge.
Jefferson, Gail
1979   "A Technique for Inviting Laughter and Its Subsequent Acceptance Declination." In G. Psathas (ed.), *Everyday Language: Studies in Ethnomethodology.* New York: Irvington: 79–96.
1984   "On the Organization of Laughter in Talk about Troubles." In J. M. Atkinson and J. Heritage (eds.), *Structures of Social Action.* Cambridge: Cambridge University Press: 346–369.
Jencks, Charles
1977   *The Language of Post-Modern Architecture.* New York: Rizzoli.

Jessop, Bob
1985   *Nicos Poulantzas: Marxist Theory and Political Strategy.* New York: St. Martin's.
Joas, Hans
1981   "George Herbert Mead and the 'Division of Labor': Macrosociological Implications of Mead's Social Psychology." *Symbolic Interaction* 4:177–190.
1985   *G. H. Mead: A Contemporary Re-examination of His Thought.* Cambridge: MIT Press.
Johnson, Chalmers
1966   *Revolutionary Change.* Boston: Little, Brown.
Johnson, Doyle Paul
1981   *Sociological Theory: Classical Founders and Contemporary Perspectives.* New York: Wiley.
Johnson, John M., and Ferraro, Kathleen T.
1984   "The Victimized Self: The Case of Battered Women." In J. A. Kotarba and A. Fontana (eds.), *The Existential Self in Society.* Chicago: University of Chicago Press: 119–130.
Johnson, Miriam M.
1989   "Feminism and the Theories of Talcott Parsons." In R. A. Wallace (ed.), *Feminism and Sociological Theory.* Newbury Park, Calif.: Sage: 101–118.
Jones, Greta
1980   *Social Darwinism and English Thought: The Interaction between Biological and Social Theory.* Atlantic Highlands, N.J.: Humanities Press.
Jones, Robert Alun
1986   "Durkheim, Frazer, and Smith: The Role of Analogies and Exemplars in the Development of Durkheim's Sociology of Religion." *American Journal of Sociology* 92:596–627.
Kalberg, Stephen
1980   "Max Weber's Types of Rationality: Cornerstones for the Analysis of Rationalization Processes in History." *American Journal of Sociology* 85:1145–1179.
1985   "The Role of Ideal Interests in Max Weber's Comparative Historical Sociology." In R. J. Antonio and R. M. Glassman (eds.), *A Weber-Marx Dialogue.* Lawrence: University Press of Kansas: 46–67.
1990   "The Rationalization of Action in Max Weber's Sociology of Religion." *Sociological Theory* 8:58–84.
Kaldor, Mary
1990   "After the Cold War." *New Left Review* 180:25–40.
Kandal, Terry R.
1988   *The Woman Question in Classical Sociological Theory.* Miami, Florida: International University Press.
Kanter, Rosabeth Moss-
1977   *Men and Women of the Corporation.* New York: Basic Books.
Karady, Victor
1983   The Durkheimians in Academe: A Reconsideration." Bernard (ed.), *The Sociological Domain.* Cambridge: Cambridge University Press.
Kasper, Anne
1986   "Consciousness Re-Evaluated: Interpretive Theory and Feminist Scholarship." *Sociological Inquiry* 56:30–49.

Kaufman, Debra R., and Richardson, Barbara L.
1982　　　*Achievement and Women: Challenging the Assumptions.* New York: Free
　　　　　　Press.
Keller, Evelyn Fox
1985　　　*Reflections on Gender and Science.* New Haven: Yale University Press.
Kellner, Douglas
1988　　　"Postmodernism as Social Theory: Some Challenges and Problems."
　　　　　　Theory, Culture and Society 5:239–269.
1990a　　"The Postmodern Turn: Positions, Problems, and Prospects." In G.
　　　　　　Ritzer (ed.), *Frontiers of Social Theory: The New Syntheses.* New York:
　　　　　　Columbia University Press: 255–286.
1990c　　*Television and the Crisis of Democracy.* Boulder, Colo.: Westview Press.
Kellner, Douglas (ed.)
1990b　　*Postmodernism: Jameson: Critique.* Washington, D.C.: Maisonneuve Press.
Kelly-Godol, Joan
1983　　　"The Social Relation of the Sexes: Methodological Implications of
　　　　　　Women's History." In E. Abel and E. K. Abel (eds.), *The Signs Reader:
　　　　　　Women, Gender and Scholarship.* Chicago: University of Chicago
　　　　　　Press.
Kemeny, Jim
1976　　　"Perspectives on the Micro-Macro Distinction." *Sociological Review*
　　　　　　24:731–752.
Kemper, Theodore
1978a　　"Toward a Sociological Theory of Emotions: Some Problems and Some
　　　　　　Solutions." *American Sociologist* 13:30–41.
1978b　　*A Social Interactional Theory of Emotions.* New York: Wiley.
1981　　　"Social Constructionist and Positivist Approaches to the Sociology of
　　　　　　Emotions." *American Journal of Sociology* 87:336–362.
Kent, Raymond A.
1981　　　*A History of British Empirical Sociology.* Aldershot, Hants, Eng.: Gower.
Kessler, Suzanne J., and McKenna, Wendy
1978　　　*Gender: An Ethnomethodological Approach.* Chicago: University of Chicago
　　　　　　Press.
Kithahara, Michio
1986　　　"Commodore Perry and the Japanese: A Study in the Dramaturgy of
　　　　　　Power." *Symbolic Interaction* 9:53–65.
Kittay, Eva Feder
1984　　　"Womb Envy: An Explanatory Concept." In Joyce Trebilcot (ed.),
　　　　　　Mothering: Essays in Feminist Theory. Totowa, N.J.: Rowman and
　　　　　　Allanheld: 94–128.
Knorr-Cetina, Karin D.
1981a　　"Introduction: The Micro-Sociological Challenge of Macro-Sociology:
　　　　　　Towards a Reconstruction of Social Theory and Methodology." In K.
　　　　　　Knorr-Cetina and A. Cicourel (eds.), *Advances in Social Theory and
　　　　　　Methodology.* New York: Methuen: 1–47.
1981b　　*The Manufacture of Knowledge: An Essay on the Constructivist and
　　　　　　Contextual Nature of Science.* Oxford: Pergamon Press.
Knox, John
1963　　　"The Concept of Exchange in Sociological Theory: 1884 and 1961."
　　　　　　Social Forces 41:341–346.

Kohn, Melvin L.
1976   "Occupational Structure and Alienation." *American Journal of Sociology*
            82:111–127.
Kolb, William L.
1944   "A Critical Evaluation of Mead's 'I' and 'Me' Concepts." *Social Forces*
            22:291–296.
Korenbaum, Myrtle
1964   Translator's preface to Georges Gurvitch, *The Spectrum of Social Time.*
            Dordrecht, Neth.: D. Reidel: ix–xxvi.
Kotarba, Joseph A.
1977   "The Chronic Pain Patient." In J. Douglas et al. (eds.), *Existential
            Sociology.* Cambridge: Cambridge University Press: 257–272.
1979   "Existential Sociology." In S. McNall (ed.), *Theoretical Perspectives in
            Sociology.* New York: St. Martin's: 348–368.
1984   "A Synthesis: The Existential Self in Society." In J. A. Kotarba and A.
            Fontana (eds.), *The Existential Self in Society.* Chicago: University of
            Chicago Press: 224–234.
Kotarba, Joseph A., and Fontana, Andrea (eds.)
1984   *The Existential Self in Society.* Chicago: University of Chicago Press.
Kronman, Anthony
1983   *Max Weber.* Stanford, Calif.: Stanford University Press.
Kuhn, Annette, and Wolpe, Ann Marie (eds.)
1978   *Feminism and Materialism.* London: Routledge and Kegan Paul.
Kuhn, Manford
1964   "Major Trends in Symbolic Interaction Theory in the Past Twenty-Five
            Years." *The Sociological Quarterly* 5:61–84.
Kuhn, Thomas
1962   *The Structure of Scientific Revolutions.* Chicago: University of Chicago
            Press.
1970   *The Structure of Scientific Revolutions.* 2nd ed. Chicago: University of
            Chicago Press.
Kurzweil, Edith
1980   *The Age of Structuralism: Lévi-Strauss to Foucault.* New York: Columbia
            University Press.
1987   "Psychoanalysis as the Macro-Micro Link." In J. Alexander et al. (eds.),
            The Micro-Macro Link. Berkeley: University of California Press: 237–254.
Lachman, L. M.
1971   *The Legacy of Max Weber.* Berkeley, Calif.: Glendessary Press.
Laclau, Ernesto
1990   "Coming Up for Air." *Marxism Today* March: 25, 27.
Laclau, Ernesto, and Mouffe, Chantal
1985   *Hegemony and Socialist Strategy: Towards a Radical Democratic Politics.*
            London: Verso.
1987   "Post-Marxism without Apologies." *New Left Review* 166: 79–106.
Lamont, Michele, and Wuthnow, Robert
1990   "Betwixt and Between: Recent Cultural Sociology in Europe and the
            United States." In G. Ritzer (ed.), *Frontiers of Social Theory: The New
            Syntheses.* New York: Columbia University Press: 287–315.

Laws, Judith Long, and Schwartz, Pepper
1977   *Sexual Scripts: The Social Construction of Female Sexuality.* Hinsdale, Ill.:
             Dryden.
Layder, Derek
1985   "Power, Structure and Agency." *Journal for the Theory of Social Behaviour*
             15:131–149.
Leach, Edmund
1974   *Claude Lévi-Strauss.* New York: Penguin.
Lefebvre, Henri
1968   *The Sociology of Marx.* New York: Vintage.
Lehman, Edward W.
1988   "The Theory of the State versus the State of Theory." *American*
             Sociological Review 53:807–823.
Lemert, Charles
1979   *Sociology and the Twilight of Man: Homocentrism and Discourse in*
             Sociological Theory. Carbondale: Southern Illinois University Press.
1990   "The Uses of French Structuralisms in Sociology." In G. Ritzer (ed.),
             Frontiers of Social Theory: The New Syntheses. New York: Columbia
             University Press: 230–254.
forthcoming "Sociological Metatheory and Its Cultured Despisers." In G. Ritzer
             (ed.), *Sociological Metatheorizing: Coming of Age.* Beverly Hills, Calif.:
             Sage.
Lemert, Charles (ed.)
1981   *French Sociology: Rupture and Renewal since 1968.* New York: Columbia
             University Press.
Lengermann, Patricia Madoo
1979   "The Founding of the *American Sociological Review*." *American*
             Sociological Review 44:185–198.
Lengermann, Patricia Madoo, and Niebrugge-Brantley, Jill
1990   "Feminist Sociological Theory: The Near-Future Prospects." In G. Ritzer
             (ed.), *Frontiers of Social Theory: The New Syntheses.* New York: Columbia
             University Press: 316–344.
Lengermann, Patricia Madoo, and Wallace, Ruth A.
1985   *Gender in America: Social Control and Social Change.* Englewood Cliffs,
             N.J.: Prentice-Hall
Lenzer, Gertrud (ed.)
1975   *Auguste Comte and Positivism: The Essential Writings.* Magnolia, Mass.:
             Peter Smith.
Lever, Janet
1978   "Sex Differences in the Complexity of Children's Play and Games."
             American Sociological Review 43:471–483.
Levidow, Les
1990   "Foreclosing the Future." *Science as Culture* 8:59–90.
Levine, Andrew, Sober, Elliot and Wright, Erik Olin
1987   "Marxism and Methodological Individualism." *New Left Review* 162:67–
             84.
Levine, Donald
1971   "Introduction." In D. Levine (ed.), *Georg Simmel: Individuality and Social*
             Forms. Chicago: University of Chicago Press: ix–xiv.

1981   "Rationality and Freedom: Weber and Beyond." *Sociological Inquiry* 51: 5–25.
1985   "Ambivalent Encounters: Disavowals of Simmel by Durkheim, Weber, Lukács, Park and Parsons." In D. Levine (ed.), *The Flight from Ambiguity: Essays in Social and Cultural Theory*. Chicago: University of Chicago Press: 89–141.
1989   "Simmel as a Resource for Sociological Metatheory." *Sociological Theory* 7:161–174.

Levine, Donald, Carter, Ellwood B., and Gorman, Eleanor Miller
1976a   "Simmel's Influence on American Sociology—I." *American Journal of Sociology* 81:813–845.
1976b   "Simmel's Influence on American Sociology—II." *American Journal of Sociology* 81:1112–1132.

Lévi-Strauss, Claude
1949   *Les Structures Elementaires de la Parente*. Paris: Presses Universitaires de France.
1963   *Totemism*. Boston: Beacon Press.
1967   *Structural Anthropology*. Garden City, N.Y.: Anchor.

Lewis, J. David, and Smith, Richard L.
1980   *American Sociology and Pragmatism: Mead, Chicago Sociology, and Symbolic Interaction*. Chicago: University of Chicago Press.

Lilienfeld, Robert
1978   *The Rise of Systems Theory: An Ideological Analysis*. New York: Wiley-Interscience.

Lipman-Blumen, Jean
1979   "Jessie Bernard." *International Encyclopedia of the Social Sciences*, Vol. 18. New York: Free Press: 49–56.
1984   *Gender Roles and Power*. Englewood Cliffs, N.J.: Prentice-Hall.

Lipset, Seymour M.
1975   "Social Structure and Social Change." In P. Blau (ed.), *Approaches to the Study of Social Structure*. New York: Free Press: 172–209.

Liska, Allen E.
1990   "The Significance of Aggregate Dependent Variables and Contextual Independent Variables for Linking Macro and Micro Theories." *Social Psychology Quarterly* 53:292–301.

Loader, Colin, and Alexander, Jeffrey C.
1985   "Max Weber on Churches and Sects in North America: An Alternative Path toward Rationalization." *Sociological Theory* 3:1–6.

Lockwood, David
1956   "Some Remarks on *The Social System*." *British Journal of Sociology* 7:134–146.

Lodahl, Janice B., and Gordon, Gerald
1972   "The Structure of Scientific Fields and the Functioning of University Graduate Departments." *American Sociological Review* 37:57–72.

Lodge, Peter
1986   "Connections: W. I. Thomas, European Social Thought and American Sociology." In R. C. Monk (ed.), *Structures of Knowing*. Lanham, Md.: University Press of America: 135–160.

Lorde, Audre
1984   *Sister Outsider: Essays and Speeches.* Trumansburg, N.Y.: Crossings Press.
Lougee, Carolyn C.
1976   *Le Paradis des Femmes: Women, Salons and Social Stratification in Seventeenth-Century France.* Princeton, N.J.: Princeton University Press.
Lukács, Georg
1922/1968   *History and Class Consciousness.* Cambridge: MIT Press.
Lukes, Steven
1972   *Emile Durkheim: His Life and Work.* New York: Harper & Row.
1977   "Power and Structure." In S. Lukes, *Essays in Social Theory.* London: Macmillan: 3–29.
Luscher, Kurt
1990   "The Social Reality of Perspectives: On G. H. Mead's Potential Relevance for the Analysis of Contemporary Societies." *Symbolic Interaction* 13:1–18.
Luxemburg, Rosa
1971   "Women's Suffrage and Class Struggle." In D. Howard (ed.), *Selected Political Writings.* New York: Monthly Review Press: 219–220.
Luxenberg, Stan
1985   *Roadside Empires: How the Chains Franchised America.* New York: Viking.
Lyman, Stanford, and Scott, Marvin
1970   *A Sociology of the Absurd.* New York: Appleton-Century-Crofts.
Lynch, Michael
1985   *Art and Artifact in Laboratory Science: A Study of Shop Work and Shop Talk in a Research Laboratory.* London: Routledge and Kegan Paul.
Lyotard, Jean-François
1984   *The Postmodern Condition.* Minneapolis: University of Minnesota Press.
MacCrae, Donald G.
1974   *Max Weber.* Harmondsworth, Eng.: Penguin.
Mackay, Robert W.
1974   "Words, Utterances and Activities." In R. Turner (ed.), *Ethnomethodology: Selected Readings.* Harmondsworth, Eng.: Penguin: 197–215.
MacKinnon, Catherine
1979   *Sexual Harassment of Working Women.* New Haven: Yale University Press.
1982   "Feminism, Marxism, Method and the State: An Agenda for Theory." In N. O. Keohane et al. (eds.), *Feminist Theory: A Critique of Ideology.* Chicago: University of Chicago Press: 1–30.
1989   *Towards a Feminist Theory of the State.* Cambridge: Harvard University Press.
Maines, David R.
1977   "Social Organization and Social Structure in Symbolic Interactionist Thought." In A. Inkeles, J. Coleman, and N. Smelser (eds.), *Annual Review of Sociology,* Vol. 3. Palo Alto: Annual Reviews: 259–285.
1988   "Myth, Text, and Interactionist Complicity in the Neglect of Blumer's Macrosociology." *Symbolic Interaction* 11:43–57.
1989a   "Repackaging Blumer: The Myth of Herbert Blumer's Astructural Bias." *Symbolic Interaction* 10:383–413.

1989b   "Herbert Blumer on the Possibility of Science in the Practice of
           Sociology: Further Thoughts." *Journal of Contemporary Ethnography*
           18:160–177.
Maines, David R., and Morrione, Thomas J.
1990   "On the Breadth and Relevance of Blumer's Perspective: Introduction to
           His Analysis of Industrialization." In H. Blumer, *Industrialization as an
           Agent of Social Change: A Critical Analysis.* New York: Aldine de
           Gruyter.
Mandelbaum, Jenny
1989   "Interpersonal Activities in Conversational Storytelling." *Western Journal
           of Speech Communications* 53:114–126.
Manis, Jerome, and Meltzer, Bernard (eds.)
1978   *Symbolic Interaction: A Reader in Social Psychology.* 3rd ed. Boston: Allyn
           and Bacon.
Mann, Michael
1986   *The Sources of Social Power,* Vol. 1. New York: Cambridge University
           Press.
Manning, Peter
1973   "Existential Sociology." *Sociological Quarterly* 14:200–225.
Manual, Frank E.
1962   *The Prophets of Paris.* Cambridge: Harvard University Press.
Marcuse, Herbert
1958   *Soviet Marxism: A Critical Analysis.* New York: Columbia University
           Press.
1964   *One-Dimensional Man.* Boston: Beacon Press.
1969   *An Essay on Liberation.* Boston: Beacon Press.
Marini, Margaret M.
1988   "Sociology of Gender." In E. F. Borgatta and K. S. Cook (eds.), *The
           Future of Sociology.* Beverly Hills, Calif.: Sage: 374–393.
Markovsky, Barry
1987   "Toward Multilevel Sociological Theories: Simulations of Actor and
           Network Effects." *Sociological Theory* 5:101–117.
Marlaire, Courtney L., and Maynard, Douglas W.
1990   "Standardized Testing as an Interactional Phenomenon." *Sociology of
           Education* 63:83–101.
Martin, Wendy
1972   *The American Sisterhood: Writings of the Feminist Movement from Colonial
           Times to Present.* New York: Harper & Row.
Marx, Karl
1842/1977 "Communism and the *Augsburger Allegemeine Zeitung.*" In D. McLellan
           (ed.), *Karl Marx: Selected Writings.* New York: Oxford University Press:
           20.
1847/1963 *The Poverty of Philosophy.* New York: International Publishers.
1852/1970 "The Eighteenth Brumaire of Louis Bonaparte." In R. C. Tucker (ed.),
           The Marx-Engels Reader. New York: Norton: 436–525.
1857–1858/ *Pre-Capitalist Economic Formations,* Eric J. Hobsbawm (ed.). New York:
1964   International Publishers.
1857–1858/ *The Grundrisse: Foundations of the Critique of Political Economy.* New
1974   York: Random House.

1859/1970   *A Contribution to the Critique of Political Economy.* New York: International Publishers.

1862–1863/   *Theories of Surplus Value,* Part I. Moscow: Progress Publishers.
1963

1862–1863   *Theories of Surplus Value,* Part II. Moscow: Progress Publishers.
1968

1867/1967   *Capital: A Critique of Political Economy,* Vol. 1. New York: International Publishers.

1869/1963   *The 18th Brumaire of Louis Bonaparte.* New York: International Publishers.

1932/1964   *The Economic and Philosophic Manuscripts of 1844,* Dirk J. Struik (ed.). New York: International Publishers.

Marx, Karl, and Engels, Friedrich

1845/1956   *The Holy Family.* Moscow: Foreign Language Publishing House.

1845–1846/   *The German Ideology,* Part 1, C. J. Arthur (ed.). New York: International
1970   Publishers.

1848/1948   *Manifesto of the Communist Party.* New York: International Publishers.

Masterman, Margaret

1970   "The Nature of a Paradigm." In I. Lakatos and A. Musgrove (eds.), *Criticism and the Growth of Knowledge.* Cambridge: Cambridge University Press: 59–89.

Masters, William, and Johnson, Virginia

1966   *Human Sexual Response.* Boston: Little, Brown.

Matthews, Fred H.

1977   *Quest for an American Sociology: Robert E. Park and the Chicago School.* Montreal: McGill University Press.

Mauss, Marcel

1954   *The Gift,* Ian Cunnison (trans.). London: Cohen and West.

Mayhew, Bruce

1980   "Structuralism versus Individualism: Part I, Shadowboxing in the Dark." *Social Forces* 59:335–375.

1981   "Structuralism versus Individualism: Part II, Ideological and Other Obfuscations." *Social Forces* 59:627–648.

Maynard, Douglas W., and Clayman, Steven E.

forthcoming "The Diversity of Ethnomethodology." *Annual Review of Sociology.*

Mazlish, Bruce

1984   *The Meaning of Karl Marx.* New York: Oxford University Press.

McCarthy, Thomas

1982   *The Critical Theory of Jurgen Habermas.* Cambridge: MIT Press.

1984   "Translator's Introduction." In J. Habermas, *The Theory of Communicative Action.* Boston: Beacon Press.

McKinney, John C.

1966   *Constructive Typology and Social Theory.* New York: Appleton-Century-Crofts.

McLellan, David

1973   *Karl Marx: His Life and Thought.* New York: Harper Colophon.

McLellan, David (ed.)

1971   *The Thought of Karl Marx.* New York: Harper Torchbooks.

McMahon, A. M.

1984   "The Two Social Psychologies: Postcrises Directions." In R. H. Turner and J. F. Short (eds.), *Annual Review of Sociology*, Vol. 10. Palo Alto: Annual Reviews: 121–140.

McMurty, John
1978   *The Structure of Marx's World-View*. Princeton, N.J.: Princeton University Press.

McPhail, Clark
1981   "The Problems and Prospects of Behavioral Perspectives." *American Sociologist* 16:172–174.

McPhail, Clark, and Rexroat, Cynthia
1979   "Mead vs. Blumer." *American Sociological Review* 44:449–467.
1980   Rejoinder: "*Ex Cathedra* Blumer or *Ex Libris* Mead?" *American Sociological Review* 45:420–430.

Mead, George Herbert
1934/1962 *Mind, Self and Society: From the Standpoint of a Social Behaviorist*. Chicago: University of Chicago Press.
1938/1972 *The Philosophy of the Act*. Chicago: University of Chicago Press.
1959   *The Philosophy of the Present*. LaSalle, Ill.: Open Court Publishing.
1982   *The Individual and the Social Self: Unpublished Work of George Herbert Mead*. Chicago: University of Chicago Press.

Mehan, Hugh, and Wood, Houston
1975   *The Reality of Ethnomethodology*. New York: Wiley.

Meltzer, Bernard
1964/1978 "Mead's Social Psychology." In J. Manis and B. Meltzer (eds.), *Symbolic Interaction: A Reader in Social Psychology*. 3rd ed. Boston: Allyn and Bacon: 15–27.

Meltzer, Bernard, Petras, James, and Reynolds, Larry
1975   *Symbolic Interactionism: Genesis, Varieties and Criticisms*. London: Routledge and Kegan Paul.

Merton, Robert K.
1949/1968 "Manifest and Latent Functions." In R. K. Merton, *Social Theory and Social Structure*. New York: Free Press: 73–138.
1968   *Social Theory and Social Structure*. New York: Free Press.
1975   "Structural Analysis in Sociology." In P. Blau (ed.), *Approaches to the Study of Social Structure*. New York: Free Press: 21–52.
1976   *Sociological Ambivalence*. New York: Free Press.
1980   "Remembering the Young Talcott Parsons." *American Sociologist* 15:68–71.
1986   "Comments." In S. Lindenberg, J. S. Coleman, and S. Nowak (eds.), *Approaches to Social Theory*. New York: Russell Sage Foundation: 61–2.

Mészáros, István
1970   *Marx's Theory of Alienation*. New York: Harper Torchbooks.

Miliband, Ralph
1972   "Reply to Nicos Poulantzas." In R. Blackburn (ed.), *Ideology in Social Science: Readings in Critical Social Theory*. London: Fontana: 253–262.

Miller, David
1973   *George Herbert Mead: Self, Language and the World*. Austin: University of Texas Press.
1981   "The Meaning of Role-Taking." *Symbolic Interaction* 4:167–175.
1982a   "Introduction." In G. H. Mead, *The Individual and the Social Self:*

Unpublished Work of George Herbert Mead. Chicago: University of Chicago Press: 1–26.

1982b   Review of J. David Lewis and Richard L. Smith, *American Sociology and Pragmatism. Journal of the History of Sociology* 4:108–114.

1985   "Concerning J. David Lewis' Response to My Review of *American Sociology and Pragmatism." Journal of the History of Sociology* 5:131–133.

Miller, Jean Baker
1976   *Toward a New Psychology of Women.* Boston: Beacon Press.

Millet, Kate
1970   *Sexual Politics.* Garden City, N.Y.: Doubleday.

Mills, C. Wright
1951   *White Collar.* New York: Oxford University Press.
1956   *The Power Elite.* New York: Oxford University Press.
1959   *The Sociological Imagination.* New York: Oxford University Press.
1960   *Listen Yankee: The Revolution in Cuba.* New York: McGraw-Hill.
1962   *The Marxists.* New York: Dell.

Mitchell, Jack N.
1978   *Social Exchange, Dramaturgy and Ethnomethodology: Toward a Paradigmatic Synthesis.* New York: Elsevier.

Mitchell, Juliet
1975   *Psychoanalysis and Feminism.* New York: Vintage.

Mitroff, Ian
1974   "Norms and Counter-Norms in a Select Group of the Apollo Moon Scientists: A Case Study of the Ambivalence of Scientists." *American Sociological Review* 39:579–595.

Mitroff, Ian, and Kilmann, Ralph
1978   *Methodological Approaches to Social Science.* San Francisco: Jossey-Bass.

Mitzman, Arthur
1969   *The Iron Cage: An Historical Interpretation of Max Weber.* New York: Grosset and Dunlap.

Miyahara, Kojiro
1983   "Charisma: From Weber to Contemporary Sociology." *Sociological Inquiry* 55:368–388.

Mizruchi, Mark
1990   "Cohesion, Structural Equivalence, and Similarity of Behavior: An Approach to the Study of Corporate Political Power." *Sociological Theory* 8:16–32.

Mizruchi, Mark S., and Koenig, Thomas
1986   "Economic Sources of Corporate Political Consensus: An Examination of Interindustry Relations." *American Sociological Review* 51:482–491.

Moi, Toril (ed.)
1986   *The Kristeva Reader.* New York: Columbia University Press.

Molm, Linda D.
1981   "The Legitimacy of Behavioral Theory as a Sociological Perspective." *American Sociologist* 16:153–166.

Mommsen, Wolfgang J.
1974   *The Age of Bureaucracy.* New York: Harper & Row.

Moore, Wilbert E.
1978   "Functionalism." In T. Bottomore and R. Nisbet (eds.), *A History of Sociological Analysis*. New York: Basic Books: 321–361.
Moraga, Cherrie, and Anzaldua, Gloria
1981   *This Bridge Called My Back: Writings by Radical Women of Color.* Watertown, Mass.: Persephone Press.
Morgan, Robin
1970   *Sisterhood Is Powerful: An Anthology of Writings from the Women's Liberation Movement.* New York: Vintage.
Morrione, Thomas J.
1988   "Herbert G. Blumer (1900–1987): A Legacy of Concepts, Criticisms, and Contributions." *Symbolic Interaction* 11:1–12.
Morris, Monica B.
1977   *Excursion into Creative Sociology*. New York: Columbia University Press.
Morse, Chandler
1961   "The Functional Imperatives." In M. Black (ed.), *The Social Theories of Talcott Parsons*. Englewood Cliffs, N.J.: Prentice-Hall: 100–152.
Mouffe, Chantal
1988   "Radical Democracy: Modern or Postmodern?" In A. Ross (ed.), *Universal Abandon? The Politics of Postmodernism*. Minneapolis: University of Minnesota Press: 31–45.
Mueller-Vollmer, Kurt
1985   "Language, Mind and Artifact: An Outline of Hermeneutic Theory since the Enlightenment." In K. Mueller-Vollmer (ed.), *The Hermeneutics Reader*. New York: Continuum: 1–53.
Mullins, Nicholas
1973   *Theories and Theory Groups in Contemporary American Sociology*. New York: Harper and Row.
1983   "Theories and Theory Groups Revisited." In Randall Collins (ed.), *Sociological Theory—1983*. San Francisco: Jossey-Bass: 319–337.
Münch, P. A.
1975   " 'Sense' and 'Intention' in Max Weber's Theory of Action." *Sociological Inquiry* 45:59–65.
Münch, Richard
1987   "The Interpenetration of Microinteraction and Macrostructures in a Complex and Contingent Institutional Order." In Jeffrey C. Alexander, et al. (eds.), *The Micro-Macro Link*. Berkeley: University of California Press: 319–336.
Münch, Richard, and Smelser, Neil J.
1987   "Relating the Micro and Macro." In Jeffrey C. Alexander, et al. (eds.), The *Micro-Macro Link*. Berkeley: University of California Press: 356–387.
Nass, Clifford I.
1986   "Bureaucracy, Technical Expertise, and Professionals: A Weberian Approach." *Sociological Theory* 4:61–70.
Natanson, Maurice
1973a   "Introduction." In A. Schutz, *Collected Papers I: The Problem of Social Reality*. The Hague: Martinus Nijhoff: xxv–xlvii.
1973b   *The Social Dynamics of George H. Mead*. The Hague: Martinus Nijhoff.

Nicolaus, Martin
1974   "Foreword." In K. Marx, *The Grundrisse.* New York: Random House: 7–
            63.
Nisbet, Robert
1959   "Comment." *American Sociological Review* 24:479–481.
1967   *The Sociological Tradition.* New York: Basic Books.
1974   *The Sociology of Emile Durkheim.* New York: Oxford University Press.
Noblit, George W. and Hare, R. Dwight
1988   Meta-Ethnography: Synthesizing Qualitative Studies. Newburg Park,
            Calif.: Sage.
Oakes, Guy
1984a   "The Problem of Women in Simmel's Theory of Culture." In G. Oakes
            (ed.), *Georg Simmel on Women, Sexuality, and Love.* New Haven: Yale
            University Press: 3–62.
Oakes, Guy (ed.)
1984b   *Georg Simmel on Women, Sexuality and Love.* New Haven: Yale
            University Press.
Oliver, Ivan
1983   "The 'Old' and the 'New' Hermeneutic in Sociological Theory." *British
            Journal of Sociology* 34:519–553.
Ollman, Bertell
1976   *Alienation.* 2nd ed. Cambridge: Cambridge University Press.
O'Neill, William L.
1971   *A History of Feminism in America.* Chicago: Quadrangle Books.
Osterberg, Dag
1988   *Metasociology: An Inquiry into the Origins and Validity of Social Thought.*
            Oslo: Norwegian University Press.
Pace, Eric
1990   "Louis Althusser, 72, a Marxist Who Harshly Criticized Moscow." *New
            York Times* Oct. 24: B6.
Pareto, Vilfredo
1935   *A Treatise on General Sociology.* 4 vols. New York: Dover.
Park, Robert E.
1927/1973   "Life History." *American Journal of Sociology* 79:251–260.
Parker, Mike, and Slaughter, Jane
1990   "Management-by-Stress: The Team Concept in the US Auto Industry."
            Science as Culture 8:27–58.
Parsons, Talcott
1934–1935   "The Place of Ultimate Values in Sociological Theory." *International
            Journal of Ethics* 45:282–316.
1937   *The Structure of Social Action.* New York: McGraw-Hill.
1942   "Some Sociological Aspects of the Fascist Movements." *Social Forces*
            21:138–147.
1947   "Certain Primary Sources and Patterns of Aggression in the Social
            Structure of the Western World." *Psychiatry* 10:167–181.
1949   *The Structure of Social Action.* 2nd ed. New York: McGraw-Hill.
1951   *The Social System.* Glencoe, Ill.: Free Press.
1954a   "The Prospects of Sociological Theory." In T. Parsons (ed.), *Essays in
            Sociological Theory.* New York: Free Press: 348–369.

1954b	"The Present Position and Prospects of Systematic Theory in Sociology." In T. Parsons (ed.), *Essays in Sociological Theory*. New York: Free Press: 212–237.
1954c	"Age and Sex in the Social Structure of the United States." In T. Parsons (ed.), *Essays in Sociological Theory*. New York: Free Press.
1960	"A Sociological Approach to the Theory of Organizations." In T. Parsons (ed.), *Structure and Process in Modern Societies*. New York: Free Press: 16–58.
1961	"Some Considerations on the Theory of Social Change." *Rural Sociology* 26:219–239.
1964	"Levels of Organization and the Mediation of Social Interaction." *Sociological Inquiry* 34:207–220.
1966	*Societies*. Englewood Cliffs, N.J.: Prentice-Hall.
1970a	*Social Structure and Personality*. New York: Free Press.
1970b	"On Building Social System Theory: A Personal History." *Daedalus* 99: 826–881.
1971	*The System of Modern Societies*. Englewood Cliffs, N.J.: Prentice-Hall.
1974	"Comment on Turner, 'Parsons as a Symbolic Interactionist.' " *Sociological Inquiry* 45:62–65.
1975	"Social Structure and the Symbolic Media of Interchange." In P. Blau (ed.), *Approaches to the Study of Social Structure*. New York: Free Press: 94–100.
1977a	"General Introduction." In T. Parsons (ed.), *Social Systems and the Evolution of Action Theory*. New York: Free Press: 1–13.
1977b	"On Building Social System Theory: A Personal History." In T. Parsons (ed.), *Social Systems and the Evolution of Action Theory*. New York: Free Press: 22–76.
1990	"Prolegomena to a Theory of Social Institutions." *American Sociological Review* 55:319–333.

Parsons, Talcott, and Platt, Gerald
1973	*The American University*. Cambridge: Harvard University Press.

Parsons, Talcott, and Shils, Edward A. (eds.)
1951	*Toward a General Theory of Action*. Cambridge: Harvard University Press.

Peel, J. D. Y.
1971	*Herbert Spencer: The Evolution of Sociologist*. New York: Basic Books.

Pelaez, Eloina, and Holloway, John
1990	"Learning to Bow: Post-Fordism and Technological Determinism." *Science as Culture* 8:15–26.

Perinbanayagam, Robert S.
1981	"Behavioral Theory: The Relevance, Validity, and Appositeness Thereof to Sociology." *American Sociologist* 16:166–169.
1985	*Signifying Acts: Structure and Meaning in Everyday Life*. Carbondale: Southern Illinois University Press.

Perrin, Robert
1976	"Herbert Spencer's Four Theories of Social Evolution." *American Journal of Sociology* 81:1339–1359.

Phillips, Derek
1973	"Paradigms, Falsifications and Sociology." *Acta Sociologica* 16:13–31.
1975	"Paradigms and Incommensurability." *Theory and Society* 2:37–62.

Piccone, Paul
1990   "Paradoxes of *Perestroika.*" *Telos* 84:3–32.
Polit, Denise F., and Falbo, Toni
1987   "Only Children and Personality Development: A Quantitative Review."
            Journal of Marriage and the Family 49:309–325.
Pollner, Melvin
1987   *Mundane Reason: Reality in Everyday and Sociological Discourse.*
            Cambridge: Cambridge University Press.
Pope, Whitney
1973   "Classic on Classic: Parsons' Interpretation of Durkheim." *American
            Sociological Review* 38:399–415.
1975   "Durkheim as Functionalist." *Sociological Quarterly* 16:361–379.
1976   *Durkheim's* Suicide: *A Classic Analyzed.* Chicago: University of Chicago
            Press.
Pope, Whitney, and Cohen, Jere
1978   "On R. Stephen Warner's 'Toward a Redefinition of Action Theory:
            Paying the Cognitive Element Its Due.' " *American Journal of Sociology*
            83:1359–1367.
Pope, Whitney, Cohen, Jere, and Hazelrigg, Lawrence E.
1975   "On the Divergence of Weber and Durkheim: A Critique of Parsons'
            Convergence Thesis." *American Sociological Review* 40:417–427.
Pope, Whitney, and Johnson, Barclay D.
1983   "Inside Organic Solidarity." *American Sociological Review* 48:681–692.
Porpora, Douglas
1989   "Four Concepts of Social Structure." *Journal for the Theory of Social
            Behaviour* 19:195–211.
Poulantzas, Nicos
1972   "The Problem of the Capitalist State." In R. Blackburn (ed.), *Ideology in
            Social Science.* London: Fontana: 238–253.
1973   *Political Power and Social Classes.* London: Verso.
1974   *Fascism and Dictatorship: The Third International and the Problem of
            Fascism.* London: NLB.
1975   *Classes and Contemporary Capitalism.* London: NLB.
1976   *The Crisis of the Dictatorships.* London: NLB.
Powers, Charles H.
1986   *Vilfredo Pareto.* Newbury Park, Calif.: Sage.
Prendergast, Christopher
1986   "Alfred Schutz and the Austrian School of Economics." *American
            Journal of Sociology* 92:1–26.
Psathas, George
1973   "Introduction." in G. Psathas (ed.), *Phenomenological Sociology: Issues and
            Applications.* New York: Wiley.
1989   *Phenomenology and Sociology: Theory and Research.* Lanham, Md.:
            University Press of America.
Puner, Helen Walker
1947   *Freud: His Life and His Mind.* New York: Dell.
Quadagno, Jill S.
1979   "Paradigms in Evolutionary Theory: The Sociobiological Model of
            Natural Selection." *American Sociological Review* 44:100–109.
Radnitzky, Gerard
1973   *Contemporary Schools of Metascience.* Chicago: Regnery.

Radway, Janice
1984   *Reading the Romance: Women, Patriarchy and Popular Literature.* Chapel
               Hill: University of North Carolina Press.
Rattansi, Ali
1982   *Marx and the Division of Labour.* London: Macmillan.
Reed, Evelyn
1970   *Women's Liberation.* New York: Pathfinder Press.
Rhoades, Lawrence J.
1981   *A History of the American Sociological Association.* Washington, D.C.:
               American Sociological Association.
Rich, Adrienne
1976   *Of Woman Born: Motherhood as Experience and Institution.* New York:
               Bantam.
1979   *On Lies, Secrets and Silences: Selected Prose 1966–1978.* New York:
               Norton.
1980   "Compulsory Heterosexual and Lesbian Experience." In C. R. Stimson
               and E. S. Person (eds.), *Women, Sex, and Sexuality.* Chicago: University
               of Chicago Press: 62–91.
Risman, Barbara, and Schwarz, Pepper (eds.)
1989   *Gender in Intimate Relationships: A Microstructural Approach.* Belmont,
               Calif: Wadsworth.
Ritzer, George
1975a   *Sociology: A Multiple Paradigm Science.* Boston: Allyn and Bacon.
1975b   "Sociology: A Multiple Paradigm Science." *American Sociologist* 10:156–
               167.
1975c   "Professionalization, Bureaucratization and Rationalization: The Views
               of Max Weber." *Social Forces* 53:627–634.
1979   "Toward an Integrated Sociological Paradigm." In W. Snizek et al.
               (eds.), *Contemporary Issues in Theory and Research.* Westport, Conn.:
               Greenwood Press: 25–46.
1980   *Sociology: A Multiple Paradigm Science.* Rev. ed. Boston: Allyn and Bacon.
1981a   *Toward an Integrated Sociological Paradigm: The Search for an Exemplar and
               an Image of the Subject Matter.* Boston: Allyn and Bacon.
1981b   "Paradigm Analysis in Sociology: Clarifying the Issues." *American
               Sociological Review* 46:245–248.
1983   "The McDonaldization of Society." *Journal of American Culture* 6:100–
               107.
1985   "The Rise of Micro-Sociological Theory." *Sociological Theory* 3:88–98.
1987   "The Current State of Metatheory." *Sociological Perspectives: The Theory
               Section Newsletter* 10:1–6.
1988   "Sociological Metatheory: Defending a Subfield by Delineating Its
               Parameters." *Sociological Theory* 6:187–200.
1989a   "Metatheorizing as a Prelude to Theory Development." Paper
               presented at the meetings of the American Sociological Association, San
               Francisco.
1989b   "Of Levels and 'Intellectual Amnesia.' " *Sociological Theory* 7:226–229.
1990a   "Micro-Macro Linkage in Sociological Theory: Applying a
               Metatheoretical Tool." In G. Ritzer (ed.), *Frontiers of Social Theory: The
               New Syntheses.* New York: Columbia University Press: 347–370.

1990b	"The Current Status of Sociological Theory: The New Syntheses." In G. Ritzer (ed.), *Frontiers of Social Theory: The New Syntheses*. New York: Columbia University Press: 1–30.
1990c	Special mini-issue on metatheory. *Sociological Forum* 5:1–74.
1990d	*Metatheorizing in Sociology*. Lexington, Mass.: Lexington Books.
1991	"Metatheorizing in Sociology." *Sociological Forum* 5:3–15.
1992	*Classical Sociological Theory*. New York: McGraw-Hill.
forthcoming a	*Big Mac Attack: The McDonaldization of Society*. New York: Lexington Books.
forthcoming b	"The Recent History and the Emerging Reality of American Sociological Theory: A Metatheoretical Interpretation." *Sociological Forum*.

Ritzer, George (ed.)

1990e	*Frontiers of Social Theory: The New Syntheses*. New York: Columbia University Press.
forthcoming c	*Sociological Metatheorizing: Coming of Age*. Newbury Park, Calif.: Sage.

Ritzer, George, and Trice, Harrison

1969	*An Occupation in Conflict: A Study of the Personnel Manager*. Ithaca, N.Y.: Cornell University Press.

Ritzer, George, and Bell, Richard

1981	"Emile Durkheim: Exemplar for an Integrated Sociological Paradigm?" *Social Forces* 59:966–995.

Ritzer, George, and Walczak, David

1986	*Working: Conflict and Change*. 3rd ed. Englewood Cliffs, N.J.: Prentice-Hall.
1988	"Rationalization and the Deprofessionalization of Physicians." *Social Forces* 67:1–22.

Ritzer, George, and Gindoff, Pamela

forthcoming	"Micro-Macro, Agency-Structure, and Individualism-Holism." In Piotr Stompka (ed.), *From Systems to Agents: The Current Reorientation of Sociological Theory*. London: Sage.

Rocher, Guy

1975	*Talcott Parsons and American Sociology*. New York: Barnes and Noble.

Rock, Paul

1979	*The Making of Symbolic Interactionism*. Totowa, N.J.: Rowman and Littlefield.

Roemer, John

1982	"Methodological Individualism and Deductive Marxism." *Theory and Society* 11:513–520.
1986a	"Introduction." In J. Roemer (ed.), *Analytical Marxism*. Cambridge: Cambridge University Press: 1–7.
1986b	" 'Rational Choice' Marxism: Some Issues of Method and Substance." In J. Roemer (ed.), *Analytical Marxism*. Cambridge: Cambridge University Press: 191–201.

Roemer, John (ed.)

1986c	*Analytical Marxism*. Cambridge: Cambridge University Press.

Rogers, Mary
1983   *Sociology, Ethnomethodology, and Experience: A Phenomenological Critique.*
            New York: Cambridge University Press.
Rollins, Judith
1985   *Between Women: Domestics and Their Employers.* Philadelphia: Temple
            University Press.
Rose, Arnold
1962   "A Systematic Summary of Symbolic Interaction Theory." In A.
            Rose (ed.), *Human Behavior and Social Processes.* Boston: Houghton
            Mifflin.
Rose, Gillian
1984   *Dialectic of Nihilism: Post-Structuralism and Law.* New York: Blackwell.
Rosenberg, Morris
1979   *Conceiving the Self.* New York: Basic Books.
1989   "Self-Concept Research: A Historical Review." *Social Forces* 68:34–44.
Rosenberg, Rosalind
1982   *Beyond Separate Spheres: Intellectual Roots of Modern Feminism.* New
            Haven: Yale University Press.
Rosenthal, Naomi, et al.
1985   "Social Movements and Network Analysis: A Case Study of
            Nineteenth-Century Women's Reform in New York State." *American
            Journal of Sociology* 90:1022–1054.
Rossi, Alice
1974   *The Feminist Papers: From Adams to de Beauvoir.* New York: Bantam.
1977   "A Biosocial Perspective on Parenting." *Daedalus* 106:9–31.
1983   "Gender and Parenthood." *American Sociological Review* 49:1–19.
Rossi, Ino
1974a   "Intellectual Antecedents of Lévi-Strauss' Notion of Unconscious." In I.
            Rossi (ed.), *The Unconscious in Culture: The Structuralism of Claude Lévi-
            Strauss in Perspective.* New York: Dutton: 7–30.
1974b   "Structuralism as a Scientific Method." In I. Rossi (ed.), *The Unconscious
            in Culture: The Structuralism of Claude Lévi-Strauss in Perspective.* New
            York: Dutton: 60–106.
Rossi, Ino (ed.)
1982   *Structural Sociology.* New York: Columbia University Press.
Roth, Guenther
1968   "Introduction." In G. Roth and C. Wittich (eds.), Max Weber, *Economy
            and Society.* 3 vols. Totowa, N.J.: Bedminster Press.
1971   "Sociological Typology and Historical Explanations." In G. Roth and R.
            Bendix (eds.), *Scholarship and Partisanship: Essays on Max Weber.*
            Berkeley: University of California Press: 109–128.
1976   "History and Sociology in the Work of Max Weber." *British Journal of
            Sociology* 27:306–318.
Rowbotham, Sheila
1973   *Women's Consciousness, Man's World.* Middlesex, Eng.: Pelican.
Rubinstein, David
1986   "The Concept of Structure in Sociology." In M. L. Wardell and S. P.
            Turner (eds.), *Sociological Theory in Transition.* Boston: Allen and Unwin:
            80–94.

Rubin, Gayle
1975   "The Traffic in Women: Notes on the Political Economy of Sex." In R.
            Reiter (ed.), *Towards an Anthropology of Women.* New York: Monthly
            Review Press.
Rubin, Lillian
1976   *Worlds of Pain: Life in the Working Class Family.* New York: Basic Books.
1979   *Intimate Strangers: Men and Women Together.* New York: Harper & Row.
1985   *Just Friends: The Role of Friendship in Our Lives.* New York: Harper &
            Row.
Ruddick, Sara
1980   "Maternal Thinking." *Feminist Studies* 6:342–367.
Runciman, W. G.
1972   *A Critique of Max Weber's Philosophy of Social Science.* London:
            Cambridge University Press.
Ryan, Mary
1990   *Women in Public: From Barriers to Ballots, 1825–1880.* Baltimore: Johns
            Hopkins University Press.
Ryan, William
1971   *Blaming the Victim.* New York: Pantheon.
Ryave, A. Lincoln, and Schenkein, James N.
1974   "Notes on the Art of Walking." In R. Turner (ed.), *Ethnomethodology:
            Selected Readings.* Harmondsworth, Eng.: Penguin: 265–275.
Salamini, Leonardo
1981   *The Sociology of Political Praxis: An Introduction to Gramsci's Theory.*
            London: Routledge and Kegan Paul.
Salomon, A.
1945   "German Sociology." In G. Gurvitch and W. F. Moore (eds.), *Twentieth
            Century Sociology.* New York: Philosophical Library: 586–614.
Sanday, Peggy Reeves
1990   *Fraternity Gang Rape: Sex, Brotherhood and Privilege on Campus.* New
            York: New York University Press.
Satoshi, Kamata
1982   *Japan in the Passing Lane.* New York: Pantheon.
Saunders, Peter
1989   "Space, Urbanism and the Created Environment." In D. Held and J. B.
            Thompson (eds.), *Social Theory of Modern Societies: Anthony Giddens and
            His Critics.* Cambridge: Cambridge University Press: 215–234.
Scaff, Lawrence
1989   *Fleeing the Iron Cage: Culture, Politics, and Modernity in the Thought of
            Max Weber.* Berkeley: University of California Press.
Scheffler, Harold
1970   "Structuralism in Anthropology." In J. Ehrmann (ed.), *Structuralism.*
            Garden City, N.Y.: Anchor: 56–79.
Schegloff, Emanuel
1979   "Identification and Recognition in Telephone Conversation Openings."
            In G. Psathas (ed.), *Everyday Language: Studies in Ethnomethodology.* New
            York: Irvington: 23–78.
1987   "Between Macro and Micro: Contexts and Other Connections." In J.
            Alexander et al. (eds.), *The Micro-Macro Link:* Berkeley: University of
            California Press: 207–234

Schluchter, Wolfgang
1981   *The Rise of Western Rationalism: Max Weber' Developmental History.*
            Berkeley: University of California Press.
Schmidt, Neal, et. al.
1984   "Meta-analyses of Validity Studies Published between 1964 and 1982
            and the Investigation of Study Characteristics." *Personnel Psychology.* 37:
            407–422.
Schneider, Louis
1967   *The Scottish Moralists: On Human Nature and Society.* Chicago: University
            of Chicago Press.
1971   "Dialectic in Sociology." *American Sociological Review* 36:667–678.
Schroeter, Gerd
1985   "Dialogue, Debate, or Dissent? The Difficulties of Assessing Max
            Weber's Relation to Marx." In R. J. Antonio and R. M. Glassman
            (eds.), *A Weber-Marx Dialogue.* Lawrence: University Press of Kansas:
            2–13.
Schroyer, Trent
1970   "Toward a Critical Theory of Advanced Industrial Society." In H. P.
            Dreitzel (ed.), *Recent Sociology: No. 2.* New York: Macmillan: 210–234.
1973   *The Critique of Domination.* Boston: Beacon Press.
Schutz, Alfred
1932/1967   *The Phenomenology of the Social World.* Evanston, Ill.: Northwestern
            University Press.
1973   *Collected Papers I: The Problem of Social Reality.* The Hague: Martinus
            Nijhoff.
1975   *Collected Papers III: Studies in Phenomenological Philosophy.* The Hague:
            Martinus Nijhoff.
1976a   *Collected Papers II: Studies in Social Theory.* The Hague Matinus Nijhoff.
1976b   "The Stranger: An Essay in Social Psychology." In A. Schutz, *Collected
            Papers II: Studies in Social Theory.* The Hague: Martinus Nijhoff: 91–105.
1976c   "The Homecomer." In A. Schutz, *Collected Papers II: Studies in Social
            Theory.* The Hague: Martinus Nijhoff: 106–119.
Schutz, Alfred, and Luckmann, Thomas
1973   *The Structure of the Life World.* Evanston, Ill.: Northwestern University
            Press.
Schwanenberg, Enno
1971   "The Two Problems of Order in Parsons' Theory: An Analysis from
            Within." *Social Forces* 49:569–581.
Schwendinger, Julia, and Schwendinger, Herman
1974   *Sociologists of the Chair.* New York: Basic Books.
Scimecca, Joseph
1977   *The Sociological Theory of C. Wright Mills.* Port Washington, N.Y.:
            Kennikat Press.
Sciulli, David
1986   "Voluntaristic Action as a Distinct Concept: Theoretical Foundations of
            Societal Constitutionalism." *American Sociological Review* 51:743–766.
Sciulli, David, and Gerstein, Dean
1985   "Social Theory and Talcott Parsons in the 1980s." *Annual Review of
            Sociology* 11:369–387.

Scully, Diana
1980   *Men Who Control Health: The Miseducation of Obstetrician-Gynecologists.*
            Boston: Houghton Mifflin.
1990   *Understanding Sexual Violence: A Study of Convicted Rapists.* Boston:
            Unwin Hyman.
Searle, John
1972   "Chomsky's Revolution in Linguistics." *New York Review of Books* 18:16–
            24.
Seidman, Steven
1983   *Liberalism and the Origins of European Social Theory.* Berkeley: University
            of California Press.
1989   "Introduction." In S. Seidman (ed.), *Jurgen Habermas on Society and
            Politics: A Reader.* Boston: Beacon Press: 1–25.
Selvin, Hanan C.
1958   "Durkheim's *Suicide* and Problems of Empirical Reseach." *American
            Journal of Sociology* 63:607–619.
Sewart, John J.
1978   "Critical Theory and the Critique of Conservative Method." *American
            Sociologist* 13:15–22.
Shalin, Dmitri
1986   "Pragmatism and Social Interactionism." *American Sociological Review* 51:
            9–29.
Sharrock, Wes, and Anderson, Bob
1986   *The Ethnomethodologists.* Chichester, Eng.: Ellis Horwood.
Sheridan, Alan
1980   *Michel Foucault: The Will to Truth.* London: Tavistock.
Shibutani, Thomas
1988   "Herbert Blumer's Contribution to Twentieth-Century Sociology."
            Symbolic Interaction 11:23–31.
Showalter, Elaine
1971   *Women's Liberation and Literature.* New York: Harcourt Brace Jovanovich.
Shreve, Anita
1989   *Women Together, Women Alone: The Legacy of the Consciousness Raising
            Movement.* New York: Viking.
Sica, Alan
1986   "Hermeneutics and Axiology: The Ethical Content of Interpretation." In
            M. L. Wardell and S. P. Turner (eds.), *Sociological Theory in Transition.*
            Boston: Allen and Unwin: 142–157.
1988   *Weber, Irrationality and Social Order.* Berkeley: University of California
            Press.
Simmel, Georg
1903/1971   "The Metropolis and Mental Life." In D. Levine (ed.), *Georg Simmel.*
            Chicago: University of Chicago Press: 324–339.
1904/1971   "Fashion." In D. Levine (ed.), *Georg Simmel.* Chicago: University of
            Chicago Press: 294–323.
1906/1950   "The Secret and the Secret Society." In K. H. Wolff (ed.), *The Sociology
            of Georg Simmel.* New York: Free Press: 307–376.
1907/1978   *The Philosophy of Money,* Tom Bottomore and David Frisby (eds. and
            trans.). London: Routledge and Kegan Paul.

1908/1950a   "Subordination under a Principle." In K. Wolff (ed. and trans.), *The Sociology of Georg Simmel.* New York: Free Press: 250–267.

1908/1950b   "Types of Social Relationships by Degrees of Reciprocal Knowledge of the Participants." In K. Wolff (ed. and trans.), *The Sociology of Georg Simmel.* New York: Free Press: 317–329.

1908/1955   *Conflict and the Web of Group Affiliations.* New York: Free Press.

1908/1959a   "How Is Society Possible?" In K. Wolff (ed.), *Essays in Sociology, Philosophy and Aesthetics.* New York: Harper Torchbooks: 337–356.

1908/1959b   "The Problem of Sociology." In K. Wolff (ed.), *Essays in Sociology, Philosophy and Aesthetics.* New York: Harper Torchbooks: 310–336.

1908/1971a   "Group Expansions and the Development of Individuality." In D. Levine (ed.), *Georg Simmel.* Chicago: University of Chicago Press: 251–293.

1908/1971b   "The Stranger." In D. Levine (ed.), *Georg Simmel.* Chicago: University of Chicago Press: 143–149.

1908/1971c   "The Poor." In D. Levine (ed.), *Georg Simmel.* Chicago: University of Chicago Press: 150–178.

1908/1971d   "Domination." In D. Levine (ed.), *Georg Simmel.* Chicago: University of Chicago Press: 96–120.

1918/1971   "The Transcendent Character of Life." In D. Levine (ed.), *Georg Simmel.* Chicago: University of Chicago Press: 353–374.

1921/1968   "The Conflict in Modern Culture." In K. P. Etzkorn (ed.), *Georg Simmel.* New York: Teachers College, Columbia University: 11–25.

1950   *The Sociology of Georg Simmel,* Kurt Wolff (ed. and trans.). New York: Free Press.

1984   *On Women, Sexuality and Love,* Guy Oakes (trans.). New Haven: Yale University Press.

Simon, Herbert
1957   *Administrative Behavior.* New York: Free Press.

Singelmann, Peter
1972   "Exchange as Symbolic Interaction." *American Sociological Review* 38:414–424.

Skinner, B. F.
1938   *The Behavior of Organisms: An Experimental Analysis.* New York: Appleton-Century-Crofts.

1948   *Walden Two.* New York: Macmillan.

1968   *Technology of Teaching.* New York: Appleton-Century-Crofts.

1971   *Beyond Freedom and Dignity.* New York: Knopf.

1983   *Matter of Consequences: Part Three of an Autobiography.* New York: Knopf.

Skocpol, Theda
1979   *States and Social Revolutions.* Cambridge: Cambridge University Press.

1986   "The Dead End of Metatheory." *Contemporary Sociology* 16:10–12.

Skotnes, Andor
1979   "Structural Determination of the Proletariat and the Petty Bourgeoisie: A Critique of Nicos Poulantzas." *Insurgent Sociologist* 9:34–54.

Slater, Phil
1977   *Origin and Significance of the Frankfurt School: A Marxist Perspective.* London: Routledge and Kegan Paul.

Smart, Barry
1983   *Foucault, Marxism and Critique.* London: Routledge and Kegan Paul.
1985   *Michel Foucault.* Chichester, Eng.: Ellis Horwood.
Smelser, Neil
1959   *Social Change in the Industrial Revolution.* Chicago: University of Chicago
              Press.
1962   *Theory of Collective Behavior.* New York: Free Press.
1987   "Depth Psychology and the Social Order." In J. Alexander et al. (eds.),
              The Micro-Macro Link. Berkeley: University of California Press: 267–286.
1988   "Sociological Theory: Looking Forward." *Perspectives: The Theory Section
              Newsletter* 11:1–3.
Smith, Dorothy
1974   "Women's Perspective as a Radical Critique of Sociology." *Sociological
              Inquiry* 44:7–13.
1975   "An Analysis of Ideological Structures and How Women Are Excluded:
              Consideration for Academic Women." *Canadian Review of Sociology and
              Anthropology.* 12:353–369.
1978   "A Peculiar Eclipsing: Women's Exclusion from Man's Culture."
              Women's Studies International Quarterly 1:281–295.
1979   "A Sociology for Women." In J. A. Sherman and E. T. Beck (eds.), *The
              Prism of Sex: Essays in the Sociology of Knowledge.* Madison: University of
              Wisconsin Press.
1987   *The Everyday World as Problematic: A Feminist Sociology.* Boston:
              Northeastern University Press.
1989   "Sociological Theory: Methods of Writing Patriarchy." In R. A. Wallace
              (ed.), *Feminism and Sociological Theory.* Newbury Park, Calif.: Sage: 34–
              64.
1990a   *The Conceptual Practices of Power: A Feminist Sociology of Knowledge.*
              Boston: Northeastern University Press.
1990b   *Texts, Facts and Femininity: Exploring the Relations of Ruling.* London:
              Routledge and Kegan Paul.
Smith, Dorothy, and Griffith, Alison
1985   "Coordinating the Uncoordinated: How Mothers Manage the School
              Day." Paper presented at the annual meeting of the American
              Sociological Association, Washington, D.C.
Smith, Norman Erik
1979   "William Graham Sumner as an Anti-Social Darwinist." *Pacific
              Sociological Review* 22:332–347.
Smith, T. V.
1931   "The Social Philosophy of George Herbert Mead." *American Journal of
              Sociology* 37:368–385.
Snitow, Ann Barr
1979   "Mass Market Romance: Pornography for Women Is Different." *Radical
              History Review* 20:141–163.
Snitow, Ann Barr, Stansell, Christine, and Thompson, Sharon
1983   *Powers of Desire: The Politics of Sexuality.* New York: Monthly Review
              Press.
Snizek, William E.
1976   "An Empirical Assessment of 'Sociology: A Multiple Paradigm
              Science.'" *American Sociologist* 11:217–219.

Snizek, William E., Fuhrman, Ellsworth R., and Miller, Michael K. (eds.)
1979   *Contemporary Issues in Theory and Research.* Westport, Conn.: Greenwood
            Press.
Snow, David
1986   "Frame Alignment Processes, Micromobilization, and Movement
            Participation: American Sociological Review 51:464–481.
Snow, David A., Zurcher, Louis A., and Peters, Robert
1984   "Victory Celebrations as Theater: A Dramaturgical Approach to Crowd
            Behavior." *Symbolic Interaction* 8:21–42.
Sokoloff, Natalie
1980   *Between Money and Love: The Dialectics of Women's Home and Market
            Work.* New York: Praeger.
Sorokin, Pitirim
1928   *Contemporary Sociological Theories.* New York: Harper.
1937–1941   *Social and Cultural Dynamics.* 4 vols. New York: American Book.
1956   *Fads and Foibles in Modern Sociology and Related Sciences.* Chicago:
            Regnery.
1963   *A Long Journey: The Autobiography of Pitirim Sorokin.* New Haven:
            College and University Press.
Speier, Matthew
1970   "The Everyday World of the Child." In J. Douglas (ed.), *Understanding
            Everyday Life.* Chicago: Aldine: 188–217.
Spender, Dale
1980   *Man Made Language.* London: Routledge and Kegan Paul.
1982   *Women of Ideas (And What Men Have Done to Them).* London: Routledge
            and Kegan Paul.
1989   *The Writing or the Sex? Or Why You Don't Have to Read Women's Writing
            to Know It's No Good.* New York: Pergamon Press.
Spender, Dale (ed.)
1983   *Feminist Theorists: Three Centuries of Key Women Thinkers.* New York:
            Random House.
Spykman, Nicholas
1925/1966   *Social Theory of Georg Simmel.* Chicago: Aldine.
Staats, Arthur W.
1976   "Skinnerian Behaviorism: Social Behaviorism or Radical Behaviorism?"
            American Sociologist 11:59–60.
Stacey, Judith, and Thorne, Barrie
1985   "The Missing Feminist Revolution in Sociology." *Social Problems* 32:301–
            316.
Stanfield, Ron
1974   "Kuhnian Scientific Revolutions and the Keynesian Revolution." *Journal
            of Economic Issues* 8:97–109.
Stanton, Donna
1985   "Language and Revolution: The Franco-American Dis-Connection." In
            H. Eisenstein and A. Hardine (eds.), *The Future of Difference.* New
            Brunswick, N.J.: Rutgers University Press.
Stockard, Jean, and Johnson, Miriam
1980   *Sex Roles: Sex Inequality and Sex Role Development.* Englewood Cliffs,
            N.J.: Prentice-Hall.

Stolte, John F.
1987   "Legitimacy, Justice, and Productive Exchange." In K. S. Cook (ed.),
            Social Exchange Theory. Beverly Hills, Calif.: Sage: 190–208.
Struik, Dirk
1964   "Introduction." In K. Marx, *The Economic and Philosophic Manuscripts of
            1844.* New York: International Publishers: 9–56.
Stryker, Sheldon
1980   *Symbolic Interactionism: A Social Structural Version.* Menlo Park, Calif.:
            Benjamin/Cummings.
Swedberg, Richard
1989   "Socioeconomics and the New Methodenstreit: On the Paradigmatic
            Struggle in Contemporary Economics." Paper presented at the
            conference on "Socio-Economics" at the Harvard Business School, Mar.
            31–Apr. 2.
Symbolic Interaction
1981   Fall. Entire issue devoted to George Herbert Mead.
1983   Review symposium on J. David Lewis and Richard L. Smith, *American
            Sociology and Pragmatism* 6:127–174.
1988   Special issue on Herbert Blumer's legacy. 11:1–160.
Szacki, Jerzy
1979   *History of Sociological Thought.* Westport, Conn.: Greenwood Press.
Sztompka, Piotr
1974   *System and Function: Toward a Theory of Society.* New York: Academic
            Press.
Takla, Tendzin, and Pope, Whitney
1985   "The Force Imagery in Durkheim: The Integration of Theory,
            Metatheory and Method." *Sociological Theory* 3:74–88.
Tar, Zoltan
1977   *The Frankfurt School: The Critical Theories of Max Horkheimer and Theodor
            W. Adorno.* London: Routledge and Kegan Paul.
Telos
1989–1990   "Does Critical Theory Have a Future? The Elizabethtown *Telos*
            Conference (February 23–25, 1990)." *Telos* 82:111–130.
Terkel, Studs
1974   *Working.* New York: Pantheon.
Thomas, William I., and Thomas, Dorothy S.
1928   *The Child in America: Behavior Problems and Programs.* New York: Knopf.
Thompson, E. P.
1978   *The Poverty of Theory.* London: Merlin Press.
Thompson, John B.
1989   "The Theory of Structuration." In D. Held and J. B. Thompson (eds.),
            Social Theory of Modern Societies: Anthony Giddens and His Critics.
            Cambridge: Cambridge University Press: 56–76.
Thompson, Kenneth
1975   *Auguste Comte: The Foundation of Sociology.* New York: Halstead Press.
Tiger, Lionel, and Fox, Robin
1971   *The Imperial Animal.* New York: Holt, Rinehart and Winston.
Tilman, Rick
1984   *C. Wright Mills: A Native Radical and His American Intellectual Roots.*
            University Park: Pennsylvania State University Press.

Tinker, Irene (ed.)
1983   *Women in Washington: Advocates for Public Policy.* Beverly Hills, Calif.:
            Sage.
Tiryakian, Edward A.
1962   *Sociologism and Existentialism: Two Perspectives on the Individual and
            Society.* Englewood Cliffs, N.J.: Prentice-Hall.
1965   "Existential Phenomenology and the Sociological Tradition." *American
            Sociological Review* 30:674–688.
1979   "The Significance of Schools in the Development of Sociology." In W.
            Snizek, E. Fuhrman, and M. Miller (eds.), *Contemporary Issues in Theory
            and Research.* Westport, Conn.: Greenwood Press: 211–233.
1981   "The Sociological Import of Metaphor." *Sociological Inquiry* 51:27–33.
1986   "Hegemonic Schools and the Development of Sociology: Rethinking the
            History of the Discipline." In R. C. Monk (ed.), *Structures of Knowing.*
            Lanham, Md.: University Press of America: 417–441.
forthcoming "Pathways to Metatheory: Rethinking the Presuppositions of
            Macrosociology." In G. Ritzer (ed.), *Sociological Metatheorizing: Coming of
            Age.* Beverly Hills, Calif.: Sage.
Toby, Jackson
1977   "Parsons' Theory of Societal Evolution." In T. Parsons, *The Evolution of
            Societies.* Englewood Cliffs, N.J.: Prentice-Hall: 1–23.
Touraine, Alain
1977   *The Self-Production of Society.* Chicago: University of Chicago Press.
Trebilcot, Joyce
1973   "Sex Roles: The Argument from Nature." Paper presented at the
            meeting of the American Philosophical Association, Western Division,
            April.
Trebilcot, Joyce (ed.)
1984   *Mothering: Essays in Feminist Theory.* Totowa, N.J.: Rowman and
            Allanheld.
Troyer, William
1946   "Mead's Social and Functional Theory of Mind." *American Sociological
            Review* 11:198–202.
Tucker, Robert C. (ed.)
1970   *The Marx-Engels Reader.* New York: Norton.
Tumin, Melvin
1953   "Some Principles of Stratification: A Critical Analysis." *American
            Sociological Review* 18:387–394.
Turner, Bryan S.
1974   *Weber and Islam: A Critical Study.* London: Routledge and Kegan Paul.
1981   *For Weber: Essays in the Sociology of Fate.* Boston: Routledge and Kegan
            Paul.
1986   "Simmel, Rationalization and the Sociology of Money." *Sociological
            Review* 34:93–114.
Turner, Jonathan
1973   "From Utopia to Where? A Strategy for Reformulating the Dahrendorf
            Conflict Model." *Social Forces* 52:236–244.
1974   "Parsons as a Symbolic Interactionist: A Comparison of Action and
            Interaction Theory." *Sociological Inquiry* 44:283–294.

| 1975 | "A Strategy for Reformulating the Dialectical and Functional Theories of Conflict." *Social Forces* 53:433–444. |

1975   "A Strategy for Reformulating the Dialectical and Functional Theories of Conflict." *Social Forces* 53:433–444.

1982   *The Structure of Sociological Theory.* 3rd ed. Homewood, Ill.: Dorsey Press.

1985   "In Defense of Positivism." *Sociological Theory* 3:24–30.

1986   *The Structure of Sociological Theory.* 4th ed. Chicago: Dorsey Press.

1987   "Social Exchange Theory: Future Directions." In K. S. Cook (ed.), *Social Exchange Theory.* Beverly Hills, Calif.: Sage: 223–238.

1989a   "Introduction: Can Sociology Be a Cumulative Science?" in J. Turner (ed.), *Theory Building in Sociology: Assessing Theoretical Cumulation.* Newbury Park, Calif.: Sage: 8–18.

1990   "The Past, Present, and Future of Theory in American Sociology." In G. Ritzer (ed.), *Frontiers of Social Theory: The New Syntheses.* New York: Columbia University Press: 371–391.

1991   *The Structure of Sociological Theory.* 5th ed. Belmont, Calif.: Wadsworth.

Turner, Jonathan (ed.)

1989b   *Theory Building in Sociology: Assessing Theoretical Cumulation.* Newbury Park, Calif.: Sage.

Turner, Jonathan, and Maryanski, A. Z.

1979   *Functionalism.* Menlo Park, Calif.: Benjamin/Cummings.

1988a   "Is 'Neofunctionalism' Really Functional?" *Sociological Theory* 6:110–121.

1988b   "Sociology's Lost Human Relations Area Files." *Sociological Perspectives* 31:19–34.

Turner, Ralph

1968   "The Self-Conception in Social Interaction." In C. Gordon and K. J. Gergen (eds.), *The Self in Social Interaction.* New York: Wiley: 93–106.

Turner, Roy

1970   "Words, Utterances and Activities." In J. Douglas (ed.), *Understanding Everyday Life.* Chicago: Aldine: 161–187.

Turner, Stephen

1983   "Weber on Action." *American Sociological Review* 48:506–519.

Udehn, Lars

1981   "The Conflict between Methodology and Rationalization in the Work of Max Weber." *Acta Sociologica* 24:131–147.

Uehara, Edwina

1990   "Dual Exchange Theory, Social Networks, and Informal Social Support." *American Journal of Sociology* 96:521–557.

Ungar, Sheldon

1984   "Self-Mockery: An Alternative Form of Self-Presentation." *Symbolic Interaction* 7:121–133.

van den Berg, Axel

1980   "Critical Theory: Is There Still Hope?" *American Journal of Sociology* 86:449–478.

van den Berghe, Pierre

1963   "Dialectic and Functionalism: Toward Reconciliation." *American Sociological Review* 28:695–705.

Veltmeyer, Henry

1978   "Marx's Two Methods of Sociological Analysis." *Sociological Inquiry* 48:101–112.

Venable, Vernon
1945   *Human Nature: The Marxian View.* New York: Knopf.
Vetter, Betty M., Babco, Eleanor, and Jensen-Fisher, Susan
1982   *Professional Women and Minorities: A Manpower Resource Service.*
            Washington, D.C.: Scientific Manpower Commission.
Vidich, Arthur J., and Lyman, Stanford M.
1985   *American Sociology: Worldly Rejections of Religion and Their Directions.*
            New Haven: Yale University Press.
Vogel, Lise
1984   *Marxism and the Oppression of Women: Towards a Unitary Theory.* New
            Brunswick, N.J.: Rutgers University Press.
Wacquant, Loïc J. D.
1989   "Towards a Reflexive Sociology: A Workshop with Pierre Bourdieu."
            Sociological Theory 7:26–63.
Wagner, Helmut
1964   "Displacement of Scope: A Problem of the Relationship between Small
            Scale and Large Scale Sociological Theories." *American Journal of
            Sociology* 69:571–584.
1983   *Alfred Schutz: An Intellectual Biography.* Chicago: University of Chicago
            Press.
Walker, Alice
1983   *In Search of Our Mothers' Gardens.* New York: Harcourt Brace
            Jovanovich.
1988   *Living by the Word.* New York: Harcourt Brace Jovanovich.
1989   *The Temple of My Familiar.* New York: Pocket Books.
Wallace, Ruth A. (ed.)
1989   *Feminism and Sociological Theory.* Newbury Park, Calif.: Sage.
Wallace, Walter
1969   "Overview of Contemporary Sociological Theory." In W. Wallace (ed.),
            Sociological Theory. Chicago: University of Chicago Press: 1–59.
1988   "Toward a Disciplinary Matrix in Sociology." In N. Smelser (ed.),
            Handbook of Sociology. Newbury Park, Calif.: Sage: 23–76.
Wallerstein, Immanuel
1974   *The Modern World-System: Capitalist Agriculture and the Origins of the
            European World-Economy in the 16th Century.* New York: Academic Press.
1980   *The Modern World-System II: Mercantilism and the Consolidation of the
            European World-Economy, 1600–1750.* New York: Academic Press.
1986   "Marxisms as Utopias: Evolving Ideologies." *American Journal of
            Sociology* 91:1295–1308.
1989   *The Modern World-System III: The Second Era of Great Expansion of the
            Capitalist World-Economy, 1730–1840.* New York: Academic Press.
Wallimann, Isidor
1981   *Estrangement: Marx's Conception of Human Nature and the Division of
            Labor.* Westport, Conn.: Greenwood Press.
Wallwork, Ernest
1972   *Durkheim: Morality and Milieu.* Cambridge: Harvard University Press.
Walum-Richardson, Laurel
1981   *The Dynamics of Sex and Gender.* Boston: Houghton Mifflin.
Wardell, Mark L., and Turner, Stephen P.
1986b   "Introduction: Dissolution of the Classical Project." In M. L. Wardell

and S. P. Turner (eds.), *Sociological Theory in Transition*. Boston: Allen and Unwin: 11–18.

Wardell, Mark L., and Turner, Stephen P. (eds.)
1986a   *Sociological Theory in Transition*. Boston: Allen and Unwin.

Warriner, Charles
1969   "Social Action, Behavior and Verstehen." *Sociological Quarterly* 10:501–511.

Warsh, David
1990   "Modern Thinkers Merge Sociology, Economics to Explain Today's World." *Washington Post* Aug. 15:D3.

Warshay, Leon, and Warshay, Diana H.
1986   "The Individualizing and Subjectivizing of George Herbert Mead: A Sociology of Knowledge Interpretation." *Sociological Focus* 19:177–188.

Wartenberg, Thomas E.
1982   " 'Species-Being' and 'Human Nature' in Marx." *Human Studies* 5:77–95.

Wax, Murray
1967   "On Misunderstanding Verstehen: A Reply to Abel." *Sociology and Social Research* 51:323–333.

Weber, Marianne
1975   *Max Weber: A Biography*, Harry Zohn (ed. and trans.). New York: Wiley.

Weber, Max
1896–1906/   *The Agrarian Sociology of Ancient Civilizations*. London: NLB.
1976
1903–1906/   *Roscher and Knies: The Logical Problems of Historical Economics*. New
1975   York: Free Press.
1903–1917/   *The Methodology of the Social Sciences*, Edward Shils and Henry Finch
1949   (eds.). New York: Free Press.
1904–1905/   *The Protestant Ethic and the Spirit of Capitalism*. New York: Scribner's.
1958
1906/1985   " 'Churches' and 'Sects' in North America: An Ecclesiastical Socio-Political Sketch." *Sociological Theory* 3:7–13.
1915/1958   "Religious Rejections of the World and Their Directions." In H. H. Gerth and C. W. Mills (eds.), *From Max Weber: Essays in Sociology*. New York: Oxford University Press: 323–359.
1916/1964   *The Religion of China: Confucianism and Taoism*. New York: Macmillan.
1916–1917/   *The Religion of India: The Sociology of Hinduism and Buddhism*. Glencoe,
1958   Ill.: Free Press.
1921/1958   *The Rational and Social Foundations of Music*. Carbondale: Southern Illinois University Press.
1921/1963   *The Sociology of Religion*. Boston: Beacon Press.
1921/1968   *Economy and Society*. 3 vols. Totowa, N.J.: Bedminster Press.
1922–1923   "The Social Psychology of the World Religions." In H. H. Gerth and C. W. Mills (eds.), *From Max Weber: Essays in Sociology*. New York: Oxford University Press: 267–301.
1927/1981   *General Economic History*. New Brunswick, N.J.: Transaction Books.

Weigert, Andrew
1981   *Sociology of Everyday Life*. New York: Longman.

Weingart, Peter
1969   "Beyond Parsons? A Critique of Ralf Dahrendorf's Conflict Theory."
            Social Forces 48:151–165.
Weingartner, Rudolph H.
1959   "Form and Content in Simmel's Philosophy of Life." In K. Wolff (ed.),
            Essays on Sociology, Philosophy and Aesthetics. New York: Harper
            Torchbooks: 33–60.
Weinstein, Deena, and Weinstein, Michael A.
1990   "The Postmodern Discourse of Metatheory." Paper presented at
            miniconference on "Metatheorizing in Sociology" at the meetings of the
            American Sociological Association, Washington, D.C., August.
Weinstein, Eugene A., and Tanur, Judith M.
1976   "Meanings, Purposes and Structural Resources in Social Interaction."
            Cornell Journal of Social Relations 11:105–110.
Weldes, Jutta
1989   "Marxism and Methodological Individualism." *Theory and Society* 18:
            353–386.
Wellman, Barry
1983   "Network Analysis: Some Basic Principles." In R. Collins (ed.),
            Sociological Theory—1983. San Francisco: Jossey-Bass: 155–200.
Wellman, Barry, and Wortley, Scot
1990   "Different Strokes for Different Folks: Community Ties and Social
            Support." *American Journal of Sociology* 96:558–588.
Wellman, David
1988   "The Politics of Herbert Blumer's Sociological Method." *Symbolic
            Interaction* 11:59–68.
Whalen, Jack, Zimmerman, Don H., and Whalen, Marilyn R.
1988   "When Words Fail: A Single Case Analysis." *Social Problems* 35:335–
            361.
Whalen, Marilyn R., and Zimmerman, Don H.
1987   "Sequential and Institutional Contexts in Calls for Help." *Social
            Psychology Quarterly* 50:172–185.
White, Harrison C., Boorman, Scott A., and Breiger, Ronald L.
1976   "Social Structure from Multiple Networks: Parts 1 and 2." *American
            Journal of Sociology* 91:730–780, 1384–1446.
White, Hayden
1973   *The Historical Imagination in Nineteenth-Century Europe*. Baltimore: Johns
            Hopkins University Press.
Wiley, Norbert
1979   "The Rise and Fall of Dominating Theories in American Sociolgy." In
            W. Snizek, E. Fuhrman and M. Miller (eds.), *Contemporary Issues in
            Theory and Research*. Westport, Conn.: Greenwood Press: 47–79.
1985   "The Current Interregnum in American Sociology." *Social Research*
            52:179–207.
1986   "Early American Sociology and *The Polish Peasant*." *Sociological Theory* 4:
            20–40.
1988   "The Micro-Macro Problem in Social Theory." *Sociological Theory* 6:254–
            261.
1989   "Response to Ritzer." *Sociological Theory* 7:230–231.

Willer, David, Markovsky, Barry, and Patton, Travis
1989   "Power Structures: Derivations and Applications of Elementary
            Theory." In J. Berger, M. Zelditch, Jr., and B. Anderson (eds.),
            Sociological Theories in Progress: New Formulations. Newbury Park, Calif.:
            Sage: 313–353.
Williams, Robin
1980   "Talcott Parsons: The Stereotypes and the Reality." *American Sociologist*
            15:64–66.
Williams, Simon Johnson
1986   "Appraising Goffman." *British Journal of Sociology* 37:348–369.
Wilner, Patricia
1985   "The Main Drift of Sociology between 1936 and 1982." *History of
            Sociology: An International Review* 5:1–20.
Wilson, Thomas P.
1970   "Normative and Interpretive Paradigms in Sociology." In J. Douglas
            (ed.), *Understanding Everyday Life*. Chicago: Aldine: 1–19.
Wiltshire, David
1978   *The Social and Political Thought of Herbert Spencer*. London: Oxford
            University Press.
Wippler, Reinhard, and Lindenberg, Siegwart
1987   "Collective Phenomena and Rational Choice." In J. Alexander et al.
            (eds.), *The Micro-Macro Link:* Berkeley. University of California Press:
            135–152.
Wolf, Frederic M.
1986   *Meta-Analysis: Quantitative Methods for Research Synthesis*. Beverly Hills,
            Calif.: Sage University Papers.
Womack, James P., Jones, Daniel T., and Roos, Daniel
1990   *The Machine That Changed the World*. New York: Rawson.
Wood, Ellen Meiksins
1986   *The Retreat from Class: The New "True" Socialism*. London: Verso.
1989   "Rational Choice Marxism: Is the Game Worth the Candle?" *New Left
            Review* 177:41–88.
Wood, Michael, and Wardell, Mark L.
1983   "G. H. Mead's Social Behaviorism vs. the Astructural Bias of Symbolic
            Interactionism." *Symbolic Interaction* 6:85–96.
Worsley, Peter
1982   *Marx and Marxism*. Chichester, Eng.: Ellis Horwood.
Wright, Erik Olin
1985   *Classes*. London: Verso.
1987   "Towards a Post-Marxist Radical Social Theory." *Contemporary Sociology*
            16:748–753.
Wright, Erik Olin, and Martin, Bill
1987   "The Transformation of the American Class Structure, 1960–1980."
            American Journal of Sociology 93:1–29.
Wuthnow, Robert, et al. (eds.)
1984   *Cultural Analysis*. Boston: Routledge and Kegan Paul.
Yamagishi, Toshio, Gillmore, Mary R., and Cook, Karen S.
1988   "Network Connections and the Distribution of Power in Exchange
            Networks." *American Journal of Sociology* 93:833–851.

Yeatman, Anna
1987   "Women, Domestic Life and Sociology." In C. Pateman and E. Gross
            (eds.), *Feminist Challenges: Social and Political Challenges*. Boston:
            Northeastern University Press: 157–172.
Zaretsky, Eli
1976   *Capitalism, the Family and Personal Life*. New York: Harper Colophon.
Zaslavsky, Victor
1988   "Three Years of *Perestroika*." *Telos* 74:31–41.
Zeitlin, Irving M.
1981   *Ideology and the Development of Sociological Theory*. 2nd ed. Englewood
            Cliffs, N.J.: Prentice-Hall.
1990   *Ideology and the Development of Sociological Theory*. 4th ed. Englewood
            Cliffs, N.J.: Prentice-Hall.
Zimmerman, Don
1978   "Ethnomethodology." *American Sociologist* 13:5–15.
1988   "The Conversation: The Conversation Analytic Perspective."
            Communication Yearbook 11:406–432.
Zimmerman, Don, and Pollner, Melvin
1970   "The Everyday World as a Phenomenon." In J. Douglas (ed.),
            Understanding Everyday Life. Chicago: Aldine: 80–103.
Zimmerman, Don, and Wieder, D. Lawrence
1970   "Ethnomethodology and the Problem of Order: Comment on Denzin."
            In J. Douglas (ed.), *Understanding Everyday Life*. Chicago: Aldine: 285–
            298.
Zuboff, Shoshana
1988   *In the Age of the Smart Machine*. New York: Basic Books.
Zurcher, Louis A.
1985   "The War Game: Organizational Scripting and the Expression of
            Emotion." *Symbolic Interaction* 8:191–206.

NAME INDEX

SUBJECT INDEX